Lecture Notes in Computer Science 9280

Commenced Publication in 1973
Founding and Former Series Editors:
Gerhard Goos, Juris Hartmanis, and Jan van Leeuwen

More information about this series at http://www.springer.com/series/7412

Vittorio Murino · Enrico Puppo (Eds.)

Image Analysis and Processing – ICIAP 2015

18th International Conference
Genoa, Italy, September 7–11, 2015
Proceedings, Part II

 Springer

Editors
Vittorio Murino
PAVIS - Pattern Analysis
   and Computer Vision
Istituto Italiano di Tecnologia (IIT)
Genoa
Italy

Enrico Puppo
Università di Genova
Genoa
Italy

and

Department of Computer Science
University of Verona
Verona
Italy

ISSN 0302-9743   ISSN 1611-3349 (electronic)
Lecture Notes in Computer Science
ISBN 978-3-319-23233-1   ISBN 978-3-319-23234-8 (eBook)
DOI 10.1007/978-3-319-23234-8

Library of Congress Control Number: 2015946761

LNCS Sublibrary: SL6 – Image Processing, Computer Vision, Pattern Recognition, and Graphics

Springer Cham Heidelberg New York Dordrecht London

Printed on acid-free paper

Springer International Publishing AG Switzerland is part of Springer Science+Business Media
(www.springer.com)

Preface

The 2015 International Conference on Image Analysis and Processing, ICIAP 2015, was the 18th edition of a series of conferences promoted biennially by the Italian Member Society (GIRPR) of the International Association for Pattern Recognition (IAPR). The conference traditionally covers both classic and the most recent trends in computer vision, pattern recognition, and image processing, addressing both theoretical and applicative aspects.

ICIAP 2015 (www.iciap2015.eu) was held in Genova, during September 7–11, 2015, in Palazzo della Borsa (the former Stock Exchange Building) conveniently located in the very center of the city, and was organized by the Pattern Analysis and Computer Vision (PAVIS) department (www.iit.it/pavis) of the Istituto Italiano di Tecnologia (IIT), with the valuable support of the University of Genova and University of Verona. Moreover, ICIAP 2015 was endorsed by the International Association for Pattern Recognition (IAPR), the Italian Member Society of IAPR (GIRPR), and the IEEE Computer Society Technical Committee on Pattern Analysis and Machine Intelligence (TCPAMI) and received the institutional support of Regione Liguria and Comune di Genova. Notable sponsorships came from several industrial partners such as Datalogic, Google, Centro Studi Gruppo Orizzonti Holding, Ansaldo Energia, EBIT Esaote, Softeco, eVS embedded Vision Systems, 3DFlow, Camelot Biomedical Systems, as well as Istituto Italiano di Tecnologia, University of Genova, and University of Verona.

ICIAP is traditionally a venue to discuss image processing and analysis, pattern recognition, computer vision, and machine learning, from both theoretical and applicative perspectives, promoting connections and synergies among senior scholars and students, universities, research institutes, and companies. ICIAP 2015 followed this trend, and the program was subdivided into seven main topics, covering a broad range of scientific areas, which were managed by two area chairs per each topic. They were: Video Analysis and Understanding, Multiview Geometry and 3D Computer Vision, Pattern Recognition and Machine Learning, Image Analysis, Detection and Recognition, Shape Analysis and Modeling, Multimedia, and Biomedical Applications.

Moreover, we hosted several prominent companies as well as start-ups to show their activities while assessing them with respect to the cutting-edge research in the respective areas: Datalogic, eVS embedded Vision Systems, 3DFlow, Camelot Biomedical Systems.

ICIAP 2015 received 234 paper submissions coming from all over the world, including Algeria, Brazil, Canada, China, Colombia, Czech Republic, Egypt, Finland, France, Germany, Italy, Japan, Korea, Lebanon, Morocco, New Zealand, Pakistan, Poland, Qatar, Romania, Russia, Saudi Arabia, Spain, Switzerland, Thailand, The Netherlands, Tunisia, Turkey, UK, USA and, Vietnam. The paper review process was managed by the program chairs with the invaluable support of 14 area chairs, together with the Program Committee and a number of additional reviewers. The peer-review selection process was carried out by three distinct reviewers in most of the cases. For the accepted papers, authors were asked to include in the final version a list of the revisions carried out on the paper, underlining the changes made according to the reviewers' comments. This ultimately led to the selection of 129 high quality manuscripts, 27 orals, and 102 posters, with an overall acceptance rate of about 55 % (about 11 % for orals). The ICIAP 2015 proceedings are published as volumes of the *Lecture Notes in Computer Science* (LNCS) series by Springer.

The program also included six invited talks by distinguished scientists in computer vision pattern recognition and image analysis. We enjoyed the plenary lectures of Arnold Smeulders, University of Amsterdam (The Netherlands), Michal Irani, Weizmann Institute of Science (Israel), Bernt Schiele, Max Planck Institute for Informatics (Germany), Kristen Grauman, University of Texas at Austin (USA), Xiaogang Wang, The Chinese University of Hong Kong (China), and Samy Bengio, Google Inc. (USA), who addressed very interesting and recent research approaches and paradigms such as deep learning, big data, search and retrieval, semantic scene understanding, visual cognition, and image enhancement.

While the main conference was held during September 9–11, 2015, ICIAP 2015 also included several tutorials and workshops, held on Monday, September 7 and Tuesday, September 8, 2015, on a variety of topics.

The organized tutorials were: "Life Long Learning in Computer and Robot Vision" by Barbara Caputo (Italy), "Structure from Motion: Historical Overview and Recent Trends" by Andrea Fusiello (Italy), "Probing Human Brain Network Architecture and Dynamics Using MRI" by Maria Giulia Preti (Switzerland), and "Deep Learning in Computer Vision" by Xiaogang Wang (China).

ICIAP 2015 also hosted seven half- or full-day satellite workshops: "International Workshop on Recent Advances in Digital Security: Biometrics and Forensics (BIO-FOR 2015)," organized by Modesto Castrilln Santana, Matthias Kirchner, Daniel Riccio, and Luisa Verdoliva; "Color in Texture and Material Recognition (CTMR 2015)," organized by Claudio Cusano, Paolo Napoletano, Raimondo Schettini, and Joost van de Weijer; "Medical Imaging in Rheumatology: Advanced Applications for the Analysis of Inammation and Damage in the Rheumatoid Joint (RHEUMA 2015)," organized by Silvana Dellepiane, Marco A. Cimmino, Gianni Viano; "Image-Based Smart City Application (ISCA 2015) by Giuseppe Pirlo, Donato Impedovo, and Byron Leite Dantas Bezerra; "First International Workshop on Multimedia Assisted Dietary Management (MADiMa 2015), organized by Stavroula Mougiakakou, Giovanni Maria Farinella, and Keiji Yanai; "Scene Background Modeling and Initialization (SBMI 2015)," organized by Lucia Maddalena and Thierry Bouwmans; "Workshop on Image and Video Processing for Quality of Multimedia Experience," organized by Nicu Sebe, Ben Herbst, and Dubravko Culibrk. Also the workshop papers were all collected in a separate volume of the LNCS series by Springer.

We thank all the workshop organizers and tutorial speakers who made possible such an interesting pre-conference program.

Several awards were conferred during ICIAP 2015. Two student support grants were provided by the International Association for Pattern Recognition (IAPR). The "Eduardo Caianiello" award was attributed to the best paper authored or co-authored by at least one young researcher (PhD student, Post Doc, or similar); a Best Paper award was also assigned after a careful selection made by an *ad hoc* appointed committee.

Unfortunately, just a few months ago, Stefano Levialdi, an eminent scientist and one of the "founders" of the Italian Chapter of the IAPR, passed away. ICIAP 2015 commemorated this scientist, colleague, and friend dedicating the Best Paper award to his memory with the aim of celebrating his pioneering activities in the early stages of Image Analysis and Pattern Recognition in Italy.

The organization and the success of ICIAP 2015 were made possible thanks to the cooperation of many people. First of all, special thanks should be given to the area chairs, who made a big effort for the selection of the papers, together with all the members of the Program Committee. Second, we also would like to thank the industrial, special session, publicity, publication, and Asia and US liaison chairs, who, operating in their respective fields, made this event a successful forum of science. Special thanks go to the workshop and tutorial chairs, as well as all workshop organizers and tutorial lecturers for making richer the conference program with notable satellite events. ASAP S.r.l., the agency that supported the registration process and the financial aspects of the conference, among many other issues, should be acknowledged for all the work done. Last but not least, we are indebted to the Local Committee, mainly colleagues from IIT-PAVIS, who covered almost every aspects of the conference when necessary and the day-to-day management issues of the ICIAP 2015 organization, notably Sara, Diego, Matteo.

Thanks very much indeed to all the aforementioned people since without their support we would have not made it.

We hope that ICIAP 2015 will serve as a basis and inspiration for the future ICIAP editions.

September 2015   Vittorio Murino
                                                           Enrico Puppo

Organization

Organizing Institution

Pattern Analysis and Computer Vision (PAVIS)
Istituto Italiano di Tecnologia (IIT), Genova, Italy
http://www.iit.it/pavis

General Chair

Vittorio Murino	Istituto Italiano di Tecnologia, Italy
	University of Verona, Italy

Program Chairs

Enrico Puppo	University of Genova, Italy
Gianni Vernazza	University of Genova, Italy

Workshop Chairs

Marco Cristani	University of Verona, Italy
Carlo Sansone	University of Napoli Federico II, Italy

Tutorial Chair

Alessio Del Bue	Istituto Italiano di Tecnologia, Italy

Special Sessions Chairs

Giuseppe Boccignone	University of Milan, Italy
Giorgio Giacinto	University of Cagliari, Italy

Finance and Industrial Chairs

Sebastiano Battiato	University of Catania, Italy
Luigi Di Stefano	University of Bologna, Italy

Publicity/Web Chair

Manuele Bicego	University of Verona, Italy
Umberto Castellani	University of Verona, Italy

Publications Chairs

Ryad Chellali   Istituto Italiano di Tecnologia, Italy
Diego Sona   Istituto Italiano di Tecnologia, Italy

US Liaison Chair

Silvio Savarese   Stanford University, USA

Asia Liaison Chair

Hideo Saito   Keio University, Japan

Steering Committee

Virginio Cantoni   University of Pavia, Italy
Luigi Cordella   University of Napoli Federico II, Italy
Alberto Del Bimbo   University of Firenze, Italy
Marco Ferretti   University of Pavia, Italy
Fabio Roli   University of Cagliari, Italy
Gabriella Sanniti di Baja   ICIB-CNR, Italy

Area Chairs

Video Analysis and Understanding

Rita Cucchiara   University of Modena e Reggio Emilia, Italy
Jordi Gonzàlez   Universitat Autònoma de Barcelona, Spain

Multiview Geometry and 3D Computer Vision

Andrea Fusiello   University of Udine, Italy
Michael Goesele   TU Darmstadt, Germany

Pattern Recognition and Machine Learning

Marcello Pelillo   University of Venice, Italy
Tiberio Caetano   NICTA, Australia

Image Analysis, Detection and Recognition

Raimondo Schettini   University of Milano-Bicocca, Italy
Theo Gevers   University of Amsterdam, The Netherlands

Shape Analysis and Modeling

Leila De Floriani   University of Genova, Italy
Gunilla Borgefors   Uppsala University, Sweden

Multimedia

Nicu Sebe   University of Trento, Italy
Cees Snoek   University of Amsterdam, The Netherlands

Biomedical Applications

Silvana Dellepiane   University of Genova, Italy
Dimitri Van De Ville   EPFL and University of Genève, Switzerland

Program Committee

Lourdes Agapito, UK
Jake Aggarwal, USA
Albert Ali Salah, Turkey
Edoardo Ardizzone, Italy
Sebastiano Battiato, Italy
Stefano Berretti, Italy
Silvia Biasotti, Italy
Manuele Bicego, Italy
Elisabetta Binaghi, Italy
Giuseppe Boccignone, Italy
Alfred Bruckstein, Israel
Joachim Buhmann, Switzerland
Francesco Camastra, Italy
Barbara Caputo, Italy
Umberto Castellani, Italy
Chen Change Loy, China
Rama Chellappa, USA
Xin Chen, UK
Carlo Colombo, Italy
Marco Cristani, Italy
Maria De Marsico, Italy
Alessio Del Bue, Italy
Adrien Depeursinge, Switzerland
Luigi Di Stefano, Italy
Aykut Erdem, Turkey
Francisco Escolano, Spain
Giovanni Farinella, Italy
Mario Figueiredo, Portugal
David Fofi, France
Ana Fred, Portugal
Giovanni Gallo, Italy
Giorgio Giacinto, Italy
Mehmet Gonen, USA
Shaogang Gong, UK

Marco Gori, Italy
Costantino Grana, Italy
Edwin Hancock, UK
Anders Hast, Sweden
Francesco Isgrò, Italy
Walter Kropatsch, Austria
Claudia Landi, Italy
Laura Leal-Taixé, Switzerland
Ales Leonardis, UK
Giosué Lo Bosco, Italy
Marco Loog, The Netherlands
Lucia Maddalena, Italy
Angelo Marcelli, Italy
Gloria Menegaz, Italy
Greg Mori, USA
Michele Nappi, Italy
Ram Nevatia, USA
Ko Nishino, USA
Francesca Odone, Italy
Pietro Pala, Italy
Alfredo Petrosino, Italy
Massimo Piccardi, Australia
Julien Prados, Switzerland
Andrea Prati, Italy
Maria Giulia Preti, Switzerland
Daniel Riccio, Italy
Jonas Richiardi, Switzerland
Bodo Rosenhahn, Germany
Samuel Rota Bulò, Italy
Amit Roy-Chowdhuri, USA
José Ruiz-Shulcloper, Cuba
Gabriella Sanniti di Baja, Italy
Carlo Sansone, Italy
Ali Shokoufandeh, USA

XII   Organization

Patricio Simari, USA
Cees Snoek, The Netherlands
Domenico Tegolo, Italy
Massimo Tistarelli, Italy
Andrea Torsello, Italy
Francesco Tortorella, Italy
Stefano Tubaro, Italy
Andrea Vedaldi, UK

Mario Vento, Italy
Alessandro Verri, Italy
Alessandro Vinciarelli, UK
Kenneth Weiss, USA
Richard Wilson, UK
Marcel Worring, The Netherlands
Tony Xiang, UK
Ramin Zabih, USA

Additional Reviewers

Patrizia Boccacci, Italy
Moazzam Butt, Germany
Alessandro Crimi, Italy
Marco Crocco, Italy
Claudio Cusano, Italy
Nikolas De Giorgis, Italy
Efstratios Gavves, The Netherlands
Fabio Ganovelli, Italy
Laura Gemme, Italy
Andrea Giachetti, Italy
Stefan Guthe, Germany
Roberto Henschel, Germany
Jian Hou, China
Federico Iuricich, USA
Mihir Jain, The Netherlands
Giuseppe Lisanti, Italy
Zhigang Ma, USA
Francesco Malapelle, Italy

Farid Melgani, Italy
Pascal Mettes, The Netherlands
Sadegh Mohammadi, Italy
Nicoletta Noceti, Italy
Elisa Ricci, Italy
Stefano Rovetta, Italy
Marco San Biagio, Italy
Enver Sangineto, Italy
Alberto Signoroni, Italy
Fabio Solari, Italy
Marco Tarini, Italy
Federico Tombari, Italy
Philipp Urban, Germany
Sebastiano Vascon, Italy
Roberto Vezzani, Italy
Radu-Laurentiu Vieriu, Italy
Michael Waechter, Germany
Pietro Zanuttigh, Italy

Local Committee

Sara Curreli
Matteo Bustreo
Nicholas Dring
Carlos Beltran

Istituto Italiano di Tecnologia
Istituto Italiano di Tecnologia
Istituto Italiano di Tecnologia
Istituto Italiano di Tecnologia

Endorsing Institutions

International Association for Pattern Recognition (IAPR)
Italian Group of Researchers in Pattern Recognition (GIRPR)
IEEE Computer Society's Technical Committee on Pattern Analysis and Machine
Intelligence (IEEE-TCPAMI)

Institutional Patronage

Istituto Italiano di Tecnologia
University of Genova
University of Verona
Regione Liguria
Comune di Genova

Sponsoring and Supporting Institutions

Istituto Italiano di Tecnologia, Italy
Datalogic, Italy
Google Inc., USA
Centro Studi Gruppo Orizzonti Holding, Italy
EBIT Esaote, Italy
Ansaldo Energia, Italy
Softeco, Italy
eVS embedded Vision Systems S.r.l., Italy
3DFlow S.r.l., Italy
Camelot Biomedical Systems S.r.l.
University of Genova, Italy
University of Verona, Italy
Camera di Commercio di Genova, Italy

Acknowledgments

We kindly acknowledge Camera di Commercio of Genova for the availability of the conference location of "Sala delle Urla" in the Stock Exchange building and for the related services.

Contents – Part II

Contents – Part I

Shape Analysis and 3D Computer Vision

Biomedical Applications

Multimedia

Image Analysis

Learning Balanced Trees for Large Scale Image Classification

Tien-Dung Mai[1]([✉]), Thanh Duc Ngo[1], Duy-Dinh Le[1,2], Duc Anh Duong[1], Kiem Hoang[1], and Shin'ichi Satoh[2]

[1] University of Information Technology, VNU-HCM, Ho Chi Minh City, Vietnam
{dungmt,thanhnd,duyld,ducda,kiemhv}@uit.edu.vn
[2] National Institute of Informatics, 2-1-2 Hitotsubashi, Chiyoda-ku, Tokyo, Japan
{ledduy,satoh}@nii.ac.jp

Abstract. The label tree is one of the popular approaches for the problem of large scale multi-class image classification in which the number of class labels is large, for example, several tens of thousands of labels. In learning stage, class labels are organized into a hierarchical tree, in which each node is associated with a subset of class labels and a classifier that determines which branch to follow; and each leaf node is associated with a single class label. In testing stage, the fact that a test example travels from the root of the tree to a leaf node reduces the test time significantly compared to the approach of using multiple binary one-versus-all classifiers. The balance of the learned tree structure is the key essential of the label tree approach. Previous methods for learning the tree structure use clustering techniques such as k-means or spectral clustering to group confused labels into clusters associated with the nodes. However, the output tree might not be balanced. We propose a method for learning effective and balanced tree structure by jointly optimizing the balance constraint and the confusion constraint. The experimental results on the datasets such as Caltech-256, SUN-397, and ImageNet-1K show that the classification accuracy of the proposed approach outperforms that of other state of the art methods.

1 Introduction

This paper considers the problem of multi-class image classification whose goal is to classify an image belongs to one of the different pre-defined classes. It is one of the essential problems in computer vision because of many potential applications such as object categorization, scene classification, and semantic image retrieval [5, 6, 13, 14].

One approach to the multi-class classification problem is to use multiple binary one-versus-all classifiers [19]. However, this approach is not scalable to large-scale datasets (e.g., ImageNet [20] which includes 21,841 concepts with each of them associated with 1,000 images), because all classifiers have to be called at run-time for every image.

One popular approach to reduce the complexity is to use label tree [2, 6, 7, 15]. In a label tree model, label of a test sample is assigned by traversing its tree.

© Springer International Publishing Switzerland 2015
V. Murino and E. Puppo (Eds.): ICIAP 2015, Part II, LNCS 9280, pp. 3–13, 2015.
DOI: 10.1007/978-3-319-23234-8_1

At each node visited, a small number of classifiers are applied to compute scores to determine which branch to follow. This tree structure causes the classification complexity to grow logarithmically, rather than linearly, with the number of classes. The balance of the learned tree structure is therefore essential to the label tree approach.

Using label tree requires two tasks of learning the tree and learning node classifiers. Existing approaches [2,7,11,15] are either to separate or combine these two tasks in one optimization framework. Although the combined methods usually have higher classification performance, they are too costly because node classifiers are trained multiple times until the algorithm is converged. In this paper, we consider the methods that separate the two tasks as in [2] and focus to the first task of learning the tree.

Given a set of class labels at each node (the root node contains all class labels, and the leaf node contains a single class label) and the number of branches k, the problem is to split these labels into k groups. There are two constraints: (i) confused class labels should be in the same group and (ii) the number of class labels of the branches should be equal. The first constraint is to reduce the tree loss and to learn node classifiers with ease. The second constraint is to create the balanced tree.

The popular method is to use clustering methods such as k-means and spectral clustering [17]. For example, in [2], the confusion matrix is computed, and spectral clustering is used to recursively split class labels. Because the objective function of spectral clustering penalizes unbalanced partitions, it encourages balanced trees. However, this method is not reliable because it assumes the high correlation among the estimated confusion matrix and the real one. In practice, this assumption is not hold, especially when binary one-versus-all classifiers have poor accuracy due to small number of training samples and curse of dimensionality. Another method is to perform k-means clustering on training samples [16]. In this method, the mean of all feature vectors of the training samples of a class is used as representation for each class. This representation implicitly enforces the balanced constraint when using with k-means clustering. However, using the mean is not an effective way for classes with high variations.

We propose a method for learning effective and balanced trees by jointly optimize the balance constraint and confusion constraint. We avoid the unreliable situation when using confusion matrix and single feature vector for class representation described above by using all feature vectors of the training samples in each class. We formulate the learning process in an optimization framework in which the balance constraint is solved using integer linear programming and the confusion constraint is solved using k-means clustering. We tested the proposed method on several benchmarks datasets such as Caltech-256, SUN-397, and ImageNet-1K, and the result shows the superiority over other state of the methods.

The rest of the paper is organized as follows. In Sec 2, related works are presented. In Sec 3, the proposed method is describe. The experimental results are presented in Sec 4. Finally, Sec 5 concludes the paper.

2   Related Work

Learning tree structure is one of the main issues of a label tree-based approach. In [2], Bengio et al. proposed an approach to learn a tree structure base on spectral clustering. The approach utilizes confusion matrix generated by applying one-versus-all classifiers to a validation set as affinity measure to split classes into disjoint subsets. Each subset is corresponding to a child node of the tree. Such splitting procedure is repeated recursively until the whole tree is created. This approach has several limitations. Firstly, to obtain confusion matrix, multiple binary classifiers are learned with one-versus-all strategy. It therefore becomes costly when the number of classes increases. Secondly, since the spectral clustering approach does not guarantee equal partitions, the tree structure can be unbalanced, which leads to a sub-optimal test efficiency. Thirdly, the similarity between classes may not be reflected correctly via the affinity matrix due to low accuracy of the one-versus-all classifiers. As a result, classifiers of child nodes which are learned by using the set of class labels split by the above spectral clustering may give incorrect prediction.

In [7], Deng et al. proposed an approach which jointly performs class partitioning and learning a classifier for each child node. The one-versus-all training step is eliminated. Learning the classifier weights and determining the partitions are formulated as an optimization problem. It is then solved by two alternative optimization steps. However, by allowing overlapping of classes among child nodes to reduce false navigation, it at the same time increases the test cost thus cannot ensure a desired speedup.

Liu et al. in [15] proposed a probabilistic approach for learning tree structure. Each node of the probabilistic label tree is associated with a categorical probability distribution and a maximum likelihood classifier defined as a multinomial logistic regression model. Training process at each node is formulated as a maximum optimization of a log likelihood function which is then solved by using alternating convex optimization. Firstly, the maximum likelihood classifiers are learned based on the categorical distribution of each child node. Then, the categorical distribution associated with each child node is learned.

There are other solutions introduced for reducing the number of classifiers such as ECOC-based methods [1,4,8,9,18]. They mainly involve designing an optimal coding matrix which requires a small number of bits for efficiency, good row and column separation for robustness, and high accurate bit predictors. Sparse random codes and random codes described in [1,8] require a large number of bit predictors ($15.log(N)$ and $10.log(N)$ respectively where N is the number of classes) to achieve a reasonable accuracy. However, it is shown in [19], the accuracy of these methods is worse than that of the one-versus-all approach. Spectral ECOC [24] is based on spectral decomposition on the normalized Laplacians of the similarity graph of the classes. The resulting eigenvectors are used to define partitions. Because it uses one-versus-one classifiers to generate the similarity matrix, it is not scalable for classification problems with large number of classes. Recently, Sparse Output Coding (SpOC) [25] is a new encoding and decoding scheme that learns coding matrix and bit predictor separately but still has good balance between error-correcting ability and bit prediction accuracy. However, it uses a predefined class taxonomy to build a semantic relatedness matrix for the both stages.

3   Learning a Balanced Tree for Image Classification

3.1   Overview of Label Tree

Following the definition in [2,7], a set of class labels $L = \{1, ..., C\}$ are organized into a label tree $T = (V, E)$ with a set of nodes V and a set of edges E. Each node $v \in V$ is associated with a set of class labels $l(v) \subseteq L$ that indicates information about class belonging to node v and a set of children $\sigma(v) \subset V$. Note, a set of class labels of the root node contains all classes $l(v = root) = L$ and a set of class labels of a leaf node only contains one class $l(v = leaf) \subseteq L, |l(v = leaf)| = 1$. The edges connect each node $v \in V$ to a set of children $\sigma(v)$.

To make a branching decision at a node v, we train $|\sigma(v)|$ one-versus-all classifiers corresponding to its child nodes.

To classify the class of a test image x in the label tree, starting from the root node, classifiers are applied to the feature vector of x to determine response values. The child node which takes the largest value will be selected to go on. This process is then repeated until a leaf node is reached. The test image is classified into the class whose label associated with this leaf node. Since we only need to evaluate classifiers of nodes along the path from the root to a leaf node, the testing complexity is sub-linear. If the tree is balanced, the complexity is the logarithm of the number of classes.

Following the notation in [7], we use $T_{Q,H}$ to denote a label tree having Q children for each non-leaf node and maximum depth H. Depth of each node is defined as the maximum distance to the root (the root has the depth 0). These two parameters should be set so that the tree structure is balanced and Q^H approximate the number of classes

3.2   The Proposed Approach

In order to create a balanced label tree, the number of class labels in each child node, which have the same parent node, need to approximate each others. For example, if node v has N class labels and we want to split them into Q child nodes. Each child node has the maximum T_{max} class labels. The value of T_{max} can be calculated with the following formula:

$$T_{max} = Q^{H-1} \tag{1}$$

where, $H = \log_Q(N)$ is maximum level. For example, if the node v has $N = 1000$ class labels and $Q = 32$, we obtain $T_{max} = 32$.

Let matrix $S_{N \times Q}$ contains splitting information of N class labels as they are split into Q children nodes. The value of $S_{i,j}$ means:

$$S_{i,j} = \begin{cases} 1, & \text{if } i^{th} \text{class belong to} j^{th} \text{child node} \\ 0, & \text{otherwise} \end{cases} \tag{2}$$

Since a class only belong to one child node, we have:

$$\sum_{i=1}^{Q} S_{i,j} = 1 \tag{3}$$

In addition, the constrain which each node has maximum T_{max} class labels can be represented as:

$$\sum_{j=1}^{N} S_{i,j} \leq T_{max} \tag{4}$$

We follow the main idea of k-means algorithm, let $F_{N \times Q}$ be a matrix with $F_{i,j}$ to be the average distance from all images of class i to the center of cluster j. Each cluster is corresponding to a child node. If class i belongs to cluster j, the value of $F_{i,j}$ is minimized. This implies that the sum of average distance of classes belongs to $\ell(j)$ must to be minimized.

$$\min_{\ell(j)} \sum_{i \in \ell(j)} F_{i,j} \tag{5}$$

In general, we find values $S_{i,j}$ so that the sum of average distances between all images of classes and its nearest cluster center is minimized.

$$\min_{S,F} \sum_{i=1}^{N} \sum_{j=1}^{Q} S_{i,j} \cdot F_{i,j} \tag{6}$$

subject to the constraints (3) and (4).

The problem (6) is a minimum optimization problem with two variables S and F. It can be solved by using two alternating convex optimizations. In the first step, F is fixed, the problem (6) can be regraded as an integer linear programming problem subject to the constraints (2), (3) and (4), where S represents the integer variable to be determined, F are coefficients. Next, S is fixed, we update the cluster centers of classes which correspond to the non-zero values in columns of S, then we can obtain F by calculating the average distance from all images to these centers. This optimization can be repeated with a fixed number of iterations t (in our implementation, we set $t = 5$) or repeated until the solution is converged.

We summarize the algorithm for splitting set of class labels at node in Algorithm 1.

4 Experiments

4.1 Datasets

We conduct experiments on several benchmark datasets including Caltech-256 [12], SUN-397 [23] and ImageNet-1K [20]. These datasets are widely used to evaluate both hierarchy-based and flat-based approaches for large-scale image classification.

Algorithm 1. Splitting set of class labels $\ell(v)$ into Q child nodes

---

Input: $X = \{(x_i, y_i)\}, \cup y_i = \ell(v), |\ell(v)| = N$: the set of training images
   Q: the number of child nodes.
   t: the fixed number of iterations
Output: The class label sets of Q child nodes.

1. Initialize: Compute the mean of all feature vectors of the training images of a class, namely, $\bar{X}$. And then, use k-means algorithm for clustering $\bar{X}$ into Q clusters with centers C_Q: $C_Q = k\text{-means}(X, Q)$.
2. For each class, compute averge distance from all feature vectors of the training images to centers C_Q. We obtain $F_{N \times Q} = ave\_distance(X, C_Q)$.
3. Fix F, solve (6) for S and update centers C_Q
4. Repeat step 2 until (6) convergence or a specified number of iterations t is reached.

- **Caltech-256** [12] dataset. This is a multi-class object recognition dataset with 29,780 images of 256 classes. Each class contains at least 80 images of varying size and quality. Most of classes are relatively independent of one another.

- **SUN-397** [23] dataset. This is a scene classification dataset. It contains 108,754 images of 397 classes well-sampled from 908 scene classes of the SUN dataset. There are at least 100 images per class.

- **ImageNet-1K** or ILSVRC2010 [20] is a subset of ImageNet. It provides images of 1,000 classes, separated into three parts. The first part is a set of 1,261,406 images for training (at least 668 images per class). The second part includes 50,000 images for validation (50 images per class). And, the third part contains 150,000 images for testing (150 images per class).

4.2   Experimental Setting

With Caltech-256 and SUN-397, we split the original dataset into three disjoint subsets as following: 50% of images are for training, 25% of images for validation, and the last 25% of images are for testing. With ImageNet-1K, we use the provided image sets for validation and testing. We randomly pick 100 images of each class for training.

For each image, we extract dense SIFT features using VLFeat toolbox [21]. These features are then encoded using LLC encoding approach [22] with two level spatial pyramid (1 × 1 and 2 × 2 grids) [13] for pooling. Using a codebook with 10,000 visual words, we obtain a 50,000 dimensional feature vector for each image. LIBLINEAR (version 1.96) library [10] is used for training linear SVM classifiers with one-versus-all strategy.

We re-implemented the approaches proposed by Liu et al. [16] and Bengio et al. [2] as a base-line for comparison. Specially, [2] is considered as the original label tree based learning approach. First, we train n classifiers independently with one-versus-all strategy. We then apply these classifiers on a validation set to obtain a confusion matrix C. For each node v of the tree, we obtain a matrix $A = \frac{1}{2}(\bar{C} + \bar{C}^T)$ with $\bar{C}_{i,j} = C_{\ell(v)_i, \ell(v)_j}$. Regarding A as the affinity matrix, a standard spectral clustering is then used to partition the label sets between classes. However, since the objective function of spectral clustering penalizes unbalanced partitions, it might generate an unbalanced tree. In our experiments, we used the constrained k-means [3] instead of the k-means in clustering step to obtain a better balanced tree.

4.3 Evaluation Measurement

We employ standard measurements, global accuracy and test speedup [7], for evaluating the proposed approach and other approaches for comparison.

Global Accuracy. The global classification accuracy (Acc) is defined following:

$$Acc = \frac{1}{m} \sum_{i=1}^{m} fi(\hat{y}_i = y_i) \tag{7}$$

where, m is the total number of testing images and $fi(\hat{y}_i = y_i)$ is an indicator function. $fi(\hat{y}_i = y_i) = 1$ if the predicted class $\hat{y}_i$ is similar to the assigned class y_i of the image x_i; otherwise, $fi(\hat{y}_i = y_i) = 0$.

Test Speedup. Test speedup (S_{te}) is measured as the test cost of one-versus-all based approach divided by the test cost of the label tree based approach. Test costs are computed as the average number of vector operations (dot-products) required for classifying a testing image. If linear classifiers are used, the values of S_{te} can be defined as following:

$$S_{te} = \frac{n * m}{N}, \tag{8}$$

where n is the number of classes, m is the total number of testing images, and N is the total number of vector operations performed for classifying m testing images. A higher value of S_{te} indicates more efficient approach in terms of computational cost. It also means less number of classifiers evaluated on a test image to give the final class decision.

4.4 Experimental Results

Experimental results are presented in Table 1, 2, 3 corresponding to dataset ImageNet-1K, SUN-379, and Caltech-256 respectively.

    To obtain stable experimental results, we trained and evaluated the approaches with different subsets selected by randomly sampling images in classes. We then reported the average classification performance with the corresponding standard

Table 1. Comparison the performance of the evaluated approaches on ImageNet-1K

Approaches	Flat		T32,2		T10,3		T6,4		T4,5	
	Acc%	S_{te}	Acc%	S_{te}	Acc%	S_{te}	Acc%	S_{te}	Acc%	S_{te}
Bengio et al. [2]			7.22 ± 0.21	15.78 ± 0.03	5.20 ± 0.03	33.33 ± 0.00	4.61 ± 0.10	42.28 ± 0.20	4.05 ± 0.06	49.89 ± 0.27
Deng et al. [7]			11.90	10.3	8.92	18.20	5.62	31.3		
Liu et al. [16]			12.12 ± 0.03	15.64 ± 0.01	9.73 ± 0.15	33.33 ± 0.00	9.39 ± 0.33	40.93 ± 1.56	8.68 ± 0.34	49.94 ± 0.22
Our approach			**13.14** ± 0.04	15.77 ± 0.00	**10.74** ± 0.07	33.33 ± 0.00	**9.85** ± 0.09	42.24 ± 0.9	**9.61** ± 0.13	50.06 ± 0.02
One-versus-All	26.01	1								

deviation. Moreover, the accuracy of multi-class classification using one-versus-all classifiers trained with LIBLINEAR [10] are also reported for reference.

We compare our proposed approach with other tree-based approaches proposed Bengio et al. [2], Deng et al. [7], and Liu et al. [16]. Each row of the table presents performance of one approach. Meanwhile, columns are related to tree configurations with different numbers of branches at a node and tree levels. For example, $T_{32,2}$ in Table 1 indicates a 2-level tree with 32 branches at a node. Note that the flat-based approach can be considered a special case of a tree-based approach. Given the number of level equals to 1, a tree becomes flat. And, the performance of a tree-based approach is strongly affected by the changes of tree configuration.

Generally, as we increase the number of level of a tree, the path from the root to a leaf node i.e. an individual class is lengthened. However, since the number of branches at a node i.e. the number of classifier evaluated at a node is decreased, the test speed up is significantly improved. But, this also results in accuracy drop. Tree configuration therefore can be adaptively selected to balance accuracy and computational cost for a specific practical need.

The essential conclusion can be drawn from the experimental results is that our proposed approach outperform other tree-based approach. At the same accuracy level, our approach is usually more efficient (i.e. higher Ste) than the other tree based approaches. Meanwhile, at the same speed up level, we achieve higher accuracy in most of the cases.

For example, as shown in Table 1, the average classification accuracy is significantly higher for the trees learned using our approach. For the tree $T_{10,3}$, there are approximately $10 * 3$ classifiers evaluated for a test image, so we achieved $1000/30 \approx 33.33$ speedup with the accuracy $10.74 \pm 0.07\%$. Meanwhile, the average accuracy of the approaches proposed by Bengio et al. [2], Deng et al. [7], and Liu et al [16] are $5.20 \pm 0.03\%$, 8.92% and $9.73 \pm 0.15\%$ respectively. As shown in Figure 1, the our method achieves comparable or significantly better classification accuracy at the same test speedup. Note that as we evaluate the approach proposed by Deng et al. [7], since it allows overlapping among child

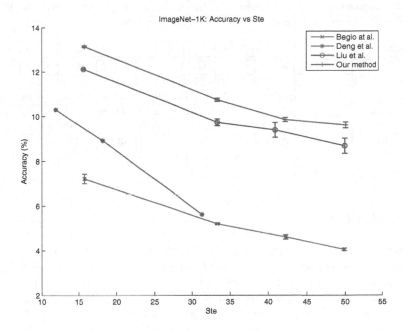

Fig. 1. Performance of the evaluated approaches on ImageNet-1K

nodes, it usually requires more evaluation cost at each level (i.e. smaller Ste in result).

Similar observation can be found in Table 2 and Table 3. The results in Table 2 show that for all types of tree configurations, our method achieves comparable or significantly better classification accuracy at the same test speedup on SUN-397 dataset. Table 3 shown the relationship between the average accuracy and the test speedup on Caltech-256 dataset. It shows that the better performance of our method compare to the others.

Table 2. Comparison the performance of the evaluated approaches on SUN-397

Approaches	Flat		T20,2		T8,3		T5,4		T2,9	
	Acc%	S_{te}	Acc%	S_{te}	Acc%	S_{te}	Acc%	S_{te}	Acc%	S_{te}
Bengio et al. [2]			30.86	9.96	25.76	17.28	22.83	20.83	15.91	22.70
			± 0.13	± 0.02	± 0.09	± 0.06	± 0.98	± 0.14	± 0.29	± 0.10
Liu et al. [16]			37.34	9.93	35.48	16.96	33.55	20.36	28.37	22.51
			± 0.27	± 0.00	± 0.37	± 0.08	± 0.55	± 0.41	± 0.92	± 0.02
Our approach			**38.32**	9.97	**35.87**	17.16	33.28	20.90	**29.46**	22.73
			± 0.41	± 0.01	± 0.57	± 0.04	± 0.28	± 0.14	± 0.31	± 0.07
One-versus-All	50.99	1								

Table 3. Comparison the performance of the evaluated approaches on Caltech-256. Our method achieves outperform accuracy than the others.

Approaches	Flat		T16,2		T7,3		T4,4		T2,8	
	Acc%	S_{te}	Acc%	S_{te}	Acc%	S_{te}	Acc%	S_{te}	Acc%	S_{te}
Bengio et al. [2]			31.79 ± 0.69	8.00 ± 0.00	27.56 ± 0.47	12.55 ± 0.07	25.47 ± 0.22	16.00 ± 0.00	22.87 ± 0.29	16.00 ± 0.00
Liu et al. [16]			37.13 ± 0.60	8.00 ± 0.00	34.07 ± 0.94	12.40 ± 0.09	31.69 ± 0.14	16.00 ± 0.00	29.15 ± 0.48	16.00 ± 0.00
Our approach			**39.13** ± 0.21	8.00 ± 0.00	**35.07** ± 0.16	12.70 ± 0.04	**33.02** ± 0.43	16.00 ± 0.00	**29.68** ± 0.68	16.00 ± 0.00
One-versus-All	50.95	1								

5　Conclusion

The label tree approach is an efficient technique for the problem of large scale multi-class image classification. We have proposed a method for learning an effective and balanced tree that jointly optimize both the balance constraint and confusion constraint. We compared our proposed method with other state of the art methods in experiments on the large datasets such as Caltech-256, SUN-397, and ImageNet-1K. The results show that our proposed method achieves the best performance among the methods.

Acknowledgments. This research is funded by Vietnam National University Ho Chi Minh City (VNU-HCM) under grant number B2015-26-01.

References

1. Allwein, E.L., Schapire, R.E., Singer, Y.: Reducing multi-class to binary: a unifying approach for margin classifiers. J. Mach. Learn. Res. (2001)
2. Bengio, S., Weston, J., Grangier, D.: Label embedding trees for large multi-class tasks. In: Advances in Neural Information Processing Systems (NIPS), pp. 163–171 (2010)
3. Bradley, P., Bennett, K., Demiriz, A.: Constrained k-means clustering, pp. 1–8. Microsoft Research, Redmond (2000)
4. Crammer, K., Singer, Y.: On the learnability and design of output codes for multiclass problems. Machine Learning (2002)
5. Datta, R., Joshi, D., Li, J., Wang, J.Z.: Image retrieval: Ideas, influences, and trends of the new age. ACM Comput. Surv. **40**(2), 5:1–5:60 (2008)
6. Deng, J., Berg, A., Fei-Fei, L.: Hierarchical semantic indexing for large scale image retrieval. In: The Twenty-Fourth IEEE Conference on Computer Vision and Pattern Recognition, Colorado Springs, CO, June 2011
7. Deng, J., Satheesh, S., Berg, A., Fei-Fei, L.: Fast and balanced: efficient label tree learning for large scale object recognition. In: Proceedings of the Neural Information Processing Systems (NIPS) (2011)
8. Dietterich, T.G., Bakiri, G.: Solving multi-class learning problems via error-correcting output codes. J. A.I. Res. (1995)

9. Escalera, S., Tax, M., Pujol, O., Radeva, P.: Subclass problem-dependent design for error-correcting output codes. PAMI (2008)
10. Fan, R.E., Chang, K.W., Hsieh, C.J., Wang, X.R., Lin, C.J.: Liblinear: A library for large linear classification. J. Mach. Learn. Res. **9**, 1871–1874 (2008)
11. Gao, T., Koller, D.: Discriminative learning of relaxed hierarchy for large-scale visual recognition. In: 2011 IEEE International Conference on Computer Vision (ICCV), pp. 2072–2079, November 2011
12. Griffin, G., Holub, A., Perona, P.: Caltech-256 object category dataset. Tech. Rep. 7694, California Institute of Technology (2007). http://authors.library.caltech.edu/7694
13. Lazebnik, S., Schmid, C., Ponce, J.: Beyond bags of features: spatial pyramid matching for recognizing natural scene categories. In: CVPR, pp. 2169–2178. IEEE Computer Society (2006)
14. Li, L., Socher, R., Li, F.: Towards total scene understanding: classification, annotation and segmentation in an automatic framework. In: 2009 IEEE Computer Society Conference on Computer Vision and Pattern Recognition (CVPR 2009), June 20–25, 2009, Miami, Florida, USA, pp. 2036–2043 (2009)
15. Liu, B., Sadeghi, F., Tappen, M., Shamir, O., Liu, C.: Probabilistic label trees for efficient large scale image classification. In: 2013 IEEE Conference on Computer Vision and Pattern Recognition (CVPR), pp. 843–850. IEEE (2013)
16. Liu, S., Yi, H., Chia, L.T., Rajan, D.: Adaptive hierarchical multi-class svm classifier for texture-based image classification. In: IEEE International Conference on Multimedia and Expo. ICME 2005, pp. 1190–1193, July 2005
17. Ng, A.Y., Jordan, M.I., Weiss, Y., et al.: On spectral clustering: analysis and an algorithm. In: Advances in Neural Information Processing Systems, vol. 2, pp. 849–856 (2002)
18. Pujol, O., Radeva, P., Vitria, J.: Discriminant ecoc: A heuristic method for application dependent design of error correcting output codes. PAMI (2006)
19. Rifkin, R., Klautau, A.: In defense of one-vs-all classification. J. Mach. Learn. Res. **5**, 101–141 (2004)
20. Russakovsky, O., Deng, J., Su, H., Krause, J., Satheesh, S., Ma, S., Huang, Z., Karpathy, A., Khosla, A., Bernstein, M., Berg, A.C., Fei-Fei, L.: Imagenet large scale visual recognition challenge (2014)
21. Vedaldi, A., Fulkerson, B.: VLFeat: An open and portable library of computer vision algorithms (2008). http://www.vlfeat.org/
22. Wang, J., Yang, J., Yu, K., Lv, F., Huang, T.S., Gong, Y.: Locality-constrained linear coding for image classification. In: IEEE Conference on Computer Vision and Pattern Recognition (CVPR), pp. 3360–3367. IEEE (2010)
23. Xiao, J., Hays, J., Ehinger, K.A., Oliva, A., Torralba, A.: Sun database: large-scale scene recognition from abbey to zoo. In: Computer Vision and Pattern Recognition (CVPR), pp. 3485–3492 (2010)
24. Zhang, X., Liang, L., Shum, H.: Spectral error correcting output codes for efficient multiclass recognition. In: ICCV (2009)
25. Zhao, B., Xing, E.P.: Sparse output coding for large-scale visual recognition. In: CVPR (2013)

Analysis of Compact Features
for RGB-D Visual Search

Alioscia Petrelli[1]([⊠]), Danilo Pau[2], and Luigi Di Stefano[1]

[1] University of Bologna, Bologna, Italy
{alioscia.petrelli,luigi.distefano}@unibo.it
http://vision.deis.unibo.it
[2] ST Microelectronics, Agrate Brianza, Italy
danilo.pau@st.com
http://www.st.com

Abstract. Anticipating the oncoming integration of depth sensing into mobile devices, we experimentally compare different compact features for representing RGB-D images in mobile visual search. Experiments on 3 state-of-the-art datasets, addressing both category and instance recognition, show how Deep Features provided by Convolutional Neural Networks better represent appearance information, whereas shape is more effectively encoded through Kernel Descriptors. Moreover, our evaluation suggests that learning to weight the relative contribution of depth and appearance is key to deploy effectively depth sensing in forthcoming mobile visual search scenarios.

Keywords: RGB-D visual search · Binary hash codes · Deep learning

1 Introduction

Nowadays almost any mobile device is equipped with an high-resolution camera and constantly connected to the Internet. This fosters development and increasing diffusion of a variety of mobile visual search tools, such as Google Goggles, Amazon Flow, CamFind, Vuforia, and WeChat Image Platform. A mobile visual search engine allows the user to easily gather information about the objects seen in the camera field of view. Purposely, she/he would just snap a picture to have the mobile device computing a representation of the image which is sent to a remote server and matched into a database to recognize image content and report back relevant information. Such scenario has been made real by the fertile research on mobile visual search [6,9,12] as well as by sensor miniaturization, which enables inexpensive integration of cameras into smartphones and tables. Alongside these progresses, the advances on 3D sensing have lead to the availability of affordable and effective RGB-D cameras, such as the Microsoft Kinect or Creative Senz3D, and, predictably, will enable depth sensing on mobile devices in the near future. Indeed, a number of solutions aimed at enhancing mobile devices with depth sensing capabilities do already exist. *Occipital* has recently released

V. Murino and E. Puppo (Eds.): ICIAP 2015, Part II, LNCS 9280, pp. 14–24, 2015.
DOI: 10.1007/978-3-319-23234-8_2

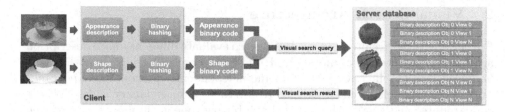

Fig. 1. Visual search architecture deployed to investigate on RGB-D features.

the *Structure Sensor*[1], a structured light depth camera that can be clipped onto a tablet. In [22], *Pelican Imaging*[2] introduced a camera array that captures light fields and synthesizes a range image, the camera being small enough to be embedded into next generation smartphones. The *HTC One (M8)* smartphone, released by *HTC* in 2014, integrates a 2-megapixel depth sensor and provides the *Dual Lens SDK* to foster the development of 3D applications on Android. Google has given green light to *Project Tango*[3], that is shipping to researchers and programmers a prototype tablet equipped with 3D sensing capabilities and up-to-date APIs. The foreseeable advent of depth sensing on mobile devices at a significant scale may pave the way to a new generation of mobile applications. In particular, we are interested in investigating on whether and how mobile visual search architectures may benefit of depth sensing capabilities.

A fundamental requirement of any mobile visual search architecture deals with compactness of the description sent to the server, so as to guarantee a satisfying user experience even in case of limited bandwidth or congestion of the network. Moreover, research on binary codes is not limited to mobile visual search but pertains the entire field of content-based image retrieval. As a matter of fact, compact and binary descriptors are key to efficient storage and matching in databases comprising millions of images. Thus, several approaches to either conceive compact image descriptors or compress existing ones have been proposed in literature [4,5,7,13]. However, research on compact representation has addressed only RGB images thus far. To the best of our knowledge, the only works that address compact description of depth information are [18], which is focused on 3D point clouds, and [19], which, instead, deals with RGB-D images. Both papers, though, propose local descriptors without addressing the issue of obtaining a compact global representation of the image.

To fill this lack, in this paper we consider next generation mobile visual search scenarios and propose an investigation on how to encode both appearance and depth information to obtain compact binary codes that properly describe RGB-D images. More precisely, within a visual search pipeline that allows to exploit both color and depth data, we analyze different image description approaches and carry out an experimental comparison aimed at evaluating their relative merits and limits.

---

[1] http://structure.io
[2] http://www.pelicanimaging.com
[3] www.google.com/atap/projecttango

2 Visual Search Architecture

Fig. 1 depicts the architecture we deployed to evaluate different image description approaches for the task of mobile RGB-D visual search. Given an RGB-D image acquired by a mobile device, the pipeline independently process the appearance and shape channels at client side, so to produce compact binary codes that are concatenated and sent to the server. Each binary code is obtained by a two step process that computes first a global encoding of the whole image and then creates the binary description through a similarity-preserving hashing stage. At server side, the received binary code is matched against a database of descriptions in order to find the most similar image.

2.1 Image Description

For global encoding of the RGB and depth images we considered the established paradigm dealing with aggregation of local features. Accordingly, local features are first extracted and described, then they are globally encoded through the *Fisher Kernel* [20] algorithm. Moreover, we considered an approach based on deep neural networks so as to address both hand-crafted and learned features.

SIFT: As a baseline local description approach we use SIFT[4] [16], which detects keypoints through DoG and produces descriptions of length $D = 128$. We apply SIFT on intensity images without any preprocessing, whereas depth images are rescaled in the range $[1, 255]$ reserving the 0 value for denoting invalid depths. As to isolate depths belonging to the searched object, we modeled the distribution of depths of database images as a gaussian, then we linearly rescaled depths falling on less than $2 \times \sigma$ from the gaussian mean and saturated all the others. Then, the *Fisher Kernel*[5] method is deployed to aggregate SIFT features into a global representation of the entire image. Fisher kernels has been introduced to combine the power of discriminative classifiers with the ability of generative models to handle representations comprising a variable number of measurement samples. The encoding vector is the gradient of the sample log-likelihood with respect to the parameters of the generative model, which, intuitively, can be seen as the contribution of the parameters to the generation of the samples. Perronnin et al. in [20] applied Fisher kernels to image classification by modeling visual vocabularies by *Gaussian mixture models* (GMM). In our setup, the parameters are the mean and covariance (assumed diagonal) of each of the N_G components of the mixture. Thus, global encodings have length $2 \times D \times N_G$. According to our experiments, best results are obtained with a number of components as small as $N_G = 3$.

Dense SIFT: To investigate on whether uniform sampling of features may turn out more beneficial than keypoint detection to visual search applications, we compute SIFT descriptors on 16×16 patches sampled across a regular grid. Then, densely computed descriptors are aggregated via *Fisher Kernel*. As $N_G = 1$ turns

---

[4] SIFT features are computed by the OpenCV implementation.

[5] We use the Fisher Kernel implementation available in the VLFeat library.

out here the best choice for the number of components, global encodings of RGB and depth images both have length $2 \times D$.

Kernel Descriptors: Given the excellent results reported on a variety of RGB-D recognition tasks, we have considered the *RGB-D Kernel Descriptors* introduced in [1,2]. Kernel descriptors are a generalization of descriptors based on orientation histograms, such as SIFT and HOG, which may suffer from quantization errors due to binning. Kernel descriptors overcome this issue by defining the similarity between two patches through kernel functions, referred to as *Match Kernels*, that average out across the continuous similarities between pairs of pixel attributes within the two patches. Local description is performed on patches sampled across a regular grid, with each patch represented by a 200-dimensional feature vector. Finally, local features are condensed into a global description by *Fisher Kernel* ($N_G = 2$). The authors propose 8 types of kernel descriptors by defining match kernels for different patch attributes such as intensity and depth gradient, local binary patterns and object size. In our experiments we used the C++ implementation made available online by the authors, which permits to apply 4 types of Kernel Descriptors. In particular, appearance information is described by kernels dealing with *Intensity Gradients* and *Color*, while shape information is captured by kernels based on *Depth Gradients* and *Spin Images*.

Deep Features: In [10], Gupta et al. address the problem of globally encoding an RGB-D image through a Convolutional Neural Network (CNN) architecture. Purposely, they exploit the so called "AlexNet" proposed in [14], that processes a 256×256 RGB image and can produce a 4096-dimensional feature vector as output of the last hidden layer. Besides describing the RGB image, the authors of [10] deploy the HHA representation to map the depth image into three channels: *H*orizontal disparity, *H*eight above ground and *A*ngle between local surface normal and inferred gravity direction. Accordingly, AlexNet is also fed with the HHA representation as if it were an RGB image. The authors ground this approach on the hypothesis that RGB and depth images share common structures due to, for example, disparity edges corresponding to object boundaries in RGB images. Moreover, the authors perform fine tuning of AlexNet based on HHA data. Our experiments indicate that slightly better results can be achieved by feeding the hashing stages with the 100 *Principal Components* of the 4096-dimensional vectors computed by both the RGB and HHA networks.

2.2 Binary Hashing

Among the several hashing approaches proposed in the last years, we considered the state-of-the-art *Spherical Hashing* (SH) method [11], which has been reported to result peculiarly effective on large datasets. Let N_b be the number of bits comprising the binary description. At training time, SH represents the data with a set of N_b hyperspheres and choose the value of the $i - th$ bit depending on whether the feature vector falls inside or outside the $i - th$ hypersphere. To determine the centers and radii of the hyperspheres, an iterative optimization process is performed so to achieve balanced partitioning of descriptions for each hashing function as well as independence between any two of them. We applied the iterative process on 1% of the training samples, such percentage turning out adequate to train SH. Furthermore, we do not exploit the *Spherical hashing distance* proposed in [11], as our experiments did not show any improvement with respect to the standard Hamming distance.

2.3 Matching

As illustrated in Fig. 1, the appearance and shape binary codes are juxtaposed to form the final binary code. This is sent to the server to be matched against a database of stored binary codes using the Hamming distance together with the weighted k-NN search approach introduced in [8]. To speed-up the search for the k-NNs, the server side database is efficiently indexed by the *multi-probe LSH* scheme proposed in [17].

3   Experimental Evaluation

This section reports the results of the experimental analysis we performed to determine the merits and limits of the considered features. For each dataset, we split the images so as to reserve a portion as the training set used to estimate the GMM required by Fisher Kernel, to find the principal components of the Deep Features extracted by the CNNs and to train SH. After that, we describe each image of the training set with the trained pipeline and build the index used in the server-side matching stage. Finally, we describe all the test images and calculate the rate of them correctly recognized in the training set. This procedure is repeated 10 times splitting differently the training and test sets and, eventually, the attained recognition rates are averaged. To compare the different types of features, we execute the pipeline by considering either the appearance information extracted from the RGB image only or the shape information extracted from the depth image only or we fuse the two kinds of information concatenating their binary codes (see again Fig. 1). For each configuration, we run the pipeline while varying the length of the final binary code from 32 to 1024 bits and plot the attained mean recognition rates as a function of the code length. In the case of kernel descriptors, both for appearance and shape description, we compute the two available kernel descriptors, perform the hashing separately and then juxtapose the resulting binary codes.

3.1   Datasets

The evaluation concerns 3 state-of-the-art datasets of household objects: the *RGB-D Object Dataset*, *CIN 2D+3D* and *BigBIRD*. The former two datasets share a two-level category/instance structure that allows us to evaluate our framework on both category and instance recognition tasks, whereas BigBIRD consists of object instances not partitioned into categories.

The **RGB-D Object Dataset** [15] is nowadays the de-facto standard for evaluating and comparing visual recognition systems relying on RGB-D sensing. For each of the 300 household objects composing the dataset, a set of acquisitions from different vantage points has been collected and segmented from the background so as to gather a total of 41,877 RGB-D images. Each object belongs to one of 51 categories based on the WordNet hierarchy. As for instance recognition, we chose the *Alternating Contiguous Frames* methodology [15].

The **CIN 2D+3D** dataset [3] consists of 18 categories, which in turn include about 10 instances each. The objects, placed on a turntable, have been acquired from 36 vantage points by rotating the turntable by 10°upon each acquisition. In [3], the authors propose a procedure aimed at evaluating simultaneously the ability to recognize both instances and categories. However, similarly to standard methodology defined with the RGB-D Object Dataset, we test the performance for the two tasks of category and instance recognition separately. Thus, for category recognition, we select a tenth of the instances for each category as test set and train the pipeline on the remaining ones. Likewise, for instance recognition, we split a different tenth of the views of each instance and uses it as test set whereas the remaining acquisitions are used for training. As suggested by the authors, we discard the "Perforator" and "Phone" categories from the evaluation as they do not include a sufficient number of instances. Instead, we do not aggregate "Fork", "Spoon" and "Knife" into the "Silverware" super-category.

The **BigBIRD** dataset [21] comprises 600 views of 125 object instances, including mostly supermarket products. The dataset includes quite challenging instances as most of them are box-shaped products recognizable only by their package textures, which sometimes are very similar (e.g. as in the case e.g. "pop secret butter" and "pop secret light butter") or distinguishable just due to color. As reliable segmentation masks are not provided for 11 objects (the majority of them being transparent bottles), we discarded them from the data used in our experiments. As the authors do not suggest a methodology to evaluate the dataset, for each of the 10 trials, we randomly select 100 acquisitions and split them so as to perform testing on a tenth of them and training based on the others.

3.2   Results

The results of our experimental evaluation are reported in Fig 2. Firstly, the charts reveal that an encoding based on SIFT keypoints (the green curves in the figure) is not effective within our visual search architecture as it provides the lowest recognition rates in all but the experiment dealing with appearance-only description on BigBIRD. Better results are scored by methods leveraging on densely computed local descriptors. Indeed, if SIFT is applied to patches extracted across a regular grid, the recognition rate raises substantially (red plots), especially in category recognition experiments (first 2 rows of the figure). Overall, the best performance are provided by representations based on Kernel Descriptors and Deep Features. Accordingly, in the remainder of the discussion we will mostly focus on these two approaches. We start by commenting the behavior of representations based on appearance information only (first column

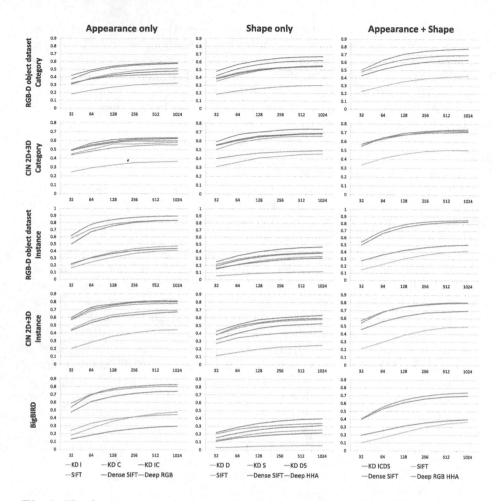

Fig. 2. The charts are organized as a table, the rows dealing with the different datasets and recognition tasks (first 2 rows: category recognition, last 3 rows: instance recognition) and the 3 columns reporting, respectively, the results obtained with appearance-based descriptions only, shape-based descriptions only and fusion of appearance and shape. Each chart reports the recognition rate as a function of the length in bits of the binary code. The different curves are identified by the legend underneath columns. Kernel Descriptors (KD) based on Intensity gradients, Color, Depth gradients and Spin Images are labeled as I, C, D and S respectively.

of Fig 2) and address the impact of the two types of Kernel Descriptors first. The charts report the recognition rates yielded by Kernel Descriptors based on either intensity gradients or color as orange and cyan curves respectively, whereas purple curves deal with the performance attained assigning half of the binary code to the former and half to the latter. In category recognition experiments, both Kernel Descriptors contribute significantly to the recognition ability of the pipeline, so that their synergistic deployment ends up in improving the recognition rate, as

Fig. 3. Examples of BigBIRD objects distinguishable by colour and texture only.

perceivable more clearly in the case of the RGB-D Object dataset. On the other hand, in case of instance recognition experiments, color seems the main cue that allows for telling apart objects in the considered datasets. This is particularly noticeable in the BigBIRD dataset, as deploying half of the binary code to represent intensity gradients turns out even detrimental with respect to spending all bits to encode color. This can be ascribed to the nature of the dataset that, as already pointed out, consists mainly of boxes and bottles distinguishable by color features only (a few examples are shown in Fig. 3). The comparison between Kernel Descriptors and Deep Features (the blue plots in the charts) highlights how, with the exception of category recognition on the CIN 2D+3D dataset, the latter approach provides quite consistently higher recognition rates.

As for the experiments addressing representation of shape information only (second column of Fig 2), it is unclear which Kernel Descriptor allows for encoding more effectively the depth channel between that relying on Depth Gradients and on Spin Image, which represented by the orange and cyan curves respectively. Nonetheless, it is clear that fusing the two contributions by splitting the code bits evenly (purple curve) does increase the recognition rates insomuch as to outperform Deep Features in 4 out of the 5 experiments. This vouches as the two types of kernel descriptors are complementary and thus the recognition ability of the pipeline can benefit significantly of their synergistic deployment. Looking now at the first two columns, it seems quite evident how shape is more relevant than appearance in category recognition experiments, the opposite being the case of instance recognition, appearance being definitely the primary cue to tell apart the different objects comprising the considered datasets.

The third column of charts in Fig 2 reports the recognition rates attained by exploiting jointly the appearance and shape information provided by RGB-D images. In the task of category recognition (first 2 rows), Kernel Descriptors (purple curve) provide the best performance whereas Deep Features (blue curve) turn out more effective in distinguishing object instances (last 3 rows). This can be explained by observing that Kernel Descriptors seem more effective to encode shape information that, in turn, is more relevant to the task of category recognition, whereas Deep Features better capture the appearance information that is key to effective instance recognition. In Table 1 we summarize the results shown in Fig 2 by highlighting the approaches providing the best performance when deploying either appearance or shape information only (first 2 columns). Furthermore, the last column of the table reports the configuration yielding the highest recognition rate when both kinds of information are available. In the

Table 1. Summary of the results reported in Fig 2. For each dataset and both types of experiment, the first two columns highlight the method providing the best recognition rate in case either only appearance or only shape information is deployed for image representation. Then, the last column highlights the approach yielding the highest possible recognition rate assuming that both kinds of information are available.

	Appearance	Shape	Best
RGB-D Object Dataset - Category	Deep RGB	KD DS	KD ICDS
CIN 2D+3D - Category	KD IC	Deep HHA	KD ICDS
RGB-D Object Dataset - Instance	Deep RGB	KD DS	Deep RGB
CIN 2D+3D - Instance	Deep RGB	KD DS	Deep RGB
BigBIRD	Deep RGB	KD DS	Deep RGB

case of category recognition, exploiting both appearance and shape information is beneficial as the best configuration involves the combined use of all Kernel Descriptors. Conversely, for the task of instance recognition, our evaluation suggests to simply discard the shape contribution for the available code bits would be best spent to encode the RGB image only by Deep Features. Puzzled by the above finding, we devised an additional type of instance recognition experiment, whereby the bits of the binary codes are no longer split evenly between appearance and shape but, instead, according to a varying ratio. We run the experiments setting the description length to 1024 bits (i.e. the lengthiest considered in Fig 2) while deploying Deep Features to encode the RGB image and Kernel Descriptors (Depth Gradient and Spin Image) to encode the depth image, i.e. the best approaches to represent appearance and shape respectively. In Fig 4 we report the obtained recognition rates: as expected, peak performance are reached with a high ratio of code bits deployed to represent appearance. Interestingly, though, the best performance are never achieved by allocating the totality of the binary code to appearance information, but, rather, by splitting properly code bits between appearance and shape. In particular, with CIN 2D+3D the best recognition rate is reached by allocating 1/4 of the binary code to shape, while

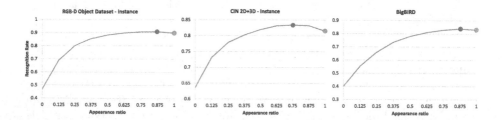

Fig. 4. Instance recognition experiments with a varying relative contribution of appearance (Deep Features) and shape (Kernel Descriptors). The horizontal axis indicates the ratio of bits of the binary code deployed to encode appearance. Accordingly, the performance of the best methods in Table 1 are denoted by blue dots (all bits encode appearance by Deep Features). The best recognition rates attainable by splitting code bits unevenly between appearance and shape are highlighted by red dots.

the optimal ratio is 1/8 for both the RGB-D Object dataset as well as BigBIRD. Indeed, a shape-to-appearance ratio of about 1/8 would provide better performance than disregarding shape with all the considered datasets. Hence, proper deployment of the depth channel associated with RGB-D images may contribute to improve instance recognition performance even in scenarios where texture and color provide the primary cues to tell objects apart.

4   Conclusion and Future Work

Our analysis on image features for RGB-D mobile visual search reveals that an approach based on Kernel Descriptors or Deep Features followed by Spherical Hashing can provide an effective and very compact image encoding. In particular, Deep Features computed through Convolutional Neural Networks seem the best choice to represent appearance, whereas shape information is better captured by Kernel Descriptors. In category recognition scenarios, both RGB and depth information contribute notably to ascertain the class to which a query object does belong. Instead, in instance recognition tasks, our experiments highlight how appearance features, like texture and colour, are key to tell apart the specific object instances stored into the database, whereas depth furnishes a limited, though still informative, contribution. Indeed, an approach based on simply juxtaposing the two representations does not take into account the different discriminative power that the two cues may convey in diverse scenarios. Hence, devising suitable strategies to learn and deploy the relative prominence of appearance and depth in diverse settings is among the key research issues to be addressed in order to leverage on depth sensing in forthcoming mobile visual search scenarios. We are currently investigating on a learning-to-rank approach aimed at deploying the weights provided by two separate k-NN classifiers associated with appearance and depth in order to better judge candidates according to the specific distinctiveness of the two cues for any query. The architecture has been ported on a *Samsung Galaxy Tab Pro 10.1* equipped with a *Structure Sensor* for the acquisition of the depth image. The pipeline, deploying the four types of Kernel Descriptors and trained on the *RGB-D Object Dataset*, spends, on average, 550 ms for producing the binary code and 2 ms to perform the matching.

References

1. Bo, L., Ren, X., Fox, D.: Kernel descriptors for visual recognition. In: Advances in Neural Information Processing Systems, vol. 23, pp. 1–9 (2010)
2. Bo, L., Ren, X., Fox, D.: Depth kernel descriptors for object recognition. In: Intelligent Robots and Systems (2011)
3. Browatzki, B., Fischer, J.: Going into depth: Evaluating 2D and 3D cues for object classification on a new, large-scale object dataset. In: International Conference on Computer Vision Workshops (2011)
4. Calonder, M., Lepetit, V., Strecha, C., Fua, P.: BRIEF: binary robust independent elementary features. In: Daniilidis, K., Maragos, P., Paragios, N. (eds.) ECCV 2010, Part IV. LNCS, vol. 6314, pp. 778–792. Springer, Heidelberg (2010)

5. Chandrasekhar, V., Makar, M., Takacs, G., Chen, D., Tsai, S.S., Cheung, N.M., Grzeszczuk, R., Reznik, Y., Girod, B.: Survey of SIFT compression schemes. In: International Conference on Pattern Recognition (2010)
6. Chandrasekhar, V., Takacs, G., Chen, D.M., Tsai, S.S., Makar, M., Girod, B.: Feature matching performance of compact descriptors for visual search. In: Data Compression Conference (2014)
7. Chandrasekhar, V., Takacs, G., Chen, D.M., Tsai, S.S., Reznik, Y., Grzeszczuk, R., Girod, B.: Compressed Histogram of Gradients: A Low-Bitrate Descriptor. International Journal of Computer Vision (2011)
8. Dudani, S.A.: The Distance-Weighted k-Nearest-Neighbor Rule. Transactions on Systems, Man, and Cybernetics, 325–327 (1976)
9. Girod, B., Chandrasekhar, V., Chen, D.M., Cheung, N.M., Grzeszczuk, R., Reznik, Y., Takacs, G., Tsai, S.S., Vedantham, R.: Mobile visual search. IEEE Signal Processing Magazine, 61–76, July 2011
10. Gupta, S., Girshick, R., Arbeláez, P., Malik, J.: Learning rich features from RGB-D images for object detection and segmentation. In: Fleet, D., Pajdla, T., Schiele, B., Tuytelaars, T. (eds.) ECCV 2014, Part VII. LNCS, vol. 8695, pp. 345–360. Springer, Heidelberg (2014)
11. Heo, J.P., Lee, Y., He, J., Chang, S.F., Yoon, S.E.: Spherical hashing. In: Conference on Computer Vision and Pattern Recognition, pp. 2957–2964 (2012)
12. Ji, R., Duan, L.Y., Chen, J., Yao, H., Yuan, J., Rui, Y., Gao, W.: Location Discriminative Vocabulary Coding for Mobile Landmark Search. International Journal of Computer Vision, 290–314 (2011)
13. Johnson, M.: Generalized descriptor compression for storage and matching. In: British Machine Vision Conference, pp. 23.1-23.11 (2010)
14. Krizhevsky, A., Sutskever, I., Hinton, G.E.: ImageNet classification with deep convolutional neural networks. In: Advances in Neural Information Processing Systems, pp. 1–9 (2012)
15. Lai, K., Bo, L., Ren, X., Fox, D.: A large-scale hierarchical multi-view rgb-d object dataset. In: International Conference on Robotics and Automation, pp. 1817–1824 (2011)
16. Lowe, D.G.: Distinctive image features from scale-invariant keypoints. Int. J. Comput. Vision **60**(2), 91–110 (2004)
17. Lv, Q., Josephson, W., Wang, Z., Charikar, M., Li, K.: Multi-probe LSH: efficient indexing for high-dimensional similarity search. In: International Conference on Very Large Data Bases (2007)
18. Malaguti, F., Tombari, F., Salti, S., Pau, D., Di Stefano, L.: Toward compressed 3D descriptors. In: International Conference on 3D Imaging, Modeling, Processing, Visualization & Transmission, pp. 176–183, October 2012
19. Nascimento, E.R., Oliveira, G.L., Campos, M.F.M., Vieira, A.W., Schwartz, W.R.: BRAND: a robust appearance and depth descriptor for RGB-D images. In: International Conference on Intelligent Robots and Systems, pp. 1720–1726, October 2012
20. Perronnin, F., Dance, C.: Fisher kernels on visual vocabularies for image categorization. In: Conference on Computer Vision and Pattern Recognition (2007)
21. Singh, A., Sha, J., Narayan, K.S., Achim, T., Abbeel, P.: BigBIRD: a large-scale 3D database of object instances. In: International Conference on Robotics and Automation, pp. 509–516 (2014)
22. Venkataraman, K., Lelescu, D., Duparr, J., McMahon, A., Molina, G., Chatterjee, P., Mullis, R.: PiCam: an ultra-thin high performance monolithic camera array. In: Siggraph Asia (2013)

Hierarchical Image Segmentation Relying on a Likelihood Ratio Test

Silvio Jamil F. Guimarães[1,2]([⊠]), Zenilton Kleber G. do Patrocínio Jr.[1],
Yukiko Kenmochi[2], Jean Cousty[2], and Laurent Najman[2]

[1] PUC Minas - ICEI - DCC - VIPLAB, Belo Horizonte, Brazil
{sjamil,zenilton}@pucminas.br
[2] Université Paris-Est, LIGM, ESIEE Paris - CNRS, Champs-sur-Marne, France
{y.kenmochi,j.cousty,l.najman}@esiee.fr

Abstract. Hierarchical image segmentation provides a set of image segmentations at different detail levels in which coarser details levels can be produced by simple merges of regions from segmentations at finer detail levels. However, many image segmentation algorithms relying on similarity measures lead to no hierarchy. One of interesting similarity measures is a likelihood ratio, in which each region is modelled by a Gaussian distribution to approximate the cue distributions. In this work, we propose a hierarchical graph-based image segmentation inspired by this likelihood ratio test. Furthermore, we study how the inclusion of hierarchical property have influenced the computation of quality measures in the original method. Quantitative and qualitative assessments of the method on three well known image databases show efficiency.

Keywords: Hierarchical image segmentation · Graph-based method · Statistical properties

1 Introduction

Image segmentation is the process of grouping perceptually similar pixels into regions. A hierarchical image segmentation is a set of image segmentations at different detail levels in which the segmentations at coarser detail levels can be produced from simple merges of regions from segmentations at finer detail levels. Therefore, the segmentations at finer levels are nested with respect to those at coarser levels. Hierarchical methods have the interesting property of preserving spatial and neighboring information among segmented regions. Here, we propose a hierarchical image segmentation in the framework of vertex-edge-weighted graphs, where the image is equipped with an adjacency graph, the cost of an edge is given by a dissimilarity between two points of the image and the cost of a vertex is the color information of the associated point. Therefore, the adjacency graph is represented by data structures in order to efficiently compute this hierarchy.

The authors are grateful to PUC Minas, CNPQ, CAPES and FAPEMIG for the partial financial support of this work.

V. Murino and E. Puppo (Eds.): ICIAP 2015, Part II, LNCS 9280, pp. 25–35, 2015.
DOI: 10.1007/978-3-319-23234-8_3

The first appearance of minimum spanning tree in pattern recognition for representing a hierarchy dates back to the seminal work of Zahn [19]. Lately, its use for image segmentation was introduced by Morris *et al.* [14] in 1986 and popularized in 2004 by Felzenszwalb and Huttenlocher [9], Noch and Nielsen [16] proposed a statistical method in which the merging order is similar to the creation of a MST. However the region-merging method [9,16] does not provide a hierarchy. Some optimality properties of hierarchical segmentations have been studied in [6,15]. New characterizations between MST and saliency maps based on quasi-flat zones have been studied in [8]. Considering that, for a given image, one can tune the parameters of the well-known method [9] for obtaining a reasonable segmentation of this image. A seminal framework to transform a non-hierarchical method to a hierarchical one has been proposed in [11] . Following a similar idea, we proposed in [12] a method for hierarchizing the approach proposed in [16] in which the image segmentation is formulated as an inference problem. In [5,17] were proposed methods, that can also be formulated as inference problems, relying on likelihood ratio test. In both cases, the regions are iteratively merged until a termination criterion is fulfilled. Unlike the method proposed in [5], a one proposed in [17] does not directly use the likelihood ratio test as similarity measure taking it as an enhancement for the merging evidence. Thus, the proposed predicate can be interpreted as a combination of consistency and similarity measures since these ones are computed from pixel values randomly sub-sampled in each pair of tested regions. The existent consistency tells whether the tested data belong to the same group, and it is measured by two hypotheses according to the sequential probability ratio test. Moreover, a Gaussian distribution model to approximate the cue distributions has been used in [17] instead of Kullback-Leibler divergence, which is used in [5]. Furthermore, the method proposed in [17] holds certain global properties, *i.e.*, by using the merging predicate the results are neither overmerged nor undermerged, which preserves the perceptual cues.

Even if the results presented in [5,17] are interesting since they have important statistical properties, the merging order is adaptive since, after each merging step, the similarity measure between all adjacent regions must be updated in order to identify the two new adjacent regions of maximum similarity value. Thus, in this work, instead of considering an adaptive merging order, we propose a hierarchical method in which the merging order (or order for evaluating the regions) is defined, a priori, by the weights of MST computed from the image. Unfortunately, the causality and the location properties are missing in [17] whether their two parameters (λ_1 and λ_2) are considered as scales, as can seen in Fig. 1. According to [17], the number of regions decreases when λ_1 increases, and the number of regions increases when λ_2 decreases, however these statements are not completely true as showed in Fig. 1. According to [10], a "scale" is considered as a true scale-parameter, when it satisfies both the causality principle and the location principle, which leads to work with a hierarchy of segmentations. In this sense, the method proposed in [17], so-called **SPRT**, does not produce a hierarchy of partitions.

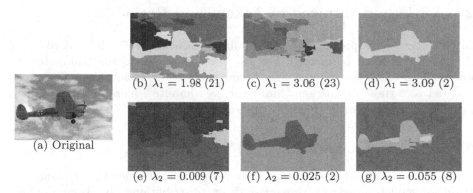

(a) Original

(b) $\lambda_1 = 1.98$ (21)   (c) $\lambda_1 = 3.06$ (23)   (d) $\lambda_1 = 3.09$ (2)

(e) $\lambda_2 = 0.009$ (7)   (f) $\lambda_2 = 0.025$ (2)   (g) $\lambda_2 = 0.055$ (8)

Fig. 1. A real example illustrating the violation of the causality and location principles by [17] in which the number of regions (in parentheses) is not monotonic, when the so-called "segmentation scale" increases. Moreover, the location of the contours are not stable in different segmentations. In first row, the parameter λ_2 is equal to 1 and in the second row, the parameter λ_1 is equal to 1.

The main contribution of this paper is the proposal of a similarity measure based on likelihood ratio test computed from a Gaussian model distribution in the context of graph-based hierarchical segmentation. Moreover, unlikely [5,17], instead of iteratively deciding whether two adjacent regions might be merged, we compute the scales for which the regions must be merged. Differently of [17], our method can be directly applied to the original image instead of computing on an over segmentation. Although, our method provides all statistical scales is more efficient than **SPRT** and according to our experiments the proposed method is statistically better, in terms of paired t-test analysis, than **SPRT**.

Furthermore, since our algorithm is a hierarchical approach, its result satisfies both the locality principle and the causality principle. Namely, the number of regions decreases when the scale parameter increases, and the contours do not move from one scale to another, as can be seen in Fig. 2.

This work is organized as follows. In Section 2, we present our hierarchical method for color image segmentation. Some experimental results performed on three well known image databases are given in Section 3. Finally, in Section 4, some conclusions are drawn and further works are discussed.

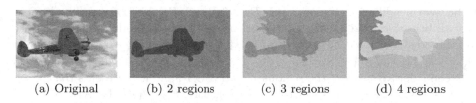

(a) Original   (b) 2 regions   (c) 3 regions   (d) 4 regions

Fig. 2. A real example illustrating the hierarchical segmentation obtained by our proposed method inspired by similarity measure proposed in [17] showing the number of regions. Moreover, the location of the contours are stable in different segmentations.

2   A Method Inspired by Likelyhood Ratio Test

In this section we present the (dis)similarity measure which is used to verify if two regions must be merged. We also propose a method that computes the low scale in which two regions must be merged without violating the likelyhood test between these two regions. Moreover, we compute a hierarchy of partitions providing all scales instead of only one segmentation.

2.1   Likelihood Ratio Test

The likehihood ratio test computed from two regions in which the Gaussian distribution model is used to approximate the cue distributions x has been proposed in [17], as follows

$$P_0(x|\theta_0) = \lambda_1 \exp(-(I_Y - I_{X\cup Y})^T S_I^{-1}(I_Y - I_{X\cup Y})) \qquad (1)$$
$$P_1(x|\theta_1) = \; 1 - \lambda_2 \exp((I_Y - I_X)^T S_I^{-1}(I_Y - I_X))$$

in which I_X and I_Y are the average color of the samples in regions X and Y, respectively, and $I_{X\cup Y}$ is the average value of the samples' union. θ is called hypothesis in which θ_0 is related to consistent regions and θ_1 is related to inconsistent regions. S_I is the covariance matrix of the regions, λ_1 and λ_2 are scalar parameters which could be considered as "scales" in the segmentation process. If each test is independent, the composition of the likelihood ratio δ is the sum of the individual $\delta_i = \log \frac{P_0(x_i|\theta_0)}{P_1(x_i|\theta_1)}$ for N iterations, in which N is the first integer for which $\delta \geq A$ (consistent regions) or $\delta \leq B$ (inconsistent regions). It is possible to see that the solution to the hypothesis is decided by the relationship between δ and a pair of upper and lower limits denoted by A and B, respectively. If δ goes out of one of these limits, the hypothesis is made, and thus, the test stops. Otherwise, the test is carried on with a new random sampling. Due to space limitations, more explanations are omitted here (see [17] for more details).

2.2   Similarity Measure

Before discussing about the similarity measure, lets remember some definitions. Let $A = \log \frac{1-\beta}{\alpha}$ be one value computed from two constants α and β, which are probabilities of the decision error and are set to 0.05 [17]. Let X and Y be two neighboring regions. Let $P_0(x|\theta_0)$ and $P_1(x|\theta_1)$ be two conditional probabilities for representing the Gaussian distribution model to approximate the cue distributions x. From Eq. 1, $P_0(x|\theta_0) = \lambda_1 \exp(-D_Y^{X\cup Y})$ in which $D_Y^{X\cup Y} = (I_Y - I_{X\cup Y})^T S_I^{-1}(I_Y - I_{X\cup Y})$ could be computed by the difference between color averages of the regions Y and $X \cup Y$, and it represents the consistency of region X with respect to Y. Analogously, $P_1(x|\theta_1) = 1 - \lambda_2 \exp(-D_Y^X)$ in which $D_Y^X = (I_Y - I_X)^T S_I^{-1}(I_Y - I_X)$. Considering that the parameters λ_1 and λ_2 control the coarseness (or "scale") of a segmentation, it is important to understand the influence of these parameters in the process. Moreover, we consider that the number of iterations, N, is equal to 1. Thus, without loss of generality, we fix λ_2, and the distribution of visual cues for producing consistent regions ($\delta \geq A$) could explicitly define the parameter λ_1, as follows:

$$\delta \geq A \tag{2}$$

$$\frac{\lambda_1 \exp(-D_Y^{X \cup Y})}{1 - \lambda_2 \exp(-D_Y^X)} \geq \frac{1 - \beta}{\alpha} \tag{3}$$

$$\lambda_1 \geq \frac{1 - \beta}{\alpha} \times \frac{1 - \lambda_2 \exp(-D_Y^X)}{\exp(-D_Y^{X \cup Y})} \tag{4}$$

Fig. 1 illustrates the missing of the location and the causality principles, for variation of both λ_1 and λ_2, which controls the so-called segmentation scale, and this shows the absence of hierarchical properties of the method **SPRT**. In fact, this work will look for a procedure to adapt the values of λ_1 according to the analyzed regions in order to guarantee that two regions are correctly merged. Then, the scale $Q_Y(X)$ of X *relative* to Y, which represents λ_1 when λ_2 is equal to 1, is defined as:

$$Q_Y(X) = \frac{1 - \beta}{\alpha} \times \frac{1 - \exp(-D_Y^X)}{\exp(-D_Y^{X \cup Y})} \tag{5}$$

Thus, the scale $Q(X, Y)$ for merging two regions X and Y could be written by

$$Q(X, Y) = \max(Q_Y(X), Q_X(Y)) \tag{6}$$

2.3   The Proposed Method

In this section we describe our method, so-called **hPRT**, to compute a hierarchy of partitions based on scales, so-called here *probability ratio scale*, as defined by Eq. 6. The main difference between this method and our previous work [12] is the application of a new measure based on likelihood probability ratio test. Let us first recall some important notions for handling hierarchies [4,6,7,14,15].

According to [8], for any tree T spanning the set V of the image pixels, to any map $w : E \to \mathbb{N}$ that relates a weight to each edge of T, one may associate the partition $\mathbf{P}_\lambda^w$ of V for a given threshold $\lambda \in \mathbb{N}$, induced by the connected components of the graph made from V and edges whose weights are below λ. It is well known [6,14] that for any two values λ_1 and λ_2 such that $\lambda_1 \geq \lambda_2$, the partitions $\mathbf{P}_{\lambda_1}^w$ and $\mathbf{P}_{\lambda_2}^w$ are *nested* and $\mathbf{P}_{\lambda_1}^w$ is *coarser* than $\mathbf{P}_{\lambda_2}^w$. Hence, the set $\mathcal{H}^w = \{\mathbf{P}_\lambda^w \mid \lambda \in \mathbb{N}\}$ is a *hierarchy of partitions induced by the weight map w*. Each element of a partition is called a *region*, and the *index* of a region A is the largest weight of the edges of the subtree induced by A from T. We also denote by $R_{\mathcal{H}^w}(x, \lambda)$ the set of all regions of $\mathcal{H}^w$ which contains x and whose index is less than λ. Our algorithm does not explicitly produce a hierarchy of partitions, instead it produces a new weight map L (scales of probability ratio values) from which the desired hierarchy $\mathcal{H}^L$ can be infered. It starts from a minimum spanning tree T of the gradient edge-weighted graph built from the image. In order to compute the scale $L(e)$ associated with each edge of T, after an initialization step, our method iteratively considers the edges of T in a non-decreasing order of their original weights w. For every edge e, the new weight $L(e)$ of e is initialized to ∞; then, for each edge e linking two vertices x and y the following steps are proceeded:

1. Compute the probability ratio scale s of e with respect to the current values of L:

$$s = \min\{\lambda \mid C(x, y, \lambda, L) \text{ is true}\} \tag{7}$$

   where $C(x, y, \lambda, L)$ is true if

$$\forall X \in R_{\mathcal{H}^L}(x, \lambda), \forall Y \in R_{\mathcal{H}^L}(y, \lambda), Q(X, Y) \leq \lambda.$$

2. Update the weight of e for L with the value s obtained at step 1:

$$L(e) = s.$$

Intuitively, the probability ratio scale at edge e corresponds to the lowest scale value λ such that we cannot find two regions in the current hierarchy (the one associate to L at the current iteration) which are linked by e and whose similarity is greater than λ (according to the similarity measure Q). Hence, the hierarchical probability ratio scale $L(e)$ is computed based on a minimization procedure related to the similarity measure Q on the set of all the possible pairs of regions linked by the edge e.

3 Experimental Analysis

In this section, we have done assessments in terms of F-measure and precision-recall curves by using six segmentation methods applied to three different image databases.

3.1 Compared Methods and Their Underlying Graphs

As mentioned before, we will compare our method **hPRT** that provides a hierarchical graph-based segmentation result with the original method **SPRT** [17] that provides a non-hierarchical graph-based segmentation result, even if in the original paper the method is presented as hierarchical, we have show that two features of hierarchical methods are missing, the location and the causality principles (see Fig. 1). We also compare the proposed method to **GB** [9], **hGB** [11], **SRG** [17] and **hSRG** [12]. The parameters of each non-hierarchical method are given below:

GB. This method depends on three parameters: (i) k; (ii) σ; and (iii) τ. The parameter k, which control the the so-called "scale" varies in $[100, 10000]$. Gaussian smoothing pre-processing with parameter σ, whose values are set to 0 (no smoothing). The area parameter τ, which is detailed ahead, is used to merge adjacent regions.

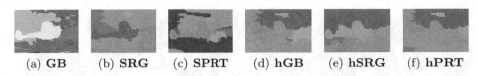

| (a) GB | (b) SRG | (c) SPRT | (d) hGB | (e) hSRG | (f) hPRT |

Fig. 3. Some results by using the compared segmentation methods (**GB**, **hGB**, **SRG**, **hSRG**, **SPRT** and **hPRT**). In order to compute these results, we consider the parameters that obtain the best F-measures for each method. Moreover, we illustrate the segmentations containing either 7 regions (easy for hierarchical methods) or as close as possible to 7 regions.

SRG. This method depends basically on the parameter q, whose values vary in $[2, 256]$.

SPRT. This method depends on two parameters, λ_1 and λ_2. In order to study the behaviour of these parameters, we tested two different configurations. In the first one, we fixed the parameter $\lambda_1 = 1$ and λ_2 varies in $[0.001, 5]$. In the second one, we fixed the parameter $\lambda_2 = 1$ and λ_1 varies in $[0.1, 10]$. However, to apply this method, a pre-processing is needed for produce a over-segmented image, in order to do that, we apply **GB** in which $k = 100$ and σ vary in $[0.1, 1]$.

For the hierarchical methods, we consider the most simple configuration by ignoring, for example, the smoothing pre-processing. In all cases, an area-filtering post-processing step with parameter τ, which is the ratio of the component size to the image size, is applied. The values of τ are set to 0.01%, 0.05% or 0.1% of image size. This post-processing is an important step since the order to analyse the edges is pre-defined and depends on the gradient values, thus small regions which contain elements with high gradient values could have high values of scales.

Before applying those methods, it is necessary to transform a given image into an edge-weighted graph for **hGB** and **GB** or into a vertex-edge-weight graph for **SRG** and **hSRG**. In this paper, we consider the following underlying graph. The graph is induced by the 8-adjacent pixel relationship, where each vertex corresponds to a pixel and each edge corresponds to a pair of adjacent pixels. Each edge is weighted by a simple color gradient: the Euclidean distance in the RGB space between the colors of the two adjacent pixels.

In order to illustrate some segmentations, Fig. 3 shows some results obtained by the compared methods. Due to the features of those methods, it was not possible to obtain exactly 7 regions, thus we present segmentations containing as close as possible the number of required regions. Fig. 4 illustrates some results using only the hierarchical methods. As can be seen, the two yellow flowers (center and right of the image) are better identified when **hPRT** is used since it is necessary only 4 segments (including the background) against 6 and 9 segments for **hSRG** and **hGB**, respectively. In other words, for this example, the proposed method is more robust than the others to obtain the single objects.

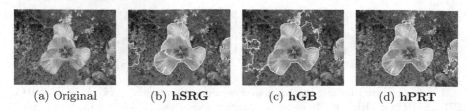

| (a) Original | (b) **hSRG** | (c) **hGB** | (d) **hPRT** |

Fig. 4. Some results by using the hierarchical compared segmentation methods (**hGB**, **hSRG** and **hPRT**). In order to compute these results, we consider the parameters that makes possible to obtain the yellow flowers (center and right of the original image).

Table 1. Performances of our method **hPRT** and the compared methods (**GB**, **hGB**, **SRG**, **hSRG** and **SPRT**) using Ground-truth Covering (GT Covering). The presented scores in (a) are optimal considering a constant scale parameter for the whole dataset (ODS) and a scale parameter varying for each image (OIS). In (b), the best method choice is presented with confidence interval for each pairwise comparison. See [3] for more details on the evaluation method.

(a)

Database	Method	GT Covering ODS OIS Best	F-Measure
BSDS500	GB	0.42 0.54 0.68	0.59
	SRG	0.51 0.57 0.68	0.63
	SPRT	0.45 0.52 0.57	0.57
	hGB	0.45 0.54 0.63	0.60
	hSRG	0.45 0.53 0.61	0.59
	hPRT	0.45 0.53 0.61	0.60
GRABCUT	GB	0.72 0.77 0.79	0.79
	SRG	0.71 0.75 0.77	0.74
	SPRT	0.72 0.76 0.78	0.77
	hGB	0.71 0.77 0.81	0.79
	hSRG	0.71 0.74 0.77	0.75
	hPRT	0.73 0.78 0.80	0.80
WI1OBJ	GB	0.67 0.75 0.78	0.75
	SRG	0.68 0.73 0.75	0.73
	SPRT	0.63 0.68 0.72	0.70
	hGB	0.64 0.72 0.76	0.74
	hSRG	0.64 0.70 0.73	0.71
	hPRT	0.65 0.71 0.74	0.73
WI2OBJ	GB	0.74 0.85 0.88	0.85
	SRG	0.78 0.84 0.86	0.84
	SPRT	0.73 0.82 0.84	0.82
	hGB	0.74 0.86 0.88	0.86
	hSRG	0.77 0.83 0.86	0.84
	hPRT	0.76 0.85 0.87	0.86

(b)

Database	Methods	F-measure for regions Confidence interval (5%)	The best method
BSDS500	GB x hPRT	[-0.0213, 0.00519]	equivalent
	SRG x hPRT	[0.0249, 0.0486]	SRG
	SPRT x hPRT	[-0.0397, -0.0163]	hPRT
	hGB x hPRT	[0.000872, 0.0171]	hGB
	hSRG x hPRT	[-0.0169, 0.000151]	equivalent
GRABCUT	GB x hPRT	[-0.0307, 0.019]	equivalent
	SRG x hPRT	[-0.115, -0.0145]	hPRT
	SPRT x hPRT	[-0.0582, 0.00445]	equivalent
	hGB x hPRT	[-0.0231, 0.0165]	equivalent
	hSRG x hPRT	[-0.078, -0.0147]	hPRT
WI1OBJ	GB x hPRT	[-0.0187, 0.0483]	equivalent
	SRG x hPRT	[-0.0286, 0.0237]	equivalent
	SPRT x hPRT	[-0.0534, -0.0112]	hPRT
	hGB x hPRT	[-0.0122, 0.0192]	equivalent
	hSRG x hPRT	[-0.035, -0.00269]	hPRT
WI2OBJ	GB x hPRT	[-0.0283, 0.0194]	equivalent
	SRG x hPRT	[-0.0396, 0.00904]	equivalent
	SPRT x hPRT	[-0.0517, -0.0149]	hPRT
	hGB x hPRT	[-0.015, 0.0219]	equivalent
	hSRG x hPRT	[-0.0407, 0.00103]	equivalent

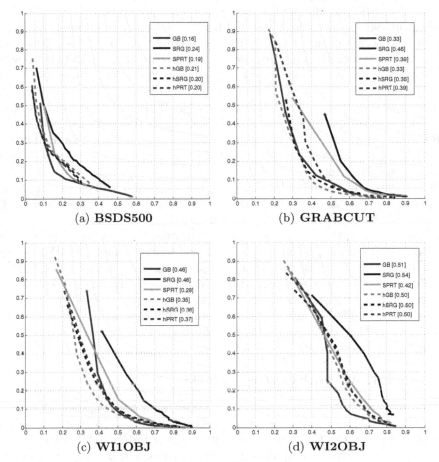

(a) **BSDS500**   (b) **GRABCUT**

(c) **WI1OBJ**   (d) **WI2OBJ**

Fig. 5. Precision-Recall curves for objects and parts computed on three databases. The curves represent the 5 (five) segmentation methods (**GB, hGB, SRG, hSRG** and **SPRT**) and the proposed method (**hPRT**). The marker on each curve is placed on the Optimal Dataset Scale (ODS). Moreover, the F-measures of the marked points on each curve is presented in brackets.

3.2 Databases

In order to provide a comparative analysis between several methods, we used three different databases: (i) the Berkeley Segmentation Dataset [13], called **BSDS500**; (ii) the database proposed in [18], called **GRABCUT**; and (iii) the database proposed in [1,2] which is divided into two groups – single and two objects – called **WI1OBJ** and **WI2OBJ**, respectively.

3.3 Quantitative Analysis

In this section, we assess the proposed method **hPRT** when compared to some other methods by using Ground-truth Covering (GT Covering) as showed in

Table 1. According to [3], the GT Covering of a segmentation S by a family of ground-truth segmentations $\{G_i\}$ is defined by first covering S separately with each human segmentation G_i, and then averaging over the different humans (see [3] for more details). Furthermore, we present the best method choice with confidence interval for each pairwise comparison. By using the F-measure, which is the harmonic mean of precision and recall, the compared methods are quite similar to the proposed one (as can be observed in Table 1(a)), however according to the pairwise comparison, the proposed method **hPRT** is always better than **SPRT**, and similar to other methods for all databases, except for **BSDS500** (as can be observed in Table 1(b)). Usually, the F-measure can be seen as a summary statistic of each method.

When the comparison is made by using the precision-recall curves for object and parts (Fig. 5), the method **hPRT** is better than or equivalent to **SPRT**. For other methods, test results are inconclusive for all databases.

In order to illustrate an example of computation time, we implemented our algorithm in C++ on a standard single CPU computer under OS X, we run it in a Intel Core i5, 4GB. For the image shown in 1 (a) (with size 321x481), the hierarchy is computed in 5 seconds, without any pre-processing. Considering that the method proposed in [17] is highly dependent on the number of regions in the over-segmented image, we present three different measurements: (i) for 722 regions the time is 3 seconds; (ii) for 1204 regions the time is 7 seconds; and (iii) for 2765 regions the time is 24 seconds.

4 Conclusions and Further Works

In this work, we propose a method for transforming a non-hierarchical method into a hierarchical one preserving the merging criterium, *i.e.*, all regions are merged according to the same probability ratio criterium. Differently of the method that iteratively computes the hierarchies and following our previous works, our method produces a weight map L (scales of probability ratio values) from which the desired hierarchy can be easily infered.

According to our results, the inclusion of the hierarchical property on this region merging approach solves the causality and the location problems which are missing in **SPRT** method, without prejudicing the quality of results, in fact, our method **hPRT** is statistically better than **SPRT** when F-measure is used for comparison, and equivalent for other compared methods in three databases and worst than **SRG** and **hGB** for **BSDS500**. Moreover, unlikely the original method, our hierarchical one is not dependent on the over-segmented image to produce the segmentation.

In all the tests performed in this paper, we filter out small regions at all levels of the hierarchies. This filtering step has a strong impact on the quality of the results, that deserves an in-depth study by itself: it is actually a transformation of the hierarchy, and as an operator acting on hierarchies, it has clearly some theoretical and practical properties. In future work, we endeavor doing such a study. Other items that sould be the topic of further studies are the robustness to noise, as well as the choice of a good hierarchical scale.

References

1. Alpert, S., Galun, M., Basri, R., Brandt, A.: Image segmentation by probabilistic bottom-up aggregation and cue integration. In: CVPR, June 2007
2. Alpert, S., Galun, M., Brandt, A., Basri, R.: Image segmentation by probabilistic bottom-up aggregation and cue integration. PAMI **34**(2), 315–327 (2012)
3. Arbelaez, P., Maire, M., Fowlkes, C., Malik, J.: Contour detection and hierarchical image segmentation. PAMI **33**, 898–916 (2011)
4. Beucher, S.: Watershed, hierarchical segmentation and waterfall algorithm. In: Proceedings of the 2nd International Symposium on Mathematical Morphology and Its Applications to Image Processing, ISMM 1994, Fontainebleau, France, September 1994, pp. 69–76 (1994)
5. Calderero, F., Marques, F.: Region merging techniques using information theory statistical measures. Trans. Img. Proc. **19**(6), 1567–1586 (2010)
6. Cousty, J., Najman, L.: Incremental algorithm for hierarchical minimum spanning forests and saliency of watershed cuts. In: Soille, P., Pesaresi, M., Ouzounis, G.K. (eds.) ISMM 2011. LNCS, vol. 6671, pp. 272–283. Springer, Heidelberg (2011)
7. Cousty, J., Najman, L.: Morphological floodings and optimal cuts in hierarchies. In: ICIP, pp. 4462–4466 (2014)
8. Cousty, J., Najman, L., Kenmochi, Y., Guimarães, S.: New characterizations of minimum spanning trees and of saliency maps based on quasi-flat zones. In: Benediktsson, J.A., Chanussot, J., Najman, L., Talbot, H. (eds.) ISMM 2015. LNCS, vol. 9082, pp. 205–216. Springer, Heidelberg (2015)
9. Felzenszwalb, P.F., Huttenlocher, D.P.: Efficient graph-based image segmentation. IJCV **59**, 167–181 (2004)
10. Guigues, L., Cocquerez, J.P., Men, H.L.: Scale-sets image analysis. IJCV **68**(3), 289–317 (2006)
11. Guimarães, S.J.F., Cousty, J., Kenmochi, Y., Najman, L.: A hierarchical image segmentation algorithm based on an observation scale. In: Gimel'farb, G., Hancock, E., Imiya, A., Kuijper, A., Kudo, M., Omachi, S., Windeatt, T., Yamada, K. (eds.) SSPR & SPR 2012. LNCS, vol. 7626, pp. 116–125. Springer, Heidelberg (2012)
12. Guimarães, S.J.F., Patrocínio Jr., Z.K.G.: A graph-based hierarchical image segmentation method based on a statistical merging predicate. In: Petrosino, A. (ed.) ICIAP 2013, Part I. LNCS, vol. 8156, pp. 11–20. Springer, Heidelberg (2013)
13. Martin, D.R., Fowlkes, C.C., Malik, J.: Learning to detect natural image boundaries using local brightness, color, and texture cues. PAMI **26**(5), 530–549 (2004)
14. Morris, O., Lee, M.J., Constantinides, A.: Graph theory for image analysis: an approach based on the shortest spanning tree. IEE Proceedings F (Communications, Radar and Signal Processing) **133**(2), 146–152 (1986)
15. Najman, L.: On the equivalence between hierarchical segmentations and ultrametric watersheds. JMIV **40**, 231–247 (2011)
16. Nock, R., Nielsen, F.: Statistical region merging. PAMI **26**(11), 1452–1458 (2004)
17. Peng, B., Zhang, D., Zhang, D.: Automatic image segmentation by dynamic region merging. IEEE Trans. on Image Processing **20**(12), 3592–3605 (2011)
18. Rother, C., Kolmogorov, V., Blake, A.: "grabcut": Interactive foreground extraction using iterated graph cuts. ACM Trans. Graph. **23**(3), 309–314 (2004)
19. Zahn, C.T.: Graph-theoretical methods for detecting and describing gestalt clusters. IEEE Trans. Comput. **20**, 68–86 (1971)

Large Scale Specific Object Recognition by Using GIFTS Image Feature

Hiroki Nakano[1(✉)], Yumi Mori[2], Chiaki Morita[1], and Shingo Nagai[1]

[1] Tokyo Laboratory, IBM Japan Ltd., Tokyo, Japan
{hnakano,cmorita,snagai}@jp.ibm.com
[2] Yokohama National University, Yokohama, Japan
moriyumi@ynu.ac.jp

Abstract. We propose GIFTS (Goods Image Features for Tree Search) which uses image local features for large-scale object recognition. Each GIFTS is a kind of keypoint feature. The feature vector consists of intensity deltas for 128 selected pixel pairs around the keypoint. By generating a KD-Tree from the GIFTS feature vectors of the training images and using the KD-Tree to search for nearest neighbor feature vectors of a query image, query times are on the order of $\log N$ for specific object recognition. We used the proposed method for book cover queries with 100,000 training images, had recognition accuracy over 99% with query times within one second.

Keywords: Object recognition · Local feature · KD-Tree · Augmented reality

1 Introduction

As performance and object recognition algorithms improve in computers, identification of various types of goods is possible using pattern recognition techniques. In bookstores, there is a strong desire to improve the efficiency of store inventory management by overlaying useful information (e.g. sales rankings and numbers of copies in stock) directly on book cover images by using tablet computers and without using barcode readers.

The authors propose a large-scale book cover image query system by using new image local features named GIFTS (Goods Image Features for Tree Search) to achieve query accuracy over 99% and response times within one second with more than 100,000 training images of books. By generating a KD-Tree (k-dimensional tree) from the GIFTS feature vectors of the training images of the books, searching for similar feature vectors in the KD-Tree, we confirmed that order of $\log N$ query time can be achieved even for huge numbers of feature vectors.

The paper is organized as follows: in Section 2 we describe the GIFTS image local features. Section 3 is about the large-scale goods image query system using GIFTS with the KD-Tree. In Section 4 we present and discuss our experimental results.

© Springer International Publishing Switzerland 2015
V. Murino and E. Puppo (Eds.): ICIAP 2015, Part II, LNCS 9280, pp. 36–45, 2015.
DOI: 10.1007/978-3-319-23234-8_4

1.1   Related Work

After the invention of SIFT image local features for specific object recognition by David G. Lowe [1], many image local features with high recognition accuracy were developed such as SURF with better computational time and PCA-SIFT with fewer dimensions in the feature vectors [2,3,4]. In contrast to SIFT-like image features using DoG (Difference of Gaussians), the ORB image local feature approach uses local corner characteristics, and the method drastically improved the computational times while maintaining the recognition accuracy [5]. However, the query times were still proportional to the number of training images. With more than 10,000 training images, computational times for query become impractical.

There are two query methods with query time that are not proportional to the number of training images. One is KD-Tree and the other is LSH (Locality Sensitive Hash), which uses a hash table [6,7]. The KD-Tree is suitable for the feature vectors with real number components, and LSH is suitable for the feature vectors with binary bit pattern components [8]. The proposed GIFTS feature vector has 128-dimension real number components, and so we used KD-Tree for the mapping of the GIFTS feature vectors. The average computational cost for queries with KD-Tree is on the order of Log N, where N is the number of feature vectors of the training images.

We found some published work using approximate nearest neighbor search methods for large-scale specific object recognition [9], but we couldn't find any prior work with recognition accuracy over 99% and response times under one second for 100,000 training images.

2   GIFTS Image Local Feature and KD-Tree

2.1   GIFTS Image Feature

A GIFTS image local feature has three components: keypoints, feature vectors, and distances for keypoint pairs. GIFTS uses oFAST (Oriented FAST) keypoints that are rotation- and scale-invariant local image features [5]. For scale invariance, we first prepared the images at eight scales, each separated by a scaling factor of $\sqrt{2}$. Then we classify 16 pixels on a circular ring of radius R around the center pixel. These 16 pixels are sorted into darker, similar, and brighter classes based on the differences in the gray levels between the center pixel and the surrounding 16 pixels. If the gray level difference is more than an experimentally determined threshold (i.e. 25), then the corresponding pixel is classified in the darker or brighter class. If 9 consecutive darker pixels or brighter pixels are found among the 16 pixels, then the center pixel is identified as a keypoint (see Fig. 1).

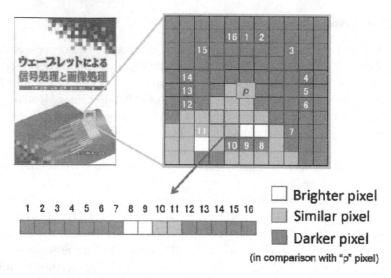

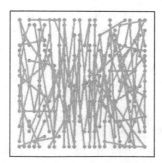

Fig. 1. GIFTS keypoints

To obtain the orientation of each keypoints, we calculate a gray level centroid for all the pixels within radius R. The offset of the coordinates of the centroid and that of the center pixel indicates the orientation of the keypoint. The intensity of the keypoint is defined as the sum of absolute values of the gray level deltas between the center pixel and the brighter or darker pixels in radius R. The intensity is used for selection of the strongest keypoints. We search the keypoints across 8 multiple resolution images for scale-invariance.

For the feature vector of each keypoint, we choose 128 pixel pairs in the rectangle of 31 ×31 pixels around the keypoint, and each component of the feature vector is the delta of the gray level of one of these pixel pairs. Fig. 2 shows the pixel pairs for generating the GIFTS feature vectors. The selection method is the greedy search algorithm described in [5].

Fig. 2. 128 pixel pairs for generating feature vectors of GIFTS keypoints

Here is how we select the 128 pixel pairs with the greedy search algorithm:

Step 1:

 Select 100,000 keypoints at random from the training image set. Calculate the variances of the differences of the gray levels of all of the pixel pairs in the 31×31 pixel patch around the keypoint. Select the pixel pair with the largest variance.

Step 2:

 Among the remaining pixel pairs, choose another pixel pair with the next largest variance and the absolute correlation with the already selected pixel pairs is less than a threshold.

Step 3:

 Repeat Step 2 until 128 pixel pairs have been selected.

By selecting pixel pairs using the test set of training images, the proper pixel pairs can be found for the object image set. In the paper [5], 256 pixel pairs were selected by using the binary differences between pairs of pixels. In our approach, 128 pixel pairs are selected by using the gray level differences of the pixel pairs. Thus we expect more accurate recognition performance with lower calculation cost compared to the approach in paper [5].

Each component of a feature vector is a 128-dimension real number, and the feature vector is invariant to in-plane rotation because we rotate the coordinates of the pixel pairs with respect to the orientation of the keypoint. For any coordinate set of 128 pixel pairs (x_i, y_i), we define the 2×128 matrix

$$S = \begin{pmatrix} x_0, \cdots, x_{127} \\ y_0, \cdots, y_{127} \end{pmatrix} \; .$$

Using the corresponding rotation matrix R_θ, we construct a rotated version S_θ of S:

$$S_\theta = R_\theta S.$$

The major parameter set for the keypoints and feature vector calculations we used (e.g. using surrounding 16 pixels for keypoint search and patch size of 31×31 pixels for feature vector calculation) are the same as the recommended values for the oFast approach in paper [5]. For the distance of two keypoints, we use the Euclidian distance of the two feature vectors after normalizing the magnitude of each feature vectors to the value one.

2.2 KD-Tree

The KD-Tree is the k-dimensional extension of a binary tree. By generating the tree structure from k-dimensional vectors, we can search for the nearest-neighbor vector of the query vector in the tree. If we use a KD-Tree, the average search time for a query image in the training images is of order of $M \times \log N$, where N is the number of keypoints of the training image set and M is the number of keypoints of the query image [6]. When the number of training images is 10,000 and the average number of keypoints for each training image is 1,000, the KD-Tree will contain 10^7 feature vectors. In the search phase, each keypoint of a query image is voted to the training image which has the nearest neighbor keypoint in the feature vector space. We take the training image with the highest rating that exceeds the predetermined threshold number as the search result. We use the FLANN library to generate and search the KD-Trees [10].

3   Large Scale Book Image Query System

In Japan, around one million distinct books are in print and on sale in bookstores. We generate several KD-Trees for the parallel processing of the divided training images. As the number of training images increase, we can add processor cores for the additional sets of training image. The design allows the target query time to be satisfied even though the number of training images increases. In our experiment, each KD-Tree handles 10,000 book cover images, and accessed by one processor core. In the query phase, we search the KD-Trees in all of the cores in parallel, and the training image with the highest score is regarded as the query result. We select the top n candidates because some of the images of book covers are quite similar to each other. Fig. 3 shows the system configuration. We assume the group of book cover images is G1, G2, ···, Gx, and each group consists of around 10,000 books in the same category from the same publisher. Thus we can select the search categories by enabling or disabling groups.

The computational steps are as follows:

(a) In the query server, the GIFTS feature vectors for each training image is calculated.
(b) KD-Trees for each training image groups is generated and stored in the memory of respective processor core.
(c) Users take photos of book covers with a tablet PC, and send them to the query server.
(d) In the query server, the GIFTS feature vectors are extracted from the query images, and matched against the feature vectors in the KD-Trees so candidate training images can be extracted.
(e) The results are sent to the tablet PC and displayed.

In this paper, the time from sending an image to the query server and receiving a query result from the server is defined as the book search time. This is from Step (c) thorough Step (e). The time between receipt of an image by the query server and return of the query result is defined as the query time, corresponding to Step (d). Fig. 4 shows an example of query results displayed on a tablet PC. The results include book names, ISBN numbers, number of copies available, and instructions for replacement in bookshelves. One of the advantages of using a tablet PC is the capability of displaying the results for several books at one time. Conventional barcode-reader-based systems don't have so much versatility.

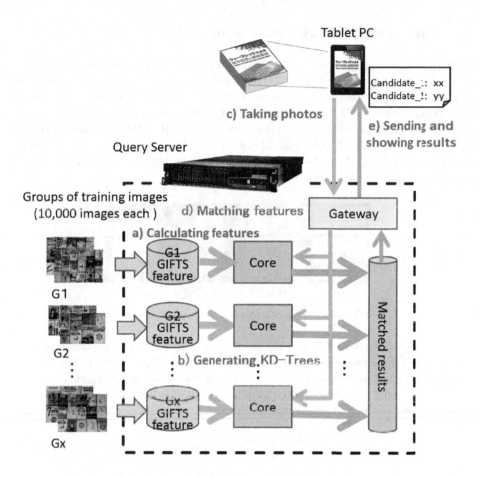

Fig. 3. System configuration

Fig. 4. An example of query results on a tablet PC

4   Experimental Results and Considerations

We measured the recognition accuracy and query times of the proposed method using
GIFTS features. We gathered 100,000 book cover images for the training images. The
sizes of the training images are between 120×180 to 300×450 pixels. We used an
IBM Power8 server (3.72 GHz, 20 cores, 512 GB of memory, running RHEL) for the
experiment. We measured the query times by assigning 10,000 book images per processor core. We prepared 1,000 query books, and each book cover has 4 images with
tilt angles of 0, 15, 22.5, and 30° (See Fig. 5). Thus a total of 4,000 images for the
book cover queries were prepared.

(a) 0°   (b)15°   (c)22.5°   (d)30°

Fig. 5. Examples of query images with 4 tilt angles

We registered the 100,000 training images and prepared the 4,000 query images,
and compared the recognition accuracies of GIFTS, GIFTS-2, and SIFT. The GIFTS-
2 version reduced the maximum number of keypoints per image (Kmax) to 300,
which was the only difference between GIFTS and GIFTS-2.

Here is our definition of percentage recognition accuracy:

$$\frac{\text{Correct queries}}{\text{Query images}} \times 100.$$

The query results consist of GIFTS (Maximum number of keypoints per image
Kmax: 1,000), GIFTS-2 (Kmax: 300), and SIFT (Kmax: 1,000) are shown in Table 1
and Fig. 6. GIFTS obtained over 99% of recognition accuracy when the tilt angle
between training image and query image is less than 22.5°. GIFTS obtained better
recognition accuracy than SIFT, but the average query time is inferior. In general,
GIFTS generates more keypoints than SIFT, so the query times are longer in proportion to the number of keypoints. With GIFTS-2 the number of total keypoints for the
training images is comparable to SIFT, and this results in query times about the half
of the SIFT times, while the recognition accuracy remains better as long as the tilt
angle is less than 30°. We believe that SIFT is less robust than GIFTS when a query
image undergoes homographic transforms, though SIFT is highly robust for in-plane
rotations and scaling [11].

Fig. 7 shows the average query time per each number of training images. The maximum number of keypoints is 1,000 for both the training and query images. We used 1
core for each 10,000 training images, so the 1000,000 images used 10 cores, resulting
in query times around 0.2 seconds. Fig. 7 indicates that the average query time of
KD-Tree is of order $M \times \log N$.

Table 1. Comparison of GIFTS, GIFTS-2, and SIFT (10,000 training images)

	GIFTS	GIFTS-2	SIFT
Max keypoints/image (Kmax)	1,000	300	1,000
Total keypoints	7,185,731	2,674,683	2,491,024
Average query time [sec]	0.148	0.044	0.112

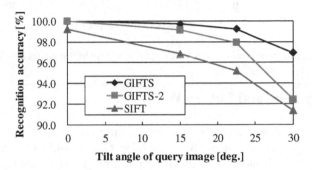

Fig. 6. Recognition accuracy against tilt angles of the query images

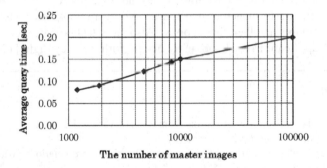

Fig. 7. Average query time by the number of training images (GIFTS)

4.1 Comparison with ORB

ORB is a well-known keypoint approach with high recognition accuracy and two orders of magnitude faster than SIFT [5]. Each feature vector of ORB is a bit pattern (256 bits), which it is suitable for LSH (Locality Sensitive Hashing). We also used the FLANN library for LSH. We measured the recognition accuracy by using 10,000 training images and 4,000 query images (Fig. 8). ORB showed over 98% recognition accuracy when the tilt angle is less than 22.5°, but the accuracy of GIFTS was superior to ORB. This may be because ORB creates its binary bit patterns for the feature vectors by binarizing the intensity deltas of pixel pairs. This means the intensity information is lost in the binary transformation. Therefore, ORB's recognition performance with similar book covers seems to be inferior to GIFTS.

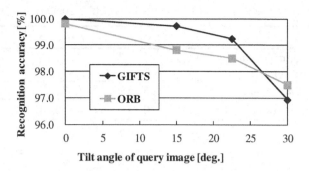

Fig. 8. Recognition accuracy against tilt angles of the query images (GIFTS vs. ORB)

5   Conclusions and Future Work

In the paper, we proposed a new image local feature named GIFTS for a large-scale book cover image query system. By combining GIFTS with KD-Trees, we could recognize images accurately and quickly. By testing the proposed system on book cover images queries with 100,000 training images, we correctly recognized more than 99% of the query images within one second. Our future work will include improvements of the performance in real-life operations in bookstores and applying the system to merchandise other than books. Also, this technology seems likely to be useful in such applications as shopping by people with weak eyesight [12].

References

1. Lowe, D.: Distinctive Image Features from Scale-Invariant Keypoints. International Journal of Computer Vision **60**(2), 91–110 (2004)
2. Ke, Y., Sukthankar, R.: PCA-SIFT: a more distinctive representation for local image descriptors. In: CVPR, vol. 2, pp. 506–513 (2004
3. Bay, H., Tuytelaars, T., Van Gool, L.: Surf: speeded up robust features. In: Leonardis, A., Bischof, H., Pinz, A. (eds.) ECCV 2006, Part I. LNCS, vol. 3951, pp. 404–417. Springer, Heidelberg (2006)
4. Juan, L., Gwun, O.: A Comparison of SIFTPCA-SIFT and SURF. International Journal of Image Processing **3**(4), 143–152 (2009)
5. Rublee, E., et. al.: ORB: an efficient alternative to SIFT or SURF. In: ICCV2011, pp. 2564–2571 (2011)
6. Arya, S., et al.: An Optimal Algorithm for Approximate Nearest Neighbor Searching in Fixed Dimensions. Journal of the ACM **45**(6), 891–923 (1998)
7. Andoni, A.: Near-optimal hashing algorithms for approximate nearest neighbor in high dimensions. In: 47th Annual IEEE Symposium on Foundations of Computer Science, pp. 459–468 (2006)
8. Muja, M., Lowe, D.: Fast matching of binary features. In: Conference On Computer And Robot Vision (CRV 2012), pp. 404–410 (2012)

9. Kise, K., Noguchi, K., Iwamura, M.: Simple representation and approximate search of feature vectors for large-scale object recognition. In: Proceedings of BMVC 2007, vol. 1, pp. 182–191 (2007)
10. Muja, M., Lowe, D.: FLANN: Fast library for approximate nearest neighbors. http://www.cs.ubc.ca/research/flann
11. Bekel, D., Teutschy, M., Schucherty, T.: Evaluation of binary keypoint descriptors. In: ICIP 2013, pp. 3652–3656 (2013)
12. Do, A.T., Ilango, K., Ramasamy, D., Kalidasan, S., Balakrinan, V., Chang, R.T.: Effectiveness of low vision services in improving patient quality of life at Aravind Eye Hospital. Indian J. Ophthalmol **62**(12), 1125–1131 (2014)

On Spatiochromatic Features
in Natural Images Statistics

Edoardo Provenzi[1]([⊠]), Julie Delon[1], Yann Gousseau[2], and Baptiste Mazin[2]

[1] Sorbonne Paris Cité, Laboratoire MAP5, UMR CNRS 8145, Université Paris Descartes, 45 rue des Saints Pères, 75006 Paris, France
edoardo.provenzi@parisdescartes.fr
[2] Télécom ParisTech, LTCI, CNRS, 46, rue Barrault, 75013 Paris, France

Abstract. In this communication, we show that two simple assumptions on the covariances matrices of color images, namely stationarity and commutativity, can explain the observed shape of decorrelated spatiochromatic elements (bases obtained by PCA) of natural color images. The validity of these assumptions is tested on a large database of RAW images. Our experiments also show that the spatiochromatic covariance decays exponentially with the spatial distance between pairs of pixels and not as a power law as it is commonly assumed.

1 Introduction

Two kind of redundancies characterize the interaction between humans and natural scenes: the spatial one, due to the fact that nearby points are likely to send similar radiance information to the eyes (unless they lie in the proximity of a sharp edge), and the chromatic one, implied by the overlapping of the spectral sensitivity functions $L(\lambda), M(\lambda), S(\lambda)$ of retinal cones. *Spatio-chromatic correlation* is the term used to define both effects at once.

While there is a large literature on opponent color spaces and it is also known that spatial stationarity imply the appearance of *Fourier-like structure* in the Principal Component Analysis (PCA), the spatio-chromatic structure of color images has been less studied. One of the most striking known empirical observation is that the spatio-chromatic covariance matrices resemble a tensor product between a Fourier basis and color opponent channels, as pointed out in section 2.

In this work, we focus on this statistical characteristic, both from a theoretical and an experimental perspective, proving that two simple assumptions on the nature of spatiochromatic covariance matrices of real-world images are enough to explain the appearance of the tensor product structure.

In this communication, due to space bounds, we will only discuss tests performed on a database of RAW images. Further results on a large database of compressed images, coherent with those obtained with RAW images, can be found in [9]. A longer and more complete version has been submitted to Vision Research.

Known results of second order statistics between pixel values are the *Fourier-like structure* of Principal Component Analysis (PCA), a result of *spatial stationarity*, and the *power-law decay* of the covariance, as a possible consequence of *scale-invariance*. Higher order statistics have also been largely investigated, for instance through wavelets or sparse coding.

On the other hand, several works have been concerned with chromatic redundancy in images, mostly through second order property and in connection with opponent color spaces.

However, the spatio-chromatic structure of color images has been less studied. One of the most striking known empirical observation is that the spatio-chromatic covariance matrices resemble a tensor product between a Fourier basis and color opponent channels, as pointed out in section 2.

In this work, we focus on this statistical characteristic, both from a theoretical and an experimental perspective, proving that two simple assumptions on the nature of spatiochromatic covariance matrices of real-world images are enough to explain the reason for the appearance of the tensor product structure.

In order to have a better perspective on this result, we will first start by recalling the most relevant results of second order natural image statistics related to this work.

2   Previous Studies on Spatial and Chromatic Natural Color Image Statistics

The literature about natural image statistics is vast and its exhaustive presentation is far beyond the scope of this paper. Here we will emphasize only the results from [2] and from [12], which are essential to understand our results.

2.1   Chromatic Redundancy in Natural Images

Buchsbaum and Gottshalk approached in [2] the problem of finding uncorrelated color features from a purely theoretical point of view.

They considered the abstract ensemble of all possible visual stimuli (radiances), i.e. $S \equiv \{S(\lambda),\ \lambda \in \mathcal{L}\}$, where $\mathcal{L}$ is the spectrum of visible wavelengths, and built the three cone activation values as follows: $L = \int_{\mathcal{L}} S(\lambda)L(\lambda)\, d\lambda$, $M = \int_{\mathcal{L}} S(\lambda)M(\lambda)\, d\lambda$, $S = \int_{\mathcal{L}} S(\lambda)S(\lambda)\, d\lambda$.

Assuming that the stimulus $S(\lambda)$ (coming from a fixed point $\bar{x}$ of a scene) is a random variable, the *chromatic covariance matrix* associated to the three random variables L, M, S is:

$$C = \begin{bmatrix} C_{LL} & C_{LM} & C_{LS} \\ C_{ML} & C_{MM} & C_{MS} \\ C_{SL} & C_{SM} & C_{SS} \end{bmatrix}, \tag{1}$$

where $C_{LL} \equiv \mathbb{E}[L \cdot L] - (\mathbb{E}[L])^2$, $C_{LM} \equiv \mathbb{E}[L \cdot M] - \mathbb{E}[L]\mathbb{E}[M] = C_{ML}$, and so on, $\mathbb{E}$ being the expectation operator.

Let $K(\lambda, \mu) = \mathbb{E}[S(\lambda)S(\mu)] - \mathbb{E}[S(\lambda)] \cdot \mathbb{E}[S(\mu)]$ be the *covariance function*, then $C_{LL} = \iint_{\mathcal{L}^2} K(\lambda, \mu) L(\lambda) L(\mu) \, d\lambda d\mu$, and so on. To be able to perform explicit calculations, the analytical form of $K(\lambda, \mu)$ must be specified. In the absence of a database of multispectral images, Buchsbaum and Gottschalk used abstract non-realistic data to compute $K(\lambda, \mu)$. They chose the easiest covariance function corresponding to monochromatic visual stimuli, i.e. $K(\lambda, \mu) = \delta(\lambda - \mu)$, δ being the Dirac distribution.

With this choice, the entries of the covariance matrix C are all positives and they can be written as $C_{LL} = \int_{\mathcal{L}} L^2(\lambda) \, d\lambda$, $C_{LM} = \int_{\mathcal{L}} L(\lambda) M(\lambda) \, d\lambda$, and so on. C is also real and symmetric, so it has three positive eigenvalues $\lambda_1 \geq \lambda_2 \geq \lambda_3$ with corresponding eigenvectors $\mathbf{v}_i$, $i = 1, 2, 3$. If W is the matrix whose columns are the eigenvectors of C, i.e. $W = [\mathbf{v}_1 | \mathbf{v}_2 | \mathbf{v}_3]$, then the diagonalization of C is given by $\Lambda = W^t C W = \mathrm{diag}(\lambda_1, \lambda_2, \lambda_3)$.

The eigenvector transformation of the cone excitation values L, M, S, in the special case of monochromatic stimuli, is then

$$\begin{pmatrix} A(\lambda) \\ P(\lambda) \\ Q(\lambda) \end{pmatrix} = W^t \begin{pmatrix} L(\lambda) \\ M(\lambda) \\ S(\lambda) \end{pmatrix}.$$

The transformed values A, P, Q are *uncorrelated* and their covariance matrix is Λ. A is the achromatic channel, while P and Q are associated to the opponent chromatic channels.

The *key point* in Buchsbaum and Gottschalk's theory is the application of *Perron-Frobenius theorem* (see e.g. [1] for more details), which assures that positive matrices, i.e. matrices whose entries are all strictly greater than zero, have one and only one eigenvector whose entries have all the positive sign, and this eigenvector corresponds to the largest eigenvalue, i.e. λ_1. So, only the transformed A channel will be a linear combination of the cone activation values L, M, S with positive coefficients, while the channels P and Q will show opponency. This is the theoretical reason underlying the evidence of post-retinal chromatic opponent behavior, following Buchsbaum and Gottschalk.

2.2 Spatio-chromatic Redundancy in Natural Images

The most influential paper in the analysis of spatio-chromatic redundancy is [12], where Ruderman, Cronin and Chiao proposed a *patch-based* spatio-chromatic coding and tested Buchsbaum-Gottschalk's theory on a database of 12 multispectral natural images of *foliage*.

The authors studied these LMS data built thanks to this database by first taking their decimal logarithm and then subtracting their average logarithmic value, building the so-called *Ruderman-Cronin-Chiao coordinates*, i.e. $\tilde{L} = \mathrm{Log}\, L - \langle \mathrm{Log}\, L \rangle$, $\tilde{M} = \mathrm{Log}\, M - \langle \mathrm{Log}\, M \rangle$ and $\tilde{S} = \mathrm{Log}\, S - \langle \mathrm{Log}\, S \rangle$. This transform is motivated with the fact that, following Weber-Fechner's law, uniform logarithmic changes in stimulus intensity tend to be equally perceptible, see [5]. Moreover, second-order statistics of log-transformed data is similar to that of linear images, see [11]. Instead, the motivation for the average substraction is to assess the data independently on the illumination level, analogously to a von Kries procedure (see [7]).

Following [12], if $\tilde{L}$, $\tilde{M}$, $\tilde{S}$, are the basis vectors in the logarithmically-transformed space, then the application of the PCA gives the following three principal axes $l = \frac{1}{\sqrt{3}}(\tilde{L} + \tilde{M} + \tilde{S})$, $\alpha = \frac{1}{\sqrt{6}}(\tilde{L} + \tilde{M} - 2\tilde{S})$, $\beta = \frac{1}{\sqrt{2}}(\tilde{L} - \tilde{M})$.

The color space spanned by these three principal axes is called $l\alpha\beta$ space.

To study spatiochromatic decorrelated features, Ruderman, Cronin and Chiao considered 3×3 patches, with each pixel containing a 3-vector color information, so that every patch is converted in a vector with 27 components that they analyzed with the PCA. The principal axes of these small patches in the logarithmic space are depicted in the figure at page page 2041 in [12]. The first principal axis shows fluctuations in the achromatic channel, followed by blue-yellow fluctuations in the α direction and red-green ones in the β direction.

The spatial axes are largely symmetrical and can be represented by Fourier features, in line with the translation-invariance of natural images, as argued in [3]. No pixel within the patches appear other than the primary gray, blue-yellow or red-green colors, i.e. no mixing of l, α, β has been found in any 3×3 patch. These means that not only the single-pixel principal axes l, α, β, but also the spatially-dependent principal axes $l(x), \alpha(x), \beta(x)$, viewed as functions of the spatial coordinate x inside the patches, are decorrelated.

These results have been confirmed by [8] and, in Section 4, we will perform similar experiments on much larger databases.

3   Relationship Between Second Order Stationarity and the Decorrelated Spatiochromatic Features of Natural Images

In this section we will analyze the consequence of second order stationarity in natural images on their decorrelated spatiochromatic features, by first considering gray-level images, where stationarity implies that the principal components are Fourier basis functions, then extending this result to the color case. The supplementary hypothesis on color covariance matrices will yields principal components given by the tensor product between Fourier basis functions and achromatic plus opponent color coordinates.

3.1   The Gray-Level Case

Let I be a gray-level natural image of dimension $W \times H$, W being the width (number of columns) and H being the height (number of rows) of I.

If we denote the H rows of I as $r^0, \ldots, r^{H-1}$, then we can describe the position of each pixel of I row-wise as follows:

$$I = \{r_k^j; \ j = 0, \ldots, H-1, \ k = 0, \ldots, W-1\}, \tag{2}$$

j is the row index and k is the column index. Each row $r^j = (r^j_0, \ldots, r^j_{W-1})$ will be interpreted as a W-dimensional random vector and each component r^j_k as a random variable.

Let us define the *spatial covariance of the two random variables* r^j_k, $r^{j'}_{k'}$:

$$\mathrm{cov}(r^j_k, r^{j'}_{k'}) \equiv c^{j,j'}_{k,k'} = \mathbb{E}[r^j_k r^{j'}_{k'}] - \mathbb{E}[r^j_k]\mathbb{E}[r^{j'}_{k'}]. \tag{3}$$

Due to the symmetry of covariance we have $c^{j,j'}_{k,k'} = c^{j',j}_{k',k}$. Then, we can write the *spatial covariance matrix of the two random vectors* r^j, $r^{j'}$ as $\mathrm{cov}(r^j, r^{j'}) \equiv C^{j,j'}$ and the *spatial covariance matrix* C of the image I, respectively, as follows:

$$C^{j,j'} = \begin{bmatrix} c^{j,j'}_{0,0} & c^{j,j'}_{0,1} & \cdots & c^{j,j'}_{0,W-1} \\ c^{j,j'}_{1,0} & c^{j,j'}_{1,1} & \cdots & c^{j,j'}_{1,W-1} \\ \vdots & \vdots & \ddots & \vdots \\ c^{j,j'}_{W-1,0} & \cdots & \cdots & c^{j,j'}_{W-1,W-1} \end{bmatrix} \tag{4}$$

$C = (C^{j,j'})_{j,j'=0,\ldots,H-1}$. Notice that C is a $HW \times HW$ matrix because each sub-matrix $C^{j,j'}$ is a $W \times W$ matrix.

Hypothesis 1. From now on, the covariance of I is assumed to be invariant under translations of the row and column index: $c^{j,j'}_{k,k'} = c^{|j-j'|}_{|k-k'|}$.

Hypothesis 1 will be tested in Section 4. We notice that it is weaker than the typical definition of second order stationarity because here we do not assume the translation invariance of the mean.

Alongside this hypothesis, we add the typical requirement of *symmetrized spatial domain with a toroidal distance* implicitly assumed in the Fourier contest, i.e. $r^j_k = r^{j'}_{k'}$ when $j \equiv j' \pmod{H}$ and $k \equiv k' \pmod{W}$.

Noticing that $c^{j,j'}_{k,k'} = c^{j,j'}_{k+1,k'+1}$, we have that the $C^{j,j'}$ are *circulant matrices*, i.e. matrices where each row vector is rotated one element to the right relative to the preceding row: $C^{j,j'} = \mathrm{circ}\left(c^{j,j'}_{0,0}, c^{j,j'}_{0,1}, \ldots, c^{j,j'}_{0,W-1}\right)$.

Now, writing $C^j \equiv C^{0,j}$, $j = 0, \ldots, H-1$ it is straightforward to see that C is block-circulant: $C = \mathrm{circ}\left(C^0, C^1, \ldots, C^{H-1}\right)$.

Thanks to the well known relationship between circulant matrices and discrete Fourier transform (DFT), see e.g. [4], the eigenvectors of the matrices C^j are the Fourier basis vectors: $\mathbf{e}_m = \frac{1}{\sqrt{W}}\left(1, e^{-\frac{2\pi i m}{W}}, \ldots, e^{-\frac{2\pi i m(W-1)}{W}}\right)^t$ and their eigenvalues are given by components of the DFT of the first row of C^j: $\hat{c}^{0,j}_{0,m} = \sum_{k=0}^{W-1} c^{0,j}_{0,k} e^{-\frac{2\pi i m k}{W}}$.

The set of eigenvalue equations $C^j \mathbf{e}_m = \lambda^j_m \mathbf{e}_m$, can be written as the following matrix equation $C^j E_W = \Lambda^j E_W$, where $\Lambda^j = \mathrm{diag}(\hat{c}^{0,j}_{0,m}; m = 0, \ldots, W-1)$ and E_W are the Vandermonde matrices:

$$E_W = \frac{1}{\sqrt{W}} \begin{bmatrix} 1 & 1 & \cdots & 1 \\ 1 & e^{-\frac{2\pi i}{W}} & \cdots & e^{-\frac{2\pi i(W-1)}{W}} \\ \vdots & \vdots & \ddots & \vdots \\ 1 & e^{-\frac{2\pi i(W-1)}{W}} & \cdots & e^{-\frac{2\pi i(W-1)^2}{W}} \end{bmatrix}. \tag{5}$$

Notice now that if we have a block-circulant matrix $M = \mathrm{circ}(M^0, \ldots, M^{H-1})$ with the property that the blocks M^j can be diagonalized on the same basis B, then it can be verified by direct computation that $E_H \otimes B$ is a basis of eigenvectors of M, where $\otimes$ denotes the Kronecker product and $E_H = [\mathbf{e}_0 | \mathbf{e}_1 | \cdots | \mathbf{e}_{H-1}]$.

In the case of our spatial covariance matrix C, all the submatrices C^j have the same basis of eigenvectors E_W, thus, if we define $E_H \otimes E_W = [\mathbf{e}_{m,l}]$ as $\mathbf{e}_{m,l} = \left(1, e^{-2\pi i \left(\frac{m}{W} + \frac{l}{H}\right)}, \ldots, e^{-2\pi i \left(\frac{m(W-1)}{W} + \frac{l(H-1)}{H}\right)}\right)^t / \sqrt{HW}$, for $m = 0, \ldots, W-1$, and $l = 0, \ldots, H-1$, then $E_H \otimes E_W$ provides a basis of eigenvectors for C. Actually, due to the symmetry of covariance matrices, the complex parts of the exponentials involving the sinus function cancel out (see [6]) and so the 2D cosine Fourier basis also constitutes a basis of eigenvectors of C.

3.2   The Color Case

Let $\mathbf{u} : \Omega \to [0, 255]^3$ be an RGB image function, where Ω is the spatial domain, and, for all $(j, k) \in \Omega$, $\mathbf{u}(j, k) = (R(j, k), G(j, k), B(j, k))$ is the vector whose components are the red, green and blue intensity values of the pixel defined by the coordinates (j, k).

We define the *spatiochromatic covariance matrix among two pixels of position* (j, k) *and* (j', k') by extending eq. (3) as follows $c_{k,k'}^{j,j'}(R, G, B)$

$$\begin{bmatrix} C_{RR}(j, j', k, k') & C_{RG}(j, j', k, k') & C_{RB}(j, j', k, k') \\ C_{GR}(j, j', k, k') & C_{GG}(j, j', k, k') & C_{GB}(j, j', k, k') \\ C_{BR}(j, j', k, k') & C_{BG}(j, j', k, k') & C_{BB}(j, j', k, k') \end{bmatrix}. \tag{6}$$

In the particular case defined by $j' = j$ and $k' = k$, we will call $c_{k,k'}^{j,j'}(R, G, B)$ '*chromatic autocovariance*' and denote it simply as $c^0(R, G, B)$. By substituting $c_{k,k'}^{j,j'}$ with $c_{k,k'}^{j,j'}(R, G, B)$ in the matrices appearing in (4), we find the *spatiochromatic covariance matrix* $C^{j,j'}(R, G, B)$ among the two random vectors r^j, $r^{j'}$ and the *spatiochromatic covariance matrix* $C(R, G, B)$ of the RGB image u, which is a $3HW \times 3HW$ matrix.

Now, supposing that all the elements of the matrices (6) are positive, thanks to the Perron-Frobenius theorem we can assure that each of these $c_{k,k'}^{j,j'}(R, G, B)$ matrices has a basis of eigenvectors that can be written as a triad of achromatic plus opponent chromatic channels. If we further *assume that the matrices (6) can be diagonalized on the same basis of eigenvectors* (A, P, Q), then, thanks to what remarked before, the eigenvectors of the spatiochromatic covariance matrix $C(R, G, B)$ can be written as the Kronecker product: $(A, P, Q) \otimes \mathbf{e}_{m,l} \in \mathbb{R}^{3HW}$, which is precisely the type of eigenvectors that have been exhibited experimentally in [10]. A standard result of linear algebra guarantees that a set of matrices can be diagonalized on the same basis of eigenvectors if and only if they commute[1]. Thanks to the hypothesis of translation invariance of covariance, this is verified if and only if the generic covariance matrix $c_{k,k'}^{j,j'}(R,G,B)$ commutes with the chromatic autocovariance matrix $c^0(R,G,B)$.

It is convenient to resume all the hypotheses made and results obtained so far in the following proposition.

Proposition 1. *Let* $u : \Omega \to [0,255]^3$ *be an RGB image function, with a periodized spatial domain* Ω, *and suppose that:*

1. *The spatiochromatic covariance matrices matrices* $c_{k,k'}^{j,j'}(R,G,B)$ *defined in (6) depend only on the distances* $|j - j'|$, $|k - k'|$, *i.e. the covariance of* u *is stationary;*
2. *All matrices* $c_{k,k'}^{j,j'}(R,G,B)$ *are positive, i.e. their elements are strictly greater than 0;*
3. *The following commutation property holds:*

$$[c^0(R,G,B), c_{k,k'}^{j,j'}(R,G,B)] = 0, \quad \forall(j,k),(j',k') \in \Omega. \tag{7}$$

Then, the eigenvectors of the spatiochromatic covariance matrix $C(R,G,B)$ *can be written as the Kronecker product* $(A,P,Q) \otimes e_{m,l}$, *where* (A,P,Q) *is the achromatic plus opponent color channels triad and* $e_{m,l}$ *is the 2D cosine Fourier basis.*

Proposition 1 defines a mathematical framework where the empirical result shown in [12] can be formalized and understood in terms of statistical properties of natural images. In the following section we will test this framework with the help of two large databases of RGB images.

4   Validations on a Natural Image Database

In this section we present the tests that we have performed to check the validity of the hypotheses of Proposition 1.

To perform our numerical experiences we have generated a databases of RAW photographs made of 1746 natural scenes, available at http://download.tsi. telecom-paristech.fr/RawDatabase/. Each 4-neighborhood of pixels in a raw image contains two pixels corresponding to the R and B channels and two pixels corresponding to the G channel. We demosaicked each RAW image to build a subsampled RGB image simply by keeping unaltered the R and B information and averaging the G channel. The advantage of this database is that RAW images are free

---

[1] We recall that, given two generic matrices A and B for which the products AB and BA is well defined, $[A,B] \equiv AB - BA$ is called the 'commutator' between them. Of course A and B commute if and only if $[A,B] = 0$.

from post-processing operations such as gamma correction, white balance or compression, thus, modulo camera noise, they provide a much better approximation of physical irradiance than common jpeg images.

4.1 $c^0(R, G, B)$ and Its Eigenvalues and Eigenvectors

The expression of the chromatic autocovariance matrix relative to the RAW database, $c^0(R, G, B)$, is:

$$c^0(R, G, B) = \begin{bmatrix} 0.0022 & 0.0021 & 0.0021 \\ 0.0021 & 0.0021 & 0.0022 \\ 0.0021 & 0.0022 & 0.0024 \end{bmatrix} \tag{8}$$

which confirm the positivity assumption on $c^0(R, G, B)$. Its eigenvectors are:

$$\begin{cases} A = (0.5679, 0.5683, 0.5954) & \longleftrightarrow & \lambda_1 = 0.0065, \\ P = (0.7210, 0.0055, -0.6930) & \longleftrightarrow & \lambda_2 = 0.0002, \\ Q = (0.3971, -0.8228, 0.4066) & \longleftrightarrow & \lambda_3 = 7.8 \cdot 10^{-7}. \end{cases} \tag{9}$$

4.2   The Exponential Decay of Spatiochromatic Covariance

To simplify the notation, from now on we will write $c_{k,k'}^{j,j'}(R, G, B) = c^d(R, G, B)$, where d is the Euclidean distance between (j, k) and j', k'. All the spatiochromatic matrices $c^d(R, G, B)$ that we have estimated turned out to be positive. Their decay with respect to increasing values of d is reported in semi-logarithmic scale in Fig. 1 for the Flickr and the RAW database, respectively.

The graphs of Fig. 1 show a linear decay for all the distances that we have tested (from 1 to 300 pixels) quantified by a coefficient of determination R^2 greater than 0.98 for all curves.

Let us now write the generic element of the matrix $c^d(R, G, B)$ as $c_{\mu\nu}^d$, $\mu, \nu \in \{R, G, B\}$. A linear behavior in the semilogarithmic domain corresponds the following exponential decay: $c_{\mu\nu}^d = c_{\mu\nu}^0 e^{\beta_{\mu\nu} d}$, $\mu, \nu \in \{R, G, B\}$, where $c_{\mu\nu}^0$ is the generic element of the chromatic autocovariance matrix and $\beta_{\mu\nu} < 0$.

The value of the coefficients $\beta_{\mu\nu}$ (i.e. the slopes of the straight lines which approximate the spatiochromatic covariance graphs in the semilogarithmic scale) are the following: $\beta_{RR} = -0.0023$, $\beta_{GG} = -0.0021$ $\beta_{BB} = -0.0020$ $\beta_{RG} = \beta_{GR} = -0.0022$ $\beta_{RB} = \beta_{BR} = -0.0022$ $\beta_{GB} = \beta_{BG} = -0.0021$.

It can be seen that the spatiochromatic covariance relative to the blue channel decreases less rapidly than that of the red and green channels. This may be explained by the fact that pictures in which the sky is present are characterized by large homogeneous areas dominated by the blue channel.

The explicit analytical expressions of $c^d(R, G, B)$ obtained provide an accurate model for the covariance that corrects the power-law decay. Moreover, they allow computing the commutators $[c^0(R, G, B), c^d(R, G, B)]$ for every distance $d > 0$. If the coefficients $\alpha_{\mu\nu}$ were all perfectly equal, then these commutators

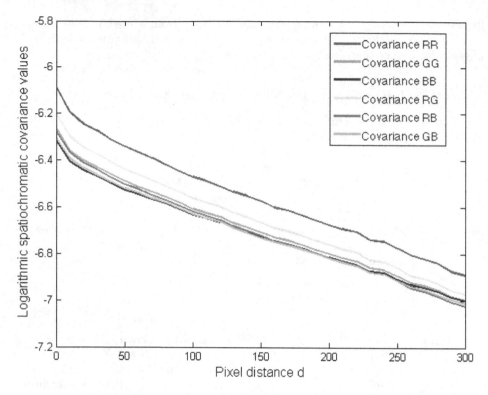

Fig. 1. The linear behavior of the six spatiochromatic covariance matrix elements in the semi-logarithmic scale as a function of d, which implies an exponential decay.

would be exactly null matrices, however, the differences in the values of the exponentials make the matrix elements of the commutators slightly different than zero. Nonetheless the highest deviation from the zero matrix that we have found can be quantified with a matrix norm of $4.5 \cdot 10^{-7}$, thus showing that the commutation hypothesis is verified with very good precision.

In proposition 1, the hypothesis of commutativity is essential to guarantee that the spatiochromatic covariance matrices can be diagonalized on the same basis of eigenvectors.

5   Discussion and Perspectives

We have provided a theoretical analysis of the relationship between translation invariance of the covariance and the decorrelated spatiochromatic features of digital RGB images, supported by several numerical tests.

Our analysis has been motivated by the will to understand the basic mathematical reasons underlying the appearance of a separable spatiochromatic basis of uncorrelated features when the PCA is performed over patches or whole natural images.

In order to investigate this property, we have built the spatiochromatic covariance matrix of an abstract three-chromatic image and we have shown that, under the assumption of spatial invariance and commutativity, their eigenvectors can be written as the Kronecker product of the cosine Fourier basis times an achromatic plus color opponent triad.

The numerical tests that we have conducted have shown that the assumptions are verified with a good degree of approximation on a quite large database of RAW images.

In particular, the analysis of the commutativity of spatiochromatic covariance matrices have led to a lateral result that it is worth underlying: our tests have shown that the spatial covariance decays exponentially and not following a power law. The failure of the power law decay has already been reported in the literature of natural image statistics, but our result on the exponential decay is novel. Moreover, we have shown that the decay speed is not the same for all the combinations of chromatic channels: the autocovariance decay of the blue channel being the slowest and the R-B covariance decay being the fastest.

References

1. Berman, A., Plemmons, R.: Nonnegative Matrices in the Mathematical Sciences. SIAM (1987)
2. Buchsbaum, G., Gottschalk, A.: Trichromacy, opponent colours coding and optimum colour information transmission in the retina. Proc. Royal Society of London B **220**, 89–113 (1983)
3. Field, D.: Relations between the statistics of natural images and the response properties of cortical cells. J. Opt. Soc. Am. **4**(12), 2379–2394 (1987)
4. Frazier, M.W.: Introduction to wavelets through linear algebra. Springer (2001)
5. Goldstein, B.: Sensation and Perception, 9th edn. Cengage Learning (2013)
6. Gray, R.: Toeplitz and Circulant Matrices: A review. Now Publishers Inc. (2006)
7. von Kries, J.: Chromatic adaptation. Festschrift der Albrecht-Ludwigs-Universität, pp. 145–158 (1902)
8. Párraga, C., Troscianko, T., Tolhurst, D.: Spatiochromatic properties of natural images and human vision. Current Biology **6**(12), 483–487 (2002)
9. Provenzi, E., Delon, J., Gousseau, Y., Mazin, B.: Second order stationarity and spatiochromatic properties of natural images. In: 2014 Tenth International Conference on Signal-Image Technology and Internet-Based Systems (SITIS), November 23–27, Marrakech, pp. 598–605. IEEE (2014)
10. Ruderman, D.: Origin of scaling in natural images. Vision Research **37**, 3385–3398 (1996)
11. Ruderman, D., Bialek, W.: Statistics of natural images: Scaling in the woods. Phys. Rev. Lett. **73**, 814–817 (1994)
12. Ruderman, D., Cronin, T., Chiao, C.: Statistics of cone responses to natural images: implications for visual coding. J. Opt. Soc. Am. A **15**(8), 2036–2045 (1998)

Real-Time Foreground Segmentation
with Kinect Sensor

Luigi Cinque[1], Alessandro Danani[2], Piercarlo Dondi[2]([✉]), and Luca Lombardi[2]

[1] Department of Computer Science,
Sapienza University of Rome, Via Salaria 113, Roma, Italy
cinque@di.uniroma1.it
[2] Department of Electrical, Computer and Biomedical Engineering,
University of Pavia, via Ferrata 5, 27100 Pavia, Italy
{piercarlo.dondi,luca.lombardi}@unipv.it, alessandro.danani@gmail.com

Abstract. In the last years, economic multichannel sensors became very widespread. The most known of these devices is certainly the Microsoft Kinect, able to provide at the same time a color image and a depth map of the scene. However Kinect focuses specifically on human-computer interaction, so the SDK supplied with the sensors allows to achieve an efficient detection of foreground people but not of generic objects. This paper presents an alternative and more general solution for the foreground segmentation and a comparison with the standard background subtraction algorithm of Kinect. The proposed algorithm is a porting of a previous one that works on a Time-of-Flight camera, based on a combination of a Otsu thresholding and a region growing. The new implementation exploits the particular characteristic of Kinect sensor to achieve a fast and precise result.

Keywords: Segmentation · Background subtraction · Kinect · Depth imagery

1 Introduction

Foreground segmentation is one of the most used technique of computer vision. It is a basic step for many kinds of applications, such as tracking, augmented reality, behavior analysis, human computer interaction. In the last years, new devices such as Time-of-Flight (ToF) camera or the recent Kinect sensor gave new impulse to the research in this field, proposing increasingly efficient solutions.

This work presents a porting on Kinect sensor of an algorithm designed to use depth data produced by a Time-of-Flight camera able to detect multiple clusters at the same time handling also short term occlusions [1]. The main limitations of this procedure are related to the high noise and low resolution (generally a QCIF, 174x144) of a ToF camera. An extension of that work involves the integration with a standard RGB camera to achieve a more accurate refinement of the border of the clusters [2]. The results is very precise but also computationally expensive

© Springer International Publishing Switzerland 2015
V. Murino and E. Puppo (Eds.): ICIAP 2015, Part II, LNCS 9280, pp. 56–65, 2015.
DOI: 10.1007/978-3-319-23234-8_6

due to the use of a non real-time matting algorithm (Soft Scissor [3]), thus it can only be applied for post production purposes.

Kinect is an efficient and economic solution to overcome this issues with few compromises: it has a good resolution (640x480), color and depth data directly synchronized, a less depth precision but a much lower noise ratio than a ToF camera. Kinect is designed for Human-Computer Interaction, thus it has a native software able to retrieve in real-time people and to track their movements. At the same time it provides an efficient and fast background subtraction tool, with a good edge precision. However the performance of this procedure is limited by the original purpose of Kinect: detecting people movements and not only their shapes. The tool is able to detect at most six people at a time, of which generally only two active, to reduce errors in movements detection and speed up the execution. These limits are not related to the hardware but only to software, thus excluding the movements detection and using the Kinect only as a sensor, it is theoretically possible to achieve a more general implementation of background subtraction.

Our goal is to achieve a background subtraction similar in accuracy to the native Kinect algorithm, but more flexible, thus it is possible to retrieve both generic objects and humans with the same level of precision and with no limits in their number.

The paper is organized as follow: section 2 provides an overview of Kinect sensor; section 3 presents a brief overview of state of art of the most recent background subtraction and matting solutions; section 4 describes the proposed method; section 5 shows the achieved results; and finally the conclusions are drawn in section 6.

2   Kinect

Kinect is a motion sensing device released by Microsoft in November 2010 for Xbox 360 console and then in February 2012 for Windows with a full developer toolkit. The Kinect sensor incorporates several sensing hardware: an infrared (IR) projector and a IR camera used to obtain a depth map, a color camera with a resolution of 640x480, and a four-microphone array for voice recognition. The most notable characteristic of Kinect is the skeletal tracking that allows to detect and understand movements of at most six people (of which only two active). A human body is segmented starting from the depth map, then a per-pixel body classification is applied to the retrieved cluster. The system hypothesizes the body joints by finding a global centroid of probability mass and then maps these joints to a skeleton using temporal continuity and a priori knowledge [4].

The most recent version of the device, Kinect 2.0, was released in November 2013 (in summer 2014 for PC), it includes a new and more precise generation of sensors that allow a better tracking of human parts, e.g. fingers, and an improved face and facial expression detection.

Our solution was tested on the first model of kinect. The porting on the new one requires only small adjustments, since the core technology is the same in both versions.

3   Previous Works

Matting algorithms focus on the obtaining of a very precise foreground segmentation able to correctly discriminate also those pixels of an image that are part of the background and of the foreground. Each pixel has a different level of opacity (alpha), that refers to its percentage of affiliation to the foreground. The set of alpha values creates the so called alpha-matte, i.e. the correct classification of all the pixels of the image, by which it is possible achieving a precise foreground extraction and a precise background substitution. Matting algorithms are extremely precise but can often be very computationally expensive, thus they are generally applied to static images or for video post-production, for a real-time application, such as a video streaming, it is better to apply different approaches with a compromise between precision and speed. A description of the principal matting methods is outside of the topic of this paper, a comprehensive survey can be found in [6].

In the last years several approaches for matting and background subtraction based on the use of the Kinect have been proposed.

A first approach toward an automatic image matting is described in [7]. The authors proposed a method that combines color and depth information from a Kinect device. Morphological operators are used to select a trimap from a depth map that is finally combined with the RGB image. A trimap is the standard input of many matting algorithms, and specifies the areas that certainly belong to background, those that certainly belongs to foreground and those that are in a indeterminate state on which the algorithm must work. The proposed solution perform very well in comparison with other similar matting solutions, but it works only on a single image at a time and not on sequences, the Kinect is used only for providing the input color/depth sequence and not for its real-time capability.

An application of 3D scene generation is considered in [8], also in this paper object boundary in depth map is enhanced fusing the depth map with a color one. The authors are considered both TOF cameras and IR cameras (a Kinect). The proposed approach enhances the depth map by propagating values along both the spatial dimensions and the temporal sequence of frames considering the RGB and the alpha channels. The quality of the final matting is however limited by several restrictions: similar foreground-background colors gives problems in trimap generation and object connected to the floor are not correctly segmented.

In [9] a new background subtraction method is described. The algorithm is based on specific characteristic of the Kinect device. The authors propose a method that handles the holes in depth map (pixel with unreliable values). The non-uniformity of the spatial distribution of noise in range images is also considered to enhance the quality of the final segmentation.

A real time video segmentation is proposed in [10]. The main contribution of the paper is the porting of the algorithm on a GPU in order to reach real time performances.

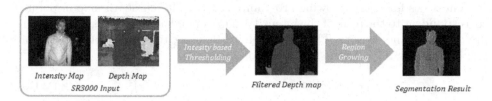

Fig. 1. Schema of the main steps of ToF based foreground segmentation. Input data are supplied by a SR3000, a modulated light ToF camera [2].

4   Foreground Segmentation

This section describes our method, from a brief overview of the original algorithm to the current Kinect implementation. Our solution it is able to achieve a good quality segmentation of multiple subjects (moving or static) in real-time. It does not need any a priori knowledge of the ambient or to generate a model of the background such as in [9]. It handles partial short time occlusions and works in the same way with humans or objects (more flexibility respect to standard Kinect solution).

4.1   ToF Based Segmentation

Time-of-Flight cameras are active imaging sensors able to provide distance measures of an environment using laser light in near-infrared spectrum, they can work with impulses or by phase delay detection. A ToF camera can provide two type of data: a depth map and an intensity map that represents the intensity of the reflected light in near infrared spectrum [11].

The foreground segmentation algorithm presented in [1,2] exploits the unique characteristics of this kind of sensor and can be subdivided in two main phases: a first thresholding of the distance map based on the corresponding values of intensity map; followed by a region growing on the filtered distance map that identifies and labels the various clusters (Fig. 1).

The thresholding step is used to exclude background and noisy pixels without deleting important part of the foreground. A depth pixel x belongs to the filtered distance image F, if it satisfies the following conditions:

$$\{I_x \geq \lambda \ \ or \ \ \forall n \in N_x, \ I_n > \beta * \lambda\} \rightarrow \{x \in F\} \tag{1}$$

where I_x is the correspondent intensity values of pixel x, λ is an intensity threshold estimated for every frame using the Otsu's method, N_x is the 8-connected neighborhood of pixel x, and β is a weight, set by the user, that can assume values between 0 and 1. These controls compensate the noise and the imprecisions on the intensity map caused by objects with low IR reflectance (such as dark hairs) or by a limited sunlight interference (e.g. the light that comes from an open window). If needed, a series of mathematical morphology operations (erosions and dilations) are applied to refine edges and to close holes.

The seeds for region growing are planted on the filtered depth map in points correspondent to the peak of the intensity map (an high intensity means a greater proximity to the sensor). Then, a pixel x belonging to a cluster C absorbs a neighbor y if it respects the following conditions:

$$\{x \in C, \ S(x,y) < \theta, \ I_y \in F\} \rightarrow \{y \in C\} \tag{2}$$

where θ is a constant parameter, experimentally estimated [12], related to clusters separation, and $S(x,y)$ is a measure of the similarity between the distance value of pixel y (D_y) and the mean distance value around pixel x (μ_x), incrementally updated at growing of the cluster:

$$S(x,y) = |\mu_x - D_y| \tag{3}$$

Every region grows excluding the analyzed pixels from successive steps. The process is iterated for all seeds in order of descending intensity. Very small regions are then discarded, to remove noise points that can pass the thresholding. The minimum acceptable dimension of a region is fixed and is related to ToF device behavior.

The final outcome is then automatically converted in a trimap applying a series of morphological operation: a dilation identifies the background samples more closed to the retrieved clusters; an erosion identifies the more stable parts of the clusters, that are labeled as foreground samples; finally the clusters edges are marked as the indeterminate zone. The trimap is used as input for the Soft Scissors, a matting algorithm that works on a correspondent color frame supplied by a RGB camera to achieve a precise refinements of the edges with sub-pixel precision (Fig. 2).

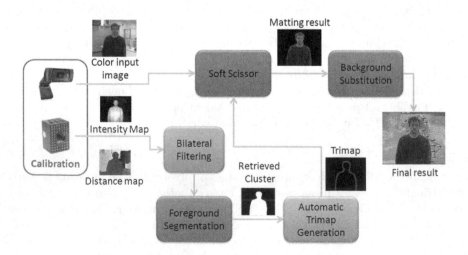

Fig. 2. Main steps of the automatic matting method [2].

As said in the introduction, this final step, even if very precise, it is also high computationally intensive (in a worst case scenario it can reach more than a minute for frame) and limits the applicability of the solution only to non real-time applications such as video post-production.

A kinect approach can provide a comparable result, slightly less accurate but definitively more practical for using a continuous stream of data.

4.2   Kinect Based Segmentation

Figure 3 shows the core steps on the new implementation on Kinect. The overall structure is similar to the previous one, thus there is a depth base segmentation followed by a refinement of the clusters and the integration with color, but there are also some adaptations and improvements granted by the new hardware. In the next paragraphs the procedure will be analyzed step by step, to highlight the differences between the two approaches.

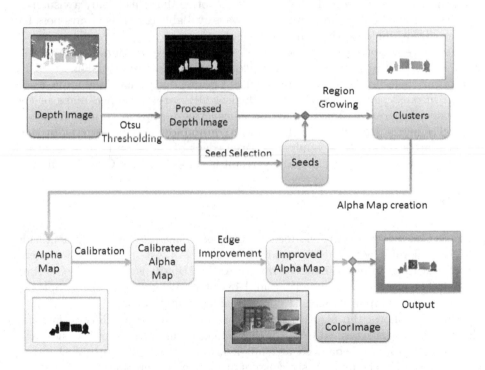

Fig. 3. Schema of the Kinect based foreground segmentation.

Thresholding and Region Growing. As in the original algorithm the segmentation is subdivided in two steps: a thresholding and a region growing. However in this case we do not need the intensity map for the thresholding, because the depth data provided by Kinect are more uniform and less noisy of those provided by a ToF camera [5], thus it is possible to apply the Otsu thresholding directly on the depth map. For the same reason also the corrections of formula 1 are overcome. This variation allows to free some computational resources and to use them to perform some new refinements.

Region growing step remains the same, but now the seeds are planted directly on the filtered depth map in the peaks of proximity to the sensor. Summarizing it is possible to collapse the formulas 1 and 2 in this new one:

$$\{x \in C, \ S(x,y) < \theta, \ D_y < \lambda_d\} \rightarrow \{y \in C\} \tag{4}$$

where λ_d is the Otsu threshold computed on the distance map.

Refinements and Visualization. The segmentation identifies a group of labeled clusters. For maintaining a correct alignment between depth and color data and to show the color only on foreground, the kinect needs an alpha map that classifies what is foreground and what is background. This map is generated combining all the clusters. It is important to notice that this is only a visualization issue, the labeling information are always available (e.g. it is always possible to visualize a single specific cluster or a subset).

The edge improvement is the crucial step to achieve an output comparable with that produced by the native background segmentation of Kinect SDK. Temporary holes in the alpha map of current frame, due to noise and imprecision of the infrared sensor, are closed by logical OR with the alpha maps of the previous three frames. Tests show that considering a sequence of four frames is a good compromise between computing performances and precision. The new alpha map is then refined applying on the edges of the clusters morphological erosions and dilations, at the end the result is smoothed by a Gaussian filter.

5   Results

This section presents some significant examples of the foreground segmentation results achievable with objects and with humans. All tests have been performed on a PC with an Intel I7-4790k @4Ghz, an AMD HD6970 as GPU, and 8GB Ram DDR3. The overall frame-rate is around 18-20fps (depending on the complexity of the scene), compatible with standard real-time applications.

Figure 4 shows the algorithm behavior applied to static objects: fig. 4(c) shows the clusters retrieved from the depth map in fig. 4(b), note that the single objects are properly separated and labeled, even if very closed to each other, and that the Kinect limit of six clusters at a time is overcome; fig. 4(d) shows the final outcome obtained applying to the clusters the refinements described in section 4.2, it can be noted that the edges are more precise and small holes present in blue and purple clusters are now closed.

A direct comparison between our solution and the default kinect background subtraction tool is presented in fig. 5 and in fig. 6. The results are very similar, in both cases there are only small imprecisions mainly focused on the edges or on the finger tips. With moving people skeleton tracking is in general slightly more

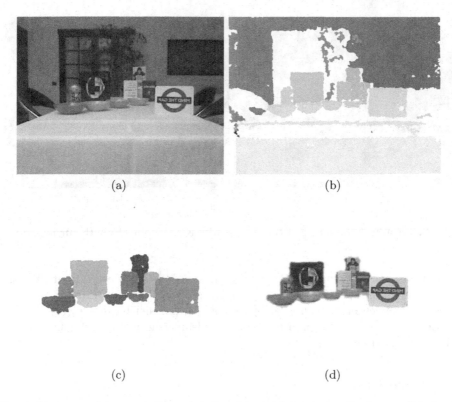

(a)   (b)

(c)   (d)

Fig. 4. Foreground segmentation of static objects: (a) input color image; (b) depth map; (c) detected clusters; (d) final result after refinements and color addition.

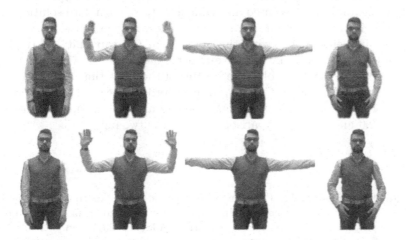

Fig. 5. Comparison between kinect background subtraction tool (top row) and the proposed solution (bottom row).

(a)   (b)

Fig. 6. Final background substitution: (a) with Kinect tool; (b) with our method.

efficient respect to our method, because it is specifically design for this task, but our solution maintains a more general approach. We are working to increase the performances moving critical operations on parallel hardware (e.g. GPU), in order to free computational power for implementing further refinements, not giving up real-time execution.

6   Conclusions

This paper proposes a new system for the automatic background removal based on the Kinect device. An alternative and more general approach to foreground segmentation is presented and compared to the standard solution of the Microsoft SDK. The new approach is comparable with the precision of the original Kinect implementation with the addition of the capability to track also generic objects. The limit in clusters number is overcome.

Future enhancements involve the porting of the most time consuming parts of the code on GPU (such as Gaussian filter) in order to reach a greater precision maintaining a full real-time execution. Then we are also considering the use of the Kinect 2.0 and a new comparison between the two outcomes.

References

1. Dondi, P., Lombardi, L.: Fast real-time segmentation and tracking of multiple subjects by time-of-flight camera. In: Proceedings of 6th International Conference on Computer Vision Theory and Applications (VISAPP 2011), pp. 582–587 (2011)
2. Dondi, P., Lombardi, L., LaRosa, A., Cinque, L.: Automatic image matting fusing time-of-flight and color cameras data streams. In: Proceedings of 8th International Conference on Computer Vision Theory and Applications (VISAPP 2013), vol. 1, pp. 231–237 (2013)

3. Wang, J., Agrawala, M., Cohen, M.F.: Soft scissors: an interactive tool for real-time high quality matting. In: ACM SIGGRAPH 2007 Papers (SIGGRAPH 2007), Article 9, pp 1–6. ACM (2007)

4. Zhang, Z.: Microsoft Kinect Sensor and Its Effect. IEEE MultiMedia **19**(2), 4–10 (2012)

5. Smisek, J., Jancosek, M., Pajdla, T.: 3D with kinect. In: 2011 IEEE International Conference on Computer Vision Workshops (ICCV Workshops), pp. 1154–1160 (2011)

6. Wang, J., Cohen, M.F.: Image and video matting: a survey. Found. Trends. Comput. Graph. Vis. **3**(2), 97–175 (2007)

7. Lu, T., Li, S.: Image matting with color and depth information. In: 2012 21st International Conference on Pattern Recognition (ICPR), pp. 3787–3790 (2012)

8. Cho, J.-H., Lee, K.H., Aizawa, K.: Enhancement of Depth Maps With Alpha Channel Estimation for 3-D Video. IEEE Journal of Selected Topics in Signal Processing **6**(5), 483–494 (2012)

9. Braham, M., Lejeune, A., Van Droogenbroeck, M.: A physically motivated pixel-based model for background subtraction in 3D images. In: 2014 International Conference on 3D Imaging (IC3D), pp. 1–8 (2014)

10. Abramov, A., Pauwels, K., Papon, J., Worgotter, F., Dellen, B.: Depth-supported real-time video segmentation with the kinect. In: 2012 IEEE Workshop on Applications of Computer Vision (WACV), pp. 457–464 (2012)

11. Kolb, A., Barth, E., Koch, R., Larsen, R.: Time-of-Flight cameras in computer graphics. Journal of Computer Graphics Forum **29**, 141–159 (2010)

12. Bianchi, L., Gatti, R., Lombardi, L., Lombardi, P.: Tracking without background model for time-of-flight cameras. In: Wada, T., Huang, F., Lin, S. (eds.) PSIVT 2009 LNCS, vol. 5414, pp. 726–737. Springer, Heidelberg (2009)

Hierarchical Image Representation Using Deep Network

Emrah Ergul[1], Sarp Erturk[1], and Nafiz Arica[2(✉)]

[1] Electronics & Communication Engineering Department of Kocaeli University,
Kocaeli, Turkey
{106103002,sertur}@kocaeli.edu.tr
[2] Software Engineering Department of Bahcesehir University, Istanbul, Turkey
nafiz.arica@eng.bahcesehir.edu.tr

Abstract. In this paper, we propose a new method for features learning from unlabeled data. Basically, we simulate k-means algorithm in deep network architecture to achieve hierarchical Bag-of-Words (BoW) representations. We first learn visual words in each layer which are used to produce BoW feature vectors in the current input space. We transform the raw input data into new feature spaces in a convolutional manner such that more abstract visual words are extracted at each layer by implementing Expectation-Maximization (EM) algorithm. The network parameters are optimized as we keep the visual words fixed in the Expectation step while the visual words are updated with the current parameters of the network in the Maximization step. Besides, we embed spatial information into BoW representation by learning different networks and visual words for each quadrant regions. We compare the proposed algorithm with the similar approaches in the literature using a challenging 10-class-dataset, CIFAR-10.

Keywords: Deep network architectures · Image classification · Unsupervised feature extraction · Bag-of-words representation

1 Introduction

The main goal of a learning algorithm is generalization which refers to the ability of having satisfactory performance on the test samples, based on what it has learned in the training phase. At this point of view, our hypothesis function should be robust to bias-variance dilemma [1] which means to construct a learning structure neither too complex for overfitting, nor too simple for underfitting. To do so, we must give our attention mainly to representation learning. This can be described as learning transformations, or posterior distributions in the case of probabilistic models, for the underlying factors of the raw data that extract useful information [2]. Furthermore, we can make the learning algorithm less dependent on the features that are extracted in an unsupervised manner by using huge amount of unlabeled data. Additionally, the source domain may not be the same as or similar to the target domain. This is where Deep Learning Architectures (DLA) proves to be the most successful learning algorithm on the shelf. Unlike hand-engineered feature extraction methods like Scale

© Springer International Publishing Switzerland 2015
V. Murino and E. Puppo (Eds.): ICIAP 2015, Part II, LNCS 9280, pp. 66–77, 2015.
DOI: 10.1007/978-3-319-23234-8_7

Invariant Feature Transform (SIFT) [3], Speeded Up Robust Features (SURF) [4], Pyramid Histogram of Oriented Gradients (PHOG) [5] or GIST [6]; DLA can extract useful features without explicitly using input data statistics.

DLA can be summarized as the multi-layer neural network structures that are formed by the composition of multiple nonlinear transformations of the input data. They aim to have more abstract intermediate features implicitly in deeper layers. By using a deep network, in the case of visual data, one can learn part-to-whole and low level-to-semantic decompositions. What makes DLA effective in representation learning is that they can extract hierarchical features from huge amount of unlabeled data that would prevent overfitting while they are sufficiently complex which might help to recover from underfitting.

In this work, we propose an unsupervised feature learning algorithm for image classification that is based on a deep architecture. Basically, we try to model the feature extraction hierarchically by using unlabeled data through the deep network. The studies based on this basic principle such as [7, 8, 9, 10] use hidden layer activations (i.e. the last layer's activations or the activations of all hidden layers in a concatenated vector) as the new feature vector to be classified. However, we claim that each hidden layer of a deep network corresponds to a different perspective of the same input in another feature space. Therefore, the concatenation alone does not improve the performance adequately. In addition, we do not use the complementary efforts of the previous layers if we consider only the last layer's activations at the supervised classification step. We, on the other hand, implement soft weighted Bag-of-Words (BoW) representations [8], [11], and [12] in the classification by simulating k-means algorithm iteratively for finding visual words at each layer of the deep network. Additionally, we associate spatial layout information by dividing each image into quadrant regions and implementing the model for each region individually. Finally, the image is represented by a pyramid of BoWs.

2   Related Work

The era of the deep networks starts in the 1940's as 'neural networks'. We can describe deep networks as the multi-layer neural structures for data modeling that imitate the most powerful learning bio-machine, brain. One of the key findings has been that the neo-cortex, associated with many cognitive abilities, is layered and hierarchical. It allows sensory signals (i.e. visual, acoustic) to propagate through a complex hierarchy [13] of computational elements (i.e. neurons) that learn to represent observations based on the regularities they expose. The hierarchical nature is that generally the upper layers represent increasingly discriminative representations and are more invariant to transformations such as illumination, scale, rotation and translation. Although it promises to approximate any complex function theoretically, it has not been used widely because of two main restrictions until 2006 when Hinton et al. propose a new approach [10], called 'greedy layer-wise unsupervised pre-training'.

First, traditional gradient based feed forward – back propagation multi-layer networks have a supervised learning objective which refers to the need of labeled data. However, labeled data are often scarce, and the quality of supervision is directly proportional to the experience of human subjects. In short, it is a labor-intensive and application specific job. Given the high expressive power of deep networks, training on insufficient labeled data would also result in overfitting. Another thing is that training a neural network at once involves solving a highly complex and non-convex optimization problem which leads to bad local optima. Because we use nonlinear computational elements (e.g. hyperbolic tangent, sigmoid) in sequential layers and initialize the parameters of the system randomly while trying to minimize them for regularization. As a result, the weights of the earlier layers change slowly, and fail to learn much.

To overcome the problems of supervision and bad local optima, greedy layer-wise unsupervised pre-training is proposed initially in [10] and [14]. The main idea is to learn a hierarchy of intermediate features layer by layer from unlabeled data. We first train a network with only one hidden layer, and only after that is achieved, we start training a network with two hidden layers while keeping the first layer's weights fixed, and so on. Finally, the set of learned layers could be combined to initialize the whole deep network. By using unlabeled data to learn a good initial value for the weights in all the layers, algorithm is now able to learn and discover patterns from massive amount of data while avoiding bad local optima. One can refer to Auto-Encoders (AEs) and Restricted Boltzmann Machines (RBMs) [15] as the primitives or building blocks of the deep learning architectures.

As mentioned above, the deep architectures consist of multiple hidden layers that are assumed to extract more abstract features at their activations when we go deeper. That would be a smart way to 'stack' AEs and RBMs to get discriminative features in the deep architectures. If we stack these two building blocks together, we produce popular deep networks, Stacked Auto Encoders (SAEs) and Deep Belief Networks (DBNs), respectively. To use these structures as classifiers combined with feature learning, we add another layer at the output (i.e. softmax classifier) and may update the parameters of the system at once. These deep networks are implemented in many computer vision problems like object recognition [7], face detection [17] and event detection [18], achieving state-of-art performances.

There is a serious problem with AEs, in that if the hidden layer is similar or greater in size than the input (i.e. over-complete) then the algorithm could simply learn the identity function. It means that we may not get discriminative features. On the other side, we can get higher accuracy in over-complete structures since we make the system more complex. One option is to input corrupted signal and train the system in a way to reconstruct the clean input, which is called De-noising Auto-Encoder (DAE). DAE is successfully implemented in [9] for digit recognition and object classification in a stacked and convolutional manner. Another rational way to get robustness into the system is masking the hidden layer's activations, instead of masking the input for corruption. This is called 'dropout' [19] in the literature where we make a variable amount v of the activations 0. The parameter v represents the percentage of masking to deactivate the outputs of the hidden layer. Finally, we introduce sparsity into the architecture. In particular, if we impose a sparsity constraint on the hidden units, then the AE will still discover interesting structure in the data, even if the number of hidden units is large [20].

Finally for comparison to our work, Gong et. al. [25] discusses the benefits of deep Convolutional Neural Networks (CNN) especially for retrieval and classification tasks. They argue that Bag-of-Words approach introduces an orderless spectrum which loses the spatial information while CNN depends on too much globally ordered spatial information which lacks especially geometric invariance. To overcome the insufficiencies of the both sides, they combine two approaches at a common platform which is called Multi-scale Orderless Pooling (MOP-CNN). They handle an image at 3 levels for multi-scale representation each of which divides its upper level into quadrants, and the level 1 is the whole image. In this configuration, level 1 is the traditional CNN activations that already preserves the global spatial layout while they implement k-means+VLAD (Vectors of Locally Aggregated Descriptors) [26] algorithm at level 2 and 3 for orderless representations of the patches in order to achieve geometric invariance in a concatenated features vector. For comparison, their start point is a pre-trained seven-layer CNN at each layer, and there is no transitional connection between CNN levels for data representation. Additionally, they use k-means to find centroids for VLAD score aggregation and PCA for dimension reduction. On the other hand, we propose connections between scale levels where the next level uses the hidden layer activations of the previous level for BoW representations; and the last layer represents again the whole image with the composite activations of the quadrants of the previous level.

So far, we have given important details of deep network architectures and their implementations. It is a common practice to use the resulting unsupervised feature representations either as input to a classifier directly, or as initialization for a supervised deep neural network. Alternatively, the outputs of the previous layer may be treated as extra inputs, with the original signal, for the next layer. Although it seems very reasonable to use the hidden layers' activations directly as a new representation, we hypothesize that the system might get poor performance because the activation values are in tight range. Assuming that there is high variance within input data and a limited number of neurons in the hidden layers, the classifier would not approximate the data satisfactorily, leading to underfitting. On the other hand, we may just replicate the data, other than learning useful structures, when we increase the complexity of the system with more neurons, leading to overfitting. To avoid both situations, we need to add randomness or sparsity into the system while adjusting the number of neurons carefully.

Instead of handling aforementioned issues, we introduce a new approach which learns visual words (i.e. code words) hierarchically while training the deep network. We use them to construct BoW representations as a new feature space, not the neuron activations itself. To do so, k-means algorithm is simulated in the deep network. We additionally use spatial information by implementing pyramid-like representations as in [12].

3   Unsupervised Feature Extraction

3.1   Deep Network Architecture

We propose a 3-hidden layer neural network that is trained in a greedy layer wise learning scheme to extract BoW representations at each layer, sequentially. After learning some features at a lower layer, we go further with these learned features and start learning the next layer's weights while keeping the previous ones fixed. Basically, we repeat the same procedure at each layer which is to update the system parameters for finding the fundamentals of a BoW representation, i.e. code words. Fig. 1 summarizes the proposed deep structure visually.

Given a set of unlabeled training images $X=\{x^{(1)}, x^{(2)}, x^{(3)}, ..., x^{(i)}\}$, $x^{(i)} \in R^{nxlxd}$, where n and l are image sizes and d is the color dimension, we first select a large number of patches randomly from the whole image set. We use them as the input signal for the first layer. Each patch has a dimension of w-by-w and has d color channels. So each patch can be represented as a vector of M (i.e. M equals to $w*w*d$) pixel intensity values. But we do not use the intensity values directly as they contain noise and correlation. In our work, we apply contrast normalization that of zero mean-unit standard deviation, and whitening for uncorrelation with the same variance, operations to the intensity values in the preprocessing stage. Given a set of z patch examples, we then define the overall cost function of a typical single-layer network to be:

$$J(W, \; b) = \frac{1}{z}\sum_{j=1}^{z} \frac{1}{2}\left\|h_{w,b}(p^{(j)}) - y^{(j)}\right\|^2 + \frac{\lambda}{2}\sum W^2 \tag{1}$$

where $h_{W,b}(p)=f(W^T*p + b)$, $f : R \rightarrow R$, is the hypothesis function (i.e. the prediction of the system for a sample patch input pattern, p), W and b are the collection of parameters to be minimized, y is the target value and λ is the regularization term. Note that the hypothesis function is nonlinear and non-convex as the activation functions, $f(\cdot)$, are nonlinear; and the parameters are initialized randomly, near to zero. To summarize, we try to find the optimum solution by minimizing the average sum-of-squares error while penalizing the high magnitude of the weights to prevent overfitting. Since this function is derivable, gradient based algorithms can be used to find the optimum parameters and back propagation method is run to calculate derivations.

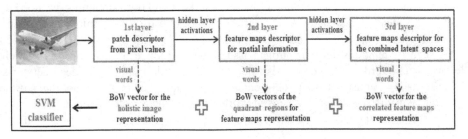

Fig. 1. Overview of the proposed image representation

As we have mentioned before, the AE neural networks optimize the parameters in an unsupervised way by setting the target values to be equal to the inputs, i.e. $y^{(j)}=p^{(j)}$. Our algorithm differs from the auto-encoder method in that we set the target values to the visual words, $c^{(i)}$. So we try to learn code words rather than identity function by simulating k-means algorithm in the network which will be detailed in the next part of this section.

3.2   Simulating K-Means in the Network

We hypothesize that we may achieve representative code words while optimizing the neural network because k-means resembles of the neural network structure in encoding-decoding and reconstruction aspects. So one can transform the input space into another space (i.e. more discriminative) by using the hidden layer activations and continue learning deeper structures while producing BoW representations from visual words for classification tasks. We first take randomly k patch instances as the initial centroids, $c^{(i)}$. Thereafter, we find the nearest centroid for each input and set the target values to the selected centroids, i.e. $y^{(j)}=c^{(i)}$. Now we can run the feed forward – back propagation algorithm in mini batches to update the system parameters by using (1). Note that we keep the centroids, $c^{(i)}$, fixed until we complete all training examples in one epoch. At the end of each epoch, we then update the centroids with the current parameters in the latent space of the current layer:

$$E - step : update \ (W,b) \ while \ keeping \ c^{(i)} \ fixed \tag{2}$$

$$\{W_1,b_1,W_2,b_2\} = \arg\min_{w,h} \frac{1}{2z}\sum_{t=1}^{z} \left\| h_{w,h}(p^{(t)}) - c^{(t)} \right\|^2 + \frac{\lambda}{2}\sum W^2$$

$$M - step : update \ c^{(i)} \ in \ latent \ space, (W_1,b_1)$$

$$f_p(p^{(t)};W_1,b_1) = W_1^T p^{(t)} + b_1 \ ; \ f_c(c^{(i)};W_1,b_1) = W_1^T c^{(i)} + b_1$$

$$\forall \ p^{(t)} \in P \ ; q_i^t \leftarrow \begin{cases} 1 \ if \ \left\| f_p - f_c \right\| = \min_i \left\| f_p - f_{c^{(i)}} \right\| \\ 0 \ otherwise \end{cases} \tag{3}$$

$$\forall \ c^{(i)}, i = 1,2,3,...,k \ ; \ c^{(i)} = \frac{\sum_t q_i^t \ p^{(t)}}{\sum_t q_i^t}$$

The activation values of the hidden layer are recorded for both inputs and centroids after updating the network parameters, W and b, in an epoch. Finally, we assign the nearest centroid to each patch in this new domain but we update the centroids in the original input space as in maximization step of (3). These two steps are followed alternately until the cost is under some threshold or the iterations reach to a predetermined number.

3.3   Hierarchical Bag-of-Words Representation

Assuming that we have learned the current layer, we can now produce BoW representations for the input image by using the tuned centroids, $c^{(i)}$. We first extract all patches with a dimension of *w-by-w* in a convolutional way by one-pixel spacing. After preprocessing, we run the network to compute the hidden layer activations which will be used as the input to the next layer. This corresponds to a valid convolution that extracts local patterns in the receptive fields. Additionally, the nonlinear voting scheme of [8] is implemented to the patches of the input image for BoW representations as it is simple to implement, and it offers a softer and sparse encoding.

After extracting global feature maps from patch descriptions for images, we now aim to get local features, again in an unsupervised manner. More formally, we coarsely segment the feature maps, the activations of the first hidden layer, spatially into quadrants and train another specific network for each quadrant. The intuition is that we may extract more abstract feature maps and BoW representations after the first layer, plus spatial information by segmentation is achieved. We follow the same procedure in the second layer. We randomly select patches from the quadrant feature maps and use them for the input to the network, respectively. We finally get another convolutional feature maps that are specific to quadrants while producing new BoW representations. Before going through the third layer, we first join the quadrant feature maps to get an integral input, and then repeat the same procedure. The intuition of the last layer is that we may correlate the spatial information that is extracted from each quadrant individually. Besides, we may get better performance in a holistic representation. Also note that we only whiten the input of the 2nd and 3rd layer as a preprocessing step. The proposed network architecture for hierarchical BoW representations is depicted in Fig. 2.

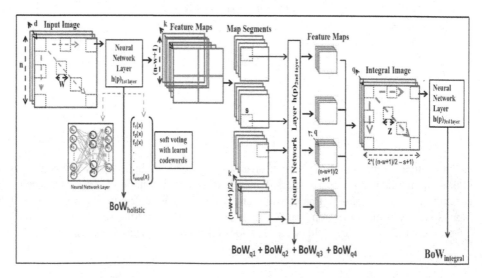

Fig. 2. The proposed three-hidden layer network for hierarchical BoW representations

We can now use the BoW feature vectors layer by layer, in pairs or concatenated at once to represent the instances in a new feature space. This pyramid like structure has been first proposed in [12] and proved to increase the performance. Given these hierarchical BoW representations extracted from the 3-hidden-layer network, we apply standard discriminant algorithms to the labeled training data. In our experiments, we use $L2$ Support Vector Machines (SVM) classification method. Cross-validation is implemented to adjust the constant factor (i.e. C) of the SVM. The experimental setup and results are explained in the next section.

4   Performance Evaluation

In the experiments, we use a very popular dataset in the literature for object classification, CIFAR-10. The detailed information about this dataset can be found at [22]. It consists of *32-by-32* 50,000 training RBG images which are divided by 5 equal batches, all of them in one of 10 object categories. The test set is already separated and it consists of 10,000 unseen images, and the task is to classify each to its category.

We construct a 3-hidden-layer network for unsupervised feature learning. Code words are found at each layer while optimizing the network parameters. We use the code words for hierarchical BoW representations, and the learned layers to transform the input into feature maps for the next layer. In detail, we use *7-by-7* patches for the first layer, *2-by-2* patches for the second and the third layers as input, with a standard stride of *1* pixel. We feed huge amount of randomly selected patches (i.e. about 500,000) at each layer to optimize the parameters. Notice that we decrease the patch size after the first layer and we have two reasons for doing so. First, the feature maps where each point is h-dimensional (i.e. the number of neurons at the previous hidden layer) are fed as the input after the first layer. Increasing the size means increasing the complexity of the network. Second, we need to have sufficiently enough sample patches to create a stable BoW representation, which is to decrease the patch size. But this would also decrease the complexity. So we offset the complexity by adding the mean values of each activation channel within the patch window, like in [17]. Besides, we use hyperbolic tangent function at the hidden layer and no function (i.e. linear) at the output neurons.

Another detail is that we use BoW representations in the classification step while the others [8, 9, 10, 18, 19] use the hidden layer activations directly to produce a new feature vector for the instances. So they usually need an over-complete structure which leads to an extra computational cost. With regards to our approach, the dimensionality of the feature vector depends on the number of code words, not related to the network structure. This is an advantage over the other works. For comparative results, we set the number of centroids sequentially to 100, 200, 400, 800, 1200, 1600 as in [8]; and the test accuracies are displayed in Fig. 3. In the experiments, we use 30 neurons in each layer which are determined by cross-validation and it is much smaller than the input. Finally, it is worth to note that we implement contrast normalization to the first layer's input, and whitening to all layers' inputs as the preprocessing steps.

We first analyze classification results of the BoW representations in pyramid form at Table 1. The experiments are repeated 30 times and the average results are noted. It shows the performance rates at single and multiple layers of the pyramid similar to format in [12]. The pyramid form refers to the BoW vectors of the previous and the current layers. It is obvious that we get better performances in deeper layers. The best single layer performance is achieved at layer two with 72.16%. We conclude that the spatial information improves the performance when we divide an image into finer sub-regions. Besides, more discriminative representations are produced as we use BoW representations together. The hierarchical BoW representations provide up to 11% increments in classification result when the pyramid forms are used. In overall, 2% increase is achieved when compared to [8] in this particular dataset.

Next, we compare the performance of our method to the similar unsupervised feature learning approaches at Table 2. They mainly use the building blocks that we have already mentioned in section 2; like AEs, RBMs and CNNs. Although our work is much less complex, except k-means [8], we slightly outperform the others at minimum about 1%. This indicates that better performances may be achieved by using the features of all layers together in a computationally efficient way.

Table 1. Classification results of the BoW Representations in pyramid form.

Layer	Pyramid of BoWs W = 1600	
	Single Layer (%)	*Pyramid Layers (%)*
1	68.24	---
2	**72.16**	77.45
3	70.17	**79.72**

Table 2. Classification performances of the algorithms on CIFAR-10 test set.

Algorithms	Accy. (%)
3-way Factorized RBM [23]	65.3
Convolutional RBM [21]	78.9
Sparse Auto-encoder [8]	73.4
Sparse RBM [8]	72.4
Triangle k-means [8]	77.9
Mean-Covariance RBM [24]	71.0
Convolutional Neural Network [9]	77.5
Concolutional Auto-Encoder [9]	78.2
Proposed 3-layer BoW Encoder	**79.7**

Later, we compare the performances of some methods by changing the dimensionality of features in Fig. 3. It is determined by the number of centroids for the k-means and our approach while it is the number of neurons in the hidden layers for AEs and RBMs. As expected, all algorithms get higher rates by learning more features. Our work is always better than single layer AE and RBM. On the other side, k-means method outperforms ours by a certain level, 400 features, but we start getting better performances from that point. We can say that the hierarchical representations improve the performance in simple structures.

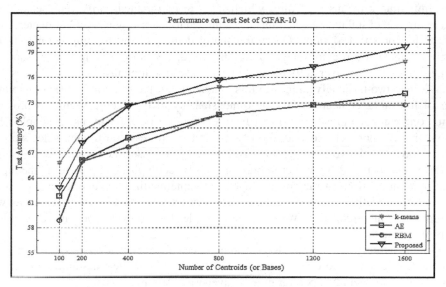

Fig. 3. Comperative results with different number of centroids (or bases)

Finally, we investigate the effect on the overall accuracy of the patches sizes that are used to feed the network. While we keep *2-by-2* size fixed for the second and the third levels, the patch size is changed as the input to the first layer for further evaluations. Also note that stride is still *1* pixel in all levels, the number of centroids is *1600*. At Table 3, we see that the patch size does not significantly impact on the overall performance which is also acknowledged in [8]. Instead, the number of features (i.e. centroids) and the stride size are more effective parameters. The intuition in here is that reasonably high dimensionality for the feature vector mostly introduces better discrimination and we get more samples for the BoW representations if the stride is reduced.

Table 3. The effect of receptive field sizes on the overall accuracy.

Patch Size	Accy. (%)
2	77.4
3	77.6
5	78.9
7	**79.7**
9	79.1
12	78.6

5   Conclusion

In this paper, we analyze the deep network structures in greedy layer-wise unsupervised feature learning. A three-hidden-layer network is learned to produce code words by simulating k-means algorithm which leads to hierarchical BoW representations. Huge amount of unlabeled patch instances are fed to learn single layer parameters and the code words in EM steps. Only after that is done, we start training the next layer while keeping the previous layer's weights fixed, and so on. Note that we do not count on the hidden layer activations directly in classification task.

We gain two basic advantages in this manner. First, the relation between the number of hidden layer neurons and the dimensionality of the feature vectors is broken. Thus one can get more dimensional feature vectors efficiently by using simple networks in our approach. Second, the feature vectors are less constrained since we use code words to achieve BoW vectors. Additionally, we associate location information with the conventional BoW representation. This is accomplished by dividing the input into quadrant regions at the second layer and implementing a network for each sub-region individually. In experiments, we see that the performance is increased as we combine the hierarchical BoW representations, leading to outperform more complex approaches in the literature.

For the future work, we plan to embed hierarchical segmentation into this approach for more discriminative code words, and to develop a holistic fine-tuning procedure for updating the parameters after greedy layer-wise training.

Acknowledgements. This work was supported in part by the Scientific and Technological Research Council of Turkey - TUBITAK 2214-B.14.2.TBT.0.06.01-214-83.

References

1. Alpaydın, E.: Introduction to Machine Learning. The MIT Press, London (2004)
2. Bengio, Y., Courville, A., Vincent, P.: Representation Learning: A Review and New Perspectives. PAMI **35**(8), 1798–1828 (2013)
3. Lowe, D.: Distinctive Image Features From Scale Invariant Keypoints. Int'l J. Computer Vision **60**(2), 91–110 (2004)
4. Bay, H., Ess, A., Tuytelaars, T., Gool, L.C.: SURF: Speeded Up Robust Features. Computer Vision and Image Understanding (CVIU) **110**(3), 346–359 (2008)
5. Bosch, A., Zisserman A., Munoz, X.: Representing shape with a spatial pyramid kernel. In: ACM International Conference on Image and Video Retrieval (2007)
6. Oliva, A., Torralba, A.: Modeling the Shape of the Scene: a Holistic Representation of the Spatial Envelope. Int'l J. Computer Vision **42**(3), 145–175 (2001)
7. Krizhevsky, A., Hinton, G.E.: Using very deep auto-encoders for content-based image retrieval. In: ESANN (2011)
8. Coates, A., Lee, H., Andrew, Y.N.: An analysis of single-layer networks in unsupervised feature learning. In: International Conference on Artificial Intelligence and Statistics (AISTATS) (2011)

9. Masci, J., Meier, U., Cireşan, D., Schmidhuber, J.: Stacked convolutional auto-encoders for hierarchical feature extraction. In: Honkela, T. (ed.) ICANN 2011, Part I. LNCS, vol. 6791, pp. 52–59. Springer, Heidelberg (2011)
10. Hinton, G.E., Osindero, S., Teh, Y.W.: A Fast Learning Algorithm for Deep Belief Nets. Neural Computation **18**(7), 1527–1554 (2006)
11. Ergul, E., Arica, N.: Scene classification using spatial pyramid of latent topics. In: ICPR, pp. 3603–3606 (2010)
12. Lazebnik, S., Schmid, C., Ponce, J.: Beyond bags of features: spatial pyramid matching for recognizing natural scene categories. In: Proc. IEEE CVPR, vol. 2, pp. 2169–2178 (2006)
13. Arel I., Rose D.C., Karnowski T.P.: Deep Machine Learning: A New Frontier in Artificial Intelligence Research. IEEE Computational Intelligence Magazine **5** (2010)
14. Bengio, Y., Lamblin, P., Popovici, D., Larochelle, H.: Geedy Layer-wise Training of Deep Networks. NIPS (2007)
15. Bengio, Y.: Learning Deep Architectures for AI. Foundations and Trends in Machine Learning **2**(1), 1–127 (2009)
16. Hinton, G.E.: A Practical Guide to Training Restricted Boltzmann Machine. University of Toronto (2010)
17. Quoc, L., Ranzato, M., Monga, R., Devin, M., Chen, K., Corrado, G., Dean, J., Andrew, N.: Building high-level features using large scale unsupervised learning. In: International Conference in Machine Learning (2012)
18. Yang, Y., Shah, M.: Complex events detection using data-driven concepts. In: ECCV, pp. 722–735 (2012)
19. Srivastava, N.: Improving Neural Networks with Dropout. Master of Science Thesis, University of Toronto (2013)
20. Raina, R., Battle, A., Honglak, L., Packer, B., Andrew Y.N.: Self-taught learning: transfer learning from unlabeled data. In: Proceedings of the 24th Int'l Conf. on Machine Learning (ICML) (2007)
21. Krizhevsky, A.: Convolutional Deep Belief Networks on CIFAR-10. Technical Report (2010)
22. The CIFAR-10 dataset. http://www.cs.toronto.edu/~kriz/cifar.html
23. Ranzato, M., Krizhevsky, A., Hinton, G.E.: Factored 3-way restricted boltzmann machines for modeling natural images. In: ASTATS 13 (2010)
24. Ranzato, M., Hinton, G.E.: Modeling pixel means and covariances using factorized third-order boltzmann machines. In: CVPR (2010)
25. Gong, Y., Wang, L., Guo, R., Lazebnik, S.: Multi-scale orderless pooling of deep convolutional activation features. In: Fleet, D., Pajdla, T., Schiele, B., Tuytelaars, T. (eds.) ECCV 2014, Part VII. LNCS, vol. 8695, pp. 392–407. Springer, Heidelberg (2014)
26. Bergamo, A., Sinha, S.N., Torresani, L.: Leveraging structure from motion to learn discriminative codebooks for scalable landmark classication. In: CVPR (2013)

Fast Image Classification with Reduced Multiclass Support Vector Machines

Marco Melis, Luca Piras$^{(\boxtimes)}$, Battista Biggio,
Giorgio Giacinto, Giorgio Fumera, and Fabio Roli

Department of Electrical and Electronic Engineering, University of Cagliari,
Piazza D'Armi, 09123 Cagliari, Italy
{marco.melis,luca.piras,battista.biggio,giacinto,
fumera,roli}@diee.unica.it
http://pralab.diee.unica.it

Abstract. Image classification is intrinsically a multiclass, nonlinear classification task. Support Vector Machines (SVMs) have been successfully exploited to tackle this problem, using one-vs-one or one-vs-all learning schemes to enable multiclass classification, and kernels designed for image classification to handle nonlinearities. To classify an image at test time, an SVM requires matching it against a small subset of the training data, namely, its support vectors (SVs). In the multiclass case, though, the union of the sets of SVs of each binary SVM may almost correspond to the full training set, potentially yielding an unacceptable computational complexity at test time. To overcome this limitation, in this work we propose a well-principled reduction method that approximates the discriminant function of a multiclass SVM by jointly optimizing the full set of SVs along with their coefficients. We show that our approach is capable of reducing computational complexity up to two orders of magnitude without significantly affecting recognition accuracy, by creating a super-sparse, budgeted set of virtual vectors.

1 Introduction

In the last decade, Support Vector Machines (SVMs) [23] have gained increasing popularity in the field of image classification, due to their high generalization capability [1,14,25]. In addition, the introduction of novel kinds of feature descriptors, like the Scale-Invariant Feature Transform (SIFT) [15] and the Histogram of Oriented Gradients (HoG) [8], extracted following the Bag-of-Words (BoW) paradigm and the spatial pyramid framework [11], has caused a significant increase in the dimensionality of the corresponding feature spaces. This change, along with the ability of SVMs to retain a high generalization capability even in high-dimensional feature spaces, has favored a wide diffusion of SVMs in image classification tasks.

Under this setting, high-dimensional image descriptors in combination with linear classifiers are used. The use of linear classifiers is usually motivated by computational efficiency reasons. This is especially important when dealing with

© Springer International Publishing Switzerland 2015
V. Murino and E. Puppo (Eds.): ICIAP 2015, Part II, LNCS 9280, pp. 78–88, 2015.
DOI: 10.1007/978-3-319-23234-8_8

a large number of classes and images, even if it may not attain a very high classification accuracy [1,14]. To overcome this drawback, the use of kernel-based approaches has become widely popular. Although being frequently used, this approach has the disadvantage of requiring a large number of computations during testing, as it requires matching each test image against a potentially large number of images in the training set. For instance, to classify a test image, an SVM requires computing the kernel values between the test image and the so-called Support Vectors (SVs), whose number increases linearly with the training set size [6,20]. Usually, in image classification, researchers aim to optimize the training phase and use parallel computing to manage the complexity at test time while preserving classification accuracy [14].

The use of nonlinear classifiers, besides bringing clear benefits in terms of classification performance, demands for a higher complexity at test time. In fact, if linear classifiers can classify a test image by simply computing a scalar product between its feature vector and the set of learned feature weights [23], the use of kernels requires a much higher number of comparisons, as mentioned above. It is thus clear that enabling the use of kernel-based methods on large image datasets while retaining a reduced computational complexity at test time can be considered a relevant open research issue. In the field of pattern recognition, diverse methods have been proposed to tackle this problem. In particular, several methods have been proposed to reduce the number of SVs in SVMs [19,21] but, to the best of our knowledge, no one has been ever exploited for image classification purposes.

Although SVMs have been designed for binary classification, in object recognition and image classification tasks they have to deal with several classes. To this end, several multiclass extensions have been considered (see Sect. 2).

In this paper, we propose a novel algorithm that can drastically reduce the number of required matchings without significantly affecting recognition accuracy. To this end, our algorithm creates a small set of virtual support vectors, and jointly optimizes the objective function of all SVMs (one for each class) at once. In particular, our algorithm optimizes a unique, budgeted set of virtual vectors along with an optimal set of coefficients for their combination (see Sect. 3). It is also worth noting that the proposed method may be exploited to speed up other non-parametric approaches besides SVMs, making it suitable for a wider range of pattern recognition tasks.

The reported results show that our approach is capable of reducing computational complexity up to two orders of magnitude, while only worsening the recognition accuracy of about 5% in the worst case (see Sect. 4).

2 Image Classification with Visual Descriptors

Classifying a scene depicted in an image amounts to labeling it among a set of categories, according to its semantic meaning. In recent years, scene classification has been an active and important research topic, ranging from computer vision to content-based image retrieval, as witnessed by the large number of related approaches proposed in the last decade [11,13,26]. Despite this, a number of challenging aspects in scene classification can be still considered open issues, including inter-class similarity, intra-class variability, and the wide range of illumination and scale changes. Along with the considerable progress made in this field, tougher challenges have been posed by researchers, in terms of more difficult benchmark datasets, *i.e.*, bigger datasets with an increasing number of images: 8-category scenes [16], 13-category scenes [13], 15-category scenes [11], and 397-category scenes (SUN-dataset) [24].

Feature extraction and classification algorithms play an important role in scene classification problems [5,18]. Regarding feature descriptors, researchers have recently employed histograms of local descriptors instead of global image features. The former are indeed able to better model the content of images in order to fill the semantic gap between low-level features and high-level concepts.

The most famous approach uses the so-called bag-of-features paradigm to model visual scenes in image collections [13]. This approach has been first exploited with SIFT descriptors [15] but it has been quickly used also with other descriptors. One of the main drawbacks of the bag-of-features representation is that it does not account for spatial information. To overcome this limitation, an efficient extension of this approach, called spatial pyramid matching (SPM), has been proposed in [11]. It exploits spatial relationships between neighboring local regions. Compared with methods based on low-level features, both the aforementioned approaches achieve very good results for multiple scene classification, although they suffer a high computational cost and generate very high-dimensional feature spaces.

Due to their good generalization ability also in the presence of high-dimensional feature spaces, SVMs are among the most used classifiers in scene classification tasks [7,24,26]. SVMs have been designed for binary classification, but they can be exploited for multiclass classification by decomposing the multiclass problem into several two-class sub-problems, *e.g.*, using the One-vs-One (OVO) and the One-vs-All (OVA) approaches. The first method trains each binary classifier on two out of N classes and builds $N(N-1)/2$ classifiers, subsequently combined through majority voting. Conversely, the second approach constructs a set of N binary classifiers, each aiming to discriminate one given class from the remaining ones. During classification, a sample is assigned to the class exhibiting the highest *support*, *i.e.*, the one corresponding to the classifier that outputs the most confident prediction.

Another important aspect of statistical learning approaches like SVMs is the choice of the kernel, since an inappropriate kernel can lead to poor performance. There are currently no techniques available to know which kernel to use, so it easy to understand why several authors exploit well-known kernels such as the polynomial kernel or the Radial Basis Function (RBF) kernel. In image classification, however, several studies have investigated this issue, reporting that histogram-intersection kernels usually outperform polynomial and RBF kernels.[2,3,7,11].

3   Reducing Multiclass Support Vector Machines

In this section, we extend the SVM reduction method originally proposed in [4] for binary classification problems to the multiclass classification case. Let us assume we are given a set $\mathcal{D} = \{\boldsymbol{x}_i, y_i\}_{i=1}^n \in \mathcal{X}^n \times \mathcal{Y}^n$ of n images along with their labels $y \in \mathcal{Y} = \{1, \ldots, c\}$, being c the number of classes.[1] Training a one-vs-all multiclass SVM on $\mathcal{D}$ amounts to learning a binary SVM for each class $k = 1, \ldots, c$, using the samples of class k as positive training samples, and the remaining ones as negative. Its decision function is then given as:

$$y^\star = \arg \max_{k=1,\ldots,c} g_k(\boldsymbol{x}) = \sum_{i=1}^n \alpha_i^k k(\boldsymbol{x}, \boldsymbol{x}_i) + b^k, \tag{1}$$

where $y^\star$ is the predicted class label, $g_k(\boldsymbol{x})$ is the kth SVM's discriminant function, and the set $\{\alpha_i^k\}_{i=1}^n$ are its *signed* dual coefficients (positive if $y_i = k$, and negative otherwise). Although each binary SVM has a sparse solution, *i.e.*, only a subset of the values in $\{\alpha_i^k\}_{i=1}^n$ are not null (corresponding to its *support* vectors), their number grows linearly with the training set size [6,20]. Furthermore, in the multiclass case, classifying an input image requires matching it against the set of SVs of each binary SVM, which yields a number of matchings (*i.e.*, kernel computations) equal to the size of the *union* of the sets of SVs of each binary SVM. In the sequel, we refer to this number as m, and, as we will see in Sect. 4, m may be very close to the full training set size n.

Our goal is to reduce the number of required matchings m to a much smaller number r, by approximating each SVM's discriminant function $g_k(\boldsymbol{x})$ with a much *sparser* linear combination $h_k(\boldsymbol{x})$, such that all functions $h_k(\boldsymbol{x})$, for $k = 1, \ldots, c$ share the *same* set of SVs $z = (z_1, \ldots, z_r) \in \mathcal{X}^r$, but have a different set of weighting coefficients $\boldsymbol{\beta}_k = (\beta_1^k, \ldots, \beta_r^k) \in \mathbb{R}^r$. In other words, we aim to approximate the decision function given by Eq. (1) as:

$$y^\star = \arg \max_{k=1,\ldots,c} h_k(\boldsymbol{x}) = \sum_{j=1}^r \beta_j^k k(\boldsymbol{x}, \boldsymbol{z}_j) + b^k \ . \tag{2}$$

To find the coefficients $\{\boldsymbol{\beta}_k\}_{k=1}^c$ and the shared SVs z, we extend our recent work in [4] to the multiclass case. In that work, inspired by the earlier work in [19], we proposed a reduction method based on the idea of minimizing the squared Euclidean distance between the values of g_k and h_k computed on the training points, with respect both to $\boldsymbol{\beta}_k$ and to the choice of the SVs z. In practice, we did not require the SVs z to be samples of $\mathcal{D}$, but allow for the creation of *novel, virtual* vectors. In the multiclass case, the initial formulation in [4] can be modified by considering k distinct SVMs that share the same SVs z, as:

$$\min_{\beta, z} \Omega = \sum_{k=1}^c \sum_{i=1}^n u_i \left(h_k(\boldsymbol{x}_i) - g_k(\boldsymbol{x}_i) \right)^2 + \lambda \boldsymbol{\beta}_k^\top \boldsymbol{\beta}_k \ , \tag{3}$$

---

[1] For simplicity, we assume here that each image can belong only to one class, *i.e.*, we focus on single-label classification. Although our approach can be easily extended to the multi-label classification case, we leave this investigation to future work.

Algorithm 1. Reduced Multiclass SVM (RMSVM), adapted from [4]

Input: the training data $\mathcal{D} = \{x_i, y_i\}_{i=1}^n$; the kernel function $k(\cdot, \cdot)$; the parameters C and λ; the initial vectors $\{z_j^{(0)}\}_{j=1}^r$; the gradient step size η; a small number ϵ.
Output: The coefficients β and the SVs $\{z_j\}_{j=1}^r$.

1: Learn a one-vs-all multiclass SVM on $\mathcal{D}$, with kernel $k(\cdot, \cdot)$ and regularizer C.
2: Compute $\{g_k\}_{k=1}^c$ by classifying $\mathcal{D}$ with each binary SVM.
3: Set the iteration count $q \leftarrow 0$.
4: Compute $\{\beta_k^{(0)}\}_{k=1}^c$ (Eq. 5) using $z_1^{(0)}, \ldots, z_r^{(0)}$.
5: **repeat**
6:      Set $j \leftarrow \mathrm{mod}(q, r) + 1$ to index a support vector.
7:      Compute $\frac{\partial \Omega}{\partial z_j}$ using Eq. (6).
8:      Increase the iteration count $q \leftarrow q + 1$
9:      Set $z_j^{(q)} \leftarrow z_j^{(q-1)} + \eta \frac{\partial \Omega}{\partial z_j^{(q-1)}}$.
10:     **if** $z_j^{(q)} \notin \mathcal{X}$, **then** project $z_j^{(q)}$ onto $\mathcal{X}$.
11:     Set $z_i^{(q)} = z_i^{(q-1)}$, $\forall i \neq j$.
12:     Compute $\{\beta_k^{(q)}\}_{k=1}^c$ (Eq. 5) using $z_1^{(q)}, \ldots, z_r^{(q)}$.
13: **until** $\left| \Omega\left(\beta^{(q)}, z^{(q)}\right) - \Omega\left(\beta^{(q-1)}, z^{(q-1)}\right) \right| < \epsilon$
14: **return:** $\beta = \beta^{(q)}$, and $z = z^{(q)}$.

---

where the scalars $u_1, \ldots, u_n$ can be used to balance the contribution of each point x_i to the empirical loss (*e.g.*, if classes are unbalanced), the regularizer $\beta_k^\top \beta_k$ controls overfitting, and λ is a regularization parameter.[2] By denoting with $g_k, h_k \in \mathbb{R}^n$ the values of g_k and h_k for the training points, and with $U \in \mathbb{R}^{n \times n}$ the diagonal matrix $\mathrm{diag}(U) = (u_1, \ldots, u_n)$, we can rewrite Eq. (3) in matrix form as:

$$\Omega(\beta, z) = \sum_{k=1}^c \left(h_k^\top U h_k - 2 h_k^\top U g_k + g_k^\top U g_k \right) + \lambda \beta_k^\top \beta_k \ . \tag{4}$$

Problem (4) can be solved by iteratively modifying β and z, as detailed below. The full procedure is given as Algorithm 1. We also report a two-dimensional example in Fig. 1, in which our algorithm reduces the number of SVs of approximately 24 times, from $m = 73$ to $r = 3$.

β-Step. The coefficients β_k for each reduced SVM are computed assuming that the SVs z are fixed. This yields a standard ridge regression, which can be analytically solved by deriving Eq. (4) with respect to β_k, assuming z constant, and then setting the gradient to zero:

$$\beta_k = \underbrace{\left(K_{xz}^\top U K_{xz} + \lambda \mathbb{I} \right)^{-1}}_{M^{-1}} \underbrace{\left(K_{xz}^\top U \right)}_{N} g_k \ , \tag{5}$$

where $\mathbb{I} \in \mathbb{R}^{r \times r}$ is the identity matrix, and $K_{xz} \in \mathbb{R}^{n \times r}$ denotes the kernel matrix computed between $x_1, \ldots, x_n$ and the set of SVs z.

---

[2] Here, for convenience, the bias values b^k are set equal to those of the initial SVMs g_k. In general, they can be jointly optimized with the coefficients β_k, with minor variations to our subsequent derivations.

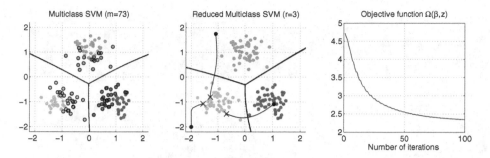

Fig. 1. A two-dimensional classification example with three classes (cyan, green, and red points). *Left:* Decision boundaries (black lines) for the one-vs-all multiclass SVM, that requires $m = 73$ SVs (circled in black). *Middle:* Decision boundaries for our reduced multiclass SVM, using only $r = 3$ SVs (black points). The path followed by each SV during the optimization is also reported (in black), starting from points denoted with '×'. *Right:* Objective function values (Eq. 3) during the minimization process.

z-**Step.** To update z, the objective can be minimized through gradient descent (no analytical solution is available). Its gradient with respect to a given z_j is:

$$\frac{\partial \Omega}{\partial z_j} = 2\sum_{k=1}^{c}\left(h_k - g_k\right)^\top \mathbf{U}\left(\beta_j^k \frac{\partial \mathbf{K}_{xz_j}}{\partial z_j} + \mathbf{K}_{xz}\frac{\partial \beta_k}{\partial z_j}\right) + 2\lambda \beta_k^\top \frac{\partial \beta_k}{\partial z_j} , \qquad (6)$$

where $\mathbf{K}_{xz_j}$ is the jth column of $\mathbf{K}_{xz}$, and we use the numerator-layout convention for matrix derivatives, *i.e.*, all the derivatives with respect to z_j are vectors or matrices with the same number of columns as the dimensionality of z_j. The term $\frac{\partial \beta}{\partial z_j}$ can be obtained by deriving Eq. (5) (before inverting $\mathbf{M}$), which yields:

$$\frac{\partial \beta_k}{\partial z_j} = -\mathbf{M}^{-1}\left(\beta_j^k \mathbf{K}_{xz} + \mathbf{S}\right)^\top \mathbf{U}\frac{\partial \mathbf{K}_{xz_j}}{\partial z_j}, \qquad (7)$$

where $\mathbf{S}$ is an $n \times r$ matrix of zeros, with the jth column equal to $(h_k - g_k)$.

Gradient of $k(x_i, z_j)$**.** Our approach can be readily applied to many numeric kernels, as most of them are differentiable. In our experiments, we will use the exponential χ^2 (exp-χ^2) kernel, given as $k(x_i, z_j) = \exp\left(-\gamma \sum_{l=1}^{d}\frac{(x_{il}-z_{jl})^2}{x_{il}+z_{jl}}\right)$, where x_{il} and z_{jl} are the lth feature of x_i and z_j, and d is the dimensionality of the input space. It is easy to see that the lth element of the gradient $\frac{\partial k(x_i, z_j)}{\partial z_j}$ is given as $\gamma(x_{il} - z_{jl})\frac{3x_{il}+z_{jl}}{(x_{il}+z_{jl})^2}k(x_i, z_j)$.

4   Experiments

In this section, we report a set of experiments to show how significantly our RMSVM algorithm can reduce computations required by a kernel-based app-roach in an image classification scenario. For a fair comparison with current state-of-the-art approaches, we reproduce the image classification setup origi-nally adopted by Xiao *et al.* [24]. The data, the extracted feature values for each

suburb (241)   coast (360)   forest (328)   highway (260)   inside city (308)

mountain (374)   open country (410)   street (292)   tall building (356)   office (215)

bedroom (216)   industrial (311)   kitchen (210)   living room (289)   store (315)

Fig. 2. Example images from the 15-category scenes dataset. We also report the number of available acquisitions for each category.

image, and the training-testing splits are publicly available [9,24] To implement the multiclass SVM classifier and our regression-based algorithm, we exploit the open-source machine-learning library `scikit-learn` [17]. We test our method by selecting a different number of virtual SVs, fixed in advance (*i.e.*, budgeted).

Dataset. According to [24], we use a widely-used benchmark dataset for image classification [11,13,16,24,26], *i.e.*, the *15-category scenes dataset*.[3] It consists of fifteen scene categories. Each class has different number of grayscale images, from 200 to 400 acquisitions, with an average size of 300×250 pixels. In Fig. 2 a selection of images of different classes is shown for reference purpose.

Experimental Setup. We consider a classification problem where each one-vs-all classifier is trained using a subset of randomly-selected images from each available class, while the remaining ones are used to build the test set. In the training set, the number of samples per category is the same for each class. In the test set, the number of samples per class is different, as it depends on the number of images belonging to each class. Results are averaged over 10 repetitions, considering different training-test pairs.

To compare our results to those obtained in [11,24], we exploit HoG descriptors as in [8,24]. Each descriptor consists of 124 feature values, obtained by stacking 2×2 neighboring HoG descriptors each consisting of 31 dimensions. The descriptors extracted from the training images are clustered using the k-means algorithm to identify 300 representative centroids (one per cluster). A histogram of 300 bins is computed from each image. Each bin represents the number of image's descriptors assigned to the corresponding centroid. A number of additional histograms are computed using the same procedure, respectively splitting the image into 2×2 and 4×4 blocks, eventually yielding a total of

---

[3] http://www-cvr.ai.uiuc.edu/ponce_grp/data/

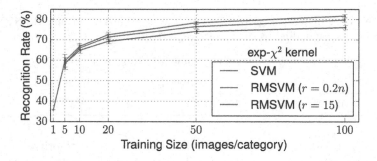

Fig. 3. Recognition rate of the unpruned SVM, and of RMSVM (with different number r of SVs) using the exp-χ^2 kernel on the *15-category scenes dataset*. Results are averaged over 10 repetitions, and reported against an increasing number of samples per class.

21 histograms per image (*i.e.*, $21 \times 300 = 6,300$ features). The exp-χ^2 kernel is used for both SVMs and regressors. According to [24], for each SVM classifier, we set the regularization parameter $C = 1$ and the exp-χ^2 kernel parameter $\gamma = (\frac{1}{n^2} \sum_{i,j}^{n} k(\boldsymbol{x}_i, \boldsymbol{x}_j))^{-1}$, yielding $\gamma \approx 0.2$ in each run. The gradient step η and the parameter λ of our RMSVM (see Algorithm 1) are set as $\eta = 0.5$ and $\lambda = 0.1$ by maximizing classification accuracy through a 3-fold cross validation.

Results. Results for the unpruned SVM and RMSVM on the *15-category scenes dataset* are reported in Fig. 3 in terms of recognition rate (*i.e.*, fraction of correctly-classified test images) against an increasing number of training samples per class. For RMSVM, we consider a different number of SVs. In particular, we consider one SV per class (yielding a total of $r = 15$ SVs), and a number of SVs corresponding to the 20% of the training set size ($r = 0.2n$).

It is easy to see that the proposed method for multiclass SVM reduction performs significantly well even when using a very small set of virtual SVs; *e.g.*, in the case of $n - 1500$ training samples (100 images per class), the RMSVM trained with $r = 15$ virtual SVs worsens the recognition rate of less than 5%. This result is exceptionally good considering the extreme reduction rate; in fact, the number of matchings needed is lowered by 100 times. All other reported cases have a proportional behavior, as the number of SVs (*i.e.*, required matchings for classification) found by the standard SVM classifier grows linearly with the training set size [6, 20]. It is worth noting also that the RMSVM with $r = 0.2n$ SVs only worsens the recognition rate of about 1%, while reducing the required number of matchings of 5 times.

In Fig. 3, we also report the performance of the multiclass SVM trained with one image per class (requiring $n = 15$ matchings at test time). Our results show that an equally-sized set of well-principled optimized SVs can significantly outperform a standard SVM; in particular, the RMSVM using only 15 virtual SVs ($r = 15$, synthesized from a larger training set) achieves recognition rates ranging from 60% to 76%, while that of the unpruned SVM is only 36%. While the training complexity of our approach is increased, computational complexity at test time remains unaffected.

Table 1. Number of matchings required by the unpruned SVM and RMSVM with $r = 0.2n$ SVs, corresponding to the results reported in Fig. 3.

					Number of Matchings	
SVM	$m =$	75	150	300	746.7 ± 1.3	1472.4 ± 4.2
RMSVM (20%)	$r =$	15	30	60	150	300

We finally report an analysis of how well the considered algorithms perform on each scene category in the dataset, by reporting the performance of each of the one-vs-all (binary) base classifiers. In particular, in Table 2 we report the Area Under the ROC Curve (AUC) for each category, and for both the SVM and our RMSVMs using a training set of $n = 1500$ samples, averaged over 10 repetitions. Although our method is able to reliably categorize most of the dataset scenes, some categories, like *store* and *industrial* exhibit higher differences in terms of AUC values with respect to the unpruned SVM. This is mainly due to a very high intra-class variability that may not be thoroughly captured by a significantly-reduced set of SVs.

Table 2. Area Under the ROC Curve (AUC %) for each category, using a training set of 100 samples per class. The performance of the unpruned SVM (requiring $m = 1472.4 \pm 4.2$ matchings per classification) is compared to the RMSVMs, respectively budgeted to $r = 15$ and $r = 300$ matchings.

	suburb	coast	open country	forest	highway	inside city	mountain	street	tall building	office	bedroom	industrial	kitchen	living room	store
SVM	100	98.8	99.6	99.0	97.3	99.1	97.1	99.4	98.8	99.8	96.4	94.5	97.7	97.6	97.0
RMSVM$_{15}$	99.9	98.3	99.5	98.1	96.6	98.7	95.7	98.9	97.9	99.6	94.1	91.5	96.9	96.8	95.4
RMSVM$_{300}$	100	98.8	99.7	98.7	96.3	98.9	96.3	99.1	98.3	99.7	96.0	90.2	95.3	94.8	95.1

5   Related Work on SVM Reduction

We have proposed a novel reduction method for *multiclass* SVMs by extending a previously-proposed method for reducing the set of SVs in binary SVMs [4]. The latter method turned out to outperform existing reduction methods [19], as it is not greedy: as ours, it iteratively modifies each SV during the optimization process, while the methods in [19] optimize one SV at a time, without modifying it when the remaining SVs change. Moreover, the former approach can also be used when the kernel function $k(\cdot, \cdot)$ does not satisfy the Mercer condition, *i.e.*, it is not a proper (positive semi-definite) kernel, but a generic similarity function, whereas the approaches in [19] are only suitable for definite kernels. There are other versions of reduced SVMs [6,10,12], which are however all devoted to the standard binary formulation of this classifier. To our knowledge, the problem of multiclass SVM reduction has only been more systematically investigated in [22]. Despite comparing this approach with ours remains an interesting future development of this work, it is worth remarking that it considers an independent reduction problem for each binary SVM in the one-vs-all scheme, then it concatenates the resulting sets of SVs, and retrains each binary SVM. Our method, conversely, jointly learns a common set of SVs for *all* the binary SVMs involved.

6 Conclusions and Future Work

The proposed image classification approach allows us to overcome the limitation of high computational complexity at test time, common to multiclass, nonlinear classification tasks that exploit kernel-based or similar methods, by jointly optimizing a unique, small set of virtual SVs along with an optimal set of coefficients for their combination. We have shown that we can *dramatically* speed up the test phase without significantly affecting the recognition rate given by the use of nonlinear (though differentiable) kernel functions, and required by large multi-category datasets. As future developments of this work, we plan to investigate the use of our multiclass reduction algorithm with *non-differentiable* and *indefinite* kernel functions, as already preliminary considered in [4]. This opens interesting research directions, considering that well-known non-differentiable kernels, like the histogram intersection kernel [3], have demonstrated high recognition rates in various image classification tasks. Another potential future investigation regards the application of our method to speed up other non-parametric approaches besides SVMs; in fact, the function $g(x)$ in Eq. 3 (and subsequent derivations) is *not* required to be an SVM's discriminant function, but can be *any* discriminant function (or target variable).

Acknowledgments. This work has been partly supported by the project "Advanced and secure sharing of multimedia data over social networks in the future Internet" (CUP F71J11000690002) funded by Regione Autonoma della Sardegna, and by the project "Computational quantum structures at the service of pattern recognition: modeling uncertainty" (CRP-59872) funded by Regione Autonoma della Sardegna, L.R. 7/2007, Bando 2012.

References

1. Akata, Z., Perronnin, F., Harchaoui, Z., Schmid, C.: Good practice in large-scale learning for image classification. IEEE Trans. Pattern Anal. Mach. Intell. **36**(3), 507–520 (2014)
2. Barla, A., Franceschi, E., Odone, F., Verri, A.: Image kernels. In: Lee, S.-W., Verri, A. (eds.) SVM 2002. LNCS, vol. 2388, pp. 83–96. Springer, Heidelberg (2002)
3. Barla, A., Odone, F., Verri, A.: Histogram intersection kernel for image classification. In: Int'l Conf. Image Processing (ICIP), pp. 513–516 (2003)
4. Biggio, B., Melis, M., Fumera, G., Roli, F.: Sparse support faces. In: Int'l Conf. Biometrics (ICB), pp. 1–6 (2015)
5. Bosch, A., Muñoz, X., Marti, R.: Which is the best way to organize/classify images by content? Image Vision Comput. **25**(6), 778–791 (2007)

6. Chapelle, O.: Training a support vector machine in the primal. Neural Comput. **19**(5), 1155–1178 (2007)
7. Chapelle, O., Haffner, P., Vapnik, V.: Support vector machines for histogram-based image classification. IEEE Trans. on Neural Networks **10**(5), 1055–1064 (1999)
8. Dalal, N., Triggs, B.: Histograms of oriented gradients for human detection. In: IEEE Conf. Computer Vision and Pattern Recognition (CVPR), pp. 886–893 (2005)
9. Felzenszwalb, P.F., Girshick, R.B., McAllester, D.A., Ramanan, D.: Object detection with discriminatively trained part-based models. IEEE Trans. Patt. Anal. Mach. Intell. **32**(9), 1627–1645 (2010)
10. Keerthi, S.S., Chapelle, O., DeCoste, D.: Building support vector machines with reduced classifier complexity. J. Mach. Learn. Res. **7**, 1493–1515 (2006)
11. Lazebnik, S., Schmid, C., Ponce, J.: Beyond bags of features: spatial pyramid matching for recognizing natural scene categories. In: IEEE Conf. on Computer Vision and Pattern Recognition (CVPR), pp. 2169–2178 (2006)
12. Lee, Y.J., Mangasarian, O.L.: RSVM: reduced support vector machines. SDM **1**, 325–361 (2001)
13. Li, F.F., Perona, P.: A bayesian hierarchical model for learning natural scene categories. In: IEEE Conf. Computer Vision and Pattern Recognition (CVPR), pp. 524–531 (2005)
14. Lin, Y., Lv, F., Zhu, S., Yang, M., Cour, T., Yu, K., Cao, L., Huang, T.S.: Large-scale image classification: fast feature extraction and SVM training. In: IEEE Conf. on Computer Vision and Pattern Recognition (CVPR), pp. 1689–1696 (2011)
15. Lowe, D.G.: Distinctive image features from scale-invariant keypoints. Int'l Journal of Computer Vision **60**(2), 91–110 (2004)
16. Oliva, A., Torralba, A.: Modeling the shape of the scene: A holistic representation of the spatial envelope. Int'l Journal of Computer Vision **42**(3), 145–175 (2001)
17. Pedregosa, F., Varoquaux, G., Gramfort, A., Michel, V., Thirion, B., Grisel, O., Blondel, M., Prettenhofer, P., Weiss, R., Dubourg, V., Vanderplas, J., Passos, A., Cournapeau, D., Brucher, M., Perrot, M., Duchesnay, E.: Scikit-learn: Machine learning in Python. J. Mach. Learn. Res. **12**, 2825–2830 (2011)
18. Rifkin, R.M., Klautau, A.: In defense of one-vs-all classification. J. Mach. Learn. Res. **5**, 101–141 (2004)
19. Schölkopf, B., Mika, S., Burges, C.J.C., Knirsch, P., Muller, K.R., Rätsch, G., Smola, A.J.: Input space versus feature space in kernel-based methods. IEEE Trans. Neural Networks **10**(5), 1000–1017 (1999)
20. Steinwart, I.: Sparseness of support vector machines. J. Mach. Learn. Res. **4**, 1071–1105 (2003)
21. Suhr, J.K., Jung, H.G.: Sensor fusion-based vacant parking slot detection and tracking. IEEE Trans. on Intelligent Transportation Systems **15**(1), 21–36 (2014)
22. Tang, B., Mazzoni, D.: Multiclass reduced-set support vector machines. In: Proc. Int'l Conf. Machine Learning, ICML 2006, pp. 921–928. ACM, New York (2006)
23. Vapnik, V.N.: Statistical Learning Theory. Wiley, New York (1998)
24. Xiao, J., Hays, J., Ehinger, K.A., Oliva, A., Torralba, A.: SUN database: large-scale scene recognition from abbey to zoo. In: IEEE Conf. Computer Vision and Pattern Recognition (CVPR), pp. 3485–3492 (2010)
25. Zhang, L., Lin, F., Zhang, B.: Support vector machine learning for image retrieval. In: Int'l Conf. Image Processing (ICIP), pp. 721–724 (2001)
26. Zhou, L., Zhou, Z., Hu, D.: Scene classification using multi-resolution low-level feature combination. Neurocomputing **122**, 284–297 (2013)

A Gravitational Model for Plant Classification Using Adaxial Epidermis Texture

André Richard Backes[1]($\boxtimes$), Jarbas Joaci de Mesquita Sá Junior[2],
and Rosana Marta Kolb[3]

[1] Faculdade de Computação, Universidade Federal de Uberlândia,
Av. João Naves de Ávila, 2121, CEP: 38408-100, Uberlândia, MG, Brazil
arbackes@yahoo.com.br
[2] Departamento de Engenharia de Computação, Campus de Sobral,
Universidade Federal do Ceará, Rua Estanislau Frota, S/N, Centro,
CEP: 62010-560, Sobral, Ceará, Brazil
jarbas_joaci@yahoo.com.br
[3] Departamento de Ciências Biológicas, Faculdade de Ciências E Letras,
Universidade Estadual Paulista, UNESP, Av. Dom Antônio,
2100, CEP: 19806-900, Assis, SP, Brazil
rosanakolb@hotmail.com

Abstract. The leaves are very informative plant organs. They are extensively used in plant anatomical studies focusing taxonomy. Their both inner and outer structures provide very discriminant features from vegetal species. In this study, we propose using images from adaxial epidermis for plant classification. The adaxial epidermis is a very variable region in a plant leaf cross-section. It differs in color, number of layers and presence/absence of hypodermis. To accomplish this task, we propose combining complexity analysis methods with a gravitational collapsing system to extract texture features from adaxial epidermis samples. Experimental results show that this combination of techniques surpasses traditional and state-of-the-art methods in both grayscale and color images of adaxial epidermis.

Keywords: Adaxial epidermis · Texture analysis · Color · Gravitational system

1 Introduction

Plant classification has been the focus of intensive research in computer vision. One of its most important goals is to explore information sources that are not used in traditional taxonomy, such as that present in leaves. This plant organ can provide features related to its venation and contour [1] and surface texture [2]. Furthermore, recent studies have proven that its tissues can provide discriminative features as well [3].

We can obtain plant features from different attributes, such as color, shape and texture, being the latter one of the most relevant. Even though there is no

© Springer International Publishing Switzerland 2015
V. Murino and E. Puppo (Eds.): ICIAP 2015, Part II, LNCS 9280, pp. 89–96, 2015.
DOI: 10.1007/978-3-319-23234-8_9

formal definition for the texture attribute, it is possible to understand it as an image composed by models that are repeated in its exact form or with small variations [4]. Such restricted definition is more suitable for artificial textures. Natural textures usually present a random and persistent pattern with a cloudlike appearance [5]. There are many methods that can extract feature vectors from grayscale and color textures, ranging from the classical methods (co-occurrence matrices [6], Gabor filters [7], wavelet descriptors [8]) to the recent or state-of-the-art methods (Bouligand-Minkowski fractal dimension [9], micro-structure descriptors [10]).

This paper aims the classification of grayscale and color images of adaxial epidermis, a very discriminative tissue, thus contributing to plant identification. This leaf tissue has already provided discriminative signatures, as seen in [11,12], proving to be very suitable for plant classification. We used eight species from the neotropical savanna of Brazil. They are: *Byrsonima intermedia* A. Juss., *Miconia albicans* (Sw.) Triana, *Tibouchina stenocarpa* (DC.) Cogn., *Vochysia tucanorum* Mart., *Xylopia aromatica* (Lam.) Mart., *Gochnatia polymorpha* (Less.) Cabrera, *Miconia chamissois* Naudin and *Jacaranda caroba* (Vell.) A. DC [12].

In this study we aim to extend the work previously published in [13–15], where we proposed and evaluated the technique in the classification of synthetic and natural texture. In this paper we focus on a biological problem in order to assess the discrimination ability of our approach. Moreover, the growing and disposal of cells in microscopic biological images are influenced by external factors. This leads to the absence of a well-defined pattern in their texture, increasing the challenge of their recognition.

2   A Gravitational System

We propose simulating a simplified gravitational system from an image I. Since different pixels present different masses, we consider each pixel (x, y) as a particle whose mass is its intensity, $m = I(x, y)$. We also set a central mass M at the center of the image. This mass works as a black hole and it attracts each particle towards it. There is no influence among the particles, only between each particle and the central mass.

Each particle has a singular movement according to its mass and distance from the image center. As a result, an image is able to produce different collapse stages for each time step t. In each collapse stage, a new texture pattern is produced based on the new positions of the particles. Each collapse stage represents a step in the evolution of the system. Complexity descriptors, such as fractal dimension and lacunarity, can be used to describe each stage, resulting in a signature for the image in collapsing process. More details about the gravitational system for grayscale and color images can be found in [13–15].

3   Complexity Analysis

Mandelbrot first developed the concept of fractal dimension to characterize the complexity of a new class of sets called fractals [16]. Nowadays, fractal dimension has been extended to describe other objects (shape and texture) in terms of their irregularity and space occupation [9,16].

Throughout the years, many methods were developed to estimate fractal dimension, here included the Bouligand-Minkowski fractal dimension. This method is known for its great sensitiveness to the structural changes of the object [4,17]. In order to apply this method to a texture pattern, we first create a surface $S \in R^3$ from the texture pattern I by using the function $f : I(x,y) \rightarrow S(x,y,I(x,y))$. In the sequence, we compute the influence volume $V(r)$ of the surface S. We perform this task by dilating each point of S using a sphere of radius r:

$$V(r) = \left| \left\{ s' \in R^3 | \exists s \in S : |s - s'| \leq r \right\} \right|. \tag{1}$$

The Bouligand-Minkowski fractal dimension D is estimated as

$$D = 3 - \lim_{r \to 0} \frac{\log V(r)}{\log r}. \tag{2}$$

Although its known ability to discriminate texture patterns, Mandelbrot realized that completely different texture patterns may present the same fractal dimension, rendering it useless to characterize such samples. To overcome this problem, Mandelbrot introduced the lacunarity. This method enables us to describe a texture pattern in terms of spatial dispersion using a specific gap size [16,18].

Different approaches exist to compute lacunarity. In this study, we consider the gliding-box algorithm [18,19]. This method glides a box of $l \times l$ pixels size to compute the distribution of gaps in the image and, thus, its lacunarity. For each box, the method computes the relative height of that portion of the image

$$h_l(i,j) = \lceil v/l \rceil - \lceil u/l \rceil, \tag{3}$$

where u and v are the minimum and maximum pixel values inside the box, respectively. From the probability density function $Q_l(H)$ of the relative height $h_l(i,j)$, the lacunarity for a box size l is defined as

$$\Lambda(l) = \sum H^2 . Q_l(H) / \left(\sum H . Q_l(H) \right)^2. \tag{4}$$

4   Proposed Feature Vector

In [14,15], we proposed a feasible feature vector to characterize an image modeled as a gravitational system in process of collapse. We used two sets of fractal dimension and lacunarity values computed at each time step t of the gravitational collapse to compose a feature vector as follows

$$\psi_{T,R,L} = [D_{t_1}(R), \ldots, D_{t_k}(R), \Lambda_{t_1}(L), \ldots, \Lambda_{t_k}(L)], \tag{5}$$

where $D_t(R)$ and $\Lambda_t(L)$ represent, respectively, the sets of fractal and lacunarity descriptors computed for a specific set of radii and box sizes, $R = \{r_1, r_2, \ldots, r_N\}$ and $L = \{l_1, l_2, \ldots, l_M\}$, at a specific time step in $T = \{t_1, t_2, \ldots, t_k\}$.

We used this approach to obtain a feature vector as each stage in the collapsing process represents a different relationship among pixels and, therefore, it is a new source of information to be explored. Moreover, fractal dimension is an excellent tool to measure structural changes in a system in collapse due to its great sensitiveness, while lacunarity is able to discriminate systems which present the same fractal dimension although the differences in their structures.

5   Experiments and Results

In our experiment we addressed the problem of plant leaf classification. More specifically, we aim plant classification from the analysis of its adaxial epidermis. We built a database containing 30 texture windows acquired from eight different plant species. Figure 1 shows examples of samples in the database. Additional details about the database can be found in [11]. Each texture window has 150 pixels height while its width is determined by the adaxial surface epidermis thickness, which can vary from species to species. To avoid an undesirable influence of thickness in the computed descriptor, we opted to use a mosaic of 150×150 pixels size. We produced this mosaic for each sample by using a scheme of copy and reflection of the texture pattern over y axis, as shown in Figure 2.

To compute the proposed feature vectors we must set up some parameters of the gravitational process: the mass of the black hole at the center of the image, M, and the gravitational constant G. According to previous studies [13–15], we set $G = 1$, so that, we do not limit, or accelerate, the movement of a particle. The mass M is a value which depends on the image size. As the width of the mosaic image is 150×150 pixels size, and according to the study performed in [13], we computed the mass as $M = 281.25$. For the feature vector parameters, we evaluated different configurations. Among all the combinations of parameters evaluated, we achieved the best results when using $R = \{3, 4\}$ and $L = \{2, 3, 4, 5, 6\}$, at a specific time step set $T = \{1, 3, 6, 9\}$

For the evaluation of our approach, we carried out two experiments. In the first experiment we used grayscale images of adaxial epidermis and we compared our approach to the following grayscale texture analysis methods: Fourier descriptors [20], co-occurrence matrices [6], Gabor filters [7] and wavelet descriptors [8]. In the second experiment, we used color images of adaxial epidermis and the following color texture analysis methods: Gabor EEE [21], HRF [22], multiLayer CCR [23], LBP + Haralick [24], and MSD [10]. The parameters of the compared methods were set up according to either their original papers or, when it was not possible, to the most common use in literature.

For the experimental evaluation, we used Linear Discriminant Analysis (LDA), a supervised statistical classification method, over the computed feature vectors, in a *leave-one-out cross-validation* scheme [25].

Table 1 shows the results obtained when we compare the gravitational approach to other important methods in the grayscale adaxial epidermis database.

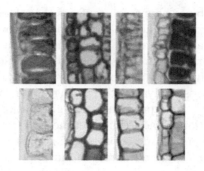

Fig. 1. Adaxial epidermis images of the eight species considered.

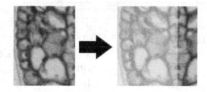

Fig. 2. Process of building a texture mosaic by copy and reflection.

We notice that the classification accuracy obtained by our approach surpasses all the other methods. As an example, our approach achieves a result 2.50% superior, while using around 42% less descriptors, when compared to the second best method (Gabor filters). This result indicates that the gravitational model associated with complexity descriptors is very suitable for discriminating grayscale images from adaxial epidermis tissue.

Table 1. Comparison results for different grayscale texture analysis methods.

Methods	Descriptors	Success rate (%)
Gravitational model	28	89.58
Fourier descriptors	74	74.58
Co-occurrence	16	83.75
Gabor filters	48	87.08
Wavelet descriptors	18	76.67
LBP	10	77.92

Table 2 shows the comparison of the gravitational model with recent and state-of-the-art color analysis methods for the classification of the adaxial epidermis database. For this comparison, we applied the gravitational approach in each channel of the RGB image. This resulted in a total of three feature vectors per image. We concatenated these feature vectors into a single one, which was used to describe the image sample.

The result obtained by our approach confirms that the gravitational model is very suitable for the analysis of adaxial epidermis. Moreover, the results clearly indicate that the color attribute must be considered in adaxial epidermis classification. When comparing the results achieved in grayscale and color images (Tables 1 and 2, respectively), we noticed an increase of 7.5% in the classification accuracy. This difference is equivalent to 18 images correctly classified.

In relation to other color approaches, the gravitational approach yields a success rate 0.83% superior to the second best method (multiLayer CCR). However, our approach uses only 84 descriptors against 640 of the multiLayer CCR method. This is, clearly, a great advantage of our approach.

Table 2. Comparison results for different color texture analysis methods.

Methods	Descriptors	Success rate (%)
Gravitational model RGB	84	97.08
Gabor EEE	192	93.75
HRF	-	45.42
MultiLayer CCR	640	96.25
LBP + Haralick	10	84.58
MSD	72	85.83

Computer vision research applied to adaxial epidermis is very recent. For instance, we know only our three previous works [3,11,12] related to this subject. Among them, only paper [11] can be used for comparison as it adopts the same database (converted into grayscale) and the same performance measurement (accuracy). In such paper, we obtained a success rate of 93.33% while in this work our approach yielded a success rate of 89.58% (see Table 1). Although our current result is inferior, it is important to consider two important facts: first, the paper [11] also proposes a very powerful texture analysis method based on Bouligand-Minkowski fractal dimension; second, in the paper [11] we used 50 descriptors while in this paper we used only 28 descriptors. Moreover, if we consider the color adaxial epidermis database, the performance increases to 97.08% (see Table 2), that is, 3.75% superior to the best result of the paper [11]. This corroborates the assumption that the gravitational model RGB is very suitable for analyzing adaxial epidermis tissue.

6   Conclusion

In this paper, we presented a study addressing the problem of leaf texture classification. By using a simplified gravitational system combined with complexity analysis methods we were able to extract discriminative features from a leaf cell tissue, from both color and grayscale images. We compared these features to other grayscale and color texture analysis methods found in literature. Results showed that these features surpass all the compared approaches and achieve high accuracy, proving to be very suitable for plant classification.

Acknowledgments. André R. Backes gratefully acknowledges the financial support of CNPq (National Council for Scientific and Technological Development, Brazil) (Grant #301558/2012-4), FAPEMIG and PROPP-UFU. Jarbas Joaci de Mesquita Sá Junior gratefully acknowledges the financial support of CNPq (National Council for Scientific and Technological Development, Brazil) (Grant #453298/2015-0).

References

1. Plotze, R.O., Pádua, J.G., Falvo, M., Bernacci, L.C., Oliveira, G.C.X., Vieira, M.L.C., Bruno, O.M.: Leaf shape analysis using the multiscale Minkowski fractal dimension, a new morphometric method: a study with Passiflora. (Passifloraceae). Canadian Journal of Botany - Revue Canadienne de Botanique **83**(3), 287–301 (2005)
2. Casanova, D., Sá Junior, J.J.M., Bruno, O.M.: Plant leaf identification using Gabor wavelets. International Journal of Imaging Systems and Technology **19**(1), 236–243 (2009)
3. Sá Junior, J.J.M., Rossatto, D.R., Kolb, R.M., Bruno, O.M.: A computer vision approach to quantify leaf anatomical plasticity: a case study on Gochnatia polymorpha (Less.) Cabrera. Ecological Informatics **15**, 34–43 (2013)
4. Backes, A.R., Casanova, D., Bruno, O.M.: Plant leaf identification based on volumetric fractal dimension. IJPRAI **23**(6), 1145–1160 (2009)
5. Kaplan, L.M.: Extended fractal analysis for texture classification and segmentation. IEEE Transactions on Image Processing **8**(11), 1572–1585 (1999)
6. Haralick, R.M.: Statistical and structural approaches to texture. Proc. IEEE **67**(5), 786–804 (1979)
7. Manjunath, B.S., Ma, W.Y.: Texture features for browsing and retrieval of image data. IEEE Trans. Pattern Anal. Mach. Intell **18**(8), 837–842 (1996)
8. Laine, A., Fan, J.: Texture classification by wavelet packet signatures. IEEE Transactions on Pattern Analysis and Machine Intelligence **15**(11), 1186–1191 (1993)
9. Backes, A.R., Casanova, D., Bruno, O.M.: Color texture analysis based on fractal descriptors. Pattern Recognition **45**(5), 1984–1992 (2012)
10. Liu, G.H., Li, Z., Zhang, L., Xu, Y.: Image retrieval based on micro-structure descriptor. Pattern Recognition **44**(9), 2123–2133 (2011)
11. Backes, A.R., de M. Sá Junior, J.J., Kolb, R.M., Bruno, O.M.: Plant species identification using multi-scale fractal dimension applied to images of adaxial surface epidermis. In: Jiang, X., Petkov, N. (eds.) CAIP 2009. LNCS, vol. 5702, pp. 680–688. Springer, Heidelberg (2009)
12. Sá Junior, J.J.M., Backes, A.R., Rossatto, D.R., Kolb, R.M., Bruno, O.M.: Measuring and analyzing color and texture information in anatomical leaf cross sections: an approach using computer vision to aid plant species identification. Botany **89**(7), 467–479 (2011)
13. Sá Junior, J.J.M., Backes, A.R.: A simplified gravitational model to analyze texture roughness. Pattern Recognition **45**(2), 732–741 (2012)
14. Sá Junior, J.J.M., Backes, A.R., Cortez, P.C.: A simplified gravitational model for texture analysis. Journal of Mathematical Imaging and Vision **47**(1–2), 70–78 (2013)
15. Sá Junior, J.J.M., Backes, A.R., Cortez, P.C.: Color texture classification based on gravitational collapse. Pattern Recognition **46**(6), 1628–1637 (2013)

16. Mandelbrot, B.: The fractal geometry of nature. Freeman & Co. (2000)
17. Tricot, C.: Curves and Fractal Dimension. Springer-Verlag (1995)
18. Allain, C., Cloitre, M.: Characterizing the lacunarity of random and deterministic fractal sets. Phys. Rev. A **44**(6), 3552–3558 (1991)
19. Du, G., Yeo, T.S.: A novel lacunarity estimation method applied to SAR image segmentation. IEEE Trans. Geoscience and Remote Sensing **40**(12), 2687–2691 (2002)
20. Azencott, R., Wang, J.P., Younes, L.: Texture classification using windowed fourier filters. IEEE Trans. Pattern Anal. Mach. Intell **19**(2), 148–153 (1997)
21. Hoang, M.A., Geusebroek, J.M., Smeulders, A.W.M.: Color texture measurement and segmentation. Signal Processing **85**(2), 265–275 (2005)
22. Paschos, G., Petrou, M.: Histogram ratio features for color texture classification. Pattern Recognition Letters **24**(1–3), 309–314 (2003)
23. Bianconi, F., Fernández, A., González, E., Caride, D., Calvino, A.: Rotation-invariant colour texture classification through multilayer CCR. Pattern Recognition Letters **30**(8), 765–773 (2009)
24. Porebski, A., Vandenbroucke, N., Macaire, L.: Haralick feature extraction from LBP images for color texture classification. In: Image Processing Theory, Tools and Applications, pp. 1–8 (2008)
25. Everitt, B.S., Dunn, G.: Applied Multivariate Analysis, 2nd edn. Arnold (2001)

Adaptive Background Modeling for Land and Water Composition Scenes

Jing Zhao[1], Shaoning Pang[1(✉)], Bruce Hartill[2],
and AbdolHossein Sarrafzadeh[1]

[1] Unitec Institute of Technology, Private Bag 92006, Auckland 1020, New Zealand
ppang@unitec.ac.nz
[2] National Institute of Water and Atmospheric Research, Private Bag 99940,
Auckland 1149, New Zealand

Abstract. In the context of maritime boat ramps surveillance, this paper proposes an Adaptive Background Modeling method for Land and Water composition scenes (ABM-lw) to interpret the traffic of boats passing across boat ramps. We compute an adaptive learning rate to account for changes on land and water composition scenes, in which the portion of water changes over time due to tidal dynamics and other environmental influences. Experimental comparative tests and quantitative performance evaluations of real-world boat-flow monitoring traffic sequences demonstrate the benefits of the proposed algorithm.

1   Introduction

Background modeling has been studied for traffic surveillance in a variety of situations including: motorways [1–3], road intersections [4–6], car parks [7–10], swimming pools [11,12], and water channels [13,14], etc. In general, we categorize different types of scenes into two groups: land scenes and water scenes, as background dynamics in these contexts differ markedly. On land, the background is usually static, with little or no change in topography. In contrast, water scenes are intrinsically dynamic, as water is a reflective surface that moves continuously, often to varying degrees. The reflection of the sun on water, coupled with the unpredictability of waves caused by the wind, moving vessels (wakes) and tidal flows in the maritime environment creates situations where background modeling is far more challenging.

In the context of maritime boat ramps surveillance, we consider background modeling for a dynamic maritime environment, at the interface between the land and the sea. Fig. 1 shows an example of maritime boat ramp which our case study is based on. As seen, the region-of-interest (ROI), identified as a polygon contains both areas of land and water. The boundary between the water and land changes over time with the rise and fall of the tide. As a consequence, the distribution of water and land varies over time in the ROI, which makes background modeling in this case extremely difficult given the varying area of water and amount of light reflected from this water at differing times of day and sun angle.

© Springer International Publishing Switzerland 2015
V. Murino and E. Puppo (Eds.): ICIAP 2015, Part II, LNCS 9280, pp. 97–107, 2015.
DOI: 10.1007/978-3-319-23234-8_10

In this paper, we propose an Adaptive Background Modeling for Land and Water composition scenes (ABM-lw), for performing real-time traffic surveillance at maritime boat ramps. The proposed ABM-lw dynamically classify areas of an image as either land or water, given ancillary tidal height data so that different strategies can be adopted to model backgrounds on land and on the water, respectively. The impact of sunrise and sunset is also specifically considered by proposed ABM-lw, to allow for changes in outdoor luminance. In particular, the use of dynamic learning rate and intelligent updating rules for areas of land and water, respectively, significantly increases the robustness of ABM-lw method. We apply the ABM-lw to real 24-hour boat-flow analysis and counting system and compare it against existing methods for background modeling, the empirical results show that the proposed ABM-lw achieves better performance.

2   Proposed Background Modeling Algorithm

To cope with this extremely challenging land and water composition scene, we classify areas of each image as either land or water, given ancillary model data on predicted tidal height, so that different strategies can be adopted to model the background on land and on the water, respectively. The proposed ABM-lw has four main components:

(1) Separation of areas of land and water: determining the optimized boundary between areas of land and water given ancillary tidal height model data.
(2) Background learning rate calculation: computing background learning rates for areas of land and water, respectively.
(3) Accounting for the influence of sunrise and sunset: adjusting current learning rates by applying the sunrise/sunset pattern.
(4) Background updating: computing background separately for land and water area, and updating the modeled background accordingly.

Before addressing the above main components, we introduce firstly the base model that we use to derive the proposed background modeling. Given $\{I_t\}_{t=1...T}$ as current set of images in observation, and polygon R as the Region Of Interest (ROI). We introduce the following signum function of image pixels as,

$$I_t(i,j) = \begin{cases} I_t(i,j) & \text{if } (i,j) \in R, \\ -1 & \text{otherwise.} \end{cases} \quad (1)$$

By (1), we are able to cast any image (or the same size matrix) and related calculations into the ROI block.

According to [15], the next background B_{t+1} is generated using the weighted average of the instantaneous background IB_t and the current background B_t:

$$B_{t+1} = \alpha IB_t + (1 - \alpha)B_t. \quad (2)$$

Here B_1 is initialized as an image of the background without any moving objects present. α is the learning rate which determines the updating speed of background. In practice, α should be big enough so that background modeling algorithms can adapt rapidly to changes in the background, but small enough so that they are not sensitive to momentary changes. Because the background is influenced by changing luminance, different weather conditions, etc., it is essential for the background modeling algorithm to adopt a dynamic learning rate to optimize performance. We have therefore adopted a dynamic learning rate in the proposed method, rather than a static rate in [15].

The instantaneous background IB_t is generated from the current image but with detected objects removed, and their regions are filled with the current background. Specifically, for each incoming image I_t, we calculate its differences to current background B_t, and threshold the resulting difference image to obtain a binary object mask,

$$O_t(x,y) = \begin{cases} 0 & \text{if } |I_t(x,y) - B_t(x,y)| < \lambda , \\ 1 & \text{otherwise} \end{cases} \tag{3}$$

where λ refers to the luminance threshold for object detection. The current instantaneous background IB_t can then be calculated as,

$$IB_t(x,y) = \begin{cases} B_t(x,y) & \text{if } O_t(x,y) = 1, \\ I_t(x,y) & \text{otherwise.} \end{cases} \tag{4}$$

Note that the above calculations are all in terms of gray-level intensity. In the case of color image, we simply transform the image to gray-level before any calculation.

2.1   Land and Water Area Separation

The goal of separation is to segment the ROI into areas of land and water. In the image coordinate system shown in Fig. 1, the distinction between areas of land and water can be simplified as a geometric problem, which is to find/fix a straight line as,

$$n = km + b \tag{5}$$

where k and b refer to the slope and intercept of straight line, respectively. Thus to determine the shoreline, the task is to search for optimal values of k and b.

Physically, we look the sea as a large container, with the amount of water determined the position of tidal boundary. In this sense, for a specific ramp, we are able to determine the optimal b^* given tidal height data H provided by an ancillary model using interpolation methods such as linear interpolation, polynomial interpolation, or spline interpolation, etc. As a result, we have the revised shoreline function as,

$$n = km + b^* \tag{6}$$

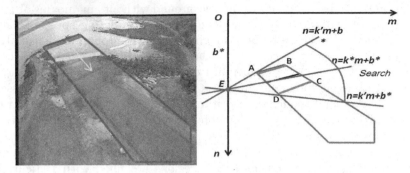

Fig. 1. Left: an example of maritime boat ramp. The region-of-interest (ROI) includes areas of land and water as seen inside the red polygon, and the boundary between water and land is shown by the yellow line. Right: an illustration of searching optimal boundary between water and land.

However, the slope k varies over time, as the direction of the boundary between the land and the water is not only determined by the shape of container, but also by the prevailing weather conditions such as the wind direction. Here, the proposed solution is to classify all ROI pixels into land and water area, then we seek the optimal slope k^* by a searching process described below.

Let D_t denote a land-water distribution matrix of current image I_t, we can find the land water border line by accurately classifying every pixel as covering either land or water. D_t can be obtained by a binary pixel classification, which can be formulated as a convex optimization problem, i.e. the task of finding a minimizer of a convex function f that depends on a variable vector ω. Formally, we formulate this as an optimization problem, where the objective function is of the form

$$f(\omega) = \frac{1}{2}\omega^T\omega + C\sum_{i=1}^{l}\max(1 - y_i\omega^T x_i, 0), \qquad (7)$$

Here the vectors $x_i \in \mathcal{R}^d$ are the training data examples, for $1 \le i \le r$, and $y_i \in [-1, 1]$ are their corresponding labels, which we want to predict. Consequently with the SVM trained, every pixel in S is classified as either land or water. It is not difficult to model a line $n = gm + l$ that gives a pixel level shoreline approximation regardless of tide change.

Consider shoreline approximation in Fig. 1, by (6) we have point E that the actual land/water boundary should have gone through, and its distance to O is b^*. Without loss of generality, we can define for every ramp in surveillance a maximum margin for all possible shorelines. In the example of Fig. 1, rectangle $ABCD$ is the margin area which we denote hereafter as S. To find the optimal slope k^*, we rotate line (6) around E by trying every possible slope k' that directs the line going through margin S. For each test line, we calculate its angle to the land-water border line comes from (7) for land and water pixel classification.

Thus, we have optimized slope k^* calculated as,

$$k^* \leftarrow \underset{k' \in \mathcal{S}}{\text{argmin}} (\arctan \frac{|k' - g|}{1 + k'g}) \qquad (8)$$

2.2   Background Learning Rate Calculation

Under the condition of land and water area distinction, we are able to model land and water backgrounds separately by applying (2) to land and water image block as,

$$\begin{aligned}
\boldsymbol{B}_{t+1}^{l} &= \alpha_l \boldsymbol{I} \boldsymbol{B}_t + (1 - \alpha_l) \boldsymbol{B}_t, \\
\boldsymbol{B}_{t+1}^{w} &= \alpha_w \boldsymbol{I} \boldsymbol{B}_t + (1 - \alpha_w) \boldsymbol{B}_t,
\end{aligned} \qquad (9)$$

where α_l and α_w represent the learning rate for land and water scenes respectively.

The proposed method adopts a dynamic learning rate for land and water area respectively rather than a static one in [15]. In practice, we maintain a 24-hour learning rate buffer, in which a pair of land and water learning rates (α_l, α_w) are stored at every minute. The process for computing learning rates is described below.

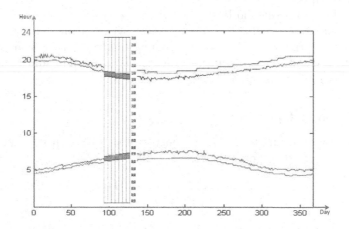

Fig. 2. Learning rate patterns for sunrise and sunset on different days

Consider in our case that, the objective is traffic analysis; more specifically, to count the number of boats/cars passing through the ramps. Thus, the number of objects is the ground truth of our background modeling. When determining the learning rate at time t, we search the optimal rates in the criterion of minimizing the error of objects counting as,

$$(\alpha_l^*, \alpha_w^*) \leftarrow \underset{\alpha_l, \alpha_w \in [0,1]}{\text{argmin}} \left\{ \| (\psi_l - \eta_l) + (\psi_w - \eta_w) \|^2 \right\}, \qquad (10)$$

where η_l and η_w are the predicted number and ψ_l and ψ_w are the actual number of objects in land and water area respectively. Here ψ_l and ψ_w can be obtained by manually viewing each frame. In practice, this is a time-consuming process. For simplicity, we implement (10) by counting the total number of objects using currently computed background regardless of water or land scene.

2.3 Accounting for the Influence of Sunrise and Sunset

In complex outdoor scenes, the level of luminance is easily influenced by several factors, such as time of day, cloud cover, time of year, available street lighting, etc. The rate of luminance change is obviously higher during sunrise and sunset than that of other time. It is therefore necessary to specifically consider the influence of sunrise and sunset as part of our background modeling.

Sunrise and sunset occur during two brief periods every 24-hours. Publicly available sunrise/sunset data provided by Land Information New Zealand (www.linz.govt.nz) gives an accurate estimate of when sunrise and sunset occur, which changes throughout the year. In practice, the influence of sunrise and sunset on the learning rate follows a specific pattern. We assume the pattern gradually changes throughout the year. Fig. 2 gives the learning rate patterns for sunrise and sunset on different days, where the top and bottom curves are for sunset and sunrise respectively.

Accordingly we refresh the learning rate for every minute during a 24-hour loop (i.e., learning rate buffer) as Fig. 2, given the shifting timing of sunrise and sunset during the year. For every incoming image, we search in the buffer suitable rates by time t, if t falls during the expected period of sunrise or sunset, the pattern learning rates are assigned to α_w and α_l.

2.4 Background Updating

Our strategy for updating background consists of two steps: firstly update land and water background respectively as,

$$\begin{aligned} \boldsymbol{B}_{t+1}^l &= \alpha_l^* \boldsymbol{I} \boldsymbol{B}_t + (1 - \alpha_l^*) \boldsymbol{B}_t, \\ \boldsymbol{B}_{t+1}^w &= \alpha_w^* \boldsymbol{I} \boldsymbol{B}_t + (1 - \alpha_w^*) \boldsymbol{B}_t. \end{aligned} \tag{11}$$

Then merge obtained land and water backgrounds into the next background,

$$\boldsymbol{B}_{(t+1)} = \boldsymbol{B}_{t+1}^w \cup \boldsymbol{B}_{t+1}^l. \tag{12}$$

Note that $\boldsymbol{B}_{(t+1)}$ here is an ROI image. To have the entire background image, we can simply merge $\boldsymbol{B}_{(t+1)}$ with the ROI residual image which can be obtained by applying a reversed function (1) on $\boldsymbol{I}_t$.

3   Experimental Results

New Zealand's National Institute of Water and Atmospheric Research (NIWA) has established a network of web cameras overlooking key boat ramps, on behalf of the Ministry for Primary Industries, to monitor trends in recreational fishing effort over time. In this monitoring system, one image is captured per minute for each web camera, providing 1440 images of a monitored ramp on each day. These images are viewed in series by a technician who manually interprets these images and records a count of returning boats for that day. In our experiments, we used 2010-2012 image series captured at Waitangi, Takapuna and Manu Bay boat ramp. We compared backgrounds generated by the ABM-lw algorithm with those generated by the SABS method [15], which is initially designed for detecting vehicles in a terrestrial situation, such as on a highway, and which is proposed ABM-lw based on. The parameter settings for the SABS algorithm were made according to the authors' recommendations [15].

3.1   Robustness to Changes in Luminance at Sunrise and Sunset

In this comparative study, we demonstrate algorithm robustness to sunrise and sunset luminance changes. As we know, the periods of sunrise or sunset last for approximately 30 minutes each day, for which a corresponding 30 frame images are collected by each web camera system. Starting from the first frame, we select frames of minutes with an interval of six and observe algorithm performance in the whole procedure of luminance changes. Fig. 3 gives the comparison matrix, in which the first column shows input frames, and the second and third column show

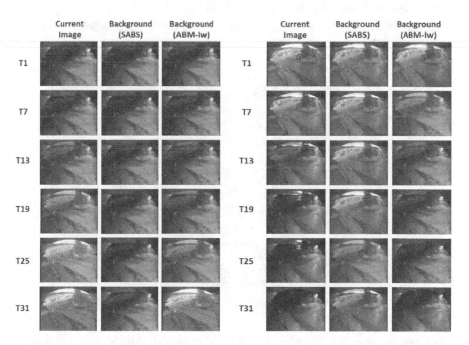

Fig. 3. Comparisons of SABS and proposed ABM-lw modelled backgrounds for a sunrise(left) and sunset(right) sequence of images.

the backgrounds modelled using the SABS and proposed ABM-lw algorithms, respectively.

As would be expected, levels of illumination increased rapidly in the sunrise sequence, being darkest in T1 to brightest in T31; whereas the reverse occurred at sunset. The background models generated by both the ABM-lw and SABS approaches adapt to changes in levels of illumination at either end of the day, but the proposed ABM-lw approach performs much more rapidly and accurately than the SABS approach. The background model luminance generated by the ABM-lw approach closely matches that of the actual image at the time, but the background images generated by the SABS approach do not track the actual change in level of luminance seen in the first column. By T31 the background model generated by the proposed ABM-ls approach is very different from that generated by the less accurate SABS method.

3.2 Robustness to Changes in Tidal Height

Background modeling in coastal situations also needs to consider changes in tidal height. In this section we compare the performance of the proposed ABM-lw and existing SABS approaches at differing tidal states at Waitangi. The results of these comparisons are shown in Fig. 4, in which SABS background and the background from proposed ABM-lw are given in the middle and right column, and the ellipses in red color highlight the shoreline area of each predicted background.

Since the moving objects presented in previous images have not yet been completely forgotten, the ghost cars and boats are evident in the land

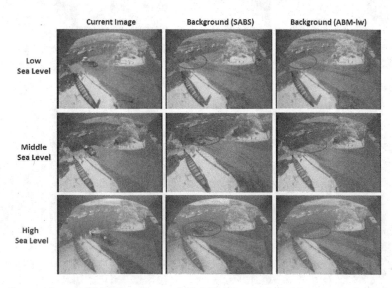

Fig. 4. Comparisons of SABS and proposed ABM-lw modelled backgrounds at different tidal states at Waitangi. (Left to right) current image, background from SABS, and background from proposed ABM-lw.

water boundary area of the SABS backgrounds, and the shoreline is blurred. This suggests that the SABS approach has difficulty with modeling backgrounds in areas where the movement of water is highly variable, whereas the dual area ABM-lw approach can readily account for this variability and generates more reliable background image for each frame. Results of moving objects detection provided by the ABM-lw approach should therefore be more accurate.

3.3 Quantitative Performance Evaluation on Real Data

The overall relative performance of the SABS and ABM-lw background modeling approaches is also evaluated quantitatively. We use the alternative backgrounds generated by the two algorithms when detecting moving objects appearing at all three boat ramps, at different times of day, under differing weather conditions, and at different tidal states. For performance evaluation, we measure object detection accuracy as the ratio of the number of objects correctly detected by the algorithm, against the manual number of objects.

Table 1. Object Detection Accuracy on Waitangi, Takapuna, and Manu Bay, respectively.

Waitangi		Detection Accuracy(%)		Takapuna		Detection Accuracy(%)	
		SABS	ABM-lw			SABS	ABM-lw
Time	Sunrise	65.48(±6.81)	**91.62(±2.31)**	Time	Sunrise	62.39(±5.83)	**90.37(±2.12)**
	Sunset	64.29(±7.12)	**91.67(±2.12)**		Sunset	61.46(±6.84)	**90.52(±2.33)**
	Daytime	75.01(±5.52)	**91.78(±2.52)**		Daytime	72.12(±7.02)	**90.73(±1.98)**
	Night	68.01(±6.96)	**91.69(±2.81)**		Night	65.34(±5.97)	**90.69(±2.03)**
Weather	Rainy	66.17(±6.37)	**91.58(±2.12)**	Weather	Rainy	63.34(±5.39)	**90.57(±2.26)**
	Foggy	63.19(±7.39)	**91.37(±2.91)**		Foggy	60.32(±6.23)	**90.21(±2.57)**
	Windy	65.01(±7.53)	**91.63(±2.13)**		Windy	62.34(±6.58)	**90.45(±2.25)**
	Sunny	74.82(±4.62)	**92.01(±1.95)**		Sunny	71.91(±5.67)	**90.96(±1.89)**
Tide	Low	66.48(±6.51)	**91.39(±2.13)**	Tide	Low	63.62(±6.72)	**90.22(±2.48)**
	Mid	71.29(±5.92)	**91.61(±2.01)**		Mid	68.42(±6.02)	**90.56(±2.36)**
	High	75.21(±4.34)	**91.92(±1.89)**		High	72.32(±3.39)	**90.91(±1.93)**

Manu Bay		Detection Accuracy(%)	
		SABS	ABM-lw
Time	Sunrise	67.56(±5.76)	**92.59(±2.01)**
	Sunset	66.44(±6.18)	**92.55(±2.23)**
	Daytime	77.23(±5.63)	**92.84(±1.78)**
	Night	70.75(±7.01)	**92.82(±1.92)**
Weather	Rainy	68.43(±5.65)	**92.66(±2.32)**
	Foggy	65.38(±7.02)	**92.25(±2.51)**
	Windy	67.32(±6.59)	**97.75(±2.33)**
	Sunny	76.98(±5.23)	**93.11(±1.83)**
Tide	Low	68.43(±7.03)	**92.28(±2.32)**
	Mid	73.45(±6.08)	**92.69(±2.17)**
	High	77.19(±5.33)	**93.08(±1.88)**

Table 1 gives the comparison results. As seen from the table, the proposed ABM-lw gives in general above 90% accuracy for all three boat ramps moving objects detection, whereas the accuracy of the SABS approach is in the range of 60% to 77%. The superiority of the ABM-lw approach relative to the SABS method is as high as 25%. Also, the average standard deviation of proposed ABM-lw approach is about 2%, which is three times lower than SABS's 6.5%. This suggests that, the ABM-lw algorithm generates a more stable background than the SABS algorithm in this context, under all conditions. Both algorithms perform worst at Takapuna which is a busier four lane ramp with a longer water line, and this causes that the background modeling for Takapuna is more difficult in practice.

4   Conclusions

In this paper, we propose a new background modeling algorithm (ABM-lw) intended to be used at maritime boat ramps where areas of both land and water are in frame. Background modeling in this context is especially challenging. The proposed ABM-lw approach attempts to classify each image into areas of land and water, and uses different strategies to model background of land and water scenes. Experimental tests and evaluations of its performance have been presented on a real 24-hour boat-flow analysis and counting system, where the proposed ABM-lw approach is compared with an existing method. These tests demonstrate that a much more stable background model is obtained by the ABM-lw algorithm in this context. The optimal learning rate α is mostly determined by the luminance threshold λ which is used in (3) for objects detection. Future work will therefore focus on how to estimate the optimal value for this luminance threshold.

Acknowledgment. The authors wish to thank New Zealand's Ministry for Primary Industry for funding provided for this work as part of project MAF2013/08, and especially Neville Smith for his support. We also wish to thank Nicola Rush and Andy Millar at NIWA for providing the manual counts used to evaluate the performance of our proposed algorithm.

References

1. Unzueta, L., Nieto, M., Cortes, A., Barandiaran, J., Otaegui, O., Sanchez, P.: Adaptive multicue background subtraction for robust vehicle counting and classification. IEEE Transactions on Intelligent Transportation Systems 13(2), 527–540 (2012)
2. Wang, W., Yang, J., Gao, W.: Modeling background and segmenting moving objects from compressed video. IEEE Transactions on Circuits and Systems for Video Technology 18(5), 670–681 (2008)
3. Cucchiara, R., Piccardi, M., Prati, A.: Detecting moving objects, ghosts, and shadows in video streams. IEEE Transactions on Pattern Analysis and Machine Intelligence 25, 1337–1342 (2003)

4. Kamijo, S., Matsushita, Y., Ikeuchi, K., Sakauchi, M.: Traffic monitoring and accident detection at intersections. IEEE Trans. Intell. Transp Syst. **1**(2), 108–118 (2000)
5. Ottlik, A., Nagel, H.H.: Initialization of model-based vehicle tracking in video sequences of inner city intersections. Int. J. Comput. Vis. **80**(2), 211–225 (2008)
6. Veeraraghavan, H., Masoud, O., Papanikolopoulos, N.: Vision-based monitoring of intersections. In: Proc. IEEE 5th Int. Conf. Intell. Transp Syst., pp. 7–12 2002
7. Park, K., Lee, D., Park, Y.: Video-based detection of street-parking violation. In: Int. Conf. Image Process. CVPR (2007)
8. Lin, S., Chen, Y., Liu, S.: A vision-based parking lot management system. In: IEEE International Conference on Systems, Man and Cybernetics, SMC 2006, pp. 2897–2902 (2006)
9. Choeychuen, K.: Automatic parking lot mapping for available parking space detection. In: IEEE International Conference on Systems, Man and Cybernetics, SMC 2006, pp. 117–121 (2013)
10. Choeychuen, K.: Available car parking space detection from webcam by using adaptive mixing features. In: 2012 International Joint Conference on Computer Science and Software Engineering (JCSSE), pp. 12–16 (2012)
11. Eng, H., Wang, J., Kam, A., Yau, W.: Novel region-based modeling for human detection within highly dynamic aquatic environment. In: CVPR 2004 Proceedings of the 2004 IEEE computer society conference on Computer vision and pattern recognition, pp. 390–397 (2004)
12. Nuno, P., Nuno, C., Jorge, C., Adriano, T., Jose, M.: A segmentation approach for object detection on highly dynamic aquatic environments. In: 35th Annual Conference of IEEE Industrial Electronics, IECON 2009, pp. 1985–1989 (2009)
13. Bloisi, D., Iocchi, L.: Argos - a video surveillance system for boat traffic monitoring in venice. International Journal of Pattern Recognition and Artificial Intelligence **23**(07), 1477–1500 (2009)
14. Bloisi, D., Pennisi, A., Iocchi, L.: Background modeling in the maritime domain. Machine Vision and Applications **25**(5), 1257–1269 (2014)
15. Gupte, S., Masoud, O., Martin, R., Papanikolopoulos, N.: Detection and classification of vehicles. IEEE Transactions on Intelligent Transportation Systems **3**(1), 37–47 (2002)

Enhancing Signal Discontinuities with Shearlets: An Application to Corner Detection

Miguel Alejandro Duval-Poo[1], Francesca Odone[1(✉)], and Ernesto De Vito[2]

[1] DIBRIS - Università Degli Studi di Genova, Genoa, Italy
francesca.odone@unige.it
[2] DIMA - Università Degli Studi di Genova, Genoa, Italy

Abstract. Shearlets are a relatively new and very effective multi-resolution framework for signal analysis able to capture efficiently the anisotropic information in multivariate problem classes. For this reason, Shearlets appear to be a valid choice for multi-resolution image processing and feature detection. In this paper we provide a brief review of the theory, referring in particular to the problem of enhancing signal discontinuities. We then discuss the specific application to corner detection, and provide a novel algorithm based on the concept of a cornerness measure. The appropriateness of the algorithm in detecting good matchable corners is evaluated on benchmark data including different image transformations.

1 Introduction

Multi-resolution methods, which are concerned with the representation and the analysis of images at multiple resolutions, are very appealing and effective in image processing since image features that are difficult to detect at one resolution may be easily detectable at another. In this general framework, Wavelets have often been chosen to represent the image content and, more specifically, to enhance signal discontinuities [14]. However, Wavelets are known to have a limited capability in dealing with directional information. In recent years, several methods were introduced to overcome these limitations (see, for instance, [2,13,18,20]). Among those, the *Shearlet representation* offers a unique combination of some highly desirable properties: it has a single or finite set of generating functions, it provides optimally sparse representations for a large class of multi-dimensional data, it allows the use of compactly supported analyzing functions both in the space and frequency domain. Last, but not less important, it has fast algorithmic implementations and it allows a unified treatment of the continuum and digital realms. For these reasons, in this work we choose Shearlets as a reference framework for feature detection.

In this paper we summarize some of Shearlets theoretical and computational properties, while referring in particular to the problem of enhancing image singularities. We then apply these findings to the corner detection problem which has not been fully addressed yet within the Shearlet framework. We take inspiration from [22], but we adopt a different algorithm to compute the digitalized

© Springer International Publishing Switzerland 2015
V. Murino and E. Puppo (Eds.): ICIAP 2015, Part II, LNCS 9280, pp. 108–118, 2015.
DOI: 10.1007/978-3-319-23234-8_11

Shearlet transform, which was first introduced in [8] for segmentation problems. With respect to the latter we choose a *mother function* which is more suitable for enhancing signal discontinuities.

There are several approaches for detecting corners in images. Since the pioneering work of Harris and Stephens [7], and later of Shi and Tomasi [21], the structure tensor of image gradients, also known as the *autocorrelation matrix*, has become popular for corner detection. A recent review on interest points, and corners in particular, is [1]. Wavelets have been applied to corner detection [3,17], although their limited capability in dealing with directional information is critical for this application. In order to overcome this limitation, orientation sensitive wavelets, such as the Log-Gabor wavelets, have been adopted [5]. Here we present an alternative way for addressing the problem effectively by selecting a more appropriate orientation selective transform.

The paper is organized as follows: in Section 2 we briefly review the Shearlet transform in the continuous and discrete case. In Section 3 we address the general issue of detecting signal discontinuities with Shearlets, while in Section 4 we propose procedures for corner detection, whose effectiveness is discussed in Section 5 following the Oxford evaluation procedure[16]. Section 6 is left to a final discussion and to an account of future works.

2   A Review of the Shearlet Transform

In this section we review the main properties of Shearlets, referring the interested reader to [11]. A shearlet is generated by the dilation, shearing and translation of a function $\psi \in L^2(\mathbb{R}^2)$, called the *mother shearlet*, in the following way

$$\psi_{a,s,t}(x) = a^{-3/4}\psi(A_a^{-1}S_s^{-1}(x-t)) \tag{1}$$

where $t \in \mathbb{R}^2$ is a translation, A_a is a *scaling* (or *dilation*) matrix and S_s a *shearing* matrix defined respectively by

$$A_a = \begin{pmatrix} a & 0 \\ 0 & \sqrt{a} \end{pmatrix} \qquad S_s = \begin{pmatrix} 1 & -s \\ 0 & 1 \end{pmatrix},$$

with $a \in \mathbb{R}^+$ and $s \in \mathbb{R}$. The anisotropic dilation A_a controls the scale of the Shearlets, by applying a different dilation factor along the two axes. The shearing matrix S_s, not expansive, determines the orientation of the Shearlets. The normalization factor $a^{-3/4}$ ensures that $\|\psi_{a,s,t}\| = \|\psi\|$, where $\|\psi\|$ is the Hilbert norm in $L^2(\mathbb{R}^2)$.

The *Shearlet transform* $\mathcal{SH}(f)$ of a signal $f \in L^2(\mathbb{R}^2)$ is defined by

$$\mathcal{SH}(f)(a,s,t) = \langle f, \psi_{a,s,t} \rangle, \tag{2}$$

where $\langle f, \psi_{a,s,t} \rangle$ is the scalar product in $L^2(\mathbb{R}^2)$. A possible classical choice for the *mother Shearlet* ψ is

$$\hat{\psi}(\omega_1, \omega_2) = \hat{\psi}_1(\omega_1)\hat{\psi}_2(\frac{\omega_2}{\omega_1}) \tag{3}$$

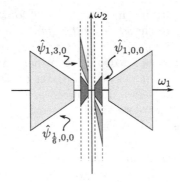

Fig. 1. Support of the Shearlets $\hat{\psi}_{a,s,t}$ in the frequency domain.

where $\hat{\psi}$ is the Fourier transform of ψ, and $\hat{\psi}_1, \hat{\psi}_2$ are usually two compactly supported functions in the one-dimensional frequency domain. The mother Shearlet in the frequency domain becomes

$$\hat{\psi}_{a,s,t}(\omega_1, \omega_2) = a^{3/4}\,\hat{\psi}_1(a\omega_1)\hat{\psi}_2\left(\frac{\omega_2 - s\omega_1}{\sqrt{a}\,\omega_1}\right)e^{-2\pi it\cdot(\omega_1,\omega_2)} \qquad (4)$$

and it has a support on two trapezoids at scale a oriented along a line of slope s (Fig. 1). The Shearlet transform can be rewritten as

$$\mathcal{SH}(f)(a,s,t) = a^{3/4}\int_{\hat{R}^2} \hat{f}(\omega_1,\omega_2)\hat{\psi}_1(a\omega_1)\hat{\psi}_2\left(\frac{\omega_2 - s\omega_1}{\sqrt{a}\,\omega_1}\right)e^{2\pi it\cdot(\omega_1,\omega_2)}d\omega_1 d\omega_2.$$

The mother function ψ satisfies some technical condition, which we do not discuss in detail, see [11]. In the following we assume that ψ_1 is a one-dimensional wavelet and $\hat{\psi}_2$ is a bump function whose support is in $[-1,1]$.

The Shearlet transform is able to capture the geometry of signal singularities through its asymptotic decay at fine scales ($a \to 0$). A group of theoretical results [6,12] show that the Shearlet transform precisely describes the geometric information of edges and other singular points of an image through their asymptotic behavior at fine scales. Explicitly, the Shearlet coefficient $\mathcal{SH}(\mathcal{I})(a,s,t)$ goes to zero faster than any power of a either if t is a regular point (for any s) or if t is an edge point and $s \neq s_0$ where s_0 is the normal orientation of the edge. If t is an edge and $s = s_0$, the decay is of the order $a^{3/4}$. A similar behaviour holds if t is a corner point and s coincides with one of the normal directions of the corner, otherwise the decay is $O(a^{9/4})$.

For numerical implementation, it is useful to restrict the range of a and s to bounded intervals. This is achieved by a suitable tiling of the frequency plane

$$\mathcal{C}_h = \{(\omega_1, \omega_2) \in \mathbb{R}^2 : |\omega_2/\omega_1| \leq 1, |\omega_1| > 1\},$$
$$\mathcal{C}_v = \{(\omega_1, \omega_2) \in \mathbb{R}^2 : |\omega_1/\omega_2| \leq 1, |\omega_2| > 1\},$$
$$\mathcal{R} = \{(\omega_1, \omega_2) \in \mathbb{R}^2 : |\omega_1|, |\omega_2| \leq 1\}.$$

For each cone $\mathcal{C}_{h,v}$ there is a corresponding mother Shearlet

$$\hat{\psi}^h(\omega_1,\omega_2) = \hat{\psi}_1(\omega_1)\hat{\psi}_2\left(\frac{\omega_2}{\omega_1}\right)\chi_{\mathcal{C}_h}$$

$$\hat{\psi}^v(\omega_1,\omega_2) = \hat{\psi}_1(\omega_2)\hat{\psi}_2\left(\frac{\omega_1}{\omega_2}\right)\chi_{\mathcal{C}_v}$$

where $\chi_{\mathcal{C}_{h,v}}$ is 1 on $\mathcal{C}_{h,v}$ and 0 outside. The low frequency region $\mathcal{R}$ can be handled by a scaling function $\hat{\phi}(\omega_1,\omega_2)$. This construction is usually called cone-adapted Shearlets.

The next step is to provide a discretization sampling of a, s and t. In the literature there are many different discretization schemes. In this paper we adopt the Fast Finite Shearlet Transform (FFST) [8] which performs the entire Shearlet construction in the Fourier domain. In this scheme, the signal is discretized on a square on size N, which is independent of the dilation and shearing parameter, whereas the scaling, shear and translation parameters are discretized as

$$a_j = 2^{-j}, \quad j = 0,\ldots,j_0 - 1,$$

$$s_{j,k} = k2^{-j/2}, \quad -\lfloor 2^{j/2}\rfloor \leq k \leq \lfloor 2^{j/2}\rfloor,$$

$$t_m = \left(\frac{m_1}{N},\frac{m_2}{N}\right), \quad m \in \mathcal{I}$$

where j_0 is the number of considered scales and $\mathcal{I} = \{(m_1,m_2) : m_1, m_2 = 0,\ldots,N-1\}$. With these notations the Shearlet system becomes

$$\psi^{\mathrm{x}}_{j,k,m}(x) = \psi^{\mathrm{x}}_{a_j,s_{j,k},t_m}(x)$$

where x = h or x = v.

The *discrete Shearlet transform* of a digital image $\mathcal{I}$ is now defined as

$$SH(\mathcal{I})(j,k,m) = \begin{cases} \langle \mathcal{I}, \phi_m\rangle \\ \langle \mathcal{I}, \psi^h_{j,k,m}\rangle \\ \langle \mathcal{I}, \psi^v_{j,k,m}\rangle \end{cases}$$

where $j = 0,\ldots,j_0 - 1$, $|k| \leq \lfloor 2^{j/2}\rfloor$, $m \in \mathcal{I}$. Based on the Plancherel formula $\langle f,g\rangle = \frac{1}{N^2}\langle \hat{f},\hat{g}\rangle$, the discrete shearlet transform can be efficiently computed by applying the 2D fast Fourier transform (`fft`) and its inverse (`ifft`). Thus, a *discrete Shearlet transform algorithm* can be summarized as

$$SH(\mathcal{I})(j,k,m) = \begin{cases} \mathtt{ifft}(\hat{\phi}(\omega_1,\omega_2)\mathtt{fft}(\mathcal{I}))(m) \\ \mathtt{ifft}(\hat{\psi}_1(2^{-j}\omega_1)\hat{\psi}_2(2^{j/2}\frac{\omega_2}{\omega_1} - k)\mathtt{fft}(\mathcal{I}))(m) \\ \mathtt{ifft}(\hat{\psi}_1(2^{-j}\omega_2)\hat{\psi}_2(2^{j/2}\frac{\omega_1}{\omega_2} - k)\mathtt{fft}(\mathcal{I}))(m) \end{cases} . \quad (5)$$

3   Detecting Discontinuities with Shearlets

In this section we discuss the ability of Shearlets to enhance local signal discontinuities.

Fig. 2. Enhancement of signal discontinuities provided by Shearlets: two example images and the results obtained by choosing the $\hat{\psi}_1$ as the Lemarie-Meyer wavelet (center) or the Mallat wavelet (right).

Shearlets for Enhancing Discontinuities. In choosing the function ψ_1 we adopt the Mallat wavelet [15], a family of one dimensional wavelets which share the same properties of the first derivative of the Gaussian:

$$\hat{\psi}_1(\omega) = i\omega \left(\frac{\sin(\omega/4)}{\omega/4} \right)^{2n+2} . \tag{6}$$

This choice is alternative to the classical Lemarie-Meyer wavelet [4,8] which is not optimal for edge detection since the Lemarie-Meyer wavelet is an even function and thus its Shearlet transforms suffer from large side-lobes around prominent edges, which interfere with the detection of the edge location (see Fig. 2). As for ψ_2, instead, any smooth function with compact support in the frequency domain can be considered. In our case we used the same bump function as in [4,8].

Enhancing Discontinuities at Fixed Scales. Signal discontinuities can be identified as those points $m \in \mathcal{I}$ which, at scale j, the function $\mathcal{E}_j(m)$ has large values, with

$$\mathcal{E}_j(m)^2 = \sum_k (\mathcal{SH}(\mathcal{I})(j,k,m))^2. \tag{7}$$

$\mathcal{SH}(\mathcal{I})(j,k,m)$ denotes the discrete Shearlet transform of $\mathcal{I}$ in Eq. (5).

Estimating the Discontinuities Orientation at Fixed Scales. The Shearlet transform provides naturally this type of information, which can be easily obtained at a fixed scale j by finding the index k that maximizes $\mathcal{SH}(\mathcal{I})(j,k,m)$,

$$\theta_j(m) = \arg\max_k |\mathcal{SH}(\mathcal{I})(j,k,m)|. \tag{8}$$

Fig. 3 shows different orientations at different scales j. The estimated directions are color coded, i.e. each color represents a specific direction summarized in the colorbar at the right of the figure. As we can observe, the Shearlet transform

Fig. 3. Image discontinuities across scales. Top: Shearlet coefficients - Eq. (7). Bottom: Orientations - Eq. (8). Coarse to fine from left to right.

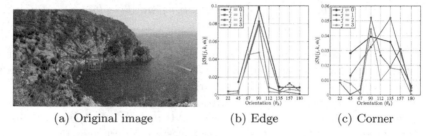

(a) Original image   (b) Edge   (c) Corner

Fig. 4. Shearlet orientation patterns for an edge (square) and a corner (circle).

accurately estimates the orientation. In addition, it can be noticed how accuracy increases at fine scales ($j \rightarrow 3$) due to the fact that at fine scales more shears k have to be considered, $-\lfloor 2^{j/2} \rfloor \leq k \leq \lfloor 2^{j/2} \rfloor$.

Analysing Discontinuities Across Scales. Orientation is an important cue to classify different types of signal discontinuities. To this purpose, we may analyze how the Shearlets coefficients vary across different orientations. Fig. 4 shows a comparison of the orientation patterns in the case of an edge (square) and a corner (circle) in a natural image. Let us first consider a fixed scale $j = 2$ (red plots). As we can observe, for the edge point a strong Shearlet response is obtained on one direction only, while for the corner point it can be observed strong Shearlet responses at two different, almost perpendicular, orientations. If we perform the analysis across scales, it can be seen how on the edge point the strongest Shearlet response is maintained on one direction only with the exception of the finest scale where two high responses are obtained on two close orientations. Instead, on the corner point, the two orientations with the strongest Shearlet response slightly vary across scales. This is an expected behavior since, depending of the scale at which the analysis is performed, a corner point can have different main orientations.

4   Corner Detection with Shearlets

Corner patterns are associated with signal discontinuities in at least two directions and it is reflected on the behavior of Shearlet coefficients across different orientations, as discussed in the previous section. In this work we favor corners assiciated with at least two large coefficients, with a preference for patterns where such coefficients are at about 90 degrees to one another (the "ideal" corner).

Considering a generic image point m, at a fixed scale we compute a weighted sum of its Shearlet coefficients across shears, where each weight is a value that represents how *perpendicular* is the orientation of the shear with the orientation of the shear with the maximum Shearlet response for that point. To this purpose, we define a *cornerness measure* $\mathcal{CM}$ for a point $m \in \mathcal{I}$ and for a fixed scale j in the following way

$$\mathcal{CM}_j(m) = \sum_{u \in W(m)} \sum_k |\mathcal{SH}(j,k,u)| \sin(|\theta_k - \theta_{k_{\max}}|)$$

where $\mathcal{SH}(j,k,u)$ represents the discrete Shearlet transform coefficient for a point u in a neighborhood of m, at scale j and shearing k, θ_k is the angle associated to the shearing k, $k_{\max} = \arg\max_k |\mathcal{SH}(j,k,m)|$ and $W(m)$ is a window centered at point m of an appropriate size. Then we may aggregate the cornerness measure at different scales: $\mathcal{CM}(m) = \sum_j \mathcal{CM}_j(m)$. In this way detected corner points that persist across scales are reinforced. Alg. 1 describes a sketch of the algorithm.

Taking the advantage of the multi-scale representation produced by the Shearlets, we may associate an appropriate scale to each detected corner $m \in \mathcal{C}$:

$$\bar{j} = \arg\max_j \ K_j \sum_k |\mathcal{SH}(j,k,m)| \tag{9}$$

where K_j is a normalization factor that depends on the scale j. Fig. 5 shows the result of the Shearlet multi-scale corner detection with automatic scale selection.

5   Experimental Results

In this section we assess the effectiveness of the corner detection procedure. The evaluation is based on the standard Mikolajczyk's software framework[1]. Image sequences are provided, each one containing 6 images of natural textured scenes with increasing geometric and photometric transformations. In our analysis we discarded those that are not applicable in our scenario that does not consider large zooming and rotations (normally addressed by appropriate descriptors). For the evaluation metrics [16] we consider:

  - The *number of correspondences* $|CR_{1i}|$, is the cardinality of the set containing all the corner points correspondences between image $\mathcal{I}_1$ and the evaluated

---

[1] http://www.robots.ox.ac.uk/~vgg/research/affine/

Fig. 5. Shearlet corner detection with automatic scale estimation - sample outputs: $j = 0$ (Blue); $j = 1$ (Green); $j = 2$ (Red); $j = 3$ (Magenta).

Algorithm 1. Shearlet Corner Detection.

Input $\mathcal{I}$: input image, j_0: number of scales considered, t: threshold.

Output $\mathcal{C}$: set of detected corner points.

1: **procedure** SMCD($\mathcal{I}, j_0, t$)
2:     $\mathcal{C} = \{\}$;
3:     $\mathcal{SH} = \mathtt{dst}(\mathcal{I})$; // Discrete Shearlet Transform as in Eq. (5)
4:     **for all** $m \in \mathcal{I}$ **do**
5:         $\mathcal{CM}(m) = \sum_j \sum_{u \in W(m)} \sum_k |\mathcal{SH}(j,k,u)| \sin(|\theta_k - \theta_{k_{\max}}|)$; //Multi-Scale Cornerness
6:     **end for**
7:     $\mathtt{nonmaxsup}(\mathcal{CM})$; // Non Maxima Suppression as in [9]
8:     **for all** $m \in \mathcal{I}$ **do**
9:         **if** $\mathcal{CM}(m) > t$ **then** // Corner detection
10:             $\mathcal{C} = \mathcal{C} \cup (m)$;
11:         **end if**
12:     **end for**
13:     **return** $\mathcal{C}$;
14: **end procedure**

---

image $\mathcal{I}_i$. To estimate it, we employ the homography H_{1i} which is provided with the images and count the number of corners of image $\mathcal{I}_i$ which are close to corners from $\mathcal{I}_1$, after H_{1i} has been applied.

– The *repeatability score* RS_i for an image $\mathcal{I}_i$ is the ratio of the number of correspondences and the minimum number of corners detected in the images:
$RS_i = \frac{|CR_{1i}|}{\min(|\mathcal{C}_1|, |\mathcal{C}_i|)}$.

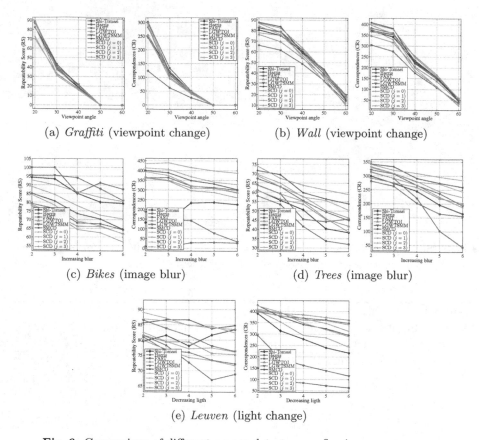

(a) *Graffiti* (viewpoint change) (b) *Wall* (viewpoint change)

(c) *Bikes* (image blur) (d) *Trees* (image blur)

(e) *Leuven* (light change)

Fig. 6. Comparison of different corner detectors on five image sequences.

In this experimental analysis we consider the corner detection algorithm across scales that we propose (Alg. 1 - reported in the following as SMCD) as well as a variant of it where j is fixed and the only change in the algorithm is the summation across scales which is not needed (henceforth SCD). As a threshold we set 10% of the cornerness measure maximum value of each image. If more than 500 detected corner points remains, only the 500 points with the maximum cornerness measure are selected. We compare our algorithms with the classical *Harris* [7] and *Shi-Tomasi* [21], the two methods *LGWTOI* and *LGWTSMM* proposed in [5] based on Log-Gabor wavelets, and the more recent *FAST* [19]. The results are reported in Fig. 6:

– *View-point changes:* in (a) different corner detection methods perform in a similar way, with a slightly higher number of correspondences in FAST slightly outperforms the rest. In (b) SMCD and SCD at scale $j = 1, 2$ obtain a higher repeatability score and number of correspondences.
– *Image blur:* in (c) Harris and LGWTSMM obtain a very high repeatability score but with the lowest number of correspondences. The best trade-off

between the two different metrics is achieved by SCD at the coarsest scale $j = 0$. Coherent results are noticeable in (d), where we also observe a remarkable performance of our multi-scale variant SMCD.

– *Illumination changes:* in (e) we see how many methods (LGWTOI, FAST, SMCD and SCD with $j = 2, 3$) obtained the high correspondences, but the best trade-off with the repetibility score is achieved by SMCD.

6   Discussion

In this paper we addressed the problem of enhancing image singularities with the Shearlet transform.

Shearlets are capable of capturing anisotropic information in multivariate functions and are thus particularly appropriate for the detection of directional sensitive features. We applied our analysis to the corner detection problem and sketched an algorithm which allowed us to detect meaningful corner features at a fixed scale and at multiple scales. The expressive power of the adopted framework allowed us also to associate a scale with each detected key point. We assessed our corner detection algorithm comparing our results with state of the art methods. The analysis illustrated the appropriateness of our algorithm in detecting matchable corners across different image transformations, with very good performances in particular for blur and illumination changes.

We are currently working on a fully multi-scale corner detection pipeline, which includes an optimal scale selection and a suppression of multiple corners across scales, comparable with the scale-space approach. The general framework adopted will allow us in the future to detect other types of image features (such as blob-like features) and space-time features (such as STIP).

Our approach relies on classical choices for the mother Shearlet, but interesting alternatives are available and would be worth investigating in future works. For instance, compactly supported Shearlets [10] have been recently shown to have nice properties for edge detection [12].

References

1. Aanes, H., Dahl, A.L., Pedersen, K.S.: Interesting interest points. IJCV (2011)
2. Candes, E.J., Donoho, D.L.: New tight frames of curvelets and optimal representations of objects with piecewise c2 singularities. Communications on Pure and Applied Mathematics **57**(2), 219–266 (2004)
3. Chen, C.H., Lee, J.S., Sun, Y.N.: Wavelet transformation for gray-level corner detection. Pattern Recognition **28**(6), 853–861 (1995)
4. Easley, G., Labate, D., Lim, W.Q.: Sparse directional image representations using the discrete shearlet transform. Applied and Computational Harmonic Analysis **25**(1), 25–46 (2008)
5. Gao, X., Sattar, F., Venkateswarlu, R.: Multiscale corner detection of gray level images based on log-gabor wavelet transform. IEEE Transactions on Circuits and Systems for Video Technology **17**(7), 868–875 (2007)

6. Guo, K., Labate, D.: Characterization and analysis of edges using the continuous shearlet transform. SIAM Journal on Imaging Sciences **2**(3), 959–986 (2009)
7. Harris, C., Stephens, M.: A combined corner and edge detector. In: Alvey Vision Conference, Manchester, UK, vol. 15, p. 50 (1988)
8. Häuser, S., Steidl, G.: Fast finite shearlet transform: a tutorial. ArXiv (1202.1773) (2014)
9. Kitchen, L., Rosenfeld, A.: Gray-level corner detection. Pattern Recognition Letters **1**(2), 95–102 (1982)
10. Kittipoom, P., Kutyniok, G., Lim, W.Q.: Construction of compactly supported shearlet frames. Constr. Approx. **35**(1), 21–72 (2012)
11. Kutyniok, G., Labate, D.: Shearlets: Multiscale analysis for multivariate data. Springer (2012)
12. Kutyniok, G., Petersen, P.: Classification of edges using compactly supported shearlets. ArXi (1411.5657) (2014)
13. Labate, D., Lim, W.Q., Kutyniok, G., Weiss, G.: Sparse multidimensional representation using shearlets. In: Optics & Photonics 2005, pp. 59140U–59140U. International Society for Optics and Photonics (2005)
14. Mallat, S., Hwang, W.L.: Singularity detection and processing with wavelets. IEEE Transactions on Information Theory **38**(2), 617–643 (1992)
15. Mallat, S., Zhong, S.: Characterization of signals from multiscale edges. IEEE Transactions on Pattern Analysis and Machine Intelligence **14**(7), 710–732 (1992)
16. Mikolajczyk, K., Tuytelaars, T., Schmid, C., Zisserman, A., Matas, J., Schaffalitzky, F., Kadir, T., Van Gool, L.: A comparison of affine region detectors. International Journal of Computer Vision **65**(1–2), 43–72 (2005)
17. Pedersini, F., Pozzoli, E., Sarti, A., Tubaro, S.: Multi-resolution corner detection. In: ICIP, pp. 881–884 (2000)
18. Po, D.D., Do, M.N.: Directional multiscale modeling of images using the contourlet transform. Image Processing **15**(6), 1610–1620 (2006)
19. Rosten, E., Porter, R., Drummond, T.: Faster and better: A machine learning approach to corner detection. IEEE Transactions on Pattern Analysis and Machine Intelligence **32**(1), 105–119 (2010)
20. Selesnick, I.W., Baraniuk, R.G., Kingsbury, N.C.: The dual-tree complex wavelet transform. IEEE Signal Processing Magazine **22**(6), 123–151 (2005)
21. Shi, J., Tomasi, C.: Good features to track. In: Proceedings of the 1994 IEEE Computer Society Conference on Computer Vision and Pattern Recognition, CVPR 1994, pp. 593–600. IEEE (1994)
22. Yi, S., Labate, D., Easley, G.R., Krim, H.: A shearlet approach to edge analysis and detection. IEEE Transactions on Image Processing **18**(5), 929–941 (2009)

Improved Human Gait Recognition

Imad Rida[1]([⊠]), Ahmed Bouridane[2], Gian Luca Marcialis[3],
and Pierluigi Tuveri[3]

[1] LITIS EA 4108 - INSA de Rouen, Saint Etienne du Rouvray, Rouen, France
imad.rida@insa-rouen.fr
[2] Department of Computer Science and Digital Technologies,
Northumbria University, Newcastle, UK
ahmed.bouridane@northumbria.ac.uk
[3] Department of Electrical and Electronic Engineering,
University of Cagliari, Cagliari, Italy
marcialis@diee.unica.it, tuveri.pierluigi@gmail.com

Abstract. Gait recognition is an emerging biometric technology which aims to identify people purely through the analysis of the way they walk. The technology has attracted interest as a method of identification because of its non-invasiveness, since it does not require the subject's cooperation. However, "covariates" which include clothing, carrying conditions, and other intra-class variations affect the recognition performances. This paper proposes a feature selection mask which is able to select most relevant discriminative features for human recognition to alleviate the impact of covariates so as to improve the recognition performances. The proposed method has been evaluated using CASIA Gait Database (Dataset B) and the experimental results demonstrate that the proposed technique yields 77.38 % of correct recognition.

Keywords: Biometrics · Gait · Model free · Feature selection

1 Introduction

Technology has invaded our lives as never before and the effectiveness of current security systems has become increasingly important. Biometric recognition aims to identify individuals using unique, reliable and stable physiological and/or behavioral characteristics such as fingerprint, palmprint, face, gait, etc. Gait recognition consists on discriminating among people by the way or manner they walk.

Gait recognition techniques can be classified into two main categories: model-based and model-free approach. Model based approach [1,2] models the person body structure, it uses the estimation over time of static body parameters for recognition (i.e. trajectory, limb lengths etc). This process is usually computationally intensive since we need to model and track the subjects body. On the other hand, the model free approach does not recover a structural model of human motion, instead it uses the features extracted from the motion or shape

V. Murino and E. Puppo (Eds.): ICIAP 2015, Part II, LNCS 9280, pp. 119–129, 2015.
DOI: 10.1007/978-3-319-23234-8_12

for recognition. Compared to a model based approach, the model free approach requires much less computation cost, furthermore dynamic information results in improved recognition performance than static counterpart [3]. These reasons have motivated the researchers to introduce new feature representations in model free approach context. The major challenges of methods belong the model free gait recognition are due to the effect of various covariates as the presence of shadows, clothing variations and carrying conditions (backpack, briefcase, handbag, etc). Moreover, segmentation and the view dependency are further causes of gait recognition errors. This has motivated the work presented in this paper which aims to mitigate the effect of the covariates and improve the recognition performance.

The rest of this paper is organized as follows: Sect. 2 summarizes the previous works. Sect. 3 gives the theoretical description of the proposed method. Sect. 4 presents the experimental results. Sect. 5 offers our conclusion.

2   Related Works

There exists a considerable amount of work in the context of model free approaches for gait recognition. Benabdelkader et al. [4] introduced a self similarity representation to measure the similarity between pairs of silhouettes. Collins et al. [5] proposed a template based silhouette matching in some key frames. Recent trends seem to favor Gait Energy Image (GEI) representation suggested by Han and Bhanu [6]. GEI is a spatio-temporal representation of the gait obtained by averaging the silhouettes over a gait cycle. This representation has already been used in several state of the art works [7–10]. Yu et al. introduced a simple template matching technique based on the euclidian distance without data reduction and feature selection [11]. It has been found that the different clothing and carrying conditions between the gallery and probe sequences influence the recognition performances [6,11]. To overcome the limitations of the GEI presentation, Bashir et al. introduced a novel gait feature selection method named Gait Entropy Image (GEnI) [12]. It consists of computing Shannon entropy for each pixel over a gait cycle; in other terms it aims to distinguish static and dynamic pixels of the GEI. In this case GEnI represents a measure of feature significance (pixels with high entropy correspond to dynamic parts which are robust against appearance changes). In the same context Bashir et al. suggested a new gait representation called flow field [13] in order to represent a weighted sum of the optical flow corresponding to each coordinate direction of human motion. Rida et al. [19,20] proposed a supervised feature extraction method based on Modified Phase-Only Correlation (MPOC) algorithm which is an improved version of the Phase Only Correlation (POC). Recently Random Subspace Method (RSM) has been been used to reduce the effect of the covariates, the results showed very good performances in the USF database [14,15].

3   Methodology

3.1   Motivations

In this paper among all available feature representations we have chosen the so-called Gait Energy Image [6]: it is an easy and simple representation to compute, thus making it an effective compromise between the computational cost and the recognition performance. Its main drawback is common to all model-free approaches: covariates makes it unreliable.

The aim of this work is to improve the GEI representation by determining a mask capable to select the robust features against the covariates. The notion of gait mask was introduced by Foster et al. [16] where several predefined masks were used to capture gait characteristics. Fig 1 shows some of such predefined masks, where the gray parts represent the features selected whereas the black parts represent the non selected ones.

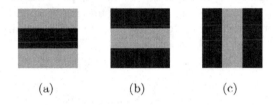

(a)   (b)   (c)

Fig. 1. Predefined masks introduced by Foster et al. to capture gait features [16].

In the current work we propose to estimate a mask instead of using a predefined one as suggested in the previous work by Foster et al. [16]. The calculation of the mask on all data will bias the results, furthermore the selection method (mask) should not be overspecialized for a particular and specific training set [17], all that has motivated to current work which has as particularity to estimate a fixed unique mask on a small feature selection set independently from training and testing sets (all selected sequences from the feature selection set were removed from the training and testing sets) capable to select relevant features from all GEIs under both carrying and clothing conditions (see Fig. 2). To calculate our mask we estimate the normal walk GEI called $\mathbf{M}$ by taking the mean of all normal walk GEIs within the feature selection set, after that we calculate the variation matrix $\mathbf{D}_k$ between each couple (estimated normal walk $\mathbf{M}$ and carrying-bag/wearing-coat GEIs) by taking the difference pixel by pixel. A mask $\{\mathbf{S}_k\}_{k=1}^{K}$ is defined for each variation matrix $\{\mathbf{D}_k\}_{k=1}^{K}$ which aims to select pixels with low variation value by assigning 1 for pixels with variation $\mathbf{D}_k(i,j)$ less than a threshold T and 0 otherwise. The masks $\{\mathbf{S}_k\}_{k=1}^{K}$ are combined together using a simple 'AND' operator to obtain our final mask $\mathbf{S}$ (see Sect. 3.3).

Our framework is divided into two main modules: the first one consists of calculating the mask on the feature selection set. The second module estimates

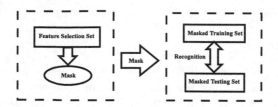

Fig. 2. Scheme of our framework.

the performance of our method (Correct Classification Rate) using GEI features selected with the resulting mask in the first module and Component Discriminant Analysis (CDA) [18] (see Sec. 3.4).

3.2   Gait Energy Image

GEI is a spatio-temporal representation of the gait patterns. It consists of representing the gait cycle using a single grayscale image obtained by averaging the silhouettes extracted over a complete gait cycle [6]. GEI is computed using the following equation:

$$\mathbf{G}(x,y) = \frac{1}{N} \sum_{t=1}^{N} \mathbf{B}(x,y,t) \tag{1}$$

where N is the number of the frames within a complete gait cycle, $\mathbf{B}$ is a silhouette image, x and y are the coordinates of the image and t is frame number in the cycle. Low and high intensity pixels of the GEI correspond to the dynamic and static parts of the body, respectively. Dynamic parts are most informative since they contain the information of the gait while static parts are sensitive since they contain the shape and contour information which can easily be influenced by the covariates [12].

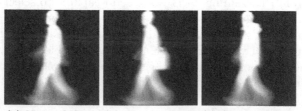

(a) Normal Walk (b) Carrying Bag (c) Wearing Coat

Fig. 3. Gait energy image of an individual under different conditions.

3.3   Feature Selection Mask

Let consider L Gait Energy Image templates $\{\mathbf{G}_l\}_{l=1}^{L}$ characterizing normal gait walking, we calculate the mean GEI normal walk as follows:

$$\mathbf{M} = \frac{1}{L} \sum_{l=1}^{L} \mathbf{G}_l \qquad (2)$$

The variation $\{\mathbf{D}_k\}_{k=1}^{K}$ for a given GEI template $\{\mathbf{G'}_k\}_{k=1}^{K}$ characterizing carrying bag or wearing coat walk is given by:

$$\mathbf{D}_k = \mathbf{G'}_k - \mathbf{M} \qquad (3)$$

$\mathbf{D}_k$ represents a measure of feature significance (i.e. discriminative power) since pixels with large variation are more suspected to be affected by the covariates (it can be seen as an inverse relationship between variation value and importance). Someone can say that $\mathbf{D}_k$ can contain negative values and we should take the square when we calculate $\mathbf{D}_k$, this is not possible for the simple reason that two pixels with same position (i, j) from two different GEI templates $\mathbf{G}_1(i, j)$ and $\mathbf{G}_2(i, j)$ with the corresponding variations $\mathbf{D}_1(i, j) < \mathbf{D}_2(i, j)$ and $|\mathbf{D}_1(i, j)| = |\mathbf{D}_2(i, j)|$ don't have the same importance because $\mathbf{G}_2(i, j)$ has more intensity value than $\mathbf{G}_1(i, j)$, as consequence it is much more suspected to be affected by the covariates. To facilitate our calculations we normalize the matrix $\mathbf{D}_k$ values between 0 and 1.

A mask defines if a feature is selected therefore a binary representation is useful: assigning a value 1 or 0 corresponding to selected or unselected features respectively. The mask based GEI template is given by:

$$\mathbf{S}_k(i, j) = \begin{cases} 1, & if\ \mathbf{D}_k(i,j) \leq T \mid T \in [0,1] \\ 0, & otherwise \end{cases} \qquad (4)$$

Where T represents the threshold. The masks $\{\mathbf{S}_k\}_{k=1}^{K}$ are combined together using a simple binary 'AND' to obtain the final mask $\mathbf{S}$ which is given by:

$$\mathbf{S} = \mathbf{S}_1 \ \&\&, \cdots, \ \&\& \ \mathbf{S}_k, \cdots, \&\& \ \mathbf{S}_K \qquad (5)$$

Algorithm 1. Mask calculaion algorithm.

1: **Input:** $\{\mathbf{G}_l\}_{l=1}^{L}$ (normal walk GEI templates)
      $\{\mathbf{G'}_k\}_{k=1}^{K}$ (carrying bag and wearing coat walk GEI templates)
      T: treshold
   Output: S (mask)
2: Calculate $\mathbf{M}$ using formula (2);
3: **for** $k = 1$ to K **do**
4:    Compute $\mathbf{D}_k$ using formula (3);
5:    Compute $\mathbf{S}_k$ using formula (4);
      $k = k + 1$;
6: **end for**
7: Compute the mask $\mathbf{S}$ using formula (5);

Where && is the binary operator. The whole process of mask calculation is summarized step by step in Alg. 1.

3.4 Canonical Discriminat Analysis

Canonical Discriminant Analysis (CDA) corresponds to Principal Component Analysis (PCA) followed by a Multiple Discriminant Analysis (MDA). The aim of the PCA is to be able to represent most of the variations of the original data using only a few principal components which are orthogonal to each others. MDA tries to maximize the distance between classes and preserve the distance inside the classes (the full explantation is found in [18]). The performance of our method is measured with the correct classification rate (CCR) which corresponds to the ratio of the number of well classified samples over the total number of samples.

Let n d-dimensional training GEI templates $\{\mathbf{g}_1, \cdots, \mathbf{g}_n\}$, where each template is a column vector obtained by concatenating the rows of the corresponding GEI. The feature selection is applied to these templates using the mask to obtain n d'-dimensional GEI templates $\{\mathbf{x}_1, \cdots, \mathbf{x}_n\}$ where $d' < d$. PCA aims to minimize the following objective function:

$$J_{d''} = \sum_{k=1}^{n} \left\| \left(\mathbf{m} + \sum_{i=1}^{d''} a_{ki} \mathbf{u}_i \right) - \mathbf{x}_k \right\|^2 \tag{6}$$

where $d'' < d' < d$, $\mathbf{m} = \frac{1}{n} \sum_{k=1}^{n} \mathbf{x}_k$, $\{\mathbf{u}_1, \cdots, \mathbf{u}_{d''}\}$ set of orthogonal unit vectors representing new coordinate system of the subspace and a_{ki} is the projection of the k-th data over $\mathbf{u}_i$.$J_{d''}$ is minimized when $\mathbf{u}_1, \cdots, \mathbf{u}_{d''}$ are eigenvectors of the largest eigenvalues of the covariance matrix $\mathbf{C}$ given by:

$$\mathbf{C} = \sum_{k=1}^{n} (\mathbf{x}_k - \mathbf{m})(\mathbf{x}_k - \mathbf{m})^T \tag{7}$$

The d''-dimensional feature vector $\mathbf{y}_k$ obtained from $\mathbf{x}_k$ is given by:

$$\mathbf{y}_k = [a_1, \cdots, a_{d''}]^T = [\mathbf{u}_1, \cdots, \mathbf{u}_{d''}]^T \mathbf{x}_k, \ k = 1, \cdots, n \tag{8}$$

As suggestion in [6] we retain $d'' = 2c$ eigenvectors after applying PCA. Suppose that the n d''-dimensional principal vectors $\{\mathbf{y}_1, \cdots, \mathbf{y}_n\}$ belong c classes, MDA is a supervised learning method which seeks a transformation matrix $\mathbf{W}$ that maximizes the ratio of the between-class scatter matrix S_B to the within-class scatter matrix S_W given by:

$$J(\mathbf{W}) = \frac{|\mathbf{W}^T S_B \mathbf{W}|}{|\mathbf{W}^T S_W \mathbf{W}|} \tag{9}$$

The within-class scatter matrix in the PCA subspace S_W is defined as $S_W = \sum_{i=1}^{c} S_i$ where:

$$\begin{cases} S_i = \sum_{\mathbf{y} \in \mathcal{D}_i} (\mathbf{y} - \mathbf{m}_i)(\mathbf{y} - \mathbf{m}_i)^T \\ \mathbf{m}_i = \frac{1}{n_i} \sum_{\mathbf{y} \in \mathcal{D}_i} \mathbf{y} \\ \{\mathcal{D}_i\}_{i=1}^{c} \; training \; data \; of \; class \; i \; of \; size \; n_i \end{cases} \qquad (10)$$

The between-class scatter in the PCA subspace S_B is given by:

$$S_B = \sum_{i=1}^{c} n_i (\mathbf{m}_i - \mathbf{m})(\mathbf{m}_i - \mathbf{m})^T \qquad (11)$$

where $\mathbf{m} = \frac{1}{n} \sum_{\mathbf{y} \in \mathcal{D}} \mathbf{y}$. $J(\mathbf{W})$ is maximized when the columns of $\mathbf{W}$ are the generalized eigenvectors that correspond to $c - 1$ nonzero eigenvalues in:

$$S_B \mathbf{w}_i = \lambda_i S_W \mathbf{w}_i \qquad (12)$$

where $\mathbf{w}_i$ is the i-th column of the matrix $\mathbf{W}$. The corresponding generalized eigenvectors are denoted by $\mathbf{v}_1, \cdots, \mathbf{v}_{c-1}$. The $(c-1)$-dimensional feature vector $\mathbf{z}_k$ in the MDA subspace is obtained from the d''-dimensional principal component vector $\mathbf{y}_k$:

$$\mathbf{z}_k = [\mathbf{v}_1, \cdots, \mathbf{v}_{c-1}]^T \mathbf{y}_k, \quad k = 1, \cdots, n \qquad (13)$$

4   Experiments

We have used CASIA database (dataset B) [11] to evaluate our method. It is a multiview gait database containing 124 subjects captured from 11 different angles. Each subject has six normal walking sequences (SetA), two carrying-bag sequences (SetB) and two wearing-coat sequences (SetC). The first four sequences of setA noted as (SetA1) are used for training. The two remaining noted as (SetA2), (SetB) and (SetC) are used for testing the effect of view angle variations, clothing and carrying conditions respectively. In our work we focus on the effect of clothing, carrying conditions and experiments are carried out under 90° view using 64 × 64 GEI resolution. We determine our mask from a feature selection set independent from training and testing sets (all selected sequences from the feature selection set were removed from the training and testing sets). To create our feature selection set we randomly select 24 subjects without replacement as follows: for each subject 3 sequences are randomly chosen corresponding to the three situations (normal, carrying bag, wearing coat) so that 72 sequences are obtained. To make our method robust and avoid the

Algorithm 2. The Evaluation Method

1: **Input:** feature selection set
2: **for** $p = 1$ to P **do**
3:      Randomly select without replacement of 15 subjects from feature selection set;
4:      Select related GEI templates corresponding to the three variants (normal, carrying bag, wearing coat);
5:      Calculate the mask based on Alg. 1 ;
6:      Estimate the best threshold value T using 3-folds Cross-Validation;
7:      Select the mask corresponding to best threshold performance;
8: **end for**

---

overspecialization we have applied the evaluation strategy described in Alg. 2 on feature selection set for $P = 5$ (The threshold T is estimated using a 3-folds Coss-Validation for $T \in [0,1]$ with a step of 0.1).

It can be seen from Fig. 4 that the threshold value $T = 0.6$ is giving the best performance for the $P = 5$ experiments, we combine the resulting $P = 5$ masks of the experiments together with a simple 'AND' operator to obtain our mask used to select relevant features and remove irrelevant ones.

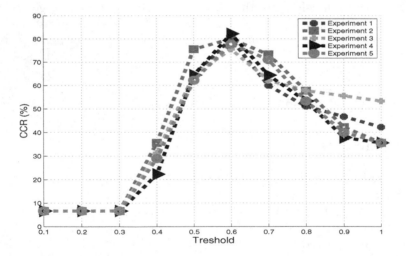

Fig. 4. Correct classification rate of the carried out experiments on the feature selection set using different threshold values.

Fig. 5 shows the calculated mask by our method as well as the masked GEI under different conditions (the white part from the mask represents the selected features). We can notice that our mask selects features from the bottom part of the GEI template which represent the dynamic movement of the legs, this part is robust against the covariates and is discriminative, our mask selects also some

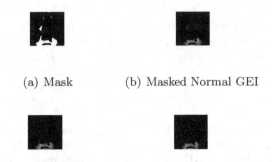

(a) Mask   (b) Masked Normal GEI

(c) Masked Carrying GEI (d) Masked Clothing GEI

Fig. 5. The mask obtained by our method and the corresponding masked GEI of an individual under different conditions.

features from the top part of the GEI corresponding the dynamic motion of the hands during the walk and head shape.

Tab. 1 represents the results obtained by our method compared to the reported results of four other state-of-the-art methods. It can be seen that our method loses slightly a bit performance in the case of normal walk condition and improves considerably the performance in the case of clothing conditions. Moreover, it makes the best compromise between gait walk conditions performance which can be seen by the mean and the standard deviation, which outperform the other ones. This can be explained by the fact that our method eliminates features from the top of the GEI template which, in turn, improve the recognition performance in the case of normal and carrying bag walks while these features are considerably affected in the presence of wearing coat covariates.

Table 1. Comparison of CCRs (In percent) from several different algorithms on CASIA database using 90° view.

Method	Normal	Carrying-Bag	Wearing-Coat	Mean	Std.Dev.
Han et al. [6]	99.60	57.20	23.80	60.20	37.99
Yu et al. [11]	97.60	32.70	52.00	60.77	33.33
Bashir et al. [12]	**100.00**	78.30	44.00	74.10	28.24
Bashir et al. [13]	97.50	**83.60**	48.80	76.63	25.09
Our Method	95.97	63.39	**72.77**	**77.38**	**16.77**

5   Conclusions

This paper has presented a feature selection mask for improved gait recognition. The proposed mask demonstrates attractive results in the presence of clothing covariates and makes the best compromise between different gait walk recognition performances.

As future work we will investigate the robustness of the mask in case of view angle variation between training and testing data and extend the results to USF database to compare our method with others using this dataset [15].

References

1. Yam, C., Nixon, M.S., Carter, J.N.: Automated person recognition by walking and running via model-based approaches. Pattern Recognition **37**(5), 1057–1072 (2004)
2. Niyogi, S.A., Adelson, E.H.: Analyzing and recognizing walking figures in XYT. In: Proceedings of the IEEE Computer Society Conference on Computer Vision and Pattern Recognition, CVPR 1994, pp. 469–474. IEEE (1994)
3. Wang, L., Ning, H., Tan, T., Hu, W.: Fusion of static and dynamic body biometrics for gait recognition. IEEE Transactions on Circuits and Systems for Video Technology **14**(2), 149–158 (2004)
4. Benabdelkader, C., Cutler, R.G., Davis, L.S.: Gait recognition using image self-similarity. EURASIP Journal on Advances in Signal Processing **2004**(721765), 572–585 (2004). doi:10.1155/S1110865704309236
5. Collins, R.T., Gross, R., Shi, J.: Silhouette-based human identification from body shape and gait. In: Proceedings of the Fifth IEEE International Conference on Automatic Face and Gesture Recognition, pp. 366–371. IEEE (2002)
6. Han, J., Bhanu, B.: Individual recognition using gait energy image. IEEE Transactions on Pattern Analysis and Machine Intelligence **28**(2), 316–322 (2006)
7. Tao, D., Li, X., Wu, X., Maybank, S.J.: General tensor discriminant analysis and gabor features for gait recognition. IEEE Transactions on Pattern Analysis and Machine Intelligence **29**(10), 1700–1715 (2007)
8. Xu, D., Yan, S., Tao, D., Zhang, L.: Human gait recognition with matrix representation. IEEE Transactions on Circuits and Systems for Video Technology **16**(7), 896–903 (2006)
9. Xu, D., Yan, S., Tao, D., Lin, S., Zhang, H.-J.: Marginal fisher analysis and its variants for human gait recognition and content-based image retrieval. IEEE Transactions on Image Processing **16**(11), 2811–2821 (2007)
10. Zhang, E., Zhao, Y., Xiong, W.: Active energy image plus 2DLPP for gait recognition. Signal Processing **90**(7), 2295–2302 (2010)
11. Yu, S., Tan, D., Tan, T.: A framework for evaluating the effect of view angle, clothing and carrying condition on gait recognition. In: 18th International Conference on Pattern Recognition, ICPR 2006, pp. 441–444. IEEE
12. Bashir, K., Xiang, T., Gong, S.: Gait recognition without subject cooperation. Pattern Recognition Letters **31**(13), 2052–2060 (2010)
13. Bashir, K., Xiang, T., Gong, S.: Gait representation using flow fields. In: BMVC, pp. 1–11 (2009)
14. Guan, Y., Wei, X., Li, C.-T., Marcialis, G.L., Roli, F., Tistarelli, M.: Combining gait and face for tackling the elapsed time challenges. In: 2013 IEEE Sixth International Conference on Biometrics: Theory, Applications and Systems (BTAS), pp. 1–8. IEEE
15. Guan, Y., Li, C.-T., Roli, F.: On reducing the effect of covariate factors in gait recognition: a classifier ensemble method. IEEE Trans. on Pattern Analysis and Machine Intelligence (2014) doi:10.1109/TPAMI.2014.2366766

16. Foster, J.P., Nixon, M.S., Prgel-Bennett, A.: Automatic gait recognition using area-based metrics. Pattern Recognition Letters **24**(14), 2489–2497 (2003)
17. Zheng, S., Zhang, J., Huang, K., He, R., Tan, T.: Robust view transformation model for gait recognition. In: 2011 18th IEEE International Conference on Image Processing (ICIP), pp. 2073–2076. IEEE
18. Huang, P.S., Harris, C.J., Nixon, M.S.: Recognising humans by gait via parametric canonical space. Artificial Intelligence in Engineering **13**(4), 359–366 (1999)
19. Rida, I., Bouridane, A., Al Kork, S., Bremond, F.: Gait recognition based on modified phase only correlation. In: Elmoataz, A., Lezoray, O., Nouboud, F., Mammass, D. (eds.) ICISP 2014. LNCS, vol. 8509, pp. 417–424. Springer, Heidelberg (2014)
20. Rida, I.: Al Maadeed, S., Bouridane, A. Gait recognition based on modified phase-only correlation. Signal, Image and Video Processing (2015). doi:10.1007/s11760-015-0766-4

Human Area Refinement for Human Detection

Rong Xu[✉], Satoshi Ueno, Tatsuya Kobayashi, Naoya Makibuchi, and Sei Naito

KDDI R&D Laboratories Inc., Fujimino-shi, Saitama 356-8502, Japan
ro-xu@kddilabs.jp

Abstract. Human detection technologies are very useful tools to understand human activity for various purposes, such as surveillance. Recently, tracking-by-detection methods have also become popular for analyzing human activity, but their performance is greatly affected by the accuracy of detected human areas because they use online learning based on the detected results. In order to improve the performance of such tracking methods, the inclination of human bodies in the image is considered as a way to refine the detected human bounding boxes. Based on background subtraction and a novel scheme of estimating human foot position, a refinement scheme is proposed to estimate a bounding box more accurately, which can better fit the contours of inclined human bodies than the conventional method. Experimental results illustrated that the bounding boxes refined by the proposed algorithm achieved a higher cover rate of 92.7 % and a smaller mean angle error of 0.7° compared with the cover rate of 83.7 % and mean angle error of 3.8° obtained using the conventional method, as determined by comparison with the ground truth, and a real-time detection speed of 32.3 fps on a 640×480 video has been realized. Thus, tracking performance is significantly enhanced by refining the human areas, with a mean improvement of 42.4 % in the F-measure when compared with the conventional method.

Keywords: Human detection · Background subtraction · Foot position estimation · Refinement scheme · Human tracking

1 Introduction

In computer vision, human detection in still images and videos has become a very hot research topic in the last few years. It is critical in applications such as surveillance systems, assisted driving, robotics, and smart homes. It can also be used in shops, supermarkets and stores to count the number of people present and to analyze customer behavior and interactions with clerks for business optimization.

In recent decades, several methods have been proposed for human detection, in which some typical descriptors include a Histogram of Oriented Gradients (HOG) feature [1], an Integral Channel Feature (ICF) [2], Local Binary Patterns (LBP) [3], and the CENTRIST feature [4]. The effectiveness of these methods has been proven in practice for the detection of upright complete humans. With the development of human detection technologies, an approach called tracking-by-detection [5] has become popular recently. This approach treats the tracking problem as a detection task applied over time. Such a method learns classifiers for tracking online using detected

© Springer International Publishing Switzerland 2015
V. Murino and E. Puppo (Eds.): ICIAP 2015, Part II, LNCS 9280, pp. 130–141, 2015.
DOI: 10.1007/978-3-319-23234-8_13

human bounding boxes (b-boxes) instead of using offline labeled data for training, and thus the quality of the classifiers is greatly affected by the accuracy of the detected human areas, which contributes to the final tracking performance.

Although most detection methods can provide a high detection rate, accurate depiction of human postures and regions still cannot be achieved, i.e., all existing methods can only detect approximate human locations denoted by upright b-boxes, and cannot deal with the contour of an inclined human body very well. In order to improve the accuracy of the detected human areas, in this paper we propose a refinement algorithm for the detected human bounding box (b-box) to fit the contour of the inclined human body based on background subtraction, human detection, and a novel scheme of estimating human head and foot position using a predefined human height.

The rest of this paper is organized as follows. Section 2 briefly introduces related work. Section 3 describes the details of the proposed approach. Section 4 presents the experimental results and discussion, and Section 5 concludes the paper.

2   Related Work

Certain features are commonly used for human detection, such as, Haar features [7], edgelet [8], Integral Channel Feature (ICF) [2], HOG feature [1], LBP [3], and the CENTRIST feature [4]. Papageorgiou et al. [7] proposed a sliding window-based target detector combined with multi-scale Harr features, which identifies the object by the SVM classifier in [9]. Wu et al. [8] treated the human body as several body parts and proposed part-detectors learned by boosting a number of weak classifiers based on edgelet features, which can detect multiple and partially occluded humans. Dollar et al. [2] studied integral channel features coupled with a standard boosting algorithm for pedestrian detection, which can efficiently extract gradient and color channels from a transformed image to represent image features by computing the cumulative integral value of special channel areas. Dalal and Triggs et al. [1] provided a feature using a histogram of oriented gradients (HOG) for pedestrian detection. This method is effective, and has reduced the missed detection ratio by at least one order of magnitude, relative to the Harr-based detector. Mu et al [3] improved the original LBP descriptor by proposing two variants of LBP: Semantic-LBP and Fourier-LBP for human detection, and achieved performance comparable to other descriptors based on the INRIA human database. In addition, real-time detection has attracted more and more attention, e.g., the CENTRIST feature [4] achieves a much higher speed than existing human detectors, and can detect humans on a 640×480 video at 20 fps using an ordinary CPU. In pursuit of a better detection rate, combining multiple information sources has become a trend, e.g., HOG-LBP [11] achieves the best detection rate in the literature (about 86%), while multiple information increases the cost in terms of detection time.

However, all current methods focus on detection rate and efficiency, and none of them can detect human body areas with sufficient accuracy to fit the contour of an inclined human body, which results in poor tracking performance for the tracking-by-detection method [5]. In order to resolve this problem, we propose a refinement system to generate human body areas more accurately using the detected b-boxes. Since detection efficiency is also a critical factor in tracking performance, the fastest existing algorithm for human detection is employed in this paper, i.e., the CENTRIST feature [4] with a detection rate of 83.5%, which is comparable to the state-of-the-art [2,11]. The refined human areas will be produced in real-time by the proposed method and applied as learning and tracking targets to improve the tracking performance of the tracking-by-detection method [5].

3   Proposed Method

3.1   Basic Ideas

There are two advantages of the proposed method compared with other methods:

(1) A novel refinement scheme is proposed to estimate human areas more accurately to fit the contour of an inclined human body;

(2) Real-time detection and refinement of human areas can be realized due to the high efficiency of the CENTRIST feature [4], and by detecting humans and computing an integral image only on the foreground extracted by the Radial Reach Filter (RRF) [6].

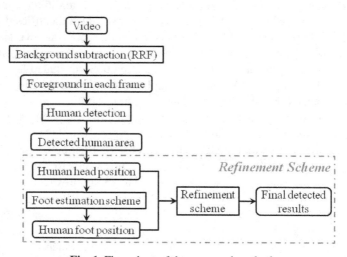

Fig. 1. Flow chart of the proposed method

The flow chart of the proposed method is shown in Fig. 1. First, RRF [6] is utilized to extract the foreground of each frame from an indoor video, which can detect new objects in a time-series image even if they stop moving after they enter the scene. Next, the CENTRIST feature [4] is applied to detect humans only in the foreground regions of each frame, to improve the computational efficiency. After human areas are detected, the corresponding human head position is estimated from the detected b-box, which is more reliable than the foot position extracted from the b-box, since feet are easily occluded by tables or other objects. Subsequently, the human foot position is calculated based on the estimated human head position and the predefined human height by the proposed foot estimation scheme. Finally, the refinement scheme will create a refined b-box to fit the contour of the inclined human body.

3.2   Coarse Foot Position Estimation

In order to estimate foot position, a coarse foot position estimation scheme is proposed based on background subtraction by RRF [6], human detection by the CENTRIST feature [4], and projection and back-projection by direct linear transformation (DLT) [13], as depicted in Fig. 2. In Step-1, the human head position in the image is extracted from the detected b-box, i.e., the top and central point of the b-box (P_h in Fig. 4 (c)). In Step-2, the human head position in a 3D world coordinate system is calculated by back-projection based on the projection matrix estimated by DLT [13]. In Step-3, a coarse foot position is estimated from the human head position in the 3D world coordinate system, which will be projected onto the image to get the coarse foot position in the image in Step-4.

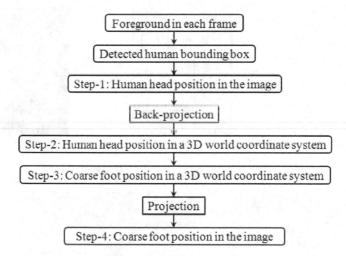

Fig. 2. Flow chart of the coarse foot position estimation

Background Subtraction. Radial Reach filter (RRF) [6] is an effective statistical measure for robust object detection. It can detect new objects in a time-series image even if they stop moving after they enter the scene.

For usual background subtraction methods, to detect new objects they simply subtract the current image from a background image. However, simple background subtraction is easily affected by illumination changes such as shadows. Furthermore, when the brightness difference between objects and a background is small, it cannot detect the difference. In order to solve such problems, the RRF method evaluates a local texture, i.e., measurement of the brightness difference between one pixel and its adjacent neighbors, and realizes robust object detection.

Fig. 3 illustrates one example of background subtraction by RRF, where (a) is the background image, (b) is one scene, and (c) is the detected foreground. Although there is some additional noise as shown in red ellipses in Fig. 3 (c), there is no negative impact on human detection since all of the persons in the scene have been successfully extracted from the background.

Human Detection. CENTRIST is short for CENsus TRansform hISTogram, and has been used for human detection by a cascade classifier called C^4 [4]. The CENTRIST visual descriptor can succinctly encode the crucial sign information (signs of local comparisons) and implicitly encodes the global human contour, and thus it is a suitable representation for detecting human contours. For CENTRIST, the histogram intersection kernel [12] is used to compute similarity scores, which will be used in the refinement scheme for selecting the best detection result described later in Section 3.3.

In this paper, the CENTRIST feature [4] is applied only to regions of interest (ROIs) extracted from the foreground in each frame by RRF [6]. Fig. 4 shows an example of detection, where (a) is the original image, and (b) is the detected results.

(a)

(b)

(c)

Fig. 3. An example of results from RRF

(a)

(b)

(c)

Fig. 4. Results of human detection

Projective Transformation. In order to perform projective transformation from a 3D world coordinate system (Fig. 5 (b), where the units are meters) to a 2D image coordinate system (Fig. 5 (a), where the units are pixels), a projection matrix is estimated in offline processing. In Eq. (1), the projection matrix [P] between the 3D world coordinate system and the 2D image coordinate system is estimated by the Direct Linear Transformation (DLT) method [13],

$$s \begin{bmatrix} u \\ v \\ 1 \end{bmatrix} = [P] \begin{bmatrix} X \\ Y \\ Z \\ 1 \end{bmatrix} = \begin{bmatrix} P_{11} & P_{12} & P_{13} & P_{14} \\ P_{21} & P_{22} & P_{23} & P_{24} \\ P_{31} & P_{32} & P_{33} & P_{34} \end{bmatrix} \begin{bmatrix} X \\ Y \\ Z \\ 1 \end{bmatrix} \qquad (1)$$

where, s is the scale factor, (u, v) gives the coordinates of one pixel in the image, and (X, Y, Z) the corresponding coordinates in the world coordinate system. About 40-50 points (red points in Fig. 5 (a)) are selected from the image, and the corresponding points in the 3D world coordinate system (blue points in Fig. 5 (b)) are measured manually. In order to simplify the estimation process, we choose a regularly shaped room, and its floor is composed of regularly shaped floor tiles each of which is 0.6m by 0.6m, as shown in Fig. 8. Then the corners of the floor tiles and other stationary objects (e.g., table, whiteboard, wall, etc.) are extracted from the image for projective transformation, which can be easily distinguished from the image and the real room. On the other hand, the 3D world coordinate system of the room is constructed as shown in Fig. 5 (b), where the origin is set at one corner of the room, the X-Y plane is the floor, the X and Y axes are parallel to the respective sides of the rectangular floor, and the Z axis is vertical to the floor. Accordingly, we measure actual distances in meters between each corresponding point in the real room and X, Y, and Z axes to get their 3D coordinates.

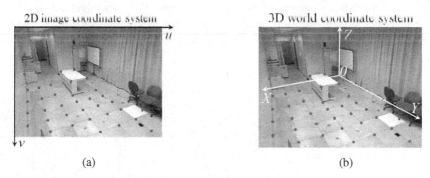

Fig. 5. 2D image coordinate system and 3D world coordinate system

Coarse Foot Position Estimation. Based on the human head position in the age($P_h(u_h, v_h)$ in Fig. 4 (c) and Fig. 6) and the estimated projection matrix [P], a human head position (V_h in Fig. 6) is calculated in the 3D world coordinate system by back-projection, using a predefined human height (1.7 meters in experiments), to define the head's z position in the 3D world coordinate system. Considering only upright humans in the scene, a coarse foot position (V_f in Fig. 6) in the world coordinate system can be estimated from the head position $V_h(\tilde{X}, \tilde{Y}, \tilde{Z})$ by setting $\tilde{Z} = 0$, i.e., the coarse foot position is $V_f(\tilde{X}, \tilde{Y}, 0)$. Finally, the coarse foot position ($P_f(u_f, v_f)$ in Fig. 6) in the image is computed from V_f by projection using the estimated projection matrix [P].

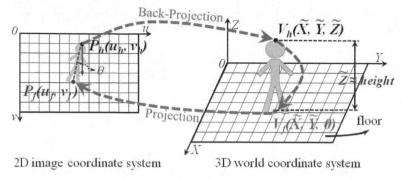

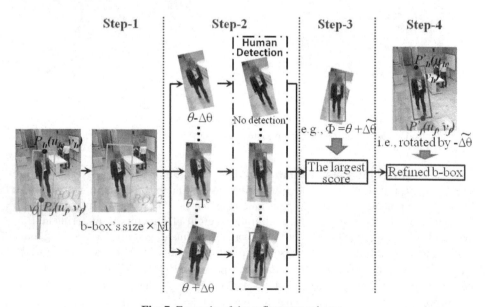

Fig. 6. Foot Estimation Scheme

Note that a predefined human height of 1.7 meters will lead to some error in estimated foot positions since actual human heights will differ. However, such errors can be removed by the refinement scheme because a human re-detection mechanism will be utilized to estimate foot positions more accurately.

3.3   Refinement Scheme

Based on the b-box initially detected by the CENTRIST feature [4], the extracted head position (P_h) and the estimated foot position (P_f), a new ROI is created the uppermost and lowermost centers of which are P_h and P_f, respectively, with a width equal to the width of the initial b-box(ROI1 in the leftmost image of Fig. 7). The steps of the refinement scheme are shown in Fig. 7 and are as follows:

Fig. 7. Example of the refinement scheme

Step 1. ROI1 is enlarged M times to obtain a new region of ROI2 for human detection, the center of which is the same as that of ROI1, and the width and height are M times larger than those of ROI1. Meanwhile, angle θ of ROI1 is calculated from the lines from P_h to P_f and the v axis in the 2D image coordinate system. Here, M = 1.2 is selected based on experimental experience.

Step 2. The area of ROI2 in the image is extracted, and rotated in the range of $[\theta - \Delta\theta, \ \theta + \Delta\theta]$ in increments of τ in a clockwise direction. Thus a number of cases corresponding to different rotation angles are examined by the CENTRIST descriptor, and their similarity scores calculated by the histogram intersection kernel [12] will be recorded if a human is detected as shown in the dashed rectangle (Human Detection) in Fig. 7. If no human is detected, the corresponding similarity score is set to 0. Here, $\Delta\theta = 15°$ and $\tau = 2°$ are selected based on experiments.

Step 3. All scores from those cases are compared, and the detected result with the largest score is selected as the best. Also, the rotation angle of the image corresponding to the best detected result is recorded as $\Phi = \theta + \widetilde{\Delta\theta}$, as shown in Fig. 7.

Step 4. The refined result is achieved by rotating the best detected result (b-box) counter-clockwise around its center by an angle of $\widetilde{\Delta\theta}$. Then a fine head position (P_h') and foot position (P_f') are extracted from the refined b-box using its uppermost and lowermost central points, as shown in the right most image of Fig. 7.

4   Experiments

In the experiments, a camera was set in each of four corners of an indoor laboratory to cover all areas of the room, the layout of which is shown in the upper right image in Fig. 8. Fig. 8 also shows a set of four captured images. To simulate the recording of customer behavior in a shop, two groups of videos were recorded for human detection and tracking, with each group containing four videos captured by the four cameras. The first group shows a simple case with four people in the scene. The second group is a more complex case with ten people in the scene. Each 9-minute video was shot at 10 fps, and thus contains about 5400 frames. For one group, all of the 2D pixels in each video can be back-projected into the same 3D world coordinate system by the estimated projection matrices. Thus, humans are detected and tracked in each video, and integrated in the 3D world coordinate system.

4.1   Evaluation of Projection Transformation

As the basis of the proposed method, the accuracy of the projective transformation is very critical for estimating coarse foot position, which contributes to the accuracy of the refinement scheme and the final results. For this reason, we use the reconstruction error to measure transformation errors, specifically the RMS distance between the reconstructed coordinates and the measured ones (i.e., the ground truth). In experiments, the estimated fine foot positions in Section 3.3 from the four cameras are back-projected into the 3D world coordinate system, and compared with the ground truth measured manually to calculate the reconstruction error, where the mid-point between the feet is considered to be the foot position. The mean and standard deviation of the reconstruction error of the cameras was $0.28 \pm 0.19\ meters$, which is sufficiently acceptable for practical applications.

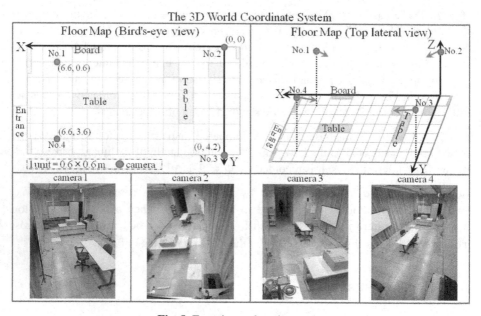

Fig. 8. Experimental environment

4.2   Evaluation of Refined B-Boxes

To evaluate the accuracy of the results, the ground truth was extracted manually for each person, and the following criteria were calculated to measure the similarity between the result and the ground truth for all videos. The *cover rate* equals the size of the overlap area of the result and the ground truth divided by the size of their union, i.e., $\frac{G \cap R}{G \cup R}$ in Fig. 9, where the blue (G) and red (R) b-boxes represent the ground truth and the result. The *mean angle error* is the mean of angle ε in Fig. 9.

Fig. 9. Similarity criteria

In Table 1, the proposed method achieves a much better accuracy than the conventional method [4] for each criterion. Meanwhile, the standard deviations of each criterion show that the proposed method is more robust than the conventional method [4]. In addition, the proposed method is highly efficient at human detection, due to the combination of the conventional method [4] and ROIs of the foreground extracted by RRF [6], which yields a mean processing time of $31 \pm 14\,ms$ (32.3 fps) on a 640×480 video using 4 processing cores of a 3.5GHz CPU. This shows that real-time detection can be achieved by running the proposed method on a common desktop PC. Moreover, it is faster than the conventional algorithm [4] (i.e., 25.5 fps on a 640×480 video by the same PC). The higher efficiency of the proposed method is attributed to detecting humans and computing an integral image, two of the most time-consuming parts of the algorithm, only on the foreground.

Table 1. Accuracy of the detected results

	Cover rate	Mean angle error
Ref. [4]	$83.7 \pm 16.6\%$	$3.8 \pm 3.5°$
The proposed method	$92.7 \pm 9.0\%$	$0.7 \pm 1.8°$

4.3   Evaluation of Tracking Performance

The performance of the tracking-by-detection [5] method is strongly affected by the detected human areas. To evaluate how the proposed method affects tracking performance, the tracking quality of the conventional method [4] and the proposed method are compared. These are frequently estimated from three fundamental measurements: precision, recall, and F-measure [14]. High values of precision, recall, and F-measure indicate good tracking quality, where the F-measure that is calculated from the harmonic mean of precision and recall is the best measurement. The ground truth of human tracking is manually generated.

Since four cameras are used for human detection and tracking, integration of detection results from different cameras is critical for human tracking. In our tracking system, we calculate physical distances between detected humans from different cameras and tracked persons in a tracking list to judge whether they are the same person. Herein, we use local and global to separate detected humans from the cameras and tracked persons in the 3D world coordinate system. For example, we suppose that local person A, B, C, and D are detected by camera 1, 2, 3, and 4, respectively. First, the local person A's foot position is estimated in the 3D world coordinate system based on the projection and back-projection transformation, as described in Section 3.2 and 3.3. Then the distances between the local person A and the global tracked persons registered in the tracking list will be computed, and the minimal distance between the local person A and some global tracked person will be selected. If such a minimal distance is smaller than one threshold (in the experiments we use 0.5 meters), then the local person A will be considered to be the same person who has been registered in the tracking list. Meanwhile, tracking information of the corresponding tracked person will be updated based on the local person A detected by camera 1. If such a minimal distance is larger than the threshold, then a new person will be added to the tracking list.

Subsequently, the local person B, C, and D will be integrated into the tracking list in the same way, and the corresponding tracking information will be updated. However, the position of the global tracked person will be updated after checking all detected results from four cameras. For example, if the local person A, B, C, and D are assumed to be the same person, then the position of the corresponding global tracked person is updated by calculating the central point of four persons' positions in the 3D world coordinate system. Therefore, as minimum conditions, our tracking system requires the synchronization of four fixed cameras, projection transformations estimated between each camera and a global 3D world coordinate system, and background images captured by each camera for object extraction.

The tracking results are listed in Table 2, and we find that compared with the tracking results of the conventional method [4], improvements of about 45.9%, 18.6%, and 32.5% for precision, recall, and F-measure, respectively, are achieved by the proposed method using in the videos of the first group, and improvements of about 63.2%, 41.4%, and 52.2% for precision, recall, and F-measure, respectively, are achieved in the videos of the second group. A mean 42.4% improvement in F-measure was achieved by the proposed method for tracking performance, compared with the conventional method [4], showing that the refined human b-boxes of the proposed method can contribute to a significant improvement in tracking performance, especially for cases involving more persons.

Table 2. Comparison of tracking accuracy

	Videos of the first group		Videos of the second group	
	Ref. [4]	Proposed method	Ref. [4]	Proposed method
Precision	0.37	**0.54**	0.19	**0.31**
Recall	0.43	**0.51**	0.29	**0.41**
F-measure	0.40	**0.53**	0.23	**0.35**

Although the proposed method has been compared with only one conventional method [4] by b-box similarity and tracking performance, this was sufficient to verify its superiority because all other detection methods are like the conventional method [4] in only providing similar upright b-boxes for human detection.

5   Conclusions

In this paper, we have proposed a novel approach to refine b-boxes to better fit the contours of inclined human bodies based on background subtraction technology, human detection technology, and a novel scheme for estimating human foot position. The results showed that the proposed approach performs well at extracting human areas accurately, i.e., a cover rate of 92.7% and a mean angle error of 0.7° compared with the ground truth, and it contributes to a roughly 42.4% improvement in tracking performance. Moreover, a real-time detection speed of $31 \pm 14 \, ms$ on a 640×480 video has been achieved. In the future, accuracy of head position estimation will be further improved by introducing human head detection technology. Also, some open datasets such as PETS 2009 will be used for evaluating the proposed approach.

References

1. Dalal, N., Triggs, B.: Histograms of oriented gradients for human detection. In: IEEE Computer Society Conference on Computer Vision and Pattern Recognition, pp. 886–893 (2005)
2. Dollár, P., Tu, Z., Perona, P., Belongie, S.: Integral channel features. In: BMVC, vol. 3, p. 5 (2009)
3. Mu, Y., Yan, S., Liu, Y., Huang, T., Zhou, B.: Discriminative local binary patterns for human detection in personal album. In: IEEE Conference on Computer Vision and Pattern Recognition, pp. 1–8 (2008)
4. Wu, J., Geyer, C., Rehg, J.M.: Real-time human detection using contour cues. In: 2011 IEEE International Conference on Robotics and Automation (ICRA), pp. 860–867 (2011)
5. Hare, S., Saffari, A., Torr, P.H.: Struck: structured output tracking with kernels. In: 2011 IEEE International Conference on Computer Vision (ICCV), pp. 263–270 (2011)
6. Satoh, Y., Tanahashi, H., Wang, C., Kaneko, S.I., Niwa, Y., Yamamoto, K.: Robust event detection by radial reach filter (RRF). In: 16th International Conference on Pattern Recognition, pp. 623–626 (2002)
7. Papageorgiou, C., Poggio, T.: A trainable system for object detection. International Journal of Computer Vision 38(1), 15–33 (2000)
8. Wu, B., Nevatia, R.: Detection and tracking of multiple, partially occluded humans by bayesian combination of edgelet based part detectors. International Journal of Computer Vision 75(2), 247–266 (2007)
9. Maji, S., Berg, A.C., Malik, J.: Classification using intersection kernel support vector machines is efficient. In: IEEE Conference on Computer Vision and Pattern Recognition, pp. 1–8 (2008)
10. Zhu, Q., Yeh, M.-C., Cheng, K.-T., Avidan, S.: Fast human detection using a cascade of histograms of oriented gradients. In: IEEE Computer Society Conference on Computer Vision and Pattern Recognition, pp. 1491–1498 (2006)
11. Wang, X., Han, T.X., Yan, S.: An HOG-LBP human detector with partial occlusion handling. In: IEEE 12th International Conference on Computer Vision, pp. 32–39 (2009)
12. Swain, M.J., Ballard, D.H.: Color indexing. International Journal of Computer Vision 7(1), 11–32 (1991)
13. Shapiro, R.: Direct linear transformation method for three-dimensional cinematography. Research Quarterly American Alliance for Health, Physical Education and Recreation 49(2), 197–205 (1978)
14. Smith, K., Gatica-Perez, D., Odobez, J.-M., Ba, S.: Evaluating multi-object tracking. In: IEEE Computer Society Conference on Computer Vision and Pattern Recognition-Workshops, pp. 36–43 (2005)

Skeletonization Algorithm Using Discrete Contour Map

Hassan Id Ben Idder$^{(\boxtimes)}$ and Nabil Laachfoubi

Department of Mathematics, IR2M laboratory Faculty of Science and Technology,
University Hassan 1st, Settat, Morocco
hassan.id.ben.idder@gmail.com

Abstract. The skeleton of a binary object can be considered as an alternative to the object itself; it describes the object in a simple and compact manner that preserves the object topology. In this paper, we introduce a new definition for discrete contour curves, and we propose a new approach for extracting a well-shaped and connected skeleton of two-dimensional binary objects using a transformation of the distance map into contour map, which allows us to disregard the nature of the distance metric used. Indeed, our algorithm can support various distances such as the city-block distance, the chessboard distance, the chamfer distance or the Euclidean distance. To evaluate the proposed technique, experiments are conducted on shape benchmark dataset.

Keywords: Image analysis · Digital topology · Distance map · Discrete Contour Map · Skeletonization

1 Introduction

The skeleton is a representation widely used for shape description and shape interpretation in several applications of image processing. There are several equivalent definitions in continuous space. For example the skeleton is defined by the set of centers of maximal disks contained in the object, by the set of ridges in the distance map, or by analogy with the fire front propagation as introduced early by Blum [9]. The skeleton of an object can also be defined as the set of centers of the disks that touch the boundary of the object in two or more locations. Skeletonization algorithms proposed in the literature are grouped into three categories: 1) approximation of the fire front propagation [7,20], 2) approximation of the continuous skeleton [10,12] or 3) extraction and interconnection of the centers of maximal disks in the distance map [11,14,19,29]. There are several algorithms that use the distance map to calculate the skeleton of an object, in common cases they involve the following steps: generating the distance map from a binary image, extracting the centers of maximal inscribed disks from the distance map and linking the centers of maximal disks to produce a connected skeleton. Algorithms using approximate distance metrics such as d_4 and d_8 are intensively considered and discussed by researchers and their theory

© Springer International Publishing Switzerland 2015
V. Murino and E. Puppo (Eds.): ICIAP 2015, Part II, LNCS 9280, pp. 142–150, 2015.
DOI: 10.1007/978-3-319-23234-8_14

is well established. However, these algorithms are not efficient for applications requiring greater precision. Using the Euclidean distance may be considered as a solution to this problem; however, it has topological disadvantages that may directly influence the resulting skeleton. In this paper, we present a new approach to extract the skeleton of binary objects based on the notion of contour map. In fact, we extended the algorithm proposed in [21] - originally developed to support only distances d_4 and d_8 - to be capable of disregarding the nature of distance metric used. Our work is based on the results of Andres and Jacob on the discrete analytical hypersphere [3] to propose a new definition of discrete contour curves, independent of the distance metric used. Based on this definition we introduce the notion of the contour map, which is a transformation of the distance map.

The main features of the proposed skeletonization approach are:

- The Contour map is an abstraction layer between the skeletonization algorithm and the distance function used.
- The algorithm is based on a new definition of discrete contour curves which is valid for several discrete distances.
- The algorithm can be, readily, extended to other distances by adapting the definition of discrete contour curves to such distances.

The remainder of the paper is organized as follows. Section 2 gives insights on the notations and some elementary definitions used in this paper. Sections 3 and 4 introduce the definition of *Discrete Contour Map* and our approach to skeletonization process. Experimental results are presented in section 5. In section 6 we present a historical walk through the skeletonization techniques. Section 7 provides some final conclusions and the impact of the suggested approach.

2   Preliminaries and Notations

We denote $\mathbb{R}$ the set of reel numbers, $\mathbb{Z}$ the set of integers and $\mathbb{N}^*$ the set of strictly positive integers. A discrete point is an element of $\mathbb{Z}^n$ denoted p, an object X is a set of discrete points. Two discrete points $p(x_p, y_p)$ and $q(x_q, y_q)$ are 4-neighbor (or 4-adjacent) if: $|x_p - x_q| + |y_p - y_q| = 1$. Similarly, they are 8-neighbor (or 8-adjacent) if: $max(|x_p - x_q|, |y_p - y_q|) = 1$. A binary image I is a function $\mathbb{Z}^2 \rightarrow \{0, 1\}$: each element of I can have the following values: 1 for object points and 0 for non-object points. Functions d_4, d_8, $d_{\langle a,b,\cdots\rangle}$ and d_E refer respectively to the city-block distance, chessboard distance, chamfer distance and the Euclidean distance. The distance of a point $p \in X$ to the border, denoted $d(p, \overline{X})$, is the minimal distance of p to the complementary of X. The distance map of an object X relative to the distance metric d, denoted DM_d is the set of points labeled with their minimal distance to the boundary of X. A point $p \in DM_d$ is a local maximum in a 8-neighborhood if all its neighbors are at a distance from the boundary lower or equal to $d(p, \overline{X})$.

3   Discrete Contour Map

In a topographic map, the contour curves are lines that connect points of equal elevation. Similarly, we consider the contour curves in a distance map d_4 or d_8 as the set of points having the same distance to the border. This definition is meaningless if we are interested in the chamfer distance or Euclidean distance. To give a general definition that characterizes the contour curves, we consider, in the continuous space, circular curves around a point (denoted $C\,(x_c, y_c) \in \mathbb{R}^2$) centered in the image. In this case a contour curve corresponds to a circle with center C and radius $r \in R$. The set of points belonging to this circle is defined by: $\left\{ P\,(x,y) \in \mathbb{R}^2 : (x - x_c)^2 + (y - y_c)^2 = r^2 \right\}$. In the discrete space several formulations have been proposed for the circle depending on the discretization scheme. In [3] for example, authors proposed a generalized definition in arbitrary dimension, which combines the continuous analytical definition and the properties specific to the discrete space.

Definition 1 (Discrete Analytical Hypersphere [3]). *A discrete analytical Hypersphere $H_n\,(C, r, \omega)$ in dimension n, of center $C \in \mathbb{R}^n$, radius $r \in R$ and thickness $\omega \in \mathbb{R}$, is the set of discrete points $P\,(x_1, \cdots, x_n) \in H_n$ such that:*

$$H_n\,(C, r, \omega) = \left\{ P \in \mathbb{Z}^n : \left(r - \frac{\omega}{2} \right)^2 \leq \sum_{i=1}^{n} (C_i - P_i)^2 < \left(r + \frac{\omega}{2} \right)^2 \right\} \qquad (1)$$

This formula defines the points that constitute the discrete circle in an open interval $[-\frac{\omega}{2}, \frac{\omega}{2}[$. For what concerns us - defining circles in dimension 2 with thickness 1 and centered on the origin point $(0,0)$ - the above inequality is reduced to:

$$H\,(r) = \left\{ P\,(x, y) \in \mathbb{Z}^2 : \left(r - \frac{1}{2} \right)^2 \leq x^2 + y^2 < \left(r + \frac{1}{2} \right)^2 \right\} \qquad (2)$$

The authors showed that for thicknesses $\omega \geq 1$, the circle is at least 8-connected and the union of circles is a tiling of the discrete space. In other words, each lattice point in $\mathbb{Z}^2$ belongs to one and only one of the concentric circles. Those properties make this definition well-suited for characterizing contour curves in a distance map computed using an arbitrary distance metric. In fact, it solves the topological issues related to the Euclidean distance in discrete space (non-connectedness of curves and the presence of gaps between two successive curves). Thus, we define the contour curve of level k as the set of points that are at a distance d from the object boundary, such that: $d \in [k - \frac{1}{2}, k + \frac{1}{2}[$

Definition 2 (Discrete contour curves). *Given an object X, the contour curve of level $k \in \mathbb{N}^*$ relative to a distance metric d is the set of points $p \in X$ which satisfy the double inequality:*

$$C\,(k) = \left\{ p \in \mathbb{Z}^2 : (m\,(2k - 1))^2 \leq 4d^2\,(p, \overline{X}) < (m\,(2k + 1))^2 \right\} \qquad (3)$$

Where $m \in \mathbb{N}^*$ is the smallest distance to the object boundary, its value is equal to 1 for distances d_4, d_8 and d_E and equal to a for chamfer distances $d_{\langle a,b,\cdots \rangle}$.

This definition is directly applicable in the discrete space and uses only integer operations and has the advantage of being valid for all distance metrics mentioned in this article ($d_4, d_8, d_{\langle a,b,\cdots \rangle}$ and d_E).

Definition 3 (Contour map). *Given an object X, its contour map, relative to a distance metric d, denoted CM_d is an image where each point $p \in X$ is labeled with the level k of the contour curve to which it belongs.*

Note that for discrete distances d_4 and d_8 we have $CM_d = DM_d$, because to each distance value corresponds a separate contour curve. Furthermore, each point at a distance d, which belongs to the contour curve of level k, is always surrounded by points belonging to a contour curve $k' \in \{k-1, k, k+1\}$. This will allow us to limit the check of the inequality 3 in the interval $[k-1, k+1]$. Figure 1 represent respectively the contour map for distances d_8, $d_{\langle 3,4 \rangle}$ and d_E. The set of local maxima points coincides with the skeleton of the object.

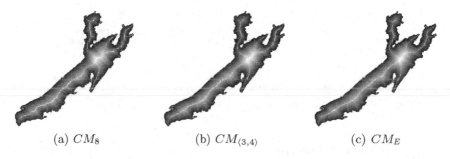

(a) CM_8 (b) $CM_{\langle 3,4 \rangle}$ (c) CM_E

Fig. 1. Contour map for distances d_8, $d_{\langle 3,4 \rangle}$ and d_E

4   Skeletonization Algorithm

The set of local maxima points extracted from contour map of an object is not connected in most cases. Therefore, the skeleton defined only by set of local maxima of contour map is not useful for shape analysis applications. To overcome this problem, we need to interconnect all groups of local maxima points and produce a connected skeleton. The skeletonization algorithm proposed in [21] is applicable only for distances d_4 and d_8, it is based on the notion of *multiple points* introduced by Pavlidis [25]. Multiple points are identified in the distance map using local configurations in a 3×3 neighborhood. These points correspond to either a folding of a contour curve on itself near local maxima, or to a shrinkage center in the object. A recursive procedure is applied to perform a steepest ascent from each multiple point until another skeleton point is met. The algorithm produces a correct skeleton with a convenient computational complexity.

We propose a variant of this algorithm, which gives rise to a new skeletonization approach. In fact, we have extended this algorithm to support chamfer distance and the Euclidean distance by replacing the distance map by the contour map introduced in this article. The new algorithm performs the following operations:

1. Generating the distance map from a binary image.
2. Generating the contour map from the distance map.
3. Extracting local maxima points from the contour map.
4. Extracting multiple points from contour map using local configurations.
5. Interconnecting groups of local maxima points by performing a steepest ascent from each multiple point until another skeleton point is met.

The local configurations used in the original algorithm to detect multiple points, do not allow the proposed algorithm to interconnect all groups of local maxima points, it is therefore necessary to introduce other configurations to insure this interconnection. Figure 2 shows the set of additional configurations that we introduced to detect multiple points, the 8 neighbors $p_{i=0,\dots,7}$ of point p are numbered with respect to the counterclockwise ordering.

·	p_2	·		·	p_2	·		·	p_2	·		·	p_2	·
·	p	p_0		·	p	·		p_4	p	p_0		p_4	p	p_0
p_5	·	·		p_5	·	p_7		·	p_6	·		·	·	·

Fig. 2. Additional configurations used to detect multiple points from contour map, the central point p is a multiple point.

5   Experimental Results

In this section we evaluate the shape topology preservation of the proposed algorithm by conducting experiments on random images from Kimia's shape dataset [28]. We compare results obtained using distances d_8 and $d_{<3,4>}$ with those obtained using the distance d_E. (See table 1). To generate the euclidean distance map we used the Shih's algorithm [30] that achieves the euclidean distance transform in two scans using a 3×3 neighborhood, the algorithm produce a correct distance map in a linear time without iterations.

In real applications, binary images are obtained from cluttered scenes, therefore the boundaries of generated binary shapes contains a lot of noise which affects substantially the resulting skeleton. As an image preprocessing, we apply an edge blurring algorithm to smooth the shape boundary before computing distance map. In fact, rough edges produce local maxima points in the boundary of the shape, these local maxima become endpoints of unwanted branches in the final skeleton.

Most of skeletonization algorithms based on distance map are developed to support only one distance function, their extension to another distance function is not a trivial task. The Contour map defined in this work allow our algorithm to overcome this problem. In fact, extending the algorithm to another distance function involves only extending the definition of the discrete contour curve. As shown in table 1, the skeletons obtained using distances d_8, $d_{\langle 3,4 \rangle}$ and d_E are well-connected, centered in the object and contain all significant branches of the shape. Except for distance d_8, where some irrelevant branches appear in the skeleton, no pruning process is required to remove redundant branches. The results obtained using distances $d_{\langle 3,4 \rangle}$ and d_E are similar, one can use either $d_{\langle 3,4 \rangle}$ or d_E without impacting the performance of the algorithm. For both distances, efficient algorithms exist for computing the distance map with linear run-time complexity.

Table 1. Binary shapes from Kimia's dataset [28] and their skeletons using contour maps CM_8, $CM_{<3,4>}$ and CM_E

6 Related Work

In this section we present the most common ideas and techniques proposed in the literature to extract skeleton of $2D$ shapes. Skeletonization algorithms first appeared in the sixties. Blum [9] presented the process of skeletonization as a transformation of the image - called *Medial Axis Transformation* - to extract a new shape descriptor. Hilditch [15,16] proposed a sequential algorithm based on the notion of the *crossing number*. When the neighbors of a pixel are traversed in sequence, the crossing number is the number of times one crosses over from a white pixel to a black pixel. Pixels are traversed and marked for deletion under conditions that maintain skeleton connectivity and preserve two-pixel thickness. Rosenfeld [27] established the necessary and sufficient conditions for preserving topology while deleting border points in parallel process of skeletonization. Arcelli proposed a parallel algorithm [5] that deletes pixels using two 3×3 masks together with their 90° rotations. Dyer and Rosenfeld [13] worked out an algorithm for extracting skeleton from gray-scale images. It uses a generalized definition of pixel connectivity: two pixels are *connected* if there is a path joining them with no pixel lighter than either of them. Pavlidis [23–26] introduced the definition of *multiple pixels*, pixels that are traversed more than once during contour tracing, points with no neighbors in the interior and points on two-pixel-wide lines. *Multiples pixels* as well as the neighbors of skeletal pixels from a previous iteration are retained to maintain the connectivity of the skeleton. Arcelli [6] proposed another sequential skeletonization algorithm. It performs a contour tracing to detect the pixels for deletion. Arcelli and di Baja [8] presented a necessary definition to satisfactorily detect *multiple pixels* introduced by Pavlidis. Later [4] they developed a sequential algorithm that uses a *4-distance* transform to find a set of skeletal pixels using one scan of the image, followed by a second scan to remove unwanted pixels. Parker et al. [22] introduced the force-based approach for skeletonization. The authors define a *skeletal pixel* as being as far from the object boundary as possible while maintaining connectivity properties. The skeleton is interpreted as a global property of a binary object, and the boundary is used to locate the skeleton pixels. Andreadis et al. [2] presented an algorithm to extract a skeleton using morphological operators on image defined in the HSV color space. Huang et al. [17] proposed another parallel thinning algorithm. Pixel elimination rules are based on 3×3 windows considering all kinds of relations formed by 8 neighbors of the object pixel. Ji and Feng [18] proposed a method that interprets the image as a $2D$ thermal conductor that consists of pixels, where pixel intensity represents the temperature. The skeletonization is considered as an inverse process of heat conduction. Tang et al. [32] proposed a skeletonization algorithm based on a wavelet transform. The algorithm extracts an initial skeleton in a regular region followed by second stage to connect the initial skeletons in the singular region. Wan et al. [31] presented an algorithm that extract a skeleton in 3 stages. In the first stage, the Euclidean distance map of the image is generated. In the second stage, the local maximal disc centers are marked as skeleton points. In the last stage, a connected skeleton is generated by linking isolated skeleton points. Recently, Abu-Ain et al. [1] proposed an algorithm for optical character recognition (OCR) consisting of three main stages; conditional contour selection stage, pixel removing stage, and one pixel width stage.

7   Conclusion

This study presents a new skeletonization approach, which is to use the contour map as an alternative to the distance map. Using this approach, we proposed an algorithm capable of disregarding the nature of distance metric used. Indeed, we were able to generalize an existing algorithm to support more distance metrics such as the chamfer distance or Euclidean distance. The skeleton obtained by this method has the essential characteristics required by applications dealing with shapes description and interpretation in image processing.

References

1. Abu-Ain, W., Abdullah, S.N.H.S., Bataineh, B., Abu-Ain, T., Omar, K.: Skeletonization Algorithm for Binary Images. Procedia Technology **11**, 704–709 (2013)
2. Andreadis, I., Vardavoulia, M.I., Louverdis, G., Papamarkos, N.: Colour image skeletonisation. In: Proceedings of the 10th European Signal Processing Conference, vol. 4, pp. 2389–2392 (2000)
3. Andres, E., Jacob, M.A.: The discrete analytical hyperspheres. IEEE Transactions on Visualization and Computer Graphics **3**(1), 75–86 (1997)
4. Arcelli, C., di Baja, G.: A one-pass two-operation process to detect the skeletal pixels on the 4-distance transform. IEEE Transactions on Pattern Analysis and Machine Intelligence **11**(4), 411–414 (1989)
5. Arcelli, C., di Baja, G.S.: On the Sequential Approach to Medial Line Transformation. IEEE Transactions on Systems, Man and Cybernetics **8**(2), 139–144 (1978)
6. Arcelli, C.: Pattern thinning by contour tracing. Computer Graphics and Image Processing **17**(2), 130–144 (1981)
7. Arcelli, C., Di Baja, G.S.: A Width-Independent Fast Thinning Algorithm. IEEE Transactions on PAMI Pattern Analysis and Machine Intelligence **7**(4), 463–474 (1985)
8. Arcelli, C., di Baja, G.S.: A contour characterization for multiply connected figures. Pattern Recognition Letters **6**(4), 245–249 (1987)
9. Blum, H.: A transformation for extracting new descriptors of shape. In: Models for the Perception of Speech and Visual Form, pp. 362–380 (1967)
10. Brandt, J.W., Algazi, V.: Continuous skeleton computation by Voronoi diagram. CVGIP: Image Understanding **55**(3), 329–338 (1992)
11. Chaussard, J., Couprie, M., Talbot, H.: Robust skeletonization using the discrete λ-medial axis. Pattern Recognition Letters **32**(9), 1384–1394 (2011)
12. Choi, W.P., Lam, K.M., Siu, W.C.: Extraction of the Euclidean skeleton based on a connectivity criterion. Pattern Recognition **36**(3), 721–729 (2003)
13. Cr, D., Rosenfeld, A.: Thinning algorithms for gray-scale picture. IEEE Trans. Pattern Anal. Mach. Intell. **1**(1), 88–89 (1979)
14. Ge, Y., Fitzpatrick, J.M.: On the generation of skeletons from discrete Euclidean distance maps. IEEE Transactions on Pattern Analysis and Machine Intelligence **18**(11), 1055–1066 (1996)
15. Hilditch, C.: An Application of Graph Theory in Fabric Design. Machine Intelligence **3**, 325–347 (1968)
16. Hilitch, C.J.: Linear skeletons from square cupboards. In: Meltzer, B., Michie, D. (eds.) Machine Intelligence, vol. 4, p. 403. Edinburgh University Press (1969)
17. Huang, L., Wan, G., Liu, C.: An improved parallel thinning algorithm. In: Proceedings of the Seventh International Conference on Document Analysis and Recognition, pp. 780–783 (August 2003)
18. Ji, X., Feng, J.: A new approach to thinning based on time-reversed heat conduction model (image processing). In: 2004 International Conference on Image Processing, ICIP 2004, vol. 1, pp. 653–656 (October 2004)
19. Latecki, L.J., Li, Q.N., Bai, X., Liu, W.Y.: Skeletonization using SSM of the distance transform. In: IEEE International Conference on Image Processing, ICIP 2007, vol. 5, pp. V-349–V-352 (September 2007)
20. Leymarie, F., Levine, M.D.: Simulating the grassfire transform using an active contour model. IEEE Transactions on Pattern Analysis and Machine Intelligence **14**(1), 56–75 (1992)

21. Montanvert, A.: Contribution au traitement de formes discrèes: squelettes et codage par graphe de la ligne médiane. Theses, Institut National Polytechnique de Grenoble - INPG; Université Joseph-Fourier - Grenoble I (October 1987)
22. Parker, J.R., Jennings, C., Molaro, D.: A force-based thinning strategy with subpixel precision. In: Vision Interface Conference, pp. 82–87 (1994)
23. Pavlidis, T.: A flexible parallel thinning algorithm. In: Proceedings of the International Conference on Pattern Recognition and Image Processing, pp. 162–167 (1981)
24. Pavlidis, T.: Algorithms for graphics and image processing. Digital system design series. Computer Science Press (1982)
25. Pavlidis, T.: A thinning algorithm for discrete binary images. Computer Graphics and Image Processing $13(2)$, 142–157 (1980)
26. Pavlidis, T.: An asynchronous thinning algorithm. Computer Graphics and Image Processing $20(2)$, 133–157 (1982)
27. Rosenfeld, A.: A characterization of parallel thinning algorithms. Information and Control $29(3)$, 286–291 (1975)
28. Sharvit, D., Chan, J., Tek, H., Kimia, B.B.: Symmetry-based Indexing of Image Databases. Journal of Visual Communication and Image Representation $9(4)$, 366–380 (1998)
29. Shih, F.Y., Pu, C.C.: A skeletonization algorithm by maxima tracking on Euclidean distance transform. Pattern Recognition $28(3)$, 331–341 (1995)
30. Shih, F.Y., Wu, Y.T.: Fast Euclidean distance transformation in two scans using a 3x3 neighborhood. Computer Vision and Image Understanding $93(2)$, 195–205 (2004)
31. Wan, Y., Yao, L., Xu, B., Zeng, P.: A distance map based skeletonization algorithm and its application in fiber recognition. In: International Conference on Audio, Language and Image Processing, ICALIP 2008, pp. 1769–1774 (July 2008)
32. You, X., Tang, Y.Y.: Wavelet-Based Approach to Character Skeleton. IEEE Transactions on Image Processing $16(5)$, 1220–1231 (2007)

Superpixel and Entropy-Based Multi-atlas Fusion Framework for the Segmentation of X-ray Images

Dac Cong Tai Nguyen[2,3], Said Benameur[2,3]([✉]), Max Mignotte[2], and Frédéric Lavoie[1,3]

[1] Orthopedic Surgery Department, Centre Hospitalier de l'Université de Montréal (CHUM), Montréal, Québec, Canada
[2] Département d'Informatique et de Recherche Opérationnelle (DIRO), Université de Montréal, Québec, Canada
[3] Eiffel Medtech Inc., Montréal, Québec, Canada
`dac.cong.tai.nguyen@umontreal.ca, benameus@iro.umontreal.ca`

Abstract. X-ray images segmentation can be useful to aid in accurate diagnosis or faithful 3D bone reconstruction but remains a challenging and complex task, particularly when dealing with large and complex anatomical structures such as the human pelvic bone. In this paper, we propose a multi-atlas fusion framework to automatically segment the human pelvic structure from 45 or 135-degree oblique X-ray radiographic images. Unlike most atlas-based approach, this method combines a data set of a priori segmented X-ray images of the human pelvis (or multi-atlas) to generate an adaptive superpixel map in order to take efficiently into account both the imaging pose variability along with the inter-patient (bone) shape non-linear variability. In addition, we propose a new label propagation or fusion step based on the variation of information criterion for integrating the multi-atlas information into the final consensus segmentation. We thoroughly evaluated the method on 30 manually segmented 45 or 135 degree oblique X-ray radiographic images data set by performing a leave-one-out study. Compared to the manual gold standard segmentations, the accuracy of our automatic segmentation approach is 85% which remains in the error range of manual segmentations due to the inter intra/observer variability.

Keywords: Consensus segmentation · X-ray images · Multi-atlas segmentation · Variation of information based fusion step · Superpixel map

1 Introduction

In clinical practice, X-Ray radiographic images are used to assist in disease diagnosis, pre-operative planning and treatment analysis. Extraction of the contours and/or regions of the bone structures (pelvis, talus, patella, etc.) from 45-degree and 135-degree oblique X-Ray radiographic images may eventually play

© Springer International Publishing Switzerland 2015
V. Murino and E. Puppo (Eds.): ICIAP 2015, Part II, LNCS 9280, pp. 151–161, 2015.
DOI: 10.1007/978-3-319-23234-8_15

an important role in the diagnosis and treatment of diseases such as osteoarthritis (e.g. joint-replacement planning) or osteoporosis (e.g. fracture detection and bone density measurements).

X-Ray segmentation of bone structures in the pelvic region is both intrinsically and extrinsically difficult. This is caused partly by the intrinsic difficulties of the system. First because of the X-Ray imaging systems: Noise in X-Ray images has a number of origins, but the most fundamental is from the X-Ray source itself. This type of noise is called quantum noise, in reference to the discrete nature of the X-Ray photons producing it. Also, bone regions in X-Ray images often overlap with soft tissues and other bones. Extrinsic difficulties are usually due to the patients: neighboring tissues inside human body may have similar X-Ray absorption rates. As a result, the boundaries of the organs may be ambiguous and there is sometimes no clear edge between two neighboring bone structures. In addition we must also consider the bone structures density variability, the inter-patient (bone structure) shape variability and the imaging pose variability. These difficulties are particularly true when dealing with large and complex anatomical structures such as the human pelvic bone which explains why the segmentation process of such anatomical structures is currently performed manually or semi-automatically and often requires human expert interaction.

To simplify and guide an automatic segmentation task, *a priori* anatomical information is essential and may be provided in different ways. For instance, with the knowledge of the luminance distributions within each different tissue or regions to be segmented [1] or in the form of deformable statistical models represented by a family of parametrized curves [2,3] or by one or several prototype templates together with their parametric spaces of deformations [4].

A recent, simple and non-parametric alternative to bring spatial prior knowledge to the segmentation process consists in defining and using a multi-atlas, *i.e.*, a set of training segmented images (possibly with the set of their associated X-ray images) [5–7]. With this latest strategy, the automatic segmentation task turns into a two step procedures; namely a first registration step where each atlas segmented (possibly with its associated X-ray image) is registered to the target image independently and the calculated transformation is then applied to the segmentation of the atlas image to obtain a segmented version of the target image and a second *fusion* or *label propagation* step where the preceding candidate segmentations, resulting from the first step, are finally fused to produce a final consensus segmentation.

More precisely, in the multi-atlas segmentation strategy, the first registration stage is usually carried out in two steps: a global rigid registration that obtains an initial rough alignment followed by a local non-rigid (and non-linear) registration to take into account the target specific deformation (mainly due to inter-patient bone structure and imaging pose variability). This latter non-linear registration is typically performed by applying a non-linear parametric transform model on the control points of a free-form deformation grid with B-spline-curves, demons, optical flows, etc. [8]. In these commonly used registration strategies, it is important to note that the parametric deformation model is generally computationally expensive, could fail in the case of complex deformations and is not learned from the multi-atlas data set. In this work, the multi-atlas allows us to generate an adaptive superpixel map which is then exploited to efficiently take into account the non linear target-specific deformations and to comprise all the non-linear variability of the multi-atlas population.

Concerning the second *fusion* or *label propagation* step, the commonly used combination strategies, proposed in the literature, include majority voting [9], (possibly locally) weighted voting [5] or Expectation-Maximization algorithm based vote procedure[10]. In this study, we propose to use a *label propagation* strategy based on the minimization of the variation of information criterion [11] between the candidate segmentations to be fused. This fusion procedure has already turned out to be very relevant for combining multiple low cost and inaccurate segmentations given by several simple algorithms of a textured natural image to achieve a final improved segmentation [11].

2   Proposed Model

2.1   Data Set and Multi-atlas Creation

Anonymised 45 and 135 degree oblique X-ray radiographic images of the full pelvic bone from 31 patients without pelvic deformity were obtained after approval by the local ethics board. Images of the pelvis were manually segmented into 14 different regions of interest (ROIs) by experts well trained in pelvic anatomy and medical image segmentation. These segmentations included the entire pelvis with all three adjoining bones, namely the left and right proximal femurs as well as the sacrum including the coccyx (tail bone). Each hemipelvis consists of the ischium, the ilium and the pubis (see Fig. 1).

2.2   Image Pre-processing

All the acquired X-Ray images to be segmented are firstly pre-processed with a histogram equalization technique and a DCT-based denoising step [12,13] to enhance the contour of the different bones of the human pelvis region. These contour cues will be then exploited in the contour-based registration step explained in the following section.

2.3   Proposed Multi-atlas Fusion Procedure

Linear Registration and Multi-atlas Selection Step. As said in Introduction, the most informative and reliable visual cues in a X-Ray image of the pelvic region remains the boundary contours between the different pelvic bone structures and particularly the external bone contour of the pelvis. Considering this, each atlas segmented image is linearly registered to the target image independently

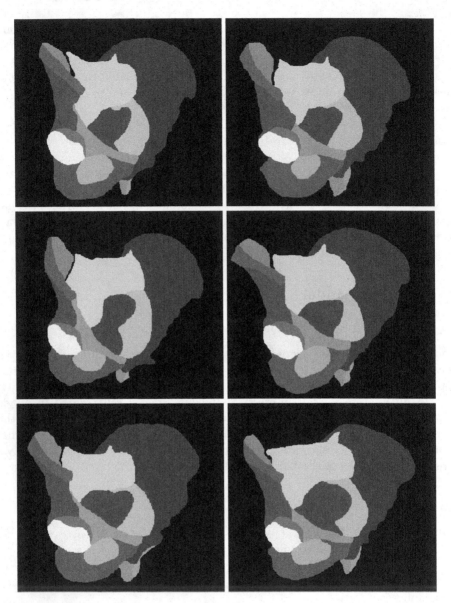

Fig. 1. 6 examples of 45-degree oblique manual segmentations of the human pelvic bone used in our multi-atlas.

using a contour-based registration technique. More precisely, a global linear registration (affine or rigid transformations) is performed to obtain an initial alignment that maximizes a measure of similarity between the external contour of the pelvis region in the segmented image of the atlas and an edge potential field (edge map) estimated on the X-Ray image by a simple Canny edge detector (allowing to

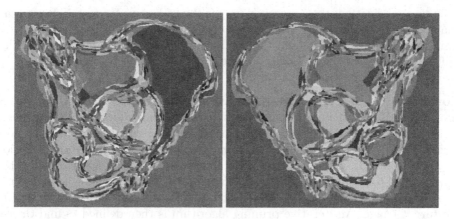

Fig. 2. Superpixel maps obtained for a given X-ray 45 and 135 degree image to be segmented.

obtain a binary edge image) [14] followed by a Gaussian blur (filter) with standard deviation σ controlling the degree of smoothness of this edge potential map [15]. The global rigid registration that maximizes the summation of this potential map over all the pixels on the boundary of the external contour of the pelvis (given by the manual segmentation) thus allows to obtain a rough alignment of each atlas image to the target image.

In addition, our contour-based similarity registration metric allows us to rank the different manual segmentations of our multi-atlas by decreasing order of similarity and consequently to select the first half of the segmented images of the multi-atlas for generating the superpixel map which will be explained in the following section.

Superpixel Map Creation. The first half of the segmented images of the multi-atlas allows us to generate a superpixel map where each defined superpixel remains a coherent unit which, in fact, contains a set of connected pixels belonging to the same label region for each segmented image of our subset (i.e., pre-selected as previously mentioned) of manual segmented images of the multi-atlas. This superpixel map is simply obtained by the intersection of all the regions (or segments) existing in the multi-atlas (see Fig. 2).

The use of superpixel was originally developed by Ren and Malik in [16] as a pre-processing step for the segmentation of natural images [16] in order to reduce the number of entities to be labeled when the segmentation is formulated as a difficult optimization problem (in the space of all possible segmentations). Let us also note that the use of superpixels in an energy-based fusion procedure has also been initially proposed in [17] with a different goal, namely the one of blending a spatial segmentation (region map) and a quickly estimated and to-be-refined application field (e.g., motion estimation/segmentation field, occlusion map, etc.) and in [18] for restoration application.

In our application, the superpixel map is thus adaptive for each X-Ray target image to be segmented and will allow us to carry out an adaptive local non-rigid registration to take into account the non linear target-specific deformations. This will be explained in the following section.

Non-linear Registration from the Superpixel Map. Each X-Ray target image allows us to generate a specific superpixel map which locally comprises all the non-linear variability (*i.e.*, inter-patient bone structure and imaging pose variability) of a selected subset of the multi-atlas population (see the selection step in section 2.3). To this end, let us recall that the subset of selected segmented images, used to generate the superpixel map, have been linearly registered to the target image. By this fact, the superpixel map is already linearly registered to the target image. An iterative pruning algorithm is then defined to find the set of connected superpixels which maximizes the contour-based similarity measure between the edge map of the target X-Ray image and the outer contour of this superpixel map[1].

More precisely, each superpixel, in a lexicographic order, which is connected with the background label (*i.e.*, which is contiguous with the external region of the pelvic bone), is considered as belonging to the pelvic region if the outer contour-based similarity metric increases and until convergence or a maximum number of iterations is reached. At convergence, this pruning algorithm allows us to find an accurate closed external contour of the pelvic bone which is then used in the following step.

Final Selection and Variation of Information Based Fusion Step. A final linear registration between the previously closed external contour allows us to select the first quarter of the manual segmentations of our multi-atlas data set, in term of a region-based similarity metric, and to fuse these segmentations in the variation of information (VoI) sense [11]. This similarity metric is the F-measure (the harmonic mean of precision and recall) between the internal region defined by the previously estimated closed external contour and the internal region of the pelvis (given by the manual segmentation).

In this *label propagation* step, the VoI-based fusion procedure allows to infer the internal region labels of the pelvis from the filtered (or selected) atlases to the final segmentation image.

---

[1] Experiments have shown that slightly better results are given if the superpixel map is scaled by a factor slightly greater than one in order to ensure that the pelvis contour of the X-Ray target image is fully contained in the superpixel map. To this end, after trial and error, a scale factor of 1.02 allows us to give the best segmentation results.

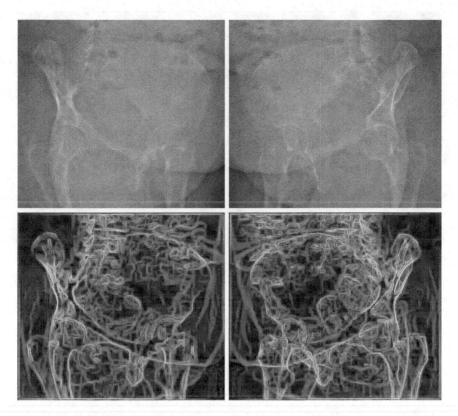

Fig. 3. Original oblique X-Ray radiographic images of pelvis before and after the pre-processing step (see Section 2.2: the pre-processing step).

3   Experimental Results

In all the experiments, we have tested our multi-atlas segmentation approach on 31 images (45 or 135-degree oblique) X-ray radiographic images of the pelvis acquired using a X-ray imaging system (see Fig. 3).

In order to validate our procedure, we have performed a leave-one-out procedure, *i.e.,* we removed each existing manual segmentation from the multi-atlas data set while other manual segmentations remained. Each X-Ray image associated to the previously removed segmentation map was then segmented by our strategy and compared, in terms of classification error rate, with its manual segmentation. Compared to the manual gold standard segmentations, the accuracy of our automatic segmentation approach was 85%. Examples of segmentations are given in Figures 4 and 5. Figure 6 shows two segmentation results from our automatic segmentation approach compared to a manual gold standard segmentation. In this example, the accuracy of our automatic segmentation approach is respectively 89% for Figure 6(g), 85% for Figure 6(h), 81% for Figure 6(i).

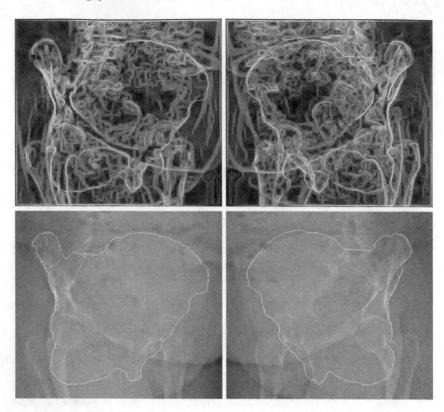

Fig. 4. Example of external pelvis contours on the corresponding 45 and 135 -degree oblique X-ray radiographic (original and gradient) images.

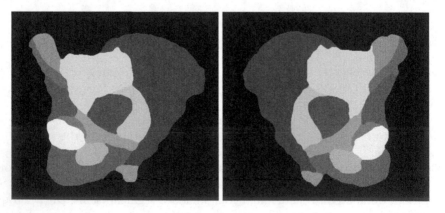

Fig. 5. Resulting fusion image estimated after the VoI-based *label propagation* step, with the estimated internal region labels of the pelvis.

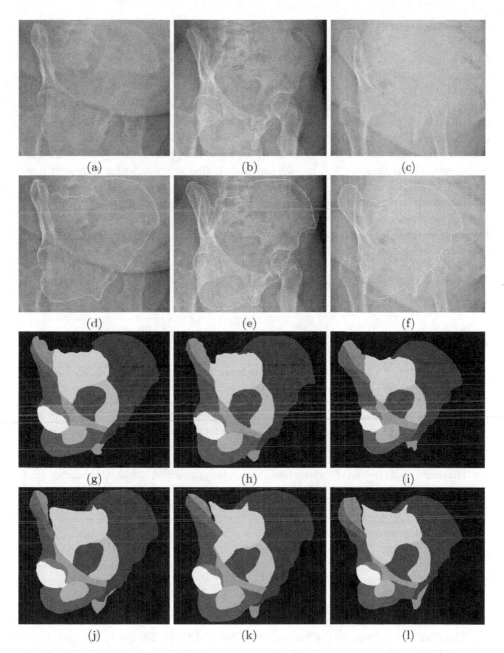

Fig. 6. Comparison of two segmentation results from our automatic segmentation app-roach and a manual gold standard. (a),(b) and (c) original oblique X-Ray radiographic images of pelvis; (d),(e) and (f) external pelvis contours on the corresponding 45 -degree oblique X-ray radiographic images; (g),(h) and (i) resulting fusion image estimated after the VoI-based *label propagation* step, with the estimated internal region labels of the pelvis; (j),(k) and (l) a manual segmentations of the corresponding 45 -degree oblique X-ray radiographic images

4   Conclusion

In this paper, a new multi-atlas based segmentation method is presented. Unlike most atlas-based approach, the proposed method includes the following contributions. First, the multi-atlas data set allows us to generate an adaptive superpixel map which comprises all the non-linear variability of the multi-atlas population and allows us to take into account the non linear target-specific deformations of our multi-atlas based segmentation approach. Second, the similarity measure used in our registration step is used in an atlas selection strategy both for the registration step and for the label propagation fusion step, which is herein performed in the variation of information sense. Third our approach allows us to consider only the most informative and reliable visual cues in a X-Ray image of the pelvic region, *i.e.*, the external bone contour of the pelvis and the *fusion* step then allows to infer the internal region labels of the pelvis from the filtered (or selected) atlases to the final segmentation image. The average classification rate, obtained with a leave-one-out method, is within the range of observer variability when compared to a semi-automatic segmentation technique that is performed by an expert.

References

1. Mignotte, M., Collet, C., Pérez, P., Bouthemy, P.: Sonar image segmentation using an unsupervised hierarchical MRF model. IEEE Trans. on Image Processing **9**(7), 1216–1231 (2000)
2. Mignotte, M., Meunier, J., Tardif, J.-C.: Endocardial boundary estimation and tracking in echocardiographic images using deformable templates and markov random fields. Pattern Analysis and Applications **4**(4), 256–271 (2001)
3. Mignotte, M., Meunier, J.: A multiscale optimization approach for the dynamic contour-based boundary detection issue. Computerized Medical Imaging and Graphics **25**(3), 265–275 (2001)
4. Destrempes, F., Mignotte, M.: Localization of shapes using statistical models and stochastic optimization. IEEE Trans. on Pattern Analysis and Machine Intelligence **29**(9), 1603–1615 (2007)
5. Artaechevarria, X., Muñoz-Barrutia, A., Ortiz-de-Solorzano, C.: Combination strategies in multi-atlas image segmentation: Application to brain MR data. IEEE Trans. Med. Imaging **28**(8), 1266–1277 (2009)
6. Aljabar, P., Heckemann, R.A., Hammers, A., Hajnal, J.V., Rueckert, D.: Multi-atlas based segmentation of brain images: Atlas selection and its effect on accuracy. NeuroImage, 726–738 (2009)
7. Dowling, J.A., Fripp, J., Chandra, S., Pluim, J.P.W., Lambert, J., Parker, J., Denham, J., Greer, P.B., Salvado, O.: Fast automatic multi-atlas segmentation of the prostate from 3D MR images. In: Madabhushi, A., Dowling, J., Huisman, H., Barratt, D. (eds.) Prostate Cancer Imaging 2011. LNCS, vol. 6963, pp. 10–21. Springer, Heidelberg (2011)
8. Morin, J.-P., Desrosiers, C., Duong, L.: A random walk approach for multiatlas-based segmentation. In: ICPR 2012, pp. 3636–3639 (2012)

9. Rohlfing, T., Brandt, R., Menzel, R., Maurer, C.R.: Evaluation of atlas selection strategies for atlas-based image segmentation with application to confocal microscopy images of bee brains. Neuroimage **21**(4), 1428–1442 (2004)
10. Rohlfing, T., Russakoff, D.B., Maurer, C.R.: Performance-based classifier combination in atlas-based image segmentation using expectation-maximization parameter estimation. IEEE Trans. Med. Imaging **23**(8), 983–994 (2004)
11. Mignotte, M.: A label field fusion model with a variation of information estimator for image segmentation. Information Fusion **20**, 7–20 (2014)
12. Mignotte, M., Meunier, J., Soucy, J.-P.: DCT-based complexity regularization for EM tomographic reconstruction. IEEE Trans. on Biomedical Engineering **55**(2), 801–805 (2008)
13. Yu, G., Sapiro, G.: DCT image denoising: a simple and effective image denoising algorithm. Image Processing On Line **1** (2011)
14. Canny, J.: A computational approach to edge detection. IEEE Transactions on Pattern Analysis and Machine Intelligence **8**(6), 679–698 (1986)
15. Benameur, S., Mignotte, M., Parent, S., Labelle, H., Skalli, W., De Guise, J.: 3d/2d registration and segmentation of scoliotic vertebrae using statistical models. Computerized Medical Imaging and Graphics **27**(5), 321–327 (2003)
16. Ren, X., Malik, J.: Learning a classification model for segmentation. In: 9th IEEE International Conference on Computer Vision, vol. 1, pp. 10–17 (October 2003)
17. Jodoin, P.-M., Mignotte, M., Rosenberger, C.: Segmentation framework based on label field fusion. IEEE Trans. on Image Processing **16**(10), 2535–2550 (2007)
18. Mignotte, M.: A segmentation-based regularization term for image deconvolution. IEEE Trans. on Image Processing **15**(7), 1973–1984 (2006)

Wavelet-Like Lifting-Based Transform for Decomposing Images in Accordance with the Inter-prediction Principles of Video Coding

Marek Parfieniuk[✉]

Department of Digital Media and Computer Graphics,
Bialystok University of Technology, Wiejska 45A, 15-351 Bialystok, Poland
m.parfieniuk@pb.edu.pl

Abstract. In this paper, an innovative approach to image analysis-synthesis is presented, which follows the prediction principles of video coding. It consists in decomposing an image into four polyphase components, which are processed like video frames. One of them is made the essential reference frame, whereas each of the remaining components is predicted using the reference or any of previously encoded components. Such hierarchical prediction is adapted, being similar to the bidirectional motion estimation-compensation using two reference frames, known of the MPEG-4 AVC standard for video coding. On the other hand, obtainable residuals are similar to the results of lifting-based subband decompositions of images, or even to wavelet transforms, if the algorithm is applied iteratively to the reference. But, surprisingly, our computational scheme is most related to the known PLT and GTD algorithms, conceptually distant from both wavelets and video coding, and thus it can be called the hierarchical adaptive spatial triangular decomposition (HASTD). Owing to implementation advantages, our solution forms an interesting basis for developing a new class of image codecs.

Keywords: Image · Decomposition · Prediction · Polyphase · Adaptive · Transform · Lifting

1 Introduction

From several works [10][15], it is known that video codecs can be used to compress still images to good effect. This has been verified mainly by applying a video codec to the single-frame sequence that consists only of a given image. But in [10], we have shown that a video codec can as well be applied to a sequence that comprises four polyphase components of the image. In the first approach, images are compressed using only the intra-coding mechanisms of the video codec, whereas the latter solution additionally allows for employing motion estimation-compensation and bidirectional inter-prediction.

The second method has given no notable advantages, but it seems possible to significantly improve its performance by adjusting inter-prediction and entropy

© Springer International Publishing Switzerland 2015
V. Murino and E. Puppo (Eds.): ICIAP 2015, Part II, LNCS 9280, pp. 162–171, 2015.
DOI: 10.1007/978-3-319-23234-8_16

coding to processing polyphase components. As this requires very deep changes in a video codec, we decided to develop from scratch a novel image codec that follows the inter-prediction principles of video coding.

In this paper we present the main part of such a codec — a transform that does that with polyphase components what happens with frames in a video encoder. A similar idea was proposed in [19], where the authors noticed analogies between motion compensation and prediction among image blocks. Block prediction was considered also in [6][18][7], but image blocks are much less correlated than blocks taken from polyphase components, which are predicted in our approach. Our solution has also some connection with adaptive lifting-based wavelet transforms [3][4][8][16][11][2][5][1], but is most similar to the prediction-based lower triangular (PLT) transform [12] and generalized triangular decomposition (GTD) [17]. For this reason, the proposed transform could be called the hierarchical adaptive spatial triangular decomposition (HASTD).

The general computational scheme of the HASTD is almost the same as for the PLT and GTD, but there are fundamental conceptual differences. Firstly, both those transforms have been developed by factorizing autocorrelation matrices and by looking for approximations of the Karhunen–Loeve transform (KLT). No analogies to video coding have been noticed. Secondly, the PLT and GTD are aimed at processing 1-D signals, and their theory cannot easily be extended to images, or to the spatial domain. Thirdly, neither adaptive nor iterative variants of the transforms have been considered. Finally, multiplications are necessary to compute both PLT and GTD.

2 Proposed Principle of Image Analysis-Synthesis

The HASTD algorithm for image analysis and synthesis can be explained using Fig. 1. In the scheme, if some symbol $\mathbf{S}$ denotes a signal, then $\underline{\mathbf{S}}$ stands for a prediction-based estimate of this signal, and $\Delta\mathbf{S} = \mathbf{S} - \underline{\mathbf{S}}$ is the prediction residual. The quantized version of the residual is denoted as $\overline{\Delta\mathbf{S}}$, and the related approximation of the signal is denoted as $\overline{\mathbf{S}} = \underline{\mathbf{S}} + \overline{\Delta\mathbf{S}}$.

In our approach, an image $\mathbf{X}$ is firstly split into four polyphase components, $\mathbf{A}$, $\mathbf{B}$, $\mathbf{C}$, and $\mathbf{D}$, in accordance with Fig. 2. Then $\underline{\mathbf{A}}$, a quantized version of $\mathbf{A}$, is used to predict $\mathbf{B}$. The prediction residual $\Delta\mathbf{B} = \mathbf{B} - \underline{\mathbf{B}}$ is quantized, and its approximate $\overline{\Delta\mathbf{B}}$ and the estimate of $\underline{\mathbf{B}}$ from $\underline{\mathbf{A}}$ are added so as to reconstruct $\overline{\mathbf{B}}$, an approximate of $\mathbf{B}$. The $\mathbf{C}$ component is processed in the same way, but being predicted using $\overline{\mathbf{A}}$, and $\overline{\mathbf{B}}$. Finally, $\mathbf{D}$ is predicted using $\overline{\mathbf{A}}$, $\overline{\mathbf{B}}$, and $\overline{\mathbf{C}}$. We do not apply any additional transform to the residuals, like in the MPEG standards for video coding [13][14], or in [9].

The analysis results comprise a quantized version of the reference component, the quantized residuals of prediction of the remaining polyphase components, and the prediction-control data. The data point out samples of approximate components used to obtain residual blocks, as explained in Section 3.

The synthesis algorithm is shown in the right-hand side of Fig. 1. The control data allow for reversing the prediction done during analysis. Given $\overline{\mathbf{A}}$ and $\overline{\Delta\mathbf{B}}$,

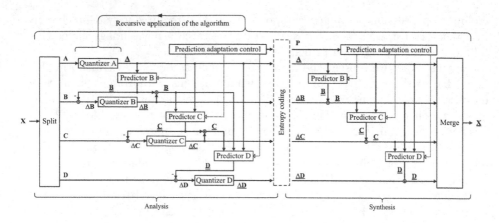

Fig. 1. Data flow graphs of the HASTD.

one can restore $\underline{\mathbf{B}}$. Then $\underline{\mathbf{C}}$ can be reconstructed from $\mathbf{A}$, $\mathbf{B}$, and $\mathbf{\Delta C}$, and $\underline{\mathbf{D}}$ — from $\mathbf{A}$, $\mathbf{B}$, $\underline{\mathbf{C}}$, and $\mathbf{\Delta D}$.

In Fig. 1, the "Split" and "Merge" blocks represent the conversions of an image into its polyphase components and vice versa, respectively. Obviously, they symbolize only conceptual reorganization of image samples, not real memory data movements.

Each quantizer in Fig. 1 represents an arbitrary algorithm for approximating samples at reduced bit rate. It is expected to produce a representation of approximated values that is more suitable to entropy coding. In particular, one can realize a hierarchical transform by using the scheme in Fig. 1 to decompose the $\mathbf{A}$ component in the same way. Thus, decompositions obtainable using our approach can be visualized as in Fig. 3, similarly to wavelet transforms.

Our solution mimics the motion estimation-compensation used in video coding, where previously encoded frames serve as references for predicting a subsequent frame. The scheme is also similar to lifting schemes that are commonly used to implement wavelet transforms, but the differences between the solutions are considerable. Firstly, prediction lifting steps are done after quantization of signals used as the prediction basis. Secondly, there is no update steps, in our approach.

It can by surprising for some people that we omit the update step in the lifting scheme and that we process polyphase components like smooth signals, even though they contain aliasing. However, from a pragmatic point of view, if a signal contains aliasing terms, then this only means that this signal is "difficult" to encode using methods that assume its smoothness, as severe artifacts are more probable in its decoded versions , and it is risky to reconstruct the original signal using its alias-contaminated quantized components. Undoubtedly, an untouched polyphase component carries useful information about an image — the values of every fourth pixel. In our transform, quantization of a polyphase component directly introduces inaccuracies to the reconstructed image, and the

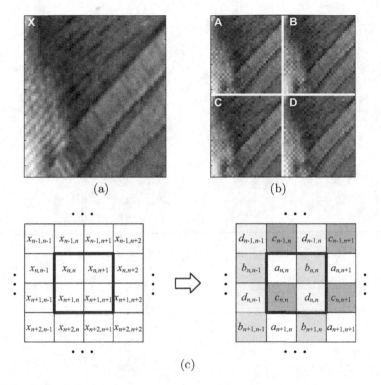

Fig. 2. Polyphase decomposition of an image: (a) a fragment of the "Lena" image, (b) its polyphase components, and (c) the relations among pixels of the image and its components.

error in a polyphase component limits reconstruction quality. But this error does not automatically spread on other polyphase components, or adjacent pixels, as in the conventional transform coders. It only increases prediction residuals among this and other components. If a residual is not quantized, then the related polyphase component can be exactly recovered regardless of what happened with the remaining components.

This establishes two important key properties of our algorithm. Firstly, the effect of coefficient quantization on the reconstruction accuracy can be determined more easily than in the known transform coders, as errors in reconstructed images are directly determined by errors in polyphase components. Secondly, each residual might be quantized in a different way, for the same reconstruction accuracy. If a component can be predicted using more other components, and/or the reference components are quantized less, then the resulting residual is smaller and can be quantized more coarsely.

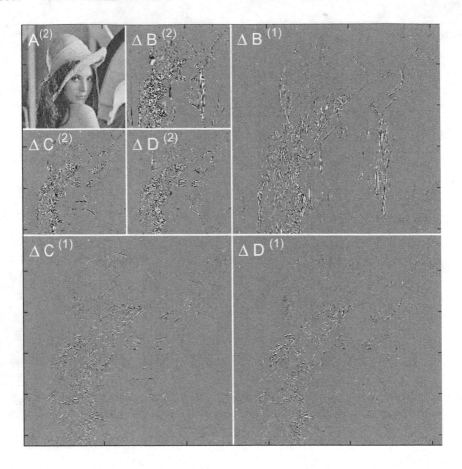

Fig. 3. Non-quantized two-level HASTD of the "Lena" image. The residuals have been amplified, so as to better show distributions of their non-zero values.

3   Adaptive Prediction Mechanisms

Predicting a polyphase component using other ones is equivalent to predicting a pixel using its neighbours, which is the well known effective means of image compression. In our algorithm, the prediction is adapted, because this allows to reduce the energies of the residuals about ten times, compared to simply taking the average of all accessible adjacent pixels. The unit of adaptation is the square block of pixels of a polyphase component. Our experiments showed that the block size is not very important and can be large, as there is no big difference between residuals obtained using 4×4 and 16×16 blocks.

We have limited the adaptation to switching reference samples that are arguments for a fixed prediction function. The function is the average of adjacent pixels, so can be computed without multiplications, using only one addition, one bit shift, and one subtraction. In the preliminary experiments, we considered the following models of a pixel block: only one prediction mode

$$b_{m,n} = \tfrac{1}{2}\left(a_{m,n} + a_{m,n+1}\right) + \Delta b_{m,n} \tag{1}$$

for the B component; three prediction modes:

$$c_{m,n} = \tfrac{1}{2}\left(a_{m,n} + a_{m+1,n}\right) + \Delta c_{m,n} \tag{2}$$

$$c_{m,n} = \tfrac{1}{2}\left(b_{m,n-1} + b_{m+1,n}\right) + \Delta d_{m,n} \tag{3}$$

$$c_{m,n} = \tfrac{1}{2}\left(b_{m,n} + b_{m+1,n-1}\right) + \Delta c_{m,n} \tag{4}$$

for the C component; and four modes

$$d_{m,n} = \tfrac{1}{2}\left(b_{m,n} + b_{m+1,n}\right) + \Delta d_{m,n} \tag{5}$$

$$d_{m,n} = \tfrac{1}{2}\left(c_{m,n} + c_{m,n+1}\right) + \Delta d_{m,n} \tag{6}$$

$$d_{m,n} = \tfrac{1}{2}\left(a_{m,n} + a_{m+1,n+1}\right) + \Delta d_{m,n} \tag{7}$$

$$d_{m,n} = \tfrac{1}{2}\left(a_{m,n+1} + a_{m+1,n}\right) + \Delta d_{m,n} \tag{8}$$

for the D component, where $m = iM + (0, \ldots, M-1)$, $n = jM + (0, \ldots, M-1)$, i and j determine a pixel block, and M denotes the block size. Thus, the algorithm predicts the pixels of a block using their horizontal, vertical, or diagonal neighbours of other polyphase components, so as to follow the direction of local changes of image intensity. This can be conceptually connected with the bidirectional prediction of video coding.

The adaptation consists in searching for the prediction variant that minimizes the Sum of Absolute Differences (SAD), the criterion that is often used in motion estimation. In the preliminary experiments, the optimum prediction settings for a block were determined by brute-force testing all possibilities. Therefore, SAD evaluations represent the main computational load related to our transform, but the quantity can be computed without multiplications, and it is possible to skip further evaluations for a given block after reaching the SAD below some threshold.

It is noteworthy that the indexes of prediction variants, which must accompany HASTD residuals, can be effectively encoded. Firstly, for large blocks, a single index codeword is shared by many pixels. In particular, the related bitrate is only $4/256 = 0.016$ bpp, if 4 bits, necessary to straightforwardly represent the index, are assigned to each 16×16 block. Secondly, the indexes of adjacent blocks are usually correlated, so they can be compressed using known methods for coding motion vectors in video compression.

It should also be mentioned that similar prediction equations can be found in many papers on adaptive wavelet transforms, see eg. [4][8], but in contexts different from our idea. In those works, contrary to our approach, prediction is usually done among rows or columns, so as to preserve the transform separability, a single pixel is the adaptation unit, and the optimum prediction model is determined by analyzing adjacent reference pixels, so that no side data must accompany transform coefficients. But, the main difference between our approach and adaptive wavelet transforms is that, in the latter, prediction, or lifting, is based on non-quantized signals, and thus the encoding order and reconstruction quality of these signals need not to be taken into account.

Table 1. Statistics of the HASTD coefficients of the "Lena" image

Category	Min	Max	Mean	Var	Entropy
$A^{(1)}$	-101,0	113,0	-4,0	2260,1	7,4
$\Delta B^{(1)}$	-56,0	73,0	0,0	40,8	4,4
$\Delta C^{(1)}$	-48,0	63,0	0,0	21,1	4,1
$\Delta D^{(1)}$	-48,0	68,0	0,0	20,7	4,0
$A^{(2)}$	-101,0	106,0	-4,0	2291,4	7,4
$\Delta B^{(2)}$	-99,0	152,0	0,0	143,5	5,0
$\Delta C^{(2)}$	-81,0	106,0	0,0	78,5	4,6
$\Delta D^{(2)}$	-76,0	100,0	0,0	78,4	4,6

Table 2. Statistics of the wavelet coefficients of the "Lena" image

Category	Min	Max	Mean	Var	Entropy
$A^{(1)}$	-207.6	228.0	-8.2	8907.8	8.4
$H^{(1)}$	-49.3	47.7	0.0	17.4	3.9
$V^{(1)}$	-74.2	63.6	0.0	42.4	4.3
$D^{(1)}$	-33.7	27.9	0.0	8.7	3.5
$A^{(2)}$	-395.8	402.8	-17.2	33651.2	9.4
$H^{(2)}$	-204.4	141.0	0.0	166.7	4.9
$V^{(2)}$	-299.6	238.1	-0.2	430.3	5.6
$D^{(2)}$	-106.4	117.6	0.1	113.1	4.8

4   Experimental Evaluation of the HASTD

The key properties of the HASTD can be demonstrated empirically. We use the "Lena" image through this paper, but we obtained similar results also for other standard test images. The presented plots and tables refer to the 2-level decomposition with the prediction adaptation block size of 16×16.

Figure 3 illustrates the results of the HASTD, in the way commonly used to wavelet transforms. The residuals generally look like ordinary wavelet subbands. The image energy is packed into the reference polyphase component at the second level, an the variance of this component is orders of magnitude greater than those of the residuals. The second-level residuals are larger than the first-level ones, but both have significant values located at the same places, related to image edges. Thus, the HASTD can be used to compress images using the principle of zero-tree coding. The main difference compared to the wavelet transform is that that the **C** and **D** residuals are very similar and cannot be identified with horizontal and diagonal details.

More information about the HASTD results is revealed in Table 1 and Fig. 4. For comparison purposes, the analogous data for the two-level wavelet transform with the "9-7" filters has been shown in Table 2 and Fig. 5, where $A^{(n)}$ stands for the approximation subband of the n-th level, whereas **H**, **V**, and **D** denote horizontal, vertical, and diagonal details, respectively.

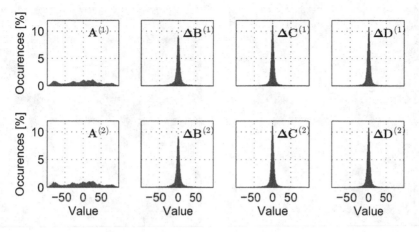

Fig. 4. Coefficient histograms of the 2-level HASTD of the "Lena" image.

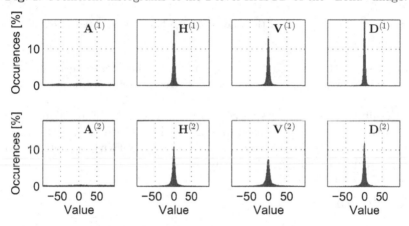

Fig. 5. Coefficient histograms of the 2-level wavelet transform obtained for the "Lena" image using the "9–7" filters.

From a compression point of view, there is not much difference between the histograms of the HASTD residuals and the histograms of wavelet coefficients. Unlike for wavelet coefficients, the dynamic range and variance of HASTD results increase only slightly from level to level. The HASTD seems to posses the property of the unit gain, which characterizes the known triangular transforms [12]. Thus, it seems possible to store HASTD results in the place of image samples, so as to save memory.

It is also of interest to evaluate the achievable accuracy of reconstruction of an image from its quantized HASTD representations. The image in Fig. 6a has been restored using only the second-level data: $\mathbf{A}(2)$ was quantized to 7 bits, whereas $\mathbf{\Delta B}(2)$, $\mathbf{\Delta C}(2)$, and $\mathbf{\Delta D}(2)$ were quantized to 3 bits (the total bitrate of 1 bpp). In Fig. 6b, the image is presented that has been restored using only $\mathbf{A}(2)$ samples quantized to 4 bits (the total bitrate of 0.25 bpp). It is notable that

(a)   (b)

Fig. 6. Reconstructions of the "Lena" image from its quantized HASTDs.

the compression artifacts are different from those that characterize the known, DCT- as well as wavelet-based codecs: they are a combination of blocking and blurring.

The results are not impressive compared to the state-of-art algorithms but prove that the HASTD can be used in image coding. Obviously, better compression ratios can be obtained using fine-tuned quantization and entropy coding algorithms, which are subjects for future works.

5   Conclusion

The HASTD is conceptually simple, even though it is difficult to describe it using mathematical notation. Nevertheless, it decorrelates image samples nearly as well as the known transforms that are based on well-developed theories or have been designed using advanced numerical optimization. Our algorithm can be implemented without multiplications, using only additions and bit shifts, and can be computed without wasting memory for intermediate results. Therefore, our transform can be very economically implemented in hardware and is able to substitute the conventional transforms in many applications.

Acknowledgments. This work was supported by the Polish National Science Centre under Decision No. DEC-2012/07/D/ST6/02454.

References

1. Blackburn, J., Do, M.N.: Two-dimensional geometric lifting. In: Proc. 16th IEEE Int. Conf. Imag. Process. (ICIP), Cairo, Egypt, pp. 3817–3820 (November 7–10, 2009)

2. Fang, Z., Xiong, N., Yang, L., Sun, X., Yang, Y.: Interpolation-based direction-adaptive lifting DWT and modified SPIHT for image compression in multimedia communications. IEEE Systems J. **5**(4), 584–593 (2011)
3. Gerek, O.N., Cetin, A.E.: Adaptive polyphase subband decomposition structures for image compression. IEEE Trans. Image Process. **9**(10), 1649–1659 (2000)
4. Gerek, O., Cetin, A.: A 2-D orientation-adaptive prediction filter in lifting structures for image coding. IEEE Trans. Image Process. **15**(1), 106–111 (2006)
5. Hattay, J., Benazza-Benyahia, A., Pesquet, J.: Adaptive lifting for multicomponent image coding through quadtree partitioning. In: Proc. 30th IEEE Int. Conf. Acoust., Speech, Signal Process. (ICASSP), Philadelphia, PA, vol. 2, pp. 213–216. (March 19–23, 2005)
6. Huang, J., Liu, S.: Block predictive transform coding of still images. In: Proc. IEEE Int. Conf. Acoust., Speech, Signal Process. (ICASSP). vol. 5, Adelaide, Australia, pp. V-333–V-336 (April 19–22, 1994)
7. Jiao, L., Wang, L., Wu, J., Bai, J., Wang, S., Hou, B.: Shape-adaptive reversible integer lapped transform for lossy-to-lossless ROI coding of remote sensing two-dimensional images. IEEE Geosci. Remote Sens. Lett. **8**(2), 326–330 (2011)
8. Kaaniche, M., Pesquet-Popescu, B., Benazza-Benyahia, A., Pesquet, J.C.: Adaptive lifting scheme with sparse criteria for image coding. EURASIP J. Advances Sig. Process. **2012**(1), 10 (2012)
9. Kamisli, F., Lim, J.: 1-D transforms for the motion compensation residual. IEEE Trans. Image Process. **20**(4), 1036–1046 (2011)
10. Parfieniuk, M.: Polyphase components of an image as video frames: a way to code still images using H.264. In: Proc. Picture Coding Symp. (PCS), Cracow, Poland, pp. 189–192 (May 7–9, 2012)
11. Peng, X., Xu, J., Wu, F.: Directional filtering transform for image/intra-frame compression. IEEE Trans. Image Process. **19**(11), 2935–2946 (2010)
12. Phoong, S.M., Lin, Y.P.: Prediction-based lower triangular transform. IEEE Trans. Signal Process. **48**(7), 1947–1955 (2000)
13. Rao, K., Kim, D., Hwang, J.: Video Coding Standards: AVS China, H.264/MPEG-4 PART 10, HEVC, VP6, DIRAC and VC-1. Springer (2014)
14. Richardson, I.: The H.264 Advanced Video Compression Standard, 2 edn. Wiley (2010)
15. Tran, T., Liu, L., Topiwala, P.: Performance comparison of leading image codecs: H.264/AVC Intra, JPEG2000, and Microsoft HD Photo. In: Proc. SPIE 6696 (Applications of Digital Image Processing XXX), 66960B (2007)
16. Vrankic, M., Sersic, D., Sucic, V.: Adaptive 2-D wavelet transform based on the lifting scheme with preserved vanishing moments. IEEE Trans. Image Process. **19**(8), 1987–2004 (2010)
17. Weng, C.C., Chen, C.Y., Vaidyanathan, P.: Generalized triangular decomposition in transform coding. IEEE Trans. Signal Process. **58**(2), 566–574 (2010)
18. Xu, J., Wu, F., Zhang, W.: Intra-predictive transforms for block-based image coding. IEEE Trans. Signal Process. **57**(8), 3030–3040 (2009)
19. Zhao, H., He, Z.: Lossless image compression using super-spatial structure prediction. IEEE Signal Process. Lett. **17**(4), 383–386 (2010)

Real-Time Age Estimation from Face Imagery Using Fisher Vectors

Lorenzo Seidenari[1]([✉]), Alessandro Rozza[2], and Alberto Del Bimbo[1]

[1] University of Florence, Firenze, Italy
{lorenzo.seidenari,alberto.delbimbo}@unifi.it
[2] Hyera Software, Coccaglio, Italy
alessandro.rozza@hyera.com

Abstract. In the last decade facial age estimation has grown its importance in computer vision. In this paper we propose an efficient and effective age estimation system from face imagery. To assess the quality of the proposed approach we compare the results obtained by our system with those achieved by other recently published methods on a very large dataset of more than 55K images of people with different gender and ethnicity. These results show how a carefully engineered pipeline of efficient image analysis and pattern recognition techniques leads to state-of-the-art results at 20FPS using a single thread on a 1.6GHZ i5-2467M processor.

Keywords: Age estimation · Face analysis · Biometrics

1 Introduction

In the last decade age estimation from facial imagery has grown its importance in the computer vision field. The process of age determination has many potential application areas, such as: age-based access control and verification, where a person's age is verified prior to physical access to a place or product being sold or virtual access to a website is granted; age-adaptive human-computer interaction, where as example, a digital sign can display advertisements based on the age of the audience walking past; age-based indexing of face images, that is the use of age as criterion for indexing into huge-scale biometric databases for faster retrieval.

To guarantee the success of all the aforementioned applications it is required to obtain fast (or real-time) estimation of the attribute of interest (the age). This requirement is particularly severe when it exists a limited window of time for a decision based on the outcome, such as when a person walks past a digital sign. Nevertheless, even in the case of the usage of age as criterion for indexing into huge-scale biometric databases, high speed of the age estimation algorithms are required to make it operationally viable.

Age estimation is usually performed as a multi-class classification problem or as a regression task. In the first case, given an image feature $\phi(I)$ computed

© Springer International Publishing Switzerland 2015
V. Murino and E. Puppo (Eds.): ICIAP 2015, Part II, LNCS 9280, pp. 172–182, 2015.
DOI: 10.1007/978-3-319-23234-8_17

from a face image I, the task is to predict the class associated to the interval (*age group*) containing the actual age. Precisely, the age labels are quantized in a set of age groups, e.g. $\{[16, 25], [26, 35] \ldots [56, 65]\}$. This approach is intuitive but has a few drawbacks. First of all, if the aim is a precise estimation the age groups must be kept small, but this comes at the cost of reducing the amount of positive samples per class and increasing the dataset imbalance. Second, if the relationship among labels is discarded, a classical classification loss function would equally penalize errors among close and distant age groups.

In the regression case the age is treated as a real number and a function age$(\phi(I))$ is estimated to minimize the age estimation error. This approach has several advantages over the multi-class classification task. First, all data can be used to fit a single model. This avoids the quantization problem and reduces the amount of models needed to estimate the age leading to higher efficiency at evaluation time. Second, the loss function can be formulated more naturally penalizing models proportionally to the error they commit.

Many related works exploit shape features based on active appearance models [1] and Biological Inspired Features (BIF). BIF are firstly proposed for age estimation by Guo *et al.* [2] combined with a linear SVM. In this work the authors employ a pyramid of Gabor filters with small sizes and they suggest to determine the number of orientations and bands with a problem-specific approach, rather than using a predefined number. In [3] Guo *et al.* investigate the variations of age estimation performance under variations across race and gender. They observe that crossing race and gender can result in significant error increases for age estimation. To leverage the aging pattern of different gender and ethnicity they employ the feature presented in their previous work [2] and they propose a 3-step method learning separate classifiers for different combinations of age and genders and applying the age estimator only after predicting the gender and ethnicity of the subject.

Guo *et al.* also propose to use the kernel partial least squares regression (KPLS) for age estimation [4]. The strength of this approach is twofold. First, the KPLS simultaneously performs the feature dimensionality reduction and learns the aging function; furthermore, since KPLS can find a small number of latent variables to reduce the dimensionality of the original space, this can improve the efficiency of the proposed approach.

In [5] a hierarchical part based representation for face age estimation has been proposed. This method identifies different facial components and extracts BIF feature vectors describing these parts; subsequently, each facial component is classified into one of four disjoint age groups using a binary decision tree based on SVM; finally, a separate SVM age regressor is trained to predict the actual age.

Chang *et al.* in [6] proposed an ordinal hyperplane ranker on Active Appearance Models (AAM [1]) exploiting the distribution of training labels. The key idea is try to obtain multiple decisions on who is the older of two people to finally determine the person's actual age. To perform this task the authors present an approach that is able to efficiently compute the input face age as the result of a series of comparisons between the target face and the training ones, and then to estimate the person's age by integrating the result. Precisely, all the facial images are separated by each ordinal hyperplane into two groups according to the relative order, and a cost-sensitive property is exploited to find better hyperplanes based on the classification costs. The actual age is inferred by aggregating a set of preferences from the ordinal hyperplanes with their cost sensitivities.

Geng *et al.* propose two algorithms exploiting the label distributions [7] of the face images. Instead of considering each face image as an instance with a single label (the age), the author consider each face image as an instance associated with a label distribution. The label distribution covers a certain number of class labels, representing the degree that each label describes the instance. This approach guarantees that one face image can contribute also to the learning of its adjacent ages. One of the main assumptions of the first proposed algorithm is that the distribution of each face image can be derivated by the maximum entropy model. Nevertheless, there is no particular evidence supporting it in the problem of age estimation. To relax this assumption the authors propose to use a three layer neural network to approximate the distributions. A comprehensive list of recent age estimation approaches can be found in [5].

(a) Landmark estimation   (b) Feature Sampling   (c) Fisher Vector

Fig. 1. Our image representation pipeline. Face detection and landmark estimation (a) followed by dense multi-scale SIFT extraction on the aligned face (b) and Fisher Vector computation (c).

In this paper we describe our age estimation system (see Fig. 1) designed with efficiency in mind. Differently from previous works we use a high-dimensional modern feature [8] that proves to be accurate yet efficient. We use regularized linear regression that is efficient to evaluate requiring a single dot product per face and allows to directly minimize the error in years.

This paper is organized as follows: in Section 2 the employed face detection approach and the alignment technique are described; in Section 3 our face representation is summarized; in Section 4 the regression approach used for age estimation is presented; in Section 5 the achieved results on a very large dataset are shown; in Section 6 our conclusions are highlighted.

2   Fast Face Detection and Alignment

The first block of our processing chain is an image pre-processing one followed by face detection. Subsequently, face alignment is performed in order to obtain a consistent geometric reference for image features. These steps will be exploited in the face representation step as explained in Sect. 3.

2.1   Features and Image Pre-processing

To avoid missing faces, especially in highly saturated images, we apply an histogram equalization to the image. Several approaches have been developed to normalize images in order to gain invariance to illumination. Usually these techniques aim at normalizing a face crop in a way that recognition does not suffer from illumination variations. In our case we are interested in reducing the effect of sensor saturation in presence of strong lighting. Our concern is to detect as many faces as possible and have a reliable landmark estimation without sacrificing real-time performance. Among many available algorithms we evaluated rank normalization and wavelet based normalization [9]. In our experiments we found that, for detection and landmark estimation purposes, i.e. to keep discriminative features from faces a basic histogram equalization is enough to guarantee high recall. As can be seen in Fig. 2 attempting to estimate landmarks without normalization may result in poor localization. Indeed, in Fig. 2a all nose landmarks are wrongly localized in the image processed without equalization.

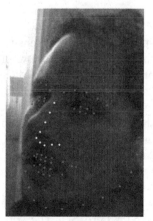 

(a) Landmarks estimated without equalization.   (b) Landmarks estimated with equalization.

Fig. 2. Face landmark detection without (a) and with (b) equalization on a challenging image. Nose landmarks, marked in yellow, are wrongly localized without equalization.

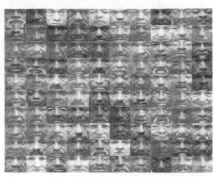
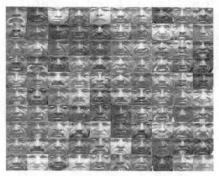

(a) Rotation alignment.   (b) Affine transform alignment.

Fig. 3. Alignment results with rotation compensation and with affine alignment. In the face marked in red the mouth is missing in the rotated image whilst using the affine compensation all important facial features are visible.

2.2 Face Detection

We use a very simple yet effective multi-pose linear classifier. The model is trained with structural SVM on ~3000 faces with 5 poses: frontal, profile-left, profile-right, frontal left-tilted and frontal right-tilted. We used the structural SVM formulation of [10], this method allows very fast training and state-of-the art results even with linear classifiers.

2.3 Face Alignment

Our face representation exploits the joint statistics of pixel intensities and locations. In order to make the representation invariant to face pose we have applied a face alignment step. To do so we rescale and align the detected faces to a common reference square. The simplest face alignment approach consists to estimate the angle of the line intersecting the eye centers and tilting the face image. As can be seen in Fig. 3(a) for many faces the mouth is not always fully visible thus discarding important features. We instead apply an affinity based alignment. The affinity, performing a non uniform scaling along the two dimensions, allows to align the whole face in a common reference. We estimate the affine transformation matrix, i.e. rotation scale and translation, mapping the triangle defined by the eye and mouth centers and a canonical triangle defined as $(0.2 \cdot S, 0.2 \cdot S), (0.8 \cdot S, 0.2 \cdot S), (0.5 \cdot S, 0.5 \cdot S)$ where S is the square size. As highlighted by Fig. 3(b) all important facial features can be recovered.

To estimate the eye and mouth centers we firstly extract the 68 landmarks provided by [11] which implements a face shape estimation using a cascade of regression trees trained on pixel intensities. Robust estimates of eyes and mouth centers are obtained using the median of the 6(eye) and 20(mouth) landmarks describing these parts of the face. Finally, we remap detected faces in a square with 100 pixel side using the aforementioned affine transformation.Our method efficiently deals with poses with little yaw (±15°) for higher pose variation a full 3D approach should be used to improve results[12]. Our face detection and alignment solution runs at 30 FPS on a i5-2467M 1.60GHz CPU using a single thread.

3 Face Representation

Our face representation is inspired by recent image classification techniques based on local features [13] and face verification [14]. After face alignment we extract the face patch and we resize it to a fixed scale (as described in Sect. 2).We sample dense SIFT [15] descriptors without orientation and scale estimation. Even if faces are rescaled at a fixed size different features may appear at different patch scales, therefore we apply multi-scale sampling. Thanks to the face alignment we are able to exploit feature location. We compute Fisher vectors over SIFT descriptors augmented with their x,y coordinate rescaled in $[-1, 1]$. Before computing Fisher vectors we learn 64 PCA components on a set of 200K randomly sampled SIFT features. The final local feature is obtained concatenating the PCA reduced SIFT descriptor and the rescaled x,y coordinates. Considering the learned dictionary employing a Gaussian Mixture Model with parameters $\mu_n, \sigma_n, \omega_n$ and given soft-assignments $\gamma_m^{(n)}$ for each of the M augmented SIFT feature $x_m \in X$, the Fisher vector is computed concatenating the following gradients:

$$\mathcal{G}_n^\mu(X) = \frac{1}{\sqrt{\omega_n}} \sum_{m=1}^M \gamma_m^{(n)} \left(\frac{x_m - \mu_n}{\sigma_n^2} \right), \tag{1}$$

$$\mathcal{G}_n^\sigma(X) = \frac{1}{\sqrt{2\omega_n}} \sum_{m=1}^M \gamma_m^{(n)} \left(\frac{(x_m - \mu_n)^2}{\sigma_n^2} - 1 \right), \tag{2}$$

where

$$\gamma_m^{(n)} = \frac{\omega_n p_n(x_m)}{\sum_{j=1}^D \omega_j p_j(x_m)}, \tag{3}$$

and p_n is the nth Gaussian of the learned mixture and X is the feature set of a face image. Considering a vocabulary of size $D = 128$, the final image feature size is $66 \times 128 \times 2 = 16896$.

4 Large Scale Learning with SGD

Most of the best performing methods for age estimation rely on regression, this is indeed the natural approach to overcome quantization errors that occur for classification based approaches. Our feature representation is extremely high dimensional, therefore a linear regressor is likely to obtain good performance with very low evaluation cost.

Table 1. MORPH-II dataset gender and ethnicity statistics.

Race	Female	Male	Female and Male
Black	5,757	36,803	42,560
White	2,601	7,999	10,600
Hispanic	100	1,651	1,751
Asia	13	146	159
India	14	43	57
Other	2	3	5
Total	8,487	46,645	55,132

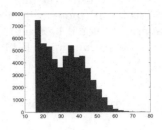

Fig. 4. MORPH-II age distribution.

From an applicative point of view, using a single linear regressor has many advantages. First, it reduces the memory footprint with respect to a multi-class classification approaches; second, avoiding kernels has also a strong impact in the evaluation time of the regressor allowing us to compare each detected face with just one hyperplane instead of computing a kernel evaluation per support vector.

Our aim is to estimate a weight vector w and a bias b given an image I and a feature function $\phi(\cdot)$ to produce an age estimate:

$$\text{age}(\phi(I)) = \langle w, \phi(I) \rangle + b \tag{4}$$

To efficiently train our regressor we apply stochastic gradient descent (SGD) to L2-regularized least square regression or ridge regression, optimizing the following equation:

$$\frac{1}{2}\lambda||w||^2 + \frac{1}{n}\sum_{i=1}^{N}\left(\langle w, \phi(I) \rangle + b - y_i\right)^2 \tag{5}$$

Considering a vast amount of training samples SGD is efficient and accurate as also noticed in [16]. We set $\lambda = 1/(C \cdot N))$, where N are the training samples, and tune the parameter C by five fold cross-validation of MAE on the training set.

5   Experimental Results

We test our approach on the MORPH-II dataset that contains more than 55K facial images with different gender and ethnicity. In Table 1 the detailed statistics of gender and ethnicity are shown, whilst in Fig. 4 the age distribution is summarized.

5.1   Timing

We run a set of benchmarks to evaluate the run time of our method. The system speed is mostly affected by the density of feature sampling both in scale and size as can be seen in Figs. 5a and 5c since the sampling step quadratically affects the amount of features extracted.

Furthermore, the number of Gaussians affects the computation time in two ways. First, with a large vocabulary single feature embeddings are slower to compute, since they need to calculate more derivatives. Second, increasing the final feature size the regression step is longer, even though the regression step time is negligible with respect to the feature computation step cost.

In Table 2 we have reported the FPS of some commercial systems presented in [17]. It is possible to notice that the best performing commercial frameworks obtain comparable performance results with those achieved by our approach but they are tested on a more powerful 6-cores Intel Xeon Processor X5690 CPU with respect to our 1.6GHZ i5-2467M processor, moreover they are implemented using multi threads. This results confirm that our method reaches state-of-the-art performance.

Table 2. FPS of commercial systems reported in [17]. Notice that the best performing commercial frameworks obtain comparable results with those achieved by our approach but they are tested on a more powerful 6-cores Intel Xeon Processor X5690 CPU and they are implemented using multi threads.

System	FPS
Our Approach	20
Junyu Tech.	15
Zhuhau-Yisheng	10
MITRE	27
Tsinghua University	11
NEC	19
Cognitech	5

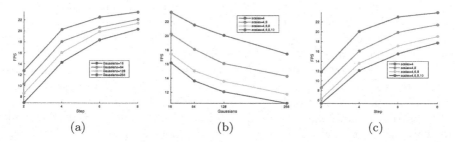

(a)   (b)   (c)

Fig. 5. Frame rate of the proposed processing pipeline for different dictionary size, sampling in space and scale. We set scales=4,8 in (a) step=4 (b) and Gaussians=128 (c). Face detection and alignment is included.

5.2 Accuracy

We have assessed the quality of our method using the Mean Absolute Error or $\text{MAE} = \frac{1}{N} \sum_{i=1}^{N} |\text{age}(\phi(\boldsymbol{I})) - y_i|$.

In order to compare our results with those achieved by recently published methods we have ran a set of experiments with different experimental setups. Results are summarized in Table 4. To compare our results with [6,18] we have used the same photos used by the authors: a set of 5,492 images taken from people of Caucasian descent. We have reported the average of MAE over 30 trials.

To compare our results with those proposed in [2–4] we have followed the procedure specified in [3]. Given the whole dataset $\mathcal{W}$ we have defined a set $\mathcal{S} \subset \mathcal{W}$ of $\sim$ 21000 images of black and white individuals keeping all the women and an amount of men to keep the proportion between males and females 1:3. We have further split this set in $\mathcal{S}_1$ and $\mathcal{S}_2$ such that $\mathcal{S} = \mathcal{S}_1 \cup \mathcal{S}_2$ and $\mathcal{S}_1 \cap \mathcal{S}_2 = \emptyset$. Moreover, we have generated $\mathcal{S}_1$ and $\mathcal{S}_2$ so that identities of people in $\mathcal{S}_1$ are not allowed in $\mathcal{S}_2$ and vice versa. We have trained the regressor on $\mathcal{S}_i$ and we have reported the average of MAE obtained on $\mathcal{W} \setminus \mathcal{S}_i$ for $i = 1, 2$.

Finally since with our approach we can leverage a huge amount of data we have split the dataset using 80% of the identities for the training and 20% for testing and we have ran a 10-fold cross-validation. We have not stratified the sampling on gender and ethnicity but an empirical check has shown that randomly sampling identities keep the subsampled sets distribution of age, ethnicity and gender similar to the distribution on the whole set. This setup is the same proposed in [7].

In Table 3 we have shown how MAE varies depending on the feature extraction step using the setup of [7]. It is possible to notice that the only parameters affecting the MAE are the sampling step and the amount of Gaussians. A sufficiently tight sampling step is critical to ensure a wide coverage of all the facial features. At the same time a dictionary with too few Gaussians is unable to capture the SIFT descriptor statistics for faces. Instead, the amount of scales is not affecting the accuracy, this is mostly due to the fact that faces are all aligned and scaled at the same size so there is no need to match image patches representing the same structure at different scales.

In Table 4 we have compared our results with those achieved by some approaches tested on MORPH Album2 dataset. The first setup [2–4] is the easiest since it employes a single ethnicity. The second and third setups deal with multiple ethnicities and gender, with the second [6,18] using only black and white people and the third using the whole dataset [7].

These results show that our method is not limited to be trained on a single ethnicity or gender, nor require any strategy to deal with cross-racial or cross-gender influence in age estimation.

Table 3. Mean absolute error varying sampling step, scales and Gaussians. We used 128 Gaussians in (a) and step=4 and scales=4,8 in (b). The algorithm is mostly affected by the sampling step.

<table>
<tr><th colspan="3">(a)</th><th colspan="2">(b)</th></tr>
<tr><th>Scales</th><th>Sampling</th><th>MAE</th><th>Gaussians</th><th>MAE</th></tr>
<tr><td>4,6,8,10</td><td>2</td><td>3.7</td><td>16</td><td>4.2</td></tr>
<tr><td>4,8</td><td>2</td><td>3.7</td><td>64</td><td>3.8</td></tr>
<tr><td>4,8</td><td>4</td><td>3.7</td><td>128</td><td>3.7</td></tr>
<tr><td>4,8</td><td>8</td><td>4.0</td><td>256</td><td>3.6</td></tr>
</table>

Table 4. Mean Absolute Error (MAE) in years compared with recently published methods. Our method obtains state-of-the-art results with a very low-weight processing pipeline.

Approach	Features	Classifier	MAE [6,18]	MAE[2–4]	MAE[7]
Our approach	**SIFT+FV**	**L2L2 Regression**	**3.8**	**4.0**	**3.7**
Geng *et al.* [7]	AAM,BIF	CPDNN	-	-	4.9
Geng *et al.* [7]	AAM,BIF	IIS-LLD	-	-	5.7
Guo *et al.* [4]	Holistic BIF	Kernel PLS	-	4.2	-
Guo *et al.* [3]	Holistic BIF	3-Step	-	4.5	-
Guo *et al.* [2]	Holistic BIF	Linear SVM	-	5.1	-
Chang *et al.* [6]	AAM	Ordinal Hyperplane Ranker	6.1	-	-
Chang *et al.* [18]	AAM	Ranking SVM	6.5	-	-

6   Conclusions

In this paper we have proposed a real-time age estimation system from face imagery. We have shown how a carefully engineered pipeline of efficient image analysis and pattern recognition techniques leads to state-of-the-art results. Our single threaded approach runs at 20 FPS on a 1.6GHZ i5-2467M processor, thus leaving room for further improvement. Furthermore, we have found that employing very densely sampled SIFT features and a large dictionary decreases the mean absolute age estimation error; nevertheless, this configuration conflicts with our real-time aim. With this in mind, we have identified another setting that obtains a low drop in performance (.1 years of MAE, for details see Sect. 5) but guaranteeing a real-time system.

To assess the quality of our framework we have tested our approach on a very large dataset of more than 55K images of people with different gender and ethnicity. We tested our method on different settings comprising the whole dataset or reducing it to a smaller single ethnicity version. Our method results compared with those achieved by other recently published approaches confirm the efficiency and the effectiveness of the proposed framework.

Acknowledgments. Lorenzo Seidenari is supported by "THE SOCIAL MUSEUM AND SMART TOURISM", MIUR project no. CTN01_00034_23154_SMST.

References

1. Cootes, T., Edwards, G., Taylor, C.: Active appearance models. IEEE Transactions on Pattern Analysis and Machine Intelligence **23**, 681–685 (2001)
2. Guo, G., Mu, G., Fu, Y., Huang, T.: Human age estimation using bio-inspired features. In: IEEE Conference on Computer Vision and Pattern Recognition, CVPR 2009, pp. 112–119 (2009)
3. Guo, G., Mu, G.: Human age estimation: What is the influence across race and gender? In: 2010 IEEE Computer Society Conference on Computer Vision and Pattern Recognition Workshops (CVPRW), pp. 71–78 (2010)
4. Guo, G., Mu, G.: Simultaneous dimensionality reduction and human age estimation via kernel partial least squares regression. In: 2011 IEEE Conference on Computer Vision and Pattern Recognition (CVPR), pp. 657–664 (2011)
5. Han, H., Otto, C., Jain, A.K.: Age estimation from face images: Human vs. machine performance. In: International Conference on Biometrics, ICB 2013, June, 4–7, Madrid, Spain (2013)
6. Chang, K.Y., Chen, C.S., Hung, Y.P.: Ordinal hyperplanes ranker with cost sensitivities for age estimation. In: 2011 IEEE Conference on Computer Vision and Pattern Recognition (CVPR), pp. 585–592 (2011)
7. Geng, X., Yin, C., Zhou, Z.H.: Facial age estimation by learning from label distributions. IEEE Transactions on Pattern Analysis and Machine Intelligence **35**, 2401–2412 (2013)
8. Snchez, J., Perronnin, F., Mensink, T., Verbeek, J.: Image classification with the fisher vector: Theory and practice. International Journal of Computer Vision 105, 222–245 (2013)
9. Shan, D., Ward, R.: Wavelet-based illumination normalization for face recognition. In: 2005 International Conference on Pattern Recognition (ICPR) (2005)
10. King, D.E.: Max-Margin Object Detection. ArXiv e-prints (2015)
11. Kazemi, V., Sullivan, J.: One millisecond face alignment with an ensemble of regression trees. In: CVPR (2014)
12. Hassner, T., Harel, S., Paz, E., Enbar, R.: Effective face frontalization in unconstrained images. In: Proc. of CVPR (2015)
13. Seidenari, L., Serra, G., Badanov, A.D., Del Bimbo, A.: Local pyramidal descriptors for image recognition. Transactions on Pattern Analisys and Machine Intelligence (2013)
14. Simonyan, K., Parkhi, O.M., Vedaldi, A., Zisserman, A.: Fisher Vector Faces in the Wild. In: British Machine Vision Conference (2013)
15. Lowe, D.G.: Distinctive image features from scale-invariant keypoints. Int. J. Comput. Vision **60**, 91–110 (2004)
16. Akata, Z., Perronnin, F., Harchaoui, Z., Schmid, C.: Good practice in large-scale learning for image classification. IEEE Transactions on Pattern Analysis and Machine Intelligence **36**, 507–520 (2014)
17. Ngan, M., Grother, P.: Face recognition vendor test (frvt) performance of automated age estimation algorithms. Technical report, NIST (2014)
18. Chang, K.Y., Chen, C.S., Hung, Y.P.: A ranking approach for human ages estimation based on face images. In: 2010 20th International Conference on Pattern Recognition (ICPR), pp. 3396–3399 (2010)

Bounded Non-Local Means for Fast and Effective Image Denoising

Federico Tombari[✉] and Luigi Di Stefano

University of Bologna, Bologna, Italy
{federico.tombari,luigi.stefano}@unibo.it
http://vision.deis.unibo.it

Abstract. Non-Local Means (NLM) is a powerful but computationally expensive image denoising algorithm, which estimates a noiseless pixel as a weighted average across a large surrounding region whereby pixels centered at more similar patches are given higher weights. In this paper, we propose a method aimed at improving the computational efficiency of NLM by quick pre-selection of dissimilar patches thanks to a rapidly computable upper bound of the weighting function. Unlike previous approaches, our technique mathematically guarantees all highly correlated patches to be accounted for while discarding dissimilar ones, this providing not only faster speed but improved denoising too.

Keywords: Non local means · Image denoising · Fast bounding method

1 Introduction and Related Work

Image denoising is a recurrent topic in image processing research due to the ubiquitous presence of noise in the image formation and acquisition process. Research on effective image denoising algorithms has brought a wealth of methods (see [2],[4] for a review). Among the several proposals, Non-Local Means (NLM) [2] has demonstrated remarkable effectiveness even in presence of high noise levels. With NLM, a noiseless pixel is estimated by averaging across image positions so that pixels centered at highly correlated patches contribute more. This conceptually simple and effective approach comes at the cost of a huge computational complexity, which is theoretically $O(n^2 r_p^2)$, n being the number of pixels in the image and r_p the size of the side of the adopted squared patch. Therefore, the search for correlated patches is limited in practice to a squared surrounding *search area* of size r_s, the computational complexity decreasing to $O(n r_s^2 r_p^2)$ accordingly.

Several algorithms aimed at speeding up NLM have been proposed in literature. In [8], a pre-selection of contributing neighboring pixels is carried out by computing each patch's average value and gradients. In [1] candidate pre-selection is accomplished by arranging the data in a cluster tree where each leaf node is constrained to a minimum size, so that each pixel can be weighted with a relatively large subset of similar patches. The method in [13] proposes to

© Springer International Publishing Switzerland 2015
V. Murino and E. Puppo (Eds.): ICIAP 2015, Part II, LNCS 9280, pp. 183–193, 2015.
DOI: 10.1007/978-3-319-23234-8_18

estimate probabilistically the dissimilarity between two patches out of a small portion of the distance function in order to terminate the computation early for highly uncorrelated patches. On completely different grounds, [11] uses PCA to project the set of neighboring candidates onto a lower dimensional subspace, thus reducing the computational burden by computing distances in the subspace rather than at full dimensionality. A fast approximated scheme based on a multi-resolution computation of the NLM weights is proposed in [5]. Finally, in [7] the computation of the distance is carried out in the Fourier domain to achieve improved efficiency when the patch size and search area size are different enough [6].

One drawback associated with methods based on quick pre-selection of mismatching image positions such as [8],[1],[13] is that they might also eliminate useful (i.e. highly correlated) candidates, thus implying computational savings to be achieved at the expense of some deterioration of the final result: e.g., in [8], a high difference in mean intensity and gradient orientation between two patches does not guarantee that their distance is always high. In our approach, instead, we aim at selecting mismatching candidates while at the same time guaranteeing that all highly correlated image positions are included in the final averaging operation. This is made possible thanks to the deployment of an efficiently computable lower bound of the dissimilarity function used in the NLM weight formulation. Moreover, discarding candidates that are guaranteed to lie - patchwise - far away from the current pixel tends not only to speed-up the computation but also to improve the accuracy of the denoising process. Another advantage of the proposed technique is that the minimum guaranteed correlation between two patches is an explicit parameter which can be easily set by the user so as to lean towards either higher speed or higher accuracy.

The paper will introduce the NLM algorithm in Section 2.1 and illustrate the proposed technique in Section 2.2. Successively, an experimental comparison including a standard benchmark dataset is carried out in Section 3. Finally, conclusions are drawn in Section 4.

2   Weighting by a Bounding Function

2.1   Original NLM

Like many denoising approaches, the NLM algorithm computes the noiseless estimate $\tilde{I}(i)$ of pixel $I(i)$ as a weighted sum within a surrounding region centered at position i:

$$\tilde{I}(i) = \sum_{j \in s(i)} w(i,j) \cdot I(j) \tag{1}$$

Notably, the *supporting pixel set* $s(i)$ in (1) may be in principle the whole image, although a squared window of size r_s is used in practice for the sake of computational tractability.

The weighting advocated in [2] consists of a decreasing function of the dissimilarity between the patch centered at position i and that centered at j, under the assumption that the noiseless estimate of $I(i)$ should be obtained by averaging the intensities of those locations featuring image patches similar to that centered at i:

$$w(i,j) = \frac{1}{Z(i)} exp\left(-\frac{\parallel I(\mathcal{N}(i)) - I(\mathcal{N}(j)) \parallel_{2,a}^2}{h^2}\right) \tag{2}$$

In (2), $\mathcal{N}(i)$ and $\mathcal{N}(j)$ are square image patches of size r_p centered at i and j, h is a parameter of the method, $\parallel \cdot \parallel_{2,a}^2$ is the L_2 norm weighted by a Gaussian function centered at the patch and with standard deviation a and Z is a normalization factor:

$$Z(i) = \sum_{j \in s(i)} exp\left(-\frac{\parallel I(\mathcal{N}(i)) - I(\mathcal{N}(j)) \parallel_{2,a}^2}{h^2}\right) \tag{3}$$

Successively, the authors publicly released an implementation of NLM[1] based on a definition of the weighting function slightly different to that originally proposed in [2]:

$$w'(i,j) = exp\left(-\frac{max\left(\parallel I(\mathcal{N}(i)) - I(\mathcal{N}(j)) \parallel_2^2 - 2\sigma^2, 0\right)}{h^2}\right) \tag{4}$$

with σ related to the estimated amount of noise affecting the image. The authors recommend now to use this new formulation as it obtains improved results[2].

2.2 Proposed Bounded NLM

The main idea underpinning our approach is that, while image positions exhibiting highly similar patches represent a valuable subset to rely upon to estimate a noiseless pixel, those yielding a low degree of similarity do not bring in any useful contribution in the averaging process formulated in (1); indeed, they tend to distort the final estimate and should thus better be discarded from the averaging process to improve the quality of the final image. An inherent advantage of such an approach deals with low-correlation patches being often high in number within the search area surrounding a pixel, so that if we are able to devise a method which is able to quickly detect mismatching patches, we would obtain both improved accuracy as well as significant computational savings.

Purposely, we define a *test* to be evaluated at each pixel $j \in s(i)$ *before* the actual computation of the weight $w'(i,j)$:

$$e(i,j) > \tau \tag{5}$$

In (5), function $e(i,j)$ is a lower bound of the L_2 distance between the patch centered at i and that centered at j, while τ is a parameter. Accordingly, we

---

[1] www.ipol.im/pub/art/2011/bcm_nlm
[2] From personal communication with A. Buades.

Algorithm 1. The Bounded-NLM denoising algorithm

$\mathbf{I} =$ image of n pixels
$s =$ search area of radius r_s
compute b, the box-filtered squared norms of r_p-sized patches $\in I$
for i $\in I$ **do**
   $Z(i) = 0$
   for j $\in s(i)$ **do**
      if $(b(i) - b(j))^2 > \tau$ **then**
         $w'(i,j) = 0$
      else
         compute $w'(i,j)$ as in (4)
         $Z(i) = Z(i) + w'(i,j)$
      end if
      $w'(i,j) = w'(i,j)/Z(i)$
      compute $\tilde{I}(i)$ as in (1)
   end for
end for

---

define a new weighting function w'_τ so that if test (5) holds at position j the associated weight is set to 0:

$$w'_\tau (i,j) = \begin{cases} 0, & e(i,j) > \tau \\ w'(i,j), & otherwise \end{cases} \tag{6}$$

As $e(i,j)$ is a lower bound of the L_2 distance, all positions at which (5) holds would have yielded a patch distance higher than τ. Hence parameter τ represents the maximum dissimilarity above which a weight is set to zero and it is guaranteed that no position j closer than τ to i is going to be discarded by test (5). In particular, we choose:

$$e(i,j) = \left(\| I\left(\mathcal{N}\left(i\right)\right) \|_2^2 - \| I\left(\mathcal{N}\left(j\right)\right) \|_2^2 \right)^2 \tag{7}$$

which turns out to be a lower bound of the L_2 distance

$$e(i,j) \leq \| I\left(\mathcal{N}\left(i\right)\right) - I\left(\mathcal{N}\left(j\right)\right) \|_2^2, \forall i,j \tag{8}$$

due to the triangular inequality. Moreover, the chosen function $e(i,j)$ is very efficiently computable because the two norms appearing in (7) can be calculated once and for all at initialization time and independently of the size of the patch via fast incremental schemes such as Box Filtering [9] or Integral Images [3]. The pseudo-code of the proposed algorithm is reported in Alg. 1.

Hence, the higher the number of positions satisfying test (5) the more substantial are the computational savings due to weights being immediately just set to zero without calculating neither the dissimilarity function, i.e. the right hand side in (8), nor (4). Remarkably, the proposed method guarantees that all pixels showing a degree of dissimilarity to i smaller than τ will be included in the averaging process required to compute its noiseless estimate. This compares favorably with respect to other approaches in literature aimed at selecting

Table 1. PSNR and efficiency comparison between NLM and bNLM on a standard benchmark dataset at increasing noise levels ($\sigma = 5, \cdots, 40$). At each noise level, the same value of $\tilde{\tau}$ is used in bNLM throughout the dataset (reported on the left). Efficiency is compared in terms of measured execution times (reported in seconds in the Table).

				Barbara (512x512)				Boat (512x512)				Fingerprint (512x512)			
				NLM		bNLM		NLM		bNLM		NLM		bNLM	
σ	r_p	r_s	$\tilde{\tau}$	PSNR	t	PSNR	t	PSNR	t	PSNR	t	PSNR	t	PSNR	t
5	1	10	4	37.04	4.69	37.07	1.79	36.58	4.82	36.61	1.99	35.14	4.19	35.08	0.68
10	1	10	6.6	33.17	5.08	33.24	2.29	32.92	5.16	33.04	2.46	31.03	4.49	31.09	1.03
15	1	10	10	30.81	5.16	30.87	2.76	30.73	5.25	30.90	2.90	28.74	4.78	28.85	1.41
20	2	10	10	30.25	9.91	30.32	5.25	29.76	10.80	29.93	5.56	27.30	9.43	27.33	2.67
25	2	10	10	29.09	9.86	29.18	5.03	28.62	9.86	28.88	5.31	26.25	9.68	26.33	2.70
30	2	10	13	28.08	9.93	28.24	5.67	27.69	9.88	28.00	5.94	25.36	9.84	25.56	3.31
35	3	17	8	27.45	45.90	27.82	16.81	26.81	45.84	27.35	19.21	24.80	46.07	25.01	12.39
40	3	17	8	26.50	46.38	27.03	16.58	26.03	45.83	26.69	18.67	24.03	46.37	24.39	12.50
				House (256x256)				Lena (512x512)				Peppers (256x256)			
				NLM		bNLM		NLM		bNLM		NLM		bNLM	
σ	r_p	r_s	$\tilde{\tau}$	PSNR	t	PSNR	t	PSNR	t	PSNR	t	PSNR	t	PSNR	t
5	1	10	4	38.59	1.23	38.63	0.72	37.90	5.00	37.96	2.23	37.30	1.17	37.34	0.39
10	1	10	6.6	34.98	1.25	34.98	0.77	34.30	5.20	34.44	2.68	33.52	1.22	33.68	0.50
15	1	10	10	32.82	1.25	32.83	0.83	32.07	5.30	32.24	3.09	31.21	1.25	31.42	0.60
20	2	10	10	32.48	2.36	32.56	1.58	31.55	9.83	31.75	5.83	30.32	2.34	30.51	1.08
25	2	10	10	31.33	2.36	31.40	1.46	30.46	9.86	30.71	5.56	29.15	2.37	29.40	1.05
30	2	10	13	30.28	2.37	30.48	1.57	29.54	9.85	29.85	6.16	28.16	2.38	28.47	1.19
35	3	17	8	29.75	10.79	30.23	5.20	28.89	45.87	29.46	19.36	27.22	10.83	27.73	3.30
40	3	17	8	28.80	10.78	29.44	4.98	28.09	45.83	28.78	18.82	26.30	10.85	26.99	3.26

a suitable subset of candidates to compute the noiseless estimate of a pixels [8],[1],[13], as previous proposals may instead discard highly correlated candidates and therefore potentially weaken the denoising process.

It is worth pointing out that more effective and complex schemes have been proposed in literature to bound dissimilarity functions derived from the L_2-norm [10]. Yet, these approaches are conceived to deliver notable computational benefits with patch sizes as large as required in typical template matching applications, whilst they can hardly provide similar advantages when applied to much smaller patches (e.g. 7×7) as those usually deployed for the purpose of image denoising in algorithms like NLM. In particular, we verified experimentally that a more advanced incremental scheme such as IDA [12]) does not provide additional advantages with respect to the simple bounding function defined in (7). Moreover, many of such methods constrain the patch size, e.g. to be even, while this is not the case of original NLM formulation.

3   Experimental Results

In this Section we compare the proposed approach, which will be referred to in these experiments as *bNLM* (*bounded*-NLM), to the NLM algorithm, so as

188   F. Tombari and L. Di Stefano

Table 2. Comparing bNLM to [8],[1],[13] according to the results reported in [1] (Table 3) and in [13] (Table 4). Results related to method [1] in Table 3 concern increasing block overlaps (a,b,c), as described in [1].

	PSNR	S.U.
NLM (2)	30.31	//
NLM (4)	30.70	//
bNLM	30.72	2.17
[8]	29.80	2.38
[1],a	30.26	1.34
[1],b	30.08	2.14
[1],c	29.83	2.9

	PSNR	S.U.
NLM (2)	27.83	//
NLM (4)	30.47	//
bNLM	30.63	2.91
[8]	27.78	2.13
[1]	27.51	2.68
[13]	27.60	4.35

Table 3. *Barbara*, $\sigma = 20$, $r_p = 4$, $r_s = 10$ **Table 4.** *Peppers*, $\sigma = 20$, $r_p = 3$, $r_s = 11$

to assess quantitatively its effectiveness in both speeding up and improving the original technique. We have chosen to use the NLM version based on the weighting function defined in (4) for two reasons. First, the chosen one is the most recent NLM formulation proposed by the authors. Second, the publicly available authors' code and suggested parameter values concern this more recent version only: using their code and parameter settings allow the comparison to be carried out with the best possible fairness. Indeed, to actually implement and evaluate our own method we have modified the authors' code only in those parts strictly related to our proposal and then run the program with exactly the same parameters as suggested by them[3], which concern specifically the patch size r_p, the search area size r_s and parameter h.

As for the parameter introduced by our method, i.e. the maximum dissimilarity τ, the experiments have been conducted using the normalized value $\tilde{\tau}$:

$$\tau = \tilde{\tau}^2 \cdot (2r_p + 1)^2 \tag{9}$$

Thus, $\tilde{\tau}$ compares directly to the average pixelwise difference and ranges within $[0, 255]$, so it is an easier parameter to interpret and set with respect to τ.

Table 1 reports the results yielded by NLM and bNLM on standard benchmark datasets, where each image is corrupted by additive Gaussian noise with standard deviation ranging from $\sigma = 5$ up to $\sigma = 40$. As for the choice of parameter $\tilde{\tau}$ for bNLM, we have set a fixed value for each noise level, chosen so to privilege denoising accuracy. Yet, depending on the application settings, other choices of this parameter may be preferred so to favor computational savings rather than denoising accuracy: this can be easily achieved by decreasing the value of τ so to increase the number of candidates being discarded by (5). The Table reports, for each image, noise level and evaluated method, the PSNR (Peak Signal-to-Noise Ratio) and the measured execution time (in seconds). To measure execution times, the same platform has been used to run both the NLM and the bNLM code, i.e. an Intel Core i7 with 64 GB RAM. As vouched by the Table, bNLM consistently outperform NLM in terms of both computational

---

[3] www.ipol.im/pub/art/2011/bcm_nlm

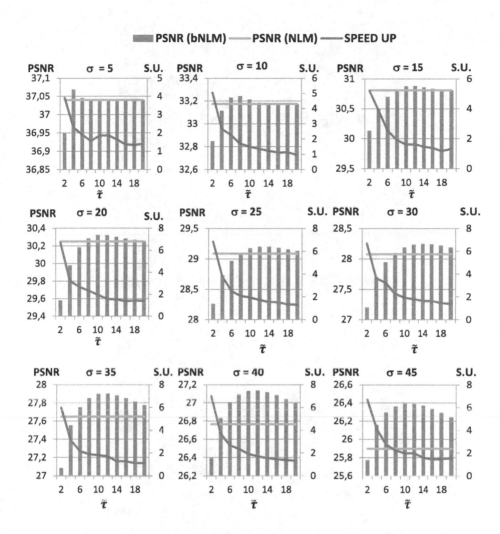

Fig. 1. Quantitative comparison between bNLM and NLM on the *Barbara* test image. Each chart is related to a different noise level and reports as a function of $\tilde{\tau}$ both the PSNR yielded by bNLM and NLM (range reported on the left vertical axis) as well as the speed-up provided by bNLM over NLM (range on the right vertical axis).

savings as well as denoising accuracy, yielding higher PSNRs and higher efficiency with all test images, the improvement in terms of PSNR ranging up to 0.91.

The experimental results provided in this Section indicate also that, when using similar patch and search area sizes, the proposed method compares favorably with respect to previous pre-selection algorithms aimed at speeding up NLM, such as [8],[1],[13]. Indeed, the results reported in Table 1 in [1] show

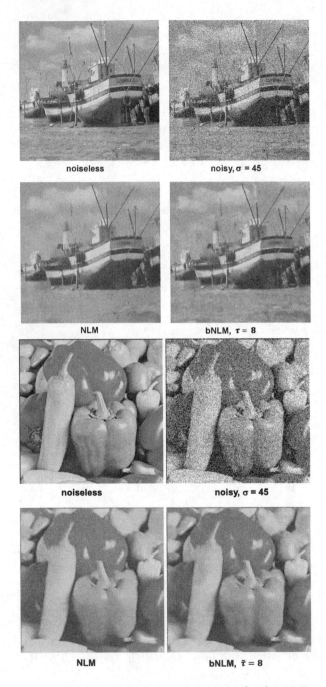

Fig. 2. Comparison between NLM and bNLM on *Boat* (top) and *Peppers* (bottom). Both figures show, respectively, the noiseless image (top left), the noisy image with $\sigma = 45$ (top right), the noiseless estimation by NLM (bottom left) and by bNLM with the suggested $\tilde{\tau}$ value as in Table 1 (reported in the bottom right part of each Figure)

Noisy image   NLM   bNLM

Fig. 3. Comparison on real noise. Upper row: qualitative comparison between bNLM and NLM on an image affected by real noise. Lower row: comparison on a zoomed detail of the original image (bottom right corner).

that on *Barbara* neither [1] nor [8] can improve the PSNR with respect to NLM. Similarly, Tables I and II in [13], show that with *Peppers* and *Lena* and a search windows of size 23x23, NLM yields always a higher PSNR with respect to [8], [1] and [13]. A more detailed comparison between bNLM and [8],[1],[13] is reported in Tables 3 and 4. To obtain this data, bNLM parameters have been set exactly as in the considered experiments in [1] and [13]. Also, the Tables report the PSNR yielded by both NLM algorithms, i.e. as based on either formula (2) or formula (4). The two Tables highlight that bNLM provides always the highest PSNR with respect to previous fast NLM-based methods while turning out either second-best (Table b) or third-best (Table a) in terms of speed-up.

To provide more insights on the behavior of our method, in Fig. 1 we consider the *Barbara* image corrupted by Gaussian noise, with $\sigma = 5$ up to $\sigma = 45$, and compare bNLM to NLM in terms of both PSNR (left vertical axis) as well as speed-up (right vertical axis) while varying $\tilde{\tau}$ values. As it can be observed from the Figure, with small τ values bNLM can report remarkable speed-ups with respect to NLM without introducing a significant deterioration of the PSNR. By increasing $\tilde{\tau}$, bNLM starts discarding a smaller number of candidates, this resulting in lower speed-ups but also higher PSNRs. It is worth highlighting how, with proper choices for $\tilde{\tau}$, in each of the experiments depicted in Fig. 1 bNLM can yield higher PSNRs than NLM, in particular at the higher noise levels, this validating the idea that discarding dissimilar patches is beneficial to improve not only efficiency but denoising accuracy as well. In the three most challenging denoising experiments considered in Fig. 1, bNLM can be tuned to deliver both a substantial speed-up (i.e. larger than 4) and a higher PSNR with respect to NLM. When $\tilde{\tau} \to \infty$, bNLM behaves exactly as NLM (no candidate is discarded), so that, by moving rightward along the horizontal axis of the charts, speed-ups get close to 1 and the PSNRs yielded by the two algorithms becomes more and more similar.

In addition to quantitative comparisons, we propose qualitative experiments aimed at assessing the perceived denoising accuracy. Accordingly, Fig. 2 compares NLM and bNLM on the *Boat* and *Peppers* test images corrupted by Gaussian noise ($\sigma = 45$). The Figure shows how the proposed algorithm can restore a higher amount of details in the estimated noiseless image, while NLM tends to introduce more over-smoothing. This is particularly evident in the ground surface and in the recovered cloud patterns in the sky of the *Boat* image, as well as on the surface of the foreground vegetables depicted in *Peppers*.

Finally, Fig. 3, addresses the case of images corrupted by real noise. In the figure, the upper row shows the original test image acquired by the camera of a Nexus 5 smartphone under indoor lighting conditions, together with the output yielded by NLM and bNLM, the parameters of the two algorithms set as in Table 1, $\sigma = 10$. The bottom row shows also a zoomed detail of the original image (taken from the bottom right corner) and the corresponding output by the two compared methods. As it can be observed, bNLM can effectively smooth out noise while preserving edges, the perceived quality being substantially equivalent for the two considered methods. bNLM, though, turns out the most efficient algorithm in these settings, running in 0.91 seconds, i.e. remarkably faster than NLM, which requires 2.11 seconds.

4 Concluding Remarks

A candidate selection scheme for the NLM image denoising algorithm has been proposed. By deploying a lower bound of the dissimilarity function employed to compute NLM weights, the proposed approach can safely discard dissimilar patches, so as to peculiarly provide both higher efficiency as well as improved denoising accuracy with respect to NLM. Experimental results show that our proposal is more beneficial as the noise level corrupting the image gets higher. Possible extensions to this approach would include exploiting more effective lower bounding function in spite of (8), so to increase the computational savings associated with the proposed algorithm, at the same time rejecting weakly correlated patches with respect to that of the current position.

References

1. Brox, T., Kleinschmid, O., Cremers, D.: Efficient nonlocal means for denoising of textural patterns. IEEE Trans. Image Processing **17**(7), 1083–1092 (2008)

2. Buades, A., Coll, B., Morel, J.: A review of image denoising methods, with a new one. SIAM Multiscale Modeling and Simulation 4(2), 490–530 (2005)
3. Crow, F.: Summed-area tables for texture mapping. Computer Graphics 18(3), 207–212 (1984)
4. Danielyan, A., Katkovnik, V., Egiazarian, K.: Bm3d frames and variational image deblurring. IEEE Trans. Image Processing 21(4), 1715–1728 (2012)
5. Karnati, V., Uliyar, M., Dey, S.: Fast non-local algorithm for image denoising. In: Proc. Int. Conf. on Image Processing (ICIP) (2009)
6. Lewis, J.: Fast template matching. Vision Interface, pp. 120–123 (1995)
7. Liu, Y., Wang, J., Chen, X., Guo, Y., Peng, Q.: A robust and fast non-local means algorithm for image denoising. J. Computer Science and Technology 23(2), 270–279 (2008)
8. Mahmoudi, M., Sapiro, G.: Fast image and video denoising via nonlocal means of similar neighborhoods. IEEE Signal Processing Letters 12(12), 839–842 (2005)
9. McDonnell, M.: Box-filtering techniques. Computer Graphics and Image Processing 17(1), 65–70 (1981)
10. Ouyang, W., Tombari, F., Mattoccia, S., Di Stefano, L., Cham, W.K.: Performance evaluation of full search equivalent pattern matching algorithms. Trans. Pattern Analysis and Machine Intelligence (PAMI) 34(1), 127–143 (2012)
11. Tasdizen, T.: Principal neighborhood dictionaries for nonlocal means image denoising. IEEE Trans. Image Processing 18(12), 2649–2660 (2009)
12. Tombari, F., Mattoccia, S., Di Stefano, L.: Full search-equivalent pattern matching with incremental dissimilarity approximations. Trans. Pattern Analysis and Machine Intelligence (PAMI) 31(1), 129–141 (2009)
13. Vignesh, R., Oh, B., Kuo, C.: Fast non-local means (nlm) computation with probabilistic early termination. IEEE Signal Processing Letters 17(3), 277–280 (2010)

i-Street: Detection, Identification, Augmentation of Street Plates in a Touristic Mobile Application

Stefano Messelodi[1], Carla Maria Modena[1(✉)], Lorenzo Porzi[1,2],
and Paul Chippendale[1]

[1] FBK-irst, Via Sommarive 18, I-38123 Povo, Trento, Italy
{messelod,modena,porzi,chippendale}@fbk.eu
[2] University of Perugia, Perugia, Italy

Abstract. Smartphone technology with embedded cameras, sensors, and powerful computational resources have made mobile Augmented Reality possible. In this paper, we present i-Street, an Android touristic application whose aim is to detect, identify and read the street plates in a video flow and then to estimate relative pose in order to accurately augment them with virtual overlays. The system was successfully tested in the historical centre of Grenoble (France), proving to be robust to outdoor illumination conditions and to device pose variance. The average identification rate in realistic laboratory tests was about 82%, remaining cases were rejected with no false positives.

Keywords: Augmented reality · Mobile devices · Text in scene images

1 Introduction

Augmented Reality (AR) is a concept that is already present in everyday life: using mobile devices with a connection to the Internet allows us to almost instantly gain access to the collective global knowledge, thus outsourcing memory [1]. In this report, we present a technology to visually augment information into the real world through portable devices, in a pervasive AR paradigm, where external available information can be presented in a *user* rather than a *device* centric way. In particular, we present a novel feature of an Android-based Smartphone Application [2] developed for a touristic scenario. The user visiting the historic centre of a city, can receive pertinent historical facts about the street in which (s)he is walking down, enriched with familiar directional indicators that highlight relevant and local points of interest.

Understanding user location cannot be completely solved solely through positional context *e.g.* GPS (Global Positioning System), as the urban canyon effect degrades reception and accuracy, particularly in historic centres, where streets are often narrow. According to experiments [3], GPS performs very badly in such environments with a median error of 6.7 mt. and only 62% of all GPS points

© Springer International Publishing Switzerland 2015
V. Murino and E. Puppo (Eds.): ICIAP 2015, Part II, LNCS 9280, pp. 194–204, 2015.
DOI: 10.1007/978-3-319-23234-8_19

falling within 10 mt of the real path. To improve location accuracy and thus inject information into the scene in the appropriate place, computer vision can help to refine position accuracy through the detection of geo-located visual pointers. In our case we will utilise street plates, which commonly lay at street intersections. We can reinforce or correct location errors by scanning for and subsequently reading the text of such plates and then by cross-referencing text strings with the known location of streets, gleaned from sources like OpenStreetMap. However, Computer vision alone cannot solve completely the problem, as multiple instances of the same plate often adorn intersections. For this reason, we also combined e-compass data from the mobile device to reduce ambiguities. Thus, by elaborating images coming from a camera, reading from the compass and GPS, and combining this with maps, it is possible to gain better self localization and orientation than pure sensor readings alone. We have integrated this strategy into a working demonstrator in the historic centre of Grenoble (France), where a user can point the device towards a street plate and obtain historical information about that street, whilst simultaneously correcting GPS location error estimates, thus improving the guidance of the user through the AR tour.

In this contribution, we present the i-Street application, developed as a part of the 3rd year demonstrator for the the European project VENTURI [4]. The intention was to demonstrate the possibility to integrate information coming from different sensors and then add visual augmentation to the video flow. The paper is organized as follow. In Sect. 2, we provide an overview of the system. In Sect. 3, we briefly explain the method adopted to localize, extract and read the text on a street plate. Section 4 reports a method to use recognized text and a-priori knowledge to identify a plate. Section 5 describes how virtual arrows are rendered into the real scene. Section 6 presents challenging situations and examples in which the system fails to provide a good result. In Sect. 7 results obtained in the laboratory and in the real demo environment are presented, and Sect. 8 concludes the paper.

2   i-Street Overview

The goal of i-Street is to fuse scenario knowledge, image analysis, and sensors data to identify street plates in a Smartphone's camera field of view and to supply augmented information to the user. In this scenario, computer vision algorithms have to cope with challenges such as harsh lighting conditions encountered in the outdoor environments, blurring of images due to motion of the device, uninteresting text presence, plate pose variation with respect to the device: Knowledge of the scenario and data coming from mobile sensors contribute to make the task of recognizing the correct street name feasible. Figure 1 depicts the main phases of the process along with the input role. The images coming from the phone camera are analyzed on the fly to detect candidate text strings that could potentially be present in the scene. Suspected text regions are segmented and filtered according to pre-defined formatting rules suggested by the real scenario. Each detected text line is de-skewed and its apparent deformation is corrected to facilitate the

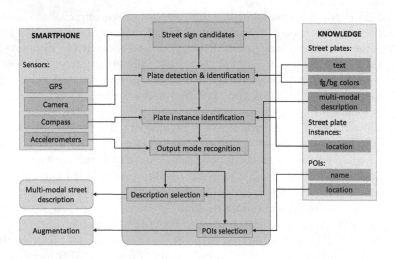

Fig. 1. i-Street architecture. The video frames are analysed taking into account specific domain knowledge and Smartphone's sensor data. Output is supplied to the user with different types of augmentation.

work of an Optical Character Recognition (OCR) module. The OCR outputs are compared to a dictionary of expected local street names (ranked according to the user's known location from GPS and a street map in the user's surroundings). A scoring function considers the spatial nearness of the lines and readability scores, thus enabling the system to determine the most probable street plate containing the read text. The live camera-stream is then augmented with information pertinent to the location. In particular, it is enriched with two virtual arrows that inform the user of some points of interest (POIs) in the right and left directions. These arrows are superimposed with the same apparent geometric deformation as the detected street plate to maintain realism. The i-Street application is articulated in the following main parts:

1. text detection and extraction from images and its recognition;
2. recognition of the plate and its location in the city;
3. augmentation of the image to supply information.

External knowledge (refer to Fig. 1) plays a fundamental role: the flexibility of the system to different scenarios is obtained by changing the content of the external knowledge. It helps the system to improve its robustness by reducing false plate detection and by driving the OCR. Furthermore it provides information for the augmentation task. Scenario knowledge is encoded inside a structured XML file that contains a list of the plates present in the city, and a list of points of interest, each one characterized by an unique identifier. The file stores, for each plate, the following data:

– code that describes roughly the pair (foreground, background) colours, *e.g.* white text on blue plate, or vice versa;

- printed text of each line that appears on the real plate;
- historical information about the location, possibly links to iconic pictures;
- number of plate instances (appearance of the same plate in the town). And for each instance:
  - approximate location (longitude, latitude);
  - identifiers of two particularly relevant POIs (optional).

Each POI is characterized by an identification number, its geo-coordinates (longitude, latitude), and its denomination to be shown on the virtual arrows. POIs can also be dynamically assigned, if none are prior associated. In this case, the two nearest (on the left and on the right) will be determined based on relative distance.

The on-board sensors providing input to the application are: *Camera* - frames to be elaborated; *GPS* - rough user location in the city map to restrict the set of street plate possibilities; *Compass* - estimate of the device direction for instance disambiguation and point of interest selection; *Accelerometer* - as a trigger to change the type of augmentation. A further operative requirement is the on-device storage of the language files needed for the OCR process. In this way, the system can operate completely off-line and in real-time.

3 Text in Scene Images

From a general point of view, text found in natural scenes can provide important contextual information. Several methods can be found in literature to cope with this problem [5,6]. We chose to use our previously proposed text detector [7,8], which provides good performance on low resolution images (640 × 480), permits us to detect skewed lines, text that exhibits positive as well as negative contrast, is easily customizable using scenario information, and is computationally efficient, therefore suitable to be ported onto a mobile device.

Each frame coming from the phone's camera is processed in order to detect potential text lines in the scene. The algorithm outputs a list of binarized regions corresponding to candidate text lines. It works through the following steps:

intensity normalization - It is applied to compensate for light variations throughout the image. Normalization is achieved by the computation of the divisive local contrast of the intensity map. This operation improves image details and the local contrast in shadowed regions.

double binarization - For the detection of positive and reverse text, two thresholds are determined by taking into account the shape of the histogram of the intensity normalized map, computing the left and right deviation from the histogram's mode. The thresholds are then used to extract two binary maps that should contain, respectively, positive and negative contrasting elements.

elementary objects - The connected components of both bitmaps are analyzed by a cascade of filters to mark likely non-text components as non-interesting. The filtering criteria relate to area, elongation, convexity of the connected components and delimitation value, *i.e.* the percentage of border pixels exhibiting a sufficiently high gradient in the colour image.

aggregation into lines - Survived elementary objects are recursively clustered according to proximity, alignment and size similarity. The alignment criterion consider the expected angular range from horizontal given by possible perspective distortions. Only clusters that satisfy certain characteristics are considered in order to discard possibly spurious lines. Lines whose aspect ratio (width/height of the minimum bounding rectangle) is below a threshold are discarded. The threshold is computed starting from the aspect ratio of the shortest string in the dictionary as typed in a sans-serif font. Furthermore, colours inside the line zone are tested, which should be concentrated on the pair (foreground, background) colours, provided by the knowledge.

deformation correction - Clusters that survive are geometrically normalized to facilitate the subsequent OCR process, by correcting the apparent deformation. The slant deformation due to perspective is corrected by searching the minimum trapezium around the text line region, whose parallel side corresponds approximately to the begin and the end of the string. The region is then stretched, using bilinear interpolation, in order to obtain a rectangular image of fixed height depicting a candidate text line.

Figure 2 provides an example of the candidate text lines extraction steps. By reducing the number of candidate lines, system processing time can be dramatically reduced as the OCR step is one of the most demanding in the whole chain. We utilise a free OCR engine released under the Apache License, called Tesseract [9,10], considered to be one of the most accurate open source OCR engines currently available. We apply Tesseract to each rectangular region with the single-line analysis option. The output is a string of characters accompanied by an index, in the range $[0-100]$, quantifying an average recognition confidence. We filter away lines with a low OCR confidence, as they are likely to be derived from noise. In Tab. 1, column one shows examples of images feed into Tesseract and column two the OCR output.

Fig. 2. Main steps of candidate text lines extraction: (from left to right) input frame, normalized contrast map, double binarization and filtering (retained components are shown in black), clustering into lines (blue, green, and red: three groups of components). Prudential criteria are used in filtering phases, in order to avoid the risk of discarding the text of interest.

4   Plate Identification

The recognition of plates is based on the OCR output, Knowledge, and GPS data. OCR output can be partial or fuzzy information: in fact, not all text lines are guaranteed to be detected, noise or out-of-plate text can also be captured and read, and text of interest can be read with errors. Strings obtained from the OCR step are therefore compared to the plate text dictionary using a string matching algorithm [11]. The dictionary is formed starting from the knowledge file, collecting expected text taking into account text/background colours. Only the OCRed lines that have a sufficient match with the dictionary are retained (Tab. 1, third column). Current geo-location, coming from the GPS, cross referenced to the city map with a tolerance radius can help to restrict the dictionary to local street names. The area has a radius of about 50 mt.

Table 1. Tesseract input/output and string matching with the known scenario words. The first line is not considered as a text plate string, as it doesn't match with any dictionary word, the two other are retained along with their matching score.

Candidate text line after rectification (OCR input)	OCR output (confidence)	Dictionary comparison and matching score
ECOLE et COLLEGE BAYAZID	ECOIE el COHIGE BAYAIB (74)	*no match*
PLACE	FLICE (65)	PLACE - 80%
du TEMPLE	du TEMPLE (80)	du TEMPLE - 100%

Text lines belonging to the same plate must exhibit the same contrast, similar height, be spatially near (with respect to their height) and placed one under the other. Using this knowledge, the detected lines are aggregated into potential plate regions. A scoring function based on spatial nearness of the candidate lines, contrast consistency, matching scores and frequency distribution of the words in the dictionary, allows us to determine the most probable street plate containing the read text. Figure 3, on the left, illustrates an example of plate identification. A string read as PLACE, though it exhibits a perfect match between the OCRed text and a dictionary word will give a small contribution to the plate score because the string is common to many plates, while the word 'TEMPLE' provides a greater contribution for the identification of the correct plate even when read with an OCR error, for example as TEMPII.

Note that the described elaboration refers to each single frame. The integration of results through subsequent frames, managed by a finite state machine, greatly improves plate identification, particularly in critical cases, avoiding hasty identification decisions.

5   Image Augmentation

The image that the user sees through the portable device's display is augmented with two AR arrows clamped to the real street plate. They direct the user to points of interest in the right and the left directions. To maintain realism, the arrows must be superimposed in a scene compliant manner. This is achieved through an estimation of the apparent dimension and geometric deformation of existing scene text.

The best recognized line of the plate is taken as a basis to determine the first arrow anchor point. Let H be the height, in pixels, of the text in its middle point. The anchor is placed on the vertical axis through the middle point of the line at a distance that depends on H and on its ordered position in the real plate. The interline space, as well as the space between the last line and the plate border, are considered to be similar to H. The height of the AR arrow is proportional to H, $e.g.$ $2H$. The second arrow anchor point is vertically positioned under the first one, at a distance of $H/2$. The minimum enveloping trapezium of the best recognized plate line is used to roughly estimate a vanishing point for the arrow's slope and its perspective deformation. This method provides a nice render under the working assumption that device roll is not far from zero. Figure 3, on the right, illustrates schematically the arrows rendering inside a frame. The rendering of the arrows is continuously adapted to match the dimensions and slope of the text in subsequent frames, thus matching user movements.

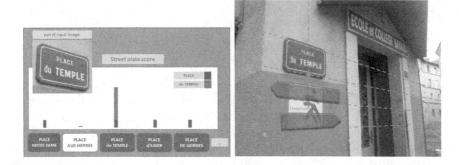

Fig. 3. On the left: example of plate scoring for plate identification. Each detected plate line contributes to assign a score to each possible plate. The contribution depends on the matching score ($e.g.$ 80%) and the number of different plates containing the line ($e.g.$ 'PLACE' appears in 4 plates - with the same contrast - while 'du TEMPLE' appears only in the plate at hand). On the right: A schematic representation to define the position of the AR-rows under the recognized plate and to estimate their deformation for their rendering inside the frame.

The text to be depicted on the virtual arrows comes from the Knowledge. Points of interest can be forced to the most interesting, depending on the opinion of the file maker, or calculated on the fly as the nearest with respect to location and orientation. A walking time to reach the POI is also calculated, based on relative distances, and added as further information on the virtual arrows. Because occurrences of identical plates can be present on both sides of a street, and they are indistinguishable simply using GPS, a POI direction is assigned to match user orientation using e-compass data as a disambiguation criterion.

Other important information that can be given to the user is a textual description of the historical significance of street, presented in a user's spoken language. It is shown in an info box only when the device is orientated parallel to the ground plane. The phone pose is estimated from data coming from the device's accelerometer that acts as a trigger to switch the type of augmentation.

6   Requirements and Criticalities

As the system is mainly vision based, the user must be situated within a distance sweet spot from a street plate to obtain a robust detection, similar to those depicted in the frames shown in Fig. 4. Low resolution images result in poor detection, but an analysis of subsequent frames can provide correct output as distance or motion blur decreases, albeit with a low OCR confidence value. In general, frontal images perform better as the distortion-free nature results in an improved character appearance, while very angular views give rise to apparently touching characters. If the device roll is far from zero (more than ten degrees) the method adopted for the rectification of the detected text works poorly, therefore it often produces a low confidence OCR output; furthermore, in this case, the virtual arrows rendering may appear inconsistent.

Fig. 4. Examples of maximum distance of the street plate in the camera field of view.

Real world plates sometimes present intrinsic difficulties due to physical damage, defacement or dirt. Examples can be seen in Fig. 5. The first plate is damaged: the lack of blue enamel gives rise to white bullets, with the result that only the third line is correctly detected and segmented. In the second one, graffiti is present and the blue plate is degraded by rust. Text segmentation is not perfect,

Fig. 5. Examples of challenging cases for text segmentation and OCR interpretation. In the case on the left, only one line is detected. In the second example, the upper line is noisily segmented and OCRed as HUE MVP. In the case on the right, a poor characters segmentation leads to a poor OCR results (the upper line is read as NUL).

giving rise to OCR errors, particularly on the first line. The third example is a challenging case, mainly for text segmentation (and therefore for the OCR), as the character font exhibits extremely thin stroke.

7   Lab Tests and Real Usage

i-Street has been tested and tuned on a database of 134 high resolution pictures of 39 plates and 14 video clips collected in the historical centre of Grenoble. The photos were used as static input for the text detection algorithms during the development phases, before the porting and integration into an Android application. The videos were used to estimate the operative distance range.

For lab testing of the application, the pictures were displayed on the workstation screen and aimed at by the Smartphone that was moved to various distances and angles in front of the screen, whilst analyzing the correspondent output during the continuous elaboration of the video flow. The text lines detected and recognized with sufficient OCR confidence were emphasized with coloured outlines to check their positions. We observed that on and off false lines arose, but the clustering of those belonging to the street plate was correct. The plate recognition at frame level occasionally produces a false alarm. In these cases, the finite state machine, avoiding hasty identification decisions, improves the system performance at the cost of a small delay for new initialisation.

We performed various test sessions aiming at 134 city scenes using a low cost Smartphone (MIZ Z1, Android 4.2), considerably different from that used for development and final project demonstration (Sony Xperia Z, Android 4.4). The system proved to be very robust: between 109 and 112 correct identifications were obtained (average identification rate is 82%). In our tests no false alarm was produced (18% average rejection rate). A particular plate, characterized by slightly bluish text on blue background, violating the white on blue assumption, proved to be particularly challenging. One third of the miss detections was occurrences of this plate. Occurrences of "Rue Brocherie" are occasionally not recognized because of the presence in the database of "Impasse Brocherie" too. Therefore, they have equal scores if the first word is not captured, causing a rejection. Finally, two other plates were often not recognized due to their narrow text font. We emphasize that in lab tests, GPS information was not utilizable, and the dictionary comprised all the words present on the 39 street plates. Tests revealed that some plates were recognised immediately, whilst others required more time (up to 2 seconds). This was due to detection uncertainty in one or more of the process phases, which forced the system to wait until successively high confidence detections were forthcoming.

The i-Street application was integrated into a multi-aspect AR demonstrator that featured in a live demo in the city of Grenoble in November 2014 providing excellent results (Fig. 6). In the final version, when the camera is pointed towards a street plate, the system detects and recognizes text on the plate, giving the user visual feedback, namely two AR brown arrows showing POIs and walking times, and an icon advising the user to turn the device parallel to the ground to see more detailed street information. Text to speech was also available.

Fig. 6. i-Street app working in a real scenario. Here the text localization has been emphasized with green outlines for demonstrative purposes only.

8   Conclusions

In this paper, we have presented i-Street, an Android touristic application. Its goal is to supply augmented information to the user by aligning real and virtual objects in a *user* rather than a *device* centric way. Computer vision algorithms enable the system by detecting and reading the plate text in the video flow and by estimating plate pose and size with respect to the device. Knowledge of the scenario and data coming from mobile sensors makes the task of recognizing the correct location feasible. The live camera-stream is then augmented with information pertinent to the location. In particular, it is enriched with two virtual arrows that appear clamped under the real street plate, informing the user of some points of interest in the neighbourhood.

The system, successfully tested in the historical centre of Grenoble, showed to be robust to outdoor illumination conditions and motion blur. Moreover, it can be easily extended to other scenarios.

Acknowledgments. This research was funded by the European 7th Framework Program, under grant VENTURI (FP7-288238).

References

1. Huang, Z., Hui, P., Peylo, C., Chatzopoulos, D.: Mobile augmented reality survey: a bottom-up approach. Technical Report arXiv:1309.4413, HKUST, Hong Kong University of Science and Technology (2013)
2. API Guide. https://developer.android.com/guide
3. Schipperijn, J., Kerr, J., Duncan, S., Madsen, T., Demant Klinker, C., Troelsen, J.: Dynamic Accuracy of GPS Receivers for Use in Health Research: A Novel Method to Assess GPS Accuracy in Real-World Settings. Frontiers in Public Health 2(21) (2014)
4. VENTURI - ImmersiVe ENhancemenT of User-woRld Interactions: EC FP7-ICTProject. http://tev.fbk.eu/projects/venturi (2011–2014)
5. Jung, K., Kim, K.I., Jain, A.K.: Text Information Extraction in Images and Video: a Survey. Pattern Recognition 37(5), 977–997 (2004)
6. Ye, Q., Doermann, D.: Text Detection and Recognition in Imagery: A Survey. IEEE Transaction on Pattern Analysis and Machine Intelligence (2015)
7. Messelodi, S., Modena, C.M.: Automatic Identification and Skew Estimation of Text Lines in Real Scene Images. Pattern Recognition 32, 791–810 (1999)
8. Messelodi, S., Modena, C.M.: Scene Text Recognition and Tracking to Identify Athletes in Sport Videos. Multimedia Tools and Applications, Special Issue on Automated Information Extraction in Media Production 63(2), 521–545 (2013)
9. Smith, R.: An Overview of the Tesseract OCR Engine. In 9th International Conference on Document Analysis and Recognition, Curitiba, Brazil, pp. 629–633 (2007)
10. Lee, D-S., Smith, R.: Improving Book OCR by Adaptive Language and Image Models. In: 10th IAPR International Workshop on Document Analysis Systems, pp. 115–119 (2012)
11. Myers, E.: An O(ND) Difference Algorithm and its Variations. Algorithmica 1(2), 251–266 (1986)

Distortion Adaptive Descriptors: Extending Gradient-Based Descriptors to Wide Angle Images

Antonino Furnari[1]([✉]), Giovanni Maria Farinella[1],
Arcangelo Ranieri Bruna[2], and Sebastiano Battiato[1]

[1] Department of Mathematics and Computer Science,
University of Catania, 95125 Catania, Italy
{furnari,gfarinella,battiato}@dmi.unict.it
http://iplab.dmi.unict.it
[2] Advanced System Technology - Computer Vision,
STMicroelectronics, 95121 Catania, Italy
arcangelo.bruna@st.com

Abstract. Gradient-based descriptors have proven successful in a wide variety of applications. Their standard implementations usually assume that the input images have been acquired using classic perspective cameras. In practice many real-world systems make use of wide angle cameras which allow to obtain wider Fields of View (FOV) but introduce radial distortion which breaks the rectilinear assumption. The most straightforward way to overcome such a problem is to compensate the distortion by unwarping the original image prior to computing the descriptor. The rectification process, however, is computationally expansive and introduces artefacts which can deceive the subsequent analysis (e.g., feature matching). We propose the Distortion Adaptive Descriptors (DAD), a new paradigm to correctly compute local descriptors directly in the distorted domain. We combine the DAD with existing techniques to correctly estimate the gradient of distorted images and hence derive a set of SIFT and HOG-based descriptors. Experiments show that the DAD paradigm allows to improve the matching ability of the SIFT and HOG descriptors when they are computed directly in the distorted domain.

Keywords: Gradient-based descriptors · Wide angle images · Gradient estimation · SIFT · HOG

1   Introduction

Most Computer Vision applications assume that the input images have been acquired using cameras employing a perspective projection model. The perspective projection has the convenient property that straight lines in the real world are mapped to straight lines in the image, producing a representation of the scene which is coherent with our perception. Unfortunately, the perspective projection

© Springer International Publishing Switzerland 2015
V. Murino and E. Puppo (Eds.): ICIAP 2015, Part II, LNCS 9280, pp. 205–215, 2015.
DOI: 10.1007/978-3-319-23234-8_20

is not suitable to build wide angle cameras covering large Fields Of View (FOV) up to 180°. Those cameras indeed require different designs which are grouped into two main categories: dioptric [2] and catadioptric [4,5]. Due to their ability to acquire a large portion of the scene, wide angle cameras are of great interest in many fields (e.g., automotive, surveillance and robotics [12,13]) as they allow to use a single wide angle camera in place of more perspective ones. However, all wide angle cameras have inherent distortion since it is not possible to form an image of an hemispheric field on a plane without distortion [2]. Under given conditions, the distortion is radially symmetric and can be modelled as an invertible function. When the distortion function is known, the wide angle images can be rectified in order to obtain data compliant with the perspective model. Unfortunately, the rectification process is computationally expansive and the undistorted images contain artefacts that may affect the subsequent computation [6]. To overcome these problems, it would be ideal to process the images directly in the distorted domain (i.e., avoiding rectification) paying attention to the geometry of the deformation affecting the images. Many endeavours towards this direction exist: in [6,8] the Scale Invariant Feature Transform (SIFT) pipeline [9] is modified in order to be used directly on wide angle images, in [7] a direct approach to detect people using omnidirectional cameras is proposed, in [1] it is studied how affine covariant features can be reliably detected on fisheye images, finally in [6,10] methods to estimate geometrically correct gradients of distorted images are investigated.

In this paper we study how gradient based descriptors can be modified in order to be computed directly in the distorted domain. We propose the Distortion Adaptive Descriptors (DAD), a new paradigm for computing local descriptors directly on the distorted images. We combine the DAD paradigm with existing methods for the correct estimation of the gradient of distorted images in order to derive distortion adaptive variants of the SIFT [9] and Histogram of Oriented Gradients (HOG) [11] descriptors. The adaptation of such descriptors to the distorted domain, virtually enables a number of applications in which they have proven to be successful, such as object and people detection [9,11], video stabilization [14], object class recognition [15] and panorama stitching [16]. Experiments show that the DAD variants significantly outperform the regular SIFT and HOG descriptors when they are applied directly in the distorted domain. Moreover, we show that there is still space for improving the gradient estimation techniques. The remainder of the paper is organized as follows: in Section 2 we discuss the distortion model adopted in this paper and briefly review the considered techniques for the gradient estimation of distorted images; in Section 3 we introduce the Distortion Adaptive Descriptors; Section 4 discusses the experimental settings, whereas Section 5 reports the results. Finally Section 6 draws the conclusions.

2   The Distorted Domain

In the rest of the paper we will assume that a distortion function $f : \Re^2 \to \Re^2$ which maps the point $\mathbf{u} \in \Re^2$ in the rectilinear space to the corresponding

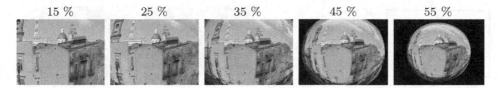

Fig. 1. Different amounts of radial distortion artificially added to a sample image.

point $\mathbf{x} = f(\mathbf{u})$ in the distorted space is known and invertible. Moreover, we will assume that both functions f and f^{-1} can be linearly approximated locally with a small error. These two conditions are easily met in real systems as pointed out in [1]. If we denote the acquired wide angle image by $\hat{I}(\mathbf{x})$, its undistorted counterpart is defined as $I(\mathbf{u}) = \hat{I}(f(\mathbf{u}))$. Since $\hat{I}$ is a discrete function, I is actually reconstructed by interpolation. In this paper we use the division model [6,17] as the distortion model. Its distortion function is defined as:

$$\mathbf{x} = f(\mathbf{u}) = \frac{2\mathbf{u}}{1 + \sqrt{1 - 4 \cdot \xi \|\mathbf{u}\|^2}} \tag{1}$$

where the distortion parameter $\xi < 0$ can be used to adjust the amount of distortion undergone by the image and the coordinates of points $\mathbf{x}$ and $\mathbf{u}$ are referred to the centre of the radial distortion. Since the effects of parameter ξ depend on the dimension of the input image, we quantify the amount of distortion independently from the image size as the percentage:

$$d_\% - 1 - \frac{\hat{r}_M}{r_M} \tag{2}$$

where r_M represents the maximum radius in the undistorted image (i.e., the distance from the image centre to the corner) and $\hat{r}_M$ represents its distorted counterpart. The parameter ξ is related to the percentage of distortion $d_\%$ by the following formula:

$$\xi = -\frac{d_\%}{[r_M(1 - d_\%)]^2}. \tag{3}$$

As shown through Fig. 1, the main advantage of dealing with the distortion percentage $d_\%$ rather than with the distortion parameter ξ is that it gives a perceptually coherent measure of the amount of distortion characterizing an image. Exploiting the local linearity assumption discussed above, a circular neighbourhood of radius r centred at the undistorted point $\mathbf{u}$ can be mapped with a small error to a circular neighbourhood centred at the distorted point $\mathbf{x}$ of radius:

$$\hat{r} = g_\mathbf{u}(r) = \frac{2r}{1 + \sqrt{1 - 4\xi r^2}}. \tag{4}$$

2.1   Gradient Estimation of Distorted Images

Since the gradients of an image are very related to the geometry of the acquired scene, employing classic estimation techniques (e.g., Sobel filters) on geometrically distorted images would lead to the estimation of distorted gradients.

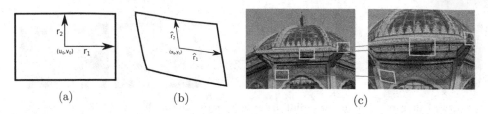

Fig. 2. (a) A rectilinear neighbourhood and (b) its distorted counterpart. (c) Examples of rectilinear neighbourhoods along with their distorted counterparts.

The most common way to compute a geometrically correct gradient is performing a rectification process and applying the classic techniques (e.g., Sobel filters) on the rectified image. Since we would like to be able to work directly in the distorted domain, consider two more approaches available in the literature. The former consists in correcting the distorted gradients using the Gradient Correction Jacobian (GCJ) matrix computed at the interested distorted locations [6]. The latter estimates the gradients using the Generalized Sobel Filters (GSF), a family of adaptive filters which takes into account the geometry of the distortion [10].

3 Distortion Adaptive Descriptors

In this Section we introduce the Distortion Adaptive Descriptors (DAD). Rather than a new set of descriptors, the DAD constitute a paradigm for correctly computing existing local descriptors directly on the distorted images. For sake of generality we consider a generic descriptor $D(\mathcal{N}, \mathcal{M}(I, \mathcal{N}))$ computed on a rectangular neighbourhood $\mathcal{N}$ using some measurements $\mathcal{M} = \mathcal{M}(I, \mathcal{N})$ performed in the locations of the input image I specified by the neighbourhood $\mathcal{N}$. The measurements can be of any kind and are related to the feature extraction process required by the specific descriptor. In the SIFT descriptor, for instance, the measurements $\mathcal{M}$ are the image gradients estimated at the relevant locations. The rectangular neighbourhood centred at point (u_0, v_0) with radii r_1 and r_2 is naturally defined as the set of points:

$$\mathcal{N}(u_0, v_0, r_1, r_2) = \{(u, v) : |u - u_0| \leq r_1 \wedge |v - v_0| \leq r_2\} \tag{5}$$

Fig. 2 (a) shows an example of rectangular local neighbourhood. When the descriptor has to be computed on a distorted image, the shape of the neighbourhood $\mathcal{N}$ depends on its position in the image. Some examples of such assertion are illustrated in Fig. 2 (c). The rectilinear neighbourhood (5) is easily mapped to its distorted counterpart centred at point (x_0, y_0) with radii $\hat{r}_1$ and $\hat{r}_2$ using the following expression:

$$\hat{\mathcal{N}}(x_0, y_0, \hat{r}_1, \hat{r}_2) = \{(x, y) : |f^{-1}(x) - f^{-1}(x_0)| \leq g_{x_0, y_0}^{-1}(\hat{r}_1) \wedge$$
$$|f^{-1}(y) - f^{-1}(y_0)| \leq g_{x_0, y_0}^{-1}(\hat{r}_2)\} \tag{6}$$

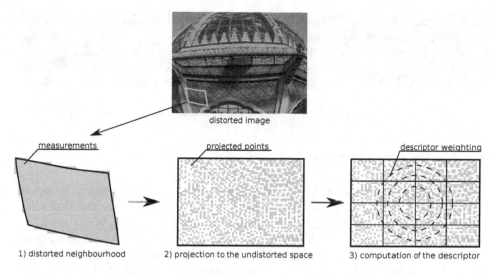

measurements   projected points   descriptor weighting

distorted image

1) distorted neighbourhood   2) projection to the undistorted space   3) computation of the descriptor

Fig. 3. A scheme of the computation of the Distortion Adaptive Descriptors. 1) The distorted neighbourhood is extracted from the input image. 2) The measurements are projected to the rectilinear space. As it can be noted, this yields to samples of non uniform density. 3) The regular descriptor is computed accounting for the correct arrangement of the measurements in the rectilinear space.

where $(x_0, y_0) = f(u_0, v_0)$ and $\hat{r}_1$ and $\hat{r}_2$ are obtained from r_1 and r_2 using equation (4). Fig. 2 (b) shows an example of distorted neighbourhood. Let be $\hat{\mathcal{M}}(\hat{I}, \hat{\mathcal{N}})$ the geometrically correct measurement performed in the locations of the distorted image $\hat{I}$ specified by the distorted neighbourhood $\hat{\mathcal{N}}$. The Distortion Adaptive Descriptor related to $\mathcal{D}$ is hence defined as:

$$\hat{\mathcal{D}} = D(f^{-1}(\hat{\mathcal{N}}), \hat{\mathcal{M}}(\hat{I}, \hat{\mathcal{N}})) \tag{7}$$

where $f^{-1}(\hat{\mathcal{N}}) = \{f^{-1}(x, y) : (x, y) \in \hat{\mathcal{N}}\}$.

The computation defined above is carried in three key steps: 1) given a point (x_0, y_0) in the distorted space and two radii $\hat{r}_1$, $\hat{r}_2$, the distorted neighbourhood $\hat{\mathcal{N}}(x_0, y_0, \hat{r}_1, \hat{r}_2)$ is considered; 2) all the coordinates of the points in $\hat{\mathcal{N}}$ are projected back to the rectilinear space $(f^{-1}(\hat{\mathcal{N}}))$; 3) the regular descriptor is computed using the geometrically correct measurements $\hat{\mathcal{M}}(\hat{I}, \hat{\mathcal{N}})$ and the projected coordinates $f^{-1}(\hat{\mathcal{N}})$. It should be noted that step 2) is important since it allows the descriptor to weigh the measurements according to their position in the undistorted space. Specifically, the projection leads to samples of non-uniform density which are correctly dislocated in the undistorted circular neighbourhood. The new locations for the considered measurements ensure a correct isotropic spatial weighting. Fig. 3 shows a scheme of the computation of the Distortion Adaptive Descriptors.

Fig. 4. Thumbnails of the images included in the dataset.

4   Experimental Settings

We argue that a combination of the gradient estimation techniques discussed in Section 2.1 and the scheme proposed in Section 3 can improve the matching ability of gradient based local descriptors on distorted images. What we want to evaluate is the invariance of the descriptors with respect to radial distortion, i. e., the ability to produce similar descriptors for two image regions representing the same physical area of the scene despite they are affected by different amounts of distortion. An ideal descriptor, for instance, would give identical results when computed on the matching neighbourhoods shown in Fig. 2 (c). In the following we discuss the experimental settings including the images used for the evaluations, the considered descriptors and the evaluation pipeline.

Wide Angle Images. We work with real-world rectilinear images to which radial distortion is artificially added as done in [1,6,7,10]. Working in this settings is convenient since it allows to control the exact amount of distortion present in the image for evaluation purpose. Moreover, the source rectilinear images can be reliably used to compute the ground truth descriptors using the standard algorithms proposed by their authors. In general, given a rectilinear image I and the percentage of distortion $d_\%$, we use the Division Model described in Section 2 to generate the distorted image $\hat{I}(\mathbf{x}) = I(f^{-1}(\mathbf{x}))$. We always consider the centre of distortion as the centre of the distorted image. We use the dataset proposed in [10] which contains 100 high resolution (5204×3472 pixels) images depicting scenes taken from different image categories including indoor, outdoor, natural, handmade, urban, car, pedestrian and street scenes.[1] Fig. 4 shows the thumbnails of the images included in the dataset. In order to obtain distorted images with variable FOV, we map the high resolution images contained in the dataset to distorted images with standard resolution of 1024×768 pixels at variable distortion rates as suggested by [10]. Fig. 1 reports some examples of output images.

Descriptors. We apply the DAD scheme to the SIFT and HOG descriptors using the gradient estimation techniques discussed in Section 2.1 to obtain the measurements. To assess the improvement due to the DAD scheme independently

---

[1] The dataset is available at the url: http://iplab.dmi.unict.it/icip2015/dataset.zip.

Table 1. The descriptors considered in the experiments.

Acronym	Description
SIFT$_{DIST}$ HOG$_{DIST}$	Regular SIFT/HOG descriptor computed on the distorted images using the distorted gradients as measurements.
SIFT$_{RECT}$ HOG$_{RECT}$	Regular SIFT/HOG descriptor computed on the rectified images using the Sobel filters to estimate the gradients.
SIFT$_{GCJ}$ HOG$_{GCJ}$	Regular SIFT/HOG descriptor computed on the distorted images using the GCJ gradients as measurements.
SIFT$_{GSF}$ HOG$_{GSF}$	Regular SIFT/HOG descriptor computed on the distorted images using the GSF gradients as measurements.
SIFT$_{IDEAL}$ HOG$_{IDEAL}$	Regular SIFT/HOG descriptor computed on the distorted images using the ground truth gradients as measurements.
DAD-SIFT$_{DIST}$ DAD-HOG$_{DIST}$	SIFT/HOG descriptor computed with the DAD scheme on the distorted images using the distorted gradients as measurements.
DAD-SIFT$_{GCJ}$ DAD-HOG$_{GCJ}$	SIFT/HOG descriptor computed with the DAD scheme on the distorted images using the GCJ gradients as measurements.
DAD-SIFT$_{GSF}$ DAD-HOG$_{GSF}$	SIFT/HOG descriptor computed with the DAD scheme on the distorted images using the GSF gradients as measurements.
DAD-SIFT$_{IDEAL}$ DAD-HOG$_{IDEAL}$	SIFT/HOG descriptor computed with the DAD scheme on distorted images using the ground truth gradients as measurements.

from the employed gradient estimation technique, we also consider an ideal estimator by warping the ground truth gradients to the distorted locations. Moreover, we consider the standard SIFT and HOG descriptors computed directly in the distorted domain (without adaptation) combined with the different gradient estimation techniques. Hence we derive the 18 descriptors summarized in Table 1. The SIFT-based descriptors are computed using the implementation provided by the VLFeat library [3], which produces standard 128-dimensional descriptors. For the HOG-based descriptors we consider the variant of HOG proposed in [23] as implemented by the VLFeat library [3]. Moreover, in our settings, the HOG-based descriptors are computed dividing the support region into 4×4 cells and the gradients are computed using 3×3 filters (in place of the non-smoothing $[-1\ 0\ 1]$ and $[-1\ 0\ 1]^T$ filters originally proposed by the authors [11]) in order to allow the gradient estimation techniques to compensate the distortion exploiting neighbourhood information. This configuration returns a 496-dimensional HOG descriptor for input support region of any size.

Evaluation Pipeline. For our evaluations, we measure the matching ability of the considered descriptors when they are densely extracted from the test images. Dense descriptors are appropriate for our analysis since they allow us to draw conclusions which are independent from any interest point detector. Moreover dense descriptors have proven powerful in a variety of tasks [19–21]. Given the reference-distorted image pair $(I, \hat{I})$, we densely extract square support regions from the reference image at a regular step of 50 pixels. To account for multiscale features, different layers of overlapping support regions are extracted considering radii ranging from 32 to 256 pixels. In this context, a support region is an entity $\mathcal{S}(\mathbf{u}, r)$ made of two elements: a centre $\mathbf{u}$ and a radius r. Each support region $\mathcal{S}$ is mapped to the corresponding support region $\hat{\mathcal{S}}$ in the distorted image using equations (1) and (4) reported in Section 2: $\hat{\mathcal{S}}(f(\mathbf{u}), g(r))$. All projected support regions which are not entirely contained in the distorted image $\hat{I}$ or which projected radius is under 16 pixels are discarded together with their undistorted counterparts. This settings lead to support regions of variable sizes ranging from 32×32 pixels to 512×512 pixels which cover the entire FOV of the distorted images. The number of support regions per image ranges from 887 to 3881 depending on the distortion rate. We refer to the set of reference support regions as $S = \{\mathcal{S}_i\}$ and to the set of projected support regions as $\hat{S} = \{\hat{\mathcal{S}}_i\}$. The reference support regions S are used to compute the standard SIFT and HOG descriptors, while the projected support regions $\hat{S}$ are used to compute the descriptors under evaluation. For instance, let be $\hat{\mathcal{D}}$ one of the SIFT-based descriptors in Table 1, we define the set of reference descriptors as $D = SIFT(S)$ and the set of test descriptors $\hat{D} = \hat{\mathcal{D}}(\hat{S})$. Similar definitions hold for the HOG-based descriptors. To evaluate the matching ability of descriptor $\hat{\mathcal{D}}$, we follow the scheme proposed in [18] to compute 1-precision vs recall curves. According to the authors of [18] two support regions $\mathcal{S}$ and $\hat{\mathcal{S}}$ match if the distance between their descriptors is below a threshold t. Each descriptor from the reference image is compared to each descriptor from the distorted one and the numbers of correct and false matches are counted. The threshold t is varied to obtain the curves. A match between two descriptors is considered correct only if they have been computed on corresponding support regions. For each threshold t, the precision and recall values are computed using the expressions:

$$Precision = \frac{\#correct\ matches}{\#matches} \tag{8}$$

$$Recall = \frac{\#correct\ matches}{\#suppport\ regions}. \tag{9}$$

The 1-precision vs recall curves have a straightforward interpretation: a perfect descriptor would give a recall equal to 1 for any precision. In practice increasing the value of threshold t increases the recall and decreases the precision. The rate at which those values vary with respect to the threshold tells how an algorithm is able to produce distinctive descriptors, which are similar for corresponding regions. As reported in [18], this kind of evaluation is independent from the matching scheme one could adopt (e.g., nearest neighbour with or without rejection of ambiguous matches) and respect the distribution of the descriptors in the space. To complement our analysis we also report threshold vs F-Measure curves. The F-Measure values are computed as reported in [22]:

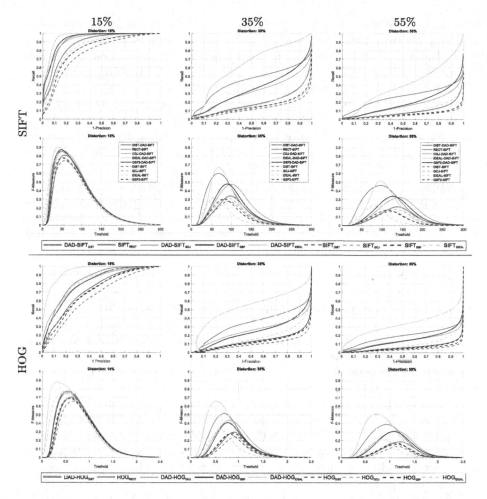

Fig. 5. The 1-precision vs recall curves (rows 1 and 3) and the threshold vs F-Measure curves (rows 2 and 4) for the SIFT-based and the HOG-based descriptors.

$$F_\beta = \frac{(1 + \beta^2) Precision \times Recall}{\beta^2 \times Precision + Recall} \qquad (10)$$

where $\beta^2 = 0.3$ to weigh precision more than recall. The threshold vs F-Measures curves can be interpreted from a retrieval point of view: a good descriptor allows to get a high number of positives with a small amount of noise. This situation is represented by a F-Measure curve with a high peak for a low threshold value.

5 Results

Fig. 5 shows the 1-precision vs recall and the threshold vs F-Measure curves of the considered descriptors for different amounts of distortion. As it can be noted, all the DAD variants systematically outperform their non-adaptive counterparts independently from the employed gradient estimation technique. Moreover, using the GCJ and GSF techniques for the measurements allows to improve the performances of all the descriptors over the distorted gradients. Interestingly such techniques, combined with the DAD paradigm, allow to reach the performances obtained through the rectification process for low amounts of distortion (15%). In general, however, the rectification provides better results for higher distortion rates at the cost of the computational time required by the unwarping. The GCJ and GSF techniques have similar performances when used both in the HOG-based and SIFT-based descriptors. The descriptors based on the ground truth gradients always have the best performances, which confirms the power of the DAD paradigm. Moreover, the gap between the performances given by the ground truth gradients and the ones given by the considered gradient estimation techniques suggests that there is still space for improvement for such techniques.

6   Conclusion

We have tackled the problem of improving the matching ability of gradient-based descriptors when they are directly computed on wide angle images. We have proposed the Distortion Adaptive Descriptors, a new paradigm for the correct computation of local descriptors in the distorted domain. Even if the proposed descriptors can be computed directly on the wide angle images, the performances obtained through the rectification process are not matched yet. The results convey that improving the gradient estimation techniques would allow to significantly improve the performances of gradient-based local descriptors on wide angle images. Further works will be devoted to quantitatively assessing the improvement in computational time of the DAD over the rectification-based techniques as well as compare the performances of the DAD against existing solutions (e.g., [6,8]).

This work has been performed in the project PANORAMA, co-funded by grants from Belgium, Italy, France, the Netherlands, the United Kingdom, and the ENIAC Joint Undertaking.

References

1. Furnari, A., Farinella, G.M., Puglisi, G., Bruna, A.R., Battiato, S.: Affine Region Detectors on the Fisheye Domain. In: IEEE International Conference on Image Processing (2014)
2. Miyamoto, K.: Fish eye lens. Journal of the Optical Society of America, 2–3 (1964)
3. Vedaldi, A., Fulkerson, B.: VLFeat: An open and portable library of computer vision algorithms. In: Proceedings of the international conference on Multimedia, pp. 1469–1472, (2010)
4. Puig, L., Guerrero, J.J.: Omnidirectional Vision Systems. Springer (2013)
5. Baker, S., Nayar, S.K.: A theory of catadioptric image formation. In: International Conference on Computer Vision, pp. 35–42 (1998)

6. Lourenço, M., Barreto, J.P., Vasconcelos, F.: sRD-SIFT: keypoint detection and matching in images with radial distortion. IEEE Transactions on Robotics **28**(3), 752–760 (2012)

7. Cinaroglu, I., Bastanlar, Y.: A direct approach for human detection with catadioptric omnidirectional cameras. In: Signal Processing and Communications Applications Conference, pp. 2275–2279 (2014)

8. Cruz-Mota, J., Bogdanova, I., Paquier, B., Bierlaire, M., Thiran, J.: Scale invariant feature transform on the sphere: theory and applications. International Journal of Computer Vision **98**(2), 217–241 (2011)

9. Lowe, D.G.: Distinctive Image Features from Scale-Invariant Keypoints. International Journal of Computer Vision 60, 91–110

10. Furnari, A., Farinella, G.M., Bruna, A.R., Battiato, S.: Generalized Sobel filters for gradient estimation of distorted images. In: The International Conference on Image Processing (submitted 2015)

11. Dalal, N., Triggs, B.: Histograms of oriented gradients for human detection. Computer Vision and Pattern Recognition **1**, 886–893 (2005)

12. Hughes, C., Glavin, M., Jones, E., Denny, P.: Wideangle camera technology for automotive applications: a review. IET Intelligent Transport Systems **3**(1), 19–31 (2009)

13. Battiato, S., Farinella, G.M., Furnari, A., Puglisi, G., Snijders, A., Spiekstra, J.: A Customized System for Vehicle Tracking and Classification, Expert Systems With Applications (2015)

14. Battiato, S., Gallo, G., Puglisi, G., Scellato, S.: SIFT features tracking for video stabilization. In: International Conference on Image Analysis and Processing, pp. 825–830 (2007)

15. Dorko, G., Schmid, C.: Selection of Scale Invariant Parts for Object Class Recognition. In: International Conference on Computer Vision, pp. 634–640 (2003)

16. Brown M., Lowe, D.: Recognising Panoramas. In: International Conference on Computer Vision, pp. 1218–1227 (2003)

17. Fitzgibbon, A.W.: Simultaneous linear estimation of multiple view geometry and lens distortion. In: Computer Vision and Pattern Recognition, vol. 1 (2001)

18. Mikolajczyk, K., Schmid, C.: Performance evaluation of local descriptors. Pattern Analysis and Machine Intelligence **27**(10), 1615–30 (2005)

19. Liu, C., Yuen, J., Torralba, A.: SIFT flow: dense correspondence across scenes and its applications. Pattern Analysis and Machine Intelligence 33(5) (2011)

20. Farinella, G.M., Allegra, D., Stanco, F.: A benchmark dataset to study the representations of food images. In: Assistive Computer Vision and Robotics in conjunction with the European Conference on Computer Vision (2011)

21. Lazebnik, S., Schmid, C., Ponce, J.: Beyond bags of features: spatial pyramid matching for recognizing natural scene categories. In: Computer Vision and Pattern Recognition, vol. 2 (2006)

22. Achanta, R., Hemami, S., Estrada, F., Susstrunk, S.: Frequency-tuned salient region detection. In: Computer Vision and Pattern Recognition, pp. 1597–1604 (2009)

23. Felzenszwalb, P.F., Grishick, R.B., McAllester, D., Ramanan, D.: Object detection with discriminatively trained part based models. Pattern Analysis and Machine Intelligence (2009)

Counting Turkish Coins
with a Calibrated Camera

Burak Benligiray[1]([✉]), Halil Ibrahim Cakir[2], Cihan Topal[1],
and Cuneyt Akinlar[3]

[1] Department of Electrical and Electronics Engineering,
Anadolu University, Eskisehir, Turkey
{burakbenligiray,cihant}@anadolu.edu.tr
[2] Department of Computer Engineering, Dumlupinar University, Kutahya, Turkey
cakirhal@dpu.edu.tr
[3] Department of Computer Engineering, Anadolu University, Eskisehir, Turkey
cakinlar@anadolu.edu.tr

Abstract. We present a computer vision application that detects all coins in a test image, classifies each detected coin and computes the total amount. Coins to be counted are assumed to be lying on a flat surface. The application starts by estimating the extrinsic parameters of the input camera relative to this flat surface ($[\mathbf{R} \,|\, t]$), whose intrinsic parameters ($\mathbf{K}$) are assumed to be known beforehand. Then, a bilateral filter is applied to the image to remove textural details and noisy artifacts. Circles in the filtered image are detected and smaller concentric circles are eliminated. Finally, the geometric parameters (the center and the diameter) of the remaining circles are computed by back-projecting the reciprocal points from the circle contours using the estimated camera parameters. Having thus computed the diameter of each detected coin, the classification is performed by comparing the computed diameter with the actual coin diameters. The experiments performed with a dataset consisting of 50 images containing different combinations of Turkish coins show that the proposed method achieves 98% accuracy rate and works even when some coins are partially occluded, as the method does not use any texture information.

Keywords: Coin detection · Circle detection · Bilateral filtering · Pose estimation · Camera calibration

1 Introduction

The detection and recognition of coins in digital images is an important problem with many applications. Vending machines and mass coin classification machines are among the many real-world applications areas where coin identification is required. In these kinds of machines, the problem is usually solved by means of a mechanical system that makes use of the diameter, weight or conductivity properties of the coins.

© Springer International Publishing Switzerland 2015
V. Murino and E. Puppo (Eds.): ICIAP 2015, Part II, LNCS 9280, pp. 216–226, 2015.
DOI: 10.1007/978-3-319-23234-8_21

In addition to such mechanical systems, there are applications that utilize image processing techniques for coin detection and recognition. Such applications usually aim to detect fraud coins, or coins that belong to a certain ancient period. The goal of these applications is not to detect all coins in a complex image containing many coins, but is rather to classify a single coin by utilizing different features extracted from the coin's texture.

Reisert et al. report a coin recognition system that utilizes the image gradient directions [1]. To determine the alignment of two coins, it is adequate to know that their gradient directions are aligned. After determining the alignment of the gradient directions, the recognition process is completed by a Fast Fourier Transform. The results are then classified using the nearest neighbor classification algorithm and false positive rate is reduced by employing different criteria.

Fuerst et al. developed a machine called Dagobert that can classify coins belonging to 100 different countries, and can count up to 10 coins per second [2]. The machine has a mechanism to capture the images of both sides of the coin, which are then processed by a vision application to recognize the coin type. Finally, the classified coin is placed into the appropriate machine bin by a mechanical key system.

Zaharieva et al. have tested their coin recognition algorithm on three different data sets, and measured the success of the their algorithm on classifying antique and modern coins [3]. They report that their algorithm can classify modern coins better, compared to antique coins. Modi and Bawa describe a coin recognition system based on artificial neural networks [4]. Their work tries to recognize coins of worth 1, 2, 5 and 10 rupis from both faces of a coin that did not go through rotation. For feature extraction, the authors use techniques such as Hough transform and pattern averaging. Finally, the obtained feature vector is fed into the artificial neural network for classification.

Shen et al. propose using local texture features for image-based coin recognition [5]. The authors use Gabor wavelets and local binary patterns (LBP) to generate a feature vector. The coin image is divided into small parts due to the concentric circular structure. Gabor coefficient statistics and LBP values are combined together to generate a feature vector representing the coin image. A circular shift operator is also proposed to make Gabor features more robust against rotation. For classification, the nearest neighbor classification method is used due to its speed. It is known that more complex classifiers such as artificial neural networks or decision support systems are slower compared to a nearest neighbor classifier. The proposed algorithm is measured to have a 74% accuracy based on the average and standard deviation of the Gabor features.

Kim and Pavlovic developed a method for automatic recognition of antique Roman coins [6]. The actual work is to recognize the Roman empire engraved on the face of the coin. The authors achieve this by concentrating on the dimensions of the coin rather than looking at the textural information. They report that using the coins' dimensions improves the recognition accuracy. The authors have also generated an antique Rome coin collection data set consisting of high quality images.

The proposed algorithms found in the literature mostly assume that the coins have already been detected and segmented from within the image either manually or by some segmentation method, and concentrate on the recognition of such segmented coins using textural features. In this paper, we concentrate on both the detection and the recognition of coins in a complex image containing an arbitrary number of coins regardless of which face of the coin is visible, and to compute the total amount of money. Although there is not a lot of work that target this problem in the literature, the authors in [7] attempt a heuristic approach by thresholding the image and counting the number of pixels above the threshold.

The obverse of all Turkish coins have the same picture of Ataturk, the founder of modern Turkey (see Table 1). Therefore, a method that makes use of textural features for coin recognition can only make use of the symbols present on the reverse of the coins. Since our goal is to design a system that detects and recognizes all coins that can be arbitrarily placed on a flat surface regardless of the side facing the camera, we aimed at determining the diameters of the coins and comparing them with the actual coin diameters. Since only geometric features are used for recognition, the proposed method works even in cases where the coins are partially occluded. Given that the textural features are not used, the proposed method is not useful for the detection of counterfeit coins.

2   The Proposed Coin Detection and Recognition Method

The proposed method concentrates on the geometric features of the coins to be detected rather than their textural features. The flow of the algorithm is presented briefly in Fig. 1. Since the difference between the diameters of different Turkish coins may be as small as 1 millimeter, the accuracy of the camera calibration will be critical (refer to Table 1). A small error in the diameter computation can easily lead to an incorrect classification. Therefore, it is important that the camera which the images are taken by is calibrated accurately.

When the application starts, the pose of the camera ($[\mathbf{R}\,|\,t]$) with respect to the plane where the coins will be placed is estimated. It is assumed that the intrinsic parameters of the camera have already been computed beforehand, and

Table 1. Turkish coins and their diameters [8].

Coin	1kr	5kr	10kr	25kr	50kr	1 TL
Diameter (mm)	16.5	17.5	18.5	20.5	23.85	26.15
Obverse (Heads)						
Reverse (Tails)						

Fig. 1. The block diagram of the proposed method.

is available to the application. The pose computation is performed once at the start of the application using a marker pattern, and is not repeated every frame because the camera is fixed throughout the application.

2.1 Bilateral Filtering

The first step in processing a captured image is to apply a filter to remove noise and unwanted artifacts. The goal here is to remove, if possible, the small internal circles resident inside 50kr and 1 TL coins, and to also remove unwanted textural details engraved over some coins so that the following circle detection algorithm works more robustly. The traditional approach to perform this is to apply a Linear Gaussian Filter with a high standard deviation. Although this would remove the unwanted details present inside the coins, it would also deteriorate the actual edges of the coins; thus affecting the accuracy of the detected coin boundary and its diameter. Therefore, to remove unwanted details present over the coins while preserving edges, we use bilateral filtering [9]. Fig. 2 shows a test image and the results of applying linear Gaussian and bilateral filters respectively. It should be clear from Fig. 2.c that the result obtained by a bilateral filter contains less texture while preserving the coin edges better compared to the result obtained by a linear Gaussian filter in Fig. 2.b.

2.2 Circle Detection and Elimination

After bilateral filter is applied to the captured image, the filtered image is fed into the recently-proposed, real-time parameter-free circle detection algorithm,

(a)   (b)   (c)

Fig. 2. (a) Test image, (b) Image after linear Gaussian filtering, (c) Image after bilateral filtering.

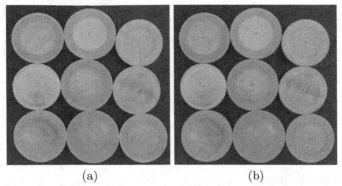

(a)   (b)

Fig. 3. (a) All detected circles, (b) Remaining circles after smaller concentric circles have been eliminated.

EDCircles [10], and a set of detected circles are obtained each in the form of center coordinates (x_m, y_m) and radii (r). Although bilateral filter removes most textural details from the coin surfaces, it is possible to detect inner circles, especially over 50kr and 1 TL coins since these coins consist of two different metallic parts having different colors. Additionally, it is possible to find double circles around the coin boundaries due to ridges, reliefs and shadows. Therefore, we go over the detected circles and eliminate the ones that have smaller radii among the set of concentric circles. Fig. 3.a shows all detected circles, and Fig. 3.b shows the remaining circles after elimination for a sample image.

2.3   Diameter Computation and Coin Classification

After the detection of the coin boundaries in the image and the computation of the coin center and radius, the next step is to compute the coordinates of this circle in the world coordinate system by means of the pre-computed camera pose. To perform this task, we compute $n = 2\pi/\alpha$ many reciprocal point pairs located over the circle's circumference as shown in Fig. 4, where α is the angular resolution of the points to be sampled. Then, for each point in the image coordinate system, its corresponding world coordinates are computed by back-projection using the camera pose $([\mathbf{R} \mid t])$ [11].

According to the pinhole camera model, the projection of point in the world coordinate system onto the image plane is performed by:

$$p_i = \mathbf{K}[\mathbf{R} \mid t]P_i \tag{1}$$

where P_i is a 3D point in the world coordinate system, and p_i is its projection onto the image coordinate system. To compute the real diameter of a coin, we need to compute the 3D coordinates of the reciprocal point pairs from the coin's boundary, and take the distance between them as the coin's diameter. For this purpose, we first compute the 3D coordinates of the camera center as follows:

$$P_k = -\mathbf{R}^{-1}t \tag{2}$$

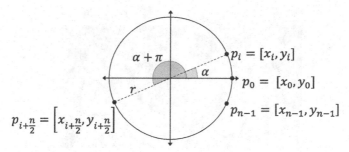

Fig. 4. Reciprocal point pairs used to estimate the diameter of a detected circle.

Then using the ray equation that originates from the camera center and passes through point p_i, the 3D point that maps to p_i is computed with respect to the depth (λ):

$$L(\lambda) = P_k + \lambda \mathbf{R}^{-1} \mathbf{K}^{-1} p_i \tag{3}$$

For a known depth Z, it is possible to find the X and Y coordinates in 3-dimensions by computing λ:

$$\lambda = \frac{Z - Z_{P_s}}{v_3} \tag{4}$$

where Z_{P_s} is the Z component of the scene camera center and $(v_1, v_2, v_3)^T = \mathbf{R}^{-1}\mathbf{K}^{-1}p_g$. For convention, the plane which the coins lie on is defined to be $Z = 0$.

As seen from Fig. 4, we compute, from the circumference of each circle, n p_i points using angular resolution $\alpha = 2\pi/n$, which corresponds to $n/2$ reciprocal point pairs:

$$\begin{aligned} x_i &= x_m + r\ cos(n\alpha) \\ y_i &= y_m + r\ sin(n\alpha) \end{aligned} \tag{5}$$

In the next step, all these points are back-projected to the world coordinate system and their 3D coordinates are computed. From each reciprocal pair of 3D points, a diameter is computed by taking the distance between the points. The final diameter of the coin is assumed to be the average of the computed diameters:

$$\bar{R} = \frac{2}{n} \sum_{i}^{\frac{n}{2}} \| P_i - P_{i+\frac{n}{2}} \| \tag{6}$$

After the diameter of a coin is computed, it is compared with the real diameters of the Turkish coins given in Table 1, and the coin whose diameter is the closest is assumed to be the detection. Since the diameter difference between some coins is a mere millimeter, it is important that the computed diameter to be of high accuracy. To improve the system's performance and make it more robust, the number of reciprocal point pairs used to compute the coin's diameter may be increased.

Fig. 5. Experimental setup. The marker pattern used during initial camera calibration (left), the system in action (right).

3   Experimental Results

The experimental setup is shown in Fig. 5. A USB camera is attached to a tripod and is facing down a flat surface (a hardcover book in the figure) located at about 30 cm above the plane. We developed a vision application that receives real-time video feed from the camera at 1280×720 resolution.

We could not compare the proposed method with other state of the art methods, because our problem can not be defined as recognizing ancient coins [3,6] or classifying different coins individually [1,2,4,5]. Our method uses an

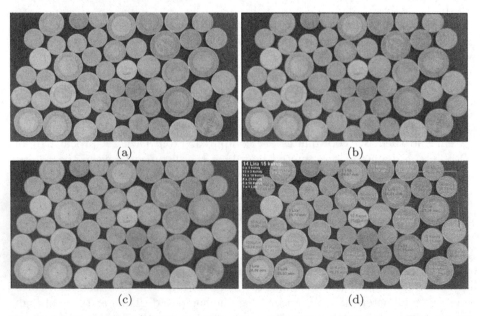

(a)   (b)

(c)   (d)

Fig. 6. (a) Test image, (b) The resulting image after bilateral filter is applied. (c) All detected circles are marked in green, the circles remaining after elimination are marked in pink. (d) Classified and marked coins.

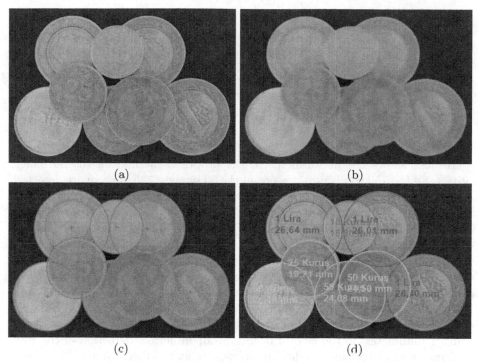

Fig. 7. (a) An image with partially occluded coins, (b) the image after bilateral filtering, (c) detected (green) and selected (pink) circles, (d) marked coins after classification.

image with multiple coins and results in a set of classificaitons, which can also be interpreted as a total amount of money.

Fig. 6 shows the performance of the proposed method for an image containing a certain number of coins placed arbitrarily over the plane. It is notable that although some coins are only partially visible in the image, they are still correctly detected and classified.

Fig. 7 shows a more complex scenario where the coins are stacked on top of each other with the coins at the top occluding a significant portion of the coins at the bottom. Even in this though test case, all coins have been correctly detected and classified. The two factors that influence the success of the proposed method the most are the employed circle detection algorithm [10], and the accurate external calibration of the camera. A demo video that shows how the system operates can be found in [12]. To measure the overall performance of the proposed method, we created a dataset consisting of 50 images each containing different combinations of 1 TL, 50kr, 25kr, 10kr and 5kr Turkish coins. The number of coins in each image is either 5, 10, 15, 20 or 25. The coins are placed on the plane to create many different scenarios ranging from simple no occlusion cases to severe occlusion cases, where some coins are placed on top the others partially blocking the coins placed at the bottom.

Table 2. Confusion matrix of the proposed method on the dataset.

Coin	No. Coins	Missed	1 TL	50kr	25kr	10kr	5kr
1 TL	145	1	142	2	0	0	0
50kr	155	1	0	154	0	0	0
25kr	150	1	0	0	149	0	0
10kr	150	3	0	0	0	143	4
5kr	150	0	0	0	0	3	147

Table 2 shows the performance of the proposed method on the 50 image dataset. Of the 750 total coins present in the 50 images, 735 of them are detected and classified correctly, with an accuracy rate of 98%. 6 coins are totally missed with no detection. Specifically, one 1 TL, one 50kr, one 25kr and three 10kr are not detected at all. Missed detections are due to severe occlusions, where several coins are placed on top of each other. As also seen from Table 2, there are some false detections and classifications. For example, two 1 TL coins are detected as 50kr coins. This is due to the inner ring present on 1 TL coins. In rare occasions, when the outer ring of 1 TL coin is not detected, the inner ring is detected and classified as 50kr. The other common false detection occurs due to similarity between 5kr and 10kr coins. Since the diameter difference between these coins is just 1 millimeter, in the case of occlusions or imperfect detection of the coin boundary due to lighting conditions, it is possible to classify 5kr as 10kr, and

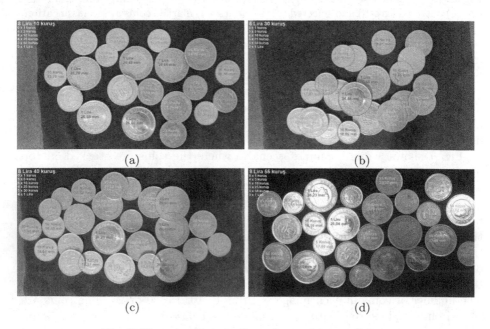

(a)   (b)

(c)   (d)

Fig. 8. Experimental results under various conditions.

Table 3. Dissection of the running times of the proposed method in different steps on an image with 1280 × 720 resolution.

Algorithm Step	Running Time
External Calibration(performed only once)	57 ms
Bilateral Filtering (9 × 9 kernel)	307 ms
Circle Detection & Elimination (EDCircles [10])	30 ms
Classification by Diameter Computation	21 ms
Total	**358 (+57) ms**

vice versa. As seen from Table 2, four 10kr are classified as 5kr, and three 5kr are classified as 10kr. See Fig. 8 for results with additional test images.

The dissection of the running time of the proposed method in different stages for an image of size 1280×720 pixels on a 3.70 GHz computer is given in Table 3. As seen from the table, bilateral filtering is the part that takes the most amount of time. If we use linear Gaussian filter instead of the bilateral filter, then the filtering time goes down to about 10 ms, but the robustness of the system decreases. But even with bilateral filtering, the method takes about 350 ms in total, and can thus run at 3 frames per second.

4   Conclusions

We present a system that reliably detects and classifies Turkish coins in images captured by a calibrated camera. The proposed system differs from the systems found in the literature in that it only makes use of geometric features of the coins, disregarding their textural features. It works even in presence of partial occlusions, since the method does not make use of the texture information as other methods in the literature. Experiments show that the proposed method is sensitive to lighting conditions, as the shadows around the coin boundaries create difficulties in coin detection and contour localization.

We plan to extend this work by incorporating a texture based classification step. The coins classified using the textural information can then be used to estimate the pose of the camera, thus removing the need for the pre-calibration step proposed in this paper. Once the pose is estimated using the coins classified using textural information, the rest of the coins on the scene can be classified using the approach proposed in this paper. The resulting system will be able to work under arbitrary camera poses.

References

1. Reisert, M., Ronneberger, O., Burkhardt, H.: An efficient gradient based registration technique for coin recognition. In: Proc. of the Muscle CIS Coin Competetion Workshop (2006)
2. Fuerst, M., Woegerer, C., Kronreif, G., Hollaender, I., Penz, H.: Intelligent high-speed, high-variant automation of universal coin sorting for charity organizations. In: ICRA (2006)

3. Zaharieva, M., Kampel, M., Zambanini, S.: Image based recognition of ancient coins. In: Kropatsch, W.G., Kampel, M., Hanbury, A. (eds.) CAIP 2007. LNCS, vol. 4673, pp. 547–554. Springer, Heidelberg (2007)

4. Modi, S., Bawa, S.: Automated Coin Recognition System using ANN. Int'l. Journal of Computer Applications **26**(4), July 2011

5. Shen, L., Jia, J., Ji, Z., Chen, W.S.: Extracting Local Texture Features for Image-Based Coin Recognition. IET Image Process. **5**(5), 394–401 (2011)

6. Kim, J., Pavlovic, V.: Ancient coin recognition based on spatial coding. In: Int'l. Conf. Pattern Recognition (ICPR), Stockholm, Sweden (2014)

7. Pendse, M., Wang, Y.: Automated Coin Recognition with Android Phone, Term Project, Dept. of Electrical Engineering, Stanford University

8. Online link: http://tr.wikipedia.org/wiki/Turkiye_Cumhuriyeti_madeni_paralari (last accessed: February 15, 2015)

9. Tomasi, C., Manduchi, R.: Bilateral filtering for gray and color images. In: IEEE Int. Conf. on Computer Vision, pp. 839–846 (1998)

10. Akinlar, C., Topal, C.: EDCircles: A real-time circle detector with a false detection control. Pattern Recognition **46**(3), 725–740 (2013)

11. Hartley, R., Zisserman, A.: Multiple View Geometry in Computer Vision, 2nd edn. Cambridge Univ. Press (2004)

12. Online link: https://www.youtube.com/watch?v=NzyxP3Mvh5M (last accessed: February 15, 2015)

Design and Implementation of a Dynamic Adaptive Video Streaming System with a Buffer Aware Rate Selection Algorithm

M. Venkata Phani Kumar$^{(\boxtimes)}$, K.C. Ravi, and Sudipta Mahapatra

Department of E & ECE, IIT Kharagpur, Kharagpur, India
venkataphanikumarm@gmail.com

Abstract. This paper proposes a novel buffer aware rate selection algorithm for adaptive video streaming. The proposed framework uses a throughput estimation module and a rate adaptation algorithm, which enhances the Quality of Experience for a viewer by maximizing the average selected bit rate with minimum quality fluctuations. Further, the paper presents a pyramid coding scheme for media content preparation that can provide media with consistent visual quality under constraints on the encoding speed and the target bit rate. The experimental evaluation carried over a test-bed validates our rate selection algorithm.

Keywords: Video streaming · Rate adaptation

1 Introduction

Currently, the reliance on traditional video streaming solutions is substituted with a steady shift towards adaptive streaming. Protocols such as RTSP, RTMP and MMS are replaced with HTTP delivery. Recently a new standard called Dynamic Adaptive Streaming over HTTP (DASH) has been developed by MPEG and 3GPP to enable high-quality streaming of media content over the internet from conventional HTTP web servers [1]. The Quality of Experience (QoE) for a viewer in adaptive video streaming can be enhanced by minimizing frequent playback interruptions. Since adaptive streaming systems are particular in their automatic switching between the quality levels, quality transitions can affect the QoE for a viewer in addition to sub-optimal quality selections. An efficient rate adaptation algorithm is required for adaptive video streaming to solve the above problems. Further, the content preparation at the server side can also be considered as one of the main parts in adaptive streaming since it can enhance the QoE for a viewer under multiple network conditions. In this paper, we propose two algorithms, namely buffer aware rate selection algorithm at the client player and pyramid coding scheme for content preparation at the server. The pyramid coding scheme can provide media with a consistent visual quality under the constraints on the encoding speed and the target bit rate. To achieve the target bit rate with the best quality, the encoding process starts with the derivation of

© Springer International Publishing Switzerland 2015
V. Murino and E. Puppo (Eds.): ICIAP 2015, Part II, LNCS 9280, pp. 227–238, 2015.
DOI: 10.1007/978-3-319-23234-8_22

an initial quantization parameter (QP) based on the spatiotemporal complexity of the sequence, its resolution, and the target bit rate. Simple linear estimation models are used to predict the number of bits that would be necessary to encode a frame for a given complexity and quantization parameter. The proposed algorithm achieves consistent visual quality while satisfying the long term bit rate constraint. Since the proposed coding scheme has a limited complexity, it is more suitable for real-time applications. The buffer aware rate selection algorithm at the client player enhances the QoE for the viewer by maximizing the average selected bit rate with minimum quality fluctuations. A dynamic adaptive video streaming system with the proposed rate adaptation algorithm is implemented over a miniature test-bed and the experimental results validate the proposed algorithm. The rest of the paper is organized as follows: Section II presents the background and related work. Section III shows the implemented video streaming system. The experimental results are discussed in Section IV. Finally, Section V concludes the paper.

2   Background and Related Work

In the past few years, some research efforts on rate adaptation algorithms for adaptive streaming have been reported [2–6]. The rate adaptation algorithms of commercial solutions such as Adobe Open Source Media Framework (OSMF), Microsoft Smooth Streaming, and Netflix client are evaluated in [2] and the experimental results reveal that none of them provides smooth quality adaptation. A buffer preserving rate adaptation mechanism is proposed in [3], which keeps the playback buffer duration up to a certain amount by continually increasing the video bit rate. However, when the available throughput drops suddenly, the algorithm aggressively decreases the representation bit rate and, therefore, causes abrupt decrease in the video quality. In [4], a representation quality aware adaptation algorithm is proposed, which minimizes sudden changes in video quality by utilizing segments at the buffer. However, this adaptation algorithm cannot perfectly resolve the quality transition problems since the algorithm does not include any buffer absorbing part that is necessary to cope up with the available throughput fluctuations.

To minimize the unnecessary quality fluctuations, a safety margin based rate adaptation scheme is proposed in [5]. The adaptation scheme uses a logistic function (LF) based throughput estimation mechanism in which a deviation parameter is used to assign a proportional weight for the recent observed throughput. The algorithm prevents the playback interruptions by selecting a sub-optimal bit rate, which is lower than the available throughput. In [4], a simple rate adaptation scheme is proposed in which the video bit rate is selected as the highest value that is smaller than or equal to the estimated throughput. The algorithm employs an exponential weighted moving average (EWMA) based throughput estimation method in which the throughput for the next instant is estimated by assigning a proportional weight for the recently observed throughput. In [6], a network-aware rate adaptation scheme is proposed. The algorithm uses a dynamic fluctuation index (DFI) based throughput estimation scheme that assigns a dynamic proportional weight for the recent observed throughput. The rate adaptation algorithm prevents the playback buffer depletion by choosing a bit rate lower than or equal to the estimated throughput. However, the existing rate adaptation schemes are still insufficient considering the frequent changes in video quality for a rapidly changing network condition.

3 The Proposed Video Streaming System

3.1 Encoding Scheme

In video streaming applications, the QoE for a viewer can be greatly enhanced by delivering the media content with a consistent visual quality. It requires the media content to be encoded not only with a good average quality, but also with fewer quality fluctuations among the adjacent frames. The use of hierarchical pictures leads to an improved coding efficiency compared to coding with the classical IBBP or IPPP structures [7]. In this paper, we propose a novel pyramid coding scheme for the hierarchical pictures. The adopted scheme for content preparation is shown in Fig. 1. In this scheme each of the frames to be encoded is assigned a unique rank, i.e., all of the I frames are assigned a rank zero, B frames are assigned the maximum rank, while ranks assigned to P frames vary from rank zero to a rank less than the maximum rank value. The QP for any frame of rank i is derived by adding a small value to the QP of the corresponding reference frames of rank $i - 1$ irrespective of the frame type.

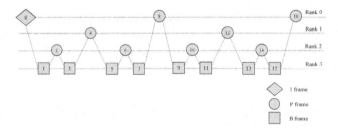

Fig. 1. Proposed Encoding Scheme

We maintain this pyramid structure of QP variation between zero rank reference frames as shown in Fig. 1. Further, the proposed scheme modulates the zero rank frame QPs according to the buffer status while the rest of the QPs are derived as above. To achieve the target bit rate with the best quality, the algorithm first calculates an initial QP value based on the complexity of the sequence, its resolution, and the target bit rate. Specifically, the proposed algorithm determines the QP for encoding a zero rank P frame as follows: Let us assume that $\bar{P}_{QP}$ is the average of the QP values of zero rank P frames encoded so far, $\overline{cplx}$ is the average spatio-temporal complexity observed so far, bit_{act} represents the total bits consumed for all the frames encoded so far, $cplx$ denotes the spatio-temporal complexity of the current frame and bit_{tgt} denotes the total target bits for all of the frames including the current frame. Then, the QP selected for encoding the frame is given by

$$P_{QP} = \frac{bit_{act} * \bar{P}_{QP} * cplx}{bit_{tgt} * \overline{cplx}} \qquad (1)$$

A Coding Group (CG) is considered to represent a set of frames from the frame succeeding the past zero rank frame to the future zero rank frame. For all the frames in the current CG, the total number of bits required for encoding are estimated using simple linear estimation models for a given QP derived from the current P_{QP}. Before encoding the zero rank P frame, the algorithm calls a buffer to project the status such that if the above derived P_{QP} and QPs corresponding to different ranks are used for encoding the entire CG. Depending on the estimated buffer status, the current P_{QP} is either left unchanged or is modified so as to achieve the desired bit rate accurately. If the estimated buffer is close to the target buffer, the current P_{QP} is used for encoding the frame. Otherwise, the algorithm derives a small increment in P_{QP} (ζ_{qp}) that needs to be applied to the current P_{QP} to achieve the desired bit rate. This increase is derived as follows:

$$\zeta_{qp} = P_{QP} * (\zeta_{qpf} - 1) \qquad (2)$$

where the step size factor, $\zeta_{qpf} = (1 + \zeta_{br}) * (1 + \zeta_{vq})$. The two quantities ζ_{br} and ζ_{vq} respectively corresponds to the bit rate constraint and the consistent visual quality constraint. After estimating the increment in P_{QP}, it is updated as follows:

$$P'_{QP} = P_{QP} + \zeta_{qp} \qquad (3)$$

where P'_{QP} is the updated P_{QP}. Whenever P_{QP} is modified, the QPs corresponding to different ranks are updated accordingly. We observe that the proposed coding scheme leads to a smoother variation in QP and hence less quality fluctuations among the adjacent frames. Compared to the existing coding scheme in Joint Model (JM) reference software, the proposed coding scheme achieves a maximum peak signal to noise ratio (PSNR) improvement of 1.5 dB and an average of 0.7 dB when different test sequences are considered. The Rate-Distortion (RD) performance of the proposed algorithm for two test sequences is shown in Fig. 2. The complexity of the proposed algorithm is also much lower than

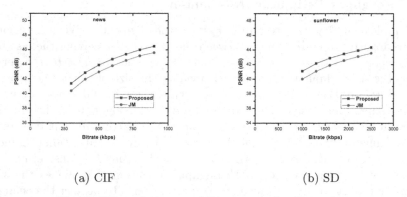

(a) CIF   (b) SD

Fig. 2. RD performance of the proposed coding scheme

that of traditional algorithm used in JM software since the proposed algorithm employs a simple linear prediction mechanism rather than the complicated MAD prediction as used in the latter.

3.2   Dynamic Adaptive Video Streaming System

The proposed encoding mechanism is used for the preparation of video content. Later the encoded content is split into video segments according to the MPEG DASH specifications. The implemented dynamic adaptive video streaming system is shown in Fig. 3. The server content is represented by a Media Presentation Description (MPD) file and a collection of segments with different representation qualities. The client requests the MPD file from the server, and the received MPD file is interpreted by the parser at the client. The extracted information from the MPD file is used for requesting the media segments from the server. The video streaming system further consists of two more modules at the client, namely the throughput estimation module and buffer aware rate selection module as shown in Fig. 3.

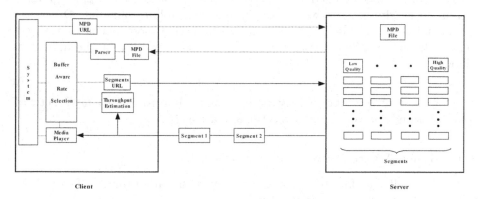

Fig. 3. Dynamic Adaptive Video Streaming System

3.3   Throughput Estimation Mechanism

In the implemented video streaming system, the segment delivery duration is considered as the time difference between the instant of receiving the last byte of the response to the instant of sending the segment request to the server. Further, the throughput is obtained by dividing the size of the segment by the delivery duration. Before fetching the next segment, the available network conditions are estimated by using the throughput estimation algorithm. The proposed throughput estimation mechanism uses a smoothing factor (ρ) that reflects the rapid changing network conditions. The proposed throughput estimation mechanism outperforms the existing throughput mechanisms by considering both absolute and smoothed values of throughput deviation that makes the algorithm more robust to short-term network fluctuations. To project the changing network conditions at each instant, we determine a throughput deviation (e_n) as follows:

$$e_n = \hat{T}_n - T_n \tag{4}$$

where $\hat{T}_n$ represents estimated throughput and T_n represents the available throughput. The absolute and smoothed values of e_n are determined as follows:

$$a_n = \gamma|e_n| + (1 - \gamma)a_{n-1} \tag{5}$$

$$b_n = \gamma\, e_n + (1 - \gamma)b_{n-1} \tag{6}$$

Finally, we compute ρ as

$$\rho = \left|\frac{a_n}{b_n}\right| \tag{7}$$

The parameters a_n and b_n measure the fluctuations in the available throughput over time and are used to dynamically update ρ. The value of ρ reflect the changing network condition as follows: The higher value of ρ indicates the network condition has changed suddenly and thus the next instant throughput is estimated by giving more weight to the past available throughput. Otherwise, the next instant throughput is determined by giving more weight to the estimated throughput. The algorithm determines the next instant throughput as follows:

$$\hat{T}_{n+1} = \rho T_n + (1 - \rho)\hat{T}_n \tag{8}$$

The value of ρ is updated dynamically according to the available network conditions and the throughput is estimated accordingly.

3.4   Buffer Aware Rate Selection Algorithm

One of the challenges for the rate adaptation algorithm arises from the fact that the end-to-end available throughput between the server and the client changes dynamically and is difficult to predict. The other challenges include maximization of QoE, minimization of start up delay and avoidance of playback interruptions. If the status of the buffer at the client player is not taken into consideration before requesting the video segment from the server, the buffer at the client player may suffer from either overflow or underflow. For example, if the available network throughput is higher than the estimated throughput, the video segment may arrive at the player before the expected time; on the other hand, if the available network throughput is lower than the estimated throughput, the video segment may arrive later than the expected time. As the status of the buffer is not taken into consideration while requesting the next segment, the buffer at the client player may endure either overflow or underflow. The viewer will experience playback interruptions in the event of buffer underflow. In the event of buffer overflow, the adaptation algorithm fails to provide the best quality video to the viewer.

If the video segments are requested in accordance with only the estimated throughput, frequent bit rate switching will occur at the client when the available throughput fluctuates. The frequent bit rate switching will adversely affect the viewer's QoE. In addition to the above, minimizing start-up delay, i.e., the time difference between the instant a video is requested until the video playback starts, also needs to be addressed in real time video streaming. The start-up delay can be minimized by selecting a lowest representation bit rate for the initial few chunks in order to produce fast playout start. As a result of this, the viewer will experience either a sudden increase in quality level or will not be able to view the best quality video for few seconds. To address the above issues we propose a novel buffer aware rate selection (BARS) algorithm with the following goals: 1)To avoid playback interruptions 2) Minimize the bit rate fluctuations 3) Minimize the start up delay.

Let Q_1, Q_2, ...Q_m be the **m** different qualities available for a given video stream. Q_1 represent the lowest quality and Q_m represent the highest quality of the video stream. The different qualities of the same video sequence are stored on a video server, as shown in Fig. 3. For **m** different video qualities the corresponding bit rates are R_1, R_2, ...R_m such that $R_1 < R_2 .... < R_m$. R_1 represents the lowest bit rate corresponding to the lowest quality Q_1 while R_m represents the highest bit rate corresponding to the highest quality Q_m. The proposed algorithm is invoked immediately once the playback starts. In order to have smooth and uninterrupted playback, the algorithm takes two arguments, namely the estimated throughput and the buffer level of the video player. The proposed rate adaptation algorithm operates as follows. Initially, the algorithm estimates a bit rate to be selected for the $(n+1)^{th}$ segment as

$$\underset{R_{n+1}^{est}}{\arg\max}\{R_{n+1}^{est} \leq \hat{T}_{n+1}\}$$
$$R_{n+1}^{est} \in \{R_1, R_2...R_m\}$$

(9)

where R_{n+1}^{est} is the initially estimated bit rate to be selected for the $(n+1)^{th}$ segment and $\hat{T}_{n+1}$ is the estimated throughput as given by Equation (5). Before requesting the $(n+1)^{th}$ segment, the algorithm verifies the status of the client buffer and updates the bit rate to be selected for the $(n+1)^{th}$ segment by estimating a weight factor, α_{n+1} according to the buffer occupancy level.

Initially, we define two thresholds for the buffer level, namely B_1 and B_2 measured in seconds such that $0 < B_1 < B_2 < B_{max}$ where B_{max} is the maximum level of the buffer in seconds. We consider an operating margin in the buffer as follows: $B_{mar} = [B_1, B_2]$. The target buffer level (B_{tar}) is considered as the midpoint of the operating margin i.e., $B_{tar} = 0.5[B_1 + B_2]$. The proposed algorithm keeps the buffer level close to B_{tar}. If a decrement/increment in buffer level is followed by an increment/decrement in the available throughput, the algorithm responds by requesting a representation quality same as the current representation quality or a representation quality slightly higher/lower than the current representation quality depending on the rate of buffer fluctuation.

The pseudo-code of the proposed algorithm is given in Algorithm 1. The proposed algorithm is more robust to short-term throughput fluctuations by not changing to any different representation quality as long as $\beta_n^{cur} \in B_{mar}$, where

---

Algorithm 1.

1: **if** $(\beta_n^{cur} \leq B_{tar})$ **then**
2:     **if** $\beta_{n-1}^{pre} \geq B_{tar}$ **then**
3:         $\varepsilon = \dfrac{B_{max} - \beta_n^{cur} - \beta_{n-1}^{pre}}{B_{max} - \beta_{n-1}^{pre}}$
4:     **else**
5:         $\varepsilon = \dfrac{|\beta_n^{cur} - \beta_{n-1}^{pre}|}{\beta_{n-1}^{pre}}$
6:     **if** $\beta_n^{cur} - \beta_{n-1}^{pre} \leq 0$ **then**
7:         $\alpha_{n+1} = \alpha_n(1 - \varepsilon)$
8:     **else**
9:         $\alpha_{n+1} = \alpha_n(1 + \varepsilon)$
10:     **if** $R_{n+1}^{est} > R_n^{cur}$ **then**
11:         $R_{n+1}^{adap} = \alpha_{n+1} R_{n+1}^{est} + (1 - \alpha_{n+1}) R_n^{cur}$
12:     **else**
13:         $R_{n+1}^{adap} = \alpha_{n+1} R_n^{cur} + (1 - \alpha_{n+1}) R_{n+1}^{est}$
14: **else**
15:     **if** $\beta_{n-1}^{pre} \geq B_{tar}$ **then**
16:         $\varepsilon = \dfrac{|\beta_n^{cur} - \beta_{n-1}^{pre}|}{B_{max} - \beta_{n-1}^{pre}}$
17:     **else**
18:         $\varepsilon = \dfrac{\beta_n^{cur} + \beta_{n-1}^{pre} - B_{max}}{\beta_{n-1}^{pre})}$
19:     **if** $\beta_n^{cur} - \beta_{n-1}^{pre} \leq 0$ **then**
20:         $\alpha_{n+1} = \alpha_n(1 + \varepsilon)$
21:     **else**
22:         $\alpha_{n+1} = \alpha_n(1 - \varepsilon)$
23:     **if** $R_{n+1}^{est} > R_n^{cur}$ **then**
24:         $R_{n+1}^{adap} = \alpha_{n+1} R_n^{cur} + (1 - \alpha_{n+1}) R_{n+1}^{est}$
25:     **else**
26:         $R_{n+1}^{adap} = \alpha_{n+1} R_{n+1}^{est} + (1 - \alpha_{n+1}) R_n^{cur}$

β_n^{cur} is the current buffer level at the time of requesting the $(n+1)^{th}$ segment. This behavior increases the viewers QoE by minimizing the frequent bit rate switching. The sensitivity of the algorithm to short term fluctuations can be enhanced by adjusting the size of B_{mar}. The proposed algorithm now estimates an adapted bit rate, R_{n+1}^{adap} from the available buffer occupancy level and the bit rate of the current representation, R_n^{cur}. R_{n+1}^{adap} is further updated as given in Algorithm 2.

Algorithm 2.

1: **if** $R_1 < R_{n+1}^{adap} < R_m$ **then**
2:     $R_{n+1}^{adap} = R_{n+1}^{adap}$
3: **else**
4:     **if** $R_{n+1}^{adap} < R_1$ **then**
5:         $R_{n+1}^{adap} = R_1$
6:     **else**
7:         $R_{n+1}^{adap} = R_m$

The proposed algorithm minimizes playback interruptions by keeping the buffer level within the operating margin B_{mar} and maximizes the QoE for the viewer. The algorithm avoids playback interruptions as follows: whenever the current buffer level, β_n^{cur} falls below the threshold level, B_{th} ($0 < B_{th} < B_1$) the proposed algorithm switches more aggressively to the lowest representation quality. This is because the probability of a buffer underflow in the presence of throughput fluctuations is high. Since the goals minimizing the start-up delay and providing the best quality at the beginning of the stream constitute a trade-off, the proposed algorithm resolves the trade-off by downloading the first segment at mid representation quality and thereby adapting the quality in a more aggressive way. The proposed rate selection algorithm finally selects a representation quality with its corresponding bit rate as follows.

$$\underset{R_{n+1}^{sel}}{\arg\max}\{R_{n+1}^{sel} \leq R_{n+1}^{adap}\}$$
$$R_{n+1}^{sel} \in \{R_1, R_2...R_m\}$$

(10)

4   Experimental Evaluation

A miniature Next Generation Wireless Internet (NGWI) test-bed is used for evaluating the performance of the proposed algorithm. The system consists of a core router (CR1), a switch (SW1), two wireless routers (WR1 and WR2), and three access points (AP1, AP2, and AP3), three laptops (L1, L2, and L3),

Fig. 4. Client Player

a smartphone (S1) and three desktop computers (PC1, PC2, and PC3). Quality of Service (QoS) parameters for clients are also set-up on the WRs such that the performance can be measured in both constant and variable bandwidth. For the experimental evaluation, we considered WiFi as the wireless broadband access technology. A rapidly changing network condition is selected for evaluating the effectiveness of the proposed algorithm. The available throughput in such a condition is measured and logged using the custom build wireless routers and was used to emulate the scenario on the NGWI test-bed. The proposed algorithm is implemented as an extension for the VLC player as shown in Fig. 4. The extension acts as a middle layer between the VLC player and the buffer. A viewer can access the extension using the **view** item in the player menu. Once the playback starts, the rate adaptation algorithm is invoked immediately and basic statistics about the streamed content, namely the available throughput and the selected representation, are displayed for the viewer. We set a 20 second client buffer to provide smooth video playback during experimentation. The server content is represented by an MPD file and a collection of segments with different representation qualities. All the video segments have the same length of 2 seconds. We considered several test sequences of various resolutions provided by xiph.org (http://media.xiph.org/video/derf) for experimentation. The available reference test video sequences are of about 500 seconds duration and all these are used in the experimental evaluation. The test video sequence is provided with ten bit rates from 400kbps to 800kbps with a step size of 40kbps. The performance of the proposed algorithm is compared with three existing algorithms namely, EWMA based throughput estimation mechanism with simple rate selection algorithm (EWMA + SRS), DFI based throughput estimation mechanism with adaptive video rate selection algorithm (DFI+AVRS) and LF based throughput estimation mechanism with safety margin based rate selection algorithm (LF + SMBRS). Fig. 5 shows the experimental results of all the algorithms.

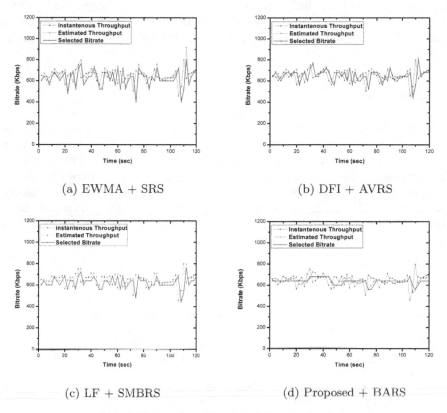

(a) EWMA + SRS   (b) DFI + AVRS

(c) LF + SMBRS   (d) Proposed + BARS

Fig. 5. Rate adaptation for different algorithms

From the results, it can be observed that EWMA + SRS has more bit rate fluctuations. This is because the video bit rate is selected as the highest value that is smaller than or equal to the estimated throughput. DFI+AVRS scheme performs better than the EWMA + SRS scheme, but it also suffers from bit rate fluctuations. This is because AVRS algorithm requests segments with the highest bit rate to avoid buffer overflow, but the buffer depletes quickly in case of a sudden decrement in the available throughput due to inflated bit rate requests. Further, there is no inherent underflow detection scheme in the AVRS algorithm due to which playback pauses are observed. The LF+SMRS scheme uses a simple safety margin for avoiding the buffer underflow, but the algorithm fails to provide to provide best quality video to the viewer. Further, there is no inherent overflow detection mechanism in SMRS algorithm due to which low-quality video is streamed. All the three algorithms suffer from bit rate fluctuations and playback discontinuities because of not considering status of the buffer at the player. The proposed algorithm minimizes frequent bit rate switching by not changing to any different representation quality for short-term throughput fluctuations. In addition, the algorithm continuously monitors the status of the buffer and avoids both buffer overflow and underflow with inherent early detection mechanisms. The proposed algorithm enhances the QoE for a viewer by maximizing the average selected bit rate while minimizing the fluctuations in quality.

5   Conclusion

A dynamic adaptive video streaming system with a buffer aware rate selection algorithm is implemented and presented in this paper. The proposed algorithm enhances the QoE for a viewer by maximizing the average selected bit rate with minimum quality fluctuations. Further, the paper presents a pyramid coding scheme for media content preparation that can provide media with consistent visual quality under the constraints of the encoding speed for a target bit rate. The experimental evaluation carried over a miniature NGWI test-bed validates the proposed rate selection algorithm.

References

1. Stockhammer, T.: Dynamic adaptive streaming over http - standards and design principles. In: Proc. ACM MMSys, pp. 133–144, February 2011
2. Akhshabi, S., Begen, A.C., Dovrolis, C.: An experimental evaluation of rate-adaptation algorithms in adaptive streaming over http. In: Proc. ACM MMSys, pp. 157–168, February 2011
3. Liu, C., Bouazizi, I., Gabbouj, M.: Rate adaptation for adaptive http streaming. In: Proc. ACM MMSys, pp. 169–174, February 2011
4. Mok, R.K., Luo, X., Chan, E.W., Chang, R.K.: QDASH: a QoE-aware dash system. In: Proc. ACM MMSys, pp. 11–22, February 2012
5. Thang, T.C., Pham, A.T.: Adaptive Streaming of Audiovisual Content using MPEG DASH. IEEE Trans. on Consumer Electronics 58(1), 78–85 (2012)
6. Kim, Y.H., Park, J.: Design and Implementation of a Network-Adaptive Mechanism for HTTP Video Streaming. ETRI Journal 35(1), 27–34 (2013)
7. Schwarz, H., Marpe, D., Wiegand, T., et al.: Hierarchical B pictures. In: Joint Video Team, Doc. JVT-P014, Poznan, Poland (2005)

Leveraging Mutual Information in Local Descriptions: From Local Binary Patterns to the Image

Tahir Q. Syed$^{(\boxtimes)}$, Sadaf I. Behlim, Alishan K. Merchant,
Alexis Thomas, and Furqan M. Khan

Visual Analytics Lab, National University of Computer and Emerging Sciences,
Karachi, Pakistan
{tahir.syed,sadaf.iqbal,k112214,k112026,furqan.khan}@nu.edu.pk

Abstract. Local image descriptors provide robust descriptions of image localities. Their geometric arrangement provides additional information about the image they describe, a fact often ignored when employing them to that wide slew of tasks from image registration to scene classification. On the premise that descriptor quality could be assessed in terms of its expressiveness of image content, we investigate the use of the described as well as that additional geometric information to the task of recovering the image from its local descriptors. This paper uses Local Binary Patterns, an operator nested in a dense geometry, to study how this additional information in the form of constraints among pixels dictates the intensity estimated for a pixel. We determine that constraints propagate from regional extrema to regions around them that observe the same constraint class, and that the intensity for any of the region's pixels influences that for all others. We build a directed constraint graph of pixel nodes such that the arcs on the graph are strongly k-consistent, and propagate intensity estimates from extremum nodes. Evaluations are run on the SIPI texture and the BSD500 datasets. The estimates preserve the local structure of the image, as shown by the Mean Absolute Error of about 15% and 18% respectively and Structural Texture SIMilarity of about 92% for both datasets, in addition to observing 100% constraint satisfaction.

1 Introduction

Local image descriptors describe image localities in compact yet rich ways, which is why they have been successfully employed in numerous computer vision applications such as image retrieval [1], action recognition [2,3], object detection and recognition [4]. The success of local descriptors is due to their expressiveness of image content, which has been quantified by seminal work [5] via precision-recall criteria on the image retrieval task. We propose to measure this expressiveness directly by investigating the fundamental question: *could we get an intensity image back given its local description?*

T.Q. Syed and S.I. Behlim—Equal contribution.

© Springer International Publishing Switzerland 2015
V. Murino and E. Puppo (Eds.): ICIAP 2015, Part II, LNCS 9280, pp. 239–251, 2015.
DOI: 10.1007/978-3-319-23234-8_23

Concretely, this *inverse problem* amounts to the estimation of an image's pixel intensities given its local description which preserves not only the perceptual semantics but is also consistent with the structure arising from image content. The manner that the descriptor patches are arranged within the image has lead to two threads of investigation: 1) where the macroscopic information (arrangement) is kept as meta-data separate from the descriptor [6,7], and 2) where densely computed local descriptors allow this information to be inferred [8,9]. The work presented here lies in the second because we find it more interesting to see whether at all the inversion problem is addressable in the absence of meta information.

In this thread of investigation, Kruse et al. [10] show that the local-structure of an image could be revealed by exploring a pixel's relationship with its 8-connected neighborhood, solving for a system of inequalities, one for each pixel. This simultaneous solution is computationally prohibitive for any meaningful image size. After the advent of local image descriptors, Lindahl et al. [11] reproduce Kruse's results by estimating pixel intensities beginning with an image of uniform intensity and then running a gradient descent procedure to arrive at a similar local description as the one supplied for the original image. Wu et al. [8] also perform reconstruction by taking a permuted version of an image as input and tweaking the pixel values until the reconstructed image produce the same description as was provided for the image before permutation. These works illustrate that the encoding mechanism of descriptors maintains the local structure of the described patch, even though they do not use this information for the purpose of reconstruction. More recent work, Waller et al. [9], takes into account the information encoded by a descriptor patch. They utilize inter-pixel intensity relationship (*greater-than* or *less-than*) information provided by the LBP descriptor to estimate the pixel intensity values in a way that is consistent with these relationships, by following the longest path uphill from image minima using a recursive procedure. Since their method does not conserve the path from the minimum to any given pixel, there is no way to update the values of the pixels along the path, including the minima, which are universally estimated as 0.

In this paper we are investigating the inversion problem in a manner that takes into account both the within-patch structure information provided by the descriptor but *also* the macroscopic information between pixels of different patches interlocked in a dense geometrical relationship. We work with a dense binary image descriptor, Local Binary Patterns (LBPs) [12] which in its original and extended form is widely used in applications ranging from segmentation [13] to gait analysis [3]. This descriptors is simple and easy to compute and encodes not only the local structural information of an image but also spatial information of patch pixels w.r.t the center pixel of the patch. Our contributions in this paper are:

1. posing image inversion from binary descriptors as a constraint satisfaction problem, i.e., reformulating the problem of estimating pixel intensities as one of domain shrinkage of constrained variables.

2. proposing a constraint graph sub-graphs of which take tree forms that encode constraints (either superiority or inferiority, defined in Sec. 2) possibly between any pair of pixels in the image. For the purpose of inversion, we work only with the constraints occurring through the longest successions of constraints.

3. proposing a method that inverts an image given its LBP codes that account for all encoded constraints being satisfied, and quantifiably recovers local image contrast.

2   Local Binary Pattern and Constraint Propagation

The Local Binary Pattern (LBP) is a dense local binary descriptor that describes the relationship between pair of pixels using a two-way comparison within a given window size. It encodes the local structure of an image within a window in terms of constraints [8]. This view at the operator level would generalize to the fact that an LBP code at any given pixel constrains the intensity of its neighbors to be either greater than (*superior to*) or less than (*inferior to*) its intensity.

The LBP code for a particular pixel is the weighted sum of a Heaviside[1] function of oriented differences around each pixel of a patch (Fig. 1(a)). These codes encode only superiority and inferiority constraints present between neighborhood pixels but do not contain any information about *how much* a pixel is superior or inferior to the center pixel, that is, they have lost all contrast information. A

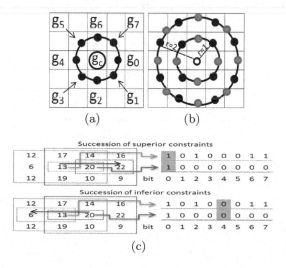

(a)   (b)

(c)

Fig. 1. (a) Neighbors of center pixel g_c participating in $LBP_{8,1}$ (b) different neighbor samplings (e.g. black pixels might be discounted) in neighborhoods of different sizes (c) succession of superiority or inferiority constraints via LBP codes

[1] $H(z) = \begin{cases} 0 & z < 0 \\ 1 & z \geq 0 \end{cases}$

pixel P_2 observes the superiority constraint, denoted by $superior(P_1, P_2)$ w.r.t pixel P_1 when the Heaviside function of difference between P_2 and P_1 results in 1, else observes the inferiority constraint denoted by $inferior(P_1, P_2)$.

$$superior(P_1, P_2) = H(P_2 - P_1) \tag{1a}$$

$$inferior(P_1, P_2) = 1 - superior(P_1, P_2) \tag{1b}$$

The LBP code could be mathematically defined in terms of the superiority constraint as:

$$LBP_{n,r}(g_c, g_i^r) = \sum_{i=0}^{n-1} superior(g_c, g_i^r) * 2^i. \tag{2}$$

where r is the radius of a circle defined on the L_∞ norm, n is the number of sampling points in the neighborhood (Fig. 1(b)), g_c is the intensity of the pixel for which the LBP code is being calculated, and g^r is a pixel at a radius r on a circle in the L_∞ space.

The LBP code could also provide information about a larger neighborhood than defined by the local patch on which it was computed, i.e. the LBP of a larger radius, $LBP_{16,2}$ could be recursively defined in terms of the $LBP_{8,1}$ primitive. The relationship between any two non-neighbor pixels can be estimated through the LBP codes if there is a succession of either superiority or inferiority constraints through any possible path i.e. relationship between pixelindex (linear index) PI-5 and PI-11 could be defined by evaluating the LBP codes of PI-5 and PI-8 as shown in Fig. 1c. Analyzing the value at bit 0 of PI-5 and PI-8 codes, which is 1, reveals that PI-8 is superior to PI-5 and PI-11 is superior to PI-8 respectively. This implies that PI-11 is superior to PI-5 by transitivity. Mathematically,

$$superior(P_i, P_j) = superior(P_i, P_k) \wedge superior(P_k, P_j) \tag{3}$$

Thus, a succession of superiority constraints, $Superior$, could be defined as:

$$Superior(g_c, g_j^r) = superior(g_c, g_i^1) \wedge superior(g_i, g_k^{1 \vee \ldots \vee r}) \wedge \ldots \wedge superior(g_k^{(r-1) \vee r}, g_j^r) \tag{4}$$

where $\wedge$ is a composition and $\vee$ is a selection operator. The succession of inferiority constraints, $Inferior$, is also defined in a dual fashion (Fig. 1(c)) where the relationship to PI-2 from PI-8 is found to be inferior.

Sometimes, it is not possible to identify the relationship between two pixels using any shared pixel i.e. In Fig. 2(a), a relationship between PI-1 and PI-16 could not be determined using any neighborhood pixels. Thus, constraint propagation comes to a halt when an inferiority constraint follows a succession of superiority constraints and vice versa i.e.

$$Superior(g_c, g_j^r) \wedge inferior(g_j^r, g_p^r) \text{ or } Inferior(g_c, g_j^r) \wedge superior(g_j^r, g_p^r)$$

These opposite constraints themselves either have g_p^r as an image extremum or propagate towards an extremum. The set P of all such successions emanating from a given extremum demarcated by pixels p defines the $propagation\ extent$ of that extremum. For instance, for minimum min_n:

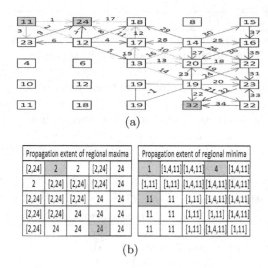

(a)

Propagation extent of regional maxima					Propagation extent of regional minima				
[2,24]	2	2	[2,24]	24	1	[1,4,11]	[1,4,11]	4	[1,4,11]
2	[2,24]	[2,24]	[2,24]	24	[1,11]	[1,11]	[1,4,11]	[1,4,11]	[1,4,11]
[2,24]	[2,24]	[2,24]	24	24	11	11	[1,11]	[1,4,11]	[1,4,11]
[2,24]	[2,24]	24	24	24	11	11	[1,11]	[1,11]	[1,4,11]
[2,24]	24	24	24	24	11	11	[1,11]	[1,4,11]	[1,11]

(b)

Fig. 2. (a) Constraint graph formed due to the arboresence expanding from the regional minimum lying at PI-1. Hotness of color encodes increasing distance from the minimum. (b) pixel memberships in multiple propagation extents of regional maxima (pink) at $PI - 6$ and $PI - 20$ and of regional minima (blue) at $PI - 1$, $PI - 3$ and $PI - 16$

$$P = \bigcup_p \{Superior(min_1, g_j^r) \wedge inferior(g_j^r, p^r)\} \tag{5}$$

Therefore, it is of interest to determine the positions of image extrema as well as their propagation extents.

3   The Directed Constraint Graph

Given any pixel g_c, we can enumerate all the neighborhood pixels that observe the superiority or the inferiority constraints, and for all of these neighborhood pixels a similar enumeration could be performed. This naturally lends itself to two kinds of constraint arborescence, one that encodes superiority constraints having regional minimum as the starting node and other one encode inferiority constraints having regional maximum as the starting node. Fig. 2(a) shows 3 regional minima and 2 regional maxima which are identified by analyzing the LBP codes of a particular image - it is observed that the LBP code for regional maxima evaluates to 0, and for regional minima to 255, discounting border effects.

Algorithm 1. MINIMA TREES

Input: A list of minima $minList = \{min_1, min_2, \ldots, min_n\}$ which
contains each minimum linear index in an image.

Output: A set of tree $treeList = \{tree_1, tree_2, \ldots, tree_n\}$. Each tree
corresponds to a minimum contains array of cell each
$tree_{no} = \{node_1, node_2, \ldots, node_n\}$ holds information of nodes
$node_n = \{nodeId, nodeValue, parNodeId, nodeLevel\}$ that
observe superiority constraints where $nodeId$ is the temporary
Id and $nodeValue$ is a value that is either a pixelindex or -1

---

1   **for** $i \leftarrow 1$ **to** $size(minList)$ **do**
2   initialize $expandNodesQueue, tree_i \leftarrow \emptyset$ and $nodesCount \leftarrow 1$
3   push $minList(i)$ in $expandNodesQueue$
4   insert root of $tree_i$ as $node_1 = \{nodesCount, minList(i), NULL, 1\}$
5   increment $nodesCount$
6   **while** $not\ empty(expandNodesQueue)$ **do**
7        $parNodeId \leftarrow$ pop(expandNodesQueue)
8        $superiorNodes$ contains $parNodeId$ neighbors that observe
         superiority constraints
9   **if** $not\ empty(superiorNodes)$ **then**
10   **for** $each\ supNode\ in\ superiorNodes$ **do**
11            $supNodeLevel$ is $parNodeLevel + 1$
12   check whether the $tree_i$ contains $supNode$
13   **if** $false$ **then**
14   insert $supNode$ in $tree_i$ as
              $\{nodesCount, supNode, parNodeId, supNodeLevel\}$
15   increment $nodesCount$
16   push $supNode$ in $expandNodesQueue$
17   **else**
18   get $nodeLevel$ of $supNode$ from $tree_i$
19   **if** $nodeLevel < supNodeLevel$ **then**
20   update supNode $parNodeId$ and $supNodeLevel$ in
                $tree_i$
21   update $nodeLevel$ of subtree associated with
                $supNode$ if exists

However, sometimes it is possible that a certain pixel observes the same
succession of constraints from either pixel g_c or from one of its children, e.g.
in Fig. 2(a) $PI\text{-}2$ could be reached from $PI\text{-}1$ and $PI\text{-}7$ where $PI\text{-}7$ and $PI\text{-}2$
are both children of $PI\text{-}1$. Therefore, a directed constraint graph emerges from
every extremum which could be lead to a number of arborescences, one for each
extremum. Fig. 2(a) shows the directed constraint graph emerges from minimum
lying at $PI\text{-}1$ and Fig. 2(b) indicates for each pixel the extremum with which
the pixel is associated.

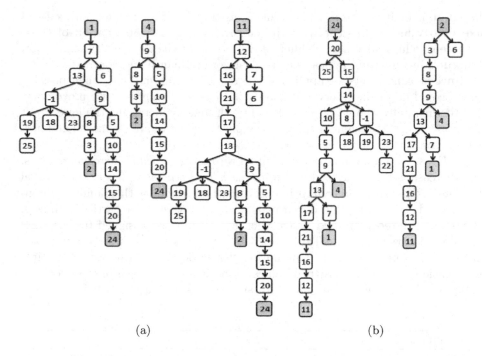

(a)   (b)

Fig. 3. Overlapping trees formed (a) regional minima; (b) regional maxima (Each node(box) of the tree shows pixelindex PI, node with value -1 is used to connect all equal nodes)

It is well known that for large constraint graph with high branching factors, 8 in our case, the complexity of constraints satisfaction significantly reduces if the graph could be reducible to a tree based on information about the problem domain [14]. Since multiple directed paths could connect a pair of nodes therefore multiple spanning trees are possible. Each of these branches enforces constraint propagation in a strongly-k-consistent manner [15,16], k being the length of the branch. A large value of k enables the encoding of a large contrast interval, and also enables the exclusion of a subset of inconsistent domain values. Therefore, the path with the largest ultrametric value of k is retained. This hierarchical representation thus formed helps in approximating contrast not onlylarge in the local 3×3 LBP window but also some contrast information in the propagation extent of that extremum. Algorithm 1 describes the formation of trees based on superiority constraints emanating from regional minima. Fig. 3(a) and 3(b) show trees formed from regional minima and maxima.

4   The Inversion Algorithm

The proposed data structure presents a new representation of an image in terms of propagation extents of regional extrema. Algorithm 1 ensures constraint propagation in a strongly k-consistent manner from the minimum to pixels defining the contour of its propagation extent. This translates to domain shrinkage of pixels' to values consistent with the constraints. Every combination of those consistent values generates a different variations of the image with same local structure, but different appearance in terms of luminance and contrast.

Since no constraints are applied at the root of all minima trees, their possible values could lie in the interval $[0, 255 - (treeDepth \times step)]$. As we move down the tree hierarchy, the set of possible values shrinks by increasing the lower limit of the interval. Algorithm 2 explains how pixel intensities are estimated and how the assignment of estimates proceeds, done in two passes.

In $Pass - 1$, all minima trees are filled with monotonically increasing values. The increase in the intensity estimate at each level (the $step$) lies in the interval $[1 - maxStep]$ where $maxStep$ is determined by dividing the range of intensity value i.e. 256 with the depth of the deepest tree for a particular image. The $Pass - 1$ reconstructed image thus has all minima assigned 0. The LBP codes at this stage are satisfied to 100% but it is possible to have a better estimate in terms of local contrast by noting that nodes that form part of multiple propagation extents are assigned values propagating from each of their sources, finally retaining the largest one. Any successor down the branch is therefore

---

Algorithm 2. IMAGE RECONSTRUCTION

Input: A set of trees $treeList = tree_1, tree_2, \ldots, tree_n$ that observes superiority constraints.

Output: Reconstructed image $reconsImg[m, n]$

1 initialize $reconsImg[m, n] \leftarrow -1$ and $step \leftarrow$ floor(256/depth of the deepest tree in $treeList$)

2 **for** $k \leftarrow 1$ **to** $size(treeList)$ **do**

3   **for** *each* $node$ in $tree[k]$ **do**

4   i, j are 2D indices of pixelindex $nodeValue$

5   **if** $(reconsImg[i, j] < ((nodeLevel - 1) * step))$ **then**

6           $reconsimg[i, j] = (nodeLevel - 1) * step$

7 **for** $k \leftarrow 1$ **to** $size(treeList)$ **do**

8     $nodeId \leftarrow nodeId$ of deepest node of $tree[k]$

9     $pixelInd \leftarrow nodeValue$ of deepest node of tree[k]

10   i, j are 2D indices of pixelindex $pixelInd$

11    $maxValue \leftarrow reconsImg[i,j]$

12    $treeDepth \leftarrow nodeLevel$ of corresponding $nodeId$

13    $updRootValue \leftarrow maxValue - ((treeDepth-1) * step)$

14    $localStep \leftarrow (255 - maxValue)/treeDepth$

15   **for** *each* $node$ in $tree[k]$ **do**

16   i, j are 2D indices of pixelindex $nodeValue$

17   **if** $(reconsImg[i, j] < (updRootValue + (nodeLevel - 1) * localStep))$ **then**

18          $reconsImg[i, j] = updRootValue + (nodeLevel - 1) * localStep$

consistent with our longest ultrametric requirement but the ancestors need updating. Therefore, a second pass of node intensity estimation is performed.

$Pass-2$ of the reconstruction updates the estimates back to the roots of the trees. In order to make the estimates consistent with local contrast, we adjust the values of all nodes using a 'local' step size that is determined using the depth of a tree. This removes the loss in local-contrast-preservation induced by the longest-ultrametric update having only been made on parts of the tree in $Pass-1$.

5   Results and Discussions

The algorithms described above ensure that the descriptor-to-image inversion is consistent with the constraints emerging from the mutual arrangement of the descriptor patches. In this section, we qualtify the goodness-of-inversion. Results are separately reported for both kind of propagation sources, minima and maxima. However, since the average of two constraints-consistent values lies in the interval of consistent values, we also report the measure on the averaged image. To show that $Pass-2$ of the inversion algorithm improves results over $Pass-1$, measures are shown on both passes.

Since the LBP is classically considered a descriptor of image texture, we work with the SIPI texture dataset, which includes images from the earlier Brodatz dataset as well. However, since our method is not limited to texture description because superiority or inferiority constraints occur due to the nature of the descriptor not the images containing significant texture, we also use the popular BSD500 dataset, containing images in the wild.

We can observe from Table 1 that the estimated images make visual sense. Edges and object silhouettes, where present, are discernable, the image content structure is respected i.e. the estimated image is dark or light where the original image was dark or light. In the Lenna image, one can observe the gradual shading on the hat, consistent with the original. But the quality of estimates need to be quantified to answer two questions: 1. whether the intensity estimated at a particular pixel matches the one in the original image, and 2. whether the local appearance of the image i.e. the contrast and luminance along the two axis is respected.

Competing work [9] uses the **Mean Absolute Error** between the original and the estimated pixel intensities to explain the efficacy of their method of inversion, so we use the MAE too for benchmarking. The MAE is given by:

$$\text{MAE}(\bar{R}, \bar{O}) = \frac{\sum_{i=1}^{m} \sum_{i=1}^{n} \bar{R} - \bar{O}}{m \times n} \tag{6}$$

where $\bar{X} = \frac{X - min(X)}{max(X) - min(X)}$ for an image with size $m \times n$, normalizes image X to lie in the interval $[0, 1]$.

Table 1. Reconstructed images using LBP codes - first 3 rows show *Pass*-1 reconstruction (*minima*, *maxima* and *average* respectively), next 3 rows show *Pass*-2 reconstruction and last row contains sample original images.

Lenna   SIPI Texture   BSD500

Table 2 shows the MAE computed on the SIPI and BSD500 dataset. The results computed on the two passes of the inversion algorithm show that the MAE calculated on images from $Pass - 1$ is higher than the $Pass - 2$ estimates. Averaging is likely to improve a measure by spreading the image intensity histogram and improving contrast. Also, the average image MAE diminishes because a generic image is not likely to have its histogram naturally skewed to either toward 0 or toward 255, under the application of the central limit theorem. MAE on average images is found to be 15% and 18% on the SIPI and BSD500 dataset respectively.

A truer measure for inversion quality would take into account the contrast of image localities, partly because the MAE is very sensitive to appearance changes while local descriptors are quasi-invariant to them, but mostly because we would be interested to know whether any of the contrast, which the LBP operator lost, has been recovered. Structural similarity measures give access to that information, and we use the **Structural Texture SIMilarity measure (STSIM)**, proposed by [17]. This measure incorporates two appearance terms, *luminance* and *contrast*, which measure the local mean and standard deviation of an image using Eq. 7, where R is the estimated image, O is the original image, l is the luminance and c is the contrast comparison term and $C_{R,O}\,(0,1)$ and $(1,0)$ are the first order auto correlation terms computed in the x and y directions.

$$STSIM(R,O) = (l_{R,O})^{1/4} \times (c_{R,O})^{1/4} \times (C_{R,O}(0,1))^{1/4} \times (C_{R,O}(1,0))^{1/4} \quad (7)$$

Table 2 shows the $STSIM$, *luminance* and *contrast* computed for both datasets. Results of $STSIM$ show that the reconstructed image retains 92% structural similarity with the original image. Although, *contrast* doesnot show remarkable change between the two passes, however, *luminance* is improved by approximately 10% in $Pass - 2$ particularly in the image reconstructed through the *maxima* tree generation, because intensity estimates are now closer to the original intensities.

Table 2. Results calculated on $SIPITexture$ and $BSD500$ dataset

	SIPI			BSD500		
	minima	maxima	average	minima	maxima	average
Pass-1						
Luminance	0.929	0.785	0.971	0.816	0.768	0.952
Contrast	0.886	0.886	0.886	0.941	0.932	0.902
STSIM	0.909	0.869	0.919	0.891	0.874	0.912
MAE	0.217	0.305	0.167	0.374	0.227	0.179
Pass-2						
Luminance	0.976	0.974	0.976	0.952	0.954	0.952
Contrast	0.854	0.868	0.867	0.928	0.928	0.931
STSIM	0.913	0.919	0.919	0.918	0.916	0.917
MAE	0.155	0.156	0.149	0.197	0.179	0.180

Another deduction which could be made from Table 2 is that both MAE and STSIM for inverted images after $Pass-2$ through either minima or maxima trees converge to those of the average case. Therefore, it would be computationally interesting to perform the inversion using either of the two kind of trees.

6   Conclusions

It is instructive to understand what information is lost when local descriptions for instance LBP codes are generated, and whether and how that information could be estimated. Descriptors such as FREAK [18] or BRIEF [19] explicitly encode geometric information, while we derive it by observing the constraints emerging from the LBP's sliding window architecture and use it to answer the inversion problem posed in the introduction.

The underlying mechanism of overlapping sliding windows provides the leverage to argue about global image structure. It also poses the question of generalizing the inference of implied information to any sliding-window operation.

References

1. Yao, C.-H., Chen, S.-Y.: Retrieval of translated, rotated and scaled color textures. Pattern Recognition **36**(4), 913–929 (2003)
2. Wang, H., Ullah, M.M., Klaser, A., Laptev, I., Schmid, C: Evaluation of local spatio-temporal features for action recognition. In: Procedings of the British Machine Vision Conference 2009, pp. 124.1–124.11 (2009)
3. Kellokumpu, V., Zhao, G., Li, S.Z., Pietikäinen, M.: Dynamic Texture Based Gait Recognition, pp. 1000–1009 (2009)
4. Zhao, G., Chen, J., Pietikäinen, M.: An improved local descriptor and threshold learning for unsupervised dynamic texture segmentation. In: Proc. 2nd IEEE International Workshop on Machine Learning for Vision-based Motion Analysis (MLVMA 2009), Kyoto, Japan, pp. 460–467 (2009)
5. Mikolajczyk, K., Schmid, C.: A Performance Evaluation of Local Descriptors. IEEE Transaction on Pattern Analysis and Machine Intelligence **27**, 1615–1630 (2005)
6. Weinzaepfel, P., Jégou, H., Pérez, P.: Reconstructing an image from its local descriptors. In: Proceedings of the IEEE Computer Society Conference on Computer Vision and Pattern Recognition, pp. 337–344 (2011)
7. Daneshi, M., Guo, J.: Image reconstruction based on local feature descriptors (2011)
8. Wu, J., Rehg, J.M.: CENTRIST: A Visual Descriptor for Scene Categorization. IEEE Transactions on Pattern Analysis and Machine Intelligence, 1–14, December 2010
9. Waller, B.M., Nixon, M.S., Carter, J.N.: Image reconstruction from local binary patterns. In: 2013 International Conference on Signal-Image Technology & Internet-Based Systems, pp. 118–123. IEEE, December 2013
10. Gudmundsson, B., Kruse, B., Antonsson, D.: PICAP and Relational Neighborhood Processing in FIP
11. Lindahl, T:. Study of Local Binary Patterns Study of Local Binary Patterns Examensarbete utfört i medieteknik Tobias Lindahl (2007)

12. Timo, O., Pietikätinen, M., Harwood, D.: A comparative study of texture measures with classification based on featured distributions. Pattern Recognition **29**(1), 51–59 (1996)
13. Qing, X., Yang, J., Ding, S.: Texture segmentation using lbp embedded region competition. Electronic Letters on Computer Vision and Image Analysis **5**(1), 41–47 (2005)
14. Mackworth, A.: Consistency in networks of relations. Artificial Intelligence **8**(1), 99–118 (1977)
15. Freuder, C.E.: Synthesizing constraint expressions. Commun. ACM **21**(11), 958–966 (1978)
16. Freuder, E.C.: A sufficient condition for backtrack-free search. J. ACM **29**(1), 24–32 (1982)
17. Zujovic, J., Pappas, T.N., Neuhoff, D.L.: Structural similarity metrics for texture analysis and retrieval. In: 2009 16th IEEE International Conference on Image Processing (ICIP), vol. 22(7), pp. 2545–2558 (2009)
18. Ortiz, R.: Freak: Fast retina keypoint. In: Proceedings of the 2012 IEEE Conference on Computer Vision and Pattern Recognition, CVPR 2012, pp. 510–517. IEEE Computer Society, Washington, DC (2012)
19. Calonder, M., Lepetit, V., Strecha, C., Fua, P.: BRIEF: Binary robust independent elementary features. In: Daniilidis, K., Maragos, P., Paragios, N. (eds.) ECCV 2010, Part IV. LNCS, vol. 6314, pp. 778–792. Springer, Heidelberg (2010)

Dominant LBP Considering Pattern Type for Facial Image Representation

Alaa Sagheer[1,2(✉)] and Shimaa Saad[2]

[1] Department of Computer Science, College of Computer Science
and Information Technology, King Faisal University, Hofuf, Saudi Arabia
asagheer@kfu.edu.sa
[2] Center for Artificial Intelligence and Robotics,
Faculty of Science, Aswan University, Aswan, Egypt
s.saad@cairo-aswu.edu.eg

Abstract. Facial image representation plays an important role in computer vision and image processing applications. This paper introduces a novel feature selection method, dominant LBP considering pattern type (DLBP-CPT), capable to capture, effectively, the most reliable and robust dominant patterns in face images. In contrast to the Dominant LBP (DLBP) approach, we take into account the dominant pattern types information. We find that pattern type represents essential information that should be included, especially, in facial image representation across illumination. We apply the proposed method with the conventional LBP and the angular difference LBP (AD-LBP) operators. It is shown in this paper, that the proposed DLBP-CPT and DAD-LBP-CPT descriptors are more reliable to represent the dominant pattern information in the facial images than either the conventional uniform LBP or other dominant LBP approaches.

Keywords: Local binary patterns · Facial representation · Feature selection · Face identification

1 Introduction

Facial image representation has the utmost importance in computer vision research, with applications like biometric identification, visual surveillance, information security and access control, human-machine interaction, video conferencing and content-based image retrieval. Face representation is included in many topics such as face detection and facial feature extraction, face tracking and pose estimation, face and facial expression, and face modeling and animation [1,6]. What makes the problem of face representation challenging is the fact that facial appearance varies due to changes in pose, expression, illumination and other factors such as age and make-up [3].

Recently, very discriminative and computationally efficient local texture descriptors have been proposed such as local binary patterns (LBP) [12], which has led to a significant progress in applying texture-based methods to

V. Murino and E. Puppo (Eds.): ICIAP 2015, Part II, LNCS 9280, pp. 252–263, 2015.
DOI: 10.1007/978-3-319-23234-8_24

different computer vision applications. While texture features have been success-fully used in different computer vision problems, only few works have considered them in facial image analysis before the introduction of LBP [2,5]. Since then, the methodology has inspired a lot of new methods in face analysis, thus reveal-ing that texture based region descriptors can be very efficient in representing and analyzing facial features.

Ideally, LBP is capable to provide a transformed output image that is invari-ant to the global intensity variations. However, when LBP is utilized in repre-senting facial features, it is sensitive to local variations that occur commonly along edge components of the human face [7,13]. Also, the basic LBP operator generates rather long histograms overwhelmingly large even for a small neighbor-hood size, leading to poor discriminative power and large storage requirements. In addition, using the complete set of histogram cannot be reliable to describe the input image, because some pattern types rarely occur. The proportions of such patterns are too small to provide a reliable estimate of the occurrence pos-sibilities of those patterns.

As such, several extensions of LBP have been proposed with an aim to increase its robustness and discriminative power. In 2002, Ojala et al. suggested an extension to LBP by considering only the so-called "uniform" patterns [12]. Uniform LBPs effectively capture the fundamental information of textures, which mainly consist of straight edges or low curvature edges [9].

In 2009, Liao et al. extended the conventional LBP approach in order to effectively capture the dominating patterns in texture images [9]. In their app-roach, they omitted the information related to the dominant pattern types, and only consider the information about pattern occurrence frequencies. In 2010, Guo et al. introduced a learning framework of image descriptor based on Fisher separation criteria to learn the most reliable and robust dominant pattern types considering intra-class similarity and interclass distance [4]. They applied their FSC-based learning framework with LBP and presented the FBL-LBP descriptor.

Recently in 2012, Liu et al. proposed new four descriptors to extend the con-ventional LBP [10], namely two local intensity-based descriptors CI-LBP and NI-LBP and two local difference-based descriptors RD-LBP and LBP-AD. How-ever, they found that, proportions of the uniform patterns of AD-LBP are too small to provide a meaningful description of texture. Broadly speaking, even though the success of the uniform patterns with some LBP variants, the pro-portions of these patterns are inadequate to provide a meaningful description of texture for some other LBP variants [10].

In this paper, we propose a new-feature selection method, dominant LBP considering patten type (DLBP-CPT), capable to capture, effectively, the most reliable and robust dominant pattern types in face images. In contrast to previous Dominant LBP approaches, we take into account the dominant pattern types information. Experimental results show that pattern type represents essential information that should be included in facial image representation. The proposed approach showed better performance comparing to other dominant approaches.

This paper is organized as follows: Section 2 shows an overview of both LBP and AD-LBP. The proposed approach is described in section 3. Experiments and results are provided in section 4. Finally, discussion and conclusion are given in section 5.

2   The Local Binary Pattern (LBP)

2.1   A Brief Overview of LBP

The original LBP operator, proposed by Ojala [11], is a powerful method for texture description due to its invariance to global intensity variations. It labels the pixels of an image by thresholding a 3 × 3 square neighborhood with the value of the center pixel and considering the result as a binary number. Later the operator was extended to use circular symmetric neighborhoods [12], that allowed considering any radius and number of pixels in the neighborhood, see Fig. 1. Given a central pixel x_c and its p neighbors x_n, the decimal form of the resulting LBP code can be expressed as:

$$LBP_{p,r} = \sum_{n=0}^{p-1} s\left(x_n - x_c\right) 2^n, \quad s\left(x\right) = \begin{cases} 0 \,, x < 0 \\ 1 \,, x \geq 0 \end{cases} \tag{1}$$

Later, Ojala et al. extended the original LBP operator to use the so-called uniform patterns [12]. The number of bitwise transitions, when the binary string is circular, gives a uniformity measure U of the pattern as follows:

$$U\left(LBP_{p,r}\right) = \sum_{n=0}^{p-1} \left| s\left(x_{r,n} - x_{0,0}\right) - s\left(x_{r,mod(n+1,p)} - x_{0,0}\right) \right| \tag{2}$$

The LBP operator is called uniform if its uniformity measure is at most 2. The notation $LBP_{p,r}^{u2}$ is used for the operator where the superscript $u2$ denotes the uniform patterns which have U values at most 2. Uniform LBP mapping gives a separate output label for each uniform pattern and all the non-uniform patterns are assigned to a single label. The uniform mapping results in $p(p-1)+3$ different output labels, leading to a much shorter histogram representation.

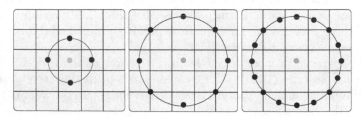

Fig. 1. The circular (4,1), (8,2) and (16,2) neighborhoods

2.2   The Angular Difference LBP (AD-LBP)

The AD-LBP descriptor uses the angular difference instead of intensity differences between the specified pixel and its neighbors, in order to have higher stability in flat image regions. Given the gray values of pairs of pixels $x_{r,n}$ and $x_{r,mod(n+\delta,p)}$, with a certain angular displacement $\delta(\frac{2\pi}{p})$, the angular difference is defined as $\Delta_{\delta,n}^{Ang} = x_{r,n} - x_{r,mod(n+\delta,p)}$, where δ is an integer such that $1 \leq \delta \leq \frac{p}{2}$. Therefore, the AD-LBP is computed as follows, see Fig. 2:

$$AD - LBP_{p,r} = \sum_{n=0}^{p-1} s\left(\Delta_{\delta,n}^{Ang}\right) 2^n, \quad s\left(x\right) = \begin{cases} 0, & x < \varepsilon \\ 1, & x \geq \varepsilon \end{cases} \qquad (3)$$

In order to increase the operator's robustness in flat areas, the differences are thresholded at a non-zero threshold value ε, that is 1% of the pixel value range. For the experiments of this paper, we set $\varepsilon = 0.01$.

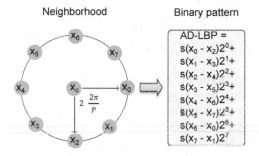

Fig. 2. Description of the AD-LBP operator with $\delta = 2$

3   Dominant LBP Considering Pattern Type (LBP)

3.1   Related Works and Motivation

Although the LBP approach is attractive for its invariance against monotonic gray level changes and its computational simplicity, the original LBP comes with disadvantages and limitations. For example, the LBP operator produces long histograms, and it can become intractable to estimate histograms due to the overwhelming dimensionality of it with large p. Also, it is demonstrated that LBP is very sensitive to noise [10].

Using uniform LBP patterns, instead of all the possible patterns has produced better recognition results in many applications. On one hand, there are indications that uniform patterns are less prone to noise, and on the other hand, the uniform mapping makes the number of possible LBP labels considerably lower and reliable estimation of their distribution requires fewer samples. Additionally, uniform LBPs detect local primitives such as spots, flat areas, edges and edge ends, which represent the majority among all LBP types [12].

However, in practice, there are some textures images have more complicated shapes and edge types. Then the uniform LBPs are not necessary to occupy the major type proportions. Also, uniform patterns will have a much smaller proportion among all LBP types, as the radius and the number of neighbors increase. Therefore, textural information cannot be effectively captured using only the uniform LBPs [4,9].

Liao et al. [9] extended the conventional LBP approach to the dominant LBP (DLBP)which make use of the most frequently occurred patterns of LBP to improve the recognition accuracy compared to the original uniform patterns.The DLBP approach considers only the pattern occurrence frequencies, regardless the information related to the dominant pattern type.

Next, Guo et al. introduced a learning framework for image descriptor design, overcomes the drawbacks of uniform LBP [4]. Considering the intra-class similarity and inter- class distance, the most reliable and robust dominant pattern types are learnt based on the Fisher separation criterion (FSC).Thus, image structures are described by the FSC-based learning (FBL) encoding method. In their experiments, FBL-LBP outperformed many other methods, including DLBP [9].

However, in some situations (e.g., large illumination variations), samples of the same class in the database may have high intra-class variations. Accordingly, the aforementioned methods suffer in terms of reliability and robustness. In case of FBL-LBP, global dominant pattern sets are constructed for each dominant region independently. For some regions the Fisher separation criterion is too hard to be applicable, as features vary greatly among samples for those regions. Thus there are no common features to be considered in the intra class similarity space, which represent those regions for some classes. In other words, some classes are not represented in the extra class similarity space. Therefore, the optimum discrimination among data cannot be guaranteed. On the other hand, neglecting the dominant pattern type, in case of DLBP [9], could probably weaken the discriminative ability under hard illumination conditions.

This motivated us to present our dominant approach for LBP considering the pattern type. The proposed approach proceeds as follows: Divide each image from the training set into m overlapping regions, and determine the most reliable dominant types for each region. Then, all the learned dominant types of each region are merged and form the global dominant types for the whole database. In this paper, we chose to apply the proposed approach on LBP and AD-LBP. The proposed approach includes two phases; learning phase and feature extraction phase as given in the following subsections.

3.2   The Learning Phase

Given a training image set of different classes, divide each image of the training set into m regions. To learn the most reliable and robust dominant pattern types for each region, initialize a record vector of 2^p entries to 0. For each region, compute the occurrence frequencies of all patterns, and then sort them in descending order. The first k most frequently occurring pattern types are sought, for each region, and the corresponding elements of the record vector are increased by 1. After all, sort the record vector of each region, and then the first k elements of each record vector are connected to be the overall dominant types for the whole database. The learning phase is described in (**Algorithm 1**).

Algorithm 1. Determininghe Dominant Pattern Types

Input: I: a training image set, m: number of regions, k: dominant number
      per regions, p: number of neighbor pixels, and r: radius
Output: Dom$_s$et: The dominant pattern types set

1. **Initialize** a reference pattern type record vector $domV_j[i] = i$, $i = 0, ..., 2^p - 1$, $j = 1, ..., m$.
2. **Initialize** pattern histogram $domH_j[0...(2^p - 1)] = 0$, $j = 1, ...m$
3. **FOR** each image I in the training image set
   (a) **Divide** the image into m overlapping regions
   (b) **FOR** $j = 0$ to $m - 1$
       i. **Initialize** the pattern histogram $H[0...(2^p - 1)] = 0$
       ii. *Initialize* a reference pattern type record vector V where $V[i] = i$, $i = 0, ..., 2^p - 1$
       iii. **FOR** each center pixel $t_c \in I$
           A. **Compute** the pattern label of t_c, l
           B. **Increase** the corresponding bin by 1, $H[l] + +$
           END FOR
       iv. **Sort** the histogram H in a descending order, Change the configuration of V according to the element switching order of H. Now the top h entries of H denote the occurrence frequencies of the top h most dominant patterns.
       v. **FOR** $i = 0$ to $k - 1$
           A. $domH_j[V[i]] + +$
           END FOR
       END FOR
   END FOR
4. **FOR** $j = 0$ to $m - 1$
   (a) **Sort** the histogram $domH_j$ in descending order. Change the configuration of doV_j according to the element switching order of $domH_j$ $dom\_set_j = \{domV_j[0], ..., domV_j[k - 1]\}$
5. **Return** $Dom\_set = \{dom\_set_0, ..., dom\_set_{m-1}\}$

3.3 Feature Extracting Phase

For a training, or testing, image and given the global dominant pattern types set obtained in the learning phase, extract occurrence histogram of pattern types of the features of this image. The feature vector for each image will not only encode the occurrence frequency of each dominant pattern type as in DLBP method [9], but also consider the pattern type information, which is the complementary discriminative information. This makes the proposed feature vectors more powerful in classification. The feature extraction phase is described in (**Algorithm 2**).

Algorithm 2.   Extracting the feature vector

Input: I: a training image set, m: number of regions, k: dominant number
        per regions, Dom_set: the dominant LBP set obtained by Algorithm 1,
        p: number of neighbor pixels, and r: radius
Output: The feature vector corresponding to image I

1. **FOR** $j = 0$ to $m - 1$
    (a) **Initialize** the pattern histogram, $H[0...(2^p - 1] = 0$
    (b) **FOR** each center pixel $t_c \in I$
        i. **Compute** the pattern label of t_c, l
        ii. **Increase** the corresponding bin by 1, $H[l] + +$
        END **FOR**
    END **FOR**
2. **Return** $H[Dom\_set_0[0], ..., Dom\_set0[k-1]...Dom\_setm - 1[0], ..., Dom\_set_{m-1}[k-1]]$ as the feature vector

---

4   Experiments and Results

4.1   Experiments Setting

We demonstrate the performance of the proposed approach in face identification using two databases; the Extended Yale Face Database B [8] and the CMU-PIE Face Database [14]. The Extended Yale B database, used in this paper, includes 28 subjects under 9 poses × 60 illumination conditions. Half of the illumination conditions are devoted for training phase, i.e. $(28 \times 9 \times 30 = 7560)$ and the other half is devoted for testing phase, as well.The testing images are divided into 5 subsets; each includes 6 illumination conditions, according to severity of illumination conditions from moderate to extreme luminance. Fig. 3 shows samples of the extended Yale B face database. A subset of the CMU-PIE database containing frontal, right-left twist and up-down tilt images of 67 subjects under 21 illumination condition(7035 in total), is used and 2 fold cross validation is performed in experiment using this database.

Images are manually cropped and resized into 48×48 pixels. We set $r = 1$ and $p = 8$, and divide each image into 3 × 3 overlapping regions. The dominant type set is determined for each database by applying **Algorithm 1** on both the LBP and AD-LBP operators. Then, a feature vector for each test image is extracted using **Algorithm 2**. The support vector machine (SVM) is used as a classifier. The multi-class face identification problem is reduced into multiple two-class problems (i.e.,$28 \times (28 - 1)$, $67 \times (67 - 1)$) using one-versus-one approach and classification is done by a max-wins voting strategy.

Fig. 3. Samples of the extended Yale B face database from moderate up to sever illumination

4.2   Experimental Results

We proceed now to the evaluation phase of the proposed approach. Toward a fair evaluation, we conduct a comparison among the proposed approach, the traditional uniform approach [12], and the other dominant approaches [9] and [4] in face identification. Fig. 4(a) shows the comparison among the four approaches with the LBP descriptor, whereas Fig.4(b) shows the comparison among the four approaches with the ADLBP descriptor using the Extended Yale B database.

As a first observation, the performance of the proposed approach with AD-LBP descriptor is better than that with LBP descriptor. Thus, applying our approach with AD-LBP instead of using uniform patterns has improved its performance given originally in [10]. Also, it is clear that the proposed approach outperforms the other three approaches either with the LBP descriptor or the AD-LBP descriptor. In addition, we can observe that the performance of both the uniform pattern approaches (LBP^{u2} and $AD-LBP^{u2}$) and the other dominant approach (DLBP and DAD-LBP) is degraded with illumination, especially, with severe illumination conditions (subset 2 - subset 5).

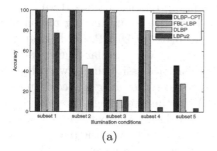

(a)

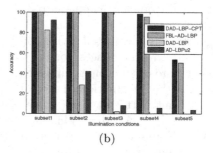

(b)

Fig. 4. Face identification rates for(a) LBP (b) AD-LBP descriptors

Table 1. Face identification rates for LBP operator using the CMU-PIE

(p,r)	$DLBP - CPT$	$FBL - LBP$	$DLBP$	LBP^{u2}
(8,1)	93.24%	76.36%	32.64%	45.74%
(8,2)	94.35%	65.91%	51.63%	45.49%

Table 2. Face identification rates for AD-LBP operator using the CMU-PIE

(p,r)	$DAD - LBP - CPT$	$FBL - AD - LBP$	$DAD - LBP$	$AD - LBP^{u2}$
(8,1)	96.52%	82.89%	19.67%	16.14%
(8,2)	96.35%	78.19%	20.87%	28.24%

In contrast, the proposed approach and the FBL approach (FBL-LBP and FBL-ADLBP) show a similar performance in case of moderate illumination conditions (subset 1- subset 2), whereas their performance starts to degrade gradually with severe illumination (subset 3 subset 5) with clear superiority for our approach over the FBL approach in these hard luminance conditions.

The expremintal results using the CMU-PIE database, again demonstrate the superiority of the proposed approach over the other approaches with both the LBP (see Table 1) and AD-LBP (see Table 2) operators.

5 Discussion and Conclusion

In the overall comparison with DLBP, FBL-LBP and uniform LBP, the proposed DLBP-CPT descriptor provides better performance in face identification task. It is clear that the pattern type has an important role in the discrimination process. For example, the DLBP [9] approach takes into account only the pattern occurrence information, and neglects the pattern type information. This affects the discriminative power and robustness of DLBP against hard illumination conditions.

To assure this conclusion, Fig. 5 shows two samples of two different subjects, where we divide each sample into 3×3 overlapping regions. The pattern occurrences of, for example, the first 11 DLBP patterns are computed per region per image. As it is illustrated in Fig. 6(a) and Fig. 6(b) for DLBP, the histograms of the pattern occurrences, for the two subjects, are very similar to each other. In other words, it becomes difficult to distinguish or classify these two subjects using only the information of the pattern occurrences. However, the corresponding dominant pattern types (x-axis in Fig. 6) for the two images are obviously different from each other. This means that, considering the pattern types, certainly, will enhance the classification task. Indeed, considering the pattern types gives our approach extra discriminative ability as it is illustrated in Fig. 7(a) and Fig 7(b).

On the other hand, however the FBL-LBP descriptor considers the dominant pattern type as complementary discriminative information, which gives it

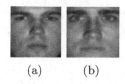

(a)   (b)

Fig. 5. Two faces of two different subjects

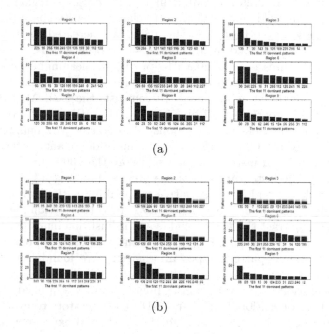

(a)

(b)

Fig. 6. The pattern occurrences of the first 11 dominant patterns of each region produced by DLBP (a) for Fig. 5(a) and (b) for Fig. 5(b)

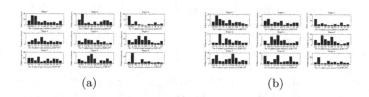

(a)   (b)

Fig. 7. The dominant pattern occurrences of each region produced by DLBP-CPT (a) for Fig. 5(a) and (b) for Fig. 5(b)

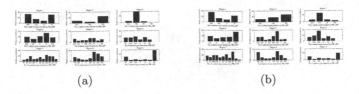

(a)   (b)

Fig. 8. The dominant pattern occurrences of each region produced by FBL-LBP (a) for Fig. 5(a) and (b) for Fig. 5(b)

superiority over the DLBP, the Fisher separation criterion may decrease its discriminative ability. As it is illustrated in Fig. 8, for some regions, the Fisher separation criterion yields inadequate extra class similarity space that does not represent all classes, even though in this paper we increased the threshold into 95% instead of 90% described by authors in [4]. In other words, this small number of selected features is inadequate to provide a meaningful description for this number of classes. Therefore, the optimum discrimination status among the input data cannot be guaranteed. In contrast, the FBL-AD-LBP descriptor produces long histograms (215 bins), as the AD-LBP operator demonstrates robustness against illumination variations. Moreover, as the number of classes increases in case of the CMU-PIE database, more dominant pattern types are selected, producing long histograms as well (more than 300 bins for FBL-LBP). On the contrary, the histogram size of the proposed approach is independent of the number of classes and is less sensitive to the illumination variations.

In conclusion, this paper introduced a novel feature selection method DLBP-CPT, capable to extract the most reliable and robust dominant patterns in face image. In contrast to the DLBP approach, the proposed approach takes into account the dominant pattern types information. We found that the pattern type represents essential information that should be included, especially, in face image representation across variation of illumination. We applied the proposed approach on the conventional LBP and AD-LBP operators to evaluate its discriminative power. It is shown through the conducted experiments, using the Extended Yale B and the CMU-PIE databases, that the proposed approach is more reliable to represent the dominating pattern information in the facial images than the conventional uniform LBP and other dominant approaches. Moreover, it is shown that applying the proposed operator with the AD-LBP operator, is more adequate than using the conventional uniform pattern approach, and has increased the its performance significantly.

References

1. Abate, A.F., Nappi, M., Riccio, D., Sabatino, G.: 2d and 3d face recognition: A survey. Pattern Recognition Letters **28**(14), 1885–1906 (2007)
2. Ahonen, T., Hadid, A., Pietikäinen, M.: Face recognition with local binary patterns. In: Pajdla, T., Matas, J.G. (eds.) ECCV 2004. LNCS, vol. 3021, pp. 469–481. Springer, Heidelberg (2004)

3. Delac, K., Grgic, M., Bartlett, M.S.: Recent advances in face recognition. Tech Publication, Crosia (2008)
4. Guo, Y., Zhao, G., Pietikäinen, M., Xu, Z.: Descriptor learning based on fisher separation criterion for texture classification. In: Kimmel, R., Klette, R., Sugimoto, A. (eds.) ACCV 2010, Part III. LNCS, vol. 6494, pp. 185–198. Springer, Heidelberg (2011)
5. Hadid, A., Pietikainen, M., Ahonen, T.: A discriminative feature space for detecting and recognizing faces. In: Proceedings of the 2004 IEEE Computer Society Conference on Computer Vision and Pattern Recognition, CVPR 2004, vol. 2, p. II–797. IEEE (2004)
6. Jain, A.K., Li, S.Z.: Handbook of face recognition, vol. 1. Springer (2005)
7. Jun, B., Kim, D.: Robust face detection using local gradient patterns and evidence accumulation. Pattern Recognition 45(9), 3304–3316 (2012)
8. Lee, K.C., Ho, J., Kriegman, D.J.: Acquiring linear subspaces for face recognition under variable lighting. IEEE Transactions on Pattern Analysis and Machine Intelligence 27(5), 684–698 (2005)
9. Liao, S., Law, M.W., Chung, A.C.: Dominant local binary patterns for texture classification. IEEE Transactions on Image Processing 18(5), 1107–1118 (2009)
10. Liu, L., Zhao, L., Long, Y., Kuang, G., Fieguth, P.: Extended local binary patterns for texture classification. Image and Vision Computing 30(2), 86–99 (2012)
11. Ojala, T., Pietikäinen, M., Harwood, D.: A comparative study of texture measures with classification based on featured distributions. Pattern Recognition 29(1), 51–59 (1996)
12. Ojala, T., Pietikainen, M., Maenpaa, T.: Multiresolution gray-scale and rotation invariant texture classification with local binary patterns. IEEE Transactions on Pattern Analysis and Machine Intelligence 24(7), 971–987 (2002)
13. Shan, C., Gong, S., McOwan, P.W.: Facial expression recognition based on local binary patterns: A comprehensive study. Image and Vision Computing 27(6), 803–816 (2009)
14. Sim, T., Baker, S., Bsat, M.: The cmu pose, illumination, and expression (pie) database. In: Proceedings of the Fifth IEEE International Conference on Automatic Face and Gesture Recognition, pp. 46–51. IEEE (2002)

Improving High Resolution Satellite Images Retrieval Using Color Component Features

Houria Sebai and Assia Kourgli[(✉)]

USTHB, Faculté D'Electronique Et D'Informatique, LTIR,
B.P.32, 16111 El-alia, Bab-ezzouar, Algeria
assiakourgli@gmail.com

Abstract. This paper highlights multi-scale color component features that improve high resolution satellite images retrieval. Color component correlation across image lines and columns is used to define a revised color space. It is designed to take simultaneously both color and neighborhood information. From this new space, color descriptors namely RIULBP (Rotation Invariant Uniform Local Binary Pattern), LV (Local Variance) and a modified version of LV (smoothed LV) are derived through Dual Tree complex wavelet transform (DT-CWT) or scale-invariant features transform (SIFT) representations. The features obtained offer an efficient way to represent both color and texture/structure information. We report an evaluation of the proposed descriptors according to different similarity distances in our CBIR (Content-based image retrieval) schemes. We, also, perform comparison with recent approaches. Experimental results show that color LV descriptor combined to SIFT representation outperforms the other approaches.

Keywords: CBIR · DT-CWT · SIFT · LBP · Opponent color · SLV

1 Introduction

The interest in fast and accurate information retrieval systems over collections of remote sensing images is increasing as the volume of the available data grows exponentially creating new challenges in different fields including processing, archiving and retrieval. Given its importance, this problem received a lot of attention in the literature. Many approaches have been proposed to retrieve low and mid-satellite images using their content such as region level semantic features mining [1], Knowledge-driven information mining (KIM) [2], texture model [3], entropy-balanced bitmap (EBB) tree [4]. High resolution satellite retrieval schemes use different features according to color (spectral) features [5], texture features [6] [7] [9], structure features [5] [9]. However, the performance of most techniques is limited by the semantic gap between low level features and high level concepts. To reduce this gap, we explore the idea of color images encoding using relevant features according to texture and structure information to describe the images contents. Usually a color component descriptor is obtained through

© Springer International Publishing Switzerland 2015
V. Murino and E. Puppo (Eds.): ICIAP 2015, Part II, LNCS 9280, pp. 264–275, 2015.
DOI: 10.1007/978-3-319-23234-8_25

the concatenation of the descriptors derived from component images in an oppo-nent color space [10] [9]. Our approach is different, we use color component cor-relation across image lines and columns to define multiscale descriptors using a proposed measure named SLV (Smoothed Local Variance). These descriptors permit to encode simultaneously local texture/shape information according to three different color plans. To assess the efficiency of these descriptors, a com-parison is made according to other color spaces usually used when dealing with satellite images retrieval. To take into account high resolution satellite images nature, two kind of multiscale approaches are considered. The former is based on DT-CWT representation that possesses a good directional selectivity for feature representation while the latter employs SIFT features that are well known for their efficiency for images retrieval. According to different similarity measures, the retrieval performances of the feature vectors obtained are compared to those reached by other studies showing that the descriptors LV and SLV computed on the color space derived permit to get more efficient retrieval schemes. Con-sequently, the paper is organized as follows : Section 2 introduces the different color component descriptors tested. Our CBIR scheme based on color component features and used through DT-CWT is presented also in this section. Section 3 introduces our bag of visual words model based on the combination of SIFT and our opponent color features. Section 4 presents the experimental results and discussions. Conclusions and future orientations constitute section 5.

2   Multiscale Opponent Color Descriptors

New descriptors obtained by combining color and texture (or shape) according to DT-CWT (or SIFT) representation are introduced. Both texture/structure and shape features such as LBP [11], HOG [12], Grey Level Co-occurrence Matrices, etc. are usually computed on each color channel separately. The features result-ing are then concatenated to constitute one single vector feature. We extended the idea of Banerji et al. [13] to derive color component features that consider simultaneously color and texture information.

2.1   Opponent Cross-Correlation

Several opponent color spaces have been proposed and used for color represen-tation based on the perceptual concepts. For high resolution satellite images retrieval, an appropriate space must be based on an intuitive combination of image characteristics (color and context). We referred to a recent work of Banerji et al [13] who suggested to define three new color plans by applying perpendic-ular encoding using the RGB color space. The first color image is the RGB_1, while the second color image RGB_2 encodes the rows across the red, green, and blue. The last image RGB_3 is obtained through columns encoding across the red, green and blue channels (more details can be found in [13]). Unlike classical color spaces that produce the same number of output images, Banerji's encoding scheme multiplies by three its outputs. This fact is prohibitive as it will induce feature vectors that would be three times larger and thus a retrieval process taking three times more. To overcome this problem, a data reduction has been considered. It is based on an adaptive grayscale transformation that is used on each color plan to produce three new images. It is a kind of adaptive luminance transformation that lets the weights in the averaging process be dependent on the actual image to be convert,.i.e., be adaptive.

$$AL_i = R_i * \frac{\sqrt{\sum R_i{}^2}}{\sum R_i{}^2 + \sum G_i{}^2 + \sum B_i{}^2} + G_i * \frac{\sqrt{\sum G_i{}^2}}{\sqrt{\sum R_i{}^2 + \sum G_i{}^2 + \sum B_i{}^2}} + B_i * \frac{\sqrt{\sum B_i{}^2}}{\sqrt{\sum R_i{}^2 + \sum G_i{}^2 + \sum B_i{}^2}}$$

(1)

where i=1,2,3.

The new space obtained through the combination of cross-correlation and adaptive luminance transformation is named cross adaptive luminance (CAL). The performances of colors descriptors derived from CAL space are compared to those [13] [10] achieved using other popular color spaces used for images retrieval.

2.2   Color Features

Feature extraction is the basis of content-based image retrieval. Extraction of color feature is carried out by computing a visual feature on color images. Because of our image nature, some invariant rotation and translation features are required to characterize spatial color distribution and thus integrate structure information. To this aim, a modified version of local variance is suggested and compared to LBP variants. However, the color feature vector dimensions of typical color feature descriptors are quite large resulting in high computational cost in distance calculation for similarity retrieval. As a solution, we suggest to compute some uncorrelated statistical moments namely mean, kustosis, L1 and the quadratic mean instead of histograms to get a compact representation. The aforementioned color features are described below.

LBP The original LBP operator is defined in a rectangular $3*3$ neighborhood. It operates with eight neighboring pixels using the center as a threshold. The final LBP code is then produced by multiplying the threshold values by weights given by powers of two and adding the results. The authors [11] gave an improved uniform gray-scale and rotation invariance operator defined as:

$$LBP_{P,R}^{riu2} = \begin{cases} \sum_{i=0}^{P-1} s(g_i - g_c) & U \leq 2 \\ P+1 & otherwise \end{cases}$$

(2)

the $LBP_{P,R}^{riu2}$ operator outputs are accumulated into a histogram of $P+2$ bins. By changing P and R, the LBP code of diverse radius and neighborhood is computed to obtain texture features. LBP images obtained are decomposed using DT-CWT and statistical moments are computed using the sub-images resulting.

LV and SLV Measures of local variance have been widely used in image processing for texture and spatial image structure measures. As, this parameter is invariant to illumination changes, we suggest to compute the average value of local variances (LV) estimated around each pixel according to our color space. The LV computed in this manner will constitute a rotation invariant feature that permits to identify localized color distributions of each color plan. Nevertheless, it is sensitive to outlier as a single pixel with a different color will induce a significant increase of LV value. To surmount this shortcoming, we propose to compute the LV on a smoothed neighborhood. Smoothing is obtained through the use of edge preserving smoothing filters (EPSF) [15] [14]. Instead of processing filtering on each neighborhood, the whole image is filtered. Then, the LV is computed to produce a smoothed local variance (SLV), by this way, local image outliers are discarded.

2.3   Feature Extraction

In our CBIR system dedicated to HRS images, a muli-scale representation of color features descriptors is used to better reflect the objects of different sizes and shapes present in HRS images. Multiresolution DT-CWT technique [16] is adopted since it allows analysis that is localized in both space and frequency. It calculates the complex transform of a signal using two separate DWT decompositions (two trees). The prime motivation for introducing the dual-tree complex wavelet was shift invariance. DT-CWT [16] is able to discriminate between positive and negative orientation of the diagonal sub-bands. The horizontal and vertical sub-bands are divided giving six distinct sub-bands in each scale at orientations $\pm15°$, $\pm45°$, $\pm75°$. DWT have three sub-bands in $0°$, $45°$, $90°$ only but DT-CWT having six sub-bands in $\pm15°$, $\pm45°$ and $\pm75°$, for this reason DT-CWT improves the directional selectivity.

Statistical moments on DT-CWT decomposed subimages obtained either from LBP or LV are computed. For both features, different moments are tested to retain only the less correlated: For the LL block we kept the mean, kurtosis and Root Mean Square (RMS). While for the details, the standard L1 also called mean deviation MDni is calculated.

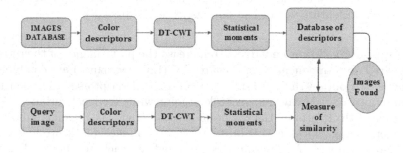

Fig. 1. CBIR schema

3 Bag of Visual Words Model

Bag of visual words is a vector of occurrence counts of a vocabulary of local image features. Representing an image using bag of visual words includes usually the following steps: Extract features, learn visual vocabulary, quantize features using visual vocabulary, represent images by frequencies of visual words. Feature representation methods deal with how to represent images as a collection of local properties calculated from a set of small sub-images named patches. These vectors are called features descriptors. One of the most famous descriptors is the Scale Invariant Feature Transform (SIFT) [17]. The final step for the BOW is to generate the code words (Word dictionary). The idea is to cluster the features descriptors of all patches based on given cluster number using K-means clustering. Codewords are then defined as the center of the learned clusters. The number of the clusters is the codebook size. Thus, each image can be represented by frequencies of visual words.

3.1 Features Extraction

SIFT. Scale invariant feature transform (SIFT) developed by David Lowe [17] to detect and describe local features in images is invariant to uniform scaling, orientation and partially invariant to affine distortion and illumination changes. To calculate SIFT feature vectors internal representation of the original image is created to ensure scale invariance. This is done by generating scale Space. Then, locations and scales of key points that are initially selected from local extrema in Difference of Gaussian (DoG) are determined. Each point needs to be compared with 8 neighboring pixels in the same scale and 18 neighboring pixels around the corresponding position of adjacent scales. The last step is to determine the orientation of key point using the direction of gradient of its neighboring pixels to assure the rotation invariance. Thus, each key point has three parameters: location, scale and orientation.

The SIFT descriptor is extracted from image patches around the interest point. To assure the rotation invariance, a key point rotation is made. Lowe suggests to describe each key point using 4x4 seed points to increase the stability of matching. The feature descriptor consists of histograms of gradient directions computed over a 4x4 spatial grid. The gradient directions are quantized into 8 bins so the final feature vector has dimension of 128 (4x4x8).

SIFT-Opponent Color Feature. To increase the performance of the retrieval system, SIFT and opponent color features LV (Local variance) are combined in our scheme. To obtain the SIFT-LV or SIFT-LBP descriptors, 128-dimensional SIFT descriptor is calculated for each key point while for local variance(LV) or LBP, region of 16x16 around the key point is considered. The region is subdivided into 9 overlapping blocks and 9 bins histograms of each block are calculated. Thus, 81-dimensional LV descriptor is obtained for each key point. The next step is to build a code books for SIFT descriptors and another one for LV

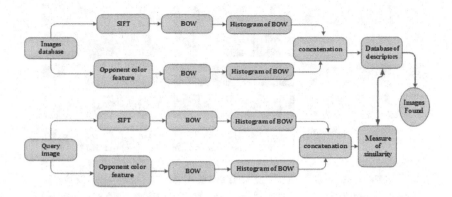

Fig. 2. CBIR schema using bag of visual words

descriptors. To consider both color and context information, LV is applied to CAL (cross adaptive luminance) images.

To evaluate the CBIR system proposed (Fig.2), other descriptors are tested. Following the CBIR scheme based on DT-CWT, different distance measures are also tested and compared.

4   Results and Discussions

The dataset [6] consists of images belonging to 21 categories: agricultural, airplane, baseball diamond, beach, buildings, chaparral, dense residential, forest, freeway, golf course, harbor, intersection, medium density residential, mobile home park, overpass, parking lot, river, runway, sparse residential, storage tanks, and tennis courts. Each category is composed of 100 samples (see Fig.3).

In a query by example scheme, we are interested in retrieving several similar images and this requires comparing two descriptors to obtain a measure of similarity (or dissimilarity) between the two image patterns. Some common similarity measures (Table 1) are tested and their performances are compared.

Table 1. Common Similarity measures

Manhattan distance(L1)	Euclidean distance(L2)	Khi square	Canberra distance
$\sum_{i=1}^{n} \lvert x_i - y_i \rvert$	$\sqrt{\sum_{i=1}^{n} (x_i - y_i)^2}$	$\sqrt{\sum_{i=1}^{n} \frac{(x_i - y_i)^2}{(x_i + y_i)}}$	$\sum_{i=1}^{n} \frac{\lvert x_i - y_i \rvert}{\lvert x_i + y_i \rvert}$

CBIR performance is measured by precision and recall.
Precision P as well as average precision and $\overline{P}$ are given as:

$$P = \frac{\text{Number of relevant images retrieval}}{\text{Total number of images retrieval}}, \overline{P} = \frac{1}{N_q} \sum_{k=1}^{N_q} P(k) \qquad (3)$$

Where Nq represents the number of queries.

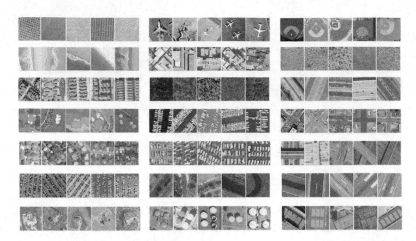

Fig. 3. Image patches of the 21 land-use/land-cover classes

Similarly recall R and average recall $\overline{R}$ are given as:

$$R = \frac{\text{Number of relevant images retrieval}}{\text{Total number of relevant images}}, \overline{R} = \frac{1}{N_q} \sum_{k=1}^{N_q} R(k) \qquad (4)$$

To evaluate the performance of the proposed CBIR scheme, many tests were conducted. They aim, among others, to determine the best color space and the most appropriate measure of similarity for satellite images indexing using color descriptors as well as the best approach. We began by comparing the color descriptors derived from the DT-CWT sub-images considering the different color spaces previously presented. According to the paper of Shao et al [9], eight LULC classes are used in our experiments. These are agricultural, airplane, beach, buildings, chaparral, dense residential, forest, and harbor. Table 2 illustrates the overall recognition rate obtained for different precision values using the similarity measure of Canberra. The choice of the latter is motivated by the fact that Canberra distance is biased for measures around the origin and very sensitive for values close to zero. Thus, it is well suited for data scattered around an origin as it is the case for details images obtained from DT-CWT decomposition. The overall average precision obtained on whole images shows that the reduction of space that we offer through the calculation of the adaptive luminance allows us to have the benefit of the same performance (65.63 % instead of 65.73 %) using three times less images.

To know whether the distance of Canberra is the most suitable for our descriptors, we considered the use of other similarity measures while considering different color spaces. Average precision values are summarized in Table 3. In all cases, the measurement of Canberra outperforms other measures.

In order to increase the performance of the CBIR system, we combined our colors features derived from CAL space with colors descriptors resulting from RIULBP(uniform invariant LBP), LV (Local variance), SLV (Smoothed Local

Table 2. Precision values using DT-CWT applied to different spaces

	P% (N=10)	P% (N=20)	P% (N=30)	P% (N=40)	P% (N=50)	P% (N=60)	P% (N=70)	P% (N=80)	P% (N=90)	P% (N=100)	Average
RGB	85.88	77.35	71.73	67.31	63.73	60.48	57.60	54.90	52.30	49.81	64.11
opp [10]	84.97	73.85	65.53	59.59	54.49	50.39	47.13	44.27	42.03	40.15	56.24
opp[13]	87	78.93	73.02	68.63	65.19	62.21	59.53	56.9	54.24	51.69	65.73
CAL (proposed)	86.08	78.1	72.34	68.37	65.23	62.41	59.73	57.19	54.66	52.19	65.63

Table 3. Average precision using different distance measures

	Euclidean	Manhattan	Khi-square	Canberra
RGB	55.78	62.76	63.95	**64.11**
opp[13]	53.99	61.13	64.31	**65.73**
opp [10]	49.19	54.32	55.99	**56.24**
CAL	52.60	62.10	63.04	**65.63**

Variance). To obtain the feature SLV, smoothing is applied using anisotropic filter. Analysis of Table 4 highlights the fact that the parameters tested namely RIULBP and LV bring nothing (a gain of just 1%), while the proposed feature SLV can reach an average precision of almost 70%.

Table 4. Comparisons of precision values using RIULBP, LV and SLV with DT-CWT representation

	P% (N=10)	P% (N=20)	P% (N=30)	P% (N=40)	P% (N=50)	P% (N=60)	P% (N=70)	P% (N=80)	P% (N=90)	P% (N=100)	Average
CAL+RIULBP(CAL)	87.06	79.95	73.04	68.66	65.42	62.22	59.58	57.44	54.60	52.11	66.01
CAL + LV(CAL)	86.22	78.06	72.72	68.98	66.06	63.60	61.13	58.59	56.05	53.48	66.49
CAL+ SLV	87.38	80.3	75.59	71.00	69.45	67.14	65.06	62.90	60.48	57.72	**69.80**

Table 5. Comparisons of precision values using SIFT representation

	P% (N=10)	P% (N=20)	P% (N=30)	P% (N=40)	P% (N=50)	P% (N=60)	P% (N=70)	P% (N=80)	P% (N=90)	P% (N=100)	Average
SIFT	80.21	76.6	74.001	72.2	70.06	68.06	66.13	64.18	61.77	59.16	69.23
SIFT+ CAL	84.23	79.21	76.22	73.34	71.01	69.18	67.38	65.40	63.13	60.34	70.94
SIFT + ULBP(CAL)	83.01	78.75	75.8	73.57	71.88	70.15	68.65	67.14	65.19	62.43	71.65
SIFT+ SLV	85.1	80.93	78.27	76.37	74.52	72.64	70.71	68.67	66.26	63.36	73.68
SIFT + LV(CAL)	85.41	81.5	78.96	77.04	75.08	73.34	71.52	69.63	67.34	64.55	**74.44**

In order to evaluate our two CBIR schemes, average precision charts as well as precision-recall curves for the different features tested in [9] are compared with our descriptor SLV and reported in Fig.4 and 5. The charts indicate that our descriptors (CAL or CAL+SLV) yields to better results on all classes compared to the best feature CGOT proposed in ref [9]. Moreover, except for dense residential class, the combination CAL+ SLV performs better than CAL alone specially for highly textured classes i.e. agricultural and beach classes. Figure 5 depicts all the precision-recall curves corresponding to our descriptors (in solid lines) and those reported (in dashed lines) in ref [9]. It can be observed that our descriptors are more efficient. Indeed, as the correct returned images increase, precision decrease rapidly with the other techniques.

To further validate our CBIR scheme, we made a comparison with the results of Yang et al [6] using Local features based on SIFT representation (Figure 6), Gabor filter, color histogram and simple statistics on the whole database(2100

Table 6. Average precision using different measure using SIFT representation

	Canberra	Euclidean	Manhattan	Khi-square
SIFT	66.45	66.16	68.41	**69.23**
SIFT-CAL	66.45	67.61	66.44	**70.94**
SIFT-CAL(LV)	66.92	69.66	72.02	**74.44**

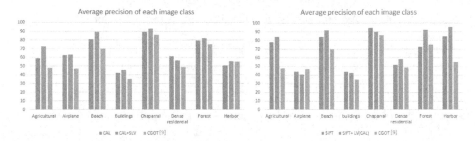

Fig. 4. Comparison of average precision for each image class for both DT-CWT and SIFT representations

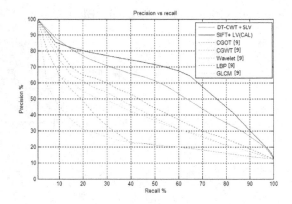

Fig. 5. Precision versus recall curves for the 8 classes

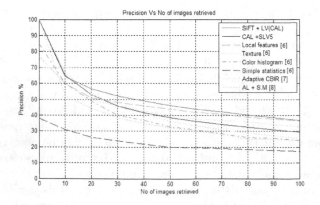

Fig. 6. Precision vs No of images retrieved for the 21 classes

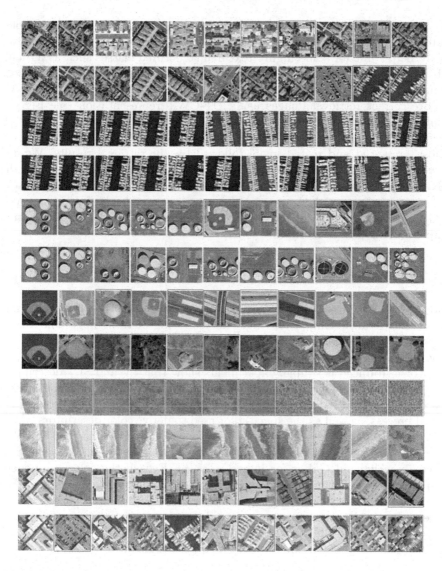

Fig. 7. Comparison of sample retrievals for different classes using local features [6] followed by ours results using SLV through DT-CWT: dense residential (72.22% [6], 63,63%), Harbor (100% [6], 100%), storage tanks (54.54% [6], 100%), baseball diamond (45.45% [6], 36.36%), beach (18.18%[6], 72.72%), building (63.63% [6], 45.45%)

images). We also made a comparison with two other studies. The first one based on 3D-LBP and HOG is adaptive [7] and the second one [8] compares different feature vectors such as statistical moments, Zernike moments, HOG, color histograms, LBP histograms extracted from wavelet decomposed images.

Considering all database images, average precisions have been computed obtaining 44.51% with local features based also on SIFT descriptors [6], 38.92%

using the Adaptive CBIR [7] and 47.01 % using our approach integrating color features. We should note that even if the CBIR scheme based on SIFT performs globally better but for some highly textured structured classes such as agricultural, beach and chaparral as well as for categories containing objects whose contours are curved such as airplane, baseball diamond and storage tanks we get more correct retrieval images using DT-CWT representation (see Fig. 4), specially in the first set of images found.

Fig. 7 gives some retrieval results obtained using local feature according to those presented and tested in [6] followed by our retrieval results. We can observe that storage tanks and beach classes are better recognized using the CBIR scheme based on DT-CWT representation. So, this second comparison, here, is in accordance with the previous comparisons, and both of them have validated the effectiveness and good performance of the proposed color descriptors to improve HRS images retrieval.

5   Conclusion

Rapid growth of remote sensed information generates a new research challenges in processing, transferring, archiving, and retrieving of these huge amounts of data. We introduced color component descriptors that are obtained through the creation of three new encoded color images. Even if the invariant to rotation color descriptor introduced is simple, experiments show that LV and SLV descriptors permit to enhance the retrieval performance of high resolution satellite images. We also quantitatively analyzed the effects of distance measures employed in the retrieval process, as well as the space color used to derive color descriptors. Comparison with other studies showed that the proposed features allied to DT-CWT and SIFT representations perform better than LBP, Grey Level co-occurrence matrices, wavelet and Gabor for image retrieval. Even if the color component descriptors perform better in all cases, for some categories, it is not sufficient. For those categories such as buildings, sparse residential and tennis-court, it would be interesting to define more appropriate descriptors taking into consideration their particularities (different shape and scale, surrounded by different classes, etc.). This should improve our CBIR system performances.

References

1. Liu, T., Zhang, L., Li, P., Lin, H.I.: Remotely sensed image retrieval based on region-level semantic mining. EURASIP Journal on Image and Video Processing, 1687–5281 (2012)
2. Daschiel, H., Pelizzar, A., Quartulli, M.: Information mining in remote sensing image archives: system concepts. IEEE Transactions on Geoscience and Remote Sensing 41, 2923–2936 (2003)
3. Aksoy, S., Yalniz, I.Z., Nick, J., Tasdemirl, K.: Automatic Detection and Segmentation of Orchards Using Very High-Resolution Imagery. IEEE Transactions on Geoscience and Remote Sensing 50, 3117–3131 (2012)

4. Scott, G., Klaric, M., Davis, C., Shyu, C.R.: Entropy-balanced bitmap tree for shape-based object retrieval from large-scale satellite imagery databases. IEEE Transactions on Geoscience and Remote Sensing **49**, 1603–1616 (2011)
5. Bao, Q., Guo, P.: Comparative studies on similarity measures for remote sensing image retrieval. In: IEEE International Conference on Systems, Man and Cybernetics, pp. 1112–1116 (2004)
6. Yang, Y., Newman, S.: Geographic image retrieval using local invariant features. IEEE Transactions on Geoscience and Remote Sensing, 818–832 (2012)
7. Sebai, H., Kourgli, A.: An adaptive CBIR system for remote sensed data. In: 12th International Workshop on Content-Based Multimedia Indexing (CBMI), Klagenfurt (2014)
8. Sebai, H., Kourgli, A.: A comparative study of feature vectors derived from wavelets applied to high resolution satellite images retrieval. In: 4th International Conference on Image Processing Theory, Tools and Applications (IPTA), Paris, France (2014)
9. Shao, Z., Zhou, W., Zhang, L., Hou, J.: Improved color texture descriptors for remote sensing image retrieval. Journal of Applied Remote Sensing (JRS) **8**(1) (2014)
10. Van de Sande, K., Gevers, T., Snoek, C.M.: Evaluating color descriptors for object and scene recognition. IEEE Transactions on Pattern Analysis and Machine Intelligence **32**(9), 1582–1596 (2010)
11. Ojala, T., Pietikainen, M., Maenpaa, T.: Multiresolution gray-scale and rotation invariant texture classification with local binary patterns. Trans. on Pattern analysis and Machine Intelligence **24**, 971 987 (2002)
12. Dala, N., Triggs, B.: Histograms of oriented gradients for human detection. In: Proceedings of the IEEE Computer Society Conference on Computer Vision and Pattern Recognition, vol. 1, pp. 886–893 (2005)
13. Banerji, S., Sinha, A., Liu, C.: New image descriptors based on color, texture, shape, and wavelets for object and scene image classification. Neurocomputing **117**, 173–185 (2013)
14. Perona, P., Malik, J.: Scale-space and edge detection using anisotropic diffusion. IEEE Transactions on Pattern Analysis and Machine Intelligence **12**(7), 629–639 (1990)
15. Tomasi, C., Manduchi, R.: Bilateral filtering for gray and color images. In: IEEE Sixth International Conference on computer Vision, pp. 839–846 (1998)
16. Kingsbury, N.G.: The dual-tree complex wavelet transform with improved orthogonality and symmetry properties. In: IEEE International Conference on Image Processing, pp. 375–378 (2000)
17. Lowe, D.G.: Object recognition from local scale-invariant features. In: ICCV, pp. 1150–1157 (1999)

The QCRI Recognition System
for Handwritten Arabic

Felix Stahlberg[(✉)] and Stephan Vogel

Qatar Computing Research Institute, HBKU, Doha, Qatar
{fstahlberg,svogel}@qf.org.qa
http://www.qcri.qa/

Abstract. This paper describes our recognition system for handwritten Arabic. We propose novel text line image normalization procedures and a new feature extraction method. Our recognition system is based on the Kaldi recognition toolkit which is widely used in automatic speech recognition (ASR) research. We show that the combination of sophisticated text image normalization and state-of-the art techniques originating from ASR results in a very robust and accurate recognizer. Our system outperforms the best systems in the literature by over 20% relative on the *abcde-s* configuration of the IFN/ENIT database and achieves comparable performance on other configurations. On the KHATT corpus, we report 11% relative improvement compared to the best system in the literature.

Keywords: Arabic · Handwriting recognition · Text image normalization

1 Introduction

Offline handwriting recognition (HWR) refers to the conversion of handwritings in a scanned image to machine-encoded text. State-of-the-art HWR systems are based on Hidden Markov Models (HMMs) which are statistical models for sequences of feature vectors. The order of the feature vectors within the sequence can represent temporal dependencies. For instance, in automatic speech recognition (ASR), the audio recording is often split into 10-15 ms chunks and a feature vector is extracted for each of these chunks [9] (Fig. 1(a)). In our work, the input for HWR are images of single text lines. Analogously to ASR, we split the image into chunks with three pixel width and extract a feature vector for each of these chunks. The sequential order of the extracted feature vectors is defined by the reading order of the script (e.g. right-to-left for Arabic in Fig. 1(b)).

Realizing the similarities between offline HWR and ASR, many groups apply tools initially develop for ASR to HWR tasks. The HTK Speech Recognition Toolkit [19] from the University of Cambridge is often used in HWR research. The RWTH Aachen University offers the optical character recognition software package *RWTH OCR* [17] which is based on their speech framework *RWTH ASR*.

© Springer International Publishing Switzerland 2015
V. Murino and E. Puppo (Eds.): ICIAP 2015, Part II, LNCS 9280, pp. 276–286, 2015.
DOI: 10.1007/978-3-319-23234-8_26

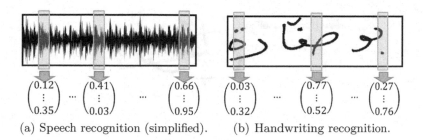

$$\begin{pmatrix} 0.12 \\ \vdots \\ 0.35 \end{pmatrix} \cdots \begin{pmatrix} 0.41 \\ \vdots \\ 0.03 \end{pmatrix} \cdots \begin{pmatrix} 0.66 \\ \vdots \\ 0.95 \end{pmatrix} \qquad \begin{pmatrix} 0.03 \\ \vdots \\ 0.32 \end{pmatrix} \cdots \begin{pmatrix} 0.77 \\ \vdots \\ 0.52 \end{pmatrix} \cdots \begin{pmatrix} 0.27 \\ \vdots \\ 0.76 \end{pmatrix}$$

(a) Speech recognition (simplified).   (b) Handwriting recognition.

Fig. 1. Feature extraction in speech recognition and handwriting recognition

The Kaldi speech recognition toolkit [15] is another project intended for use by speech recognition researchers.

In this paper, we describe the Arabic HWR system developed at the Qatar Computing Research Institute (QCRI) based on Kaldi. We adapted the training recipes in Kaldi to make them work with HWR. We show that training procedures and feature transforms popular for ASR are also applicable to HWR. Additionally, we use dedicated *connector* and *space* models as proposed in [1] to capture the distinction between connecting and non-connecting Arabic letters. We also integrated *glyph dependent model lengths* as described in [4] to address the varying complexity of characters. Both approaches are explained in Sec. 4.

The main focus of this paper, however, is the investigation of text line image normalization and feature extraction for Arabic. We demonstrate that the recognition performance can be improved by normalizing the text line image to cope with variations due to different writers and writing styles. We propose the following normalization procedure prior to the feature extraction:

1. The baseline of Arabic handwritings is often not horizontal. Longer text lines even feature curved or discontinuous baselines. This leads to characters translated along the vertical axis which obviously poses problems when using pixel gray values as features. In order to reduce these artefacts, we slice the line image vertically (i.e. along the horizontal axis) and estimate the baseline in each sub image. The slices are translated and rotated separately according the estimated baseline, and then concatenated to obtain an image with a rectified straight baseline at a predefined vertical position.
2. Even with a straight baseline, Arabic handwritings are often italic. The slant varies largely across script images. We estimate the slant of the text and apply a shear transform to remove artefacts due to this variation.
3. The resolution and the size of the letters differ among images. Therefore, we rescale the images to a fixed height while retaining the aspect ratio above the baseline.
4. The thickness of the lines is the last variation we address. The thickness varies due to different pens or the the previous rescaling operation. We apply a line thinning algorithm to obtain the script skeleton, and then increase the thickness to a normalized value with a dilate operation.

The proposed normalization steps lead to a very robust system which can cope with a wide variety of writing styles. We report 11.5% word error rate on

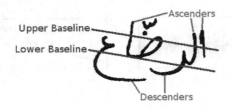

Fig. 2. Upper and lower baselines in Arabic script

the *abcde-s* configuration of the IFN/ENIT database [14] with a simple feature extraction method based on pixel grayscale intensity values. We thereby outperform the best system in the literature [1] by 23% relative. On the KHATT [11] corpus we achieve 11% relative improvement compared to the best system in the literature [8]. Additionally, we propose a novel segment-based approach to feature extraction which conveys enough information to fully recover the written script image from a sequence of low dimensional feature vectors (i.e. the original image is still reconstructible from the feature vector sequence). The resulting features are similar to *Autonomously Normalized Horizontal Differential Features* [6] but are more suitable for using them within the HMM paradigm. Segment-based features lead to comparable or better results in all configurations of the IFN/ENIT database compared to the respective state-of-the art systems of other researchers.

2   Text Line Image Normalization

2.1   Baseline Estimation

We describe our baseline estimation in [18]. Our method assumes that the zone between the lower and the upper baseline (core zone) usually includes a large fraction of all foreground pixels – i.e. is a dense foreground region in the image (Fig. 2). It is justified by the fact that ascenders and descenders usually contribute relatively little to all foreground pixels compared to the core zone. We search for the narrowest stripe in the image that contain a certain fraction of all foreground pixels. We detect the lower baseline at the bottom border of the stripe. Our method outperforms a previous method by 22.4% relative for the task of finding acceptable baselines in Tunisian town names in the IFN/ENIT database [14]. However, if the baseline is curved or discontinuous, our method fails since it tries to fit a straight dense stripe to the image. We propose in [18] to vertically split the image into smaller segments. Our splitting procedure ensures that we do not cut any foreground stroke (Fig. 3). We estimate the baseline for each of the segments separately and rotate/translate them such that the baseline is horizontal at a predefined height. Concatenating all segments results in a normalized image with a rectified straight and horizontal baseline. This procedure has proved effective on the KHATT database [11].

Fig. 3. Image of curved text lines into smaller segments

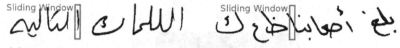

(a) Text features only slight slant.   (b) Text is heavily skewed to the left.

Fig. 4. Different slants in Arabic handwriting.

2.2 Slant Correction

Arabic handwriting is usually italic, i.e. the letters tend to tilt to the left or right instead of being perfectly aligned with the vertical axis. Fig. 4 shows two text images with different slants. The variation in slant heavily affects the feature vectors. For example, the Arabic letter *alif* ("أ") usually stands out from the surrounding letters due to its vertical orientation and its non-connecting characteristic. However, with a high degree of slant, the letter does not fit in a single sliding window and the resulting feature vector is fundamentally different. We reduce these artefacts by applying a shear transform with angle $-\sigma$ to the image. As illustrated in Fig. 5 we estimate the slant angle σ as follows:

1. First, we apply the Hough [5] transform to the text image. In order to avoid quantization errors, we use the modified version of the Hough transform suggested in [18] that represents lines with angle $\Theta + 90°$ and position ρ of its intersection with the x-axis instead of using polar coordinates. We shift Θ by 90° such that an orthogonal intersection is represented with $\Theta = 0°$.

2. Straight lines in σ-direction (e.g. caused by the Arabic letters "أ", "ل", "ط", ...) trigger sharp peaks in the projection as shown in Fig. 6(a). In contrast, the projection profile in other directions is blurred (Fig. 6(b)). Therefore, we expect large variations and sudden changes in the Hough transformed image along the ρ-axis in slant direction ($\Theta = \sigma$). Consequently, we take the derivative in ρ-direction of the Hough transformed image using the Sobel filter.

3. Both positive and negative derivatives indicate large and sharp jumps in the projection profile. Therefore, we take the element-wise square.

4. For each angle Θ we sum over all elements in the corresponding row. We set σ to the angle which maximizes this sum.

5. The original text image is corrected with a shear transform with angle $-\sigma$.

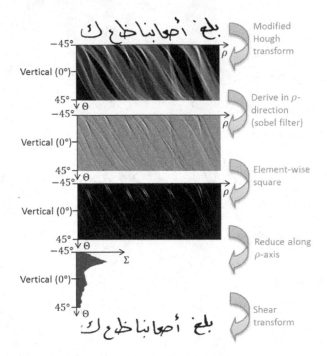

Fig. 5. Slant normalization

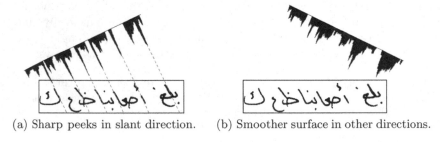

(a) Sharp peeks in slant direction.   (b) Smoother surface in other directions.

Fig. 6. Slant angle estimation using projection profiles

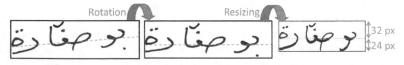

Fig. 7. Image size normalization

2.3   Size Normalization

In order to use pixel values in a sliding window as features, all images need
to have the same height because the dimensionality of all feature vectors needs
to be constant. Even for segment-based features, image size normalization is

beneficial as it reduces the impact of different glyph sizes on the feature vectors. Therefore, we rescale the image to a height of 48 pixels and enforce that the baseline is positioned at a height of 32 pixels: First, we calculate the scaling factor for resizing the partial image over the baseline to a height of 32 pixels with fixed aspect ratio. Then we rescale the entire image with this factor. If the resulting image does not have a height of 48 pixels, we stretch or shrink the area below the baseline accordingly in the vertical direction.

2.4   Pen Size Normalization

Different pen sizes also influence the feature vectors without contributing useful information for the recognition. Additionally, the previous step can introduce undesirable variations in line thickness. Therefore, we apply the line thinning algorithm described in [20] to the image. A dilation operation with ellipse shaped 3x3 kernel followed by a convolution with a 5x5 Gauss filter rethick the lines to a normalized width and blur them to reduce the impact of small variations in line positions. Fig. 8 shows a complete overview of our image normalization steps.

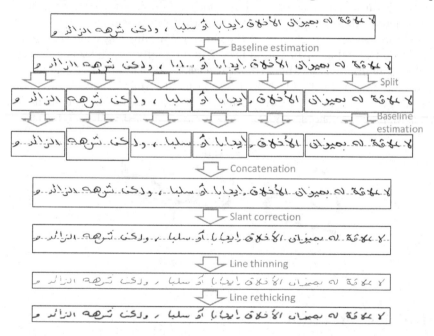

Fig. 8. Overview of all text image normalization steps

3   Feature Extraction

We investigate two different feature extraction strategies: pixel-based and segment-based features. In both methods, feature vectors are derived from a sliding window shifted in reading direction over the normalized text line image (window width: 3 pixels, window shift: 2 pixels). Pixel-based features utilize the raw grayscale intensity values of the pixels within the window. Since the image height is normalized to 48 pixels and the window width is set to 3 pixels, the dimensionality of pixel-based feature vectors is $48 \cdot 3 = 144$.

The high dimensionality of pixel-based features requires rigorous dimensionality reduction with standard techniques like principal component analysis (see Sec. 4). In contrast, the author in [6] proposed a low dimensional feature vector representation which is able to fully recover the original binarized image – i.e. given the feature vector sequence, the original text image can be reconstructed without any loss. In this work, we extend his method with a more natural way to represent connectivity of foreground segments in adjacent windows. As shown in Fig. 9, our segment-based features consist of six centroid features $c_{1...6}$ plus six segment height features $h_{1...6}$ (i.e. 12 dimensions). An area of consecutive foreground pixels within the sliding window is called *segment*. Suppose that there are n segments in the window. If $n = 6$, we set c_i to the y-coordinate of the centroid of the i-th segment, and h_i to height of that segment. In Arabic, the number of segments within a window usually does not exceed six. If the current window contains more than six segments due to binarization or segmentation errors, we discard the lowest $n - 6$ segments. If the window contains less than six segments, we distribute the values over the indices 1 to 6 equally. For instance, in case of only two segments, c_1, c_2, and c_3 hold the centroid of the upper segment, and c_4, c_5, c_6 contain the centroid of the lower segment. Analogously, h_1, h_2, and h_3 are the height of the upper segment, and h_4, h_5, and h_6 the height of the lower segment. Windows without any segments are represented with the 0-vector.

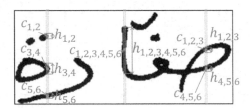

Fig. 9. Extraction of segment-based features

4   Training Procedure

Our recognition system is based on the Kaldi speech recognition toolkit [15]. The Arabic script features 28 letters with two to four contextual forms which we treat separately. As suggested in [1], we insert dedicated *sil* states after each non-connecting character, and *conn* states after each connecting character. We added punctuation symbols and numbers and ended up with a glyph set size of 133 for the KHATT corpus and 126 for the IFN/ENIT database (corresponding to the phoneme set size in speech recognition). We follow a common training scheme

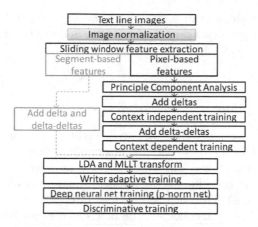

Fig. 10. Overview of the training procedure

specified in Kaldi's example scripts (Fig. 10): First, we normalize the input images (Sec. 2) and extract the 144-dimensional pixel-based feature vectors as described in Sec. 3 (right path in Fig. 10). Note that even if we use segment-based features later on, the early training stages are always based on pixel features. We empirically found out that segment-based features are not useful to start with. A principal component analysis reduces the dimensionality to 8. We add the dynamic delta features and train the context independent system with 40k Gaussians. Then we add the second order dynamic features (delta-deltas) and train a context dependent system with 55k Gaussians in total (context width of 3, i.e. *triphone* in speech recognition terms). We stopped the decision tree splitting at 500 leaves. The tree includes questions regarding the shape of characters [10].

The forced-alignments of the context dependent system are used for deriving linear discriminant analysis (LDA) and maximum likelihood linear transform (MLLT) features [7] with 12 dimensions. At this point, the training differs depending on the selected feature set for the final recognizer (segment-based versus pixel-based). In our experiments with pixel-based features, the LDA and MLLT transforms are estimated on the original pixel features (before applying the principle component analysis). In case of segment-based features, the LDA and MLLT transforms are estimated on the raw segment-based features (left path in Fig. 10 highlighted in blue). On top of the resulting features we apply writer adaptive training (known as *speaker adaptive training* [2] in speech recognition). For deep neural network based optical modelling, we use Kaldi's *nnet2* recipe [16] which supports discriminative training of the network.

Arabic characters differ largely in their complexity. Therefore, authors in [4] use a small number of HMM states for simple characters, and model complex characters with more HMM states. First, we train a context-dependent system with a 3-state left-to-right HMM topology. Then, we estimate the best number of states for each glyph using the forced-alignments of this initial system. Lastly, the final system is trained from scratch with the adjusted HMM topology. This method known as *glyph dependent model lengths* is described in detail in [4].

5   Experiments

5.1   Data Description

We evaluate our recognition system on two different Arabic handwriting recognition tasks. The IFN/ENIT database [14] is a freely available collection of hand-written Tunisian town names and was used in a number of competitions [13]. Images contain one of 937 different town names (i.e. no out-of-vocabulary words and no language model). The corpus is divided into the subsets a, b, c, d, e, f, s (Tab. 1). The s set has been collected in a different region with different writing styles and posses the most challenges to the recognizer.

Table 1. Data statistics for the IFN/ENIT database

	Set a	Set b	Set c	Set d	Set e	Set f	Set s	$\sum$
Number of words	6,537	6,710	6,477	6,735	6,033	8,671	1,573	42,736

The KHATT corpus [11] consists of line images extracted from text areas in forms filled out by a large variety of writers with different origin, educational background, age, and handedness. For the KHATT corpus, we use a trigram language model trained on the KHATT training set. Tab. 2 contains information about the corpus size. The out-of-vocabulary rate on the test set is 11%.

Table 2. Data statistics for the KHATT corpus

	Train set	Dev set	Test set	$\sum$
Number of lines	9,462	1,899	1,996	13,357
Number of word tokens	131,716	26,635	26,921	185,272

5.2   Results

Tab. 3 and 4 compare our recognition system with the best results reported so far on the respective data sets. The best word error rate (WER) for each configuration is written in bold font. Tab. 3 shows four different *train set - test set* configurations for the IFN/ENIT database. Our recognizer performance is comparable to state-of-the-art systems on the *abc-d*, *abcd-e*, *abcde-f* configurations with both pixel-based and segment-based features. Discriminative training usually improves the WER slightly. However, training on sets a, b, c, d, e and testing on the set s (*abcde-s* configuration) leads to our largest gains compared to the best system in the literature. Using pixel-based features and discriminative training results in 11.5% WER which constitutes a relative gain of 23%, but it is

Table 3. Word error rate on the IFN/ENIT database (in %)

	abc-d	abcd-e	abcde-f	abcde-s
UPV-PRHLT [12]	4.8	**6.1**	7.8	15.4
Azeem and Ahmed [3]	**2.3**	6.6	6.9	15.2
Ahmad et al. [1]	2.8	6.5	7.8	14.9
This work				
Pixel-based features	2.7	6.9	7.3	12.3
Segment-based features	2.5	6.3	6.9	12.5
Pixel-based features + discriminative training	2.9	6.6	7.0	**11.5**
Segment-based features + discriminative training	2.4	**6.1**	**6.8**	11.9

Table 4. Word error rate on the KHATT corpus (in %)

	Dev set	Test set
Hamdani et al. (baseline for constrained task) [8]	33.6	34.1
This work		
Pixel-based features	**29.4**	**30.5**
Segment-based features	29.5	30.9
Pixel-based features + discriminative training	30.3	31.6
Segment-based features + discriminative training	29.9	30.9

not optimal for the other configurations. Segment-based features with discriminative training still outperform the best system so far by 20% (11.9% WER) on the *abcde-s* configuration, but also achieve state-of-the-art performance on the other configurations.

To the best of our knowledge, the best handwritten text recognizer for the KHATT corpus is described in [8]. In contrast to [8] we do not focus on language modelling. Therefore, we compare our system to the baseline of the restricted task in [8]. Pixel-based features work slightly better than segment-based features and lead to our best WER on the test set of 30.5% (11% relative gain). Discriminative training does not improve recognition accuracy in this case.

6 Conclusion

In this work, we described our recognition system for handwritten Arabic developed at the Qatar Computing Research Institute. We achieve a high degree of robustness with intensive text image normalization. Feature extraction was done either using the raw pixel grayscale intensity values, or a novel method based on foreground segments (segment-based). The recognizer was developed with the Kaldi toolkit and used discriminatively trained deep neural networks for optical modelling. We outperform the best system in the literature by 23% relative on the *abcde-s* configuration of the IFN/ENIT database. On the KHATT corpus, we report a relative gain of 11% compared to the state-of-the-art.

References

1. Ahmad, I., Fink, G.A., Mahmoud, S.A.: Improvements in sub-character HMM model based arabic text recognition. In: ICFHR (2014)
2. Anastasakos, T., McDonough, J., Schwartz, R., Makhoul, J.: A compact model for speaker-adaptive training. In: ICSL. IEEE (1996)
3. Azeem, S.A., Ahmed, H.: Effective technique for the recognition of offline Arabic handwritten words using hidden Markov models. IJDAR 16(4), 399–412 (2013)
4. Dreuw, P., Rybach, D., Gollan, C., Ney, H.: Writer adaptive training and writing variant model refinement for offline arabic handwriting recognition. In: ICDAR. IEEE (2009)
5. Duda, R.O., Hart, P.E.: Use of the Hough transformation to detect lines and curves in pictures. Communications of the ACM 15(1) (1972)
6. El-Mahallawy, M.S.M.: A Large Scale HMM-Based Omni Font-Written OCR System for Cursive Scripts. Ph.D. thesis, Faculty of Engineering, Cairo University Giza, Egypt (2008)
7. Gales, M.: Semi-tied covariance matrices for hidden Markov models. Transactions on Speech and Audio Processing 7(3), 272–281 (1999)
8. Hamdani, M., Mousa, A.D., Ney, H.: Open vocabulary arabic handwriting recognition using morphological decomposition. In: ICDAR. IEEE (2013)
9. Huang, X., Acero, A., Hon, H.W., R., R.: Spoken language processing: a guide to theory, algorithm, and system development. Prentice Hall PTR (2001)
10. Likforman-Sulem, L., Mohammad, R.A.H., Mokbel, C., Menasri, F., Bianne-Bernard, A., Kermorvant, C.: Features for HMM-based arabic handwritten word recognition systems. In: Guide to OCR for Arabic Scripts. Springer (2012)
11. Mahmoud, S.A., Ahmad, I., Alshayeb, M., Al-Khatib, W.G., Parvez, M.T., Fink, G.A., Märgner, V., Abed, H.E.: KHATT: arabic offline handwritten text database. In: ICFHR (2012)
12. Margner, V., Abed, H.E.: ICFHR 2010-arabic handwriting recognition competition. In: ICFHR. IEEE (2010)
13. Märgner, V., El Abed, H.: Arabic handwriting recognition competitions. In: Guide to OCR for Arabic Scripts, pp. 395–422. Springer (2012)
14. Pechwitz, M., Maddouri, S.S., Märgner, V., Ellouze, N., Amiri, H., et al.: IFN/ENIT-database of handwritten arabic words. In: CIFED (2002)
15. Povey, D., Ghoshal, A., Boulianne, G., Burget, L., Glembek, O., Goel, N., Hannemann, M., Motlicek, P., Qian, Y., Schwarz, P., Silovsky, J., Stemmer, G., Vesely, K.: The kaldi speech recognition toolkit. In: ASRU (2011)
16. Povey, D., Zhang, X., Khudanpur, S.: Parallel training of Deep Neural Networks with Natural Gradient and Parameter Averaging. CoRR (2014)
17. Rybach, D., Gollan, C., Heigold, G., Hoffmeister, B., Lööf, J., Schlüter, R., Ney, H.: The RWTH Aachen university open source speech recognition system. In: Interspeech (2009)
18. Stahlberg, F., Vogel, S.: Detecting dense foreground stripes in arabic handwriting for accurate baseline positioning. In: ICDAR. IEEE (2015) (to be published)
19. Young, S., Woodland, P., Evermann, G., Gales, M.: The HTK Toolkit 3.4. 1 (2013)
20. Zhang, T.Y., Suen, C.Y.: A fast parallel algorithm for thinning digital patterns. Communications of the ACM 27(3), 236–239 (1984)

Optimized Parallel Model of Covariance Based Person Detection

Nesrine Abid[1(✉)], Kais Loukil[1], Walid Ayedi[1], Ahmed Chiheb Ammari[2,3], and Mohamed Abid[1]

[1] Laboratory of Computer and Embedded Systems, National School of Engineering of Sfax, Sfax University, Sfax, Tunisia
nesrineabid88@gmail.com
[2] MMA Laboratory, National Institute of the Applied Sciences and Technology, Carthage University, Carthage, Tunisia
[3] Renewable Energy Group, Department of Electrical and Computer Engineering, Faculty of Engineering, King Abdulaziz University, Jeddah 21589, Saudi Arabia

Abstract. Covariance descriptor has good performance for person detection systems. However, it has high execution time. Multiprocessors systems are usually adopted to speed up the execution of these systems. In this paper, an optimized parallel model for covariance person detection is implemented using a high-level parallelization procedure. The main characteristics of this procedure are the use of Khan Process Network (KPN) parallel programming model of computation, and the exploration of both task and data levels of parallelism. For this aim, a first KPN parallel model is proposed starting from the block diagram of the covariance person detection application. This model is implemented through the Y-Chart Application Programmers Interface (YAPI) C++ library. To ensure the best workload balance of the optimized model, communication and computation workload analysis are considered. Based on these results, both task merging and data-level partitioning are explored to derive an optimized model with the best communication and computation workload balance. The optimized parallel model obtained has three times lower execution time in comparison with the sequential model.

Keywords: Covariance descriptor · Person detection · Mpsoc · KPN · Parallel model

1 Introduction

Person detection is exploited as a key operation in video surveillance, and in many other fields. The large variability of the target, which is subjected to occlusions, pose, appearance and shape variations, presents a hard issue. To solve these problems, many solutions have been proposed. Among these solutions, a classifier that operates by means of a sliding window over the image is used. This classifier can be fed with heterogeneous features, e.g. Wavelet-based features [1], Haar-like characteristics [2], Histograms of oriented gradients (HOG) based features [3].

© Springer International Publishing Switzerland 2015
V. Murino and E. Puppo (Eds.): ICIAP 2015, Part II, LNCS 9280, pp. 287–298, 2015.
DOI: 10.1007/978-3-319-23234-8_27

The experiments in [3] show that the HOG descriptor is an excellent alternative of many others antecedent descriptors. In [4] authors proposed a region covariance descriptor technique for person detection that outperforms the previous approaches. Authors in [5] show that person detection with covariance (COV) even outperforms the HOG based solution. The covariance descriptor combines location, shape and color information such as pixel coordinates intensity, gradients, etc. and is invariant to color, luminance and pose. Recently, COV approaches have received the attention of many researchers [6] that are looking for detectors capable to achieve high accuracy. Nevertheless, in video surveillance the processing speed required for person detection is also a primary issue. To achieve real time detection, multiprocessing approaches are motivated to enable for sharing the system execution time between several processing elements. Any processing element can be either a processor that is executing a software (SW) task or any hardware accelerator that is implementing the needed task directly in hardware [7]. Now, prior to any multiprocessing implementation, a parallel specification of the system application is required. This parallel model has to have the best characteristics in terms of process workload and inter-process communication balances. In this paper, we propose an optimized parallel model for the covariance person detection using a high-level independent target-architecture parallelization procedure. The main characteristics of this procedure are the use of Khan Process Network (KPN) parallel programming models of computation [8], the exploration of task and data levels of parallelism with the minimal communication granularity, and the analysis of both communication and computation workloads for the best balance of the parallel model under investigation. For this aim, a first KPN parallel model is proposed starting from the block diagram of the covariance person detection application. This model is implemented through the Y-Chart Applications Programmers Interface (YAPI) C++ library [9]. Both communication and computation workloads analysis are then considered. Based on these results, task merging and data-level task splitting are explored to get the best communication and computation workload balance.

The paper is organized as follows: the following section 2 presents the covariance based person detection algorithm. In section 3, we will discuss the different steps of the parallelization procedure implemented to get the optimized parallel model. Finally, conclusions of the paper are given in Section 4.

2   Person Detection Based on Covariance Descriptor

The person detection system we are targeting is based on a covariance descriptor [4] followed by a Support Vector Machine (SVM) classification [10].

The block diagram of the covariance person detection system is shown in Fig.1. It is composed by four modules. The first module extracts features from the image. The second module exploits the fact that covariance may be computed by adopting integral representations under the form of first-order and second-order P and Q tensors [4]. These tensors are exploited by the third module. A sliding window scans

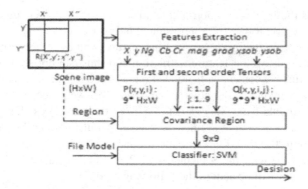

Fig. 1. Schematic of the covariance person detection application

the entire image to calculate a covariance matrix for each window. Final the fourth module builds the entire object model to perform the classification. Next, more details are given to better explain the role of each module and our first optimization for the sequential code.

2.1   Features Extraction

On the scene image we perform feature extraction, sequentially for each pixel, in a row wise fashion. The choice of the desired features and their number (d = 9), is based on Michael et al.study [11] where F(x,y) feature is extracted from each pixel such that: F(x,y)=[x y Ng Cb Cr mag $grad$ $xsob$ $ysob$]^T where :

x: x location; y: y location; Ng: Grayscale intensity value; Cr: Read component value; Cb: Bleu component value; xsob and ysob: Norm of the first order derivatives in x and in y; grad: Sobel Gradient; mag: Sobel Magnitude.

Given the feature extraction principle, the x and y locations, the Grayscale intensity, and the Cr and Cb color component values can be computed in parallel. Once the Grayscale intensity value is extracted, the first order derivatives (xsob and ysob) can be computed in parallel. Using the first order derivatives, the second-order derivatives (grad and mag) can also be computed in parallel. The Sobel filters are designed to produce pixel by pixel output, as long as consecutive local areas. Pixels processed by this module will be forming a feature vector to be sent to the next module.

2.2   First and Second Order Tensors

In this task, the first-order integral tensor P and the second-order integral tensor Q are computed. P is a 9-dimensional vector encoding the sum of each feature defined by equation (1). Q is 9x9 array defined by equation (2) as given next.

$$P(x',y',i) = \sum_{x<x',y<y'} F(x,y,i) \qquad\qquad i=1..9 \qquad\qquad (1)$$

$$Q(x',y',i,j) = \sum_{x<x',y<y'} F(x,y,i)\, F(x,y,j) \qquad i,j=1..9 \qquad\qquad (2)$$

Where (x', y') is the upper left coordinate and (x", y") is the lower right coordinate of the rectangular region R(x',y';x",y") presented in Fig 1.

For each pixel from the image scene, nine features values are generated. The tensor processing will be using the feature extraction and thus can not start performing unless the first feature vector is available. Taking advantage from the major "symmetric characteristic" advantage of the covariance descriptor, we propose first to reduce the number of Q elements from 81(=9x9) to 45 (=9* (9 +1) / 2) as shown in Fig.2. To speed up processing, a coarse-grained task level parallelism can be implemented to separately compute the P and Q elements. In particular, the 45 elements of Q can be calculated in parallel with the 9 elements of P. At the end, a total of 54 vector elements for each pixel will be sent to the following modules.

Original code	Our optimized code

For(y=0;y<9;y++)
  For (x=0;x<9;x++)
    Q[y][x]=integral(F[x],F[y])
	For(y=0;y<9;y++)
	  For (x=0;x<5;x++)
	    Q[y][x]=integral(F[x],F[y])

Fig. 2. First optimization

2.3   Covariance Region

For each sliding widow region R (x', y'; x", y"), a covariance matrix of 9x9 elements is computed as follows:

$$Cr(x',y';x",y") = \frac{1}{n-1}[Q_{x",y"} + Q_{x',y'} - Q_{x",y'} - Q_{x',y"} - \frac{1}{n}(P_{x",y"} + P_{x',y'} - P_{x",y'} - P_{x',y"}) \quad (3)$$

where n = (x' − x")·(y' − y").

Taking advantage from the symmetric characteristic we propose also to compute only 45 elements of the covariance as shown in Fig.3.

Original code	Our optimized code

For each image region:
  For(y=0;y<9;y++)
    For (x=0;x<9;x++)
      cov[y][x]=Cr(x',y',x",y")
	For each image region:
	  For(y=0;y<9;y++)
	    For (x=0;x<5;x++)
	      cov[y][x]=Cr(x',y',x",y")

Fig. 3. Second optimization

Each descriptor is transformed to Euclidean space to be fed to the classifier.

2.4   The Classifier

The SVM classifier classifies unlabeled descriptors based on their similarity with descriptors in their training sets. Two classes are considered one for person and the other class is for no person.

3   Parallelization Procedure

Implementing a covariance based person detection application for an embedded System-on-Chip is a big challenge. First, we start by the software implementation of this application using a mono processor architecture running on a stratixII_2s60_RoHS Altera FPGA. The computation has taken 44 s to detect persons from a 150X99 image. To achieve faster processing for real time detection, a multiprocessing approach is motivated and a parallel model of the application is required. In this case, we will be using the KPN parallel programming models of computation. In addition, an appropriate partitioning analysis is performed to ensure for the best computation and communication balance of the proposed parallel model.

3.1   Kahn Process Networks

Prior to any multiprocessor implementation, a parallel specification is required to functionally describe the studied application as a set of processes exchanging data according to an appropriate model of computation. Many dataflow process network models of computation have been used in several parallelization studies of signal processing applications. Examples include Kahn process networks(KPN) [9], dynamic data flows [12], synchronous data flows [13], etc. Among all these models, the KPN is the most often used for dataflow oriented applications [14]. The KPN model of computation assumes a network of concurrent autonomous processes that communicate over first-in-first-out (FIFO) channels using particular blocking-read and write synchronization primitives. Several frameworks for designing multi-processor systems are based on the KPN model, such as C-heap, Cic [15], DaedalusR [16], Space Codesign [17], Dal [18],[19]. For all these frameworks, system level design tools are used to facilitate the mapping of a behavioral application specification to an architecture platform model. The applicability of these frameworks to the multimedia domain comes essentially from the use of KPN model of computation in which parallel processes, implemented in a high-level language, communicate with each other via unbounded FIFO channels. It is demonstrated that the execution of a KPN model is deterministic, meaning that for a given input always the same output is produced and the same workload is generated, irrespective of the execution schedule.

To execute the KPN in a parallel fashion, several implementations are provided. Since the most language chosen for writing image processing programs is the C/C++, we choose to implement the KPN process using the C++ library YAPI [10].

3.2   The Initial Parallel Model

The application blocks diagram presented in Fig.1 is used for extracting the maximum task-level parallelism. The application is decomposed in separate blocks. Each block defines one single task or process that runs a separate stage of an algorithm. The sequential covariance person detection algorithm is thus split into separate concurrent blocks that will be executed as independent processes. Next, the inter-process communication is established using message passing KPN primitives. Going through this procedure, the Initial proposed model shown in Fig.4 is obtained and then implemented using the YAPI multi-threading runtime environment.

This model performs as follows: the "Ng", "Cb" and "Cr" processes collect image data from the input file. The "X_sob", "Y-sob", "mag" and "grad" processes calculate the sobel first and second derivatives. The outputs of these processes represent the features. Each feature is sent to "Pi" and "qij" (i: 0..8; j:0..8) to calculate first and second Tensors. The obtained Tensors are forwarded to "ComputCovregion" process to get covariance descriptors. Finally each descriptor is classified by "SVM" process.

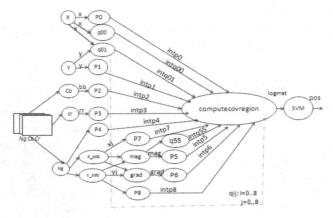

Fig. 4. Initial parallel model of the covariance person detection application

For YAPI implementation purposes, we started with the sequential code of the covariance based person detection application. This code is modified and restructured manually to describe the KPN in C++. Each KPN process is described by a set of associated functions extracted from the original C code. Appropriate FIFO communication channels are then added to enable for data exchange and communication between processes. The implemented parallel KPN model of Fig.5 is validated by high level functional simulation. First, using the same test benches for the sequential and parallel code, a same detection results are obtained. This gives a proof of correctness of the parallel code. Second, for performance evaluation of the proposed parallel model, the amount of data exchange over FIFO channels and the processing time are evaluated using communication and computation workload profiling. These characteristics define the concurrency properties of the model and measure the efficiency of the computation division over the different processes. In fact, a parallel model with good concurrency proprieties should have a balanced computation workload for all the network processes together with a balanced communication workload over its different FIFO communication channels.

The Communication Workload. The obtained communication workload for an image of 640x422 resolution is shown in Fig.5. The Initial model has 171 FIFO channels, 169 of these channels are transmitting 270080 Tsize elements (Tsize= 4 bytes) making the total number of bytes communicated over each one of these 169 channels equal to 270080*4*1 bytes. This amount of data is generally received through read instructions and then transmitted back over a write instruction ("Wtokens" = "Rtoken"). This represents a very big amount of data to be processed which will require the connected processes to spend a lot of the time dealing with communication. In addition, some other channels are exchanging only few amounts of data. All this makes the communication workload of this starting model completely unbalanced and thus we should be looking for a better model with a communication behavior using data level parallelism using task level splitting or merging techniques.

Communication Workload:

	Size	Tsize	Wtokens	Wcalls	T/W	Rtokens	Rcalls	T/R
Covdetect.rr[0]	270080	4	270080	270080	1	270080	1	270080
Covdetect.bb[0]	270080	4	270080	270080	1	270080	1	270080
Covdetect.xi[0]	270080	4	270080	270080	1	270080	1	270080
Covdetect.y1[0]	270080	4	270080	270080	1	270080	1	270080
Covdetect.i[0]	270080	4	270080	270080	1	270080	1	270080
Covdetect.ii	270080	4	270080	270080	1	270080	270080	1
Covdetect.X[0]	270080	4	270080	270080	1	270080	270080	1
Covdetect.Y[0]	270080	4	270080	270080	1	270080	270080	1
Covdetect.mag[0]	270080	4	270080	270080	1	270080	1	270080
Covdetect.grad[0]	270080	4	270080	270080	1	270080	1	270080
Covdetect.intg0	270080	4	270080	1	270080	270080	270080	1
Covdetect.intg00	270080	4	270080	1	270080	270080	270080	1
Covdetect.c	128	4	62937	777	81	62937	777	81
Covdetect.logmat	128	4	62937	777	81	62937	777	81
Covdetect.pds	128	4	1554	777	2	1554	777	2

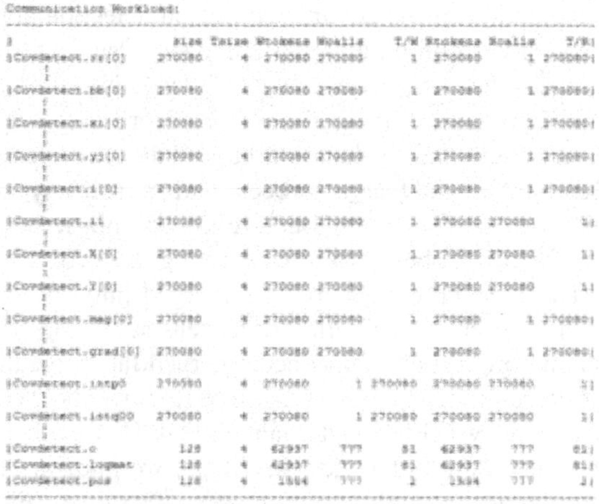

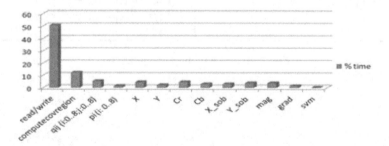

Fig. 5. Communication workload of the Initial parallel model

Computation Workload Analysis. Generally, different tasks need different amount of processing time. For this purpose, a computational workload analysis is considered using the "Gprof" GNU [20] profiling tool. The obtained results are represented in Fig 6 in terms of the CPU time percentage spent in the execution of each process.

Fig. 6. Parallel computational profiling of the first proposed model

Given the profiling results of Fig.6, it is clear that the computational workload of this Initial model is too much unbalanced. More than 50% of the execution time is spent in reading and writing data. In addition, the majority of the implemented processes have negligible load. It is thus clear, using the obtained communication and computation workload results, that the proposed Initial model has very poor concurrency properties and this outlines the potential of its optimization for a better computation and communication workload balance. For this aim, we propose to use data level parallelism and task level splitting or merging approaches.

3.3   The Optimized Parallel Model

This section presents the different steps that have been used to derive in a structured way a parallel implementation of the covariance person detection application that has a balanced workload and good communication behavior. Using the profiling results of Fig.5 and Fig.6, it is clear that the process "x_sob", "y_sob", "cb", "cr", "ng", "grad", "mag", "X", "Y", the 9 processes "$p_{i(i:0..8)}$" and the 45 processes "$q_{ij(i:0..8;j:0..8), i<j}$" have negligible computations loads and exchange a large data structures. So we propose to merge "cb", "cr", "X" and "Y" in "feat_4" process and "x_sob", "y_sob", "grad", "Ng", and "mag" in "sobel" process. For more concurrency optimization, we propose also to perform data splitting for the "sobel" task thus splitting this process into two processes "sob1" and "sob2". The nine processes "p_i" are merged into one process called "pregion" that computes the 9 vectors of the first order tensor. The 45 processes that calculate vectors of the second order tensor have been merged into 5 parallel processes. Each process calculates 9 vectors of the second order tensor. The "computecovRegion" process has initially too many FIFO input channels (54*H*W, where H= 422 and W= 640). To reduce the related communication workload, we integrate the computation of covariance matrix into "pregion" and "qiregion" $_{(i: 0..4)}$ processes. Fig.7 presents an example of calculation in "qregion" and "q1region" processes.

Original code	Our optimized code

For(x=0;x<9;x++)
   | Q[0][x]=integral(F[0],F[x]);
 For each image region:
   For (x=0;x<9;x++)
    | cov[0][x]=Q(x',y';x",y");
	For(x=1;x<9;x++)
	   | Q[1][x]=integral(F[1],F[x]);
	   Q[8][8]=integral(F[8],F[8]);
	 For each image region:
	     For (x=1;x<9;x++)
	      | cov[1][x]=Q(x',y';x",y");
	     cov[8][8]=Q(x',y';x",y");

Fig. 7. Example of proposed processes

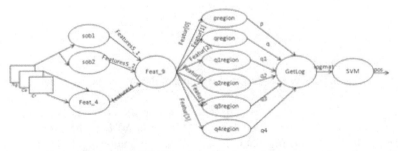

Fig. 8. Proposed optimized parallel KPN model of the covariance person detection application

The transmission of data between these processes is performed by an "image" type structure. "feature4" and "feature5" transmits respectively 4*h*w and 5*h*w image vector characteristics. "p" and "q_i" are exchanging respectively 9x9 and 1x9 data elements. In this case, all the communications channels associated with the exchange of large amounts of data (Fig 5) are removed.

Concurrency Results of the Optimized Model. The optimized parallel model obtained is given in Fig.8. This figure shows the data-partitioning "sob1" and "sob2" and also the task-merging of the "pregion", "qregion", "q1region", "q2region", "q3region", "q4region", and "feat4" processes. This model has been implemented and validated at the YAPI system level. The communication workload results are obtained and shown in Fig.9 for the 640x422 image. A computational "gprof" profiling is also performed and the obtained results are reported in Fig.10.

```
Communication Workload:
                         size  Tsize Wtokens Wcalls T/W Rtokens Rcalls T/R
| detect.features4    1080320      4       4      1    4       4      4   1|
| detect.features5_1  1350400      4       5      1    5       5      5   1|
| detect.features5_2  1350400      4       5      1    5       5      5   1|
| detect.featur[0]    2430720      4       9      1    9       9      1   9|
| detect.featur[1]    2430720      4       9      1    9       9      1   9|
| detect.featur[2]    2430720      4       9      1    9       9      1   9|
| detect.featur[3]    2430720      4       9      1    9       9      1   9|
| detect.featur[4]    2430720      4       9      1    9       9      1   9|
| detect.featur[5]    2430720      4       9      1    9       9      1   9|
| detect.p                 82      4     777    777    1     777    777   1|
| detect.q                 10      4     777    777    1     777    777   1|
| detect.q1                10      4     777    777    1     777    777   1|
| detect.q2                10      4     777    777    1     777    777   1|
| detect.q3                10      4     777    777    1     777    777   1|
| detect.q4                10      4     777    777    1     777    777   1|
| detect.signal           148      1     777    777    1     777    777   1|
| detect.pos              128      4     777    777    1     777    777   1|
```

Fig. 9. Communication workload of the optimized parallel model

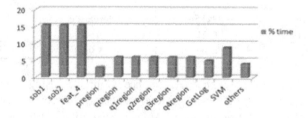

Fig. 10. Parallel computational profiling of the final model

It is clear from Fig.9 that the optimized proposed model has better communication behavior compared to the Initial model. The total number of tokens communicated from/to "feature extraction" and "covariance region" processes has been reduced. Effectively, the number of tokens transmitted over the "p", "q", "q1", "q2", "q3" and "q4" connecting the input of the "pregion" and "$q_i$region" $_{(i:0..4)}$ processes has been reduced to 777 tokens. The total bytes number communicated over these channel is 4*777*1 bytes. In addition, as indicated in Fig.10, merging tasks decreased the time processes spent in read/write data. Also this better distributes the complexity over processes. The final proposed model has obviously better communication and computational behavior compared to the Initial model.

Results Discussion. To evaluate the effectiveness of the used procedure and the proposed model, we compare the execution time performance of the proposed model with the initial model and the sequential model of 640x422 image resolution. Measurements have been done on the YAPI interface using Gprof tool.

Table 1. Comparative table using 640x422 image resolution

	execution time (s)	Speed-up
Sequential	15.782	-
Initial model	10.93	1,44
Optimized model	5.701	2,767

As shown in Table1, the obtained optimal model outperforms the two previous models. The only use of tasks partitioning mechanism in initial model improves execution time performance by decreasing processing time from 15.782 s to 10.93 s per image. However, using data splitting and task merging, the processing time of the optimized model is reduced to 5.70 s per image. This is three times accelerated execution time in comparison with the original sequential reference code (15.782 s). So depending on the computational and communication workload and the execution time, the initial model is spending a lot of time dealing with communication rather than computation.

To evaluate the feasibility of this procedure, we vary the resolution of the used image. So we apply this procedure to a standard image resolution, a lower resolution and a higher resolution. It is clear from Table 2 that the used procedure decrease significantly the execution time regardless of image resolution.

Table 2. Execution time of varied images resolutions

Resolution	99x150	640x480	1024x676
Sequential	0.21	16.1	41.342
Optimized model	0.03	5,967	18.737

Consequently, much more better performance is obtained using task level merging and data level splitting for the best workload balance of the covariance based person detection parallel model. In addition, the smaller resolution is used, the higher speedup is obtained. So at certain image resolution the use of this procedure accelerate the computation without achieving real time. This require the use of more performing processor or a hardware accelerator.

4   Conclusion

In this paper an optimized parallel model of a covariance based person detection system is developed. First, an Initial KPN parallel model is proposed using only task level parallelism. This model is then validated using the YAPI multi-threading environment. Analysis of the communication and computation workload results showed the very poor concurrency properties of the initial model. In this context, data level parallelism and task level merging are applied to improve the concurrency properties. At the end, an optimized process network parallel model of the person detection system based on covariance descriptor is obtained. This model has fast processing time and considerable computation and inter process communication workload balance.

References

1. Strickland, R., Ilhahn, H.: Wavelet transform methods for object detection and recovery. IEEE Transaction. Image Processing **6**(5), 724–735 (1997)
2. Lienhart, R., Maydt, J.: An extended set of haar like features for rapid object detection. IEEE Proceedings. Image processing **1**, 900–903 (2002)
3. Dalal, N., Triggs, B.: Histograms of oriented gradients for human detection. IEEE computer society. computer vision and pattern recognition **1**, 886–893 (2005)
4. Tuzel, O., Porikli, F., Meer, P.: Pedestrian Detection Via Classification on Riemannian Manifolds. IEEE Transactions on Pattern Analysis and Machine Intelligence **30**, 1713–1727 (2008)
5. Paisitkriangkrai, S., Shen, C., Zhang, J.: Performance evaluation of local features in human classification and detection. IET Computer Vision **2**, 236–246 (2008)
6. Qin, L., Snoussi, H., Abdallah, F.: Adaptive covariance matrix for object region representation. In: SPIE Fifth International Conference on Digital Image Processing (2013)
7. Abid, N., Ayedi, W., Ammari, A.C., Abid, M.: SW/HW implementation of image covariance descriptor for person detection system. In: IEEE Advanced Technologies for Signal and Image Processing, pp. 115–119 (2014)
8. Kahn, G.: The semantics of a simple language for parallel programming. In: Proceedings of IFIP. vol. 74 (1974)
9. Kock, E., Essink, G., Smits, W., Wolf, P., Brunel, J.-Y., Kruijtzer, W.M., Lieverse, P., Vissers, K.A.: YAPI: application modeling for signal processing system. In: IEEE Procceeding Design Automation Conference, pp. 402–405 (2000)
10. Fradkin, D., Muchnik, I.: Support vector machines for classification. Mathematics subject classification (2000)
11. Metternich, M.J., Worring, M., Smeulders, A.W.: Color based tracing in real-life surveillance data. In: Shi, Y.Q. (ed.) Transactions on DHMS V. LNCS, vol. 6010, pp. 18–33. Springer, Heidelberg (2010)
12. Kangkook, J., Kemerlis, P., Keromytis, D., Georgios, P.: Shadowreplica: efficient parallelization of dynamic data flow tracking. In: Proceedings of the 2013 ACM SIGSAC conference on Computer & communications security, pp. 235–246 (2013)
13. Canelhas, D., Stoyanov, T., Lilienthal, J.: SDF Tracker: A parallel algorithm for on-line pose estimation and scene reconstruction from depth images. IEEE Intelligent Robots and Systems 3671–3676 (2013)
14. Lee, E., Parks, T.: Dataflow Process Networks. IEEE Proceeding **83**(5), 773–801 (1995)
15. Kwon, S., Kim, Y., Jeun, W., Ha, S., Paek, Y.: A Retargetable Parallel-Programming Framework for MPSoC. ACM Trans. on Design Automation of Electronic Systems **13**, 39:1–39:18 (2008)
16. Bamakhrama, M., Zhai, J., Nikolov H., Stefanov, T.: A methodology for automated design of hard-real-time embedded streaming systems. In: Design, Automation Test in Europe Conference Exhibition, pp. 941–946 (2012)

17. Bailey, B., Martin, G.: Codesign experiences based on a virtual platform. In: ESL Models and their Application, Ser. Embedded Systems. Springer US, pp. 273–308 (2010)
18. Schor, L., Bacivarov, I., Rai, D., Yang, H., Kang, S.: Scenario-based design flow for mapping streaming applications onto on-chip many-core systems. In: International conference on Compilers, Architectures and Synthesis for Embedded Systems, pp. 71–80 (2012)
19. Corre, Y., Diguet, J.-P., Lagadec, L., Heller, D., Blouin, D.: Fast template-based heterogeneous MPSoC synthesis on FPGA. In: Brisk, P., de Figueiredo Coutinho, J.G., Diniz, P.C. (eds.) ARC 2013. LNCS, vol. 7806, pp. 154–166. Springer, Heidelberg (2013)
20. Arora, H.: Gprof Tutorial. How To Use Linux Gnu Gcc Profiling Tool (2012)

Face Recognition from Robust SIFT Matching

Massimiliano Di Mella and Francesco Isgrò[✉]

Dipartimento di Ingegneria Elettrica E Delle Tecnologie Dell'Informazione,
Università Degli Studi di Napoli Federico II, Napoli, Italy
francesco.isgro@unina.it

Abstract. This paper presents a face recognition algorithm based on the matching of local features extracted from face images, namely SIFT. Some of the earlier approaches based on SIFT matching are sensitive to registration errors and usually rely on a very good initial alignment and illumination of the faces to be recognised. The method is based on a new image matching strategy between face images, that first establishes correspondences between feature points, and then uses the number of correct correspondences, together with the total number of matches and detected features, to determine the likelihood of the similarity between the face images.

The experimental results, performed on different datasets, demonstrate the effectiveness of the proposed algorithm for automatic face identification. More exhaustive experiments are planned in order to perform a fair comparison with other state of the art methods based on local features.

Keywords: Face recognition · Feature matching

1   Introduction

Automatic face recognition from digital still images has attracted much attention [12,31] in the research community because of its large number of applications. Formally the problem can be defined as follows: given an input face image and a database of face images of known individuals, determine the identity of the face in the input image. Despite of the vast literature on the topic to date face recognition it is still an unsolved problem, although some recent work has reported good results on difficult datasets [28].

Face recognition methods can be classified as either holistic or feature based. Holistic face recognition makes use of global information from the images of faces to perform face recognition. The global information is represented by a small number of features which are directly derived from the pixel information of face images. These features capture the variance among different faces. The Eigenfaces method [29] and the Fisher's Linear Discriminate (FLD) [30] belong to this class. Local feature based methods started being proposed more recently, as an alternative to the holistic method, and are currently an area of active research in the face recognition field. Among the various local feature used we

V. Murino and E. Puppo (Eds.): ICIAP 2015, Part II, LNCS 9280, pp. 299–308, 2015.
DOI: 10.1007/978-3-319-23234-8_28

remind Local Binary Patterns [2], Histogram of Oriented Gradients [27], and Gabor Wavelets [19].

From Lowe's work on object recognition using SIFT (Scale Invariant Feature Transform) descriptors [20], multiple authors have applied such descriptors in other fields, like robot navigation [26], scene classification [25], and also face recognition [5,8,13,14,22]. The general approach first extracts a number of key-points in the images, and then compute a local descriptor for each key-point. Recognition is performed matching each point descriptor in the test image against all descriptors extracted from all the images in the database. The input image is assigned to a class in the database depending on the output of the matching procedure.

One important thing that must be taken into account when using local features for face recognition are false matched key-points. Most of the local feature approaches to face recognition tackle this problem adopting a grid-based matching strategy [7] that works establishing a few sub-regions on the face images: only descriptors between corresponding sub-regions are compared for matching. This local matching help to reduce (without eliminating) the number or wrong matches, but requires that the images are somewhat preregistered, making it difficult the application on databases with arbitrary poses and image sizes as PubFig [15]. Moreover variable illumination still has significant influence on the detection of keypoints, since the keypoint detector intrinsic to the SIFT technique is not really invariant to illumination [14].

In this work we present an improvement on the standard method for face recognition using local features using matching. The proposed method instead of relying on the fact that the images are pre-aligned, exploits the fact that images can have different poses, and that the existence of a large number of wrong matches between two face images is likely to mean that the two persons are different. Observing that many parts of a face nearly lie on a plane, wrong matches are determined assuming a homographic transformation between faces, that is computed using a standard RANSAC [11] procedure.

The use of an outlier detection step assuming an homographic model has been already discussed in [7], where it was more used as a post-processing step for a grid matching, and for a RANSAC-based system combination for combining different descriptors. In [16] is proposed a system where a robust estimation of the fundamental matrix is used to refine the output of a battery of SVM classifiers.

The paper is structured as follows. The next Section briefly reminds how SIFT key-points and descriptors are computed. Section 3 presents the proposed face recognition strategy. The experimental results are shown and discussed in Section 4. Section 5 is left to the final remarks.

2   Features Detection in Scale-Space

SIFT key-points were first proposed in [20] and attracted the attention of the computer vision community for their tolerance to scale changes, illumination variations, and image rotations. These features are also claimed robust to affine distortion, change of viewpoints and additive noise.

The process of building SIFTs [21] is heavily inspired by the scale-space framework, but it keeps all the information related to the different levels of resolution. The process can be sketched in two phases: the first is key-points detection in scale-space pyramid and the second is key-points description using the image gradient at the right level of resolution.

SIFT features have always been known for being computationally intensive, so that less expensive features (e.g., SURF [4] and BRIEF [6]) have been proposed. In fact, when considering one of the many C/C++ SIFT implementations available on the Internet that run on standard CPU, it is true that it is not possible to extract features at a high frame rate. On the other hand, for applications where computational performance is an issue, it is possible to consider the GPU-based implementation provided in the library OpenVIDIA [1]. It exploits the processing power of the graphics card to achieve a significant speedup (10x) over traditional software versions. In [17] it is reported that speeds around 60 frames per second (640 × 480 pixels in size) have been reached with an off-the-shelf nVIDIA graphics board that carried out both feature extraction and matching while, at the same time, relieving the main CPU.

3   Proposed Method

The strategy proposed in the paper is depicted in the pseudo-code given in Algorithm 1. The procedure takes as an input a face image P and a gallery $\mathcal{G}$ of face images the identity of which is known. The system assigns an identity to the unknown person.

In a nutshell the method first extract the SIFT features from all the images, and then find robust feature correspondences between P and the images in the gallery assuming a homographic model. The quantities of matches returned is used into a scoring function that gives a measure of similarity between two faces.

Algorithm 1. Pseudo-code of the face recognition strategy proposed in this paper.

---

identity Face Recognition(SingleImage P, Gallery $\mathcal{G}$)

   $descSiftProbe \leftarrow extractSift(P)$
   for all image $\in \mathcal{G}$ **do**
      $descSiftImage \leftarrow extractSift(image)$
      $matchPoints \leftarrow match(descSiftProbe, descSiftImage)$
      $inlier \leftarrow RansacHomography(matchPoint)$
      $score \leftarrow getScore(matchPoint, inlier, descSift)$
      $evalVector(image) \leftarrow score$
   end for
   $image \leftarrow searchMaxScoreInVector(evalVector)$
   $identity \leftarrow getIdentity(image)$

Fig. 1. Two examples of face images with detected key-points.

The identity of the image in the gallery most similar to the unknown image P is returned.

The first step of the procedure is extracting the SIFT key-points and descriptors (see Figure 1) from the face image P. Then each image in the gallery is compared to the input image P determining the correspondences between the features extracted from P and the ones extracted from the image in the gallery, that were precomputed. The similarity measure used for the matching between SIFT descriptor is the one proposed by Lowe in [21]: a feature vector f_i in the image P is matched to a feature vector g_j in the image from the gallery if the Euclidean distance d_{ij} between the two vectors is such that

$$d_{ij} = \min(D_i) < 0.6 \min(D_i - \{d_{ij}\})$$

where $D_i = \{d_{ih} = d(f_i, g_h), \forall g_h\}$.

As it can be seen from the image in Figure 2(left) even when matching images of the same person wrong matches can occur. The presence of wrong matches between the two face images can lead to errors when computing the similarity if they are not taken into account properly. This can be particularly true when comparing face images of different individuals. This is evident when looking at Figure 3, where three face images are matched against the same one: the last two matches, that are between faces of different persons, return worst matches than the first one, where different face images of the same person are compared.

The strategy we propose is actually very simple. We assume that the most of the face is nearly planar, therefore there is a homography [11] between two face images, that can be estimated from at least four point correspondences, as an homography depends on 8 free parameters. In this way we assume that there is a parametric model θ linked to the point correspondences, therefore we can use robust estimation methods [24] to detect all the wrong correspondences, that are the outliers for the estimated model.

The *Random Sample Consensus* (RANSAC) selects random subsets of the data set. It proceeds as follows:

1. randomly selects a subset L of 4 correspondences and estimate the model θ;
2. computes the subset L' of correspondences that are within some error tolerance from the estimated model θ; L' is called the *consensus* set of L;

3. if the number of correspondences in L' is larger than a given threshold then L' is used to compute the model using Least Squares and exit;
4. if the number of observations in L' is smaller than a given threshold goto 1

Having a reliable estimation of the model, wrong matches can be determined using an outlier rejection rule [24].

The similarity score between the unknown face image P and each image in the gallery takes into account the results of the wrong matches feature matching step described above. Exploiting the fact that face images of different person should return a larger number of wrong matches than images of the same person, we investigated the use of different score function between two face images P, the unknown probe image, and G, one of the images in the gallery. For this study we compared the performance of the following scores:

$$M_2(P, G) = \frac{I_{PG}}{M_{PG}}$$
$$M_1(P, G) = \frac{I_{PG}}{M_{PG}} + \frac{M_{PG}}{N_P}$$
$$M_3(P, G) = \frac{M_{PG} * I_{PG}}{N_P^2}$$

(1)

where M_{PG} is the number of matches between the two images, I_{PG} is the number of correct matches determined by the robust estimation of the homography between P and G, and N_P is the number of feature point detected in the image P.

The scores are maximised when $M_{PG} = I_{PG} = N_P$, that can happen, for instance, when the two images are identical. M_2 is the simplest one, and consider as score only the ratio of inliers. The other two also consider the portion of points of interest detected in the image P for which a match in the image G is found. In practice the second one considers the sum of the two components, while the last proposed score function weighs the ratio $\frac{M_{PG}}{N_P}$, that gives already an idea of similarity between faces [3], with the ratio $\frac{I_{PG}}{N_P}$, that is the fraction of feature points in the unknown image that can be considered good matches.

After iterating the process for each image in the gallery, the recognition is then performed determining the image $\hat{G}$ such that

$$\hat{G} = \underset{G \in \mathcal{G}}{\operatorname{argmax}} M_h(P, G)$$

(2)

where M_h is any of score functions defined in Equation (1), and then assigning to P the identity of $\hat{G}$.

4   Experimental Assessment

In this Section we report a preliminary assessment of the method proposed in this paper. As a measure of the goodness of the method we adopted the widely used recognition rate. For the experiments we considered two different data-sets: ORL, and Extended Yale B [10].

Fig. 2. Feature matching for face images of the same person. Left image shows correspondences obtained directly, there is a wrong match. Right image shows only correct matches after the outlier rejection from RANSAC.

Fig. 3. Top row point matches before the RANSAC procedure. Bottom row matches determined as correct after the RANSAC procedure. Notice how the inliers determined in the case of different persons may still contain wrong matches, due to the number of wrong matches larger than 50% of the all matches.

ORL contains 400 images of 40 subjects taken at different times, varying the lighting, facial expressions (e.g., open or closed eyes, smiling or not smiling) and facial details (e.g., glasses or no glasses). The images of two subjects from the ORL database are shown in Figure 4.

The Extended Yale B contains 38 subjects and each subject has approximately 64 frontal view images taken under different illuminations conditions. Because of time reason we did not manage to run experiments on the whole data-set. The experiments shown in this paper were run on a randomly selected subset of 15 subjects for 10 illumination conditions, randomly chosen among the set of relatively good lighting conditions. The images used in the experiment for two subjects are shown in Figure 5.

The experiments were run as follows. For each subject j we randomly divided the data-set into a gallery $\mathcal{G}_j$ and a test set $\mathcal{P}_j$, with the size of the gallery $N_{\mathcal{G}_j}$ increasing from 2 to 9, and computed the recognition rate for each $N_{\mathcal{G}_j}$. We run this procedure 2500 times for each gallery size, and returned the mean recognition rate and standard deviation.

In Figure 7 the results returned on the ORL data-set are shown. The graph shows that the score M_1 returns very bad results, while with the other two scores a good recognition rate is achieved, with better results obtained with $M-3$, for which we have a recognition rate above 90% with a gallery of at least 4 images for each subject. Of course the performance improve with the gallery size.

Our results are compared with recent algorithms based on SIFT matching reporting results on the ORL data-set. In [23] it is reported a recognition rate of 93.5 on a single run with a gallery size of 5 for each subject. Under similar experimental conditions [8] report a recognition rate of 95.5. The recognition rate returned by our algorithm with a gallery of the size of 5 images for each subject is 95.06 with a standard deviation of 1.5. A gallery consisting of a single sample for subject is used in [9] reporting a recognition rate of 77.72 averaged over 10 runs, with a standard deviation of 1.64. The closest condition we can report is with a gallery size of 2, for which we obtain an average recognition rate of 77.85 with a standard deviation of 2.67. The comparative results are summarized in Table 1. In [18] are reported experiments on the ORL data-set using a simple matching strategy where performance close to the one returned by our experiments are obtained using less standard metrics for the matching.

The results on the Yale data-set are reported in Figure 6. For the comparison among the three score we have results similar to the ORL data-set, with M_1 performing poorly, and MM_3 returning the best results. For M_3 we have a recognition rate above the 98% with a gallery size as small as 3 samples per subject. Similar results are reported in [14], where a similar experiment run using all the subjects, and dividing the best lighting conditions into a gallery of around 7 images per subject (exact figures are not reported), and around 4 test images per subject. The recognition rate reported is 100%, as in our case.

The much better performance on the Yale data-set are probably due to the fact that the images, in this case, are all well cropped frontal views.

Among the three scores considered in this work, M_3 is the one returning the best results, as it is the one which mixes in a better way both the ratios involved in M_2 and M_3. What it is worth commenting at this point is the poor results returned by M_1. This is mainly due to the fact that, as it is possible to see from the examples in Figure 3, two images of the same face can return a very small number of matches, so that even a small set of inliers (say four) is returned by the RANSAC procedure, this can produce a large value for M_1, causing an erroneous recognition.

Table 1. Comparison with recent literature using SIFT matching on the ORL data-set. See text for more details.

	N_G	Reported	Our result
[9]	1	77.22	77.85
[8]	5	95.5	95.06
[23]	5	93.5	95.06

Fig. 4. The images of two subjects included in the ORL data-set.

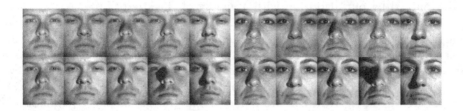

Fig. 5. The images of two subjects included in the Yale data-set.

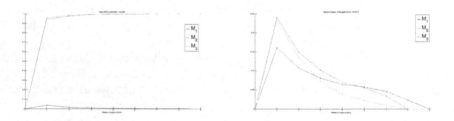

Fig. 6. Results on the Yale data-set. On the left the average recognition rate plotted against the size of the gallery N_G. The recognition rate has been averaged over 2500 run for Each gallery size. On the left the graph of the standard deviation.

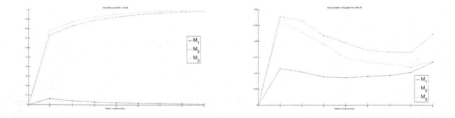

Fig. 7. Results on the ORL data-set. On the left the average recognition rate plotted against the size of the gallery N_G. The recognition rate has been averaged over 2500 run for each gallery size. On the left the graph of the standard deviation.

5   Conclusions

In this paper we presented a face recognition system based on SIFT features. The method first establishes correspondences between feature points extracted from the face images, and then uses the number of correct correspondences, obtained assuming an homographic transform between the images, to build measurement to determine the likelihood of the similarity between the face images. The recognition is then performed using a rank-1 approach.

The result reported are comparable with recent result with other algorithms based on SIFT matching, showing that the method is promising. However more experiment are still needed for a definitive analysis of the performance of the method. The algorithm must be validated on the whole Extended Yale data-set. Further exhaustive experiments on the Feret data-set, and on the more difficult LFW data-set are planned.

Further work needs also to be done exploring how the performance change using local features different from the SIFT.

Acknowledgments. This work has been partially supported by the Smart Health 2.0 Project - PON04a2_C, funded by the Italian government (MIUR) in the program PON R&C 2007-2014.

References

1. OpenVIDIA: Parallel GPU computer vision. http://openvidia.sourceforge.net
2. Ahonen, T., Hadid, A., Pietikäinen, M.: Face description with local binary patterns: Application to face recognition. IEEE Transactions on Pattern Analysis Machine Intelligence 28(12), 2037–2041 (2006)
3. Aly, M.: Face recognition using sift features. CNS/Bi/EE report 186 (2006)
4. Bay, H., Ess, A., Tuytelaars, T., Van Gool, L.: Speeded-up robust features (surf). Computer Vision and Image Understanding 110(3), 346–359 (2008)
5. Bicego, M., Lagorio, A., Grosso, E., Tistarelli, M.: On the use of sift features for face authentication. In: Proceedings of the 2006 Conference on Computer Vision and Pattern Recognition Workshop, pp. 35–41 (2006)
6. Calonder, M., Lepetit, V., Strecha, C., Fua, P.: BRIEF: binary robust independent elementary features. In: Daniilidis, K., Maragos, P., Paragios, N. (eds.) ECCV 2010, Part IV. LNCS, vol. 6314, pp. 778–792. Springer, Heidelberg (2010)
7. Dreuw, P., Steingrube, P., Hanselmann, H., Ney, H.: SURF-face: face recognition under viewpoint consistency constraints. In: Proceedings of the British Machine Vision Conference, pp. 1–11 (2009)
8. Geng, C., Jiang, X.: Face recognition using SIFT features. In: Proceedings of the International Conference on Image Processing, pp. 3313–3316 (2009)
9. Geng, C., Jiang, X.: Face recognition based on the multi-scale local image structures. Pattern Recognition 44(10), 2565–2575 (2011)
10. Georghiades, A., Belhumeur, P., Kriegman, D.: From few to many: Illumination cone models for face recognition under variable lighting and pose. IEEE Trans. Pattern Anal. Mach. Intelligence 23(6), 643–660 (2001)
11. Hartley, R.I., Zisserman, A.: Multiple view geometry. Cambrige University Press (2000)
12. Jafri, R., Arabnia, H.R.: A Survey of Face Recognition Techniques. Journal of Information Processing Systems 5(2), 41–68 (2009)

308   M. Di Mella and F. Isgrò

13. Kisku, D., Rattani, A., Grosso, E., Tistarelli, M.: Face identification by SIFT-based complete graph topology. CoRR abs/1002.0411 (2010)
14. Križaj, J., Štruc, V., Pavešić, N.: Adaptation of SIFT features for robust face recognition. In: Campilho, A., Kamel, M. (eds.) ICIAR 2010. LNCS, vol. 6111, pp. 394–404. Springer, Heidelberg (2010)
15. Kumar, N., Berg, A., Belhumeur, P., Nayar, S.: Attribute and simile classifiers for face verification. In: Proceedings of the International Conference on Computer Vision, pp. 365–372 (2009)
16. Kuo, C.H., Lee, J.D.: A two-stage classifier using SVM and RANSAC for face recognition. In: Proceedings/TENCON IEEE Region 10 Annual International Conference, pp. 1–4 (2007)
17. Lalonde, M., Byrns, D., Gagnon, L., Teasdale, N., Laurendeau, D.: Real-time eye blink detection with GPU-based SIFT tracking. In: Proceedings of the Canadian Conference on Computer and Robot Vision, pp. 481–487 (2007)
18. Lenc, L., Král, P.: Novel matching methods for automatic face recognition using SIFT. In: Iliadis, L., Maglogiannis, I., Papadopoulos, H. (eds.) AIAI 2002. IFIP AICT, vol. 381, pp. 254–263. Springer, Heidelberg (2012)
19. Liu, C.: Capitalize on dimensionality increasing techniques for improving face recognition grand challenge performance. IEEE Transactions on Pattern Analysis and Machine Intelligence 28(5), 725–737 (2006)
20. Lowe, D.G.: Object recognition from local scale-invariant features. In: Proceedings of the International Conference on Computer Vision, pp. 1150–1157 (1999)
21. Lowe, D.G.: Distinctive image features from scale-invariant keypoints. International Journal of Computer Vision 60(2), 91–110 (2004)
22. Luo, J., Ma, Y., Takikawa, E., Lao, S., Kawade, M., Lu, B.L.: Person-specific SIFT features for face recognition. In: IEEE International Conference on Acoustics, Speech and Signal Processing, vol. 2 (2007)
23. Majumdar, A., Ward, R.K.: Discriminative sift features for face recognition. In: Electrical and Computer Engineering, CCECE 2009. Canadian Conference on, pp. 27–30 (2009)
24. Meer, P., Mintz, D., Rosenfeld, A., Kim, D.Y.: Robust regression methods for computer vision: a review. International Journal of Compuer Vision 6(1), 59–70 (1991)
25. Pham, T., Waillot, N., Lim, J., Chevallet, J.: Latent semantic fusion model for image retrieval and annotation. In: Proceedings of the ACM Conference on Information and Knowledge Management, pp. 439–444 (2007)
26. Se, S., Lowe, D., Little, J.: Vision-based mobile robot localization and mapping using scale-invariant features. In: Proceedings of the IEEE Conference on Robotics and Automation, pp. 2051–2058 (2001)
27. Shu, C., Ding, X., Fang, C.: Histogram of the oriented gradient for face recognition. Tsinghua Science and Technology 16(2), 216–224 (2011)
28. Taigman, Y., Yang, M., Ranzato, M., Wolf, L.: Deepface: closing the gap to human-level performance in face verification. In: Conference on Computer Vision and Pattern Recognition (CVPR), pp. 1701–1708 (2014)
29. Turk, M., Pentland, A.: Eigenfaces for recognition. Cognitive Neuroscience 3(1), 71–86 (1991)
30. Xiang, C., Fan, X., Lee, T.: Face recognition using recursive Fisher linear discriminant. IEEE Transactions on Image Processing 15(8), 2097–2105 (2006)
31. Zhao, W., Chellappa, R., Philips, P., Rosenfeld, A.: Face recognition: A literature survey. ACM Computing Survey, 399–458 (2003)

Optimized Intra Mode Decision for High Efficiency Video Coding

Anis BenHajyoussef[✉] and Tahar Ezzedine

Ecole Nationale D'Ingénieurs de Tunis, Université de Tunis El Manar,
LR-99-ES21 Sys'Com, 1002 Tunis, Tunisie
anis.hajyoussef@gmail.com, tahar.ezzedine@enit.rnu.tn

Abstract. In order to reach higher coding efficiency, the design of the newest video compression standard - High Efficiency Video Coding (HEVC) - is relying on many improved coding tools and sophisticated techniques. Such a complexity leads to the vital need of video encoders for fast algorithms to overcome the real-time encoding constraint and memory limits. In this context, we propose a gradient based pre-processing stage that will help decreasing the complexity of the encoder and will speed up the Intra mode decision. For that purpose, we investigate the potential of a Prewitt operator instead of the famous Sobel operator used to generate the gradient. In addition and in order to enhance the gradient potential of Intra mode detection without adding a significant complexity, we propose an optimized Intra mode selection through a neighbor mode extension as well as an adapted cost function to take into account the appearing number of modes and the gradient magnitudes. The obtained results demonstrate that we can reduce the encoding time for All Intra configuration by 31.9% with a loss in BD-rate of only 1.1%.

Keywords: HEVC · Intra mode decision · Pre-processing · Image gradient · Sobel · Prewitt · Differential operator

1   Introduction

The emergence of the previous standard, the H.264/AVC, has contributed to an expansion of the video applications. Such an expansion has led to an increasing need for better video quality and higher compression especially with the applications dealing with high and Ultra-High resolutions.

In 2013, HEVC has been developed by the Joint Collaborative Team on Video Coding (JCT-VC), a team of experts from the ITU-T Video Coding Experts Group (VCEG) and the ISO/IEC Moving Picture Experts Group (MPEG). The new standard keeps the same high-level design as its predecessor but relies on many improved coding tools and techniques that offer higher coding efficiency but at the cost of more encoding complexity. The block structure is one of the most important new features that contributes to this complexity and directly affects all the other features.

© Springer International Publishing Switzerland 2015
V. Murino and E. Puppo (Eds.): ICIAP 2015, Part II, LNCS 9280, pp. 309–319, 2015.
DOI: 10.1007/978-3-319-23234-8_29

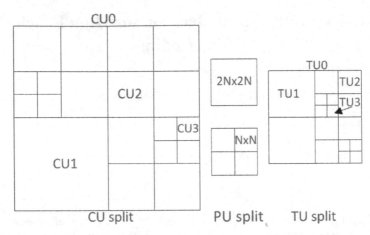

Fig. 1. Example of CUk, PUk and TUk recursive split structures for intra case with k as depth index

In, fact, HEVC relies on a coding tree block (CTB) structure. Unlike the AVC Macrobloc with the size of 16x16, the large coding unit (LCU) defined in HEVC, allows to use block sizes of 8x8 up to 64x64. The LCU can then be partitioned into coding units (CUs) with a quad-tree structure.

At the prediction stage, each CU can be split into one or more prediction units (PUs) [1][2]. Moreover at the transform stage, each CU can be split into one or more recursive transform units (TUs). Figure 1 illustrates a description of the possible recursive splits of a CU. Particularly, at the Intra prediction level, HEVC supports 33 angular prediction modes in addition to DC and planar modes, which is much more than the maximum of 8 angular modes proposed by H.264/AVC. Furthermore, the new standard allows deriving the "most probable mode" from neighbor blocks. In the case of the Chroma component, the same mode as the Luma can be used. Moreover, HEVC supports additional reference sample smoothing as well as a boundary smoothing.

These sophisticated prediction features offer a better coding efficiency, but at the cost of significant complexity at the encoder side. This complexity gives a special importance to developing fact mode decisions, especially for some applications and devices that do not support huge resources and that need to deal with real time encoding. In this context, we propose, in this paper, to investigate the potential of the gradient based Intra prediction.

A such gradient approach offers the possibility to estimate mathematically the gradient direction at each pixel position. This estimation is offering an interesting solution to take advantage of the large number of the angular Intra modes.

To generate the gradient information, the well-known Sobel operator is widely used in many video and image algorithms and applications. The reason behind this is the fact that this operator has one of the best edge detection performances over all the existing gradient operators.

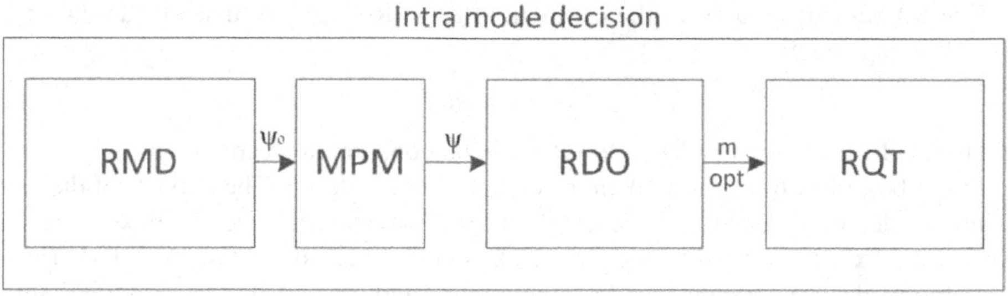

Intra mode decision

Fig. 2. Four stage Intra prediction

The related works that proposed a gradient stage to speed up the intra prediction use the 3-dimentonal Sobel operator like Pan et. al for H.264/AVC [3] and Jiang for HEVC [4]. In [5], we have investigated the potential of the Prewitt filter, presenting simpler coefficients than Sobel. In that work, we have generated a granular gradient map to reduce the preprocessing complexity coupled with a mode selection approach based on pixel neighbor extension.

In this work, we propose to investigate on HEVC Intra modes detection potential of the Roberts operator, a 2-dimensional operator as well as the complexity reduction that it can offer for hardware implementation. To be able to use such less accurate operator, we propose two approaches that allow enhancing the gradient decision on the Intra mode decision without introducing a significant complexity.

The remaining of this paper is structured as follows. The Section 2 presents an overview of the HEVC Intra prediction algorithm. Thereafter, Section 3 exposes the gradient based Intra prediction algorithm. We present then, in the Section 4 the proposed optimization approaches dealing with a pre-selection of Intra mode as well as an optimized mode selection at PU level, generated from the gradient information.

Section 5, then, exposes the approach of exploiting the gradient information to speed up the Intra prediction. Thereafter, the section6 presents an analysis of the complexity reduction offered by the Roberts operator. Then, Section 7 presents the experimental evaluation of the proposed algorithm. And finally, we present the conclusion in Section 7.

2   HEVC Intra Prediction

To speed up the Intra prediction, the HEVC test model (HM) [6], adopted a simplified Intra prediction algorithm which goes through 4 stages process for each PU [7] as presented in Figure 2. In the first stage, referred to as the rough mode decision (RMD), the HM performs a Hadamard Transform for each PU possible size, for all the 35 possible Intra modes, to generate the Sum of Absolute Transform Difference (SATD).

The SATD will be used in the estimation of the R-D cost of that PU, as shown in the following equation:

$$J = SATD + \lambda.R \tag{1}$$

where λ is Lagrangian multiplier and R is the bit consumption estimation.

The n best intra modes are taken to form the candidate set. The number of the candidate modes n, is set to 3, 3, 3, and 8 respectively for PU sizes of 64x64, 32x32, 16x16 and 8x8. At a second stage, a check is performed for additional MPMs (most probable modes) that are derived from neighbors, and are added to the candidate set if they are not already included. Then, a rate-distortion optimized quantization (RDO) is performed, at a third stage, for the modes of the candidate set at only the maximum size of TU, to pick the best intra mode for the PU as well as the best PU split structure at rate-distortion wise. In the last stage, for each PU, the best intra mode found previously is used in order to find the optimal Residual Quadtree (RQT) structure.

3   Gradient Based Pre-processing

To calculate the gradient, a discrete differentiation operator is used. The most widely used operator is the Sobel. This operator has two 3x3 kernels S_x and S_y shown in equations (2) and (3), used to approximate the horizontal and vertical derivatives of a two dimensions matrix. At each pixel position on the original image represented here as a matrix A, we perform a convolution through the two kernels, as shown in (4) and (5), to generate two matrices G_x and G_y which represent respectively an approximation of the horizontal and vertical derivatives at each pixel.

$$S_{x(Sob)} = \begin{bmatrix} -1 & 0 & 1 \\ -2 & 0 & 2 \\ -1 & 0 & 1 \end{bmatrix} \tag{2}$$

$$S_{y(Sob)} = \begin{bmatrix} 1 & 2 & 1 \\ 0 & 0 & 0 \\ -1 & -2 & -1 \end{bmatrix} \tag{3}$$

$$G_x = S_x \times A \tag{4}$$

$$G_y = S_y \times A \tag{5}$$

$$\Phi = artan(G_y/G_x) \tag{6}$$

Equation (6) is then used to generate the corresponding gradient direction. In each pixel position, this direction points to the most important variation of pixels intensity.

That means that in the case of a pixel located on an edge, the gradient direction goes across that edge. For our case, we have to take the perpendicular direction to the gradient as it represents the similarity of pixels intensity. We simplify the direction computation presented in equation 6 to simply computing G_y/G_x. We define a lookup table with HEVC intra directions and correspondent G_y/G_x values. We pick from the look-up table the supported Intra direction that is the nearest to the obtained Φ value. And we affect the corresponding Intra mode to the current pixel location.

For complexity reduction, the gradient magnitudes can be roughly approximated by:

$$M = |G_x| + |G_y| \tag{7}$$

At the end of this pre-processing step, we will have a matrix of modes where each mode corresponds to a pixel location in the original picture. We mention here that the generated mode matrix contains only angular modes. DC and planar modes are not represented and as these two modes have great probability to be the best modes at the end of the Rate-Distortion evaluation, we include them automatically in the candidate set.

To reduce the complexity of the convolution calculation, a process that is generated at each pixel position, we propose to use here the Roberts operator.

$$S_{x(Rob)} = \begin{bmatrix} 1 & 0 \\ 0 & -1 \end{bmatrix} \tag{8}$$

$$S_{y(Rob)} = \begin{bmatrix} 0 & 1 \\ -1 & 0 \end{bmatrix} \tag{9}$$

As shown in the equations 8 and 9, the Roberts operator is based on 2x2 kernels that allow generating diagonal differences. So for the implementation, the gradient direction becomes:

$$\Phi_{Roberts} = artan(G_y/G_x) + \pi/4 \tag{10}$$

The smaller kernel size of the operator is offering an option to more simplify the gradient algorithm and so motivates our investigation in this work. But to enhance the gradient based solution and especially when using Roberts, less accurate operator than the wildly used Sobel, we propose in the next section some approaches that would improve the gradient performance.

4   Optimization of Intra Mode Detection

4.1   Optimal Mode Selection

Jiang has considered the accumulated gradient magnitudes M_m for each mode in the current PU, as a criterion to choose the best modes for the candidate set:

$$M_m = \Sigma_{i \in PU} M_{m,i} \tag{11}$$

where $M_{m,i}$ is the gradient magnitude of a point i that have the mode direction m.

We propose, in this work, to take into account one more factor in the selection, which is N_m, the number of appearance of a mode in the current PU. In fact, we can have, in some cases, a mode that appears in many points in the PU but with small magnitudes representing a spread variation of pixel intensity but with very small values.

And we can have, in other cases, a mode that exists in few points but with high gradient magnitudes reflecting a limited but high variation of pixel intensity. So as both the most appearing modes and the modes with high gradient values would approach the optimal Intra mode, we investigate the following cost function for each angular mode m:

$$Cost_m = N_m + \Sigma_{i \in PU} M_{m,i} \tag{12}$$

4.2   Mode Pre-selection

As the generated modes are just approximations, we propose in this section to extend, at each pixel position, the detection of a mode m, to consider two more angular modes if they exit. These two modes are the neighbor modes m+1 and m-1 of the detected mode m.

To farther investigate this extension, we express the cost function $Cost_m$ considering $Cost_{m,i}$, the cost of a gradient point i in the current PU which correspond to the Intra mode m :

$$Cost_m = \Sigma_{i \in PU} Cost_{m,i} \tag{13}$$

As expressed in the equation (15), for each detected mode m, we increase the $Cost_{m,i}$ by a bonus value b_m used to favor the detected mode against its neighbors. Similarly, the $Cost_{m-1}$ and $Cost_{m+1}$ of the neighbor modes $m + 1$ and $m - 1$ are increased by a neighboring bonus value b_n, used to favor the two neighbor modes against the other modes. For investigation on the best bonus values, we consider for different values of b_m and b_n the percentage of matching the best theoretical best mode in the candidate set for each PU.

$$\begin{cases} Cost_{m-1} = (1 + M_{m,i}) \times b_n \\ Cost_{m,i} = (1 + M_{m,i}) \times b_m \\ Cost_{m+1} = (1 + M_{m,i}) \times b_n \end{cases} \tag{14}$$

where b_m and b_n are the used bonus values so that $b_m > b_n$.

As we noticed favorable results for the bonus values $(b_m; b_n)$ equal to (3;2), so in the remaining of this paper, we continue working with these bonus values.

5   Fast Mode Decision

As mentioned before, all the 35 modes will be tested, in the RMD stage through a Hadamard Transform encoding in order to choose the best modes for the current PU. The idea here relies on a selection of the most probable modes, in order to limit the number of Intra modes to be tested and so speed up the Intra prediction process. In fact, the gradient generated histogram, for each PU, includes the costs $Cost_m$ of each of the Intra modes.

These costs will reflect a kind of probabilities for the modes to match the optimal mode for the current PU. Therefore, instead of going through all the modes, only a limited list of modes will be investigated. We refer to this list as the gradient candidate set, ψ_i^G where $0 \leq i \leq N_G$, N_G being the number of modes in the candidate set. The gradient modes are ordered from most probable to least probable.

The gradient generated modes are more precise for higher sizes of PU as it has more points to approximate the most representative gradient of the PU. Thus, the number of modes N_G has to be set accordingly. We set this number to 15, 14, 8, 6 and 5 for respectively PU sizes of 4x4, 8x8, 16x16, 32x32 and 64x64, as we noticed that under theses settings, we have good tradeoff between time saving and encoding performance.

The best modes obtained through the RMD will form the RMD candidate set referred to as ψ_i^R, where $0 \leq i \leq N_R$, N_R being the number of modes. We keep the number of modes N_R as it set in HM12.0, i.e. 8, 8, 3, 3 and 3 for respectively PU sizes of 4x4, 8x8, 16x16, 32x32 and 64x64.

In order to speed up the RDO process, the heaviest stage in the Intra prediction, we propose to reduce even more the number N_R for PU sizes of 8x8 and 4x4, based on the gradient stage performance of detecting the theoretical optimal mode. So, we reduce the number N_R according to different confidence scenarios.

These scenarios are set by comparing the candidate set ψ_G, result of gradient stage, to the candidate set ψ_R result of the RMD stage. The idea relies on the hypothesis that the more the results are similar, the more the gradient stage is approaching the theoretical optimal mode. So if the best RMD mode and best gradient mode are neighbors, we reduce the tested modes to only the best RMD one:

$$\text{if } |\psi_0^G - \psi_0^R| \leq 1 \quad \text{then } N_R = 1 \tag{15}$$

6   Complexity Analysis

We analyze in this section, the complexity of the implementation for both operators. The implementation difference concerns the convolutions process expressed for both operator in the equations below:

$$G_{x(i,j)}^{Sobel} = A_{(i+1,j-1)} - A_{(i-1,j-1)} + (A_{(i+1,j)} - A_{(i-1,j)}) \ll 2 + A_{(i+1,j-1)} - A_{(i-1,j-1)} \tag{16}$$

$$G_{y(i,j)}^{Sobel} = A_{(i-1,j-1)} - A_{(i-1,j+1)} + (A_{(i,j-1)} - A_{(i,j+1)}) \ll 2 + A_{(i+1,j-1)} - A_{(i+1,j-1)} \tag{17}$$

$$G_{x(i,j)}^{Roberts} = A_{(i-1,j-1)} - A_{(i,j)} \tag{18}$$

$$G_{y(i,j)}^{Roberts} = A_{(i-1,j)} - A_{(i,j-1)} \tag{19}$$

The multiplication for Sobel can be replaced by simple binary shifts. Despite this simplification, from software complexity wise, the convolution with Sobel operator needs 14 operations for each pixel position. However, the Robert operator needs only 2 operations, which is much less than the Sobel one.

In addition to the reduced software complexity offered by Roberts, this operator is a quite interesting solution hardware-wise.

In fact, in addition to the fact that Roberts based solution presents much less instructions, it offers some key points which make it even more interesting and by far a more friendly hardware solution.

- Data loading: For one gradient point, the Roberts based solution needs two pixel lines loading while the Sobel operator solution needs 3 lines loading.
- Line-based data: For the convolution, the Roberts based solution needs only a rotation instruction to be able to apply multi data-subtraction. However, to benefit from the multi data instructions, the Sobel based solution needs to convert the line-based loaded data to column-based one, which is a heavy process for the implementation.
- Coefficients: the 2 and -2 coefficients, in the Sobel kernels, make the convolution implementation need to apply additional masks to isolate the pixels to be multiplied by these coefficients and also need to apply then extra addition/subtraction instructions.

7   Experimental Results

For performance evaluation, the proposed algorithm was integrated in HM 12.0, and simulations were performed conforming to common test condition specified in [8].

To compare the time effect of the algorithm, we consider the time gain:

$$\Delta T = (T_{HM12} - T_{Prop})/T_{HM12} \tag{20}$$

where T_{HM12} is the encoding time of HM12.0 and T_{Prop} is that of the proposed solution integrated on HM12.0. As the implemented feature concerns mainly the intra coding, we present the results for an All Intra (AI) coding for 8 bit depth coding.

As cited previously, we have set the number of modes in the candidate set to be tested in the RMD to 15, 14, 8, 6 and 5 for respectively the PU sizes of 4x4, 8x8, 16x16, 32x32 and 64x64 and for the RDO, we kept these numbers as defined in the HM12.0 (8, 8, 3 , 3 and 3 accordingly).

In the table 1, we present the Bjontegaard Delta rate (BD-rate) [9] measurement and time saving performance of the proposed gradient solution over that of HM12.0. We can see from the table, that the proposed Intra perdition algorithm provides a time reduction for all the sequences with an average value of 31.9% with an average increase in BD-rate of only 1.1%.

For better evaluation of the proposed features, we present in the table 2 a comparison with the Jiang work [4]. Also, in order to evaluate the proposed features, we consider 3 configurations of the proposed algorithm with different combinations of the proposed features. We obtained almost the same BD-rate performances as in [4] but with some difference in time reduction.This difference is related to the fact that Jiang has used different mode numbers in candidate sets for both rough mode decision as well as the rate distortion optimization stage. In this work, we have chosen the RMD mode numbers according to the HM mode numbers of RDO candidate set [7].

Table 1. Comparison of best mode matching mode

Class / Sequence		Y	U	V	ΔT
Class A	Traffic	1.0	0.0	-0.5	30.7
	PeopleOnStreet	1.1	-1.0	-0.1	29.6
	Nebuta	0.2	0.3	0.2	29.7
	SteamLocomotive	0.1	-0.5	0.0	31.2
Class B	Kimono	0.3	0.1	0.0	34.7
	ParkScene	0.7	-0.6	-0.6	33.8
	Cactus	1.3	-0.1	0.2	31.5
	BasketballDrive	1.7	1.1	0.5	34.1
	BQTerrace	0.9	-0.5	-0.3	34.2
Class C	BasketballDrill	1.0	0.4	-0.1	29.8
	BQMall	1.3	-0.5	0.0	29.3
	PartyScene	1.3	-0.9	-0.8	30.6
	RaceHorses	0.9	-0.4	-0.9	29.9
Class D	BasketballPass	1.2	-0.2	-0.2	37.3
	BQSquare	1.6	0.1	0.0	33.4
	BlowingBubbles	1.3	-0.6	-0.7	29.3
	RaceHorses	1.4	-0.4	0.2	29.2
Class E	FourPeople	1.1	0.0	-0.4	33.7
	Johnny	1.3	0.0	-0.1	33.5
	KristenAndSara	1.4	0.1	-0.8	33.4
Ave.		1.1	-0.2	-0.2	31.9

The first proposed configuration presents the gradient solution using Roberts operator instead of Sobel. The second configuration deals with a Robert based gradient solution combined with the mode decision optimizations. And the third configuration includes, in addition to the former cited features, the early RDO option. We can see from the table 2 that the basic Sobel gradient algorithm achieves an average time reduction of 11.7% with an increase of 0.6% in BD-rate.

The first proposed configuration offers almost the same time reduction but with 0.8% as an increase in the BD-rate. Such configuration shows the impact in coding efficiency of using a less accurate operator. However the second configuration, while offering also almost the same time reduction as the two former configurations, allows just 0.4% increase in BD-rate.

Table 2. Performance comparison

Class	[4] (Sob.)		Prop. (Rob.)		Prop. (Rob., opt.)		Prop. (Rob., opt., Fast Intra)	
	Y	ΔT	Y	ΔT	Y	ΔT	Y	ΔT
A	0.4	9.6	0.5	9.1	0.2	9.1	0.6	30.3
B	0.5	12.9	0.9	12.2	0.6	12.1	1.0	33.7
C	0.5	9.6	0.8	10.0	0.2	9.8	1.1	29.9
D	0.8	12.4	0.9	12.4	0.4	12.7	1.4	32.3
E	0.7	14.0	1.1	13.7	0.5	13.3	1.3	33.5
Ave.	0.6	11.7	0.8	11.5	0.4	11.4	1.1	31.9

So the optimizations on the mode decision allows the Robert solution to make up the precisions difference and even offers 0.2% in BD-rate, better than the Sobel basic solution. The third configuration, including early RDO option, allows to reach 31.9% as an average time reduction with 1.1% in BD-rate. This result confirms the interesting option of exploiting the gradient information in order to speed up the Intra prediction algorithm with a small loss in BD-rate. But what makes this solution quite interesting is that it achieves better performances while offering important potential for a hardware complexity reduction.

We precise here that the time execution profiling computed as shown in equation 22 aims to estimate the complexity reduction achieved by the gradient based algorithms compared to the Hadamard transform based prediction and not for comparing the two operators. This is due to the fact that the pre-processing stage is about 2% of the whole Intra encoding. We precise that further investigation can be done on the number of modes in the candidate sets to optimize it for better trade-off of time gain/BD-rate loss for the proposed solution.

8   Conclusions

In this paper, we have presented a pixel-based gradient Intra prediction for HEVC. The proposed algorithm uses the Roberts operator as a discrete differentiation operator in order to approximate the gradient of the concerned block in the original picture.

The algorithm generates a preferred direction for each pixel in the block, from which we select a candidate set of modes to be tested in a Rate-Distortion optimization level. The mode election can be optimized through neighbor mode extension and adapted cost function to take into account both the most appearing modes and those with higher gradient magnitudes. A comparison with the Hadamard transform based algorithm used in HM12, shows that the proposed algorithm achieves a time saving of 31.9% with an average increase in BD-rate of just 1.1%.

References

1. Sullivan, G.-J., Ohm, J.-R., Han, W.J., Wiegand, T.: Overview of the high efficiency video coding (HEVC) standard. IEEE Transactions on Circuits and Systems for Video Technology **22**(12), 1649–1668 (2012)
2. Lainema, J., Bossen, F., Han, W.J., Min, J., Ugur, K.: Fast mode decision algorithm for intra prediction in H.264/AVC video coding. IEEE Transactions on Circuits and Systems for Video Technology **15**(7), 813–822 (2005)
3. Pan, F., Lin, X., Rahardja, S., Lim, K., Li, Z., Wu, D., Wu, S.: Fast mode decision algorithm for intra prediction in H.264/AVC video coding. IEEE Transactions on Circuits and Systems for Video Technology **15**(7), 813–822 (2005)
4. Jiang, W., Ma, H., Chen, Y.: Gradient based fast mode decision algorithm for intra prediction in HEVC. In: International Conference on Consumer Electronics, Communications and Networks (2012)
5. BenHajyoussef, A., Ezzedine, T., Bouallegue, A.: Fast Gradient Based Intra mode decision for High Efficiency Video Coding. International Journal of Emerging Trends & Technology in Computer Science **3**(3), 223–228 (2014)
6. HEVC reference model. http://hevc.hhi.fraunhofer.de/svn/svnHEVCSoftware/
7. Zhao, L. Zhang, L., Zhao, X.: Further encoder improvement of intra mode decision. In: JCT-VC Meeting, Doc., vol. D283 (2011)
8. Bossen, F.: Common HM test conditions and software reference configurations. In: JCT-VC Meeting, Doc., vol. L1100 (2013)
9. Bjontegaard, G.: Calculation of average PSNR differences between R-D curves. In: ITU-T VCEG 13th Meeting, Doc. VCEG-M33 (2001)

Towards Learning Free Naive Bayes Nearest Neighbor-Based Domain Adaptation

Faraz Saeedan[1] and Barbara Caputo[1,2 (✉)]

[1] Sapienza University, Rome, Italy
caputo@dis.uniroma1.it
[2] Idiap Research Institute, Martigny, Switzerland

Abstract. As of today, object categorization algorithms are not able to achieve the level of robustness and generality necessary to work reliably in the real world. Even the most powerful convolutional neural network we can train fails to perform satisfactorily when trained and tested on data from different databases. This issue, known as domain adaptation and/or dataset bias in the literature, is due to a distribution mismatch between data collections. Methods addressing it go from max-margin classifiers to learning how to modify the features and obtain a more robust representation. Recent work showed that by casting the problem into the image-to-class recognition framework, the domain adaptation problem is significantly alleviated [23]. Here we follow this approach, and show how a very simple, learning free Naive Bayes Nearest Neighbor (NBNN)-based domain adaptation algorithm can significantly alleviate the distribution mismatch among source and target data, especially when the number of classes and the number of sources grow. Experiments on standard benchmarks used in the literature show that our approach (a) is competitive with the current state of the art on small scale problems, and (b) achieves the current state of the art as the number of classes and sources grows, with minimal computational requirements.

Keywords: Naive Bayes Nearest Neighbor · Domain adaptation · Transfer learning

1 Introduction

In the last years the attention of the visual recognition community has been driven towards the existence of differences across predefined image datasets, and the necessity to recompose these idiosyncrasies. The main reason behind this need is the increasing amount of available image data sources and the absence of a unique general learning method that can perform well across all of them. In practice, training a classifier on a dataset (e.g. Flicker photos) and testing on another (e.g. images captured with a mobile phone) produces very poor results although the task (i.e. the set of depicted object categories) is the same.

In this context the notion of *domain*, already used in machine learning for speech and language processing, has been extended to visual problems. A source

© Springer International Publishing Switzerland 2015
V. Murino and E. Puppo (Eds.): ICIAP 2015, Part II, LNCS 9280, pp. 320–331, 2015.
DOI: 10.1007/978-3-319-23234-8_30

domain (S) usually contains a large amount of labeled images, while a target domain (T) refers broadly to a dataset that is assumed to have different characteristics from the source, and few or no labeled samples. Formally we can say that two domains differ when for their probability distributions it holds $P_S(x,y) \neq P_T(x,y)$, where $x \in \mathcal{X}$ indicates the generic image sample and $y \in \mathcal{Y}$ the corresponding class label. Specific annotator tendencies may influence the conditional distributions, implying $P_S(y|x) \neq P_T(y|x)$. Other typical causes of visual domain shift include changes in the acquisition device, image resolution, lighting, background, viewpoint and post-processing [27]. Most of these information are directly encoded in the descriptor space $\mathcal{X}$ chosen to represent the images and may induce a difference among the marginal distributions $P_S(x) \neq P_T(x)$.

In 2013, Tommasi and Caputo showed that by casting the domain adaptation problem into the Naive Bayes Nearest Neighbor framework (NBNN, [5]) one could achieve a very high level of generalization, thanks to the intrinsic properties of NBNN classifiers [23]. The proposed approach used distance metric learning to leverage over the source knowledge at the local patch level. This brought strong results in the semi-supervised and unsupervised domain adaptation scenarios, but the method is computationally expensive and thus not suitable to work on real-time systems, like smatphones or robots.

Here we propose a simple, learning free domain adaptation method that makes it possible to exploit the generalization power of NBNN in the domain adaptation setting. We leverage over the source patches by randomly selecting a subset of them, and adding them to the target patches. To further increase the descriptive power of the descriptors, we perform data augmentation both on the source and the target data, as it is standard practice in the convolutional neural network literature [8]. The combined effect of these two simple actions is remarkable: on commonly used benchmark databases, our approach is on par with the current state of the art when there is a single source from which to adapt, and when the number of classes is limited. In the more challenging and more realistic settings of multiple sources, combined with a large number of classes, our algorithm achieves the state of the art.

The rest of the paper is organized as follows: after reviewing previous work (section 2) we revise the basic definitions for domain adaptation (section 3.1) and the NBNN framework (section 3.2). Section 4 introduces our approach, while section 5 presents a thorough experimental evaluation. We conclude with a summary discussion and outlining possible future avenues for research.

2 Related Work

The problem of domain adaptation stems from the fact that supervised learning methods fail to generalize across datasets [27]. Although this problem exists in various applications [2,4,9,20], the visual recognition community has just recently shown interest in dealing with it [3,14,21,25]. Failure to generalize across datasets has been attributed to the mismatch among various characteristics of the considered databases, and is usually referred to as the 'dataset bias' problem [27]. The fact that different image datasets vary considerably in quality, point of view and image contents, reveals that addressing the domain adaptation problem can significantly improve the performance of visual recognition applications.

Several approaches have been adopted for reducing the distance between datasets. These approaches vary from transferring source data to the target domain [21] or transferring both source and target to a third space [14]. Unfortunately, despite all efforts, [12] showed that sophisticated learning methods, aiming at learning the optimal subset of source data to transfer to the target set, in practice do not offer significant improvement over random transfers. Alternative approaches to the instance-based strategy have been explored in [6, 10, 16, 28].

While the image-to-image paradigm is the dominant approach in the methods mentioned above, recent work suggested that an alternative classification paradigm, called image-to-class, achieves higher generalization across databases compared to the very popular Bag-of-Words (BoW) approach [17,19]. This classification paradigm, whose most popular algorithm is the Naive Bayes Nearest Neighbor classifier, has been tested on several visual learning applications. Still, its use in domain adaptation has been limited. Only in 2013, Tommasi and Caputo [23] exploited its potential in a metric learning approach, and showed that using NBNN, one can easily surpass the state of the art among BOW-based algorithms presented so far. A drawback of the algorithm is its computational complexity: once the amount of classes, the number of sources and the number of data for each class and source grow, using DA-NBNN becomes computationally prohibitive. Our approach overcomes these computational limitations while preserving, and often significantly surpassing, the performance of DA-NBNN, proposing the first learning free NBNN-based domain adaptation method in the literature.

3   Problem Setting and Definitions

In this section we set the scene by introducing formal definitions for the domain adaptation problem (section 3.1) and NBNN (section 3.2).

3.1   Domain Adaptation

Domain Adaptation is the problem where knowledge from the source domain $\mathcal{D}^s$ is used to enrich and hence improve the performance in the target domain $\mathcal{D}^t$. The souce knowledge might be in the form of instances or data, or model parameters, or metric induced by the source. It is usually implicitly assumed that labeled data on the target domain does not exist (unsupervised setting) or it is scarce (semi-supervised setting). Although the source and the target domains are different, they use equal label sets $\mathcal{Y}^s = \mathcal{Y}^t$ [26].

The core cause of mismatch between the two domains is attributed to the difference in the distribution of these labels. The conditional probability of the labels, for a given feature representation, are not completely coincident

$P^s(Y|X) \sim P^t(Y|X)$; the marginal data distributions are not equal either $P^s(X) \neq P^t(X)$. In this paper, we will focus exclusively on the semi-supervised setting.

3.2   Naive Bayes Nearest Neighbor

In the NBNN classification framework, it is assumed that for each class there exists a distribution from which local descriptors are drawn independently of one another. This leads to the use of a Naive Bayes maximum a posteriori classifier [5] where each feature m votes for one of the classes in $c = \{1, ..., C\}$. This voting is realized using the local distance between each feature and its nearest neighbor in class c. $D_f2C(m, c) = ||f_m - f_m^c||$. The generalization of this distance concept to image to class distance is straightforward:

$$D_I2C(F_i, c) = \sum_{m=1}^{M_i} D_f2C(m, c).$$

The output of the classifier would then be

$$p = \operatorname*{argmin}_c D_I2C(F_i, c) \tag{1}$$

The distance to this optimum class p is called the positive distance while the distances to the rest of the classes $n : \{c \neq p\}, D_I2c(F_i, n)$ are called the negative distances.

4   Learning Free NBNN-Based Domain Adaptation

As outlined above, the problem of domain adaptation emerges when the training data for the target task is scarce. Should it not be the case, any supervised learning algorithm would be capable of learning a classifier, according to its learning abilities. It is also assumed that there exists at least another dataset with enough samples to learn a good classifier (the source), but since the two datasets have been acquired in two different domains, the performance obtained training on the source and testing on the target is weak.

The NBNN algorithm builds support sets for each class from the collection of all the features computed from patches extracted from each of the training examples. Due to the scarcity of the data on the target, the support sets that can be built solely using features from the target samples will not contain enough features to guarantee a solid performance. In order to enrich these support sets, *our proposal is to use also features extracted from the patches of the source images.*

How to select such patches-based features? In [12], the authors investigated a domain adaptation approach based on the idea of landmark samples from the source domain, which are relevant for the modeling of the target classifier.

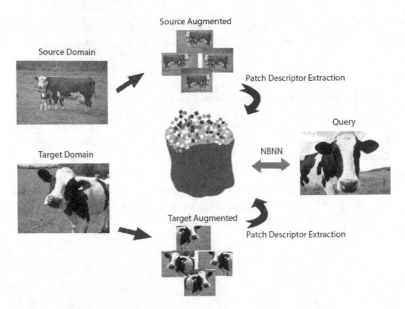

Fig. 1. An overview of our proposed learning free, NBNN-based domain adaptation approach for the class'cow': after performing data augmentation on both the source and target data, patches-based features are extracted from both, and a new target data set is created by merging the whole patches-based features extracted from the target with a fraction of those of the source, randomly selected from the whole sample data. This new pool of patches-based features is then used to build an NBNN classifier in the target domain.

Although their approach is theoretically sound, experiments show that the learning method proposed to select such landmarks is often statistically on par, and otherwise within a two percent range of performance, with a random selection of the learning samples. Motivated by this result, we apply the same philosophy here to the patches-based features, and we propose to achieve domain adaptation in an NBNN-based framework by randomly sampling a percentage of the patches-based features from the source, adding them to the patches-based features of the target. We will show with experiments in the next section that this extremely simple and learning free strategy achieves amazingly good results on standard domain adaptation benchmark databases, while being reasonably stable with respect to the amount of features to be sampled.

To further improve performance, we have tested the effect of performing data augmentation on the source and target data. Data augmentation is a technique that, since the spectacular success of convolutional neural network in the visual classification arena, has been shown to be very effective in general for any classification algorithm [8]. Again, our experiments confirm the effectiveness of this strategy, even more so combined with the instance-based domain adaptation approach based on random sampling of patches-based features from the source. A schematic representation of the overall approach for the class 'cow' is given in figure 4. Note that adding the data augmentation step to our overall approach does not significantly increase the almost non-existent computational load in training. This characteristic, combined with the remarkably good performances achieved especially as the number of classes and sources grow, makes our approach potentially attractive for applications where computational complexity should be low, like mobile robot or online, wearable systems. To the best of our knowledge, there are no previous instance-based, NBNN-based domain adaptation methods in the literature, nor the random sampling strategy has been ever tested in the NBNN learning framework for any learning to learn approach.

5 Experiments

In this section we describe the experiments we performed to assess our approach. We first describe the data, features and experimental setup used (section 5.1), then we report the results obtained (section 5.2). We discuss our findings in section 5.3.

5.1 Datasets, Features and Setup

Datasets. We used the Office dataset, the standard test bed in domain adaptation which addresses the problem of object categorization between any two datasets of objects usually found in offices [21]. This test bed consists of three domains namely Amazon, Webcam and Dslr. The Amazon dataset contains images obtained from online merchants. The images are centered and usually on a white background. Webcam and Dslr are respectively low resolution and high resolution images obtained from web cam and SLR cameras. Unlike Amazon, they could be subject to various environmental disturbances such as lighting or background changes. The Office dataset contain 31 classes of images for each domain.
Having chosen 10 of the original 31 classes from office, [13] suggested that we can add images of the same 10 classes from Caltech-256 [15] and form the Office+Caltech test bed in order to add a fourth domain in the office dataset.

Features. Following the protocol of [23], images were all resized to a common width (256px) and then converted to grayscale. SURF features were extracted according to [1]. The final result was a set of features of length 64 that were consequently fed to a 1-nearest neighbor classifier.
The effect of data augmentation on both domains has also been studied. To this end, we have duplicated the exact procedure suggested in [8] and each image is converted into 10 images through the procedure of cropping and flipping.

Setup. Different pairs of datasets are chosen to act as the source and the target from the Office+Caltech group. From the source dataset, 20 images were selected to represent the source data but only 3 were chosen from the target in every class. When the target was Webcam, 15 images were selected instead of 20 as described in [23]. At this stage, since the Dslr dataset behaves very similarly to Webcam

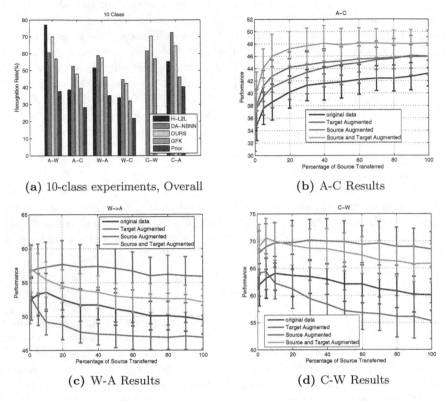

(a) 10-class experiments, Overall   (b) A-C Results

(c) W-A Results   (d) C-W Results

Fig. 2. Results for the 10 class experiments. Figure 2a shows the overall results obtained by our method compared against state of the art algorithms. Figure 2b shows the change in recognition rate on the Amazon-Caltech experiment of our method as the percentage of source data transferred to the target set increases, for the cases no augmentation, only source data augmentation, only target data augmentation and both source and target data augmentation. Analogous results are shown in figure 2c and figure 2d for the Webcam-Amazon and Caltech-Webcam settings respectively.

and it contains a lower number of images, we decided not to include it in our benchmarking. The same sample selection protocol has been adopted for the 31 class adaptation experiments. The third setup that we considered is domain adaptation from more than one source with one target. To this end, all possible combinations of two sources to one target have been examined and benchmarked against the existing reported results in the literature.

5.2   Results

The first set of experiments was done on a subset of Office+Caltech consisting of 10 classes as explained in [23]. Figure 2 shows the results in comparison to the state of the art and some baseline algorithms.

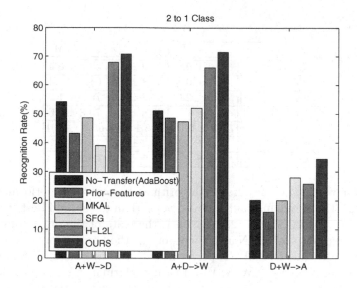

Fig. 3. Accuracy on target domains with multiple sources (A:Amazon, W:Webcam, D:DSLR), 31 class, semi-supervised

Figures 2b, 2c and 2d show the changes in the recognition rate with the increase of the percentage of descriptors, randomly transferred to the target from the source. For a better understanding of the effects of different factors, four cases have been demonstrated together. Original data is where there is no augmentation done neither on the target nor on the source domains. The cases where only the source and only the target domains have been augmented are referred to as Source augmented and Target Augmented respectively. Source and Target Augmented is where both domains have been over-sampled.

The second set of experiments is done on the 31 class Office dataset. The experiments are done exactly inline with what explained and done in [23]. Table 1 shows the results with comparison to the state of the art both using NBNN and the state of the art based on a method other than NBNN. Some further baselines are also included for better comparison.

The Third and last set of experiments are those run using more than one source domain. The Results can be seen in Figure 3. Not all Algorithms can be extended to cover the case of several sources and so only those who had this advantage were included in the comparison. For the experiments the exact test set of [18] has been used.

5.3 Discussion

The biggest advantage of our proposed method is its simplicity combined with its strong performance over growing number of classes and source domains. It also performs surprisingly well in comparison to other algorithms. The results

Table 1. 31 class Office dataset experiments, semi-supervised setting

Algorithm	$A \longrightarrow W$	$W \longrightarrow D$	$D \longrightarrow W$
BOW	34.9 ± 0.6	48.9 ± 0.5	38.4 ± 0.4
GFK	46.4 ± 0.5	66.3 ± 0.4	61.3 ± 0.4
NBNN	40.0 ± 2.0	67.2 ± 2.5	70.7 ± 1.2
I2CDML	47.9 ± 1.3	72.8 ± 2.1	73.8 ± 1.6
$H - L2L(hp - \beta)$	$\mathbf{76.2 \pm 0.02}$	67.8 ± 0.05	66.0 ± 0.01
DA-NBNN	52.8 ± 3.7	76.2 ± 2.5	76.6 ± 1.7
OURS	55.0 ± 3.3	$\mathbf{77.5 \pm 2.0}$	$\mathbf{78.2 \pm 1.4}$

in Figure 2 show that while different algorithms have varying performances on various test settings, our method is never worse than the second best. In particular, compared to DA-NBNN [23] (which is the state of the art among all the methods that exploit an NBNN approach), our method outperforms it in 2 cases (A-W and C-W), while DA-NBNN performs better in two cases (C-A and A-C). In the remaining two cases (W-A, W-C) their performance is close. In fact, the p test shows that in these two experiments there is no statistical evidence of superiority for either of the algorithms.

Our method performs significantly better than L2L [18] where L2L is the state of the art among methods that do not use NBNN. In four of the experiments, L2L achieves inferior results than ours, while only in one setting shows superiority. Note that the accuracy values reported for L2L have been taken from [18], where no result was reported for the C-W experiment.

Using the 31 class Office setting, one can study and compare the scalability of the algorithms with respect to the number of classes. Addressing this type of scalability for our method appears very straightforward. The fact that there is no training, makes things very easy and faster. Table 1 shows that, performance-wise, our method scores higher than DA-NBNN in all three experiments and better than L2L in two out of three cases.

Figure 3 compares the recognition rate for all possible combinations of two sources and one target in the Office dataset. For DA-NBNN it is not clear how it could be extended to this case and no experiments of the kind have been reported by its authors. L2L supports this case and it has been included in the benchmark. It can be seen that our method outperforms all the others for all three cases of experiments. All methods used on the setting $D + W \rightarrow A$ achieve a performance lower than what obtained in the other two settings. This is due to the similarities among the D, W domains, both picturing objects in domestic settings, as opposed to the A domain, which contains images of objects from a commercial website.

An open issue in our method is of course which percentage of the source data should be randomly selected and then added to the target data, in relation to the data augmentation procedure. Results shown in figures 2b-2d show that in general the combination of source plus target data augmentation and random sampling of around 20% of patches-based features from the source seems to achieve strong performance, always better than the original data. Still, as it can be seen from the figures, the actual optimal performance might vary in terms of percentage of sampling and/or data augmentation strategy for different settings. Although accuracy results are on average quite stable, and therefore the algorithm could be used in online systems even in its current form with good expectations about performance, it would be desirable to explore further the issue of the data selection and find principled ways of selecting the patches to transfer from the source to the target so to have guarantees about the optimality of the procedure. This could be done by learning about the most informative patches in the source, borrowing ideas from [22,24]. An alternative route might be to borrow acritically all patches, and then use enhanced versions of NBNN to learn what patches are informative for the task at hand, as in [11]. Of course, that would come at the expenses of the current negligible computational cost of the approach.

6 Conclusions

The contribution of this paper is a learning free Naive Bayes Nearest Neighbor based domain adaptation method that is competitive with the current state of the art on the standard Office-Caltech benchmark database, and that achieves the state of the art when the number of classes and sources grows. The method consists in performing a random selection of patches-based local features from the source to the target, combined with a data augmentation strategy mutated from the CNN literature. The resulting algorithm is extremely simple but also remarkably effective, especially when the number of classes and sources grows. An open challenge is how to select the best percentage of source data to add to the target: even though our experimental evaluation indicates that as a rule of thumb sampling around twenty percent of the overall sample data (i.e. after data augmentation) in general leads to very good results, future work will focus on how to determine how much to sample in a principled manner, while at the same time not increasing excessively the computational cost of the approach. This will be investigated on domain adaptation scenarios of increasing complexity, as those presented in [7], which are closer to application needs.

References

1. Bay, H., Ess, A., Tuytelaars, T., Gool, V.: SURF: Speeded up robust features. CVIU **110**, 346–359 (2008)
2. Ben-David, S., Blitzer, J., Crammer, K., Pereira, F.: Anaylsis of representations for domain adaptation. In: NIPS (2007)
3. Bergamo, A., Torresani, L.: Exploiting weakly-labeled web images to improve object classification: a domain adaptation approach. In: NIPS (2010)
4. Blitzer, J., McDonald, R., Pereira, F.: Domain adaptation with structural correspondence learning. In: EMNLP (2006)
5. Boiman, O., Shechtman, E., Irani, M.: In defense of nearest-neighbor based image classification. In: CVPR (2008)

6. Bruzzone, L., Marconcini, M.: Domain adaptation problems: A DASVM classification technique and a circular validation strategy. IEEE PAMI **32**(5), 770–787 (2010)
7. Caputo, B., Müller, H., Martinez-Gomez, J., Villegas, M., Acar, B., Patricia, N., Marvasti, N., Üsküdarlı, S., Paredes, R., Cazorla, M., Garcia-Varea, I., Morell, V.: ImageCLEF 2014: overview and analysis of the results. In: Kanoulas, E., Lupu, M., Clough, P., Sanderson, M., Hall, M., Hanbury, A., Toms, E. (eds.) CLEF 2014. LNCS, vol. 8685, pp. 192–211. Springer, Heidelberg (2014)
8. Chatfield, K., Simonyan, K., Vedaldi, A., Zisserman A.: Return of the Devil in the Details: Delving Deep into Convolutional Nets
9. Daume III., H.: Frustratingly easy domain adaptation. In: ACL (2007)
10. Duan, L., Tsang, I.W.-H., Xu, D., Maybank, S.J.: Domain transfer svm for video concept detection. In: CVPR (2009)
11. Fornoni, M., Caputo, B.: Scene recognition with naive bayes non-linear learning. In: Proc. ICPR (2014)
12. Gong, B., Grauman, K., Sha, F.: Connecting the dots with landmarks: discriminatively learning domain-invariant features for unsupervised domain adaptation. In: JMLR (2013)
13. Gong, B., Shi, Y., Sha, F., Grauman, K.: Geodesic flow kernel for unsupervised domain adaptation. In: CVPR (2012)
14. Gopalan, R., Li, R., Chellappa, R.: Domain adaptation for object recognition: an unsupervised approach. In: ICCV (2011)
15. Griffin, G., Holub, A., Perona, P.: Caltech 256 object category dataset. Technical Report UCB/USD-04-1366, California Institute of Technology (2007)
16. Khosla, A., Zhou, T., Malisiewicz, T., Efros, A.A., Torralba, A.: Undoing the damage of dataset bias. In: Fitzgibbon, A., Lazebnik, S., Perona, P., Sato, Y., Schmid, C. (eds.) ECCV 2012, Part I. LNCS, vol. 7572, pp. 158–171. Springer, Heidelberg (2012)
17. Ni, J., Qiu, Q., Chellappa, R.: Subspace interpolation via dictionary learning for unsupervised domain adaptation. In: CVPR (2013)
18. Patricia, N., Caputo, B.: Learning to learn, from transfer learning to domain adaptation: a unifying persspective. In: CVPR (2014)
19. Qiu, Q., Patel, V.M., Turaga, P., Chellappa, R.: Domain adaptive dictionary learning. In: Fitzgibbon, A., Lazebnik, S., Perona, P., Sato, Y., Schmid, C. (eds.) ECCV 2012, Part IV. LNCS, vol. 7575, pp. 631–645. Springer, Heidelberg (2012)
20. Quionero-Candela, J., Sugiyama, M., Schwaighofer, A., Lawrence, N.: Dataset Shift in Machine Learning. The MIT Press (2009)
21. Saenko, K., Kulis, B., Fritz, M., Darrell, T.: Adapting visual category models to new domains. In: Daniilidis, K., Maragos, P., Paragios, N. (eds.) ECCV 2010, Part IV. LNCS, vol. 6314, pp. 213–226. Springer, Heidelberg (2010)
22. Tommasi, T., Caputo, B.: The more you know, the less you learn: from knowledge transfer to one-shot learning of object categories. In: Proc. BMVC (2009)
23. Tommasi, T., Caputo, B.: Frustratingly easy NBNN domain adaptation. In: ICCV (2013)
24. Tommasi, T., Orabona, F., Caputo, B.: Learning categories from few examples with multi model knowledge transfer. IEEE Transaction on PAMI **36**(5), 928–941 (2014)
25. Tommasi, T., Orabona, F., Castellini, C., Caputo, B.: Improving control of dexterous hand prostheses using adaptive learning. IEEE Transaction on Robotics, pp. 1–13 (2013)

26. Tommasi, T., Quadrianto, N., Caputo, B., Lampert, C.H.: Beyond dataset bias: multi-task unaligned shared knowledge transfer. In: Lee, K.M., Matsushita, Y., Rehg, J.M., Hu, Z. (eds.) ACCV 2012, Part I. LNCS, vol. 7724, pp. 1–15. Springer, Heidelberg (2013)
27. Torralba, A., Efros, A.A.: Unbiased look at dataset bias. In: CVPR (2011)
28. Yang, J., Yan, R., Hauptmann, A.G.: Cross-domain video concept detection using adaptive svms. In: ACM Multimedia (2007)

A Gravitational Model for Grayscale Texture Classification Applied to the *pap-smear* Database

Jarbas Joaci de Mesquita Sá Junior[1] and André R. Backes[2](✉)

[1] Departamento de Engenharia de Computação, Campus de Sobral - Universidade
Federal do Ceará, Rua Estanislau Frota, S/N, Centro,
Sobral, Ceará CEP: 62010-560, Brazil
jarbas_joaci@yahoo.com.br
[2] Faculdade de Computação, Universidade Federal de Uberlândia,
Av. João Naves de Ávila, 2121, Uberlândia, MG CEP: 38408-100, Brazil
arbackes@yahoo.com.br

Abstract. This paper presents the application of a novel and very discriminative texture analysis method based on a gravitational model to a relevant medical problem, which is to classify *pap-smear* cell images. For this purpose, the complexity descriptors Bouligand-Minkowski fractal dimension and lacunarity were employed to extract signatures from the gravitational collapsing process. The obtained result was compared to other texture analysis methods. Additionally, AUC measure performance was computed and compared to several LBP based descriptors presented in two recent papers. The performed comparisons demonstrate that texture analysis based on gravitational model is suitable for discriminating *pap-smear* images.

Keywords: *pap-smear* database · Gravitational model · Bouligand-Minkowski fractal dimension · Lacunarity

1 Introduction

Computer vision has been successfully applied to many medical problems, such as discriminating normal and abnormal tissues, segmenting a region of interest (e.g., a tumor image), associating a determined image pattern to a disease etc. These applications contribute significantly to medical diagnosis, sometimes reinforcing the specialist's opinion or providing information that cannot be perceived by the human eye. One can cite as instances from the large set of works of computer vision applied to medical purposes: paper [1] classifies breast tissues into normal and abnormal tissues, and these abnormal tissues into benign and malignant cancer; paper [2] uses texture measures for meningioma classification of histopathological images; and paper [3] classifies dermoscopy images to differentiate between melanomas and benign melanocytic lesions.

© Springer International Publishing Switzerland 2015
V. Murino and E. Puppo (Eds.): ICIAP 2015, Part II, LNCS 9280, pp. 332–339, 2015.
DOI: 10.1007/978-3-319-23234-8_31

Among the several attributes that can be analyzed in a medical image, such as color and shape, texture is surely one of the most important. Texture concept can be understood as the distribution and spatial dependency among pixels in a determined local area [4]. This description, however, is more suitable for artificial textures. Natural textures (e.g., images of smoke, leaf, wood) present persistent quasi-periodic patterns, resulting in a cloud-like appearance [5]. There is a great variety of methods for texture analysis, ranging from classical approaches, such as co-occurrence matrices [4] and wavelet descriptors [6], to state-of-the-art methods, such as tourist walk [7] and shortest paths in graphs [8].

This work aims to apply a texture analysis method based on a simplified gravitational system to grayscale images from the *pap-smear* dataset. This dataset is composed by human cell images obtained from the cervix [9]. This is an extension of the works previously published in [10,11]. Here we focus on the application of the technique in a new variety of digital images and not in the development or refinement of the method. This is a way of measuring the applicability of our method in biological problems, thus aiming to contribute to the diagnosis of diseases.

The paper is organized as follows: Section 2 briefly describes the gravitational system for images. Section 3 presents the procedure to obtain an image signature based on two complexity descriptors (Bouligand-Minkowski fractal dimension and lacunarity), which are extracted from the gravitational collapse process. Section 4 describes the experiments performed on the grayscale *pap-smear* database. Section 5 shows the superior performance of the presented method in comparison to other important texture analysis methods. Finally, Section 6 establishes some considerations of this work.

2   Gravitational Model

The gravitational model applied in this work aims to extract additional information from images in order to construct more discriminative feature vectors. For this purpose, each pixel is interpreted as a particle whose mass is its own intensity. Next, a central mass M located at the image center is used to attract each pixel towards itself. This mass M is calculated for each image according to the mean of its dimensions. This is performed because images from the *pap-smear* database are rectangular. Moreover, there is no interaction among the pixels, only between each pixel and the central mass. Also because *pap-smear* images are rectangular, no tangential velocity is established to the image pixels. Thus, all the pixels have an acceleration a_{pix} toward the image center according to the following equation

$$a_{pix} = \begin{cases} G.M/\|r\|^2 & \text{if } I(x,y) \neq 0 \\ 0, & \text{if } I(x,y) = 0, \end{cases} \quad (1)$$

where G is the gravitational constant, r is the distance vector between the pixel and the image center, and $I(x,y)$ is the pixel intensity. The distance covered by the pixel is $S = (1/2).\|a_{pix}\|.t^2$, where t is the time step.

Adopting this procedure it is possible to simulate a collapsing gravitational process from the original image. Each image that represents a stage of this collapsing process (i.e., the collapsing process in a determined time step t) can be explored by complexity descriptors, such as Bouligand-Minkowski fractal dimension and lacunarity. A detailed description of the gravitational approach can be found in the papers [10,11].

3   Signature for Grayscale Textures

Different images produce different gravitational systems, and each one will collapse in its own way. So, it is interesting to measure each collapsing state in order to achieve a multiscale signature for the original image. In previous studies [10,11], we proposed to represent a collapsing image computed at time t using fractal dimension and lacunarity values. Fractal dimension is a widely used tool to describe objects (shape and texture) in terms of theirs irregularity and space occupation [12,13]. For this task we used the Bouligand-Minkowski fractal dimension. This method uses a function $f : I(x,y) \rightarrow S(x,y,I(x,y))$ to create a surface $S \in R^3$ from a texture pattern I. Then, it computes the influence volume $V(r)$ of this surface by dilating each point of S with a sphere of radius r:

$$V(r) = \left| \left\{ s' \in R^3 | \exists s \in S : |s - s'| \leq r \right\} \right|. \tag{2}$$

The Bouligand-Minkowski fractal dimension D is estimated as

$$D = 3 - \lim_{r \to 0} \frac{\log V(r)}{\log r}. \tag{3}$$

There are cases where different texture patterns present the same fractal dimension, thus making this method inefficient. To solve this problem Mandelbrot introduced the lacunarity: a method that describes a texture pattern in terms of spatial dispersion using a specific gap size [12,14]. For this study, we use the gliding-box algorithm to compute the lacunarity [14,15]. Basically, this algorithm uses a box of $l \times l$ pixels size to compute the distribution of gaps in the image. As this box glides over the image, the algorithm calculates the relative height for that portion of the image

$$h_l(i,j) = \lceil v/l \rceil - \lceil u/l \rceil, \tag{4}$$

where u and v are the minimum and maximum pixel values inside the box, respectively. From the probability density function $Q_l(H)$ of the relative height $h_l(i,j)$, the lacunarity for a box size l is defined as

$$\Lambda(l) = \sum H^2 . Q_l(H) / \left(\sum H . Q_l(H) \right)^2. \tag{5}$$

Since we are able to compute more than one collapsing stage per image, we propose a feature vector which is the concatenation of these values computed for a set of time steps $T = \{t_1, t_2, \ldots, t_k\}$, as described as follows:

$$\psi_{T,R,L} = [D_{t_1}(R), \ldots, D_{t_k}(R), \Lambda_{t_1}(L), \ldots, \Lambda_{t_k}(L)], \tag{6}$$

where $D_t(R)$ and $\Lambda_t(L)$ represent, respectively, the set of fractal and lacunarity descriptors computed for a specific set of radii and box sizes, $R = \{r_1, r_2, \ldots, r_N\}$ and $L = \{l_1, l_2, \ldots, l_M\}$.

By using both fractal dimension and lacunarity we improve the discrimination of the collapsing process. This is due to the great sensitiveness to measure structural changes from the fractal dimension combined to the ability of the lacunarity to discriminate systems that are similar in terms of fractal dimension although different in their structures.

4 Experiments

4.1 *pap-smear* Database

The *pap-smear* [9] database is composed by 917 images extracted from the cervix. This images are divided into the following cell types: normal superficial squamous epithelial (74 images); normal intermediate squamous epithelial (70 images); normal columnar epithelial (98 images); mild squamous non-keratinizing dysplasia (182 images); abnormal moderate squamous non-keratinizing dysplasia (146 images); abnormal severe squamous non-keratinizing dysplasia (197 images); and abnormal squamous cell carcinoma in situ intermediate (150 images). Two categories can be used to classify these images: normal (242 images) and abnormal (675 images). Figure 1 shows a sample from each cell type as well as their classifications. In the experiments, we considered only these two classes, as the 7-classes problem is still difficult to deal with texture analysis methods. Moreover, we converted all the images into grayscale by considering only its luminance.

4.2 Methods and Classification

To perform a more accurate evaluation of our approach, we compared the gravitational model to other important texture analysis methods using the highest obtained accuracy as criterion. The compared methods are:

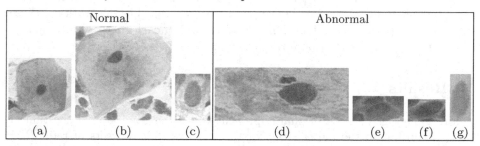

Fig. 1. Samples of the *pap-smear* database: a - superficial squamous epithelial, b - intermediate squamous epithelial, c - columnar epithelial, d - mild squamous non-keratinizing dysplasia, e - moderate squamous non-keratinizing dysplasia, f - severe squamous non-keratinizing dysplasia, g - squamous cell carcinoma in situ intermediate.

Tourist walk [7]: this method interprets each pixel as a tourist that visits cities (i.e., other pixels) adopting as criterion to choose the closest (or farthest) city not visited in the last μ (tourist memory parameter) time steps. In the experiments, we used the time steps $\mu = \{0, 1, 2, 3, 4, 5\}$ for the minimum and maximum distance. This resulted in a feature vector of 48 attributes for each tourist histogram.

Wavelet descriptors [6,16]: a multilevel 2D wavelet decomposition is performed with three dyadic decompositions using daubechies 4. Energy and entropy were computed from horizontal, vertical and diagonal details, resulting in a feature vector of 18 attributes.

Co-occurrence matrices [4]: this method quantifies the co-occurrence of a pair of pixels i and j in a determined direction θ and distance d. In the experiments, we used the directions $\theta = \{0°, 45°, 90°, 135°\}$ and distances $d = \{1, 2\}$. We also used non-symmetric matrices. For each matrix, we computed energy and entropy descriptors. This resulted in an image signature of 16 features.

For the classification of the samples, we used Linear Discriminant Analysis (LDA) [17]. This supervised statistical method aims to maximize the inter-class variance and minimize the intra-class variance. In the experiments with this classifier, the leave-one-out cross validation scheme was employed. This strategy consists of using one sample for validation and the remainder $N - 1$ samples for training, where N is the total of samples. This process is repeated N times, each time with a different sample for testing.

Additionally, we performed a comparison against two recent papers [18,19] using Area Under the ROC Curve (AUC) [20] as performance measurement. The paper [18] applies a total of nine LBP variants to the *pap-smear* database, and the paper [19] presents a large list of LBP based descriptors applied to this same database (more than 50 different tests were performed). These two papers use a Linear Support Vector Machine (SVM) for classification and the strategy 5-fold cross-validation. This validation scheme consists of dividing the dataset into five subsets, one subset used for testing and the remainder four subsets for training. This process is repeated five times, each time with a different subset for testing. The paper [18] does not describe which parameters C and γ were used in SVM, but the paper [19] uses the default values of C and γ of LIBSVM, a public library for SVM [21]. The experiments performed in this work use these same default parameter values. The highest AUC of each paper was compared to the gravitational model performance.

5   Results

Before applying the gravitational approach, we set the gravitational constant G to 1, according to the paper [10]. Next, we tested different sets of radii $R = \{3, 4, \ldots, 8\}$ and window sizes $L = \{2, 3, \ldots, 19\}$, for the same set of time steps $T = \{1, 3, 6, 9\}$ in order to find the combination that yields the highest accuracy, as can be seen in Table 1. We chose to use non-sequential time steps as they minimize the amount of redundant information that two sequential values of t

Table 1. Accuracy (%) of the gravitational model method on the *pap-smear* database for sets $R = \{3, \ldots, r_{max}\}$ and $L = \{2, \ldots, l_{max}\}$ values and the same time set $T = \{1, 3, 6, 9\}$

l_{max}	r_{max}			
	5	6	7	8
10	85.71	85.82	85.49	85.82
12	86.80	86.25	86.15	86.36
14	87.13	87.24	87.35	87.56
16	86.80	87.35	87.89	87.56
18	88.11	88.11	87.89	88.44
20	87.02	87.45	87.78	87.89

may share, thus improving the discrimination ability of the method. We also noticed that there is a small but consistent increase in the success rate as we increase the number of fractal and lacunarity descriptors used. We obtained the highest accuracy with the following parameter values: $R = \{3, 4, \ldots, 8\}$ and $L = \{2, 3, \ldots, 18\}$.

Table 2 shows the comparison of the gravitational model with other grayscale texture analysis methods using accuracy as measurement performance. The gravitational approach surpassed all the other methods. Moreover, the obtained accuracy is 2.07% superior to the second best method (wavelet descriptors). This represents an amount of more 19 images corrected classified. This corroborates the efficiency and the discrimination power of the presented method, as the *pap-smear* database is hard to classify and any improvement is desirable.

Table 2. Comparison results of different methods applied to the *pap-smear* database

Methods	No of descriptors	Accuracy (%)
Gravitational model	92	88.44
Wavelet descriptors	18	86.37
Tourist walk	48	85.82
Co-occurrence matrices	16	79.83

The comparison with LBP based descriptors confirms the high performance of the gravitational model, as can be seen in Table 3. The results of the presented method surpassed all the results presented in the [18]. Moreover, it yields AUC value superior to more than 90% of the LBP based descriptors presented in the paper [19].

Table 3. Comparison of the gravitational model with LBP based descriptors applied to the *pap-smear* database

Methods	AUC
Gravitational model	0.8915
ENS (Highest AUC in the paper [18])	0.8840
MAG1 (Highest AUC in the paper [19])	0.9080

6   Conclusion

This work presented an application of a powerful texture analysis method to a challenging medical database, which consists of *pap-smear* images. The obtained accuracy and AUC values were superior to almost all the compared methods, demonstrating that the gravitational approach is suitable for this specific set of medical images. The results indicated that future improvements in the gravitational model will lead to still better classification rates in the *pap-smear* database.

Acknowledgments. André R. Backes gratefully acknowledges the financial support of CNPq (National Council for Scientific and Technological Development, Brazil) (Grant #301558/2012-4), FAPEMIG and PROPP-UFU. Jarbas Joaci de Mesquita Sá Junior gratefully acknowledges the financial support of CNPq (National Council for Scientific and Technological Development, Brazil) (Grant #453298/2015-0).

References

1. Braz Junior, G., Paiva, A.C., Silva, A.C., Oliveira, A.C.M.: Classification of breast tissues using Moran's index and Geary's coefficient as texture signatures and SVM. Computers in Biology and Medicine **39**(12), 1063–1072 (2009)
2. Al-Kadi, O.S.: Texture measures combination for improved meningioma classification of histopathological images. Pattern Recognition **43**(6), 2043–2053 (2010)
3. Abbas, Q., Celebi, M., Serrano, C., García, I.F., Ma, G.: Pattern classification of dermoscopy images: A perceptually uniform model. Pattern Recognition **46**(1), 86–97 (2013)
4. Haralick, R.M.: Statistical and structural approaches to texture. Proceedings of the IEEE **67**(5), 786–804 (1979)
5. Kaplan, L.M.: Extended fractal analysis for texture classification and segmentation. IEEE Transactions on Image Processing **8**(11), 1572–1585 (1999)
6. Chang, T., Kuo, C.J.: Texture analysis and classification with tree-structured wavelet transform. IEEE Transactions on Image Processing **2**(4), 429–441 (1993)
7. Backes, A.R., Gonçalves, W.N., Martinez, A.S., Bruno, O.M.: Texture analysis and classification using deterministic tourist walk. Pattern Recognition **43**(3), 685–694 (2010)
8. Sá Junior, J.J.M., Backes, A.R., Cortez, P.C.: Texture analysis and classification using shortest paths in graphs. Pattern Recognition Letters **34**(11), 1314–1319 (2013)
9. Jantzen, J., Norup, J., Dounias, G., Bjerregaard, B.: Pap-smear benchmark data for pattern classification. In: Proc. NiSIS 2005, Albufeira, Portugal, NiSIS, pp. 1–9 (2005)
10. Sá Junior, J.J.M., Backes, A.R.: A simplified gravitational model to analyze texture roughness. Pattern Recognition **45**(2), 732–741 (2012)
11. Sá Junior, J.J.M., Backes, A.R., Cortez, P.C.: A simplified gravitational model for texture analysis. Journal of Mathematical Imaging and Vision **47**(1-2), 70–78 (2013)
12. Mandelbrot, B.: The fractal geometry of nature. Freeman & Co. (2000)

13. Backes, A.R., Casanova, D., Bruno, O.M.: Color texture analysis based on fractal descriptors. Pattern Recognition **45**(5), 1984–1992 (2012)
14. Allain, C., Cloitre, M.: Characterizing the lacunarity of random and deterministic fractal sets. Phys. Rev. A **44**(6), 3552–3558 (1991)
15. Du, G., Yeo, T.S.: A novel lacunarity estimation method applied to SAR image segmentation. IEEE Trans. Geoscience and Remote Sensing **40**(12), 2687–2691 (2002)
16. Daubechies, I.: Ten lectures on wavelets. Society for Industrial and Applied Mathematics, Philadelphia (1992)
17. Everitt, B.S., Dunn, G.: Applied Multivariate Analysis, 2nd edn. Arnold (2001)
18. Nanni, L., Lumini, A., Brahnam, S.: Local binary patterns variants as texture descriptors for medical image analysis. Artificial Intelligence in Medicine **49**(2), 117–125 (2010)
19. Nanni, L., Lumini, A., Brahnam, S.: Survey on LBP based texture descriptors for image classification. Expert Systems with Applications **39**(3), 3634–3641 (2012)
20. Fawcett, T.: An introduction to ROC analysis. Pattern Recognition Letters **27**(8), 861–874 (2006)
21. Chang, C.C., Lin, C.J.: LIBSVM: A library for support vector machines. ACM Transactions on Intelligent Systems and Technology **2**, 27:1–27:27 (2011)

Combining ARF and OR-PCA for Robust Background Subtraction of Noisy Videos

Sajid Javed[1], Thierry Bouwmans[2], and Soon Ki Jung[1]($\boxtimes$)

[1] School of Computer Science and Engineering, Kyungpook National University,
80 Daehak-ro, Buk-gu, Daegu 702-701, Republic of Korea
`sajid@vr.knu.ac.kr, skjung@knu.ac.kr`
[2] Laboratoire MIA (Mathematiques, Image et Applications),
Université de La Rochelle, 17000 La Rochelle, France
`thierry.bouwmans@univ-lr.fr`

Abstract. Background subtraction is a fundamental pre-processing step
for many computer vision applications. In addition to cope with dynamic
background scenes, bad weather conditions such as rainy or snowy environments and global illumination conditions such as light switch on/off
are still major challenging problems. Traditional state of the art methods,
such as *Robust Principal Component Analysis* fail to deliver promising
results under these worst conditions. This is due to the lack of global pre-
processing or post-processing steps, incorrect low-dimensional subspace
basis called *low-rank* matrix estimation, and memory or computational
complexities for processing high dimensional data and hence the system does not perform an accurate foreground segmentation. To handle
these challenges, this paper presents an input video denoising strategy
to cope noisy videos in rainy or snowy conditions. A real time *Active
Random Field* constraint is exploited using probabilistic spatial neighborhood system for image denoising. After that, *Online Robust Principal Component Analysis* is used to separate the *low-rank* and *sparse*
component from denoised frames. In addition, a color transfer function
is employed between the *low-rank* and the denoised image for handling
abruptly changing lighting conditions, which is a very useful technique for
surveillance agents to handle the night time videos. Experimental evaluations, under bad weather conditions using two challenging datasets such
as I-LIDS and Change Detection 2014, demonstrate the effectiveness of
the proposed method as compared to the existing approaches.

1 Introduction

Video background modeling and subtraction is a very crucial step in many
image processing applications such as video registration, inpainting, compression and segmentation [1]. This pre-processing step consists of segmenting the
moving foreground objects from the static scene called "background". But existence of undesirable weather conditions such as rain, fog, snow or haze is still
major challenge for many applications, in addition to bootstrapping and dynamic
background subtraction issues, which may cause performance problems in visual
surveillance systems.

© Springer International Publishing Switzerland 2015
V. Murino and E. Puppo (Eds.): ICIAP 2015, Part II, LNCS 9280, pp. 340–351, 2015.
DOI: 10.1007/978-3-319-23234-8_32

A number of interesting frameworks have been developed to tackle the problems of background subtraction in videos [2] and several implementations are available in BGS[1] and LRS[2] libraries. *Robust Principal Component Analysis* (RPCA) based *low-rank* matrix decomposition algorithms using Principal Component Pursuit (PCP) provide encouraging performance for background/foreground separation [2]. RPCA decomposes the original data matrix, as a sum of low-dimensional subspace having intrinsic structure called *low-rank* matrix (corresponds to the background) and correlated outliers called *sparse* component (constitutes the foreground objects). For example, 1st row in Fig. 1 shows an example of background subtraction using RPCA of original image taken from I-LIDS dataset [3].

However, due to the batch optimization processing and partial SVD computation at each major loop, RPCA suffers from memory and computational complexities and hence the *low-rank* matrix can not be estimated correctly due to the lack of constraints. Moreover, earlier RPCA methods also do not provide satisfactory performance under bad weather conditions as depicted in the 2nd and 3rd rows of Fig. 1 of sequences taken from I-LIDS [3] and Change Detection (CDnet) 2014 dataset [4].

In order to tackle these challenges, this paper presents a robust background subtraction algorithm via *Online Robust PCA* (OR-PCA) on denoised video frames (noise free). We briefly explain our methodology here. First, the continuous constraints such as *Active Random Field* (ARF) based on the combination of *Markov Random Field* (MRF) and *Conditional Random Field* (CRF), are employed on noisy or rainy video frames. Then, OR-PCA is applied on denoised images for background modeling. Since ARF based image denoising technique provides encourging results against noisy pixels. Therefore, our methodology improves the quality of foreground via OR-PCA under mild weather environments. Moreover, without detecting the global illumination conditions, a color transfer function is used between the source and input image to maintain the abruptly changing lighting conditions of current frame when the light switch is turned off. It can be a useful functionality for surveillance agents to select the color transfer option for night time surveillance or illumination changing conditions. Finally, a very nice comparison of ARF based background subtraction with other methodologies is presented in detail.

The rest of this paper is organized as follows. In Section 2, the related work is reviewed. Section 3 describes our methodology in detail. Experimental results are discussed in Section 4. Finally, conclusions are drawn in Section 5.

2 Related Work

In the literature, a number of encouraging methods have been proposed for robust background subtraction. Due to the over growing demand of processing high dimensional data, subspace learning models such as RPCA [5] attract a

---

[1] https://github.com/andrewssobral/bgslibrary
[2] https://github.com/andrewssobral/lrslibrary

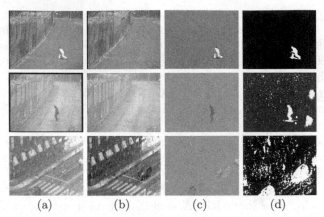

$$\begin{array}{cccc} \text{(a)} & \text{(b)} & \text{(c)} & \text{(d)} \end{array}$$

Fig. 1. An example of background subtraction using RPCA. From left to right: (a) input, (b) *low-rank*, (c) *sparse* component, and (d) foreground mask. From top to bottom: non-noisy, rainy, and snowy scene.

lot of attention. Excellent surveys on background modeling using RPCA can be found in [2]. All these RPCA approaches discussed in [2] work according to batch optimization and therefore they are not applicable for real-time systems.

In contrast, Feng and Xu [6] proposed OR-PCA that alleviates most of the ealier RPCA limitations. OR-PCA processes one frame per time instance via online (also called iterative or stochastic) optimization. In [6], it is argued that OR-PCA converges to the optimal solution and achieves the comparative performance as compared to its batch counterparts. However, no encouraging results over video background subtraction are reported. Therefore, S. Javed *et. al* [7] modified OR-PCA [6] for background/foreground segmentation. A number of encouraging results are presented in [7]. But annoying parameters tuning is the main drawback in their approach.

All these RPCA methods discussed above perform the *low-rank* recovery which is robust to *sparse* corruptions but it gets fail to handle worst weather conditions such as rainy or snowy. To address rain removal from videos using RPCA, A. Hakim [8] proposed a novel framework for rainy video restoration using exact *low-rank* recovery, but the system performance was degraded as the hard constraints were applied in the *low-rank* part, which is not useful for online processing. In this study, we propose an integrated framework based on ARF for image denoising, and OR-PCA along with color transfer scheme for robust background subtraction of noisy image sequences.

3   Proposed Approach

In this section, we discuss our scheme for background subtraction of noisy videos in detail. Our methodology consists of several components which are described as a system diagram in Fig. 2.

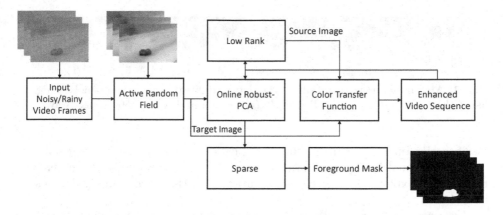

Fig. 2. Block diagram of our proposed scheme

Our methodology consists of three main stages: ARF, background subtraction, and color transfer function. In this work, instead of applying any mild constraints on *low-rank* component, we first denoise the input video frames using the continuous ARF, and then, OR-PCA [7] is applied on filtered frames to get the improved foreground segmentation. To handle the global illumination conditions, we use the color transfer scheme for illumination stability without detecting the global changes in a scene. We propose an integrated framework for both bad weather conditions and night time surveillance or abruptly changing lighting conditions . One very useful benefit of our approach is that, the surveillance agent is able to select the color transfer function for night time surveillance. In addition, a very effective comparison is presented in detail with earlier methods using ARF based initialization, and we show that ARF with OR-PCA provides the best results. In the following sections, we will describe each module in detail.

3.1   Real Time Acive Random Field (ARF) for Image Denoising

In this work, the rain/snow filtering problem is analyzed using input video restoration method. The original video frame, say Z_t, is assumed to be three dimensional e.g., *width* × *height* × *color*, at a time t. This noise free input frame is then corrupted by some noise (rain/snow drops) represented by y_t. The main goal is to restore this original frame using the continuous constraints like ARF, and then, the background subtraction is performed for improved foreground detection.

The ARF [9,10] model is a combination of probabilistic MRF/CRF model which shows a very nice potential for many computer vision applications such as image segmentation, denoising and stereo disparity using the Fields of Experts MRF model [11] and simple gradient descent inference algorithm. In [9], a very interesting real time image denoising application is proposed.

The main idea of ARF model is that, through an appropriate training of MRF/CRF prior model, and a fast inference algorithm with an optimization of

(a)	(b)	(c)	(d)	(e)	(f)

Fig. 3. ARF based image denoising. From left to right: (a) input, and denoised image using (b) $\sigma = 10$, (c) $\sigma = 15$, (d) $\sigma = 20$, (e) $\sigma = 25$, and (f) $\sigma = 50$, respectively.

loss function on a given image, the model perform very well for image denoising on a suboptimal inference algorithm. In this work, rainy video is denoised or restored by exploiting the ARF information with the same training data used in [9,10].

Let each pixel be a node in a directed graph $G = (V, E)$, where a set of vertices V stands for all pixels in the image and a set of edges E denotes 4-connected spatially neighboring pixels. Let C be a set of cliques of G which is fully connected subgraphs. Then, the main goal is to recover an image x_t which is both smooth and close to y_t using the gradient descent having energy minimization function given by

$$E_{x_t} = E_{data}(x_t) + E_{FOE}(x_t, \theta), \tag{1}$$

where the term $E_{data}(x_t)$ is a cost function for assigning labels to x_t and is given by

$$E_{data}(x_t) = \frac{1}{2\sigma^2} \sum_j (y_t^j - x_t^j)^2, \tag{2}$$

where x_t^j and y_t^j is the value of pixel j of image x_t and y_t, and σ is a smoothing factor. Similarly $E_{FOE}(data)$ is the energy of Fields of Experts which is an MRF prior model having convolution kernels called filters as $J_f, f = 1, ..., N$ with corresponding coefficients α_f, which is given by

$$E_{FOE}(x_t, \theta) = \sum_j \sum_{f=1}^{N} \alpha_f \log(1 + \frac{1}{2}(J_f x_t^k)^2), \tag{3}$$

where $\sum_j$ is the sum over the cliques k of the denoised image x_t and x_t^k are the corresponding pixels of clique k. Solving (1) takes thousands of iterations, which is really a hard task for real time systems. A. Barbu [9] designed a loss function with its online optimization available in his homepage[3], and it normally takes less than a second with four iterations to minimize the energy function and hence applicable for real-time processing. Fig. 3 (b) to (f) show the ARF based denoised images taken from CDnet [4] with different values of σ. This σ value in Fig. 3 (b) to (f) makes the smoothed restored images using the same training data used in [9,10].

---

[3] http://www.stat.fsu.edu/abarbu/ARF/index.html

3.2   Background Subtraction

In this paper, OR-PCA [6] is applied on each denoised video frame for robust *low-rank* and *sparse* error separation. OR-PCA basically decomposes the nuclear norm of the objective function of the traditional PCP algorithms into an explicit product of two matrices, i.e., the basis and coefficient.

In [6], an iterative or stochastic optimization scheme is designed for OR-PCA and it is proved that the method converges to the global optimal solution of the original PCP formulation. OR-PCA can be formulated as

$$\min_{L\in\Re^{p\times d},R\in\Re^{n\times d},E} \left\{ \frac{1}{2}\|D - LR^T - E\|_F^2 \right.$$
$$\left. + \frac{\lambda_1}{2}(\|L\|_F^2 + \|R\|_F^2) + \lambda_2\|E\|_1 \right\}, \tag{4}$$

where D is the column-vector of denoised images e.g., $D \in \Re^{p\times n}$, p is the number of pixels with three color features, e.g. (*width* × *height* × 3), n denotes the number of samples (video frames), d is a rank, L is the optimum basis of each individual color channel, R is a basis coefficient, and E is a *sparse* error. λ_1 controls the basis and coefficients for *low-rank* matrix, whereas λ_2 controls the sparsity pattern, which can be tuned according to video analysis. In addition, *basis* and *coefficients* depend on the value of *rank* r, which is tuned carefully to speed up the stochastic optimization process.

In particular, the OR-PCA optimization consists of two iterative updating components. First, every incoming restored image is projected onto current initialized basis L and we separate the *sparse* noise component, which includes the outliers contamination. Then, the basis L is updated with a new denoised color image individually. More details can be found in [6].

The background sequence for each image is then modeled by a multiple of basis L and its coefficient R, e.g., $X = LR^T$, whereas the sparse component E for each image constitutes the foreground objects which is then thresholded to get the binary mask using hard thresholding scheme.

3.3   Color Transfer Method

The *low-rank* component is not always consistent and needs to be updated at a time t, especially for abruptly changing lighting conditions, such as turning off the light switched in indorr scenes. The surveillance system always show a very weak performance due to rapid lighting variations.

Many approaches have been developed to detect change of global illumination conditions such as in [12]. However, the delay always arise when the new pixels are updated which is the main drawback in earlier approaches. Color transfer between images has shown to be a very efficient strategy, initially developed for computer graphics applications [13,14] to transfer the desired colors into an input image.

In this work, we transfer the color between the *low-rank* and input denoised images, without detecting the intense lighting variations, and this can be done by taking the bright colors from *low-rank* matrix, and then, transform the color map of the input video sequence. The OR-PCA is then employed on enhanced video sequence for improved foreground segmentation. This color transfer scheme is very important especially for night time surveillance, when a bright day time *low-rank* scene is computed online using OR-PCA, and then, it is used to transform the colormap of the night time scene for video enhancement. However, we have not stored any bright time *low-rank* scene in this study, but a series of these images can be stored if not available during night time surveillance, and then, the weighted *low-rank* component which can be computed using the linear combinations of these images, can be adopted as a source image for color transfer function.

E. Reinhard *et. al* [14] proposed a very efficient and simple color transfer algorithm using decorrelated color space between the source and target image. Let say that I_s and I_t be an RGB source (*low-rank* component obtained from OR-PCA) and target image (current denoised video frame).

The I_s and I_t images are first converted into $l\alpha\beta$ color space using the formulation presented in [14]. Then, $l_s\alpha_s\beta_s$ and $l_t\alpha_t\beta_t$ are each source and target $l\alpha\beta$ color spaces after conversion. Next, the mean value is subtracted from each individual axis and standard deviation is divided from the source image with a multiple of enahanced source $l\alpha\beta$ axis. The standard deviation of each I_t axis is added separately, and finally the enhanced $l'\alpha'\beta'$ space is then converted back into the RGB color space after the color transfer function given by

$$l' = \frac{\sigma_t^l}{\sigma_s^l}l^* + \mu_{l,t}, \; \alpha' = \frac{\sigma_t^\alpha}{\sigma_s^\alpha}\alpha^* + \mu_{\alpha,t}, \; \beta' = \frac{\sigma_t^\beta}{\sigma_s^\beta}\beta^* + \mu_{\beta,t} \tag{5}$$

where $l^* = l_s - \mu_{l,s}$, $\alpha^* = \alpha_s - \mu_{\alpha,s}$ and $\beta^* = \beta_s - \mu_{\beta,s}$. Similary the μ and σ are the mean value and standard deviations of each source and target $l\alpha\beta$ axis in (5). More details can be found in [14]. Fig. 4 (a) to (e) show the enhanced video results using ARF with color transfer scheme for improved background subtraction. The average RGB pixel is also computed for evaluation purpose and Fig. 4 (f) depicts that the color transfer video has more stable illumination condition.

4   Experimental Evaluations

In this section, experimental results are reported for bad weather conditions and night videos category, taken from the two well-known challenging datasets such as CDnet [4] 2014 and I-LIDS [3] dataset.

We have also evaluated and studied several state of the art approaches by integrating ARF with Mixture of Gaussians [15] (ARF-MOG), PBAS [16] (ARF-PBAS), Codebook [17] (ARF-CB) and some recent methods, e.g., FTSG [18], Bin Wang Apr [1], and MSTB model [19] with results publicly available in CDnet[4].

---

[4] http://www.changedetection.net/

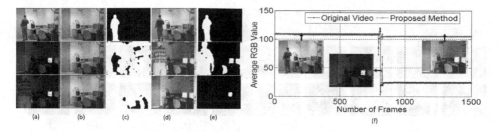

Fig. 4. Color transfer between *low-rank* and input denoised image. From left to right: (a) input, (b) *low-rank*, (c) binary mask without color conversion, (d) video sequence using color conversion, (e) foreground mask with color conversion, and (f) comparison of RGB pixel values between original and restored video using color transfer function

We use the parameters in (4) as $d = 6$, $\lambda_1 = 0.01$, $\lambda_2 = 0.05$, and $\sigma = 20$ for ARF video denoising. First the qualitative results are presented, and then, quantitative study is described in details.

4.1 Qualitative Results

The visual results are presented on some selected video sequences from each dataset due to the space limitations . The proposed approach is implemented on Matlab R2013a with 3.40 GHz Intel core i5 processor and 4 GB RAM. Moreover, a 5x5 median filtering is applied on binary mask.

CDnet [4] 2014 is a well-known real-time challenging dataset, which contains the category called *Bad weather condition* and *Night* videos. The 1st category contains 4 major video sequences called *Blizzard, Skating, Snow fall*, and *Wet snow*. The 2nd one consists of 6 videos, but only two sequences called *Bridge entry* and *Tram station* are presented. In this dataset, the *Night* videos do not contain any day time scene so we directly apply our approach without color transfer sheme. The image size of 1st category is 720×480, whereas the other videos contain 540×360 and 720×540 frame sizes, and half of the resolution is used in our experiments.

We have also tested some non-noisy videos under stable illumination condition from CDnet dataset [4] using the *Baseline* category. This category contains 4 basic videos namely: *Highway, Office, Pedestrians*, and *PETS2006*. These non-noisy sequences that contain stable lighting condition are also pre-processed using the ARF constraints, and then, the background subtraction is performed. Due to the denoised non-noisy images satisfactory smoothing properties, a small moving pixels are suppressed that eradicates most of the false alarms from the binary mask. However, the color transfer scheme has no affect in this case, since the source image i.e., the *low-rank* component and denoised non-noisy image contains the same bright scene. Fig. 5 (a) to (d), show the results on *Bad Weather Condition* videos, whereas the visual results of *Night Videos* are shown in Fig. 5 (e) to (f). In addition, the results on *Baseline* video sequences are also reported in Fig. 5 (g) to (j).

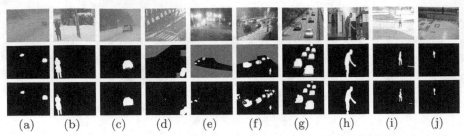

Fig. 5. Results of the proposed method. From left to right: (a)-(d) *Bad Weather* videos: (a) *Blizzard*, (b) *Skating*, (c) *Snow fall*, and (d) *Wet snow*. (e)-(f) *Night* videos: (e) *Bridge entry*, and (f) *Tram station*. (g)-(j) *Baseline* category: (g) *Highway*, (h) *Office*, (i) *Pesdestrians*, and (j) *Pets2006*. From top to bottom: input, ground truth, and our results.

I-LIDS [3] is the *Imagery Library for Intelligent Detection Systems* dataset which consists of about 213 video sequences. Among them, the category SZTRA104b contains 10 videos of worst weather environment. The image size of each sequence is 576×720. Fig. 6 depicts the visual results of 5 sequences using I-LIDS dataset.

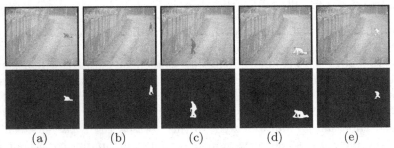

Fig. 6. I-LIDS category *SZTRA104b*. From left to right: (a) *SZTRA104b01*, (b) *SZTRA104b04*, (c) *SZTRA104b06*, (d) *SZTRA104b08*, and (e) *SZTRA104b09*. From top to bottom: input and results of our method.

4.2   Quantitative Results

For quantitative evaluations, we have computed the F-*measure* score for all sequences, by comparing our results with their available corresponding ground truth data. The *F-measure* is given as

$$F_{measure} = \frac{2 \times Recall \times Precision}{Recall + Precision}, \tag{6}$$

where *Recall* and *Precision* are computed based on true positives, false positives, and false negatives. CDnet [4] is quantitatively evaluated according to this criteria by comparing our results with available ground truth image of each sequence. However, I-LIDS dataset is evaluated according to the process described in [3] as the ground truth images are not available.

According to I-LIDS evaluation process, any alarm events presented in the first 5 minutes will be ignored and it will not effect the system performance. The detection is performed, which is compared with its ground truth data to generate the number of true positives, false positives, and false negative alarms. The detailed evaluation process can be found in [3].

Table 1, 2, and 3 show the performance of our proposed method using CDnet [4] and I-LIDS [3] dataset as compared to other approaches. In Table 1 and 2, our method outperforms in *Bad Weather* and *Night* video sequences, as compared with the state of the art algorithms. However, a comparative performance is observed for simple cases such as *Baseline* category in table. 1. Moreover, the *F-measure* score in Table 1 and 2, depicts that we are the 4th top best performer in *Bad Weather* and *Night* videos category, according to the online results reported in CDnet [4] website.

Time comlexity is also observed during our evaluations. The time is recorded in CPU time as $[hh : mm : ss]$ and we have $[00 : 00 : 56]$ for the first 100 frames having image resolution of 576×720. Since RPCA methods are not stable to process high dimensional data or they take longer time, which is not useful for real-time systems. In this study, we have achieved almost a real-time processing, in addition smoothing or suppressing the snow pixels using ARF constraints improved the background subtraction results. These good experimental evaluations are the evidence of introducing a real-time image denoising constraints together with OR-PCA.

Table 1. Qualitative results of CDnet dataset [4]: Average *F-measure* score of each video sequence with earlier approaches.

Method	Change Detection dataset [4]									
	Bad Weather				Average	Baseline				Average
	Blizzard	Skating	SnowFall	WetSnow		Highway	Office	Pedestrians	PETS2000	
ARF-MOG [15]	0.7532	0.7020	0.7899	0.7154	0.7406	0.7741	0.3260	0.7120	0.4566	0.5671
ARF-PBAS [16]	0.8020	0.7230	0.7555	0.7564	0.7573	0.8266	0.2855	0.7562	0.6822	0.6376
ARF-CB [17]	0.7564	0.7860	0.7966	0.7852	0.7810	0.8056	0.7120	0.7751	0.7789	0.7679
FTSG [18]	**0.8503**	**0.9147**	0.8197	0.7066	0.8228	0.9446	**0.9338**	0.9323	**0.9212**	**0.9330**
Bin Wang Apr [1]	0.7177	0.9103	0.7874	0.6538	0.7673	0.9452	0.7863	0.9250	0.8688	0.8813
MSTBM Model [19]	0.7136	0.5862	0.7141	0.5343	0.6370	**0.9535**	0.7541	0.8709	0.8017	0.8450
Ours	0.8496	0.7880	**0.8913**	**0.8502**	**0.8447**	0.9166	0.8850	0.9010	0.8230	0.8814

Table 2. Qualitative results of CDnet [4]: Average *F-measure* score of each video sequence with earlier approaches.

Method	Change Detection dataset [4]						
	Night Videos						Average
	BridgeEntry	BussyBoulvard	FluidHighway	StreetCornerAtNight	TramStation	WinterStreet	
ARF-MOG [15]	0.3460	0.3792	0.3987	0.4063	0.3860	0.4420	0.3960
ARF-PBAS [16]	0.4222	0.346	0.442	0.4063	0.412	0.4677	0.4160
ARF-CB [17]	0.3445	0.2930	0.3555	0.3111	0.2890	0.4599	0.3421
FTSG [18]	0.4213	0.3457	0.4169	**0.5897**	0.7017	**0.6030**	0.5130
Bin Wang Apr [1]	0.1806	0.3508	0.1924	0.4971	0.5909	0.4032	0.3802
MSTBM Model [19]	0.0256	0.3308	**0.5045**	0.2911	0.6443	0.5049	0.4164
Ours	**0.4758**	**0.3916**	0.3575	0.5601	**0.8499**	0.4944	**0.5215**

Table 3. Qualitative results of I-LIDS dataset [3]: Average *F-measure* score of each video sequence with earlier approaches.

Method	I-LIDS dataset [3]										
	SZTRA104b										Average
	01	02	03	04	05	06	07	08	09	10	
ARF-MOG [15]	0.5602	0.7452	0.6022	0.7145	0.6233	0.4856	0.7566	0.7784	0.7968	0.7475	0.6856
ARF-PBAS [16]	0.6032	0.8122	0.7466	0.7630	0.5820	0.5560	0.7720	0.7120	0.7502	0.7030	0.7062
ARF-CB [17]	0.8030	0.7820	0.7136	0.7820	0.7030	0.7844	0.8032	0.8430	0.8530	0.8830	0.7950
FTSG [18]	0.8460	0.8010	0.7563	0.7760	0.7065	0.7936	0.8230	0.8566	0.7930	0.8030	0.8125
Bin Wang Apr [1]	0.6450	0.7720	0.6630	0.8030	0.6460	0.8530	0.7256	0.7964	0.7460	0.7974	0.7447
MSTBM Model [19]	0.7488	0.8770	0.5633	0.7489	0.7687	0.7861	**0.8156**	**0.8888**	0.8654	0.9025	0.8087
Ours	**0.8632**	**0.9120**	**0.8931**	**0.8560**	**0.8870**	**0.8752**	0.8065	0.8668	**0.9450**	**0.9380**	**0.8842**

5   Conclusion

In this paper, an integrated framework for improved background subtraction is presented using real time continuous constraints ARF together with OR-PCA. Basically, the proposed scheme is divided into two stages. The first part shows the robustness against intensive weather situations such as snow or rain, whereas in the second stage, where day time scene is our assumption, which is very advantageous for the night time surveillance agents to choose it for monitoring different activities. However, we just performed small evaluations on color transfer strategy due to unavailability of datasets. Therefore, our future work is mainly focus on a more robust color transfer technique which is independent of day time bright scene and this work will be further extended for moving camera case.

Acknowledgments. This work is supported by the World Class 300 project, Development of HD video/network-based video surveillance system(10040370), funded by the Ministry of Trade, Industry, and Energy (MOTIE), Korea.

References

1. Wang, B., Dudek, P.: A fast self-tuning background subtraction algorithm. In: 2014 IEEE Conference on Computer Vision and Pattern Recognition Workshops (CVPR), pp. 401–404. IEEE (2014)
2. Bouwmans, T., Zahzah, E.H.: Robust PCA via Principal Component Pursuit: A review for a comparative evaluation in video surveillance. Computer Vision and Image Understanding, 22–34 (2014)
3. Branch, H.O.S.D.: Imagery library for intelligent detection systems I-LIDS. In: The Institution of Engineering and Technology Conference on Crime and Security, pp. 445–448, June 2006
4. Goyette, N., Jodoin, P., Porikli, F., Konrad, J., Ishwar, P.: Changedetection.net: a new change detection benchmark dataset. In: IEEE Computer Society Conference on Computer Vision and Pattern Recognition Workshops (CVPRW), pp. 1–8, June 2012
5. Candès, E.J., Li, X., Ma, Y., Wright, J.: Robust Principal Component Analysis? Journal of the ACM (JACM) **58**(3), 11–37 (2011)
6. Feng, J., Xu, H., Yan, S.: Online robust PCA via stochastic optimization. In: Advances in Neural Information Processing Systems, pp. 404–412 (2013)

7. Javed, S., Oh, S.H., Sobral, A., Bouwmans, T., Jung, S.K.: OR-PCA with MRF for robust foreground detection in highly dynamic backgrounds. In: Cremers, D., Reid, I., Saito, H., Yang, M.-H. (eds.) ACCV 2014. LNCS, vol. 9005, pp. 284–299. Springer, Heidelberg (2015)

8. Hakim, A.E.A.: A novel approach for rain removal from videos using low-rank recovery. In: Proceedings of the 5th IEEE International Conference on Intelligent Systems, Modelling and Simulation, pp. 13–18 (2014)

9. Barbu, A.: Learning real-time MRF inference for image denoising. In: IEEE Conference on Computer Vision and Pattern Recognition. CVPR 2009, pp. 1574–1581. IEEE (2009)

10. Barbu, A.: Training an active random field for real-time image denoising. IEEE Transactions on Image Processing $18(11)$, 2451–2462 (2009)

11. Roth, S., Black, M.: Fields of experts. International Journal of Computer Vision $82(2)$, 205–229 (2009)

12. Shah, M., Deng, J.D., Woodford, B.J.: Video background modeling: recent approaches, issues and our proposed techniques. Machine vision and applications $25(5)$, 1105–1119 (2014)

13. Hwang, Y., Lee, J.Y., Kweon, I.S., Kim, S.J.: Color transfer using probabilistic moving least squares. In: 2014 IEEE Conference on Computer Vision and Pattern Recognition (CVPR), pp. 3342–3349. IEEE (2014)

14. Reinhard, E., Ashikhmin, M., Gooch, B., Shirley, P.: Color transfer between images. IEEE Computer graphics and applications $21(5)$, 34–41 (2001)

15. Stauffer, C., Grimson, W.E.L.: Adaptive background mixture models for real-time tracking. In: IEEE Computer Society Conference on Computer Vision and Pattern Recognition, vol. 2. IEEE (1999)

16. Hofmann, M., Tiefenbacher, P., Rigoll, G.: Background segmentation with feedback: The pixel-based adaptive segmenter. In: 2012 IEEE Computer Society Conference on Computer Vision and Pattern Recognition Workshops (CVPRW), pp. 38–43 (2012)

17. Kim, K., Chalidabhongse, T.H., Harwood, D., Davis, L.: Background modeling and subtraction by codebook construction. In: 2004 International Conference on Image Processing. ICIP 2004, vol. 5, pp. 3061–3064. IEEE (2004)

18. Wang, R., Bunyak, F., Seetharaman, G., Palaniappan, K.: Static and moving object detection using flux tensor with split gaussian models. In: 2014 IEEE Conference on Computer Vision and Pattern Recognition Workshops (CVPRW), pp. 420–424. IEEE (2014)

19. Lu, X.: A multiscale spatio-temporal background model for motion detection. In: 2014 IEEE International Conference on Image Processing (ICIP), pp. 3268–3271. IEEE (2014)

Image Clarification Method Based on Structure-Texture Decomposition with Texture Refinement

Masato Toda$^{(\boxtimes)}$, Kenta Senzaki, and Masato Tsukada

NEC Corporation, 1753 Shimonimabe, Kawasaki 211-8666, Japan
m-toda@ap.jp.nec.com, k-senzaki@bp.jp.nec.com,
m-tsukada@cj.jp.nec.com

Abstract. This paper presents a high quality and low complexity image clarification method, which restores the visibility of images captured in bad weather and poor lighting conditions. A sequential processing of conventional dehazing and backlit correction methods has a problem that textures and noises are over-emphasized by the corrections. The proposed method first decomposes a captured image into two components: a structure component forming smooth regions and strong edges and a rest component for fine textures and noises. Image enhancement is conducted based on analyses of the first component, while controlling an amplification factor of the texture component. The utilization of the structure component for the enhancement enables pixel-wise corrections without local area analysis which results in lower computational cost. Experimental results demonstrate that the proposed method can successfully enhance image qualities and its computational cost is reasonable for real-time video processing.

Keywords: Video surveillance · Image clarification · Image dehazing · Backlit correction

1 Introduction

Recently, video surveillance for outdoor purpose has attracted attention due to the fear of terrorism and violent criminals. In a surveillance system, operators catch occurrences of crimes or suspicious behaviors from the captured images. The performance of the system depends on the visibility of the images. To achieve a high security surveillance system and comfortable operations, captured images are required to be of high quality.

Image degradations in outdoor scenes are mainly caused by two kinds of environmental conditions. There are lighting conditions and weather conditions. The lighting condition affects brightness and the weather condition affects contrast of objects in an image (figure 1). Since it is difficult to control these environmental conditions physically, image restoration techniques are required.

Many methods have been proposed to enhance the image quality in poor lighting conditions, which modifies the dynamic range of the captured image virtually and provides high visibility [5, 10, 17, 19, 20]. These methods change tone-mapping curves for each pixel according to local area analysis. The image restoration in poor

© Springer International Publishing Switzerland 2015
V. Murino and E. Puppo (Eds.): ICIAP 2015, Part II, LNCS 9280, pp. 352–362, 2015.
DOI: 10.1007/978-3-319-23234-8_33

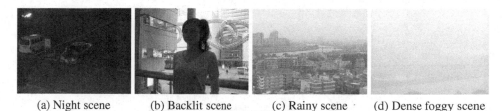

  (a) Night scene   (b) Backlit scene   (c) Rainy scene   (d) Dense foggy scene

Fig. 1. Images in bad environmental conditions.

lighting conditions is an established technique, it is widely used in many applications such as consumer digital cameras and imaging software.

The restoration of images in bad weather conditions is called "haze removal" or "image dehazing" and has been studied actively [2-4, 6-9, 11, 12, 16, 18]. Narashiman and Nayer proposed a physics-based scattering model, which can represent the light path in bad weather conditions, and showed that the scene structure can be recovered by captured images in different weather conditions [11, 12]. Schechner *et al.* proposed a dehazing method from two or more images with different polarized angles [16]. Single image dehazing is a more challenging problem, since there is fewer information available to estimate the haze-free scene. However, significant advances have been seen in recent years [2-4, 7-9, 18]. These advances are achieved based on the physics-based model with new prior about the scene. Tan proposed a method which restores the image by maximizing its local contrast [18]. Fattal proposed a retrieval method by using the relationship between the surface shading and the scene transmission that these are locally uncorrelated [2]. He *et al.* found that most local patches in haze-free images contain a pixel which has low intensity in at least one color channel and based on the prior, which is called dark channel prior, they recover vivid color images [3]. Refined methods based on the dark channel prior have been proposed [4, 8], because the dark channel prior is a simple but a effective prior. Since single image dehazing is conducted based on assumptions about the imaging model and the prior, it is quite possible that the image retrieval fails in some regions. As a result, the restored image tends to be dark and over-saturated [7].

Li *et al.* [7] proposed a post enhancement method after a single image dehazing to recover the degradation in the restored image using local area luminance. Their post enhancement is conducted with the similar concept to the enhancement in poor lighting conditions. Their work suggests that it is possible to achieve an image restoration in poor lighting and bad weather conditions, when a processing is executed in the order of a bad weather correction to a lighting correction, the lighting correction recovers the failure of the bad weather correction.

There are several problems still remain when the conventional methods are simply proceeded sequentially. One of the problems is the overemphasized textures by the correction. Since these corrections work as contrast enhancement, textures in captured images are emphasized by the corrections. The poor lighting correction recovers the failure in the bad weather correction in luminance level, however, it conducts an unnecessary enhancement in terms of textures. As a result, the corrected images become too sharp at these regions. The presence of noise in captured images is also an issue in

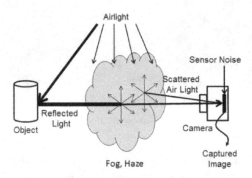

Fig. 2. Imaging model.

the corrected images. The noise is also emphasized by the corrections, and sometimes the noise becomes significantly visible by the enhancement even if it is hard to see in the original image. In addition, the computational cost becomes a problem, considering the case of implementation for image applications, because at least two local analyses are needed for the restoration.

To overcome these problems, this paper presents a new image clarification method based on structure-texture decomposition. The proposed method first decomposes a captured image into two components: a structure component forming smooth regions and strong edges and a rest component for fine textures and noises. A correction for bad weather and poor light is conducted based on analyses the structure component, while suppressing overemphasis in texture component. The utilization of the structure component for the enhancement enables pixel-wise corrections without local analyses which results in lower computational cost.

2   Imaging Model

In this section, the imaging model is presented. Figure 2 illustrates the path of lights which reach to an image sensor. In this model, an object is irradiated with airlight, and a reflected light is produced. The reflected light is attenuated by particles in the air before reaching the image sensor. The image sensor also captures airlight scattered by the particles. Finally the image sensor creates a captured image from these mixed lights with additive sensor noise.

It is well known that radiance of reflected light is related to irradiance of light and surface reflectance characteristics of object such as shape and albedo [13.14]. The radiance J is represented as equation (1), where x, c, l, A and R denote pixel position, color channel, irradiance of the incoming light, color composition of the airlight and the surface reflectance characteristics, respectively.

$$J^c(x) = l(x)\, A^c\, R^c(x) \tag{1}$$

The physics-based scattering model by Narasimhan and Nayer [11] is employed to represent the behavior of light passing through the air. Their model is simplified as equation (2) [2,3], where H denotes the intensity of mixed light irradiating the image sensor, t denotes the transmission for the scattering.

$$H^c(x) = t(x)J^c(x) + (1 - t(x))A^c \qquad (2)$$

Assuming that the additive sensor noise is white gaussian noise with a variance σ, the intensity in captured image I is represented as equation (3), where η represents an intensity of the noise.

$$I^c(x) = \big(t(x)l^c(x)R^c(x) + (1 - t(x))\big)A^c + \eta^c(x) \qquad (3)$$

In this imaging model, the change in lighting conditions is represented by l, and the change in weather conditions is represented by t. The degradation by image sensor noise and the effect by the color of the airlight are represented by η and A, respectively. Our target is to restore the captured image into an image in a good lighting and a fine weather condition represented as equation (4), where l_{ideal} denotes irradiance in a good lighting condition.

$$I^c_{ideal}(x) = l^c_{ideal}(x)R^c(x) \qquad (4)$$

3 Proposed Method

3.1 Structure-Texture Decomposition

The proposed method first decomposes a captured image into two components: a structure component forming smooth regions and strong edges and a rest component for fine textures and noises. In general, irradiance and transmission change smoothly in an object and the significant changes occur at the boundaries of objects, which correspond to image edges. Therefore, an extraction of smooth regions preserving strong edges is useful for the analyses of these variables.

In this paper, total variation (TV) norm minimization [15] is employed for the decomposition, which can extract geometric features such as flat areas, monotonic changes, and steps in an input image, while separating oscillating signals such as fine textures, specular reflection light and noises. The processed image after the TV norm minimization is configured as the structure component and the residual is regarded as texture component in this paper. Processed images are shown in figure 3, where the texture component is amplified to five times.

The structure component and the texture component are approximately represented as equation (5) and (6), respectively, where R_s represents the body color of an object and R_t represents its textures. Since the noises are separated into the texture component, we can conduct noise-free analyses using the structure component.

$$S^c(x) = \big(t(x)\,l^c(x)R^c_s(x) + (1 - t(x))\big)A^c \qquad (5)$$

$$T^c(x) = t(x)\,l^c(x)R^c_s(x)A^c + \eta^c(x) \qquad (6)$$

| (a) Input Image | (b) Structure component | (c) Texture component |

Fig. 3. Structure-texture decomposition.

The structure-texture decomposition enables to predict the occurrence of overemphasized textures after corrections by observing the change in the texture component. The structure component contains much information about a surrounding region for each pixel. Therefore, utilization of the structure component enables pixel-wise corrections without local analysis which takes computational costs, just by sharing the change in the structure component during processing.

3.2 Airlight Correction

The effect by the airlight is removed as preprocessing in this paper. This processing is a kind of an automatic white balance correction. The airlight A is estimated by taking the top 1% brightest pixel for each color channel from the structure component where little specular reflection light is included. The captured image, the structure component and the texture component are corrected as equation (7).

$$I_1^c(x) = \frac{I^c(x)}{A^c} \ , \ S_1^c(x) = \frac{S^c(x)}{A^c} \ , \ T_1^c(x) = \frac{T^c(x)}{A^c} \tag{7}$$

The variance of the image sensor noise in the corrected image is also emphasized by the correction as equation (8).

$$\sigma_1^c = \sigma^c / A^c \tag{8}$$

3.3 Bad Weather Correction

An image dehazing is proceeded with a non-linear function based on the structure component in the proposed method. To conduct the image dehazing, the transmission t should be estimated for each pixel. In this paper, the transmission t is calculated as equation (9), which means strength of scatting in the air in an image is represented by a sum of a uniform coefficient α and regionally changing coefficient β.

$$t(x) = 1 - \big(\alpha + \beta(x)\big) \tag{9}$$

Since the dark channel prior is satisfied enough when it is applied to whole region in an image, α can be detected by equation (10) with high accuracy.

$$\alpha = \min_{\forall c}(\min_{\forall x}(I_1^c(x))) \tag{10}$$

β is estimated as equation (11) under an assumption that a residual of a dark channel in the structure component include the airlight with constant ratio k.

$$\beta(x) = k \cdot \min_{\forall c}(S_1^c(x) - \alpha) \tag{11}$$

The proposed method reduces the degradation by α and β separately. Since α can be detected with high accuracy as already mentioned, the restoration based on the physics-based scattering model works well. So proposed firstly remove the effect by coefficient α as equation (12) and creates a processed image I_2.

$$I_2^c(x) = \frac{1}{1-\alpha}(I_1^c(x) - \alpha) \tag{12}$$

The accuracy of the estimate value β is relatively lower than α, and the value of β includes a prediction error which causes dark and color over-saturated regions in a restored image. The degradation tends to be significant when it is applied to dark regions, because the correction amount by the scattering model increases while the region becomes dark. To avoid the problem, the proposed method conduct a restoration to reduce the effect by errors in β using a refined non-linear function represented in equation (13), and create a haze-free image I_3.

$$I_3^c(x) = (I_2^c(x))^{1/(1-\beta(x))} \tag{13}$$

This function has a characteristic that when it is applied to bright areas it works similar to the restoration using the physics-based scattering model like equation (12), and when it is applied to dark areas it reduces the correction amount not to make the area too dark. The proposed method conduct a restoration of structure component by the same procedure and create a haze-free structure component S_3.

3.4   Poor Lighting Correction

The haze-free structure component S_3 represents a brightness of a surrounding region at an interest pixel after the bad weather correction, including the effect by the failure of the bad weather correction. Thus, a poor lighting correction is conducted using the component S_3. The irradiance is estimated by taking the maximum value of each color channel in S_3 as equation (14). A scaling factor γ for the correction is calculated as equation (15), with the similar concept to a method in [20]. In equation (15), as the estimated irradiance l_{est} decreases, the scaling factor γ increases according to parameters a and b.

$$l_{est}(x) = \max_{\forall c}(S_3^c(x)) \tag{14}$$

$$\gamma(x) = max(-a\, l_{est}(x) + b, 1) \tag{15}$$

A corrected image I_4 is created as equation (16), while ensuring that the corrected image does not cause saturation.

$$I_4^c(x) = 1 - \left(1 - I_3^c(x)\right)^{\gamma(x)} \tag{16}$$

The proposed method also conducts a restoration of structure component by using the same way and create a processed structure component S_4.

3.5   Texture Refinement

Finally, the proposed method refines textures of the processed image after the poor lighting correction. The change in the texture component by the bad weather and the poor lighting correction is represented as equation (17).

$$r_c(x) = (I_4^c(x) - S_4^c(x))/T_1^c(x) \tag{17}$$

In order to suppress the excessive amplification of the texture component, the proposed method sets an upper limit value of the amplification factor r_{max} and modifies the texture component as equation (18) and (19).

$$T_2^c(x) = p(x)\, r^c(x)\, T_1^c(x) \tag{18}$$

$$p(x) = \begin{cases} r_{max}/\max_{\forall c}(r^c(x)) & if\ \max_{\forall c}(r^c(x)) > r_{max} \\ 1 & otherwise \end{cases} \tag{19}$$

Since the noise variance in the refined texture component T_2 can be estimated as equation (20), the proposed method conducts a soft threshold shrinkage for the noise reduction as equation (21).

$$\sigma_2^c(x) = p(x)\, r^c(x)\, \sigma_1^c \tag{20}$$

$$T_3^c(x) = \begin{cases} \mathrm{sgn}(T_2^c(x)) \cdot (|T_2^c(x)| > \sigma_2^c(x)) & if\ |T_2^c(x)| > \sigma_2^c(x) \\ 0 & otherwise \end{cases} \tag{21}$$

Finally, an output image I_{out} is created by combining the corrected structure component S_4 and the refined texture component T_3.

$$I_{out}^c(x) = S_4^c(x) + T_3^c(x) \tag{22}$$

4   Evaluation

Evaluations of the proposed method were` conducted using captured images in bad environmental conditions. Table 1 shows the parameter sets used for the evaluations. The same parameters are used for the restorations except for the noise variance in a night scene. In this paper, digital TV filter [1] is employed for the structure-texture decomposition, which can efficiently minimize the TV norm.

Table 1. Parameter sets for the evaluation.

Parameter	Value	Parameter	Value
Noise variance σ	0.005	Bad lighting correction parameter a	5.0
Noise variance σ (night scenes)	0.015	Bad lighting correction parameter b	4.0
Bad weather correction parameter k	0.85	Texture refinement parameter r_{max}	3.0

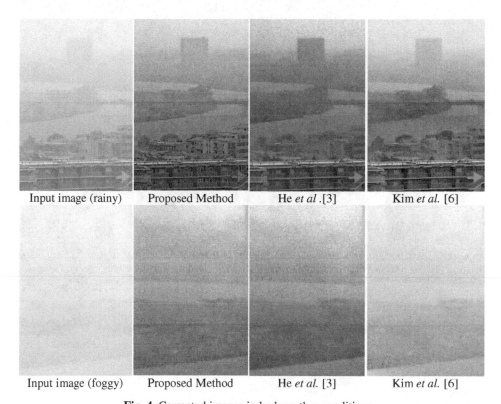

Input image (rainy)	Proposed Method	He *et al*.[3]	Kim *et al*. [6]
Input image (foggy)	Proposed Method	He *et al*. [3]	Kim *et al*. [6]

Fig. 4. Corrected images in bad weather conditions.

Figure 4 shows restored images in different bad weather conditions by the proposed method. The results by He *et al*. [3] and Kim *et al*. [6] are also shown in figure 4 for a comparison. The corrected images by He *et al*. [3] tends to be dark and color over-saturated as reported in [7] and noises in the captured image become significantly visible. The method by Kim *et al*. [6] does not cause dark or color over-saturated regions in the corrected images, however, the strength of the correction is very weak in the captured image in the foggy scene. On the other hand, our method successfully restores the image contrast failure in the bad weather condition, and create comfortable images, because our method recovers the failure in the bad weather correction while suppressing overemphasized textures and noises in the corrected images.

| Input Image | Our result | Our result without texture refinement |

Fig. 5. Details of corrected images in bad weather conditions.

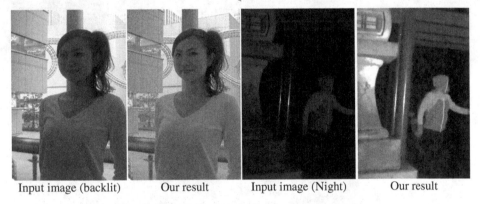

| Input image (backlit) | Our result | Input image (Night) | Our result |

Fig. 6. Corrected images in bad weather conditions.

Figure 5 represents the differences of corrected images by the presence of the texture refinement procedure in the proposed method. The corrected images without the texture refinement indicate the corrected images when the conventional bad weather correction and the poor lighting correction are simply proceeded sequentially. In the corrected images without the texture refinement, the textures are overemphasized and become like a result of applying an unsharp mask which is not intended. The noises are also emphasized and become significantly visible. The proposed method adequately suppresses these overemphasized textures and noises.

Figure 6 demonstrates corrected images in poor lighting conditions by the proposed method. These results present that the proposed method also can successfully correct images in poor lighting conditions with the same parameters.

Table 2 shows the processing times of the proposed method to a VGA size image (640×480 pixels) on a CPU (Intel Xeon E5-1650 3.2GHz). The proposed method is

Table 2. Processing times of the proposed method.

Function	Processing time (ms)
Structure-texture decomposition	8.8
Airlight correction	2.0
Bad weather correction	5.0
Poor lighting correction	3.0
Texture refinement	1.5
Total	20.3

implemented using Intel AVX. The total time of the correction is 20.3 milliseconds. This result suggests that the proposed method can be embedded as software in actual imaging applications which require real-time video processing. The computational time is almost the same as the method by Kim *et al.* [6] (48.5 fps for VGA size video) which conducts only image dehazing. The notable point is that the computation of the bad weather and the poor lighting corrections takes less than 10 milliseconds. A sequential processing of the conventional dehazing and backlit correction methods requires filtering or optimization processes for local analyses which take relatively high computational costs in each correcting procedure. On the other hand, the enhancement based on the structure component in the proposed method enables pixel-wise corrections without any local analysis after the decomposition.

5   Conclusion

This paper has proposed a new image clarification method based on structure-texture decomposition, which can restore images captured in bad weather and poor lighting conditions. Image enhancement is conducted by an analysis of the structure component, while suppressing overemphasized textures and noises. Experiments demonstrated that the proposed method can successfully enhance image qualities and its computational cost is reasonable for real-time video processing.

Future studies include detailed subjective evaluation of the corrected images by the proposed method, in comparison with other conventional methods.

References

1. Chan, T.F., Osher, S., Shen, J.: The digial TV filter and nonlinear denoising. IEEE Transactions on Image Processing **10**(2), 231–241 (2001)
2. Fattal, R.: Single image dehazing. In: Proc. ACM SIGGRAPH 2008, pp. 1–9 (2008)
3. Huang, S.-C., Chen, B.-H., Wang, W.-J.: Visibility restoration of single hazy images captured in real-world weather conditions. IEEE Transactions on Circuits and Systems for Video Technology **24**(10), 1814–1824 (2014)

4. He, K., Sun, J., Tang, X.: Single image haze removal using dark channel prior. In: IEEE conference on Computer Vision and Pattern Recognition (CVPR) 2009, pp. 1956–1963 (2009)

5. Jobson, D.J., Rahman, Z.-U., Woodell, G.A.: A multiscale retinex for bridging the gap between color images and the human observation of scenes. IEEE Transactions on Image Processing 6(7), 965–976 (1997)

6. Kim, J.-H, Jang, W.-D., Park, Y., Lee, D.-H., Sim, J.-Y., Kim, C.-S.: Temporally x real-time video dehazing. In: 19th IEEE International Conference on Image Processing, ICIP 2012, pp. 969–972 (2012)

7. Long, J., Shi, Z., Tang, W., Zhang, C.: Single remote sensing image dehazing. IEEE Geoscience and Remote Sensing Letters 11(1), 59–63 (2014)

8. Li, B., Wang, S., Zheng, J., Zheng, L.: Single image haze removal using content-adaptive dark channel and post enhancement. IET Computer Vision 8(2), 131–140 (2014)

9. Meng, G., Wang, Y., Duan, J., Xiang, S., Pan, C.: Efficient image dehazing with boundary constraint and contextual regularization. In: 2013 IEEE International Conference on Computer Vision (ICCV), pp. 617–624 (2013)

10. Monobe, Y., Yamashita, H., Kurosawa, T., Kotera, H.: High dynamic range compression for digital video camera using local contrast enhancement. In: International Conference on Consumer Electronics (ICCE) 2015, Digest of Technical Papers, pp. 217–218 (2005)

11. Narasimhan, S.G., Nayer, S.K.: Vision and the Atmosphere. International Journal on Computer Vision 48(3), 233–254 (2002)

12. Narasimhan, S.G., Nayer, S.K.: Contrast Restoration of Weather Degraded Images. IEEE Transactions on Pattern Analysis and Machine Intelligence 25(6), 713–724 (2003)

13. Oren, M., Nayer, S.K.: Generalization of lmbert's reflectance model. In: ACM SIGGRAPH 1994, pp. 239–246 (1994)

14. Phong, B.T.: Illumination for computer generated pictures. Commun. ACM 18(6), 311–377 (1975)

15. Rudin, L.I., Osher, S., Fatemi, E.: Nonlinear total variation based noise removal algorithms. Physica D: Nonlinear Phenomena 60(1–4), 259–268 (1992)

16. Shimoyama, S., Igarashi, M., Ikebe, M., Motohisa, J.: Local adaptive tone mapping with composite multiple gamma functions. In: 16th IEEE International Conference on Image Processing (ICIP 2009), pp. 3153–3156 (2009)

17. Schechner, Y.Y., Narasimhan, S.G., Nayer, S.K.: Polarization-Based Vision through Haze. Applied Optics, Special issue 42(3), 511–525 (2009)

18. Tan, R.T.: Visibility in bad weather from a single image. In: IEEE Conference on Computer Vision and Pattern Recognition (CVPR) 2008, pp. 1–8 (2008)

19. Toda, M., Tsukada, M.: High dynamic range rendering method for YUV images with global luminance correction. In: IEEE International Conference on Consumer Electronics (ICCE) 2011, pp. 255–256 (2011)

20. Toda, M., Tsukada, M., Inoue, A., Suzuki, T.: High dynamic range rendering for YUV images with a constraint on perceptual chroma preservation. In: 16th IEEE International Conference on Image Processing (ICIP 2009), pp. 1817–1820 (2009)

Detecting and Tracking the Tips of Fluorescently Labeled Mitochondria in U2OS Cells

Eero Lihavainen[1]($\boxtimes$), Jarno Mäkelä[1], Johannes N. Spelbrink[2], and Andre S. Ribeiro[1]

[1] Tampere University of Technology, Tampere, Finland
{eero.lihavainen,jarno.makela,andre.ribeiro}@tut.fi
[2] Nijmegen Centre for Mitochondrial Disorders,
Radboud University Medical Center, Nijmegen, The Netherlands
hans.spelbrink@radboudumc.nl

Abstract. We present a method for automatically detecting the tips of fluorescently labeled mitochondria. The method is based on a Random Forest classifier, which is trained on small patches extracted from confocal microscope images of U2OS human osteosarcoma cells. We then adopt a particle tracking framework for tracking the detected tips, and quantify the tracking accuracy on simulated data. Finally, from images of U2OS cells, we quantify changes in mitochondrial mobility in response to the disassembly of microtubules via treatment with Nocodazole. The results show that our approach provides efficient tracking of the tips of mitochondria, and that it enables the detection of disease-associated changes in mitochondrial motility.

Keywords: Mitochondria · Detection · Tracking · Image analysis

1 Introduction

Mitochondria are involved in many cellular processes, and their dysfunctions have been linked to several diseases. In particular, abnormal mitochondrial dynamics such as an increased rate of fission, have been reported in the case of neurodegenerative diseases (see [2]).

In order to better understand the underlying mechanisms behind abnormal mitochondrial dynamics, it is necessary to analyze time-lapse image data from a large number of cells. So far, studies have relied on qualitative descriptions of mitochondrial movement [3] and manual image analysis [11], which limit the amount of data that can be analyzed. For more detailed studies, e.g. focusing on how interactions may affect the mobility, automatic image analysis methods are needed.

Previously described methods for automatic quantification of mitochondrial motion have mostly been restricted to measuring instantaneous velocity distributions using e.g. Optical Flow estimation [9] among other techniques [1]. Such methods yield no information about long-term dynamics of individual mitochondria. For tracking individual mitochondria, Silberberg et al. [12] applied a

© Springer International Publishing Switzerland 2015
V. Murino and E. Puppo (Eds.): ICIAP 2015, Part II, LNCS 9280, pp. 363–372, 2015.
DOI: 10.1007/978-3-319-23234-8_34

particle tracking method, consisting of the detection of mitochondria and a subsequent tracking step. A limitation of their detection method is that it assumes that the mitochondria appear globular, which is not true in general, as mitochondria often exhibit elongated and networked morphologies.

As mitochondria are similar in appearance to other elongated cellular structures, such as cytoskeletal filaments, when imaged with a fluorescence microscope, methods for tracking such filaments should be applicable to tracking mitochondria as well. For tracking cytoskeletal filaments, active contour tracking methods have been used [13]. These methods have the disadvantage of requiring the adjustment of several, non-intuitive parameters. In addition, methods for tracking the tips of microtubules have recently been proposed [5,6], but they rely on an initial manual detection of the tips.

In this work, we present a novel, automatic approach for detecting the tips of mitochondria, and apply the tracking framework of [8] to track the detected tips. Our detection method is based on supervised learning, namely a Random Forest classifier. Previous methods for automatically detecting the tips of microtubules [10] or mitochondria [9] have relied on segmentation, by applying filters that enhance curvilinear structures, binarizing the filtered image via thresholding, and extracting the tips from the morphological skeleton of the binarized image. Often such approaches will either over- or undersegment parts of the mitochondrial structure, which leads to false positives and misses. In contrast, directly detecting the tips should lead to a more robust method.

Here, we present the method and its validation using synthetic data. We also present a comparison of the method to a segmentation-based approach, and find it more reliable. Finally, we demonstrate the applicability of the method to experimental data, by measuring changes in mitochondrial motility caused by treatment with Nocodazole [14,15].

2   Materials and Methods

2.1   Image Acquisition

We transfected U2OS cells with a vector expressing mitoDsRED2, a red fluorescent protein targeting the mitochondrial matrix. The nuclei were labeled with the Hoechst 33342 fluorescent dye. The images were acquired with a Nikon Eclipse Ti-E with 100x Apo, a Wallac-Perkin Elmer Ultraview spinning-disk confocal system, Andor EMCCD camera, and a Nikon PFS autofocus system.

Prior to imaging, the cells were treated with $5\mu g/ml$ Nocodazole. We then selected four cells to be imaged. At 0, 30, 60, 90, 120 and 180 minutes after the application of Nocodazole, we imaged one optical slice of each cell every 3 seconds, for 10 minutes. This resulted in 6 movies of 10 minutes for each cell.

2.2   Training and Test Data

We selected one representative image of a cell not affected by Nocodazole, in which the sizes and appearances of mitochondria varied widely. In this image, we manually marked 50 points at the tips of mitochondria, and extracted square patches of size 9×9 around them; we will refer to these as *positive* patches. Next, we extracted 1000 patches at random points, to serve as *negative* examples. This random selection was justified, because less than 1% of the points in the image contain tips of mitochondria. Finally, we manually marked 50 points at non-tip locations that shared visual features with tips: points along the mitochondria filaments, borders between two mitochondria, and curved edges of mitochondria. Figure 1 shows examples of each of these three subsets of the training data.

Although we estimated that 50 patches suffice to cover most of the variation in the appearance of the tips of mitochondria, as well as of the non-tip regions, any particular appearance may be represented in few orientations. In order to make our detector invariant to orientation, we augmented the data set with transformed versions of each manually selected patch. In particular, we applied each of the symmetries of a square to the patch: First, we mirrored the patch horizontally. Second, we rotated both the original patch and its mirrored version by 90, 180 and 270 degrees. This amounted to 7 new patches for each old patch. The reason we selected these transformations instead of, e.g., rotations of arbitrary angles, is that they require no interpolation, and thus do not introduce artifacts to the patch.

After extracting the training data, we further manually extracted 25 positive and 25 negative patches to serve as test data.

2.3   Detecting the Tips of Mitochondria Using a Random Forest Classifier

Our detection method works by classifying each sub-patch of the image in a sliding window, using a binary Random Forest (RF) classifier. As features for the classifier, we use the pixel values of the patches, read in column-major order, and normalized to zero mean and unit variance, in order to achieve invariance to intensity scaling. That is, for an image patch $P_k = \{p_{ij}\}$, where $i \in 1..9$ and $j \in 1..9$ are the row and column indices, respectively, the corresponding unnormalized feature vector is

$$x_k = [p_{11}, p_{21}, \ldots, p_{91}, p_{12}, p_{22}, \ldots, p_{19}, p_{29}, \ldots p_{99}], \tag{1}$$

and the final, normalized feature vector is obtained as

$$y_k = \frac{x_k - \langle x_k \rangle}{\text{std}(x - \langle x_k \rangle)}, \tag{2}$$

where $\langle \cdot \rangle$ denotes the sample mean, *std* denotes the sample standard deviation.

This detection procedure results in a binary image, where each connected component (CC) corresponds to one tip of a mitochondrion. However, the image will also contain some CCs that are false positive detections. We verified by visual inspection that these are typically small, approximately $1 - 2$ pixels in size. Noting that there is some uncertainty to the exact location of a manually marked tip, true positive CCs should contain more pixels in the tip region.

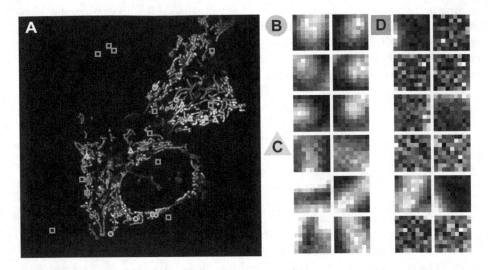

Fig. 1. Panel A shows the image from which the training data was extracted. The markers denote different types of training samples: manually picked positive samples (orange circles), manually picked negative samples (green triangles) and randomly selected negative samples (blue squares). The corresponding patches are visualized in panels B, C and D, where the colors and shapes correspond to the training sample types in panel A.

This is evident from the example classification results shown in Figure 2. Thus, as a post-processing step, we remove connected components that contain less than 3 pixels.

From the remaining CCs, we compute the centroids, which we use as the estimates of the tip locations. Examples of the final detection results are shown in Figure 2C.

2.4   Tracking

For tracking, we adopted the framework of [8], and used the authors' publicly available MATLAB implementation. In short, the method constructs tracks for detected objects in two steps: First, in each pair of subsequent frames, the objects are linked by solving a Linear Assignment Problem (LAP). If an object disappears temporarily, this procedure results in track segments instead of a complete track. Thus, as a second step, another LAP is solved to link track segments from the first step. A more detailed description of the method can be found in [8].

2.5   Generation of Synthetic Image Data

In order to test the performance of the method quantitatively, we needed movies for which the ground-truth location of each tip is known in each frame. To this end, we generated movies with simulated mitochondria. The advantages of using

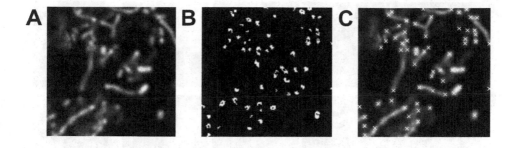

Fig. 2. A. Cropped region of a test image. B. Classification result. C. Tip locations (white crosses) detected as centroids of the connected components in B.

simulated images over manually-analyzed real images are that the ground-truth locations are free from human error, and that all parameters of the simulation can be varied to produce diverse test data.

To generate these synthetic movies, we modeled mitochondria as cubic splines, and subjected them to both brownian-like "wiggling" motion, and translation by applying a single random displacement vector to all control points of a mitochondrion. To simulate the wiggling, we first generated a random displacement vector for each control point. We then averaged the displacement vectors of nearby control points, in order to restrict the movements of the mitochondrial filaments to a realistic level of rigidity. To simulate the flat morphology of the U2OS cells, the distances moved by the mitochondria in the z-dimension were on average 1% of the distances they moved in the x- and y-dimensions.

The imaging process was modeled as follows: first, we rasterized the splines. To the resulting three-dimensional binary image, we added Poisson noise in order to generate variability in intensity inside the mitochondria filaments. Next, we convolved the noisy image with a Gaussian approximation of a fluorescence microscope point-spread-function. Finally, we added Gaussian noise to the image to simulate noise from the imaging system. Figure 3 shows example frames from one synthetic movie, as well as the locations of the true and detected tips.

3   Results

3.1   Performance of Tip Detection

For the RF, we trained 50 trees, and the number of features per split was selected to be 8. The latter parameter was selected using cross validation, by maximizing the area-under-ROC-curve. On the test data set, the classifier correctly classified 20/25(80%) of the positive examples, and 24/25(96%) of the negative examples.

We also compared the detection performance to that of a previous approach [9] based on segmentation. Briefly, the alternative method, here referred to as *SEG*, finds tips in 3 steps: first, it applies a median filter and a morphological

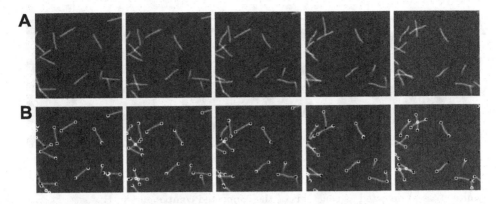

Fig. 3. A. Frames 0, 10, 20, 30 and 40 from a synthetic movie. B. The same frames with ground truth points (black crosses) and detected tips (white circles) overlaid.

top-hat filter to the image, to enhance the mitochondria structures. Next, it segments the image via Otsu's thresholding. Finally, it applies morphological thinning to find the morphological skeleton, from which the tips can be uniquely identified.

The methods were compared by generating 11 synthetic images, each containing approximately 20 tips, and comparing the locations of the detected tips to the ground truth tip locations. Specifically, the detected tips were paired with the ground truth tips via a Linear Assignment Problem (LAP); pairings were only made when the distance between the points was less than X pixels – points lacking such a real pair were paired with dummy points in the LAP. From the pairings, we obtained false positives as unpaired detections, true positives as paired detections, and false negatives as unpaired ground truth points. From these, we computed the true positive rate (TPR) and positive predictive value (PPV), and the F1-score defined as the harmonic mean of PPV and TPR. The results for both methods are shown in Table 1. The proposed method had only a slightly smaller TPR compared to SEG, but a significantly larger PPV. Consequently, the proposed method also yielded a larger F1-score.

Table 1. Detection performance of proposed method and alternative method (SEG) on synthetic images

	Proposed	SEG
TPR	0.91	0.92
PPV	0.89	0.79
F1	0.90	0.85

3.2 Accuracy of Tracking

For validating the method, we generated 11 synthetic movies of 101 frames each, and stored the locations of the mitochondrial tips, to serve as the ground truth data. We quantified the tracking accuracy on the synthetic data using a similar approach to [4]: we paired each ground truth track with a *hypothesis track* generated by the tracking method. This was done via solving a Linear Assignment Problem (LAP), where the cost c of each pairing is defined as

$$c(g,h) = \sum_{i \in G \cap H} \min(||g_i - h_i||_2, d_{max}) + |G \ominus H| \cdot d_{max} \qquad (3)$$

Here, we used the following definitions: $|\cdot|$ denotes set cardinality, and $\ominus$ is the symmetric difference between sets. We defined $d_{max} = 2$ pixels to be the maximum distance between a ground truth point and a hypothesis point at which we can consider a point detected. G and H are sets that contain the indices of the movie frames in which a ground truth track and the paired hypothesis track are present (the former corresponding to frames where the object is visible, i.e. in focus), g and h are ground truth and hypothesis tracks, and the track points in frame i are denoted by g_i and h_i.

The effect of the latter summand in Eq. 3 is to increment c by d_{max} for all ground truth points that do not have a matching hypothesis point (misses), and all the hypothesis points that do not have a matching ground truth point (false detections). In the solution of the LAP, a pairing was not allowed between tracks that had no points less than d_{max} pixels apart; unpaired tracks were handled by assigning them to dummy elements in the LAP.

From the paired tracks, we wanted to answer the following questions: How likely is a hypothesis track to be paired with a ground truth track? Also, how likely is a true object track to be detected by the tracking method? To address these questions, we defined the following error measures, which were calculated over all the tracks in the data set:

$$E_1 = 1 - \frac{\#\{\text{hypothesis tracks paired with a ground truth track}\}}{\#\{\text{hypothesis tracks}\}} \qquad (4)$$

$$E_2 = 1 - \frac{\#\{\text{ground truth tracks paired with a hypothesis track}\}}{\#\{\text{ground truth tracks}\}}. \qquad (5)$$

In addition, we wanted to quantify the quality of the detected tracks. To this end, we asked: in a correctly detected true track, how likely is a point to be missed or assigned to the wrong object? For this, we calculated the following:

$$E_3 = \frac{\sum_{i \in G} \mathcal{I}(i \notin H)}{|G|} \qquad (6)$$

$$E_4 = \frac{|H \setminus G| + \sum_{i \in G \cap H} \mathcal{I}(||g_i - h_i||_2 > d_{max})}{|H|}. \qquad (7)$$

Here, $\mathcal{I}$ denotes the indicator function. The quantity E_3 measures the fraction of ground truth points that were missed, and E_4 measures the fraction of hypothesis points that were assigned to a wrong object.

The results from the experiment were as follows: E_1, 0.09; E_2, 0.29; E_3, 0.4 and E_4, 0.09. Thus, 9% of the hypothesis tracks were not paired; 29% of the true tracks were not detected; 40% of the ground truth points were missed; and 9% of the hypothesis points were assigned to a wrong object. We confirmed by visual inspection that the high values for E_2 and E_3 were largely due to failures of the detection method. Another source of missed points was that some track segments were not linked by the tracking method.

3.3   Quantification of Mitochondrial Motion in U2OS Cells

After validating the method on synthetic data, we tested whether it can quantify changes in mitochondrial movement caused by Nocodazole, which causes the depolymerization of microtubules (see e.g. [14]). Since intracellular transport of mitochondria occurs, at least to some extent, along microtubules (see [7]), the application of Nocodazole should result in reduced mobility of mitochondria. Such a reduction in mobility has been observed in various cell types [14,15]. We can quantify this effect with the proposed method.

To this end, we computed the mean speed for each track as the mean displacement between movie frames. Figure 4 shows the distributions of the mean speeds in each cell, for the first and the last movie, and the medians of these distributions in all movies. Between the first and the last movie, the median speed has decreased by 14–44%, with the difference being statistically significant for each cell ($P < 0.01$, Wilcoxon rank-sum test, N=416–755).

4   Discussion

With the ongoing development of live, single-cell time-lapse imaging techniques, the objective analysis of the kinetics of mitochondria is expected to play a significant role in the detection of mitochondria-related diseases, among other. This will require the use of image analysis tools capable of automatic detection and tracking mitochondria.

We demonstrated that our method can detect the tips of fluorescently labeled mitochondria with reasonable accuracy. In addition, we showed that the direct detection of tips using the new method results in fewer false positives than a segmentation-based approach, as indicated by the higher PPV.

In our tests with synthetic data, we found that the detection and tracking approach proposed here tends to result in incomplete tracks, as well as completely missed tracks. This is in part due to some tips being missed by the detection method, and also due to the tracking method sometimes failing to link track segments. Still, as long as the application does not require complete tracks, or unique tracks for each object, the method produces reliable results in this regard.

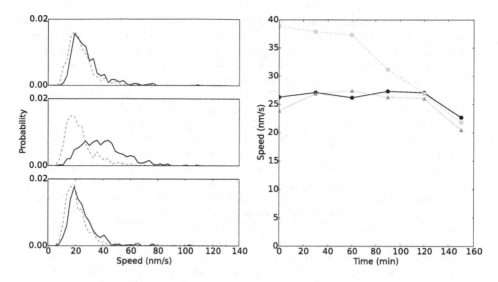

Fig. 4. Left: normalized histograms of mean speeds for cells 1-3 (top to bottom). The solid and dashed lines correspond to the movies captured 0 minutes and 180 minutes after application of Nocodazole, respectively. Right: medians of mean speeds for cells 1 (circles), 2 (squares) and 3 (triangles); each data point corresponds to one movie.

The results also showed that, for a correctly identified track, although many points will be missed (relating to the aforementioned issues), the tracks consist mainly of correctly identified points. This, along with the previous result, suggests that the method's results can be trusted.

Finally, by applying the method to images of U2OS cells treated with Nocodazole, we detected a decrease in mitochondrial motility in all cells; this result is consistent with previous studies [14, 15].

For a more complete characterization of mitochondrial dynamics, it would be useful to keep track of not only the tips, but the whole mitochondrial filaments. This should be feasible by, for example, coupling the present method with an active contour segmentation method.

Finally, we expect our approach to be applicable to tracking other subcellular structures with similar shapes, such as microtubules and other cytoskeletal filaments, as well.

References

1. Beraud, N., Pelloux, S., Usson, Y., Kuznetsov, A.V., Ronot, X., Tourneur, Y., Saks, V.: Mitochondrial dynamics in heart cells: very low amplitude high frequency fluctuations in adult cardiomyocytes and flow motion in non beating HL-1 cells. Journal of bioenergetics and biomembranes **41**(2), 195–214 (2009)
2. Chen, H., Chan, D.C.: Mitochondrial dynamics-fusion, fission, movement, and mitophagy-in neurodegenerative diseases. Human Molecular Genetics **18**(R2), R169–76 (2009)

3. Chen, H., Detmer, S., Ewald, A.J., Griffin, E.E., Fraser, S.E., Chan, D.C.: Mitofusins Mfn1 and Mfn2 coordinately regulate mitochondrial fusion and are essential for embryonic development. The Journal of cell biology **160**(2), 189–200 (2003)

4. Chenouard, N., Smal, I., Chaumont, F.D.: Objective comparison of particle tracking methods. Nature Methods **11**(3), 281–289 (2014)

5. Demchouk, A.O., Gardner, M.K., Odde, D.J.: Microtubule Tip Tracking and Tip Structures at the Nanometer Scale Using Digital Fluorescence Microscopy. Cellular and molecular bioengineering **4**(2), 192–204 (2011)

6. Hadjidemetriou, S., Toomre, D., Duncan, J.: Motion tracking of the outer tips of microtubules. Medical image analysis **12**(6), 689–702 (2008)

7. Hales, K.G.: The machinery of mitochondrial fusion, division, and distribution, and emerging connections to apoptosis. Mitochondrion **4**(4), 285–308 (2004)

8. Jaqaman, K., Loerke, D., Mettlen, M.: Robust single-particle tracking in live-cell time-lapse sequences. Nature methods **5**(8), 695–702 (2008)

9. Lihavainen, E., Mäkelä, J., Spelbrink, J.N., Ribeiro, A.S.: Mytoe: automatic analysis of mitochondrial dynamics. Bioinformatics **28**(7), 1050–1 (2012)

10. Saban, M., Altinok, A., Peck, A., Kenney, C., Feinstein, S., Wilson, L., Rose, K., Manjunath, B.S.: Automated tracking and modeling of microtubule dynamics. In: 3rd IEEE International Symposium on Biomedical Imaging: Nano to Macro, pp. 1032–1035 (2006)

11. Saunter, C.D., Perng, M.D., Love, G.D., Quinlan, R.A.: Stochastically determined directed movement explains the dominant small-scale mitochondrial movements within non-neuronal tissue culture cells. FEBS letters **583**(8), 1267–73 (2009)

12. Silberberg, Y.R., Pelling, A.E., Yakubov, G.E., Crum, W.R., Hawkes, D.J., Horton, M.A.: Tracking displacements of intracellular organelles in response to nanomechanical forces. In: 2008 5th IEEE International Symposium on Biomedical Imaging: From Nano to Macro, pp. 1335–1338, May 2008

13. Smith, M.B., Li, H., Shen, T., Huang, X., Yusuf, E., Vavylonis, D.: Segmentation and tracking of cytoskeletal filaments using open active contours. Cytoskeleton **67**(11), 693–705 (2010)

14. Steinberg, G., Schliwa, M.: Organelle movements in the wild type and wall-less fz; sg; os-1 mutants of Neurospora crassa are mediated by cytoplasmic microtubules **564**, 555–564 (1993)

15. Yi, M., Weaver, D., Hajnóczky, G.: Control of mitochondrial motility and distribution by the calcium signal: a homeostatic circuit. The Journal of cell biology **167**(4), 661–72 (2004)

Recognition of the Human Fatigue Based on the ICAAM Algorithm

Konrad Rodzik and Dariusz Sawicki[✉]

Warsaw University of Technology, Warsaw, Poland
konrad.rodzik@gmail.com, dasa@iem.pw.edu.pl

Abstract. The international statistics show that a large number of road accidents are caused by driver fatigue. A system that can detect oncoming worker fatigue could help in preventing many accidents. Many researchers focused to measure separately different physiological changes like eye blinking or head movement. Uncomfortable EEG analysis is also discussed in this field. In presented paper, we describe a simple, non-intrusive system for detection of worker fatigue. The system, based on Inverse Compositional Active Appearance Models (ICAAM) method, allows for comprehensive analysis of the face shape and its basic elements.

Keywords: Fatigue detection · Worker fatigue · ICAAM · Yawning · Eyes blinking

1 Introduction

Fatigue is one of the most important factors determining the performance and safety on a variety of workplaces. Overall fatigue is the most frequently mentioned work-related problem, and even more so for transport workers [1]. Statistical data summarizing the accidents are very sad. Drivers and doctors (surgeons) are professions where the dangerous consequences of fatigue can be very serious. In many countries tiredness and falling asleep while driving was found to explain almost 20 % of the traffic accidents causing deaths [2]. Symptoms and effects of fatigue are obviously dependent on individual predisposition and age. It depends also on the time of day or night, and the circadian cycle of work and rest. Early and fast recognition of fatigue can prevent accidents in many cases. In addition, identification and assessment of fatigue can be used in many scientific fields.

The aim of this study was to develop a simple and effective system for fatigue detection based on facial image analysis. Additionally the usefulness and implementation possibility of Active Appearance Models (AAM) and Inverse Compositional Active Appearance Models (ICAAM) methods in extracting facial features needed to assess the fatigue were analyzed.

Rapid technological development causes, that attempts to auto-evaluation of the multivariate condition (and thus also the fatigue) are increasingly being used in various fields. A good example is the automotive industry, where the newer types of cars

© Springer International Publishing Switzerland 2015
V. Murino and E. Puppo (Eds.): ICIAP 2015, Part II, LNCS 9280, pp. 373–382, 2015.
DOI: 10.1007/978-3-319-23234-8_35

are equipped with a variety of sensors and driver assistance systems. Attempts to detect fatigue in such systems are based on the analysis of driver activity. Most often analyzed are: the driver's eye movements and the timing and frequency of eyelid closure [3] or the physical activity (movements of the body, hands, facial muscle movements) [4]. Despite the fact that work on the described technology have been carried out for more than 10 years, it still imperfections of such solutions and the complexity of the problem does not allow to put it into the mass (inexpensive and commonly used) production.

Fatigue tests for detection are carried out in different directions. In many papers eye tracking system is used for detection of sleep symptoms [5,6,7,8,9]. Devi and Bajaj [5], focused on the state of eyes (open or closed) in 5 consecutive frames of video. In [6] blinking analysis (frequency and duration) was used and also the Karolinska Sleepiness Scale (KSS) was discussed.

Singh and Papanikolopoulos in paper [8] determine driver fatigue by analysis of eyes movements and looking for micro-sleep symptoms. The yawning analysis can be added effectively to the eye tracking [10]. In the paper [11] the authors try to use global analysis of the physiological state of fatigue, but in order to achieve real-time performance they focused on a single visual cue – the state of the eye. In [12] a Support Vector Machine (SVM) classifier is used. It allows recognize the state of fatigue in the face image after proper SVM training. EEG analysis has been also used in detection the level of sleepiness [13,14,15]. There is very interesting method but in our opinion it is today unpractical in a real work of drivers. We can find also well prepared surveys of the fatigue and sleep symptoms [6], [16,17]. Very interesting example of the review is the industrial publication [18] where the set of systems for detecting fatigue in the mining industry has been described.

2   Behaviors That Demonstrate the Appearance of Fatigue

Recognizing of the fatigue and sleep symptoms is the important tasks of psychology of work. Research on a sleep is conducted by the National Sleep Foundation [19]. It is nonprofit organization whose stated objectives are not only to focus on comfort of the sleep but also to improve public health and safety in context of sleep problems. When we analyze the behavior of human fatigue, we should focus on the three main parts of the face (eyes, eyebrows, mouth) and the whole head [19]. Most of the fatigue recognition systems use one selected item of the face. Most often it is the analysis of eye movement / blinking. It should be noted, however, other factors, including the impact of working / activity time. The impact of sleep deprivation on skill based cognitive functions and the degradation of performance of responding to unexpected disturbances was also analyzed in the literature [20].

The most important items that indicate changes of the fatigue level include:

- **The eyes.** It stands out, mainly, a smaller opening of the eyelids and increased frequency of eye blinking. In addition the movements of the eyelid (blinking), in this case, become much slower than those in the state of the rest. Attention should also be paid to the viewing direction. While the state of fatigue, people often look for a long time at one point, it is the so-called state of "suspension".

- **The mouth.** The basic and reliable response of the mouth, which proves fatigue, is yawning. Assuming that the default position is closed or slightly open mouth, it is enough to analyze the opening of the upper and lower lips. In addition, it is worth noting that while yawning, in the moment of maximum mouth opening, a person also frequently closes his eyes and frowning.
- **The eyebrows.** Eyebrows are closely related to human eyes. Rested man performs small movements of the eyebrows in accordance with the movements of the eyes (eyelids). Fatigue causes "stillness" of the eyebrows.
- **The head.** The behavior of the head is also important. Tired man has difficulty keeping his head straight and vertical. In the final stage of fatigue (and indeed at the moment of falling asleep), the head falls forward or deviates far to the rear or to any side. Tired person starts also more likely to touch his face, as well as over-comb his hair.

It is worth noting that all behaviors mentioned above can be analyzed in a similar manner using methods of shape recognition for the face.

3   Image Processing in the Fatigue Detection

Separation of facial features can be performed using multiple algorithms. Frequently used method for analyzing medical or mechanical images, as well as images of the face is an Active Shape Model (ASM) [21,22]. In this method, the shapes are described by a set of so-called landmark points. In the learning phase, a statistical model is constructed for a given object. In the recognition phase the attempt is made to match the analyzed object model. The combination of using the Active Appearance Models (AAM) [23] allows additionally analyzing the texture. Statistical models of shape and appearance are powerful tools for interpreting medical images. We assume a training set of images in which corresponding landmark points have been marked on every image. From this data we can compute a statistical model of the shape variation, a model of the texture variation and a model of the correlations between shape and texture [24]. AAM is an iterative algorithm, the iteration followed by matching shapes to the shape of the reference. Inverse Compositional Active Appearance Models (ICAAM) [25] is an improved version of the AAM algorithm.

ICAAM method was used in the proposed solution in this article. Analysis is performed using images captured by a video camera. On the face from the image the grid points was applied to describe the shape. Tracking changes in the position of the grid points allows us to analyze changes in the shape of the face, and thus analyze the changes of the shape and position of the individual face elements. In accordance with Chapter 2 changes recognized as closing eyes and yawning are taken into account. The analysis of the relevant changes leads to attempt of fatigue detection.

The main problem of facial image processing for detecting fatigue is to identify the appropriate shape of the lips. The main difference between yawning and standard mouth that is in open state is that the yawning state is recognized based on time. Our algorithm checks if the distance between mouth upper and lower lips is greater than width of the mouth. Based on the landmark points the maximum width and height of mouth is calculated in each iteration. That gives us the accurate comparison parameters. When the correct criteria for yawning are met, algorithm starts tracking how long yawning is taking. Fatigue level increases more with time. It means that more fatigue points will be added to the overall fatigue level for example in the 3rd second of the yawning than in the first second. That gives us nice advantage against faulty recognition when human just open his mouth to speak something. Even if criteria are met (distance of the lips higher than width of the mouth), this state will last for very limited period of time, that means it will not impact overall fatigue level in the meaningful way. This same rules are applied when algorithm track eyes. Both eyes, at the same time need to be in a closing state. The distance between upper and lower eyelid needs to be equal or lower than one of the third of width of the eye. And again maximum height and width of the eye are calculated in each recorded frame.

4   Assessment of the Fatigue Condition

In order to facilitate the final evaluation, the simple percentage measure of fatigue has been proposed. We assume that the initial level (initial measure) of the human fatigue is 0%. Along with the ongoing tracking and analysis the level of fatigue may rise or fall. But it will be always situated in the range from 0% to 100%. In the algorithm, the different weights for individual events have been used. We proposed simple formulas (1), (2) describing the changes of the fatigue condition in the best way.

For increasing the fatigue level:

$$CFL = CFL + 0.5(LEC + REC) + 0.75MO \tag{1}$$

For reducing the fatigue level:

$$CFL = CFL - \frac{\sqrt{ET}}{ET} \tag{2}$$

where:

CFL - current fatigue level (in percent 0-100%), LEC - left eye closed, REC - right eye closed, MO - mouth opened, ET - elapsed time when no single fatigue symptoms were detected (in seconds). The values of LEC, REC can be: 0, 1, 2, 3, etc. – in proportion to the time of closing eyes in seconds. The value of MO can be 0 or 1.

At the start of analysis $CFL=0$. After every change of fatigue level, the value of CFL is corrected if it is out of the range (0-100).

The formulas (1) and (2) were developed empirically. We performed set of experiments and many versions of the equations were analyzed. The main idea behind this equation was that single evidence of fatigue detected from eyes is greater than single evidence detected from mouth. However this is only valid when both eyes are closed with the given criteria. That means when only one eye is closed the fatigue level will increase less dynamically than when yawning is detected. But when both eyes are closed, fatigue level will increase more rapidly than during yawning. Of course all the value parameters can be adjusted for the further experiment purposes. Current values were giving the best results for the experiments performed on the face database. During the time that algorithm doesn't detect any symptoms of fatigue; the overall level of fatigue is decreased. But it's decreasing a lot slower than it can increase when fatigue symptoms are detected.

The rules of "fatigue behavior" (described above) are simple and obvious but not so easy to describe by simple equation. Many versions of equation with different weight were taken into account. To find the right weight for individual events and provide the best work of the algorithm many trials and comparative studies have been conducted.

5   Implementation and Tests of the System

The project was written in XCode and Qt-Creator environment for MacOS X platform using C++ and OpenCV library. There is of course the possibility to move the project to other operating system like Windows or Linux because Qt-Creator and OpenCV are multiplatform. Due to the long time involved in the learning process of the system, the phase responsible for this process was written in a way that allows parallelization of operations on multiple processor units. The whole project can operate in four modes. In learning mode, the recognition mode, preview mode and test mode. Of course, the first two modes are standard modes of operation (fatigue analysis).

The algorithm described in this paper has been subjected to many tests. We used public face database The IMM Face Database [26]. It contains 240 face images of different people in different positions. The first half of the images was used to train the algorithm, the second for testing the matching algorithm.

The fatigue detection experiment covered two steps: learning process performed on the public face database and fatigue detection from live camera stream.

Learning process was done for colorful face images as well as grayscale images. The output file from the learning process differs between color and gray scale images. For the colorful images it was approximately 3 times greater in size than in gray scale. Learning time for the colorful input frames took also approximately 3 times more. There is also one important problem in this step. It's a scale of the image during learning process. Algorithm is creating mipmaps of the reference images. It's scaling down reference image always by the factor of two (x1, x2, x4, x8). Time of the learning process (as well as size of the output file) increases with every mipmap scale.

The fatigue detection was tested using live camera stream. It was conducted on the images of authors' faces. We performed four kinds of tests:

- Without any extraordinary lighting conditions (directional point lighting etc).
- With strong left and right directional lighting.
- Colorful recording frames.
- Grayscale recording frames.

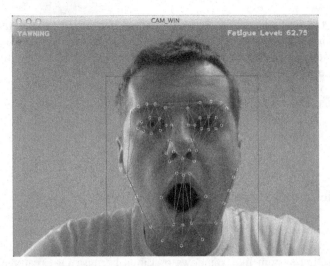

Fig. 1. Image of author's face. The result of the matching algorithms. The net of landmark point is shown. The visible rectangle represents the part of image where face has been found

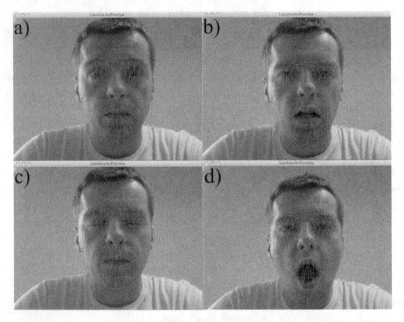

Fig. 2. Image of author's face. The result of the fatigue analysis. a) standard shape of mouth and a little wider opened eyes, decision: no fatigue symptoms, b) standard shape of eyes and a little wider opened mouth, decision: no fatigue symptoms. c) standard shape of mouth and closed eyes, decision: fatigue, d) standard shape of eyes and yawning, decision: fatigue

The matching problem was observed when the image from live camera stream and the strong left and right directional light was used. Landmarks grid not always proper-ly fit into the image frame. In such a case the algorithm could not perform real fatigue test on input frame images. For other test cases 90% match was observed. It confirmed the correctness of the program. In the Figure 1. the result of proper matching is shown. The result of the fatigue analysis for the author's is shown in the Figure 2.

6   Results and Analysis

In the analysis of the proposed algorithm, attention was drawn primarily on learning mode of the system. The more test data is entered, the better description of the changes the shape of the face will be included in the algorithm. However, not only the amount of data is important. The obvious problem is the quality of the images – the better technical quality (sharpness, exposure) and improved image resolution allows for more accurate matching grid. The study also showed that the training set should cover the different lighting options as well as face settings. This allows extending the scope of the analysis of fatigue. Independent problem is the decision of the usage of color images (RGB palette) or black and white (grayscale) in the learning process. Grayscale fatigue detection was performed faster than colorful one and could work on wider range of image data (lower resolutions, small differences in light conditions etc). Good quality color photos provide a better description of the learning process. Research showed, however, that if the test images are much lower quality (or e.g. black and white); they result in errors in the recognition of the shape which leads to poor fit of landmark points. This will result in incorrect operation of fatigue analysis algorithm. It seems that the problem of correlation of image quality between learning and testing modes is an independent serious problem and requires additional study later.

An important problem was the lighting conditions. The strong left / right directional light creates difficult conditions to recognize fatigue effectively. It is caused by matching problem. The developing of the matching algorithm or extended light recognition is needed. This required, however, additional study and future research.

The ICAAM method turned out to be effective for applications in fatigue detection. On the one hand the same algorithm allows detecting shape changes in mouth image as well as in eyes images. On the other hand the tests showed good performance of the iterative algorithm. The best results were observed after 4-5 iterations of the algorithm. After that, no real improvements could be observed in the fitting process. Good quality images make it possible to obtain high quality results in the learning mode. As a result, in the recognition mode, fatigue diagnosis is possible after approx. 5 iterations. In this way the processing of one frame of the video stream takes approx. 0.05s. This gives the ability of analysis up to 20fps (frames per second). This would mean fatigue recognition in real time. Unfortunately, experiments have shown that keeping so fast work of algorithm is very difficult. Temporary change of lighting was enough to extend the matching process more than ten times. In this case, temporary speed of analysis is at level of 2-3fps.

7   Summary

In this paper the use of methods of shape assessment (ICAAM) for fatigue analysis has been proposed. It turned out that the application of ICAAM method was very effective. This gave the opportunity to comprehensive approach to the analysis of the shape of the face. As a result, the same mechanism can detect local changes in the position and shape of the different elements of the face. The study focused on two factors associated with fatigue: on yawning and on closing eyes (Figure 2.). In both cases was carried out the same analysis of changes in the position of the mesh nodes describing the shape of the face. In this way, the addition of another element (e.g. changes in the position of the eyebrows) does not require new algorithm. It is enough to collect proper images of the new behavior and to learn the system. This is a very important advantage of the introduced method.

The proposed solution also has disadvantages. Matching grid using ICAAM creates problems in situations of environmental change (e.g. lighting). Also, the image quality of learning and recognition mode has a very strong impact on the correctness of the analysis. These problems require additional research, and this work will be continued. After a series of experiments, on the basis of the properties of two different symptoms of fatigue, a simple multifactorial formula for assessment of fatigue level has been proposed. Of course, adding another symptom requires an additional modification of the formula.

The results – processing capabilities at up to 20fps offer an opportunity, after optimization and solving the above problems, to implement the proposed algorithm in practice.

References

1. Osh in figures: Occupational Safety and Health in the Transport Sector - an Overview, Report of the European Agency for Safety and Health at Work. Publications Office of the European Communities, Luxembourg (2011)
2. Osh in figures: Annex to Report: Occupational Safety and Health in the Road Transport sector: An Overview. National Report: Finland. Report of the European Agency for Safety and Health at Work. Publications Office of the European Communities, Luxembourg (2011)
3. von Jan, T., Karnahl, T., Seifert, K., Hilgenstock, J., Zobel, R.: Don't sleep and drive – VW's fatigue detection technology. In: Proc. of 19th International Technical Conference on the Enhanced Safety of Vehicles, Washington, DC, USA (2005). http://www-nrd.nhtsa.dot.gov/pdf/esv/esv19/05-0037-O.pdf (retrieved March 18, 2015)
4. Bosch Driver Drowsiness Detection. http://www.bosch-presse.de/presseforum/details.htm?txtID=5037&locale=en (retrieved March 18, 2015)
5. Devi, M.S., Bajaj, P.R.: Driver fatigue detection based on eye tracking. In: Proc. of ICETET 2008. First International Conference on Emerging Trends in Engineering and Technology, Nagpur, Maharashtra, pp. 649–652 (2008). doi:10.1109/ICETET.2008.17
6. Friedrichs, F., Yang, B.: Camera-based drowsiness reference for driver state classification under real driving conditions. In: Proc. of 2010 IEEE Intelligent Vehicles Symposium, San Diego USA, pp. 101–106 (2010). doi:10.1109/IVS.2010.5548039

7. Rahman, A.S.M.M., Azmi, N., Shirmohammadi, S., El Saddik, A.: A novel haptic jacket based alerting scheme in a driver fatigue monitoring system. In: Proc. of 2011 IEEE International Workshop on Haptic Audio Visual Environments and Games (HAVE), Hebei, pp. 112–117 (2011). doi:10.1109/HAVE.2011.6088406

8. Singh, S., Papanikolopoulos, N.P.: Monitoring driver fatigue using facial analysis techniques. In: Proc. of 1999 IEEE/IEEJ/JSAI International Conference on Intelligent Transportation Systems, Tokyo Japan, pp. 314–318 (1999). doi:10.1109/ITSC.1999.821073

9. Jiao, Y., et al.: Recognizing slow eye movement for driver fatigue detection with machine learning approach. In: Proc. of 2014 International Joint Conference on Neural Networks (IJCNN), Beijing China, pp. 4035–4041 (2014). doi:10.1109/IJCNN.2014.6889615

10. Liu, W., Sun, H., Shen, W.: Driver fatigue detection through pupil detection and yawning analysis. In: Proc. of 2010 International Conference on Bioinformatics and Biomedical Technology (ICBBT), Chengdu China, pp. 404–407 (2010). doi:10.1109/ICBBT.2010.5478931

11. Branzan Albu, A., Widsten, B., Wang, T., Lan, J., Mah, J.: A computer vision-based system for real-time detection of sleep onset in fatigued drivers. In: Proceedings of 2008 IEEE Intelligent Vehicles Symposium, Eindhoven, The Netherlands, pp. 25–30 (2008)

12. Ji, Q., Zhu, Z., Lan, P.: Real-Time Nonintrusive Monitoring and Prediction of Driver Fatigue. IEEE Transactions on Vehicular Technology 53(4), 1052–1068 (2004). doi:10.1109/TVT.2004.830974

13. Papadelis, C., Kourtidou-Papadeli, C., Bamidis, P.D., Chouvarda, I.: Indicators of sleepiness in an ambulatory EEG study of night driving. In: Proc. of the 28th IEEE EMBS Annual International Conference, New York, USA, pp. 6201–6204 (2006).

14. Michail, E., Kokonozi, A., Chouvarda, I., Maglaveras, N.: EEG and HRV Markers of Sleepiness and Loss of Control During Car Driving. In: Proc. of EMBS 2008. 30th IEEE Annual International Conference on Engineering in Medicine and Biology Society, Vancouver, Canada, pp. 2566–2569 (2008). doi:10.1109/IEMBS.2008.4649724

15. Borghini, G., et al.: Assessment of mental fatigue during car driving by using high resolution EEG activity and neurophysiologic indices. In: Proc. of 2012 IEEE Annual International Conference on Engineering in Medicine and Biology Society (EMBC), San Diego USA, pp. 6442–6445 (2012). doi:10.1109/EMBC.2012.6347469

16. Wang, Q., Yang, J., Ren, M., Zheng, Y.: Driver fatigue detection: a survey. In: Proc. of WCICA 2006. The Sixth World Congress on Intelligent Control and Automation, Dalian, vol. 2, pp. 8587–8591 (2006). doi:10.1109/WCICA.2006.1713656

17. Coetzer, R.C., Hancke, G.P.: Driver fatigue detection : a survey. In: Proc. of AFRICON 2009 Nairobi, Kenya, pp. 1–6 (2009). doi:10.1109/AFRCON.2009.5308101

18. Operator Fatigue - Detection Technology Review. CATERPILAR report (2008). https://safety.cat.com/cda/files/771871/7/fatigue_report_021108.pdf (retrieved March 18, 2015)

19. National Sleep Foundation. http://sleepfoundation.org/ (retrieved March 18, 2015)

20. Yang, J.H., et al.: Detection of Driver Fatigue Caused by Sleep Deprivation. IEEE Trans. on Man and Cybernetics, Part A: Systems. Systems and Humans 39(4), 694–705 (2009). doi:10.1109/TSMCA.2009.2018634

21. Cootes, T.F.: An Introduction to active shape models. apears as a chapter 7 (model-based methods in analysis of biomedical images). In: Baldosk, R., Graham, J. (ed) Image Processing and Analysis. Oxford University Press, pp. 223–248 (2000). http://personalpages.manchester.ac.uk/staff/timothy.f.cootes/Papers/asm_overview.pdf (retrieved March 18, 2015)

22. Cootes, T.F., Taylor, C.J., Cooper, D.H., Graham, J.: Active Shape Models - Their Training and Application. Computer Vision and Image Understanding **61**, 38–59 (1995)
23. Cootes, T.F., Edwards, G.J., Taylor, C.J.: Active Appearance Models. IEEE Trans. on Pattern Analysis and Machine Intelligence **23**(6), 681–685 (2001). doi:10.1109/34.927467
24. Cootes, T.F., Taylor, C.J.: Statistical models of appearance for medical image analysis and computer vision. In: Proc. SPIE 4322, Medical Imaging 2001: Image Processing, vol. 236 (2001). doi:10.1117/12.431093 http://personalpages.manchester.ac.uk/staff/timothy.f.cootes/Papers/asm_aam_overview.pdf (retrieved March 18, 2015)
25. Matthews, I., Baker, S.: Active Appearance Models Revisited. Intern. Journal of Computer Vision **60**(2), 135–164 (2004). doi:10.1023/B:VISI.0000029666.37597.d3
26. Stegmann, M.B., Ersbøll, B.K., Larsen, R.: FAME – a Flexible Appearance Modeling Environment. IEEE Trans. on Medical Imaging **22**(10), 1319–1331 (2003)

Rich QR Code for Multimedia Management Applications

Iuliia Tkachenko[1,2]([✉]), William Puech[1], Olivier Strauss[1],
Christophe Destruel[2], Jean-Marc Gaudin[2], and Christian Guichard[2]

[1] LIRMM, UMR CNRS 5506, University of Montpellier, Montpellier, France
[2] Authentication Industries, Montpellier, France
iuliia.tkachenko@lirmm.fr

Abstract. The Quick Response (QR) code is the most popular graphical code in the world today. These codes are used for storage of information, but they have a limited storage capacity. In this paper, we present a two level QR (2LQR) code, which stores information on two levels. The first (public) level is accessible to everyone and can be read by any classical QR code reader. The second (supplementary) level is readable only by a selected group of users, which have a specific reader application. This code increases storage capacity of standard QR code. We use specific textured patterns for construction of a second level. We also suggest a blind pattern recognition method, which is based on maximization of correlation values.

Keywords: QR code · Two level stored information · Pattern recognition · Print-and-scan process · Multimedia management application

1 Introduction

Today, Quick Response (QR) codes are used in many applications, reaching more and more users: from consumers who look for information (reference to an URL from a smartphone) to professionals who think about quality of its product information (information storage - serial number, date - for market control and quality management). One of the popular application of QR codes is multimedia management [12]. This interest is due to several interesting characteristics of QR code: small size, high coding and error correction capacities, robustness against geometrical distortion, easy generation and reading process. Nevertheless, these codes have a limited storage capacity. Moreover, the information that is stored in these codes, is accessible to everyone who has the standard reading QR application. So, in standard QR codes we can only store public information.

In this paper we suggest a two level QR (2LQR) code, that can be used, for example, for automatic tracing and tracking of printed documents (bills, tax forms, reports). This code allows to split information into public (first level of information storage), which is accessible to all users, who have the standard QR code reading application, and supplementary information (second level of

© Springer International Publishing Switzerland 2015
V. Murino and E. Puppo (Eds.): ICIAP 2015, Part II, LNCS 9280, pp. 383–393, 2015.
DOI: 10.1007/978-3-319-23234-8_36

information storage), which is useful only for administrative purposes. This supplementary information is accessible only to authorized users, who have a specific reading application, that permits to read and decode this information. Thus, this 2LQR code add new capacities to standard QR code:

1. Supplementary reading level, which does not disrupt the standard QR code reading process.
2. Increasing storage capacity of initial QR code.

The standard QR code used as first level of our 2LQR code stays fully functional: it can be read by all standard application, without any restriction; all standard features stays optimal, for example, the error tolerance of the QR code stays maximal; it is not perturbed by the second level information which is not present at this first level. Thus, our 2LQR code ensure privacy of data stored in the second level not only by applying a classic numeric ciphering, but also by a physical separation, between levels and reader application abilities.

The second level of information storage is performed by using specific textured patterns, which are distinguished one from another after printing and scanning processes.

The paper is organized as follows. Section 2 introduces the QR code features and the existing rich graphical codes. The proposed two level QR code as well as the proposed recognition methods are presented in Section 3. Section 4 looks at the experimental results and we conclude in Section 5.

2   Related Work

Graphical codes are very popular now, because of easy generation and fast reading process. Standard graphical codes are black-and-white (or with two contrasting colors) as EAN-13 barcodes [1], QR code [3], DataMatrix [2]. But today, a lot of research projects and researchers suggest improvements to these graphical codes by using colors or time. These improved graphical codes can be named as *rich graphical codes*. In this paper we propose a new type of rich QR code, thus in Section 2.1 we present the main characteristics and structure of standard QR code and the existing rich QR codes are discussed in Section 2.2.

2.1   QR Code Features

The QR code was invented for the Japanese automotive industry by Denso Wave[1] corporation in 1994. The important characteristics of this code are small printout size and high speed reading process. The certification of the QR code was performed by International Organization of Standardization (ISO). That is why, all specifications can be found in [3].

A QR code encodes the information in binary form. Each information bit is represented by a black or white module. The Reed-Solomon error correction code (RS-ECC) [10] is used for data encoding. Thus, one of 4 error correction levels has to be chosen during QR code generation. The lowest level can restore nearly 7% of damaged information, the highest level can restore nearly 30%. Today,

---

[1] http://www.qrcode.com/en/index.html

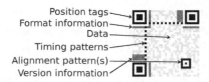

Fig. 1. Specific QR code structure consists of position patterns, alignment patterns, timing patterns, format information and version information patterns.

there are 40 QR code versions depending on storage capacity. The maximum number of information bis, that can be stored in standard QR code, is equal to 7089.

The QR code has a specific structure for geometrical correction and high speed decoding. All specific patterns are illustrated in Fig. 1.

2.2 Rich Graphical Codes

In order to improve the QR code properties, the rich QR codes have recently been introduced. These rich QR codes aim to add visual significance, to personalize the stored information and to increase the storage capacities. The most simple rich QR code is the design QR code[2], where we change the colors, shape of modules or add an image into the QR code. The target of these codes is to improve the aesthetic view of QR codes. But this kind of code reduces the error correction capacity of standard QR codes. A rich QR code, which adds the significance without losing error correction capacity, was introduced in [4]. The authors proposed a novel method of blending a color image into the QR code, which modifies the QR code source pixels so that the white (rsp. black) module pixels are transformed from white (rsp. black) to any RGB values and whose luminance value is considered as white (rsp. black) pixel by QR code binarization method. The HCC2D code [8] is a rich QR code which significantly increases the storage capacity of standard QR codes. The authors increased the density and storage capacity of standard QR code by replacing binary colored modules by RGB colored modules. The HCC2D code encodes information using 4, 8 or 16 module colors. This code inherits all the strong properties of standard QR codes, but it is not readable by a standard QR code reading application and needs to be printed using a color printer. One of the application scenarios for HCC2D code is facial biometrics [9]. The QR code steganography aims to embed a secret message into a QR code [6,7]. The message insertion is performed by using Reed-Solomon error correction code (RS-ECC) capacity of the QR code, that does not disturb the reading process of the standard QR code.

The main difference between the 2LQR code and all existing techniques is focused on the 2 level functionality. Most of existing techniques can be

---

[2] For example: https://www.unitag.io/qrcode

considered as a new code format (HCC2D). On the other hand, several codes add a supplementary messages (visual or hidden) to a standard QR code [4,6,7]. This kind of code uses the RS-ECC to add this supplementary information that implies, by construction, a very constrained storage. The 2LQR code do not have this very strong limit and do not alter the standard QR code reading. This short discussion shows the rich graphical codes popularity, research interest and variety of application scenarios.

3   Rich QR Code with Two Stored Levels

In this section we aim to present a rich QR code with two stored levels. In Section 3.1, we explain the generation steps of 2LQR code, and the recognition method is introduced in Section 3.2.

3.1   Two Level QR (2LQR) Code Generation

As it was mentioned in Section 1, the proposed 2LQR code have all the strong characteristics of the standard QR code [3] such as: small code size, high encoding capacity, high density, error correction capacity, easy code construction and quick reading process. In addition, the 2LQR code has two information levels. The first level contains public information and can be read by any QR code application, i.e. iOS, Android and scanner applications. That is why the proposed 2LQR code satisfies all standard QR code features. The second level contains supplementary information and is realized by replacing black modules in QR code with two specific textured patterns. The combination of these textured patterns allows to encode and afterwards, to reconstruct the supplementary information. Fig. 2 shows the difference between a standard QR code and the proposed 2LQR code. To increase robustness of this second level information, it is encoded using a binary error correction code. As illustrated in Fig. 3, the 2LQR code generation consists of the following steps: 1) Generation of standard QR code with a public information M_{pub}; 2) Generation of codeword C_{sup} with a supplementary information M_{sup}; 3) Selection of textured patterns P_1, P_2; 4) Replacement of black modules in standard QR code by textured patterns P_1, P_2, respecting codeword C_{sup}.

Standard QR Code Generation: in this step we store a public information M_{pub} in a standard QR code using the method described in ISO standard [3]. The QR code generation algorithm includes the following steps. Firstly, the input

(a)   (b)

Fig. 2. Comparison between: a) Standard QR code, b) Proposed 2LQR code.

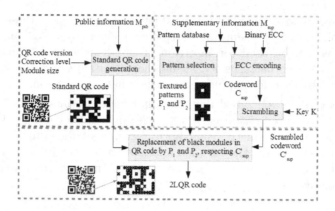

Fig. 3. Overview of the proposed 2LQR code generation steps.

data is encoded with the RS-ECC [10] with error setting correction level. The bit streams are formed and divided into codewords, which have an 8 bit length. The codewords form the blocks, in which the error correction codewords have been added. Then, the mask pattern is used for codewords masking. The codewords are placed from the right-bottom corner to the left-top corner in a zigzag pattern. A more complex codeword placement is used for the highest QR code versions due to the alignment pattern presence and interleaved error-correction blocks. At the last step, the function patterns are placed into the QR code.

Generation of Codeword C_{sup}**:** we encode the supplementary information M_{sup} using a binary error correction code (ECC) such as Golay code, BCH code or Reed-Solomon code [10]. The classical encoding function $\mathbb{C} : \mathbb{F}^k \rightarrow \mathbb{F}^n$ for linear codes is defined as follows. Let G be the $k \times n$ generator matrix of linear ECC with elements in $\mathbb{F}$ and $M_{sup} = (m_{sup}^1, ..., m_{sup}^k) \in \mathbb{F}^k$. Then, the codeword is calculated as $C_{sup} = M_{sup} \cdot G$. After, that we apply a scrambling operation with key K in order to mix codewords and add the supplementary protection to specific information. Thus, we obtain the scrambled codeword C'_{sup}.

Selection of Textured Patterns P_1, P_2**:** the textured patterns are the squared images $P_i, i = 1, 2$ of size $p \times p$ pixels. This kind of patterns was used in textured image generation [11]. These patterns are chosen from a pattern database, which contains $N, N >> 2$ patterns, and have the particular properties: 1) Images are binary, 2) The number (density) of black pixels is constant and equal to d, 3) The spectra are related among them. These criteria are important: any variation of density in pattern modules will introduce a distortion in the correlation computation during the detection step. The classification of patterns could be skewed and the result could not be validated.

As the proposed recognition method is based on maximization of correlation values, the textured patterns have to respect two conditions [11]: 1) Each pattern has to be better correlated with its Print-and-Scan (P&S) degraded version than with all other P&S degraded pattern versions; 2) The P&S degraded version of each pattern has to be better correlated with its original pattern than with all other original patterns. Only the textured patterns that respect these conditions can be combined among them and can be recognized after P&S process, thus these patterns can be used for insertion of supplementary information M_{sup} into 2LQR code. Let patterns P_1, P_2 be chosen with respect to all described conditions and be used for supplementary information insertion.

Replacement of Black Modules: the black modules in standard QR codes are replaced by textured patterns P_1, P_2, respecting codeword C'_{sup}. We start to insert codeword C'_{sup} from the right-bottom corner of the standard QR code. Note, that we do not insert the encoded information into the modules in QR code position patterns. These patterns are reserved for the storage of used textured pattern templates.

3.2   Recognition Methods

The QR code reproduction implies the printing process and the scanning process. The Print-and-Scan (P&S) process is a difficult process, which modifies the output image. These visible and invisible image modifications can be introduced by sampling inherent to the P&S process, inhomogeneous lighting conditions, ink dispersion, varying speed of the scanning device [5]. The modifications inserted by the printer are not separable from modifications added by the scanning process, that is why the distortions belong to each other [13]. Let S_i be the P&S degraded version of textured pattern P_i. The Fig. 4 illustrates all steps of the 2LQR code reading process. First of all, we apply the standard QR code preprocessing into the P&S 2LQR. The standard process [3] of position pattern localization is applied in order to determine the position coordinates. Then, the standard re-sampling method using bilinear interpolation is applied. As an output we have 2LQR code with correct orientation and original code size.

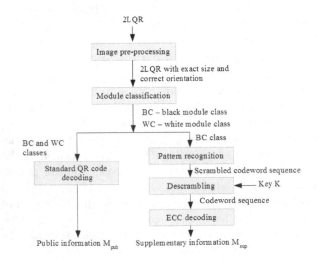

Fig. 4. 2LQR code reading process.

Then the module classification step is performed by any binarization method, either global threshold methods (standard ISO binarization method or Otsu's binarization method) or local threshold methods. In this paper, we set a global threshold equal to mean value of whole image. When the modules are classified in two (white and black) module classes, we can decode the public information M_{pub} using standard QR code decoding algorithm and use the black module class for pattern recognition and supplementary information decoding.

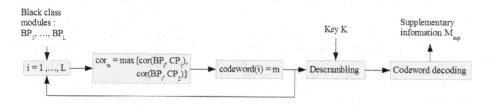

Fig. 5. Supplementary information decoding algorithm.

The blind pattern recognition, illustrated in Fig. 5, does not need any particular information in input. We define this method for combination of two patterns P_1, P_2. During the 2LQR generation, we replaced all black modules of left-top position pattern and right-top position pattern by textured patterns P_1 and P_2, respectively. These patterns are used for generation of characterization models of original textured patterns P_1 and P_2. Each position pattern consists of $t = 33$ black modules (for any QR code version). We calculate characterization models as:
- the *mean images* obtained by averaging the t P&S textured patterns : $CP_l = \frac{1}{t} \sum_{\tau=1}^{t} S_l^\tau, l = 1, 2$;
- the *median image*: $CP_l = median(S_l^1 \cdots S_l^t), l = 1, 2$. During the recognition step, we use the Pearson correlation between a pattern P_i and a pattern S_i, which is defined by:

$$cor(P_i, S_i) = \frac{\sum_r \sum_c (P_i^*(r,c))(S_i^*(r,c))}{\sqrt{\sum_r \sum_c (P_i^*(r,c))^2}\sqrt{\sum_r \sum_c (S_i^*(r,c))^2}}, \tag{1}$$

where $P_i^*(r,c)$ (rsp. $S_i^*(r,c)$) are the central values of P_i (rsp. S_i) defined by $P_i^*(r,c) = P_i(r,c) - \mu_{P_i}$ (rsp. $S_i^*(r,c) = S_i(r,c) - \mu_{S_i}$) with $\mu_{P_i} = \frac{1}{k} \sum_r \sum_c P_i(r,c)$ (rsp. $\mu_{S_i} = \frac{1}{k} \sum_r \sum_c S_i(r,c)$).

Let $BP_1, ..., BP_L$ be black information modules from the 2LQR code. For each module BP_i, we calculate correlation value with CP_1 and CP_2 (values cor_1 and cor_2 respectively). The maximal correlation value corresponds to the type of inserted pattern. That is why, if $cor_1 > cor_2$, the $codeword(i) = 1$, else $codeword(i) = 0$. When the $codeword$ is determined, we apply, firstly, the descrambling operation with key K, and, secondly, the ECC decoding algorithm in order to extract the supplementary information M_{sup}.

4   Experimental Results

In this section, we illustrate both the generation steps of the proposed 2LQR code and the recognition algorithm. The application scenario is as follows. We store information in the public level: Surname, Name, Date of Birth and Place of Birth. In the second level, we encode the security number of this person. We use the version V2 of QR code using Low error correction level. The version V2 of QR code has 25×25 module size and can store 272 bits of the message in the low error correction level. For supplementary information encoding, we use the binary Golay code $[23, 12, 7]$. It means, that the codeword length is 23 bits, where the length of the encoded information is 12 bits and 11 bits are used for error correction. In QR code version V2, we have 216 black modules (we do not take into account the black modules used in position pattern construction), thus we can store about 216 bits of encoded information (including error correction bits) in the second level of the 2LQR code. Therefore, we can store 108 bits of a supplementary information in second level of 2LQR code version V2. In Table 1, we determine the storage capacities of both standard QR code and 2LQR code.

Table 1. Storage capacity information of standard QR code and 2LQR code.

	Standard QR code V2 Low	2LQR code V2 $[23, 12, 7]$ code
Modules	625	312
Encoded bits	324	216
Message bits	272	108

4.1   Generation of 2LQR Code

We generate the standard QR code of version V2 with the public M_{pub} information: "John Doe - 13/05/1958 - New York" by using any QR code application, see Fig. 6. Then, we define the supplementary information M_{sup} with a length of 108 bits and the used textured patterns. As we decide to use the binary Golay code we create the codeword C_{sup} of 207 bits, where we will store 108 bits of the

(a)

(b)

Fig. 6. The example of a) Standard QR code with public information M_{pub}, b) Standard QR code of real size defined at 600 dpi.

Fig. 7. The used textured patterns: a) Pattern 1, b) Pattern 2.

supplementary information. The last 9 accessible bits were defined randomly. Then, after scrambling, we obtain the codeword C'_{sup}.

We choose two textured patterns P_1 and P_2 (see Fig. 7.a - Fig. 7.b). These patterns have a size of 12×12 pixels and respect 3 mentioned properties, the number of black pixels is equal to $d = 72$.

We encode the second level of 2LQR code placing these patterns with respect to codeword C'_{sup}, starting from right-bottom corner of the QR code. We replace black modules by textured patterns P_1 and P_2 in the top-left and top-right position patterns, respectively. The example of 2LQR code is illustrated in Fig. 8. We set the size of 2LQR code equal to 1.2×1.2 cm^2. The examples of 2LQR code in real size is illustrated in Fig. 8.c. The standard QR code, as well as, the public level of 2LQR code are readable by standard smartphone application in Fig. 6.b and Fig. 8.c.

Fig. 8. The example of a) 2LQR code with both public M_{pub} and supplementary M_{sup} information, b) P&S 2LQR with two levels of stored information c) 2LQR code of real size defined at 600 dpi and d) P&S 2LQR code of real size defined at 600 dpi.

4.2   Message Extraction

We printed the same 2LQR code 30 times in 600 dpi using Brother HL-4150 printer. Then, we scanned each printed 2LQR code in 600 dpi using Canon LIDE 210 scanner. After several experiments with P&S samples, we have concluded that the database of 30 samples is enough to perform the correct statistical tests due to random impact of P&S process. An example of P&S 2LQR code is illustrated in Fig. 8.b and Fig. 8.c. We can note the image blur and changes of colors in comparison with original 2LQR code Fig. 8.a. In spite of these changes the public level is readable by standard QR code applications. For each P&S 2LQR, we apply the blind detection method both with mean and median characterization patterns. We present the detection results in Table 2. The error probability of pattern detection using proposed blind method is 1.64% with mean characterization patterns and 1.23% with median characterization patterns.

Table 2. Pattern detection results after P&S process.

	Mean	Median
% of P_1 detected as P_2	0.95%	1.33%
% of P_2 detected as P_1	2.28%	1.14%
Error probability of pattern detection	1.64%	1.23%

Table 3. Error probability of incorrect message decoding after error correction algorithm.

Error probability of incorrect bit decoding after ECC	Mean	Median
	0.65%	0%

After the detection step, we apply the descrambling, error correction and decoding algorithms. In the end, we find the encoded supplementary information M_{sup}. Sometimes, due to bad pattern recognition results, the supplementary message was decoded incorrectly. The error probabilities of incorrect bit decoding are presented in Table 3. We had some errors in message decoding process after pattern detection using mean characterization patterns. At the same time, we did not have errors during message decoding process after pattern detection using median characterization patterns.

5   Conclusion

In this paper we propose a new efficient rich code called two level QR (2LQR) code, which can be used for automatic tracing and tracking of printed documents. This rich QR code has two levels. The first level can be read by any QR code reading application. On the contrary, the second level needs a specific application. The second level is created by using specific binary textured patterns, which are distinguishable from one another after P&S process and are considered as black modules by standard QR code reading applications. Thus, the second level does not affect at all the reading process of first level. The experimental results were performed for QR code version V2, the supplementary information has a length of 108 bits and was encoded using binary Golay $[23, 12, 7]$ error correction code. The pattern detection was performed for mean characterization models and median characterization models. The probability of correct bit decoding after ECC is equal to 99.35% after pattern detection using mean characterization models, and to 100% after pattern detection using median patterns. In future we plan to study the capacities of 2LQR code, depending on both QR version and pattern size, as well as, to propose other pattern recognition algorithms, that will be less sensitive to P&S impact.

References

1. 15420:2009, I.: Information technology - Automatic identification and data capture techniques - EAN/UPC bar code symbology specification (2009)
2. 16022:2006, I.: Information technology - Automatic identification and data capture techniques - Data Matrix bar code symbology specification (2006)
3. 18004:2000, I.: Information technology - Automatic identification and data capture techniques - Bar code symbology - QR Code (2000)
4. Baharav, Z., Kakarala, R.: Visually significant QR codes: Image blending and statistical analysis. In: IEEE International Conference on Multimedia and Expo, ICME 2013, July 15–19, pp. 1–6, San Jose, California, USA (2013)
5. Baras, C., Cayre, F.: 2D bar-codes for authentication: A security approach. In: The 20th European Signal Processing Conference, EUSIPCO 2012, August 27–31, pp. 1760–1766. Bucharest, Romania (2012)
6. Bui, T.V., Vu, N.K., Nguyen, T.T., Echizen, I., Nguyen, T.D.: Robust message hiding for QR code. In: 2014 Tenth International Conference on Intelligent Information Hiding and Multimedia Signal Processing (IIH-MSP), pp. 520–523. IEEE (2014)
7. Lin, P.Y., Chen, Y.H., Lu, E.J.L., Chen, P.J.: Secret hiding mechanism using QR barcode. In: 2013 International Conference on Signal-Image Technology & Internet-Based Systems (SITIS), pp. 22–25. IEEE (2013)
8. Querini, M., Grillo, A., Lentini, A., Italiano, G.F.: 2D color barcodes for mobile phones. IJCSA 8(1), 136–155 (2011)
9. Querini, M., Italiano, G.F.: Facial biometrics for 2D barcodes. In: IEEE Federated Conference on Computer Science and Information Systems, FedCSIS 2012, September 9–12, pp. 755–762, Wroclaw, Poland (2012)
10. Sklar, B.: Digital communications, vol. 2. Prentice Hall, NJ (2001)
11. Tkachenko, I., Puech, W., Strauss, O., Gaudin, J.M., Destruel, C., Guichard, C.: Fighting against forged documents by using textured image. In: The 22nd European Signal Processing Conference, EUSIPCO 2014, September 1–5, pp. 790–794, Lisbon, Portugal (2014)
12. Villán, R., Voloshynovskiy, S., Koval, O., Pun, T.: Multilevel 2d bar codes: Towards high capacity storage modules for multimedia security and management. IEEE Transactions on Information Forensics and Security 1(4), 405–420 (2006)
13. Yu, L., Niu, X., Sun, S.: Print-and-scan model and the watermarking countermeasure. In: Image and Vision Computing, vol. 23, pp. 807–814. Elsevier (2005)

Panel Tracking for the Extraction and the Classification of Speech Balloons

Hadi S. Jomaa[✉], Mariette Awad, and Lina Ghaibeh

Electrical Engineering Department, American University of Beirut, Beirut, Lebanon
hsj04@mail.aub.edu, {mariette.awad,lg00}@aub.edu.lb

Abstract. Searching for texts inside a full comic strip may be exhaustive, and can be simplified by restricting the scope of the search to single panels, and better yet to within individual speech balloon. In this paper, a novel approach is devised where a tracking algorithm is employed for panel extraction, and speech balloons are identified using 'Roberts' edge detection operator as well as a classifier to find the number of balloons within every panel using a non-exhaustive projection method. Two main objectives in the field of comic strip understanding are achieved through our panel tracking for the extraction and classification of speech balloons (PaTEC). PaTEC may be incorporated as a precursor to text extraction and recognition reducing the computational time and effort of searching the whole image to the speech balloon area itself. PaTEC accuracy for panel extraction is *88.78%* while balloon classification accuracy is *81.49%* on a homegrown comic database.

Keywords: Comic strip · Panel · Classification · Speech balloon extraction · Comic page segmentation · Text detection

1 Introduction

Comic books represent a cultural expression and have been known as a cultural heritage for many countries. Most of the well-known comics are American, Japanese, and European from which animated movies have been made. They have been around for more than a century serving as means of entertainment and gathering an audience that ranges from kids to adults with content that expands from satirical caricatures to drama, mystery and erotica. With the growth of the mobile industry and digitization that is happening worldwide, comic books are falling behind in the race to be present in the digital world.

For user convenience, a significant number of newspapers can be now read online. Following in their footsteps, comic companies are starting to do the same. People like to view comics on their electronic devices, on the go, without the hassle of carrying around the hard copy. However, viewing the comic strip as a whole image on mobile electronic devices is not always convenient. The visual information present in the comic strip, along with the expressions of the characters in the frames and the text in balloons may be deteriorated if the comic strip page was to be fitted without proper processing. This problem can be solved through segmenting the comic strip to its

© Springer International Publishing Switzerland 2015
V. Murino and E. Puppo (Eds.): ICIAP 2015, Part II, LNCS 9280, pp. 394–405, 2015.
DOI: 10.1007/978-3-319-23234-8_37

individual panels, and extracting the text before fitting the panels to the electronic screen. This way, instead of viewing the comic strip as whole and having to zoom in, the user can scroll through the panels while reading the extracted texts typed below each one, or the text can pop out by tapping on the panels.

Recently, comic digitization field has gained growing attention, and presented here are some approaches that deal differently with the presented problem. Morphological operations were applied in [1] followed by region growing to highlight the background from the panels, whereas [2] employed a recursive algorithm that detects uniform color stripes and kept on segmenting the strip into sub regions until no more stripes were detected. The regions that can no longer be segmented were saved as panels. [3] proposed an ACS that also uses the X-Y recursive cut algorithm to segment the page into frames, which are then fitted to the size of the mobile screen. In [4], Rigaud et al. formulated the problem of speech balloon detection as fitting of a closed contour around text areas where the outline is not always confined to the image. However they assumed that the text location is already known. In [5] a watershed segmentation algorithm extracted the panels and the comic strips were preprocessed to classify the panels with uniform solid colors differently from that of the white background. Ishii et al in [6] detected separation lines through calculating the total gradient of the lines to get the basic shape of the panel. The corner candidates were then detected using Harrison's corner detection technique while Sobel filter calculated the image gradient. Frame lines were shifted in parallel until they reach the corner candidates. Evaluation values of all possible rectangular combinations were calculated based on the average density of gradient values of the quadrangle formed between each line and the intersection. Combinations with the highest evaluation values were kept as frames.

Using the pre-described XY recursive cut algorithm in [7], candidate points are detected for segmenting the frames and then these candidates are classified by a multilayer perceptron as corners of panels or not. In [8], screen division is applied using the density gradient after filling the quadrangle regions in each image with black. All possible lines that pass by every pixel are generated and an evaluation term of the density gradient is created. Based on an exhaustive criterion, the separation lines are detected.

In this paper, we propose a panel extraction technique followed by speech balloon extraction and classification, hereafter PaTEC, The mean-shift tracking algorithm is applied to a processed comic strip, after which every panel undergoes edge detection coupled with filtering and morphological operation to remove all but the speech balloons. The accuracy of panel extraction topped Burie's method [1], which showed better results than those in the literature, by more than 10%, while the speech balloon classification resulted in 81.49% accuracy. The differences between PaTEC and the existing approaches proposed in the literature are many: 1) it doesn't include recursions, such as the X-Y cut algorithm, 2) requires less computation and showed better results than region growing, and 3) doesn't require calculating the gradient of the image along different orientations. The remaining of this paper is as follows: section 2 deals with the methodology while experimental results are detailed in section 3. Section 4 concludes the paper along with possible future work.

2   Methodology

Throughout this paper, some comic book terminology described in Fig. 1 will be used. The comic strip corresponds to the page, the panel refers to the block which contains information on a specific event, and the gutter is the space separating the panels.

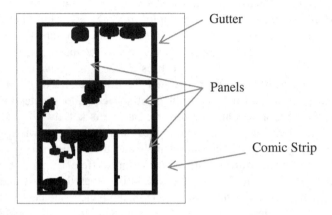

Fig. 1. Comic book terminology

An overview of PaTEC is represented in Fig. 2. As mentioned earlier, a tracking algorithm is applied to detect individual panels within the processed comic strip. Every panel is then treated individually. The speech balloons are extracted through "Roberts" edge detection operator coupled with a set of morphological operations and filtering, and then using histogram projections, they are classified. PaTEC workflow hence has four major steps, namely: Pre-Processing, Tracking, Extraction and Classification.

Fig. 2. PaTEC flowchart

2.1   Pre-processing

The input to the system is a colored image, size (m, n), of the comic strip that is first transformed to grayscale. The image is then binarized based on a grayscale threshold of *253*, chosen heuristically, since the white background has a value ranging between *253* and *255* A morphological operation, *N-dilations*, is applied to the image to widen the separation between the panels. The number "*N*" varies from one strip to another, and is chosen by user visual inspection to be the smallest number that ensures proper separation between the panels. Hence slight user interaction is required in setting the value of "N" which results in the optimal separation of the panels from the background. The user is also required to visually check the horizontal projection of the panel and save the value corresponding to the maximum number of pixels a gutter may have in the horizontal projection (Hp_{thresh}). In Fig. 3a, a binarized image is presented, with the horizontal projection in Fig. 3b. The value circled in Fig. 3b is the maximum number of pixels a gutter may have in the horizontal direction. The shorter the gutter in the comic, the larger the threshold.

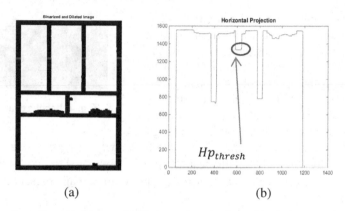

(a)   (b)

Fig. 3. (a) Binarized image (b) Horizontal projection with circled threshold

The horizontal gutters are considered as the spaces with zero vertical projections and their ordinates are saved automatically ($y_{horizontalgutter,i}$). They represent the separation lines between the panels.

2.2   Tracking

The tracker initiates from the top left part of the image, a couple of pixels before the beginning of the upper left panel at point P_1 (x_1, y_1). The mean shift algorithm (MSA) is initialized with center ($c_1 = P_1$) and horizontal direction ($d_1 = [1\ 0]$). The mean of the valid points within the specified semi-ellipse, i.e. the points that belong to the gutter and/or background, is calculated, and is saved as the new center, c_i of the semi-ellipse. The direction is also updated to be the difference between the old and the new center ($d_i = c_i - c_{i-1}$). After every iteration, the tracker checks whether or not it should initiate a change in direction, i.e. turn down. The decision is based on the value of the horizontal projection at the corresponding pixel coordinates (Hp_i). If the value is less than the pre-specified threshold, ($Hp_i < Hp_{thresh}$), and no obstacles are present between the center and the nearest horizontal gutter ($y_{horizontalgutter,i}$), this means that the tracker reached the edge of the panel, and should start rotating downwards. The horizontal gutter can be considered the first point whose vertical projection ($Vp_i = 0$) is zero. The turndown point is saved, $Td_i(xd_i, yd_i)$. After the change in direction is applied, i.e. turn downwards, the tracker proceeds until it reaches the nearest horizontal gutter separating the panel being tracked from the one below it, and then turns right. The turn right point is saved, $Tr_i(xr_i, yr_i)$. The tracker proceeds until it reaches the lower edge of the panel and when it goes past the abscissa (x_0) of the origin, rotates upwards. Notice that the rotation of the tracker is in a clockwise manner and it ends when the point is a couple of pixels near the initial point $(|y_i - y_0| < thresh)$. The order in which the tracker extracts panels is displayed in Fig. 4.

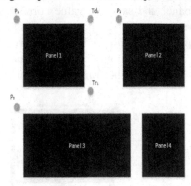

Fig. 4. Panel extraction order

The initial point for the second panel is considered a couple of pixels away from the turn-down point of the previous panel if it is still far from the end of comic strip. If not, the tracker jumps down to the second block of panels, and initiates from the same abscissa of the one above it. The vertical level of the new initial point is just a few pixels below the turn-right point of the panel above. $(if \ |n - xd_i| \gg 0, P_2 \ (xd_i + x_1, yd_i); else \ P_2 \ (x_i, yr_i - y))$. The pseudo code of extracting a single panel is presented in Fig. 5 followed by a pictorial depiction of panel extraction for a typical comic page present in the home-grown dataset in Fig. 6.

1	Initiate tracker at point P_1
	$d_1 = [1 \ 0]$
	Set $done = false$
	While $\neg done$ **do**
2	Create semi ellipse
3	Get valid point coordinates v_i for all $i \in gutter$
4	Calculate the mean m_i
5	Update center $c_{i+1} = m_i$
	If $Hp_i < thresh \ \wedge \sum_{j=i}^{y \, horizontal \, gutter, i} I(x, y) = 0$ **then**
	$d_{i+1} = [0 - 1]$
	$(xd_i, yd_i) = c_{i+1}$
	Repeat steps 2,3,4,5 **until** $y_i = y_{horizontal \, gutter}$
	$d_i = [-1 \ 0]$
	Repeat steps 2,3,4,5 **until** $|y_i - y_1| < thresh$
	Connect the final point c_i and initial point P_1
	Set $done = true$
	Else
	Update the direction vector $d_{i+1} = c_{i+1} - c_i$

Fig. 5. Panel tracking algorithm

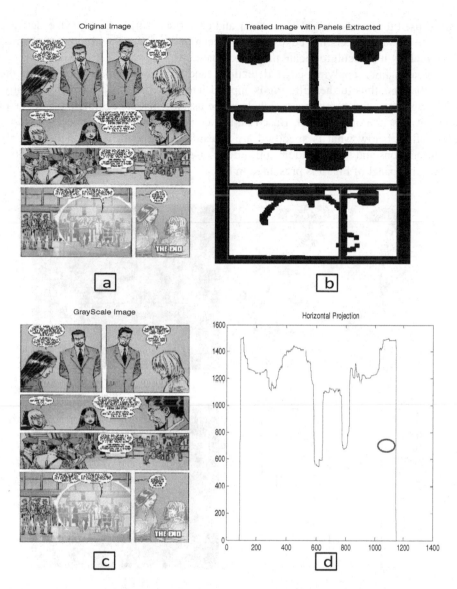

Fig. 6. (a) Original Image (b) Treated image with panels extracted (c) Grayscale image (d) Horizontal projection of treated image

2.3   Extraction

Speech balloons are extracted using the 'Roberts' operator for edge detection. The "Roberts" operator is effective in extracting speech balloons, since it calculates the gradient of the pixels through convolving them with a diagonal matrix, and keeping the ones with a gradient greater than an automatically set threshold. Other edge detection operators such as 'Prewitt' or 'Sobel' fail in detecting curved objects, and are mainly used to detect straight horizontal and/or vertical edges. Canny edge detector on the other side detects the edges of the speech balloon along with other unwanted edges making it difficult to locate the speech balloons.

Typically, after applying edge detection, random noises appear along with the speech balloon, thus further filtering is applied. The edge panel is projected vertically, and using connected components, labeled. We assume that speech balloons cover in length at least *3%* of the panel. Based on this empirical threshold, connected components falling below what is specified are discarded. The result is a panel with only speech balloons and some random unfiltered noise. A sample balloon extraction done on the same panel of Fig. 5 is presented in Fig 7.

Fig. 7. (a) Original image (b) Edge image pre-filtering (c) Projection of edge image before and after filtering (d) Exracted balloons dilated

2.4   Classification

Classification is needed in order to get the real number of balloons within the panels. A non-exhaustive way to classify balloons is based on projections. Start by getting the horizontal and vertical limits of where balloons may be present based on the respective projections. Based on these limits, rectangular combinations are formed to explore the presence of bubble. Every rectangle hence may contain a bubble, noise, or nothing based on its content. The decision is based on the content of the rectangle. If the rectangle contains high density of pixels, above a certain threshold, it is considered as having a bubble, and added to the count; otherwise, the rectangle is considered to contain noise and consequently no balloons. The value of the threshold was taken to be 20% of the rectangular area, and was chosen heuristically based on the assumption that at least one fifth of the area covered by the balloon is filled with text.

3   Experimental Results

3.1   Experimental Setup

A data set consisting of 38 pages extracted from 5 different issues of 2 distinct comic books has been created. The pages were selected from the issues based on the following criteria: the comic strip should have white background, any comic strip with more than one irregular panel is discarded, and the panels should include round-shaped speech balloons. This data set contains *205* panels with various sizes and shapes. The result of panel extraction is expressed and compared using two methods, Page and Panel. A Page is considered well segmented when all the panels have been correctly extracted. The Panel section represents the accuracy of extracting any panel in the page. The script used was written and executed in *MATLAB R2014a*.

3.2   Panel Extraction

The results of the tracker are validated manually. [1]'s method was reproduced and tested on our dataset for the sake of comparison. In their paper, Burie *et al's* approach showed better results than others in the literature. Table 1 represents the accuracy of our method versus Burie *et al's* [1]. PaTEC failed to detect irregular panels, i.e. slanted panels and panels with more than 4 corners, present within the comic image that lead to this gap in accuracy.

Table 1. Accuracy of Panel Extracion

Method	PaTEC	Burie *et al.*
Page (%)	**89.05**	72.24
Panel (%)	**88.78**	75.63

PaTEC outperforms Burie's on both Panel and Page scale. The accuracy of extracting all the panels in the comic strip is considerably high. Looking also at the standard deviation of the results, our approach has a standard deviation *(18.88%)* less than that of Burie's *(32.11%)*. It means that in some cases Burie's method either extracted most of the panels in the page, or extracted none. The figure below displays a comic strip treated by the region growing method followed by *N-dilations* and *N-erosions* Fig. 8a compared to the same comic strip treated by PaTEC, Fig. 8b.

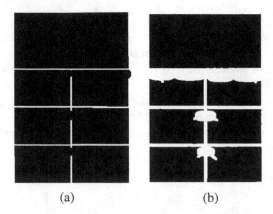

(a)   (b)

Fig. 8. (a) Burie (b) PaTEC

Applying connected components to the left will result in extracting 4 panels, while on the right, applying the tracker yields 6 out of 6 panels. Since the balloons connected two separate panels, region growing failed in extracting each one individually. The balloons however where emphasized as part of the gutter after we applied our thresholding method, and broke the connection between joining panels.

3.3   Speech Balloon Classification

The panels successfully extracted contain a total of 335 speech balloons, where a balloon is considered to be a closed contour surrounding texts in the panel. The content-based classification process applied to the different rectangular combinations resulted in identifying 273 balloons (*81.49%* accuracy), which were visually inspected. The accuracy of the extraction is considerably high, and resulted in misclassification at certain instances when speech balloons overlapped, in which case more than one balloon are identified as one, or when there is significant unfiltered noise, adding a non-existent balloon to the count.

3.4   Discussion

PaTEC has certain limitations. Notably, the tracker can't extract all the panels in comic strips where panels exist on different horizontal levels *without* slight user intervention. The user must limit the scope of the image to that of the panel, before applying the tracker, because when projecting the whole image vertically, the small horizontal gutter is masked, and passed over by the tracker. Fig. 9a displays a comic strip that requires such user interference. Fig. 9b shows the result of extracting the panels automatically, while Fig. 9c displays the result with slight intervention. Notice how all three panels to the right of the Eiffel tower are extracted as one in Fig. 9b, while they are detected separately in Fig. 9c.

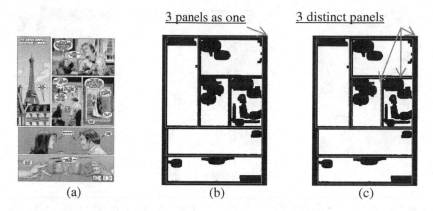

Fig. 9. (a) Original panel (b) No intervention (c) Slight user intervention

Slanted panels are not extracted since the vertical projection of the comic strip doesn't recognize the slanted gutters. In Fig 10b, the slanted gutter is masked by the pixels of the panel, preventing the tracker from identifying a horizontal gutter. Such failure results in extracting slanted panels as a part of a larger panel such as in Fig. 10c.

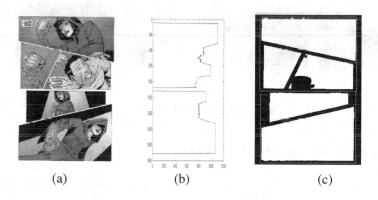

Fig. 10. (a) Slanted image (b) Vertical projection (c) Extracted panels not added to count

Other comic strips in which not all panels are extracted include panels that extend to the border of the image, panels with more than 4 corners and panels that are formed by objects rather than in blocks. Examples on such situations are found in Fig. 11.

Fig. 11. Sample failures

Image processing of the comic strip varies from one to another since every image has different sized gutters. Hence the number of dilations which is directly related to the original size of the gutter between panels can't be fixed to constant value.

When speech balloons overlap, i.e. boundaries are almost connected to each other; the classifier fails to detect them as separate, and ends up classifying them as one. Some panels may end up with scattered noise that looks like a speech balloon and hence misclassified as one, Fig. 12a. In others, not all speech balloons survive the edge operator, and are overlooked by the classifier such as in the panel of Fig. 12b.

 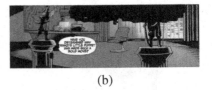

(a)   (b)

Fig. 12. (a) Noise augmented with balloon (b) Missed balloon

4   Conclusion and Future Work

In this paper, we proposed panel tracking for speech balloon extraction. The comic strip is preprocessed through several image processing techniques. A tracker is employed to extract the panels of the image and then every panel undergoes other processing techniques for speech balloon extraction and classification. The results of panel extraction reached *88.78 %* and speech balloon classification accuracy was *81.49 %*.

PaTEC doesn't apply to irregular panels. Improved image processing techniques might be able to enhance the speech balloon preservation. Preprocessing, tracking and extraction, applied in PaTEC can be dealt with separately as any optimization in one step contributes to overall better results.

References

1. Ho, A.K.N., Burie, J.-C., Ogier, J.: Panel and speech balloon extraction from comic books. In: 2012 10th IAPR International Workshop on Document Analysis Systems (DAS). IEEE (2012)
2. Chan, C.H., Leung, H., Komura, T.: Automatic panel extraction of color comic images. In: Ip, H.H.-S., Au, O.C., Leung, H., Sun, M.-T., Ma, W.-Y., Hu, S.-M. (eds.) PCM 2007. LNCS, vol. 4810, pp. 775–784. Springer, Heidelberg (2007)
3. Han, E., Chun, S., Park, A., Jung, K.: Automatic conversion system for mobile cartoon contents. In: Fox, E.A., Neuhold, E.J., Premsmit, P., Wuwongse, V. (eds.) ICADL 2005. LNCS, vol. 3815, pp. 416–423. Springer, Heidelberg (2005)
4. Rigaud, C., et al.: An active contour model for speech balloon detection in comics. In: 2013 12th International Conference on Document Analysis and Recognition (ICDAR). IEEE (2013)
5. Ponsard, C., Fries, V.: An accessible viewer for digital comic books. Springer, Heidelberg (2008)
6. Ishii, D., Watanabe, H.: A study on frame position detection of digitized comics images. In: Proc. Workshop on Picture Coding and Image Processing, PCSJ2010/IMPS2010, Nagoya, Japan (2010)
7. Han, E., Kim, K., Yang, H.-K., Jung, K.: Frame segmentation used MLP-based X-Y recursive for mobile cartoon content. In: Jacko, J.A. (ed.) HCI 2007. LNCS, vol. 4552, pp. 872–881. Springer, Heidelberg (2007)
8. Tanaka, T., et al.: Layout Analysis of Tree-Structured Scene Frames in Comic Images. In: IJCAI, vol. 7 (2007)

Combining Hardwaremetry and Biometry for Human Authentication via Smartphones

Chiara Galdi[1(✉)], Michele Nappi[2], and Jean-Luc Dugelay[1]

[1] EURECOM, Sophia Antipolis, France
{galdi,dugelay}@eurecom.fr
[2] Università degli Studi di Salerno, Fisciano, SA, Italy
mnappi@unisa.it

Abstract. The role of smartphones in our life is ever-increasing. They are used to store and share sensitive data and to perform security critical operation online e.g. home banking transaction or shopping. This leads to the need for a more secure authentication process via mobile phones. Biometrics could be the solution but biometric authentication systems via mobile devices presented so far still do not provide a good trade-off between ease of use and high security level. In this paper we analyze the combination of sensor recognition (hardwaremetry) and iris recognition (biometry) in order to provide a double check of user's identity in one shot, i.e. a single photo of the eye captured by the Smartphone, without the need of additional or dedicated sensors. To the best of our knowledge, this is the first attempt to combine these two aspects.

Keywords: Hardwaremetry · Biometry · Sensor recognition · Iris recognition · Mobile device

1   Introduction

Performing biometric recognition via mobile devices is an important issue due to the need of a secure use of critical services (e.g. home banking) and to protect sensitive data that nowadays are mostly stored on our personal smartphones or tablets.

Biometry is very suitable for human recognition on mobile devices in fact the users are used to employ the frontal camera of their personal mobile devices to capture pictures of themselves, the so called "selfie". One of the biometric traits that assures the highest recognition accuracy is the iris [25]. However, iris recognition performance on mobile phones suffers from several noise factors, e.g. specular reflections, out of focus images, occlusions, low resolution, etc. To improve the accuracy of an iris recognition system, it is possible to combine the iris with another user's distinctive feature.

Authentication can be performed based on one or a combination of the following items [1]:

- Something the user knows (e.g., password, personal identification number (PIN), secret answer, pattern);
- Something the user has (e.g., smart card, ID card, security token, software token);
- Something the user is or does (e.g. fingerprint, face, gait).

© Springer International Publishing Switzerland 2015
V. Murino and E. Puppo (Eds.): ICIAP 2015, Part II, LNCS 9280, pp. 406–416, 2015.
DOI: 10.1007/978-3-319-23234-8_38

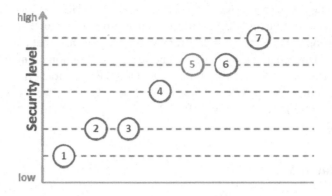

Fig. 1. Security levels. (1) Something the user knows; (2) Something the user has; (3) Something the user knows + something the user has; (4) Something the user is or does; (5) Something the user has + something the user is or does; (6) Something the user knows + something the user is or does; (7) Something the user knows + something the user has + something the user is or does.

One possible solution to improve a system's accuracy, is to combine different biometric traits, such systems are called multi-biometric systems. They could require to perform several acquisition phases, one for each biometric trait. In this paper we propose to combine iris recognition with sensor recognition, i.e. the recognition of the Smartphone employed by the user to get authenticated, this combination can assure an higher security level as shown in Fig. 1, (5) something the user has + something the user is [1], with respect to the use of biometric recognition only (4) something the user is or does. This kind of system is known as multimodal system.

The advantage in using the Smartphone is two-sided: first, the smartphone is a very personal object that nowadays is used to store and exchange sensitive data, this lead to a strict relation between the user and his/her smartphone, more than a simple smart card or a token generator. Secondly, Smartphones are equipped with high resolution cameras that can be used to perform biometric recognition (e.g. face, iris, etc.) without the need of additional or dedicated sensors.

In this paper we present a technique that combines the recognition of the iris (Biometry), with the recognition of the Smartphone (Hardwaremetry) that captured the photo containing the biometric trait. In one single shot, it is possible to authenticate both the user and his/her Smartphone in order to provide a double check of user's identity. The objective is to provide a system more robust to security flaws and spoofing attacks, e.g. if somebody capture a photo of a person's iris and try to access the system, the device recognition module will detect that the smartphone used for the authentication is not the one belonging to the authentic user. In a hypothetical usage scenario of the system, first an enrollment phase is exploited in which the user register his/her iris and his/her smartphone providing few eye photos. Then, at authentication time, only the couple user-smartphone previously enrolled is accepted as genuine user. In case the user changes his/her Smartphone, a new enrollment is required.

We tested our approach on the available online MICHE database [2, 3], and it is worth to notice that this is the first database that provides pictures of irises of a large number of people, captured with different mobile devices and that allows to perform a realistic performance assessment of iris and device recognition on mobile phones. We assessed performance in terms of Receiver Operating Characteristic (ROC) curve, Cumulative Match Score (CMS) curve, Area Under ROC Curve (AUC), Equal Error Rate (EER), False Rejection Rate (FRR), False Acceptance Rate (FAR), and Recognition Rate (RR).

2   Related Works

Biometric recognition on mobile devices is an issue already addressed in few works that we will briefly list in this section.

The biometric trait firstly chosen for biometric recognition on mobile phones, leveraging the presence of embedded cameras, is of course the face. In fact face recognition algorithms do not require high resolution images, and for this reason face was more suitable than iris at the beginning, when the resolution provided by mobile phone embedded cameras was limited. Some example of works on face recognition on mobile phones are presented in [4] and [5], the latter also address the problem of performing complex face-recognition tasks on a mobile terminal. This could shorten the battery lifetime, while it is better to use the mobile phone only as an interface and perform all computationally heavy operations on the server side. In [6] the face recognition system presented also addresses the issue of using biometric recognition for security-critical operations, e.g. home banking, providing also an anti-spoofing module and the opportunity of performing continuous recognition.

Nowadays Smartphones provide built-in high resolution imaging sensors. This gave the researchers the green light to study proper solutions to perform all the phases of iris recognition on mobile phones. For what concerns iris detection, in [7] and [8] methods for pupil and iris boundaries detection are presented, in these two works however, the databases employed were collected respectively with a Samsung SPH-S2300 and Samsung SPH-2300 [9] (in [7] only 132 images were captured with the mobile phone and the others were from CASIA database [10]) which embed a 3.2 megapixel digital camera with a 3X optical zoom, which is a very specific imaging sensor that cannot commonly be found in the most popular Smartphones. Toward the aim of providing a solution suitable for any kind of mobile devices, in [11] and [12] a database acquired with different mobile devices, namely MICHE database [3], is employed to test the iris segmentation algorithm.

One of the first works investigating the possibility to optimize iris segmentation and recognition for mobile phones is [13], the authors propose a method for computing the iris code based on Adaptive Gabor Filter. In [14], Park et al. present a recognition method based on corneal specular reflections, while Kang in [15] presents a method to pre-process iris in order to remove the noise related to occlusions of eyelids and improve system performance. In [16] and [17] authors presents an iris recognition system based on Spatial Histograms. Finally, in [18], authors present a face and iris recognition system for mobile devices that also provides an anti-spoofing module.

3   Method

The system is made up by two main modules: sensor recognition module and iris recognition module. When a picture of the eye is captured, it is employed to check both device's and user's identity. In our experiments, we observed that selecting a sub-region (512x512 pixel) of the picture is sufficient to perform sensor recognition with high accuracy and it also speeds up the recognition process. In Fig. 2 the architecture of the system is shown. In this section we will describe the algorithms employed to perform sensor recognition, iris recognition and the fusion technique used to improve system's reliability.

Fig. 2. System architecture.

3.1   Sensor Recognition Module

In order to recognize the sensor that captured a given photo, we implemented the Enhanced Sensor Pattern Noise (ESPN) based algorithm presented by Li in [19]. This method extracts from a picture the noise pattern of the sensor that acquired the photo, it can also be used to distinguish cameras of the same model [20, 21] [24]. The approach presented by Li, is based on a previous work by Lukás et al. [20] in which the authors present the algorithm for extracting the Sensor Pattern Noise (SPN).

In order to compute the ESPN, first the Sensor Pattern Noise (SPN) is extracted accordingly with the formula presented in [20]:

$$n = DWT(I) - F(DWT(I)) \tag{1}$$

where $DWT()$ is the discrete wavelet transform to be applied on image I and $F()$ is a denoising function that filters out the SPN in the DWT domain. For $F()$ we used the filter proposed in appendix A in [20]. Then the SPN is enhanced as suggested in [19] with the following formula:

$$n_e(i,j) = \begin{cases} e^{-0.5n^2(i,j)/\alpha^2}, & \text{if } 0 \le n(i,j) \\ -e^{-0.5n^2(i,j)/\alpha^2}, & \text{otherwise} \end{cases} \tag{2}$$

where n_e is the ESPN, n is the SPN, i and j are the indices of the components of n and n_e, and α is a parameter that we set to 7, as indicated in [19].

To determine which sensor captured a given photo, we have to compare the ESPN extracted from the picture with the Reference Sensor Pattern Noise (RSPN) of the sensor. The RSPN is obtained by averaging the SPN over N photos acquired with the given camera (see section 4.2 for details):

$$n_r = \frac{1}{N} * \sum_{k=1}^{N} n_k \tag{3}$$

Finally, the correlation between the ESPN and the RSPN is computed as follows:

$$\mathrm{corr}(n_e, n_r) = \frac{(n_e - \overline{n_e}) * (n_r - \overline{n_r})}{\|n_e - \overline{n_e}\| \|n_r - \overline{n_r}\|} \tag{4}$$

where the bar above a symbol denotes the mean value.

3.2   Iris Recognition Module

The iris recognition module employs the Cumulative SUMs (CSUM) algorithm [22]. This method analyzes the local variation in the gray levels of an image. The image is first normalized transforming the Cartesian coordinates in polar ones, obtaining a rectangular shape. Then the image is subdivided in cells and, for each cell, the representative value X is computed as the average gray level. Then the cells are grouped (horizontally and vertically in turn) and the average value $\overline{X}$ of the representatives of the cells of each group is computed. The cumulative sums are computed over each group as follows:

$$S_0 = 0$$

$$S_i = S_{i-1} + (X_i - \overline{X}) \qquad \text{for } i = 1, 2, \ldots, N$$

where N is the size of the group.

Finally, the iris code is generated comparing each pair of consecutive sums and assigning values 1 or 2 to a cell if the value of the corresponding sum contributes respectively to an upward slope or to a downward slope. Otherwise, value 0 is assigned to the cell.

The matching of the iris codes computed as explained before, is performed by Hamming distance.

3.3   Fusion Technique

The choice of the fusion strategy mostly depends on the application scenario of the system. For example it could be preferable to have a high security access to restricted areas, or just to provide a privileged access to a sub-set of users (e.g. fast track in airports).

We performed fusion at score level and employed the weighted sum technique with the aim of improving system performance (high security scenario).

In next section we will explain in detail these approaches and we will show the results obtained.

4   Experimental Results

Performing iris recognition on mobile devices may introduce many noise factors during the acquisition phase due to the fact that:

- the user may need to get authenticated at any time and in any place, with different illumination conditions, while walking, standing or sitting;
- the user holds the mobile device by his hand and may involuntarily move the device;
- the acquisition device characteristics may influence the acquisition: resolution of the sensor, presence of the frontal camera, possibility of using voice control to take the picture, etc.

In order to develop a robust solution for iris recognition on mobile devices, the database used for testing should simulate the uncontrolled acquisition conditions described above.

For this reason, for the experiments we used the MICHE database [2, 3], a database composed by 75 subjects, with at least 40 images per subject, captured in different illumination conditions and with, when possible, different cameras (front and rear) of the three mobile devices employed for the acquisition.

This database perfectly fits our problem because it contains pictures of the same subjects captured with different mobile devices. Performances were assessed in terms of ROC curve, CMS curve, AUC, EER, FRR, FAR, RR.

4.1   Data Set

MICHE database contains photos captured indoor and outdoor with three different mobile devices: Samsung Galaxy S4 (hereinafter GS4), iPhone 5 (hereinafter iP5) and Samsung Galaxy tab 2. As we performed iris recognition, among the three devices, we selected the two with highest resolution cameras: GS4 and iP5. Both the front and the rear cameras of these two devices were used. For our experiments we selected 2 photos acquired with the front camera and 2 photos acquired with the rear camera for each device, for a total of 8 pictures per subject, for a total of about 600 images.

Some examples of MICHE database are shown in Fig. 3.

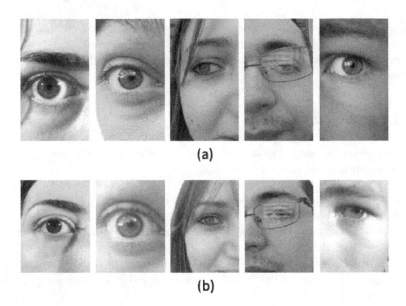

(a)

(b)

Fig. 3. Examples of images in MICHE database: (a) captured from Galaxy S4; (b) captured from iPhone 5. In both rows are shown, in corresponding positions, the same subjects acquired in the same conditions (i.e. indoor/outdoor, front/rear camera).

4.2   Sensor Recognition

To extract the ESPN, in appendix A of [20], it is suggested to process large images by blocks of 512x512 pixel, but during our experiments we observed that using just one block is sufficient to obtain a RR of 98%, for this reason, in our experiments we extracted from all the images a block of size 512x512 starting from the top-left corner of the photo.

In order to extract the RSPN for each camera, we computed the average SPN, as explained in section 3.1, over around 100 photos of the blue sky. We employed this kind of images because they do not contain details that, as the noise, are located in the high frequencies of the image and can be confused with the sensor's noise [20].

We used the RSPNs extracted from the four cameras as Gallery set and the ESPNs extracted from each photo as Probe set.

It must be noted that the iPhone 5 was changed with another device of the same model during the acquisition process of the MICHE database. This means that starting from the subject with ID=49, the photos were acquired with an iP5 but with a different sensor and thus they integrate a different SPN. Since we extracted the RSPN from the new iP5 device, pictures relative to IDs less than 49, should be detected as unenrolled subjects. The presence of unenrolled subjects in the probe, i.e. pictures captured with a device of which we do not have the corresponding RSPN ("old" iP5) in the Gallery, makes the system performance assessment more reliable.

The system obtained a RR equal to 98% and a very low average FAR of about 5%. Results for sensor recognition are shown in Fig. 4 and the performance values are reported in Table 1.

Table 1. Sensor recognition performance

Exp.	EER	avg. FAR	avg. FRR	AUC	RR
Sensor	0.04	0.05	0.56	0.99	0.98

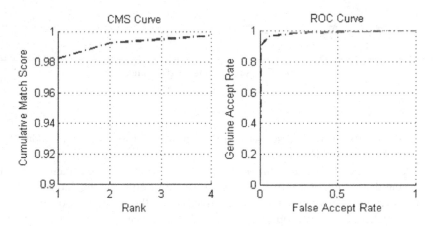

Fig. 4. Sensor recognition performance

4.3 Iris Recognition

To assess the performance of the iris recognition algorithm, we employed the same dataset used for the sensor recognition experiment but in this case we split the images so that for each subject half of the pictures (4 images) are in the Probe and the remaining are in the Gallery. Then, to better test the reliability of the system, we removed half of the subjects from the Gallery in order to simulate the attempt of unenrolled users to access the system.

It must be noted that MICHE is a very challenging database, containing pictures affected by many noise factors. Iris recognition system performances could be improved by preprocessing iris images to remove the noise. However, since this goes beyond the aim of the paper, we have not addressed the noise problem.

The system has an 85% RR and an AUC of 77%. Results for iris recognition are shown in Fig. 5 and the performance values are reported in Table 2.

Table 2. Iris recognition performance

Exp.	EER	avg. FAR	avg. FRR	AUC	RR
Iris	0.29	0.27	0.60	0.77	0.85

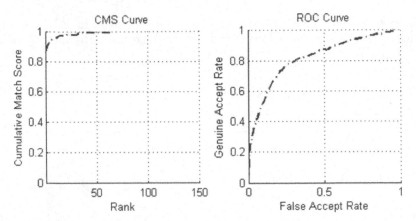

Fig. 5. Iris recognition performance

4.4   Fusion

To test the fusion of iris and sensor recognition, we split the dataset into Gallery and Probe so that in each set we had for each subject four pictures, one for each sensor: GS4 front camera, Gs4 rear camera, iP5 front camera and iP5 rear camera. In Fig. 6 we present the results of the fusion obtained combining the device and the iris recognition scores via the weighted sum technique. To set the weights associated with the scores, we choose values proportional to the RR obtained by each system. The combination device-iris recognition obtained a RR of 86% and AUC = 98%. The performance values are reported in Table 3.

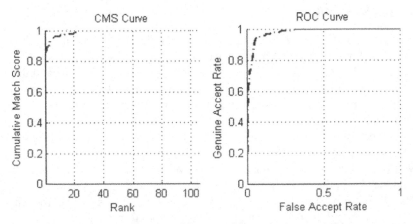

Fig. 6. Fusion performance: iris recognition + device recognition

Table 3. Experimental results. Fusion of the sensor recognition scores with the iris recognition ones.

Exp.	EER	FAR avg.	FRR avg.	AUC	RR
Fusion	0.09	0.26	0.37	0.98	0.86

5   Conclusions

Combining the output of a device recognition module with the output of an iris recognition module, we provided an approach that, based on a single image captured with a mobile device, can assure a higher security level with respect to an authentication system based only on biometrics. In addition, our approach does not require any additional or dedicated sensors as it leverages the presence of high resolution imaging sensors embedded in common Smartphones. In further works we will study the development of a complete system combining hardwaremetry and biometry, further improving the security level adding a liveness detection module. Another aspect that can be improved is the extraction of the RSPN, currently obtained from images of the blue sky, which could be replaced by the technique presented in [23], where the images employed are of any kind, e.g. landscapes, indoor or outdoor photos, etc. Finally, to properly test the system, a biometric database acquired with different sensors is needed, the MICHE database is rich enough to analyze the advantages of combining sensor and iris recognition, but would be interesting to analyze the possibility of developing a multi-biometric system, e.g. iris + face, face + voice, iris + voice, etc., towards the aim of providing higher security through a simple authentication process.

References

1. http://www.ffiec.gov/pdf/authentication_guidance.pdf
2. http://biplab.unisa.it/MICHE/database/
3. De Marsico, M., Nappi, M., Riccio, D., Wechsler, H.: Mobile Iris Challenge Evaluation - MICHE - 1, Biometric iris dataset and protocols. Pattern Recognition Letters (2015). doi:10.1016/j.patrec.2015.02.009
4. Chen, B., Shen, J., Sun, H.: A fast face recognition system on mobile phone. In: 2012 International Conference on Systems and Informatics (ICSAI), pp. 1783–1786. IEEE (2012)
5. Imaizumi, K., Moshnyaga, V.G.: Network-based face recognition on mobile devices. In: IEEE Third International Conference on Consumer Electronics?? Berlin (ICCE-Berlin), ICCE Berlin 2013, pp. 406–409 (2013)
6. Barra, S., De Marsico, M., Galdi, C., Riccio, D., Wechsler, H.: FAME: face authentication for mobile encounter. In: IEEE Workshop on Biometric Measurements and Systems for Security and Medical Applications (BIOMS), pp. 1–7 (2013)
7. Cho, D.H., Park, K.R., Rhee, D.W., Kim, Y.G., Yang, J.H.: Pupil and iris localization for iris recognition in mobile phones. In: Proceedings of the SNPD, pp. 197–201 (2006)
8. Cho, D.H., Park, K.R., Rhee, D.W.: Real-time iris localization for iris recognition in cellular phone. In: International Conference on Software Engineering, Artificial Intelligence, Networking and Parallel/Distributed Computing, pp. 254–259 (2005)
9. http://www.samsung.com/
10. http://www.sinobiometrics.com
11. Frucci, M., Galdi, C., Nappi, M., Riccio, D., Sanniti di Baja, G.: IDEM: Iris DEtection on Mobile devices. In: 22nd International Conference on Pattern Recognition, ICPR, August 24–28 (2014)

12. Abate, A.F., Frucci, M., Galdi, C., Riccio, D.: BIRD: watershed Based IRis Detection for mobile devices. Pattern Recognition Letters (available online November 14, 2014. doi:10.1016/j.patrec.2014.10.017

13. Jeong, D.S., Park, H.-A., Park, K.R., Kim, J.H.: Iris recognition in mobile phone based on adaptive gabor filter. In: Zhang, D., Jain, A.K. (eds.) ICB 2005. LNCS, vol. 3832, pp. 457–463. Springer, Heidelberg (2005)

14. Park, K.R., Park, H., Kang, B.Y., Lee, E.C., Jeong, D.S.: A study on iris localization and recognition on mobile phone. Eur. J. Adv. Signal Process., 1–12 (2007)

15. Kang, J.S.: Mobile iris recognition systems: an emerging biometric technology. In: International Conference on Computational Science (ICCS) (2010)

16. Barra, S., Casanova, A., Narducci, F., Ricciardi, S.: Ubiquitous iris recognition by means of mobile devices. Pattern Recognition Letters (available online 28 October 2014). doi:10.1016/j.patrec.2014.10.011

17. Abate, A.F., Nappi, M., Narducci, F., Ricciardi, S.: Fast Iris recognition on smartphone by means of spatial histograms. In: Cantoni, V., Dimov, D., Tistarelli, M. (eds.) BIOMET 2014, LNCS 8897. LNCS, vol. 8897, pp. 66–74. Springer, Heidelberg (2014)

18. De Marsico, M., Galdi, C., Nappi, M., Riccio, D.: FIRME: face and iris recognition for mobile engagement. Image Vis. Comput. **32**(12), 1161–1172 (2014)

19. Li, C.-T.: Source camera identification using enhanced sensor pattern noise. IEEE Transactions on Information Forensics and Security **5**(2), 280–287 (2010)

20. Lukás, J., Fridrich, J., Goljan, M.: Digital camera identification from sensor pattern noise. IEEE Trans. Inf. Forensics Security **1**(2), 205–214 (2006)

21. Chen, M., Fridrich, J., Goljan, M., Lukás, J.: Determining image origin and integrity using sensor noise. IEEE Trans. Inf. Forensics Security **3**(1), 74–90 (2008)

22. Ko, J.-G., Gil, Y.-H., Yoo, J.-H., Chung, K.-I.: A novel and efficient feature extraction method for iris recognition. ETRI J. **29**(3), 399–401 (2007)

23. Taktak, W., Dugelay, J.-L.: Digital Image Forensics: A Two-Step Approach for Identifying Source and Detecting Forgeries. The Era of Interactive Media, pp. 37–51. Springer, New York (2013)

24. Redi, J.A., Taktak, W., Dugelay, J.-L.: Digital image forensics: a booklet for beginners. Multimedia Tools and Applications **51**(1), 133–162 (2011)

25. Daugman, J.: How iris recognition works. In: 2002 International Conference on Image Processing. Proceedings, vol. 1, pp. I-33–I-36 (2002)

Multi-scale Opening – A New Morphological Operator

Subhadip Basu[1]([✉]), Eric Hoffman[2], and Punam K. Saha[2,3]

[1] Department of Computer Science and Engineering, Jadavpur University,
Kolkata 700032, India
subhadip@cse.jdvu.ac.in
[2] Department of Radiology and the Department of Biomedical Engineering,
The University of Iowa, Iowa City, IA 52242, USA
eric-hoffman@uiowa.edu
[3] Department of Electrical and Computer Engineering, The University of Iowa,
Iowa City, IA 52242, USA
pksaha@engineering.uiowa.edu

Abstract. Theoretical properties of multi-scale opening (MSO), a new mathematical morphological operator, are established and its application to separation of conjoined fuzzy objects is presented. The new MSO operator accounts for distinct intensity properties of individual objects inside the assembly of two conjoined fuzzy objects by combining fuzzy distance transform (FDT), a morphologic feature, with fuzzy connectivity, a topologic feature, to iteratively open two objects starting at large scales and progressing toward finer scales. Results of application of the new mathematical morphological operator to separate conjoined arterial structures in mathematically generated phantoms and for segmentation of arteries and veins in a physical cast phantom of a pig lung are presented. Performance of the MSO operator is also evaluated in terms of patients' pulmonary non-contrast CT data for separating arteries and veins and for complete carotid vascular segmentation for patient's CTA data set.

Keywords: Fuzzy distance transform · Morphology · Multi-scale opening

1 Introduction

Knowledge extraction over varying scales or multiple layers in two- and higher-dimensional images has remained a front-line research objective over several decades [1–5]. Object segmentation in images is one of the major challenges in many such applications[6–11]. It is difficult to design general purpose segmentation methods and, often, we face a new segmentation challenge that may not be efficiently solved the using existing methods. Design of the mathematical morphological operators play a key role in the success of many segmentation methods. In case of multi-layered extraction of knowledge, the segmentation results are often found to be extremely sensitive to the choice of the structure size of the morphological operators. In this work, we present multi-scale opening (MSO) as a new mathematical morphological operator, capable of separating two conjoined fuzzy objects over varying scales. We also present the theoretical validations for the new morphological operator and

© Springer International Publishing Switzerland 2015
V. Murino and E. Puppo (Eds.): ICIAP 2015, Part II, LNCS 9280, pp. 417–427, 2015.
DOI: 10.1007/978-3-319-23234-8_39

present the results with respect to both mathematical and vessel-cast phantoms and patients' data. Two different situations may arise here regarding the intensity distribution of the conjoined structures, 1) segmentation of fused iso-intensity objects and, 2) segmentation in shared intensity space.

The developed MSO operator use fuzzy distance transform (FDT) [16], a morphologic feature, with topologic fuzzy connectivity [17–20] algorithm to develop a multi-scale opening operator for separating two conjoined fuzzy objects fused at different locations and scales. The proposed method for multi-scale opening starts with a fuzzy segmentation of the assembly of two conjoined objects, and two sets of seed points (one for each object). The method outputs spatially separated objects. It is designed under the assumption that fusions of the two objects are locally separable using a suitable morphological opening operator. The method uses a novel approach to solve the following two fundamental challenges: 1) how to find local size of morphological operators and, 2) how to trace continuity of locally separated regions. These challenges are met by combining FDT, a morphologic feature with a topologic fuzzy connectivity, and a constrained dilation to iteratively open finer and finer details starting at large scales and progressing toward smaller scales.

2   Theory of Multi-Scale Opening of Conjoined Fuzzy Objects

A three dimensional (3D) cubic grid, is represented by $Z^3 |$ Z is the set of integers. A grid point, often referred to as a point or a voxel, is an element of Z^3 and is represented by a triplet of integer coordinates. Standard 26-adjacency [21] is used here, i.e., two voxels $p = (x_1, x_2, x_3), q = (y_1, y_2, y_3) \in Z^3$ are adjacent if and only if $\max_{1 \leq i \leq 3} |x_i - y_i| \leq 1$, where $|\cdot|$ returns the absolute value. Two adjacent voxels are often referred to as neighbors of each other; the set of 26-neighboors of a voxel p excluding itself is denoted by $\mathcal{N}^*(p)$. An object $\mathcal{O}$ is a fuzzy set $\{(p, \mu_O(p)) | p \in Z^3\}$ of Z^3, where $\mu_O: Z^3 \rightarrow [0,1]$ is the membership function. The support $\Theta(\mathcal{O})$ of an object $\mathcal{O}$ is the set of all voxels with non-zero membership, i.e., $\Theta(\mathcal{O}) = \{p \mid p \in Z^3 \text{ and } \mu_O(p) \neq 0\}$; $\bar{\Theta}(\mathcal{O}) = Z^3 - \Theta(\mathcal{O})$ is the background. Images are always acquired with a finite field of view. Thus, we will assume that an object always has a bounded support. Let S denote a set of voxels; a path π in S from $p \in S$ to $q \in S$ is a sequence $\langle p = p_1, p_2, \cdots, p_l = q \rangle$ of voxels in S such that every two successive voxels on the path are adjacent. A link is a path $\langle p, q \rangle$ consisting of exactly two mutually adjacent voxels $p, q \in Z^3$. The length of a path $\pi = \langle p_1, p_2, \cdots, p_l \rangle$ in a fuzzy object $\mathcal{O}$, denoted by $\Pi_O(\pi)$, is defined as the sum of lengths of all links along the path, i.e.,

$$\Pi_O(\pi) = \sum_{i=1}^{l-1} \frac{1}{2} \left(\mu_O(p_i) + \mu_O(p_{i+1}) \right) \| p_i - p_{i+1} \|. \tag{1}$$

The *fuzzy distance* between two voxels $p, q \in Z^3$ in an object $\mathcal{O}$, denoted by $\omega_\mathcal{O}(p, q)$, is the length of one of the shortest paths from p to q, i.e.,

$$\omega_\mathcal{O}(p, q) = \min_{\pi \in \mathcal{P}(p,q)} \Pi_\mathcal{O}(\pi)| \, \mathcal{P}(p, q), \tag{2}$$

where, $\mathcal{P}(p, q)$ is set of all paths from p to q. The *fuzzy distance transform* or *FDT* of an object $\mathcal{O}$ is an image $\{(p, \Omega_\mathcal{O}(p))| p \in Z^3\}$, where $\Omega_\mathcal{O}: Z^3 \to \Re^+ | \Re^+$ is set of positive real numbers including zero, is the fuzzy distance from background. i.e.,

$$\Omega_\mathcal{O}(p) = \min_{q \in \Theta(\mathcal{O})} \omega_\mathcal{O}(p, q). \tag{3}$$

Local scale is defined as the depth (i.e., the FDT value) at the nearest locally-deepest voxels. Let $S_{\max} \subset \Theta(\mathcal{O})$ be the set of locally-deepest voxels, i.e., $S_{\max} = \{p \mid p \in \Theta(\mathcal{O}) \text{ and } \forall q \in \mathcal{N}_l(p), \ \Omega_\mathcal{O}(q) \leq \Omega_\mathcal{O}(p)\}$, where $\mathcal{N}_l(p)$ is the $(2l + 1)^3$ neighborhood of p; here, $\mathcal{N}_2(p)$ is used to avoid noisy local maxima. Local scale at a voxel p, denoted by $\delta_\mathcal{O}(p)$, is defined as the FDT value of the voxel in $S_{\max}$ nearest to p. Now onward, both "FDT" and $\Omega_\mathcal{O}$ will refer to "scale-normalized FDT".

Let us assume two fuzzy objects $\mathcal{O}_\mathcal{A}$ and $\mathcal{O}_\mathcal{B}$, which are fused at various unknown locations and scales. The segmentation of the two fuzzy objects is solved using a new MSO operator in two sequential steps – Step 1: segmentation of the combined region $\mathcal{O}_\mathcal{A} \cup \mathcal{O}_\mathcal{B}$ from the background, and Step 2: separation of $\mathcal{O}_\mathcal{A}$ and $\mathcal{O}_\mathcal{B}$. The first step may trivially be achieved using simple thresholding [22, 23] and connectivity analysis [24, 25]. Let $\mathcal{O}$ be the fuzzy segmentation of the combined region obtained in Step 1. All subsequent analyses will be confined to the support $\Theta(\mathcal{O})$ of $\mathcal{O}$; let $I: \Theta(\mathcal{O}) \to [I_{\min}, I_{\max}]$ be image intensity function over $\Theta(\mathcal{O})$.

In the second step, segmentation is modeled as opening of two fuzzy objects mutually fused at different unknown regions and scales. Often, a simple fuzzy connectivity or edge analysis may not be suitable to separate the two structures. On the other hand, the two objects may frequently be locally separable using a suitable morphological opening operator. The challenges here are – (1) how to determine local size of suitable morphological operators and (2) how to combine the locally separated regions. The MSO operator combines fuzzy distance transform (FDT) [26], [16] a morphologic function with a topologic fuzzy connectivity [17, 18, 27] to iteratively open the two objects starting at large scales and progressing toward finer scales.

2.1   Optimal Erosion Using Morpho-Connectivity

Here, we define the algorithm during the first iteration.   It starts with two sets of seed voxels $S_\mathcal{A}$ and $S_\mathcal{B}$ and a set of common separators S_S. The initial FDT map $\Omega_{\mathcal{A},0}$ for the first object is computed from $\mathcal{O}$ except that the voxels in $S_\mathcal{B} \cup S_S$ are added to the background; it is worth mentioning that the local scale map $\delta_\mathcal{O}$, derived from the original assembled object $\mathcal{O}$, is used for normalization. FDT map $\Omega_\mathcal{B}$ for the other object is computed similarly. It is reasonable to assume that the sets $S_\mathcal{A}$, $S_\mathcal{B}$, and S_S are mutually exclusive.

Fuzzy morpho-connectivity strength of a path $\pi = \langle p_1, p_2, \cdots, p_l \rangle$ in a fuzzy object $\mathcal{O}$, denoted as $\Gamma_O(\pi)$, is the minimum FDT value along the path:

$$\Gamma_O(\pi) = \min_{1 \le i \le l} \Omega_O(p_i) . \tag{4}$$

Fuzzy morpho-connectivity between two voxels $p, q \in \mathcal{Z}^3$, denoted as $\gamma_O(p, q)$, is the strength of one of the strongest morphological paths between p and q, i.e.,

$$\gamma_O(p, q) = \max_{\pi \in \mathcal{P}(p,q)} \Gamma_O(\pi). \tag{5}$$

Definition 2.1. Optimum erosion for a fuzzy object $\mathcal{A}$ represented by the set of seed voxels $S_{\mathcal{A}}$ with respect to its co-object $\mathcal{B}$ represented by the set of seed voxels $S_{\mathcal{B}}$ and a set of common separator S_s is the set of all voxels p such that there exists an erosion scale that disconnects p from $\mathcal{B}$ while leaving it connected to $\mathcal{A}$, i.e.,

$$R_{\mathcal{A},0} = \left\{ p \mid \max_{a \in S_{\mathcal{A}}} \gamma_{\mathcal{A},0}(a, p) > \max_{b \in S_{\mathcal{B}}} \gamma_{\mathcal{B},0}(b, p) \right\}, \tag{6}$$

where, the fuzzy morpho-connectivity functions $\gamma_{\mathcal{A},0}$ and $\gamma_{\mathcal{B},0}$ are defined from the FDT maps $\Omega_{\mathcal{A},0}$ and $\Omega_{\mathcal{B},0}$, respectively The optimum erosion $R_{\mathcal{B},0}$ for the object $\mathcal{B}$ is defined similarly.

Proposition 2.1. For any fuzzy object $\mathcal{O}$ in $\mathcal{Z}^3$, for any two mutually exclusive sets of seeds $S_{\mathcal{A}}$ and $S_{\mathcal{B}}$, representing two different objects, and a set of common separator S_s disjoint to both $S_{\mathcal{A}}$ and $S_{\mathcal{B}}$, the separated regions $R_{\mathcal{A},0}$, $R_{\mathcal{B},0}$, after optimum erosion, are always disjoint, i.e., $R_{\mathcal{A},0} \cap R_{\mathcal{B},0} = \emptyset$.

Proof. To prove this proposition by contradiction, let us assume that the proposition is not true, i.e., $R_{\mathcal{A},0} \cap R_{\mathcal{B},0} \ne \emptyset$. Let us consider a voxel p in $R_{\mathcal{A},0} \cap R_{\mathcal{B},0}$ and from Eqn. (6) the voxel p belongs to $R_{\mathcal{A},0}$ since, $\max_{a \in S_{\mathcal{A}}} \gamma_{\mathcal{A},0}(a, p) > \max_{b \in S_{\mathcal{B}}} \gamma_{\mathcal{B},0}(b, p)$. But since the voxel p also belongs to $R_{\mathcal{B},0}$, following the same equation, $\max_{b \in S_{\mathcal{B}}} \gamma_{\mathcal{B},0}(b, p) > \max_{a \in S_{\mathcal{A}}} \gamma_{\mathcal{A},0}(a, p)$. Hence contradiction.   ∎

2.2   Constrained Dilation

The two optimally eroded regions $R_{\mathcal{A},0}$ and $R_{\mathcal{B},0}$ (Fig. 1(a)) separates the two target objects using morpho-connectivity. However, each of these two separated regions captures only an eroded version of the target objects over respective local regions and dilation is needed to further improve the delineation results (Fig. 1(b)). Also, the annular left-over of optimal erosion (Fig. 1(a)) wrongly permits path leakages from one separated region into the other. It is crucial to block such leakages in order to proceed with the separation process to the next finer scale. Both objectives are fulfilled by local dilation of the two separated objects and we refer to it as a "constrained dilation" Constrained dilation is applied over a "morphological neighborhood" to ensure that the dilation is locally confined.

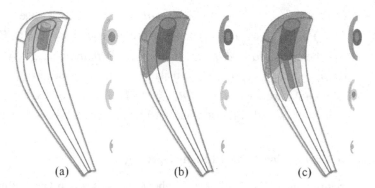

Fig. 1. A schematic illustration of the results of different steps in the MSO algorithm – (a) optimal erosion, (b) constrained dilation, and (c) iterative progression to the next iteration.

Definition 2.2. Morphological neighborhood of a set of voxels X in an object $\mathcal{O}$, denoted by $N_{\mathcal{O}}(X)$, is a set of all voxels $p \in \Theta(\mathcal{O})$ such that $\exists\, q \in X$ for which $\omega_{\mathcal{O}}(p,q) < \Omega_{\mathcal{O}}(q)$ and p is connected to q by a path $\pi = \langle p = p_1, p_2, \cdots, p_l = q \rangle$ of monotonically increasing FDT values.

To define morphological neighborhood, original FDT map without scale normalization is used as morphological neighborhood should capture original un-normalized scale and geometry of the local structure.

Definition 2.3. *Constrained dilation* of $R_{\mathcal{A},0}$ with respect to its co object $R_{\mathcal{B},0}$ within the fuzzy object $\mathcal{O}$, denoted as $M_{\mathcal{A},0}$, is the set of all voxels $p \in N_{\mathcal{O}}(R_{\mathcal{A},0})$ which are strictly closer to $R_{\mathcal{A},0}$ than $R_{\mathcal{B},0}$ (Fig. 1(b)), i.e.,

$$M_{\mathcal{A},0} = \left\{ p \mid p \in N_{\mathcal{O}}(R_{\mathcal{A},0}) \wedge \max_{a \in R_{\mathcal{A},0}} \omega_{\mathcal{O}}(a,p) > \max_{b \in R_{\mathcal{B},0}} \omega_{\mathcal{O}}(b,p) \right\}, \qquad (7)$$

where, the fuzzy distance function $\omega_{\mathcal{O}}$ is defined over the fuzzy object $\mathcal{O}$ in $\mathcal{Z}^3$. The region $M_{\mathcal{B},0}$ is defined similarly.

It may be noted that, gaps between the separated regions visible in Fig. 1(a) are filled in Fig. 1(b) after constrained dilation and, thus, undesired paths running through those gaps are blocked enabling separation at the next finer scale. The two steps of optimal erosion and constrained dilation lead to an "optimal opening" operation preparing the ground for separation at next finer scales.

Proposition 2.2. For any fuzzy object $\mathcal{O}$ in $\mathcal{Z}^3$, for any two mutually exclusive sets of seeds $S_{\mathcal{A}}$ and $S_{\mathcal{B}}$, representing two different objects, and a set of common separator $S_{\mathcal{S}}$ disjoint to both $S_{\mathcal{A}}$ and $S_{\mathcal{B}}$, the constrained dilations $M_{\mathcal{A},0}$ $M_{\mathcal{B},0}$ are always disjoint, i.e., $M_{\mathcal{A},0} \cap M_{\mathcal{B},0} = \emptyset$.

Proof. To prove this proposition by contradiction first let us assume that the proposition is not true, i.e., $M_{\mathcal{A},0} \cap M_{\mathcal{B},0} \neq \emptyset$. Let us consider a voxel p in $M_{\mathcal{A},0} \cap M_{\mathcal{B},0}$.

Following $p \in M_{\mathcal{A},0}$ and *Definition* *2.3*, we have $\max_{a \in R_{\mathcal{A},0}} \omega_O(a,p) > \max_{b \in R_{\mathcal{B},0}} \omega_O(b,p)$. Therefore p is strictly closer to $R_{\mathcal{A},0}$. But since p also belongs to $M_{\mathcal{B},0}$, following *Definition* *2.3*, we have $\max_{a \in R_{\mathcal{B},0}} \omega_O(a,p) > \max_{b \in R_{\mathcal{A},0}} \omega_O(b,p)$, making p strictly closer to $R_{\mathcal{B},0}$ as well. But from *Proposition 2.1* we have, $R_{\mathcal{A},0} \cap R_{\mathcal{B},0} = \emptyset$. Therefore the voxel p cannot be strictly closer to both $R_{\mathcal{A},0}$ and $R_{\mathcal{B},0}$ simultaneously. Hence contradiction.   ∎

2.3   Iterative Progression to Multi-Scale Opening

The optimal opening algorithm, as described above, separates two target objects at a specific scale and the purpose of the current step is to freeze the boundary of previous separation enabling propagation to the next finer scale. This step operates in a fashion similar to the iterative strategy described in references [19, 28] for intensity based fuzzy connectivity. For each of the two objects, we set the FDT values to zero over the region currently acquired by its rival object. Specifically, after each iteration, the FDT image of object $\mathcal{A}$ is updated as follows:

$$\Omega_{\mathcal{A},i}(p) = \begin{cases} 0, & \text{if } p \in N_O(R_{\mathcal{B},i-1}) - M_{\mathcal{A},i-1}, \\ \Omega_{0,i-1}(p), & \text{otherwise}. \end{cases} \tag{8}$$

The FDT map of the other object is updated similarly. The seed voxels $S_{\mathcal{A}}$ and $S_{\mathcal{B}}$ for the two objects are replaced by $M_{\mathcal{A},i-1}$ and $M_{\mathcal{B},i-1}$, respectively (Fig. 1(c)). Then, the morphological separations $M_{\mathcal{A},i}$ and $M_{\mathcal{B},i}$ are derived using the Eqns. (6-8) and *Definition 2.1* to *Definition 2.3*.

Proposition 2.3. For any fuzzy object O in Z^3, for any two mutually exclusive sets of seeds $S_{\mathcal{A}}$ and $S_{\mathcal{B}}$, representing two different objects, and a set of common separator S_S disjoint to both $S_{\mathcal{A}}$ and $S_{\mathcal{B}}$, for any positive integer i, the separation results $M_{\mathcal{A},i}$, $M_{\mathcal{B},i}$ of the MSO algorithm are always disjoint, i.e., $M_{\mathcal{A},i} \cap M_{\mathcal{B},i} = \emptyset$.

Proof. This proposition will be proved by induction. From *Proposition 2.1* we have $R_{\mathcal{A},0} \cap R_{\mathcal{B},0} = \emptyset$ and from *Proposition 2.2* we have $M_{\mathcal{A},0} \cap M_{\mathcal{B},0} = \emptyset$. This ensures disjoint separation of the two fuzzy objects after the first iteration of the MSO algorithm. Let us assume that this proposition is true after $(i-1)^{\text{th}}$ iteration, for some $i > 1$. To complete the proof, we will show that the proposition remains true after the ith iteration. During the ith iteration of multi-scale opening, the following changes take place in the optimum erosion and iterative progression steps as compared to the first iteration: $\Omega_{\mathcal{A},0}$ (or, $\Omega_{\mathcal{B},0}$) is replaced by $\Omega_{\mathcal{A},i}$ (respectively, $\Omega_{\mathcal{B},i}$) in Equation (6) and the set seeds $S_{\mathcal{A}}$ is replaced by $M_{\mathcal{A},i-1}$ instead of $M_{\mathcal{A},0}$ while $S_{\mathcal{B}}$ is replaced by $M_{\mathcal{B},i-1}$, instead of $M_{\mathcal{B},0}$. Therefore, following *Proposition 2.1* and *Proposition 2.3*, the results of optimum erosion and constrained dilation, the output separation of the ith iteration remain disjoint, i.e., $M_{\mathcal{A},i} \cap M_{\mathcal{B},i} = \emptyset$.   ∎

Proposition 2.4. For any fuzzy object O in Z^3, for any two mutually exclusive sets of seeds $S_{\mathcal{A}}$ and $S_{\mathcal{B}}$, representing two different objects, and a set of common separator S_S disjoint to both $S_{\mathcal{A}}$ and $S_{\mathcal{B}}$, for any positive integer i, the separation results $M_{\mathcal{A},i} \subset M_{\mathcal{A},i+1}$.

Proof. Following iterative progression of multi-scale opening, during the $(i+1)^{\text{th}}$ iteration, $M_{\mathcal{A},i}$ is used as the set of seeds for the object $\mathcal{A}$. Following *Definition 2.3*, $M_{\mathcal{A},i} \subset N_O(R_{\mathcal{A},i})$; following *Proposition 2.3*, $M_{\mathcal{A},i} \cap M_{\mathcal{B},i} = \emptyset$. Therefore, $p \in M_{\mathcal{A},i} \subset M_{\mathcal{A},i} - M_{\mathcal{B},i} \subset N_O(R_{\mathcal{A},i}) - M_{\mathcal{B},i}$. Thus, following Equation (8), $\forall p \in M_{\mathcal{A},i}$, $\Omega_{\mathcal{B},i+1}(p) = 0$. Hence, following Equation (6), $M_{\mathcal{A},i} \subset R_{\mathcal{A},i+1} \subset M_{\mathcal{A},i+1}$.   ∎

Proposition 2.5. For any fuzzy object O in Z^3 with a finite support $\Theta(O)$, for any two mutually exclusive sets of seeds $S_{\mathcal{A}}$ and $S_{\mathcal{B}}$, representing two different objects, and a set of common separator S_S disjoint to both $S_{\mathcal{A}}$ and $S_{\mathcal{B}}$, the MSO algorithm terminates in a finite number of iterations.

Proof. For all voxels, $p \in \bar{\Theta}(O)$, for any $i \geq 0$, the FDT maps $\Omega_{\mathcal{A},i}(p) = \Omega_{\mathcal{B},i}(p) = 0$. Therefore, following Eqn. (6), $R_{\mathcal{A},i}, R_{\mathcal{B},i} \subset \bar{\Theta}(O)$. Following *Definition 2.2*, the morphological neighborhoods $N_O(R_{\mathcal{A},i}), N_O(R_{\mathcal{B},i}) \subset \bar{\Theta}(O)$. Therefore, the results of constrained dilation $M_{\mathcal{A},i}$ and $M_{\mathcal{B},i}$ are confined to the finite set. Again, following *Proposition 2.4*, $M_{\mathcal{A},i}$ and $M_{\mathcal{B},i}$ are monotonically non-contracting. Therefore, after a finitely many iterations, both these sets converge when MSO algorithm terminates.   ∎

3   Experimental Results

In this section, we describe our experimental plans, methods, and qualitative results to examine the accuracy of segmentation results with the MSO operator, both in isointesity and shared intensity space. Performance of the system is first evaluated on two different types of phantom images, 1) conjoined mathematical phantoms in iso-intensity space, 2) CT images of a pig pulmonary vessel cast phantom with contrast separated A/V trees in shared intensity space. Another experiment is conducted on two different sets of patients' data, i.e., 1) pulmonary non-contrast CT data for separating arteries and veins in iso-intensity space and, 2) for complete carotid vascular segmentation for patient's CTA data in shared intensity space.

At first, four mathematical phantoms are computer-generated where each phantom is an assembly of two cylindrical objects running quasi-parallel across the slice direction with different geometry and varying levels of fuzziness, overlap, scale and noise. These phantom images were initially generated at high resolution after assigning a pure intensity values for the two structures. Subsequently, each of these images was down sampled using $3 \times 3 \times 3$ window to simulate partial volume effects. Each down-sampled image was further degraded with additive white Gaussian noise at SNR of 12. Using a graphical user interface, exactly one seed point was placed for each object near its center on the top-most slice at the largest-scale level. Fig. 2 shows that, even in the presence of significant overlap, down sampling and random noise, the method can separate the two conjoined structures. Note that the method of multi-scale opening has successfully removed the partial volume effects.

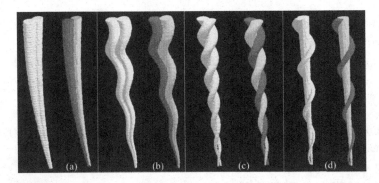

Fig. 2. Results of application of the MSO operator on four computer-generated phantoms after 3x3x3 down-sampling are shown. Each block shows the original phantom (left) of two mutually fused objects and the color-coded results of the separation using the multi-scale opening operator.

Fig. 3. Results of artery/vein (A/V) separation on a pulmonary pig vessel cast phantom are shown. (a) Photograph of the phantom. (b) 3-D rendering of the optimum thresholding result. (c) 3-D rendering of the A/V separation results using the MSO algorithm.

Results of application of the algorithm to a CT image of a pig lung cast phantom with different CT contrasts for arterial and venous trees are presented in Fig. 3. The vessel cast was scanned on a Siemens Somatom Definition Flash 128 CT scanner using the following protocol – 120 kV, 115 effective mAs, 1-s rotation speed, pitch factor: 1.0, nominal collimation: 16 mm × 0.3 mm, image matrix: 512 × 512 and (0.34 mm)2 in-plane resolution, and 0.75 mm slice thickness. Two CT intensity values I_{min} and I_{artery} segmenting the background and pure artery regions were manually selected by three independent users. Therefore, the intensity range $[I_{min}, I_{artery}]$ was used as the shared intensity space. The superiority of the new MSO operator lies in its ability to trace fine structures of individual objects despite the presence of partial voluming and intensity sharing. For this experiment, two seed voxels were used for arteries and another three seed voxels were used for veins using our custom 2D/3D graphical interface.

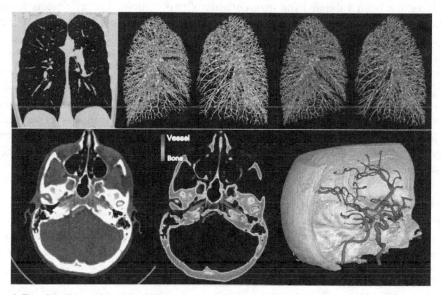

Fig. 4. Results of applying the MSO operator on patients' data. (top) artery/vein separation on a pulmonary non-contrast CT data, (bottom) carotid vessel segmentation in a patient's CTA data.

The effectiveness of the MSO operator has also been examined qualitatively on clinical pulmonary multidetector CT images. A result of application of the method separating pulmonary arteries/veins in a non-contrast thoracic CT image of a healthy subject is qualitatively illustrated in Fig. 4 (top row). The thoracic region of the patient is imaged using a Siemens Sensation 64 multidetector CT scanner at 120 kVp and 100 mA. The subject was scanned in feet-first supine position. The image was acquired at 0.75 mm slice thickness and was reconstructed with 0.5 mm slice thickness and in-plane resolution. 25-30 seed points for each of the arteries and veins were manually selected by an expert using a 2-D-slice-display graphical interface followed by the application of the MSO operator.

In case of carotid CT angiogram it is evident that carotid vasculature and soft/thin bones appear with similar CT intensities. In a CTA data, bone receives high intensity values while contrast enhanced vascular trees appear with intermediate intensity values. Although the intensity characteristics are different for bone and vascular tree, there is a significant overlap between the two due to the presence of partial voluming, noise and soft/thin bones. To evaluate the performance of the MSO operator, CTA data sets were collected using Siemens Somatom Sensation 16 scanner at 120 kV, rotation time of 0.5 second, 0.75 pitch and 0.75 mm collimation. The contrast medium used was 75 cc of Omipaque 300. Bone/vessels separation result using the new MSO operator is illustrated in Fig. 4 (bottom row). The half-skull representation displays the vascular structure in the context of bone geometry.

4   Conclusion

In this paper, the theoretical properties of the multi-scale opening have been established as new mathematical morphological operator. The applicability of the MSO operator has been validated for segmentation of two conjoined fuzzy objects having similar or shared intensity characteristics, which are fused at different scales and locations. The current work extends our previous work [13], [14] on artery-vein separation in 3-D non-contrast pulmonary CT imaging which was formulated as a separation task for two similar-intensity conjoined objects. Qualitative segmentation results of application of the new mathematical morphological operator to mathematical phantoms and artery/vein separation in a physical cast phantom of a pig lung have been illustrated. Elegant segmentation results have been observed from our experiments with the patients' data on non-contrast pulmonary CT and cerebral CTA. High accuracy and reproducibility at the cost of moderate user efforts demonstrates that the new MSO operator is suitable for a wide range of clinical and research studies.

Acknowledgment. Research work of Subhadip Basu is supported by the BOYSCAST fellowship (SR/BY/E-15/09) and FASTTRACK grant (SR/FTP/ETA-04/2012) by DST, Government of India. This study was supported in part by the NIH under Grants R01 AR-054439, R01 HL-083475 and R01 HL-064368. Authors are grateful to Prof. M.L. Raghavan, The University of Iowa and Dr. Robert E. Harbaugh, Penn State Hershey Medical Center for sharing the CTA data used in this study.

References

1. Udupa, J.K., Herman, G.T.: 3D imaging in medicine. CRC Press, Boca Raton (1991)
2. Sonka, M., Hlavac, V., Boyle, R.: Image processing, Analysis, and Machine Vision. Thomson Engineering, Toronto (2007)
3. Sonka, M., Fitzpatrick, J.: Handbook of Medical Imaging: Medical image processing and analysis, vol. 2. SPIE, Bellingham (2000)
4. Bushberg, J.T., Boone, J.M.: The essential physics of medical imaging. Lippincott Williams & Wilkins (2011)
5. Cho, Z.H., Jones, J.P., Singh, M.: Foundations of medical imaging. Wiley, New York (1993)
6. McInerney, T., Terzopoulos, D.: Deformable models in medical image analysis: a survey. Med. Image Anal. **1**, 91–108 (1996)
7. Pham, D.L., Xu, C., Prince, J.L.: Current methods in medical image segmentation 1. Annu. Rev. Biomed. Eng. **2**, 315–337 (2000)
8. Heimann, T., Meinzer, H.-P.: Statistical shape models for 3D medical image segmentation: A review. Med. Image Anal. **13**, 543–563 (2009)
9. Bezdek, J.C., Hall, L.O., Clarke, L.P.: Review of MR image segmentation techniques using pattern recognition. Med. Phys. **20**, 1033 (1993)
10. Olabarriaga, S.D., Smeulders, A.W.M.: Interaction in the segmentation of medical images: A survey. Med. Image Anal. **5**, 127–142 (2001)

11. Saha, P.K., Liang, G., Elkins, J.M., Coimbra, A., Duong, L.T., Williams, D.S., Sonka, M.: A New Osteophyte Segmentation Algorithm Using the Partial Shape Model and Its Applications to Rabbit Femur Anterior Cruciate Ligament Transection via Micro-CT Imaging. Biomed. Eng. IEEE Trans. **58**, 2212–2227 (2011)
12. Van Bemmel, C.M., Spreeuwers, L.J., Viergever, M.A., Niessen, W.J.: Level-set-based artery-vein separation in blood pool agent CE-MR angiograms. IEEE Trans. Med. Imaging **22**, 1224–1234 (2003)
13. Lei, T., Udupa, J.K., Saha, P.K., Odhner, D.: Artery-vein separation via MRA-an image processing approach. IEEE Trans. Med. Imaging **20**, 689–703 (2001)
14. Buelow, T., Wiemker, R., Blaffert, T., Lorenz, C., Renisch, S.: Automatic extraction of the pulmonary artery tree from multi-slice CT data. Medical Imaging, pp. 730–740. International Society for Optics and Photonics (2005)
15. Yonekura, T., Matsuhiro, M., Saita, S., Kubo, M., Kawata, Y., Niki, N., Nishitani, H., Ohmatsu, H., Kakinuma, R., Moriyama, N.: Classification algorithm of pulmonary vein and artery based on multi-slice CT image. Medical Imaging, p. 65142E–65142E. International Society for Optics and Photonics (2007)
16. Saha, P.K., Wehrli, F.W., Gomberg, B.R.: Fuzzy Distance Transform: Theory, Algorithms, and Applications. Comput. Vis. Image Underst. **86**, 171–190 (2002)
17. Rosenfeld, A.: Fuzzy Digital Topology. Inf. Control. **40**, 76–87 (1979)
18. Udupa, J.K., Samarasekera, S.: Fuzzy Connectedness and Object Definition: Theory, Algorithms, and Applications in Image Segmentation. Graph. Model. Image Process. **58**, 246–261 (1996)
19. Saha, P.K., Udupa, J.K.: Iterative relative fuzzy connectedness and object definition: theory, algorithms, and applications in image segmentation. In: Proceedings IEEE Workshop on Mathematical Methods in Biomedical Image Analysis, MMBIA-2000 (Cat. No.PR00737), pp. 28–35. IEEE Comput. Soc.
20. Udupa, J.K., Saha, P.K., Lotufo, R.A.: Relative fuzzy connectedness and object definition: theory, algorithms, and applications in image segmentation. IEEE Trans. Pattern Anal. Mach. Intell. **24**, 1485–1500 (2002)
21. Saha, P.K., Chaudhuri, B.B.: 3D Digital Topology under Binary Transformation with Applications. Comput. Vis. Image Underst. **63**, 418–429 (1996)
22. Saha, P.K., Udupa, J.K.: Optimum image thresholding via class uncertainty and region homogeneity (2001). http://www.computer.org/portal/web/csdl/doi?doc=abs/trans/tp/2001/07/i7toc.htm
23. Otsu, N.: A threshold selection method from gray-level histograms. IEEE Trans. Syst. Man, Cybern. **8**, 62–66 (1978)
24. Kong, T.Y., Rosenfeld, A.: Digital topology: Introduction and survey. Comput. Vis. Graph. Image Process. **48**, 357–393 (1989)
25. Saha, P.K., Chaudhuri, B.B.: Detection of 3-D simple points for topology preserving transformations with application to thinning. Pattern Anal. Mach. Intell. IEEE Trans. **16**, 1028–1032 (1994)
26. Saha, P.K., Wehrli, F.W.: Measurement of trabecular bone thickness in the limited resolution regime of in vivo MRI by fuzzy distance transform. IEEE Trans. Med. Imaging. **23**, 53–62 (2004)
27. Saha, P.K., Udupa, J.K., Odhner, D.: Scale-Based Fuzzy Connected Image Segmentation: Theory, Algorithms, and Validation. Comput. Vis. Image Underst. **77**, 145–174 (2000)
28. Ciesielski, K.C., Udupa, J.K., Saha, P.K., Zhuge, Y.: Iterative Relative Fuzzy Connectedness for Multiple Objects with Multiple Seeds. Comput. Vis. image Underst. CVIU **107**, 160–182 (2007)

Level-by-Level Adaptive Disparity Compensated Prediction in Wavelet Domain for Stereo Image Coding

Shigao Li[✉] and Liming Jia

School of Mathematic & Computer Science, Wuhan Polytechnic University,
Wuhan 430023, Hubei, China
sg51@163.com

Abstract. Disparity compensation prediction and transform coding are incorporated into a hybrid coding to reduce the bit-rate of multi-view images. However, aliasing and inaccurate displacement impair the performance of disparity compensation, especially in wavelet domain. In this paper, we propose a level-by-level adaptive disparity compensated prediction scheme for scalable stereo image coding. To get spatial scalable feature, wavelet transform is first applied to the target image of a stereo image pair. A separable 2-D filter applied to the reference image is optimized for each resolution layer by minimizing the energy of the prediction high-bands of the target image. To form a multi-resolution representation, similar processes are then applied to the low-band image pairs generated by the prior resolution layer iteratively. Experimental results show that the proposed scheme can provide significant coding gain compared to other scalable coding scheme.

Keywords: Disparity compensation · Image compression · Stereo image coding · Wavelet image coding

1   Introduction

Stereoscopic imaging systems are extensively applied in photogrammetry, entertainment and machine vision. Especially in the field of digital photogrammetry, stereo image pairs are used to generate Digital Elevation Model (DEM). However, a mass of image data bring a challenge to image storage and transmission. Especially, how to cater to the capacity of wireless channel for those stereo sensors set on satellites is a strenuous task. Compression techniques are usually used to solve the problem. Stereo image compression techniques have thus received attention of many researchers [1-6].

It's well known that there exists high correlation between two view images. The correlation (or redundancy) can be removed by inter-view prediction using disparity estimation (DE) and disparity compensation (DC). How to perform efficiently DE and DC gets the key of coding methods and many different methods are thus developed. In [2-3], spatial domain DC-based methods are proposed. In general, these methods can be briefed as follows. First, one image of an image pair as a reference is used to

This work was supported by the Chinese Natural Science Foundation (61201452).

V. Murino and E. Puppo (Eds.): ICIAP 2015, Part II, LNCS 9280, pp. 428–437, 2015.
DOI: 10.1007/978-3-319-23234-8_40

predict another image called target image and a residue image is then generated. Second, a transform coding is applied to the reference and the residue independently. In last two decades, discrete wavelet transform (DWT) applied to image and video compression has achieved a great success [7-8]. A typical coding method (or coder) is EBCOT [9]. It's remarkable that wavelet-based methods can produce scalable code stream. However, DC in spatial domain violates the resolution scalability.

In [1], M.Kaaniche et al. proposed a novel vector lifting schemes (VLS), in which the DC process is incorporated into the decomposition procedure of target images. Because the information of the reference image directly joins the lifting process of target images level by level, no residue images are generated. Experiment results in [1] indicate that VLS achieves a significant coding gain compared to the conventional lifting scheme of wavelet. Due to the DC in multiple resolution levels, VLS can produce scalable code stream.

To get a scalable video coding, in-band prediction compensation were proposed by many researchers [10]. Nantheera Anantrasirichai applied the scheme to multi-view image coding [11]. The in-band compensation directly predicts the sub-bands of target images by using the sub-bands of reference images level by level based on the relation of subbands with different phases [10]. Although in-band compensation provides the scalable feature, aliasing introduced by the critically-sampled DWT and inaccurate displacement estimation impair the performance of DC/MC. In [12], a scheme called in scale compensation were proposed to scalable compression for video. Due to the fixed analysis filters are applied to generated prediction compensation frames, in scale compensation are similar with in-band compensation in the essence.

In recent years, adaptive interpolation filter (AIF) and adaptive loop filter (ALF) are introduced into video compression by many researchers [13-15]. In these AIF methods [13-14], filters have been designed to eliminate aliasing and to interpolate subpixel data so that more exact displacement vectors can be obtain. Thanks to the adaptivity, AIFs provide significant coding gains compare to fixed interpolation filter.

In this paper, we propose a multi-layer adaptive disparity compensation scheme for scalable stereo image coding. To get spatial scalable feature, 2-D wavelet transform (2D-DWT) is first applied to the target image of a stereo image pair. The reference image rather than subbands is used to predict the target subbands at each resolution layer. That is to say, the prediction is performed between the reference image (or the low-frequency approximation at low resolution layers) and the high-subbands of the target image at corresponding level. Although the in-scale motion compensation scheme for spatially scalable video coding is similar with ours, we adopt adaptive prediction filters instead of fixed analysis filters. In addition, considering occulsion between reference images and target images, a piecewise selection procedure is designed to exclude those pixels in occlusion region. Alternatively, original coefficients of DWT are reserved and encoded. When compared to the VLS, because a better scheme and more accurate displacement vectors are adopted, the proposed scheme obtain less high-frequency sub-band energy of target image.

This paper is organized as follows. In Section 2, we introduce the general layer-based prediction compensation formulation. In the fact, the in-band scheme and the in-scale are specific instance. The proposed structure is described and the problem to be solved is formulated in Section 3. The fourth section is devoted to occlusion culling. Experimental results show that the proposed outperforms other related schemes in terms of coding efficiency in Section 5. Section 6 provides brief conclusions.

2   Layer-Based Prediction Compensation Formulation

Many researchers applied DWT to video compression. In general, DWT is first applied to multi-frame group at temporal direction. And 2D-DWT is applied to each sub-band frame generated at the first step. This scheme is called t+2D scheme. However, when this scheme is used in scalable video coding, drifting impairs the coding efficiency [16]. To avoid the drifting, in-band MC/DC and in-scale MC are proposed. Generally, to get a scalable scheme, these methods carry out the prediction compensation level by level. A general decomposition can be depicted as Fig.1. The compensation process can be given by

$$\hat{d}_n^t = d_n^t - \mathcal{P}_n\big(\mathcal{DC}_{n-1}(I_{n-1}^r)\big)$$

$$\cdots\cdots$$

$$\hat{d}_j^t = d_j^t - \mathcal{P}_j\Big(\mathcal{DC}_{j-1}(I_{j-1}^r)\Big)$$

$$\cdots\cdots$$

$$\hat{d}_1^t = d_1^t - \mathcal{P}_1\big(\mathcal{DC}_0(I_0^r)\big) \tag{1}$$

where $\mathcal{DC}$ denotes disparity compensation operations used to form the disparity compensated image (DCI) $\tilde{I}_{j-1}^t$ as a prediction of I_{j-1}^t and $\mathcal{P}_j$ denotes the prediction compensation operations used to predict the high-frequency sub-bands at the j-th level. Varied $\mathcal{P}_j$ forms various scheme. For instance, the $\mathcal{P}_j$ used in in-band MC based on low-bands shifting (LBS) [17] consist of inverse DWT, over-complete DWT by translating. Being similar with in-band MC, in-scale MC adopts fixed predictors.

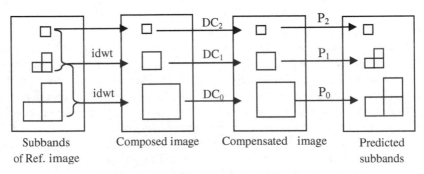

| Subbands | Composed image | Compensated image | Predicted |
| of Ref. image | | | subbands |

Fig. 1. Level-by-level Prediction Compensation

Fractional-pixel disparity accuracy can be adopted to enhance the correlation between target images and prediction images generated from reference images in the DC process. However residual translation errors still exist and impair the performance of compensation in bands because of fixed filters. In order to improve the coding efficiency by considering the non-stationary statistical properties resulting from residual translation errors and illumination differences between two different views, adaptive prediction filters are introduced in this paper. In the next section, we'll give the proposed scheme and the design of adaptive predictors $\mathcal{P}_j$'s for each level.

3   Proposed Scheme

3.1   Separable Level-by-Level Adaptive Disparity Compensation Scheme

This subsection presents the proposed level-by-level lifting scheme by using adaptive predictors. The proposed scheme can be depicted as Figure 2. At first, the conventional 2D-DWT is applied to target images at the j-th level and three high-frequency sub-bands $d_{V,j}^t$, $d_{H,j}^t$, $d_{D,j}^t$ and a low-frequency approximation image I_j^t are generated. To exploit the correlation between reference images and target images, three prediction compensation processes are carried out for the three high-frequency sub-bands independently. As a result, three new high-frequency sub-bands, i.e. prediction residue images, are formed. The decomposition process of target images can be formulated as follows,

$$I_j^t = \mathcal{A}_{LL}(I_{j-1}^t)$$

$$d_{V,j}^t = \mathcal{A}_{LH}(I_{j-1}^t)$$

$$d_{H,j}^t = \mathcal{A}_{HL}(I_{j-1}^t)$$

$$d_{D,j}^t = \mathcal{A}_{HH}(I_{j-1}^t)$$

$$\hat{d}_{V,j}^t = d_{V,j}^t - \mathcal{P}_{V,j}\left(\mathcal{DC}_{j-1}(I_{j-1}^r)\right)$$

$$\hat{d}_{H,j}^t = d_{H,j}^t - \mathcal{P}_{H,j}\left(\mathcal{DC}_{j-1}(I_{j-1}^r)\right)$$

$$\hat{d}_{D,j}^t = d_{D,j}^t - \mathcal{P}_{D,j}\left(\mathcal{DC}_{j-1}(I_{j-1}^r)\right) \tag{2}$$

where $\mathcal{A}_{LL}$, $\mathcal{A}_{LH}$, $\mathcal{A}_{HL}$, $\mathcal{A}_{HH}$ denotes the analysis operators of 2D-DWT, and $\mathcal{P}_{V,j}$, $\mathcal{P}_{H,j}$, $\mathcal{P}_{D,j}$ denotes the adaptive predictors for $d_{V,j}^t$, $d_{H,j}^t$, $d_{D,j}^t$ respectively. $\hat{d}_{V,j}^t$, $\hat{d}_{H,j}^t$, $\hat{d}_{D,j}^t$ denotes the new high-frequency sub-bands. To simplify the problem, separable and symmetric filters can be adopted for adaptive predictors $\mathcal{P}_{V,j}$, $\mathcal{P}_{H,j}$, $\mathcal{P}_{D,j}$.

At last, 2D-DWT are applied to reference images, new approximation reference image and three high-frequency sub-bands are produced. Similar operations can be applied to the low-frequency approximation images of the reference image and target image for further decomposition.

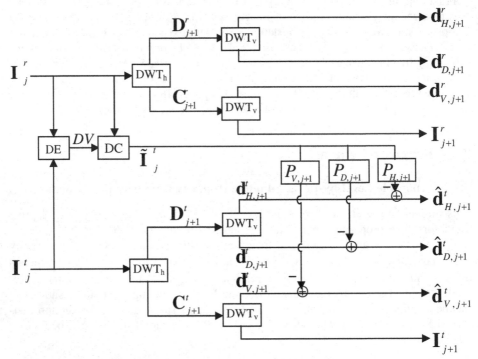

Fig. 2. Adaptive disparity compensation scheme

3.2   Separable Adaptive Prediction Filters for Target High-Bands

It's critical to obtain those adaptive predictors in the last subsection. However, we should strike a balance between prediction performance and complexity. Therefore, in this sub-section, separable and symmetric filters are designed for those adaptive predictors. The separable prediction processes can be formulated as follows:

$$C_j^t = \mathcal{A}_L^h\left(I_{j-1}^t\right)$$

$$D_j^t = \mathcal{A}_H^h\left(I_{j-1}^t\right)$$

$$\tilde{C}_j^t = q_{j,L}^h\left(\mathcal{D}C_{j-1}\left(I_{j-1}^r\right)\right)$$

$$\tilde{D}_j^t = q_{j,H}^h\left(\mathcal{D}C_{j-1}\left(I_{j-1}^r\right)\right)$$

$$\hat{d}_{V,j}^t = d_{V,j}^t - q_{j,V}^v\left(\tilde{C}_j^t\right)$$

$$\hat{d}_{H,j}^t = d_{H,j}^t - q_{j,H}^v\left(\tilde{D}_j^t\right)$$

$$\hat{d}_{D,j}^t = d_{D,j}^t - q_{j,D}^v\left(\tilde{D}_j^t\right) \tag{3}$$

where q's denote the one dimensional prediction operators whose superscript 'h' denotes horizontal direction and 'v' denotes vertical direction. It's clear that 5 prediction vectors should be designed for each level. We can estimate the coefficients of the prediction vectors by minimizing the energy of the prediction error

$$\hat{q}_{j,L}^h = \arg\min_{q_{j,L}^h}\left\{\left\|C_j^t - \tilde{C}_j^t\right\|^2\right\}$$

$$\hat{q}_{j,H}^h = \arg\min_{q_{j,H}^h}\left\{\left\|D_j^t - \tilde{D}_j^t\right\|^2\right\}$$

$$\hat{q}_{j,H}^v = \arg\min_{q_{j,H}^v}\left\{\left\|\hat{d}_{H,j}^t\right\|^2\right\}$$

$$\hat{q}_{j,V}^v = \arg\min_{q_{j,V}^v}\left\{\left\|\hat{d}_{V,j}^t\right\|^2\right\}$$

$$\hat{q}_{j,D}^v = \arg\min_{q_{j,D}^v}\left\{\left\|\hat{d}_{D,j}^t\right\|^2\right\}. \tag{4}$$

4   Occlusion Culling

In occlusion regions, there exists no correlation between reference images and target images. In this case, the proposed scheme will bring a bad effect in the prediction. Clearly, the wavelet transform should be used to exploit intra-view correlation instead. To correct the prediction method when necessary, conventional 2D-DWT is incorporated into the proposed scheme. In order to make a proper choice of prediction, a piecewise decision method is proposed. That is to say, the pixels in the same block use a same prediction method. As a result, only one bit is necessary to record the choice of an entire block. Bit '0' expresses the prediction result of the proposed scheme is used and bit '1' denotes the result of 2D-DWT is used. The choice of Block k can be determined as the following formulation

$$f(x) = \begin{cases} 0, & \sum_{(x,y)\in\mathcal{B}(k)}\left(\hat{d}_j^t(x,y)\right)^2 \leq \sum_{(x,y)\in\mathcal{B}(k)}\left(d_j^t(x,y)\right)^2 \\ 1, & \text{else} \end{cases}. \tag{5}$$

To seek a balance between accuracy and bitrate cost, different block sizes are used in different decomposition levels. As the subbands in the first level have the least energy weight, a block size of 16×16 is used in the first decomposition level. A block size of 8×8 is used in the second decomposition level. For higher decomposition level, smaller block size is used. Due to the effect of low-pass filters, the correlation between left and right views at the higher level is very high. As to the decomposition levels higher than the third, the prediction result of the proposed scheme is always used. Assuming a three-level decomposition are used, the cost of recording the flag for each block is negligible (about 0.0117BPP). If a entropy encoder is used, lower bitrate can be obtained.

After culling those pixels within occlusion regions labeled with bit '1', prediction filters q's are recalculated again to obtain more accurate results.

5   Experiments and Results

This section designs several experiments to test the mention-above algorithm. Following Kaaniche et al. (2009), we use 5/3 wavelet. In the following experiments, we used the MQ-coder to encode the transform coefficients, which is used in EBCOT as a part of JPEG2000. We have compared the proposed method with other two compression methods. The first is independent encoding method using JPEG2000. We use OpenJ-PEG software (version 1.3) that is an open source JPEG2000 codec. Another one is VLS proposed by Kaaniche et al. (2009).

We have used three image pairs called "Tile1", "Tile2" and "Tile3" with the size of 512×512 extracted from a big image pairs, which are downloaded from http://www.isprs.org/data/ikonos_hobart/default.aspx and derived from the high-resolution satellite Ikonos. Tile1 and Tile2 are extracted from urban areas while Tile3 is extracted from the region covered with vegetation.

A fixed block size of 8x8 and a simple block matching method are adopted in disparity estimation. We adopt displacement vectors with integer pixel accuracy. To lower the bitrate of side information, the DPCM and arithmetic coding method are used to encode the parallax vector.

5.1   The Performance of Prediction

The experiments of this subsection are designed mainly to compare the proposed to the VLS proposed by Kaaniche et al.. The variances of subbands of target images are estimated. As shown in Table 1-3, the proposed scheme obtains smaller subband variances than the VLS. It's clearly that the proposed scheme can improve the prediction performance.

Table 1. The variance of subbands of the target image of Tile1

Level	VLS			Proposed		
	LH	HL	HH	LH	HL	HH
1	6632.2	6603.4	5916.4	5308.2	6195.3	5509.0
2	19423.9	18749.7	29494.3	12070.1	13417.4	24497.4
3	34794.3	32244.3	61611.9	17813.5	17238.7	44839.1

Table 2. The variance of subbands of the target image of Tile2

Level	VLS			Proposed		
	LH	HL	HH	LH	HL	HH
1	7805.0	7321.2	7811.6	6207.8	6919.3	7181.7
2	19061.5	16574.2	43542.4	13107.7	12300.0	37343.9
3	26520.5	24355.4	55883.4	13505.3	15330.0	41814.3

Table 3. The variance of subbands of the target image of Tile3

Level	VLS			Proposed		
	LH	HL	HH	LH	HL	HH
1	1408.8	1342.7	1456.3	1207.1	1276.8	1388.4
2	3521.2	3013.5	5398.7	2276.8	2298.5	4643.4
3	6379.8	5123.7	10732.5	2923.2	2877.7	7469.1

5.2   The Performance of Lossy Compression

In this subsection, several experiments are designed to compare the compression performance. Fig. 3, Fig. 4 and Fig. 5 present the test results of the images above-mentioned respectively. The PSNR expresses the joint peak signal-to-noise ratio that is calculated by the following formulation.

$$PSNR = 10\log_{10}\left(\frac{(2^{BP}-1)^2}{(MSE^{(t)}+MSE^{(r)})/2}\right) \tag{6}$$

where BP is the bit number of each sample, $MSE^{(t)}$ and $MSE^{(r)}$ expresses the mean square error of the reconstruct of reference and target images respectively.

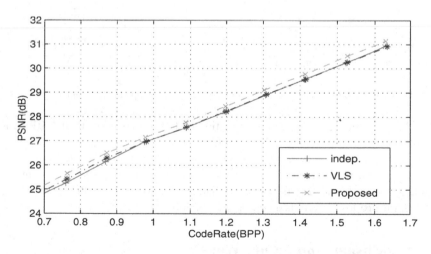

Fig. 3. Comparison performance of the proposed, VLS and independent compression for Tile 1

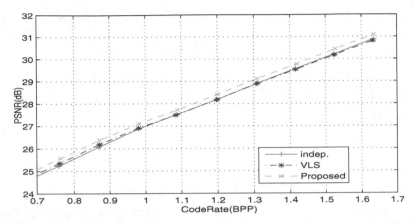

Fig. 4. Comparison performance of the proposed, VLS and independent compression for Tile 2

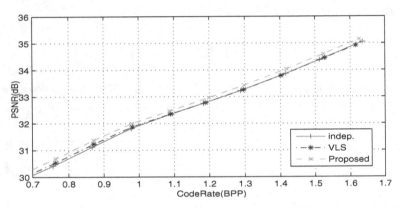

Fig. 5. Comparison performance of the proposed, VLS and independent compression for Tile 3

As shown in Fig. 3-5, under the condition of low bitrate (less than 1 BPP), joint compression methods including VLS and the proposed significantly are superior to the independent compression method. The lower the code-rate is, the more obvious the advantage is. Under the condition of high bit rate, the proposed can maintain the advantage while the VLS gets no better than the independent method. Compared to the VLS, the proposed obtains a coding gain of about 0.2 dB.

6   Conclusions and Future Work

This paper proposed a level-by-level adaptive disparity compensated prediction scheme for scalable stereo image coding. To get spatial scalable feature, 2-D wavelet transform is first applied to the target image of a stereo image pair. A separable 2-D filter applied to the reference image is optimized for each resolution layer by minimizing the energy of the high-bands of the target image. To form a multi-resolution representation, similar processes are then applied to the low-band image pairs generated by the prior resolution layer iteratively. And a piecewise decision method is used to choose the better prediction result from the proposed scheme and 2D-DWT. Experimental results show that the proposed scheme can provide significant coding gain compared to other scalable coding scheme.

Because the proposed scheme are easy extended to much more views, in the future, we'll use this scheme to compress multiview images.

References

1. Kaaniche, M., et al.: Vector Lifting Schemes for Stereo Image Coding. IEEE Trans. Image Process 18(11), 2463–2475 (2009)
2. Perkins, M.G.: Data Compression of Stereopairs. IEEE Trans. Communications 40(4), 684–696 (1992)
3. Moellenhoff, M.S., Maier, M.W.: Transform coding of stereo image residuals. IEEE Trans. Image Processing 7(6), 804–812 (1998)
4. Jiang, Q., Lee, J.J., Hayes, M.H.: A wavelet based stereo image coding algorithm. In: International Conference on Acoustics, speech, and signal processing, Phoenix, pp. 684–696. Arizona State University, Arizona (1999)
5. Boulgouris, N.V., Strintzis, M.G.: A Family of Wavelet-Based Stereo Image Coders. IEEE Trans. Circuits Syst. Video Technol. 12(10), 898–904 (2002)
6. Edirisinghe, E.A., Nayan, M.Y., Bez, H.E.: A wavelet implementation of the pioneering block-based disparity compensated predictive coding algorithm for stereo image pair compression. Signal Processing: Image Communication 19, 37–46 (2004)
7. Sweldens, W.: The lifting scheme: A construction of second generation wavelets. SIAM J. Math. Anal. 29(2), 511–546 (1998)
8. Daubechies, I., Sweldens, W.: Factoring wavelet transforms into lifting steps. J. Fourier Anal. Appl. 4(3), 247–269 (1998)
9. Taubman, D.S.: High performance scalable image compression with EBCOT. IEEE Trans. Image Proc. 9, 1158–1170 (2000)
10. Andreopoulosa, Y., Munteanu, A.: In-band motion compensated temporal filtering. Signal Processing: Image Communication 19, 653–673 (2004)
11. Anantrasirichai, A., Canagarajah, C.N.: In-Band Disparity Compensation for Multiview Image Compression and View Synthesis. IEEE Transactions On Circuits And Systems For Video Technology 20(4), 473–484 (2010)
12. Xiong, R., Xu, J., Wu, F., Li, S.: In-scale motion aligned temporal filtering. In: IEEE International Symposium on Circuits and Systems, pp. 3017–3020 (2007)
13. Ye, Y., Motta, G.: Enhanced Adaptive Interpolation Filters for Video Coding. Data Compression Conference, Snowbird, UT, USA, pp. 24–26 (2010)
14. Vatis, Y., Ostermann, J.: Adaptive Interpolation Filter for H.264/AVC. IEEE Transactions On Circuits And Systems For Video Technology 19(2), 179–187 (2009)
15. Yoo, Y.J., Seo, C.W., Han, J.K.: Enhanced Adaptive Loop Filter for Motion Compensated Frame. IEEE Transactions On Image Processing 20(8), 2177–2188 (2011)
16. Xiong, R., Xu, J., Wu, F., Li, S.: Studies on spatial scalable frameworks for motion aligned 3D wavelet video coding. In: VCIP 2005, Beijing, vol. 5960, pp. 189–200 (2005)
17. Park, H.W., Kim, H.S.: Motion estimation using lowband-shift method for wavelet-based moving picture coding. IEEE Trans. Image Process. 9(4), 577–587 (2000)

Logo Recognition Using CNN Features

Simone Bianco, Marco Buzzelli, Davide Mazzini$^{(\boxtimes)}$, and Raimondo Schettini

DISCo (Dipartimento di Informatica, Sistemistica E Comunicazione),
Universitàdegli Studi di Milano-Bicocca, Viale Sarca 336, 20126 Milano, Italy
{simone.bianco,davide.mazzini,schettini}@disco.unimib.it,
marco.buzzelli@unimib.it

Abstract. In this paper we propose a method for logo recognition based on Convolutional Neural Networks, instead of the commonly used keypoint-based approaches. The method involves the selection of candidate subwindows using an unsupervised segmentation algorithm, and the SVM-based classification of such candidate regions using features computed by a CNN. For training the neural network we augment the training set with artificial transformations, while for classification we exploit a query expansion strategy to increase the recall rate. Experiments were performed on a publicly-available dataset that was also corrupted in order to investigate the robustness of the proposed method with respect to blur, noise and lossy compression.

1 Introduction

Logo recognition in images and videos has been gaining considerable attention in the last decade, with such applications as copyright infringement detection, intelligent traffic-control systems, and automated computation of brand-related statistics. Such problems are typically addressed with keypoint-based detectors and descriptors like SIFT [1–3]. These methods are in fact best suited for well-defined shapes and affine transformations, like those found in the domain of logos. Since in many real applications the logo images could be highly degraded, in this paper we investigated Convolutional Neural Networks [4] as an alternative approach that is not based on keypoint detection. CNNs fall in the category of Deep Learning techniques, which have been employed in others fields such as speech recognition [5] and action recognition [6]. However, they are relatively new to logo recognition. The only relevant contribution is [7], where the authors trained a network to classify a custom dataset of vehicle logos and employed some very specific heuristics to localize the vehicle logo position. We instead make use of an object proposal algorithm [8,9] to produce a higher number of candidate windows, while drastically reducing the number of candidates obtainable from a multiscale sliding window approach. The underlying idea is similar to what was used in [10] for object recognition.

We report some experiments on the publicly available FlickrLogos-32 dataset [11] and show that our approach is able to achieve near-state-of-the-art performance on high-quality images, and still achieves good results on degraded

© Springer International Publishing Switzerland 2015
V. Murino and E. Puppo (Eds.): ICIAP 2015, Part II, LNCS 9280, pp. 438–448, 2015.
DOI: 10.1007/978-3-319-23234-8_41

images. More precisely, we tested our detection system after applying different types of image distortions to decrease the image quality in a controlled fashion. The proposed method can deal with JPEG compression of high intensity, and with noise and blur of medium intensity. Performance decrease with higher levels of blurriness, and further decrease with high-variance gaussian noise.

2   Proposed Method

In this section we outline the recognition pipeline used in this work. We follow the idea first investigated by Girshick et al. [10]. Given an input image, we extract regions which are more likely to contain an object. These regions are called object proposals. The algorithm used for the extraction of the objects proposals is class-agnostic, therefore it extracts regions of different aspect-ratios that can be used to recognize objects under different kinds of geometric transformation. These proposal are then warped to a common size (see Section 5.1) and processed for query expansion in order to increase recall. Finally we use a pre-trained CNN as feature extractor and a linear SVM for logo recognition and classification. Figure 1 shows the main steps of the recognition pipeline.

Fig. 1. Outline of the recognition pipeline: (1) Candidate objects regions are extracted from the image. (2) Regions are warped to a common size and multiplied through Query Expansion. (3) CNN features are computed over each region. (4) Classification is performed using linear SVMs.

3   Selective Search

Selective Search has been introduced by van de Sande et al. [8,9] to enable the use of more expensive features and classifiers in object detection, eliminating the need of computing them for every possible sliding window.

The authors exploit a hierarchical grouping algorithm, in order to naturally generate locations at all scales, by continuing the grouping process until the whole image becomes a single region. They first use [12] to create initial regions, then, instead of using a single clustering technique, they use a variety of complementary grouping criteria to account for as many image conditions as possible. Such criteria include color similarity, texture similarity, and measures that encourage merging of small regions and overlapping regions. The final set of candidate locations is then obtained by combining the locations of these complementary partitionings.

4   Query Expansion

When working with object detection and classification, usually we have to deal with two kinds of variability. The *intrinsic* variability corresponds to the fact that two instances of the same object class can be visually different, even when viewed under similar conditions (e.g. different versions of a logo may differ for some details or colors). The *extrinsic* variability refers to those differences in appearance that are not specific to the object class (e.g. different viewpoints, lighting conditions, image compression artifacts).

The FlickrLogos-32 dataset exhibits high levels of extrinsic variability. To cope with this, we transform, at test time, each candidate location extracted with Selective Search, thus producing an expanded query. The candidate location is then assigned to the class with maximum confidence over all the expanded query.

5   Convolutional Neural Networks

Convolutional Neural Networks were first presented by Kunihiko Fukushima in [4] as a tool for visual pattern recognition. However, only in recent years they have become widespread in the scientific community, thanks to the development of high-performing architectures working on GPU [13].

A CNN takes an input image, which usually has undergone some minor preprocessing, processes it with a cascade of different transformation layers, to finally produce a prediction of the image class. Convolutional layers are the main type of layer used in CNNs. These are designed to perform a convolutional operation on the input data (which can be either the original image, or the result of hidden layers). The kernel involved in this operation, however, is not hand-encoded, but automatically learned through the backpropagation algorithm used to train the network. Non linearities are implemented in the CNN by activation functions and pooling layers. The most used activation function is ReLU (Rectified Linear Units), which keeps only the positive part of the input without applying any kind of upper bound to the signal. Pooling layers work as average or maximum filters, and as such are used to reduce the impact of small variations in the signal. Furthermore, they allow for a dimensionality reduction of the input data. Their effect depends on the filter size and stride. Dropout layers are used to reduce overfitting, which can occur when the number of training examples and number of CNN parameters are unbalanced, with the second one being greater than the first one. This is done, at every training iteration, by randomly dropping some neurons with probability p. At testing time instead, all the neurons are used, but their responses are weighted by p itself.

5.1   CNN Features

Instead of learning an ad-hoc CNN for the logo recognition problem, we investigate how a pre-trained one works on this problem. It is in fact known that the features produced by CNNs in the last layers before the class assignment work effectively on other problems as well [14]. To this end, we employ a Caffe [13] implementation of the CNN described by Krizhevsky et al. [15] to extract a 4096-dimensional feature vector from each 227×227 RGB image. This is done by subtracting a previously computed mean RGB image, and forward-propagating the result through five convolutional layers and two fully connected layers. More details about the network architecture can be found in [13,15]. The CNN was originally trained on a large dataset (ILSVRC 2012) with image-level annotations to classify images into 1000 different classes. Features are obtained by extracting activation values of the last hidden layer. The extracted features for each candidate location are then used as input to a Support Vector Machine (SVM) [16] for classification as no-logo or as belonging to a specific logo class. We employed a multiclass one-vs-all linear SVM with regularization hyperparameter $C = 1$.

5.2   Transformation Pursuit

Since the Flickr-logo dataset has been collected to evaluate SIFT-like recognition algorithms [11] the training set contains only few examples for each logo (see Table 1). To handle the large extrinsic variability of the dataset and to prevent the learning algorithm to overfit, we significantly increase the training set following Transformation Pursuit [17]. For each region proposal extracted from images which overlaps with the groundtruth annotation we apply a set of predefined image transformations. In particular the applied tranfomations include: translation, scale, shear on the y axis and shear on the x axis. With this set we take into account also rotation transformation which is a combination of the two shear transform. By applying only the two extrema values of each of the complete set of geometric transformations we can increase the number of examples by a factor of ~ 250. In figure 2 is depicted a subset of the geometric transformations applied.

6   Experimental Setup and Results

Experiments were performed on the publicly-available FlickrLogos-32 dataset [11]. This is a collection of photos showing 32 different logo brands, and is meant for the evaluation of logo retrieval and multi-class logo detection/recognition systems on real-world images. All logos have an approximately planar or cylindrical surface. The whole dataset is split into three disjoint subsets P_1, P_2, and P_3 as reported in Table 1, each containing images of all 32 classes.

6.1   Selective Search Evaluation

The Selective Search algorithm [9] can extract the candidate object regions upon different color spaces. In this section we report an evaluation of Selective Search object proposals quality using different color spaces on the FlickrLogos-32 dataset.

Fig. 2. Representative subset of geometric tranformations applied to an extracted region proposal. The original image is in the lower-right corner.

Table 1. FlickrLogos-32 dataset partitions

Partition	Description	Images	Total
P_1 (training set)	Single logo images, clean background	10 per class	320 images
P_2 (validation set)	Images showing at least a single logo Non-logo images	30 per class 3000	3960 images
P_3 (test set)	Images showing at least a single logo Non-logo images	30 per class 3000	3960 images

Hosang et al. [18] introduced a class agnostic metric to evaluate the effectiveness of an object proposal algorithm: the Recall versus IoU (Intersection over Union). It is computed by varying the IoU rejection threshold, then for each threshold value, the number of overlapping bounding-boxes is counted.

In Figure 3 we report the curves for five different color spaces: HSV, Lab, rg plus the Intensity channel, the Hue channel and the Intensity channel only.

We also report in Table 2 the list of the mean number of object proposals extracted and the Average Recall for each colorspace tested. The Average Recall was computed for levels of IoU from 0.5 to 1. Lower levels haven't been considered because we are only interested in high levels of overlap.

Finally we chose to use the Selective Search based on the HSV colorspace as building-block for our pipeline because it shows the higher recall among all the others colorspaces.

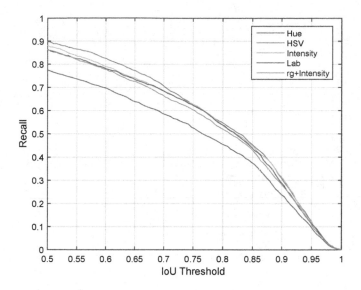

Fig. 3. Recall versus IoU threshold for different color spaces on Flickr-Logos dataset.

Table 2. Mean Number of Object Proposals per image and Average Recall value for each color space

Color space	#Proposals/image	Average Recall
Hue	486	0.472
HSV	642	0.566
Intensity	412	0.552
Lab	292	0.545
rg + Intensity	352	0.535

6.2   Results

The system was trained on FlickrLogos-32 P_1 set, and validated on P_2 for hyperparameters selection with a target precision of 98% (for better comparison with the state of the art [1,11,19]). Finally, it was tested on P_3 with the selected hyperparameters.

Figure 4 shows the performance level obtained by the proposed method in terms of precision and recall, on validation set and test set. For the test set we report both performance with and without Query Expansion, showing the significant gain obtained with this step.

Table 3 reports a comparison with other state of the art approaches. [11] and [1] are based on the bundling of neighboring SIFT-based visual words into

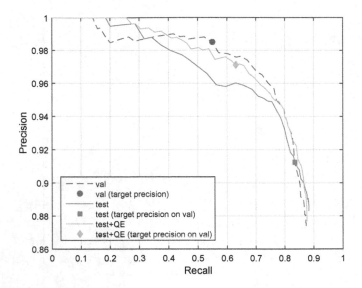

Fig. 4. Precision-Recall curve on validation set, test set, and test set with Query Expansion. Selected points are obtained by setting target precision at 98% in validation set.

unique signatures. [19] uses a statistical model for identifying incorrect detections output by keypoint-based matching algorithms.

Results show how even though the underlying CNN was trained for recognition in a different domain, it is still able to achieve near-state-of-the-art performance.

Table 3. Performance comparison with other approaches

Method	Precision	Recall
Romberg et. al [11]	0.98	0.61
Revaud et. al [19]	≥ 0.98	0.73
Romberg et. al [1]	0.999	0.832
Proposed method	0.91	0.84
Proposed method + QE	0.97	0.63

7   Results under Image Distortions

We want to test the robustness of the proposed method with respect to three kinds of image distortion as reported in Table 4 and Figure 5.

Table 4. Types of distortions applied to the images of the FlickrLogos-32 dataset.

Type	Amount
Gaussian Blur	Filter Size 10px
Gaussian Blur	Filter Size 20px
JPEG Compression	Quality 20%
JPEG Compression	Quality 10%
Gaussian Noise	$\sigma^2 = 0.005$
Gaussian Noise	$\sigma^2 = 0.02$

Fig. 5. Types of distortions applied to the images of the FlickrLogos-32 dataset.

7.1 Selective Search Evaluation

Figure 6 shows values of the Recall versus IoU threshold for the original and distorted images.

Image distortion has a low impact on the overall quality of the extracted Object Proposals. Blur has the biggest impact especially for low levels of IoU but in the worst case performance dropped by 10% only. On the other hand, jpeg compression seems to have a very low impact on the Object Proposals quality even at high levels of compression. Our tests confirm the results obtained by Hosang et al. in [18] which found the Selective Search to be one of the most robust Object Proposals algorithms.

7.2 Results

In order to test the complete recognition pipeline on the distorted images, we augmented the training set by a factor of six. For each original image we add six deformed images, each with a single distortion applied. The magnitude of each distortion, shown in table 4, is the same for train and test. We run the recognition pipeline on images of the Flickr-logo test set modified with a single distortion at a time. This controlled environment makes it possible to check the impact of every single distortion without masking effects.

Figure 7 shows the results of the performed tests. Gaussian noise and blur with high magnitude ($\sigma^2 = 0.02$ and $size = 20px$) have the highest impact on the overall results. The results on the complete recognition pipeline reflect those on the Selective Search part: the same types of distortions having the highest impact on the overall performance affect also the Recall measure of the Selective Search evaluation. This clue leads us to consider the quality of the Object Proposals as one of the most important aspects to care about in our recognition pipeline.

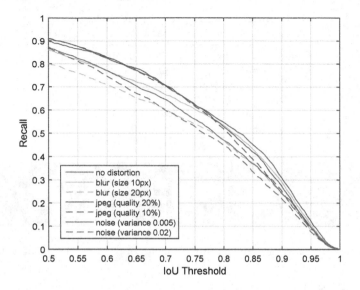

Fig. 6. Recall versus IoU threshold for 6 different types of image distortion on the Flickr-Logos dataset. Only the best overlapping bounding-box for each groundtruth annotation is considered.

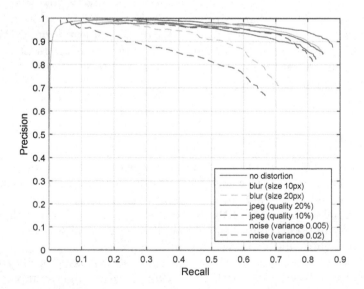

Fig. 7. Precision-Recall curves on the Flickr-logo test dataset. Different image distortions have been applied to obtain different curves.

8   Conclusions

In this work we treated the problem of logo recognition. This is usually addressed with keypoint-based methods on high-quality images. We instead used Convolutional Neural Networks as a robust alternative for low-quality images. The proposed pipeline involved selecting candidate subwindows using Selective Search, augmenting the training set using Transformation Pursuit, and performing Query Expansion for increasing recall. The method proved to be effective even with CNN features that were trained for a different task, producing results close to the state of the art. The robustness of the method has been investigated with respect to three different kinds of distortion: blur, noise and lossy compression. Results showed that noise was the most affecting one, while lossy compression produced little to no performance loss.

As future developments, we will investigate the use of a Viola-Jones-like AdaBoost detector [20] for object proposal in place of Selective Search. In order to further improve the recognition performance, we will also investigate the application of a pre-processing step to the image aimed to obtain a faithful color description [21].

References

1. Romberg, S., Lienhart, R.: Bundle min-hashing for logo recognition. In: Proceedings of the 3rd ACM conference on International conference on multimedia retrieval, pp. 113–120. ACM (2013)
2. Bianco, S., Schettini, R., Mazzini, D., Pau, D.P.: Quantitative review of local descriptors for visual search. In: IEEE Third International Conference on Consumer Electronics Berlin (ICCE-Berlin), ICCEBerlin 2013, pp. 98–102. IEEE (2013)
3. Bianco, S., Schettini, R., Mazzini, D., Pau, D.P.: Local detectors and compact descriptors: a quantitative comparison. Digital Signal Processing (2015) (accepted)
4. Fukushima, K.: Neocognitron: A self-organizing neural network model for a mechanism of pattern recognition unaffected by shift in position. Biological Cybernetics 36(4), 193–202 (1980)
5. Abdel-Hamid, O., Mohamed, A.-R., Jiang, H., Deng, L., Penn, G., Yu, D.: Convolutional neural networks for speech recognition. IEEE/ACM Transactions on Audio, Speech and Language Processing (TASLP) 22(10), 1533–1545 (2014)
6. Foggia, P., Saggese, A., Strisciuglio, N., Vento, M.: Exploiting the deep learning paradigm for recognizing human actions. In: 2014 11th IEEE International Conference on Advanced Video and Signal Based Surveillance (AVSS), pp. 93–98. IEEE (2014)
7. Pan, C., Yan, Z., Xu, X., Sun, M., Shao, J., Wu, D.: Vehicle logo recognition based on deep learning architecture in video surveillance for intelligent traffic system (2013)
8. van de Sande, K.E.A., Uijlings, J.R.R., Gevers, T., Smeulders, A.W.M.: Segmentation as selective search for object recognition. In: IEEE International Conference on Computer Vision (2011)
9. Uijlings, J.R.R., van de Sande, K.E.A., Gevers, T., Smeulders, A.W.M.: Selective search for object recognition. International Journal of Computer Vision 104(2), 154–171 (2013)

10. Girshick, R., Donahue, J., Darrell, T., Malik, J.: Rich feature hierarchies for accurate object detection and semantic segmentation. In: 2014 IEEE Conference on Computer Vision and Pattern Recognition (CVPR), pp. 580–587. IEEE (2014)
11. Romberg, S., Pueyo, L.G., Lienhart, R., Van Zwol, R.: Scalable logo recognition in real-world images. In: Proceedings of the 1st ACM International Conference on Multimedia Retrieval, p. 25. ACM (2011)
12. Felzenszwalb, P.F., Huttenlocher, D.P.: Efficient graph-based image segmentation. International Journal of Computer Vision **59**(2), 167–181 (2004)
13. Jia, Y., Shelhamer, E., Donahue, J., Karayev, S., Long, J., Girshick, R., Guadarrama, S., Darrell, T.: Caffe: Convolutional architecture for fast feature embedding. In: Proceedings of the ACM International Conference on Multimedia, pp. 675–678. ACM (2014)
14. Sharif Razavian, A., Azizpour, H., Sullivan, J., Carlsson, S.: Cnn features off-the-shelf: An astounding baseline for recognition. In: The IEEE Conference on Computer Vision and Pattern Recognition (CVPR) Workshops, June 2014
15. Krizhevsky, A., Sutskever, I., Hinton, G.E.: Imagenet classification with deep convolutional neural networks. In: Advances in Neural Information Processing Systems, pp. 1097–1105 (2012)
16. Cortes, C., Vapnik, V.: Support-vector networks. Machine Learning **20**(3), 273–297 (1995)
17. Paulin, M., Revaud, J., Harchaoui, Z., Perronnin, F., Schmid, C.: Transformation pursuit for image classification. In: 2014 IEEE Conference on Computer Vision and Pattern Recognition (CVPR), pp. 3646–3653. IEEE (2014)
18. Hosang, J., Benenson, R., Dollár, P., Schiele, B.: What makes for effective detection proposals? (2015). arXiv preprint arXiv:1502.05082
19. Revaud, J., Douze, M., Schmid, C.: Correlation-based burstiness for logo retrieval. In: Proceedings of the 20th ACM International Conference on Multimedia, pp. 965–968. ACM (2012)
20. Viola, P., Jones, M.: Rapid object detection using a boosted cascade of simple features. In: Proceedings of the 2001 IEEE Computer Society Conference on Computer Vision and Pattern Recognition, CVPR 2001, vol. 1, pp. I-511. IEEE (2001)
21. Bianco, S., Bruna, A., Naccari, F., Schettini, R.: Color space transformations for digital photography exploiting information about the illuminant estimation process. Journal of the Optical Society of America A **29**(3), 374–384 (2012)

Person Re-identification Using Robust Brightness Transfer Functions Based on Multiple Detections

Amran Bhuiyan[(✉)], Behzad Mirmahboub, Alessandro Perina,
and Vittorio Murino

Pattern Analysis and Computer Vision (PAVIS),
Istituto Italiano di Tecnologia, Genova, Italy
amran.bhuiyan@iit.it

Abstract. Re-identification systems aim at recognizing the same individuals in multiple cameras and one of the most relevant problems is that the appearance of same individual varies across cameras due to illumination and viewpoint changes. This paper proposes the use of *Minimum Multiple Cumulative Brightness Transfer Functions* to model this appearance variations. It is multiple frame-based learning approach which leverages consecutive detections of each individual to transfer the appearance, rather than learning brightness transfer function from pairs of images. We tested our approach on standard multi-camera surveillance datasets showing consistent and significant improvements over existing methods on two different datasets without any other additional cost. Our approach is general and can be applied to any appearance-based method.

Keywords: Re-identification · Brightness transfer function · Video surveillance

1 Introduction

Person re-identification (ReID) refers to the problem of recognizing individuals at different times and locations. A schematic illustration of the problem is given in Fig. 1a, where the task is to match detections of the same person acquired by the two cameras. Re-identification involves different cameras, views, poses and illuminations and it has recently drawn a lot of attention due to its significant role in visual surveillance systems, including person search and tracking across disjoint cameras.

The core assumption in re-identification is that individuals do not change their clothing so that appearances in the several views are similar, nevertheless it still consists in a very challenging task due to the non-rigid structure of the human body, the different perspectives with which a pedestrian can be observed, and the highly variable illumination conditions (as an example see the images of the same lady on the top of Fig. 1a).

© Springer International Publishing Switzerland 2015
V. Murino and E. Puppo (Eds.): ICIAP 2015, Part II, LNCS 9280, pp. 449–459, 2015.
DOI: 10.1007/978-3-319-23234-8_42

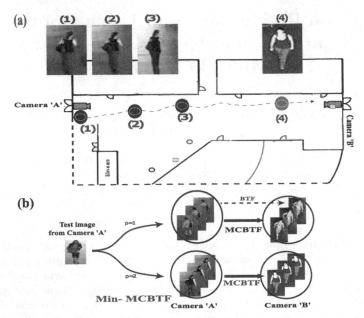

Fig. 1. (a) Typical indoor system; (b) Overview of our approach.

Re-identification approaches can mainly be organized in two classes of algorithms: direct and learning-based methods. In the former group, algorithms search for the most discriminant features to form a powerful descriptor for each individual [1–6]. In contrast, learning-based methods have techniques that learn metric spaces where to compare pedestrians, in order to guarantee a high re-identification rates [7–12]. Finally, we find methods that learn the transformation that the appearance of a person undergoes when passing from one domain to another [13–17].

This work lies in the latter, camera-specific, category, which is very relevant in large video surveillance networks where individuals are observed using various cameras across a large environment.

A thorough review of the state-of-the-art shows how these approaches mainly aim to model a function to transfer "appearance" cues between cameras. For example, [13] estimate the brightness transfer function, in short BTF, to transfer the appearance for object tracking. By employing a set of N labeled pairs $\{(I_A^p, I_B^p)\}$, where I_X^p represents an observation of pedestrian p acquired by camera X, they learn multiple BTFs, one for each pedestrian and then rely on a *Mean-BTF*(MBTF) [13]. Porikli [18] used the same setup previously but estimate the transfer function in the form of color. Later, Prosser [14] proposed the *Cumulative-BTF*(CBTF) amalgamating the training pairs before computing the transfer function. In contrast to MBTF and CBTF which end up with a single transfer function, Datta [15] proposed a *Weighted-BTF* (WBTF) that assigns different weights to test observations based on their proximity to training observations. The latter approach showed a remarkable improvement over [14,18] and therefore we will consider it as our main comparison.

This paper makes another step forward and taking inspiration from real scenarios it bridges the works of [13] and [14]. Actually, most of the state-of-the-art methods learn a single BTF from a pair of images, but nowadays we have powerful tools for person tracking and we robustly have access to at least 5-10 detections of the same individual in consecutive frames [19]. A mild criticism of single pair-based method lies in how they choose labeled pairs. Fig. 1a shows 3 detections from camera A and the detection from camera B. It is easy to figure out how a transfer function learned from the pair (1)-(4) would behave differently from the one learned from the pair (3)-(4). The question we pose here is that if and how these very similar sets of images can be exploited to learn more robust and principled transfer functions. Examples of detections for the same pedestrian are shown in Fig. 1b and, although at a first glance it may appear they do not add anything, we will show that considering all of them is indeed useful. More specifically, we propose here the use of the *Minimum Multiple Cumulative Brightness Transfer Function* (Min-MCBTF). Our approach assigns minimum distance for ReID from the distances calculated using all the MCBTFs individually which, exploiting multiple detections, is more robust of the previous approach based on single pairs. To be more specific, our approach showed the cumulative effect of multiple detections for learning BTF on ReID performance. Our technique is general and strongly outperforms previous appearance transfer function based methods [14,15,18] and the basic framework upon which we built it. Unlike previous work, we also considered the effect of increasing the number of pedestrian in the validation set.

The rest of the paper is organized as follows: Sec. 2 describes the proposed algorithm, Sec. 3 illustrates the re-identification framework in which it is used, Sec. 4, we present an exhaustive experimental session and, finally, concluding remarks are drawn in Sec. 5.

2   Minimum Cumulative Brightness Transfer Function

Our goal is to find the correspondence between multiple observations of an pedestrian across a camera pair C_i and C_j. As in previous work, we assume a limited validation set of labeled detections that can be used to calculate an inter-camera MCBTF. Subsequently the MCBTF of each pedestrian in the validation set are used to transform the test pedestrian and consider the minimum distance to form the final Min-MCBTF.

We assume to have $N \leq 10$ subsequent frames for each of the P pedestrians in the validation set which we used to learn the transfer functions. To obtain such images, we assume the reliability of a tracking algorithm able to detect single pedestrians for less then a second[1], or alternatively one could simply propagate the detected bounding box for $\frac{N}{2}$ before and after the "labeled" detection, as illustrated by Fig. 2a. In this sense, our approach does not increase the amount of labeled data needed.

---

[1] In standard conditions trackers run at 25 FPS.

To compute the Min-MCBTF, it is necessary to understand the extraction procedure of brightness transfer function, proposed by Javed et al. [13]. In principle, it would be necessary to estimate the pixel-to-pixel correspondences between the pedestrian images in the two camera views, however this is not possible due to self-occlusion and pose difference. Thus, to be robust to occlusions and pose differences, normalized histograms of object brightness values are employed for the BTF calculation under the assumption that the percentage of the image pixels on the observed image I_i with brightness less than or equal to ρ_i is equal to the percentage of image points in the observation I_j with brightness less than or equal to ρ_j. Now, let H_i and H_j be the normalized cumulative histograms of observations I_i and I_j respectively. More specifically, for H_i each bin of brightness value $\rho_1, \ldots, \rho_m, \ldots, \rho_M$ related to one of the three color channels is obtained from the color image I_i as follows:

$$H_i(\rho_m) = \sum_{k=1}^{m} I_i(\rho_k) \tag{1}$$

where $I_i(\rho_k)$ is the pixel count of brightness value ρ_k in I_i. $H_i(\rho_i)$ represents the proportion of H_i less than or equal to ρ_i, then $H_i(\rho_i) = H_j(\rho_j)$ and the BTF function $H_{i \rightarrow j}$ can be defined:

$$H_{i \rightarrow j}(\rho_i) = H_j^{-1}(H_i(\rho_i)) \tag{2}$$

with H^{-1} representing the inverted cumulative histogram.

As the first step of our approach, we compute a cumulative normalized version of the MCBTF. The cumulative histogram cH_i^p considering the N detection of a pedestrian p in camera view i, can be computed from the brightness values as:

$$cH_i^p(\rho_m) = \frac{1}{M \cdot N} \sum_{m=1}^{M} \sum_{n=1}^{N} I_n^p(\rho_m) \tag{3}$$

being M the number of different brightness levels. The normalization is necessary as bounding boxes can have different sizes. Then, similarly to Eq. 2, its MCBTF is computed as follows:

$$CH_{i \rightarrow j}^p(\rho_i) = cH_j^{-1}(cH_i(\rho_i)) \tag{4}$$

We use these MCBTFs to map the illumination from C_i to C_j. In this way, a given test image is transformed into a number of same test images based on the number of MCBTFs specified by the pedestrians present in the validation set.

At this point, we extract the features and compute the distances (described in the section 3.2) of all the transformed test images from the gallery and consider the minimum distance to calculate the ReID score. Mathematically,

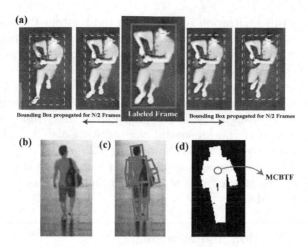

Fig. 2. (a) Bounding Box propagation (red) and actual tracking result (green); (b) One image from the SAIVT-SoftBio; (c) Custom Pictorial Structure (CPS); (d) Segmentation mask M_z derived its CPS.

$$d\left(S_i, S_j\right) = \min_p \{d\left(\tilde{S}_i^p, S_j\right)\}_{p=1}^p \qquad (5)$$

where, '$\sim$' indicates the transformed version of the main context after applying MCBTF, S represents the signatures extracted from the respective images and d is the respective feature distances for calculating ReID score.

3   Re-Identification with Min-MCBTF

The aim of this section is to summarize the framework we used for re-identification, nevertheless our method is clearly independent from any appearance direct method employed. The goal of re-identification is to assign to a test image seen in camera C_i an "identity" choosing among the G identities present in the gallery at camera C_j which acts as training set. We summarize our approach by the following three steps: *i)* first, we calculate $CH_{i \to j}^p$ to transfer the appearance from C_i to C_j using validation set and transformed the test images accordingly as explained in the previous section, *ii)* second, we isolate the actual body appearance from the rest of the scene and we extract a feature signature from its foreground, and *iii)* third, we match the transformed signatures with the gallery and select top matching identities as explained in the previous section. In the following we detail the second and the last steps.

3.1   Pedestrian Segmentation

In previous section, we showed how transfer functions are learned from the whole image, however to increase the robustness, we apply the transfer function to the foreground normalized histogram only.

We performed this separation by exploiting the Custom Pictorial Structure (CPS) [1]. CPS is based on the framework of [20] where the parts are initially located by general part detectors, and then a full body pose is inferred by solving their kinematic constraints.

In CPS [1], the Histogram of Oriented Gradient (HOG) [21] feature based part detector and a linear discriminant analysis (LDA) [22] classifier is used. Moreover, CPS [1] also used the belief propagation algorithm to infer MAP body configurations from the kinematic constraints, isolated as a tree-shaped factor graph. An example of CPS is shown in Fig. 2b-c.

Finally, we generate a segmentation mask M_z employing the following rule $M_z = 1$ if z belongs to at least one of the foreground parts, otherwise $M_z = 0$; this is shown in Fig. 2d.

3.2 Feature Extraction and Matching

The feature extraction stage consists in distilling complementary aspects from each body part in order to encode heterogeneous information, so capturing distinctive characteristics of the individuals. There are many possible cues useful for a fine visual characterization. We use standard ReID features: color histogram and maximally stable color regions (MSCR) already considered in [1,2,4,23].

As for feature matching to calculate re-id score, we use the combination of Bhattacharyya distance for histogram signature and the MSCR distance for MSCR feature, as previously done in [4].

4   Experiment

In this section, we compare the performance of Min-MCBTF with the base framework upon which they are applied, e.g., [1] and the state-of-the-art in transfer functions [14,15,18]. It is important to note that *i)* all the transfer functions are applied to the same framework and *ii)* MCBTF can in principle be applied to any other appearance-based direct approach. So comparison with other methods makes little sense.

Datasets: Two publicly available person re-identification benchmarks datasets were used for our experiments, including SAIVT-SoftBio [24] and PRID 2011 [25].

- **SAIVT-SoftBio:** As first dataset, we considered SAIVT-SoftBio [24]. It includes annotated sequences (704 × 576 pixels, 25 frames per second) of 150 people, each of which is captured by a subset of eight different cameras placed inside an institute, providing various viewing angles and varying illumination conditions. A coarse box indicating the location of the annotated person in each frame is provided. We chose this dataset because it provides consecutive frames of same person which is suitable to evaluate the performance of our approach. We considered one pair of similar view cameras (3-8) and one pair of dissimilar view (5-8) (see [24] for more details).

- **PRID 2011:** To further evaluate our approach, we considered PRID 2011 [25] dataset. The dataset consists of images extracted from trajectories recorded from two static outdoor cameras. Images from these cameras contain a viewpoint change and a stark difference in illumination, background and camera characteristics. We considered first 200 persons who appear in both camera views. It also provides consecutive frames of same person like previous one which is suitable to evaluate the performance of our approach.

Evaluation: For each camera pair, we fixed the number of identities in the gallery to $G = 50$. In all our experiments the gallery and the validation set are kept disjoint and we repeated each task 10 times by randomly picking the identities in validation and gallery. We varied the number of pedestrian $P = [0, 2, 3, 4, 5]$ in the validation set, picking $N = 5$ consecutive frames for each pedestrian (we used the bounding boxes provided by a tracking algorithm). When $P = 0$, no transfer function is used and our framework becomes the same as [1].

We quantify re-identification performance using two standard measures, i.e. Cumulative Matching Characteristic (CMC) curve and normalized area under CMC curve (nAUC). Cumulative Matching Characteristic (CMC) curve is a plot of the recognition performance vs. the ReID ranking score. It represents the expectation of finding the correct match in the top k matches. To compare the results numerically at-a-glance, we relied on the normalized area under the CMC ($nAUC$). We report all the CMC curves setting P=5, consistently with [15]. We further quantified ReID performance using the graphs with P-vs-$nAUC$.

As first experiment, we used our approach to compare with the state-of-the-art of transfer functions as well as the base ReID framwork. Fig. 3 and Fig. 4 report the experimental findings for both datasets respectively. In the legend we also report the nAUC for each method, which gives an idea of the trend of the curves across all the ranks. Our approach handily outperforms the base CPS [1] ReID framework, as well as CBTF [14], WBTF [15], and MBTF [13]. The improvement over the state-of-the-art at first rank is particularly noticeable: there is 10-30% differences at the position of rank-1 in the CMC curves between our performance and competing methods. Furthermore, our proposed approach works consistently for all the datasets unlike other methods. Note that considering limited number of pedestrians P in the validation set, we have been able to learn the robust brightness transfer function.

As second test, we evaluated the robustness of our approach to transfer function; in the specific, we considered the *Inter-Camera Color Calibration*- ICC of Porikli et al. [18]. Working in the exact same way of Sec. 2, we adapted (for the first time) [13–15] and we compared with our *Minimum-Multiple-Cumulative-ICC* (Min-MCICC). The results of color calibration for all the dataset is shown in Fig. 5.

Fig. 5 shows the experimental results of the color calibration method for all the datasets. Again our proposed approach yields the best performance. Note that WBTF [15], CBTF [14] and MBTF [13] techniques do not yield the base ReID performance upon which we apply our method consistently, but applying

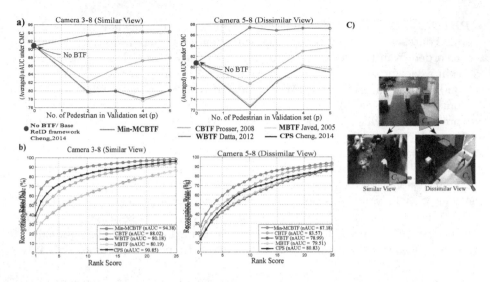

Fig. 3. (a) P-vs-$nAUC$ for two camera pairs of SAIVT-SoftBio; (b) CMC and nAUC; (c) Example frames of a person in the selected similar and dissimilar cameras [24].

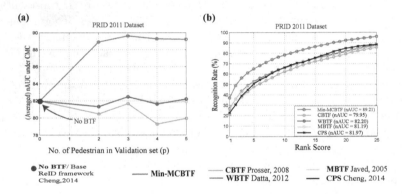

Fig. 4. (a) P-vs-$nAUC$ PRID 2011 dataset; (b) CMC and nAUC of PRID 2011 dataset.

color calibration method in the same ways gives us WICC, CICC and MICC which work better than the base CPS [1] ReID framework as shown in Fig. 5.

As final test, we tested our approach using the signature that has been proposed by Listanti et al. [6]. The authors designed a descriptor of person appearance for re-identification based on coarse, striped poling local features. It does not require sophisticated background or body part modeling, instead used a central point kernel to approximately segment foreground from background. It should be mentioned that, we did not implement the iterative sparse basis expansion as did on [6], instead we use the Bhattacharyya distance for feature matching to calculate the ReID score.

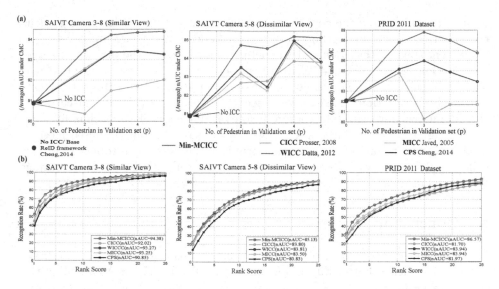

Fig. 5. (a) P-vs-$nAUC$ of all the datasets; (b) CMC and nAUC of all the datasets.

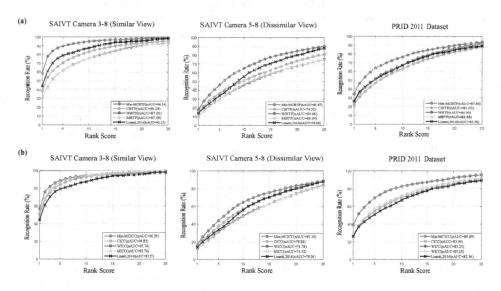

Fig. 6. (a) CMC for brightness transfer function (BTF) of all the datasets ; (b) CMC for inter-camera color calibration (ICC) for all the datasets.

Fig. 6 reports the CMC curves for above mentioned descriptor using our approach. The improvement over the state-of-the-art using our approach for this descriptor is clearly visible both for brightness transfer and color calibration function. In the legend we also report the nAUC for each method, which gives an idea of the trend of the curves across all the ranks. Again, it has been evident the effectiveness of our method for any appearance-based ReID problems.

All the state-of-the-art use single detection for learning the brightness transfer function. The CBTF [14] also use single detection of each observation and then accumulate all the observations before computing a BTF. In contrast, our approach use multiple consecutive detections of each individual and calculate the cumulative normalized histogram before calculating BTF for each individual. Analyzing all the experimental findings, we can say that our proposed method is able to transfer appearance in the form of brightness more robust than any other methods and works consistently for all the ReID datasets, outperforming the state-of-the-art.

5   Conclusion

This paper proposes the use of cumulative histograms from multiple consecutive detections to learn better and more robust transfer functions. Augmenting the pool of labeled data *within* a camera can be easily carried out by relying on tracking algorithms or simply by propagating the label for few frames. Our results clearly demonstrate a significant improvement over previous ways to model appearance variations. Moreover, our propose approach is general and can be applied to model appearance variation problems beyond person re-identification.

References

1. Cheng, D., Cristani, M.: Person re-identification by articulated appearance matching. in person re-identification, isbn 978-1-4471-6295-7. Springer (2014)
2. Farenzena, M., Bazzani, L., Perina, A., Murino, V., Cristani, M.: Person re-identification by symmetry-driven accumulation of local features. In: CVPR (2010)
3. Bazzani, L., Cristani, M., Perina, A., Farenzena, M., Murino, V.: Multiple-shot person re-identification by hpe signature. In: ICPR, pp. 1413–1416 (2010)
4. Bhuiyan, A., Perina, A., Murino, V.: Person re-identification by discriminatively selecting parts and features. In: Agapito, L., Bronstein, M.M., Rother, C. (eds.) ECCV 2014 Workshops. LNCS, vol. 8927, pp. 147–161. Springer, Heidelberg (2015)
5. Kviatkovsky, I., Adam, A., Rivlin, E.: Color invariants for person re-identification. IEEE Transactions on Pattern Analysis and Machine Intelligence, 99 (2012)
6. Lisanti, G., Masi, I., Bagdanov, A., Bimbo, A.: Person re-identification by iterative re-weighted sparse ranking. IEEE Transactions on Pattern Analysis and Machine Intelligence **PP**(99) (2014)
7. Dikmen, M., Akbas, E., Huang, T.S., Ahuja, N.: Pedestrian recognition with a learned metric. In: Kimmel, R., Klette, R., Sugimoto, A. (eds.) ACCV 2010, Part IV. LNCS, vol. 6495, pp. 501–512. Springer, Heidelberg (2011)
8. Gray, D., Tao, H.: Viewpoint invariant pedestrian recognition with an ensemble of localized features. In: Forsyth, D., Torr, P., Zisserman, A. (eds.) ECCV 2008, Part I. LNCS, vol. 5302, pp. 262–275. Springer, Heidelberg (2008)
9. Liu, C., Gong, S., Loy, C.C., Lin, X.: Person re-identification: what features are important? In: Fusiello, A., Murino, V., Cucchiara, R. (eds.) ECCV 2012 Ws/Demos, Part I. LNCS, vol. 7583, pp. 391–401. Springer, Heidelberg (2012)

10. Ma, B., Su, Y., Jurie, F.: Local descriptors encoded by fisher vectors for person re-identification. In: Fusiello, A., Murino, V., Cucchiara, R. (eds.) ECCV 2012 Ws/Demos, Part I. LNCS, vol. 7583, pp. 413–422. Springer, Heidelberg (2012)
11. Prosser, B., Zheng, W.S., Gong, S., Xiang, T.: Person re-identification by support vector ranking. In: BMVC (2010)
12. Zheng, W., Gong, S., Xiang, T.: Person re-identification by probabilistic relative distance comparison. In: CVPR, pp. 649–656 (2011)
13. Javed, O., Shafiq, K., Shah, M.: Appearance modeling for tracking in multple non-overlapping cameras. In: CVPR (2005)
14. Prosser, B., Gong, S., Xiang, T.: Multi-camera matching using bi-directional cumulative brightness transfer functions. In: BMVC (2008)
15. Datta, A., Brown, L.M., Feris, R., Pankanti, S.: Appearance modeling for person re-identification using weighted brightness transfer functions. In: ICPR (2012)
16. Brand, Y., Avraham, T., Lindenbaum, M.: Transitive re-identification. In: BMVC (2013)
17. Avraham, T., Gurvich, I., Lindenbaum, M., Markovitch, S.: Learning implicit transfer for person re-identification. In: Fusiello, A., Murino, V., Cucchiara, R. (eds.) ECCV 2012 Ws/Demos, Part I. LNCS, vol. 7583, pp. 381–390. Springer, Heidelberg (2012)
18. Porikli, F.: Inter-camera color calibration using cross correlation model function. In: ICIP (2003)
19. Chen, X., Bhanu, B.: Soft biometrics integrated multi-target tracking. In: ICPR (2014)
20. Andriluka, M., Roth, S., Schiele, B.: Pictorial structures revisited: people detection and articulated pose estimation. In: CVPR (2009)
21. Dalal, N., Triggs, B.: Histogram of oriented gradients for human detection. In: CVPR (2005)
22. Forssen, P.E.: Maximally stable color regions for recognition and matching. In: CVPR (2007)
23. Bazzani, L., Cristani, M., Murino, V.: Symmetry-driven accumulation of local features for human characterization and re-identification. Computer Vision and Image Understanding 117, 130–144 (2013)
24. Bialkowski, A., Denman, S., Lucey, P., Sridharan, S., Fookes, C.C.: A database for person re-identification in multi-camera surveillance networks. In: Digital Image Computing: Techniques and Application (DICTA 2012), pp. 1–8 (2012)
25. Hirzer, M., Beleznai, C., Roth, P.M., Bischof, H.: Person re-identification by descriptive and discriminative classification. In: Heyden, A., Kahl, F. (eds.) SCIA 2011. LNCS, vol. 6688, pp. 91–102. Springer, Heidelberg (2011). www.springerlink.com

Analysis of HOG Suitability for Facial Traits Description in FER Problems

Marco Del Coco[1]([✉]), Pierluigi Carcagnì[1], Giuseppe Palestra[2], Marco Leo[1], and Cosimo Distante[1]

[1] National Research Council - National Institute of Optics, Arnesano, LE, Italy
marco.delcoco@ino.it
[2] Department of Computer Science, University of Bari, Bari, Italy

Abstract. Automatic Facial Expression Recognition is a topic of high interest especially due to the growing diffusion of assistive computing applications, as Human Robot Interaction, where a robust awareness of the people emotion is a key point. This paper proposes a novel automatic pipeline for facial expression recognition based on the analysis of the gradients distribution, on a single image, in order to characterize the face deformation in different expressions. Firstly, an accurate investigation of optimal HOG parameters has been done. Successively, a wide experimental session has been performed demonstrating the higher detection rate with respect to other State-of-the-Art methods. Moreover, an online testing session has been added in order to prove the robustness of our approach in real environments.

Keywords: Facial expression recognition · HOG · SVM

1 Introduction

Facial expression is one of the most common non-verbal way that humans use to convey internal emotion states and consequentially it plays a fundamental role in interpersonal interaction. Although there exists a wide range of possible face expressions, psychologists have identified six basic ones (happiness, sadness, fear, disgust, surprise, and anger) that are universally recognized [8]. It is straightforward that a system capable to perform an automatic recognition of the human emotion is a desirable task in the Human Computer Interaction (HCI) field (humanoid robots or digital signage applications). Unfortunately, the design of a system with an high recognition rate is a non trivial challenge, due to the subjects variability in terms of appearance and running expression.

A robust FER system should deal with the intrinsic variation of the same expression among different subjects in order to keep good performance with the unseen ones. Computer vision interest in the FER field has exponentially grown-up in the last years leading to a wide range of possible solutions.

There are two main approaches to FER; the first one uses image sequences while the second one is based on the analysis of a single image.

V. Murino and E. Puppo (Eds.): ICIAP 2015, Part II, LNCS 9280, pp. 460–471, 2015.
DOI: 10.1007/978-3-319-23234-8_43

The use of image sequences means that many information are available for the analysis. Usually the neutral expression is used as the baseline face and then tracked in order to analyse the evolving expression over time [4,9,17]. Anyway, this approach shares a common lack: the dependence on a video sequence that evolves from the neutral expression to the expressive one. This constrain limits the use in real world environments where the evolution of facial expression is completely unpredictable. For this reason a more suitable solution for practical applications it to perform facial expression recognition on a single image. The approaches in literature that work on a single image can be conveniently categorized, depending on the strategies they use to lead to the recognition of the emotions, in two categories: Component Based Approaches and Global Approaches.

Component Based approaches preliminary extract some facial components and then try to classify the emotions on the basis of the matching among corresponding components or comparing the geometrical configuration among different components [7,14,19]. Unfortunately, even if in this kind of solutions the whole classification performances are not completely satisfactory due to the challenging alignment of components in different facial images (especially in case of extreme expressions) and to the computational burden if low-power systems are involved.

The above mentioned problems can be overcome by using "Global Approaches", i.e. approaches that directly try to extract a representation of the emotions from the appearance of the global face. This research area has been deeply investigated but there is still much effort to do, since it is very challenging to find a global set of descriptors able to robustly characterize human emotion traits. Many works exploiting most recent and reliable local descriptors have been proposed in recent years. Locally Binary Pattern (LBP) is used in [20] with kernel-based manifold approach, whereas directional information by the use of compass masks is exploited in [15]. Curvelet transform and online sequential extreme learning machine (OSELM) is instead proposed in [16].

As revealed in the previous discussion, FER problem is clearly related to the face deformation. Different persons could express the same emotion with some differences but the majority of the involved muscles work in such a way to give a coherent characterization of that emotions among different people of different ethnicity and gender.

This paper proposes a novel FER automatic pipeline based on the exploitation of the Histogram of Oriented Gradients (HOG) descriptor. It is a powerful shape description technique that counts occurrences of gradient orientations, in localized portions of an image, and that is intuitively useful to model the facial muscles shape by means of an edge analysis. To the best of our knowledge, HOG descriptors have been used as a tool for FER purposes only in [6] where authors just investigated the alignment perturbations for different descriptors and demonstrated that the best FER performances were obtained using LBP.

This paper proposes instead an in-depth analysis of how the HOG descriptors could be effectively exploited for facial expression recognition purposes and it demonstrates, by extensive experimental proofs, that the achieved FER performances outperform those of the leading state of the art approaches. Another important contribution of the paper is the introduction of an innovative algorithmic pipeline that takes as input a single facial image, performs a preliminary face detection and registration [1], apply the HOG descriptors and finally classify the facial expression by a group of Support Vector Machines (SVMs).

The rest of the paper is organized as in the followings: in section 2, the proposed methodology is detailed; in section 3 the optimization of the HOG parameters is experimentally performed; results, comparison against the state of the art approaches and tests on video streams are demanded to section 4. Conclusions are summarized in section 5.

2   Proposed Methodology

Facial expression recognition from generic images requires an algorithmic pipeline that involves different operative blocks. The scheme in Figure 1 has been used in this work: the first step detects the human faces in the image under investigation and then detected faces are cropped and registered [1]. These preliminary operations allow to get the quite similar position for eyes and in this way the subsequent HOG descriptor may be applied using a coherent spatial reference. The vector of features extracted by HOG is finally used for the classification of the facial emotions by SVM strategies. Each operative step is detailed in the following.

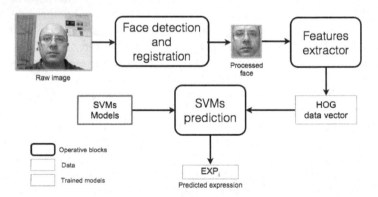

Fig. 1. Proposed system pipeline: faces are cropped and registered and then HOG descriptor is applied to build a data vector that is finally provided as input to a SVM bank that gives the estimation of the observed facial expression.

In *Face detection and registration* step human faces are detected in the input images and then registration and cropping operations are performed (Figure 2). Face detection makes use of both implicit and explicit knowledge: the explicit knowledge is based on the face geometry, color and appearance. On the other side, the implicit knowledge is integrated using the general object detection framework proposed by [18], which combines increasingly more complex classifiers in a cascade. Whenever a face is detected by a Viola Jones detector [18], it is fitted with an elliptical shape in order to rotate it to a vertical position. Successively a Viola-Jones based eye detector searches the eyes and exploits their position to scale the frontal face to a standard size of 65 × 59 pixels (registration).

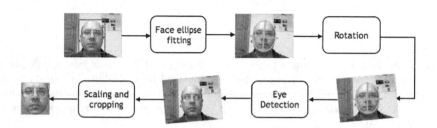

Fig. 2. Face registration: the detected face is fitted in an ellipse used to rotate the face in a perfectly vertical position; successively eyes are detected and used to scale the image and crop the zone of interest.

HOG descriptor is then applyed to the detected face region. Local object appearance and shape can often be characterized rather well by the distribution of local intensity gradients or edge directions, even without precise knowledge of the corresponding gradients or edge positions. This statement led to the definition of the HOG technique that has been used in its mature form in Scale Invariant Features Transformation [11] and it has been widely exploited in human detection [3]. HOG descriptor is based on the accumulation of gradient directions over the pixels of a small spatial region referred as "cell" and in the subsequent construction of a 1D histogram whose concatenation supplies the feature vector to be considered for further purposes. Let L be the image to be analysed. The image is divided into cells of size $N \times N$ pixels (as in Figure 3 (a)) and the orientation $\theta_{x,y}$ of the gradient in each pixel is computed (Figure 3 (b-c)).Successively the orientations θ_i^j $i = 1...N^2$, i.e. belonging to the same cell j are quantized and accumulated in a M-bins histogram (Figure 3 (d-e)). Finally, all the achieved histograms are ordered and concatenated in a unique HOG histogram (Figure 3 (f)) that is the final outcome of this algorithmic step, i.e. the feature vector to be considered for the subsequent processing.

The feature vectors extracted by HOG descriptors are then given as input to a group of *Support Vector Machines* (SVMs). SVM is a discriminative classifier defined by a separating hyperplane. Given a set of labelled training data (supervised learning), the algorithm computes an optimal hyperplane (the trained model) which categorizes new examples in the right class. Anyway, such an approach is suitable only for a two classes problem whereas FER is a multi-class problem. It can be treated through the "one-against-one" [10]. Let k be the number of classes, then $k(k-1)/2$ classifiers are constructed where each one trains data from two classes. The final prediction is returned by a voting system

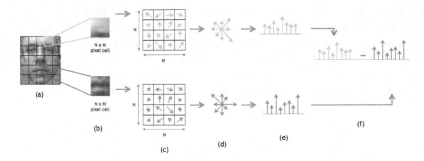

Fig. 3. HOG extraction features process: image is divided in cells of size $N \times N$ pixels. The orientation of all pixels is computed accumulated in an M-bins histogram of orientations. Finally, all cell histograms are concatenated in order to construct the final features vector. The example reports a cell size of 4 pixels and 8 orientation bins for the cell histograms.

among all the classifiers. In particular, the multi C-support vector classification (multi C-SVC) learning task implemented in the LIBSVM library[2] was used in the following experiments. Radial Basis Function (RBF) was used as kernel with penalty parameter $C = 1000$ and $\gamma = 0.05$.

3   Experimental Setup

The evaluation of the proposed method has been performed on the Chon-Kanade dataset (CK+) [12], one of the most used to test the accuracy of FER solutions. It is made up by image sequences of people performing 6 facial expressions. Each sequence starts with a neutral face expression and ends with the expressive face.

In order to extract a balanced subset (quite the same number of instances for each considered expression) of images containing expressive faces, from the available sequences the following images were selected: the last image for the sequences related to the expression of anger, disgust and happiness; the last image for the first 68 sequences related to expression of surprise; the last and the fourth to the last images for the sequences related to the expression of fear and sadness. At the end, a set of 347 images was obtained with the following distribution among the considered classes of expressions: anger (45), disgust (59), fear (50), happiness (69), sadness (56) and surprise (68). An additional configuration of the previous subset was also introduced in order to test the accuracy performance with 7 classes and in this case 60 neutral faces were add to the aforementioned one. In Figures 4 some examples in the considered subsets of images are reported.

Once the datasets have been built up, the next step it to select the optimal value for the internal HOG parameters, i.e. the best configuration to capture the most discriminative information for the FER problem. HOG descriptor is characterized by two main parameters, the cell size and the number of orientation bins. Cell size represents the dimension of the patch involved in the single

(a) An   (b) Di   (c) Fe   (d) Ha   (e) Ne   (f) Sa   (g) Su

Fig. 4. Examples of expressions for the CK+ dataset. An=Anger, Di=Disgusted, Fe=Fearful, Ha=Happy, Ne=Neutral, Sa=Sad, Su=Surprised.

histogram computation. Using a large cell size the appearance information of a significant region is squeezed into a single cell histogram and then some details, useful for subsequent classification, can be lost. On the other hand, with a small cell size, high resolution analysis can be carried out, but this way the discrimination between useful and useless information could affect the classification step. The number of orientation bins refers instead to the quantization levels of the gradient information. A low number of orientations could drive to some loss of information and a consequent reduction in FER accuracy. On the contrary, an high number of quantization levels could spread-out the information along the bins, decreasing the FER accuracy as well. For these reasons, the choice of these parameters have to be carefully made taking into consideration the goal to be reached in the particular application context. How this choice was made for FER purposes is described in the following.

First of all, concerning cell size, a qualitative assessment can be made: in Figure 5 the normalized version of a neutral and a surprised face expressions is shown with the related processing outcomes obtained by HOG descriptor with a fixed number of 8 orientations and different values of cell size (3, 8 and 15 pixels). From figure could be deduced that the most discriminative representation is given, instead, by the use of a middle cell size (in the examples 8 pixels) whereas other cell size led to crowded bins distribution (3 pixels) or to a loss of correspondences between facial traits and HOG histogram (15 pixels).

The above qualitative evaluation can be also strengthened by a quantitative analysis of the FER accuracy sensitivity to both cell size and number of orientation bins. To perform this evaluation the proposed algorithmic pipeline was tested using a 10-fold cross validation with 12 possible values of the cell size (from 4 to 15 pixels) and different number of orientation bins (3, 5, 7, 9, 12, 15 and 55).

FER results for different numbers of orientation bins are graphically reported onto the y-axis in Figure 6 where the x-axis reports instead the cell size. From the figure it is possible to infer that a cell size of 7 pixels led to the best FER accuracy. Concerning the choice of the number of orientations, the best results were obtained with value set to 7 even if also with 9 or 12 orientations the FER accuracy did not change significatively.

Choosing the optimal parameter configuration (cell size of 7 pixels and 7 orientation bins) the proposed pipeline is able to correctly classify an average of 95.8% of the images supplied as input during the 10-fold cross validation process.

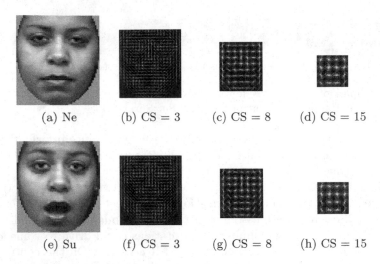

(a) Ne   (b) CS = 3   (c) CS = 8   (d) CS = 15

(e) Su   (f) CS = 3   (g) CS = 8   (h) CS = 15

Fig. 5. Examples of HOG (9 orientation) processing on normalised face images (Ne=Neutral, Su=Surprised.). CS is the cell size of the processed images.

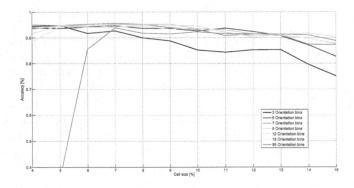

Fig. 6. FER results using different cell sizes and number of orientation bins for HOG descriptor (6 expressions): the x-axis report the cell size in pixel and the y-axis refers to the average accuracy percentage.

In order to verify that the best configuration of the selected HOG parameters keeps still valid also with different testing sets, the optimization carried out for the 6-expressions CK+ dataset has been extended to the the CK+ with 7 expressions. Results (showed in Figure 7) demonstrate that a cell size of 7 pixels and 7 orientation bins are the best configuration also for the 7-expressions CK+ dataset leading to a FER accuracy of 95.4%.

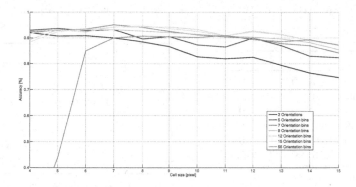

Fig. 7. FER results using different cell sizes and number of orientation bins for HOG descriptor (7 expressions): the x-axis report the cell size in pixel and the y-axis refers to the average accuracy percentage.

4   Experimental Results

In this section a wide experimental session is presented. Firstly, a detailed discussion of FER accuracy (in from of confusion matrices) is reported in subsection 4.1 whereas subsection 4.2 is aimed to the comparison with different techniques in the state of the art. Lastly, in subsection 4 3, an analysis of the behavior of the proposed pipeline when applied to video streams is presented.

4.1   Confusion Matrices for All the Datasets

Once established, in previous subsection, that there is a unique best configuration of the HOG parameters, the performance of the proposed approach are better analyzed by means of the confusion tables reported in Tables 2a and 2b. In particular, in a multi-class recognition problem as the FER one, the use of confusion tables makes possible a more detailed analysis of the results that can point out the missclassification cases and the interpretation of their possible causes. First of all, from tables it is possible to observe that, in the case of the CK+ dataset with 6 expressions, the accuracy was of 95.8% but, as expected, after the addition of the neutral expression it decreased to 95.4% (table 2b) due to the consequently increase of problem complexity.

These are very encouraging results considering the challenging benchmark used for testing.

Going into details, Tables 2a and 2b highlight the ambiguity between anger, disgusted and sad expressions. This becomes quite reasonable if the examples in Figure 4 are observed: for all aforementioned expressions, strict lips and low position of eyebrows are in fact very similar, in both location and appearance. For the same reasons, the neutral expressions introduced additional missclassifications in table 2b. Similarly, the sad expression experimented some erroneous

Table 1. Accuracy performance for proposed approach. (orientation bins = 7, cell size = 7). Ne=neutral, An=Anger, Di=Disgusted, Fe=Fearful, Ha=Happy, Sa=Sad, Su=Surprised.

	An	Di	Fe	Ha	Sa	Su
An	**88.6**	4.5	2.4	0	4.5	0
Di	5.5	**89.1**	1.8	1.8	0	1.8
Fe	0	0	**100**	0	0	0
Ha	0	0	0	**100**	0	0
Sa	0	0	0	0	**100**	0
Su	1.3	0	1.3	0	0	**97.4**

(a) CK+ (6-expressions): average accuracy = 95.8%

	Ne	An	Di	Fe	Ha	Sa	Su
Ne	**89.6**	1.8	0	0	0	8.6	0
An	4.4	**86.8**	4.4	0	0	4.4	0
Di	0	5.4	**92.9**	1.7	0	0	0
Fe	0	0	0	**93.9**	4.1	0	2.0
Ha	0	0	0	0	**100**	0	0
Sa	0	0	1.8	0	0	**98.2**	0
Su	1.3	0	0	1.3	0	0	**97.4**

(b) CK+ (7-expressions): average accuracy = 95.4%

classification in the anger face expression due to the strict lips and low position of eyebrows that are very similar for the two expressions.

4.2 Comparison with the State of the Art

In this subsection the proposed pipeline is compared with the leading State-of-the-Art solutions in literature. In order to proceed in the fairest way, the comparison was performed with all those solutions that used an evaluation protocol based on the CK+ dataset with 6 expressions. Table 2 reports the comparison results demonstrating that the proposed approach gave the best average recognition rate. In particular it is worth noting that the performance achieved by the proposed approach exceed also those of the recent work in [7] that represents the reference point for the FER problem. A deeper analysis of the Table 2 evidences that the proposed method suffers more than competitors to recognize the expression of disgust. This drawback could be due to the fact that, while performing this expression, the facial muscles shape is quite similar to that of the expression of anger (see Figure 4) then the edge analysis performed by HOG

Table 2. Performance comparison of our approach versus different State-of-the-Art approaches (CK+ 6 expressions). An=Anger, Di=Disgusted, Fe=Fearful, Ha=Happy, Sa=Sad, Su=Surprised.

	[17]	[14]	[19]	[7]	PROPOSED
An	82.5	87.1	87.1	87.8	88.6
Di	97.5	91.6	90.2	93.3	89.1
Fe	95.0	91.0	92.0	94.3	100
Ha	100	96.9	98.1	94.2	100
Sa	92.5	84.6	91.5	96.4	100
Su	92.5	91.2	100	98.5	97.4
AV	93.3	90.4	93.1	94.1	**95.8**

sometimes cannot be able to bring to light differences as other approaches based on texture analysis can instead highlight. However, this is a limitation only for the recognition of the expression of disgust since for all the remaining expressions the FER performances of the proposed method largely exceed those of the comparing methods highlighting that the analysis of the edges is the best method for the FER problem.

4.3   Tests on Video Streams

The experiments reported in previous subsections were relative to the recognition of facial expressions in a single image containing a clearly defined expression. In common application contexts, the automatic systems have to perform FER by analyzing image sequences in which not all the image contain a clear expression, or where there are transitions between expressions. This section aims thus at analyzing the behavior of the proposed pipeline when applied to a continuous video streaming.

To make the system suitable for video streams analysis, a decision making strategy based on the temporal consistency of FER outcomes has been introduced. The decision about the expression in a video is taken by analyzing a temporal window of size m and verifying if at least n ($n < m$) frames in the window are classified as containing the same facial expression. In the experiments the following setting was used: $n = 4$, $m = 5$,

Subjects of different gender and age have been involved in the experiment. More specifically, all subjects were asked to sit in front of the camera and perform, without a particular order, some of the aforementioned expressions. It is worth noting that, in this way, no constraints, about the passage from the neutral expression to the expressive one have been introduced, leaving the tester free to perform every possible transition among different expressions. The testing system was configured with a webcam with a resolution of 640×480 pixels

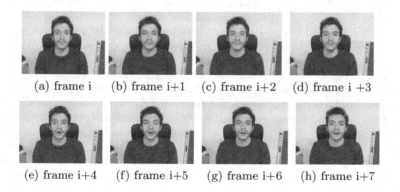

(a) frame i   (b) frame i+1   (c) frame i+2   (d) frame i +3

(e) frame i+4   (f) frame i+5   (g) frame i+6   (h) frame i+7

Fig. 8. Example of expression detection performed by the proposed system: the expression evolves over time; once the decision making rule is satisfied, the prediction is printed out.

and a PC customized by an i5 processor (2,66 GHz) and 4 GB RAM where the system worked in real-time.

The system, evaluated from a qualitative point of view, exhibited a good capacity to recognize all the emotions performed by the testing subjects with a quite low presence of false positive thanks to the filtering performed by the temporal windows and the decision rule above mentioned. One example of the system output is reported in Figure 8. The subject performs a particlular expression that is recognized and showed when a sufficient number of similar classifications are counted in the time window.

5   Conclusions

In this paper, a novel FER automatic pipeline, based on the exploitation of the Histogram of Oriented Gradients (HOG) descriptor, has been proposed. An in-depth analysis, of how the HOG descriptor can be effectively exploited for facial expression recognition purposes, has been supplied. Extensive experiments on CK+ publicly available dataset have been carried out demonstrating that the achieved FER performances outperform those of the leading state of the art approaches. Finally, additional experiments on video streams demonstrated the suitability of the proposed approach for real application contexts. Future works will deal with the test of the presented system in the field of assistive technologies. A social robot will be equipped with the proposed FER solution in order to acquire the awareness about the emotional state of an interacting subject and consequentially adopt an adequate reaction. An additional step will be provided by the coupling with face recognition and re-identification strategies [5,13] aided to keep a temporal consistence of the emotion of different subject among successive interaction sessions.

References

1. Castrillón, M., Déniz, O., Guerra, C., Hernández, M.: Encara2: Real-time detection of multiple faces at different resolutions in video streams. Journal of Visual Communication and Image Representation 18(2), 130–140 (2007)
2. Chang, C.C., Lin, C.J.: Libsvm: a library for support vector machines. ACM Transactions on Intelligent Systems and Technology (TIST) 2(3), 27 (2011)
3. Dalal, N., Triggs, B.: Histograms of oriented gradients for human detection. In: Computer Vision and Pattern Recognition, CVPR 2005, vol. 1, pp. 886–893 (2005)
4. Dornaika, F., Lazkano, E., Sierra, B.: Improving dynamic facial expression recognition with feature subset selection. Pattern Recognition Letters 32(5), 740–748 (2011)
5. Farinella, G.M., Farioli, G., Battiato, S., Leonardi, S., Gallo, G.: Face re-identification for digital signage applications. In: Distante, C., Battiato, S., Cavallaro, A. (eds.) VAAM 2014. LNCS, vol. 8811, pp. 40–52. Springer, Heidelberg (2014)
6. Gritti, T., Shan, C., Jeanne, V., Braspenning, R.: Local features based facial expression recognition with face registration errors. In: 8th IEEE International Conference on Automatic Face Gesture Recognition, FG 2008, pp. 1–8 (2008)

7. Happy, S., Routray, A.: Automatic facial expression recognition using features of salient facial patches. IEEE Transactions on Affective Computing **PP**(99), 1–1 (2015)

8. Izard, C.: The face of emotion. Century psychology series. Appleton-Century-Crofts (1971)

9. Khan, R.A., Meyer, A., Konik, H., Bouakaz, S.: Framework for reliable, real-time facial expression recognition for low resolution images. Pattern Recognition Letters **34**(10), 1159–1168 (2013)

10. Knerr, S., Personnaz, L., Dreyfus, G.: Single-layer learning revisited: a stepwise procedure for building and training a neural network. Neurocomputing **68**, 41–50 (1990)

11. Lowe, D.G.: Distinctive image features from scale-invariant keypoints. Int. J. Comput. Vision **60**(2), 91–110 (2004)

12. Lucey, P., Cohn, J., Kanade, T., Saragih, J., Ambadar, Z., Matthews, I.: The extended cohn-kanade dataset (ck+): a complete dataset for action unit and emotion-specified expression. In: Computer Vision and Pattern Recognition Workshops (CVPRW), pp. 94–101 (2010)

13. Martiriggiano, T., Leo, M., D'Orazio, T., Distante, A.: Face recognition by kernel independent component analysis. In: Ali, M., Esposito, F. (eds.) IEA/AIE 2005. LNCS (LNAI), vol. 3533, pp. 55–58. Springer, Heidelberg (2005)

14. Poursaberi, A., Noubari, H., Gavrilova, M., Yanushkevich, S.: Gauss–laguerrewavelet textural feature fusion with geometrical information for facial expression identification. EURASIP Journal on Image and Video Processing **2012**(1), 17 (2012)

15. Rivera, R., Castillo, R., Chae, O.: Local directional number pattern for face analysis: Face and expression recognition. IEEE Transactions on Image Processing **22**(5), 1740–1752 (2013)

16. Uddin, M., Lee, J., Kim, T.S.: An enhanced independent component-based human facial expression recognition from video. IEEE Transactions on Consumer Electronics **55**(4), 2216–2224 (2009)

17. Uçar, A., Demir, Y., Güzeliş, C.: A new facial expression recognition based on curvelet transform and online sequential extreme learning machine initialized with spherical clustering.Neural Computing and Applications, 1–12 (2014)

18. Viola, P., Jones, M.: Robust real-time face detection. International Journal of Computer Vision **57**(2), 137–154 (2004)

19. Zhang, L., Tjondronegoro, D.: Facial expression recognition using facial movement features. IEEE Transactions on Affective Computing **2**(4), 219–229 (2011)

20. Zhao, X., Zhang, S.: Facial expression recognition based on local binary patterns and kernel discriminant isomap. Sensors **11**(10), 9573–9588 (2011)

Difference-Based Local Gradient Patterns for Image Representation

Shimaa Saad[2] and Alaa Sagheer[1,2]([✉])

[1] Department of Computer Science, College of Computer Science and Information Technology, King Faisal University, Hofuf, Kingdome of Saudi Arabia
asagheer@kfu.edu.sa
[2] Center for Artificial Intelligence and Robotics, Faculty of Science, Aswan University, Aswan, Egypt
s.saad@cairo-aswu.edu.eg

Abstract. This paper aims to examine the impact of pixel differences on local gradient patterns (LGP) for representing facial images. Two difference-based descriptors are proposed, namely, the angular difference LGP (AD-LGP) and the radial difference LGP (RD-LGP) descriptors. For evaluation purpose, two experiments are conducted. The first is face/non face classification using samples from CMU-PIE and CBCL databases. The second is face identification under illumination variations using the extended Yale face database B and the CMU-PIE face database. The experimental results show that both descriptors demonstrate, generally, a higher capability in discriminating face patterns from non-face patterns than the standard LGP. However, in face identification, the AD-LGP descriptor shows robustness against illumination variations, while the performance of the RD-LGP descriptor degrades with hard illuminations. Furthermore, we enhance the RD-LGP descriptor using the Average-Before-Quantization (ABQ) approach in order to increase its robustness toward illumination changes.

Keywords: Local gradient patterns · Face identification · Face non-face classification

1 Introduction

Automatic face analysis has the utmost importance in computer vision research, with applications like biometric identification, visual surveillance, information security and access control, human-machine interaction, video conferencing and content based image retrieval. Face analysis includes many topics such as face detection and facial feature extraction, face tracking and pose estimation, face and facial expression, and face modeling and animation [1,6]. What makes the problem of face analysis challenging is the fact that facial appearance varies due to changes in pose, expression, illumination and other factors such as age and make-up [3].

Recently, very discriminative and computationally efficient local texture descriptors have been proposed such as local binary patterns (LBP)[11], which

© Springer International Publishing Switzerland 2015
V. Murino and E. Puppo (Eds.): ICIAP 2015, Part II, LNCS 9280, pp. 472–482, 2015.
DOI: 10.1007/978-3-319-23234-8_44

has led to a significant progress in applying texture-based methods to different computer vision applications. While texture features have been successfully used in different computer vision problems, only few works have considered them in facial image analysis before the introduction of the LBP [2,5]. Since then, the methodology has inspired a lot of new methods in face analysis, thus revealing that texture based region descriptors can be very efficient in representing and analyzing facial features.

LBP is capable to provide a transformed output image that is invariant to the global intensity variations. However, when LBP is utilized in representing facial features, it is sensitive to local variations that occur commonly along edge components of the human face [7,13]. As such, several extensions of LBP have been proposed with an aim to increase its robustness and discriminative power. Recently, Jun et al. proposed a novel image representation method called local gradient patterns (LGP) generates constant patterns irrespective of local intensity variations [7].

Although LGP is based on calculating the local difference between a pixel and its neighbor pixels, in practice, the calculation of LGP may be affected by some irrelevant situations, for example, varying viewpoint, or local curvature [4]. Local image curvature has many reasons such as illumination variations, edge components, and so on. Motivated by the work of Liu et al. [10], in this paper, we propose two simple, yet powerful difference-based descriptors, generalizing the standard LGP approach. More specifically, we present two descriptors; the angular difference LGP (AD-LGP) and the radial difference LGP (RD-LGP) in angular and radial directions of a circular grid respectively.

As the AD-LGP descriptor is concerned with the angular differences, the most prominent advantage of the AD-LGP is the capability to recover the local curvature cased by illumination variations. Also, AD-LGP is designed to have higher stability with monotonic gray scale transformations at the pixel levels. It considers the gray level differences with a given angular displacement between pairs of evenly spaced pixels on the circular neighborhood, which makes AD-LGP more tolerant with illumination variations.

In a similar way, RD-LGP considers the gray level differences between pairs of pixels of evenly spaced pixels in the same radial direction. Thus RD-LGP is capable to capture the edge information between different circumferences. However, we found experimentally that RD-LGP is sensitive to illumination changes. Thus, we incorporate the Average-Before-Quantization (ABQ) approach [9], in order to enhance the robustness of the RD-LGP descriptor through illumination variations. In this combination, we limit the number of neighboring pixels to be a multiple of four, and then local averaging along an arc is used, such that the number of neighbors is always four.

Two experiments are conducted in order to evaluate the proposed descriptors. The first experiment is face/non face classification problem, using face samples from CMU-PIE database [14] and face/non-face samples from CBCL database [15]. The experimental results demonstrate that both AD-LGP and RD-LGP descriptors have a higher capability, in discriminating face patterns from non-face patterns, than the standard LGP. The second experiment is face identification problem across illumination, using samples form the Extended Yale Face Database B[8] and CMU-PIE Database[14]. The experimental resutls asserts the robustness of the AD-LGP and the enhanced RD-LGP (ERD-LGP) descriptors against illumination variations over the standard LGP.

This paper is organized as follows: Section 2 shows an overview of the standard LGP approach. Also, a description of the proposed descriptors AD-LGP, RD-LGP, and the enhanced ERD-LGP are provided in section 2. Experimental results are shown in section 3. Section 4 shows conclusion and future work of this paper.

2 Proposed Descriptors

2.1 A Brief Overview of Local Gradient Patterns(LGP)

The LGP operator first introduced by Jun et al. [7], uses the gradient values of the eight neighboring pixels of a specified pixel, which are calculated as the absolute values of intensity differences between the specified pixel and its neighboring pixels. Then, the average of the gradient values of the eight neighbors is allocated to the specified pixel and is used as a threshold value for LGP encoding as follows. A pixel is assigned a value of 1 if the gradient value of its neighbor is higher than the threshold; otherwise it is assigned a value of 0. The LGP code for the specified pixel is then obtained by the concatenation of the binary 1s and 0s into a binary code (see Fig. 1). Here, we consider a circular neighborhood of radius r centered on a specified pixel and take p neighboring pixels on the circle. Whenever, the sampling point is not in the center of a pixel, bilinear is necessary (see Fig. 2). The gradient value between a central pixel x_c and its neighbor x_n is set as follows:

$$g_n = |x_n - x_c|, \tag{1}$$

where the average of the p gradient values is given as:

$$\bar{g} = \frac{1}{p} \sum_{n=0}^{p-1} g_n \tag{2}$$

Then, the $LGP_{p,r}$ descriptor is defined as:

$$LGP_{p,r} = \sum_{n=0}^{p-1} s(g_n - \bar{g}) 2^n, \quad s(x) = \begin{cases} 0, & x < 0 \\ 1, & x \geq 0 \end{cases} \tag{3}$$

Motivated by the coding strategy and properties of LGP we propose the following two different descriptors based on pixel differences in both the radial and angular directions on a circular grid. The proposed descriptors are different from the traditional pixel differences, which are computed in horizontal and vertical directions. In these descriptors, we modified the scheme of comparing pixels in the neighborhood of the standard LGP descriptor.

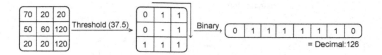

Fig. 1. The original LGP operator

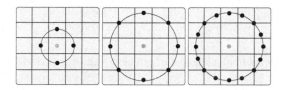

Fig. 2. The circular (4,1), (8,2) and (16,2) neighborhoods

2.2 AD-LGP Descriptor

In this descriptor, instead of calculating the gradient values as the absolute values of the intensity differences between the specified pixel and its neighboring pixels, we use the angular differences with a given angular displacement $\delta(\frac{2\pi}{p})$, where δ is an integer value such that $1 \leq \delta \leq \frac{p}{2}$. Then, the gradient values of the neighbors of the given pixel can be calculated as:

$$\Delta_{\delta,n}^{Ang} = x_{r,n} - x_{r,mod(n+\delta,p)} \tag{4}$$

where $x_{r,n}$ and $x_{r,mod(n+\delta,p)}$ correspond to the gray values of pairs of pixels of δ evenly spaced pixels on a circle of radius r, and the function $mod(x,y)$ computes x modulus y. The average of the gradient values is set as:

$$\mu = \left(\frac{1}{p}\right) \sum_{n=0}^{p-1} \Delta_{\delta,n}^{Ang} \tag{5}$$

Furthermore, toward robustness on possible flat image regions we use a small threshold value ε for the sign function (in this paper, we set $(\varepsilon = 0.01)$. Then, $AD-LGP_{p,r,\delta,\varepsilon}$ descriptor can be written as, see Fig. 3 for calculation example:

$$AD - LGP_{p,r,\delta,\varepsilon} = \sum_{n=0}^{p-1} s\left(\Delta_{\delta,n}^{Ang} - \mu\right) 2^n, \quad s\left(x\right) = \begin{cases} 0, & x < \varepsilon \\ 1, & x \geq \varepsilon \end{cases} \tag{6}$$

2.3 RD-LGP Descriptor

In the RD-LGP descriptor, the gradient values of a given pixel are computed as the absolute values of the radial differences with a given integer radial displacement δ such that:

$$\Delta_{\delta,n}^{Rad} = |x_{r,n} - x_{r-\delta,n}| \tag{7}$$

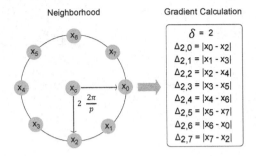

Fig. 3. Illustration of calculating the gradient values for AD-LGP with $\delta = 2$

where $x_{r,n}$ and $x_{r-\delta,n}$ correspond to the gray values of pairs of pixels of δ evenly spaced pixels of the same radial direction as illustrated at Fig. 4. The average value of the gradient values of a given pixel is defined as:

$$\mu = \left(\frac{1}{p}\right) \sum_{n=0}^{p-1} \Delta_{\delta,n}^{Rad} \tag{8}$$

Then, the $RD - LGP_{p,r,\delta}$ descriptor can be expressed as:

$$RD - LGP_{p,r,\delta} = \sum_{n=0}^{p-1} s\left(\Delta_{\delta,n}^{Rad} - \mu\right) 2^n, \quad s(x) = \begin{cases} 0, & x < 0 \\ 1, & x \geq 0 \end{cases} \tag{9}$$

Fig. 4. Illustration of radial differences of pixels

2.4   ERD-LGP Descriptor

During the experiments of this paper, we noticed that RD-LGP outperformed the standard LGP in some situations and degraded in other situation. The degradation in the performance of RD-LGP occurs in case of hard illumination variations. Since the nature of RD-LGP is close, to some extent, to standard LGP, it inherits the sensitivity of LGP to large illumination variations. Then, a further enhancement is needed to increase the robustness of the RD-LGP descriptor against change in illumination conditions.

Thus, we use the Average-Before-Quantization (ABQ) strategy [9] in order to extend the RD-LGP descriptor. The enhanced RD-LGP (ERD-LGP) descriptor

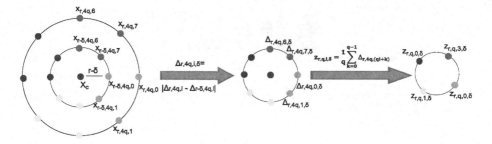

Fig. 5. Illustration of the proposed ERD-LGP descriptor

works as follows: we limit the number of points sampled around the central pixel x_c to be a multiple of the value four, thus $p = 4q$ for a positive integer q. So the neighbors of x_c sampled on the radius r can be gathered in the vector $\mathbf{X}_{r,4q} = [x_{r,4q,0}, ..., x_{r,4q,4q-1}]^T$. Then, we compute the local radial differences as:

$$\Delta_{r,4q,i,\delta} = |x_{r,4q,i} - x_{r-\delta,4q,i}|, \quad i = 0, ..., 4q - 1. \tag{10}$$

where $x_{r,4q,i}$ and $x_{r-\delta,4q,i}$ correspond to the gray values of pairs of pixels of δ evenly spaced pixels of the same radial direction. $\Delta_{r,4q,\delta}$ is transformed into:

$$z_{r,q,i} = (\frac{1}{q}) \sum_{l_\delta=0}^{q-1} \Delta_{r,4q,(qi+k),\delta}, \quad i = 0, .., 3. \tag{11}$$

Then, we compute a binary pattern based on $\mathbf{Z}$ via:

$$ERD - LGP_{p,r,\delta} = \sum_{n=0}^{3} s\left(z_{r,q,n} - \mu_{r,q}^l\right) 2^n, \quad s(x) = \begin{cases} 0, & x < 0 \\ 1, & x \geq 0 \end{cases} \tag{12}$$

where μ^l is the local thresholding value:

$$\mu_{r,q}^l = (\frac{1}{4}) \sum_{n=0}^{3} z_{r,q,n} \tag{13}$$

The construction of the ERD-LGP descriptor is illustrated in Fig. 5.

3   Experiments and Results

In this section we show the experimental results to evaluate the performance of the proposed descriptors; AD-LGP, RD-LGP, and ERD-LGP. The first experiment shows the classification rates of the first two descriptors compared to standard LGP in discriminating face from non-face patterns. The second experiment shows the recognition rates of the three descriptors compared to the standard LGP in discriminating faces of different subjects under variety of illumination conditions. In both experiments, we used the support vector machine (SVM) as a classifier. SVM is a well-founded classifier in statistical learning theory and has been successfully utilized in various classification problems [16].

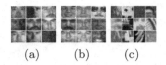

(a)   (b)   (c)

Fig. 6. Samples of the images used in training and testing phase (a) CMU-PIE face (b) CBCL face (C) CBCL non-face

3.1   Face/Non-face Classification

Face/Non-face classification problem is one of the essential problems in face analysis domain. It is simple enough to the extent that we can judge fairly the classification power of the proposed approaches. The experiment of face/non-face classification can be used separately or, mostly, is used as a part of overall face detection or face recognition applications.

In the training phase for this experiment, we use 1215 frontal face samples from the CBCL face database, 2142 frontal, right twist, and up tilt face samples from the CMU-PIE database, namely poses 27, 05 and 07, and 4548 non-face samples from the CBCL database. In the testing phase, we use 3486 frontal, right twist and up-down tilt faces from CMU-PIE database, namely poses 27, 05, 07 and 09, including subjects not used in the training set and 10328 non-face samples from the CBCL database. Fig. 6 shows samples of the face and non-face images used in training and testing phases. All training and testing images, from the CMU-PIE database, are manually cropped and resized into a resolution of 19×19 pixels. During experiments, two scenarios are adopted: Scenario #1, we build a holistic description of image where $r = 2$ and $p = 8$ to obtain a 256-bin histogram. Scenario #2, we divide the input image into nine overlapping regions each with 10×10 pixels. From each region, we compute a 16-bin histogram using $r = 2$ and $p = 4$ and concatenate the results into a single 144-bin histogram. In this scenario, we choose $p = 4$ to avoid statistical unreliability due to long histograms computed over small regions [12]. All the resulted 7905 face and non-face histograms are used to train the SVM. Table 1 shows results of the face/non-face classification problem for both scenarios.

Table 1. Classification accuracy for the proposed descriptors against LGP via the two scenarios

Scenario	LGP	AD-LGP	RD-LGP
#1	93.47%	93.64%	95.98%
#2	92.25%	94.88%	95.48%

As it is shown in Table 1, both the proposed descriptors outperform the standard LGP in the two scenarios. Also, the RD-LGP outperforms both AD-LGP and LGP. It seems that, the scenario #2 is better, for AD-LGP, than scenario #1. In the scope of each descriptor shown in section 2, these results are expected. As long as input image does not include large variations, the radial differences will work better than the angular differences. In the next experiment where illumination is included, the situation will be different, as we will see shortly.

It is clear that, both the proposed descriptors outperform the standard LGP in the two scenarios. Also, the RD-LGP outperforms both AD-LGP and LGP. It seems that, the scenario #2 is better, for AD-LGP, than scenario #1. In the scope of each descriptor shown in section 2, these results are expected. As long as input image does not include large illumination variations, radial differences will work better than angular differences. In the next experiment where illumination varies greatly among samples, the situation will be different, as we will see shortly.

3.2 Face Identification across Illumination

In this experiment, we examine the performance of the standard LGP and the proposed descriptors in discriminating faces of different subjects using two databases; the Extended Yale Face Database B [8] and the CMU-PIE Face Database[14]. The Extended Yale B database, used in this paper, includes 28 subjects under 9 poses × 60 illumination conditions. Half of the illumination conditions are devoted for training phase, i.e. $(28 \times 9 \times 30 = 7560)$ and the other half is devoted for testing phase, as well. Fig. 7 shows samples of the extended Yale B face database. A subset of the CMU-PIE database containing frontal, right-left twist and up-down tilt images of 67 subjects under 21 illumination condition(7035 in total), is used and 2 fold cross validation is performed in experiment using this database.

In the experiment settings, we choose $r = 2$ and $p = 4$ for the same reason mentioned in previous experiment. All images are manually cropped, resized to 48×48 pixels and divided into 3 overlapping regions each with 19×19 pixels. From each region, we compute a 16-bin histogram and concatenate the results into a single 144-bin histogram for each descriptor. Regarding the SVM classifier, the multi-class face identification problem is reduced into multiple two-class problems (i.e.,$28 \times (28 - 1), 67 \times (67 - 1)$) using one-versus-one approach and classification is done by a max-wins voting strategy.

Fig. 7. Samples of the extended Yale B face database

Fig. 8 shows a comparison between performance of the standard LGP from one side and performance of the proposed descriptors from the other side using the extended Yale B database. The performance comparison is conducted across

5 subsets; each includes 6 illumination conditions, according to severity of illumination conditions from moderate to extreme luminance. It is clear that, the AD-LGP descriptor shows a significant improvement in recognition accuracy compared to either LGP or even RD-LGP. The three descriptors start with optimum accuracy, 100%, using subset 1 and subset 2. In case of moderate illumination conditions (subset 3), the three descriptors, show good performance, whereas their performance starts to degrade gradually with severe illuminations (subset 4 and subset 5) with clear superiority for the AD-LGP descriptor over LGP.

Although, the RD-LGP descriptor showed a better performance compared to the AD-LGP descriptor in face/non-face classification, its performance degraded here. Since the nature of the RD-LGP descriptor is close, to some extent, to the standard LGP, it inherits the sensitivity of LGP to large illumination variations. In contrast of previous experiment, the superiority of angular differences over radial differences is reasonable in case of large illumination variations. As computing the pixel differences, in the angular direction increases the capability of the AD-LGP descriptor to recover the local curvature cased by illumination variations.

The enhanced ERD-LGP descriptor shows, less sensitivity to changes in illumination conditions than RD-LGP or LGP itself. This is due to the integration of the circular averaging before quantization strategy, which increases the robustness of the descriptor against illumination changes.

Table 2 shows the performance of the LGP and the proposed descriptor in face identification using the CMU-PIE database. Again results demonstrate the superiority of the AD-LGP descriptor over both LGP and RD-LGP descriptors. However, the ERD-LGP descriptor outperform the AD-LGP descriptor here, as illumination variation in this case is less than in case of the Extended Yale B database.

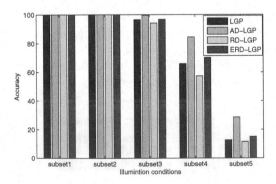

Fig. 8. Comparison between LGP, AD-LGP, RD-LGP and ERD-LGP descriptors performance using the Extended Yale B database

Table 2. Comparison between LGP, AD-LGP, RD-LGP and ERD-LGP descriptors performance using the CMU-PIE

LGP	AD-LGP	RD-LGP	ERD-LGP
81.86%	87.36%	79.98%	90.77%

4   Conclusion and Future Work

This paper proposes an extension to local gradient patterns (LGP) in order to increase its robustness and overall performance. Two difference-based descriptors are presented, namely, the angular difference LGP (AD-LGP) and the radial difference LGP (RD-LGP). Both descriptors are discriminative and showed better performance in face analysis. For evaluation, two experiments are conducted in this paper. The first is a face/non face classification using samples from CMU-PIE and CBCL databases. The second experiment is face identification across illumination, using the Extended Yale face Database B and the CMU-PIE Database. The experimental results showed that both descriptors demonstrate a higher capability in discriminating face patterns from non-face patterns than the standard LGP.

However, in face identification, the AD-LGP descriptor shows robustness against illumination variations, while the performance of the RD-LGP descriptor degrades with hard illuminations. Thus, we enhanced the RD-LGP descriptor using the Average-Before-Quantization (ABQ) strategy, which limits the number of pixels taken around the central pixel to be a multiple of a certain number. This guaranteed to increase the robustness of RD-LGP descriptor toward illumination variations. In future work, we are planning to combine, both AD-LGP and RD-LGP descriptors for a robust image representation. As they capture true complementary texture information, in that the AD-LGP descriptor measures the variations of the neighbors with angular displacement on the same circumference, while the RD-LGP captures the edge information between circumferences.

References

1. Abate, A.F., Nappi, M., Riccio, D., Sabatino, G.: 2d and 3d face recognition: A survey. Pattern Recognition Letters **28**(14), 1885–1906 (2007)
2. Ahonen, T., Hadid, A., Pietikäinen, M.: Face Recognition with local binary patterns. In: Pajdla, T., Matas, J.G. (eds.) ECCV 2004. LNCS, vol. 3021, pp. 469–481. Springer, Heidelberg (2004)
3. Delac, K., Grgic, M., Bartlett, M.S.: Recent advances in face recognition. Tech Publication, Crosia (2008)
4. Fischer, P., Brox, T.: Image descriptors based on curvature histograms. In: Jiang, X., Hornegger, J., Koch, R. (eds.) GCPR 2014. LNCS, vol. 8753, pp. 239–249. Springer, Heidelberg (2014)

5. Hadid, A., Pietikainen, M., Ahonen, T.: A discriminative feature space for detecting and recognizing faces. In: Proceedings of the 2004 IEEE Computer Society Conference on Computer Vision and Pattern Recognition, CVPR 2004, vol. 2, pp. II-797. IEEE (2004)
6. Jain, A.K., Li, S.Z.: Handbook of face recognition, vol. 1. Springer (2005)
7. Jun, B., Kim, D.: Robust face detection using local gradient patterns and evidence accumulation. Pattern Recognition 45(9), 3304–3316 (2012)
8. Lee, K.C., Ho, J., Kriegman, D.J.: Acquiring linear subspaces for face recognition under variable lighting. IEEE Transactions on Pattern Analysis and Machine Intelligence 27(5), 684–698 (2005)
9. Liu, L., Long, Y., Fieguth, P., Lao, S., Zhao, G.: Brint: Binary rotation invariant and noise tolerant texture classification. IEEE Transactions on Image Processing 23 (2013)
10. Liu, L., Zhao, L., Long, Y., Kuang, G., Fieguth, P.: Extended local binary patterns for texture classification. Image and Vision Computing 30(2), 86–99 (2012)
11. Ojala, T., Pietikainen, M., Maenpaa, T.: Multiresolution gray-scale and rotation invariant texture classification with local binary patterns. IEEE Transactions on Pattern Analysis and Machine Intelligence 24(7), 971–987 (2002)
12. Pietikäinen, M., Hadid, A., Zhao, G., Ahonen, T.: Computer vision using local binary patterns, vol. 40. Springer Science & Business Media (2011)
13. Shan, C., Gong, S., McOwan, P.W.: Facial expression recognition based on local binary patterns: A comprehensive study. Image and Vision Computing 27(6), 803–816 (2009)
14. Sim, T., Baker, S., Bsat, M.: The cmu pose, illumination, and expression (pie) database. In: Proceedings of the Fifth IEEE International Conference on Automatic Face and Gesture Recognition, 2002, pp. 46–51. IEEE (2002)
15. Cbcl face database, mit center for biological and computation learning. http://cbcl.mit.edu/software-datasets/FaceData2.html
16. Wu, X., Kumar, V., Quinlan, J.R., Ghosh, J., Yang, Q., Motoda, H., McLachlan, G.J., Ng, A., Liu, B., Philip, S.Y., et al.: Top 10 algorithms in data mining. Knowledge and Information Systems 14(1), 1–37 (2008)

Non-local Sigma Filter

Nikolay Ponomarenko[1], Vladimir Lukin[1], Jaakko Astola[2], and Karen Egiazarian[2(✉)]

[1] Department of Transmitters, Receivers and Signal Processing, National Aerospace University,
17 Chkalova St., Kharkiv 61070, Ukraine
nikolay@ponomarenko.info, lukin@ai.kharkov.com
[2] Department of Signal Processing, Tampere University of Technology,
P.O. Box-553 FIN-33101, Tampere, Finland
{jaakko.astola,karen.egiazarian}@tut.fi

Abstract. This paper proposes a non-local modification of well-known sigma filter, Nonlocal Sigma filter (NSF), intended to suppress additive white Gaussian noise from images. Similarly to the Nonlocal Mean Filter (NLM), every output pixel value is computed as a nonlocal weighted average of pixels coming from similar patches to the patch around the current pixel. The main difference between the proposed NSF and NLM is in the following: there are pixels in NSF not used in a weighted averaging (if the difference between them and the central pixel value is above a predefined threshold value, and if the distance between patch neighborhood and the central patch neighborhood is greater than a second threshold value). The weights used to estimate the output pixel depend on the patch size as well as on a distance between considered and reference patches. The proposed filter is compared to its counter parts, namely, the conventional sigma filter and the NLM filter. It is shown that NSF outperforms both of them in PSNR and visual quality metrics values, PSNR-HVS-M and MSSIM. In this paper, a novel filtering quality criterion that takes into account distortions introduced into processed images due to denoising is proposed. It is demonstrated that, according to this criterion, NSF has similar edge-detail preservation property as the conventional sigma filter but has better noise suppression ability.

Keywords: Image denoising · Non-local methods · Similarity-based methods · Sigma filter · Human perception · Visual quality metrics · Image self-similarity

1 Introduction

Noise suppression is one of the main problems in image processing during several decades [1]. Recently, non-local image denoising has become very popular image filtering technique. It is based not only on statistical and spatial information extracted from a given pixel neighborhood but uses similarity of image fragments [2-4]. In turn, this leads to a better separation of image from noise compared to local image denoising methods. Besides, recent studies in the field of visual image quality assessment [5] show that human perception uses a self-similarity in images. Then, one can expect that the use of this self-similarity in image denoising can result in improved visual quality of filtered images.

© Springer International Publishing Switzerland 2015
V. Murino and E. Puppo (Eds.): ICIAP 2015, Part II, LNCS 9280, pp. 483–493, 2015.
DOI: 10.1007/978-3-319-23234-8_45

Alongside with the design of rather complex non-local filters processing data in several iterations and/or use of orthogonal transforms in the search of similar patches and their joint processing [3], a special attention is paid to the design of non-local versions of simple (basic) filters as, e.g., the mean filter [4]. Such investigations are important [2] since they allow better understanding of "bricks" put into basis of more complex methods. To our surprise, well known sigma filter [6] still does not have a non-local version and our goal in this paper is to design and study such a filter.

Here it is worth mentioning the following. The requirement to preserve important information in images while filtering them was and continues to be very essential. Any image filter introduces certain distortions (e.g. smears edges and fine details, destroys textures) in less or greater extent [1]. Then, in practice, despite an increase of signal-to-noise ratio due to filtering, an efficiency of solving the final task (e.g., image interpreting) using filtered images can decrease [7]. Customers of digital cameras with embedded filtering are often unsatisfied by denoising outcome. Many of them switch off image filtering mode since processed images often occur to be smeared and important details appear visually worse than those before processing.

Thus, a traditional formulation "better noise suppression under a condition of acceptable information preservation" permanently changes to "less introduced distortion under a condition of sufficient noise suppression". Conditionally, this can be treated as a "distortion-free image denoising".

Among filters preserving an important information (edges, details, texture) conventional sigma filter is one of the best. As its drawbacks, insufficient noise suppression in homogeneous image regions is usually regarded. Taking this into account, several modifications of the conventional sigma filter have been designed to improve its noise suppression efficiency [8] and to provide robustness [9]. In this paper, a non-local version of the sigma filter is proposed. We check a hypothesis that the use of patch similarity is able to improve noise suppression without worsening information preservation ability. The proposed filter is compared to its closest counter-parts: conventional sigma-filter and non-local mean filter using PSNR values for output images and visual quality metrics PSNR-HVS-M [10] and MSSIM [11]. Besides, a new quality criterion is introduced where more attention is paid to distortions introduced to images.

2   Calculation of Non-local Sigma Filter

Recall that for the conventional sigma filter the output I^s_{kl} for a given distorted value I^n_{kl} which is the center of a sliding window in kl-th pixel is calculated as an average of sliding window pixel values that fall into interval $I^n_{kl}-2\sigma \dots I^n_{kl}+2\sigma$, where σ denotes a noise standard deviation, assumed a priori known or pre-estimated [12]. The value I^n_{kl} also takes part in averaging which is not weighted (all weights are equal).

Let us modify this filter taking into account similarity of image patches.

For each image block (patch) A of size NxN pixels, let us estimate its similarity with respect to each block B in a given spatial neighborhood. A spatial neighborhood is determined by a present width M of a search area around the block A (see Fig. 1). A total number of blocks in the search area is equal to $(2M+N-1)^2-1$ whilst a total number of values potentially able to take part in averaging is equal to $(2M+N)^2-1$.

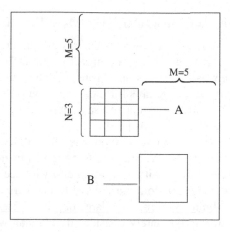

Fig. 1. Area of similar block search for the block *A* for *N=3, M=5*. Block *B* is one for which it's similarity to the block A is assessed.

Let us calculate the distance (similarity measure) for the blocks *A* and *B* as:

$$Diff(A,B) = \sum_{i=1}^{N}\sum_{j=1}^{N}(A_{ij} - B_{ij})^2 .$$

(1)

Then, for each pixel A_{ij}, it is possible to perform an estimation using the pixel B_{ij} with the weight W_{ij} as

$$W_{ij} = \begin{cases} 0, & |A_{ij} - B_{ij}| > T\sigma \quad \vee \quad D_{ij} > \sigma^2 \\ 1/max(D_{ij} + P,\sigma^2), & |A_{ij} - B_{ij}| \leq T\sigma \quad \wedge \quad D_{ij} \leq \sigma^2 \end{cases},$$

(2)

where *T* is a coefficient that determines the size of averaging σ-neighborhood (we have set *T=3*), D_{ij} is an estimate of MSE difference between the patches of pixels A_{ij} and B_{ij}, and *P* denotes a stabilizing term determined by the patch size *N*.

In the paper [4], an exponentially weighted aggregation of estimates is employed. Here, we use inverse proportionality calculation of weights depending on D_{ij} as it is done in [3]; such weighting seems to be more reasonable.

Let us explain the setting *T=3*. Recall that for the conventional sigma filter it is recommended to use *T=2* which restricts its noise suppression ability. Meanwhile, the use of *T=3* for the conventional sigma filters leads to worse preservation of an important information. In the modified version, we exploit image fragment similarity and the use of an additional restriction $D_{ij} \leq \sigma^2$ which allows expecting acceptable edge/detail preservation even for *T=3*.

To calculate D_{ij}, we use *Diff(A,B)* subtracting contribution of the pixels A_{ij} and B_{ij}:

$$D_{ij} = \frac{Diff(A,B) - (A_{ij} - B_{ij})^2}{2(N^2 - 1)}$$

(3)

In [2, 4], D_{ij} is calculated without subtracting $(A_{ij} - B_{ij})^2$ as it is done in (3), i.e. a filtered pixel value is taken into account as well. To our opinion, this is not reasonable since in this case a larger weight W_{ij} is assigned to "similar" A_{ij} and B_{ij} which may result in less efficient noise suppression. There are also suggestions to use some kernels in (1) [4] to increase the weights for those pixels in the patch that are closer to the filtered one. However, we prefer not to use a multiplication by a kernel to avoid increased smearing of edges and details [2, 4].

The parameter P is introduced to compensate the influence of fluctuations of $Diff(A,B)$ that increase for smaller N. Suppose that a given image contains only noise and it has a Gaussian distribution with zero mean and variance σ^2. Then, it is easy to show that $Diff(A,B)/(N^2-1)$ is a random variable with the distribution $\chi^2(N^2-1)$. Taking into account the central limit theorem, for a large degree of freedom ($N^2>30$) the distribution $\chi^2(N^2-1)$ can be approximately considered Gaussian with the mean $2\sigma^2$ and the variance $8\sigma^4/(N^2-1)$.

Therefore, the obtained D_{ij} are random variables with variance $2\sigma^4/(N^2-1)$ and standard deviation $\sqrt{\dfrac{2\sigma^4}{N^2-1}}$. As the parameter P, we propose to use:

$$P = 2\sqrt{\frac{2\sigma^4}{N^2-1}}. \tag{4}$$

Each filtered pixel I^n_{kl} for different positions of a sliding window (block A) can occupy different positions in the block A. Then, after processing of the entire image, one obtains $U=(2M+N)^2-1$ estimates of B_{ij} with weights W_{ij} for this pixel. Let us group all these estimates and corresponding weights into arrays B^{all} and W^{all}, respectively. Then, the output of the non-local sigma-filter for the pixel I^n_{kl} is determined as:

$$I^{NLS}_{kl} = \frac{I^n_{kl}/\sigma^2 + \sum_{u=1}^{U} B^{all}_u W^{all}_u}{1/\sigma^2 + \sum_{u=1}^{U} W^{all}_u}. \tag{5}$$

Here $1/\sigma^2$ denotes the weight for the filtered pixel for which it is a priori known that it is corrupted by an additive white Gaussian noise with variance σ^2. In the paper [4], the authors propose to use the largest among W_u^{all} but, to our experience, the weighting in (5) works better.

3   Performance Comparison of Filtering Methods

In this section we compare a performance of the proposed filter to its counter-parts, conventional sigma-filter and non-local mean filter [4]. Three modifications of the non-local Sigma with $N=2$ (NLS2), $N=3$ (NLS3), $N=5$ (NLS5) are considered. For all three modifications we set $M=5$. In our comparison we use two variants of the non-local mean filter having patch sizes 3x3 pixels (denoted as NLM3) and 5x5 pixels (denoted as NLM5) with the same area of similar patch search as for NLS. Let us also consider conventional sigma filters with sliding window sizes *5x5* pixels (*Sig5*) and *7x7* pixels (*Sig7*) as well as a version of sigma filter with the neighborhood ±3σ and the window size *7x7* pixels (*Sig73*). The filter *Sig73* is included into our analysis to demonstrate that for the conventional sigma filter the neighborhood increase leads to worse filtering.

Nine test images have been used in the experiments. Four of them are standard ones: 'Cameraman', 'Barbara', 'Baboon', and 'Lena'. To this list we have added homogeneous (constant level) image ('Homogeneous'), the gradient image ('Gradient') and three artificially created images, presented in Fig. 2. The image 'Patterns' contains different textures, gradients and small-size objects. The images 'Cartoon' and 'Text' have many sharp transitions (objects are inserted into background without antialiasing).

Fig. 2. Artificially created test images 'Patterns', 'Cartoon' and 'Text'

The image 'Cameraman' is of size *256x256* pixels, all others are of size *512x512* pixels. All images are grayscale (they can be downloaded from http://ponomarenko.info/iciap2015set.zip).

Each test image has been corrupted by AWGN with variances σ^2 equal to *25, 100* and *400* and then processed by the considered filters. As it has been mentioned above, performance analysis is carried out using conventional criterion PSNR as well as two visual quality metrics PSNR-HVS-M and MSSIM, which are among the best for grayscale images.

Besides, to characterize distortions due to filtering, we have introduced the metric NAE (new aggregate distortions) and its derivatives, NMSE (new mean square error) and percentage of pixels that are more distorted after filtering (I_{kl}^{f}) than before filtering (denoted as NDP) with respect to the true value I_{kl}^{et} .

$$\text{NDP} = \frac{100}{KL}\sum_{k=1}^{K}\sum_{l=1}^{L}\delta_{kl}, \quad \delta_{kl} = \begin{cases} 1, & \left|I_{kl}^{et} - I_{kl}^{n}\right| < \left|I_{kl}^{et} - I_{kl}^{f}\right| \\ 0, & \left|I_{kl}^{et} - I_{kl}^{n}\right| \geq \left|I_{kl}^{et} - I_{kl}^{f}\right| \end{cases},$$

$$\text{NAE} = \frac{1}{KL}\sum_{k=1}^{K}\sum_{l=1}^{L}\delta_{kl}\left(\left|I_{kl}^{et} - I_{kl}^{f}\right| - \left|I_{kl}^{et} - I_{kl}^{n}\right|\right)^{2}, \quad \text{NMSE} = 100\,\text{NAE/NDP}.$$

(6)

Table 1 lists PSNR values for all filtered images. The best PSNR in each row is marked by **Bold**. As it is seen, the proposed filter *NLS2* outperforms *Sig5* and *Sig7* by *1...2* dB for standard test images and by *6...7* dB for artificial test images and the image 'Homogeneous'. The filter *Sig73* has PSNR smaller than for *NLS2* by *0.5...1* dB for all test images. The filter *NLM5* is sometimes the best, its PSNR can be larger than for *NLS2* by up to *1* dB (this happens for some standard test images in the cases of intensive noise). However, the difference in PSNR for *NLS2* and *NLM5* can be *10* dB and more for images with sharp transitions and small σ^2. In such cases, *NLM5* can even have smaller PSNR than before filtering. Interestingly, *NLS5* suppresses noise better than *NLM5* in homogeneous regions. This evidences in favor of weighted averaging methods determined by (2).

Fig. 3 presents PSNR averaged for all nine test images. As it is seen, the best results are provided by the proposed filter *NLS5*, other considered filters can be ranked as *Sig73*, *NLM5*, and *Sig7*. The reason why we present data for *NLS5* (but not for *NLS2* which usually has the better PSNR) will follow from the analysis of data presented in Tables 2 and 3 for the metrics PSNR-HVS-M and MSSIM, respectively.

Table 1. Comparison of analyzed methods, PSNR, dB (average of 100 experiments)

σ^2	Test image	none	Sigma filter			Non-local Mean		Non-local Sigma		
			Sig5	Sig7	Sig73	NLM3	NLM5	NLS2	NLS3	NLS5
	Cameraman	34.1	36.8	36.9	36.8	34.8	33.9	37.5	**37.6**	37.4
	Barbara	34.1	35.7	35.8	35.7	36.6	36.7	36.8	**36.9**	36.5
	Lena	34.2	36.6	36.6	36.7	37.6	37.5	37.6	**37.7**	37.2
	Baboon	34.1	34.3	34.4	34.0	31.0	30.0	34.5	**34.6**	34.4
25	Cartoon	36.1	41.3	41.7	42.5	32.3	30.5	**42.7**	42.5	41.7
	Patterns	35.0	38.6	38.9	39.4	31.5	30.2	41.6	**41.7**	41.2
	Text	34.1	41.4	42.3	47.2	38.6	36.5	**48.4**	47.8	45.5
	Gradient	34.2	41.6	42.4	47.9	46.4	48.3	**49.0**	**49.0**	48.9
	Homogeneous	34.1	41.7	42.5	48.2	46.7	48.7	49.5	**49.6**	**49.6**
	Cameraman	28.3	32.0	32.1	32.4	32.4	32.0	33.2	**33.3**	32.9
	Barbara	28.1	30.8	31.0	31.3	33.4	**33.9**	32.8	33.2	32.7
	Lena	28.1	32.3	32.2	33.2	34.6	**34.9**	34.2	34.5	34.2
	Baboon	28.1	29.4	29.5	29.2	29.1	28.6	**29.7**	**29.7**	29.3
100	Cartoon	30.0	35.1	35.4	36.0	31.3	29.6	**36.4**	36.3	35.7
	Patterns	29.0	32.7	33.0	33.4	30.4	29.4	35.9	**36.1**	35.7
	Text	28.1	35.2	36.0	41.1	36.0	34.7	**42.1**	41.6	39.5
	Gradient	28.1	35.4	36.2	42.2	40.8	42.9	43.4	**43.5**	**43.5**
	Homogeneous	28.1	35.4	36.3	42.3	40.9	43.0	43.6	**43.7**	**43.7**
	Cameraman	22.5	27.2	27.5	28.4	29.3	**29.4**	29.3	29.5	29.4
	Barbara	22.1	26.2	26.4	27.2	29.3	**30.0**	28.9	29.6	29.7
	Lena	22.1	27.6	27.8	29.9	30.8	**31.5**	30.8	31.1	31.1
	Baboon	22.1	24.9	25.0	24.9	**26.0**	25.8	25.7	25.7	25.1
400	Cartoon	24.1	28.9	29.1	29.3	28.1	27.2	**30.0**	30.0	29.6
	Patterns	23.1	27.2	27.3	27.9	27.7	27.3	29.9	**30.4**	30.1
	Text	22.1	29.0	29.7	34.0	31.6	31.6	**35.4**	35.1	33.4
	Gradient	22.1	29.3	30.1	36.2	34.9	37.0	37.5	**37.6**	**37.6**
	Homogeneous	22.1	29.3	30.1	36.2	34.9	37.0	37.5	**37.6**	**37.6**

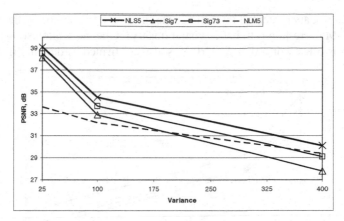

Fig. 3. PSNR averaged for all test images for three noise variances

Table 2. Comparison of analyzed methods, PSNR-HVS-M, dB

σ^2	Test image	none	Sigma filter			Non-local Mean		Non-local Sigma		
			Sig5	Sig7	Sig73	NLM3	NLM5	NLS2	NLS3	NLS5
25	Cameraman	38.2	40.6	40.9	39.8	39.3	38.2	40.8	41.3	**41.4**
	Barbara	39.0	40.5	40.5	39.2	39.9	39.6	40.1	40.5	**40.7**
	Lena	38.3	40.2	40.2	38.7	39.9	39.7	39.5	40.1	**40.4**
	Baboon	41.3	41.1	40.9	38.7	36.5	35.1	40.1	40.9	**41.4**
	Cartoon	38.0	39.8	40.0	40.0	37.2	36.3	**40.2**	**40.2**	**40.2**
	Patterns	40.2	42.9	43.5	42.8	36.6	35.0	44.5	45.1	**45.5**
	Text	37.5	42.1	43.8	45.9	45.3	44.1	48.9	**48.9**	48.6
	Gradient	36.2	40.9	42.7	45.3	46.5	47.6	**48.0**	47.9	47.8
	Homogeneous	36.1	40.8	42.6	45.3	46.8	47.9	**48.3**	**48.3**	**48.3**
100	Cameraman	31.5	34.3	34.8	33.7	34.7	34.1	34.9	35.5	**35.8**
	Barbara	31.7	33.8	34.0	33.0	34.7	34.9	34.1	34.7	**35.0**
	Lena	31.3	34.1	34.3	33.3	34.7	34.8	34.0	34.6	**35.2**
	Baboon	32.9	**33.6**	33.4	31.3	32.1	31.4	32.4	33.1	33.5
	Cartoon	31.7	33.5	33.8	33.7	33.5	32.7	**34.0**	**34.0**	**34.0**
	Patterns	33.6	36.2	36.7	35.8	34.4	33.1	37.8	38.5	**38.9**
	Text	31.3	35.8	37.4	39.5	40.2	39.7	42.2	**42.4**	42.1
	Gradient	30.1	34.7	36.5	39.3	40.8	42.0	**42.3**	**42.3**	**42.3**
	Homogeneous	30.1	34.7	36.5	39.4	41.0	42.2	**42.5**	**42.5**	**42.5**
400	Cameraman	25.2	28.3	28.9	28.1	29.8	29.6	29.4	29.8	**30.1**
	Barbara	24.9	27.6	28.1	27.5	29.4	29.5	28.8	29.3	**29.9**
	Lena	24.7	28.1	28.6	28.2	29.6	29.7	29.0	29.5	**30.0**
	Baboon	25.4	**27.0**	26.9	24.9	26.6	26.1	26.0	26.5	26.9
	Cartoon	25.3	27.1	27.3	26.9	**27.7**	27.3	27.5	27.6	27.5
	Patterns	26.7	29.2	29.6	28.4	29.8	29.3	30.6	31.6	**32.1**
	Text	24.9	29.4	31.0	32.7	34.0	34.2	35.5	**35.7**	35.2
	Gradient	24.1	28.7	30.4	33.2	34.9	36.0	**36.3**	**36.3**	**36.3**
	Homogeneous	24.0	28.6	30.3	33.2	34.8	36.0	36.2	**36.3**	**36.3**

According to data presented in Table 2, the filter *NLS5* is obviously the best (larger PSNR-HVS-M corresponds to better visual quality). One more interesting observation is that *Sig73* is often worse than *Sig7*, this is also confirmed by data in Fig 4.

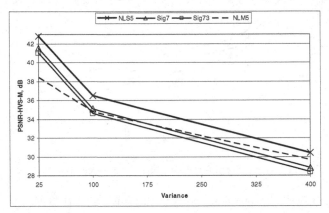

Fig. 4. PSNR-HVS-M averaged for all test images for three noise variances

Table 3. Comparison of analyzed methods, MSSIM

σ^2	Test image	none	Sigma filter			Non-local Mean		Non-local Sigma		
			Sig5	*Sig7*	*Sig73*	*NLM3*	*NLM5*	*NLS2*	*NLS3*	*NLS5*
25	Cameraman	0.977	0.990	0.991	0.991	0.991	0.990	**0.992**	**0.992**	**0.992**
	Barbara	0.984	0.991	0.991	0.990	**0.992**	**0.992**	**0.992**	**0.992**	**0.992**
	Lena	0.979	0.989	0.989	0.988	**0.990**	**0.990**	0.989	**0.990**	**0.990**
	Baboon	0.992	0.992	0.992	0.989	0.988	0.985	0.991	0.992	0.992
	Cartoon	0.991	0.998	0.999	0.999	0.998	0.997	**1.000**	0.999	0.999
	Patterns	0.989	0.996	0.997	0.998	0.996	0.994	0.998	**0.999**	**0.999**
	Text	0.974	0.993	0.995	0.998	0.998	0.998	**0.999**	**0.999**	**0.999**
	Gradient	0.948	0.985	0.989	0.995	0.995	0.996	**0.997**	**0.997**	**0.997**
	Homogeneous	0.947	0.984	0.988	0.995	0.995	**0.997**	**0.997**	**0.997**	**0.997**
100	Cameraman	0.928	0.969	0.973	0.976	0.979	0.979	0.980	0.982	**0.983**
	Barbara	0.947	0.973	0.975	0.976	0.981	**0.983**	0.980	0.982	**0.983**
	Lena	0.930	0.969	0.971	0.974	0.978	**0.979**	0.976	0.978	**0.979**
	Baboon	0.970	**0.977**	**0.977**	0.968	0.974	0.971	0.973	0.975	**0.977**
	Cartoon	0.972	0.993	0.995	0.997	0.996	0.995	**0.998**	**0.998**	**0.998**
	Patterns	0.965	0.987	0.989	0.993	0.991	0.991	0.995	0.995	**0.996**
	Text	0.923	0.974	0.980	0.991	0.992	0.993	**0.995**	**0.995**	**0.995**
	Gradient	0.838	0.943	0.957	0.980	0.983	0.988	**0.989**	**0.989**	**0.989**
	Homogeneous	0.834	0.940	0.955	0.979	0.983	0.987	0.988	**0.989**	**0.989**
400	Cameraman	0.825	0.916	0.928	0.944	0.953	0.955	0.955	0.957	**0.958**
	Barbara	0.856	0.922	0.931	0.939	0.953	0.958	0.952	0.958	**0.961**
	Lena	0.818	0.912	0.923	0.944	0.949	0.953	0.950	0.953	**0.955**
	Baboon	0.907	0.936	0.936	0.915	0.935	0.927	0.925	0.931	**0.937**
	Cartoon	0.925	0.976	0.981	0.984	0.987	0.986	**0.989**	**0.989**	**0.989**
	Patterns	0.911	0.959	0.965	0.976	0.978	0.979	0.983	**0.985**	**0.985**
	Text	0.828	0.919	0.935	0.968	0.970	0.977	**0.980**	**0.980**	**0.980**
	Gradient	0.616	0.814	0.855	0.927	0.939	0.955	0.958	**0.959**	**0.959**
	Homogeneous	0.605	0.803	0.846	0.920	0.934	0.951	0.954	**0.955**	**0.955**

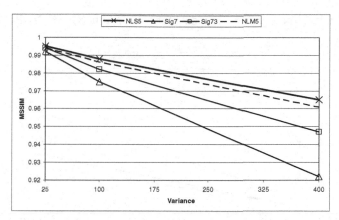

Fig. 5. MSSIM averaged for all test images from three noise variances

According to MSSIM (see Table 3 and Fig. 5, MSSIM=1 relates to perfect quality), the filter *NLS5* is again the best although the second place is occupied by *NLM5*.

Table 4. Comparison of analyzed methods, NMSE (NDP)

σ^2	Test image	Denoising method							
		Sigma filter			Non-local Mean		Non-local Sigma		
		Sig5	*Sig7*	*Sig73*	*NLM3*	*NLM5*	*NLS2*	*NLS3*	*NLS5*
25	Cameraman	5.1 (24)	4.8 (23)	9.9 (28)	36 (27)	47 (28)	7.1 (24)	6.0 (18)	**5.2 (14)**
	Barbara	5.2 (30)	4.3 (29)	8.4 (34)	12 (28)	13 (29)	6.7 (29)	6.2 (24)	**5.8 (17)**
	Lena	4.6 (25)	**4.2 (25)**	8.2 (30)	9.6 (26)	11 (27)	7.3 (28)	6.9 (25)	6.3 (21)
	Baboon	6.2 (39)	5.1 (38)	11 (44)	47 (51)	63 (53)	8.0 (34)	8.0 (17)	**6.7 (7)**
	Cartoon	3.1 (45)	**3.1 (44)**	3.8 (45)	75 (44)	118 (44)	3.7 (45)	3.7 (45)	3.7 (44)
	Patterns	3.7 (31)	3.4 (30)	4.6 (33)	130 (28)	189 (28)	3.7 (28)	3.8 (27)	**3.9 (25)**
	Text	1.6 (7)	**1.2 (4)**	1.6 (5)	110 (5)	146 (7)	1.4 (3)	1.6 (4)	1.9 (4)
	Gradient	1.5 (7)	1.2 (4)	1.3 (5)	**1.0 (3)**	**1.0 (3)**	1.1 (3)	1.1 (3)	1.1 (4)
	Homogeneous	1.5 (6)	1.1 (4)	1.2 (4)	**1.0 (2)**	**1.0 (2)**	1.0 (3)	1.1 (3)	1.1 (3)
100	Cameraman	15 (21)	15 (20)	34 (24)	48 (21)	64 (22)	28 (22)	24 (20)	**17 (16)**
	Barbara	14 (26)	**12 (25)**	27 (30)	19 (22)	20 (21)	21 (24)	19 (23)	16 (20)
	Lena	11 (20)	**10 (20)**	22 (23)	16 (18)	18 (19)	18 (21)	17 (21)	15 (19)
	Baboon	17 (36)	15 (35)	36 (41)	55 (39)	70 (41)	29 (38)	25 (29)	**23 (15)**
	Cartoon	12 (47)	**12 (46)**	15 (48)	71 (46)	115 (46)	14 (47)	15 (47)	14 (46)
	Patterns	12 (34)	**11 (33)**	17 (35)	120 (30)	173 (30)	13 (30)	13 (29)	14 (28)
	Text	3.8 (9)	**2.7 (6)**	3.9 (7)	86 (7)	115 (8)	3.8 (5)	4.1 (5)	4.9 (6)
	Gradient	3.4 (9)	2.2 (6)	2.5 (6)	**1.5 (3)**	**1.5 (3)**	1.7 (4)	1.8 (4)	1.9 (4)
	Homogeneous	3.3 (8)	2.1 (5)	2.4 (6)	**1.5 (3)**	**1.5 (3)**	1.6 (4)	1.7 (4)	1.8 (4)
400	Cameraman	41 (18)	**41 (17)**	84 (21)	76 (16)	93 (16)	80 (18)	75 (18)	70 (17)
	Barbara	40 (22)	**35 (21)**	92 (25)	45 (17)	49 (17)	63 (20)	55 (19)	50 (18)
	Lena	25 (16)	**25 (15)**	53 (17)	32 (14)	37 (14)	46 (16)	43 (16)	40 (15)
	Baboon	52 (29)	**50 (29)**	131 (35)	97 (30)	122 (31)	106 (32)	98 (31)	74 (24)
	Cartoon	**44 (49)**	45 (48)	62 (51)	100 (48)	136 (48)	59 (49)	59 (49)	59 (48)
	Patterns	42 (35)	**41 (34)**	67 (36)	141 (31)	188 (31)	54 (33)	52 (31)	52 (29)
	Text	12 (11)	**8.6 (8)**	18 (9)	81 (8)	118 (8)	17 (6)	18 (7)	21 (7)
	Gradient	11 (10)	6.1 (7)	7.0 (7)	**3.5 (4)**	**3.4 (4)**	4.1 (5)	4.3 (5)	4.6 (5)
	Homogeneous	11 (10)	6.0 (7)	7.0 (7)	**3.5 (4)**	**3.4 (4)**	4.1 (5)	4.3 (5)	4.7 (5)

Finally, Table 4 and Fig. 6 contain data for new criteria NMSE, NDP and NAE.

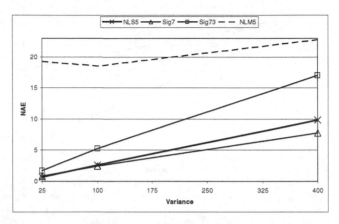

Fig. 6. Averaged values of NAE

According to these criteria characterizing information preservation (both tend to zero for ideal preservation), the best filter is *Sig7*. However, the proposed filter *NLS5* is only slightly worse and only for $\sigma^2=400$ although there are cases when *NLS5* is better (for example, for the test image 'Baboon' for $\sigma^2=25$).

Therefore, the obtained data allow concluding that the designed filter demonstrates better performance than the analyzed counter-parts. It suppresses noise better (especially, in images with sharp edges) whilst edge/detail preservation is practically the same as for the conventional sigma-filter.

4   Conclusions and Future Work

This paper presents a novel non-local Sigma filter. It is shown that this filter provides noise suppression efficiency at the same level as the non-local means filter whilst edge/detail preservation is practically similar to the conventional sigma filter.

Further studies might deal with a use of iterative filtering, orthogonal transforms as in [3], etc. Besides, it seems possible to use soft and adaptive thresholds [13], different sizes of patches and search area, combine different size patches, etc.

In this paper also new criteria of filtering efficiency are proposed. They are based on estimating level of distortions introduced by denoising.

References

1. Astola, J., Kuosmanen, P.: Fundamentals of nonlinear digital filtering, vol. 8. CRC Press (1997)
2. Deledalle, C.A., Duval, V., Salmon, J.: Non-Local Methods with Shape-Adaptive Patches (NLM-SAP). Journal of Mathematical Imaging and Vision **43**(2), 103–120 (2012).

3. Dabov, K., Foi, A., Katkovnik, V., Egiazarian, K.O.: Image denoising by sparse 3-D transform-domain collaborative filtering. IEEE Trans. Image Process. **16**(8), 2080–2095 (2007)
4. Buades, A., Coll, B., Morel, J.M.: A non-local algorithm for image denoising. IEEE Computer Society Conference on Computer Vision and Pattern Recognition **2**, 60–65 (2005)
5. Ponomarenko, N., Jin, L., Lukin, V., Egiazarian, K.: Self-similarity measure for assessment of image visual quality. In: Blanc-Talon, J., Kleihorst, R., Philips, W., Popescu, D., Scheunders, P. (eds.) ACIVS 2011. LNCS, vol. 6915, pp. 459–470. Springer, Heidelberg (2011)
6. Lee, J.S.: Digital Image Smoothing and the Sigma Filter. Computer Vision, Graphics, and Image Processing, 255–269 (1983)
7. Lukin, V., Ponomarenko, N., Zelensky, A., Astola, J., Egiazarian, K.: Automatic design of locally adaptive filters for pre-processing of images subject to further interpretation. In: Proceedings of 2006 IEEE Southwest Symp. on Image Analysis and Interpretation, Denver, USA, pp. 41–45 (2006)
8. Lukin, V.V., Zelensky, A.A., Ponomarenko, N.N., Kurekin, A.A., Astola, J.T., Koivisto, P.T.: Modified sigma filter with improved noise suppression efficiency and spike removal ability. In: Proceedings of the 6-th Intern. Workshop on Intelligent Signal Processing and Communication Systems, Melbourne, Australia, pp. 849–853 (1998)
9. Alparone, L., Baronti, S., Garzelli, A.: A hybrid sigma filter for unbiased and edge-preserving speckle reduction. In: Proceedings of International Geoscience and Remote Sensing Symposium, pp.1409–1411 (1995)
10. Ponomarenko, N., Silvestri, F., Egiazarian, K., Carli, M., Astola, J., Lukin, V.: On between-coefficient contrast masking of DCT basis functions. In: Proc. of the Third International Workshop on Video Processing and Quality Metrics, USA, p. 4 (2007)
11. Wang, Z., Simoncelli, E.P., Bovik, A.C.: Multi scale structural similarity for image quality assessment. In: IEEE Asilomar Conference on Signals, Systems and Computers, pp. 1398–1402 (2003)
12. Lukin, V., Abramov, S., Ponomarenko, N., Uss, M., Zriakhov, M., Vozel, B., Chehdi, K., Astola, J.: Methods and automatic procedures for processing images based on blind evaluation of noise type and characteristics. SPIE Journal on Advances in Remote Sensing (2011). doi:10.1117/1.3539768
13. Van De Ville, D., Kocher, M.: SURE-based non-local means. IEEE Signal Processing Letters **16**(11), 973–976 (2009)

A New Multi-resolution Affine Invariant Planar Contour Descriptor

Taha Faidi, Faten Chaieb$^{(\boxtimes)}$, and Faouzi Ghorbel

CRISTAL Laboratory, ENSI, La Manouba University, Manouba, Tunisia
taha.faidi@ensi-uma.tn, {faten.chaieb,Faouzi.ghorbel}@ensi.rnu.tn

Abstract. In this paper, a novel affine invariant shape descriptor for planar contours is proposed. It is based on a multi-resolution representation of the contour. For each contour resolution, a shape signature is defined from the contour points and the initial contour centroid and points. Finally, Fourier descriptors are computed for each signature. The proposed descriptor is invariant to affine transformations. Experiments carried on the MPEG-7 coutour database and the Multiview Curve Dataset (MCD) show that our proposed descriptor outperforms other contour shape descriptors proposed in the literature.

1 Introduction

The recognition of planar shapes that are subjected to certain viewing transformations has an increasing interest in many computer vision applications such as robotic vision, content-based image retrieval, registration and 3D reconstruction. Three dimensional objects could be also considered as planar when the camera is far away from the object and distances within the object are negligible.

The use of shape descriptors to deal with such problem seems to be the most efficient method. The main challenging task of shape descriptors is to provide an accurate representation of shape information that deals with two critical problems : (a) viewpoint invariance since object shapes can change as the viewpoint changes due to perspective transformation and (b) parametrization invariance.

The viewpoint is usually described by a group of geometric transformations. The main groups of interest for pattern recognition and image analysis applications are Euclidean, affine and projective. Most work have considered the affine transformations group, which is a pretty good approximation when the object is far from the camera, since the slight distortion that may result from the more general projection can be regarded as part of a deformation.

Furthermore, the shape parametrization is chosen arbitrarily and would not be necessary the same for different views. Thus, an isotropic representation invariant to the geometric transformations group should be considered.

Many shape descriptors have been proposed in the literature and could be classified into two main classes : contour-based shape descriptors and region-based shape descriptors methods [14].

© Springer International Publishing Switzerland 2015
V. Murino and E. Puppo (Eds.): ICIAP 2015, Part II, LNCS 9280, pp. 494–505, 2015.
DOI: 10.1007/978-3-319-23234-8_46

Region-based descriptors are obtained from all the pixels within a shape. They include the angular radial transform (ART) descriptor [6], geometric moments [11], Zernike moments [12] and affine moment invariant [8], etc. In contour-based approach, planar shapes are generally assumed to have a piecewise smooth boundary that is represented by a bidimensional (2D) continuous contour.

Many contour-based descriptors have been proposed in the last decades [9]. Early work is based on the well-known Fourier descriptors (FD) which are derived from Fourier transform of shape signatures [5,13]. The main drawback of such descriptors is that Fourier transform does not provide local shape information. Hence, they are known to be inaccurate in the case of small contour variations and sensitive to the contour extraction method. Multi-scale theory based shape descriptors are considered as a good solution to deal with this drawback. Furthermore, these descriptors are more robust to noise since prevalent features are preserved across scales. Many multi-scale contour based descriptors have been developed in the literature [1–3]. The ISO/IEC MPEG-7 shape descriptor based on the curvature scale space (CSS) representation has been proposed in [1,2]. It is based on the multi scale space theory where the arc-length parametrized contour is convolved with increasing values of Gaussian kernel. The CSS image of each boundary is computed and then the maxima of the curvature zero-crossing are used as a shape descriptor for each object. This descriptor is very compact and quite robust with respect to noise, scale and orientation changes of objects. However, it fail to distinguish shallow concavity from deep concavity on the shape boundary. Furthermore, it is only robust to local variations and it is not robust in global sense. Many extensions of the proposed CSS descriptor have been developed in order to overcome its main drawbacks. In particular, MPEG-7 recommends combing the CSS descriptor with global shape descriptors such as eccentricity and circularity (CSS+). The triangle area representation (TAR) computes the areas of the triangles formed by the boundary points to measure the convexity/concavity of each point at different scales [4]. The area value of every triangle measures the curvature of corresponding contour point and the sign of the area indicates if a contour point is convex, concave or on a straight line. Unlike CSS descriptors, scale levels are obtained by considering different triangle side lengths.

In this work, we propose a new multi-scale planar contour based signature descriptor invariant to affine transformations. The proposed descriptor, is based on the Fourier Descriptors of a multi-scale shape signature from a progressive contour representation. In order to achieve representation isotropy, an affine arc-length based reparametrization is carried out [10].

The remainder of the paper is organized as follows. In Section 2, we briefly recall the affine arclength reparametrization method. The proposed descriptor, also called Fourier Descriptors of Affine invariant Progressive signature (*FD-APS*), is described in Section 3. Experimental results are reported in section 4. Finally, conclusions and future work are presented in Section 5.

2 Affine Arc-Length Reparametrization

In this work we focus on planar shapes represented by simple and closed 2D continuous parametric curve. A curve parametrization $\gamma(t)$ of a geometric curve Γ is an 1-periodic function of a continuous parameter t defined by:

$$\begin{aligned} \gamma : [0,1] &\longrightarrow \mathbb{R}^2 \\ t &\longmapsto \gamma(t) = [x(t), y(t)]^t. \end{aligned} \tag{1}$$

It's well known that a same parametric curve may have different parameterizations. The invariant-descriptors computed from two different parameterizations of the same geometric curve are generally different. This is due to parametrization dependance on transformations. One solution to this problem consist in performing a $\mathbb{G}$-invariant reparametrization of the curve where $\mathbb{G}$ is the geometric transformations group. A reparametrization of (t, γ), noted $(\widehat{t}, \gamma)$, is defined as follows :

$$\gamma(\tilde{t}) = \gamma(\tau(t)) = [x(\tau(t)), y(\tau(t))]^t, \ t \in [0,1]. \tag{2}$$

where τ is an increasing function defined on $[0,1]$.

Let (t_1, γ_1) and (t_2, γ_2) two parameterizations of a geometric curve Γ and its image by a geometric transformation g. After $\mathbb{G}$-invariant reparametrization, both curve parametrizations verify the following equation :

$$\gamma_2(\widehat{t}) = g(\gamma_1(\widehat{t} + t_0)), \ t_0 \in \mathbb{Z} \text{ et } g \in \mathcal{G}, \tag{3}$$

where t_0 is departure points difference between the contours.

In the case of affine transformations group, we carry out a reparametrization by the normalized affine arc-length defined as:

$$\bar{s}_a(t) = \frac{1}{L_a} \int_0^t (||\det(\gamma'(t), \gamma''(t))||)^{\frac{1}{3}} dt, \ t \in [0, T]. \tag{4}$$

where L_a is the curve affine length. In figure 1, an affine arc-length reparametrization of a contour and its image by an affine transformation is shown. It's important to notice that after affine arc-length parametrization, a point to point matching between a curve and its image under an affine transformation could be performed up to an overall shift due to different starting points.

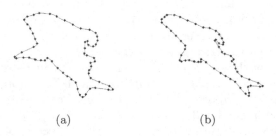

(a)   (b)

Fig. 1. Affine arc-length reparametrization of a contour (a) and its image by an affine transformation.

3 Fourier Descriptors of Affine Invariant Progressive Signature

Figure 2, shows the main steps performed to obtain the proposed descriptor, denoted *FD-APS*. First, the contour centroid is computed and translated to the origin. Then, an affine arc-length reparametrization is performed to meet parametrization invariance constraint. After, a progressive contour representation is defined and a multi-scale shape signature is generated. Finally, Fourier descriptors of the multi-scale signature are obtained.

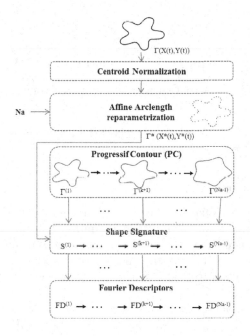

Fig. 2. Block diagram of *FD-APS* descriptor.

3.1 Progressive Contour

Let us consider the discrete parametric representation of a closed curve: $\Gamma = \{m_i = (x_i, y_i)\}_{i=1\cdots N_a}$ where N_a is a number of contour points after affine arclength reparametrization.

An initial contour can be transformed into a coarser contour Γ^N by applying a sequence of n successive elementary operations called *MiddleArc*. This former, replaces two consecutive points by their medium point:

$$MiddleArc(m_i, m_{i+1}) = \frac{m_i + m_{i+1}}{2}.$$

Thus, N contour resolutions $\{\Gamma^{(k)}\}_{k=1\cdots N}$ are generated as follows :

$$
\begin{cases}
\Gamma^{(0)} = \Gamma \\
\Gamma^{(k)} = \{MiddleArc(m_i^{(k-1)}, m_{i+1}^{(k-1)})\}_{i=1\cdots N_a-1} \bigcup , \\
\quad \{MiddleArc(m_{N_a}^{(k-1)}, m_1^{(k-1)})\}
\end{cases}
\tag{5}
$$

An example of contour resolutions is illustrated in figure 3. It's important to

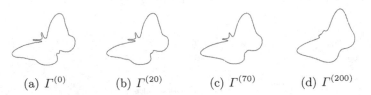

(a) $\Gamma^{(0)}$ (b) $\Gamma^{(20)}$ (c) $\Gamma^{(70)}$ (d) $\Gamma^{(200)}$

Fig. 3. A contour with different resolutions.

note that the *MiddleArc* operation preserves the affine transformation between two contours at different resolutions.

3.2   Shape Signature

Basically, our proposed signature is conceived around the linearity of triangular area under affine transform. A multi-scale approach is used to compute the area between the centroid point from the original contour and two given points from respectively original contour and the contour at scale k. By this definition, the signature is expected to preserve the affine invariance and strengthen its discrimination capability.

Therefore, the shape signature $S^{(k)}(t)$ of a given contour $\Gamma^{(k)}$ at resolution k is based on the area of triangles $T(k,t) = (m_t^{(0)} \ m_t^{(k)} \ G)$ where $m_t^{(0)} = (x^{(0)}(t), y^{(0)}(t))$ is a point of $\Gamma^{(0)}$, $m_t^{(k)} = (x^{(k)}(t), y^{(k)}(t))$ is a point of $\Gamma^{(k)}$ and G the centroid of the initial contour (see figure 4). It is given by the following equation:

$$
S^{(k)}(t) = \frac{|x^{(0)}(t)\, y^{(k)}(t) - y^{(0)}(t)\, x^{(k)}(t)|}{2}
\tag{6}
$$

where $x^{(k)}(t)$ and $y^{(k)}(t)$ are defined as:

$$
x^{(k)}(t) = \frac{1}{2^{(k)}} \sum_{i=0}^{k} \binom{k}{i} x^{(0)}(r_i)
$$

$$
y^{(k)}(t) = \frac{1}{2^{(k)}} \sum_{i=0}^{k} \binom{k}{i} y^{(0)}(r_i)
$$

Where $r_i = (t+i) \ Mod \ N_a \ and \ t = 0, \cdots, N_a - 1.$

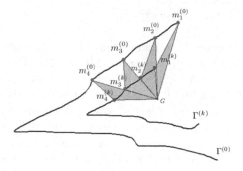

Fig. 4. Shape signature at a given scale.

3.3 Fourier Descriptors

The Fourier Descriptors are obtained by applying Fourier transform to the shape signature. The discrete Fourier transform of the signature $S^{(k)}(t)$ is given by:

$$a_n^{(k)} = \frac{1}{N_a} \sum_{t=0}^{N_a-1} S^{(k)}(t) \exp(\frac{-j2\pi nt}{N_a}), n = 0, \cdots, N_a - 1$$

The Fourier descriptors of the signature $S^{(k)}$ are derived from the Fourier coefficients $a_n^{(k)}$ as follows:

$$DF^{(k)} = DF^{(k)}(S^{(k)}) = \left\{ \frac{|a_n^{(k)}|}{|a_0^{(k)}|} \right\}_{n=1\cdots p}, \tag{7}$$

where p is the number of Fourier coefficients. Therefore, the proposed *FD-APS* descriptor is defined by $\{J_k\}_{k=1\cdots N}$:

$$\{J_k\}_{k=1\cdots N} = \{DF^{(k)}\}_{k=1\cdots N}, \tag{8}$$

where N is the number of scales. In this work, we consider N_a scales.

In order to prove the invariance property of the proposed descriptor, let us consider a contour Γ_1 and its image by an affine transformation Γ_2 characterized by its matrix A.

It's easy to verify that $S_2^{(k)}(t) = det(A) \, S^{(k)}(t)$ where $det(.)$ is the determinant. Hence, the affine transformation applied to a contour is mapped to a scaling between correspondent signatures. As the Fourier descriptor of the signature is invariant to scaling and starting point, the proposed descriptor is invariant to affine transformations and starting point.

The similarity measure used to compare two shape contours $\Gamma 1$ and $\Gamma 2$ can be formalized as follows:

$$d(\Gamma 1, \Gamma 2) = \frac{1}{N} \sum_{k=1}^{N} \frac{\|J1_k - J2_k\|_2}{\max(\|J1_k\|_2, \|J2_k\|_2)} \tag{9}$$

where N is the number of contour resolutions and $\|.\|_2$ is the L_2 norm.

4   Experimental Results

Our experimentations were conducted on two databases: MPEG-7 shape database and the Multiview Curve dataset (MCD) [15]. The MPEG-7 database consists of three parts, Set A and Set B. Set A has two parts, Set A1 and Set A2, each contain 420 shapes of 70 classes. Set A1 is for scale invariance and Set A2 is for rotation invariance. Set B has 1400 shapes classified into 70 classes. Set B is for similarity-based retrieval and shape descriptors robustness under various arbitrary shape distortions, that include rotation, scaling, arbitrary skew, stretching, defection, and indentation. The Multiview Curve dataset is composed of 40 shape classes taken from MPEG-7 database. Each class contains 14 curve samples that correspond to different perspective distortions of the original curve.this database is used to test shape descriptors under affine transformation. Samples of shapes from the MPEG-7 (set A and B) and MCD databases are shown in figures 5 and 6.

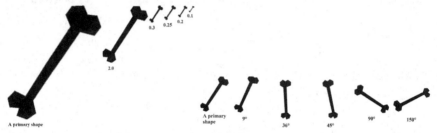

(a) MPEG-7 SetA1 (Scale: 0.1 to 2)   (b) MPEG-7 SetA2 (Rotation: 9 to 150)

Fig. 5. Samples of shapes from the MPEG-7 database (Set A1 and Set A2).

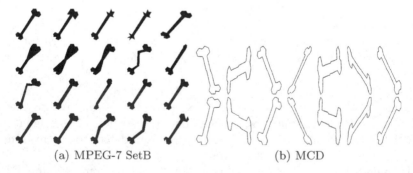

(a) MPEG-7 SetB   (b) MCD

Fig. 6. Samples of shapes from the MPEG-7 database (Set B) and MCD database.

To evalute the performance of shape descriptors techniques in terms of image retrieval efficiency, a precision-recall curve are the most commonly used measure. The precision is defined as the number of relevant shapes retrieved divided by the total number of shapes retrieved and the recall is defined as the number of relevant shapes retrieved divided by the total number of relevant shapes in the class (size of a class). The precision recall curve is plotted by averaging precision and recall over all database shapes.

In the case of rigid transformations, the proposed descriptor is compared with Fourier Descriptors (FD), Curvature Scale Space (CSS) and the Affine Invariant Fourier Descriptor (AIFD) [7] on the MPEG-7 Set A and MCD databases. The precision-recall curves of the above mentioned descriptors conducted respectively on MPEG-7 parts A1, A2 and MCD are respectively shown in the figures 7, 8 and 9. The results for MPEG-7 database part A, used to evaluate descriptors under scale and rotation invariance, show that our descriptor outperforms FD, CSS and AIFD descriptors.

Regarding robustness to arbitrary shape distortions described in the MPEG-7 database part B, a comparison with some commonly used descriptors is performed [9]. In particular, we consider the farthest points distance (FPD), radius

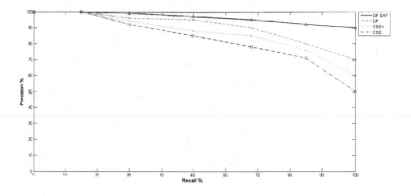

Fig. 7. Average precision and recall of retrieval on Set A1

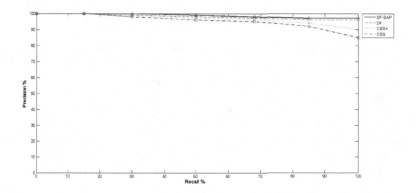

Fig. 8. Average precision and recall of retrieval on Set A2

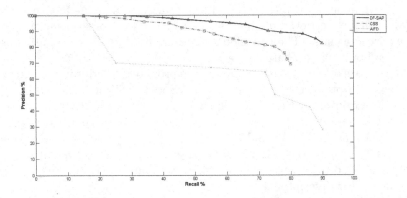

Fig. 9. Average precision and recall of retrieval on MCD

distance (RD), triangle centroid area (TCA), complex coordinates (CC), polar coordinates (PC), angular radial coordinates (ARC), triangular area representation (TAR) [4], chord length distance (CLD) and angular function (AF).

Table 1 shows the average retrieval precision scores for low and high recalls for the proposed descriptor and above mentioned descriptors from literature. The results of the other descriptors are reported from [9]. The average retrieval precision of our descriptor is respectively 78.69 and 44.46 for low and high recall rates and is higher than that in the other methods. Figures 10 and 11, show respectively the retrieval results of 10 random queries from MPEG-7 part B and MCD databases based on our proposed descriptor. It's easy to notice that the proposed descriptor performs better on the MCD database than on the MPEG-7 part B database. In fact, this is due to the theoretical invariance property of our

Table 1. The average precision for low and high recalls for the DF-SAP descriptor and other signatures using MPEG-7 database setB.

Signature	Low Recall The average precision for recall rate <= 50 %	High Recall The average precision for recall rate >= 50%
DF-SAP	78.69	44.46
FPD	75.82	42.13
RD	75.69	41.77
TCA	73.4	38.5
CC	64.76	22.59
PC	64.4	35.12
ARC	58.93	26.83
TAR	58.7	23.54
CLD	57.8	24.00
AF	57.39	27.88

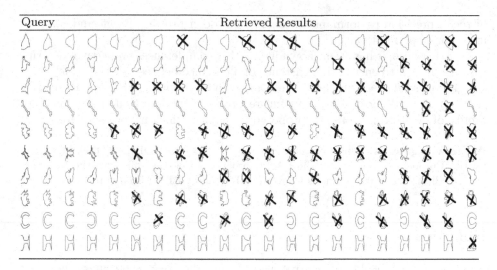

Fig. 10. 10 random retrieval results from MPEG-7 SetB database.

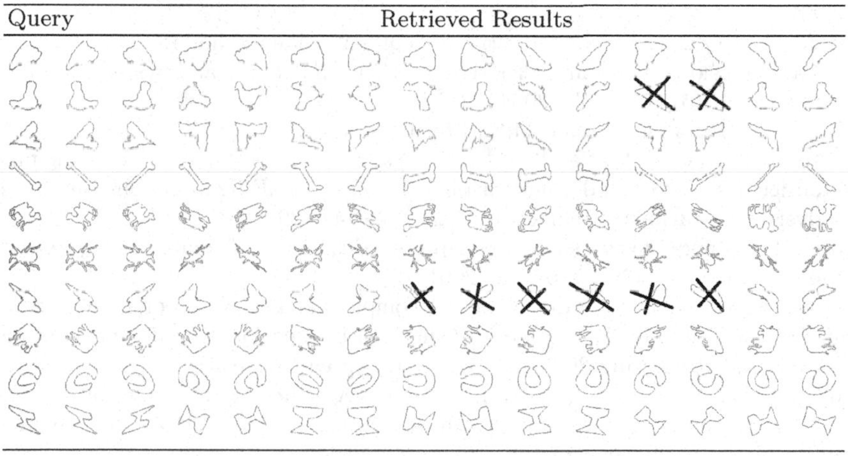

Fig. 11. 10 random retrieval results from MCD database.

descriptor under affine transformations. Furthermore, multi-scale used approach makes our descriptor robust to small distortions.

5   Conclusion

In this paper, a novel multi-scale and affine shape descriptor is proposed. The performance of this descriptor is evaluated using the MPEG-7 and MCD database and compared with other shape descriptors. Results show that in terms of recall-precision performance measures, our descriptor is efficient and competitive for shape retrieval.

Furthermore, it has been shown in [10] that completeness property of descriptors is required to ensure the existence of a distance between shapes which have a right physical mean. In fact, the completeness property allows us to recover shape from its descriptors. In our future work, we will aim to derive a complete family of descriptors from the proposed descriptor which is not complete.

Acknowledgments. This work is carried out as part of a MOBIDOC thesis financed by the European Union under the PASRI program in partnership with the Research and Studies Telecommunications Center (CERT) and CRISTAL laboratory.

References

1. Abbasi, S., Mokhtarian, F., Kittler, J.: Curvature scale space image in shape similarity retrieval. Multimedia Syst. **7**(6), 467–476 (1999)
2. Abbasi, S., Mokhtarian, F., Kittler, J.: Enhancing css-based shape retrieval for objects with shallow concavities. Image and Vision Computing **18**(3), 199–211 (2000)
3. Adamek, T., O'Connor, N.: A multiscale representation method for nonrigid shapes with a single closed contour. IEEE Transactions on Circuits and Systems for Video Technology **14**(5), 742–753 (2004)
4. Alajlan, N., Rube, I., Kamel, M.S., Freeman, G
5. Bartolini, I., Ciaccia, P., Patella, M.: Warp: accurate retrieval of shapes using phase of fourier descriptors and time warping distance. IEEE Transactions on Pattern Analysis and Machine Intelligence **27**(1), 142–147 (2005)
6. Bober, M.: Mpeg-7 visual shape descriptors. IEEE Trans. Circuits and Systems for Video Technology **11**(6), 716–719 (2001)
7. Chaker, F., Bannour, M., Ghorbel, F.: A complete and stable set of affine-invariant fourier descriptors. In: Proceedings of the 12th International Conference on Image Analysis and Processing 2003, pp. 578–581, September 2003
8. Chong, C.W., Raveendran, P., Mukundan, R.: An efficient algorithm for fast computation of pseudo-zernike moments. International Journal of Pattern Recognition and Artificial Intelligence **17**(06), 1011–1023 (2003)
9. El-ghazal, A., Basir, O., Belkasim, S.: Farthest point distance: A new shape signature for fourier descriptors. Signal Processing: Image Communication **24**(7), 572–586 (2009)
10. Ghorbel, F.: Towards a unitary formulation for invariant images description; application to images coding. Annales des télécommunications **53**(5,6), 242–260 (1998)
11. Hu, M.K.: Visual pattern recognition by moment invariants. IRE Transactions on Information Theory **8**(2), 179–187 (1962)
12. Lin, T.W., Chou, Y.F.: A comparative study of zernike moments. In: Proceedings of the IEEE/WIC International Conference on Web Intelligence WI 2003, pp. 516–519, October 2003

13. Zhang, D., Lu, G.: A comparative study of fourier descriptors for shape representation and retrieval. In: Proceedings of the Fifth Asian Conference on Computer Vision (ACCV02), pp. 646–651. Melbourne, Australia, January 2002
14. Zhang, D., Lu, G.: Review of shape representation and description techniques. Pattern Recognition **37**(1), 1–19 (2004)
15. Zuliani, M., Kenney, C., Bhagavathy, S., Manjunath, B.S.: Drums and curve descriptors. In: In British Machine Vision Conference (2004)

Image Manipulation on Facebook
for Forensics Evidence

Marco Moltisanti[1][(✉)], Antonino Paratore[1], Sebastiano Battiato[1],
and Luigi Saravo[2]

[1] Image Processing Laboratory – Dipartimento di Matematica e Informatica,
Università degli Studi di Catania, Catania, Italy
{moltisanti,battiato,battiato@dmi.unict.it}@dmi.unict.it
[2] Arma dei Carabinieri – Reparto Investigazioni Scientifiche, Naples, Italy

Abstract. The growth of popularity of Social Network Services (SNSs)
opened new perspectives in many research fields, including the emerging
area of Multimedia Forensics. In particular, the huge amount of images
uploaded to the social networks can represent a significant source of evidence for investigations, if properly processed. This work aims to exploit
the algorithms and techniques behind the uploading process of a picture
on Facebook, in order to find out if any of the involved steps (resizing,
compression, renaming, etc.) leaves a trail on the picture itself, so to infer
proper hypotheses about the authenticity and other forensic aspects of
the pipeline.

1 Introduction

One of the most common problems in the image forensics field is the reconstruction of the history of an image or a video [3]. The data related to the
characteristics of the camera that carried out the shooting, together with the
reconstruction of the (possible) further processing, allow us to have some useful
hints about the originality of the visual document under analysis. For example, if
an image has been subjected to more than one JPEG compression, we can state
that the considered image is not the exact bitstream generated by the camera
at the time of shooting. In a digital investigation that includes JPEG images
(the most widely used format on the network [4] and employed by most of cameras [1], [5]) as evidences, the classes of problems that we have to deal with, are
essentially related to the authenticity of the visual document under analysis and
to the retrieval of the device that generated the image under analysis. About the
possibility to discover image manipulations in JPEG images, many approaches
can be found in literature, as summarized in [6] and [7]. A first group of works
(JPEG blocking artifacts analysis [8], [9], hash functions [10], JPEG headers
analysis [5], thumbnails analysis [11], Exif analysis [12], etc.) proposes methods
that seek the traces of the forgeries in the structure of the image or in its meta-
data. In [13] some methods based on PRNU (Photo Response Non-Uniformity)
are exposed and tested. This kind of pattern characterizes, and allows to distinguish, every single camera sensor. Other approaches, as described in [14] and

V. Murino and E. Puppo (Eds.): ICIAP 2015, Part II, LNCS 9280, pp. 506–517, 2015.
DOI: 10.1007/978-3-319-23234-8_47

[15], [16] take care of analyzing the statistical distribution of the values assumed by the DCT coefficients. The explosion in the usage of Social Network Services (SNSs) enlarges the variability of such data and presents new scenarios and challenges.

The remainder of this paper is structured as follows: in Sec. 2 we present two possible scenarios where the information retrieved in this study can be applied. In Sec. 3 we explain the methodology used to build a coherent dataset and run the experiments. In Sec. 4 we analyze some aspects affected by the manipulation operated by the selected social network, and specifically the resizing algorithm, the variability of the Bits Per Pixels (BPP) and Compression Ratios (CR) on the images exposed to the uploading process. In Subsec. 4.3 we consider the quantization tables used to operate the compression and in Subsec. 4.4 the metadata manipulation is presented. Finally, in Sec. 5 we discuss our conclusions and talk about the possible future works on this subject.

2   Motivation and Scenarios

Investigators nowadays make extensive use of social networks activities in order to solve crimes[1][2]. A typical case involves the need to identify a subject: in such a scenario, the information provided by the naming conventions of Facebook[3], jointly with the possible availability of devices, can help the investigators in order to confirm the identity of a suspect person. More about Social Network Forensic can be read in [18]. Another interesting scenario consider the detection of possible forgeries, in order to prove the authenticity of a picture. Kee and Farid in [5] propose to model the parameters used in the creation of the JPEG thumbnail[4] in order to estimate possible forgeries, while Battiato *et al.* in [10] use a voting approach for the same purpose. For this task, the information inferred from this study can provide some priors to exclude or enforce such hypotheses.

Our analysis will focus on Facebook, because its pervasive diffusion[5] makes it the most obvious place to start for such a study.

3   Dataset

As previously stated, we refer in this phase to the Facebook environment, taking into account capabilities, data and related mobile applications available during the experimental phase.

---

[1] http://edition.cnn.com/2012/08/30/tech/social-media/
  fighting-crime-social-media/
[2] http://www.usatoday.com/story/news/nation/2015/03/20/
  facebook-cracks-murder-suspect/25069899/
[3] http://facebook.com
[4] http://www.w3.org/Graphics/JPEG/
[5] http://newsroom.fb.com/company-info/

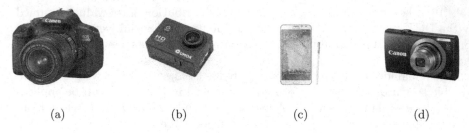

(a)   (b)   (c)   (d)

Fig. 1. The cameras used to build the dataset

In order to exploit how Facebook manages the images uploaded by the users, we decided to build a dataset, introducing three types of variability: the acquisition device, the input quality (in terms of resolution and compression rate) and the kind of scene depicted. Specifically we used the following imaging devices (see Fig. 1), which are respectively a reflex camera, a wearable camera, a camera-equipped phone and a compact camera:

- Canon EOS 650D with 18-55 mm interchangeable lens - Fig. 1a;
- QUMOX SJ-4000 - Fig. 1b;
- Samsung Galaxy Note 3 Neo - Fig. 1c;
- Canon Powershot A2300 - Fig. 1d.

The considered scenes are 3 (i.e. indoor, natural outdoor, artificial outdoor); for each scene we choose 10 frames, keeping the same point of view when changing the camera. Moreover, we took each frame 2 times, changing the camera resolution (see Fig. 1). The whole dataset is composed by 240 pictures.

Table 1. Resolution settings for the different devices (in pixels)

Camera	Low Resolution (LR)	High Resolution (HR)
Canon EOS 650D	720 × 480	5184 × 3456
QUMOX SJ4000	640 × 480	4032 × 3024
Samsung Galaxy Note 3 Neo	640 × 480	3264 × 2448
Canon Powershot A2300	640 × 480	4608 × 3456

Facebook actually provides two uploading options: the user can choose between low quality (LQ) and high quality (HQ). We uploaded each picture twice, using both options, and subsequently we downloaded them.

The whole dataset with both original pictures and their downloaded versions is available at http://iplab.dmi.unict.it/UNICT-SNIM/index.html. A subset is shown in Fig. 2.

4   Social Network Image Analysis

4.1   Facebook Resizing Algorithm

Our first evaluation focus on if and how Facebook rescales the uploaded images. We implemented a tool to ease the upload/download process of the images. The

Fig. 2. Column 1: indoor, column 2: outdoor artificial, column 3: outdoor natural. Row 1: Canon EOS 650D, Row 2: QUMOX SJ4000, Row 3: Samsung Galaxy Note 3 Neo, Row 4: Canon Powershot A2300

different resolutions, related to the devices, are shown in Tab. 1. Performing a fine-grained tuning using synthetic images, we found out that the resizing algorithm is driven by the length in pixels of the longest side of the uploaded image coupled with the high quality option (on/off).

Figure 3 report the overall flow of the resizing pipeline. Let I be a picture of size $M \times N$. If $max\,(M, N) \leq 960$, I will not be resized; if $960 \leq max\,(M, N) \leq 2048$ and the user selected the HQ upload option, I will not be resized; if the user did not select the HQ option, then I will be scaled in such a way that the resulting image I' will have its longest side equal to $max\,(M', N') = 960$ pixels. If $max\,(M, N) > 2048$ Facebook scales I both in the case the HQ option is switched on or not. In the first case, the scaled image I' will have its longest side equal to 2048 pixels; in the second case, the longest side will be scaled down to 960 pixels.

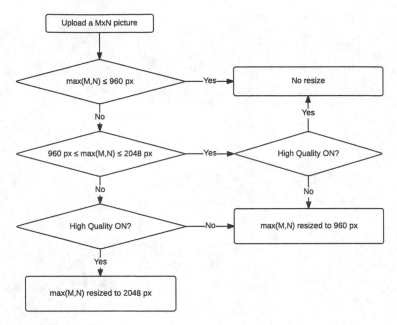

Fig. 3. Workflow of Facebook resizing algorithm for JPEG images

Naming of the Files. Facebook renames the image files after the upload. Nevertheless, it is still interesting to do a brief analysis on how this renaming is performed, in order to discover patterns in the name of the file and potential relationships among the different elements involved in the upload process: the user, the image itself, the options.

We found that the generated name is composed by three numeric parts: the first e and the third ones are random generated IDs, while the second part corresponds to the photo ID (see Fig. 4).

$$\underbrace{10996172}_{\text{Random}}\_\underbrace{745317175583308}_{\text{Photo ID}}\_\underbrace{271105793478350229}_{\text{Random}}\_(n|o)].jpg$$

Fig. 4. The filename generated for an uploaded picture

The photo ID can be used to retrieve several information about the picture, using for instance the Facebook OpenGraph tool[6]. Just using a common browser and concatenating the photo ID to the OpenGraph URL, it is possible to discover:

- The direct links to the picture;
- The description of the picture;
- The URL of the server where the picture is hosted;
- The date and time of the creation;

---

[6] http://graph.facebook.com

- The date and time of last modification;
- The name and the ID of the user (both personal profile or page) who posted the photo;
- The name(s) and ID(s) of the user(s) tagged in the picture;
- Likes and comments (if any).

Moreover, OpenGraph shows the locations of all the copies at different resolutions of the picture, created by Facebook algorithms to be used as thumbnails to optimize the loading time.

It is also interesting to note that the resizing algorithm adds a suffix to the name of the file, depending on the original dimensions and on the upload quality option. Specifically, if the dimensions are beyond the thresholds set in the resizing algorithm and the high quality option is selected, the suffix "_o" will be added; otherwise the added suffix will be "_n".

4.2 Quantitative Measures

In this Section, we show how the processing done after the upload modify the Bits Per Pixel and the Compression Ratio for the images in the dataset. BPP are calculated as the ratio between the number of bits divided by the number of pixels (Eq. 1); CR, instead, is computed as the number of bits in the final image divided by the number of bits in the original image (Eq. 2). It is possible to compute the CR of a single image simply considering the uncompressed 24-bit RGB bitmap version.

$$BPP = \frac{\text{\# bits in the final image}}{\text{\# pixels}} \tag{1}$$

$$CR = \frac{\text{\# bits in the final image}}{\text{\# bit in the original image}} \tag{2}$$

Eq. 3 is a trivial proof that BPP and CR are proportional.

$$BPP \cdot \text{\# pixels} = CR \cdot \text{\# bits in the original image} =$$
$$= \text{\# bits in the final image}$$
$$BPP = CR \cdot \frac{\text{\# bits in the original image}}{\text{\# pixels}} \tag{3}$$

The charts in Fig. 5 report the average BPPs for the images, grouped by scene, which have been taken with the same camera, distinguished depending on the acquisition resolution. Since BPP and Compression Rate are proportional, we refer the reader to the supplementary material [7] for the charts related to CR.

In Fig. 6 and 7 we reported the relation of the number of pixels respectively with the BPP and the Quality Factor (QF) as estimated by JPEG Snoop[8].

---

[7] http://iplab.dmi.unict.it/UNICT-SNIM/index.html
[8] http://www.impulseadventure.com/photo/jpeg-snoop.html

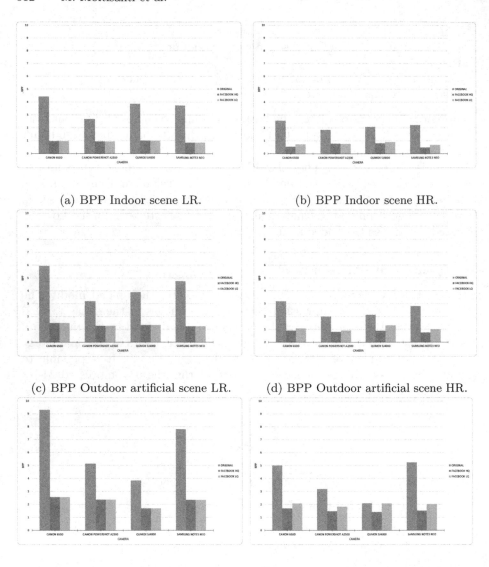

(a) BPP Indoor scene LR.

(b) BPP Indoor scene HR.

(c) BPP Outdoor artificial scene LR.

(d) BPP Outdoor artificial scene HR.

(e) BPP Outdoor natural scene LR.

(f) BPP Outdoor natural scene HR.

Fig. 5. BPP comparison with respect to scene and original resolution

Observing the graph in Fig. 6, it emerges a relation of inverse proportionality between the number of pixels and the maximum BPP; this would support the hypothesis of a maximum allowed size for the uploaded images.

A more interesting observation can be deducted from Fig. 7: trivially, we observe the same six vertical lines corresponding to the different sizes of the images, but all the points are vertically distributed in 17 discrete positions, corresponding to the quality factors reported in Tab. 2. Thus, we suppose there

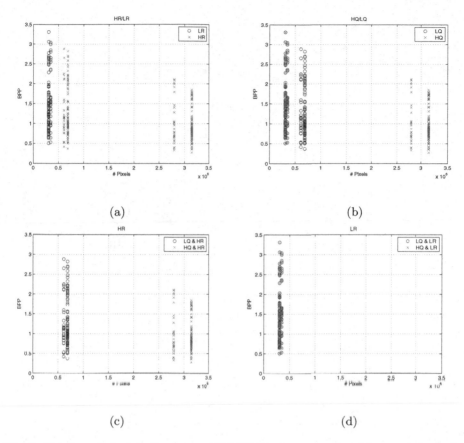

Fig. 6. Number of pixels in the images VS BPP. 6a: images grouped by input resolution (HR/LR); 6b: images group by upload quality (HQ/LQ); 6c: HR input images grouped by upload quality; 6d: LR input images grouped by upload quality.

should be 17 different Quantization Table used in the upload process of the pictures belonging to the proposed dataset. A further discussion about the quantization tables follows in Subsec. 4.3.

4.3   Quantization Tables

The images considered in our dataset are all in JPEG format, both the original versions and the downloaded ones. Thus, we want to find out how the JPEG compression affects the pictures, focusing on the Discrete Quantization tables used for that purpose. In fact, the Discrete Quantization Tables (DQT) can, in some way, certify that an image has been processed by some specific tool ([5]). We extracted the tables using JPEGSnoop. In Tab. 3 we report the DQTs for Luminance and Chrominance relative to the lowest and the highest quality factor.

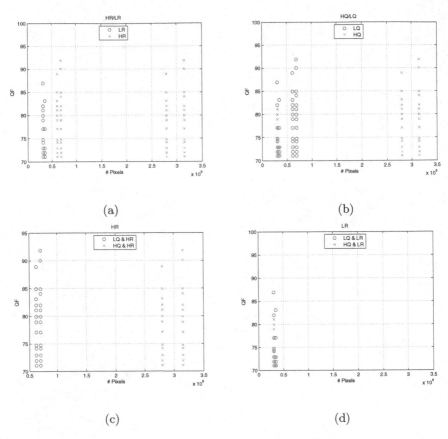

Fig. 7. Number of pixels in the images VS Quality Factor. 7a: images grouped by input resolution (HR/LR); 7b: images group by upload quality (HQ/LQ); 7c: HR input images grouped by upload quality; 7d: LR input images grouped by upload quality

Moreover, we performed the same operation on some pictures belonging to the authors that were uploaded previously, to check if the tables changed over the years.

Together with this paper, we provide some supplementary material where we reported all the charts related to BPP and CR, and the complete description of the statics computed over each image in the dataset.

4.4   Metadata

Among others, Exif data[17] contain some additional information about the picture, such as camera settings, date, time and generic descriptions. Moreover, a thumbnail of the picture is included. These kind of data has been used for forensic purposes, because it can provide evidences of possible forgeries (e.g. the thumbnail is different from the actual photo). Often, if the camera is equipped

Table 2. Quality Factors of the JPEG Compression applied by Facebook (estimated by JPEG Snoop)

Quality Factor			
1	71.07	10	81.99
2	71.93	11	83.11
3	72.91	12	84.06
4	74.16	13	84.93
5	74.75	14	86.93
6	77.09	15	88.93
7	78.93	16	90.06
8	79.94	17	91.86
9	81.09			

Table 3. DQTs for minimum and maximum QF

DQT Luminance	DQT Chrominance
9 6 6 9 14 23 30 35	10 10 14 27 57 57 57 57
7 7 8 11 15 34 35 32	10 12 15 38 57 57 57 57
8 8 9 14 23 33 40 32	14 15 32 57 57 57 57 57
8 10 13 17 30 50 46 36	27 38 57 57 57 57 57 57
10 13 21 32 39 63 60 45	57 57 57 57 57 57 57 57
14 20 32 37 47 60 66 53	57 57 57 57 57 57 57 57
28 37 45 50 60 70 70 59	57 57 57 57 57 57 57 57
42 53 55 57 65 58 60 57	57 57 57 57 57 57 57 57

(a) DQT corresponding to QF = 71.07

DQT Luminance	DQT Chrominance
3 2 2 3 4 6 8 10	3 3 4 8 16 16 16 16
2 2 2 3 4 9 10 9	3 3 4 11 16 16 16 16
2 2 3 4 6 9 11 9	4 4 9 16 16 16 16 16
2 3 4 5 8 14 13 10	8 11 16 16 16 16 16 16
3 4 6 9 11 17 16 12	16 16 16 16 16 16 16 16
4 6 9 10 13 17 18 15	16 16 16 16 16 16 16 16
8 10 12 14 16 19 19 16	16 16 16 16 16 16 16 16
12 15 15 16 18 16 16 16	16 16 16 16 16 16 16 16

(b) DQT corresponding to QF = 91.86

with a geo-tagging system, it is possible to find the GPS coordinates of the location where the photo has been captured.

Using JPEGSnoop, we extracted the Exif data from the downloaded images, and we found that Facebook completely removes them. Since no specification is available, our best guess is that, since removing the Exif data reduces the size in byte of the image, this procedure allows to save space on the storing servers, given the huge amount of pictures uploaded in the social network.

5 Conclusions

In this paper we introduced two different scenarios useful to infer forensic evidence starting from images publicly available on the most common social network platforms. We claim that, in almost all cases, knowing the involved processing acted during the uploading phase, is possible to infer evidence with respect to authentication and integrity of multimedia data.

Among others, we collected information about resolution and compression changes (quantization tables, metadata, compression ratio) applied to the uploaded image with respect to the input one.

Future works will be devoted to analyze the robustness of such changes with respect to the overall quality of the picture (recent versions of the Facebook mobile app allow to enhance the quality, in some way) and respect to the overall robustness of methods based on PRNU analysis.

Moreover, we plan to extend the involved study to other social networking platforms, such as Twitter, Instagram, Google+, considering also different kind of data (e.g. audio, video).

References

1. Battiato, S., Moltisanti, M.: The future of consumer cameras. In: Proceedings of the SPIE Elecronic Imaging, Image Processing: Algorithms and Systems XIII, PANORAMA special session, San Francisco, California, USA, February 8–12 (2015)
2. Jang, Y. J., Kwak., J.: Digital forensics investigation methodology applicable for social network services. Multimedia Tools and Applications, 1–12 (2014)
3. Oliveira, A., Ferrara, P., De Rosa, A., Piva, A., Barni, M., Goldenstein, S., Dias, Z., Rocha, A.: Multiple parenting identification in image phylogeny. In: IEEE International Conference on Image Processing (ICIP), pp. 5347–5351 (2014)
4. Usage of Image File Formats for Websites. http://w3techs.com/technologies/overview/image_format/all
5. Kee, E., Johnson, M.K., Farid, H.: Digital image authentication from JPEG headers. IEEE Transactions on Information Forensics and Security 6(3), 1066–1075 (2011)
6. Piva, A.: An overview on image forensics. Proceedings of ISRN Signal Process., p. 496701 (2013)
7. Stamm, M.C., Wu, M., Liu, K.J.R.: Information forensics: An overview of the first decade. IEEE Access 1, 167–200 (2013)
8. Bruna, A.R., Messina, G., Battiato, S.: Crop Detection through Blocking Artefacts Analysis. In: Maino, G., Foresti, G.L. (eds.) ICIAP 2011, Part I. LNCS, vol. 6978, pp. 650–659. Springer, Heidelberg (2011)
9. Luo, W., Qu, Z., Huang, J., Qiu G.: A novel method for detecting cropped and recompressed image block. In: Proceedings of IEEE International Conference on Acoustic, Speech and Signal Processing (ICASSP), vol. 2, pp. II217–II220 (2007)
10. Battiato, S., Farinella, G.M., Messina, E., Puglisi, G.: Robust image alignment for tampering detection. IEEE Transactions on Information Forensics and Security 7(4), 1105–1117 (2012)
11. Kee, E., Farid, H.: Digital image authentication from thumbnails. In: Proceedings of SPIE, vol. 7541 (January 2010)
12. Gloe, T.: Forensic analysis of ordered data structures on the example of JPEG files. In: Proceedings of IEEE International Workshop on Information Forensics and Security (WIFS), pp. 139–144 (2012)
13. Chen, Y., Thing, V.L.L.: A study on the photo response nonuniformity noise pattern based image forensics in real-world applications. In: Proceedings of IEEE International Conference on Image Processing, Computer Vision, Pattern Recognit. (IPCV) (July 2012)
14. Battiato, S., Messina G.: Digital forgery estimation into DCT domain: A critical analysis. In: Proceedings of ACM Workshop on Multimedia Forensics (MiFor), pp. 37–42 (2009)
15. Redi, J.A., Taktak, W., Dugelay, J.L.: Digital image forensics: A booklet for beginners. Multimedia Tools and Applications 51(1), 133–162 (2011)
16. Galvan, F., Puglisi, G., Bruna, A.R., Battiato, S.: First Quantization Matrix Estimation From Double Compressed JPEG Images. IEEE Transactions on Information Forensics and Security 9(8), 1299–1310 (2014)

17. Camera & Imaging Products Association: Standardization Committee - Exchangeable image file format for digital still cameras: Exif Version 2.3. http://www.cipa.jp/std/documents/e/DC-008-2012_E_C.pdf
18. Pratama, S.F., Pratiwi, L., Abraham, A., Muda, A.K.: Computational Intelligence in Digital Forensics. In: Muda, A.K., Choo, Y.-H., Abraham, A., N. Srihari, S. (eds.) Computational Intelligence in Digital Forensics. SCI, vol. 555, pp. 1–16. Springer, Heidelberg (2014)

Improved Performance in Facial Expression Recognition Using 32 Geometric Features

Giuseppe Palestra[1]([✉]), Adriana Pettinicchio[2], Marco Del Coco[2],
Pierluigi Carcagnì[2], Marco Leo[2], and Cosimo Distante[2]

[1] Department of Computer Science, University of Bari, Bari, Italy
giuseppe.palestra@gmail.com
[2] National Institute of Optics, National Research Council, Arnesano, LE, Italy

Abstract. Automatic facial expression recognition is one of the most interesting problem as it impacts on important applications in human-computer interaction area. Many applications in this field require real-time performance but not all the approach are suitable to satisfy this requirement. Geometrical features are usually the most light in terms of computational load but sometimes they exploits a huge number of features and do not cover all the possible geometrical aspect. In order to face up this problem, we propose an automatic pipeline for facial expression recognition that exploits a new set of 32 geometric facial features from a single face side covering a wide set of geometrical peculiarities. As a results, the proposed approach showed a facial expression recognition accuracy of 95,46% with a six-class expression set and an accuracy of 94,24% with a seven-class expression set.

Keywords: Facial expression recognition · Human-computer interaction · Geometric features · Random forest

1 Introduction

In communication and interaction between people, facial expression become essential for immediate transmission of emotion and social intentions. During the last decades, the field of facial expression has received growing interest from research community because of the rapidly development in computer technologies.

An automatic system for Facial Expression Recognition (FER) should be able to recognize the six basic face expression defined in by Facial Action Coding System (FACS) developed by Ekman and Friesen [2], that probably represents the most spread study on facial activity.

This kind of system usually consists of three basic modules as presented in many surveys such as [1]: Face Detection, Features Extraction, Facial Expression Classification.

Face Detection is a two-class problem related to the presence or not of the face in the shown image [17]. Several recent works, in this field, make use of the well known Viola-Jones face detector [3], a quite generic and widely spread

© Springer International Publishing Switzerland 2015
V. Murino and E. Puppo (Eds.): ICIAP 2015, Part II, LNCS 9280, pp. 518–528, 2015.
DOI: 10.1007/978-3-319-23234-8_48

algorithm that minimizes computational time while achieving high detection accuracy.

Feature Extraction represents the most important phase in the procedural pipeline as it is able to influence the whole accuracy of the system because of the fact that facial features allowed us to identify and describe the different parts of the face, such facial contour, eyebrows, eyes, nose and mouth .

Basically, there are two types of features: appearance and geometrical features. Appearance features concern skin features, fold and wrinkles whereas geometrical features are obtained from landmarks of the face (eyes, eyebrows, mouth, nose, cheeks, lips and chin).

Appearance methods are exploited in many works in recent years. For instance a Local Binary Pattern descriptor is used by Zhao et al. in [10] and Zhao, G. et. al. [11]. In [12] Jabid et al. chose to work with local directional pattern features (LDPA). Anyway appearance based methods involves a huge amount of data and could be too complex for a real time features extraction. In order to reduce the features extraction complexity some works have been oriented to the use of hybrid models defined from geometrical and appearance features, such as in [16]. Even so, noise issue introduced by the combination of the two approaches could lead to a non satisfying recognition accuracy.

On the other hand geometrical methods are characterized by low computational complexity and good accuracy. In [9] the authors propose a set of 125 geometrical features to perform the classification on facial expression. Geometrical features in association with Neural Network on an image sequence are exploited by [14]. Active Shape Model (ASM) was used to define many approaches to facial expression recognition: in Bevilacqua et al. [5], polygonal features were used, in particular, the areas of five polygons was calculated whereas in Loconsole et al. [4], linear and eccentricity features using facial landmarks and differential features were considered, the latter were defined by subtraction neutral expression features from one the six primary expression features.

Anyway, to the best of our knowledge, a combination of linear, eccentricity, polygonal and slope features was not yet used.

In this paper we propose an innovative and automatic pipeline aided to recognize facial expression from a static image exploiting the combination of features derived by geometrical information. In particular the joint use of linear eccentricity, polygonal and angular features has been adopted in order to improve the recognizing accuracy respect the most recent works. As a first step the face is detected and 20 facial landmarks are automatically extracted by means of the automatic facial keypoints extractor proposed in [7]. Successively the detected landmarks are processed in order to construct a set of 32 geometrical facial features based on linear, eccentricity, polygonal and angular information. Successively the set of features is given as input to the classifier that supplies the predicted facial expression.

Moreover we also focused attention on the classification stem by analyzing the performance with three different methods usually adopted for this task. More specifically performances with Support Vector Machines (SVM's), Random Forest and k-Nearest Neighbours (k-NN) have been tested. All the experiments were performed on the Extended Cohn-Kanade (CK+) facial expression database [8].

The rest of the paper is organized as follows: Section 2 deeply describes the proposed methodology; Section 3 is aimed to build a suitable testing dataset and to find the best configuration for the proposed pipeline; Section 4 reports the experimental results of the presented approach on both static images and video sequences and, finally, Section 5 gives conclusions and introduces future works.

2   Proposed Metodology

This section is aimed to present a detailed description of the pipeline proposed for FER classification and reported in Figure 1. As a first step an algorithm oriented to the *face detection* is applied and then a *facial landmarks extraction* module is applied. Once the facial landmarks are available they are given as input to the *geometrical feature computation* step that computes 32 geometrical features; finally the computed features are analyzed by a *classification* module in order to get a prediction of the facial expression. In the followings each step is further detailed.

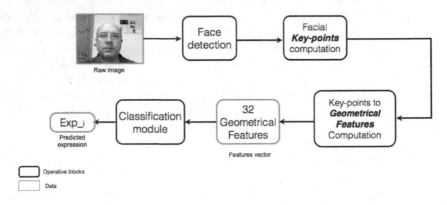

Fig. 1. Proposed pipeline: the face is detected and then facial key-points are extracted and used to compute the 32 geometrical features. Finally the vector of features is sent to the classification module.

Face detection and facial landmarks extraction are the first steps. Face detection is achieved by a Viola-Jones based face detector [3]. The detected face is then processed with a facial landmarks extractor exploiting the STaked Active Shape Model (STASM) approach. STASM uses Active Shape Model for locating 77 facial landmarks with a simplified form of SIFT descriptors and it operates with Multivariate Adaptive Regression Splines (MARS) for descriptor matching. This modified ASM is fast and it has been proved to perform better than existing techniques for automatic face landmarking on frontal faces [7].

32 geometrical features are then computed. More specifically, considering the study of Ekman et al. [2], an accurate observation of facial expression and landmark points extracted from STASM, a set of 32 features, useful to recognize facial expressions, has been defined.

In order to reduce the whole computational costs a face symmetry with respect the vertical axis passing through the center of the face has been assumed and 20 STASM landmarks have been used. More specifically, for the upper part of the face, that involves features related to eyebrows, eyes and cheeks, just one side has been considered (the left side). On the other hand, for the lower part of the face, features related to nose and mouth have been chosen involving both face sides.

The proposed features are shown in the Figure 2) and detailed in the followings. *Linear features* are defined by the Euclidean distance between 2 points. More precisely 15 linear features are used in the proposed approach:

- 3 for left eyebrow,
- 2 for left eye
- 1 for cheeks;
- 1 for nose
- 8 for mouth.

Polygonal features are determined by the area of irregular polygons constructed on three or more facial landmark points. This area is computed by the Gauss equation:

$$A = \frac{1}{2} \cdot \left| \sum_{i=1}^{n} (x_i \cdot y_{i+1} - x_{i+1} \cdot y_i) \right| \tag{1}$$

where x_i and y_i are the Cartesian coordinates of the i-th facial landmark point and n represents the number of sides of the polygon. In this case 3 polygonal features have been defined:

- 1 for the left eye;
- 1 between corners of left eye and left corner of mouth;
- 1 for mouth.

Elliptical features are defined by the major and minor ellipse axes ratio. In particular, 7 ellipses among landmarks point are chosen.

- 1 for left eyebrow;
- 3 for the left eye: eye, upper and lower eyelids;
- 3 for mouth: upper and lower lips.

Slope features are defined by the slope (m) of the line joining two facial points a and b .

$$m = \frac{y_b - y_a}{x^a - y_a} \tag{2}$$

More specifically the slope features are used in order to define 7 of the proposed features

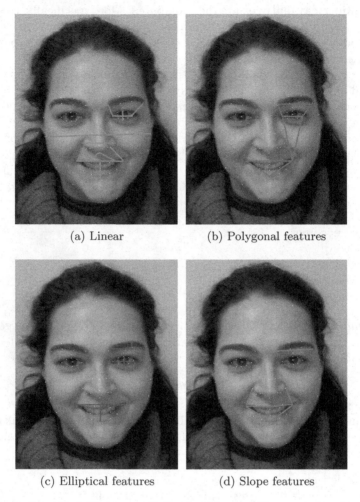

(a) Linear   (b) Polygonal features

(c) Elliptical features   (d) Slope features

Fig. 2. Geometrical Facial Features of left side of the face. Features related to eyebrows, eye and cheeks, only one side involves just the left side of the face.

- 1 for left eyebrow;
- 6 for mouth corners.

Classification module is the last step that analyzes the features vector in order to get a prediction in terms of facial expression. In recent years a huge amount of possible classifiers has been proposed. However every classifier shows variable performance depending on the peculiarities of the input data. In this work a new set of features has been proposed introducing an uncertainty about the best way to perform the classification step. With the idea to give an answer to this issue three different classifiers have been tested: a bank of Support Vector Machines (SVMs), Random Forest (RF), and the k-NN.

3 Experimental Setup

In this section the selection of a suitable set of images to test and optimize the proposed pipeline is initially carried-out. Then the best classification algorithm among the considered ones is experimentally defined.

All the evaluation tests have been conducted on the Extended Cohn-Kanade (CK+) data set, a facial image database of 123 individuals of different gender, race and age [8]. 8-bit grayscale image sequences from neutral to peak expression were digitized into 640 by 490 pixels of resolution. More specifically just 97 individuals have been considered, as suggested in [10]. This reduction was related both to the lack of emotional labels for several subjects that could affect the classification phase, severe lighting conditions of images and to the necessity to balance the data set. This way 2 different subsets have been built by the selection of static images among the 593 sequences of the 97 subjects. The first one was a 6 expression subset with the following distribution among different expressions: anger (86), disgust (95), fear (98), happiness (86), sadness (81) and surprise (101) with a total number of images of 547. A second subset with 7 expression has been built by adding 87 images with neutral expression.

Once a suitable testing dataset has been selected the next step is the selection of the best classification strategy for the proposed geometrical features set. As previously highlighted three different classification methods, Support Vector Machines, k-Nearest Neighbors (with k=1 to obtain high accuracy) and Random Forest have been compared. More specifically a k-fold validation on both the built subsets (6 and 7 expression) has been used with a k=10 as already found in previous studies. The use of both the subsets is a key point that allows the results to be more general and then to avoid all possible ambiguities related to the dataset constraints.

The experimental results, summarized in Table 1, show that in both the experiments, Random Forest experienced the best classification performed. Moreover these results confirmed the ability of the proposed solution to fully recognize facial expressions from a small set of geometric features.

Going into details of the 6 expressions results, the recognition rates were: 82,41%, 74,76% and 95,46% using respectively Multi-SVM, k-Nearest Neighbors and Random Forest. Whereas, taking into account 7 expression classification Multi-SVM reached 70,94%, whereas k-Nearest Neighbors achieved 71,96% and Random Forest reached 94,24%.

4 Experimental Results

Once the best pipeline settings have been found the next step is to perform a more accurate experimental session in order to deeply investigate the potentially of the proposed approach. To this aim the confusion tables are presented and discussed in subsection 4.1 and then the performance obtained are compared with those of the the most relevant works presented in the literature and illustrated in subsection 4.2. Finally the behavior on video sequences is highlighted and discussed.

Table 1. Table of results for six-class and seven-class expression recognition using Multi-SVM, Random Forest and k-NN on one side (left) of the face (Unit: %).

Expression	Six-class Expression			Seven-class Expression		
	Multi-SVM	Random Forest	k-NN	Multi-SVM	Random Forest	k-NN
Anger	44.71	88.24	68.24	71.76	87.06	61.18
Disgust	88.42	93.68	81.05	80.23	96.84	78.95
Fear	77.55	97.96	74.49	58.02	96.94	72.45
Happiness	98.84	95.35	81.40	78.95	97.67	82.56
Sadness	93.83	97.53	69.14	77.55	90.12	60.49
Surprise	91.09	100.00	74.26	73.27	99.01	74.26
Neutral	-	-	-	56.82	92.05	73.86
Accuracy	**82.41**	**95.46**	**74.76**	**70.94**	**94.24**	**71.96**

4.1 Discussion on Confusion Tables

This subsection compares and discusses the performance of the proposed approach choosing features from the left or the right side of the face. As described in Section 2, some of the 32 proposed geometrical features exploit the face symmetry and they are computed on the left side of the face in order to reduce the computational complexity. With the aim to prove the symmetry hypothesis, the same set of features, developed on the right side of the face, has been considered. All experiments have been performed on both the 6 and 7 expression subsets with the Random Forest classifier and the previously mentioned k-fold validation system with k=10. Tables 2 and 3 show confusion matrices, respectively for the 6 and 7 expressions subsets, summarizing both the results obtained with the use of the features from left or right side of the face. Regarding the 7 expressions subset, the proposed approach achieved 95,46% on left side and 94,36% on right side, while with the 6 expressions subset, it reached 94,24% on left side, 93,32% on right side. Despite a difference less than 1,5%, the proposed approach consistently achieved high recognition rates when applied to the left side of the face as well as if applied to the right one. Going into details, this deeper investigation highlights an ambiguity between anger, disgusted and sad expressions. This seems quite reasonable, for all these types of expressions, where strict lips and low position of eyebrows are very similar in location and shape.

4.2 Comparison with State-of-the-Art Methods

In this section, the accuracy of the proposed system was compared against common feature-based approaches. Unfortunately, there exist many different evaluation protocols in literature that make the comparison very challenging. In order to perform a comparison as fair as possible, the competitors were chosen among those solutions that use an evaluation protocol based on the CK+ dataset with 6 expressions.

Considering geometrical methods, in [9] the authors showed a graph of the number of features versus recognition accuracy, for both training and testing

Table 2. Confusion matrix of six-class expression recognition using the left and the right side of the face (Unit: %).

Expression	Anger	Disgust	Fear	Happiness	Sadness	Surprise	Side
Anger	88.24	5.88	0.00	0.00	5.88	0.00	Left
	88.24	5.88	0.00	1.18	4.71	0.00	Right
Disgust	4.21	93.68	1.05	0.00	1.05	0.00	Left
	3.16	90.53	3.16	0.00	3.16	0.00	Right
Fear	0.00	0.00	97.96	1.02	0.00	1.02	Left
	0.00	0.00	95.92	3.06	0.00	1.02	Right
Happiness	0.00	0.00	4.65	95.35	0.00	0.00	Left
	0.00	0.00	2.33	97.67	0.00	0.00	Right
Sadness	1.23	1.23	0.00	0.00	97.53	0.00	Left
	4.94	1.23	1.23	0.00	92.59	0.00	Right
Surprise	0.00	0.00	0.00	0.00	0.00	100.00	Left
	0.00	0.00	0.00	0.00	0.00	100.00	Right

Table 3. Confusion matrix of seven-class expression recognition using the left and the right side of the face (Unit: %).

Expression	Anger	Disgust	Fear	Happiness	Neutral	Sadness	Surprise	Classifier
Anger	87.06	5.88	0.00	0.00	2.35	4.71	0.00	Left
	88.24	5.88	0.00	1.18	2.35	2.35	0.00	Right
Disgust	2.11	96.84	0.00	0.00	1.05	0.00	0.00	Left
	2.11	90.53	3.16	0.00	1.05	3.16	0.00	Right
Fear	0.00	0.00	96.94	2.04	0.00	0.00	1.02	Left
	0.00	0.00	96.94	2.04	1.02	0.00	0.00	Right
Happiness	0.00	0.00	2.33	97.67	0.00	0.00	0.00	Left
	0.00	0.00	3.49	96.51	0.00	0.00	0.00	Right
Neutral	3.41	0.00	0.00	0.00	92.05	4.55	0.00	Left
	3.41	1.14	0.00	0.00	90.91	4.55	0.00	Right
Sadness	1.23	3.70	0.00	0.00	4.94	90.12	0.00	Left
	6.17	3.70	0.00	0.00	0.00	90.12	0.00	Right
Surprise	0.00	0.00	0.99	0.00	0.00	0.00	99.01	Left
	0.00	0.00	0.00	0.00	0.00	0.00	100.00	Right

data. The highest classification accuracy of 95,17% was achieved with a minimum of 125 feature vectors, so three times the number of features we proposed in the present paper (only 32). In [14], a 81% recognition rate has been achieved for 4 emotions, using a geometric features extraction method and Neural Network classifications on sequence of images. In another work [15], authors use static images and geometrical methods as in our approach and obtain their 90,33% of accuracy. Youssif and Asker [16] reach a 93,5% six-classes recognition rate combining geometrical and appearance methods (an hybrid method).

On the other hand, concerning appearance methods, recently, Zhao et al. [10] obtained 94,88% of recognition accuracy. Their selected static images of 96 subjects, using for each sequence, one neutral image and three peak faces, thus the data set results unbalanced on neutral emotion. Zhao, G. and Pietikäinen, M. [11] reached 96,26% of accuracy, using local binary patterns and SVM classifiers but it was only tested on manually aligned image sequences. In Jabid et al. [12], they achieved 93,69% of recognition accuracy, using local directional pattern features, which are similar to the LBP feature with SVM. The best average recognition accuracy of the different methods proposed by researchers is around 95%, on the Cohn-Kanade facial expression database, but one limitation of the existing facial expression recognition methods is that they attempt to recognize facial expression from sequence of images where facial expression evolves from a neutral state to a fully expressed state. In the current study, we randomly chose static images from the CK+ data set in order to avoid any possible calibration of the system. Table 4 reports the comparison with the State-of-the-Art demonstrating that the proposed approach gave the best average recognition rate and this represents an important advancement in the field of automatic recognition of facial expressions.

Table 4. Performance comparison with State-of-the-Art Methods (CK+ 6 expressions) (Unit: %).

Appearence/Hybrid			Geometrical			
[10]	[12]	[16]	[9]	[14]	[15]	Proposed
94.88	93.69	93.50	95.17	81.00	90.33	**95.46**

4.3 Tests on Video Sequences

This section aims at analyzing the behavior of the proposed pipeline when applied to image sequences. The experiments reported in previous sections were relative to the recognition of facial expressions in a static image containing a peak expression whereas, in common application contexts, the automatic systems have to perform FER by analyzing image sequences in which not all the images contain a clear expression, or where there are transitions between expressions. In order to obtain a quantitative accuracy evaluation of the capability to recognize the expressions embedded in image sequences, the proposed pipeline has been tested on the sequences of the 97 subjects selected from the CK+ dataset. Each CK+ sequences start with a neutral face expression that bring to peak expression and the number of frames, for a particular expression, changes for every subject. With the purpose to make the proposed pipeline suitable to work with video sequences, the following rule has been introduced: a sequence i was considered correctly recognized if in the first m_1 frames there exist at least n_1 images classified as containing the neutral expression and, at the same time, in the last m_2 frames there exist at least n_2 images classified as containing the expression which the sequence is labeled with. Moreover, a test with the purpose to test the classification just for the expressive face was carried out. In this case a sequence i was considered correctly recognized if in the last m_2 frames there exist at least n_2 images classified as containing the expression which the sequence is labeled with. In the experiments the following setting parameters were chosen: $m_1 = 3, n_1 = 1$, $m_2 = 5$, $n_2 = 4$ after a carefully experimental evaluation. Over the tested sequences, the percentage of correct classification was of 73.56% for six-class classification and 69.23% for seven-class classification that are very encouraging outcomes.

5 Conclusions and Future Works

In this work, a new pipeline for facial expression recognition has been proposed. More specifically, this study adopts a set of 32 geometrical features exploiting the face symmetry in order to save computational load and keep high accuracy performances. In order to optimize the potential of the proposed set, three different classification approaches have been tested leading to choose the Random Forest approach as the most suitable for this specific features vector. Experimental sessions have been performed on publicly available dataset, experiencing recognition robustness also in real world environments.

To give an idea of the complexity of the algorithm, the actual CPU time taken to process 1 image of the CK+ database was measured. The proposed approach, in the implemented version, recognizes the facial expression in about 1 second, working in R2014a Matlab environment and using an Intel Core i3 (1.8 GHz) with 4 GB of RAM. Future works will address the implementation in a intermediate-level language in order to speed-up the procedure. Where appropriate, processor supplementary instructions will also be used to achieve real-time processing. Furthermore, will be explored the proposed approach with other very challenging problems including more severe head pose variations and occlusions. Spontaneous facial expressions, common in many practical applications, will also be studied.

Acknowledgments. This work has been supported in part by Italian Ministry for Education, University and Research (MIUR) in the framework of "2007-2013 NOP for Research and Competitiveness" under Grants SARACEN with code PON04a3_00201.

References

1. Pantic, M., Rothkrantz, L.: Automatic analysis of facial expressions: The state of the art. IEEE Trans. Pattern Anal. Mach. Intell. **22**, 1424–1445 (2000)
2. Ekman, P., Friesen, W.: In Facial Action Coding System: A Technique for the Measurement of Facial Movement. Consulting Psychologists Press, Palo Alto (1978)
3. Viola, P., Jones, M.: Robust real-time face detection. Int. J. Comput. Vision. **57**, 137–154 (2004)

4. Loconsole, C., Runa Miranda, C., Augusto, G., Frisoli, A., Orvalho, V.: Real-time emotion recognition: a novel method for geometrical facial features extraction. In: Proc. of 9th International Joint Conference on Computer Vision, Imaging and Computer Graphics Theory and Applications, January 5–8, Lisbon, Portugal (2014)

5. Bevilacqua, V., D'Ambruoso, D., Mandolino, G., Suma, M.: A new tool to support diagnosis of neurological disorders by means of facial expressions. In: Proceedings of IEEE 2011 International Workshop on Medical Measurements and Applications Proceedings, May 30–31, Bari, Italy pp. 544–549 (2011)

6. Asthana, A., Saragih, J., Wagner, M., Goecke, R.: Evaluating AAM Fitting Methods for Facial Expression Recognition. In: Proc. of the Inter. Conf. on Affective Computing and Intelligent Interaction, September 10–12, Amsterdam, pp. 1–8 (2009)

7. Milborrow, S., Nicolls, F.: Active Shape Models with SIFT Descriptors and MARS. In: Proceedings of the 9th International Conference on Computer Vision Theory and Applications, January 5–8, Lisbon, Portugal (2014)

8. Lucey, P., Cohn, J.F., Kanade, T., Saragih, J., Ambadar, Z.: The Extended Cohn-Kanade Dataset (CK+): A Complete Dataset for Action Unit and Emotion-Specified Expression. In: Proc. of the 3rd IEEE Workshop on CVPR for Human Communication Behavior Analysis, June 13–18, San Francisco, CA, USA, pp. 94–101 (2010)

9. Ghimire, D., Lee, J.: Geometric Feature-Based Facial Expression Recognition in Image Sequences Using Multi-Class AdaBoost and Support Vector Machines. Sensors **13**, 7714–7734 (2013)

10. Zhao, X., Zhang, S.: Facial expression recognition based on local binary patterns and kernel discriminant isomap. Sensors **11**, 9573–9588 (2011)

11. Zhao, G., Pietikäinen, M.: Dynamic texture recognition using local binary patterns with an application to facial expressions. IEEE Trans. Pattern Anal. Mach. Intell. **29**, 915–928 (2007)

12. Jabid, T., Kabir, M.H., Chae, O.: Robust facial expression recognition based on local directional pattern. ETRI J **32**, 784–794 (2010)

13. Shan, C., Gong, S., McOwan, P.: Facial expression recognition based on local binary patterns: A comprehensive study. Image Vis. Comput. **27**, 803–816 (2009)

14. Rao, K.S., Saroj, V.K., Maity, S., Koolagudi, S.G.: Recognition of emotions from video using neural network models. Expert Systems with Applications **38**, 13181–13185 (2011)

15. Khanum, A., Mufti, M., Javed, M.Y., Shafiq, M.Z.: Fuzzy case-based reasoning for facial expression recognition. Fuzzy Sets and Systems **160**, 231–250 (2009)

16. Youssif, A.A., Asker, W.A.: Automatic facial expression recognition system based on geometric and appearance features. Computer and Information Science **4**, 115–124 (2011)

17. Martiriggiano, T., Leo, M., D'Orazio, T., Distante, A.: Face Recognition by Kernel Independent Component Analysis. In: Ali, M., Esposito, F. (eds.) IEA/AIE 2005. LNCS (LNAI), vol. 3533, pp. 55–58. Springer, Heidelberg (2005)

A Selection Module for Large-Scale Face Recognition Systems

Giuliano Grossi, Raffaella Lanzarotti$^{(\boxtimes)}$, and Jianyi Lin

Dipartimento di Informatica, Università degli Studi di Milano,
Via Comelico 39/41, Milano, Italy
{grossi,lanzarotti,lin}@di.unimi.it

Abstract. Face recognition systems aimed at working on large scale datasets are required to solve specific hurdles. In particular, due to the huge amount of data, it becomes mandatory to furnish a very fast and effective approach. Moreover the solution should be scalable, that is it should deal efficiently the growing of the gallery with new subjects. In literature, most of the works tackling this problem are composed of two stages, namely the selection and the classification. The former is aimed at significantly pruning the face image gallery, while the latter, often expensive but precise, determines the probe identity on this reduced domain. In this article a new selection method is presented, combining a multi-feature representation and the least squares method. Data are split into sub-galleries so as to make the system more efficient and scalable. Experiments on the union of four challenging datasets and comparisons with the state-of-the-art prove the effectiveness of our method.

1 Introduction

Face Recognition (FR) problem has been largely studied during the last decades [24], and the more it was investigated the more challenging developments were wished for. FR systems (FRSs) have been interested by progressively less controlled acquisition conditions concerning illumination, image quality and indoor/outdoor acquisition [17]. Also the constraints on the face appearance have been more and more relaxed: at present, a FRS is desired to work well on faces with different expressions and poses [1,6] and even having partial occlusions [13,22]. A last challenge recently risen concerns with large-scale datasets: high interest is devoted to systems able to deal with thousands of subjects [7,8], as it could happen either in security contexts [18,25] or in retrieval applications [16,21,23]. As deepened in section 2, several works have already been proposed to tackle this hurdle. Many of them are based on a two-stage scheme, consisting in a first *selection* of a subset of subjects, followed by the proper *classification* of the test image. Clearly, the behaviour of the selection step, strongly influences the system performances both in terms of recognition rate and computational costs, thus deserving an in-depth analysis.

In this paper we propose a new selection method, namely *fg-LS*, based on the least squares (LS) technique, and characterized by two key attributes: it works on

© Springer International Publishing Switzerland 2015
V. Murino and E. Puppo (Eds.): ICIAP 2015, Part II, LNCS 9280, pp. 529–539, 2015.
DOI: 10.1007/978-3-319-23234-8_49

multi features (f), and organizes data in sub-galleries (g). These characteristics together guarantee effectiveness, robustness and efficiency. Experiments show that *fg-LS* outperforms both baseline and state-of-the-art methods.

The remainder of the paper is organized as follows. Section 2 summarizes related works, section 3 presents the selection method we propose. The experimental analysis is detailed in section 4, while section 5 draws some conclusions.

2   Related Works

Two-stage FRSs apply subsequently the *selection* and the *classification* steps. The former aims at strongly shrinking the gallery in order to preserve the target subject with high confidence. Notice that, dealing with huge data, it is desirable that the selector be computationally efficient. The classification step determines the identity of the probe image referring to the reduced gallery and adopting a technique such as nearest neighbour (NN), Support Vector Machines (SVM), or Sparse Representation (SR). In the following FRSs are categorized according to the adopted selection technique.

A first category worth to be mentioned concerns the systems adopting the clustering method for the selection stage, aiming at implementing the *divide et impera* paradigm. In such approaches the image representation is crucial: raw data are often projected in some convenient feature space (PCA, LDA, ...) thus reducing noise, attenuating misalignment problems or better discriminating the subject classes. For example, in [11] the k-means clustering applied on PCA projected data is adopted to partition the gallery subjects according to a maximum-similarity criterion. Given a test image, the method searches for the most similar cluster, and then within it, the identity of the probe image. In [9] the authors propose an iterative approach that subsequently reduces the search space. The method repeats a LDA-projection of both the training and test data, a k-means clustering to partition the search space into K clusters, and a nearest-neighbour classifier to select K' clusters closest to the probe image. The process ends when $K' = 1$. Lu et al. in [12] partition the subjects into K maximal-separability clusters by a LDA-like technique, and adopt a two-level nearest-neighbour classifier to select firstly K subjects, one from each cluster, and attaining on them the final classification decision. Although the use of both the clustering and the dimensional reduction are very pertinent in case of large-scale databases, they both require to reorganize the gallery for each incoming of new subjects, making the training process too cumbersome [23].

A second category of selector approaches consists in applying the K-Nearest Neighbor (K-NN) method to select the training samples closer to a test image. In [10,14] K-NN is adopted to reduce the search domain for the subsequent l1-solvers. In [25] the K-NN selector is followed by the nonnegative SR classifier. These approaches proved good performances and remarkable speed-up.

Very recently Ortiz and Becker [16] proposed the adoption of the speed least-squares approach to reduce the search gallery to feed to a SR classifier. The authors claimed that linear regression (LR) approximates l1-minimization better than K-NN.

As an example of one-stage face identification on large datasets, it is worth to be mentioned the one proposed in [18]. It is based on a large set of feature descriptors using partial least squares (PLS) to perform multichannel feature weighting.

3   The *fg-LS* Selection Method

Given a huge gallery of face images, the selection method presented here aims at "pruning" a large part of subjects in order to make the classification stage more effective on a rather small gallery. The method relies on highly discriminative features projected on LDA subspaces. Residual errors, obtained by the least squares technique, are used for deciding which subjects to make boiling up to the classifier. As an automatic approach, all face images are cropped and normalized by means of the landmark localization method presented in [4], and then characterized extracting a pool of features $\mathcal{F}$. This characterization could be attained considering for instance simple raw data or a single feature only. However it has been proven that multi-features enrich the data description allowing one to capture more information [16,18,19]. We extend this consideration also to the illumination correction methods, each one being able to extract different discriminative characteristics from images acquired in various illumination conditions. Thus, we resort to a combination of illumination corrections (IC) and feature extractors (FE), so that $\mathcal{F} = \text{IC} \times \text{FE}$ is a collection of transformations $f^1, f^2, ..., f^J$, $J = |\mathcal{F}| = |\text{IC}| \cdot |\text{FE}|$, where each f^j maps an image I to the corresponding illumination-corrected feature vector $f^j(I) \in \mathbb{R}^{n_j}$.

Consider a large set of reference images $\mathcal{G} = \{I_1, ..., I_m\} \subset \mathbb{R}^N$ corresponding to the subjects (or classes) $\mathcal{C} = \{1, ..., c\}$. Based on a divide et impera approach, the main idea is to work on non-overlapping sub-galleries $\mathcal{G}_1, ..., \mathcal{G}_S \subset \mathcal{G}$. The first step of preprocessing consists in the construction of the matrix for the s-th sub-gallery in the j-th feature space by concatenating the feature column vectors: $G_s^j = [f^j(I)]_{I \in \mathcal{G}_s}$, $s = 1, ..., S$, $j = 1, ..., J$.

To perform dimensionality reduction while preserving as much as possible the class discriminative information, we apply the LDA projection. For each matrix G_s^j (i.e. each sub-gallery and feature) we construct the LDA projection matrix W_s^j, so maintaining lower computational costs (dominated by generalized eigenvalue problems) w.r.t. considering the gallery $\mathcal{G}$ all at once. Hence, the reference sub-galleries in LDA space are $\Phi_s^j = W_s^j G_s^j$, whose columns are feature-vectors in LDA space $\phi_s^j = \phi_s^j(I) = W_s^j f^j(I)$, for $I \in \mathcal{G}_s$.

Now, given a test image T, the same preprocessing is applied, locating and normalizing the face, extracting and projecting the features $f^j(T)$ onto the LDA spaces corresponding to every sub-gallery, hence obtaining $\tau_s^j = W_s^j f^j(T)$.

The selection is attained by evaluating the least squares residuals. Given a subject $i \in C$ in the s-th sub-gallery ($s = s(i)$ uniquely determined by i), let us denote the set of columns in sub-gallery Φ_s^j belonging to i by $\Phi^j(i)$. We then compute the ℓ_2-distance between the test image vector τ_s^j and the column-space of $\Phi^j(i)$ associated to every subject $i \in \mathcal{C}$:

$$R_i^j = \min_x \|\tau_s^j - \Phi^j(i)x\|_2 = \|\tau_s^j - \Phi^j(i)[\Phi^j(i)]^\dagger \tau_s^j\|_2 \qquad \text{for } j = 1, ..., J$$

where $A^\dagger$ is the Moore-Penrose pseudo-inverse of a matrix A. Since these distances are calculated in several inhomogeneous spaces, we perform a z-score standardization z_i^j of R_i^j (over all R_h^j, h appearing in sub-gallery s) for each feature j; we then combine them into one residual $r_i = \sum_{j=1}^J z_i^j$ for every subject $i \in C$.

Final selection is obtained gathering the K subjects in C with smallest residuals. We summarize this process in Alg. 1.

Algorithm 1. fg-LS

Input: Image gallery $\mathcal{G} = \{I_1, ..., I_m\} \subset \mathbb{R}^N$; test image T; integer K
Output: Subjects $i_1, ..., i_K \in C$ with minimum residual for T
- **Gallery construction (off-line):**
Preprocessing of $\mathcal{G}$: cropping and normalization
Sub-galleries construction: $\mathcal{G}_1, ..., \mathcal{G}_S$
for $s = 1, ..., S$ **do**
    for $j = 1, ..., J$ **do**
        Computation of feature vectors: $f^j(I)$, for all I in $\mathcal{G}_s$
        Matrix construction: $G_s^j = [f^j(I)]_{I \in \mathcal{G}_s}$
        Compute LDA transformations: W_s^j
        Galleries in LDA spaces: $\Phi_s^j = W_s^j G_s^j$
    end
end
- **Testing phase:**
Preprocessing of T: cropping and normalization
for $j = 1, ..., J$ **do**
    Computation of feature vectors: $f^j(T)$
    LDA projections: $\tau_s^j = W_s^j f^j(T)$, $s = 1, ..., S$
    for $i \in C$ **do**
        Computation of submatrices $\Phi^j(i)$ and pseudo-inverses $[\Phi^j(i)]^\dagger$
        Residuals: $R_i^j = \|\tau_s^j - \Phi^j(i)[\Phi^j(i)]^\dagger \tau_s^j\|_2$
    end
    for $i \in C$ compute $z_i^j = \text{z-score}(R_i^j)$ over subjects h in gallery $s(i)$
end
Cumulative residuals: $r_i = \sum_{j=1}^J z_i^j, i \in C$
Sort $\{r_1, ..., r_c\}$
Return indices $i_1, i_2, ..., i_K$ of the smallest residuals $r_{i_1}, r_{i_2}, ..., r_{i_K}$

---

4 Experimental Analysis

The experiments reported in this section show that the idea of filtering out a substantial number of subjects from a huge gallery, while preserving the target one with high confidence, plays a relevant role in FR task. This is mainly due to the fact that the most effective classification techniques are complex in nature while being highly discriminative when dealing with small galleries.

To show the robustness of the selector, we carry out experiments in challenging conditions, referring to a large pool of subjects, poorly represented in the gallery, and acquired in uncontrolled conditions, including variations in the environmental conditions (lighting, clutter background), variations of the face expression, and variation in the quality of the acquisition (focus/blurred).

4.1 Datasets

We collect the images of four public available databases acquired in uncontrolled conditions, thus obtaining a pool of $c = 725$ subjects[1], and thousands of images. For each experiment we randomly select 3 images per subject for the gallery construction, while the remaining images are used for testing. Specifically, we refer to the Extended Yale B (frontal), the BANCA Avderse, the FRGC v.2 Uncontrolled, and the Multi-PIE (frontal). In Table 1 we synthesize their peculiar characteristics, and in Fig. 1 some examples of face images are shown.

Table 1. Databases and their characteristics: **N. sbj**, **N. Images**, **Background**, **Illumination** (*varies*: oriented light, *good*: homogenous light, *poor*: image underexposure), **Expression** (*varies*: different face expressions, *reading*: reading subjects, *neutral*), **Timing** (*no*: single acquisition section, *yes*: several sessions spanning over several months), **Img quality** (*good*: high resolution, focused images, *bad*).

Database	N. sbj	N. Images	Background	Ill.	Expr.	Timing	Quality
Ext. YaleB (frontal)	38	2432	homogeneous	varies	neutral	no	good
BANCA Adv.	52	2.080	clutter	varies	reading	yes	bad
FRGC v.2 Uncontr.	289	5.248	clutter	varies	varies	yes	bad
Multi-PIE (frontal)	337	≈ 50.000	homogeneous	varies	varies	yes	good

4.2 Feature Extraction

The method requires the image preprocessing consisting in face detection and normalization of both the gallery and test images. This is accomplished by applying the method presented in [4] that allows us to crop the portion of the image corresponding to the face precisely, and to rescale it to 80x70 pixels (Fig. 1).

The pool of features corresponding to IC and FE has been chosen as a trade-off between performances and computational costs. In particular we adopt a pool of three illumination corrections, that is the linear stretching, the MSQ (Multi-Scale Quotient) and ASSR (Adaptive Single-Scale Retinex) techniques [20], aiming at solving various illumination problems (low contrast, strong shadows, over/under-exposure). Also the FE pool consists of three methods, that is

---

[1] We consider only those subjects with at least four images correctly, or at least approximately localized.

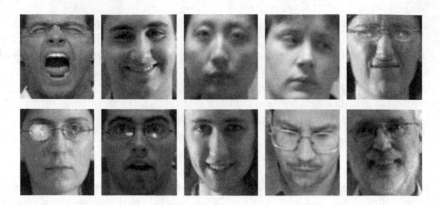

Fig. 1. Examples of original images automatically cropped. Images show some of the possible hurdles present in the database: variations in expression, pose, lighting, and focus.

the HoG (Histogram of Oriented Gradients) [5], Shearlet [3] and MSLBP (Multi-Scale Local Binary Pattern) features [15], each one able to catch a specific image property, that is the discontinuities, the granularity, and the texture respectively. This choice leads to nine combined-feature spaces.

The parameters used in illumination correction and feature extraction have been set as follows. In MSQ we adopt Gaussian filters with four standard deviations in the range $\sigma \in (1, 1.6)$. In ASSR the number of iterative convolutions is set to 10 and the weights needed for the filter are $\delta = 10e^{-\mathbb{E}_{x,y}[\|\nabla I(x,y)\|]/10}$ (that is based on the expected value of the image gradient), and $h = 0.1e^{-10\tau}$, with τ being the normalized average of local intensity differences. Concerning the HoG features, we refer to 15×15 patches, concatenating the obtained 8-bin histograms. In MSLBP we maintain the same window and histogram sizes as in HoG, setting the circle radius equal to $1, 3, 5$, respectively. The shearlet feature has been implemented using the Meyer-type filter, and adding together the detail coefficients, while excluding the first scale (low frequencies).

4.3   Tests on the fg-LS and Other Assessed Methods

The fg-LS method essentially depends on two parameters, the first is the number $M = \lceil c/S \rceil$ of subjects per sub-gallery, and the second is the number $K \in \{1, \ldots, c\}$ of subjects yielded by the selector. We analyse their impact on the selector setting-up two experiments. The first aims at studying the behaviour of fg-LS method varying M, the latter addresses a comparison with some assessed methods varying K. In addition we carry out a last experiment aiming at highlighting the effects of our selector on a complete FR system.

Experiment 1. We run fg-LS varying M between 50 and 725, the last being the number c of subjects available in the referred dataset. In Fig. 2 we report for each tested M the performances achieved by the system in terms of the percentage ρ of presence of the target subjects in the selected pools. Formally, given the test images $T_1, ..., T_n$ with corresponding labels $\ell_1, ..., \ell_n \in \mathcal{C}$, and denoting by $\mathcal{C}_T = \text{fg-LS}(\mathcal{G}, T, K)$ the output of the selector, such percentage is computed as

$$\rho = \frac{\#\{i : \ell_i \in \mathcal{C}_{T_i}, i = 1, ..., n\}}{n}.$$

From these graphs, we can observe that the system behaves better when the sub-galleries have intermediate sizes. Specifically to these experiments, sub-galleries with M between one and two hundreds of subjects (about 14-28% of all subjects) behave better than adopting bigger or smaller values for M. Recalling that the operations carried out at sub-gallery domain concern the LDA projection and the z-score standardization, these results highlight the opportunity to work in a sufficiently expressive domain. Indeed, adopting big values of M restricts the LDA capability of separating the different classes, while too small M's would make the standardized residuals too uniform across sub-galleries (for instance think about the limit $M = 1$; in this case all the cumulative residuals r_i^j would be very concentrated), making their comparison meaningless.

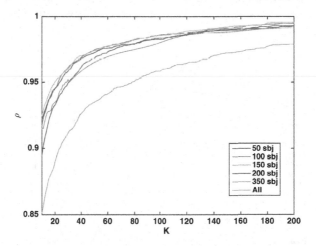

Fig. 2. Experimental analysis of the fg-LS method for different value of M (number of subjects per sub-gallery, 'sbj' in the legend) varying the selector parameter K. Performances are expressed by the percentage ρ of presence of the target subjects in the selected pools.

Concerning the computational cost of the online testing phase, the dependence of the time consumption on the gallery size (Fig. 3) is mainly due to the cost of multiplication with the LDA transform matrices W_s^j, making it convenient referring to small sub-galleries. As a trade-off between performances and computational costs, for the subsequent experiments, we set $M = 150$.

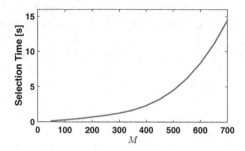

Fig. 3. Computational time (in seconds) of the fg-LS selection method, varying M.

Experiment 2. For comparisons, we set up an experimental analysis aiming at evaluating the performances of different selectors varying the number of selected subjects K. In particular we assess two baseline methods, namely the K-NN and LS approaches, both projecting data into the LDA space, and two state-of-the-art methods, namely the f-LS [16] and the f-PLS [18]. Both these systems represent data in a multi-feature space, varying the selection criterion: in f-LS the linear regression is applied on the PCA projection of the concatenation of LBP, HoG, and Gabor features. In f-PLS the features are extracted locally, and then the PLS (Partial Least Squares) is applied to derive a weighted model for each subject.

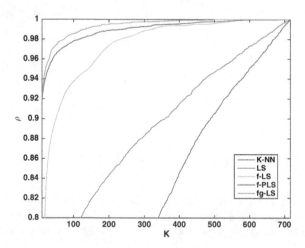

Fig. 4. Comparison of different selectors, varying the parameter K. Specifically, K-NN, and LS are well-known baseline methods, f-LS corresponds to the method presented in [16], f-PLS to the one introduced in [18], and fg-LS is ours. Performances are expressed by the percentage ρ of presence of the target subjects in the selected pools.

In Fig. 4 we plot for each assessed method the percentage ρ of presence of the target subjects in the selected pools, varying K over a challenging range. The results prove the effectiveness of the LS approach, above all if associated to multi-feature representation. In particular our selector, fg-LS, exceeds the more sophisticated f-PLS method that requires a training for each subject, simply combining the multi-feature representation with the LDA projection and the partitioning into sub-galleries.

Experiment 3. Aiming at highlighting the selection effects on a complete FR system, we adopt the FR classifier we presented in [2], namely k-LiMapS, that is a sparsity-based classifier. Note that in principle any other could be exploited (e.g. NN, LS, SRC, ...). In Fig. 5 we report the results obtained varying K. The blue line corresponds to the selector, plotting the percentage ρ of success achieved setting $M = 150$, as explained above. The curve corresponding to the classifier (red line) expresses the success ratio of the k-LiMapS when applied onto subsets correctly produced by fg-LS of K subjects, that is when they include the target one. So doing we break down the possible errors between the selector and the classifier. As already argued, the selector increases its percentage of success when increasing K. Contrarily, the classifier takes advantage of the pruning, showing a rapid drop of performance with the increase of the selected pool size. The overall recognition ratio (yellow line) is obtaining as a product between these two partial performances, thus being influenced by these two opposite trends simultaneously. Obviously, adopting a too strict selector (e.g. $K = 30$) it penalizes the total ratio because of the low ρ, while a high K makes more difficult (and also computationally expensive) the classifier's task. This suggests that the choice of the selection parameter K should above all take into account the overall system behaviour.

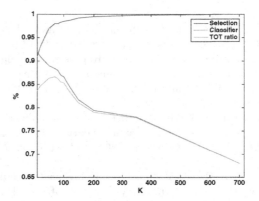

Fig. 5. Analysis of a Selection+Classifier FRS, namely fg-LS + k-LiMapS. *Blue line*: partial performances of the fg-LS selector. *Red line*: partial performances of the classifier k-LiMapS. *Yellow line*: overall system performances.

5   Conclusions

In this article we presented a new selection method, namely fg-LS, conceived as first step for any two-stage large scale FRS. The method exploits the richness of the description given by multi-feature representation, the discriminative power given by the LDA projection, and the efficiency given by the divide et impera paradigm. The characteristic of the last method is crucial also for easily dealing with new incoming subjects, that can be added to any sub-gallery, requiring the re-computation of the only corresponding LDA and feature normalization, while leaving unaltered most of the gallery information. The method is based on the least squares technique, applied on small sub-galleries of face image character-ized with multi-features. In order to test the method on large and challenging datasets, we collected the face images of four public databases, considering the images acquired in uncontrolled conditions.

The experimental analysis proves that multi-features actually give a powerful description of the data, and that the partitioning is advantageous specially if well tuned: neither too small nor too big sub-galleries are adequate in facing the selection problem. Concerning the parameter K, we have shown how it influences inversely the selection and the classifier, thus its setting should above all take into account the overall system behaviour. Comparisons proved that fg-LS is effective and efficient, performing better than well-known methods in the field.

Acknowledgments. The research was carried out as part of the project "Interpret-ing emotions: a computational tool integrating facial expressions and biosignals based shape analysis and bayesian networks", supported by the Italian Government, managed by MIUR, financed by the *Future in Research* Fund.

References

1. Abate, A.F., Nappi, M., Riccio, D., Sabatino, G.: 2d and 3d face recognition: A survey. Pattern Recognition Letters **28**(14), 1885–1906 (2007)
2. Adamo, A., Grossi, G., Lanzarotti, R.: Sparse Representation Based Classification for Face Recognition by k-LiMapS Algorithm. In: Elmoataz, A., Mammass, D., Lezoray, O., Nouboud, F., Aboutajdine, D. (eds.) ICISP 2012. LNCS, vol. 7340, pp. 245–252. Springer, Heidelberg (2012)
3. Borgi, M.A., Labate, D., El'Arbi, M., Ben Amar, C.: Shearlet Network-based Sparse Coding Augmented by Facial Texture Features for Face Recognition. In: Petrosino, A. (ed.) ICIAP 2013, Part II. LNCS, vol. 8157, pp. 611–620. Springer, Heidelberg (2013)
4. Cuculo, V., Lanzarotti, R., Boccignone, G.: Using sparse coding for landmark localization in facial expressions. In: Proc. of Int'l Conf. EUVIP. IEEE (2014)
5. Dalal, N., Triggs, B.: Histograms of oriented gradients for human detection. In: IEEE Comp. Soc. Conf. on Computer Vision and Pattern Recognition, CVPR 2005, vol. 1, pp. 886–893 (2005)
6. Gross, R., Matthews, I., Cohn, J., Kanade, T., Baker, S.: Multi-PIE. Image Vision Comput. **28**(5), 807–813 (2010)

7. Huang, G.B., Ramesh, M., Berg, T., Learned-Miller, E.: Labeled faces in the wild: A database for studying face recognition in unconstrained environments. Tech. Rep. 07–49, University of Massachusetts, Amherst (October 2007)

8. Kumar, N., Berg, A.C., Belhumeur, P.N., Nayar, S.K.: Attribute and Simile Classifiers for Face Verification. In: IEEE Int'l Conf. on Computer Vision (ICCV) (2009)

9. Kyperountas, M., Tefas, A., Pitas, I.: Face recognition via adaptive discriminant clustering. In: Proc. of the Int'l Conf. on Image Processing, ICIP 2008, pp. 2744–2747 (2008)

10. Li, C., Guo, J., Zhang, H.: Local sparse representation based classification. In: 20th International Conference on Pattern Recognition, ICPR 2010, pp. 649–652 (2010)

11. Liu, W., Wang, Y., Li, S., Tan, T.: Null space-based kernel fisher discriminant analysis for face recognition. In: Int'l Conf. on Automatic Face and Gesture Recognition, pp. 369–374. IEEE (2004)

12. Lu, J., Plataniotis, K.: Boosting face recognition on a large-scale database. In: Int'l Conf. on Image Processing, pp. 109–112. IEEE (2002)

13. Martinez, A., Benavente, R.: The AR face database. CVC Tech. Rep. 24 (1998)

14. Nan, Z., Jian, Y.: K nearest neighbor based local sparse representation classifier. IEEE 2010 Chin. Conf. on Pattern Recognition, CCPR, pp. 1–5 (2010)

15. Ojala, T., Pietikainen, M., Maenpaa, T.: Multiresolution gray-scale and rotation invariant texture classification with local binary patterns. IEEE Transactions on Pattern Recognition and Machine Intelligence 24(7), 971–987 (2002)

16. Ortiz, E.G., Becker, B.C.: Face recognition for web-scale datasets. Computer Vision and Image Understanding 118, 153–170 (2014)

17. Phillips, P., Flynn, P., Scruggs, T., Bowyer, K.: Overview of the face recognition grand challenge. Proc. IEEE Conf. CVPR 1, 947–954 (2005)

18. Schwartz, W., Guo, H., Choi, J., Davis, L.: Face identification using large feature sets. IEEE Transactions on Image Processing 21(4), 2245–2255 (2012)

19. Tan, X., Triggs, B.: Enhanced local texture feature sets for face recognition under difficult lighting conditions. Trans. on Image Processing 19, 1635–1650 (2010)

20. Štruc, V., Pavešić, N.: Photometric normalization techniques for illumination invariance. In: Zhang, Y. (ed.) Advances in Face Image Analysis: Techniques and Technologies, pp. 279–300. IGI-Global (2011)

21. Wolf, L., Hassner, T., Taigman, Y.: Descriptor based methods in the wild. In: European Conference on Computer Vision (ECCV) (2008)

22. Wright, J., Yang, A.Y., Ganesh, A., Sastry, S.S., Ma, Y.: Robust face recognition via sparse representation. IEEE Trans. Pattern Analysis and Machine Intelligence 31(2), 210–27 (2008)

23. Yan, J., Lei, Z., Yi, D., Li, S.: Towards incremental and large scale face recognition. In: Proc. of Int'l Joint Conference on Biometrics (IJCB 2011), pp. 1–6 (2011)

24. Zhao, W., Chellappa, R., Phillips, P., Rosenfeld, A.: Face recognition: A literature survey. ACM Computing Surveys 35(4), 399–458 (2003)

25. Zheng, W., Hu, B., Kong, X.: Two-stage nonnegative sparse representation for large-scale face recognition. IEEE Trans. on Neural Networks and Learning Systems 24(1), 35–46 (2013)

A Classification-Selection Approach for Self Updating of Face Verification Systems Under Stringent Storage and Computational Requirements

Pierluigi Tuveri, Valerio Mura[(✉)], Gian Luca Marcialis, and Fabio Roli

Department of Electrical and Electronic Engineering,
University of Cagliari, Cagliari, Italy
{pierluigi.tuveri,valerio.mura,marcialis,roli}@diee.unica.it

Abstract. Nowadays face recognition systems have many application fields. Unfortunately, lighting variations and ageing effects are still open issues. Moreover, face changes over time due to ageing. A further problem is due to occlusions, for example the glass presence. Re-enrolling user's face is time-consuming and does not solve above problems. Therefore, unsupervised template update has been proposed, and named self update. Basically, this algorithm adapts/modifies templates or face models by collecting samples during system operations. The most effective variant of self update is based on the collection of multiple templates. However, this approach has been evaluated and tested in conditions under which the possible number of collectable templates is uncostrained. Actually, available resources are limited in memory and computational power, thus it is likely that it is not possible to have more than a pre-set number of templates. In this paper, we propose a classification-selection approach, based on the combination of self update and C-means algorithms, which keeps constant the number of templates and improve the ratio between intra-class variations and inter-class variations for each user. Experimental results show the effectiveness of this method with respect to standard self update.

1 Introduction

Face recognition is not a time-invariant process, because traits change over time, for instances due to expressions, illumination environment, and so on. In order to recognize a face the system needs to have a set of templates for each user to cover all the possible variations. A periodical re-enrollment phase can only partially follows these variations, and is time-consuming. The idea that the system can be automatically updated without the users cooperation has been addressed in the self update algorithm and its variants [9]. Basically, the system adds a new template if the match score is over a pre-calculate "updating" threshold t^*. This is a fundamental parameter, that biases the performance of the system. A low t^* allows the collection of more templates, but there is a high probability that

© Springer International Publishing Switzerland 2015
V. Murino and E. Puppo (Eds.): ICIAP 2015, Part II, LNCS 9280, pp. 540–550, 2015.
DOI: 10.1007/978-3-319-23234-8_50

the system associates the template to a wrong user. When the threshold is more selective it does not allow adding a face template with high variation respect to stored ones.

Self update has been always applied under the hypothesis that the potential number of possible templates is infinite [4]. This allows to point out at which extent self update can be useful; on the other hand, it is not a realistic hypothesis. Moreover, during collection, noisy and redundant samples can be added to the system. Therefore, we believe that self update should be analyzed under more realistic conditions. For example under limited storage and computational resources. The comparison between a large amount of templates makes slow the identification module. Another problem is the management of the memory, that is a precious and critical resource.

Actually, state of the art is aware of points above. With regard to the limited storage and the computational resources, it has been proposed to combine more templates [3], or to use replacement algorithms when the maximum number of templates is reached [4]. With regard to the problem of noisy, redundant or wrong samples, a dual stage method that collect and select the best templates has been proposed [5].

In this paper, we propose a classification-selection method dealing with both issues. First stage the system acts as standard self update, by collecting a set of possible templates under a stringent updating threshold. Second stage adopts the C-means algorithm, under the assumption that the templates of the users are probabilistically and geometry paritional in mono-modal clusters. Centroids of these clusters are assumed to be the centroid of the population associated to a given user. Experimental results on a standard benchmark data set show the effectiveness of the proposed method.

The paper is organized as follow. After a brief review of the self update approach and its variants (Section 2), we present our method (Section 3). Experiments are described in Section 4, and conclusions are reported in Section 5.

2   State of the Art of Self-Update

Let $T = \{t_{1,1}, t_{1,2}, ..., t_{l,j}, ..., t_{k,p}\}$ be a set of enrolled users in the system, named gallery. Where the pair l, j indicates $l - th$ user and $j - th$ template, p is the maximum allowed number of face templates per user, and k the number of enrolled users which are listed in the set $u = \{u_1, ..., u_j, ..., u_k\}$.

Let $b_i = \{x_{i_{1,1}}, x_{i_{1,2}}, ..., x_{i_{l,j}}, ..., x_{i_{k,n_k}}\}$ be a batch of input faces collected during system's operations, at a certain time. We added the i pedix in order to mean that b_i is collected before b_{i+1}.

The standard self-update algorithm estimates t^* through T. Usually the threshold is set such that only a small percentage of impostors can be wrongly classified (false accepptance rate or FAR). This operating point estimates how many genuines users and impostors can pass the verification process. If a certain input sample exhibits a distance from the template $d < t^*$, it is added to the gallery of the claimed user. Obviously if t^* is such that $FAR(t^*) > 0$, a small percentage of impostors may be included in the user's gallery, thus dropping the system's performance over time. In other words, self update algorithm is as follows:

estimate the update threshold t^* using T
for all e element in u_i **do**
    if $distance(x \in u_i, T) < t^*$ **then**
        $T_{new} = T \cup x$
    end if
end for

This algorithm iterates at each collected batch of samples.

Rattani et al. [5] introduced a system composed by two stages. Firstly, samples are classified on the basis of a minimum energy function. Secondly, accepted samples are selected on the basis of a pre-defined and minimized risk function. This two-stages approach is finalized at limiting the number of impostors in the user's gallery, under the usual condition that $p \rightarrow inf$ [5].

In [4] the authors take into account the problem that p is finite by replacing the less frequently used samples in order to maintain p samples in each user's gallery. Unfortunately, using these protocols we risk replacing the useful template, in this case we don't care about the intra-class variation, because we have a rules about the time of face template [4].

3   The Proposed Method

Our method is two-staged. The first stage classifies samples of u_i for inclusion in the user's gallery as usually by standard self update, and the second one selects the best p templates among them. Selection is based on unsupervised clustering by the C-means method.

Main hypothesis behind our method is that users are clusterized in overlapping subsets as follows:

$$p(x) = \sum_{i=1}^{k} p(x|x \in c_i) \cdot P(x \in c_i) \tag{1}$$

Where c_i is the cluster associated to a well-defined user u_j. We hypothesize that the samples distribution $p(x|x \in c_i)$ is mono-modal, thus only one user at a time can be associated to a certain cluster. In order to find these clusters, we use the C-means algorithm aimed to maximize the intra-cluster/inter-clusters ratio variability. Cluster c_i is associated to a user u_j if this user exhibits the maximum number of samples in c_i.

The overall algorithm is as follows:

First stage
estimate the update threshold t^* using T
for all e element in u_i **do**
    if $distance(x \in u_i, T) < t^*$ **then**
        $T_{new} = T \cup x$
    end if
end for
Second stage
generate k clusters by C-means algorithm on T_{new}, where $C = k$ being k the number of enrolled users
for each i in $[1, .., k]$ **do**
    let c_i be the $i - th$ cluster generated by C-means (with $C = k$)
    let u_j the user with the highest number of samples in c_i
    select the p nearest samples to the centroid of c_i and update the gallery of u_j accordingly
end for

Even in this case, the algorithm is repeated once a novel batch u_{i+1} is collected.

Our system is supposed to work by accepting that hypothesis about users distributions is true. In case it is false, we may have two problems: (1) more than one cluster is associated to the same user, (2) one cluster can be associated to more than one user. However, if the matcher is working at a very stringent operational point, namely, zeroFAR, it is expected the classified samples are very close each other. Therefore, our basic hypothesis may hold in this case.

4   Experimental Result

4.1   Dataset

The dataset used to simulate our method is the Multimodal-DIEE. It is made up of 49 users with 60 images per user. The period of the acquisition is about one year and half per user. The dataset presents variations of lighting, face pose, expression and occlusions (glasses). An example is in Figure 1. Each face image is rotated in order to align eyes, then cropped and normalized at the size 128x128 pixels in order to keep the same interocular distance.

4.2   Experimental Protocol

The dataset is randomly subdivided into seven parts at incremental period of time. The first part is the initial gallery T, and the last part is the test set used to measure the performance of the system at each update cycle. In each update cycle, the intermediate five parts are submitted to the system. An independent

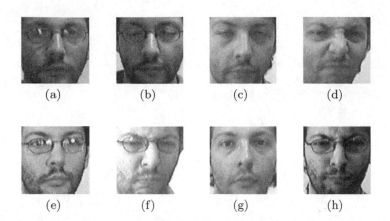

Fig. 1. Example of variation of a face in the Multimodal DIEE.

test-set allows us to appreciate the benefits of self update and proposed variant in order to have a precise reference and the same for all cycles.

Initial gallery varies from five to seven samples per user. This number also defines the maximum number of storable samples for our method, namely, the value of p, whilst for standard self update $p \to inf$.

Finally, we briefly describe the adopted facial features. After a pre-processing based on DoG [7] in order to alleviate the illumination variations problem, the resulting image is divided into non-overlapped blocks of 7x7 pixels. A set of Binarized Statistically Independent Features (BSIFs) is extracted from each block and concatenated in order to form the final feature vector [8]. This matcher is created for European MAVEN Project.

4.3   Results

In this Section, we show some experimental results about the application of standard self update and the proposed method under realistic constraints of keeping p samples in the users gallery. Updating threshold is set at the operational point such that $FAR = 0.1\%$.

The EER plots 2(a), 2(b), 2(c) show that the standard self update start dropping the performance, with average and standard deviation per user, after some batches. This is due to the fact that the more the wrongly impostors inserted into the system gallery, the more the error rate. On the contrary, the selection stage strongly reduce the error rate (Figs. 4(a), 4(b), 4(c)).

We may see that our algorithm exhibits the same behaviour independently on the investigated values of p that we kept very low in order to meet the stringent requirement of our working hypothesis. EER is substantially reduced with respect to standard self update which uses the same number of p samples.

AUC values are shown in plots 3(a), 3(b), 3(c). The proposed method exhibits the best performance even in this case, thus suggesting a substantial improvement for all operational points.

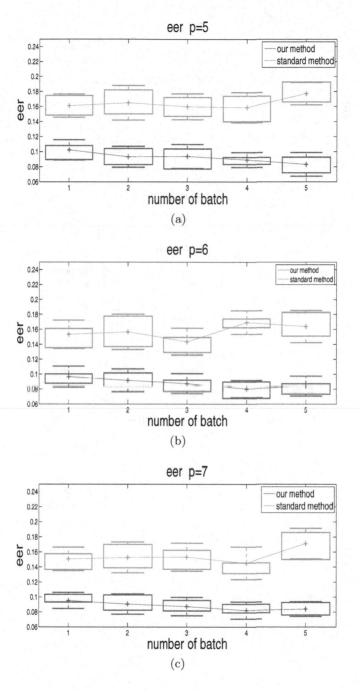

Fig. 2. Equal Error Rate comparison between state of the art system and the new proposed method by varying p.

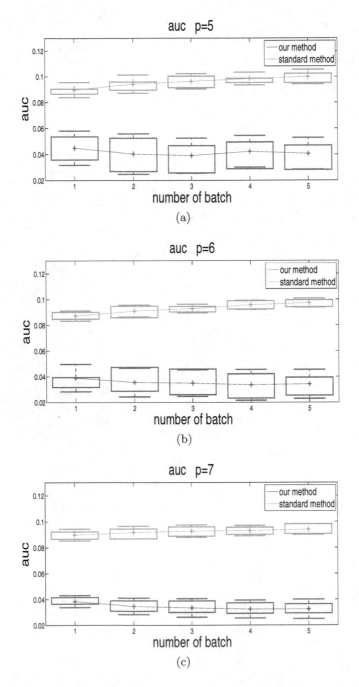

Fig. 3. AUC comparison between state of the art system and the new proposed method by varying p.

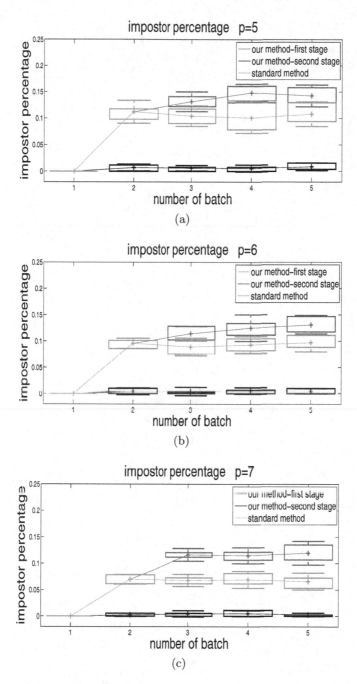

Fig. 4. Comparison between state of the art system and the new proposed method by varying p on rate of undetected impostors.

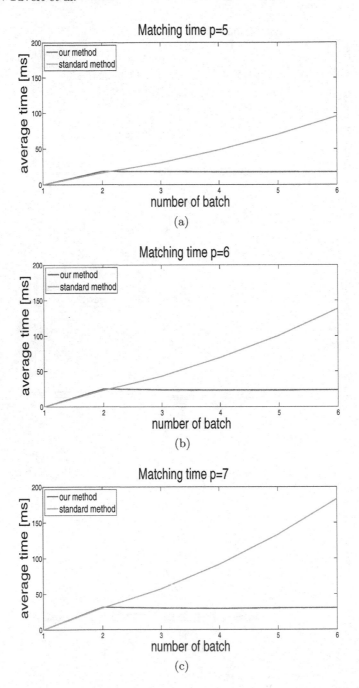

Fig. 5. Matching time comparison among the standard self-update system and the new proposed method by varying p.

The Figs. 4(a), 4(b), 4(c) show the average and standard deviation percentage of impostors in the users gallery. This percentage is always near to zero for all batches: the effectiveness of the selection approach can be appreciated by looking at the decrease of impostors number from first to second stage. This is an intrinsic confirmation about the hypothesis of users clusterization behind the rationale of our algorithm in the investigated data set.

Finally Figs. 5(a), 5(b), 5(c) show the matching time of the standard method, and the proposed one. We can appreciate that our method has a quite constant time at varying of p, because the variation of this parameter among the experiments is small. The standard self-update shows a linear matching time with number of templates. At varying of the variable p, the time increases for self-update, due to the fact that there is not a selection stage, which prunes the redundant templates. All the experiments were performed with a desktop PC with operating system Ubuntu 14.04 LTS 64bit,16 GB RAM, intel core i7-4790@3,60GHzx8, using MatLab v.R2013a.

The same arguments can be used to the memory issue, as matter of fact, our method has only p templates to every cycle. Instead in the standard self-update the number increase every time that there is a new batch of users, thus we have a linear proportionality between number of templates and occupied memory.

On the other hand, standard self update exhibit a higher number of impostors. This explains why both EER and AUC are worse than that of our method. It is important to notice that, potentially, the number of templates after first iteration is much superior than p. Despite this fact, the two-staged approach showed a more stable performance and a reduced number of impostors in the users galleries. As claimed in the introduction, this allows maintaining less complex the overall system architecture in order to be implemented even in systems with small storage and computational resources.

5   Conclusions

In this paper, we proposed an adaptive face recognition system based on two stages. First one is aimed to select a possible set of templates for each user's gallery. Second one is aimed to identify the user's cluster based on the hypothesis that the distribution of feature spaces is mono-modal for each user. Finally, the p samples nearest to each cluster's centroid are included into the clients gallery.

This approach has the ability of limiting the impostors introduction and keeping constant the number of samples in the user's gallery, by maximizing intra-class/inter-classes variations ratio.

Reported results are encouraging but experiments are limited to only one data set. Future works will be focused on extensive experiments and on a deep investigation on when and where the hypothesis behind our approach is verified.

Acknowledgement. The research leading to these results has received funding from the European Unions Seventh Framework Programme managed by REA - Research Executive Agency http://ec.europa.eu/research/rea (FP7/2007-2013) under Grant Agreement n 606058.

References

1. Yun, F., Guo, G., Huang, T.S.: Age Synthesis and Estimation via Faces: A Survey. IEEE Transactions on Pattern Analysis and Machine Intelligence **32**(11), 1955–1976 (2010)
2. Uludag, U., Ross, A., Jain, A.: Biometric Template Selection: A Case Study in Fingerprints. In: Kittler, J., Nixon, M.S. (eds.) AVBPA 2003. LNCS, vol. 2688, pp. 335–342. Springer, Heidelberg (2003)
3. Jiang, X., Ser, W.: Online fingerprint template improvement. IEEE Transactions on Pattern Analysis and Machine Intelligence **24**(8), 1121–1126 (2002)
4. Freni, B., Marcialis, G.L., Roli, F.: Replacement Algorithms for Fingerprint Template Update. In: Campilho, A., Kamel, M.S. (eds.) ICIAR 2008. LNCS, vol. 5112, pp. 884–893. Springer, Heidelberg (2008)
5. Rattani, A., Marcialis, G.L., Granger, E., Roli, F.: A Dual-Staged Classification-Selection Approach for Automated Update of Biometric Templates. In: IAPR/IEEE 21th Int. Conf. on Pattern Recognition (ICPR 2012), Tsukuba, Japan, November 11 15, pp. 2972–2975 (2012) ISBN: 978-4-9906441-1-6
6. Ryu, C., Kim, H., Jain, A.K.: Template adaptation based fingerprint verification. In: 18th International Conference on Pattern Recognition, ICPR 2006, vol. 4, pp. 582–585. IEEE (2006)
7. Tan, X., Triggs, B.: Enhanced local texture sets for face recognition under difficult lighting conditions. IEEE Transactions on Image Processing **19**(6), 1635–1650 (2010)
8. Kannala, J., Rahtu, E.: BSIF: Binarized statistical image features. In: 2012 21st International Conference on Pattern Recognition (ICPR), November 11–15, pp. 1363–1366 (2012)
9. Roli, F., Didaci, L., Marcialis, G.L.: Adaptive biometric systems that can improve with use. In: Ratha, N., Govindaraju, V. (eds.) Advances in Biometrics: Sensors, Systems and Algorithms, pp. 447–471. Springer (2008) doi:10.1007/978-1-84628-921-7 ISBN 978-1-84628-920-0

Super-Sparse Regression for Fast Age Estimation from Faces at Test Time

Ambra Demontis, Battista Biggio$^{(\boxtimes)}$, Giorgio Fumera, and Fabio Roli

Department of Electrical and Electronic Engineering,
University of Cagliari, Piazza d'Armi, 09123 Cagliari, Italy
{ambra.demontis,battista.biggio,fumera,roli}@diee.unica.it
http://prag.diee.unica.it

Abstract. Age estimation from faces is a challenging problem that has recently gained increasing relevance due to its potentially multi-faceted applications. Many current methods for age estimation rely on extracting computationally-demanding features from face images, and then use non-linear regression to estimate the subject's age. This often requires matching the submitted face image against a set of face prototypes, potentially including all training face images, as in the case of kernel-based methods. In this work, we propose a super-sparse regression technique that can reach comparable performance with respect to other nonlinear regression techniques, while drastically reducing the number of reference prototypes required for age estimation. Given a similarity measure between faces, our technique learns a sparse set of virtual face prototypes, whose number is fixed a priori, along with a set of optimal weight coefficients to perform linear regression in the space induced by the similarity measure. We show that our technique does not only drastically reduce the number of reference prototypes without compromising estimation accuracy, but it can also provide more interpretable decisions.

1 Introduction

Human faces naturally convey information about people's identity, age, gender, health, and emotional state. Earlier approaches have exploited this information for improving face recognition systems, as well as for law enforcement and statistical analysis [9,10]. With the advent of the Internet of Things, many other application scenarios have emerged, due to the increase of applications based on human-computer interactions. In particular, smart devices may change their behavior depending on the inferred user's age from their face image; *e.g.*, televisions may deny watching adult programs to children, web browsers may deny access to adult websites, and medicine cabinets may not open [9,11,21]. However, age estimation is a very difficult problem, as each individual ages differently, and the aging process does not only depend on one's genes, but also on various factors such as health state, stress, living environment, smoke and living style. Generally, the face aging process consists of two main phases: during childhood, the head grows significantly, changing the *geometry* of the face and distances

© Springer International Publishing Switzerland 2015
V. Murino and E. Puppo (Eds.): ICIAP 2015, Part II, LNCS 9280, pp. 551–562, 2015.
DOI: 10.1007/978-3-319-23234-8_51

between fiducial points like eyes, nose, *etc.*; during adulthood, instead, the aging process involves the formation of wrinkles, changing the image *texture* [9,10].

Current approaches for age estimation from faces have addressed this problem by exploiting and combining several feature representations, as well as classification and regression algorithms, to successfully cope with the intrinsic complexity and nonlinearity of this problem (Sect. 2); in particular, kernel methods like Support Vector Regression (SVR) and Support Vector Machines (SVM) [7,12]. Despite these techniques may naturally yield a sparse solution, *i.e.*, they require matching the submitted face image only against a small subset of the training face images (*e.g.*, the *support vectors* in SVR and SVM), the retrieved solutions may not be sparse enough. In particular, the number of support vectors tends to grow linearly with the training set size [5,19], causing an increase of the computational complexity at test time, and hindering the suitability of these approach for real-time, *online* age estimation [9,13]. Some methods that exhibit a reduced complexity have also been proposed, based on the exploitation of manifold learning algorithms to map input images onto more compact, reduced feature spaces, and then applying classification or regression more efficiently in that space. However, they are mostly devoted to improve prediction accuracy rather than speed at test time [12,17]. Furthermore, there are two other related issues: (i) the proposed systems are often very complicated, and it is thus difficult to interpret their decisions and understand why they predict a given age value (*e.g.*, it is not easy to understand which characteristics from face images are exploited by the system to discriminate between young and old people); and (ii) their inherent complexity poses a serious risk of overfitting to specific datasets.

In this paper, we propose an approach aimed to overcome these limitations (Sect. 3). It is inspired to a well-principled SVM reduction method that we recently proposed in [1] to reduce the number of face templates (*i.e.*, prototypes) in face verification systems, through the creation of a super-sparse, budgeted set of virtual vectors, *i.e.*, a fixed number of artificially-generated face templates. In this work, we extend that method and propose a super-sparse regression technique that can reach comparable performance with respect to other nonlinear regression techniques, while requiring a much smaller number of reference prototypes for age estimation at test time. Assuming that a similarity measure between faces is given, our technique jointly learns a very sparse set of virtual face prototypes, whose number is fixed a priori, and a set of optimal weight coefficients to linearly combine the similarities computed between the submitted face images (from which we aim to estimate the subject's age) and the set of reference prototypes. This allows our technique to drastically reduce the number of required prototypes without almost compromising estimation accuracy, while also providing more interpretable decisions. Our experimental analysis shows that our approach can achieve comparable performances to other state-of-the-art techniques on two well-known benchmark datasets for age estimation, while reducing of more than one order of magnitude the complexity at test time (Sect. 4). We conclude the paper by discussing contributions, limitations, and future developments of this work (Sect. 5).

2   Age Estimation from Faces

During the last years, the problem of age estimation from faces has received an increasing interest. Several works have been published since the pioneering work by Kwon and Lobo [15], in which an anthropometric model and wrinkle analyses were exploited to discriminate babies from adults. Most of the recent work nowadays exploits complex feature representation that account for geometry, shapes and textures of face images, like appearance active models [4,8,12], local binary patterns [7,22], and several other visual descriptors [3,6,12,13,16]. Few works have also shown that suitable projection techniques (*e.g.*, principal component analysis, or locality preserving projection) in conjunction with well-principled learning techniques (*e.g.*, SVM for classification, and SVR for regression) can even infer useful information for age estimation directly from the raw, gray-level pixel values [10,12]. In a similar fashion, very recent approaches have applied deep-learning methods to the same end [21].

Limitations and Open Issues. In the majority of the cases, the aforementioned work has focused on improving the performance of age estimation on benchmark datasets, without considering constraints deriving from the application of the proposed methods in real-time applications. Notably, in [13], a sparse kernel-based projection and learning technique have been proposed *also* to speed up age estimation at test time. Besides the issue of computational complexity at test time, the proposed methods outputs decisions which are difficult to interpret. Even for sparse methods, that rely on computing tens of features or prototype matchings, as in [13], this can be a problem. Last but not least, there is a third issue, motivated by the continuously-observed improvement of performances on benchmark datasets, *i.e.*, the need of verifying whether current methods tend to overfit on such specific datasets.

To overcome these three issues, we propose a super-sparse regression method, that can reliably estimate a person's age by matching his or her face image against a very small, budgeted set of reference prototypes, without significantly affecting estimation accuracy. Given its super-sparsity, our method provides more interpretable decisions to end-users and system administrators, and, for the same reason, it should also be less prone to overfit on the specific datasets.

3   Super-Sparse Regression for Fast Age Estimation

In this section, we illustrate our approach. We assume that a set $\mathcal{D} = \{x_i, y_i\}_{i=1}^n \in \mathcal{X}^n \times \mathbb{R}_+^n$ of n face images x_i is given, along with the corresponding ages y_i. We do not set any constraint on the representation of faces: we consider them to be objects in an abstract space $\mathcal{X}$, *i.e.*, they can be represented either as feature vectors or as structured objects (*e.g.*, graphs, or bags of visual descriptors). We further assume that a similarity function $k : \mathcal{X} \times \mathcal{X} \mapsto \mathbb{R}$ between two faces is given. For instance, it can be a kernel function (which is positive semi-definite), or any other similarity function, including functions that are not Mercer kernels.

Within this setting, the underlying idea of our approach is to estimate the age of a subject x as a function $f(x)$ defined as a *sparse* linear combination of similarities between x and a *small* set of face prototypes $z = (z_1, \ldots, z_m) \in \mathcal{X}^m$, whose number m is *budgeted*, *i.e.*, fixed a priori:

$$f(x) = \sum_{j=1}^m \beta_j k(x, z_j) + b ,\tag{1}$$

where $\beta = (\beta_1, \ldots, \beta_m) \in \mathbb{R}^m$ is the vector of coefficients and $b \in \mathbb{R}$ the bias, which have to be learnt *together with* the prototypes z. This can be formulated as the following optimization problem:

$$\min_{\beta, b, z} \Omega = \sum_{i=1}^n u_i \left(f(x_i) - y_i \right)^2 + \lambda \beta^\top \beta ,\tag{2}$$

where the scalars $u_1, \ldots, u_n$ balance the contribution of each sample x_k to the empirical loss (*e.g.*, if the distribution of samples per age in the training set is not uniform), the quadratic regularizer $\beta^\top \beta$ controls overfitting, and λ is a regularization parameter. Due to the presence of a quadratic regularizer, as in ridge regression, we name our approach *Super-Sparse Ridge* (S^2R) regression. This approach is clearly linear in the space induced by the similarity function, but not necessarily in the input space $\mathcal{X}$, *i.e.*, the similarity mapping can be used to induce nonlinearity as in kernel methods. Problem 2 turns out to be very similar to that resulting from the novel face verification approach that we recently developed in [1], except for the fact that we are considering an explicit bias term b here, and performing regression on a generic target variable (*i.e.*, not on an SVM's discriminant function to reduce its support vectors). We thus exploit a similar algorithm to compute its solution, as described below.

The objective function of problem (2) can be rewritten in matrix form:

$$\Omega(\beta, b, z) = \left(f^\top U f - 2 y^\top U f + y^\top U y \right) + \lambda \beta^\top \beta ,\tag{3}$$

where the column vectors $f, y \in \mathbb{R}^n$ contain the values of f and y for the training samples, $U \in \mathbb{R}^{n \times n}$ is a diagonal matrix with $\mathrm{diag}(U) = (u_1, \ldots, u_n)$, and $f = K_{xz} \beta + b$, being $K_{xz} \in \mathbb{R}^{n \times m}$ the similarity matrix computed between $x_1, \ldots, x_n$ and the prototypes z. The objective function (3) can be iteratively minimized by modifying β, b and z, by first randomly initializing the initial prototypes $\{z_j^{(0)}\}_{j=1}^m$ with m training samples from $\mathcal{D}$, and then alternating the two steps described in the following.

(1) **β-step.** We compute the optimal coefficients β by keeping the prototypes z fixed. This amounts to a standard ridge regression problem, which can be analytically solved by deriving Eq. (3) with respect to β and b (with z constant), and then setting the corresponding gradients to zero:

$$\underbrace{\begin{bmatrix} K_{xz}^\top U K_{xz} + \lambda \mathbb{I} & K_{xz}^\top U 1 \\ 1^\top U K_{xz} & 1^\top U 1 \end{bmatrix}}_{M} \begin{bmatrix} \beta \\ b \end{bmatrix} = \begin{bmatrix} K_{xz}^\top \\ 1^\top \end{bmatrix} U y ,\tag{4}$$

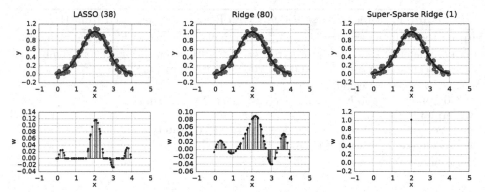

Fig. 1. A simple mono-dimensional, nonlinear regression problem. Plots in the top row show the estimated regression function (solid black line) for LASSO, Ridge, and our Super-Sparse Ridge regression, all trained on the RBF kernel matrix computed between the displayed (red) points, to yield linear functions in the kernel space. The number of selected prototypes is reported in parentheses. The non-zero weight coefficients assigned to the selected prototypes are reported in the plots in the bottom row. As one may reasonably expect, our method only requires one prototype to reliably estimate the given Gaussian-like function, thus significantly reducing complexity at test time.

where $\mathbb{I} \in \mathbb{R}^{m \times m}$ is the identity matrix. The system (4) can be iteratively solved without necessarily inverting $\mathbf{M}$, e.g., using stochastic gradient descent [23].
(2) z-step. We update z by iteratively minimizing (3) through gradient descent (no closed-form solution exists). Deriving with respect to a given z_j, and using the numerator-layout convention for matrix derivatives, we obtain:

$$\frac{\partial \Omega}{\partial z_j} = 2 \left(h - y \right)^\top \mathbf{U} \left(\beta_j \frac{\partial \mathbf{K}_{xz_j}}{\partial z_j} + \mathbf{K}_{xz} \frac{\partial \beta}{\partial z_j} + 1 \frac{\partial b}{\partial z_j} \right) + 2\lambda \beta^\top \frac{\partial \beta}{\partial z_j} \, , \quad (5)$$

where $\mathbf{K}_{xz_j}$ is the j-th column of $\mathbf{K}_{xz}$. Accordingly, all the derivatives with respect to z_j are vectors or matrices with the same number of columns as the dimensionality of z_j. In Eq. (5) we need to compute $\frac{\partial \beta}{\partial z_j}$ and $\frac{\partial b}{\partial z_j}$, which can be obtained by deriving Eq. (4). The final gradient is thus given as:

$$\begin{bmatrix} \frac{\partial \beta}{\partial z_j} \\ \frac{\partial b}{\partial z_j} \end{bmatrix} = -\mathbf{M}^{-1} \left(\beta_j \begin{bmatrix} \mathbf{K}_{xz}^\top \\ 1^\top \end{bmatrix} + \begin{bmatrix} \mathbf{S}^\top \\ 0^\top \end{bmatrix} \right) \mathbf{U} \frac{\partial \mathbf{K}_{xz_j}}{\partial z_j} \, , \quad (6)$$

where $\mathbf{S} \in \mathbb{R}^{n \times m}$ is a matrix consisting of all zeros except for the jth column which is equal to $(f - y)$, and $0, 1 \in \mathbb{R}^n$ are column vectors of n zeros and n ones, respectively.

Derivative of $\mathbf{K}_{xz_j}$. In (6), the computation of the derivative of $k(x_1, z_j), \ldots, k(x_n, z_j)$, with respect to the corresponding z_j, depends on the given similarity measure k. If k has an analytical representation, as in the case of kernels, the derivative can be easily computed; e.g., for the RBF kernel, $k(x_i, z_j) = \exp(-\gamma\|x_i - z_j\|^2)$, and thus $\frac{\partial k(x_i, z_j)}{\partial z_j} = -2\gamma \exp(-\gamma\|x_i - z_j\|^2)(x_i - z_j)$. Otherwise, numerical optimization techniques can be used.

Algorithm 1. Super-Sparse Ridge (S^2R) Regression (adapted from [1])

Input: the training set $\mathcal{D} = \{\boldsymbol{x}_i, y_i\}_{i=1}^n$; the similarity function $k(\cdot, \cdot)$; the regularization parameter λ; the initial prototypes $\{\boldsymbol{z}_j^{(0)}\}_{j=1}^m$; the step size η; a small number ϵ.
Output: The coefficients $\boldsymbol{\beta}$, b and the virtual prototypes $\{\boldsymbol{z}_j\}_{j=1}^m$.

1: Set the iteration count $q \leftarrow 0$.
2: Compute $\boldsymbol{\beta}^{(0)}$ and $b^{(0)}$ for $\boldsymbol{z}_1^{(0)}, \ldots, \boldsymbol{z}_m^{(0)}$ and $\mathcal{D}$ using Eq. (4).
3: **repeat**
4:     Set $j \leftarrow \text{mod}(q, m) + 1$ to index a virtual face prototype.
5:     Compute $\frac{\partial \Omega}{\partial \boldsymbol{z}_j}$ using Eq. (5).
6:     Increase the iteration count $q \leftarrow q + 1$
7:     Set $\boldsymbol{z}_j^{(q)} \leftarrow \boldsymbol{z}_j^{(q-1)} + \eta \frac{\partial \Omega}{\partial \boldsymbol{z}_j^{(q-1)}}$.
8:     **if** $\boldsymbol{z}_j^{(q)} \notin \mathcal{X}$, **then** project $\boldsymbol{z}_j^{(q)}$ onto $\mathcal{X}$.
9:     Set $\boldsymbol{z}_i^{(q)} \leftarrow \boldsymbol{z}_i^{(q-1)}$, $\forall i \neq j$.
10:    Compute $\boldsymbol{\beta}^{(q)}$ and $b^{(q)}$ for $\boldsymbol{z}_1^{(q)}, \ldots, \boldsymbol{z}_m^{(q)}$ and $\mathcal{D}$ using Eq. (4).
11: **until** $\left| \Omega \left(\boldsymbol{\beta}^{(q)}, b^{(q)}, \boldsymbol{z}^{(q)} \right) - \Omega \left(\boldsymbol{\beta}^{(q-1)}, b^{(q-1)}, \boldsymbol{z}^{(q-1)} \right) \right| < \epsilon$
12: **return:** $\boldsymbol{\beta} = \boldsymbol{\beta}^{(q)}$, $b = b^{(q)}$ and $\boldsymbol{z} = \boldsymbol{z}^{(q)}$.

The above optimization procedure is shown as Algorithm 1. We also report a simple graphical example to show how our algorithm works in Fig. 1, in comparison with popular regression methods like LASSO [20] (which induces sparsity through ℓ_1 regularization) and ridge regression [14].

4   Experiments

In this section we report an experimental analysis to show how the proposed super-sparse regression can: (i) drastically reduce the number of reference prototype, speeding up age estimation at test time; (ii) provide more interpretable decisions; and (iii) avoid the risk of overfitting on cross-database evaluations.

Datasets. For our empirical evaluation, we have used two well-known, public benchmark databases, described below.

FG-Net Aging. This database consists of 1002 images of 82 subjects, including from 6 to 18 images per subject. Images exhibit a variable resolution; some of them are grayscale, many are blurred. For each image, 68 manually-labeled face landmark points are provided to facilitate face normalization and feature extraction. However, we decided not to use them, to simulate a more realistic experimental setting (in which, of course, test images are not manually labeled).

FRGC. This database includes 49,228 frontal images of 568 different subjects (241 female and 327 male subjects) belonging to 7 different ethnicity groups. The minimum and the maximum age values reported in this database are respectively 17 and 69, and there are multiple images per subject. Images were acquired during different time sessions (one per month). On average, 6 images per user

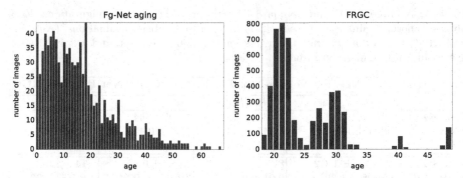

Fig. 2. Number of images per age for Fg-Net (*left*) and FRGC (*right*).

were acquired during a single session. To keep the complexity of our experiments manageable, we randomly select a subset of about 5,000 images.

For the sake of completeness, we report the distributions of ages for the two considered datasets in Fig. 2.

Experimental Setup. We normalize face images by first detecting the eye positions with a (trained) detector originally proposed in [24]; then, we align faces to have eyes into a fixed position, normalize illumination, and use an ellipse-based normalization to eliminate irrelevant background information, as described in [2]. Similarly to previous work in age estimation, our results are averaged using a 5-fold cross-validation procedure (using different subjects in each fold), and reported in terms of the Mean Absolute Error (MAE), given as:

$$\text{MAE} = \frac{1}{n} \sum_{i=1}^{n} |f(\boldsymbol{x}_i) - y_i| \tag{7}$$

where $f(\boldsymbol{x}_i)$ is the regression estimate of the true subject's age y_i for the test image $\boldsymbol{x}_i$, and n the test set size (*i.e.*, the size of the test fold).

We adopt three different feature representations for face images: (i) the grey-level values of pixels (pixel values), (ii) principal component analysis (PCA-based mapping), and (iii) linear discriminant analysis (LDA-based mapping). To obtain (ii) and (iii), we start from the pixel representation of images and apply the two aforementioned projection techniques, retaining the first 100 components for the PCA-based mapping (approximately capturing 90% of the variance in the data), and $K - 1$ components for the LDA-based mapping, being K the number of distinct ages in the training data.

We use these three representations as features, and, after linearly rescaling them in $[-1, 1]$, we apply LASSO, SVR (with linear kernel), and Ridge regression. We then consider the RBF kernel (with $\gamma = 1/d$, being d the number of dimensions in the input space) and use the same methods trained using the kernel values as input features. The regularization parameter for LASSO, SVR and Ridge regression were set through an inner 2-fold cross-validation, to optimize the expected MAE value. We consider the proposed approach for super-sparse ridge (S^2R) regression with $m = 5$ and $m = 15$ virtual reference prototypes,

Table 1. Average MAE and standard deviation for the given configurations. Each column reports training/test sets, including cross-database evaluations (*e.g.*, Fg-Net/FRGC means that we train the regression function on Fg-Net, and test on FRGC). Best results are highlighted in bold.

Regressor	Fg-Net/Fg-Net	Fg-Net/FRGC	FRGC/Fg-Net	FRGC/FRGC
Pixel values				
LASSO	9.16 ± 1.41	13.63 ± 0.23	14.05 ± 0.4	6.51 ± 0.6
SVR	9.1 ± 1.39	12.45 ± 0.38	13.6 ± 0.41	6.02 ± 0.79
Ridge	9.21 ± 1.39	13.63 ± 0.23	14.05 ± 0.4	6.53 ± 0.62
LASSO RBF	$\mathbf{6.92 \pm 1.62}$	8.76 ± 0.65	12.87 ± 0.33	4.14 ± 1.09
SVR RBF	6.98 ± 1.79	9.01 ± 0.49	$\mathbf{12.58 \pm 0.29}$	$\mathbf{3.87 \pm 1.33}$
Ridge RBF	6.94 ± 1.62	8.74 ± 0.66	12.87 ± 0.32	4.13 ± 1.09
S^2R RBF (5)	10.09 ± 1.07	6.93 ± 0.8	15.96 ± 1.11	5.48 ± 1.22
S^2R RBF (15)	8.92 ± 1.58	$\mathbf{6.89 \pm 0.21}$	13.01 ± 0.16	5.44 ± 2.30
PCA-based mapping				
LASSO	7.83 ± 1.68	10.93 ± 0.77	13.46 ± 0.61	4.9 ± 0.68
SVR	7.21 ± 1.96	8.98 ± 0.63	12.76 ± 0.29	$\mathbf{3.76 \pm 1.28}$
Ridge	9.06 ± 1.07	11.09 ± 1.27	13.41 ± 0.81	5.25 ± 0.46
LASSO RBF	8.22 ± 1.65	8.69 ± 1.5	12.75 ± 0.32	4.33 ± 1.13
SVR RBF	$\mathbf{7.05 \pm 1.96}$	8.95 ± 0.72	$\mathbf{12.48 \pm 0.31}$	3.93 ± 1.54
Ridge RBF	8.23 ± 1.65	8.67 ± 1.51	12.76 ± 0.31	4.32 ± 1.13
S^2R RBF (5)	7.92 ± 1.3	9.09 ± 0.84	14.02 ± 0.39	5.37 ± 0.89
S^2R RBF (15)	7.86 ± 1.3	$\mathbf{7.76 \pm 0.40}$	12.87 ± 0.34	5.90 ± 2.49
LDA-based mapping				
LASSO	8.72 ± 1.6	11.98 ± 0.91	13.78 ± 0.47	5.79 ± 0.73
SVR	8.63 ± 1.38	11.48 ± 0.37	13.77 ± 0.47	5.79 ± 0.73
Ridge	8.71 ± 1.6	11.98 ± 0.91	13.78 ± 0.47	5.78 ± 0.73
LASSO RBF	$\mathbf{7.92 \pm 1.87}$	10.92 ± 0.74	13.55 ± 0.32	5.93 ± 0.9
SVR RBF	8.06 ± 1.78	10.57 ± 0.7	13.7 ± 0.38	$\mathbf{5.08 \pm 0.92}$
Ridge RBF	7.92 ± 1.87	10.92 ± 0.75	13.55 ± 0.32	5.93 ± 0.9
S^2R RBF (5)	8.49 ± 1.62	11.56 ± 0.35	16.84 ± 2.06	9.56 ± 2.19
S^2R RBF (15)	8.37 ± 1.62	$\mathbf{9.93 \pm 0.40}$	$\mathbf{13.28 \pm 0.5}$	7.30 ± 1.89

for which we set the gradient step size η at each iteration by selecting the best value $\eta \in \{0.3, 0.1, 0.01, 0.001\}$. In general, the number m of prototypes could also be tuned through a cross-validation procedure. We finally evaluate all the aforementioned approaches on a cross-database scenario, where we replace the test fold of the dataset used for training with the full dataset used for testing.

Results. Results are shown in Table 1, for the given configurations (pixel values, PCA- and LDA-based mappings), linear methods (LASSO, SVR, and Ridge), RBF-based methods (LASSO RBF, SVR RBF, Ridge RBF), and S^2R regression with 5 and 15 prototypes. First, note that linear methods exhibit lower performances, confirming that the problem of age estimation is better tackled by nonlinear approaches. It is then clear that S^2R regression can achieve

Table 2. Average number of prototypes (*i.e.*, required matchings for testing) and standard deviation for nonlinear regression methods, for the different considered configurations. Note how the number of matchings is always significantly higher than 5 or 15, *i.e.*, the number of prototypes used by our S^2R regression.

Regressor	Fg-Net	FRGC
Pixel values		
LASSO RBF	758.4	3977.8
SVR RBF	759.0	3974.0
Ridge RBF	760.8	4000.0
PCA-based mapping		
LASSO RBF	758.8	3928.2
SVR RBF	759.4	3975.4
Ridge RBF	760.8	4000.0
LDA-based mapping		
LASSO RBF	758.2	3975.8
SVR RBF	753.4	1584.8
Ridge RBF	760.8	4000.0

comparable performances with the other nonlinear regressors, although using only a very small number of prototypes (*cf.* Table 2). SVR RBF and LASSO RBF outperform occasionally the other techniques. As expected, due to its super-sparsity, S^2R regression also exhibits good performance on the cross-database evaluations (*cf.* second and third column in Table 1). Sometimes, cross-database learning may be difficult due to the presence of unbalanced distributions of ages between the two considered datasets. Consequently, one method may tend to overfit and predict the age value with the highest prior probability in the training set. Our method naturally allows to compensate for this problem by using non-uniform values in $\mathbf{U}$ (see Eq. 2), *e.g.*, by assigning a value that is inversely-proportional to the prior probability of observing the corresponding age value in the training set. We leave however a more detailed cross-database analysis to future work, also from a more theoretically-sound perspective.

Interpretability. As mentioned before, interpretability of decisions is another important property to understand whether the regression algorithm has properly learned some aging pattern, and, thus, if it may correctly predict images from different datasets. In Fig. 3, we report two examples of the prototypes learned by S^2R regression on Fg-Net and FRGC, respectively. As one may appreciate, our method assigns correctly lower age values to "smaller" faces (*i.e.*, faces of children), and higher values to images which exhibit textures characterized by higher frequencies, *i.e.*, by the presence of wrinkles.

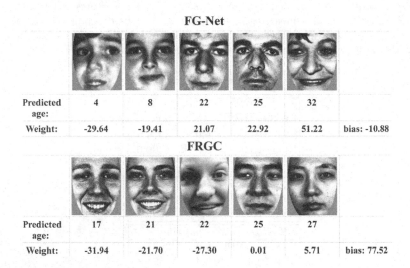

Fig. 3. Virtual reference prototypes learned by our S^2R regression method for FG-Net and FRGC, along with the corresponding weights β, bias b, and predicted age $f(x)$.

5   Conclusions and Future Work

We have proposed a novel super-sparse regression method, inspired by our recently-proposed SVM reduction technique in the context of face verification [1]. That method was in turn inspired by existing reduction methods [18], and capable of outperforming them, for the following reasons: (i) it is not greedy (*i.e.*, it iteratively modifies each prototype during the minimization process), and (ii) it can also be trained with similarity functions that are not necessarily positive semi-definite (*i.e.*, Mercer) kernels. Our results have shown that the proposed method can achieve comparable performances to other popular regression techniques, either sparse (*e.g.*, SVR, LASSO) or not (*e.g.*, Ridge), while reducing the number of prototypes required for age estimation at test time of orders of magnitude. Furthermore, thanks to its super-sparsity property, the proposed approach provides decisions which are easier to interpret for system administrators and end-users of the age estimation system, and it has also exhibited promising results on cross-database evaluations. Future research directions therefore include finding a theoretically-sound explanation to this behavior, to gain more interesting insights on this property. Another interesting line of work consists of evaluating the proposed method on more complex feature representations and visual descriptors, in order to empirically validate whether age estimation accuracy can be improved on benchmark datasets while keeping a super-sparse solution, *i.e.*, while dramatically reducing complexity at test time.

Acknowledgments. This work has been supported by the project "Computational quantum structures at the service of pattern recognition: modeling uncertainty" (CRP-59872) funded by Regione Autonoma della Sardegna (RAS), L.R. 7/2007, Bando 2012, and by the project "Security of pattern recognition systems in future internet" (CRP-18293) funded by RAS, L.R. 7/2007, Bando 2009.

References

1. Biggio, B., Melis, M., Fumera, G., Roli, F.: Sparse support faces. In: Int'l Conf. on Biometrics (ICB), pp. 208–213 (2015)
2. Bolme, D.S., Beveridge, J.R., Teixeira, M., Draper, B.A.: The CSU Face Identification Evaluation System: Its Purpose, Features, and Structure. In: Crowley, J.L., Piater, J.H., Vincze, M., Paletta, L. (eds.) ICVS 2003. LNCS, vol. 2626, pp. 304–313. Springer, Heidelberg (2003)
3. Chang, K.Y., Chen, C.S.: A learning framework for age rank estimation based on face images with scattering transform. IEEE Trans. Image Processing **24**(3), 785–798 (2015)
4. Chao, W.L., Liu, J.Z., Ding, J.J.: Facial age estimation based on label-sensitive learning and age-oriented regression. Patt. Rec. **46**(3), 628–641 (2013)
5. Chapelle, O.: Training a support vector machine in the primal. Neural Comput. **19**(5), 1155–1178 (2007)
6. Chen, Y.L., Hsu, C.T.: Subspace learning for facial age estimation via pairwise age ranking. IEEE Trans. Inf. Forensics and Security **8**(12), 2164–2176 (2013)
7. Choi, S.E., Lee, Y.J., Lee, S.J., Park, K.R., Kim, J.: Age estimation using a hierarchical classifier based on global and local facial features. Patt. Rec. **44**(6), 1262–1281 (2011)
8. Cootes, T.F., Edwards, G.J., Taylor, C.J.: Active appearance models. IEEE Trans. Patt. Anal. Mach. Intell. **23**(6), 681–685 (2001)
9. Fu, Y., Guo, G., Huang, T.: Age synthesis and estimation via faces: A survey. IEEE Trans. Patt. Anal. Mach. Intell. **32**(11), 1955–1976 (2010)
10. Fu, Y., Huang, T.: Human age estimation with regression on discriminative aging manifold. IEEE Trans. Multimedia **10**(4), 578–584 (2008)
11. Guo, G., Fu, Y., Dyer, C., Huang, T.: Image-based human age estimation by manifold learning and locally adjusted robust regression. IEEE Trans. Image Processing **17**(7), 1178–1188 (2008)
12. Guo, G., Fu, Y., Dyer, C., Huang, T.: A probabilistic fusion approach to human age prediction. In: Computer Vision and Pattern Recognition Workshops, CVPRW 2008, pp. 1–6 IEEE CS (2008)
13. Guo, G., Mu, G.: Simultaneous dimensionality reduction and human age estimation via kernel partial least squares regression. In: IEEE Conf. Computer Vision and Pattern Recognition (CVPR), pp. 657–664 (2011)
14. Hoerl, A.E., Kennard, R.W.: Ridge regression: Biased estimation for nonorthogonal problems. Technometrics **12**(1), 55–67 (1970)
15. Kwon, Y.H., Lobo, N.D.V.: Age classification from facial images. In: IEEE Conf. Computer Vision and Pattern Recognition (CVPR), pp. 762–767 (1999)
16. Li, C., Liu, Q., Dong, W., Zhu, X., Liu, J., Lu, H.: Human age estimation based on locality and ordinal information. IEEE Trans. Cybernetics (99), 1 (2014)
17. Li, Z., Park, U., Jain, A.: A discriminative model for age invariant face recognition. IEEE Trans. Inf. Forensics and Security **6**(3), 1028–1037 (2011)

18. Schölkopf, B., Mika, S., Burges, C.J.C., Knirsch, P., Muller, K.R., Rätsch, G., Smola, A.J.: Input space versus feature space in kernel-based methods. IEEE Trans. Neural Networks **10**(5), 1000–1017 (1999)
19. Steinwart, I.: Sparseness of support vector machines. J. Mach. Learn. Res. **4**(11), 1071–1105 (2003)
20. Tibshirani, R.: Regression shrinkage and selection via the lasso. Journal of the Royal Statistical Society (Series B) **58**, 267–288 (1996)
21. Wang, X., Guo, R., Kambhamettu, C.: Deeply-learned feature for age estimation. In: IEEE Winter Conf. Applications Computer Vision (WACV), pp. 534–541 (2015)
22. Ylioinas, J., Hadid, A., Hong, X., Pietikäinen, M.: Age Estimation Using Local Binary Pattern Kernel Density Estimate. In: Petrosino, A. (ed.) ICIAP 2013, Part I. LNCS, vol. 8156, pp. 141–150. Springer, Heidelberg (2013)
23. Zhang, T.: Solving large scale linear prediction problems using stochastic gradient descent algorithms. In: 21st Int'l Conf. Mach. Learning (ICML), pp. 919–926. Omnipress (2004)
24. Zhu, X., Ramanan, D.: Face detection, pose estimation, and landmark localization in the wild. In: IEEE Conf. Computer Vision and Pattern Recognition (CVPR), pp. 2879–2886. IEEE (2012)

Video Analysis

Automated Recognition of Social Behavior in Rats: The Role of Feature Quality

Malte Lorbach[1,2]($\boxtimes$), Ronald Poppe[1], Elsbeth A. van Dam[2],
Lucas P.J.J. Noldus[2], and Remco C. Veltkamp[1]

[1] Department of Information and Computing Sciences,
Utrecht University, Utrecht, The Netherlands
`m.t.lorbach@uu.nl`
[2] Noldus Information Technology, Wageningen, The Netherlands

Abstract. We investigate how video-based recognition of rat social behavior is affected by the quality of the tracking data and the derived feature set. We look at the impact of two common tracking errors – animal misidentification and inaccurate localization of body parts. We further examine how the complexity of representing the articulated body in the features influences the recognition accuracy. Our analyses show that correct identification of the rats is required to accurately recognize their interactions. Precise localization of multiple body points is beneficial for recognizing interactions that are described by a distinct pose. Including pose features only leads to improvement if the tracking algorithm can provide that data reliably.

Keywords: Social behavior · Action recognition · Tracking quality

1 Introduction

We investigate the automated recognition of social interactions between rats. Rat social behavior is of interest for biologists who look for indicators for neurological and psychiatric disorders such as Huntington's disease. Such indicators can be abnormalities in how often and how long the animals engage in specific social interactions. Currently, these studies involve laborious and error-prone manual coding of interactions and thus automating the coding is desired.

Video-based recognition of rat interactions typically requires three problems to be solved, namely: tracking and identifying the animals in the presence of occlusions, deriving meaningful features from these tracks, and classifying the features into interaction categories. Previous work on recognizing interactions has mainly focused on these steps in isolation, in particular by assuming perfect tracking when computing features. The effects of mistaken identities and noisy tracking on the classification have received less attention. As a consequence, we yet lack the ability to trace back recognition errors to either tracking or classification.

With this paper we aim at unraveling the links between feature quality and recognition accuracy. We derive trajectory features from tracking data with

V. Murino and E. Puppo (Eds.): ICIAP 2015, Part II, LNCS 9280, pp. 565–574, 2015.
DOI: 10.1007/978-3-319-23234-8_52

varying degrees of common errors, and compare the performance using off-the-shelf classifiers. This work can be seen as a thorough investigation of the factors involved in automated rat social behavior analysis.

The remainder of this work is structured as follows. In Section 2 we discuss related work. Sections 3 and 4 introduce our data set and the analysis pipeline. The results are presented in Section 5 and discussed in Section 6. We conclude in Section 7.

2   Rodent Action Recognition

Action recognition has been applied not only to rodents [4] but also to humans. In contrast to human action recognition, the recognition of rodent actions is characterized by confined spaces, less articulated, similar looking animals, and a combination of need-driven and playful behavior. The common procedure in rodent action recognition is to split the recognition into three tasks: tracking the position of the animals, deriving features from those tracks, and classifying the actions using the features.

Different tracking solutions have been presented. Some require that the animals are uniquely marked [9] or have an implanted RFID tag [12]. Others attempt to identify the animals based on their thermal [6] or visual appearance [10]. Recently, the use of depth cameras has been proposed to enhance the visual segmentation in contact situations [8]. A pronounced difference of the solutions is whether only one [1,2],[12] or more body parts [3],[6] are tracked. Tracking multiple body parts has been shown to improve solitary behavior recognition [5].

The location data obtained by the tracking algorithm is used to derive a feature set. This set often comprises individual features such as velocities and accelerations [7], and pairwise features such as the distance between animals and their relative orientation [2]. In addition, one may add features derived directly from the image data. Exploiting spatio-temporal interest points in a bag-of-words setup has been shown to yield only minor improvements over a trajectory-only feature set [2].

At the classification level, differences can be found in the way temporal information is considered. If the video frames are considered samples that have to be assigned a class label, then temporal information may be included by collecting statistical values across neighboring frames using a sliding window [4],[7]. To model temporal information in a more structural way, for example, to incorporate transition probabilities between interactions, one can deploy hidden Markov models [1]. The classification problem is then formulated so as to find the optimal temporal segmentation of the video into labeled action segments.

Most recognition systems are trained using a subset of the data. Exceptions are rule-based classifiers [3],[12], and the Janelia Automatic Animal Behavior Annotator (JAABA) [7]. The latter pursues an active learning approach in which the user trains a classifier by iteratively annotating a number of action events.

Tracking, feature extraction, and classification clearly depend on each other. Despite advances in all three areas, it has not been analyzed systematically how errors in one task affect the final classification.

3   Rat Social Behavior Data Set

The Rat Social Behavior Data Set (RSBD), which we use throughout our analyses, was obtained in a study on play behavior of young rats [11]. In 40 sessions, two male Sprague Dawley rats, 5-6 weeks old, were placed together in a Noldus PhenoTyper 9000 cage (90 cm × 90 cm) and were recorded by an infrared camera at 25 fps from a top-view perspective for about 30 min. The actions of one focal animal were labeled using Noldus Observer XT 10. From the 14 original labels, we removed actions that are too subtle to be captured by trajectory features (e.g., biting and kicking). The remaining classes capture seven interactions and one class that covers all solitary actions. Short descriptions of the classes are given in Table 1.

For our analyses we chose five videos from which we randomly selected ten events of each interaction per video (400 segments in total). Every segment includes a 0.6 s margin before and after the interaction. In total this yields 12.6 min of footage. We further chose four of the five videos at random to be used for training our system. The remaining video was considered a validation set and has never been used other than for the results presented in this paper.

Rat interactions have different temporal properties. Their durations have different means and often large inner-class variances as we can see in Table 1. This difference leads to a highly unbalanced data set. Note that our data is unbalanced regarding the number of frames but balanced in the number of interaction events.

Table 1. Left: mean, standard deviation, minimum, and maximum of the durations (in s) of the selected interactions in the training set. Right: the distribution of classes in both training and validation set.

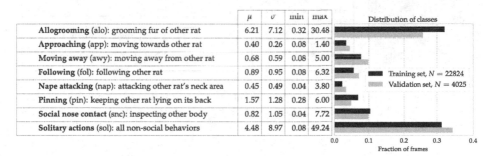

	μ	σ	min	max
Allogrooming (alo): grooming fur of other rat	6.21	7.12	0.32	30.48
Approaching (app): moving towards other rat	0.40	0.26	0.08	1.40
Moving away (awy): moving away from other rat	0.68	0.59	0.08	5.00
Following (fol): following other rat	0.89	0.95	0.08	6.32
Nape attacking (nap): attacking other rat's neck area	0.45	0.49	0.04	3.80
Pinning (pin): keeping other rat lying on its back	1.57	1.28	0.28	6.00
Social nose contact (snc): inspecting other body	0.82	1.05	0.04	7.72
Solitary actions (sol): all non-social behaviors	4.48	8.97	0.08	49.24

Distribution of classes: Training set, $N = 22824$; Validation set, $N = 4025$. Fraction of frames (0.0, 0.1, 0.2, 0.3, 0.4).

4   Feature Quality in Social Behavior Recognition

Our goal is to highlight how the feature quality influences the recognition performance. We vary the quality in two ways. First, we incrementally correct two types of tracking errors. Second, we derive three feature sets from those tracks capturing the rat's articulated body at varying degrees of detail.

4.1   Eliminating Systematic Tracking Errors in RSBD

The video tracking system used in this experiment (Noldus EthoVision XT 11)
tracks three points on the animal bodies: the nose point, the center of gravity, and the tail-base. We incrementally eliminate two types of tracking errors
and thus introduce three data set versions. We denote the initial, uncorrected
version as RSBD. In the first step (denoted as RSBD-ID), we corrected identity
swaps. Identities were not changed during fast, close-contact situations. In those
situations, the positions provided by the tracker are occasionally wrong and
thus identity assignment becomes arbitrary. In the second step (RSBD-ID+Loc),
we additionally corrected all body point locations. This decreases the amount
of noise in the positions, eliminates body part confusions (swaps of nose and
tail-base points), and yields reliable orientation values.

4.2   Extracting Features from the Data Set Versions

From the tracked body points, we compute, per animal, a number of pose,
motion, and distance variables as well as their derivatives. The values are aggregated over time computing mean, minimum, and maximum values in a sliding
window of 0.52 s. Figure 1 illustrates the extraction pipeline. The variants of the
feature set are created by varying how detailed the articulated body is captured
by the features.

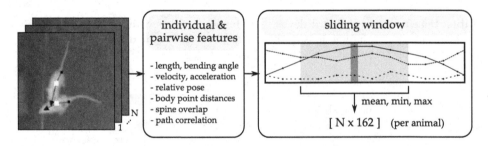

Fig. 1. From nose, center, and tail-base points we derive individual and pairwise features that describe the pose, motion, and distances of the animals in each of the
N frames. In a window centered at the current frame various statistics are computed.

Feature Set Variants. We compare three sets with ascending number of features. In the first set (CP), we only exploit the position (x, y) of the animals'
center-of-gravity. This corresponds to the approach taken by a number of previous works, e.g., [2],[12]. Features include velocity and acceleration, the distance
between the animals, and the correlation between the animals' paths. In the
second set (CP+Ori), we add orientation information (x, y, φ) which allows us
to compute the velocity vector with respect to the animal's orientation and
the relative orientation between the animals. The third set (Full) exploits all

three tracked body points $((x_0, y_0), (x_1, y_1), (x_2, y_2))$ and additionally incorporates pose features such as body length and bending, several body point distances and the degree of body overlap.

To facilitate the generalization of the features to other setups and rats, we standardize the features of all sets with respect to size of the specific rat. That is, distances, velocities, and accelerations are scaled to animal length units.

4.3   Experiment Setup

To analyze the links between feature quality and recognition accuracy, we examine the effects of tracking errors on the accuracy alone (using the `Full` feature set) as well as in combination with the different feature sets. We assess the recognition accuracy in terms of the overall and the per-class classification performance. We mainly look at the F1 score and, if appropriate, at precision, recall and confusions between specific classes. When averaging the F1 score, we average across classes. Compared to averaging across frames, the class average puts higher weight on short or rare events and thus represents unbalanced data sets like ours better.

For overall performance measures, we apply a 5-fold cross-validation scheme where each fold corresponds to one of the five videos in the data set. If we look at per-class performance, we train on the four training videos and test on the validation video. When we compare different tracking errors, we train and test using data of the same error level.

To find a suitable classifier for the analyses, we compare six off-the-shelf classifiers and then stick to one classifier for the remaining experiments. We compare the following classifiers: Linear Discriminant Classifier (LDC); Linear Discriminant Analysis with subsequent One-vs-All Quadratic Discriminant Classifier (LDA+QDC); Support Vector Machines with Gaussian (SVM-RBF) and linear (SVM-Lin) kernels; LDA with k-Nearest-Neighbors (LDA+kNN); and Random Forest (RF). Where applicable, classifier parameters are found empirically by optimizing the F1 score in the same cross-validation scheme as described above.

5   Results

5.1   Tracking Errors

The comparison of the classifiers (Tab. 2) shows that all six classifiers perform comparably on all three data set versions. Given the range of classifiers tested, this emphasizes that feature quality, rather than the classifier, largely determines the performance. The remaining experiments are conducted with the simplest of the classifiers: LDC. We further see in Table 2 that fewer tracking errors lead to higher average accuracy. With each additional error eliminated, the average per-class F1 score increases by approximately 0.12.

Looking at the F1 scores per interaction (Tables 3, 4, and 5) and confusions (Figures 2, 3, and 4), we notice that not all interactions are affected by tracking

Table 2. The average per-class F1 scores achieved by the six classifiers on the three data set versions with increasing degree of tracking quality

Classifier	Parameters	RSBD		RSBD-ID		RSBD-ID+Loc	
		μ_{F1}	σ	μ_{F1}	σ	μ_{F1}	σ
LDC	–	0.51	0.05	0.63	0.05	0.75	0.03
LDA+QDC	–	0.50	0.04	0.62	0.05	0.74	0.03
SVM-RBF	$C = 1, \gamma = .00625$	0.51	0.04	0.65	0.03	0.74	0.02
SVM-Lin	$C = 0.001$	0.50	0.04	0.63	0.04	0.74	0.03
LDA+kNN	$k = 10$	0.48	0.04	0.61	0.04	0.73	0.02
RF	$n = 100, d_{max} = 16$	0.52	0.05	0.68	0.04	0.76	0.02

errors in the same way. The accuracies are generally high for solitary actions and approaches (in which the animals are separated by definition). Contact interactions are not recognized well in the RSBD version but improve gradually as errors are corrected. Let us look at each correction step separately.

The correction of identity swaps (RSBD → RSBD-ID) leads to two major improvements. Firstly, the confusion of *following* with *moving away* is largely resolved although some confusion persists. The F1 score for *following* increases from 0.27 to 0.56 and for *moving away* from 0.47 to 0.72. Secondly, virtually all *nape attacks* that had been mistaken as *following* are now corrected. Consequently, the recall of *nape attacking* improves from 0.39 to 0.56. Notably, precision stays at a low level of 0.29.

Correcting the body point locations (RSBD-ID → RSBD-ID+Loc) increases the precision of *nape attacking* from 0.29 to 0.46, and the recall of *pinning* from 0.3 to 0.72. Confusions remain between these two classes and also between *following* and *approaching*. A number of small improvements across all classes eventually leads to higher average F1 scores at both frame level (+0.07) and class level (+0.11).

5.2   Feature Set Variants

Figure 5 shows the F1 scores of the combinations of data set versions and feature sets. There is an upwards trend across the data set versions irrespective of which feature set is used. In RSBD, the F1 score remains at approximately 0.5 for all feature sets. In both RSBD-ID and RSBD-ID+Loc, the F1 score increases with richer feature sets. The standard deviation of the accuracy decreases by approximately 50% using Full on RSBD-ID+Loc compared to RSBD-ID.

6   Discussion

On the overall performance level, we have seen that eliminating tracking errors leads to better classification. This pattern occurred for all tested classifiers, which suggests that the effect is indeed inherent to the underlying data and not to the classifier. We further showed that orientation and pose features are important

Table 3. Per-class results: RSBD

	Prec.	Recall	F1	#
alo	0.86	0.71	0.78	1038
app	0.55	0.80	0.65	184
awy	0.48	0.46	0.47	398
fol	0.33	0.24	0.27	288
nap	0.29	0.39	0.33	139
pin	0.24	0.35	0.28	200
snc	0.40	0.61	0.48	399
sol	0.98	0.87	0.92	1379
μ_{frames}	0.72	0.67	0.69	4025
$\mu_{classes}$	0.52	0.55	**0.52**	8

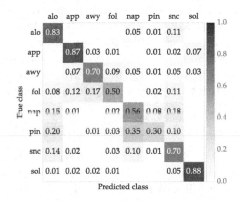

Fig. 2. Confusion matrix: RSBD

Table 4. Per-class results: RSBD-ID

	Prec.	Recall	F1	#
alo	0.85	0.83	0.84	1038
app	0.62	0.87	0.72	184
awy	0.75	0.70	0.72	398
fol	0.65	0.50	0.56	288
nap	0.20	0.56	0.30	130
pin	0.65	0.30	0.41	200
snc	0.50	0.70	0.58	399
sol	0.98	0.88	0.93	1379
μ_{frames}	0.80	0.76	0.77	4025
$\mu_{classes}$	0.66	0.67	**0.65**	8

Fig. 3. Confusion matrix: RSBD-ID

Table 5. Per-class results: RSBD-ID+Loc

	Prec.	Recall	F1	#
alo	0.92	0.92	0.92	1038
app	0.67	0.83	0.74	184
awy	0.73	0.87	0.79	398
fol	0.89	0.59	0.71	288
nap	0.46	0.69	0.55	139
pin	0.74	0.72	0.73	200
snc	0.63	0.67	0.65	399
sol	0.97	0.90	0.93	1379
μ_{frames}	0.85	0.84	0.84	4025
$\mu_{classes}$	0.75	0.77	**0.76**	8

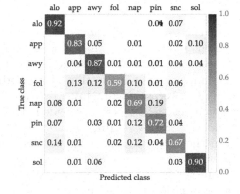

Fig. 4. Confusion matrix: RSBD-ID+Loc

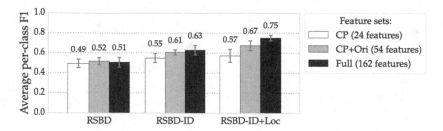

Fig. 5. The average per-class F1 score using three different feature sets, tested on all three data set versions

for the recognition. If those features are correct, they lead to better classification. If they are not, that is, if the tracking algorithm fails to provide stable pose information, we induce the risk of overfitting to the noise in the features. As a consequence, the classification accuracy stagnates or even decreases. A potential way to overcome this limitation is to include more training data, which are particularly expensive to obtain. Moreover, when we trained the classifier with corrected data but used uncorrected data to test it, we failed to achieve competitive performance ($\mu_{\text{classes}} = 0.42$, $\sigma = 0.05$, 5-fold cross-validation). For that reason, we do not benefit from corrected, clean features as long as we cannot guarantee that we can generate them without expensive, manual intervention.

6.1   Difference between Interactions

On the class level, we observed that the classes are affected differently by tracking errors and the choice of features. By which type of tracking error an interaction is most affected is determined by its characteristics. Interactions such as *following* and *pinning* rely more on the identity assignment than, for example, *solitary actions*. Because most of our interactions are indeed sensitive to the correct role assignment, we see large gains in F1 score after correcting identity swaps. Clearly, maintaining the correct identities is a necessity for social behavior recognition.

Another characteristic of the interactions is how important the relative pose is for the recognition. *Nape attacking*, *pinning*, and *following* events have a very distinct relative pose while it is less relevant for other interactions. For example, for *social nose contact* the pose can be different in every event because the class includes the inspection of all body parts. Therefore, we expect that the more an interaction is defined by the pose, the better it should be recognized if correct pose features are provided. We find supporting evidence in the results. *Nape attacking* (+0.16), *pinning* (+0.32), and *following* (+0.15) benefit most from the correction of body part locations and thus pose. Accordingly, adding uncorrected orientation and pose features results in only a small improvement (RSBD-ID: CP → Full = +0.08). We conclude that the accuracy of social behavior recognition can be improved by incorporating reliable orientation and pose features.

6.2   Unresolved Confusions

There are some confusions that persist even with perfect tracking. The predominant confusions occur between *following* and *appoaching*, and among the four classes *allogrooming*, *nape attacking*, *pinning*, and *social nose contact*.

There are two reasons for the confusions. First, *approaching* often evolves into *following* but the transition is not clearly defined. As a result, the predictions around the transition point become arbitrary. We see the same effect to a lesser degree for *awy* → *sol* and *sol* → *app*. Second, the four confused interactions can be very ambiguous in their appearance. The classifier cannot separate the classes properly and hence makes mistakes.

As for solving the transition ambiguity, we need to find more clues to when one behavior changes into another. A potential direction is to explicitly learn the temporal structure of the transitions and to incorporate the other rat's reaction.

To improve the separability of ambiguous interactions, we may want to increase the diversity of the features. The four confused interactions are ambiguous because they are close-contact situations for which the animal's trajectories and poses appear similar. However, differences may arise if we incorporate which animal is on top or below (e.g., by exploiting 3D trajectories) and capture fine-grained motion with image features (e.g., optical flow or histogram of gradients).

7   Conclusion

In this paper we investigated the effects of feature quality on video-based recognition of rat social behavior. We looked at the impact of two types of tracking errors – misidentification and inaccurate localization – as well as the type of features that are derived from the tracking data.

From the analysis of the classification accuracy across interaction classes, we observed that although correcting tracking errors improves the classification, each class is affected differently. Correctly identifying the animals is required to recognize virtually all interactions, whereas correctly tracking body parts has a larger impact on classes that are defined by a distinct relative pose. Hence, including orientation and pose features is advantageous under the condition that the tracking algorithm can provide them reliably.

We have further found that perfect tracking alone is insufficient for recognizing ambiguous behavior. Exploiting temporal context and reaction patterns alongside with features that go beyond 2D trajectories are directions that seem worth pursuing in the future.

Acknowledgments. We would like to thank Suzanne Peters and Johanneke van der Harst (Delta Phenomics) for their annotation work. The experiments were performed in adherence to the legal requirements of Dutch legislation on laboratory animals (WOD/Dutch Experiments on Animals Act) and were reviewed and approved by an Animal Ethics Committee (Lely-DEC). This work was funded by the European Commission under the 7th Framework Programme (FP7) as part of the Marie Curie Initial Training Network "PhenoRat" (GA no. 317259).

References

1. Arakawa, T., Tanave, A., Ikeuchi, S., Takahashi, A., Kakihara, S., Kimura, S., Sugimoto, H., Asada, N., Shiroishi, T., Tomihara, K., Tsuchiya, T., Koide, T.: A male-specific QTL for social interaction behavior in mice mapped with automated pattern detection by a hidden Markov model incorporated into newly developed freeware. J. Neurosci. Meth. **234**, 127–134 (2014)
2. Burgos-Artizzu, X.P., Dollár, P., Lin, D., Anderson, D.J., Perona, P.: Social behavior recognition in continuous video. In: Proc. CVPR, pp. 1322–1329 (2012)
3. de Chaumont, F., Coura, R.D.S., Serreau, P., Cressant, A., Chabout, J., Granon, S., Olivo-Marin, J.C.: Computerized video analysis of social interactions in mice. Nat. Methods **9**(4), 410–417 (2012)
4. van Dam, E.A., van der Harst, J.E., ter Braak, C.J.F., Tegelenbosch, R.A.J., Spruijt, B.M., Noldus, L.P.J.J.: An automated system for the recognition of various specific rat behaviours. J. Neurosci. Meth. **218**(2), 214–224 (2013)
5. Decker, C., Hamprecht, F.A.: Detecting individual body parts improves mouse behavior classification. In: Proc. of the Workshop on Visual Observation and Analysis of Vertebrate and Insect Behavior, Stockholm, Sweden (2014)
6. Giancardo, L., Sona, D., Huang, H., Sannino, S., Managò, F., Scheggia, D., Papaleo, F., Murino, V.: Automatic visual tracking and social behaviour analysis with multiple mice. PLoS One **8**(9), e74557 (2013)
7. Kabra, M., Robie, A.A., Rivera-Alba, M., Branson, S., Branson, K.: JAABA: Interactive machine learning for automatic annotation of animal behavior. Nat. Methods **10**(1), 64–67 (2012)
8. Matsumoto, J., Urakawa, S., Takamura, Y., Malcher-Lopes, R., Hori, E., Tomaz, C., Ono, T., Nishijo, H.: A 3D-video-based computerized analysis of social and sexual interactions in rats. PLoS One **8**(10), e78460 (2013)
9. Ohayon, S., Avni, O., Taylor, A.L., Perona, P.: Roian Egnor, S.: Automated multi-day tracking of marked mice for the analysis of social behaviour. J. Neurosci. Meth. **219**(1), 10–19 (2013)
10. Pérez-Escudero, A., Vicente-Page, J., Hinz, R.C., Arganda, S., de Polavieja, G.G.: idTracker: Tracking individuals in a group by automatic identification of unmarked animals. Nat. Methods **11**(7), 743–748 (2014)
11. Peters, S.M., Pinter, I., de Heer, R.C., van der Harst, J.E., Spruijt, B.M.: Automated classification of rat social behavior. In: Proc. of Measuring Behavior, Wageningen, The Netherlands (2014)
12. Weissbrod, A., Shapiro, A., Vasserman, G., Edry, L., Dayan, M., Yitzhaky, A., Hertzberg, L., Feinerman, O., Kimchi, T.: Automated long-term tracking and social behavioural phenotyping of animal colonies within a semi-natural environment. Nat. Commun. 4, Article No. 2018 (2013)

Scale and Occlusion Invariant Tracking-by-Detection

Andrea Mazzeschi, Giuseppe Lisanti$^{(\boxtimes)}$, Federico Pernici,
and Alberto Del Bimbo

Media Integration and Communication Center (MICC),
University of Florence, Viale Morgagni 65, 50134 Firenze, Italy
andrea.mazzeschi@gmail.com,
{giuseppe.lisanti,federico.pernici,alberto.delbimbo}@unifi.it

Abstract. In this paper we present a solution for tracking-by-detection that is able to handle both scale variations and occlusions of the tracked object. We build upon the framework proposed in [7] based on structured output SVM and improve it in order to deal with both variations of target scale and occlusions. We first propose to modify the original solution to include the scale variations both in the patch sampling stage and in the structured output state. Then in order to deal with occlusions we introduce an incremental classifier to discriminate the target from the context. This classifier combines a learning phase with a unlearning one that help to avoid drift in the model of the tracked object. The proposed solution outperforms the method in [7] for sequences that present scale variations or occlusions while maintaining comparable performance on those sequences with none of these issues. Moreover, we outperform other state-of-the-art solutions on publicly available sequences commonly used in literature.

1 Introduction

Tracking is a fundamental problem in computer vision. Several aspects of this difficult task have been considered in literature. Generally speaking, difficulties arise depending on the type of information that needs to be tracked: 3D pose, imaged 2D location, imaged 2D shape, 3D shape, imaged 2D articulated body shape, 3D articulated body shape, etc. Besides dealing with the inherent difficulties related to the specific information of interest, effective methods must also provide robust object representation coping with nuisance factors that affect the image formation process. For example objects may have non-rigid shape or may be made of translucent or reflective materials and camera sensors may suffer from the effects of noise, sensor quantization and motion blur. In addition to these intrinsic problems, practical requirements such as: 1) long-term tracking; and 2) object reacquisition after partial or total occlusion, may prevent correct tracking. In some applications, the object to be tracked is known in advance and it is possible to incorporate specific prior knowledge when designing the tracker to alleviate some of these issues. However, the general case of tracking

© Springer International Publishing Switzerland 2015
V. Murino and E. Puppo (Eds.): ICIAP 2015, Part II, LNCS 9280, pp. 575–585, 2015.
DOI: 10.1007/978-3-319-23234-8_53

arbitrary objects by simply specifying a single (one-shot) training example at runtime, is a challenging open problem which deserves particular attention. In this scenario, the tracker must be able to model the appearance of the object on-the-fly by generating and labeling image features and learning the model of the object appearance.

In this paper we propose to exploit structured output SVM, extending the work proposed in [7], in order to be able to deal with some classical nuisance factors. In particular, we introduce scale sampling in the prediction of the target state in order to be able to manage target scale variations. Then we introduce an incremental classifier that act as validator of the structured output SVM in order to handle occlusions and out of view of the scene. Experimental results show that the proposed scale and occlusion handling allows to improve performance while preserving the adaptability of [7].

1.1   Related Work

A number of methods have been developed in which tracking is considered as 2D image bounding box localization, each one dealing with different nuisance factors.

However, not all nuisance factors are equal; a distinction should be made in order to better understand the problem. When we are facing occlusions, we are dealing with presence or absence of a signal while in the case of illumination and pose variations the signal is changing but still remains strongly correlated. The former nuisance factors are not invertible and do not admit invariant representations while the latter will. The latter case is generally well captured by features like HoG, Haar or LBP while the former is much more complex and cannot be explicitly modeled through the feature representation [15] invariance. MILTrack [2], for example, adopting bag of image patches can cope with misalignments and occlusions by adding novel examples as new instances for the object representation.

Recently, three methods have received a lot of attention for their positive performance and for their algorithmic design and image representation peculiarity [2,8,12]. They mainly differ on how they consider the *template update problem* which primarily impacts on the drift of the tracker [11]. Babenko et al. [2] address the problem by building an evolving boosting classifier that tracks bags of image patches. Kalal et al. [8] combine a optic flow tracker with a online random forest. This solution has been succesively extended in [9] with the TLD-Predator tracking framework where the tracking task is decomposed into tracking, learning and detection and a P-N learning method is exploited. In Mei and Ling [12] the tracking problem is formulated as finding a sparse representation of the candidate object, combining trivial templates which are primarily responsible for the presence or the absence of certain object regions.

Our work as many others [2,4,6,8,10,17] makes use of context information to extract the features of the background surrounding the target. Features are then used to improve the distinction of the target against its background, either by feature selection or by training classifiers as in [1,3]. In [18] the CT-Tracking

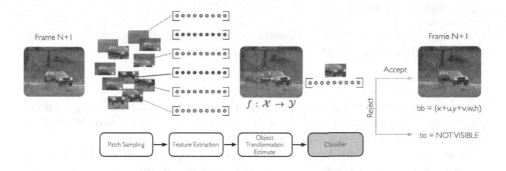

Fig. 1. Scheme of the proposed solution. The classifier (green box) validates the prediction of the structured output SVM and controls the target position change and the model update.

exploits an appearance model based on features extracted from foreground and background at multiple scales of the image and employs non-adaptive random projections to preserve the structure of the image feature space. A critical issue here is in the accuracy between foreground and background image regions. Generally they are divided by the bounding box of the object; such a partition is too rough and it could happen that background regions are treated as part of the foreground. This typically causes a gradual degradation in object appearance representation which results in template drift.

2 Scale and Occlusion Invariant Tracking-By-Detection

Hare et al. proposed a novel tracking approach [7] that directly estimates the object transformation between frames rather than performing a detection. In this solution structured output SVM has been used to learn a prediction function $f : \mathcal{X} \rightarrow \mathcal{Y}$, which maps the target features into the space of the in-plane translations:

$$\mathcal{Y} = \{(u,v) \mid u^2 + v^2 \leq r_s^2\} \tag{1}$$

where (u, v) are respectively the x and y translation components.

This solution, however, suffers from some limitations. Firstly, the tracker cannot handle target scale and this mostly affects the tracking quality. Moreover, no occlusions and out-of-field detection mechanisms are present and this can introduce erroneous data into the appearance model, compromising the long term performance.

To overcome these limitations we propose to slightly modify the original formulation of [7] in order to be able to handle target scale variations. Moreover, we introduce a detector that is able to overcome occlusion and out-of-view during the tracking. A scheme of the whole approach is shown in Fig. 1.

2.1 Scale Invariance

In order to manage the target scale variation it is necessary to extend the output space of the prediction function in Eq. 1 as follows:

$$\tilde{\mathcal{Y}} = \{(u, v, s) \mid u^2 + v^2 \leq r_s^2; s \in \{s_{min} \ldots s_{max}\}\} \tag{2}$$

where s represents the percentage variation of the target's bounding box dimension compared to the previous frame. The values s_{min} and s_{max} are the smallest and the greatest change allowed between two consecutive frames.[1]

A feature vector of 4288 elements, obtained as concatenation of HOG (4096) and Haar-like (192) features, is adopted as patch descriptor.

2.2 Occlusion and Out-of-View Handling

An occlusion and out-of-view detection mechanism is crucial in order to be able to manage complex tracking situations. Our main idea is to introduce a classifier to discriminate the target from the context [5,14]. This classifier acts as a validator of the structured output SVM prediction by accepting or rejecting the target model update and therefore the target position update, see Fig. 1.

The classifier initialization phase lasts for the first K frames of the sequence. During this period the classifier is not considered and it is assumed that the target is completely visible in the scene. Positive and negative examples are collected at every frame. The positive examples are chosen as warped versions of the region of interest (roi) of the target position. The negative samples are chosen, instead, from eight patches around the current target location.

The classifier is incrementally trained during the sequence. In particular, at every frame a prediction of the position of the target is performed, following Eq. 2, and the classifier evaluates if the predicted region contains the tracked target or not. When the classifier is not able to identify the target in any of the τ_c consecutive frames, the tracking procedure is interrupted and the reacquisition phase starts. During the reacquisition, a whole image target search is accomplished and neither the structured output SVM model nor the classifier model are updated, in order to prevent degradation of the target model.

A huge number of examples and their variability can corrupt the classifier decision boundary. To avoid this problem, similarly to [5], we integrated an unlearning phase during which a defined percentage of training examples, randomly picked every M frames, is removed. In [5] this was done following a temporal window mechanism that keeps only the latest examples. We argue that this choice produces a classifier which focuses only on the latest target appearances. This may limit the reacquisition ability for all of these cases where the target appearance differs from the latest seen. For this reason we perform a uniform random sampling in order to prevent the data distribution corruption.

---

[1] We chose to handle only fixed aspect ratio scale changes mainly due to computational limits.

In order to decide if the prediction is correct or not we need to report the classifier output in a probabilistic form following [13], such as:

$$p(\mathbf{T} \mid f(\mathbf{x})) = \frac{1}{1 + \exp(Af(\mathbf{x}) + B)} \qquad (3)$$

where $f(\mathbf{x})$ is the SVM output value and A, B are the sigmoid parameters. Eq. 3 gives the probability that $\mathbf{x}$ is an instance of the target ($\mathbf{T}$) given the SVM output $f(\mathbf{x})$. The sigmoid parameters (A and B) are updated during the tracking procedure every M frames as described in [13] in order to be able to adapt the tracker to the visual changes.

The target prediction will be classified as correct if the 80% of the positive examples of the training set are correctly classified:

$$\frac{\sum_{\mathbf{x}_i \, s.t. \, y_i = 1} \mathbb{1}(\frac{1}{1 + \exp(Af(\mathbf{x}) + B)} \geq \theta)}{N^+} \geq 0.8 \qquad (4)$$

where $\mathbb{1}(d)$ returns 1 if the inequality d is satisfied and 0 otherwise, N^+ is the amount of positive examples in the training set and θ is a threshold automatically estimated every M frames from the observed samples (in order to adapt the learned model to the new observed examples).

3   Experiments

We performed a series of experiments to show the effectiveness of the proposed solution. In particular, we first show how managing scale variations allows to improve the performance of [7] (we refer to this method as Struck); then we show the effectiveness of the occlusion handling mechanism; finally we report a comparison against some of the state-of-the-art tracking-by detection methods [2,7,9,18].

Tests were conducted on 21 public available sequences from the dataset in [16].

3.1   Parameters

In our experiments we set the scale sampling values s_{min} and s_{max} to 0.8 and 1.2 respectively. We found that these values are a good tradeoff between the computational burden and the fact that in the reality the target scale does not change abruptly between consecutive frames. Before extracting HOG and Haar-like features, every patch is preliminary resized to a fixed resolution of 32×96 pixels.

As regards the classifier for occlusion detection we set the initialization to $K = 8$ frames in order to be able to collect sufficient information about the target appearance. For the unlearning phase we decided to remove the 20% of training examples randomly picked every $M = 70$ frames. All these parameters were set accordingly to [5,13] and considering the validation reported in Fig. 2.

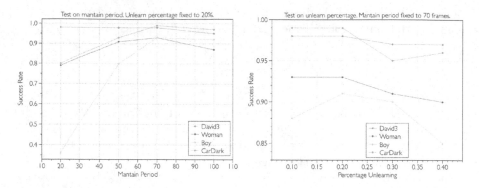

Fig. 2. *Left* The success rate variation according to the maintain period. *Right* The success rate variation according to the unlearn percentage.

3.2   Scale Handling Test

With these experiments we evaluate the performance of the scale handling as described in 2.1. For this test we chose four different video sequences in which the scale changes is the main nuisance factor. During these tests the classifier component for occlusion handling was not ran.

In Table 1 we report this comparison in terms of Success Rate and Average Overlap. Clearly handling scale variations increases both the tracking ability (higher success rate) and the tracking quality (higher avg. overlap).

Table 1. Success Rate and Average Overlap comparison for the Struck with and without our scale handling on four test sequences. Best results in bold.

		Success Rate		Avg. Overlap	
Sequence	Frames	Struck	Struck+Scale	Struck	Struck+Scale
CarScale	252	0.34	**0.63**	0.36	**0.52**
Jogging	307	0.25	**0.95**	0.16	**0.63**
Singer1	351	0.30	**0.99**	0.36	**0.62**
Walking2	500	0.42	**0.99**	0.50	**0.82**
Mean	-	0.32	**0.89**	0.34	**0.65**

In Fig. 3 we also show the percentage of frame associated to the overlap score, for the Jogging and Walking2 sequences. It is possible to appreciate that our solution with scale handling obtains an overlapping score between 0.5 and 0.7 for the Jogging sequence and between 0.7 and 0.9 for the Walking2 sequence, for a large number of frames. On the contrary, Struck is not able to track the target for a large number of frames in the Jogging sequence, while for the Walking2 sequence it presents a decreasing overlapping score.

3.3   Occlusion Handling Test

To evaluate the re-acquisition ability of the classifier component we used synthetic sequences to overcome the problem of the limited number of video sequences where out-of-field cases occur. In particular, we used 5 sequences and split them in clips of 50 frames each. Then, for each clip we replaced the 30 central frames with a synthetic image obtained by removing the target from the original scene in order to simulate an out-of-field scenario. A total of 31 cases have been analysed. In Table 2 we report the number of splits generated from the sequence, the number of cases in which the target is correctly tracked after the synthetic occlusion, the number of cases in which the target is missed after the synthetic occlusion and the number of cases in which the target is wrongly tracked during the occlusion. We assume that the target is correctly tracked if the Pascal Overlap Score is greater than 0.5.

Table 2. Reacquisition performance on synthesized sequences.

Sequence	# Splits	# Tracked	# Missed	# F. Alarm
Clutter	10	8	2	0
Couple	3	3	0	0
Jumping	5	3	1	1
Subway	3	2	1	0
Sylvester	10	4	6	0
Total	31	20	10	1

It can be observed that most of our *Missed* cases come from the Sylvester sequence. This is mainly due to the change in appearance that occurs when the target re-enter in the scene (after the synthetic out-of-field) in an extremely different pose with respect to the latest one observed by the tracker.

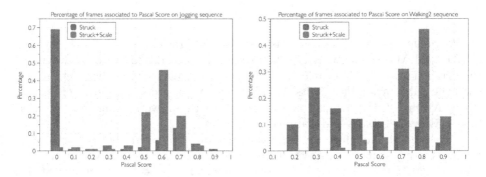

Fig. 3. Percentage of frames associated per Pascal Score for the sequences Jogging (*Left*) and Walking2 (*Right*) for Struck without (red) and with scale handling (blue).

3.4   Final Test

In this section we report the experiments performed with our full solution over various tracking conditions. Illumination changes, occlusions, out of plane rotations and scale changes are some of the issues present in the 21 sequences that we chose from the dataset in [16].

Table 3. Success Rate/Average Location error(px) - Bold numbers indicate the best score, underlined numbers indicate the second best.

Sequence	Frames	Struck	Our	CT	TLD	MIL
Boy	602	**0.98/3.21**	0.93/6.77	0.68/8.75	0.93/7.93	0.38/13.15
Car4	659	0.40/25.58	0.70/**17.28**	0.27/87.03	**0.78**/19.90	0.27/40.21
CarDark	393	**1/2.21**	0.99/3.54	0.01/119.10	0.52/28.32	0.18/42.88
CarScale	252	0.34/70.90	**0.72**/24.95	0.45/63.68	0.43/28.52	0.45/**11.26**
Couple	140	0.63/32.51	0.83/8.12	0.68/32.79	**1/4.82**	0.67/33.80
Crossing	120	0.86/3.25	**1/1.80**	0.98/3.33	0.52/22.70	0.98/2.30
David2	537	**1/1.32**	0.77/4.70	0.01/76.84	0.95/5.86	0.32/11.01
Deer	71	**1**/8.71	0.90/8.55	0.04/243.10	0.73/**3.16**	0.12/94.83
Dudek	1145	**0.94**/18.70	0.86/**16.10**	0.85/20.17	0.84/22.20	0.85/24.70
Fish	476	**1/3.70**	1/3.71	0.89/10.91	0.96/10.60	0.38/26.66
FleetFace	707	**0.69**/62.74	0.64/**38.34**	0.63/67.47	0.56/55.56	0.53/71.63
Freeman1	326	0.20/13.60	**0.64/11.74**	0.10/121.45	0.21/42.22	0.15/19.22
Jogging	307	0.21/89.49	**0.97/3.28**	0.22/93.22	0.97/5.72	0.22/93.03
Lemming	1336	0.64/33.86	**0.83/7.08**	0.68/32.58	0.59/19.95	0.81/13.59
MountainBike	228	**0.98/6.60**	0.98/6.72	0.17/216.62	0.26/96.38	0.57/74.39
Singer1	351	0.30/79.19	**1/8.81**	0.24/74.39	0.99/17.91	0.27/76.54
Subway	175	0.38/108.29	0.76/**4.92**	0.7/10.86	0.23/50.43	**0.79**/7.62
Suv	945	0.73/28.94	**0.90/4.13**	0.22/62.91	0.83/7.76	0.13/72.04
Sylvester	1345	0.80/14.88	0.81/**3.94**	0.83/10.98	**0.93**/11.97	0.54/16.13
Walking	412	0.55/8.18	**0.99/4.05**	0.50/18.75	0.38/7.16	0.54/13.69
Walking2	500	0.42/7.45	**0.97/2.87**	0.38/50.32	0.34/27.43	0.38/50.10
Mean	-	0.67/29.68	**0.86/9.12**	0.45/68.30	0.67/23.65	0.46/38.51

We compare our solution against Struck, CT-Tracking (CT), TLD-Predator (TLD) and MILTrack (MIL). In particular, Struck results are obtained using the original source code provided by the authors while for the other methods we used the public available results[2]. Performance are expressed in terms of Success Rate, Average Center Location Error and Average Overlap and are reported respectively in Table 3 and Table 4.

Experiments show how the proposed solution obtains state-of-the-art results in almost every sequence under test. In terms of Success Rate the average increase is about 20%. It's also worth to note that in all the sequences where Struck achieves best results, our solution produces similar performances. This fact

---

[2] http://cvlab.hanyang.ac.kr/tracker_benchmark/v1.0/tracker_benchmark_v1.
0_results.zip

Table 4. Average Overlap - Bold numbers indicate the best score, underlined numbers indicate the second best.

Sequence	Struck	Our	CT	TLD	MIL
Boy	**0.77±0.10**	0.66±0.11	0.59±0.18	0.66±0.09	0.49±0.21
Car4	0.49±0.19	0.55±0.20	0.21±0.30	**0.63±0.22**	0.26±0.31
CarDark	**0.80±0.07**	0.76±0.10	0.00±0.05	0.44±0.35	0.19±0.25
CarScale	0.36±0.28	**0.59±0.25**	0.43±0.31	0.42±0.24	0.40±0.31
Couple	0.48±0.35	0.65±0.20	0.46±0.32	**0.77±0.08**	0.49±0.34
Crossing	0.63±0.11	**0.76±0.06**	0.68±0.09	0.40±0.35	0.72±0.11
David2	**0.86±0.04**	0.66±0.13	0.00±0.04	0.69±0.12	0.45±0.21
Deer	**0.73±0.07**	0.67±0.10	0.03±0.18	0.59±0.36	0.12±0.24
Dudek	**0.72±0.14**	0.67±0.22	0.64±0.13	0.64±0.15	0.70±0.15
Fish	**0.87±0.06**	0.83±0.05	0.71±0.14	0.80±0.14	0.45±0.19
FleetFace	0.57±0.25	**0.58±0.23**	0.52±0.23	0.48±0.25	0.49±0.23
Freeman1	0.38±0.18	**0.52±0.23**	0.14±0.19	0.27±0.28	0.34±0.18
Jogging	0.16±0.31	**0.80±0.15**	0.17±0.32	0.76±0.14	0.18±0.33
Lemming	0.49±0.31	**0.65±0.29**	0.54±0.26	0.53±0.22	0.64±0.18
MountainBike	0.67±0.10	**0.69±0.07**	0.14±0.30	0.19±0.32	0.45±0.30
Singer1	0.36±0.25	**0.79±0.08**	0.34±0.24	0.72±0.08	0.35±0.25
Subway	0.28±0.34	**0.59±0.14**	0.57±0.10	0.18±0.33	0.64±0.14
Suv	0.62±0.38	**0.71±0.24**	0.23±0.27	0.67±0.24	0.20±0.26
Sylvester	0.63±0.27	0.62±0.30	**0.66±0.16**	0.67±0.16	0.52±0.23
Walking	0.56±0.16	**0.70±0.09**	0.52±0.13	0.44±0.21	0.54±0.15
Walking2	0.50±0.19	**0.77±0.14**	0.26±0.29	0.29±0.34	0.28±0.34
Mean	0.57	**0.70**	0.37	0.53	0.42

underlines how the introduction of the classifier does not compromise Struck's adaptive ability. A similar observation can be also made for the Average Center Location Error results and the Average Overlap, respectively in Table 3 and Table 4.

In Fig. 4 we report some sample frames for four different sequences and in comparison with [2,7,9,18]. Compared to other methods only TLD can reach similar results in terms of precision. For the Jogging sequence at the 77-th frame the tracking procedure is interrupted by the classifier due to an occlusion. In Lemming, again, the classifier stops the tracking due to a strong out-of-plane rotation. In both cases our method is able to correctly reacquire the target after some frames.

Fig. 4. Tracking results sample frames. From top to bottom: Singer1, Jogging, Lemming and Suv sequences. In each frame the results color are: Our, Struck, TLD, MIL, CT, in black the ground-truth (GT). In Singer1 the scale variation handling of our method is highlighted.

4   Conclusion

In this paper we have proposed a tracking-by-detection solution, starting from [7], that is able to deal with both variations of target scale, occlusions and out-of-view. We have shown how including scale information during the tracking allows us to achieve better performance compared to [7]. After that we have introduced a classifier to discriminate the target from the context. The proposed solution outperforms the method in [7] for those sequences that present scale variations or occlusions while it maintains comparable performance on those sequences with none of these issues.

References

1. Avidan, S.: Ensemble tracking. IEEE Trans. Pattern Anal. Mach. Intell. **29**, 261–271 (2007)
2. Babenko, B., Yang, M.H., Belongie, S.: Robust object tracking with online multiple instance learning. Pattern Analysis and Machine Intelligence **33**(8), 1619–1632 (2011)

3. Collins, R., Liu, Y.: On-line selection of discriminative tracking features. In: Proc. of ICCV (2003)
4. Dinh, T.B., Vo, N., Medioni, G.: Context tracker: Exploring supporters and distracters in unconstrained environments. In: Proc. of CVPR (2011)
5. Dinh, T.B., Yu, Q., Medioni, G.: Co-trained generative and discriminative trackers with cascade particle filter. Computer Vision and Image Understanding **119**, 41–56 (2014)
6. Gu, S., Zheng, Y., Tomasi, C.: Efficient Visual Object Tracking with Online Nearest Neighbor Classifier. In: Kimmel, R., Klette, R., Sugimoto, A. (eds.) ACCV 2010, Part I. LNCS, vol. 6492, pp. 271–282. Springer, Heidelberg (2011)
7. Hare, S., Saffari, A., Torr, P.H.: Struck: Structured output tracking with kernels. In: Proc. of ICCV (2011)
8. Kalal, Z., Matas, J., Mikolajczyk, K.: P-n learning: Bootstrapping binary classifiers by structural constraints. In: Proc. of CVPR (2010)
9. Kalal, Z., Mikolajczyk, K., Matas, J.: Tracking-learning-detection. Pattern Analysis and Machine Intelligence **34**(7), 1409–1422 (2012)
10. Li, H., Shen, C., Shi, Q.: Real-time visual tracking using compressive sensing. In: Proc. of CVPR (2011)
11. Matthews, I., Ishikawa, T., Baker, S.: The template update problem. In: Proc. of BMVC (2003)
12. Mei, X., Ling, H.: Robust visual tracking using 1 minimization. In: ICCV 2009, pp. 1436–1443 (2009)
13. Platt, J., et al.: Probabilistic outputs for support vector machines and comparisons to regularized likelihood methods. Advances in Large Margin Classifiers **10**(3), 61–74 (1999)
14. Santner, J., Leistner, C., Saffari, A., Pock, T., Bischof, H.: Prost: Parallel robust online simple tracking. In: Proc. of CVPR (2010)
15. Soatto, S.: Actionable information in vision. In: Proc. of ICCV (2009)
16. Wu, Y., Lim, J., Yang, M.H.: Online object tracking: A benchmark. In: Proc. of CPVR (2013)
17. Yu, Q., Dinh, T.B., Medioni, G.G.: Online Tracking and Reacquisition Using Co-trained Generative and Discriminative Trackers. In: Forsyth, D., Torr, P., Zisserman, A. (eds.) ECCV 2008, Part II. LNCS, vol. 5303, pp. 678–691. Springer, Heidelberg (2008)
18. Zhang, K., Zhang, L., Yang, M.-H.: Real-Time Compressive Tracking. In: Fitzgibbon, A., Lazebnik, S., Perona, P., Sato, Y., Schmid, C. (eds.) ECCV 2012, Part III. LNCS, vol. 7574, pp. 864–877. Springer, Heidelberg (2012)

Ensemble of Hankel Matrices
for Face Emotion Recognition

Liliana Lo Presti[✉] and Marco La Cascia

DICGIM, Universitá Degli Studi di Palermo,
V.le delle Scienze, Ed. 6, 90128 Palermo, Italy
liliana.lopresti@unipa.it

Abstract. In this paper, a face emotion is considered as the result of
the composition of multiple concurrent signals, each corresponding to
the movements of a specific facial muscle. These concurrent signals are
represented by means of a set of multi-scale appearance features that
might be correlated with one or more concurrent signals. The extraction of these appearance features from a sequence of face images yields
to a set of time series. This paper proposes to use the dynamics regulating each appearance feature time series to recognize among different
face emotions. To this purpose, an ensemble of Hankel matrices corresponding to the extracted time series is used for emotion classification
within a framework that combines nearest neighbor and a majority vote
schema. Experimental results on a public available dataset show that the
adopted representation is promising and yields state-of-the-art accuracy
in emotion classification.

Keywords: Emotion · Face processing · LTI systems · Hankel matrix ·
Classification

1 Introduction

Emotion recognition deals with the problem of inferring the emotion (i.e. fear,
anger, surprise, etc.) given a sequence of face images. Due to strong inter-subject
variations, especially in some kind of emotions (such as fear or sadness), and
the difficulty to extract reliable feature representations because of illumination
changes, biometric differences, and head pose changes, emotion recognition is a
challenging problem. Nonetheless, recognition of face expressions and emotions
is of great interest in many fields such as assistive technologies [21], [10], socially
assistive robotics [23], computational behavioral science [25], [18], [35], and the
emerging field of audience measurement [11].

A vast literature on affective computing [35], [27], [21], has shown that an
emotion can be identified by a subset of detected action units. This suggests
that face emotion results as combination of movements of various facial muscles.
Therefore in this paper we assume that a composition of multiple concurrent
signals yields to a face emotion. We use a restricted set of appearance features

© Springer International Publishing Switzerland 2015
V. Murino and E. Puppo (Eds.): ICIAP 2015, Part II, LNCS 9280, pp. 586–597, 2015.
DOI: 10.1007/978-3-319-23234-8_54

– computed on a frame-per-frame basis – that may be correlated with one or more of these concurrent signals. Given a sequence of face images corresponding to an emotion, the extraction of these appearance features yields to a set of time series, one for each appearance feature. Considering that face emotions are not instantaneous, we aim at using the dynamics regulating each sequence of appearance features to recognize among different emotions.

We propose to model a sequence of face appearance feature as the output of a Linear Time Invariant (LTI) system. Motivated by the success of works in action recognition [12], [17], that represent action-dynamics in terms of Hankel matrices, in this paper we explore the use of Hankel matrices to represent emotion-dynamics. We adopt a multi-scale Haar-like feature based appearance representation to obtain a set of time series (one for each spatial scale and Haar-like feature). Hence we represent a sequence of face images by means of an ensemble of Hankel matrices where each Hankel matrix embeds the dynamics of one of the extracted Haar-like feature time series. Nearest-Neighbor classifier combined with a majority vote schema is used for classification purposes.

We validated our work on the publicly available extended Cohn-Kanade dataset [20]. Our experiments show that there is a clear advantage in adopting a dynamics-based emotion representation over using the raw measurements. Furthermore, our experiments highlight that the dynamics of different appearance features contribute differently to the emotion recognition. Overall, our novel emotion representation permits to achieve state-of-the-art accuracy values in comparison to works that use accurate face landmarks.

The plan of the work is as follows. In Section 2, we present works that are related to our emotion-dynamics representation. In Section 3 we describe how we extract a multi-scale face appearance description; Section 4 introduces the Hankel matrix-based representation and describes how to build an ensemble of Hankel matrices to describe face appearance dynamics; Section 5 presents details about the adopted classification framework. Finally, in Sections 6 and 7, we present experimental results, and conclusions and future directions respectively.

2   Related Work

Face detection [31], face recognition [37], [14] and facial expression analysis [6] have been deeply studied in past years, resulting in a vast literature reviewed in [35], [27]. In this section, we focus on works that embed the temporal structure of the face image sequence in the feature representation or in the emotion model.

Dynamics-based emotion recognition has been proposed in [5] where horizontal and vertical movements of tracked landmarks of different face parts such as eyebrows, eyelids, cheeks, and lip corners jointly with spatio-temporal appearance features are used to describe a sequence of face images. Temporal changes in the face appearance are described by means of the Complete Local Binary Patterns from Three Orthogonal Planes (LBP-TOP) [36] and classification is performed by SVM. While [5] attempts to embed information about the dynamics at a feature representation level, works such as [19], [28] account for the temporal structure of the sequences of descriptors in the emotion model. In [22], restricted Boltzmann machine with local interactions (LRBM) is used to capture the spatio-temporal patterns in the data. RBM is used as a generative model for data representation instead of feature learning, and data need to be pre-aligned. In [19] time-series kernel methods are used for emotional expression estimation using landmark data only. The work shows that emotion recognition may be done by adopting either the Dynamic Time Warping (DTW) kernel or the Global Alignment (GA) kernel [3], [4]. In [28], a Bayesian approach is used to model dynamic facial expression temporal transitions. Facial appearance representation is computed in terms of Local Binary Patterns (LBP), and an expression manifold is derived for multiple subjects. A Bayesian temporal model (similar to HMM with a non parametric observation model) of the manifold is used to represent facial expression dynamics.

Works such as [9], [32] use landmarks located on face parts such as eyes, eyebrows, nose and mouth to describe an emotion. In [9], a Constrained Local Model (CLM) is used to estimate facial landmarks and extract a sparse representation of corresponding image patches. Emotion classification is performed by least-square SVM. Wang et al. [32] propose to use Interval Temporal Bayesian Network (ITBN) to capture the spatial and temporal relations among the primitive facial events.

Hankel matrices have been already adopted for action recognition in [12], which adopts a Hankel matrix-based bag-of-words approach, and in [17], which models an action as a sequence of Hankel matrices and uses a set of HMM trained in a discriminative way to model the switching between LTI systems. In [16], we have showed how the dynamics of tracked facial landmarks can be modeled by means of Hankel matrices and can be used for facial expression analysis.

Whilst it is possible to obtain a reasonably accurate estimate of the face region [31], getting a reliable estimation of facial landmarks is still an open problem despite the remarkable progress described in [2], [38]. The adoption of appearance feature extracted from the detected face region to describe an emotion, as done indeed in [24], [28], [35], [27], might be a convenient choice. Therefore, in this paper we adopt appearance features to represent a face expression. In contrast to [16], we do not model landmark trajectories but we use an ensemble of Hankel matrices to describe the dynamics of sequences of appearance features computed at multiple spatial scales. We demonstrate that, without an accurate estimation of facial landmarks, our novel representation can achieve state-of-the-art accuracy in emotion recognition.

3   Multi-Scale Face Appearance Representation

Given a face image, we need to extract a proper appearance representation for the shown face expression. Considering the success of Haar-like features in face detection we adopt this kind of features to build our face appearance descriptor.

Haar-like features resemble Haar wavelets and have been developed by Viola and Jones for face detection [31]. A Haar-like feature is computed by considering adjacent rectangular regions in a detection window. The pixel intensities in each

Fig. 1. The set of six Haar-like features used in this paper.

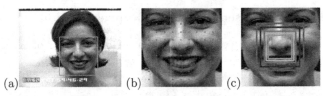

(a)   (b)   (c)

Fig. 2. Haar-like features are extracted from the face region at different spatial scales: (a) the face region is detected and cropped; (b) centers of the sliding window used to compute the Haar-like features; (c) multiple scales used to calculate Haar-like features.

region are summed up and the difference between these sums yields the Haar-like feature. In [31], Haar-like features are compared against a threshold and used to detect the face; therefore they are used as weak classifiers and a high number of features are considered in order to build a strong classifier. The key advantage of a Haar-like feature over most other features is that it can be calculated in constant time due to the use of integral images.

A number of Haar-like features have been used in literature [13], [8], and Haar-like features and/or simple variations have been formerly used in literature for emotion recognition [27],[33],[34] within boosting approaches.

In this paper we only use the six most common features depicted in Figure 1. Intuitively, a multi-scale approach might account for different intensity of the emotion, which may change from subject-to-subject. Therefore we extract Haar-like features at different spatial scales. In this preliminary work, we do not model the weights of each extracted feature; modeling these weights/performing feature selection remains a topic of future investigations. The main steps we perform to extract our face appearance representation are:

- we detect the face region (as shown in Fig. 2 (a));
- within the face region, we consider a set of uniformly sampled points (red dots in Fig. 2 (b));
- we center windows of varying spatial scales at each of these sampled points (Fig. 2 (c) shows the windows centered at a representative point on the subject's nose. Each color indicates a different scale.);
- we extract our Haar-like features from each of the selected windows. Whenever the sliding window exceeds the size of the face region (especially along the boundary), the window is cropped so to consider only the pixels within the face area. In our implementation, the white and black rectangular regions of each Haar-like feature are computed in proportion to the window size, therefore the cropping does not affect the computation of the Haar-like features.

4   Ensemble of Hankel Matrices for Emotion-Dynamics

In this section, first we briefly review LTI systems and Hankel matrix, then we describe our ensemble of Hankel matrices for emotion-dynamics representation.

4.1   Hankel Matrix-Based Dynamics Representation

In a LTI system, two linear equations regulate the behavior of the system:

$$
\begin{aligned}
x_{k+1} &= A \cdot x_k + w_k; \\
y_k &= C \cdot x_k.
\end{aligned}
\tag{1}
$$

The first equation is known as the *state equation* and involves the variable $x_k \in R^u$, which represents the u-dimensional internal state of the LTI system. The second equation is known as the *measurement equation* and provides a link between the state of the system x_k and the v-dimensional observable measurement y_k. In such equations the matrices A and C are constant over time, and $w_k \sim N(0, Q)$ is uncorrelated zero mean Gaussian measurement noise.

It is well known [30] that, given a sequence of output measurements $[y_0, \ldots, y_\tau]$ from Eq. 1, its associated truncated block-Hankel matrix is

$$
\widetilde{H} =
\begin{bmatrix}
y_0, & y_1, & y_2, & \cdots, & y_m \\
y_1, & y_2, & y_3, & \cdots, & y_{m+1} \\
\cdots & \cdots & \cdots & \cdots & \cdots \\
y_n, & y_{n+1}, & y_{n+2}, & \cdots, & y_\tau
\end{bmatrix},
\tag{2}
$$

where n is the maximal order of the system, τ is the temporal length of the sequence, and it holds that $\tau = n + m - 1$.

The Hankel matrix embeds the observability matrix Γ of the system, since $\widetilde{H} = \Gamma \cdot X$, where $X = [x_0, x_1, \cdots, x_\tau]$ is a matrix formed by the sequence of internal states of the LTI system.

As previously done in [12], [17], we normalize the Hankel matrix $\widetilde{H}$ as follows:

$$
H = \frac{\widetilde{H}}{\sqrt{||\widetilde{H} \cdot \widetilde{H}^T||_F}}.
\tag{3}
$$

and compare two Hankel matrices H_p and H_q by the following similarity score:

$$
s(H_p, H_q) = ||H_p^T \cdot H_q||_F,
\tag{4}
$$

which can be easily derived from the dissimilarity score in [12]. We have experimentally found that our similarity score is numerically more stable and fast to compute than the dissimilarity score. Such score can be regarded as an approximation of the cosine of the subspace angle between the spaces spanned by the columns of the Hankel matrices. As such, it can convey the degree to which two Hankel matrices may correspond to the same dynamical system.

4.2   Emotion-Dynamics Representation

The simple and fast appearance feature extraction described in Section 3 yields to a set of time series $Y = \{y^{i,j}\}_{i=1,j=1}^{i=N,j=S}$ where $y^{i,j} = \{y_1^{i,j}, \cdots y_T^{i,j}\}$ is the time series corresponding to the i-th Haar-like feature at the j-th spatial scale (N is the number of Haar-like features, and S is the number of scales). Each element $y_t^{i,j}$ of this time series is a vector of features computed at the uniformly sampled points and representing the t-th face in the face image sequence.

We use the set of time series Y to build an ensemble of Hankel matrices $H = \{H^{i,j}\}_{i=1,j=1}^{i=N,j=S}$ where each Hankel matrix $H^{i,j}$ is built upon the time series $y^{i,j}$ and, therefore, is associated with the i-th Haar-like feature and the j-th spatial scale. Before calculating the Hankel matrix, the sequence $y^{i,j}$ is made zero mean. We note the following:

- each vector $y_t^{i,j}$ is an ordered set of appearance features extracted from different parts of the face region. The set of Hankel matrices $H^{i,j}$ captures the dynamics of the Haar-like features over the whole face;
- each Hankel matrix is built upon a single Haar-like feature;
- each Hankel matrix is built upon a single scale;
- modeling separately Haar-like features at different spatial scales has computational advantages in terms of memory and time complexity;
- Hankel matrices can be obtained by a simple and fast reordering of the elements in the vector $y_t^{i,j}$. Therefore, from a computational point of view, the adoption of Hankel matrices over other time series representation is particularly appealing.

5   Emotion Classification

To test the effectiveness of our novel representation we have adopted the simple and widely used nearest-neighbor classifier (NN). We compare Hankel matrices by using the similarity score in Eq. 4. Given an ensemble of Hankel matrices, each Hankel matrix contributes to the emotion classification by voting for a class (predicted by NN). Comparison of Hankel matrices is done on equal terms of Haar-like feature and scale (we compare only Hankel matrices that share the same scale and Haar-like feature). Decision on the predicted class is performed considering a majority vote schema.

Other classification frameworks might be used, such as an LTI system codebook based representation similar to that proposed in [12], or a state-based approach similar to that in [17]. Alternatively, system identification techniques such as the ones applied in [29], [26] can be adopted at the cost of an increased overall time complexity. Even if stronger classification frameworks might be adopted as well, NN allows us to study the effectiveness of our representation without introducing further classifier-dependent parameters.

Table 1. Accuracy in Emotion Classification on the CK+ dataset. Red font indicates the best accuracy value per emotion, while bold font highlights the second best performance. **Different validation protocol (10-fold cross validation)

Features	Method	An.	Con.	Disg.	Fear	Hap.	Sad	Surp.	Avg
	DTW + NN	37.8	55.6	55.9	16	73.9	21.4	73.5	47.7
	DTW + NN	40	38.9	32.2	20	69.6	10.7	54.2	37.9
	DTW + NN	40	44.4	22	20	63.8	14.3	50.6	36.4
	DTW + NN	42.2	66.7	62.7	12	78.3	10.1	73.5	49.4
	DTW + NN	35.6	38.9	54.2	12	65.2	10.7	66.3	40.4
	DTW + NN	57.8	61.1	59.3	16	68.1	14.3	72.3	49.8
	DTW + NN	53.3	55.6	62.7	16	72.5	10.7	81.9	50.4
	DTW + NN	46.7	72.2	52.5	20	79.7	7.1	67.5	49.4
	DTW + NN	48.6	55.6	50.8	24	78.3	17.9	65.1	48.6
	DTW + NN	60	55.6	59.3	16	76.8	14.3	80.7	51.8
	DTW + NN	53.3	66.7	57.6	20	78.3	7.1	79.5	51.8
	DTW + NN	44.4	61.1	50.8	24	84.1	10.7	73.5	49.8
all	DTW + NN	42.2	72.2	59.3	20	87	14.3	83.1	54
	Hankel + NN	62.2	72.2	88.1	40	100	42.9	92.8	71.2
	Hankel + NN	71.1	61.1	81.4	44	94.2	64.3	87.9	72
	Hankel + NN	57.8	61.1	81.4	44	97.1	53.6	84.3	68.5
	Hankel + NN	44.4	66.7	84.7	40	**98.5**	21.4	94	64.3
	Hankel + NN	77.8	83.3	83	48	97.1	42.9	90.4	74.6
	Hankel + NN	71.1	**77.8**	91.5	48	100	60.7	96.4	77.9
	Hankel + NN	68.9	**77.8**	93.2	44	100	57.1	96.4	76.8
	Hankel + NN	82.2	83.3	91.5	44	100	**78.6**	91.6	81.6
	Hankel + NN	75.6	83.3	89.8	48	100	71.4	92.8	80.1
	Hankel + NN	60	72.2	89.8	40	100	53.6	94	72.8
	Hankel + NN	**84.4**	**77.8**	89.8	**56**	100	64.3	95.2	81.1
	Hankel + NN	62.2	**77.8**	89.8	44	100	57.1	91.6	74.6
all	Hankel + NN	86.7	83.3	96.6	52	100	71.4	**97.6**	**83.9**
CAPP	SVM [20]	70	21.9	**94.7**	21.7	100	60	98.7	66.7
LDN	RBF-SVM [24]**	71.7	73.7	93.4	90.5	95.8	78.9	**97.6**	85.9
Shape (SPTS)	SVM [20]	35	25	68.4	21.7	98.4	4	100	50.4
Shape+CAPP	SVM [1]	70.1	52.4	92.5	72.1	94.2	45.9	93.6	74.4
Shape	ITBN [32]	91.1	78.6	94	83.3	89.8	76	91.3	86.3
Shape	LRBM [22]	97.8	72.2	89.8	84	100	78.6	97.6	88.6
Shape + Hankel	NN [16]	91.1	83.3	94.9	84	100	71.4	98.8	89.1

Table 2. Confusion Matrix on the CK+ dataset when all the six Haar-like features are used. True labels are on rows, and predicted labels are on columns.

Tr. vs Pr.	Angry	Contempt	Disgust	Fear	Happy	Sadness	Surprise
Angry	**86.67**	0	2.22	2.22	0	6.67	2.22
Contempt	0	**83.33**	0	0	5.56	5.56	5.56
Disgust	0	0	**96.61**	0	1.69	0	1.69
Fear	12	4	0	**52**	24	4	4
Happy	0	0	0	0	**100**	0	0
Sadness	7.14	3.57	0	0	3.57	**71.43**	14.29
Surprise	0	1.20	0	0	1.20	0	**97.59**

6   Experimental Results

We have performed experiments in emotion recognition on the widely adopted Extended Cohn-Kanade dataset (CK+) [20]. This dataset provides facial expressions of 210 adults. Participants were instructed to perform several facial displays representing either single or combinations of action units. Based on the coded action units and by means of a validation procedure of the assigned label, the segmented recording of the participants' emotions were classified into 7 categories (in brackets the number of available samples): *angry (45), contempt (18), disgust (59), fear (25), happy (69), sadness (28), surprise (83)*. In total there are 327 sequences of the 7 annotated emotions, performed by 118 different individuals. The number of frames of these sequences ranges in $[6, 71]$ with an average value of about 18 ± 8.6. The dataset provides landmark tracking results obtained by active appearance model, which we use in our experiments only to detect the face region. We adopted the validation protocol suggested in [20], which is leave-one-subject-out cross validation.

When extracting the Haar-like features, we sample the center location uniformly with a step equals to 10% of the size of the detected face region, yielding a 81 dimensional vector for each Haar-like feature. The spatial scales (size of the window used to calculate the Haar-like feature) are also computed in proportion to the face region size and the percentage ranges in $\{30, 35, 40, 50, 60\}$. The order of each Hankel matrix has been empirically set to 2. To extract the Haar-like features we have modified the implementation used in [7], [15].

6.1   Results

We have performed an extensive validation of the dynamics-based emotion representations whose results are reported in Table 1. The table reports the per-class classification accuracy values for each of the emotion classes, and the average accuracy. The table is divided in 4 parts. The first part presents accuracy values in classification when the raw features are adopted (namely Haar-like features). In this case, as the face image sequences have different lengths, dynamic time warping (DTW) is used to align the sequences and nearest-neighbor classifier is used over the aligned sequences. For a fair comparison, also when adopting the raw features, different Haar-like features and spatial scales are compared separately and a majority vote schema is used to predict the final class.

The second part of the table presents results when an ensemble of Hankel matrices is used. Both the first and second part of the table report performance when a single Haar-like feature is used, when a pair of Haar-like features is used and, finally, when all the six Haar-like features are used.

By comparing the first and second part of the table, there is a clear advantage in using an ensemble of Hankel matrices to represent the emotions over using directly the Haar-like features. On average, the increase of performance in using the dynamics-based representation with respect to the raw measurements is of about 60.3%.

Looking at the performance of each single Haar-like feature, the most informative one is the concentric squared regions (the last of the six features). Therefore we have performed experiments to study the performance of this feature when coupled with another Haar-like feature. As the table shows, there is an improvement with three of the five Haar-like features. There is no improvement when the Haar-like feature is coupled with the first Haar-like feature and a degradation of the performance when coupled with the vertical bands Haar-like feature. What is striking is that in all the experiments, the emotion Happy is always correctly recognized 100% of times. This suggests that our ensemble of Hankel matrices can be appropriate for smile detection. A further improvement of the performance is obtained when all the Haar-like features are used together, at the cost of an higher computational complexity. We suspect that not all the features are actually contributing to the recognition of the emotion, and feature and scale selection techniques may help to achieve more accurate results.

The third part of the table reports accuracy values of state-of-the-art methods adopting only appearance features. The class for which our method seems to fail the most is the emotion *Fear*. If we ignore this class, our method achieves even better accuracy values of the most competitive method in [24]. For completeness, the fourth part of the table reports the performance of techniques adopting accurate estimation of facial landmarks (provided together with the dataset). Even if these methods are not directly comparable with the ones that use only appearance information, we note that our appearance-based representation competes already very well against these techniques.

Finally, Table 2 reports the confusion matrix of our method. The class *Fear* is confused mostly with the class *Happy*. Some confusion is also present between the classes *Sadness* and *Surprise*. We believe that these ambiguities might be probably solved with fine-grained appearance descriptors, such as the Local Directional Number (LDN) pattern introduced in [24].

7   Conclusions and Future Work

In this paper we have proposed to use an ensemble of Hankel matrices to represent the dynamics of face appearance features, where each Hankel matrix embeds the dynamics of a single appearance feature at a given spatial scale.

We have tested our novel emotion representation on a widely used publicly available benchmark (CK+). Our experiments demonstrate that, on equal terms of classification framework and feature representations, the dynamics-based emotion representation achieves about 60.3% of increase in the accuracy values with respect of using directly the raw measurements. Overall, our approach achieves competitive performance with respect to more sophisticated machinery or methods that use accurate shape information.

Our formulation is general and it is not limited to the adopted face appearance representation. We therefore aim at extending our work by considering other appearance features. Moreover, we believe that feature and scale selection techniques (i.e. boosting) might led to an increase of the accuracy of our approach. In this paper, we have focused on the problem of classifying segmented emotion sequences. In future works we aim at tackling with the problem of emotion intensity estimation and emotion detection in face image sequences. In this sense, we will explore how face appearance feature dynamics correlate with the intensity of face emotions and if they can help in detecting subtle changes in face expressions.

Acknowledgments. This work was partially supported by Italian MIUR grant PON0101687, SINTESYS - Security and INTElligence SYStem.

References

1. Chew, S.W., Lucey, P., Lucey, S., Saragih, J., Cohn, J.F., Sridharan, S.: Person-independent facial expression detection using constrained local models. In: Conf. and Workshop on Automatic Face & Gesture Recognition (FG), pp. 915–920. IEEE (2011)
2. Cootes, T.F., Edwards, G.J., Taylor, C.J.: Active appearance models. IEEE Trans. on Pattern Analysis and Machine Intelligence (PAMI) **23**(6), 681–685 (2001)
3. Cuturi, M.: Fast global alignment kernels. In: Int. Conf. on Machine Learning (ICML), pp. 929–936 (2011)
4. Cuturi, M., Vert, J., Birkenes, O., Matsui, T.: A kernel for time series based on global alignments. In: Int. Conf. on Acoustics, Speech and Signal Processing (ICASSP), vol. 2, pp. II-413. IEEE (2007)
5. Dibeklioğlu, H.: Enabling dynamics in face analysis. Ph.D. thesis, University of Amsterdam (2014)
6. Fasel, B., Luettin, J.: Automatic facial expression analysis: a survey. Pattern Recognition **36**(1), 259–275 (2003)
7. Hare, S., Saffari, A., Torr, P.H.: Struck: Structured output tracking with kernels. In: Int. Conf. on Computer Vision (ICCV), pp. 263–270. IEEE (2011)
8. Huang, C., Ai, H., Li, Y., Lao, S.: High-performance rotation invariant multiview face detection. IEEE Trans. on Pattern Analysis and Machine Intelligence **29**(4), 671–686 (2007)
9. Jeni, L.A., Girard, J.M., Cohn, J.F., De La Torre, F.: Continuous AU intensity estimation using localized, sparse facial feature space. In: Conf. on Automatic Face & Gesture Recognition (FG), pp. 1–7. IEEE (2013)

10. Lacava, P.G., Golan, O., Baron-Cohen, S., Myles, B.S.: Using assistive technology to teach emotion recognition to students with asperger syndrome a pilot study. Remedial and Special Education 28(3), 174–181 (2007)

11. Lee, H.Y., Lee, W.H.: A study on interactive media art to apply emotion recognition. International Journal of Multimedia & Ubiquitous Engineering 9(12) (2014)

12. Li, B., Camps, O.I., Sznaier, M.: Cross-view activity recognition using Hankelets. In: Conf. on Computer Vision and Pattern Recognition (CVPR), pp. 1362–1369. IEEE (2012)

13. Lienhart, R., Maydt, J.: An extended set of haar-like features for rapid object detection. In: Int. Conf. on Image Processing, vol. 1, pp. I-900. IEEE (2002)

14. Lo Presti, L., La Cascia, M.: An on-line learning method for face association in personal photo collection. Image and Vision Computing (2012)

15. Lo Presti, L., La Cascia, M.: Tracking your detector performance: how to grow an effective training set in tracking-by-detection methods. In: Int. Conf. on Computer Vision Theory and Applications (VISAPP), pp. 1–8 (2015)

16. Lo Presti, L., La Cascia, M.: Using Hankel matrices for Dynamics-based Facial Emotion Recognition and Pain Detection. In: Int. Conf. on Computer Vision and Pattern Recognition Workshops (CVPRW), pp. 1–8 (2015)

17. Lo Presti, L., La Cascia, M., Sclaroff, S., Camps, O.: Gesture modeling by hanklet-based hidden markov model. In: Cremers, D., Reid, I., Saito, H., Yang, M.-H. (eds.) ACCV 2014. LNCS, vol. 9005, pp. 529–546. Springer, Heidelberg (2015)

18. Lo Presti, L., Sclaroff, S., Rozga, A.: Joint alignment and modeling of correlated behavior streams. In: Int. Conf. on Computer Vision-Workshops (ICCVW), pp. 730–737 (2013)

19. Lorincz, A., Jeni, L.A., Szabó, Z., Cohn, J.F., Kanade, T.: Emotional expression classification using time-series kernels. In: Conf. on Computer Vision and Pattern Recognition Workshops (CVPRW), pp. 889–895. IEEE (2013)

20. Lucey, P., Cohn, J.F., Kanade, T., Saragih, J., Ambadar, Z., Matthews, I.: The Extended cohn-kanade dataset (CK+): a complete dataset for action unit and emotion-specified expression. In: Conf. on Computer Vision and Pattern Recognition Workshops (CVPRW), pp. 94–101. IEEE (2010)

21. Lucey, P., Cohn, J.F., Prkachin, K.M., Solomon, P.E., Matthews, I.: Painful data: the UNBC-McMaster shoulder pain expression archive database. In: Conf. and W. on Automatic Face & Gesture Recognition (FG), pp. 57–64. IEEE (2011)

22. Nie, S., Wang, Z., Ji, Q.: A generative restricted Boltzmann machine based method for high-dimensional motion data modeling. Computer Vision and Image Understanding (2015)

23. Rabbitt, S.M., Kazdin, A.E., Scassellati, B.: Integrating socially assistive robotics into mental healthcare interventions: Applications and recommendations for expanded use. Clinical Psychology Review 35, 35–46 (2015)

24. Ramirez Rivera, A., Castillo, R., Chae, O.: Local directional number pattern for face analysis: Face and expression recognition. IEEE Transactions on Image Processing (TIP) 22(5), 1740–1752 (2013)

25. Rehg, J.M., et al.: Decoding children's social behavior. In: Conf. on Computer Vision and Pattern Recognition (CVPR), pp. 3414–3421. IEEE (2013)

26. Sankaranarayanan, A.C., Turaga, P.K., Baraniuk, R.G., Chellappa, R.: Compressive acquisition of dynamic scenes. In: Daniilidis, K., Maragos, P., Paragios, N. (eds.) ECCV 2010, Part I. LNCS, vol. 6311, pp. 129–142. Springer, Heidelberg (2010)

27. Sariyanidi, E., Gunes, H., Cavallaro, A.: Automatic analysis of facial affect: A survey of registration, representation and recognition. EEE Trans. on Pattern Analysis and Machine Intelligence (PAMI) (2014)
28. Shan, C., Gong, S., McOwan, P.W.: Dynamic facial expression recognition using a Bayesian temporal manifold model. In: BMVC, pp. 297–306 (2006)
29. Slama, R., Wannous, H., Daoudi, M., Srivastava, A.: Accurate 3D action recognition using learning on the Grassmann manifold. Pattern Recognition (PR) **48**(2), 556–567 (2015)
30. Viberg, M.: Subspace-based methods for the identification of linear time-invariant systems. Automatica **31**(12), 1835–1851 (1995)
31. Viola, P., Jones, M.J.: Robust real-time face detection. International Journal of Computer Vision **57**(2), 137–154 (2004)
32. Wang, Z., Wang, S., Ji, Q.: Capturing complex spatio-temporal relations among facial muscles for facial expression recognition. In: Conf. on Computer Vision and Pattern Recognition (CVPR), pp. 3422–3429. IEEE (2013)
33. Yang, P., Liu, Q., Metaxas, D.: Similarity features for facial event analysis. In: Forsyth, D., Torr, P., Zisserman, A. (eds.) ECCV 2008, Part I. LNCS, vol. 5302, pp. 685–696. Springer, Heidelberg (2008)
34. Yang, P., Liu, Q., Metaxas, D.N.: Boosting coded dynamic features for facial action units and facial expression recognition. In: Conf. on Computer Vision and Pattern Recognition (CVPR), pp. 1–6. IEEE (2007)
35. Zeng, Z., Pantic, M., Roisman, G.I., Huang, T.S.: A survey of affect recognition methods: Audio, visual, and spontaneous expressions. IEEE Trans. on Pattern Analysis and Machine Intelligence (PAMI) **31**(1), 39–58 (2009)
36. Zhao, G., Pietikainen, M.: Dynamic texture recognition using local binary patterns with an application to facial expressions. IEEE Trans. on Pattern Analysis and Machine Intelligence (PAMI) **29**(6), 915–928 (2007)
37. Zhao, W., Chellappa, R., Phillips, P.J., Rosenfeld, A.: Face recognition: A literature survey. ACM Computing Surveys (CSUR) **35**(4), 399–458 (2003)
38. Zhu, X., Ramanan, D.: Face detection, pose estimation, and landmark localization in the wild. In: IEEE Conf. on Computer Vision and Pattern Recognition (CVPR), pp. 2879–2886. IEEE (2012)

A New Approach to Detect Use of Alcohol Through Iris Videos Using Computer Vision

Hedenir Monteiro Pinheiro[1], Ronaldo Martins da Costa[1,4(✉)],
Eduardo Nery Rossi Camilo[2], Anderson da Silva Soares[1], Rogerio Salvini[1,3],
Gustavo Teodoro Laureano[1], Fabrizzio Alphonsus Soares[1], and Gang Hua[4]

[1] Instituto de Informtica, Universidade Federal de Goias, Goiania, Goias, Brazil
{hedenir,ronaldocosta,anderson,rogeriosalvini,
gustavo,fabrizzio}@inf.ufg.br
[2] Ophthalmologist, Goiania, Goias, Brazil
eduardo_nery@hotmail.com
[3] University of Porto, Porto, Portugal
[4] Stevens Institute of Technology, Hoboken, NJ, USA
ghua@stevens.edu

Abstract. In all modern society the increase in alcohol consumption has caused many problems and the potential harmful effects of alcohol on human health are known. There are some ways to identify alcohol in a person, but they are invasive and embarrassing for people. This work proposes a new non-invasive and simple test to detect use of alcohol through of pupillary reflex analysis. The initial results present rates near 85% in the correct identification using algorithms for pattern recognition, demonstrating the efficacy of the test method.

Keywords: Pupillometer · Blood alcohol · Iris · Alcohol

1 Introduction

Alcohol consumption has been associated with human social activities since the start of recorded history. In modern society, the increase in alcohol consumption has caused many social problems [22]. Alcohol use disorders (AUDs) affect an estimated 8.5% of the US population over the age of 18, and problems associated with AUDs cost the United States economy up to $185 billion per year [18].

There are immediate risks from such causes such as injury, driving accidents, unwanted pregnancy, and death due to overdose. There are also longer-term risks from repeated episodes of binge drinking consequent to neurotoxicity, as well as adverse consequences to heart, liver, immune system, bone health, and other organ systems [10].

The potential harmful effects of alcohol on human health are a concern [22]. Pupil examination offers an objective evaluation of the visual function as well

---

R. M. da Costa—The author thanks FAPEG and CNPQ for providing support for the development of this research.

V. Murino and E. Puppo (Eds.): ICIAP 2015, Part II, LNCS 9280, pp. 598–608, 2015.
DOI: 10.1007/978-3-319-23234-8_55

as the vegetative pathways to the eye. Essential information is gathered within a short time. This makes pupillary inspection a valuable part of the ophthalmological, neurological, and general medical examinations routine. [17] obtained results of 80% accuracy in alcohol identification through pupil exams, using existing values in the literature and the cops tests to identify consul of alcohol, this consist in follow horizontal movements of pupil. They affirm be need more experiments to a correct determination in low doses of alcohol.

In spite of technological advances and substantial progress in the understanding of the central nervous system (CNS) pathophysiology, routine pupil examination with a conventional light source has undergone no significant changes in the last 100 years [16]. Pupillary examination involves recording the size, symmetry, and light reactivity of both pupils. The analysis of these parameters is affected by significant interobserver variability due to the influence of factors such as differences in ambient lighting, the examiners own visual acuity and experience, the intensity of the light stimulus, and the method used to direct this stimulus [16].

Numerous pathologic conditions can disrupt the neural pathways responsible for orbital control or for the visual reflex centers and can manifest as a variety of entities, including ophthalmoplegia, oculosympathetic syndrome, Parinaud syndrome, and ptosis. In general medical exam, pupillary examination provides a convenient and simple method for the evaluation of autonomic function. Most patients with autonomic disorders show evidence of sympathetic or parasympathetic deficits in the pupil [3].

Ferrari et al. [11] conducted a study to investigate the movement of the pupil in healthy volunteers and in volunteers with diabetes. The work consisted of constructing a device to capture digital images from the pupil. The stimulus light and recording was applied to the same eye and external light was not isolated. Ferrari concluded that by studying the movements of the pupil it was possible to perform screening in diabetic patients.

In human subjects, acute administration of alcohol produces euphoria and feelings of intoxication with decreased response time and accuracy on neuropsychological tests measuring memory, attention, and psychomotor performance [18]. Alcohol reduces brain efficiency, reduces night vision by 25% and reduces reaction time by 30%. These effects are more intense with a lower alcohol tolerance [10]. Alcoholic beverages give drivers a false sense of confidence, damaging skills such as attention, coordination and reaction time. Chances of accidents increase even though only small alcohol amounts were ingested which were below legal limits.

Over the last few years, infrared devices included in digital cameras led to the development of digital systems which enable outside researchers to carry out repeatable non-invasive studies of pupil size and light reactivity using an objective method [4,16,21]. However, it is not a portable device capable of helping examination and blood alcohol detection through a direct and consensual pupillary reflex test.

In the literature, there are studies evaluating changes of the pupil diameter and characteristics of iris to help a diagnostic, most of these studies affirm the need to improve the robustness of the methods to improve the recognition systems proposed [6,11,13,17,20].

The purpose of this work is to develop a portable device and a method of testing pupillary reflex (direct and consensual) to detect blood alcohol. Through 206 videos from 40 volunteers recorded in an environment with light controlled solely by a pupillometer, the preliminary results prove the method efficacy. This study proposes the use of light in a controlled environment coupled with recording dynamic videos of the pupillary movements and applying algorithms for pattern recognition. This work can also open a way to new studies involving computer-aided diagnosis (CAD).

1.1 Anatomy of the Human Ocular System

A major challenge when working with human eye images is the correct technique for image capture. This task is not trivial, mostly because the visible structure of the human eye, composed of sclera and iris, reflect visible light exceptionally well. These reflections form white spots that overlap images, preventing correct measurements of contraction and pupil dilation movement.

Moreover, research in the biometrics area has proposed equipment with special Near Infra-Red (NIR) lighting to capture human eye images [5,9,12]. This type of lighting is not visible to the human eye and thus does not offer visual stimulus for the pupil to execute its miosis and mydriasis movements.

To apply the right technique, it is necessary to understand the human optical system. The human optic nerve carries the afferent visual signals captured through the eyes to the Edinger-Westphal nucleus region, whose axons are directed to the right and left oculomotors. Thus, any inadvertent movements performed by an eye are reproduced in the other eye [7,8,14,15].

2 Material and Methods

2.1 Pupillometer Construction

To apply the blood alcohol test methodology, a pupillometer was built based on consensual human optics reflection. The pupillometer has a lighting system with visible light that grad ually goes from 0 (zero) to 38 lux, positioned at 3 centimeters distance from one of the eyes.

While the lighting system provides stimuli for pupil contraction and dilation, a set of four infrared LEDs provide invisible light to the human eye, allowing the camera to record images. These LEDs operate on an 850 nm wavelength, not providing stimulus for pupil contraction and dilation. The camera that records the images is a Point Grey Firefly MV 0.3 MP Mono USB 2.0 (Microm MTV022).

Figure 1 shows a picture of a pupillometer being used by a volunteer and examples of images captured with different light stimuli.

 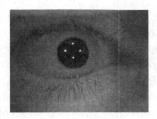 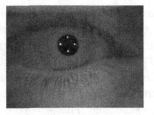

Fig. 1. Different stages of pupillary contraction and dilation.

2.2 Construction of a Video Database

The built pupillometer has a circuit that is controlled by software developed in C++ that allows setting the following recording parameters like recording time, start time for visual stimuli, visual stimulus length and visual stimulus intensity.

Were selected 40 volunteers with no pre-existing disease, either ocular or systemic. Each healthy volunteer was placed in a dark testing room for approximately 5 minutes, to adapt to darkness. Before the recording started, the volunteer was asked not to blink.

Experiments were performed with the recording of 50 seconds videos, at a recording rate of 30 frames per second. The 30 frames recording rate is the approximate number of frames that a human being can identify in movie frames. At every 10 seconds, a 1 lux visual stimulus was applied for 10 seconds. Therefore, in each video recorded, were registered three intervals without visual stimulus and two intervals with visual stimulus. The adopted visual stimulus methodology is shown in Table 1.

Each visual stimulus time was set to ensure the complete capture of the pupil contraction or dilation movement with a safety margin. Intensity of visual stimulus 1 lux is sufficient to stimulate the pupil to a full contraction without causing discomfort to the person being filmed. Unlike other studies in the literature [6], the white light source is positioned 3 centimeters away from the stimulated eye and any external lighting was completely sealed, as shown in Figure 1.

Verification of blood alcohol level on volunteers was conducted with a Mercury breathalyzer, which records alcohol milligrams number per liter of exhausted air (mg/L), and has an electrochemical sensor that reacts to alcohol in the range of 0.0 mg /L to 2.0 mg/L.

Table 1. Visual stimulus specifications

Frames	Visual Stimulus
1 300	OFF
301 600	ON
601 900	OFF
901 1200	ON
1201 1500	OFF

During the test, the volunteer was measured by a breathalyzer before taking any alcoholic beverages. After an observed value of 0.0 mg/L in the breathalyzer, filming was performed. The volunteer was measured by breathalyzer and filmed several times and the data gathered were recorded.

After the volunteer ingested alcohol, and before breathalyzer measurement, a ten minute wait time was initiated before performing breathalyzer measurement and the shooting. This was to ensure that any residual alcohol in the volunteers mouth would not distort the measurement.

2.3   Characteristics Extraction

The constructed pupillometer in this work completely seals illumination, as seen in Figure 1, and visual stimuli were of 0 lux to stimulate a full pupil dilation and 1 lux to stimulate a maximum pupil contraction, without discomfort for the volunteer.

To segmentation and get the values of diameter to create the characteristics vector with the six metrics, was applied the algorithm proposed by [19], which applies the properties width and height in the red channel of the smoothed image. Applied this algorithm is possible found the correct diameter of pupil as presented in Figure 2.

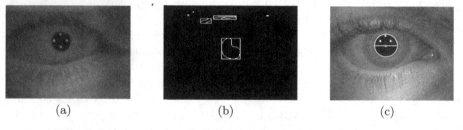

(a)   (b)   (c)

Fig. 2. (a) Channel Red. (b) Pupil segmented (c) Pupil Diameter

In order to evaluate results, six metrics similar to the tests performed by Chang et al. [6] were applied. They used visual stimuli ranging from 0.6 to 2.1 seconds long. The volunteer was not in a sealed lighting environment, but in a room with partial lighting, so the applied visual stimuli ranged from 25 lux in the dark, to stimulate pupil dilation, to 35 lux in the clearest stimulus, to stimulate pupil contraction.

- Maximum Mydriasis - demonstrates the largest pupil diameter before contraction. This is the value of maximum pupil diameter one second before apply the visual stimulus. This value is found between frames 270-300 (first visual stimulus) and between frames 870-900 (second visual stimulus);
- Maximum Miosis - demonstrates the smallest pupil diameter after contracting. This is the value of minimum pupil diameter three seconds after apply the visual stimulus. This value is found between frames 301-390 (first visual stimulus) and between frames 901-990 (second visual stimulus).;

- Amplitude (Amp) - shows in percentage how much the pupil constricts after applying 1 lux visual stimulus. This value is calculated by equation 1.

$$Amp = \frac{Miosis}{Mydriasis} \qquad (1)$$

- Latency (Lat) - shows the time in the 10 seconds of light stimulation that the pupil takes to start contraction after visual stimulus application. This value is found between frames 301-390 (first visual stimulus) and between frames 901-990 (second visual stimulus). The time is calculated from frame 300 or 900 considering the frame rate 30 fps;
- Time to maximum contraction (TMC) - demonstrates at what time in the 10 seconds stimulus the pupil reaches its maximum contraction. This is the value of minimum pupil diameter three seconds after apply the visual stimulus. This value is found between frames 301-390 (first visual stimulus) and between frames 901-990 (second visual stimulus). The time to reach minimum diameter is calculated from frame 300 or 900 considering the frame rate 30 fps;
- Time to maximum dilation (TMD) - demonstrates at what time in the 10 seconds of light stimulation absence the pupil reaches maximum dilation. This is the value of maximum pupil diameter three seconds after supply the visual stimulus. This value is found between frames 601-690 (first visual stimulus) and between frames 1201-1290 (second visual stimulus). The time to reach maximum diameter is calculated from frame 600 or 1200 considering the frame rate 30 fps.

The authorization to carry out this footage was submitted and approved by the Ethics Committee in Research (CEP), in a submitted project in Plataforma Brasil, under the number CAAE 23723213.0.0000.5083.

3   Results

206 videos were carried out, with 3 to 10 videos for the 40 volunteers. 10 volunteers were females (25%) and 30 males (75%). The individuals average age was of 29.0 8.2 years. All videos were normalized by Z-Score.

It is possible to observe the effect of alcohol in the volunteer, causing the pupil to become more dilated in the mydriasis mode versus miosis. The pupil reaction time, demonstrated by Latency (Lat) is also slower after alcohol consumption. Table 2 shows the average values and its standard deviations for all videos of the volunteers. The 1st period corresponds to frames 301 600 and 2nd period corresponds to frames 901 1200 when the light is switch on.

Figure 3a shows the pupil diameter of one person in two stages: before drinking alcohol and after drinking alcohol. As can be seen, the presence of alcohol produces a slow pupil reaction time when the light is switch on or off.

The request for the volunteers not to blink and keep their eyes fixed on the pupillometer bright points was not always followed. In some cases, the volunteer

Table 2. Metrics used for validation

	Sober				Inebriate			
	1st Period		2nd Period		1st Period		2nd Period	
	Mean	SD[1]	Mean	SD	Mean	SD	Mean	SD
Mydriasis	1.42	0.27	1.38	0.26	1.51	0.25	1.39	0.29
Miosis	0.04	0.01	0.10	0.03	0.05	0.02	0.13	0.08
Amp	0.02 %	-	0.09 %	-	0.03 %	-	0.07 %	-
Lat	0.33 seg	0.45 seg	0.26 seg	0.13 seg	0.34 seg	0.36 seg	0.28 seg	0.13 seg
TMC	1.73 seg	0.34 seg	1.60 seg	0.40 seg	1.73 seg	0.35 seg	1.48 seg	0.44 seg
TMD	1.89 seg	0.24 seg	1.90 seg	0.22 seg	1.85 seg	0.30 seg	1.85 seg	0.30 seg

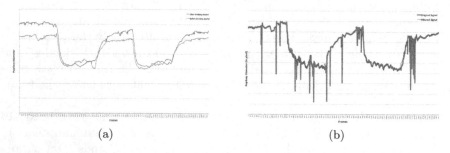

(a)   (b)

Fig. 3. (a) Pupillary diameter with different alcohol levels. (b) Pupillary diameter with noises and filtered.

movements caused failures in targeting the pupil and therefore, caused noise in the signal. Figure 3b shows an example of an original signal with noise and the same signal filtered by the neighborhood average algorithm.

3.1 Pattern Recognition

In this work, we used two algorithms for pattern recognition: Support Vector Machine (SVM) and k-Nearest Neighbors (KNN). SVM tries to model input variables by finding the separating boundary called the hyperplane to achieve classification of the input variables [1]. SVM training was performed using a linear kernel function and the C parameter was set to 1 (default of SVM). KNN is a supervised learning technique introduced by Aha [2]. The general idea of this technique is to find the k closest labeled examples to unlabeled; based on the labeling of the closest examples, the decision of which is the unlabeled example class. The value of k in this work was 3 and Euclidean distance was used.

We applied cross-validation to measure the accuracy of the classifiers. In this technique, samples are divided into n mutually exclusive partitions. In each iteration, a different partition is used to test the classifier, and all the other n-1 partitions are used to train the classifier. The hit rate and error is the average of all rates calculated for the n iterations. In this work, n equals to 10 was used.

---

[1] SD - Standard Deviation.

Table 3. Values obtained through SVM and KNN application

Volunteer	Videos	KNN	SVM
1	10	80.00	80.00
2	5	100.00	80.00
3	5	80.00	80.00
4	5	80.00	80.00
5	9	88.89	77.78
6	6	50.00	83.33
7	9	75.00	87.50
8	6	83.00	100.00
9	6	83.00	83.33
10	9	100.00	100.00
	Average score ⇒	**80.28**	**85.19**

Table 3 shows the results obtained by KNN and SVM for ten volunteers with higher amounts of videos.

4   Discussion

The pupillometer constructed proved to be an effective, non-invasive, objective, and portable pupillary change identification method based on alcohol intake. Images captured were carried out efficiently, without the need to repeat examination by measurement error. In some cases, the volunteer movements caused failures on pupil segmentation and, therefore, caused noise in the signal. To correct them, the software used the neighborhood average algorithm. The built pupillometer completely seals lighting, and visual stimuli were of 0 lux to stimulate the pupil to full dilation, and 1 lux to stimulate the pupil to a maximum contraction, without discomfort to the individual.

The developed method proved to be better than the breathalyzer, since an individual can refuse to blow on the breathalyzer. In addition, in this proposed method there is no contact with body secretions. Matching airflow with blood flow is critical for normal gas exchange and requires a delicate balance between the blood and air distribution systems.

Through the evaluation of filming results, it is observed that the pupil diameter reacts differently when the volunteer drinks alcoholic beverages. In the results general average observed in Table 3, it is noted that the maximum mydriasis value of a person remains stable between the first period (first visual stimulus frame 301 to 600) and second period (second visual stimulus frame 901 to 1200) when he/she has not ingested alcoholic beverages. When the person ingested alcoholic beverages, the pupil is dilated and unstable. It is noted by the difference in the maximum mydriasis values from one period to the other that pupillary reflexes are compromised. The same can be observed for miosis, indicating lack of control and stability reflexes when a person is under alcohol influence.

Through the evaluation of filming results, it is observed that the pupil diameter reacts differently when the volunteer drinks alcoholic beverages. The authors did not find similar research assessing alcohol and pupillary reflex.

In the results general average observed in Table 2, it is noted that the maximum mydriasis value of a person remains stable between the first period (first visual stimulus frame 301 to 600) and second period (second visual stimulus frame 901 to 1200) when he/she has not ingested alcoholic beverages. When the person ingested alcoholic beverages, the pupil is dilated and unstable. It is noted by the difference in the maximum mydriasis values from one period to the other that pupillary reflexes are compromised. The same can be observed for miosis, indicating lack of control and stability reflexes when a person is under alcohol influence.

Amplitude values, which show how the pupil constricts while receiving visual stimulus, are also unstable and higher when a person is under alcohol influence. It is also observed that the reaction times (latency) for maximum mydriasis and maximum miosis are also more stable and regular when the person has not ingested alcoholic beverages.

The results observed in Table 3 show rates for KNN and SVM algorithms in volunteers with a sufficient amount of videos. The figures show the possibility to use such algorithms to develop the identification of a blood alcohol method based on the pupillary reflex.

5   Conclusion

The pupillometer allowed the evaluation of size, symmetry, and light reactivity of pupils. Test interference factors were eliminated such as: ambient lighting, observer experience, light stimulus intensity, and the method used to direct this stimulation.

The pupillometer proved to be an effective, non-invasive, objective, and portable pupillary reflex test method based on light stimulus. It is a useful tool that can be used by companies to check the presence of blood alcohol levels in a person.

The methodology developed was efficient for identifying alcohol in volunteers with 5 or more videos. It will be necessary to conduct more experiments to determine the minimum amount of videos necessary for identification. However the lack of contact with blood or any type of secretion makes this a safe, non-invasive, and very helpful method for this kind of examination.

This work can also open a way to new studies involving computer-aided diagnosis (CAD). Changes in the software could possibility enable studies to identify signals of a probable disease. Therefore, further research is warranted to standardize dark adaptation time before the start of the test, the light intensity, duration of the light stimulus, and the interval between them.

References

1. Abe, S.: Support Vector Machines for Pattern Classification. Springer (2010)
2. Aha, D.W., Kibler, D., Albert, M.K.: Instance-based learning algorithms. Machine Learning **6**(1), 37–66 (1991)
3. Bär, K.J., Schulz, S., Koschke, M., Harzendorf, C., Gayde, S., Berg, W., Voss, A., Yeragani, V.K., Boettger, M.K.: Correlations between the autonomic modulation of heart rate, blood pressure and the pupillary light reflex in healthy subjects. Journal of the Neurological Sciences **279**(1), 9–13 (2009)
4. Bergamin, O., Zimmerman, M.B., Kardon, R.H.: Pupil light reflex in normal and diseased eyes: diagnosis of visual dysfunction using waveform partitioning. Ophthalmology **110**(1), 106–114 (2003)
5. Bittner, D.M., Wieseler, I., Wilhelm, H., Riepe, M.W., Müller, N.G.: Repetitive pupil light reflex: potential marker in Alzheimer's disease? Journal of Alzheimer's Disease **42**(4), 1469–1477 (2014)
6. Chang, D.S., Arora, K.S., Boland, M.V., Supakontanasan, W., Friedman, D.S.: Development and Validation of an Associative Model for the Detection of Glaucoma Using Pupillography. American Journal of Ophthalmology **156**(6), 1285–1296 (2013)
7. Chen, Y., Adjouadi, M., Han, C., Wang, J., Barreto, A., Rishe, N., Andrian, J.: A highly accurate and computationally efficient approach for unconstrained iris segmentation. Image and Vision Computing **28**(2), 261–269 (2010)
8. Chen, Y., Wang, J., Han, C., Wang, L., Adjouadi, M.: A robust segmentation approach to iris recognition based on video. In: 37th IEEE Applied Imagery Pattern Recognition Workshop, AIPR 2008, pp. 1–8. IEEE (2008)
9. da Costa, R.M., Gonzaga, A.: Dynamic features for iris recognition. IEEE Transactions on Systems, Man, and Cybernetics, Part B: Cybernetics **42**(4), 1072–1082 (2012)
10. Crabbe, J.C., Harris, R.A., Koob, G.F.: Preclinical studies of alcohol binge drinking. Annals of the New York Academy of Sciences **1216**(1), 24–40 (2011)
11. Ferrari, G.L., Marques, J.L.B., Gandhi, R.A., Emery, C.J., Tesfaye, S., Heller, S.R., Schneider, F.K., Gamba, H.R.: An approach to the assessment of diabetic neuropathy based on dynamic pupillometry. In: 29th Annual International Conference of the IEEE Engineering in Medicine and Biology Society, EMBS 2007, pp. 557–560. IEEE (2007)
12. Giza, E., Fotiou, D., Bostantjopoulou, S., Katsarou, Z., Gerasimou, G., Gotzamani-Psarrakou, A., Karlovasitou, A.: Pupillometry and 123I-DaTSCAN imaging in Parkinson's disease: a comparison study. International Journal of Neuroscience **122**(1), 26–34 (2011)
13. Hollingsworth, K., Bowyer, K.W., Flynn, P.J.: Pupil dilation degrades iris biometric performance. Computer Vision and Image Understanding **113**(1), 150–157 (2009). http://dx.doi.org/10.1016/j.cviu.2008.08.001
14. Jan, F., Usman, I., Agha, S.: Iris localization in frontal eye images for less constrained iris recognition systems. Digital Signal Processing **22**(6), 971–986 (2012)
15. Kawasaki, A., Crippa, S.V., Kardon, R., Leon, L., Hamel, C.: Characterization of pupil responses to blue and red light stimuli in autosomal dominant retinitis pigmentosa due to NR2E3 mutation. Investigative Ophthalmology and Visual Science **53**(9), 5562–5569 (2012)

16. Martinez-Ricarte, F., Castro, A., Poca, M.A., Sahuquillo, J., Exposito, L., Arribas, M., Aparicio, J.: Infrared pupillometry. Basic principles and their application in the non-invasive monitoring of neurocritical patients. Neurología (English Edition) **28**(1), 41–51 (2013)
17. Meunier, F., Laperriere, D.: A video-based image processing system for the automatic implementation of the eye involuntary reflexes measurements involved in the drug recognition expert (dre). In: IEEE/ACS International Conference on Computer Systems and Applications, AICCSA 2008, pp. 599–605. IEEE (2008)
18. Pava, M.J., Woodward, J.J.: A review of the interactions between alcohol and the endocannabinoid system: implications for alcohol dependence and future directions for research. Alcohol **46**(3), 185–204 (2012)
19. Pinheiro, H., Costa, R., Laureano, G., Romero, R., Soares, F., Galdino, L.: Human iris segmentation on videos obtained via natural lighting from smartphones. In: Proceedings of X Workshop of Computer Vision. Uberlandia: Facom, vol. 1, pp. 230–236. WVC (2014)
20. Tapia, J.E., Perez, C.a., Bowyer, K.W.: Gender Classification from Iris Images using Fusion of Uniform Local Binary Patterns pp. 1–13
21. Volpe, N.J., Plotkin, E.S., Maguire, M.G., Hariprasad, R., Galetta, S.L.: Portable pupillography of the swinging flashlight test to detect afferent pupillary defects. Ophthalmology **107**(10), 1913–1921 (2000)
22. Wang, S., Wang, J.J., Wong, T.Y.: Alcohol and eye diseases. Survey of Ophthalmology **53**(5), 512–525 (2008)

Selection of Temporal Features
for Event Detection in Smart Security

Niki Martinel[1]([⊠]), Danilo Avola[1], Claudio Piciarelli[1], Christian Micheloni[1],
Marco Vernier[1], Luigi Cinque[2], and Gian Luca Foresti[1]

[1] Department of Mathematics and Computer Science, University of Udine,
Via delle Scienze 206, 33100 Udine, Italy
niki.martinel@uniud.it
[2] Department of Computer Science, Sapienza University of Rome,
Via Salaria 113, 00198 Rome, Italy

Abstract. Scene understanding in smart surveillance and security is
one of the major fields of investigation in computer vision research and
industry. The ability of a system to automatically analyze and learn
the events that occur within a scene (e.g., a running person, a parking
car) is conditioned by several complex aspects such as feature extraction,
tracking and recognition. One of the most important aspects in the event
learning process is the detection of the time interval in which an event
occurs (i.e., when it starts and ends). The present paper is focused on
the learning of temporal correlated events. In particular, a formalized
description of the features associated with each event and the linked
strategy to define the event time-line are provided. The paper also reports
preliminary tests carried out on videos related to a reference outdoor
environment which validate the proposed strategy.

1 Introduction

Nowadays, intelligent video surveillance systems (e.g., [1,2]) are becoming increasingly important due to their strategic role in monitoring sensitive targets (e.g., [3,4]), as well as in supporting the safety and security of the people, environments [5] and objects. The main task of these systems is to automatically interpret the behavior of the agents (e.g., persons, vehicles) that act within the scenario in order to detect suspicious events [6]. In fact, a first basic classification of the events can be defined by considering usual events and unusual events (e.g., anomalies or novelties) [7,8]. The first class takes into account all those events which are consistent with the monitored environment or, in other words, which are statistically more frequent. An unusual event belongs to the second class. In most situations, the primary objective of a smart security system is to provoke a reaction (e.g., alarm, feedback, action) when unusual events are perceived since they can potentially cause security violations [9]. It should be noted that an event considered to be usual in one environment could be an unusual event in other sites. Moreover, within the same event may be behaviors attributable to one or the other class. The introduced issues implicitly highlight two crucial aspects of the event detection

V. Murino and E. Puppo (Eds.): ICIAP 2015, Part II, LNCS 9280, pp. 609–619, 2015.
DOI: 10.1007/978-3-319-23234-8_56

process. The first one regards the set of key features chosen to represent an event and its temporal evolution. The last one concerns the recognition of the time interval in which the event occurs. Note that, as previously mentioned, the same event (e.g., a moving car) can present, at different time intervals, features attributable to usual or unusual events thus complicating the already complex task of the event classification. From an abstract point of view, an algorithm for event detection and classification [10–13] consists of two main steps:

- The selection of the key features (i.e., feature selection technique [14]) through which to understand the semantic of the interesting events;
- The design of the classifier (i.e., machine learning technique) adopted to recognize the events. Note that, a classifier can be binary (distinguishing usual events from unusual events), or multiclass (characterizing type and meaning of each event within a set of specified classes).

The present paper has two main aims. The first one is to introduce a formalization related to the key features associated to any event. The last one is to exploit this formalization to introduce a time interval based strategy through which automatically recognize when an event starts and ends. The proposed approach was stressed by using a reference scenario in which different agents interacted forming a wide range of events. The obtained qualitative and quantitative results shown the effectiveness and the accuracy of the method.

2   Related Work

Due to the heterogeneity and vastness of the literature on the event representation and key feature extraction, the section will focus only on these works which are more directly related to the proposed approach. A first interesting work is presented in [15], where the authors address the problem of trajectory analysis for anomaly detection using SVMs. In their approach the key features are represented by a set of fixed-dimension vectors which correspond to the paths traveled by agents within the monitored scenario. The trajectories having similar features are clustered together forming the class of the usual events, while the other trajectories (i.e., outliers) will form the class of the unusual events. In [16], the role of the temporal feature for detecting unusual events is highlighted. The representation of the time is achieved by a Gaussian Mixture Model (GMM) which describes the temporal evolution of each agent involved within the scenario. Another challenging work is proposed in [17], where the authors describe a system for image understanding of complex scenarios. In particu-lar, the authors primarily adopt two key features (i.e., color and texture) to determinate the individual components of the images, subsequently they use another key feature (i.e., shape) to identify the important characteristic traits of the image and hence help in better descriptive analysis of the scene. The authors of the work shown in [18] adopt a classifier based on a set of DBNs to develop a situation assessment framework. In particular, they present a method for an automatic definition of the parameters that can be easily used by a human operator when designing a new net-work. The key features adopted within the framework come from a supervised data-base (VIRAT [19]) able to provide a semantic interpretation (labels) of the observed scenes, while the authors introduce an interesting use of the temporal feature. The temporal key feature is used to correlate different actions related to different agents with the aim to derive a more complex inter-pretation of the events. This work has the great advantage of being particularly adaptable to different application contexts. Other three interesting works are proposed in [20–22]. The first one presents an algorithm for learning the event categorizations in a given scene. In particular, the authors propose a Stochas-tic Context-Free Grammars (SCFG) for event detection in challenging outdoor video sequences. A similar work is introduced by the authors of the second one, which show an algorithm for recognizing usual and unusual events in complex video sequences. A technique of the same type is adopted by the authors of the last work, which propose both standard visual key features and domain-specific in-formation to semantically interpret different actions from video sequences. In each work the temporal feature is used to correlate spatial events and/or identify the sequence of complex actions.

3 Preliminaries

Let consider a monitored environment $\mathcal{S}$ in which n_A agents (i.e., objects), interact with it or among them. The k-th agent of class c, which is observed in the scenario at time instant t, is denoted as $\mathbf{a}_{(c,k)}(t)$ and it is composed of a set of n different features such that:

$$\mathbf{a}_{c,k}(t) = \{\mathbf{x}_k^{(1)}, \mathbf{x}_k^{(2)}, \ldots, \mathbf{x}_k^{(j)}, \ldots, \mathbf{x}_k^{(n)}\} \tag{1}$$

where $\mathbf{x}_k^{(j)} \in \mathbb{R}^d$ indicates the j-th feature type (e.g., color histogram, histogram of oriented gradients, etc.) extracted at time instant t (omitted to ease the nota-tion). Notice that, since different features can be adopted to represent an agent, then it is not a necessary condition that the i-th and j-th features span the same feature space, i.e. $|\mathbf{x}_k^{(i)}| = |\mathbf{x}_k^{(j)}|$. In the following we assume all the features to be normalized in the interval $[0, 1]$.

3.1 Events

An event is generated by the action performed by a single agent. Therefore, it con-siders no interactions between agents. More formally, let $\mathbf{e}_{(c,k)} \in \varepsilon_c = \{1, \ldots, N\}$ denote the type of an event of interest generated by the action of an agent $\mathbf{a}_{c,k}$ (e.g., a moving person, a parked car, etc.), and ε_c is the set of all N possible events associated with the c-th class agent. The set ε_c is defined off-line by the sys-tem operator and stored in an event database. Also, let $T^s = [t_0^s, t_{end}^s]$ denote the temporal interval during which an agent $\mathbf{a}_{c,k}$ performs an action of interest that fires an event. Given the set of all available features collected during the temporal interval T^s, denoted as:

$$\mathcal{A}_{c,k} = \{\mathbf{a}_{c,k}(t)\}_{t=t_0^s}^{t_{end}^s} \tag{2}$$

it is generally the case that only a subset of them is relevant to detect the event of interest. Such a subset is denoted as:

$$\tilde{\mathcal{A}}_{c,k} = \{\tilde{\mathbf{a}}_{c,k}(t)\}_{t=t_0^s}^{t_{end}^s} \subset \mathcal{A}_{c,k} \tag{3}$$

where $\tilde{\mathbf{a}}_{c,k}(t) \subset \mathbf{a}_{c,k}(t)$. Therefore a simple event generated by the k-th agent of class c, can be defined as:

$$\mathbf{e}_{c,k} = f_c(\tilde{\mathcal{A}}_{c,k}) \tag{4}$$

where $f_c(\cdot)$ is an agent class dependent function of the relevant features in $\mathcal{A}_{c,k}$ and which output in ε_c denotes the event type for the c-th class. For instance, the function $f_c(\cdot)$ can be the output of a classification algorithm (e.g., a Support Vector Machine, a Random Forest of Decision Trees, etc.).

4   Temporal Event Learning

One of the most important tasks that are required to properly learn and recognize an event of interest is to determine the time interval $T^s = [t_0^s, t_{end}^s]$ in which the event occur. To determine such a time interval we formulate the following hypothesis. Let t_0^s be the time instant in which the agent $\mathbf{a}_{(c,k)}$ enters the environment or the time instant following the last time instant of another event produced by the same agent. To establish the time instant t_{end}^s at which the event ends, we suppose that the given relevant features $\mathbf{a}_{(c,k)}$ do not vary over a given threshold. More formally, t_{end}^s is computed by taking the time instant t_i^s as follows:

$$\begin{cases} t_{end}^s = t_i^s & \text{if } h_c = 1 \\ t_i^s = t_{i+1}^s & \text{otherwise} \end{cases} \tag{5}$$

where

$$h_c = \left(\tilde{\mathbf{a}}_{c,k}(t_i^s), \tilde{\mathbf{a}}_{c,k}(t_{i-1}^s)\right), j = 1, \dots, N \tag{6}$$

is a function that compares the value of the given relevant features to determine when the variation between two consecutive time instants t_i^s and t_{i-1}^s is outside the allowed range of $K_c^j = [\epsilon_{c,\min}^j, \epsilon_{c,\max}^j]$ which describes the behavior of the agent $\mathbf{a}_{(c,k)}$, hence the main characteristics of the event. For example, let us consider the detected agent $\mathbf{a}_{\text{person},1}(t)$ being a person in the environment. Let consider the following events belonging to the scenario:

- Event 1: A walking person (moving at approximately constant speed);
- Event 2: A running person;
- Event 3: A static person.

In such a case we can defined the function h_{person} as:

$$h_{\text{person}} = \left(\tilde{\mathbf{a}}_{\text{person},1}(t_i^s), \tilde{\mathbf{a}}_{\text{person},1}(t_{i-1}^s), \epsilon_{\text{person}}^j \right)$$

$$= \tilde{\mathbf{a}}_{\text{person},1}(t_i^s) - \tilde{\mathbf{a}}_{\text{person},1}(t_{i-1}^s) \in K_{\text{person}}^j$$

where t_i^s is the sampling instant. In such a case the sampling interval $t_i^s - t_{i-1}^s$ is the 1sec. The value of the thresholds intervals for K_c^j, for $j = 1, \ldots, 3$ (in this example) should be selected according to the definitions of simple events. Here, the most significant feature characterizing the events is the speed of the person expressed as the distance traveled between consecutive frames measured in pixel or meters (if camera calibration is adopted). So, the set $\mathbf{a}_{\text{person},1}$ contains the agent position features only. The intervals K_c^j accounts for the minimum and maximum distance traveled between two consecutive frames for the j-th event of the agent of class c. For the given example, assuming that a walking person is normally moving at a speed lower than 2m/sec (i.e., covering a distance lower than 2m between consecutive samples), and that a running person is normally moving at a speed higher than 2m/sec, the following intervals can be defined by the operator for the event related to the agent $\mathbf{a}_{\text{person},1}$:

- Event 1: A walking person (moving at approximately constant speed): $\epsilon_{\text{person,min}}^1 = 0.25$ and $\epsilon_{\text{person,max}}^1 = 2$;
- Event 2: A running person: $\epsilon_{\text{person,min}}^2 = 2$ and $\epsilon_{\text{person,max}}^2 = 10$;
- Event 3: A static person: $\epsilon_{\text{person,min}}^3 = 0$ and $\epsilon_{\text{person,max}}^3 = 0.25$;

4.1 Temporal Feature Extraction

Typical features describing an event are the class of the agent, the size of the blob representing the agent, its position projected on a 2D top view map, the agent speed and the color histogram (see Fig. 1). In addition, to capture the shape of the agent [23] PHOG features are used. Such as features are extracted every time instant t and pooled in the time interval The PHOG feature [24] captures the local shape and the spatial layout of the shape in a given image exploiting the pyramidal framework proposed in [25]. As shown in Fig. 2, in a spatial pyramid framework, the given image is divided into a sequence of spatial grid cells. The PHOG feature vector is computed as a concatenation of all the HOG vectors computed for all the cells at each level of the spatial pyramid representation. Fig. 2 illustrates this principle showing the PHOG features computed for different values of spatial pyramid levels L.

4.2 Neural Tree Learning

A Neural Tree is a hierarchical classifier with a tree structure. Each node of the tree is an Artificial Neural Network (ANN) and each leaf corresponds to a class label (in this case, to an event). In a NT, the classification of a given

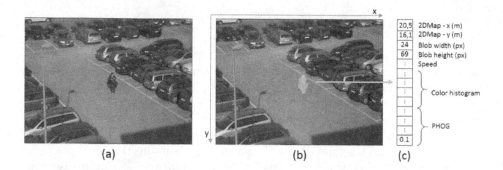

Fig. 1. An example of the considered features extracted from a given frame. (a) Shows the input frame; (b) The processed frame by a change detection algorithm localizing the agent; (c) The extracted feature vector.

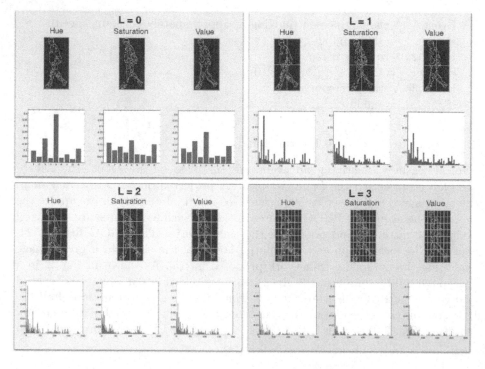

Fig. 2. Effects of the number of levels (L) in the PHOG feature extraction process. For each of the four blocks, the top row shows the grid cells (in green) at which the HOG features are extracted. Bottom rows show the final PHOG features computed concatenating the HOG features extracted at each level of the pyramid.

pattern is conducted by presenting the pattern to the ANN in the root node. Then, it follows the path determined by the ANN output. The process continues until a leaf node is reached. Due to the its classification capabilities, in this work the AHNT proposed in [26] has been used to obtain the classification function $f_c(\cdot)$. In an AHNT, each node can be a first-order or a high order perceptron (HOP) according to the complexity of the local training set. First order perceptrons split the training set by hyperplanes, while n-order perceptrons use n-dimensional surfaces. An adaptive procedure decides the best order of the HOP to be applied at a given node of the tree. The AHNT is grown automatically during the learning phase: its hybrid structure guarantees a reduction of the number of internal nodes with respect to classical neural trees and reaches a greater generalization capability. Moreover, it overcomes the classical problems of feed-forward neural networks (e.g., multilayer perceptrons) since both types of perceptrons does not require any a-priori information about the number of neurons, hidden layers, or neuron connections.

5 Experimental Results

In order to evaluate the performances of the proposed event learning and detection system in a real-world outdoor scenario, we considered the premises of the Department of Mathematics and Computer Science at the University of Udine and their surroundings, as shown in Fig. 3.

The environment consists of two main buildings, three parking lots, several roads and road joints, three main pedestrian-only paths and green areas. These areas have been manually labeled on the map (see again Fig. 3) and they compose the prior static knowledge available on the monitored environment. The area is monitored by six PTZ IP color cameras manufactured by Axis (outdoor model Q6032-E). The cameras have been oriented using the algorithm proposed in [27] to maximize their visual coverage avoiding overlaps, in order to acquire data from the largest area possible. The list of possible agents is defined as $A = \{person, car, bus\}$ and for each agent the list of features is defined as:

- $\mathbf{a} = \{position, speed, width, height, colorhistogram, PHOG\}$.

In order to learn the simple events with the AHNT [26] we considered the video sequences acquired over a 6-hours time range; the sequences have a resolution of 382×288 pixels. The experiments have been conducted to recognize three types of simple events, namely:

- Person walking on the pedestrian paths;
- Car entering/leaving the parking lot;
- Bus stopping/starting at the bus stop.

As previously mentioned, simple events are learnt using a neural tree architecture, using the most appropriate features among the available ones. The training set consisted in 451 sequences of walking person, 92 of car entering/exiting the

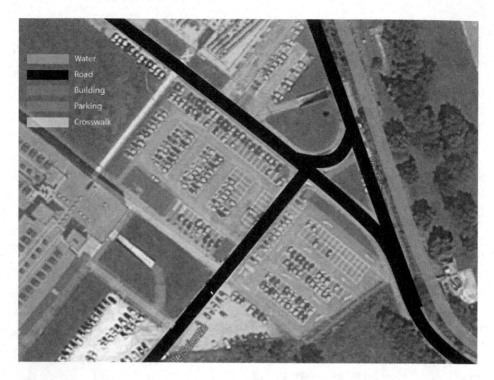

Fig. 3. The outdoor environment used as a test bed for simple/complex event learning and detection evaluation.

(a)   (b)   (c)

Fig. 4. Three frames from one of the parking lot sequences.

parking lot, and 12 of the stopping/starting bus. Fig. 4 shows few frames from a sequence in the parking lot.

The trained Neural Tree has 25 perceptron nodes and a maximum depth of 4. It has been used to classify respectively 50, 20 and 10 sequences for each of the three event classes (the test sequences are different from the training ones). The final classification result is show in Table 5. The table is a confusion matrix where the rows are the ground truth classification of the test video sequences, while the rows are the results obtained with the trained neural tree.

		Predicted Event Class		
		Person Walking	Car in the Parking Lot	Bus at the Bus Stop
Ground Truth	Person Walking	47	2	1
	Car in the Parking Lot	0	18	2
	Bus at the Bus Stop	1	2	7

From the table we can see that the neural tree recognized the "person walking on pedestrian paths" with a success rate of 94%, the "car entering/leaving the parking lot" with a success rate of 90%, and the "bus stopping/starting at the bus stop" with a success rate of 70%. The lower rate on the bus stop class can be motivated by the small number of training and test sequences, since during the acquisition time range of 6 hours the number of buses passing in the monitored environment is significantly lower than the number of detected cars and people.

6   Conclusions

Within the current state of the art one of the major problems that afflict the automatic systems of video surveillance is their ineffectiveness in recognizing the time interval in which an event occurs. Moreover, the actual systems are not oriented in distinguishing the possible different characters of a same event. The proposed paper faces the mentioned issues by means of a novel event learning process. The preliminary tests carried out on a set of videos related to a reference outdoor scenario have proven the implemented strategy.

As future works, we are currently evaluating the performance of our approach on more complex and challenging datasets. We are also investigating re-identification [28,29] methods allowing us to recognize events that span large time windows and wide areas that are only partially covered by sensors.

References

1. Martinel, N., Micheloni, C., Piciarelli, C.: Pre-Emptive camera activation for Video Surveillance HCI. In: Intenational Conference on Image Analysis and Processing, Ravenna, RA, pp. 189–198, September 2011
2. Martinel, N., Micheloni, C., Piciarelli, C., Foresti, G.L.: Camera Selection for Adaptive Human-Computer Interface. IEEE Transactions on Systems, Man, and Cybernetics: Systems 44(5), 653–664 (2014)
3. Martinel, N., Micheloni, C.: Sparse matching of random patches for person Re-identification. In: International Conference on Distributed Smart Cameras (2014)
4. Martinel, N., Micheloni, C.: Classification of Local Eigen-Dissimilarities for Person Re-Identification. IEEE Signal Processing Letters 22(4), 455–459 (2015)
5. Piciarelli, C., Micheloni, C., Martinel, N., Vernier, M., Foresti, G.L.: Outdoor environment monitoring with unmanned aerial vehicles. In: International Conference on Image Analysis and Processing (2013)

6. Fookes, C., Denman, S., Lakemond, R., Ryan, D., Sridharan, S., Piccardi, M.: Semi-supervised intelligent surveillance system for secure environments. In: IEEE International Symposium on Industrial Electronics, pp. 2815–2820 (2010)

7. Zhong, H.Z.H., Shi, J.S.J., Visontai, M.: Detecting unusual activity in video. In: Proceedings of the 2004 IEEE Computer Society Conference on Computer Vision and Pattern Recognition, CVPR 2004, vol. 2 (2004)

8. Zhao, B., Fei-Fei, L., Xing, E.P.: Online detection of unusual events in videos via dynamic sparse coding. In: Proceedings of the IEEE Computer Society Conference on Computer Vision and Pattern Recognition, pp. 3313–3320 (2011)

9. Xu, J., Denman, S., Fookes, C., Sridharan, S.: Unusual event detection in crowded scenes using bag of LBPs in spatio-temporal patches. In: Proceedings - 2011 International Conference on Digital Image Computing: Techniques and Applications, DICTA 2011, pp. 549–554 (2011)

10. Ghanem, N., DeMenthon, D., Doermann, D., Davis, L.: Representation and recognition of events in surveillance video using petri nets. In: 2004 Conference on Computer Vision and Pattern Recognition Workshop (2004)

11. Nevatia, R., Hobbs, J., Bolles, B.: An ontology for video event representation. In: 2004 Conference on Computer Vision and Pattern Recognition Workshop (2004)

12. Hakeem, A., Shah, M.: Learning, detection and representation of multi-agent events in videos. Artificial Intelligence 171(8–9), 586–605 (2007)

13. Lin, L., Gong, H., Li, L., Wang, L.: Semantic event representation and recognition using syntactic attribute graph grammar. Pattern Recognition Letters 30(2), 180–186 (2009)

14. Vernier, M., Martinel, N., Micheloni, C., Foresti, G.L.: Remote feature learning for mobile Re-identification. In: International Conference on Distributed Smart Cameras, pp. 1–6. Palm Springs, CA, IEEE, October 2013

15. Piciarelli, C., Micheloni, C., Foresti, G.L.: Trajectory-Based Anomalous Event Detection. IEEE Transactions on Circuits and Systems for Video Technology 18(11), 1544–1554 (2008)

16. Micheloni, C., Snidaro, L., Foresti, G.L.: Exploiting Temporal Statistics for Events Analysis and Understanding. Image and Vision Computing 27(10), 1459–1469 (2009)

17. Agarwal, C., Sharma, A.: Image understanding using decision tree based machine learning. In: ICIMU 2011 : Proceedings of the 5th international Conference on Information Technology & Multimedia, pp. 1–8 (2011)

18. Fischer, Y., Beyerer, J.: Defining dynamic Bayesian networks for probabilistic situation assessment. In: International Conference on Information Fusion, pp. 888–895 (2012)

19. Oh, S., Hoogs, A., Perera, A., Cuntoor, N., Chen, C.C., Lee, J.T., Mukherjee, S., Aggarwal, J.K., Lee, H., Davis, L., Swears, E., Wang, X., Ji, Q., Reddy, K., Shah, M., Vondrick, C., Pirsiavash, H., Ramanan, D., Yuen, J., Torralba, A., Song, B., Fong, A., Roy-Chowdhury, A., Desai, M.: A large-scale benchmark dataset for event recognition in surveillance video. In: International Conference on Computer Vision and Pattern Recognition, pp. 3153–3160 (2011)

20. Veeraraghavan, H., Papanikolopoulos, N., Schrater, P.: Learning dynamic event descriptions in image sequences. In: Proceedings of the IEEE Computer Society Conference on Computer Vision and Pattern Recognition (2007)

21. Joo, S.W., Chellappa, R.: Attribute grammar-based event recognition and anomaly detection. In: Proceedings of the IEEE Computer Society Conference on Computer Vision and Pattern Recognition, vol. 2006 (2006)

22. Moore, D., Essa, I.: Recognizing multitasked activities from video using stochastic context-free grammar. In: AAAI National Conf. on AI, pp. 770–776 (2002)
23. Martinel, N., Micheloni, C., Foresti, G.L.: Robust Painting Recognition and Registration for Mobile Augmented Reality. IEEE Signal Processing Letters **20**(11), 1022–1025 (2013)
24. Bosch, A., Zisserman, A., Munoz, X.: Image classification using random forests and ferns. In: International Conference on Computer Vision, Ieee, pp. 1–8 (2007)
25. Lazebnik, S., Schmid, C., Ponce, J.: Beyond bags of features: spatial pyramid matching for recognizing natural scene categories. In: International Conference on Computer Vision and Pattern Recognition (CVPR) vol. 2, pp. 2169–2178 (2006)
26. Foresti, G.L., Dolso, T.: Adaptive High-Order Neural Trees for Pattern Recognition. IEEE Transactions on System, Man and Cybernetics Part B **34**(2), 988–996 (2004)
27. Piciarelli, C., Micheloni, C., Foresti, G.L.: PTZ Camera Network Reconfiguration. In: Third ACM/IEEE International Conference on Distributed Smart Cameras, Como, Italy (2009)
28. Martinel, N., Micheloni, C., Piciarelli, C.: Distributed Signature Fusion for Person Re-identification. In: International Conference on Distributed Smart Cameras, Hong Kong, pp. 1–6 (2012)
29. Garcia, J., Martinel, N., Foresti, G.L., Gardel, A., Micheloni, C.: Person orientation and feature distances boost Re-identification. In: International Conference on Pattern Recognition (2014)

Detection of Human Movements
with Pressure Floor Sensors

Martino Lombardi, Roberto Vezzani[✉], and Rita Cucchiara

Softech-ICT, University of Modena and Reggio Emilia, Modena, Italy
{martino.lombardi,roberto.vezzani,rita.cucchiara}@unimore.it
http://imagelab.ing.unimore.it

Abstract. Following the recent Internet of Everything (IoE) trend, several general-purpose devices have been proposed to acquire as much information as possible from the environment and from people interacting with it. Among the others, sensing floors are recently attracting the interest of the research community. In this paper, we propose a new model to store and process floor data. The model does not assume a regular grid distribution of the sensing elements and is based on the ground reaction force (GRF) concept, widely used in biomechanics. It allows the correct detection and tracking of people, outperforming the common background subtraction schema adopted in the past. Several tests on a real sensing floor prototype are reported and discussed.

Keywords: Human-computer interaction · Sensing floor · Pressure analysis · Center of pressure · Ground reaction force

1 Introduction

In the last years, the research on non-invasive human-computer interaction systems has attracted a wide interest. Therefore, a lot of systems based on video cameras [2], depth sensors [7], wearable devices [3], and sensing environments [5] have been proposed for interactive media applications. In particular, the adoption of *sensing floors* plays a key role in the development of sensing environments thanks to two significant properties: low invasiveness and high invisibility (i.e., the sensing layer is invisible to the users and the floor appears similar to traditional floors to avoid the "observer effect").

Their applications are manifold in several fields, including both public and private environments. For example, smart buildings can include sensing floors to detect the presence of people and to automatically switch on/off the lighting or the heating systems. In the e-health field, these devices can be used to detect dangerous situations such as an elder falling or getting out of his/her bed. Furthermore, sensing floors can be used for people counting or to monitor crowd movements during public events, exhibitions, and so on. In comparison with other traditional technologies such as video cameras, sensing floors provide less information but have two undoubted advantages. First, they are completely

© Springer International Publishing Switzerland 2015
V. Murino and E. Puppo (Eds.): ICIAP 2015, Part II, LNCS 9280, pp. 620–630, 2015.
DOI: 10.1007/978-3-319-23234-8_57

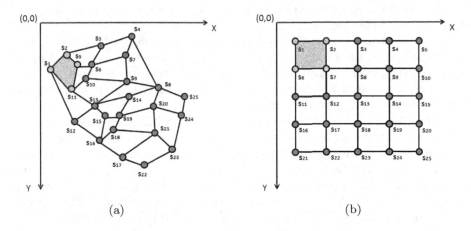

Fig. 1. Schema of two different placement of 25 sensors with (a) a random distribution or (b) a grid. Examples of Floor Cells with 4 sides and 4 vertices are colored in red.

privacy compliant as above mentioned. In fact, it is not feasible to recognize and identify users from floor data only. Installations on very private places such as toilets or bedrooms are allowed. Second, sensing floors data are not affected from occlusions, a typical issue of visual camera systems.

Since 1997, when J. Paradiso [12] at MIT presented the first example of a sensing floor, several prototypes have been proposed and designed. The adopted sensors exploit different physical characteristics, such as the pressure as measurable quantity, and the proximity effect related with the electrical properties of a human body. A complete analysis of these differences can be found in [15] and in [20].

Regardless of the technology adopted to build the sensing floor, this paper aims at focusing on the data model and the corresponding processing algorithms. The prevalent approach has been borrowed from the image processing field. Each sensing element is related to a pixel of an image. The pressure applied on top of a sensor is translated to a corresponding pixel intensity. In the following, we refer to this approach as PIM (*Pressure Image Model*). At each sampling instant, the sensing floor generates a sort of *pressure image*, where each *pixel* corresponds to a spatial portion of the floor and the *pixel value* is related to the pressure applied on the top of it. Consecutive temporal pressure images can be collected as frame sequences to generate a *pressure video*, whose analysis allows to detect and determine spatio-temporal events on sensing floors [9].

Two different types of image can be generated, depending on the physical sensor capabilities, i.e., *binary* and *grey-level* pressure images, respectively. Binary pressure images are generated by sensing floors made using matrix of switch sensors, such as those proposed in [10] or in [19]. When a switch sensor is activated, the corresponding pixel value is triggered to on. Binary images only provide information related to people or object positions on the sensing area.

Additional information related to the object/person weight or to the dynamical interaction with the floor are lost.

On the contrary, grey-level pressure images are generated by floors made using regular distribution of continuous sensors, such as those described in [18] and in [1]. In this case, each sensor response and the corresponding pixel values are changing as a function of the applied pressure. Grey-level images are characterized by a higher information content.

Despite its simplicity, PIM allows to use common video processing and analysis techniques to provide people detection and the further classification of their behaviors [9]. In particular, background subtraction techniques based on Gaussian or median distributions of the pixel values are used to extract the foreground regions, position-based trackers are employed to follow sensed people in the course of time, while machine learning classifiers are implemented for the high level action or interaction analysis as in [16], [8] and [11]. As a consequence, sensor floors can be adopted as input devices in a plethora of applications, spanning from multimedia content access to surveillance, from entertainment to medical rehabilitation.

Nevertheless, two major drawbacks characterize traditional approaches. First, their implementation is not straightforward in absence of a regular spatial distribution of the sensors. Second, symmetric and pixel-wise statistical models (such as Gaussian or median distributions) are not suitable for floor sensors.

In gait-postural analysis, the exploitation of force platforms made of piezo-electric sensors, capacitance gauges, strain gauges, or FSR can be considered a common practice. Kinesiologists can estimate the *Ground Reaction Force* (GRF) and the *Center of Pressure* (COP) of a person standing or moving on these measuring instruments. The first is the vector sum of the normal components of the forces exerted on the top of the measuring platform. The second is the point location of the vertical GRF vector and represents a weighted average of all the pressures over the surface of the area in contact with the platform [21]. The temporal analysis of GRF variations and COP displacements allows to detect people (see [20], [13], [4] and [6]).

For these reasons, starting from the concepts of COP and GRF, the aim of this work is to describe a model which overcomes the above mentioned drawbacks.

The paper is structured as follows: in Section 2 we introduce a COP based data model and we propose a possible implementation of a detection and tracking algorithm developed on the basis of it. Section 3 describes the experimental setup, the obtained results and a comparison with the traditional PIM model. Finally, conclusions and future works are drawn in Section 4.

2   The COP MODEL

2.1   Data Model

As a reference technology, we have adopted the sensing floor solution described in Lombardi et al. [9]. The device is composed of a sensing layer covered by a grid of ceramic tiles. The sensing layer is obtained by disposing on the ground plane a set of sensing elements. Differently from the PIM approach, a free distribution of the sensing elements is allowed and is not imposed to follow a grid. Each sensor s_i is thus identified by its real position on the floor (X_s, Y_s), instead of its indexes on the grid. The tiles coverage has been included to preserve the integrity of the sensors and, at the same time, to diffuse the pressures exerted on a single point of the floor to a neighbor area.

At each capturing interval t, all the sensors $s \in S$ provide a corresponding discrete response $V_s(t)$. The whole area covered by the set of sensors can be partitioned into convex polygonal cells, having the sensors as vertices. The type of polygonal decomposition strictly depends on the sensor layout and the spatial resolution. Two very different cases are reported in Figure 1. If the sensors are placed with a regular grid distribution as usual, a possible decomposition is composed by rectangular cells as reported in Figure 1(b). The obtained areas are called **Floor Cells** hereinafter, and are represented by the set of sensors placed at the vertices: $FC_i \subset S, (i = 1, 2, \cdots, M)$.

The state of a Floor Cell FC_i is represented by a $3D$ point P_i $(i = 1, 2, \cdots, M)$ as follows:

$$
P_i(t) = \begin{bmatrix} P_i^x(t) \\ P_i^y(t) \\ P_i^z(t) \end{bmatrix} = \begin{bmatrix} \dfrac{\sum\limits_{\forall s \in FC_i} X_s \cdot V_s(t)}{\sum\limits_{\forall s \in FC_i} V_s(t)}, & \dfrac{\sum\limits_{\forall s \in FC_i} Y_s \cdot V_s(t)}{\sum\limits_{\forall s \in FC_i} V_s(t)}, & \sum\limits_{\forall s \in FC_i} V_s(t) \end{bmatrix}^T . \quad (1)
$$

The first two coordinates P_i^x, P_i^y are respectively equivalent to the plane coordinates of the COP, while the third one P_i^z is the intensity of the GRF associated to the floor cell.

When no pressures is exerted on a floor cell FC_i, the location P_i^{eq} of the 3D point is only influenced by the sensor calibration and the dead weight of the tiles. Instead, when a person walks on the floor, the corresponding pressure moves the point P_i from the equilibrium state P_i^{eq} toward a new position $P_i(t)$. From Eq. 1, the projection of P_i on the ground plane falls within the FC_i convex-hull.

At time t, a floor cell FC_i can be considered in an excited state (i.e., a person or an object is located on the corresponding region) if the following condition occurs:

$$
||N_i \cdot (P_i(t) - P_i^{eq})||_2 \geq TH \quad (2)
$$

where TH is an application defined threshold, $|| \cdot ||_2$ is the Euclidean norm, N_i indicates the following normalization matrix:

$$
N_i = diag\left(d_{x,i}^{-1}, d_{y,i}^{-1}, d_{z,i}^{-1}\right). \quad (3)
$$

The normalization matrix is defined for each floor cell FC_i and takes into account the geometrical extent of the cell itself. $d_{x,i}$ and $d_{y,i}$ are the dimensions of the FC_i convex-hull, while $d_{z,i}$ is the maximum variation of the GRF intensity and is estimated during a calibration phase of the capturing board. As a consequence of the random spatial distribution of the sensors, even a single person may trigger more than one floor cell. Thus, a cluster of neighbor floor cells will switch to a non-equilibrium condition for each person located on the sensing floor. The temporal analysis and tracking of these clusters allows to detect and

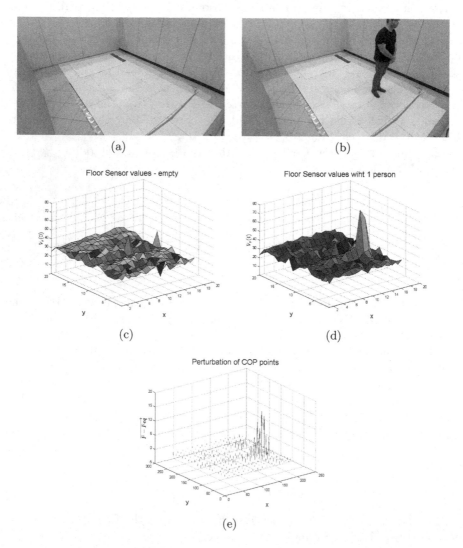

Fig. 2. Visual example of the COP vectors. (a) and (b) pictures of the empty floor and with a walking person. The sensor values captured at the equilibrium (c) and with the walking person (d). On the right (e), a plot of the vectors $P_i(t) - P_i^{eq}$ evaluated in equation 2.

track people on the floor, as detailed in the following section. A visual example is reported in Figure 2. The sensor values captured at the equilibrium and with a walking person are reported on the left and center graphs. On the right, a plot of the vectors $P_i(t) - P_i^{eq}$ evaluated in equation 2 are shown.

2.2   People Detection and Tracking

Let $C_j(t) = \{FC_k\}$ be a cluster of neighbor floor cells which are simultaneously excited at time t. Eq. 2 filters out contributions due to the noise and assures that the cluster has been generated by a person on the floor. His position $(B_j^x(t), B_j^y(t))$ on the floor at time t can be estimated from the 3D points P_i associated to the floor cells included in the cluster as in equation (4):

$$M_j(t) = \sum_i P_i^z(t)$$
$$B_j^x(t) = \frac{1}{M_j(t)} \sum_i P_i^x(t) \cdot P_i^z(t) ,$$
$$B_j^y(t) = \frac{1}{M_j(t)} \sum_i P_i^y(t) \cdot P_i^z(t)$$

$$(4)$$

The set of clusters is obtained with a connected component labeling of all the excited cells. Two FCs are defined as connected if their intersection contains at least one sensor. For a uniform grid distribution, this assumption is similar to the 8-connection of pixels (See Fig. 1(b)).

Successive detections of the same person are temporally tracked with a nearest neighbor matching based on positions only. The main purpose of the tracking step is the recovering of people's positions in some short temporal slots, during which the floor is not able to detect them. For example, when a person changes the front feet during a walking or, more clearly, during a jump, the pressure exerted on the floor is null.

Given the detections D_i at frame t and the current set of tracks T_j, we first compute the Euclidean distance matrix $\Gamma(i,j) = D_2(D_i, T_j)$. The detection-to-track association is provided using the schema proposed in [14]. For each frame, some detections may be assigned to tracks, while other detections and tracks may remain unassigned. The assigned tracks are updated using the corresponding detections. The unassigned tracks are marked invisible. Finally, unassigned detections begin new tracks. Each track keeps count of the number of consecutive frames where it remained unassigned. If the count exceeds a specified threshold, the tracking algorithm assumes that the object left the floor and it deletes the track.

Since the applications described in this paper are not required to work in very crowd situations, the implemented tracking algorithm does not handle groups (i.e., people closer to each other than a foot step) nor abrupt position changes (e.g., people leaping around). The reader can refer to [17] for more complex tracking schemes, if required by the application.

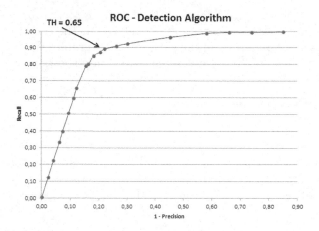

Fig. 3. ROC curve at different thresholds of the detection algorithm proposed in Section 2.2 on a calibration sequence with a person of 45 Kg on the sensing floor.

3   Experimental Evaluation

3.1   Experimental Setup

To evaluate the proposed method, we have exploited a *Florimage Device* distributed by Florim Ceramiche SpA[1] and described in [9]. The device is covered by tiles of $600\,mm \times 600\,mm$, thin enough ($4.5\,mm$) to allow the sensing elements below them to capture the presence of walking people. The sensors are distributed on a regular grid of 16 rows by 20 columns. The 320 sensing units covers a rectangular area of 4 square meters.

The experimental environment is also equipped with a Microsoft Kinect sensor. The acquisition of the floor data and of the Kinect sensor are synchronized with an external trigger (set to work at 10Hz in these experiments). The people detection and tracking capabilities of the Kinect subsystem have been exploited to automatically generate the ground truth, composed by the set of people positions on the floor. The Extrinsic calibration parameters of the Kinect device with respect to the floor have been estimated to transform the 3D coordinates of people feet joints into floor coordinates.

Using the experimental setup, 6 data sequences[2] of walking people have been acquired, involving 1 to 7 individuals. People weights are also ranging from 45 Kg to 100 Kg.

The algorithm has been evaluated counting the number of True Positive (TP), False Positive (FP) and False Negative (FN) detections. A detection provided using the algorithm reported in Section 2.2 is counted as a TP if the Kinect sensor provides a corresponding person position closer than 25 cm. The precision

---

[1] http://www.slim4plus.it/en/floor-sensor-system/
[2] Dataset available at http://imagelab.ing.unimore.it/go/sensingFloor

Table 1. Detection algorithm results

	Seq1		Seq2		Seq3		Seq4		Seq5		Seq6	
	PIM	COP	PIM	COP	PIM	COP	PIM	COP	PIM	COP	PIM	COP
Nframes	2353		1936		1504		1060		1311		1901	
Precision	0.79	**0.91**	0.53	**0.87**	0.77	**0.95**	**0.79**	0.76	0.79	**0.89**	0.71	**0.87**
Accuracy	0.86	**0.92**	0.53	**0.86**	0.78	**0.96**	**0.83**	0.81	0.81	**0.91**	0.65	**0.84**
TP	1245	1204	1333	1253	1287	1286	699	699	1028	1027	1793	1921
FP	326	121	1161	192	393	65	183	218	280	126	737	285
TN	861	1024	18	479	87	173	210	220	157	271	88	314
MD (cm)	20.68	**20.44**	24.56	**20.37**	17.37	**14.63**	19.70	**19.02**	**15.40**	15.69	21.03	**19.11**

Table 2. Tracking algorithm results

	Seq1		Seq2		Seq3		Seq4		Seq5		Seq6	
	PIM	COP	PIM	COP	PIM	COP	PIM	COP	PIM	COP	PIM	COP
Nframes	2353		1936		1504		1060		1311		1901	
Precision	0.84	**0.94**	0.57	**0.90**	0.80	**0.96**	**0.82**	0.79	0.83	**0.91**	0.75	**0.90**
Accuracy	0.88	**0.94**	0.56	**0.88**	0.81	**0.97**	**0.85**	0.83	0.85	**0.92**	0.68	**0.86**
TP	1232	1203	1305	1249	1284	1286	698	699	1026	1027	1768	1920
FP	239	82	999	143	326	48	157	190	213	105	598	223
TN	905	1027	35	482	95	174	217	221	173	272	106	318

$Pr = TP/(TP + FP)$ and accuracy $Ac = TP/(TP + FN)$ metrics are also computed as usual.

Thanks to the regular distribution of the sensing elements on a grid, $M = 285$ floor cells FC_i of 4 sensors each have been generated using the schema reported in Figure 1. For each floor cell FC_i, the coordinates of the equilibrium state point P_i^{eq} were estimated by averaging a short sequence of sensor values captured with the empty floor. The threshold TH of Equation 2 has been set to 0.65 by maximizing the precision and recall of the detection algorithm proposed in Section (2.2) on a calibration sequence. The corresponding ROC curve obtained at different threshold values is reported in Figure 3.

3.2 Reference PIM Method

As a baseline, we have implemented a PIM based detection and tracking algorithm, following the recommendations provided in [9].

Let $I(x, y, t)$ be the pressure image obtained at time t in the PIM based approach. Each pixel intensity is proportional to the value $V_s(t)$ captured by the corresponding sensor. In order to filter the contributions due to the dead weight of the tiles coverage, each pressure images is pre-processed using a background subtraction approach as follows:

$$I^{\dagger}(x, y, t) = I(x, y, t) - I_{eq} \tag{5}$$

where I_{eq} is the pressure image acquired when no people are walking on the sensing floor. Peaks on the image $I^\dagger(x, y, t)$ that are higher than a threshold are considered as activated (i.e., generated by a person or an object moving on the sensing floor). The detections $D(t)$ are obtained through a mean-shift clustering of the activated sensors. Similarly to the COP based system, a nearest-neighbor tracking algorithm is included in the processing chain (see Section 2.2).

3.3   Quantitative Results

We tested and compared the proposed method and the baseline PIM algorithm on the six sequences described in section 3.1. Table 1 and Table 2 report the values of all the estimated performance parameters for each sequence, with or without the tracking stage, respectively. In each table, the best results in term of precision and accuracy are highlighted. The precision and accuracy obtained with the COP model are higher than those obtained with the PIM one, except for the 4-th sequence.

The mean distance between the detection and the ground truth positions is also reported in the last row of Table 1. The closest mean distances are those obtained with the COP based detection algorithm.

4   Conclusion and Future Works

In this paper, we proposed a new data model for storing and processing information acquired by sensing floor. Due to the customary regular distribution of the sensor units, their values are usually stored as pressure images and processed with common computer vision algorithms [9,10]. These methods are difficult to apply to a general sensor distribution.

Instead, the proposed COP model does not assume a regular grid distribution of the sensing elements and is based on the ground reaction force (GRF) concept, widely used in biomechanics. It allows the correct detection and tracking of people, outperforming the common background subtraction schema exploited in the past. Several tests on a real sensing floor prototype confirm the validity of the model and the outperforming capabilities on people detection and tracking.

As future work, we plan to deeply address the Floor Cell creation step, taking into account different shapes and sizes of the floor cells. In addition, we want to extent the method to the case of overlapping cells, which requires a new definition of connection between cells for the clustering task. Finally, a more sophisticated detection and tracking algorithm based on both the module and the direction of the COP vectors will be handled.

Acknowledgments. This work was supported by Florim Ceramiche S.p.A. (Italy)

References

1. Anlauff, J., Großhauser, T., Hermann, T.: Tactiles: a low-cost modular tactile sensing system for floor interactions. In: Proceedings of the 6th Nordic Conference on Human-Computer Interaction: Extending Boundaries, pp. 591–594. ACM, New York (2010)
2. Betke, M., Gips, J., Fleming, P.: The camera mouse: visual tracking of body features to provide computer access for people with severe disabilities. IEEE Transactions on Neural Systems and Rehabilitation Engineering 10(1), 1–10 (2002)
3. Blake, J., Gurocak, H.: Haptic glove with mr brakes for virtual reality. IEEE/ASME Transactions on Mechatronics 14(5), 606–615 (2009)
4. Headon, R., Curwen, R.: Recognizing movements from the ground reaction force. In: Proceedings of the 2001 Workshop on Perceptive User Interfaces, PUI 2001, pp. 1–8. ACM, New York (2001)
5. Hsu, J.M., Wu, W.J., Chang, I.R.: Ubiquitous multimedia information delivering service for smart home. In: International Conference on Multimedia and Ubiquitous Engineering, pp. 341–346, April 2007
6. Jung, J.W., Sato, T., Bien, Z.: Dynamic footprint-based person recognition method using a hidden markov model and a neural network. International Journal of Intelligent Systems 19(11), 1127–1141 (2004)
7. Lai, K., Konrad, J., Ishwar, P.: A gesture-driven computer interface using kinect. In: IEEE Southwest Symposium on Image Analysis and Interpretation (SSIAI), pp. 185–188, April 2012
8. Leusmann, P., Mollering, C., Klack, L., Kasugai, K., Ziefle, M., Rumpe, B.: Your floor knows where you are: sensing and acquisition of movement data. In: 12th IEEE International Conference on Mobile Data Management (MDM), vol. 2, pp. 61–66, June 2011
9. Lombardi, M., Pieracci, A., Santinelli, P., Vezzani, R., Cucchiara, R.: Human behavior understanding with wide area sensing floors. In: Salah, A.A., Hung, H., Aran, O., Gunes, H. (eds.) HBU 2013. LNCS, vol. 8212, pp. 112–123. Springer, Heidelberg (2013)
10. Middleton, L., Buss, A., Bazin, A., Nixon, M.: A floor sensor system for gait recognition. In: Fourth IEEE Workshop on Automatic Identification Advanced Technologies, pp. 171–176, October 2005
11. Murakita, T., Ikeda, T., Ishiguro, H.: Human tracking using floor sensors based on the markov chain monte carlo method. In: Proceedings of the 17th International Conference on Pattern Recognition, vol. 4, pp. 917–920 , August 2004
12. Paradiso, J., Abler, C., Hsiao, K., Reynolds, M.: The magic carpet: physical sensing for immersive environments. In: Extended Abstracts on Human Factors in Computing Systems, pp. 277–278 (1997)
13. Qian, G., Zhang, J., Kidane, A.: People identification using floor pressure sensing and analysis. IEEE Sensors Journal 10(9), 1447–1460 (2010)
14. Rangarajan, K., Shah, M.: Establishing motion correspondence. CVGIP: Image Understanding 54(1), 56–73 (1991)
15. Rangarajan, S., Kidane, A., Qian, G., Rajko, S., Birchfield, D.: The design of a pressure sensing floor for movement-based human computer interaction. In: Kortuem, G., Finney, J., Lea, R., Sundramoorthy, V. (eds.) EuroSSC 2007. LNCS, vol. 4793, pp. 46–61. Springer, Heidelberg (2007)
16. Rimminen, H., Lindstrom, J., Linnavuo, M., Sepponen, R.: Detection of falls among the elderly by a floor sensor using the electric near field. IEEE Transactions on Information Technology in Biomedicine 14(6), 1475–1476 (2010)

17. Smeulder, A., Chu, D., Cucchiara, R., Calderara, S., Deghan, A., Shah, M.: Visual tracking: an experimental survey. IEEE Transactions on Pattern Analysis and Machine Intelligence **36**(7), 1442–1468 (2014)
18. Srinivasan, P., Birchfield, D., Qian, G., Kidané, A.: A pressure sensing floor for interactive media applications. In: Proceedings of the 2005 ACM SIGCHI International Conference on Advances in Computer Entertainment Technology, ACE 2005, pp. 278–281. ACM, New York (2005)
19. Valtonen, M., Maentausta, J., Vanhala, J.: Tiletrack: capacitive human tracking using floor tiles. In: IEEE International Conference on Pervasive Computing and Communications, pp. 1–10, March 2009
20. Vera-Rodriguez, R., Mason, J., Fierrez, J., Ortega-Garcia, J.: Comparative analysis and fusion of spatiotemporal information for footstep recognition. IEEE Transactions on Pattern Analysis and Machine Intelligence **35**(4), 823–834 (2013)
21. Winter, D.: Human balance and posture control during standing and walking. Gait & Posture **3**(4), 193–214 (1995)

Object Detection and Tracking from Fixed and Mobile Platforms

Giovanni B. Garibotto[1] and Francesco Buemi[2(✉)]

[1] Vision technology consultant, Genova, Italy
giovanni.garibotto@gmail.com
[2] Aitek S.p.A., Genova, Italy
francesco.buemi@aitek.it

Abstract. Computer Vision technology plays a fundamental role in Video Surveillance applications with the possibility to detect different categories of objects (human beings, faces, vehicles, car plates etc) in a regular stream of video recorded by surveillance cameras. Moreover, the detection process must be validated for a sufficiently long time interval (by tracking), to provide more instances of the same object/subject, and increase the rate of successful recognition/identification (including the possibility of human supervision). The paper address the problem of object detection and tracking and the proposed solution is based on visual appearance model learning during the tracking process. Simplified HOG-like texture features are used, to achieve computationally effective solutions to be applied in practical applications of video analytics. A contrast gradient normalization solution has been adopted, with adaptive threshold estimation, to increase tracking capability along the video flow. Performance of the tracking processing chain is evaluated using the public available TLD dataset [1], to achieve quantitative and comparable data.

Keywords: Object detection · Visual tracking · Appearance model learning · Adaptive processing

1 Introduction

Object detection and tracking represents a fundamental processing step in any implementation of video analysis. In security applications it is used to collect multiple views of the same object as a support to classification and recognition. It represents a topic of great interest in the vision community with many publications and research studies. A recent tutorial paper [2] describes the state of the art of this technology and the most promising lines of research under investigation.

Our research has been developed within the context of industrial video surveillance to improve the performance of Aitek Video Analytics solution [3] with the primary objective to deal with real every-day life constraints, like poor video quality and the availability of low processing power in embedded camera applications. We intend to face the problem of generic object detection and tracking from fixed cameras (with possible calibration tools) as well as from mobile platforms, including PTZ sensors

© Springer International Publishing Switzerland 2015
V. Murino and E. Puppo (Eds.): ICIAP 2015, Part II, LNCS 9280, pp. 631–642, 2015.
DOI: 10.1007/978-3-319-23234-8_58

and surveillance cameras installed on-board of security vehicles and police cars. The driving line of our research study comes from a security application of supervised detection and tracking of humans and vehicles from video recorded sequences. The final objective is hiding-blurring some selected targets, to prevent their identification in the output video stream (privacy constraints). This operation is performed in a supervisory mode (man-in-the-loop), with a selection of the initial position, and the bounding box, of the target object (it may be the face, the full body of a person, a car or a plate in the scene). The tracking process should be able to follow the target, trying to manage most of its variability including light, scale, translation and 3D pose. The initial information alone is often not sufficient to track the target for long, which means increasing the cost of human supervisor involvement, to select again the target for a next step of the tracking process. The best solution will be a fully autonomous process, able to learn different appearance models along the processing chain and keep track of the selected target as long as possible without human intervention. These are typical specifications of most advanced tracking solutions in the computer vision community, where tracking performance has significantly improved in the last decade.

Among the wide scientific literature on the subject we refer to the most recent results obtained in [4], marketed as "Predator", which exhibits superior performance level as compared to other tracking-by-detection methods. The TLD framework combines together a detector and an optical flow tracker (based on Lucas Kanade technique [5]). The purpose of the detector is to prevent the tracker from drifting away from the object as well as to recover tracking after temporary occlusions. Updates of the learning classifier are accepted only if the discovered image patch is similar to the initial object box, which represents the only prior information about the object.

In the paper the tracking task is addressed as a search problem, at the object level, where the appearance model of the object is searched in the following frames of the video sequence, to recover a consistent trajectory with time and space constraints. The main objective is to demonstrate that a model matching approach, where the appearance model of the object is continuously updated along the tracking process, can be successful in object tracking with competitive performance w.r.t. the most advanced solutions. The choice of a continuous model update and matching process, instead of classical optical flow analysis [6], is motivated by the noisy nature of most commonly used video surveillance data, the possible occurrence of sharp motion displacements between consecutive frames, and the irregularity of intensity image differences at pixel level, mainly due to motion blurring. In [7] HOG based feature descriptors have been already used to deal with large displacement motion, but the research objective, in that case, was to recover an estimation of the continuous optical flow.

In our approach, after an early detection phase of the candidate object (a rectangular patch in the image), there is a continuous loop of tracking search (i.e. the identification of the most likely object patch in the following frames of the video sequence), followed by a learning step, with a continuous update of the target model to be used in the detection and re-initialization phase.

In section 2 we discuss the appearance model which is based on a modification of the widely used texture HOG features. Section 3 describes the forward-backward tracking process and the adopted acceptance-rejection criteria. The process of object appearance model updating is referred in section 4. In spite of the apparent simplicity of the process, the achieved results are quite encouraging, as briefly discussed in section 5, using some of the video sequences collected in [1]. Then, a critical discussion is devoted to the sensitivity to processing parameters and the stability and robustness of the results.

2   HOG Features and the Matching Process

The descriptive features of the both tracking and detection models are selected as a collection of histograms of oriented gradients, HOG, following the basic approach as proposed in [8], with the introduction of some minor modifications. The normalization proposed in [8] was found not appropriate when dealing with a very limited number of learning examples, as it happens in the implementation of an on-line tracking process. As such, we have modified the HOG feature representation as follows:

- The object model is divided in a predefined number of cells (NC); the cell-size (Cx, Cy) has a squared aspect ratio (Cx = Cy) and is not fixed a-priori; rather, it depends on the overall size of the selected sample patch (scale factor of the initial model). The resulting appearance-model size (Nx*Cx, Ny*Cy) may differ by a few pixels from the initial selection, due to cell-size quantization effects.
- Cells are not grouped in blocks, and there is no block overlapping; the reason of this choice is to improve specialization capability over the generalization properties of standard HOG models, since we are not planning to use an SVM classifier. Moreover, the 4 corner cells are not considered in the feature representation, to reduce background interference in the tracking process. This choice does not affect the performance even in case of box-like shapes like cars or trucks, since the corner cells do not contain useful information due to projected shape onto the image plane.
- 1-D local histograms of gradient directions are computed for each cell, following the standard scheme of [8]. As usual, each pixel in the cell casts a weighted vote for an orientation, within a pre-defined range of discrete angles. The weight is the gradient magnitude itself, above a suitable noise threshold (as discussed in the following subsection). In our implementation we are using signed-gradient representation, with 8 direction channels in the local 3x3 neighbourhood, for maximum computational efficiency. No histogram normalization is performed at cell-level,
- The local histograms of the different cells are collected together in lexicographic order to obtain a vector of features. This vector is normalized to the overall sum of all features to achieve histogram-like properties (unitary integral value) and the similarity matching between the image patch hypothesis and the running appearance model is computed using a standard Bhattacharyya distance [www.opencv.org].

2.1   Gradient Contrast Normalization

Gradient based features are strongly affected by the contrast variability of the video sequence. For that reason it is always necessary to perform some kind of gradient normalization. In our implementation the spatial gradient function is computed on the luminance component of the video signal, as briefly summarized in the following.

Local Contrast Gradient. Spatial derivatives are computed using a Sobel mask in a 3 x 3 neighbourhood and they are normalized to the average grey intensity (in the same local window). In this way it is possible to achieve a better contrast normalization across the whole image frame. At this level, signed-edge orientations are also computed, on the same local window (3 x 3) in the quantized range of 8 directions (0°, 45°, 90°, 135°, 180°, 225°, 270°, 315°). Tracking performance is not much affected by this approximation, as shown in the experimental results of section 5.

Dynamic Range Expansion. An additional normalization is performed on the computed contrast gradient in order to fill the available dynamic range of the signal (0-255 level) for each frame in the video sequence. As such, even relevant contrast variations during time can be successfully managed by the tracking process.

Adaptive Threshold Estimation. Instead of using a fixed threshold of the contrast-gradient magnitude, an adaptive value is computed to track signal changes along the video flow. The histogram distribution of the image gradient magnitude can be roughly approximated by an exponential decreasing function, and a good estimate of a noise threshold can be computed as the median value of this function.

3   Tracking as a Search Problem

Due to the presence of noise and possible large displacements of the object trajectory, a classical optical flow approach [6], based on time differences was found not suitable. Moreover, it is necessary to perform a robust and early detection of any deviation from the right object tracking, to avoid unrecoverable drifts.

The adopted solution is a *forward-backward* implementation of a HOG-feature tracker. The best estimate of the target position in the other frame of the video sequence is computed by searching, in a pre-defined search space, centred on the previous target position, the target patch which exhibits the best matching score with the current object features. Starting from object O_{t-1} (at time t-1) we obtain an estimate of the target position O_t (in the frame at time t). The same search procedure is repeated in the backward direction from target O_t to achieve an estimate $\hat{O}_{t-1}$ (in the past frame at time t-1). The matching overlap measure IoU (intersection over Union) is computed between the starting object O_{t-1} and the back-projected object $\hat{O}_{t-1}$. Any drop of the IoU measure is a clear hint of failure which determines the activation of a local detector to re-instantiate the tracking process. As mentioned before, the similarity measure between two HOG feature vectors $\{H_v(n)\}$ and $\{H_w(n)\}$ is the Bhattacharyya distance dB and is computed as:

$$dB = (1 - cb) \tag{1}$$

where

$$cb = [\sum_{n \in (0, NF)} (H_v(n) * H_w(n))^{1/2}] / (\sum_{n \in (0, NF)} H_v(n) * \sum_{n \in (0, NF)} H_w(n))^{1/2} \quad (2)$$

NF is the length of the overall feature vector. This distance measure is defined in the range (0 – 1) where zero means full match and 0.5 is already representative of large dissimilarities between the two descriptive vectors. To achieve a processing speed-up, each tracking step is performed in a hierarchical way.

- A first *Search space bucketing* is performed, by segmenting the search space into non-overlapping blocks having the same size of the target cells (Cx, Cy) at the current tracking step (reference scale factor). Local 1-D histogram features are computed for each bucket and are stored in a working memory {W}. The best-matching target position (minimum distance (1)) is computed by a sliding-window scanning of the search space, with integer steps (Cx, Cy). The computation of the normalized HOG descriptive feature vectors is based on the stored values {W} with significant computational savings. During the tracking process this search area around the previous target object is extended of a few cells in all directions (3 cells in the experimental tests of section 5).
- *A refinement step* is repeated in the neighbourhood of the best match with decreasing sampling step (half size at each step until unit shift), by tracking always the minimum score target. During this phase HOG features are fully computed on the contrast-gradient map for each new window shift (without using the stored values in {W}), although some kind of interpolation might be possible [9], with further potential improvements.
- Finally, a *scale search* is performed, around the minimum-score target, to check if a zoomed version of it (± 1 in the cell size) may exhibit a better match (i.e. a lower distance score) with the previous object model. In this way it is possible to track expansion/compression effects of the target-object in the video stream. This approximation is quite acceptable due to the short time distance between consecutive frames.

3.1 Acceptance/Rejection Criteria

In any visual tracking implementation it is extremely important to manage the risk of drift from the real trajectory. An early and reliable missed-target detection is needed, to stop the tracking process and activate a new boot-strap detection procedure on a wider search area of the image. In our approach the following parameters are used to classify a positive matching candidate:

- The IoU measure between objects O_{t-1} and $\hat{O}_{t-1}$ in forward-backward tracking is a already strong and reliable measure of tracking failure. In case of success it should be very close to 1. Smaller values below 98% are already representative of possible drifts which cannot be corrected by a simple displacement of the pre-dicted object coordinates.
- A grey level image patch is collected for each output box of the tracked object in the frame sequence. It is obtained as a projection of the image pixels onto a small size box (typically 20 x 20 pixels) which is normalized to the maximum dynamic

range and is masked to reduce the peripheral border effects of the background. A Normalized Cross Correlation (NCC) measure is computed between such image box and the reference image patch which has been acquired from the initial target object at the beginning of the tracking process. When the NCC value falls below a confidence level (in the experimental results such threshold was 0.9) the tracking process is considered to fail and a detection search is issued. Since the starting image patch is quickly evolving and modifying during the video flow (due to light changes and 2D - 3D shape variations) and the NCC is a rigid similarity measure, a buffer of image patches is stored and updated for each successful tracking (high IoU of the forward-backward estimates), to keep track of the object evolution.

- Additional structural constraints are used like the distance to the border of the image (the selected processing region) and the tracking displacement from frame to frame of the target trajectory; it must be smaller than a threshold maximum value, which is context dependent (either fixed or mobile platforms).

If the previous constraints are not satisfied, a detection search has been implemented, to manage temporarily occlusions or disappearance of the target and re-initialize the tracking process. Ultimately, if the previous conditions persist, tracking is definitely stopped and a new start-object-detection process is issued (manual or automatic procedures)

4   Object Detection by HOG Model Appearance Updating

The use of an adaptive appearance model, which evolves during the tracking process, has proved to be the right choice in many applications of visual tracking [10]. In our approach, due to the choice of the descriptive HOG feature vector {Hv}, such model updating is computed as

$$Av_i = \lambda \, Hv + (\, 1 - \lambda \,) \, Av_{i-1} \qquad (4)$$

where {Av_i} represents the appearance model at step (i); the parameter λ represents a learning-rate of the new validated tracking features {Hv}. $\lambda = 0.5$ has been selected in all experimental results referred in section 5. This short-term estimate of the appearance model gives more weight to the last validated instance of the tracked object and it ensures a good continuity of the tracking process.

As mentioned before, the detection process is activated only when the continuous forward-backward tracking fails. Beside the appearance model update, as in (4), the average size of the target is estimated during the phase of successful tracking, as well as the predicted area of activity. This information provides a useful constraint for the search space and scale of the detection. The detector implementation follows a scheme quite similar to the one-step tracking process as before.

- The search region is defined around the target missing area, and will be expanded progressively in the following video frames, up to a maximum selected size. The range of search scales (cell size) are defined according to the tracking history

- For each selected scale a search region bucketing is performed, with non-overlapping blocks having the same size of the target cells (Cx, Cy) and the histogram features are stored.
- The best target hypothesis is computed again in two consecutive phases: the first one by a sliding window scanning of the search region with integer steps (Cx, Cy) on the stored feature cells, and the second refinement step up to the pixel level.

Once the minimum distance target has been found at multiple scales, a suitable acceptance-rejection criterion is needed. Since we are using positive models only, we must establish a threshold of the distance measure (1). In all examples of section 5 a lower threshold of 0.2 has been used. In our reference video privacy application the presence of the human supervisor plays an important role to fix any possible matching error and reduce the risk of error propagation.

4.1   Boot-Strap and First Model Selection

The first instance of the object-target in the scene has particular relevance for the tracking process, since it provides the necessary information to build the first instance of the appearance model. In the experimental results of section 5 the initial object patch is always taken from the ground-truth list of the dataset [1]. In video security applications the automatic detection of the first object instance in the scene is often based on a selected object category (human body, head shape, car-plate, size/type of vehicle, etc.).

In this domain human detection has become a quite consolidated line of research with many contributions mainly based on the use of generalized HOG models [8], [9] [11]. When dealing with fixed surveillance cameras it is possible to take advantage of foreground-background detection to focus the attention on the foreground blobs only, like in security applications of Video Analytics technology [3]. Moreover, using camera calibration constraints, there is an additional possibility to reduce the search space, by prediction of the object size and scale [12].

5   Experimental Results

This section is devoted to the evaluation of our approach, by comparing our experimental results with reference solutions from the scientific literature. From dataset [1] we have selected 3 test video sequences, namely *david*, *jumping* and *car*, which seem more related to our reference application and quite representative of challenging motion conditions for a tracking task.

5.1   Dataset and Performance Evaluation

For each video sequence, the dataset contains a list of ground-truth box coordinates, as well as additional lists of bounding box results, obtained by the different algorithms which have been tested in that challenge [1]. The comparative results referred in table 1 are based on such data lists, considering only the best solution in that dataset, namely TLD1.0 [1].

Table 1. Comparison of results of our system (AI-T) with the list of bounding boxes named TLD1.0 as provided in the dataset [1]

Sequence		TP	P	R	F_M	ACLE	IoU
david	761 frames						
	TLD1.0	761	1,00	0,999	0,999	2,75	0,75
	AI-T	688	0,91	0,90	0.90	7,32	0,67
car	945 frames						
	TLD1.0	832	0,98	0,97	0,97	13,70	0,66
	AI-T	784	0,83	0,91	0,87	17,02	0,64
jumping	313 frames						
	TLD1.0	311	0,99	0,99	0,99	3,84	0,73
	AI-T	297	0,95	0,95	0,95	7,53	0,59

Performance evaluation is based on the computation of the PASCAL overlap measure IoU (Intersection over Union) considering the bounding boxes of the tracking result and the ground-truth. In the following, a tracking result is considered successful (true positive TP) when IoU > 0.5, a quite challenging goal as compared to the lower value (0.25) which is often adopted in other recent papers. The overall system performance is evaluated using standard precision P, recall R and F-measure statistics. Precision P is the rate of valid (IoU successful) boxes, among all target predictions; recall R is the rate of correct detections over the number of object occurrences that should have been detected. The value ACLE (Average centre Location Estimation) was used in [10] to measure the deviation of the target box with respect to the ground truth. IoU stands for the average overlap measure along the tracking sequence.

5.2   Detailed Performance Analysis

The results obtained for the first sequence (*david*: 761 frames length) are shown in table 1 as well as in fig 1; this video exhibits significant contrast variations from the initial frames (in the dark side of the room) to the last ones (the subject moving in full light). During the video sequence there is a consistent pose variation of the face, from frontal to lateral view and return. A total number of 52 cells has been selected for the target, with 8-bin signed gradient directions, for a descriptive vector of 416 elements (corner cells removed). During visual tracking the cell size was varying from a minimum of (6 x 6) pixels to a maximum value of (10 x 10) pixels. The appearance model has been updated (on-line learning) 413 times. The average value of IoU along the full sequence has been 0.67, and the number of correctly tracked frames, TP (IoU > 0.5), has been 688, with an F-Measure 0.90. Fig. 2 shows two different frames of the sequence (at the beginning and towards the end) with the bounding boxes of the ground truth data (blue color) and the tracking result (red color).

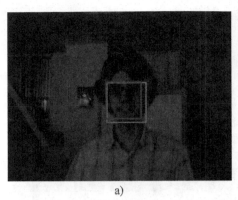 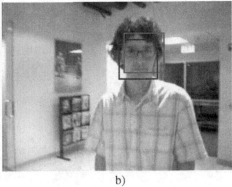

a)   b)

Fig. 1. Video sequence "david"; ground-truth box are displayed in (blue) and tracking result (red) a) frame n.92 b) frame n. 512

The same experimental test has been performed with the "car" sequence (945 frames length). This is a low-contrast video sequence, with partial and temporary occlusions of the vehicle by waving trees. The selected target model is made of 78 cells, the length of the vector feature is 592, and the cell dimensions remain quite unchanged through the full tracking sequence, with an average size of (7 x 7) pixels.

During the tracking process the appearance model has been updated 73 times. A sample of the tracking results is referred in fig.2, with an average score of IoU = 0.64, as computed along the whole sequence. The number of correctly tracked frames was TP = 784 (IoU > 0.5) with an F-Measure of 0.87.

The results in fig 3 are referred to the "jumping" sequence (313 frames). In this video the object-face trajectory is quite irregular due to the up-and-down motion of the subject. Many frames are also affected by motion blur, which makes more difficult to perform model matching. Anyway, the constraints applied to the learning-updating process of the appearance model, are sufficient to achieve satisfactory tracking results: the number of appearance model updating has been 63; the average IoU has been 0.59 along the whole sequence, and the number of corrected tracking frames has been 297, with an F-Measure 0.95.

Fig. 2. Video sequence "car"; ground-truth box is displayed in blue color and tracking result in red; a) frame n.26 b) frame n.568

Fig. 3. Video sequence "jumping"; ground-truth box (blue) and tracking result (red) a) frame n.150 b) frame n.300, c) IoU profile along the video sequence

Finally, the "motocross" sequence has been considered, as shown in fig. 4. The image contrast is quite good through all video frames in the sequence, with strong irregularities in the visual trajectory due to the relative motion of both the on-board camera sensor and the target-motocross. In this case we could not use the ground truth of the dataset, because it was limited to a small subset of the target (the driver shoulders).

By selecting a bounding box around the entire motocross object, it was possible to track almost all visual instances of the target during the video sequence (more than 3000 frames) with a total of 65 updating steps of the appearance model. The selected structure of the target object was made of 72 cells, with variable size from a minimum of (6 x 6) pixels to a maximum of (12 x 12) pixels for close-up views.

5.2.1 Discussion
A limitation of our approach is that only positive examples are used during the appearance model updating. As such it is particularly important to select reliable samples to feed the learning process. Some additional experimental tests have been performed, to evaluate the effects caused by small deviations from the ground-truth box, in term of spatial translation and scale factor, during the phase of the initial object selection and the corresponding appearance model. In general such deviations have no significant impact in the continuity of the tracking process. A small increase of the scale factor (object patch size) was always beneficial to capture wider properties of the object. On the contrary a significant shift on the image plane of the initial object detection may produce a wrong starting model which propagates along the full tracking chain. The most critical part of the process is the classification of a tracking result as a positive sample to contribute to the appearance model update. Misclassification results may lead to unstable learning and an early rejection of the tracking process.

Fig. 4. Video sequence "motocross"; a) frame n.234 b) frame n.667

The current AI-T version is a research component still under development, and it is not yet optimized for optimal performance, so that we cannot provide precise figures in terms of processing speed. Regarding the computational cost of our approach we may consider the two most demanding components: the complexity of the target features and the search space (the number of search instances in the scene). The simplified version of the HOG features (small size of the descriptive vector) and the hierarchical search at different scale (cell size and pixel size) allow to achieve satisfactory results of near real-time on small-size video (640 x 480) on a 2.5 Ghz Intel i5 processor. In the referred experimental tests a few thousand vector distance measures are required, as compared to the hundred thousand windows needed by a standard sliding window approach at multiple scales.

In the paper we have shown results of single target tracking, being that the available scenario in the TLD dataset. Actually, our approach has been already successfully tested with multiple-target tracking in the security field, where an industrial application of the AiVu technology [3] has been developed to detect and hide recognizable human faces and car-plates from a standard surveillance video stream, for privacy protection.

6   Conclusions

The paper describes an approach to object tracking using adaptive appearance models based on HOG features, with performance results which are comparable with the most successful solutions recently published in the scientific literature. The main contributions of our research are the use of a modified version of the HOG feature descriptor, with a global normalization at target level, and the use of contrast gradient normalization and adaptive threshold. The forward-backward tracking scheme represents a simple and computationally very effective solution to achieve stable tracking results in a set of challenging video sequences.

References

1. Kalal, Z., Matas, J., Mikolajczyk, K.: P-N learning: bootstrapping binary classifiers by structural constraints. In: 23th IEEE Conf. on Computer Vision and Pattern Recognition CVPR (2010)
2. Smeulders, A.W.M., Chu, D.M., Cucchiara, R., Calderara, S., Delghan, A., Shah, M.: Visual Tracking: an Experimental Survey. IEEE Trans. On Pattern Analysis and Machine Intelligence, PAMI (2013)
3. AiVu Video Analytics Technology. www.aitek.it
4. Kalal, Z., Mikolajczyk, K., Matas, J.: Tracking-learning-detection. IEEE Trans. on Pattern Analysis and Machine Intelligence 34(7), 1409–1422 (2012)
5. Lucas, B.D., Kanade, T.: An iterative image registration technique with an application to stereo vision. In: Proceedings of the International Joint Conference on ArtificialIntelligence, pp. 674–679 (1981)
6. Shi, J., Tomasi, C.: Good features to track. In: IEEE Conf. on Computer Vision and Pattern Recognition, CVPR 1994, Seattle, June 1994
7. Brox, T., Malik, J., Flow, L.D.O.: Descriptor Matching in Variational Motion Estimation. PAMI 33(3), 500–513 (2011)
8. Dalal, N., Triggs, B.: Histograms of oriented gradients for human detection. In: Proc. of CVPR 2005
9. Dollar, P., Belongie, S., Perona, P.: The fastest pedestrian detector in the west. In: Proceedings of the British Machine Vision Conference, pp. 68.1–68.11. BMVA Press, September 2010
10. Babenko, B., Yang, M.-H., Belongie, S.: Visual tracking with online multiple instance learning. In: CVpPR (2009)
11. Felzenszwalb, P.F., Girshick, R.B., McAllester, D., Ramanan, D.: Object detection with discriminatively trained part-based models. IEEE Trans. on Pattern Analysis and Machine Intelligence, PAMI 32(9), 1627–1645 (2010)
12. Zhao, T., Nevatia, R.: Tracking multiple humans in complex situations. IEEE PAMI 26(9), 1208–1221 (2004)

Audiovisual Liveness Detection

Aleksandr Melnikov[2]([✉]), Rasim Akhunzyanov[1], Oleg Kudashev[2],
and Eugene Luckyanets[1,2]

[1] ITMO University, St. Petersburg, Russia
`rasim.akhunzyanov@niuitmo.ru`
[2] STC-innovations Ltd., St. Petersburg, Russia
{`melnikov-a,kudashev,lukyanets`}`@speechpro.com`

Abstract. Although multi-modal (e.g. voice and face) biometric verification systems were in active development and showed impressive performance they need to be protected from spoofing attacks. In this paper we present methods for verifying face liveness based on estimation of synchrony between audio stream and lips movements track during the pronunciation of passphrase. The passphrase consists of a random set of the predetermined English words that are generated dynamically for each verification attempt. Lip movements extraction is performed by using of so-called Constrained Local Model of face shape. Audio stream is used to determine time intervals of pronounced words by means of automatic segmentation. Estimation of synchrony is done by analysis of lip movements for each word by employing a feedforward neural network and a Gaussian naive Bayes classifier. Finally, liveness score assessment is performed by averaging of individual word predictions during verification phrase utterance. For GRID corpus dataset average EER of 4.38% was achieved.

Keywords: Bimodal · Liveness detection · Anti-spoofing · Voice features · Face features

1 Introduction

In context of increasing advance of biometric security systems the importance of their spoofing attacks reflection is very high. In this paper we consider two biometric modalities: face and voice. Facial biometrics has developed increasingly in recent years. Some state-of-art systems show recognition quality comparable with the human recognition level [28]. However, such systems are susceptible to spoofing attacks that apply user photo or video. There are a large number of works devoted to the detection of such spoofing attacks [5]. It uses a variety of methods: frequency and texture based [10,12,20,21], variable focusing based [13,33], movement of the eyes based [1], optical flow based [3,15,16], blinking based [27], 3D face shape based [19,30], binary classification based [24,29], scenic clues based [23,32], lip movement based [6,17], context based [18].

Development of voice verification systems vulnerability to spoofing attacks has greatly increased recently. A lot of works [14,25] examine effects of voice

© Springer International Publishing Switzerland 2015
V. Murino and E. Puppo (Eds.): ICIAP 2015, Part II, LNCS 9280, pp. 643–652, 2015.
DOI: 10.1007/978-3-319-23234-8_59

synthesis and voice conversion to speaker recognition performance as well as propose countermeasures to these attacks [22,31].

There are a few works devoted to the bimodal liveness detection. In paper [6] authors determines lip region and mouth fiducial points via color segmentation. MFCC features are extracted from the speech signal. The resulting audiovisual features are classified using GMM. Method requires model parameters optimization for each individual user.

Research of [26] present algorithm that finds the degree of synchronization between the audio and image recordings of a human speaker. It uses canonical correlation to find the best direction to combine all the audio and image data, projecting them onto a single axis. Then it uses Pearson's correlation to measure the degree of synchronization between the audio and image data. However anti-spoofing is out of scope of this paper and authors were not provided tests of described algorithm in sense of ability to determine face spoofing attacks.

In [7] authors combine mouth fiducial points with PCA eigenlips features. Authors of [4] describes the bimodal system for user verification. It uses MFCC features obtained from voice. 2D-DCT textural features are extracted from the lips region. Optical flow estimated as well. These features are fused using reliability weighted summation and then are used in standard approaches to speaker recognition (HMMs for text-dependent and GMMs for text-independent speaker identification). The similar approach is described in [11].

Here we introduce bimodal anti-spoofing system based on markup of voice signal and lips movements. Voice is processed by automatic audio segmentation, that determines boundaries of words in phrase. Lips movements are catched by fiducial points model for facial images. Phrases content was limited by the predefined number of words (so-called dictionary). We used digits because their utterance were provided by GRID dataset [8], but in real-life system it might be expanded as well.

Evaluation results on GRID corpus dataset show good performance of our system. Also we estimated our algorithm on the internal dataset, witch has been collected by frontal camera of several smartphones in real life conditions.

The remainder of this paper is organized as follows. Section 2 describes bimodal liveness detection. Experimental work is described in Section 3. Finally, our conclusions are presented in Section 4.

2   Text-dependent Bimodal Liveness Detection

The general audio-video synchronization task can be complicated. In order to simplify it we limit contents of passphrase by predefined dictionary containing several words. Then password phrase needed for biometric verification randomly assembled from dictionary. If phrase has enough length it is suitable for audio verification. Potentially this approach can reduce complexity of video processing and simplify synchrony detection. However, such method has several drawbacks:

1. it is required to gather new bimodal dataset for training that might be time consuming;

2. training and adjustments are needed when new language is added;
3. it is possible that liveness performance varies with language.

2.1   Audio Segmentation

The audio segmentation task consists of automatic time mapping between audio stream and pronounced phrase. We used Hidden Markov Models (HMM) to solve this task. Each word of the target phrase was represented as a set of hidden states. Each state had 0.04 sec. average length and was defined by single diagonal Gaussian. The 12 first MFCC without energy were used for signal parametrization. Also we used two additional hidden states, "pause" and "mean speech", to represent audio segments which are not a part of the target phrase. The Viterbi algorithm was used to decode hidden states and to construct segmentation. This method provides high accuracy for pronounced phrase correctness estimation. Thus, we consider only cases with correct pronounces.

Time boundaries of the each state were used for further audio-visual features construction.

2.2   Visual Features

It is necessary to determine the consistency of the facial movements with the utterance of a passphrase. In Audio-Visual Automatic Speech Recognition (AVASR) systems similar problem is solved by analyzing the movements of the lips. Our problem is easier, so we decided to use simple features — the relative change in the shape of the lips. We use anthropometric points detector (landmark detector), which is based on the face points distribution model (PDM). Such models were under active development in recent years. One of the most successful methods presented so far is the Constrained Local Model (CLM) initially proposed by Cristinacce and Cootes [9].

Constrained Local Model for Landmark Detection. CLM mainly consists of three components: PDM, Patch Experts (PE) and algorithm for PDM parameters fitting. Point Distribution Model describes non-rigid shape variations and global rigid transformation. After parameters of PDM are estimated it's possible to compute location $\mathbf{x}_i = [x_i, y_i]$ of each facial landmark:

$$\mathbf{x}_i = sR(\overline{\mathbf{x}_i} + \Phi_i q) + t,$$

where s, R and t terms are rigid parameters responsible for global shape scaling, rotation and translation accordingly and a set of non-rigid parameters q which are responsible for deformation of mean-shape (points $\overline{\mathbf{x}_i}$).

For details about CLM implementation please refer to [2]. Further in this section we concentrate only on details specific to our work.

Facial Landmarks. Liveness detection was designed to work mainly on mobile platforms with near to real-time performance. However image processing is computationally-intensive by its nature and minimization of computation complexity is crucial due to low energy, memory and processing platform capacities.

It's possible to sacrifice flexibility of CLM by reducing the number of points in the model. But we can't discard all points that are not related to the mouth because it reduce the reliability of detection. We conducted series of experiments and reduced the number of points as shown on Fig. 1. Left picture presents original model, while right introduces reduced one.

Thus, the frame processing time is decreased by:

- reducing of the computation of patch experts feedback about twice;
- simplification of the model to reduce the number of local parameters of PDM, which simplifies the optimization problem.

Such model stably and accurately describes facial geometry, while the temporary frame processing costs are reduced almost twice.

Fig. 1. Full 2D face shape model used in [2] and face shape model with reduced set of points.

2.3 Audio-visual Features Extraction

Given a video of N frames length, facial landmarks are extracted from each frame. Since the shape of lip contour looks like an ellipse, it was decided to use ellipse semi-diameters as characteristic features. Euclidean distances between two pairs of landmarks points are calculated as shown at Fig. 2 and stored in vector of length N. Since time of word utterance varies across sessions, vectors may have different length. Therefore vector lengths are aligned to number of hidden states of audio segmentation results by performing linear interpolation as shown on Fig. 3. After that, each word of utterance represented by fixed-length vector of semi-diameters W_x, where $x \in \{\text{'zero'}, \ldots, \text{'nine'}\}$ and $N_x = \text{length}(W_x)$. This vectors are used as audio-visual features for further classification.

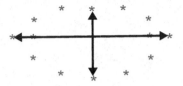

Fig. 2. Vertical and horizontal distances used as video features.

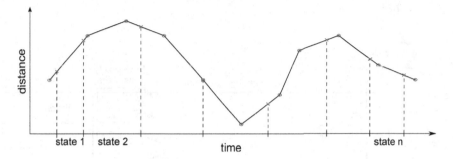

Fig. 3. State interpolation for word 'seven'.

2.4   Decision System

Classification. Training of the system requires two datasets: dataset for training and dataset for fusion optimisation. Train dataset consists of target (synchrony) and impostor (asynchrony) subsets. Impostor sessions were created from target ones by mixing audio and visual features from different utterances. From the train dataset the audio-visual features W_x^{target} and W_x^{impostor} were collected for each word in dictionary.

Obtained dataset is used for training of two classifiers: neural network and gaussian naive Bayes. We used a neural network with N_x inputs and scalar output. Such binary classifier distinguishes visual word for a specific digit from the rest.

For gaussian naive Bayes classifier two hypotheses for audiovisual features W_x are considered: H_x^s — the audio and video are synchrony, H_x^d — the audio and video are asynchrony. As the decision score a log of likelihood ratio $\ln P(W_x|H_x^s) - \ln P(W_x|H_x^d)$ is used, where $P(W_x|H_x^s)$ and $P(W_x|H_x^d)$ are represented by a single gaussian with full covariance matrices.

Resulting Score. Passphrase consists of N_w words pronunciations. For each word from passphrase prediction score is obtained by corresponding classifier. As result we have N_w scores s_k, one for each word. Using these scores we estimate equal error rate threshold T_k and the standard deviation of the impostors distribution σ_k.

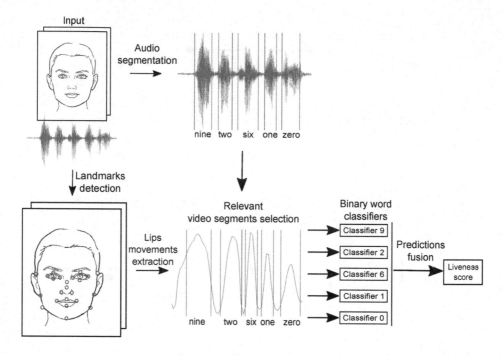

Fig. 4. Method workflow.

Fusion score s was calculated as follows:

$$s = \frac{1}{N_w} \sum_{k=0}^{N_w-1} \frac{T_k - s_k}{\sigma_k}$$

To select the optimal parameters of T_k simulated annealing optimization method was used. The initial values for this method were obtained from equal error rate threshold described below. EER value is chosen to be a quality function in result fusion system. Overall system workflow is shown on fig.4.

3   Experimental Results

In this section we present experimental results produced for GRID corpus dataset [8]. This dataset consists of 34 speakers, 1000 sessions for each. However, one speaker has no video sessions, so we did not use them. Digits from 'zero' to 'nine' were chosen from dataset to evaluate algorithm. Dataset were splitted into train and test parts by speakers. In oder to increase train dataset size we chose only one speaker for testing at each time. So, we provide 33 train-test cycles with 32 speakers for training and 1 for testing. All results were averaged to obtain final EER result.

We tested two system: gaussian naive Bayes based and neural networks based that were described in section 2.4. Also, two types of speech segmentation were used: our segmentation and segmentation provided by GRID dataset. In table 1 EER results for different passphrase lengths obtained by concatenation of several speaker sessions are shown. As it can be seen EER decreases with increasing number of digits in passphrase. Neural networks based system shows slightly better results than gaussian naive Bayes based system. It should be noted that our segmentation outperforms ground truth segmentation in current task. Fig. 3 demonstrates bad performance of our system for speaker 26. It happened because CLM algorithm worked bad on this speaker and as a result audiovisual features were wrong.

Our implementation of the facial landmarks extractor allows to achieve necessary performance and use proposed system on modern smartphones with hi-end chipsets in real-time.

We performed one more evaluation on the manually collected dataset in Russian. It contains 3 sessions of 77 male and 76 female subjects, recorded on 3 different mobile devices. Each session consists of several digit phrases. Satisfying results (table 2) approved that our method works good on essentially different datasets.

Table 1. EER results for fusion system on digits, %

num. of digits		2	3	4	5
GRID seg	NeuralNet	14.71	10.44	7.1	5.68
	GNB	15.35	10.74	7.82	5.86
our seg	NeuralNet	12.37	8.29	5.82	4.38
	GNB	13.27	8.75	6.27	4.61

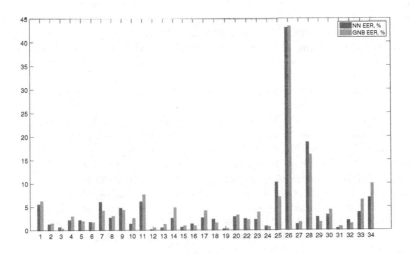

Fig. 5. EER per speaker for our segmentation, %

Table 2. EER results for fusion system on Russian dataset, %

num. of digits		2	3	4	5
our seg	NeuralNet	10.53	7.11	4.32	3.64
	GNB	12.85	8.06	5.51	4.17

4   Conclusion

In this paper we have introduced the new method for liveness detection. Through experiments on GRID dataset, we have shown that it is efficient in resolving liveness detection task with average EER of 4.38%. In future work we intend to use more complex information from facial features, such as optical flow changing, more accurate lip contour tracking and etc. Also, more robust facial PDM algorithm may be used.

Acknowledgments. The authors would like to thank the anonymous reviewers for their comments, which have significantly improved quality of the the manuscript.

References

1. Ali, A., Deravi, F., Hoque, S.: Liveness detection using gaze collinearity. In: 2012 Third International Conference on Emerging Security Technologies (EST), pp. 62–65. IEEE (2012)
2. Baltrusaitis, T., Robinson, P., Morency, L.: 3d constrained local model for rigid and non-rigid facial tracking. In: 2012 IEEE Conference on Computer Vision and Pattern Recognition (CVPR), pp. 2610–2617. IEEE (2012)
3. Bao, W., Li, H., Li, N., Jiang, W.: A liveness detection method for face recognition based on optical flow field. In: International Conference on Image Analysis and Signal Processing, IASP 2009, pp. 233–236. IEEE (2009)
4. Çetingül, H.E., Erzin, E., Yemez, Y., Tekalp, A.M.: Multimodal speaker/speech recognition using lip motion, lip texture and audio. Signal Processing **86**(12), 3549–3558 (2006)
5. Chakraborty, S., Das, D.: An overview of face liveness detection (2014). arXiv preprint arXiv:1405.2227
6. Chetty, G., Wagner, M.: Automated lip feature extraction for liveness verification in audio-video authentication. Proc. Image and Vision Computing, 17–22 (2004)
7. Chetty, G., Wagner, M.: Multi-level liveness verification for face-voice biometric authentication. In: 2006 Biometrics Symposium: Special Session on Research at the Biometric Consortium Conference, pp. 1–6. IEEE (2006)
8. Cooke, M., Barker, J., Cunningham, S., Shao, X.: An audio-visual corpus for speech perception and automatic speech recognition. The Journal of the Acoustical Society of America **120**(5), 2421–2424 (2006)
9. Cristinacce, D., Cootes, T.F.: Feature detection and tracking with constrained local models. In BMVC, vol. 2, pp. 6. Citeseer (2006)
10. Das, D., Chakraborty, S.: Face liveness detection based on frequency and micro-texture analysis. In: 2014 International Conference on Advances in Engineering and Technology Research (ICAETR), pp. 1–4. IEEE (2014)

11. Dean, D., Sridharan, S.: Dynamic visual features for audio-visual speaker verification. Computer Speech & Language **24**(2), 136–149 (2010)
12. Kim, G., Eum, S., Suhr, J.K., Kim, D.I., Park, K.R., Kim, J.: Face liveness detection based on texture and frequency analyses. In: 2012 5th IAPR International Conference on Biometrics (ICB), pp. 67–72. IEEE (2012)
13. Kim, S., Yu, S., Kim, K., Ban, Y., Lee, S.: Face liveness detection using variable focusing. In: 2013 International Conference on Biometrics (ICB), pp. 1–6. IEEE (2013)
14. Kinnunen, T., Wu, Z.-Z., Lee, K.A., Sedlak, F., Chng, E.S., Li, H.: Vulnerability of speaker verification systems against voice conversion spoofing attacks: The case of telephone speech. In: 2012 IEEE International Conference on Acoustics, Speech and Signal Processing (ICASSP), pp. 4401–4404, March 2012
15. Kollreider, K., Fronthaler, H., Bigun, J.: Evaluating liveness by face images and the structure tensor. In: Fourth IEEE Workshop on Automatic Identification Advanced Technologies, 2005, pp. 75–80. IEEE (2005)
16. Kollreider, K., Fronthaler, H., Bigun, J.: Non-intrusive liveness detection by face images. Image and Vision Computing **27**(3), 233–244 (2009)
17. Kollreider, K., Fronthaler, H., Faraj, M.I., Bigun, J.: Real-time face detection and motion analysis with application in "liveness" assessment. IEEE Transactions on Information Forensics and Security **2**(3), 548–558 (2007)
18. Komulainen, J., Hadid, A., Pietikainen, M.: Context based face anti-spoofing. In: 2013 IEEE Sixth International Conference on Biometrics: Theory, Applications and Systems (BTAS), pp. 1–8. IEEE (2013)
19. Lagorio, A., Tistarelli, M., Cadoni, M., Fookes, C., Sridharan, S.: Liveness detection based on 3d face shape analysis. In: 2013 International Workshop on Biometrics and Forensics (IWBF), pp. 1–4. IEEE (2013)
20. Määttä, J., Hadid, A., Pietikäinen, M.: Face spoofing detection from single images using texture and local shape analysis. IET Biometrics **1**(1), 3–10 (2012)
21. Maatta, J., Hadid, A., Pietikainen, M.: Face spoofing detection from single images using micro-texture analysis. In: 2011 International Joint Conference on Biometrics (IJCB), pp. 1–7. IEEE (2011)
22. Marcel, S., Nixon, M.S., Li, S.Z.: Handbook of Biometric Anti-Spoofing. Springer (2014)
23. Pan, G., Sun, L., Zhaohui, W., Wang, Y.: Monocular camera-based face liveness detection by combining eyeblink and scene context. Telecommunication Systems **47**(3–4), 215–225 (2011)
24. Peixoto, B., Michelassi, C., Rocha, A.: Face liveness detection under bad illumination conditions. In: 2011 18th IEEE International Conference on Image Processing (ICIP), pp. 3557–3560. IEEE (2011)
25. Shchemelinin, V., Topchina, M., Simonchik, K.: Vulnerability of voice verification systems to spoofing attacks by TTS voices based on automatically labeled telephone speech. In: Ronzhin, A., Potapova, R., Delic, V. (eds.) SPECOM 2014. LNCS, vol. 8773, pp. 475–481. Springer, Heidelberg (2014)
26. Slaney, M., Covell, M.: Facesync: a linear operator for measuring synchronization of video facial images and audio tracks. In: NIPS, pp. 814–820 (2000)
27. Sun, L., Pan, G., Wu, Z., Lao, S.: Blinking-based live face detection using conditional random fields. In: Lee, S.-W., Li, S.Z. (eds.) ICB 2007. LNCS, vol. 4642, pp. 252–260. Springer, Heidelberg (2007)
28. Taigman, Y., Yang, M., Ranzato, M.A., Wolf, L.: Deepface: closing the gap to human-level performance in face verification. In: 2014 IEEE Conference on Computer Vision and Pattern Recognition (CVPR), pp. 1701–1708. IEEE (2014)

29. Tan, X., Li, Y., Liu, J., Jiang, L.: Face liveness detection from a single image with sparse low rank bilinear discriminative model. In: Daniilidis, K., Maragos, P., Paragios, N. (eds.) ECCV 2010, Part VI. LNCS, vol. 6316, pp. 504–517. Springer, Heidelberg (2010)

30. Wang, T., Yang, J., Lei, Z., Liao, S., Li, S.Z.: Face liveness detection using 3d structure recovered from a single camera. In: 2013 International Conference on Biometrics (ICB), pp. 1–6. IEEE (2013)

31. Zhizheng, W., Evans, N., Kinnunen, T., Yamagishi, J., Alegre, F., Li, H.: Spoofing and countermeasures for speaker verification: A survey. Speech Communication **66**, 130–153 (2015)

32. Yan, J., Zhang, Z., Lei, Z., Yi, D., Li, S.Z.: Face liveness detection by exploring multiple scenic clues. In: 2012 12th International Conference on Control Automation Robotics & Vision (ICARCV), pp. 188–193. IEEE (2012)

33. Yang, L.: Face liveness detection by focusing on frontal faces and image backgrounds. In: 2014 International Conference on Wavelet Analysis and Pattern Recognition (ICWAPR), pp. 93–97. IEEE (2014)

Foreground Detection Robust Against Cast Shadows in Outdoor Daytime Environment

Akari Sato[✉], Masato Toda, and Masato Tsukada

Information and Media Processing Laboratories, NEC Corporation, Tokyo, Japan
a-sato@cw.jp.nec.com, m-toda@ap.jp.nec.com,
m-tsukada@cj.jp.nec.com

Abstract. This paper proposes a novel foreground detection method which estimates the color changes in shadow regions by using a solar spectral model. In conventional method, since it is assumed that only brightness changes from background in shadow regions, shadow regions are extracted falsely as foreground in the case where color in the shadow region also changes in outdoor daytime environment. The proposed method estimates the color changes in shadow regions by calculating colors of direct and ambient illuminance which radiate to the captured scene using a solar spectral model. By estimating the color changes, the proposed method can robustly distinguish foreground and shadow regions in outdoor daytime environment. Experimental results demonstrate that the proposed method successfully estimates the changes of background color in shadow regions and improves F measure of foreground detection compared with the conventional methods.

Keywords: Video surveillance · Background subtraction · Solar spectral model · Foreground detection · Shadow detection

1 Introduction

Recently, video surveillance for outdoor purpose has attracted attention due to the fear of terrorism and violent criminals. In a surveillance system, operators catch occurrences of crimes or suspicious behaviors from captured images. To achieve a high security surveillance system and comfortable operations, it is quite expected that image recognition techniques assist the operators by automatically recognizing target objects in real-time and with high accuracy.

Background subtraction is widely used for extracting foreground regions as the first step for object recognition [9]. The background subtraction conducts a comparison between a captured image and a background image data and extracts regions which have differences as foreground. The size and shape of each foreground region are utilized as cues for an identification of objects such as "human" or "vehicle". One of the general problems of the background subtraction is that cast shadows on background are also detected as foreground.

To solve this problem, background subtraction with shadow detection which enables to divide the extracted foreground regions into the actual foreground regions

© Springer International Publishing Switzerland 2015
V. Murino and E. Puppo (Eds.): ICIAP 2015, Part II, LNCS 9280, pp. 653–664, 2015.
DOI: 10.1007/978-3-319-23234-8_60

and shadow regions are studied [10][12]. These methods try to detect the shadow regions by setting a constraint about change of chromaticity of shadow regions or by installing a physical illumination condition model which enables to predict the color change of shadow regions. However, the conventional methods are insufficient for applying to outdoor daytime environment. There are two kinds of illuminant in daylight scene; one is a direct illumination of the sun and another is an ambient illumination such as sky. These illuminant colors are different, and the strength and the color of each illuminant changes constantly according to the time and the weather condition. Therefore, the change in background color caused by shadows also fluctuates variously.

In this paper, we propose foreground detection method which is applicable to outdoor daytime environment, suppressing the affection of cast shadows. The proposed method utilizes a solar spectral model which can describe the illuminant color of both of direct and ambient illuminations in the daylight scene and extracts foreground regions by estimating the color change of background regions caused by cast shadows.

The rest of the paper is organized as follows. In the next section, we review related works and explain its problems. We describe the proposed method in Section 3. We detail some experimental results in Section 4. Finally we conclude the paper in Section 5.

2   Related Work

It is well known that cast shadows on background tend to be extracted as foreground and it causes inaccurate object detection and decrease of tracking performance. Therefore, detecting cast shadows from the extracted foreground regions has become an important step for realizing robust tracking system and has been widely studied [10][12].

The most famous approach for the cast shadow detection is chromaticity based approach. This approach uses an assumption that regions under shadow become darker but their chromaticity does not change significantly. Various color space are used to evaluate the chromaticity, for example normalized RGB [2], HSV [3] and c1c2c3 [13]. The main advantage of this approach is its easiness of implementation. However, this approach is not effective since the assumption does not match to daylight conditions. In daylight conditions, there are two kinds of illuminant, a direct illumination of the sun and an ambient illumination such as sky, which have different illuminant colors. Since regions in a sunny place are irradiated by these two illuminant lights and the cast shadows are generated by obstructions of the direct illumination light, the chromaticity of the shadow regions changes significantly.

Another approach for the detection is learning based approach, which predicts the color change of shadow regions based on an illumination model of the scene. This approach can represent the color change of shadow regions in daylight conditions and can successfully detect the cast shadows when the illumination property of the scene which represents direct and ambient illuminant colors is correctly given. This approach has a difficulty to conduct appropriate setting of the illumination property. In recent years, several methods try to estimate the illumination properties or the specific color appearances of shadows which are the best fit to the captured scene using machine learning [5]. However, in daylight scene, the strength and the color of the direct and the ambient illumination changes constantly according to the time and the weather condition. So their estimated illumination color properties become invalid unless the learning process is repeated again and again, which takes high computational cost. Furthermore, the learning process needs data sets in stable illuminant condition which is sometimes difficult to obtain in actual daylight scenes. The other approaches use regional texture correlations [7][11] and discriminate target regions as shadow if the texture correlation between the target region and background is high.

There is another approach which uses geometrical properties such as sizes and shapes of the shadows [4]. However, this approach lacks versatility since the performance strongly depends on the feature of target objects and background.

We propose foreground detection method robust against cast shadows outdoor daytime environment.

3   Proposed Method

3.1   The Concept of the Proposed Method

The proposed method detects foreground regions suppressing the affection of cast shadows by estimating the color changes in background. Since colors of cast shadows changes in outdoor daytime environment it is difficult to estimate the regions of shadows. The proposed method estimates these color changes in background using spectrums of direct and ambient illuminants calculated by a solar spectral model [6] and enables to distinguish the foreground regions and the shadow regions.

3.2   Solar Spectral Model

A solar spectral model by Bird and Riordan [1] is a physics based simulation model to represent a daylight spectrum at the earth's surface under cloudless condition. In this model, the diffusion and the attenuation of sunlight passing through the atmosphere under cloudless condition are simulated and spectral power distributions of the direct illumination and the ambient illumination are calculated. In order to calculate the spectral power distributions, solar zenith angle and atmospheric conditions of the scene are needed. Since the affection by the atmospheric conditions such as water vapor, air pressure, turbidity and aerosol is much less than the solar zenith angle, a daylight spectrum is estimated with the solar zenith angle and a priori determined constant parameters of atmospheric conditions under a clear sky. The solar zenith angle is determined by the date of the year, the time of the day, and the latitude and the longitude of the place, which can be easily obtained in actual operations.

The solar spectral model is extended by Kaneko et al. to apply under weather conditions from clear sky to cloudy [6]. This model takes the behavior of light passing through clouds into consideration and represents a daylight spectrum under cloudy condition as a linear combination of the direct and the ambient illuminant spectrum under cloudless condition. Their experimental results show that their model can successfully represent daylight spectrum in cloudless, cloudy and shady conditions in the range of the wavelength from 350nm to 1000nm which includes visible wavelength.

Based on the model, illuminant colors of direct and ambient light in a captured scene L_d and L_a are represented by using the illuminant colors of direct and ambient light under the cloudless condition I_d and I_a as follows:

$$L_d^c = m\, I_d^c, \quad L_a^c = n I_d^c + l\, I_a^c \tag{1}$$

where c denote color channels in RGB color space and m, n, and l is coefficient parameters which describe the intensity of each illuminant. The illuminant colors I_d and I_a are obtained from the spectral power distributions of the direct and the ambient illumination by applying color matching functions.

3.3   Color Change Model in Background

Changes of color in shadow regions are estimated using the direct and ambient illuminance color by solar spectral model. By estimating the changes of background color, possible background colors are obtained. The changes of background color are described as followed. By using direct and ambient illuminant colors L_d^c and L_a^c, color information of background B^c is represented by

$$B^c = r^c(L_d^c + L_a^c) = r^c\big((m+n)I_d^c + lI_a^c\big) \tag{2}$$

where r is the surface reflectance.

In the shadow region, it is assumed that direct light is occluded by the object and decays, so color information of shadow region B_{sh}^c is represented by

$$B_{sh}^c = r^c(\alpha L_d^c + L_a^c) = r^c\big((\alpha m + n)I_d^c + lI_a^c\big) \tag{3}$$

where α is the parameter which represents the intensity of occluded direct light in the captured scene.

$$B_{sh}^c = \frac{(\alpha m+n)I_d^c+lI_a^c}{(m+n)I_d^c+lI_a^c} B^c = \frac{q I_d^c+I_a^c}{p I_d^c+I_a^c} B^c \tag{4}$$

where

$$p = \frac{m+n}{l}, q = \frac{\alpha m+n}{l}. \tag{5}$$

B_{sh}^c is the possible shadow colors which varies according to parameters p and q. By minimizing the color difference between B_{sh}^c and color information in captured image J^c, shadow color is estimated uniquely. Then energy function E defined as followed must be minimized for parameters p and q.

$$E = \Sigma_c(J^c - B_{sh}^c)^2 \tag{6}$$

where J^c represents the color information of input image. By minimizing E, p and q are determined and shadow color B_{sh}^c in the equation (4) is estimated uniquely.

3.4   Extract Foreground Region

Foreground likelihood for each pixel is calculated from the matching rate with the color change model. The estimated background color represents the changed color information of a pixel if its behavior follows the color changes in background (shadow). So foreground likelihood becomes high if the difference between the color information of the pixel and that of estimated background is large.

The proposed method can extract only foreground regions by using these features. To extract foreground regions, some threshold need to be set and if the foreground likelihood is higher than the threshold it is extracted as foreground region. Threshold is needed to be set appropriately to extract foreground but to suppress shadow.

3.5   The Overview of the Proposed Method

In proposed method, foreground regions are extracted by estimating the background color changes using solar spectral model. Fig. 1 shows the overall flow of the proposed method. First, from the date and position of the captured scene, spectral of direct and ambient illuminants are derived by using solar spectral model. Next, change of color information from input background image by the shadow in the captured scene is estimated from captured image and input background image. By using estimated background, foreground likelihood is calculated. As a result, foreground regions (object regions) can be extracted which have the property whose color information is highly different from that of estimated background.

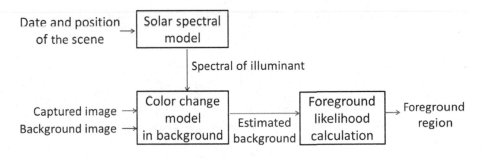

Fig. 1. Flow of the proposed method

4   Evaluations

4.1   Evaluation of Color Change Model

In the first experiment, the validity of the proposed color change model in background is confirmed compared with the model used in the chromaticity based method [3].

Fig. 2 shows the model of the chromaticity based method in RGB color space. Red line represents the possible colors of shadow. If the target pixel color is close to the line, the pixel is discriminated as shadow. In the shadow pixel, the distance between the pixel value and estimated shadow color value represents the model error of chromaticity based method. And the intersection point with the possible shadow color line (red line) and perpendicular line drawn from the pixel color point to the red line can be considered as estimated shadow color point. By using estimated shadow color C_{sh}, the model error of the chromaticity based method E_C is represented as followed.

$$E_C = \sum_c (J^c - C_{sh}^c)^2 \tag{7}$$

where J^c is corresponding pixel value of input image in shadow region.

Fig. 3 shows the proposed color change model in RGB color space. Red curved surface represents the possible colors of shadow. The target pixel color is also discriminated as shadow if the color point is close to the curved surface. The intersection point with curved surface and perpendicular line drawn from the pixel color point is the estimated background color point and the model error of the proposed method is represented by E in equation (6).

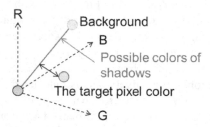

Fig. 2. Possible shadow colors under the chromaticity based method

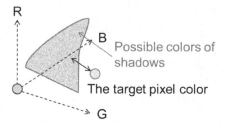

Fig. 3. Possible shadow colors under the proposed method

The experiment conducted in outdoor daytime environment and on three types of ground, lawn, artificial lawn and asphalt. Fig. 4 shows captured images and the model errors of the chromaticity based method E_C and the proposed method E calculated using the shadow pixels. Horizontal axis represents imgV/bgV, where

$$\text{imgV} = R + G + B \tag{8}$$

for each shadow pixel in input image and bgV is also the sum value of RGB of corresponding pixel in background image. Vertical axis represents the value of the model errors and red dots and blue dots represent E and E_C of each pixel in shadow region respectively. From Fig. 4 it is obvious that proposed method has the smaller model error compared to the chromaticity based method and it is confirmed that the color change model used in the proposed is valid to estimate the color changes occurred in shadow regions. In Fig. 4 (b), the shadow region is much darker than background and model errors in some shadow pixels are large. This means that if shadows become quite dark, it doesn't match the proposed color change model because the proposed model assumes that ambient illuminance doesn't attenuate even in shadow regions. So if not only direct illuminant but ambient illuminant is considerably occluded by the object, the colors in the shadow region tend not to follow the proposed color change model. In spite of this feature, the model errors are small compared with the chromaticity based method. If this feature will be solved in the future work, the performance of estimating the color changes in shadow regions can be much more improved.

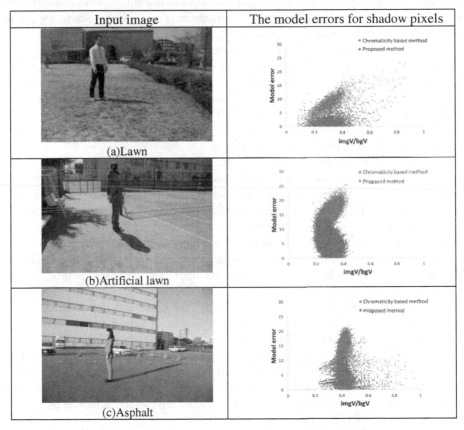

Fig. 4. Model errors in shadow pixels from captured images

4.2   Evaluation of Foreground Region Detection Performance

Other experiments were conducted to evaluate the performance of detecting foreground region by the proposed model and compare with the conventional methods, the chromaticity based method [3] and two texture based methods [7][11]. In the conventional based methods, at first it needs to extract the region which includes both foreground and shadow regions. Then extracted regions were analyzed and distinguished to foreground and shadow regions. As mentioned in the survey research by Sanin et al. [12], it is difficult to make masks manually for evaluation which include foreground and shadow regions because the boundary of shadows is ambiguous. So we first applied the background subtraction technique by using a Gaussian mixture model (GMM) of OpenCV 2.0 to extract foreground and shadow regions as Sanin et al. have done in their survey. To evaluate the chromaticity based method and the texture based method, we used the open source codes by them[1].

To evaluate impartially, we should use some classical database such as Hallway, Highway series, Campus, Room CAVIAR, etc. But our model needs latitude, longitude and time corresponding to the captured images to use solar spectral model. Also our model can only apply to the outdoor environment. From above reasons, we cannot use the well-used database and alternatively we used the images captured by ourselves which latitude, longitude and time is known.

Fig. 5 and Fig. 6 show examples of results of foreground region detection. In Fig 5 and Fig 6, (a)input captured image, (b)input background image, (c)ground truth of foreground region, (d)result image by chromaticity based method [3], (e)result image by the small region texture based method [7], (f)result image by large region texture based method [11], (g)estimated background image by the proposed method and (h)result image by proposed method are shown.

From these results it is confirmed that the proposed method detected foreground regions successfully compared with the chromaticity based method [3] and the texture based methods [7][11]. The chromaticity based method and the texture based methods detected some shadow pixels as foreground falsely, also some foreground pixels were not detected successfully. Fig. 5 demonstrated that shadows on the flat ground like asphalt can be easily estimated by both the conventional and the proposed methods. But it is shown by Fig. 6 shadows on complicated textured ground like lawns are difficult to discriminate by the conventional methods. The proposed method handled both types of ground and extracted only foreground regions robustly.

Another evaluation was conducted to confirm the numerical improvement of the foreground region detection. In the evaluation images of fifteen scenes whose date, time, place and illuminant condition are different. Table 1 shows the average precision, recall and F-measure of the proposed method, the chromaticity based method and the texture based methods, compared with the ground truth of foreground regions. From this result, it is demonstrated that F-measure of the proposed method is the highest in four methods and confirmed that the proposed method achieved the highest foreground detection performance.

The precision of the proposed method is highest and it means the proposed method successfully suppressed cast shadows and excluded them from foreground regions. But the recall of the proposed method was lowest in four methods and the conventional methods achieved high recall. This is because the conventional methods

---

[1] http://arma.sourceforge.net/shadows/

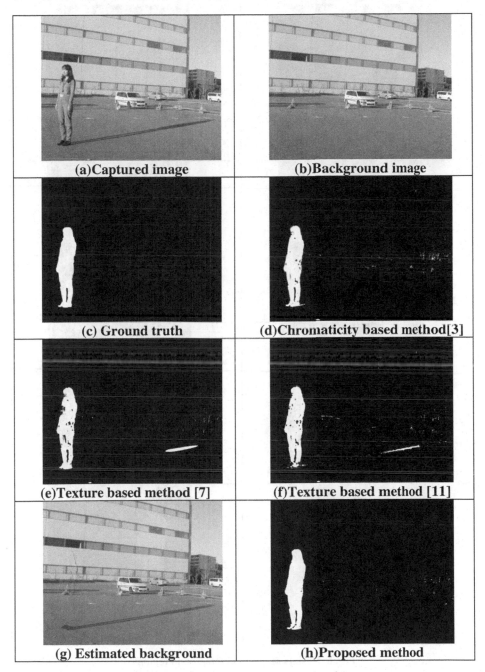

(a)Captured image

(b)Background image

(c) Ground truth

(d)Chromaticity based method[3]

(e)Texture based method [7]

(f)Texture based method [11]

(g) Estimated background

(h)Proposed method

Fig. 5. Results of detected foreground regions

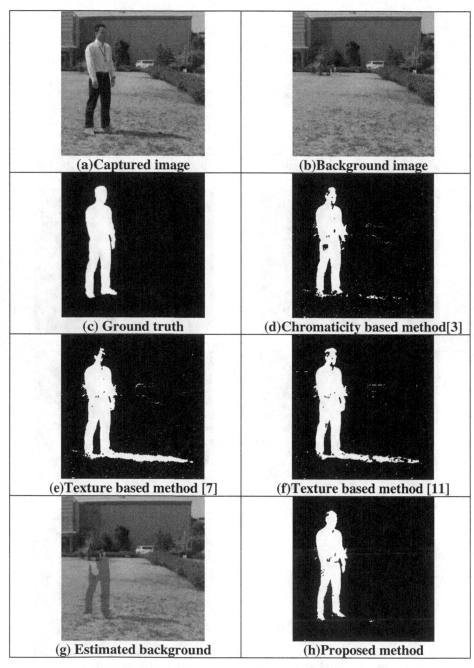

(a)Captured image

(b)Background image

(c) Ground truth

(d)Chromaticity based method[3]

(e)Texture based method [7]

(f)Texture based method [11]

(g) Estimated background

(h)Proposed method

Fig. 6. Results of detected foreground regions

Table 1. Evaluation results of foreground detection

	Precision	Recall	F-measure
Chromaticity based method[3]	0.4386	0.7625	0.5370
Texture based method [7]	0.3907	0.8874	0.5183
Texture based method [11]	0.5044	0.8691	0.6242
Proposed method	0.8100	0.6859	0.6863

extracted not only foreground but also background components such as shadows caused by illuminant changes. So the extracted regions were much larger than ground truth foreground. We tested many parameters to improve this phenomenon but it didn't work well. The extracted regions included ground truth foreground so the recall became high, but the precision become low. Conversely the proposed method could exclude extra background components from extracted foreground regions but it became difficult to include ground truth foreground in extracted region perfectly, so the recall became low. There is still room for discuss to decide which to emphasize precision or recall, but it can be said that the proposed method has the highest performance in foreground detection because it achieved the highest F-measure.

5   Conclusion

We proposed the foreground detection method which estimates the color changes in shadow regions using solar spectral model. The proposed method detects foreground region robustly against cast shadows in outdoor daytime environment by estimating the color changes in background using the direct and ambient spectral which fluctuate variously. Evaluation result demonstrated that the proposed color change model in shadow region is accurate compared with conventional only chromaticity based model. Also from accuracy evaluation, it was confirmed that the proposed method improved foreground detection performance compared with the conventional methods.

References

1. Bird, R.E., Riordan, C.: Simple Solar Spectral Model for Direct and Diffuse Irradiance on Horizontal and Tilted Planes at the Earth's Surface for Cloudless Atmospheres. Journal of Climate and Applied Meteorology **25**(1), 87–97 (1986)
2. Cavallaro, A., et al.: Shadow-aware object-based video processing. IEEE Proceedings on Vision, Image and Signal Processing **152**(4), 398–406 (2005)
3. Cucchiara, R., et al.: Detecting Moving Objects, Ghosts, and Shadows in Video Streams. IEEE Transactions on Pattern Analysis and Machine intelligence **25**(10), 1337–1342 (2003)
4. Hsieh, J.W., et al.: Shadow elimination for effective moving object detection by Gaussian shadow Modeling. Image and Vision Computing **21**(6), 505–516 (2003)

5. Huang, J.B., Chen, C.S.: Moving cast shadow detection using physics-based features. In: IEEE Conference on Computer Vision and Pattern Recognition, pp. 2310–2317 (2009)

6. Kaneko, E., et.al.: Daylight spectrum model under weather conditions from clear sky to cloudy. In: Proc. of ICPR, pp. 1438–1435 (2012)

7. Leone, A., Distante, C.: Shadow detection for moving objects based on texture analysis. Pattern Recognition 40(4), 1222–1233 (2007)

8. Nadimi, S., Bhanu, B.: Physical models for moving shadow and object detection in video. IEEE Transactions on Pattern Analysis and Machine Intelligence 26(8), 1079–1087 (2004)

9. Piccadi, M.: Background subtraction techniques: a review. IEEE International Conference on Systems, Man and Cybernetics 4, 3099–3104 (2004)

10. Prati, A., et al.: Detecting moving shadows: algorithms and evaluation. IEEE Transactions on Pattern Analysis and Machine Intelligence 25(7), 918–923 (2003)

11. Sanin, A., Sanderson, C., Lovell, B.C.: Improved shadow removal for robust person tracking in surveillance scenarios. In: International Conference on Pattern Recognition, pp. 141–144 (2010)

12. Sanin, A., Sanderson, C., Lovell, B.C.: Shadow Detection: A Survey and Comparative Evaluation of Recent Methods. Pattern Recognition 45(4), 1684–1695 (2012)

13. Salvador, E., et al.: Cast shadow segmentation using invariant color features. Computer Vision and Image Understanding 95(2), 238–259 (2004)

A Tool to Support the Creation of Datasets of Tampered Videos

Edoardo Ardizzone and Giuseppe Mazzola[✉]

Dipartimento di Ingegneria Chimica, Gestionale, Informatica, Meccanica (DICGIM),
Università degli Studi di Palermo, Viale delle Scienze bd.6, 90128 Palermo, Italy
{edoardo.ardizzone,giuseppe.mazzola}@unipa.it

Abstract. Digital Video Forensics is getting a growing interest from the Multimedia research community, as the need for methods to validate the authenticity of a video content is increasing with the number of videos freely available to the digital users. Unlike Digital Image Forensics, to our knowledge, there are not standard datasets to test video forgery detection techniques. In this paper we present a new tool to support the users in creating datasets of tampered videos. We furthermore present our own dataset and we discuss some remarks about how to create forgeries difficult to be detected by an observer, to the naked eye.

Keywords: Copy move forgery · Video forensics · Object tracking

1 Introduction

Nowadays, the widespread use of mobile devices has drastically increased the number of videos available online through several web channels, e.g. Flickr, Facebook, Twitter, YouTube, Vimeo, Dailymotion. The huge amount of available videos improved the free flow of information around the world, but raised the problem of the validation of such information. The content of a video may be altered either with funny purposes, or for malicious goals, e.g. to modify the evidences of a legal process, to support a political campaign or to emphasize a scoop of a TV news.

Unlike the image processing tools, which have been very popular in the digital users' community for a long time, video processing tools need more skill, above all if the goal is to alter the content of the video by deleting or adding objects to the scenes. Furthermore, in scientific literature, to our knowledge, there are not standard datasets to test the ability of Digital Forensics techniques in detecting tampered videos.

In this paper we present a tool to support digital users in creating tampered digital videos, in particular to clone objects from a video sequence to another, or to the same, video sequence. The goal is to build a dataset of tampered videos, which can be used by the Digital Forensics community to test their video tampering detection techniques. The paper is organized as follows: in section 2 we discuss some state of the art methods about Video Forensics; in section 3 we present our method for cloning objects in a video; in section 4 we present our dataset and remark some points and of our experimental tests; a conclusive section ends the paper.

© Springer International Publishing Switzerland 2015
V. Murino and E. Puppo (Eds.): ICIAP 2015, Part II, LNCS 9280, pp. 665–675, 2015.
DOI: 10.1007/978-3-319-23234-8_61

2   State of the Art

Multimedia Forensics is a relatively new branch of the Multimedia Processing research field, and focuses on verifying the authenticity or detecting the source of a multimedia file. While Digital Image Forensics has been widely explored in the last ten years[1], Video Forensics issues have been rather less studied [2,3]. Regarding Video Forgery Detection techniques, they can be subdivided into active and passive approaches. Active approaches [4] exploit superimposed information, as watermarks or signatures, to verify the integrity of a video file. Passive approaches use internal features to detect if a video has been tampered in some ways. Some methods propose to use noise characteristics [5] to detect possible forgeries. Other works try to detect proofs of the evidence of a double compression [6,7]. Wang and Farid [8] proposed a method to detect duplicated frames used to remove people or objects from a video.

Video forgeries may be classified [9] into: spatial domain alterations; temporal domain alterations; spatio-temporal domain alterations. Spatial alterations modify the pixels of one or more frames of a video sequence, without modifying its duration. Temporal alterations change the video sequence duration. This is the case of frame dropping or frame repetition techniques [10,11], used typically to alter the content of surveillance videos. Spatio-temporal alterations combine both of them.

Tampering methods for video sequences may be further classified into inter-frame, intra-frame and inter-video. Intra-frame forgeries are duplication of a part of a frame into the same frame and are very similar to image copy-move forgeries. Inter-frame forgeries are duplication of a part of a video into another part of the same video. Inter-video forgeries are obtained merging the content of two different videos.

In our previous works we dealt with the problem of identifying copy move forgeries in still images [12-15]. In this work we present a tool which is able to support a user in the creation of all these types of alterations (intra-frame, inter-frame and inter-video forgeries).

3   Proposed Method

The whole cloning process can be subdivided into several steps, as shown in fig. 1: Selection, Tracking, Transformation, and Blending.

3.1   Selection

The first step is the only one in which the user intervention is required. The system requires the user to select, from a frame of the Source Video, a Region of Interest (ROI), to choose the object to be cloned (fig. 2.1). The system automatically extract the centroid of the input mask, as the average value of the points of its bounding box, which will be used into the blending phase.

The system requires also a destination point into the Destination Video, where (coordinates) and when (the frame) the selected object has to be pasted. The object can be cloned into the same frame of the same video (Intra-frame), into another frame of the same video (Inter-frame), or into another video (Inter-video) .

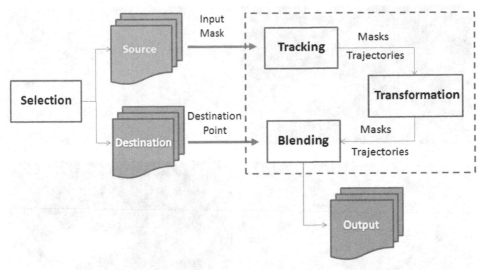

Fig. 1. Schema of the proposed method

Fig. 2. Object selection and centroid extraction

This is the most tricky part of the whole process, as a good result depends on the skill of the user. In fact, the tracking algorithm performs better if the starting mask is properly selected, depending on the object visual content. Furthermore, the choice of a proper destination point may limit the presence of artifacts when pasting the selected object. These issues will be further discussed in the next sections.

The user has to select also the maximum number of frames along which the input object has to be tracked, and copied into the destination video.

3.2 Tracking

Our tracking method is based on the SURF [16] extraction algorithm, as its ability to describe the local properties of an object well fits with our goals. After the ROI R_P is selected in the previous step from the source video, we extract the SURF points

Fig. 3. Tracking process. Input object into R_P of the Previous Frame F_P, with superimposed points (a). Next frame F_N with superimposed matching points (b). Image matching (c). The new ROI R_N (d).

from the whole starting frame F_P, where the object to be cloned is. We use R_P to filter all the SURF points of the selected object. These, and only these, points are matched to all the points of the next frame F_N, by using the related SURF descriptors. We then select only the matching points, which all probably belong to the input object, and try to estimate the geometrical transformation T between the points into R_P, and the matching points in F_N, using the RANSAC [17] algorithm (which furthermore filters out the outliers). If enough points match, and T has been estimated, we apply it to the R_P vertices, obtaining a new ROI from the next frame R_N. In the next step of the tracking algorithm, R_N turn into the new R_P, and the F_N into F_P, and the whole process is repeated until the object quits the scene, or if it is heavily occluded by some other objects in the scene, or if the maximum number of frames is reached.

Note that we could have choosen the SIFT [18] algorithm, instead of the SURF one, as it has been widely shown that it is more robust to the geometrical transformations. We decided to use SURF for two reasons. First, SURF is less computational expensive than SIFT, and the execution time is strongly reduced. Second, when considering an object into two consecutive frames, there are very small differences in terms of its geometrical aspect. In this case, the matching process between SURF points is very robust against the distortion introduced by the object movement.

Fig. 4. Handling the trajectory of the copied object in different ways. Copied object without transformation (a). Object rotated by 50° counterclockwise (b). Object position after 10 frames, if the original trajectory is kept (c). Object position after 10 frames, if the rotation is applied also to its trajectory (d).

3.3   Transformation

In the simplest case, the selected object is pasted into the destination frame as it is. Optionally, users may apply some transformations to the selected object, to adapt the cloning to the destination scene or to create more complex forgeries.

Two different types of transformations may be applied: Geometrical; Luminance and Chrominance. Regarding the geometrical transformation we considered the full transformation matrix:

$$M = \begin{bmatrix} S_x * cos\theta + S_x * H_y * sin\theta & S_x * H_y * cos\theta - S_x * sin\theta & 0 \\ S_y * sin\theta + S_y * H_x * cos\theta & -S_y * H_x * sin\theta + S_y * cos\theta & 0 \\ 0 & 0 & 1 \end{bmatrix} \quad (1)$$

where S_x and S_y are the scaling factors, H_x and H_y the shearing factors and θ is the rotation angle w.r.t. the image plane. Note that setting S_x and/or S_y as negative values, the transformed object is flipped horizontally, vertically or both sides.

When applying a transformation, it is possible to select to modify also to the object trajectory. Two options can be selected in this step: applying the transformation only to the object, which will follow the original trajectory; modify also the trajectory of the object. In this second case, we further apply a translation matrix to the transformed image. The translation values are computed as the displacement between the

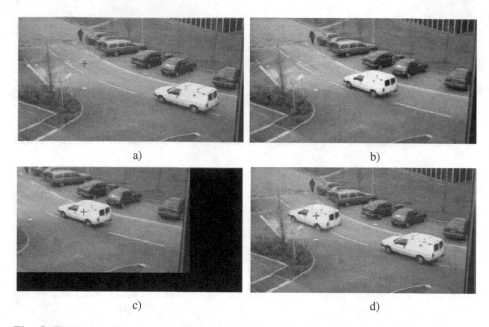

Fig. 5. The registration process. Destination Frame with superimposed destination point (a). Source frame (b). Source frame, translated according to the offset (c). Merged frame (d)

Fig. 6. The Blending phase. The two images to blend, filtered by the ROI masks (a,b). The resulting image, without (c) and with (d) blending.

centroid of the original ROI cloned into the destination point without any transformations, and the centroid of the ROI, after the applied transformation. Note that the displacement between the original trajectory and the transformed one accumulates during each step of the cloning process.

The Luminance and Chrominance changes are allowed simply by adding values to each RGB channel. Tuning these values it is possible to change the luminance or the color of the selected object, e.g. to adapt it to the scene brightness or color tone of the destination frame.

3.4 Blending

The first part of the blending module is a registration phase. We compute the offset between the two images to be merged as the displacement between the user selected destination point and the centroid of the actual ROI, and we apply the related translation to the source image, in order to be ready for the blending phase (see fig. 5). We also register, as well, the input ROI, in order to mark out the pixels of the two images for the next blending phase.

To achieve the most natural results, the two images, after the registration step, have to be merged as best as possible (fig. 6). It is desirable that the selected object contours will be harmonized with the background of the destination frame, to avoid evident and annoying artefacts. For this goal we used the technique proposed by Hsu and Wu [19], which is based on the Laplacian Pyramid decomposition. The quality of the results depends on the number of chosen decomposition levels, above all if the brightness of the source and the destination frame are very different. On the other hand, the higher the number of levels, the higher is the execution time. Then we select, as a good tradeoff between efficiency and quality of the results, a number of levels equal to 6.

4 Experiments

The goal of this work is to create a tool to support users in cloning objects in digital videos. It is very difficult to give an objective evaluation to the results of a cloning method, as no proper metrics can be used in this case. On the other hand, using a subjective criterion to evaluate the results may be meaningless, as the quality of the output videos strongly depends on the user ability: selecting the most accurate ROI; choosing a good destination zone into which copy the cloned object, in order to make it less detectable; selecting the best transformation to adapt the object aspect to the destination scene. A subjective evaluation of the results would be an evaluation of the user cloning ability, rather than our method's potential.

Then, in this section we present our own dataset of tampered videos, which we created with the proposed tool, and which is available on demand to test video forgery detection techniques. Furthermore we will also discuss how to use our tool to obtain the best results, in terms of undetectability, to the naked eye, of the cloned areas.

Table 1. Input Video Features

VIDEO	N° Frames	Frame rate	Duration	rows	Columns
v1	172	25	6,88 s	360	640
v2	334	25	13,36 s	576	768
v3	98	25	3,92 s	540	960
v4	259	30	10,36 s	540	960
v5	554	30	18,47 s	240	320
v6	104	25	4,16 s	576	768

Table 2. The number of videos in our dataset, for each applied transformation.

Transformation	v1	v2	v3	v4	v5	v6
None	5	5	5	5	5	5
Scaling	3	2	2	2	1	5
Shearing	2	2	1	1	2	2
Rotation	2	2	1	2	5	10
Flipping	2	3	1	1	3	5
Luminance	4	4	3	1	4	4
RGB	3	3	2	2	3	5
Combination	5	5	5	5	5	5

4.1 Dataset

We created our dataset from six different videos harvested by SULFA[20] and CANTATA[21] video datasets. All the videos represent scenes of traffic control, or parking surveillance. Five of the six videos are acquired with fixed cameras, while the last one is a scene of a camera following a car along a road. Note that our implemented tracking method works, as well, with fixed and not fixed cameras, as it focuses only onto the object features, regardless of the background. We prefer to use fixed camera videos just as in these scenes the movements of the objects are more evident and, as well, cloned objects are more interesting. Tab.1 shows the principal features of the chosen reference videos. Starting from these dataset of videos, we created 160 tampered videos, with different types of cloning, as shown in table 2. Within this dataset, the average duration of a cloned slot into a destination video is of 30 frames.

Regarding the efficiency, using a Windows 7 (64 bit) machine with an Intel Core i5 2.4 GHz processor, and 4 GB RAM, the execution time is about 1,7 seconds per cloned frame then, on average, less than 1 minute for the whole process. Most of the time (65% ca) is spent in the blending phase, which is nevertheless needed to achieve good quality results.

In our dataset we created both videos with invisible and visible, to the naked eye, cloned objects, as we are interested in building a dataset with a lot of possible transformations, rather than perfect cloning results. However, on the basis of our experiments, in the next subsection we will present some suggestions to obtain forgeries that will be difficult to be detected to the naked eye.

This dataset is available at [22] (or by contacting the authors by email) to researchers who want to test their forgery detection techniques.

4.2   Remarks

In this section we present some suggestions, based on our experimental tests, to create an "invisible" cloned object:

- First of all, choosing an object full of **details**. In this case, the selected object will have a lot of interest points and the tracking method will perform better. Of course, if a homogenous area is selected, our method fails, as no SURF points can be extracted and no tracking can be performed, not even with other algorithms.
- The **object trajectory** has to be as much rigid as possible. In fact when the object changes its trajectory in a non rigid way (e.g. a car along a road with turns right or left), the number of matching points between two consecutive frames decreases (see section 3.2), the estimated transformation between the object in the two frames is less accurate, and so the relative transformed mask. Therefore the tracked object may be deformed or may have lacking portions, even if correctly tracked. The same problem occurs when the tracked object starts exiting the scene, as a lower number of interest points are extracted.
- An accurate **ROI selection** is very important. When creating the mask to select the object to be copied, the ROI polygon must be as close as possible to the object edges, to discard background information which will influence the blending phase. On the other hand, if the ROI is too close to the object boundaries, some of the interest points of the object could be not included in the mask, resulting a lower performance of the tracking algorithm.
- Selecting a good **destination point**. If the area into which we want to copy the desired object is too full of details, when pasting the object, also after the blending step, the difference between the source and the destination areas will be very evident, and the cloning more easily detectable. On the other hand, pasting the select object onto homogenous areas will create more visually convincing results.
- As well, above all in case of inter-video forgeries, the source and the destination areas should have similar **luminance** values, otherwise, in spite of the blending phase, the cloned area will be evident. Alternatively, the luminance difference may be corrected by using the luminance transformation function.

- A cloned moving object must be **consistent** to the other objects into the scene. For example, if we consider a scene with a lot of cars along a street and we decide to clone another car which crosses that street orthogonally, even if no cloning artefacts are revealed, any observer will be able to detect the forgery, as the object "behaviour" is highly suspicious.
- Respect the **perspective** rules. For example, if we apply a magnification to a cloned object and we put it backward with respect to the other objects in the scene, considering the camera position, it will be very evident that the object is a fake, as the size difference will reveal the forgery.

5   Conclusions

Digital Video Forensics can be considered still a new research field, even if digital watermarking techniques have been proposed for a long time to validate the authenticity of a video content. Nevertheless, active techniques, as well known, cannot be used in most of the real cases, then passive techniques are preferable for real applications. Regarding passive Video Forensics techniques, on the other hand, a lot of work has still to be done to solve the related problems, above all if we compare the actual results to those of the existing Image Forensics methods. It is then important for the researchers to have common and standard datasets to test their algorithm and compare their results with those of the same scientific community. With this work we aim to meet these needs and to give to the Multimedia researchers both a new tool to create their own testing videos, and a reference dataset to compare their results to those of the other researchers.

In our future works we plan to improve our tool to better support users, e.g. helping them to better select the desired object, suggesting to them the best areas into which pasting it into the destination frame, automatically adjusting brightness differences between the copied and destination areas, etc. We further plan to extend our dataset, including more videos and other different types of transformation. We are also working on a new forgery detection method that will be able to detect and localize the cloned areas of tampered videos.

Acknowledgements. The authors wish to acknowledge Mr. Giorgio Vaccaro for his collaboration during the implementation and the testing phases of this work.

References

1. Sencar, H.T., Memon, N.: Overview of State-Of-The-Art in Digital Image Forensics. Algorithms, Architectures and Information Systems Security **3**, 325–348 (2008)
2. Rocha, A., Scheirer, W., Boult, T., Goldenstein, S.: Vision of the Unseen: Current Trends and Challenges in Digital Image and Video Forensics. ACM Comput. Surv. **43**(4), 42 (2011). Article 26

3. Milani, S., Fontani, M., Bestagini, P., Barni, M., Piva, A., Tagliasacchi, M., Tubaro, S.: An Overview on Video Forensics. APSIPA Transactions on Signal and Information Processing 1, e2 (2012). (18 pages)
4. Lee, S.J., Jung, S.H.: A survey of watermarking techniques applied to multimedia. In: Proc. IEEE Int. Symp. Industrial Electronics, vol. 1, pp. 272–277 (2001)
5. Kobayashi, M., Okabe, T., Sato, Y.: Detecting video forgeries based on noise characteristics. In: Wada, T., Huang, F., Lin, S. (eds.) PSIVT 2009. LNCS, vol. 5414, pp. 306–317. Springer, Heidelberg (2009)
6. Liao, D.D., Yang, R., Liu, H.M., et al.: Double H.264/AVC compression detection using quantized nonzero AC coefficients. In: Conference on Media Watermarking, Security, and Forensics, San Francisco, CA, vol. 7880, Article number: 78800Q (2011)
7. Sun, T., Wang, W., Jiang, X.: Exposing video forgeries by detecting MPEG double compression. In: 2012 IEEE International Conference on Acoustics, Speech and Signal Processing (ICASSP), pp. 1389–1392. IEEE, March 2012
8. Wang, W., Farid, H.: Exposing digital forgeries in video by detecting duplication: In: Proc. Workshop on Multimedia & Security Int. Multimedia Conf., New York, NY, pp. 35–42 (2007)
9. Upadhyay, S., Singh, S.K.: Video Authentication: Issues and Challenges. International Journal of Computer Science Issues 9(1), 409–418 (2012). No. 3
10. Malekesmaeili, M., Fatourechi, M., Ward, R.K.: Video copy detection using temporally informative representative images. In: Proc. International Conference on Machine Learning and Applications (ICMLA 2009), pp. 69–74, December 13–15, 2009
11. Chao, J., Jiang, X., Sun, T.: A novel video inter-frame forgery model detection scheme based on optical flow consistency. In: Shi, Y.Q., Kim, H.-J., Pérez-González, F. (eds.) IWDW 2012. LNCS, vol. 7809, pp. 267–281. Springer, Heidelberg (2013)
12. Ardizzone, E., Mazzola, G.: Detection of duplicated regions in tampered digital images by bit-plane analysis. In: Foggia, P., Sansone, C., Vento, M. (eds.) ICIAP 2009. LNCS, vol. 5716, pp. 893–901. Springer, Heidelberg (2009)
13. Ardizzone, E., Bruno, A., Mazzola, G.: Copy-move forgery detection via texture description. In: Proceedings of the 2nd ACM workshop on Multimedia in Forensics, Security and Intelligence (MiFor 2010), pp. 59–64
14. Ardizzone, E., Bruno, A., Mazzola, G.: Detecting multiple copies in tampered images. In: International Conference on Image Processing, pp. 2117–2120 (2010)
15. Ardizzone, E., Bruno, A., Mazzola, G.: Copy-move forgery detection by matching triangles of keypoints. IEEE Transactions on Information Forensics and Security (2015, in press)
16. Bay, H., Tuytelaars, T., Van Gool, L.: SURF: speeded up robust features. In: Leonardis, A., Bischof, H., Pinz, A. (eds.) ECCV 2006, Part I. LNCS, vol. 3951, pp. 404–417. Springer, Heidelberg (2006)
17. Fischler, M.A., Bolles, R.C.: Random Sample Consensus: A Paradigm for Model Fitting with Applications to Image Analysis and Automated Cartography. Comunications of the ACM 24(6), 381–395 (1981)
18. Lowe, D.G.: Distinctive Image Features from Scale-Invariant Keypoints. International Journal of Computer Vision 60(2), 91–110 (2004)
19. Hsu, C.T., Wu, J.L.: Multiresolution Mosaic. IEEE Transactions on Consumer Electronics 42(4), 981–990 (1996)
20. http://sulfa.cs.surrey.ac.uk/index.php
21. http://www.multitel.be/cantata/
22. http://www.dicgim.unipa.it/cvip/

Cognition Helps Vision: Recognizing Biological Motion Using Invariant Dynamic Cues

Nicoletta Noceti[1]([✉]), Alessandra Sciutti[2], and Giulio Sandini[2]

[1] DIBRIS, Università di Genova, Genova, Italy
nicoletta.noceti@unige.it
[2] RBCS, Istituto Italiano di Tecnologia, Genova, Italy
{alessandra.sciutti,giulio.sandini}@iit.it

Abstract. This paper considers the problem of designing computational models of the primitives that are at the basis of the visual perception of motion in humans. The main contribution of this work is to establish a connection between cognitive science observations and empirical computational modeling. We take inspiration from the very first stage of the human development, and address the problem of understanding the presence of biological motion in the scene. To this end, we investigate the use of coarse motion descriptors composed by low-level features inspired by the Two-Thirds Power Law. In the experimental analysis, we first discuss the validity of the Two-Thirds Power Law in the context of video analysis, where, to the best of our knowledge, it has not found application so far. Second, we show a preliminary investigation on the use of a very simple motion model for characterizing biological motion with respect to non-biological dynamic events.

1 Introduction

The interactions with other people or with the surrounding environment are easy and natural tasks for human beings, triggered by an innate predisposition. Nevertheless, it is well accepted in the cognitive science community that a mature social awareness is subject to the acquisition of a sequence of temporally-ordered perceptual and social skills, going from the detection of target of potential interest [10], to the capability of inferring the intentions of other people and the goals of their actions [8].

This work considers the development of visual perception capabilities in humans, and tries to establish a connection between the observations coming from the cognitive science world and the computational modeling side. The long-term goal of our research is the design of computational vision models able to replicate on an artificial system the developmental stages of motion perception in humans. This is of particular interest, for instance, in the robotics field, where the design of methods for a natural human-robot interaction is one of the great challenges of the research nowadays.

In this paper we specifically refer to the earliest stages of human development, and consider in particular the capability of understanding the presence

© Springer International Publishing Switzerland 2015
V. Murino and E. Puppo (Eds.): ICIAP 2015, Part II, LNCS 9280, pp. 676–686, 2015.
DOI: 10.1007/978-3-319-23234-8_62

of biological motion in the surrounding environment, a skill humans, and not only, exhibit early after birth [20]. This ability triggers the development of social interaction, since it allows the detection of potential interaction partners in the scene.

We consider a binary classification setting in which characterizing biological movements with respect to non-biological dynamic events. As for the first class, we are particularly interested in sequences of human actions typical of interactions, as repositioning objects or pointing towards a certain 3D location.

Given a video stream, we initially detect the regions where the motion is occurring using the optical flow, then we extract a set of low-level features inspired by the *Two-Thirds Power Law*, which has been experimentally proved to be an invariant property of biological motion, and human movements in particular [18,23,24,26]. We adopt a coarse motion representation leveraging on the fact that if humans show a predisposition for biological motion right after birth, when the amount of visual information is still very limited, then *it is likely* that it may depend on very simple motion information.

We consider two different levels of compression of such information over time – computing a point-based and a region-based descriptor – and evaluate their use with binary SVMs classifiers equipped with appropriate Multi-Cue kernels [21].

Related Works. Since we are primarily interested in capturing abilities typical of the early months of human development, we do not address classical action recognition tasks (very fertile disciplines in fields as video surveillance, video retrieval and robotics [4,16,28]), abilities which are likely to be gained at later stages of development, also thanks to the infants' prior motor experience [3]. Within this contexts, an approach sharing similarities with our work is [19] where the authors consider the problem of biological motion classification using joints trajectories. However, they refer to the characterization of a single class of human motion (walking) with respect to others (as boxing or jumping).

Instead, works on human perception of biological motion can be traditionally found in the field of cognitive science, where particular interest has been posed on the relative importance of visual features that are (presumably) at the basis of this strong ability [1,7,22]. In most of such works *point-light displays* or motion caption systems are adopted.

The Two-Thirds Power Law has been related to the motion perception of humans [6,24,26], and it is considered a well-known invariant property of human movements [12,18,25]. Its applicability has been empirically verified mostly for upper-limb movements, but also for eye motion [27], locomotion [23], and to the purpose of movement prediction [9]. The relation between motion and the quantities involved in the law has been also deeply analysed [12,25]. In [13] the authors show that white Gaussian noise also obeys this power-law.

To the best of our knowledge, this is the first attempt of applying the Two-Thirds Power Law in the context of video analysis, on data measured from video stream and thus, by construction, less controlled. Also, with respect to previous works, we consider a broader range of possible human movements.

The remainder of the paper is organized as follows. In Sec. 2 we briefly review the theory of the Two-Thirds Power Law, which is used as an inspiration to introduce the low-level features we consider, in Sec. 3. Sec. 4 describes the motion representation we adopt and sets the scene for the learning problem. We report the experimental analysis in Sec. 5 and we leave the final discussion to Sec. 6.

2   The Two-Thirds Power Law

Each dynamic physical event can be easily described by its spatial trajectory – which defines the *shape* of the motion – as well as many other quantities – as the evolution of length, velocity or direction. All of them represent evidences of the dynamics, and are in general interconnected with each other.

For the specific case of human motion, it is acknowledged the validity of an exponential relation between functions measured from the motion [6,23,26]. The relation can be formulated as

$$V(t) = K(t) \left(\frac{R(t)}{1 + \alpha(t)R(t)} \right)^{\beta} \tag{1}$$

where $V(t)$ is the tangential velocity, $R(t)$ is the radius of curvature, $\alpha(t) \geq 0$ depends on the average motion velocity (and is null in absence of points of inflection in the trajectory), $K(t) \geq 0$, depends on tempo and length of the motion [25]. In case $\alpha(t) = 0$ the law can be written in the alternative, yet equivalent, form

$$A(t) = K(t)C(t)^{1-\beta} \tag{2}$$

where $A(t) = \frac{V(t)}{R(t)}$ and $C(t) = \frac{1}{R(t)}$. In adults, the value of β (estimated most often for drawing movements) is very close to $\frac{1}{3}$, and so the law in Eq. 2 is usually referred to as *Two-Thirds Power Law*.

Although this relation has been deeply investigated in the fields of human motion perception analysis and cognitive science, the application in the context of artificial intelligence and computer vision is still unexplored. In the following, thus, we consider the use of a motion descriptor guided by the law and discuss its adoption in a video analysis setting.

3   From the Law to the Features

Inspired by the Two-Thirds Power Law, our idea is to describe an observed motion with a vector of low-level spatio-temporal features, computational counterparts of the variables involved in the mathematical formulation.

At each time instant t, we start by evaluating the optical flow with a dense approach (as [5]) and detecting the regions of interest $\mathcal{R}(t)$ – i.e. the regions where the motion is occurring – with a hysteresis thresholding on the magnitude. Notice that, in general, at each time instant we may detect more than one

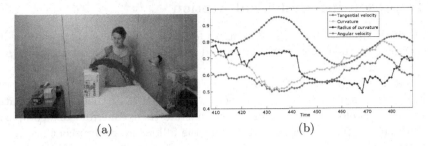

(a)   (b)

Fig. 1. Left: an example of the trajectory of a point describing the dynamic of a sequence of lifting actions. Right: the temporal series of the low-level features we computed on a sub-part of the sequence.

region. They can correspond to different portions of a single common event (e.g. when gesticulating with both hands), or they may indicate the co-occurrence of multiple events.

We then associate each point $\mathbf{p}_i(t) \in \mathcal{R}(t)$ with a feature vector

$$\mathcal{F}(\mathbf{p}_i(t)) = [\hat{V}_i(t), \hat{C}_i(t), \hat{R}_i(t), \hat{A}_i(t)] \qquad (3)$$

where the features denote, respectively, tangential velocity, curvature, radius of curvature and angular velocity estimated for the point as follows. Let $(u_i(t), v_i(t))$ be the optical flow components. We define the spatio-temporal velocity of the point as $\hat{\mathbf{V}}(t) = (u_i(t), v_i(t), \Delta_t)$, where Δ_t is the temporal displacement between observations of two adjacent time instants. The velocity magnitude is computed as $\hat{V}(t) = \sqrt{u_i(t)^2 + v_i(t)^2 + \Delta_t^2}$. The spatio-temporal acceleration can be derived as the derivative of the velocity: $\hat{\mathbf{A}}_i(t) = (u_i(t) - u_i(t-1), v_i(t) - v_i(t-1), 0)$.
The curvature, following [15,17], is computed as

$$\hat{C}_i(t) = \frac{\|\hat{\mathbf{V}}_i(t) \times \hat{\mathbf{A}}_i(t)\|}{\|\hat{\mathbf{V}}_i(t)\|^3}. \qquad (4)$$

The remaining two quantities are derived as $\hat{R}_i(t) = \frac{1}{\hat{C}_i(t)}$ and $\hat{A}_i(t) = \frac{\hat{V}_i(t)}{\hat{R}_i(t)}$. Fig. 1 shows an example of the computed quantities for repetitive lifting actions. For the sake of clarity we focus on the trajectory of a single point (the centroid of the region, see Fig. 1(a)). In Fig. 1(b) the trend of the tangential velocity shows the presence of the well-known bell shape, typical of biological motion [14]. Notice the uneven level of noise in the features estimation: the velocity magnitude, directly measured from the optical flow, is the smoothest, while the other quantities, derived with further approximations, show a lower regularity.

4   Representing Biological Motion

Now that we have defined the low-level features, we may set up a procedure to describe and then classify the observed motion as instance of a biological or non-biological event.

At each time instant, we consider a regular grid of points for each region of interest segmented according to Sec. 3. With each of them we associate a feature vector following Eq. 3, and then combine their contributions comparing two different simple strategies, detailed in the following, reminiscent of possible coarse approaches to average the visual motion information.

4.1   Centroid-Based Descriptor

We first consider a coarse description obtained collapsing the whole information within a region $\mathcal{R}(t)$ in a single vector, i.e. the centroid, henceforth denoted (with an abuse of notation with respect to the previous use) as $\bar{\mathcal{F}}(\mathcal{R}(t)) = \bar{\mathcal{F}}$. Similarly to the original feature vectors, the centroid is a vector of heterogeneous features, that when compared should be appropriately handled. A way to deal with it is to normalize the data to a common range. A better alternative is to adopt a convex combination of kernel-based similarity functions, often referred to as Multi-Cue Integration in the supervised learning literature [21], and successfully applied to the problem of dynamic events modeling [16]. Let $\mathcal{R}$ and $\mathcal{R}'$ be two regions represented with their centroids $\bar{\mathcal{F}} = (\bar{V}, \bar{C}, \bar{R}, \bar{A})$ and $\bar{\mathcal{F}}' = (\bar{V}', \bar{C}', \bar{R}', \bar{A}')$. The Multi-Cue kernel $K_{MC} : \mathbb{R}^4 \times \mathbb{R}^4 \to \mathbb{R}$ can be computed as the weighted sum of kernel-based functions $K : \mathbb{R} \times \mathbb{R} \to \mathbb{R}$ on each feature:

$$K_{MC}(\bar{\mathcal{F}}, \bar{\mathcal{F}}') = w_v K(\bar{V}, \bar{V}') + w_c K(\bar{C}, \bar{C}') + \\ w_r K(\bar{R}, \bar{R}') + w_a K(\bar{A}, \bar{A}') \tag{5}$$

where the w's sum up to 1.

4.2   Histogram-Based Descriptor

We also consider a representation based on computing a histogram for each single feature, collecting the contributions of all points from a region. To this purpose, we first normalize each feature set so that all values are in the $[0 \ldots 1]$ range, then populate the 4 histograms and finally concatenate them to collect the final region descriptor. Henceforth, we will refer to the global region histogram as $\mathcal{H}(\mathcal{R}) = [\mathcal{H}_V \mathcal{H}_C \mathcal{H}_R \mathcal{H}_A]$.

Similarly to Sec. 4.1 we can treat each feature histogram independently, fusing their similarities in a single value while associating with them different weights. More formally, given two histograms $\mathcal{H}(\mathcal{R}) = \mathcal{H}$ and $\mathcal{H}(\mathcal{R}') = \mathcal{H}'$, a Multi-Cue kernel $K_{MC}^{\mathcal{H}} : \mathbb{R}^M \times \mathbb{R}^M \to \mathbb{R}$, with M the total number of bin of the composed histogram, can be defined as

$$K_{MC}^{\mathcal{H}}(\mathcal{H}, \mathcal{H}') = w_v K^{\mathcal{H}}(\mathcal{H}_V, \mathcal{H}_V') + w_c K^{\mathcal{H}}(\mathcal{H}_C, \mathcal{H}_C') \\ w_r K^{\mathcal{H}}(\mathcal{H}_R, \mathcal{H}_R') + w_a K^{\mathcal{H}}(\mathcal{H}_A, \mathcal{H}_A') \tag{6}$$

where $K^{\mathcal{H}} : \mathbb{R}^{\frac{M}{4}} \times \mathbb{R}^{\frac{M}{4}} \to \mathbb{R}$ is an appropriate measure to compare histograms.

5   Experimental Analysis

In this section we report the experimental analysis we conducted on a dataset acquired in-house. We structured the experimental analysis in two parts. On the first, we aim at validating the Two-Thirds Power Law in our setting, while evaluating the relative importance of each low-level feature we consider. On the second part, we focus instead on the biological motion classification problem, comparing the performances of the two descriptors introduced in Sec. 4 in combination with different kernels adopted in combination with SVM classifiers.

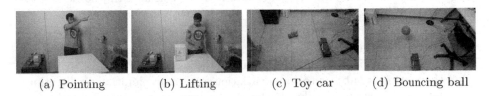

(a) Pointing   (b) Lifting   (c) Toy car   (d) Bouncing ball

Fig. 2. Samples from the acquisitions of a subject from a single viewpoint (Fig. 2(a) and 2(b)), and of non biological motion events (Fig. 2(c) and 2(d)).

5.1   Data Set

We acquired indoor videos of two subjects observed from two slightly different viewpoints, performing repetitions of given actions from a *repertoire* of dynamic movements typical of an interaction setting, the one we have in mind. More in details, we consider *Gesticulating* while talking, *Pointing* a finger towards a certain 3D location (see Fig. 2(a)); *Waving* the hand from left to right and vice-versa; *Lifting* and object from the table to place it on a box (Fig. 2(b)); *Throwing* an object away; *Transporting* an object from and to different positions on the table. The latter is instantiated in two versions, with left-right and random object repositioning. Each video consists of 20 repetitions of the same atomic action (e.g. move the object from left to right); for each subject we acquired two videos in each view for each action, ending up with more than $20K$ frames.

As for the non-biological counterpart, we consider videos of a toy car (Fig. 2(c)), bouncing and rolling balls (Fig. 2(d)), a pendulum and a lever, for a total of about $10K$ data.

We split the set of videos in training set – used for model estimation – and test set – only adopted for performance evaluation. Model selection is based on K-fold cross validation with a grid search over the ranges of the parameters.

5.2   Proof of Concepts

On the Validity of the Two-Thirds Power Law. To assess the validity of the Two-Thirds Power Law for video analysis, we represent, for the sake of simplicity, the motion as a trajectory $\{\bar{\mathcal{F}}_t\}_{t=1}^{T}$ of centroids described according to Sec. 4.1. To correctly apply the law, we analyse the temporal sequences of their

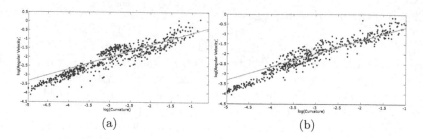

(a)   (b)

Fig. 3. Velocity *versus* curvature (log-log) measured on segments of trajectories describing sequences of lifting action performed by two different subjects.

velocity values, and then segment the trajectories in sub-parts considering portions between a maximum and a minimum in the sequence (dynamic instants in which the motion is subject to some variation, e.g. in acceleration or direction).

Following the seminal works [11,26], we analyse average velocity and curvature in each segments and show the obtained point in a log-log reference system. Fig. 3 reports two plots in which we collect observations from lifting actions performed by the two subjects in our dataset. They show a high correlation with the reference slope (i.e. $\frac{2}{3}$) in green.

We then fit each segment with an exponential function and estimate the exponents for both the biological and non-biological events. More in details, the average exponent for the biological population on the first view amounts to 0.65, and becomes 0.63 on the second view. A *two-sample t-test* confirms the high separation between average exponents for biological and non biological distributions (P-value < 0.0001).

On the Importance of the Features. In this section we investigate the relative importance of our motion features to characterize biological motion, despite their redundancy. To this purpose we consider a simple K-NN binary classifier and evaluate its accuracy for different feature vectors configurations – corresponding to using one or more features – and as the value of K increases. Since here we focus on the importance of each single feature of the vector, we adopt the centroid-based descriptor. To nullify the contribution of a feature we simply set to zero its weight in Eq. 5. From the results in Fig. 4(a) it is apparent the tangential velocity is the most relevant feature. The performances further increase when it is used in combination with other measures (see e.g. Fig. 4(b) and 4(c)).

A pros of the Multi-Cue Kernel is the fact that prior knowledge on the feature importance can be easily included in the model by appropriately tuning the weights. However, not always such information is available. An alternative is to learn the most appropriate weights from the data. We reported in Fig. 4(d) the weights selected as the best performing for increasing K values. There is a first range of Ks (from 1 to around 40) in which all the features are assigned an average importance, while for higher numbers of neighbors the curvature seems to be more relevant, but always if used in combination with some other information.

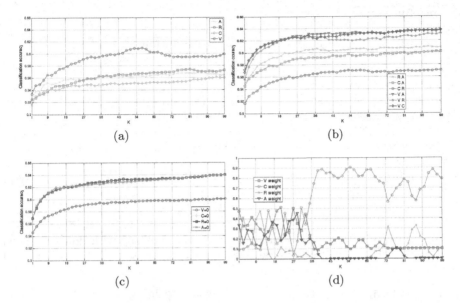

Fig. 4. An analysis of the relative importance of each feature.

To summarize, there is an empirical evidence of the relevance of all such features to the purpose of biological motion characterization. Since their *relative* importance may change depending on the specific category of human actions under analysis, the best option is to design an appropriate description by learning their importance (i.e. their weights) from the data. Nevertheless, the observation that all of them concur to best characterize our problem may be interpreted as a further evidence of the validity of the Two-Thirds Power Law: although relevant per-se, it is not the single feature that makes the difference, but its co-presence with the other measures, which are related to it by the law.

5.3 Experiments on Classification

We now focus more specifically on the problem of binary classification between biological and non-biological observations. To this end, we analyse the use of the two descriptors of Sec. 4 in combination with SVM classifiers.

Centroid-Based SVMs. We compare in the table of Fig. 5(a) the use of our instantaneous centroid-based description with different kernel functions, considering the mean accuracy computed on 5 different sampling of the input data set. As for the Multi-Cue similarities, we compare the case in which all the features are equally weighted with the values selected as best performing for some value of K using a K-NN on the training set (see previous section). The best performance is achieved with a Multi-Cue similarity function. We further test the ability of such kernel functions in classifying test data observed from the second

Kernel function	Acc.
Linear	56.66
Poly, $d = 2$	57.26
Poly, $d = 3$	56.90
Poly, $d = 4$	57.11
Radial basis, $\gamma = 0.1$	57.48
Sigmoid, $\gamma = 0.1$	55.01
(*) Multi-cue gaussian	65.42
$\mathbf{w} = [0.25\ 0.25\ 0.25\ 0.25]$	
(**) Multi-cue gaussian	66.17
$\mathbf{w} = [0.5\ 0.2\ 0.2\ 0.1]$	
(***) Multi-cue gaussian	64.41
$\mathbf{w} = [0.1\ 0.7\ 0.1\ 0.1]$	

(a)

Kernel function	Acc.
Linear	75.41
Histogram Inters.	75.69
Multi-Cue + Linear	76.37
$\mathbf{w} = [0.5\ 0.2\ 0.2\ 0.1]$	
Multi-Cue + Hist. Inters.	73.84
$\mathbf{w} = [0.5\ 0.2\ 0.2\ 0.1]$	
Multi-Cue + Gauss.	76.15
$\mathbf{w} = [0.1\ 0.7\ 0.1\ 0.1]$	

(b)

Fig. 5. Classification accuracy obtained with SVMs combined with different kernel methods. Left: using the centroid-based description. Right: using the histogram-based description.

viewpoint, obtaining 64.55 ± 1.54 for (*), 63.49 ± 2.46 for (**) and 64.3 ± 1.25 for case (***). Interestingly, the model is tolerant to viewpoint variation.

Furthermore, we may take into explicit account the temporal component by considering as input data series of temporally adjacent centroids. This requires and adaptation of the Multi-Cue function. Let $\mathcal{T} = [\bar{\mathcal{F}}_1 \ldots \bar{\mathcal{F}}_T]$ and $\mathcal{T}' = [\bar{\mathcal{F}}'_1 \ldots \bar{\mathcal{F}}'_T]$ be two sequences of centroids, then their Multi-Cue similarity is defined as

$$K_{MC}^{time}(\mathcal{T}, \mathcal{T}') = \sum_{t=1}^{T} K_{MC}(\bar{\mathcal{F}}_t, \bar{\mathcal{F}}'_t) \tag{7}$$

We consider as weights the best performing combination from the analysis of the single centroid (the one marked with (**)). We achieved the highest performace for $T = 20$, with accuracy 71.72 ± 1.45 on test data from view 1, and 65.49 ± 1.03 on test data from view 2 (training data are in both cases from view 1).

Histogram-Based SVMs. We conducted a similar analysis on the histogram-based descriptor, obtaining the performances reported on the table of Fig. 5(b). A first observation refers to the fact that the classification of instantaneous histograms outperforms the classification of centroids, even when they are supported by the temporal analysis. Also, the use of Multi-Cue kernel functions has a lower impact here, where the linear kernel is confirmed to be an appropriate choice, similarly to what happens in other classification problems built on top of histograms-like representations (see e.g. [2]). Even from a computational standpoint, the use of a linear kernel guarantees a high efficiency. The capability of handling a variation of the viewpoint is confirmed here, since the accuracy of classifying samples from view 2 using models trained on view 1 remains rather stable (76.02).

Extending the analysis to include temporal sequences of histograms (thus adapting the kernel, similarly to what done in Eq. 7) we obtain an accuracy of 89.03, which remains almost the same for view 2.

6   Final Discussion

In this paper we investigated the design of computational models of the primitives that are at the basis of the visual perception of motion in humans. Our inspiration roots on the very first stage of the human development, where the limited amount of visual information suggests that human beings have the capability of accomplishing certain perceptual tasks on the basis of rather coarse motion models. We took inspiration from the Two-Thirds Power Law, validating its applicability to video analysis problems. Moreover, we showed that a simple vector of low-level motion features, appropriately organized and handled in a learning framework, allows us to characterize biological motion against dynamic events due to non biological phenomena.

Our current investigations are devoted to the design of a hierarchical framework to replicate the developmental stages of human motion perception. On this respect, the capability of recognizing biological motion can be interpreted as the very first stage of such a system, to the purpose of localizing the possible target of interest before being able to interact with it.

A second stage in the refinement of human perception is the capability of understanding classes of actions, to focus on the important properties depending on the action. So, for manipulation actions, the relevant information may reside on the object. Alternatively, one may be interested on the environment, in presence of actions producing some kind of alteration on it. A preliminary investigation in this direction may be found in [15]. The aforementioned tasks set the scene for a more complete social awareness, that allows a subject to decode an action with respect to the final goal and the user intentions. For this task, more refined perception skills – and thus computational models – are required.

Acknowledgments. This research has been conducted in the framework of the European Project CODEFROR (FP7-PIRSES-2013-612555).

References

1. Casile, A., Giese, M.: Critical features for the recognition of biological motion. Jour. of Vision **5**, 348–360 (2005)
2. Dalal, N., Triggs, B.: Histograms of oriented gradients for human detection. In: CVPR, vol. 2, pp. 886–893 (2005)
3. Falck-Ytter, T., Gredeback, G., von Hofsten, C.: Infants predict other people's action goals. Nature Neuroscience **9**(7), 878–879 (2006)
4. Fanello, S.R., Gori, I., Metta, G., Odone, F.: Keep it simple and sparse: Real-time action recognition. JMLR **14**(1), 2617–2640 (2013)
5. Farnebäck, G.: Two-frame motion estimation based on polynomial expansion. In: Bigun, J., Gustavsson, T. (eds.) SCIA 2003. LNCS, vol. 2749, pp. 363–370. Springer, Heidelberg (2003)
6. Flach, R., Knoblich, G., Prinz, W.: The two-thirds power law in motion perception. Visual Cognition **11**(4), 461–481 (2004)

7. Hogan, N., Sternad, D.: On rhythmic and discrete movements: reflections, definitions and implications for motor control. Exp. Brain Res. **181**(1), 13–30 (2007)
8. Kanakogi, Y., Itakura, S.: Developmental correspondence between action prediction and motor ability in early infancy. Nat. Commun. **2**, 341 (2011)
9. Kandel, S., Orliaguet, J.P., Viviani, P.: Perceptual anticipation in handwriting: The role of implicit motor competence. Perc. and Psych. **62**(4), 706–716 (2000)
10. Kaplan, F., Hafner, V.: The challenges of joint attention. In: Int. Work. on Epigenetic Robotics (2006)
11. Lacquaniti, F., Terzuolo, C.: The law relating the kinematic and figural aspects of drawing movements. Acta Psychologica **54**, 115–130 (1983)
12. Lacquaniti, F., Terzuolo, C., Viviani, P.: The law relating the kinematic and figural aspects of drawing movements. Acta Psychologica **54**(13), 115–130 (1983)
13. Maoz, U., Portugaly, E., Flash, T., Weiss, Y.: Noise and the two-thirds power law. In: NIPS (2005)
14. Morasso, P.: Spatial control of arm movements. Experimental Brain Research **42**(2), 223–227 (1981)
15. Noceti, N., Sciutti, A., Rea, F., Odone, F., Sandini, G.: Estimating human actions affinities across views. In: VISAPP (2015)
16. Noceti, N., Odone, F.: Learning common behaviors from large sets of unlabeled temporal series. Image Vision Comput. **30**(11), 875–895 (2012)
17. Rao, C., Yilmaz, A., Shah, M.: View-invariant representation and recognition of actions. IJCV **50**(2), 203–226 (2002)
18. Richardson, M., Flash, T.: Comparing smooth arm movements with the two-thirds power law and the related segmented-control hypothesis. Jour. of Neuroscience **22**(18), 8201–8211 (2002)
19. Sigala, R., Serre, T., Poggio, T.A., Giese, M.A.: Learning features of intermediate complexity for the recognition of biological motion. In: Duch, W., Kacprzyk, J., Oja, E., Zadrożny, S. (eds.) ICANN 2005. LNCS, vol. 3696, pp. 241–246. Springer, Heidelberg (2005)
20. Simion, F., Regolin, L., Bulf, H.: A predisposition for biological motion in the newborn baby. Proc. of the National Academy of Sciences **105**(2), 809–813 (2008)
21. Tommasi, T., Orabona, F., Caputo, B.: Discriminative cue integration for medical image annotation. PR Letters **29**(15) (2008)
22. Troje, N.F., Westhoff, C.: The inversion effect in biological motion perception: Evidence for a life detector? Current Biology **16**(8), 821–824 (2006)
23. Vieilledent, S., Kerlirzin, Y., Dalbera, S., Berthoz, A.: Relationship between velocity and curvature of a human locomotor trajectory. Neuroscience Letters **305**(1), 65–69 (2001)
24. Viviani, P., Baud-Bovy, G., Redolfi, M.: Perceiving and tracking kinesthetic stimuli: further evidence of motor-perceptual interactions. J. Exp. Psychol. Hum. Percept. Perform. **23**(4), 1232–1252 (1997)
25. Viviani, P., McCollum, G.: The relation between linear extent and velocity in drawing movements. Neuroscience **10**(1), 211–218 (1983)
26. Viviani, P., Stucchi, N.: Biological movements look uniform: evidence of motor-perceptual interactions. J. Exp. Psych. Hum. Perc. Perf. **18**(3), 603–623 (1992)
27. Viviani, P.: The relationship between curvature and velocity in two-dimensional smooth pursuit eye movements. Jour. of Neuroscience, 3932–3945 (1997)
28. Wang, X., Ma, X., Grimson, W.: Unsupervised activity perception in crowded and complicated scenes using hierarchical bayesian models. PAMI **31**(3), 539–555 (2009)

Egocentric Object Tracking: An Odometry-Based Solution

Stefano Alletto$^{(\boxtimes)}$, Giuseppe Serra, and Rita Cucchiara

University of Modena and Reggio Emilia, Modena, Italy
{stefano.alletto,giuseppe.serra,rita.cucchiara}@unimore.it
http://imagelab.ing.unimore.it

Abstract. Tracking objects moving around a person is one of the key steps in human visual augmentation: we could estimate their locations when they are out of our field of view, know their position, distance or velocity just to name a few possibilities. This is no easy task: in this paper, we show how current state-of-the-art visual tracking algorithms fail if challenged with a first-person sequence recorded from a wearable camera attached to a moving user. We propose an evaluation that highlights these algorithms' limitations and, accordingly, develop a novel approach based on visual odometry and 3D localization that overcomes many issues typical of egocentric vision. We implement our algorithm on a wearable board and evaluate its robustness, showing in our preliminary experiments an increase in tracking performance of nearly 20% if compared to currently state-of-the-art techniques.

Keywords: Visual tracking · Wearable computing · Egocentric vision

1 Introduction and Related Work

The rapid progresses in the development of systems based on wearable cameras and embedded computing devices have created the conditions to allow computer vision technologies to augment experience in everyday life activities such sport, education, social interactions, cultural heritage visits etc. The new and challenging setting that results from the adoption of an egocentric perspective in the video analysis provides a unique insight into many problems that have already been addressed by the traditional computer vision.

Egocentric vision (or ego-vision) is a recent topic that aims at augmenting human visual capabilities and perception by enhancing our field of view [3], analyzing social interactions [4], localizing objects [6] or extracting salient moments from our daily lives [10] based on what we see.

The adoption of an egocentric perspective creates new challenges for traditional computer vision, in particular when facing the task of tracking moving objects. It is a complex field in which many results have been achieved [11], but there still are open issues. A working tracker should handle scale, illumination changes, background clutter, partial occlusions and keep track of the object of interest overcoming these challenges. A notable solution is the Fragments-based

© Springer International Publishing Switzerland 2015
V. Murino and E. Puppo (Eds.): ICIAP 2015, Part II, LNCS 9280, pp. 687–696, 2015.
DOI: 10.1007/978-3-319-23234-8_63

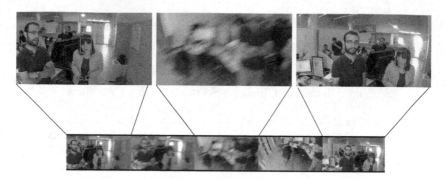

Fig. 1. An example an ego-vision sequence where fast camera motion causes objects and people to exit the camera field of view.

Robust Tracking (FRT) [1] that addresses the problem of partial occlusions representing the object template by multiple image patches. While being very fast and accurate in the case of small changes in object appearance, this method tends to worsen its performances if challenged with severe changes in appearance. To address this issue, tracking approaches that employs discriminative classifiers to identify the target opposed to the background have been proposed. The Hough-Based Tracker (HBT) by Godec *et al.* proposed in [7] is a tracker that aims at non-rigid targets in a discriminative classifier with segmentation of the object itself. The Structured Output Tracking with Kernels (STR) [8] algorithm employs a structured output supervised classifier to acquire training data directly from the image integrating the labeling procedure and its learner. Tracking Learning and Detection (TLD) [9] combines the results of an optical flow tracker and a detector, which can identify errors and learn from them.

Despite being a core component of many algorithms based on video analysis, very few works use visual tracking applied to ego-vision settings. Alletto *et al.* [2] employ HBT with some adjustments to better suit the first person perspective. Fan *et al.* [3] track features clustering motion based on the optical flow of the scene. However, these works employ trackers for a specific task in very constrained settings and lack generality.

In this work, we address the problem of tracking a single object of interest from a first person perspective. A typical example is to follow the detected shape of a friend walking with the camera wearer, which is one of the most challenging situations in visual tracking. Due to the novelty of the task if applied to a first-person wearable camera view, this work first discusses the main issues of egocentric tracking such as fast camera motion, see Fig. 1. Then, we propose a 3D localization method based on monocular visual odometry that is used to enforce a tracking framework. By intervening on its detection phase predicting the location where to expect to see the object after it re-enters the field of view following a loss or a total occlusion, we can re-initialize the tracker even when the appearance of the object differs from the learned model in a way the would have otherwise prevented the detection.

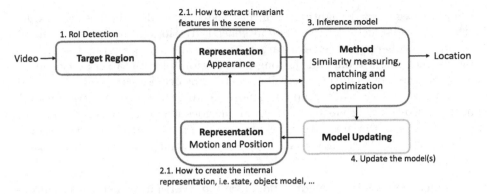

Fig. 2. The typical schema of a tracking algorithm. Each block, represented in different colors, is usually implemented in various ways thus differentiating trackers from one another.

We show that the proposed method outperforms state-of-the-art techniques by nearly 20% and, while being an initial study on the matter of visual augmentation via egocentric object tracking, it provides promising results and encourages further research on the topic. We also implement the described technique on a wearable embedded device coupled with a head mounted camera capable of acquisition and processing.

2 Motivations

In this section, we consider the typical approach to tracking a single moving object and discuss the challenges posed by the setting of first person camera views. Here, tracking-by-detection methods, since they need a specific detector for a specific target (e.g. a people detector) are not taken into account; in fact they cannot be used if the targets are unknown, as in this context.

The typical workflow of a tracking algorithm is shown in Figure 2: after a detection step, several candidate Regions of Interest (RoIs) are automatically selected by the tracker (e.g. around the previous position, with Gaussian scattering, etc) and visual features like appearance, position, and motion are extracted and used both for the frame under evaluation (step 2.1) and for the internal model (step 2.2). Then tracker (step 3), is characterized by an inference method that associates candidate RoIs to model(s), solving an optimization problem or performing a classification. The trackers often differ from each-other in the methods used to update the model (step 4): some of them do not modify the model at all, others keep more models of the target object, updating their short-term and long-term memory with some learning step.

Since the issues that make tracking so difficult are many, there is no tracker that can outperform the others regardless of the setting. In [11], thirteen different problems which can potentially lead a tracker to failure have been considered. In order to analyze them from an egocentric perspective, we could divide them in three categories: i) Lighting: lighting conditions and variations, the target surface, transparency and its shape in general; ii) Motion: motion smoothness, the motion coherence (between target, camera and background), the camera motion, the camera zoom and the long-term motion (of both target and camera); iii) Scene: the scene clutter, confusion, contrast or occlusions.

All these issues can occur simultaneously making the problem of tracking still unsolved. Considering videos taken from an egocentric perspective, our experiments show that the most crucial characteristic of this setting are the peculiar motion patterns. We can state that in egocentric tracking the main motion issues can be summarized as

- Camera motion: the camera is moving as the head of its owner, thus is unconstrained and often unpredictable. Trackers based on motion estimation alone (e.g. optical flow tracking) are likely to fail due to the significant amount of noise introduced by the ego-motion.
- The long-term motion: since the camera is not fixed, a long-term component of motion must be considered. In fact, the tracked object can change its appearance substantially due to a different point of view of the observer derived from his motion. This results in the need to keep a complex object model capable of recognizing different appearances of the same object, e.g. TLD object model.
- The motion coherence: the complexity of human attention patterns lead to very challenging situations in ego-vision. The motion coherence between the target, the background or the camera is indeed far from granted. Even a still object could bounce in and out of the camera field of view due to ego-motion, or a still background can be all but still, having significant apparent motion. Trackers that rely on robust training such as Struck, utterly fail in this setting due to the impossibility to learn an effective representation of the object vs background motion or appearance.

For these reasons, this work focuses on analyzing some of the most promising trackers currently available [11], highlighting their limitations when challenged with ego-vision sequences. Furthermore, instead of focusing on one of the issues and developing a new tracker to handle that particular situation, we develop a module based on visual odometry that can enhance the tracking performance of existing algorithms, a more general solution to a problem which is still to be solved.

3   Proposed Method

In order to overcome the issues of egocentric tracking, we develop a method that integrates 3D target localization into the detection component of the tracking algorithm. Based on experimental results (see the following section) we extend the recent tracker TLD [9] with a module that supports detection with 3D information. However, our approach can be adapted to other visual tracking techniques such as Struck [8], by introducing in its Structured SVM inference procedure a set of weights learned using 3D target localization.

TLD framework features three main components: a *Tracker* which estimates the object's motion based on a Median-Flow algorithm. This component of the framework is likely to fail if the object exits the camera field of view and it is not able to resume the tracking by itself. A *Detector* intervenes treating each frame independently and performs the detection localizing the appearances of the object which have been observed and learned in the past, recovering tracking after the *Tracker* fails. The *Learning* component observes the performance of both *Tracker* and *Detector*, estimates their error and adds training samples to its object model.

A typical ego-vision characteristic is that the camera wearer can have very fast head motion, e.g. when he is looking around for something. Another example is the object of interest being a person walking with the subject wearing the camera, resulting in him looking at the path they are walking as often as to his companion. With these characteristics in mind, it is clear how important the detection phase of the tracking process is, since the object of interest can be outside of the field of view for a significant part of the sequence.

In particular, the TLD detector is based on a sequence of classifications. Patches are densely sampled in the image at different scales obtaining a large set of candidates which is iteratively reduced by following rejection steps. First all patches with low gray-scale values variance are rejected to rapidly eliminate a large set of non-object candidates. Then patches that passed the first step are classified by an ensemble of classifiers based on pixel comparison trained offline.

The final step is a NN classifier that compares the patches with the learned object model M. This model is composed by a set of positive p^+ and negative p^- patches that respectively encode object and background parts. A patch p is recognized as the object of interest if its *relative similarity* with the model is

t

Fig. 3. Example sequence of the proposed approach.

greater than a threshold $S^r(p, M) > \theta_{NN}$. The *relative similarity* is defined as $S^r = \frac{S^+}{S^+ + S^-}$ where

$$S^+(p, M) = max_{p_i^+ \in M} S(p, p_i^+) \quad and \quad S^-(p, M) = max_{p_i^- \in M} S(p, p_i^-) \quad (1)$$

are the similarity with the positive and negative nearest neighbors.

However, detection based on the appearance encoded in the learned model M can fail if the object changes too fast or the change takes place out of the camera view. To deal with this issue we extend the detection component by adding 3D motion estimation of the head and the object to model its behavior when it is not visible.

To compute the head motion we use "Semi-Direct Visual Odometry" (SVO) algorithm [5] that can be run in real-time on an on-board embedded computer, since it eliminates the need of costly feature extraction for motion estimation operating directly on pixel intensities. SVO estimates the rigid body transformation between two consecutive camera poses $G_{k,k-1}$ minimizing the negative log-likelihood of the intensity residual:

$$G_{k,k-1} = \arg \min_{G} \int \int_{R} \rho[\delta I(G, \mathbf{u})] d\mathbf{u}. \quad (2)$$

where δI is the photometric difference between pixels observing the same 3D point and $\rho := \frac{1}{2} \|\cdot\|^2$.

When the object is visible and tracked, given the bounding-box at the frame k and the head motion estimation $G_{k+\Delta t,k}$ provided by the SVO algorithm, we can estimate its 3D motion model and use it to predict the image coordinates where the target should appear after a loss. In particular, let $c_k = (x_k, y_k)$ be the center of the bounding-box at the frame k, we can predict the image point coordinates where the center should be located when it becomes visible again after an interval Δt:

$$\hat{c}_{k+\Delta t} = P(G_{k+\Delta t,k} \cdot (P^{-1}(c_k, d) + \Delta C(t))). \quad (3)$$

where P is the projection model that maps 3D points to the image coordinates, d is an approximation of the depth based on the scale of the detection at the frame k and ΔC is the 3D target motion that we define, assuming a linear velocity, as:

$$\Delta C_{\Delta t} = C_k + V_k \Delta t \quad (4)$$

where V_k is the velocity vector of the center of the bounding-box at the frame k. While the assumption of linear velocity may appear limiting, the setting of ego-vision often requires the tracking of objects that are somehow related to the person wearing the camera, e.g. people walking beside him, and thus the assumption is often satisfied.

Based on this estimation the we extend the *relative similarity* including the displacement between the estimated center of the bounding-box $\hat{c}_{k+\Delta t}$ and the

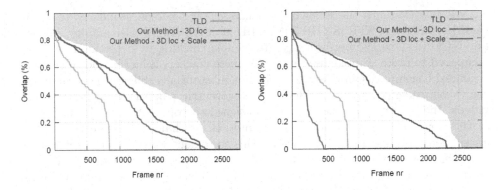

Fig. 4. Comparison between TLD and the two variations of our approach. On the left: the results of our method using the SLAM localization. On the right: SLAM data perturbed with gaussian noise. The displayed results are obtained concatenating and sorting the frames of the different video sequences.

center of the candidate patch p in the image coordinates. The new similarity function is defined as:

$$S^r(p, M, \hat{c}_{k+\Delta t}) = (1 + e^{-(\frac{d_x^2 + d_y^2}{2\sigma^2})}) \cdot S^r(p, M) \qquad (5)$$

where d_x and d_y are the displacement components in x and y, and σ is the variance of two-dimensional Gaussian function center in $\hat{c}_{k+\Delta t}$ (based on preliminary experiments we fix $\sigma = 20$). This new similarity is used to identify whether the patch is recognized as the object of interest by comparing it to the threshold θ_{NN}.

We observed that patches where the relation $S^r(p, M) < \theta_{NN} < S^r(p, M, \hat{c}_{k+\Delta t})$ is satisfied are likely to contain a detail of the target. While these patches are sufficient to restart the *Tracker*, they are not suitable to provide an accurate localization of the object of interest due to scale errors. To address this issue we adjust the scale considering the size of the patch and the dimension of the bounding-box at the frame k. This allows us to resume tracking with a more robust initialization and follow the target more properly.

Figure 3 presents an example of our method applied to ego-vision sequence. The green bounding box is the chosen detection, the blue ones represent the image patches obtained from the NN classifier. The cyan patch in the last frame satisfies $S^r(p, M, \hat{c}_{k+\Delta t}) > \theta_{NN}$ and is used as input in the scale adjustment step to compute green detection. The two-dimensional Gaussian function, that predicts the center of the object of interest c_k, is represented in shades of red and yellow.

4   Experimental Results

We described the differences and challenges posed by egocentric perspective compared to the traditional tracking setting.

We now evaluate the following trackers on first-person sequences to show their performance: STR [8], HBT [7], TLD [9], FRT [1]. We also employ a baseline NCC to show the performance of a simple tracking by detection approach compared to more complex methods. All these trackers achieve good results on standard benchmarks and datasets [11], but substantially different performances are to be expected when considering the egocentric perspective of first person videos. Indeed, these trackers are not designed to cope with the abrupt losses of the target due to head and camera motion, or changes in scale that are a consequence of movement. To validate this statement we collected a set of five ego-vision sequences that contain people interactions in both indoor and outdoor environment. Videos are recorded and processed using a wearable Odroid-XU board, that embeds the ARM Exynos 5 SoC, and a glass-mounted Matrix Vision BlueFox global shutter camera. We add a 3000 mAh battery pack to make it portable.

Figure 5 shows the results of this evaluation of the aforementioned trackers on one of the ego-vision sequences that contains changes in illumination and fast camera motion induced by head motion and walking.

It can be noticed how the challenging aspects of the ego-vision scenario, namely the fast camera motion and the target exiting the camera field of view after very few frames, significantly worsen the performance of state-of-the-art trackers. In particular, HBT and FRT fail due to the lack of the ability to cope with the exit of the target from the frame. STR, while trying to adapt to such a situation, does not perform any loss detection and quickly adapts its model to the background. A simple tracking by detection approach (NCC) can recover tracking if the appearance of the object becomes close to the initial template but it is shown to be unable to provide sufficient results in most cases. Among the evaluated trackers, due to its hybrid framework of tracking and detection, TLD results in being the more robust to the recurring loss of the target but still presents a low overlap measure. In fact its detector, while often being able to resume tracking after a loss, requires the new appearance to have already been

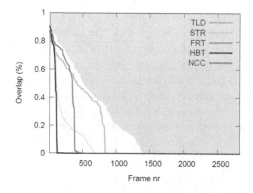

Fig. 5. Tracking results on the ego-vision sequences.

observed and encoded in the model. In egovision it often occurs that the target can change its appearance out of the camera field of view thus compromising its ability to detect the object.

Furthermore, consider the tracking upper bound of Figure 5, which is the performance obtained by the combination of the evaluated trackers by taking at each frame the best result in terms of overlap. This upper bound shows little room for improvement and demonstrates the requirement of a different approach to the task of egocentric visual tracking.

Figure 4 shows the improvement tied to the enforcing of visual tracking with 3D localization. In particular, we present a comparison between the TLD tracker and two variations of our approach: 3D localization estimation with no additional scale adjustment (Our Method - 3D loc) and improved scale estimation considering the size of the patch and the dimension of the bounding-box at the previous frames (Our Method - 3D loc + Scale). Our complete approach can achieve an average overlap of 35.26% while on the same data TLD scores a 15.28%, featuring an increase of 19.98%.

It can be noticed how if the prediction of the 3D position of the center of the object is accurate enough, performing the scale adaptation step is not strictly required since it only slightly improves results. On the other hand, if the localization results are less precise, not taking into account the errors in the scale of the detection severely impact of the performance of our method. As Fig. 4 shows, adding a gaussian noise of $\sigma = 15px$ to the predicted position requires the scale adjustment step to work properly. This is due to the error introduced by the noise excessively perturbing the localization resulting in the impossibility to resume tracking.

5   Conclusions

In this paper we presented a method that uses a semi-direct monocular visual odometry algorithm to infer the head motion of the camera wearer and subsequently compute the 3D location of the target. This allows us to build a target motion model used to predict the image coordinates where to expect it to reappear after a loss. By exploiting this information we can intervene in the detection component of a tracker and effectively leading it to a more robust detection. While this is an initial study on the matter, our preliminary results validate our method by showing a significant improvement of the state-of-the-art performance.

References

1. Adam, A., Rivlin, E., Shimshoni, I.: Robust fragments-based tracking using the integral histogram. In: Proc. of CVPR (2006)
2. Alletto, S., Serra, G., Calderara, S., Solera, F., Cucchiara, R.: From ego to nos-vision: detecting social relationships in first-person views. In: Proc. of CVPR Workshops (2014)

696   S. Alletto et al.

3. Fan, K., Huber, J., Nanayakkara, S., Inami, M.: Spidervision: extending the human field of view for augmented awareness. In: Proc. of ACM Augmented Human (2014)
4. Fathi, A., Hodgins, J., Rehg, J.: Social interactions: a first-person perspective. In: Proc. of CVPR (2012)
5. Forster, C., Pizzoli, M., Scaramuzza, D.: Svo: fast semi-direct monocular visual odometry. In: Proc. of ICRA (2014)
6. Funk, M., Boldt, R., Pfleging, B., Pfeiffer, M., Henze, N., Schmidt, A.: Representing indoor location of objects on wearable computers with head-mounted displays. In: Proc. of ACM Augmented Human (2014)
7. Godec, M., Roth, P.M., Bischof, H.: Hough-based tracking of non-rigid objects. Computer Vision and Image Understanding $117(10)$, 1245–1256 (2012)
8. Hare, S., Saffari, A., Torr, P.H.: Struck: structured output tracking with kernels. In: Proc. of ICCV (2011)
9. Kalal, Z., Mikolajczyk, K., Matas, J.: Tracking-learning-detection. IEEE Transactions on Pattern Analysis and Machine Intelligence $34(7)$, 1409–1422 (2012)
10. Lee, Y.J., Ghosh, J., Grauman, K.: Discovering important people and objects for egocentric video summarization. In: Proc. of CVPR, vol. 1, pp. 1346–1353 (2012)
11. Smeulders, A., Chu, D., Cucchiara, R., Calderara, S., Dehghan, A., Shah, M.: Visual tracking: An experimental survey. IEEE Transactions on Pattern Analysis and Machine Intelligence $36(7)$, 1442–1468 (2014)

En Plein Air Visual Agents

Marco Gori[1], Marco Lippi[2]($\boxtimes$), Marco Maggini[1], Stefano Melacci[1], and Marcello Pelillo[3]

[1] DIISM, University of Siena, Siena, Italy
{marco,maggini,mela}@diism.unisi.it
[2] DISI, University of Bologna, Bologna, Italy
marco.lippi3@unibo.it
[3] ECLT/DAIS, University of Venice,Venice, Italy
pelillo@dais.unive.it

Abstract. Nowadays, machine learning is playing a dominant role in most challenging computer vision problems. This paper advocates an extreme evolution of this interplay, where visual agents continuously process videos and interact with humans, just like children, exploiting life–long learning computational schemes. This opens the challenge of *en plein air visual agents*, whose behavior is progressively monitored and evaluated by novel mechanisms, where dynamic man-machine interaction plays a fundamental role. Going beyond classic benchmarks, we argue that appropriate crowd-sourcing schemes are suitable for performance evaluation of visual agents operating in this framework. We provide a proof of concept of this novel view, by showing methods and concrete solutions for en plein air visual agents. Crowdsourcing evaluation is reported, along with a life–long experiment on "The Aristocats" cartoon. We expect that the proposed radically new framework will stimulate related approaches and solutions.

1 Introduction

Nowadays, most computer vision algorithms are designed to successfully tackle specific tasks, such as image classification, object detection and localization, tracking, semantic segmentation, scene parsing [11,12,19,20,22]. The remarkable scientific results achieved in the last few years have fueled the diffusion of computer vision technologies even in commercial devices such as cameras, tablets, or smartphones.

However, there seems to be a lack of general results when considering the capability of an automatic agent to acquire and successfully exploit vision skills in unrestricted video environments. In particular, the basic task of semantic labeling of pixels in a given video stream has mostly been approached at the frame level, as the outcome of well-established pattern recognition methods working on images. This modality is far from the natural visual interaction experienced by humans with the surrounding environment. The acquisition of visual concepts would have been more difficult if the human cognitive processes had to analyze a stream of shuffled frames: the extraction of symbolic information from images

© Springer International Publishing Switzerland 2015
V. Murino and E. Puppo (Eds.): ICIAP 2015, Part II, LNCS 9280, pp. 697–709, 2015.
DOI: 10.1007/978-3-319-23234-8_64

that are not frames of a temporally coherent visual stream would have been extremely harder than in the natural visual experience. Pursuing this idea, we propose studying agents which develop visual skills through a life–long learning process that takes place following a protocol inspired by a human-like communication scheme to deal with unrestricted video. A similar idea is tackled down by the NEIL project [1], but working in the context of images only. In this scenario we propose an in-depth re-thinking of the role of machine learning in computer vision. We argue that a new perspective should be followed facing the challenge of disclosing the computational basis of vision by regarding it as a truly learning field that needs to be attacked by an appropriate *vision learning theory*. In particular, we think that the first step in this direction is to move the target to unrestricted visual environments, and to consider a human-like communication protocol, instead of focusing on brute–force learning on massive labeled datasets of images. We refer to this learning protocol as *learning to see like children* (L2SLC) to stress our view on how visual skills should be acquired. In this framework, there is no neat distinction between learning and test sets, but there is just a visual environment (a video stream) where the agent lives and receives its stimuli.

As pioneer examples of agents implementing the proposed protocol, we describe *Developmental Visual Agents* (DVAs). In these agents, learning is driven by several factors that can be unified under the general concept of *constraint*. The theory of *learning from constraints* [2,5,8,18] allows to incorporate different rich contributions, such as parsimony principles, external supervisions, and complex dependencies among the developed concepts. In particular, we consider motion coherence as a fundamental constraint to reduce the complexity for learning visual skills [7,10]. In fact, this constraint imposes that any label attached to a moving pixel has to be the same during its motion, thus significantly extending the provided supervisions. This aspect is essentially ignored in most machine learning approaches working on datasets of tagged images. Moreover, DVAs undergo developmental stages, that very much resemble those featured in humans [6], by exploiting a life–long computational scheme[1].

In the L2SLC scenario, the assessment of visual agents by classical benchmark approaches[2] seems unnatural, and, hence, we propose to explore a different experimental validation that seems to resonate perfectly with the considered life–long learning protocol. DVAs are to be tested in unrestricted environments and contexts during their lives. An evaluation scheme based on crowdsourcing is proposed, named *En plein air*. In this open on-line lab, any subscribed user is able to monitor and rate the performance of the currently deployed visual agents. In this paper we show two possible scenarios of assessment: an explicit rating of the performances of different agents in given environments, and the

---

[1] The acronym DVA was introduced in [9,17] in the context of low-level feature extraction and image classification. Here we are extending those agents to the life-long learning processing of video streams, performing semantic labeling.

[2] The risk of biases in vision benchmarks, always recognized, was explicitly pointed out in [23].

possibility to monitor a set of agents during their learning process. A prototype of our crowdsourcing initiative, our implementation of DVAs, and their outcome in several visual world are collected at http://dva.diism.unisi.it.

2   Learning Protocol

We consider visual agents performing scene semantic labeling on a video stream. Given a set $\mathcal{T}$ of semantic categories (*tags*), the agent labels each pixel in a video frame with a subset of $\mathcal{T}$ (i.e. it performs *multi-tag prediction*). Pixel tagging is performed continuously by the visual agent as time flows. The tag set is created by a human supervisor in an incremental way, so that new tags can be added in any moment of the agent's life. The supervisor also provides supervisions to specific patterns in the observed scenes and possibly also semantic constraints among the defined tags. Hence, at each time step a tag set $\mathcal{T}_t = \{t_1, \ldots, t_{k_t}\}$ is given, along with a set of constraints $\mathcal{C}_t = \{C_1, \ldots, C_{c_t}\}$ defined on the elements of $\mathcal{T}_t$, possibly depending on the environment configuration (i.e. spatio-temporal variables in the video stream). We do not assume any particular requirement on the nature of constraints, except that they can be specified with a given mathematical formalism. For instance, using First Order Logic we can express ontological constraints among tags, such as the relationship between categories modeled by the *is-a* predicate. Motion coherence can instead constrain the tags assigned to corresponding pixels, given the perceived motion, in a sequence of consecutive frames.

Once the agent is *born*, it starts analyzing the input video stream and to develop its internal model of the experienced environment. Learning begins as soon as the agent is deployed, initially following the constraints imposed by its own architecture and by a set of basic behaviors, such as those deriving from parsimony principles and motion coherence. The learning protocol assumes supervisors to intervene at the symbolic level, by attaching tags to visual patterns in a given frame. Supervisions can be provided at any time step and they are managed asynchronously by the agent as it continues to output predictions on the incoming frames. We consider two different kinds of supervisions to be fed to the agent: (i) *strong*, that specify one or more tags for a specific (group of)

Fig. 1. Interaction of a supervisor with a running visual agent. A semantic label is provided for a region of pixels (highlighted in pink). ("The Aristocats" cartoon, © The Walt Disney Company).

pixel(s) in a certain frame, and (ii) *weak*, that express the *presence* of an object, regardless of its specific location in the frame. Figure 1 shows such alternatives in the current version of our interface: the tag *Duchess* can be associated with strong supervision by selecting a region (*here is Duchess*), whereas weak supervision is provided at frame level (*in this frame there is Duchess*). Clearly, weak supervisions require the agent to detect the object to be supervised, and thus they are effective only after enough strong supervisions have been provided, as a reinforcement of visual concepts in their initial stages. Weak supervisions can be useful in real-time scenarios, for example if users provide spoken supervisions through a microphone. Visual agents are also expected to take the initiative by *asking for* supervision, thus exploiting an active learning scheme.

The proposed learning protocol is mainly inspired by the observation that children can learn to recognize objects and actions from a few supervised examples, whereas nowadays machine learning approaches strive to achieve this task without the availability of massive labeled datasets. This difference seems to be deeply rooted in the communication protocol at the basis of the acquisition of visual skills in children and machines. For this reason we refer to the proposed protocol as *learning to see like children* (L2SLC). The visual agent *lives* in its learning environment (its specific video stream), experiencing a life–long learning process that involves the exploitation of both natural constraints and externally provided teaching signals. Among the natural constraints it seems to be important to include parsimony principles, that constrain the complexity of the solution to be as low as possible, and the need to take coherent decisions with respect to the *perceived motion* of the pixels in the video stream. The linguistic process of attaching symbols to objects takes place at a later stage of children development, when they have already developed strong pattern regularities. We conjecture that, regardless of biology, the enforcement of the motion coherence constraint is a high level computational principle that plays the fundamental role for discovering pattern regularities.

3   *En Plein Air* Assessment

The impressive progress of computer vision has strongly benefited from the massive diffusion of benchmarks which, by and large, are regarded as fundamental tools for performance evaluation. Nowadays, the majority of researchers assume to have access to huge collections of labeled data to evaluate their algorithms, and, when they are not available, they are created from scratch. Despite their apparent indisputable dominant role in the advancements in computer vision, some criticisms have been recently raised [23]. Moreover, this methodology may not always be applicable to the setting of Section 2, at least not in a straightforward way, or it would require overwhelming efforts.

As a matter of fact, the proposed learning protocol involves visual agents operating in dynamic environments. Differently from the case of classical batch data sets, there is no clear distinction between training set and test set. This situation raises a very important question: *which is the right method to evaluate these visual agents?* It is clearly impossible to give a definitive answer, but the previous considerations suggest that the time has come to open the mind towards new approaches. The benchmark–oriented attitude, nowadays dominating the computer vision community, bears some resemblance to the influential testing movement in psychology which has its roots in the turn-of-the-century work of Alfred Binet on IQ tests (see e.g. [21]). Both cases consist in attempts to provide a rigorous way of assessing the performance or the aptitude of a (biological or artificial) system, by agreeing on a set of standardized tests which, from that moment onward, become the ultimate criterion for validity. The IQ testing movement has been severely criticized not only for the social and ethical implications deriving from the idea of ranking human beings on a numerical scale but also, more technically, on the grounds that, irrespective of the care with which such tests are designed, they are inherently unable to capture the multifaceted nature of real-world phenomena. Related concerns were given in the seminal paper by David McClelland [15], that sets the stage for the modern competency movement in the U.S. Motivated by analogous concerns, we maintain that the time is ripe for the computer vision community to adopt a similar grade-in-life attitude towards the evaluation of its systems and algorithms. Clearly, we do not intend to diminish the importance of benchmarks, as they are indeed invaluable tools for the progress of the field. The recently proposed "Visual Turing Tests" [4,13] share similar ideas, by proposing to assess whether machines can perform scene understanding as well as humans, for example by answering a list of yes/no questions regarding a given image (i.e., is the boy with the red hat drinking?).

It is clear that the skills of any visual agent can be quickly evaluated and promptly judged by humans, simply by observing its behavior. Thus, we propose a *crowdsourcing performance evaluation scheme* where registered people can inspect and assess the performance of software agents. We use the term *en plein air* ("in the open air"), mimicking the French Impressionist painters of the 19th-century and, more generally, the act of painting outdoors. This term suggests that visual agents should be evaluated by allowing people to see them in action, virtually opening the doors of research labs. A prototype of such evaluation scheme can be experimented at http://dva.diism.unisi.it. Registered users can observe the quality of visual agent predictions, and rate them (from 0 up to 5). Scores are then averaged over all the users. Clearly, this kind of mechanism does make sense when the judges have access to the setting in which the agent operates, to better evaluate the difficulty of the task and the impact of the presented results. For this reason, each agent comes with a short description of the experimental setting. This evaluation procedure also allows the users to monitor sets of agents during their life, verifying their progresses in the learning process. This is well-suited for the life–long learning protocol of Section 2, and the first case study will be described in Section 5.

The *en plein air* proposal allows others to test our algorithms and to contribute to this evaluation method by providing their own data, their own results, or the comparisons with their own algorithms. Our web site hosts a software package with a graphical interface which can be used to interact with the agents

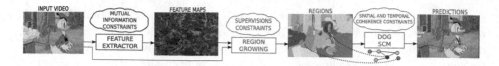

Fig. 2. The pipeline of a Developmental Visual Agent.

that we will be describing shortly (Section 4), by providing supervisions and observing the resulting predictions.

4   Pioneer Visual Agents

The learning protocol and the *en plein air* framework allow us to define a general variety of visual agents, designed so as to perform scene understanding in unrestricted domains, following a life–long learning paradigm. Here we introduce a first implementation of pioneer agents within this context, named Developmental Visual Agents (DVAs) [9,17]. The DVA architecture is hierarchically organized, starting with feature extraction from input visual streams, up to symbolic layers where user interaction occurs. Figure 2 depicts the system pipeline. The learning principles of DVAs are rooted in the theory of *learning from constraints* [5], that allows us to model the interaction of intelligent agents with the environment by means of constraints on the tasks to be learned, and gives foundations and algorithms to discover tasks that are consistent with the given constraints and minimize a parsimony index. The notion of constraint is well-suited to express both visual and linguistic granules of knowledge. Visual constraints can just encode supervisions on a labeled pixel, but the same formalism can represent also motion coherence, or complex dependencies on real-valued functions, including abstract logic formalisms [2]. While this is an ideal view to embrace different visual constraints in the same mathematical and algorithmic framework, we also consider life–long learning computational schemes where the system adapts gradually to the incoming visual stream.

Let $\mathcal{V}$ be a video stream, and $\mathcal{V}_t$ the frame processed at time t. DVA first extracts a stack of L layers of hierarchical scale- and rotation-invariant features, that are developed following the ideas described in [9,17]. Basically, for each pixel x, the goal is to learn a code of d_ℓ features (for the ℓ-th layer) by fulfilling a constraint driven by information-theoretic principles, that aims at maximizing the mutual information of the code with respect to the observed input, with no interactions with external supervisors. Features are computed over a neighborhood of x at the different levels of the hierarchy, by modeling a *receptive field* of x with a set of $\mathcal{N}$ Gaussians g_k, $k = 1, \ldots, \mathcal{N}$, located nearby the pixel. Thus, higher layers in the hierarchy virtually observe larger input portions. The features of each layer are encoded with probability scores, and the L feature codes are stacked into a single descriptor for pixel x. While in [9,17] feature extraction injects invariance to geometric transformations by processing image sets, here we follow the strategy of [7] to handle on-line video streams: the data covered by the receptive fields, also referred to as *receptive inputs*, are compared with an internal (geometrically invariant) representation of the video receptive inputs up to time t. This induces a pixel-wise *motion estimation*, a strong basis over which DVAs can learn invariant features.

On top of this unsupervised feature extraction process, DVAs partition the input frame into homogeneous superpixels (regions) to reduce the computational burden of pixel-based tagging. We extend the graph-based region-growing algorithm in [3] by progressively merging pixels according to a dissimilarity score based both on color similarity (as in [3]) and on motion coherence. The dissimilarity is decreased (increased) for those pixels whose estimated motion is (is not) coherent, so that neighbor pixels locally moving in the same direction will more likely belong to the same region. The partitioning obtained for frame $\mathcal{V}_t$ contains a set of R^t regions which correspond to visual patterns that users can tag. Region $r \in R^t$ is described with a histogram z_r, exploiting average feature pooling on the pixels belonging to it. During the agent's life, descriptors are progressively accumulated as vertices (nodes) of a graph, named *Developmental Object Graph* (DOG). We indicate with V_t the set of vertices at time t. To avoid storing duplicate nodes in the DOG, and also to meet practical memory budget requirements, a user-defined tolerance τ between vertices is employed. In detail, after having computed the descriptor z_r, its nearest-neighbor within the current set of DOG vertices is retrieved by the χ^2 distance d_{χ^2}: if $d_{\chi^2} > \tau$ then a new vertex is added to the DOG, otherwise z_r is mapped to (or "hits") its nearest-neighboring vertex. Thus, each region $r \in R^t$ is associated to a node, while the same node can be associated to multiple regions over the video. To meet real-time requirements, we exploit search space partitioning and we allow sub-optimal solutions to speed up nearest-neighbor search.

Two vertices v_i and v_j can be linked by two categories of edges, if one of the following conditions occurs: (i) they are spatially similar; (ii) the agent collected evidence that motion estimation is connecting them. For the first condition, we link nodes whose distance is smaller than a pre-defined threshold γ_s. The *spatial* weight of an edge is computed as $w_{ij}^s = \exp(-\chi^2(v_i, v_j)/2\sigma_\tau^2)$. The second condition involves two consecutive frames $\mathcal{V}_{t-1}$ and $\mathcal{V}_t$. If a region belonging to $\mathcal{V}_{t-1}$ and a similar-sized region of $\mathcal{V}_t$ are such that most of their pixels are connected by the motion estimation procedure, then the *motion-based* weight w_{ij}^m between their associated vertices (v_i and v_j) should be increased. We ignore cases where the number of connected pixels is too small (given a threshold γ_m) with respect to region sizes. During the agent's life, we update w_{ij}^m as long as we accumulate new evidence of motion-based connections between v_i and v_j[3].

The last computational block of Figure 2 involves the symbolic decision mechanism. Labels can be attached by users to the visual patterns stored in the DOG as classic supervisions. For each new semantic tag t_k introduced by a supervisor, a new function $f_k(v_j)$ is created, operating on the space of DOG vertices (we hereby discard the time index, for the sake of simplicity). These functions are defined within the framework of *learning from constraints* [5], which is based

---

[3] w_{ij}^m is averaged over all the accumulated evidences.

on the notion of *constraint*, to model interactions with the environment, and on the parsimony principle. The degree of parsimony of $f = [f_1, \ldots, f_{t_k}]$ is defined by means of a given norm $\|f\|$ [5]. Functions $f_k(v_j)$ have to satisfy coherence constraints defined over the spatio-temporal manifold induced by the DOG structure, as well as supervision constraints. We indicate the penalty associated to supervision constraints with $\mu_{\mathcal{S}}^{(1)}$, and that of coherence constraints as $\mu_{\mathcal{M}}^{(2)}$. Thus, the problem of learning f from (soft) constraints can be formulated as:

$$f^* = \arg\min_f \left\{ \|f\|^2 + \mu_{\mathcal{S}}^{(1)}(f) + \mu_{\mathcal{M}}^{(2)}(f) \right\} . \tag{1}$$

It is possible to prove a representer theorem which extends the classical kernel-based representation of traditional learning from examples, leading to the so-called Support Constraint Machine (SCM) [5]. The solution of eq. 1 is then: $f_k^* = \sum_{i=1}^{N} \zeta_{ik} K(x_i, \cdot)$, being $K(\cdot, \cdot)$ the kernel associated with the selected norm (exponential χ^2 kernel) and ζ_{ik} the parameters to be optimized. Being $\mathcal{S}_k = \{(v_i, y_{i,k}), \ i = 1, \ldots, l_k\}$ the set of supervised DOG nodes for function f_k, and being $y_{i,k} \in \{-1, +1\}$ the label attached to some node $v_i \in V$ for function f_k, the supervision constraint can be expressed as:

$$\mu_{\mathcal{S}}^{(1)}(f) = \sum_{k=1}^{t_k} \sum_{(v_i, y_{i,k}) \in \mathcal{S}_k} \beta_{ik} \max(0, 1 - y_{i,k} f_k(v_i))^2 .$$

where t_k is the number of classes for which the agent has received supervisions until time t, and the scalar $\beta_{ik} > 0$ is the *belief* [5] of each point-wise constraint. When a new constraint is added, its belief is set to a fixed initial value. Then, β_{ik} is increased as the same constraint is provided multiple times, while decreased in case of mismatching supervisions, keeping $\sum_i \beta_{ik} = 1$. This mechanism allows the agent to better focus on frequently-provided supervisions, and to give less weight to noisy and incoherent labels. Coherence constraints instead enforce smooth decisions over DOG nodes connected by any kind of edges, leading to an instance of classic manifold regularization [16]:

$$\mu_{\mathcal{M}}^{(2)}(f) = \sum_{k=1}^{t_k} \sum_{i=1}^{|V|} \sum_{j=i+1}^{|V|} w_{ij}(f_k(v_i) - f_k(v_j))^2 ,$$

The *belief* of each coherence constraint is a linear combination of edge weights: $w_{ij} = \lambda_{\mathcal{M}} \left(\alpha_{\mathcal{M}} \cdot w_{ij}^s + (1 - \alpha_{\mathcal{M}}) \cdot w_{ij}^m \right)$, where $\lambda_{\mathcal{M}} > 0$ is the global weight of the coherence constraints, and $\alpha_{\mathcal{M}} \in [0, 1]$ balances spatial/motion-based contributions.

As DVAs are expected to react and make predictions at any time, while learning evolves asynchronously, we assume f to operate in a *transductive environment* on the space of DOG nodes[4]. The life–long learning procedure operates by caching values $f_k(v_h)$ over each $v_h \in V$ after each update of ζ_{ik}: in this way

---

[4] Note that this happens also for feature functions [7].

Fig. 3. DVA sample predictions on four visual worlds (left-to-right). Only regions with confidence greater than zero are highlighted (best viewed in colors) and labeled with the most-confident class.

agents can continuously make predictions, while the underlying optimization process is still ongoing. To avoid abrupt changes of f, parameters ζ_{ik} associated with newly introduced representatives are set to zero. As memory restrictions are clearly imposed, we must define both a memory budget and a removal policy when the DOG is full: we chose to remove vertices with a small number of hits over a time window. Node hits are also used as frequency indicators for visual patterns, to select vertices upon which *ask* users for supervision.

5   Case Studies

We now describe two different case studies where visual agents that follow the learning protocol of Section 2 are evaluated in the *en plein air* framework described in Section 3. We employ DVAs, but we remark that our proposal can be extended to other instances of visual agents, encouraging other laboratories to promote their own implementations and evaluate them using the principles addressed in this work.

In the first experiment, we aim to compare five DVAs on a set of videos taken from four different visual worlds: a Donald Duck cartoon, a Pink Panther cartoon, a set of (merged) clips from the movie "Get Shorty" (taken from the HoHA2 database [14]) and another real-world video recorded with a fixed webcam in our lab (all of them processed at 240×180 resolution, 25 fps). We chose four heterogenous videos, but DVAs can process any kind of video source. We defined 4–6 semantic classes (from frequently observed objects) for each world[5], and we provided the four DVAs very few supervisions for each class (from 5 up to 10, only positive). Only a first portion (≈ 2 minutes) of each sequence was used to provide supervisions, while the remaining parts (≈ 1 minute) were used to assess the generalization capability of each agent. We asked users to rate each agent on each possible world (independently) with a score in the range 0–5, by evaluating the ability of the system to identify and tag elements in the video stream. Currently, over 40 users, including AI/CV researchers and Computer Science students, were involved in the rating process, but anyone can register on

---

[5] Donald Duck: {hat, coat, paw, pluto, collar, beak}; Pink Panther: {pink panther, pillow, blanket, blue bird, cuckoo clock}; Get Shorty: {face1, face2, face3, face4}; Webcam: {face1, monitor1, journal, bottle, poster1}. Classes ending with a digit refer to specific instances.

Table 1. Results obtained by the crowdsourcing evaluation process on five DVAs, averaged on all rates (from 0 up to 5) obtained in all four worlds, rescaled as percentages in the last column.

Agent	Description	Rate	Rate %
A1	BA (Base Architecture)	3.16	63.2%
A2	BA without motion constraints, i.e., $\alpha_{\mathcal{M}} = 1$ (see Section 4)	2.55	51.0%
A3	BA with a larger DOG, storing up to 20,000 nodes	2.47	49.4%
A4	BA with double amount of supervisions for each class	3.26	65.2%
A5	BA which processed a ~2x longer sequence	3.36	67.2%

Fig. 4. Sample prediction on two frames without (left) or with (right) motion constraints.

the website and contribute. Figure 3 shows samples of DVA predictions for the four worlds, as shown to the subscribed users: each region was labeled with the most-confident class, highlighting only those regions over which the confidence was greater that zero.

While all the agents share the same settings on the low-level feature extractors[6], they were diversified by high-level characteristics. The first agent (A1) exploits a Base Architecture (BA) designed to store up to 10,000 nodes in the DOG, including spatial and motion-based connections. The settings of the other agents, described in the second column of Table 1, were chosen to evaluate the impact of some specific DVA components: the effect of motion constraints (A2), the use of a larger DOG (A3), a higher number of supervisions (A4), and a longer duration of the agent's life (A5). Table 1 reports the votes collected with this first crowdsourcing evaluation, averaged on all the rates obtained in the four considered worlds. Motion constraint results to be crucial to improve the quality of the agents (A1 vs. A2), as motion constraints can propagate supervisions over DOG nodes connected by motion links. This happens both for moving instances, but also for static objects undergoing small changes in appearance due to illumination or occlusions (see Figure 4). Not surprisingly, also more supervisions (A4) improve the performance, whereas doubling the DOG size (A3) was badly rated. A possible explanation is that a more densely sampled DOG would require appropriate parameter adjustments (e.g., kernel width, spatial/motion

---

[6] The model settings were chosen to fulfill real-time processing on an ordinary multi-core CPU: 5×5 receptive fields, 1 layer/feature-category, spatial scales in $\{1, 1.5\}$, 8 in-plane rotation angles, 800 features. See [9,17] for a detailed description of each parameter.

Fig. 5. Sample predictions by DEVA on the same scene at different life stages (top to bottom: 1 day old, 5 days old). Better skills are acquired as long as the agent "grows up".

constraints weights). Processing longer sequences (A5) also yields better DVAs, because motion links become more stable with time and noisy DOG nodes are filtered out by the long–term removal policy.

The second experiment we present is inspired by life–long learning principles and guided by the protocol of Section 2. In this case, the so called agent DEVA was developed, by continuously processing[7] the cartoon "The Aristocats" (© The Walt Disney Company), and by receiving every day new supervisions from a set of selected supervisors. The outcome of DEVA processing can be monitored online for each day in its life (http://dva.diism.unisi.it/demo_aristocats.html), to check its evolution, its improvements and common mistakes[8]. A web inter-face allows to select the day, the semantic classes to visualize, and the agent's sensitivity. Figure 5 shows a result extrapolated from this experiment, where DEVA was tested on the same video sequence at different life stages (1 vs. 5 days old). Despite some errors (Toulouse and O'Malley, both reddish, and Duchess and Marie, both white, are easy to confuse) we can clearly appreciate how DEVA progressively acquires better visual skills during its life. This exper-iment addresses two distinct issues: (1) we publicly share results on a life–long experiment monitoring the gradual development of an agent; (2) we present a dynamic scenario where the number of classes incrementally grows over time, while existing classes keep receiving supervisions. The experiment lasted about three months.

6   Conclusions

This paper introduced a new perspective in the design and evaluation of agents that acquire visual skills simply by living in their own visual environment and by interacting with humans. A crowd-sourcing based evaluation scheme is proposed that can be instantiated by exploiting different human interaction modalities.

---

[7] DEVA actually processes a few minutes of video per day, to allow performance analysis.
[8] Processing at 320×240, 25fps, 20k DOG nodes, low-levels as in crowdsourcing experiments.

En plein air visual agents open the doors of research labs all over the world, by allowing any subscribed user to monitor and rate the performance of the currently deployed visual agents. Developmental Visual Agents turn out to be a proof of concept of the general principles outlined in this paper. DEVA, one of these agents, has been watching "The Aristocats" cartoon for months, interacting with humans who provided supervision. Future releases will include the possibility to supervise DEVA by registered users. While this paper reports the first attempt of pioneering the proposed idea, this general scheme is likely to be exploited in other labs by different approaches.

References

1. Chen, X., Shrivastava, A., Gupta, A.: NEIL: Extracting visual knowledge from web data. In: The IEEE Int. Conf. on Computer Vision (ICCV), December 2013
2. Diligenti, M., Gori, M., Maggini, M., Rigutini, L.: Bridging logic and kernel machines. Machine learning **86**(1), 57–88 (2012)
3. Felzenszwalb, P.F., Huttenlocher, D.P.: Efficient graph-based image segmentation. International Journal of Computer Vision **59**(2), 167–181 (2004)
4. Geman, D., Geman, S., Hallonquist, N., Younes, L.: Visual turing test for computer vision systems. In: Proceedings of the National Academy of Sciences (2015)
5. Gnecco, G., Gori, M., Melacci, S., Sanguineti, M.: Foundations of support constraint machines. Neural computation **27**(2), 388–480 (2015)
6. Gori, M.: Semantic-based regularization and piaget's cognitive stages. Neural Networks, 1035–1036 (2009)
7. Gori, M., Lippi, M., Maggini, M., Melacci, S.: On-line video motion estimation by invariant receptive inputs. In: CVPR workshops, pp. 712–717 (2014)
8. Gori, M., Melacci, S.: Constraint verification with kernel machines. IEEE Transactions on Neural Networks and Learning Systems **24**(5), 825–831 (2013)
9. Gori, M., Melacci, S., Lippi, M., Maggini, M.: Information theoretic learning for pixel-based visual agents. In: Fitzgibbon, A., Lazebnik, S., Perona, P., Sato, Y., Schmid, C. (eds.) ECCV 2012, Part VI. LNCS, vol. 7577, pp. 864–875. Springer, Heidelberg (2012)
10. Horn, B.K., Schunck, B.G.: Determining optical flow. In: 1981 Technical Symposium East, pp. 319–331. International Society for Optics and Photonics (1981)
11. Krizhevsky, A., Sutskever, I., Hinton, G.E.: Imagenet classification with deep convolutional neural networks. In: Advances in NIPS, pp. 1097–1105 (2012)
12. Liu, C., Yuen, J., Torralba, A.: Nonparametric scene parsing via label transfer. IEEE Transactions on Pattern Analysis and Machine Intelligence **33**(12), 2368–2382 (2011)
13. Malinowski, M., Fritz, M.: Hard to cheat: A turing test based on answering questions about images. CoRR, abs/1501.03302 (2015)
14. Marszalek, M., Laptev, I., Schmid, C.: Actions in context. In: CVPR, pp. 2929–2936. IEEE (2009)
15. McClelland, D.C.: Testing for competence rather than for intelligence. American psychologist **28**(1), 1 (1973)
16. Melacci, S., Belkin, M.: Laplacian Support Vector Machines Trained in the Primal. Journal of Machine Learning Research **12**, 1149–1184 (2011)

17. Melacci, S., Lippi, M., Gori, M., Maggini, M.: Information-based learning of deep architectures for feature extraction. In: Petrosino, A. (ed.) ICIAP 2013, Part II. LNCS, vol. 8157, pp. 101–110. Springer, Heidelberg (2013)

18. Melacci, S., Maggini, M., Gori, M.: Semi–supervised learning with constraints for multi–view object recognition. In: Alippi, C., Polycarpou, M., Panayiotou, C., Ellinas, G. (eds.) ICANN 2009, Part II. LNCS, vol. 5769, pp. 653–662. Springer, Heidelberg (2009)

19. Oquab, M., Bottou, L., Laptev, I., Sivic, J.: Learning and transferring mid-level image representations using convolutional neural networks. In: CVPR, pp. 1717–1724. IEEE (2014)

20. Sermanet, P., Eigen, D., Zhang, X., Mathieu, M., Fergus, R., LeCun, Y.: Overfeat: Integrated recognition, localization and detection using convolutional networks. arXiv preprint arXiv:1312.6229 (2013)

21. Terman, L.M.: Merrill, M.E.: Measuring intelligence. ACC (1961)

22. Tighe, J., Niethammer, M., Lazebnik, S.: Scene parsing with object instances and occlusion ordering. In: CVPR, pp. 3748–3755 (2014)

23. Torralba, A., Efros, A.A.: Unbiased look at dataset bias. In: CVPR, pp. 1521–1528. IEEE (2011)

Modalities Combination for Italian Sign Language Extraction and Recognition

Bassem Seddik[(⊠)], Sami Gazzah, and Najoua Essoukri Ben Amara

SAGE Laboratory, National Engineering School of Sousse,
Sousse University, Sousse, Tunisia
bassem.seddik.tn@ieee.org, sami_gazzah@yahoo.fr,
najoua.benamara@eniso.rnu.tn

Abstract. We propose in this work an approach for the automatic extraction and recognition of the Italian sign language using the RGB, depth and skeletal-joint modalities offered by Microsoft's Kinect sensor. We investigate the best modality combination that improves the human-action spotting and recognition in a continuous stream scenario. For this purpose, we define per modality a complementary feature representation and fuse the decisions of multiple SVM classifiers with probability outputs. We contribute by proposing a multi-scale analysis approach that combines a global Fisher vector representation with a local frame-wise one. In addition we define a temporal segmentation strategy that allows the generation of multiple specialized classifiers. The final decision is obtained using the combination of their results. Our tests have been carried out on the Chalearn gesture challenge dataset, and promising results have been obtained on primary experiments.

Keywords: Motion spotting · Action recognition · Fisher vector · Modalities combination · Classification fusion

1 Introduction

With the introduction of the Kinect sensor by Microsoft, a growing interest within the computer vision community has been conducted towards the improvement of human-action recognition solutions. The aimed applications range from education and entertainment to medical rehabilitation and sign language recognition [10]. As the Kinect sensor generates several types of spatial modalities, including the RGB, the depth and the skeletal joint pose streams of Shotton *et al.* [24], the challenge of optimally combining all of them is still open.

This paper is positioned in the context of multi-modal Italian sign language recognition. It aims to combine the different Kinect data streams in order to recognize a predefined set of actions in a continuous streaming real-world-like scenario. The samples of the considered actions are presented in Fig. 1. Human action can manifest in an infinite set of consecutive poses. In a continuous captured stream, we can find the resting poses where the actions are limited, the

© Springer International Publishing Switzerland 2015
V. Murino and E. Puppo (Eds.): ICIAP 2015, Part II, LNCS 9280, pp. 710–721, 2015.
DOI: 10.1007/978-3-319-23234-8_65

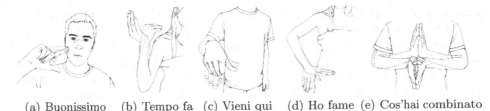

(a) Buonissimo   (b) Tempo fa   (c) Vieni qui   (d) Ho fame   (e) Cos'hai combinato

Fig. 1. Sample illustrations[1] of the Italian sign language vocabulary considered by the Chalearn gesture dataset [5] used in this paper

vocabulary action used for recognition and the rest of the non-significant actions that can be present within the streams.

Recently, efforts have been carried by a number of competitions for the creation of Kinect based dataset taking in consideration both spotting and recognizing actions. The competitive aspect of challenges such as [8] and [5] resulted in a multitude of works that have mainly focused on a dedicated type of modality to rapidly produce their results.

In this paper, we put forward both the combination of the different modalities offered by our sensor and the temporal extraction of motion before recognition. In this context, we propose an approach for the fusion of local feature decisions with global ones. We also contribute by a fusion strategy of multiple specialised SVM classifiers.

The organisation of the following writings will be turning around (1) the feature representation tools, (2) the action-extraction, and (3) the action-recognition solutions. They will be investigated in the next section of the literature review, then there will be dedicated related sections (sections (3) to (5)) detailing our own approach stages for each of them. Our experiments, conclusions and perspectives will be presented afterwards consecutively.

2   Related Works

We present in what follows the noticeable approaches of feature extraction, temporal segmentation and action recognition within the literature.

Feature Representation: For the RGB video streams, a first trend of human-action descriptors relied on region-of-interest gradient features [4,14] or spatio-temporal analysers such as [12]. More recently, global representations relying on sparse supervised [27] and unsupervised [20] encoders have gained growing interest.

For the joint modality, the first families of works focused on the recognition of actions using motion-capture signals from dedicated sensors [2]. Many new research works have used the Kinect joint stream and proposed dedicated measures related to the position, rotation, inter-joint relations and within-time

---

[1] http://www.theguardian.com/travel/series/learn-italian

behaviour [6,23]. It is noticeable that most of the joint-related representations belong to the hand-crafted feature type.

More recently, a number of research works have focused on the creation of features related to the depth streams. Most of them have relied on the binning of the orientations relative to the depth normals[17], the contextualisation of the point clouds [3] and the quantification of the motion's temporal differences [13].

Action Extraction: Also known as action spotting or temporal segmentation, it allows the delimitation of the beginning and the end of an action within a continuous stream of motion. The fastest methods for on-line human-action extraction belong to the heuristic family. In this case, a threshold is applied on a computed measure in order to capture 1D signal changes [1]. Similar thresholds can be found in [18] to evaluate the hand distance from a deduced resting position. Another one is applied in [13] to find whether the left or right hand is in action.

Other works try to analyse the behaviour of computed energy functions using different modalities. The solutions using sliding windows of specified temporal lengths and progressing steps can be found in [6] and [11]. More classic approaches rely on dynamic-programming-derived analysis in order to find temporal cuts within the continuous streams [8]. While more advanced solutions try to combine the advantages of the pre-listed approaches, as in [23], most of them are destined only for the binary classification between actions and resting positions.

Action Recognition: The work of Neverova *et al.* [16] can be considered as a frame-wise decision approach. While they used different sampling resolutions for the description of their frame contents with steps of 2,3 and 4, their final decision was on frame-scale. Similar works operating at local frame scale used hand-crafted features in combination with SVM classifiers. A joint-quadruplet descriptor has been proposed in [6] and a motion-trail based one has been presented in [13].

On the other hand, different types of works have focused on the use of global descriptors operating at the scale of the whole sequences concerned by recognition. Sparse representations derived from Bag of Words'(BoW) related representation proved their efficiency within the state of the art winning dense descriptor used in [18]. While the most classic BoW approach is related to vector-quantization global features derived form Fisher vectors have also been widely used [21].

Our Proposed Approach: We propose in this work a solution to generate segments with additional content knowledge from the temporal segmentation stage in order to improve recognition afterwards. This allows us to adopt a classification specialisation procedure that uses an adequate recogniser for every type of action. We distinguish in this context between the bi-handed and one-handed action labels.

By analysing the feature representations, we can highlight that while a many works have been interested in global representations of human actions using sparse features derived from BoW-like approaches [18], recent works focusing more on local scale descriptions have proved their efficiency [16].

We also suggest in this work an approach that combines the strengths of both global and local representations for different modalities. We proceed by a bottom-up analysis using classifiers learned at a frame scale. Then, we apply a fusion with a second up-down analysis derived from the Fisher vector's [19] representation of Gaussian Mixture Model (GMM) probability distributions. The combination of both global and local scales is performed using the weighted sum of the frame-wise recognition probabilities generated by the SVM classifiers.

3   Feature Representation

We start in this section by presenting the local features extracted from the different modalities following the stages of our previous work detailed in [22], then we present our introduced global representation.

3.1   Frame-wise Feature Representation

We have designed our features for complementarity. We have used the stabilized hand-joint positions to delimit the hand 3D poses from RGB and depth sub-windows. The dynamics of the whole upper body have been deduced afterwards from the 11 upper joints.

RGB Features: We used the video colour streams in order to deduce the poses of both hands using the HoG [4] descriptor. To achieve this, we exploited the positions indicated by the joints to extract the bounding boxes around the hands and saved 32 descriptive bins (i.e. 8 orientations x 4 cells) per hand.

Depth Features: We have utilised the depth information so as to bring the evolution of the 2D HoG features along the Z axis. For this purpose, we have subtracted the background and evaluated the depth motion $DM(t)$ differences in time, as presented in equation (1):

$$\text{DM}(t) = \gamma[(d(t+1).m(t+1) - d(t-1).m(t-1)] \tag{1}$$

where $m(t)$ is the actor mask stream offered by our dataset at each frame t, $d(t)$ is the depth and γ a downscaling factor. The difference is computed between the next $t+1$ and the past $t-1$ frames. From this stage, we have saved 16 features per hand bounding region obtained from the joint positions.

Joint Features: The joint descriptors have been designed to complete the pose captured by the HoG hand features with others relative to the whole upper body's precise position and rotation information. These features have been extracted using the normalised 3D joint positions $J_p^i = [x, y, z]$ in addition to the four quaternion angles $J_q^i = [q_x, q_y, q_z, q_w]$, where $i = 1...11$ is the upper body joint index. Also, similar to the shape-context description [15], we have analysed the joint pair-wise distances J_d of the 11x11 size, given by equation (2), and subtracted the constantly null ones:

$$J_d = \| J_p^i - J_p^j \|_2 \quad , with \ i \neq j \tag{2}$$

Finally, the dynamic evolution of the joint speed J_s and acceleration J_a have been computed using equations (3) and (4) respectively, at the frame instants t:

$$J_s(t) = J_p(t+1) - J_p(t-1) \tag{3}$$

$$J_a(t) = J_p(t+2) - 2J_p(t) + J_p(t-2) \tag{4}$$

The obtained feature vector $J = [J_p, J_q, J_d, J_s, J_a]$ has a size of 251 descriptors.

3.2   Global Feature Representation

In order to generate a wider feature representation scale, we have opted for the Fisher vector representation. This feature-space transformation has proven its efficiency, especially in the case of human-action extraction and recognition [18, 21]. It generates a sparse one-dimensional feature vector for each video stream and allows rapid SVM classification afterwards.

Considering a set of training feature vectors $F = [f_1, ..., f_t]$, extracted from t learning frames using a number of D features, we start by learning a GMM using expectation maximization approach [26]. The generated parameters $\Theta = \{\pi_k, \mu_k, \Sigma_k; k = 1, ..., K\}$ are saved such that π_k, μ_k and Σ_k are respectively the prior probabilities, means and diagonal covariance matrices of every cluster k. To initialise the GMM K centroids, we have applied a K-means clustering and considered 3 Gaussian mixtures per action label as presented in [9]. Thus, for a set of 5 bi-handed actions, we have extracted $K = 15$ centroids. They are associated to each f_i sample by the posteriori probability given in equation (5):

$$\Gamma_{ik} = \frac{exp[-\frac{1}{2}(f_i - \mu_k)^T \Sigma_k^{-1}(f_i - \mu_k)]}{\sum_{l=1}^{K} exp[-\frac{1}{2}(f_i - \mu_l)^T \Sigma_k^{-1}(f_i - \mu_l)]} \tag{5}$$

where i and k denote respectively the frame indices and the k-means centroids. The Fisher generated vector of an action sequence S is given by equation (6) where $j \in \{1, ..., D\}$ refers to the feature dimension:

$$\Phi(S) = [u_{j1}, v_{j1}, ..., u_{jK}, v_{jK}] \tag{6}$$

It is constructed using the concatenation of the mean and covariance's partial derivatives given in equations (7) and (8) respectively:

$$u_{jk} = \frac{1}{t\sqrt{\pi_k}} \sum_{i=1}^{t} \Gamma_{ik} \left[\frac{f_{ji} - \mu_{jk}}{\sigma_{jk}} \right] \tag{7}$$

$$v_{jk} = \frac{1}{t\sqrt{2\pi_k}} \sum_{i=1}^{t} \Gamma_{ik} \left[\left(\frac{f_{ji} - \mu_{jk}}{\sigma_{jk}} \right)^2 - 1 \right] \tag{8}$$

The generated Fisher vector of size $2KD$ is further improved using the function $f(x) = |x|sign(x)$ and applying l^2 normalisation [19].

4   Action-Segment Spotting

Our temporal segmentation methodology is similar to the one presented in [23], with many additional improvements. The common steps are related to the bi-processing stages going first into the heuristic joint analysis and then applying the SVM classification in order to robustly extract the motion segments. As presented in Fig. 2, the newly adopted steps have been related to the identification of the motion family out of 4 cases: the non-motion (i.e. label 0), the left-handed, the right-handed and the bi-handed actions (i.e. labels 1, 2 and 3 consecutively). We have been able to introduce this pre-classification using the following tests :

$$
\begin{cases}
Both\ hands : \mathbf{3}\ if\ \ (J_p^{lh} - J_p^{rest}) > \tau\ \ and\ \ (J_p^{rh} - J_p^{rest}) > \tau \\
Right\ hand : \mathbf{2}\ if\ \ (J_p^{lh} - J_p^{rest}) > \tau \\
Left\ \ hand : \mathbf{1}\ if\ \ (J_p^{rh} - J_p^{rest}) > \tau \\
No\ motion : \mathbf{0}\ if\ \ (J_p^{lh} - J_p^{rest}) \leqslant \tau\ \ or\ \ (J_p^{rh} - J_p^{rest}) \leqslant \tau
\end{cases}
$$

where J_p^{rest} is the resting position identified by analysing the joint's most visited cell into a 200x200 grid. We have also saved the binary vector flags indicating whether we have a motion performed by the left hand, the right hand or both. The two first plots (a) and (b) presented in Fig. 2 show the considered thresholds for these vectors. Using the SVM classification, we have been able to extract different types of enriched motion positions. The obtained labels have allowed us to apply a fusion strategy between multiple classifiers with kernels tuned for every motion type.

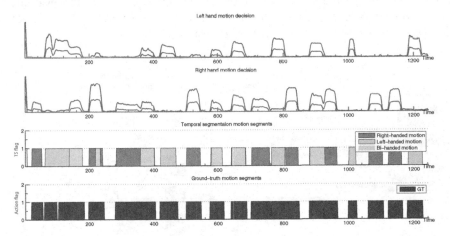

Fig. 2. Illustration of the motion spotting results: a- and b- plots showing the motion varition limit considered for the left and right hands respectively, c- the flags deduced from the left and right hand motion analysis, d- the ground-truth manual segmentation

5   Action Recognition Strategy

As presented in Fig. 3, our approach starts by grouping the RGB-D features with an order determined by the dominant hand first. This is obtained by looking at the cumulative motion of both hand joints. During the action recognition, the outputs of the previous segment-labelling stage have been used for classifier specialisation. We have deduced from the label-3 dominance that we had a bi-handed action and from the labels 1 and 2 that we have had a one-handed action. We have then redirected the generated descriptors to two classification pools. The first is related to the bi-handed actions (i.e. 'cheduepalle', 'chevuoi', 'daccordo', 'combinato' and 'basta') and the second (presented in section 6) is dedicated to the lasting one-handed ones. This specialization has reduced the inter-variability within the population of descriptors and allowed us to gain recognition improvements.

On a second level of decision, we use the SVM classifiers with the RBF kernels for the local descriptors and linear ones for the global descriptors. We have combined them using a weighted sum of the probability outputs P_{gl} of the SVM classifiers, as in equation 9:

$$P_{gl} = \alpha P_g \oplus (1 - \alpha) P_l \tag{9}$$

where α is an empirically determined weighting value and $\oplus$ denotes the element-wise addition of the global label probability P_g to each of the obtained local frame probabilities P_l. A similar fusion process has been repeated for the outputs of the RGB-D and joint decision pools. The obtained frame-wise labels have been grouped following a major voting of the central frame labels, as detailed in [22], to produce a unique global label for each extracted action segment. The evaluation of our approach performance on the ground truth and the temporally segmented partitions is going to be presented in the next section.

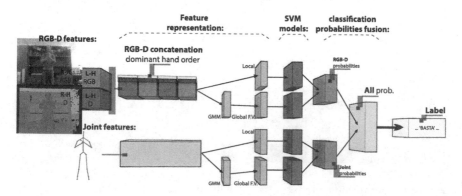

Fig. 3. Our approach learns different SVM models: those at a frame-wise local scale and those at a global scale using the Fisher vectors (F.V.). It first fuses global decisions with local ones, then combines the RGB-D probabilities with those of the joints

6   Experiments and Results

We present hereafter our used dataset, then evaluate our combined local-global approach using the ground truth and finish with the overall positioning of our solution within the state of the art.

Used Dataset: The experiments presented in this work have been carried out on a subset of the Chalearn gesture challenge 2014 dataset [5]. It is organised into 3 subsets relative to learning, validation and test stages. Each of them contains multi-modal data relative to the RGB, depth and user mask videos in addition to the skeletal joints streams as shown in Fig. 4. Each recording is associated to one person performing Italian sign language actions in front of the Kinect sensor. The considered action vocabulary is at a number of 20 different actions. They are labelled as follows: *1.'vattene', 2.'vieniqui', 3.'perfetto', 4.'furbo', 5.'cheduepalle', 6.'chevuoi', 7.'daccordo', 8.'seipazzo', 9.'combinato', 10.'freganiente', 11.'ok', 12.'cosatifarei', 13.'basta', 14.'prendere', 15.'cenepiu', 16.'fame', 17.'tempofa', 18.'buonissimo', 19.'messidaccordo', and 20.'sonostufo'.*

Performance Evaluation: The evaluation of our approach performance has been carried out using a learning set of 80 folders and a test set of 20 other ones (i.e. *Sample0081* to *Sample0100*). Our experiments have led us to choose an empirical value for the weight $\alpha = 0.4$ to allow more influence for the local decision probabilities. Then, the fusion of the decisions relative to both RGB-D and joint probabilities has been applied with equal weights (i.e. $\alpha = 0.5$). The obtained performances using the ground truth action-segments are summarised in Table 1.

The behaviour of the learned global classifiers has allowed the generation of 100% frame-rates if the action is recognised or of 0% if not. This explains the relative superiority of the local-scale classifier (84.21% against 57.06% for the

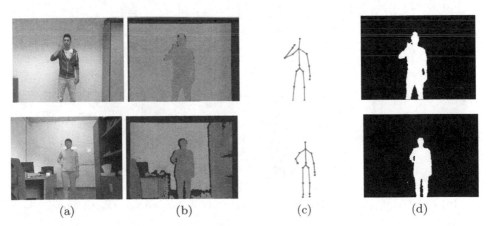

(a)   (b)   (c)   (d)

Fig. 4. Illustrations of the modalities offered by the Chalearn gesture 2014 dataset: a-RGB, b- depth, c- skeleton and d- user mask for the case of the actions: 'buonissimo' and 'ho fame'

Table 1. Evaluation of our approach processing stages using the ground truth in the case of bi-handed actions

	RGB-D local	RGB-D global	Joint local	Joint global
Per modality RR	84.21%	57.06%	75.46%	51.51%
Loc. and Glob. RR	93.33%		75.88%	
Multi-modal RR	94.58%			

RGB-D samples given in Table 1). The combination of both local and global probabilities has noticeably improved the performances, as shown in the confusion matrices of Fig. 5. The fusion of the decisions obtained from both RGB-D and joint classifiers has further improved the results to reach 94.58% in the case of the bi-handed action labels.

As demonstrated in Fig. 5, we have been able to obtain recognition gains for both global-local and multi-modal fusion stages. Compared to the results obtained in [22] using the same set of descriptors, the performances have risen from 81.01% on the ground truth to reach 94.58%. In comparison to the works presenting performance evaluation on the Chalearn 2014 dataset ground truth [6,13,18], our solution presents the advantage of reaching 100% recognition rates for multiple action classes. This is, for example, the case for the labels 9 and 13 in Fig. 5-g.

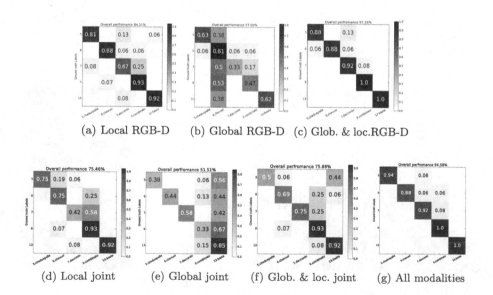

(a) Local RGB-D   (b) Global RGB-D   (c) Glob. & loc.RGB-D

(d) Local joint   (e) Global joint   (f) Glob. & loc. joint   (g) All modalities

Fig. 5. Evaluation of the performance gain for the different labels through the confusion matrices generated using the RGB-D and joint streams for the bi-handed action family

The developed method has proved to be efficient for recognition improvement compared to similar methods [13, 22]. Our solution brings two major advantages. The first is related to the exploitation of the action extraction stage for the service of classification specialisation. The second is related to the combination of the local and global classifier decisions. The presented rates are dedicated to the bi-handed actions and similar improvements can be obtained for the one-handed actions.

7   Conclusion and Perspectives

We have presented in this paper an approach for the extraction and the recognition of human actions from continuous streams of multi-modal data. We have contributed by proposing a fusion of the decisions offered by the Fisher vector's global representation with those obtained from the frame-wise local descriptions of actions. We have also put forward a combination strategy for features extracted from the RGB, depth and joint data streams offered by the Kinect sensor beside a specialisation approach of the classifiers for the one-handed and bi-handed actions. The experiments on the Chalearn gesture challenge dataset have proven the effectiveness of our approach for the recognition improvement.

Future perspectives for our work include the evaluation over the whole test dataset offered by the Chalearn gesture challenge using the Jaccard index [5] and the investigation of more advanced fusion strategies derived from the probabilistic theory [28]. In addition, we are in the process of considering data regulation strategies [7] as the extra classes of non-vocabulary and non-motion segments come with over-balanced learning population rates within our dataset.

References

1. Alippi, C., Boracchi, G., Roveri, M.: Just-In-Time Classifiers for Recurrent Concepts. IEEE Transactions on Neural Networks and Learning Systems **24**, 620–634 (2013)
2. Bao, L., Intille, S.S.: Activity recognition from user-annotated acceleration data. In: Ferscha, A., Mattern, F. (eds.) PERVASIVE 2004. LNCS, vol. 3001, pp. 1–17. Springer, Heidelberg (2004)
3. Belongie, S., Malik, J., Puzicha, J.: Shape Matching and Object Recognition Using Shape Contexts. IEEE Transactions on Pattern Analysis and Machine Intelligence **24**, 509–522 (2002)
4. Dalal, N., Triggs, B.: Histograms of oriented gradients for human detection. In: CVPR, pp. 886–893. IEEE Press, San Diego (2005)
5. Escalera, S., Baró, X., Gonzàlez, J., Bautista, M.A., Madadi, M., Reyes, M., Ponce-López, V., Escalante, H.J., Shotton, J., Guyon, I.: ChaLearn looking at people challenge 2014: dataset and results. In: Agapito, L., Bronstein, M.M., Rother, C. (eds.) ECCV 2014 Workshops. LNCS, vol. 8925, pp. 459–473. Springer, Heidelberg (2015)
6. Evangelidis, G.D., Singh, G., Horaud, R.: Continuous gesture recognition from articulated poses. In: Agapito, L., Bronstein, M.M., Rother, C. (eds.) ECCV 2014 Workshops. LNCS, vol. 8925, pp. 595–607. Springer, Heidelberg (2015)

7. Gazzah, S., Essoukri Ben Amara, N.: Writer identification using modular MLP classifier and genetic algorithm for optimal features selection. In: Wang, J., Yi, Z., Żurada, J.M., Lu, B.-L., Yin, H. (eds.) ISNN 2006. LNCS, vol. 3972, pp. 271–276. Springer, Heidelberg (2006)
8. Guyon, I., Athitsos, V., Jangyodsuk, P., Escalante, H.J.: The ChaLearn Gesture Dataset (CGD 2011), MVA (2013)
9. Hernandez-Vela, A., Bautista, M.A., Perez-Sala, X., Ponce-Lpez, V., Escalera, S., Bar, X., Pujol, P., Angulo, C.: Probability-based Dynamic Time Warping and Bag-of-Visual-and-Depth-Words for Human Gesture Recognition in RGB-D. Pattern Recognition Letters **50**, 112–121 (2014)
10. Ibanez, R., Soria, A., Teyseyre, A., Campo, M.: Easy gesture recognition for kinect. AES **76**, 171–180 (2014)
11. Ortiz Laguna, J., Olaya, A.G., Borrajo, D.: A dynamic sliding window approach for activity recognition. In: Konstan, J.A., Conejo, R., Marzo, J.L., Oliver, N. (eds.) UMAP 2011. LNCS, vol. 6787, pp. 219–230. Springer, Heidelberg (2011)
12. Laptev, I.: On space-time interest points. IJCV **64**(2–3), 107–123 (2005)
13. Liang, B., Zheng, L.: Multi-modal gesture recognition using skeletal joints and motion trail model. In: Agapito, L., Bronstein, M.M., Rother, C. (eds.) ECCV 2014 Workshops. LNCS, vol. 8925, pp. 623–638. Springer, Heidelberg (2015)
14. Lowe, D.G.: Distinctive image features from scale-invariant keypoints. IJCV **60**(2), 91–110 (2004)
15. Mori, G., Malik, J.: Recovering 3d Human Body Configurations Using Shape Contexts. IEEE Transactions on Pattern Analysis and Machine Intelligence **7**, 1052–1062 (2006)
16. Neverova, N., Wolf, C., Taylor, G.W., Nebout, F.: Multi-scale deep learning for gesture detection and localization. In: Agapito, L., Bronstein, M.M., Rother, C. (eds.) ECCV 2014 Workshops. LNCS, vol. 8925, pp. 474–490. Springer, Heidelberg (2015)
17. Oreifej, O., Zicheng, L.: HON4D: Histogram of oriented 4D normals for activity recognition from depth sequences. In: CVPR, pp. 716–723. IEEE Press, Los Alamitos (2013)
18. Peng, X., Wang, L., Cai, Z., Qiao, Y.: Action and gesture temporal spotting with super vector representation. In: Agapito, L., Bronstein, M.M., Rother, C. (eds.) ECCV 2014 Workshops. LNCS, vol. 8925, pp. 518–527. Springer, Heidelberg (2015)
19. Perronnin, F., Sánchez, J., Mensink, T.: Improving the fisher kernel for large-scale image classification. In: Daniilidis, K., Maragos, P., Paragios, N. (eds.) ECCV 2010, Part IV. LNCS, vol. 6314, pp. 143–156. Springer, Heidelberg (2010)
20. Pigou, L., Dieleman, S., Kindermans, P.-J., Schrauwen, B.: Sign language recognition using convolutional neural networks. In: Agapito, L., Bronstein, M.M., Rother, C. (eds.) ECCV 2014 Workshops. LNCS, vol. 8925, pp. 572–578. Springer, Heidelberg (2015)
21. Rostamzadeh, N., Zen, G., Mironică, I., Uijlings, J., Sebe, N.: Daily living activities recognition via efficient high and low level cues combination and fisher kernel representation. In: Petrosino, A. (ed.) ICIAP 2013, Part I. LNCS, vol. 8156, pp. 431–441. Springer, Heidelberg (2013)
22. Seddik, B., Gazzah, S., Essoukri Ben Amara, N.: Hands, face and joints for multi-modal human-actions spotting and recognition. In: EUSIPCO (2015)
23. Seddik, B., Gazzah, S., Chateau, T., Essoukri Ben Amara, N.: Augmented skeletal joints for temporal segmentation of sign language actions. In: IPAS, pp. 1–6. Hammamet (2014)

24. Shotton, J., Fitzgibbon, A., Cook, M., Sharp, T., Finocchio, M., Moore, R., Kipman, A., Blake, A.: Real-time human pose recognition in parts from a single depth image. In: CVPR (2011)

25. Sung, J., Ponce, C., Selman, B., Saxena, A.: Unstructured human activity detection from RGBD images. In: ICRA, pp. 842–849 (2012)

26. Vedaldi, A., Fulkerson, B.: VLFeat: An Open and Portable Library of Computer Vision Algorithms (2008)

27. Wang, H., Schmid, C.: Action recognition with improved trajectories. In: ICCV, pp. 3551–3558 (2013)

28. Yazid, H., Kalti, K., Essoukri Ben Amara, N.: A performance comparison of the Bayesian graphical model and the possibilistic graphical model applied in a brain MRI cases retrieval contribution. In: SSD, pp. 16. IEEE Press, Hammamet (2013)

Abnormality Detection with Improved Histogram of Oriented Tracklets

Hossein Mousavi[1]($\boxtimes$), Moin Nabi[1], Hamed Kiani Galoogahi[1],
Alessandro Perina[1], and Vittorio Murino[1,2]

[1] Pattern Analysis and Computer Vision Department (PAVIS), Istituto Italiano di
Tecnologia (IIT), Genova, Italy
{Hossein.Mousavi,Moin.Nabi,Kiani.Galoogahi,
Alessandro.Perina,Vittorio.Murino}@iit.it
[2] Dipartimento di Informatica, University of Verona, Verona, Italy

Abstract. Recently the histogram of oriented tracklets (HOT) was
shown to be an efficient video representation for abnormality detection
and achieved state-of-the-arts on the available datasets. Unlike standard
video descriptors that mainly employ low level motion features, e.g. optical flow, the HOT descriptor simultaneously encodes magnitude and orientation of tracklets as a mid-level representation over crowd motions.
However, extracting tracklets in HOT suffers from poor salient point
initialization and tracking drift in the presence of occlusion. Moreover,
count-based HOT histogramming does not properly take into account
the motion characteristics of abnormal motions. This paper extends the
HOT by addressing these drawbacks introducing an enhanced version
of HOT, named Improved HOT. First, we propose to initialize salient
points in each frame instead of the first frame, as the HOT does. Second,
we replace the naive count-based histogramming by the richer statistics of crowd movement (i.e., motion distribution). The evaluation of
the Improved HOT on different datasets, namely UCSD, BEHAVE and
UMN, yields compelling results in abnormality detection, by outperforming the original HOT and the state-of-the-art descriptors based on optical
flow, dense trajectories and the social force models.

Keywords: Histogram of oriented tracklets · Abnormality detection ·
Tracklets · Crowd motion analysis

1 Introduction

The study of human behavior has become an active research topic in the areas
of human-computer interaction, robot learning, user interface design, intelligent
surveillance and crowd analysis. The task of crowd behavior detection refers to
identifying the behavioral patterns of individuals involved in a crowd scenario.
It is well noted in the sociological literature that a crowd goes beyond a set of
individuals that independently display their personal behavioral patterns [1,2].
In other words, the behavior of each individual in a crowd may be influenced

© Springer International Publishing Switzerland 2015
V. Murino and E. Puppo (Eds.): ICIAP 2015, Part II, LNCS 9280, pp. 722–732, 2015.
DOI: 10.1007/978-3-319-23234-8_66

by "crowd factors" (e.g., dynamics, goal, environment, event, etc.), thus, the individuals behave in a different way than if they were alone.

Based on the above explanation, existing computer vision techniques designed for the detection of individual behavioral patterns are not suitable for modeling and detecting events in crowd scenes. This has encouraged the vision community to design tailored techniques for modeling and understanding behavioral patterns in crowd scenarios. A large portion of recent works is dedicated to model and detect abnormal behaviors in video data. Existing works in the literature are basically different in terms of the type of abnormal behavior (e.g. panic [3], violence [4], escape [5]), types of features (histograms of low level features [6–8], optical flow [9,10], trajectories [11], spatio-temporal features [12,13], etc.), modeling frameworks and learning techniques such as markov model based [10], bayesian models [14], clustering based [15,16], commotion measure [17] and social force models [9].

Recently, a new video descriptor called Histogram of Oriented Tracklets, HOT, is proposed to detect abnormality in crowd scenarios [18]. The HOT descriptor encodes the motion patterns in the form of 2-dimensional histogram utilizing the magnitude and orientation of tracklets. The extensive experiments over abnormality datasets showed the superiority and simplicity of the HOT compared to the state-of-the-art descriptors. The promising performance achieved by HOT is mainly provided by: i) exploiting tracklets as mid-level motion representation, and ii) the capability of HOT descriptor to simultaneously encode the statistics of tracklet's orientation and magnitude in a unified descriptor.

This approach, however, suffers form two major drawbacks. **First**, the most of tracklets are extracted by tracking the salient points initialized in the first frame. Therefore, it is not able to extract new tracklets corresponded to salient points appearing in the next frames. Besides, since the tracklets are generated over long term salient points tracking, there is always the possible danger of drifting in the presence of occlusion. For instance, tracklets corresponded to an individual's hand can be wrongly drifted to another individual's hand due to the occlusion of hand shaking. **Second**, crowd motion statistics are naively encoded by counting the number of tracklets fall into each HOT bin. Such histogramming strategy has shown to be effective for feature description. In HOT, however, we empirically observed that it can drastically degrade the effect of magnitudes belong to abnormal motions. The dilemma here is to efficiently address these disadvantages by proposing Improved HOT.

Contribution. The major contributions of this work are listed as below:

1. We propose to extract tracklets by initializing salient points in each frame (i.e., frame level initialization), instead of the first frame (i.e., video level initialization) applied in HOT [18]. In this strategy, the potential salient points are detected at each frame and then tracked over the next L frames.
2. we propose to construct HOT histograms by exploiting richer statistics of crowd motions. In particular, the magnitude distribution (mean and vari-

ance) of tracklets are exploited in histogramming as opposed to the simple counting in the original HOT.

We extensively conduct a set of experiments over abnormal detection datasets including USCD [19], UMN [9] and Behave [20]. The results demonstrate the superiority of Improved HOT compared to HOT and the state-of-the-arts descriptors. The paper is organized as follows. Section 2 introduces the improved HOT and a short overview of the original HOT. Section 3 presents the experimental results followed by conclusions in Section 4.

2   Improved HOT

In order to have a comprehensive study, we recognize two main components in HOT including tracklet extraction and HOT histogram computation. For each component, we first briefly explain the original HOT and elaborate its drawbacks. Then, we introduce new strategies to improve the existing limitations.

2.1   Tracklet Extraction

The existing approaches for motion representation in crowds can be generally classified into two main categories: local motion based (e.g., optical flows) [9,10,14] and complete trajectories of objects [21,22] based. Both have some limitations. Without tracking objects, the information represented by local motions is limited, which weakens the models power. The crowd behavior recognized from local motions are less accurate, tend to be in short range and may fail in certain scenarios. The other type of approaches assumed that complete trajectories of objects were available and crowd video can be represented using the point trajectories. The accurate long-term observation is hard to be guaranteed due to scene clutter and tracking errors, but can effectively capture the global structure of crowd motions [23].

Tracklets exploited in the HOT [18], however, are mid-level representations between the two extremes discussed above. A tracklet is a fragment of a trajectory and is obtained by a tracker within a short period. Tracklets terminate when ambiguities caused by occlusions and scene clutters arise. They are more conservative and less likely to drift than long trajectories [23].

The tracklet extraction strategy employed in the original HOT is illustrated in Fig. 1(top). In this strategy, called video-level initialization [18], tracklets are initialized using the salient points detected in the first frame of the video, and then tracked until the tracker fails. The main drawback of this strategy is that tracklets are limited to the salient points which were extracted from the first frame or the salient points detected over re-initialization process (which only happens when tracker fails). This means that the new salient points appearing in the subsequent frames will not be fully detected, and thus, not considered for tracklet extraction. Moreover, such long term salient point tracking may lead to "drifting" problem. The drifting problem mainly occurs if a salient point miss-detected/tracked in presence of two particles occlusion. Such occlusions are not avoidable in real world crowd scenarios.

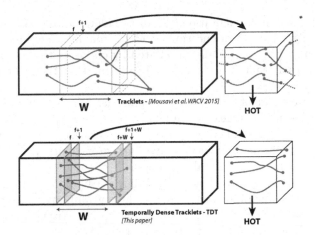

Fig. 1. Top: Video level tracklet initialization in HOT [18]. Bottom: Frame level tracklet extraction which is called Temporally Dense Tracklets.

We, on the other hand, proposed to re-initialize salient points in each single frame of the video and track the points over W frames, we called this Temporally Dense Tracklets (TDT) (Fig. 1(bottom)). This strategy is not limited to the points detected at the first frame and is capable of detecting all possible salient points over a given video. In other words, no matter how long is the captured video, this strategy is able to detect the salient points of all the appearing objects/individuals over the time. This results in producing a large pool of tracklets which can summarize the motion-patterns observed in the scene in each frame. we reset interest points in each frame and track it over W frames. In video-based tracklet extraction in HOT, on the other hand, an initial set of points are detected at the first frame of the video and tracked for the entire length of the tracklet.

2.2   Histogram of Tracklets Computation

The process of HOT computation explained in [18] starts by splitting the video in spatio-temporal cuboids. The magnitude $(M^{i,s})$ and orientation $(\theta^{i,s})$ of tracklet i passing from cuboid s are computed as:

$$M^{i,s} = \max_{t \in T}\left\{m_t^{(i,s)}\right\} \qquad \theta^{i,s} = \arctan\frac{(y_{end}^{i,s} - y_{begin}^{i,s})}{(x_{end}^{i,s} - x_{begin}^{i,s})} \qquad (1)$$

where (x_t, y_t) indicates the two-dimensional coordinates of the tth point of the tracklet i and T indicates the length of each tracklet. m_t is the magnitude of the tth point computed as $m_t = \sqrt{(x_{t+1} - x_t)^2 + (y_{t+1} - y_t)^2}$. $(x_{begin}^{i,s}, y_{begin}^{i,s})$ and $(x_{end}^{i,s}, y_{end}^{i,s})$ respectively show the entry and exit points of tracklet i in/from cuboid s. More details can be found in [18].

The magnitudes and orientations of all tracklets across cuboid s are independently quantized in O orientations and M magnitudes bins. The bins of the 2D-histogram $H_{o,m}^{s,f}$ are finally populated by counting the occurrence of the magnitude-orientation pairs in cuboid s. The frame that the HOT is computed for is indexed by f [18].

The major problem of such histogramming is, however, ignoring the magnitude characteristics of tracklets and only take into account the number of occurrences (by counting). Due to the fact that tracklets belong to abnormal motions exhibit strong magnitudes, simple histogramming degrades the weight of magnitudes belong to abnormal motions.

We differently encode the tracklets in each bin via motion magnitude distribution (mean and variance). In fact, the new histogramming technique, referred to as *weighted histogramming*, preserves the magnitude strength (mean) and the commotion (variance) of motion patterns in each HOT bin.

Given a set of J magnitude-orientation pairs $\{(\theta^{j,s}, M^{j,s})\}_{j=1}^{J}$ fall in the orientation bin o and magnitude bin m, the weighted histogramming returns two 2D histograms called mean-HOT and variance-HOT computed as:

$$mH_{o,m}^{s,f} = \frac{1}{J} \sum_{j=1}^{J} M^{j,s} \qquad vH_{o,m}^{s,f} = \frac{1}{J} \sum_{j=1}^{J} (M^{j,s} - mH_{o,m}^{s})^2 \qquad (2)$$

where $mH_{o,m}^{s,f}$ and $vH_{o,m}^{s,f}$ respectively states the mean-HOT and variance-HOT corresponded to the cuboid s at frame f (following the original HOT we compute the Improved HOT per frame).

3   Abnormality Detection

Following the original HOT [18], we applied two approaches to compute the mean-HOT and variance-HOT per frame namely Fully bag of words (BW) and Per-frame, Per-sector (FS). Similarly, we employed the latent Dirichlet allocations (LDA) generative model for learning and classification.

Given a set of two-dimensional mean-HOT $mH_{om}^{s,f}$ and variance-HOT $vH_{o,m}^{s,f}$ for all cuboids s temporary centered at frame $f = 1, \ldots, F$, we construct the LDA training corpus $\mathcal{D}$ based on two different detection strategies:

Fully bag of words (BW). In the first case, mean-HOTs and variance-HOTs are summed across spatial sectors:

$$(mD)^f = \sum_{s} (mH)_{o,m}^{s,f} \quad \text{and} \quad (vD)^f = \sum_{s} (vH)_{o,m}^{s,f} \qquad (3)$$

The LDA training corpus $\mathcal{D}$ is then constructed by concatenating the vectorized $(mD)^f$ and $(vD)^f$ at each frame as $\mathcal{D} = \{[(mD)^f | (vD)^f]\}_{f=1}^{F}$, where the operator | concatenates two vectors.

Per-frame, Per-sector (FS). In the second case, mean-HOTs and variance-HOTs from all the different sectors of a frame are concatenated in a single descriptor to preserve the spatial information of each frame:

$$(mD)^f = \{(mH)_{o,m}^{1,f} | (mH)_{o,m}^{2,f} | \ldots | (mH)_{o,m}^{S,f}\}$$
$$(vD)^f = \{(vH)_{o,m}^{1,f} | (vH)_{o,m}^{2,f} | \ldots | (vH)_{o,m}^{S,f}\} \qquad (4)$$

Similarly, the LDA training corpus $\mathcal{D}$ is constructed by concatenating the vectorized $(mD)^f$ and $(vD)^f$ at each frame as $\mathcal{D} = \{[(mD)^f | (vD)^f]\}_{f=1}^F$. When training/testing data of normal and abnormal actions is available, the corpus of both positive(normal) and negative(abnormal) clips are constructed and fed into a linear SVM for learning and classification.

4   Experimental Evaluation

We compare the Improved HOT (iHOT) descriptor with the original HOT state-of-the-art descriptors in the literature, mainly the mixtures of dynamic textures framework [19] and leading optical flows based approaches [4,11,24,25]. To have a more comprehensive investigation, we conducted two different experiments. First, we evaluate the improvement provided by only TDT extraction strategy over the UMN and BEHAVE datasets. In the second experiment, we extensively evaluate the full framework of iHOT (namely, TDT tracklet extraction + weighted histogramming) over the UCSD dataset.

4.1   Crowd Datasets

Three publicly available datasets are employed for the evaluation, including USCD [19], UMN [9] and BEHAVE [20].

   UCSD Dataset[1] The dataset contains two smaller subsets corresponded to two different scenes. The first, denoted by "ped1" contains clips of 158×238 pixels, which depict groups of people walking toward and away from the camera, with a certain degree of perspective distortion. The second, denoted by "ped2" has spatial resolution of 240×360 pixels and depicts a scene where most pedestrians move horizontally. The video footage of each scene is sliced into clips of 120-200 frames. We only considered anomaly at the frame level for this dataset.

   BEHAVE Dataset[2] consists of a set of complex group activities including *meeting, splitting up, standing, walking together, ignoring each other, escaping, fighting* and *running*. Following [18], the *fighting* activity is selected as abnormalities (50 clips) and the rest as normal activities (271 clips).

   UMN Dataset[3] includes 11 different scenarios of a panic and normal situations in three different indoor and outdoor scenes.

---

[1] Available at http://www.svcl.ucsd.edu/projects/anomaly/
[2] Available at http://groups.inf.ed.ac.uk/vision/behavedata/interactoins/
[3] http://mha.cs.umn.edu/movies/crowdactivity-all.avi

Table 1. AUC on the UMN dataset.

Dataset	iHOT-TDT	HOT [18]	SFM [9]	SR [26]	OF [9]	CI [27]
scene-1	**0.998**	0.993	0.990	0.995	0.964	n/a
scene-2	**0.991**	0.984	0.949	0.975	0.906	n/a
scene-3	**0.998**	0.991	0.989	0.964	0.967	n/a
all scenes	**0.994**	0.991	0.960	0.978	0.840	0.990

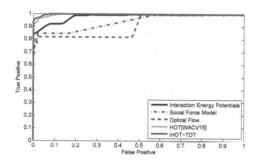

Fig. 2. ROC curve on BEHAVE dataset.

4.2   Evaluating TDT Tracklet Extraction

In this experiment, we evaluate the Improved HOT with TDT tracklet extraction (iHOT-TDT) comparing with the original HOT (video level initialization) and the state-of-the-arts on the UMN and BEHAVE datasets. The parameters are fixed to trackelt length $W = 11$, magnitude bins $M = 16$ and orientation bins $O = 8$. The classification strategy for the original HOT and the Improved HOT is limited to fully bag of words (BW).

Evaluation on UMN Dataset. In this experiment, we compared the iHOT-TDT with HOT [18], social force model (SFM) [9], sparse reconstruction (SP) [26], optical flow (OF) [9], Chaotic Invariants(CI) [27] following the standard evaluation of [9]. To have a finer evaluation, we deployed a protocol by consideration of UMN three scenes separately. We found this protocol so helpful to analyses the effect of proposed descriptor in each scene individually. The results on each scene (*scene-1, scene-2, scene-3*) and the whole dataset (*all scenes*) are reported in Table 1 in terms of AUC (Area Under the ROC Curve). The result demonstrates the superiority of our approach on this dataset for both scene-based and all scenes evaluations.

Evaluation on Behave Dataset. This experiment compares the iHOT-TDT with the optical flow based method, social force model [9] and interaction energy potential [11]. Following settings in [11], we used half of normal and abnormal videos for training and the rest for testing. We used BW classification strategy along with linear kernel SVM for frame level classification. The results are reported by the means of ROC as shown in Fig 2.

Table 2. Equal Error Rates on UCSD dataset using standard testing protocol. The results of the previous approaches are borrowed from [19]. The results of our approach and the original HOT are the best performance obtained at the parameter tuning experiment.

ped1		ped2	
Method	EER	Method	EER
MDT [19, 29]	22.9%	MDT [19, 29]	27.9%
SFM [9]	36.5%	SFM [9]	35.0%
LMH [24]	38.9%	LMH [24]	45.8%
HOT: BW [18]	23.84%	HOT: BW [18]	20.42%
HOT: FS [18]	22.53%	HOT: FS [18]	21.84%
iHOT: BW	**19.37%**	iHOT: BW	**8.59%**
iHOT: FS	22.27%	iHOT: FS	16.5%

4.3   Complete iHOT: TDT and Weighted Histogramming

We evaluate different parameter settings of the complete iHOT including spatial tessellation of the frame S, length of tracklets W and the quantization bins O and M. Following [18], we quantized tracklets orientation in $O = 8$ uniform bins [18]. We varied the temporal window of $W = \{5, 11, 21\}$ frames setting the tracklet length to W. Moreover, we varied the number of quantization levels for magnitude $M \in \{3, 5, 8, 16, 24, 32\}$. we considered three different spatial tessellations, called as *coarse* $S = 2 \times 3$, *medium* $S = 4 \times 6$ and *fine* $S = 8 \times 12$. The LDA topics number is fixed to $Z = 30$. This experiment was conducted on the UCSD dataset, ped1 and ped2, comparing our approach with the original HOT in [18] using two different classification sensations: *Fully bag of words(BW)* and *Per-frame, Per-sector (FS)*. For our method, we considered complete iHOT (TDT + weighted histogramming).

The LDA likelihood [28] of the test frames was used to compute the EERs for our approach and the original HOT [18]. Results (EER, the smaller the better) for ped1 and ped2 are reported in Fig. 3 showing the robustness of both the original HOT and the Improved HOT. However, the EERs obtained by the Improved HOT for all the parameter combinations are obviously lower than those of the original HOT.

Table.2 compares the Improved HOT with the HOT and the state-of-the-arts descriptors. EERs of competitors are taken from [19] where the authors reported *best* results across all the model-method configurations. Despite such comparison cannot statistically highlight a clear winner, we limit ourselves to acknowledge how the new tracklet extraction strategy (TDT) and the weighted histogramming improves the performance of the original HOT [18] and, surely, outperforms the prior leading methods in the literature. Particularly, our improvement achieved superior performance than the original HOT for both classification strategies, BW and FS, on ped1 and ped2. Please note that the EERs of the original HOT reported in Table 2 are slightly different than those obtained in the reference paper [18]. Since, here we fixed the LDA topics $Z = 30$, while, the results in [18] were the best achieved by varying $Z \in \{2, 4, 6, ..., 80\}$.

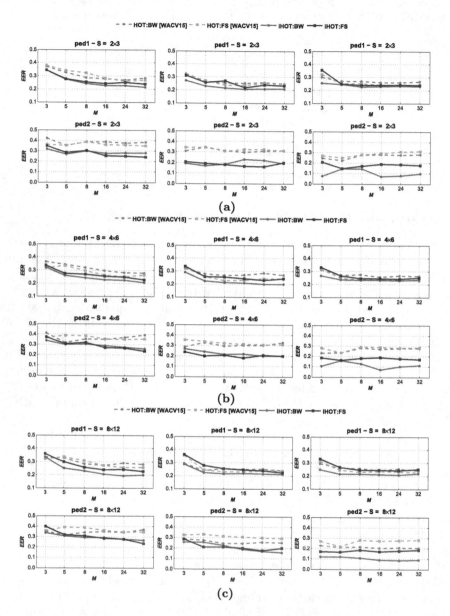

Fig. 3. Results for ped1 and ped2 varying the number of magnitude bins, tracklet length and spatial tessellation. (a) coarse tessellation, (b) medium tessellation, (c) fine tessellation. The first, second and third column respectively corresponded to the tracklet length of 5, 11 and 21.

5   Conclusion

In this paper, we introduced a modified version of histogram of oriented tracklets (HOT) descriptor for the task of abnormality detection in crowd scenes. We discussed and empirically showed that video level tracklet extraction employed by the original HOT which include poor initialization of salient points and tracking drift. To address this drawback we proposed Temporally Dense Tracklets to initialize the salient points in each frame. Moreover, we analyzed that the counting-based naive histogramming in the HOT is not capable of capturing statistics of abnormal motions. We proposed weighted histogramming to deal with this disadvantage by exploiting the distribution of crowd motions (mean and variance). The enhanced version of HOT is called Improved HOT (iHOT). The evaluations demonstrated the superiority of the Improved HOT compared to the original HOT and the prior video descriptors.

References

1. Wijermans, N., Jorna, R., Jager, W., Vliet, T.v.: Modelling crowd dynamics, influence factors related to the probability of a riot. In: Proceedings of the Fourth European Social Simualtion Association Conference (ESSA), Toulouse University of Social Sciences (2007)
2. Junior, S.J., et al.: Crowd analysis using computer vision techniques. IEEE Signal Processing Magazine **27**(5), 66–77 (2010)
3. Haque, M., Murshed, M.: Panic-driven event detection from surveillance video stream without track and motion features. In: 2010 IEEE International Conference on Multimedia and Expo (ICME), pp. 173–178. IEEE (2010)
4. Hassner, T., Itcher, Y., Kliper-Gross, O.: Violent flows: real-time detection of violent crowd behavior. In: CVPRW, pp. 1–6. IEEE (2012)
5. Wu, S., Wong, H.S., Yu, Z.: A bayesian model for crowd escape behavior detection. IEEE Transactions on Circuits and Systems for Video Technology **24**(1), 85–98 (2014)
6. Zhong, H., Shi, J., Visontai, M.: Detecting unusual activity in video. In: Proceedings of the 2004 IEEE Computer Society Conference on Computer Vision and Pattern Recognition. CVPR 2004, vol. 2, p. II-819. IEEE (2004)
7. Xiang, T., Gong, S.: Video behavior profiling for anomaly detection. IEEE Transactions on Pattern Analysis and Machine Intelligence **30**(5), 893–908 (2008)
8. Reddy, V., Sanderson, C., Lovell, B.C.: Improved anomaly detection in crowded scenes via cell-based analysis of foreground speed, size and texture. In: 2011 IEEE Computer Society Conference on Computer Vision and Pattern Recognition Workshops (CVPRW), pp. 55–61. IEEE (2011)
9. Mehran, R., Oyama, A., Shah, M.: Abnormal crowd behavior detection using social force model. In: IEEE Conference on Computer Vision and Pattern Recognition. CVPR 2009, pp. 935–942. IEEE (2009)
10. Kim, J., Grauman, K.: Observe locally, infer globally: a space-time mrf for detecting abnormal activities with incremental updates. In: IEEE Conference on Computer Vision and Pattern Recognition. CVPR 2009, pp. 2921–2928. IEEE (2009)
11. Cui, X., Liu, Q., Gao, M., Metaxas, D.N.: Abnormal detection using interaction energy potentials. In: 2011 IEEE Conference on Computer Vision and Pattern Recognition (CVPR), pp. 3161–3167. IEEE (2011)

12. Kratz, L., Nishino, K.: Anomaly detection in extremely crowded scenes using spatio-temporal motion pattern models. In: IEEE Conference on Computer Vision and Pattern Recognition. CVPR 2009, pp. 1446–1453. IEEE (2009)

13. Boiman, O., Irani, M.: Detecting irregularities in images and in video. International Journal of Computer Vision 74(1), 17–31 (2007)

14. Wang, X., Ma, X., Grimson, W.E.L.: Unsupervised activity perception in crowded and complicated scenes using hierarchical bayesian models. IEEE Transactions on Pattern Analysis and Machine Intelligence 31(3), 539–555 (2009)

15. Fu, Z., Hu, W., Tan, T.: Similarity based vehicle trajectory clustering and anomaly detection. In: IEEE International Conference on Image Processing. ICIP 2005, vol. 2, p. II-602. IEEE (2005)

16. Alvar, M., Torsello, A., Sanchez-Miralles, A., Armingol, J.M.: Abnormal behavior detection using dominant sets. Machine Vision and Applications, 1–18 (2014)

17. Mousavi, H., Nabi, M., Kiani, H., Perina, A., Murino, V.: Crowd motion monitoring using tracklet-based commotion measure. In: IEEE International Conference on Image Processing (ICIP). IEEE (2015)

18. Mousavi, H., Mohammadi, S., Perina, A., Chellali, R., Murino, V.: Analyzing tracklets for the detection of abnormal crowd behavior. In: 2015 IEEE Winter Conference on Applications of Computer Vision (WACV), pp. 148–155. IEEE (2015)

19. Mahadevan, V., Li, W., Bhalodia, V., Vasconcelos, N.: Anomaly detection in crowded scenes. In: 2010 IEEE Conference on Computer Vision and Pattern Recognition (CVPR), pp. 1975–1981. IEEE (2010)

20. Blunsden, S., Fisher, R.: The behave video dataset: ground truthed video for multi-person behavior classification. Annals of the BMVA 4, 1–12 (2010)

21. Makris, D., Ellis, T.: Learning semantic scene models from observing activity in visual surveillance. IEEE Transactions on Systems, Man, and Cybernetics, Part B: Cybernetics 35(3), 397–408 (2005)

22. Hu, W., Xiao, X., Fu, Z., Xie, D., Tan, T., Maybank, S.: A system for learning statistical motion patterns. IEEE Transactions on Pattern Analysis and Machine Intelligence 28(9), 1450–1464 (2006)

23. Zhou, B., Wang, X., Tang, X.: Random field topic model for semantic region analysis in crowded scenes from tracklets. In: 2011 IEEE Conference on Computer Vision and Pattern Recognition (CVPR), pp. 3441–3448. IEEE (2011)

24. Adam, A., Rivlin, E., Shimshoni, I., Reinitz, D.: Robust real-time unusual event detection using multiple fixed-location monitors. IEEE Transactions on Pattern Analysis and Machine Intelligence 30(3), 555–560 (2008)

25. Kim, J., Grauman, K.: Observe locally, infer globally: a space-time mrf for detecting abnormal activities with incremental updates. In: CVPR, pp. 2921–2928. IEEE (2009)

26. Cong, Y., Yuan, J., Liu, J.: Sparse reconstruction cost for abnormal event detection. In: 2011 IEEE Conference on Computer Vision and Pattern Recognition (CVPR), pp. 3449–3456. IEEE (2011)

27. Wu, S., Moore, B.E., Shah, M.: Chaotic invariants of lagrangian particle trajectories for anomaly detection in crowded scenes. In: 2010 IEEE Conference on Computer Vision and Pattern Recognition (CVPR), pp. 2054–2060. IEEE (2010)

28. Blei, D.M., Ng, A.Y., Jordan, M.I.: Latent dirichlet allocation. The Journal of machine Learning research 3, 993–1022 (2003)

29. Li, W., Mahadevan, V., Vasconcelos, N.: Anomaly detection and localization in crowded scenes. IEEE Transactions on Pattern Analysis and Machine Intelligence 36(1), 18–32 (2014)

Author Index